God and Uncle Sam

God and Uncle Sam

Religion and America's Armed Forces in World War II

Michael Snape

THE BOYDELL PRESS

First published 2015
The Boydell Press, Woodbridge

ISBN 978 1 84383 892 0

The Boydell Press is an imprint of Boydell & Brewer Ltd
PO Box 9, Woodbridge, Suffolk IP12 3DF, UK
and of Boydell & Brewer Inc.
668 Mt Hope Avenue, Rochester, NY 14620–2731, USA
website: www.boydellandbrewer.com

A catalogue record for this book is available
from the British Library

The publisher has no responsibility for the continued existence or accuracy
of URLs for external or third-party internet websites referred to in this book,
and does not guarantee that any content on such websites is,
or will remain, accurate or appropriate

This publication is printed on acid-free paper

For Katy and Helena

Contents

Illustrations

Acknowledgements

America's armed forces in World War II were the largest fighting forces ever to be raised by a self-consciously Christian – or 'Judeo-Christian' – society. Given the size of these hosts, the staggering diversity of American religious life, the vastness of this global conflict and the previous neglect of this subject, a study of the present length seemed both warranted and unavoidable. If it was a British wartime witticism that GIs were 'overpaid, oversexed and over here', this book shows that, even in Britain, there was a very different side to the American experience of war than sex, alcohol, nylon stockings, chewing gum and the jitterbug. This study is to a large extent a natural extension of my previous work on religion in the British Army c.1700 to 1950; however, it also arises from several decades of casual exposure to one major aspect of the American experience of World War II that has long been hiding in full view. More than thirty years ago, and fresh from seeing *A Bridge Too Far* (1977), the head teacher at my Catholic primary school told a school assembly of how an American officer (Major Julian A. Cook, played by Robert Redford) had survived a bullet-swept crossing of the River Waal by repeating 'Hail Mary, full of grace' – a true story, in actual fact. Years later, and during a prolonged, wintry lunch break at secondary school, the conversation turned to the previous night's television schedules, and in particular to the film *Attack* (1956), and to similar invocations of the Virgin Mary by Lieutenant Costa, played by Jack Palance. If the US was a largely Protestant country, we wondered, why were its World War II films so full of Catholics? Little did we realise that many wartime and post-war American Protestants asked much the same question, though with more asperity. In shedding light on this vexation, and on many other issues, research for this book has drawn from a great variety of sources, from the testimony of the devout believer to the avowed secularist, from that of the Jewish army chaplain to the Catholic naval rating. In addition to this, and to the published work of historians, sociologists and pollsters, it has been heavily informed by the massive and labyrinthine records of American army chaplaincy in World War II, and coloured by the short recollections and reflections of hundreds of army, navy and marine veterans. These, when given, were prompted by the item on religion in the questionnaire for the World War II Veterans Survey undertaken by the US Army Military History Institute, now part of the US Army Heritage and Education Center at Carlisle, Pennsylvania:

Q. 31 a. How and to what extent were religious convictions expressed in your unit?

Q. 31 b. How, if at all, did these convictions seem to influence performance?

Although it was impossible – given the vagaries of collection, the incompleteness of so many questionnaires, the spread of units represented or not represented, and the problems inherent in the questions themselves – to base this study simply on the answers they elicited, these responses provided some useful sidelights on the religious attitudes of veterans then and now.

In the course of my research for this project I have become hugely indebted to many hosts and friends in the United States. For their unstinting hospitality over the course of three extended visits to the US Army Heritage and Education Center, I would like to thank Rich and Iris Baker, who were generously seconded by Colonel Jim Scudieri, Professor Mike Neiberg, Chaplain Jim Carter, Chaplain David Reese, Dr Douglas V. Johnson, Dr Mike LoCicero, Professor Brian Linn and Colonel David M. Glantz, Ret. My research in Washington DC was greatly assisted by the memorable kindness and hospitality of Andrew Rawson, Reverend Gerald Kisner, Reverend Dr Joseph Evans and Senate Chaplain Reverend Dr Barry Black. In terms of invaluable archival assistance, I am grateful for the help of Dr Richard J. Sommers, Rich Baker and Tom Buffenbarger at the United States Army Heritage and Education Center, and to Megan Harris, the Collection Specialist of the Veterans History Project at the Library of Congress. I am also very grateful to the various members of the Research Room staff at the National Archives, College Park, who were able to steer me through the relevant record groups and who assisted with the often tricky reproduction of contemporary posters and photographs. In terms of ideas, references, interpretations and interest, I have benefited from contact with Professor Colleen McDannell, Professor Tim Larsen, Dr Tim Demy, Dr Patrick Houlihan and Dr Jonathan Ebel. This research was greatly facilitated by a kind invitation to speak at the US Army War College Strategy Conference 'American Society and its Profession of Arms' in April 2011, and by the generous award of a General and Mrs Matthew B. Ridgway Research Grant by the US Army Military History Institute of the US Army Heritage and Education Center in 2012. In 2013 and 2014, I was very fortunate to be invited by Professor David Hempton and Professor Hugh McLeod to participate in successive conferences on Comparative Secularization in Europe and the United States, conferences that were held at Harvard's Radcliffe Institute for Advanced Study and at Harvard Divinity School. Their support for my work over many years has been invaluable, and I very much hope that this book serves, to some extent at least, to justify their kindness.

In terms of my collaborators at Boydell, I have been lucky to work with Michael Middeke and Megan Milan, who have proved to be timely sources of guidance and support, besides reservoirs of patience. Despite the slings and arrows of an increasingly busy teaching and administrative life, the production of this book has been helped by the friendship and support of my immediate colleagues, staff and postgraduates alike, connected with the War Studies group in the School of History and Cultures at the University of Birmingham. Thus, I would like to extend my warm thanks to Dr Peter Gray, Dr Jonathan Boff, Dr John Bourne, Dr Bob Watt, Dr Jonathan Gumz, Dr Victoria Henshaw and Dr Dan Whittingham, as well as to my current and former research students, notably Reverend Stuart Bell, John Broom and Reverend Eleanor Rance. Besides the University of Birmingham's War Studies seminar, another great stimulant has been its more occasional History of Religion seminar, and also the annual Amport Conference on religion and war held at the Armed Forces Chaplaincy Centre, Amport House. My long-standing collaboration with the Royal Army Chaplains' Department continues to inspire my research into the remarkably understudied field of religion and the experience of war, and I would like to thank David Blake, Padre Andrew Totten, Padre Nick Cook, Padre David Barrett and Padre Paul Wright for their unfailing interest and insights into the nature of chaplaincy and religious faith in the military.

Last but by no means least, I would like to express my tremendous gratitude to my family for their continued love and support. My late father, Edward Snape, was one of those many thousands of British children who were feted and entertained by GIs during World War II, being inspired by wartime visits to the AAF base at Warton, Lancashire, to draw doodles of P-38s in his school textbooks, and to picture himself as a native of California rather than Clitheroe. I think he would have liked to have read this book. I remain, as ever, grateful to Andrew, John and to Angela, but above all to my wife, Rachel, and to my daughters Katy and Helena, who have had to put up with long periods of an all-too closeted and absent life. This book is, at last, dedicated to them, my greatest blessings, with much love.

Copyright Acknowledgements

by permission of Dutton, an imprint of Penguin Publishing Group, a division of Penguin Random House LLC; excerpts from PACIFIC WAR DIARY, 1942–1945 by James J. Fahey. Copyright© 1963, and renewed 1991 by James J. Fahey. Reprinted by permission of Houghton Mifflin Harcourt Publishing Company. All rights reserved. Extracts from all articles in the *Marine Corps Gazette* are reprinted courtesy of the *Marine Corps Gazette*. Copyright retained by the *Marine Corps Gazette*; material from 'The True Story of the Patton Prayer' http://pattonhq.com/prayer.html is republished by permission of The Patton Society and by Charles Province; extracts reprinted by permission of the publisher from RELIGION OF SOLDIER AND SAILOR, edited by Willard L. Sperry, contributions by Paul D. Moody, Lucien Price, John E. Johnson, William D. Cleary, and Elisha Atkins, pp. 48–49, 72–75, 85–94, 97–98, 105, Cambridge, Mass: Harvard University Press, Copyright ©1945 by the President and Fellows of Harvard College; excerpts from the *Stars and Stripes* newspaper are reprinted courtesy of *Stars and Stripes* © 1942–45;extracts from LETTERS FROM THE PACIFIC reprinted by kind permission of Dick Austin, ©2000 by The Curators of the University of Missouri, now distributed at CreeksidePress.com; Brian and Craig S. Wansink, 'Are There Atheists in Foxholes? Combat Intensity and Religious Behavior', *Journal of Religion and Health*, forthcoming, is available at http://ssrn.com/abstract=2277773 or http://dx.doi.org/10.2139/ssrn.2277773 and is cited by kind permission of Prof. Brian and Prof. Craig S. Wansink; extracts from W. Wyeth Willard, THE LEATHERNECKS COME THROUGH, Revell, a division of Baker Publishing Group, © 1944, used by permission; extracts from Israel I. Yost, COMBAT CHAPLAIN, © 2006 University of Hawaii Press (www.uhpress.hawaii.edu), reprinted with permission; 'Soldiers of God' by Hy Zaret and Benjamin A. Machan is cited by kind permission of Warner/Chappell Music Ltd. Material from the George C. Marshall Papers is cited by kind permission of the George C. Marshall Foundation, Lexington, Virginia, 24450 and material from the World War II Veterans Survey, by kind permission of the Army Heritage and Education Center, Carlisle, Pennsylvania, 17013. Picture credits are given in the plate sections of this book.

The author and publishers are grateful to all the organisations, institutions and individuals listed above for permission to reproduce the materials in which they hold copyright. Every effort has been made to trace copyright holders and apologies are extended for any omission, including those of permissions that arrived too late to be acknowledged here. The publishers will be pleased to add any necessary acknowledgements in subsequent editions and the author would be grateful for any information that would lead to further copyright acknowledgements. In seeking permissions, he would like to note the kindness of Rich Baker, Paul B. Barron, Lyndsey Claro, Christine Cullen, Dave Gardiner, Ron Hussey, Catharine Giordano, Megan Harris, John Kempton, Catherine Kramer, Sarah Laskin, Marlea Leljedal, Mack McCormick, Chaplain Michael Milton, Sharon Rubin,

Phyllis Shapiro, Samuel C. Shearin, Julia Simpkins, and Claire Weatherhead, and the assistance given by The American Jewish Archives; Behrman House Inc.; The Catholic University of America Press; *The Christian Century*; Farrar, Straus and Giroux, LLC; McGraw-Hill Education; Moody Publishers; Simon and Schuster, Inc.; University of Nebraska Press and Westminster John Knox Press. Finally, thanks also to Rosie Pearce, Megan Milan and Rohais Haughton at Boydell and Brewer for their patience and understanding.

Note on Spelling

This book uses conventional English spelling, except in the case of quotations and in the names of places, organisations and institutions.

Abbreviations

AAF	Army Air Forces
ABS	American Bible Society
AEF	American Expeditionary Forces
AEFP	Allied Expeditionary Force Programme
AFN	American Forces Network
AGF	Army Ground Forces
AGCT	Army General Classification Test
AIPO	American Institute of Public Opinion
AME	African Methodist Episcopal
ASF	Army Service Forces
ATIS	Allied Translator and Interpreter Section
BBC	British Broadcasting Corporation
BD	Bachelor of Divinity
CANRA	Committee on Army and Navy Religious Activities
CARLDL	Combined Arms Research Library Digital Library
CBI	China–Burma–India Theatre
CBS	Columbia Broadcasting System
CCC	Civilian Conservation Corps
CE	Christian Endeavor
CIO	Committee for Industrial Organization
CMTC	Citizens' Military Training Camps
CRC	Christian Reformed Church
DP	Displaced Person
ETO	European Theater of Operations
FCC	Federal Council of Churches of Christ in America
GHQ	General Headquarters
GI	Government Issue
JWB	Jewish Welfare Board
LDS	Latter-Day Saints
LST	Landing Ship, Tank
MCWR	Marine Corps Women's Reserve
MPs	Military Policemen
MTO	Mediterranean Theater of Operations
NAACP	National Association for the Advancement of Colored People
NARA	National Archives and Records Administration
NBC	National Broadcasting Company

NCCJ	National Conference of Christians and Jews
NCO	Non-Commissioned Officer
NMAJMH	National Museum of American Jewish Military History
OSS	Office of Strategic Services
Pfc	Private first class
POW	Prisoner of War
RAF	Royal Air Force
RAAF	Royal Australian Air Force
SMCL	Service Men's Christian League
SWCL	Service Women's Christian League
SPARS	Coast Guard women's reserve, from motto *Semper Paratus*
SVM	Student Volunteer Movement
Tec 5	Technician 5th Grade
USAAF	United States Army Air Forces
USAHEC	United States Army Heritage and Education Center
USO	United Service Organizations
VA	Veterans Administration
VE	Victory in Europe
VHP	Veterans History Project
VJ	Victory over Japan
WAAC/WAC	Women's Army Auxiliary Corps/Women's Army Corps
WAFS	Women's Auxiliary Ferrying Squadron
WASP	Women's Airforce Service Pilots
WAVES	Women Accepted for Volunteer Emergency Service
WPA	Works Progress Administration
YMCA	Young Men's Christian Association
YWCA	Young Women's Christian Association

Chronology

1937   7 July. Incident at Marco Polo Bridge, near Peking, ignites Sino-Japanese War.

1939   1 September. Germany invades Poland.

3 September. Britain and France declare war on Germany.

5 September. President Roosevelt issues Neutrality Proclamations.

8 September. President Roosevelt declares state of 'Limited National Emergency'.

1940   10 May. Germany launches offensive in Western Europe; Holland, Belgium and Luxembourg invaded.

16 May–3 June. Evacuation of nearly 340,000 British and French troops from Dunkirk.

10 June. Italy declares war on Britain and France.

20 June. President Roosevelt appoints Henry L. Stimson as Secretary of War and Frank Knox as Secretary of the Navy.

22 June. France signs armistice with Germany.

Mid-June to mid-September. Battle of Britain.

19 July. President Roosevelt signs Two-Ocean Navy Expansion Act.

27 August. Congress authorises President Roosevelt to call out the National Guard for a period of twelve months.

16 September. Congress approves Selective Training and Service Act, America's first peacetime draft.

27 September. Germany, Italy and Japan sign Tripartite Pact.

16 October. Selective Service Registration Day.

29 October. Commencement of the draft.

5 November. President Roosevelt is elected for a third term.

17 December. Opening of first Civilian Public Service camp for conscientious objectors.

1941   6 January. President Roosevelt advocates Lend-Lease support for Britain in State of the Union address and states national objective of upholding the 'four freedoms': freedom of speech, freedom of worship, freedom from want and freedom from fear.

4 February. Creation of United Service Organizations.

11 March. President Roosevelt signs Lend-Lease Act, with Britain as prime beneficiary.

10 April. President Roosevelt announces occupation of Greenland by American forces.

27 May. President Roosevelt issues 'Proclamation of Unlimited National Emergency'.

22 June. Germany invades Soviet Union.

25 June. Executive Order 8802 is issued, forbidding racial and other discrimination in civilian government and defence industries, but does not apply to the armed forces.

7 July. American troops occupy Iceland.

27 July. Japanese begin occupation of French Indo-China.

9 August. Placentia Bay conference commences, involving signing of Atlantic Charter by President Roosevelt and Winston Churchill.

14 August. President Roosevelt announces the Atlantic Charter.

18 August. President Roosevelt signs Selective Service Extension Act.

27 October. Following submarine attacks on American shipping and on American warships in the Atlantic, President Roosevelt's Navy Day address announces Nazi plan to 'abolish all existing religions' and to create 'an International Nazi Church'.

30 October. USS *Reuben James* torpedoed and sinks off the coast of Iceland; President Roosevelt offers Lend-Lease aid to Soviet Union.

7 December. Japan attacks Pearl Harbor without a prior declaration of war; air attacks on the Philippines and on American possessions in the Pacific.

8 December. United States declares war on Japan; Japan commences invasion of the Philippines.

11 December. Germany and Italy declare war on the United States; Guam falls to the Japanese.

20 December. Japan begins invasion of Netherlands East Indies.

23 December. Wake Island falls to the Japanese.

27 December. Australian premier John Curtin declares that Australia looks to the United States for protection.

1942 2 January. Manila is captured by the Japanese as American forces on Luzon retreat to Bataan Peninsula.

26 January. American troops begin to arrive in Britain. The number of American service personnel in Britain will exceed 1.6 million by June 1944.

March. Tenth Air Force in India begins flying Lend-Lease supplies to China over the Himalayas.

8 March 1942. Japanese forces land in Papua; fighting on the island of New Guinea will continue until the end of the war in the Pacific.

10 March 1942. General Joseph W. Stilwell appointed chief of staff to Chiang Kai-shek.

13 March. Japanese land on the Solomon Islands, threatening communications with Australia.

9 April. Bataan falls to the Japanese, American survivors withdraw to fortress island of Corregidor.

18 April. Doolittle Raid on Tokyo sees first American bombs dropped on Japanese home islands.

4–8 May. Battle of Coral Sea represents strategic setback for Japanese operations in New Guinea.

6 May. Corregidor falls to the Japanese.

14 May. Women's Army Auxiliary Corps (WAAC) established by Congress.

4–6 June. Japanese attack on Midway Island results in heavy defeat for Imperial Japanese Navy, which loses four of its large aircraft carriers.

7 June. Japanese capture Aleutian Islands of Attu and Kiska.

17 June. Publication of *Yank* magazine.

30 July. Women Accepted for Voluntary Emergency Service (WAVES) established by Congress.

7 August. American forces land on Guadalcanal, in the Solomon Islands, commencing a six-month air, sea and land campaign for possession of the island.

17 August. American bombers attack railway yards in Rouen, the first American heavy bombing raid on a target in Western Europe.

26–27 October. Battle of Santa Cruz Island, off Guadalcanal.

8 November. Anglo-American forces land in French North Africa (Operation Torch).

11–15 November. Naval Battle of Guadalcanal.

13 November. Draft age lowered to eighteen.

21 November. Alcan International Highway, running from Alberta to Alaska, is officially opened.

23 November. Coast Guard women's reserve (SPARS) established by Congress.

17 December. Army and navy announce plans to use almost three hundred college and university campuses as training facilities.

1943   2 January. Buna, in Papua, falls to American and Australian forces.

27 January. American bombers raid submarine works and port facilities at Wilhelmshaven and Emden, the first American heavy bombing raids on Germany.

8 February. Japanese evacuation of Guadalcanal completed.

19–25 February. American forces are mauled in Tunisia at the Battle of Kasserine.

2–4 March. A large Japanese convoy is destroyed off New Guinea in the Battle of the Bismarck Sea.

18 April. Admiral Yamamoto is killed in aerial ambush over the Solomon Islands.

11–29 May. American forces retake Attu.

13 May. Remnants of Axis forces in Tunisia capitulate.

21–23 June. Race riots in Detroit.

10 July. Allied invasion of Sicily.

19 July. Commencement of American bombing raids on Rome.

25 July. Mussolini is overthrown and is succeeded by Marshal Badoglio, Italy's new prime minister.

1–2 August. Race riots in Harlem.

15 August. American and Canadian forces retake Kiska after its evacuation by the Japanese.

17 August. Sicily secured with fall of Messina. American bombers suffer heavy losses in attacks on ball-bearing plant at Schweinfurt and aircraft plant at Regensburg.

3 September. First Allied troops land on Italian mainland.

8 September. Italy's unconditional surrender is announced.

9–16 September. American-led landings in the Gulf of Salerno, south of Naples, entail heavy fighting to secure the beachheads.

1 October. Naples falls to the Allies; induction of pre-Pearl Harbor fathers commences.

13 October. Marshal Badoglio's government declares war on Germany.

14 October. American bombers suffer heavy losses in second mass raid on Schweinfurt; suspension of American deep-penetration raids into Germany.

9 November. United Nations Relief and Rehabilitation Administration formed at Atlantic City, New Jersey.

20–24 November. Heavy casualties are sustained as American forces capture Tarawa and Makin atolls in the Gilbert Islands.

15 December. American forces land on New Britain, in the Bismarck Archipelago.

1944 22 January. Allied landings at Anzio, south-west of Rome, result in deadlock.

20 February. Commencement of 'Big Week' air offensive against Germany signals a growing Allied dominance of the skies above occupied Europe.

22 April. American forces land at Hollandia, New Guinea.

18 May. Fall of Monte Cassino follows the failure of three earlier Allied offensives.

4 June. American troops enter Rome.

6 June. Operation Overlord. Allies land in Normandy.

15 June. Operating from China, American B-29s commence strategic air offensive against Japan; American forces invade Saipan in the Mariana Islands, resulting in a three-week battle for the island.

22 June. President Roosevelt signs Servicemen's Readjustment Act ('GI Bill'), which had passed unanimously in Congress.

26 June. American forces capture Cherbourg.

21 July. American forces invade Guam in the Mariana Islands.

24 July. Americans invade Tinian in the Mariana Islands.

25 July. American forces begin break-out from Normandy bridgehead in Operation Cobra.

4 August. Allied forces enter Florence.

15 August. Allied landings in the French Riviera.

25 August. Paris is surrendered by its German garrison.

September–December. American forces are checked on the German border in the Battle of Hürtgen Forest.

15 September. American forces land on Peleliu in Palau Islands.

17–25 September. American airborne forces push into Holland as part of Operation Market-Garden.

20 October. American forces land on Leyte in the Philippines.

21 October. Aachen falls to American forces, Germany's first major city to be captured by the Allies.

24–25 October. Naval Battle of Leyte Gulf.

28 October. General Stilwell recalled to United States.

6 November. President Roosevelt is elected for a fourth term.

24 November. Bombing of Japan commences from the Mariana Islands.

16 December. German offensive against American forces in Belgium and Luxembourg results in the month-long 'Battle of the Bulge', the largest land battle in American history.

1945 9 January. American forces land on Luzon.

19 February. American forces land on Iwo Jima; the capture of the island takes more than a month.

3 March. Japanese resistance ends in Manila.

7 March. American troops cross the Rhine at Remagen.

1 April. American forces land on Okinawa, triggering nearly three months of fighting for the island.

10 April. American troops liberate Buchenwald.

12 April. Death of President Roosevelt; President Harry S. Truman is sworn-in.

22 April. American troops take Bologna.

25 April. American and Red Army troops meet at Torgau, on the River Elbe.

29 April. Surrender of all German forces in Italy; American forces liberate Dachau.

30 April. Hitler commits suicide.

4 May. German forces in northern Germany, the Netherlands and Denmark surrender to Field Marshal Montgomery.

7 May. Unconditional surrender of Germany signed at General Eisenhower's headquarters in Reims.

5 July. General MacArthur announces liberation of the Philippines.

6 August. Atom bomb dropped on Hiroshima.

9 August. Atom bomb dropped on Nagasaki.

14 August. Emperor Hirohito announces unconditional surrender of Japanese forces.

2 September. Ceremony marking surrender of Japan is held on battleship *Missouri* in Tokyo Bay.

Introduction

FAITH IN GOD was not a casual part of the lives of the World War II generation. The men and women who went off to war, or stayed home, volunteer that their spiritual beliefs helped them cope with the constant presence of possible death, serious injury, or the other anxieties attendant to the disruptions brought on by war.... On the front lines, chaplains were not incidental to the war effort. Some jumped with the Airborne troops on D-Day and others risked their own lives to administer last rites or other comforting words to dying and grievously wounded young men wherever the battle took them. The very nature of war prompted many who participated in it to think more deeply about God and their relationship to a higher being once they returned home.[1]

So wrote Tom Brokaw, NBC journalist and broadcaster, in the first of three hugely successful paeans of praise to 'the greatest generation'.[2] Appealing to the 'simple, shining legend of the Good War',[3] and to its sense of national unity and purpose undimmed by the doubts and traumas of Vietnam and even Korea, here Brokaw firmly identified a strong religious faith as one of the four distinguishing virtues of the peerless generation born around 1920, namely 'personal responsibility, duty, honor, and faith'.[4] Captured – with a touch of irony – in the title of Studs Terkel's pioneering oral history *The Good War* (1984) and celebrated by Stephen E. Ambrose in books such as *Band of Brothers* (1992) and *Citizen Soldiers* (1997); by Steven Spielberg in films and television productions such as *Saving Private Ryan* (1998), *Band of Brothers* (2001) and *The Pacific* (2010); and by the acclaimed documentary-maker Ken Burns in *The War* (2007) – the comfortable assumptions and abiding myths of 'the good war' and 'the greatest generation' have inevitably triggered a chorus of conflicting narratives and a lengthening list of gainsayers. Impelled by the deception and duplicity inherent in such myth-making, among its most notable and authoritative critics was the late Paul Fussell, an American infantry officer in North-West Europe in 1944–45 and a distinguished literary scholar and public intellectual in later life. Fortified by a strongly felt affinity with Siegfried Sassoon and Wilfred Owen, the most famous of Britain's officer-poets of World War I,[5] Fussell's scepticism, and acid reflections on 'the good war' and 'the greatest generation', inspired and coloured works such as 'Thank God for the Atom Bomb' (1981), *Wartime: Understanding and Behavior in the Second World War* (1989), *Doing Battle: The Making of a*

Skeptic (1996) and *The Boys' Crusade: American GIs in Europe: Chaos and Fear in World War Two* (2003). For Fussell, the pitiful and sordid realities of 'what has been misleadingly termed the Good War'[6] were risibly obvious. 'Thank God the troops, most of them, didn't know how bad we were', he wrote: 'It's hard enough to be asked to die in the midst of heroes, but to die in the midst of stumble-bums led by fools – intolerable. And I include myself in this indictment.'[7] Again, and this time inveighing against Spielberg's representation of the Normandy campaign, Fussell fulminated:

> I'd like to recommend the retention of and familiarity with the first few minutes of Steven Spielberg's *Saving Private Ryan* depicting the landing horrors. Then I'd suggest separating them to constitute a short subject, titled *Omaha Beach: Aren't You Glad You Weren't There*? Which could mean, 'Aren't you glad you weren't a conscripted working-class or high school boy in 1944?' The rest of the Spielberg film I'd consign to the purgatory where boys' bad adventure films end up.[8]

Nor did the religious assumptions inherent in the myths of 'the good war' and 'the greatest generation' escape Fussell's attention. In his view, this not-so-good war was far from being a triumph of steadfast faith: 'The Second World War was a notably secular affair. When superstitions that could be considered "religious" do surface, they are likely to carry with them a taint of scepticism, or at least wariness.'[9] A relatively rare example of a confirmed pre-war American agnostic, and the product of a Presbyterian upbringing that put him off church 'for life',[10] Fussell's existing religious views were ultimately unchanged by his wartime experiences. However, historians who share Fussell's doubts have been happy to advance even bolder claims about the marginality of religion to America's fighting men; as Kenneth Rose put it in *Myth and the Greatest Generation: A Social History of Americans in World War II* (2008), 'if there were no atheists in foxholes, it was only because troops were too indifferent to religion to bother becoming atheists.'[11] However, and as Rose concedes,[12] the strength of these opposing narratives obscures the fact that neither are necessarily true or false, but that elements of both were present to varying degrees in the myriad patchwork of the war experience. What has not helped our understanding of the religious experience of World War II – especially for Americans in the military, given that civilian society was practically insulated from the fighting by two oceanic moats – is its chronic and surprising neglect in scholarly circles. Even the exceptional, book-length study of the American churches and World War II, Gerald L. Sittser's *A Cautious Patriotism: The American Churches and the Second World War* (1997), skirts the issue of personal faith and deals with the military only tangentially. Other than some books that are decidedly devotional in tone,[13] and apart from several studies of military chaplaincy and of the effects of combat on personal faith,[14] there is little published work available to illustrate the wider religious impact of their country's bloodiest foreign war, and the greatest man-made catastrophe in history, upon those millions of Americans who experienced it most directly. While in 1998 Sittser hinted at the light this might shed 'on postwar commitment, organization, and ministry',[15] in a 2014 article in the *Journal of American Studies*, Jenel Virden complained that 'religion is rarely discussed in books about the wartime experience of servicemen except for the oft-repeated, and often refuted, idea that there were "no atheists in foxholes"', adding that, 'This simplistic view is overturned when the archival record of the [army's] Chaplains' Corps is examined. Religion had a significant role to play in fighting World War II if for no other reason than that the chaplains were there to provide religious services.'[16] So far, and although a 2013 doctoral dissertation by Kevin L. Walters may soon be published,[17] only Deborah Dash Moore's admirable study *GI Jews: How World War II Changed a Generation* (2004), which deals with only 5 per cent of America's armed forces, shows what can be achieved in terms of studying the far-reaching impact of wartime military experience on religious faith and identity.

The prevailing neglect of American religion and World War II is remarkable for other historiographical reasons. First, given the mountainous literature on the history of religion in America, it stands in marked contrast to the attention given to other conflicts, notably the Civil War and the Cold War but also the Revolutionary War, World War I and even the War of 1812.[18] Second, the war years represent a key period in the history of American religion in the twentieth century, acting as a pivotal phase between the troubled years of the interwar decades and the booming religiosity of the late 1940s and 1950s. This study seeks to examine the experience of military service in World War II as an agent of this change. In doing so it draws on a broad range of religious and secular sources, both published and archival, including the records of the army's Corps of Chaplains (much of the navy's were – remarkably – simply destroyed after the war),[19] poll data, census records, social and religious commentary, newspapers, periodicals, films, commemorative volumes, memoirs, veterans' questionnaires and oral history interviews. In combination with published secondary sources ranging from official biographies to unit histories, this study will demonstrate the importance of World War II as a key moment in the history of American religion and, in particular, the importance of military organisations and military experience as catalysts for religious change in an era of total war. However, before proceeding it is necessary to survey the diversity and complexity of America's pre-war religious landscape and to address those key features of the American armed forces in World War II that have a direct bearing on this study.

In 1922, in his book *What I Saw in America*, G.K. Chesterton famously described the United States as 'a nation with the soul of a church'.[20] And that soul was distinctly troubled in the 1920s and 1930s. In many different and disturbing ways, this was a lean period for 'mainline' American Protestantism, that broad alliance of Anglophone churches and denominational groupings that functioned as the nation's de facto Protestant establishment, and whose mainly liberal leadership reflected and embodied the zeitgeist of the Progressive Era.[21] Although the term 'mainline' was not contemporary, and lists of its constituents can vary, at the heart of this coalition stood the so-called 'Seven Sisters', namely the Methodists, the Episcopalians, the Presbyterians, the Congregationalists, the Northern Baptists, the Disciples of Christ and the United Lutherans. After its formation in 1908, these groupings represented more than half of those Protestants notionally embraced by the Federal Council of Churches, and the often liberal aspirations of their leadership found a unifying voice in Charles Clayton Morrison's magazine *The Christian Century*, a publication recently described as one of the 'key institutions' of the Protestant 'mainline'.[22] However, some major Protestant groups, notably the black Baptists, Southern Baptists and the Missouri Synod Lutherans (who were divided, in the latter case, by language as well as by theology) remained outside this alliance, and much of its internal unity was deceptive. The various groupings associated with the 'mainline' could embrace many subdivisions, the Methodists and Baptists being good illustrations,[23] and the range of theological opinion within each grouping could be broad. Furthermore, and as Elesha J. Coffman has argued, the avowedly 'undenominational' and progressive *Christian Century* basically traded on its 'cultural capital' rather than on a wide basis of popular support, the views of its educated ministerial subscribers often being at variance with those of the men and women who filled their pews.[24] The fragile unity of the 'mainline' and its components was further undermined by the ongoing strife between 'modernists' and 'fundamentalists', a struggle over questions of doctrinal orthodoxy and biblical interpretation that was trumpeted by Harry Emerson Fosdick, 'the leading pulpiteer of the time', in his famous 1922 sermon 'Shall the Fundamentalists Win?', and one that affected in particular the Disciples of Christ, the Northern Baptists and the Presbyterians in the interwar years.[25] Besides causing a succession of schisms, as rebellious fundamentalists voted with their feet in response to liberal dominance of denominational institutions, the fundamentalist controversy loosened denominational ties in other respects, as even those who remained within their old denominations 'surged out of the bonds of older denominational structures to create flexible, dynamic institutions, such as independent mission agencies, radio programs and Bible schools'.[26] Despite the national embarrassment of the notorious Scopes trial in Dayton, Tennessee, in 1925 (in which the eponymous John Thomas Scopes, a high-school biology teacher, was fined $100 for breaching a state law that proscribed the teaching of evolution) fundamentalism survived the stigma of 'know-nothing absurdity',[27] building its forces as 'a viable grassroots religious movement' for a dramatic resurgence on the national stage in the 1940s.[28]

Although Robert T. Handy's diagnosis of an 'American Religious Depression' in the interwar years requires heavy qualification,[29] it was not that wide of the mark, for this was indeed a 'bleak period' for the Protestant mainline. As we shall see, this situation was strongly reflected in the data yielded by the decennial federal Census of Religious Bodies of 1926 and 1936. If census data was complicated by a range of factors, including different membership criteria, non-cooperation and even deliberate under-reporting (prompting Claris Edwin Silcox and Galen M. Fisher to observe 'there are lies, damned lies, statistics, and *church statistics*'), they nonetheless provided an approximate guide to contrasting denominational fortunes in this period.[30] Despite some landmark mergers and reconciliations, notably between the Congregational and Christian churches in 1931, and the Northern, Southern and Protestant Methodists in 1939,[31] the ecumenical dynamic could not disguise some worrying signs of decline for the mainline churches. Riven by tensions between modernists and fundamentalists, they also saw falling attendances and Sunday school enrolments, a decline in Sunday services, and a cooling of missionary ardour at home and abroad.[32] The impact of the Depression only served to worsen a bad situation;[33] in the words of Robert M. Miller: 'Memberships dropped, budgets were slashed, benevolent and missionary enterprises set adrift, ministers fired, and chapels closed.'[34] Because the Depression greatly weakened 'American religious institutions' power to face social crisis and alleviate individual suffering', the advent of the New Deal signalled 'the transfer of that power from church to state'.[35] If the Roosevelt administration was therefore responsible for 'an important transition in the relative importance of the Protestant establishment and in the roles of church and state in assessing and meeting the needs of the nation's population',[36] the implications of this long-term development were much less obvious than the signal failure of Prohibition, 'the Protestant crusade *par excellence*', and in itself 'an attempt by dominant Protestants to impose their standards on immigrants'.[37] The repeal of the Eighteenth Amendment in 1933 – according to Sydney E. Ahlstrom 'the greatest blow to their pride and self-confidence that Protestants as a collective body had ever experienced' – spelt the defeat of a cause around which all shades of Protestant opinion could rally and added to the manifold woes of Protestant America.[38]

However, in the fragmented and kaleidoscopic world of American Protestantism, the situation looked decidedly better outside of the white, Anglophone mainstream. Under the impact of the Depression and of internal migration from the southern 'Dust Bowl' states, conservative, fundamentalist and Pentecostal churches grew numerically and spread geographically,[39] expansion that was attributed in the aftermath of World War II to the flagging spirit of revivalism 'in the large evangelical churches' and to two decades of 'deep distress and uncertainty'.[40] The growth of such 'revivalist sects', or 'churches of the disinherited',[41] was a remarkable feature of the American religious landscape. Although still small in relative terms (according to the 1936 Census of Religious Bodies, nearly 90 per cent of America's church members belonged to the country's nineteen largest denominations),[42] the proliferation and growth of 'sects' (a loaded term),

and of 'evangelistic sects' in particular, was phenomenal. The census of 1936 identified no fewer than 256 denominations, as it described them,[43] in comparison to
145 in 1890, 186 in 1906, 202 in 1916, and 213 in 1926. This, as Charles S. Braden
– a Methodist minister, professor of religion at Northwestern University and
mainline expert on the sectarian threat – pointed out in 1944, represented 'a gain
of 73.7 per cent in forty-six years, the sharpest rise in the whole period being
in the most recent decade – 1926–36'. Furthermore, those very years had shown
'the largest sectarian gains [and] the fewest reunions of sects'.[44] According to
Braden, of the new sects or denominations that had emerged between 1890 and
1936, most were 'definitely of the Pentecostal-holiness-evangelistic type',[45] with
many of these (such as the Church of the Nazarene and the Assemblies of God)
doubling their memberships between 1926 and 1936.[46] This growth continued
between 1937 and 1945, with thirteen of the fourteen fastest-growing churches
being of this ilk, and one of them, the Pentecostal Church of God in America,
registering an increase of 785.6 per cent.[47] Significantly, of the larger denominations, only one, the Southern Baptist Convention, experienced growth of more
than 20 per cent over the same period, the cause of its 29 per cent increase
being explained by Braden in terms of the fact that this denomination was 'in
some respects … not so far removed from the Pentecostal-holiness-evangelistic
type'.[48] According to Braden, among the common factors that accounted for the
appeal of these groups, especially among the nation's 'lower income groups', was
their biblicism, their emphasis on personal experience, their evangelistic urgency
(usually born of premillennial expectation), their other-worldliness, and their
lively and uninhibited styles of worship.[49]

Of course, and as Braden recognised, the nation's broad sectarian spectrum
was also occupied by groups that were neither theologically orthodox, in traditional terms, nor recognisably Christian. Because they were markedly 'out of
line with the principal beliefs of the majority faiths on a number of points', the
Church of Jesus Christ of Latter-Day Saints (LDS) (or Mormons) and the Church
of Christ, Scientist were widely regarded as sects although they embodied the
institutional characteristics of a church, not least in terms of their size and their
national representation.[50] Despite various Mormon secessions since the death of
Joseph Smith in 1844, the growth of the Salt Lake City-based LDS was impressive, registering rates of 25 per cent between 1926 and 1936, and 28 per cent
from 1936 to 1945.[51] Benefiting from a missionary system that required a year of
missionary commitment from all its members, 'sects' that commanded similar
dedication met with equivalent success. Spurred by their powerful conviction of
Christ's imminent return, in 1948 it was noted that the Seventh-Day Adventists
had been 'particularly active throughout the world during the troubled years
since 1930' and were 'growing rapidly', partly due to 'their principal stress upon
the "soon appearing of the Lord"' but also because of the resources they devoted
to missionary work (almost $800,000 per annum by 1936).[52] Between 1926 and

1936 America's Seventh-Day Adventists grew by 20 per cent.[53] More troublesome, however, was the growth of the Jehovah's Witnesses, branded as 'the present day's most extreme expression of the millennial hope', and as 'the most persistently propagandistic of any present-day religious group'. With all members expected to devote themselves to witnessing, whether on a part-time or a full-time basis, the number of Witnesses may well have doubled between 1939 and 1946, despite being the most persecuted religious group in contemporary America due to their objectionable missionary techniques and their refusal to salute the flag or submit to the draft.[54] Beyond these, of course, were the devotees of more arcane sects and humanist societies, running the gamut from the Father Divine Peace Mission (which held its founder to be God), through the 'I Am' movement (a syncretic mix of 'theosophy, New Thought, and Christianity'), to the American Ethical Union, a small confederation of humanists and Unitarians active in a handful of American cities.[55] There was even one group, the Brooklyn-based Mayan Temple, dedicated to the 'restoration of the pristine faith catholic, practiced by the Mayas in prehistoric America and common to all North and South America, prior to the coming of the white man'.[56]

Whatever their theology and orientation, the Protestant mainline did not view the sectarian boom with equanimity, especially given the evident decline in its own fortunes. For example, in 1944 Braden published a series of articles in *The Christian Century* under the title 'Why Are the Cults Growing?', and an essay 'Sectarianism Run Wild', in a high-profile, mainline symposium on Protestantism. As part of the former, Braden considered the significance of deviant beliefs and tendencies such as spiritualism and astrology,[57] and concluded that their appeal and the success of 'these marginal groups' was due to the fact that they attempted to satisfy 'legitimate needs of which the church should take account and in much greater degree attempt to meet'.[58] The cost of neglect was already clear. According to Braden's calculations:

> [T]he net gain of all the churches in 1936 over 1926 was 2.3 per cent. For a group of the larger churches, including the Methodist – there was a *loss* of 8 per cent. The Methodist Episcopal lost 14 per cent, the Methodist South, 17.1 per cent; the Presbyterian, 5.1. per cent; the Southern Baptist, 23 per cent; the Disciples of Christ, 13.2 per cent.[59]

In addition to a noted failure to supply sufficient data in 1936,[60] the fact that there was such an oscillation in Southern Baptist fortunes between 1926 and 1936, and between 1937 and 1945, was in part due to economic and demographic factors. Indeed, a persistent plaint among mainline churchmen about their current situation turned on the question of social class, and on the difficulty of appealing to the poor and to the migrant. As Braden lamented in 1944, 'our churches are to an alarming degree class institutions'.[61] In contextualising the rise and rise of the 'Churches of the Dispossessed', Braden explained that: 'Many in humbler circumstances do not feel at home in the comfortable middle class churches of the community'. It was not simply a question of their apparel, or the kind of motor cars they drove, but also that they were 'unable to participate in church social affairs', 'to contribute to all the good causes for which contributions are sought', and even 'to contribute what seems to them their proper share for the normal maintenance of the church'. Consequently, 'Pastors reported again and again during the depression period that members, when they could no longer pay as they had been accustomed, dropped out of the church'. If this was the fate of church members, the situation acted as a powerful deterrent to the unchurched, and especially to those who saw 'the obvious difference between the economic and social standards of the congregation as a whole and their own'.[62]

Such fears were confirmed in several case studies. For example, in a study of 'Class Denominationalism in Rural California Churches', published in 1944 in the *American Journal of Sociology*, Walter R. Goldschmidt explained how, in one community in the San Joaquin Valley, four Protestant churches served the white immigrant labourers 'on the social peripheries' who had 'come to the community in search of work and settled there'.[63] Whereas well-established Congregational, Methodist, Baptist and Seventh-Day Adventist churches served the 'nuclear' population, ministering to congregations in which skilled or unskilled labourers were in a minority, the Nazarene, Assembly of God, Church of God, and Pentecostal churches catered for congregations that were mainly composed of labourers, overwhelmingly so in the latter case.[64] Significantly, the uprooted from older denominations had little desire to rub shoulders with their former co-religionists. A female labourer said, 'they are good members, but we are poor people and everybody that goes there is up-to-date'. Another, now a Pentecostal, said: 'I don't like the Baptists here because they are a different class of people and I'd rather stay around my own class'. Of '51 recent immigrant white workers interviewed' for Goldschmidt's study, twenty-five had been church members 'in their former residence', chiefly Baptists or Methodists, and only one had retained their original affiliation. Of the rest, '12 have joined or are attending the outsider denominations and 12 report no attendance whatsoever'.[65]

In national terms, and while Protestantism could still lay claim to be 'the religion of the ruling and advantaged groups in the United States',[66] there were considerable variations in the social constituencies of its numerous components. Although there were problems in defining social class, especially on a national level, a slew of local studies conducted in the 1920s and 1930s pointed to a conspicuous degree of 'social stratification' in American Protestantism.[67] Not only were individual churches liable to be 'class churches', with their membership and/or management drawn from a predominant social class, but whole denominations were identified with specific social groups. As Liston Pope, professor of social ethics at Yale, put the situation in 1948:

Protestant denominations in their total outreach touch nearly all sections of the population. But each denomination tends also to be associated with a particular social status. Such denominations as the Congregational, Episcopal, and Presbyterian are generally associated in local communities with the middle and upper classes; the Methodist, Baptist, and Disciples of Christ denominations are more typically associated with the middle classes. The Lutheran denominations are harder to classify, because of their closer association with farmers, with particular ethnic backgrounds, and with skilled workers.[68]

Given this overall context, Pope concurred that there was a strong element of social as well as religious rebellion in the rise of more marginal groups:

Though all of these major denominations have adherents from the lower classes, the religious expression of the latter has increasingly taken place in the last quarter-century through the new Pentecostal and holiness sects, which represent on the one hand a protest (couched in religious form) against social exclusion and on the other a compensatory method (also in religious form) for regaining status and for redefining class lines in religious terms.[69]

These patterns of growing sectarianism and of religious and social differentiation were also felt among the African American churches. In 1936, almost 90 per cent of African American churches were located in the South, home to nearly 80 per cent of African Americans in 1930,[70] but the ongoing 'Great Migration' from the rural South drove their expansion in the cities of the industrial North.[71] Generally speaking, church membership was unusually high among African Americans; estimated at roughly 'five-sevenths of the total Negro population' in 1948, this was 'a considerably larger proportion than among the country's white population'. In denominational terms, Baptists and Methodists predominated, and 'about eight-ninths' of African American church members 'identified with these two denominational families'. Nevertheless, in 1936 Baptists led the field in every state outside Delaware, Montana and Washington,[72] outnumbering Methodists by almost four to one and accounting for nearly 70 per cent of African American church members in overall terms.[73] Characteristic of African American church life was its highly segregated nature, a function not only of white prejudice but of the key role of the self-standing, black-led church in African American society. In such an environment, and in a societal context of discrimination and disadvantage, African Americans governed their own affairs, developed their own modes of leadership and practised their distinctive styles of worship.[74] The 1936 Census of Religious Bodies identified no fewer than thirty-three denominations that were 'exclusively Negro in membership' and, even among the minority of African

Americans who were members of 'predominantly white denominations' (notably Methodists, Catholics and Episcopalians) the degree of racial intermingling was negligible. According to Liston Pope, there was 'almost no mixing of white and Negroes at the level of the individual congregation'. In fact, less than 1 per cent of white congregations had any African American members, and less than 0.5. per cent of African Americans who belonged to largely white denominations worshipped 'regularly with white persons'.[75]

However, and despite its overwhelmingly Protestant and evangelical temper, uniformity was by no means characteristic of African American Christianity in the interwar years. Like their white counterparts, individual churches and denominations were often identified with particular social groups; as Ralph Abernathy, a celebrated Baptist minister and civil rights activist, put it: 'You can tell the class of people who go to a black church by how much noise they make during the sermon. The less noise, the higher the class'.[76] Although this maxim applied to the South as much as to the North, it was vividly confirmed by a 1942 study of forty African American churches in Chicago's South Side, which found that larger, well-established black churches with a more sober, liturgical and ceremonial style of worship attracted more middle-class congregations. However, and while the black middle classes were drawn to Congregational, Episcopalian, Presbyterian 'and some of the Methodist and Baptist churches', their comparatively sedate worship and environment was usually alien to recently arrived 'migrants from the rural South', who 'developed pentecostal, spiritual, and spiritualist churches in which they celebrated the Christian tradition with an abandon which led to an ecstasy that had a more satisfactory effect upon them'.[77] Hence, it could be shown that in Chicago by 1942 'the most frequent lower class religious group is a sect, characterized by emotional demonstrativeness, and usually housed in a store-front building'.[78] Clearly, the effects of the Depression and the Great Migration served to splinter the religious world of African Americans still further. While some, appreciating the potential of Catholic schooling, converted to Catholicism in northern cities such as Chicago,[79] others were drawn to the highly eclectic world of the Spiritual Movement, which 'thrived in urban black neighborhoods between 1920 and 1950'. With their comparatively liberal mores, and chiefly dispensing advice, good luck and healing to their adherents, Spiritual churches drew promiscuously from Catholic and from Protestant forms of worship.[80] Furthermore, it is notable that one of the most accomplished black sectarians of his day, George Baker, aka 'Father Divine', or even 'God', was a Southern migrant and itinerant preacher who built a considerable following among urban blacks, and whites, through the activities of his 'Peace Mission Movement' and his singular synthesis of 'positive thinking … socialism and racial integration'.[81] Whatever else, the fissiparous nature of African American Christianity (or what Miles Mark Fischer, a black Baptist pastor and church historian described in 1937 as 'the Negro's attack upon organized Christianity')[82] made it very hard to judge the extent of overall growth in the black churches between 1926 and 1936. Writing in 1935, Fischer observed that: 'The "cults" have made it difficult to say who is a church member',[83] and the Census of Religious Bodies of 1936 duly noted that the detectable rate of growth, a meagre 2.3 per cent, seemed simply to reflect 'the result ... of relatively incomplete reporting in 1936 on the part of a number of denominations'.[84]

Although there were elements within the African American population that openly disregarded Christianity, and even viewed the churches as a positive hindrance to full emancipation,[85] the power of the ministry in the larger, more established and generally urban African American churches could not be gainsaid. As Patrick Allitt has written:

> They were often among the few black professionals not dependent on the goodwill and patronage of the white elite. They were, in addition, usually more highly educated than most of their flock, and more highly paid. They often mediated conflicts among their parishioners, supervised mutual assistance programs, and acted as go-betweens in solving interracial problems. If they preached well they could gather large, loyal congregations.[86]

If their churches could be criticised in northern cities for being more concerned with 'the things of the sanctuary' than with 'the urgent, vital needs of a struggling humanity',[87] such ministers remained central figures in African American communities, and not least in terms of political mobilisation and union organization.[88] Significantly, in the celebrated 1944 Hollywood film *The Negro Soldier*, producer Frank Capra and director Stuart Heisler chose to frame African American achievements and support for the war effort in the context of a sermon preached by a young African American minister in a large and dignified urban church setting. While such influence led the black nationalist Marcus Garvey to steer clear of confrontation with the established churches, and dictated caution in the promotion of a new African Orthodox Church as an auxiliary to his Universal Negro Improvement Association in the 1920s,[89] it tended to stand for a broadly conservative approach to social and economic issues, especially in the hard years of the Depression, which 'had a devastating impact in black communities' and upon the 'social outreach activities sponsored by black churches'.[90] In any event, and as C. Eric Lincoln and Lawrence H. Mamiya have emphasised: 'Prior to the civil rights movement, many black church leaders sometimes courted low visibility, preferring a behind the scenes approach towards civil rights and economic issues. They attempted nonconfrontational negotiations with the local white employers for access to jobs in hospitals, schools, factories, and department stores for black workers.' Given this approach, and the challenges of the time, the interwar years were inevitably 'a relatively quietistic time for black church leadership'.[91]

This could not be said of America's growing Catholic minority, however. Despite the tightening of immigration controls in the 1920s, in the interwar years Catholicism flourished in its northern and Midwestern urban heartlands. Whereas Protestantism was largely associated with small-town, rural America, by 1936 Catholicism was well on the way to becoming the religion of America's big cities, especially given 'the fabled Catholic enclaves of Boston and New York, Chicago and St. Louis'. [92] In 1936, when the American population was roughly 56.2 per cent urban and 43.8 per cent rural,[93] the Census of Religious Bodies found that 80.6 per cent of American Catholics lived in urban areas (i.e. towns with a population of more than 10,000, and with a population density of more than 1,000 per square mile), and that the urban Catholic Church had an average membership of almost 2,000.[94] In contrast, the membership of the Methodist Episcopal Church, the nation's largest single Protestant denomination, was more in keeping with national norms; 58.6 per cent lived in urban areas, but its urban churches had an average membership of only 440.[95] If Catholic numbers stabilised in the interwar years with the curbing of immigration from eastern and southern Europe in particular, Catholic growth continued. According to the 1936 census, the pace slackened from a dramatic 18.3 per cent in 1916–26 to a more modest 7 per cent in 1926–36.[96] Although America's reported 19,914,937 Catholics represented only 15.5 per cent of the estimated population in 1936,[97] they amounted to just over one-third of the nation's church membership (then put at 55,807,366), while the comparative strength and cohesion of American Catholicism was reflected in the fact that Catholics represented the largest group of church members in the District of Columbia and in thirty-four of the forty-eight states, including all of the states in four of the nation's nine census divisions (namely New England, East North Central, Middle Atlantic and Pacific).[98] Nevertheless, the Depression took its toll on Catholic finances and infrastructure. Although the Catholic clergy were not liable to be fired by their flocks, between 1926 and 1936 the number of Catholic churches declined, the amount of debt on church property increased by 50 per cent, and the average expenditure per church fell by one-third.[99] Furthermore, many Catholic charitable endeavours were affected by the expansion of 'governmental agencies' involved in relief, leading to a heavier emphasis in Catholic circles on 'the study and eradication of social causes through social action'.[100] The Depression also saw the rise of Dorothy Day's Catholic Worker Movement, whose radical communitarianism illustrated the striking breadth of American Catholicism in the interwar period.

Despite its ideological breadth, and an ethnic diversity that embraced Irish, Poles, Germans, Cajuns, Italians, Mexicans, African Americans and a mixture of other national groups, American Catholicism retained and even augmented its essential unity. Spurred by continuing Protestant hostility, whether overt or covert, the interwar years were a period of 'aggressive self-ghettoizing', which saw the continued development of Catholic schools, hospitals, colleges and other charitable foundations, and the further proliferation of Catholic publications, professional associations, recreational organisations and devotional societies.[101] With the National Catholic Welfare Conference symbolising the fundamental unity of Catholic organisation and purpose,[102] American Catholicism was naturally immune from the theological strife that beset mainline Protestantism, and nor was it as socially stratified as wider, Protestant America. Although far from being simply a church of the urban poor, surveys conducted by the American Institute of Public Opinion and by the Office of Public Opinion Research in 1939–40 showed that even the growth of a Catholic middle class could not obscure the fact that the Catholic Church had 'a larger percentage of lower-class adherents', and a much larger percentage if the South (where very few Catholics lived) was disaggregated from the national picture.[103] Despite growing levels of ethnic intermarriage, the declining number of foreign-born Catholics, and sporadic attempts at 'Americanisation' by the episcopate, the principal fault lines within American Catholicism in the interwar period remained ethnic, divisions epitomised in the mainly Irish leadership of the church and in the institution of the Catholic 'national parish'.[104] As Liston Pope explained in 1948:

> Internal differentiation in the Catholic Church tends to follow ethnic lines more largely than economic lines. Ethnic divisions cut across the organization of Catholic parishes by geographical districts, though the latter have often themselves reflected the residential propinquity of immigrants from a particular country. Thus the local Catholic churches in a community may include a French Catholic church, a Polish Catholic church, an Irish Catholic church, and the like.[105]

Likewise concentrated in the north-east and the Midwest, America's Jewish communities also witnessed significant growth in the interwar years. However, they were even more of an urban phenomenon. The 1936 Census of Religious Bodies identified only 142 Jewish congregations in rural areas across America in contrast to 3,586 in urban centres,[106] and went on to report that 99.1 per cent of Jews were urban dwellers.[107] The concentrated settlement pattern of American Jews was reflected in the fact that, by the outbreak of World War II, almost half lived in New York City, chiefly residents of Brooklyn or the Bronx.[108] According to the Census of 1936, they numbered 4,641,184, an increase of roughly 13.7 per cent over the previous decade,[109] representing around 3.6 per cent of the total population.[110] Although rampant anti-Semitism in American society and the pervasive Jewishness of Jewish neighbourhoods helped to sustain a sense of identity in the interwar period, American Jews were deeply divided along ethnic, linguistic and religious lines. The great majority of American Jews were first- or second-generation immigrants from Eastern Europe, Yiddish-speaking and, if they observed their faith at all, overwhelmingly Orthodox.[111] Although there were strong signs of movement out of the ghettoes (to the extent that, by the end of World War II, Jews were much more likely to be 'business and professional' or 'white collar' workers rather than 'urban manual workers')[112] assimilation and social mobility came at a price. In 1935, a survey of Jewish youth in New York City showed that, despite a common element of religious schooling, 72 per cent of young Jewish men and 78 per cent of young Jewish women had not attended a synagogue service for over a year, and that weekly attendance in either category stood at around 10 per cent.[113] Besides the inconveniences of traditional observance, Orthodox Judaism had to compete in 'a vigorous market-place of political ideas', with leftist ideologies and secular Zionism offering alternative allegiances.[114] In addition, there was the long-standing divide between these new arrivals and America's much smaller, more established Jewish community. Largely of German stock, during the later nineteenth century America's Jews had given rise to Reform and to Conservative Judaism, which in Will Herberg's words represented 'two forms of an Americanized Judaism substantially similar in pattern though different in temper and ideology'.[115] Despite their differences, both represented alien forms of Judaism to the great bulk of Jewish immigrants from Eastern Europe.

Despite their internal divisions and mutual antagonisms, both Catholics and Jews were the objects of heightened 'nativist' hostility among America's white, Protestant majority, especially in the 1920s. Symbolised by the dramatic, nationwide revival of the Ku Klux Klan, whose membership exceeded three million in 1926,[116] many Protestants suspected that Catholics and Jews – both essentially immigrant groups as well as the adherents of alien, minority faiths – had their own nefarious agendas for the republic. In the case of the Catholics, it was a case of imposing the influence of Rome on American public life, regardless of popular sensitivities and constitutional norms; in the case of the latter, it was a question of shadowy conspiracies of Jewish leftists or financiers bent on subverting the established order – paranoia manifested by Henry Ford's publication of *The Protocols of the Elders of Zion* in 1920.[117] While the Emergency Quota Act of 1921 and the National Origins Act of 1924 clearly carried the overtones of religious as well as racial prejudice,[118] countermeasures did not stop there. For American Jews, the 1920s were years of exclusionary housing covenants, of enrolment quotas at major universities, job discrimination, occasional violence and a steady stream of anti-Semitic propaganda.[119] While Catholics experienced much of the same, including the fatal shooting of a Catholic priest by a deranged Methodist minister in Birmingham, Alabama, in 1921,[120] the culmination came in 1928 with the presidential campaign of Al Smith, a Catholic and the Democrat governor of New York. Given his pro-labour, anti-Prohibition views, and the contemporary prosperity of the nation, Smith's chances of success were slim, but his Catholicism was clearly a factor in his heavy defeat, losing forty of the forty-eight states, including New York.[121] If more highbrow debate centred on the threat of Smith's vulnerability to Vatican diktat, Smith's campaign trail was marked with fiery crosses, and schoolchildren in Daytona Beach, Florida, were even sent home with a card that warned: 'If he is chosen President, you will not be allowed to have or read a Bible.'[122] However, the extent to which Catholics had failed to penetrate the higher levels of government prior to the Roosevelt years was reflected by the profile of the 73rd Congress in 1933; just five Catholics were in the Senate and only forty-four in the House of Representatives, the equivalent of just over 5 and 10 per cent of their membership respectively. The disparity among the nation's state governors was even worse, amounting to only two Catholics out of forty-eight.[123]

Nevertheless, and at least for American Catholics, there were signs of improvement in the 1930s. As Mark Noll has pointed out, with their electoral muscle flexed in Smith's very nomination, 'Smith's candidacy pointed to perhaps the most important religious development of the decade – the growing awareness that American life was no longer exclusively dominated by white, Anglo-Saxon, Protestant culture.'[124] Heavily reliant on the urban vote, the Roosevelt years saw the appointment of an unprecedented number of Catholics to senior judicial and governmental posts. Whereas only eight Catholics had been appointed as federal judges by the previous three administrations, a mere 4 per cent of the total, Roosevelt appointed fifty-one, more than one-quarter. Furthermore, and whereas only five Catholics had served in cabinet positions prior to Roosevelt's election – none in the past twenty-nine years, and none under a Democrat since the Civil War – Roosevelt's original cabinet included two.[125] The 1930s also saw a positive development for the image of American Catholicism in the form of Hollywood's growing fascination with the Catholic Church, and with its clergy in particular. This represented a 'radical transformation in Hollywood-Catholic relations', one brought about by convergence over censorship regulations, by the commercial success of 'Catholic movies' and by the broad appeal of their underlying themes. As Charles R. Morris has put it: 'The social mirror held up by the Catholic movies – close-knit communities, strong values, solid families, simple patriotism, self-sacrificing, morally impelled leaders – was one in which all Americans could find a reflection of their better selves.'[126] Consequently, and from the success of Spencer Tracy in *Boys' Town* (1938) to that of Gregory Peck in *The Keys of the Kingdom* (1945) and beyond, a slew of 'Catholic' films presented a new and consistently favourable image of the Catholic Church to a wider America, one that was dominated by the Hollywood figure of 'the "superpadre," virile, athletic, compassionate, wise'.[127] Furthermore, it was a context in which even the image of the urban ghetto could be redeemed; whereas Pat O'Brien grappled with innate criminality in *Angels with Dirty Faces* (1938), six years later Bing Crosby presided over an idealised vision of Catholic ghetto life for the amusement of war-weary Americans in *Going My Way* (1944).[128] By the eve of war, the Catholic Church in America, at least, was edging closer to acceptability. In March 1940, an election year, and only twelve years after the Al Smith debacle, an AIPO poll found that 61 per cent of American voters were prepared to vote for a 'generally well-qualified' Catholic if selected by their party.[129] Nevertheless, mistrust of the wider Catholic Church remained. The Spanish Civil War (1936–39), and the alignment of the Spanish Church with the Nationalist insurgents, seemed to vindicate suspicions of the dictatorial, anti-democratic character of international Catholicism.[130] Moreover, hostility towards papal pretensions remained a potent force among American Protestants, resulting in serious rumblings when President Roosevelt appointed a personal representative, Myron Taylor, to the Vatican in 1939.[131]

If the 1930s were a decade of mixed progress for American Catholics, they unfolded much less favourably for American Jews. Even more closely associated with the Democrats than were Catholics,[132] although there were no Jewish senators and only eight Jewish representatives in the 73rd Congress,[133] the Jewish presence around Roosevelt was highly controversial. According to Gary Scott Smith, Jews accounted for 'about 15 per cent of his top appointments', including, in 1934, Henry Morgenthau as Secretary of the Treasury, and Roosevelt's other Jewish appointees included speech-writers, policy advisors and a supreme court judge.[134] In a nation gripped by the Depression, increasingly troubled by the course of international affairs, and prey to immigrant as well as to nativist strains of anti-Semitism, the presence of so many Jews so close to the seat of power aroused the ire of America's many anti-Semites. According to Kevin Schultz: 'Between 1933 and 1941, more than one hundred antisemitic groups were founded nationwide.'[135] By the late 1930s, the towering figure among this motley band of hate-mongers was the Catholic radio priest and demagogue Charles E. Coughlin, whose 'Christian Front' organisation, routine attacks on Roosevelt's 'Jew Deal' and pro-fascist views led to his forced retirement from public life following the outbreak of war.[136] However, and as Martin E. Marty has pointed out, it was no mean achievement for Coughlin, as a Catholic priest, to conjure a popular following of 'Protestant and Catholic malcontents who together hoped for better days'.[137] Whatever else, Coughlin's high-profile career fuelled a wider climate of public opinion in which anti-Semitic attitudes were rife. Whereas a majority of Americans claimed they could endorse a Catholic candidate for the presidency by the late 1930s, this was not the case with a Jewish alternative; when asked by AIPO pollsters in 1937 whether they could 'vote for a Jew for President who was well qualified for the position', 51 per cent of respondents flatly said no.[138] The following year, in another AIPO poll, 58 per cent of those questioned stated that the persecution of Jews in Europe had been 'partly' or 'entirely' their own fault.[139] Nor did the outbreak of war serve to moderate attitudes in the short term. In July 1942, the Office of Public Opinion Research found that 44 per cent of Americans thought that 'the Jews have too much power and influence in this country'[140] and, at the end of 1943, one-third of all respondents in an AIPO poll still thought that the president had appointed 'too many' Jews to 'jobs in Washington'.[141]

Nevertheless, amidst the clamour of tribal and sectarian enmities, a new kind of inter-confessional alliance was emerging in interwar America, one that in the long term was to have a transformative effect on American public life. Originating in the early years of the 1920s, the National Conference of Christians and Jews (NCCJ), as it had become by 1938, was the flagship organisation of a growing Goodwill Movement that arose out of mutual recognition of the evil effects of internecine religious strife. A conscious reaction to the Klan's aggressive bid to maintain 'Native, white, Protestant supremacy',[142] the Goodwill Movement built on a spirit of cooperation that had been fostered on a local and a national level, especially among army chaplains and other Americans during World War I. Significantly, Everett R. Clinchy, the first president of the NCCJ, was a Presbyterian minister and a veteran of the Western Front, while Newton D. Baker, its first Protestant co-chairman, was an Episcopalian and a Secretary of War under Woodrow Wilson.[143] As their example serves to illustrate, the initial impetus for the NCCJ came from liberal Protestants, with the Federal Council of Churches of Christ in America (FCC) establishing a Committee on Good Will after conducting an investigation in 1924 into the question 'What makes a person join the Ku Klux Klan?'[144] Premised on the conviction that it should be truly 'tri-faith' and not merely a cat's paw for enlightened Protestants, and convinced from the outset that ignorance was the seedbed of bigotry, from its inception in 1927 the primary role of the NCCJ was educational.[145] Rapidly emerging as 'the nation's premier goodwill organization',[146] it was co-chaired by Protestant, Catholic and Jewish representatives and was guided by the slogan 'the brotherhood of man under the Fatherhood of God'.[147] Although the NCCJ did not stand for shared worship, the growth and cooperation it achieved was remarkable enough in the context of the Depression and its tensions, while its repudiation of Protestant hegemony was sufficiently radical to seem as if 'the liberal Protestant establishment was turning over the keys to its own castle, and doing so in order to fulfill its own highest ideals and aspirations'.[148] Under the guidance of Everett R. Clinchy, who had been appalled and inspired in equal measure by the proselytising zeal of Hitler's Stormtroopers,[149] from 1933 the principal ambassadors of the NCCJ were its so-called 'Tolerance Trios' composed of Catholics, Protestants and Jews who criss-crossed America holding public '"trialogues" to discuss religious stereotypes, obstacles to cooperation, and the need for unity in the light of current affairs'.[150] Such was the success of this approach that, by 1939, the NCCJ could claim that its trios had presided 'at ten thousand meetings in two thousand communities in all forty-eight states' in the space of a single year.[151] To complement these efforts, in 1934 the NCCJ established the Religious News Service, which by 1939 was not only circulating 'tri-faith' material to scores of newspapers and radio stations across America but was also scripting its own weekly radio show.[152]

Given the persistence of American anti-Semitism, and the stimulus it derived from the growth of anti-Semitism in Europe, at the heart of the NCCJ's efforts – and those of the Goodwill Movement as a whole – was an appeal to America's 'Judeo-Christian' identity, a new vision of national selfhood that was implicitly anti-fascist and was deployed in opposition to the narrowly 'Christian' identity of many anti-Semitic groups, and not least Coughlin's Christian Front.[153] Although the NCCJ was simply 'a private interfaith organization' on the eve of World War II, its efforts played a major role in shaping the religious identity of wartime America and in building a general consensus that: 'The religion of American democracy was "Judeo-Christian".[154] In 1942, for example, it issued a much-trumpeted, jointly authored 'Declaration of Fundamental Religious Beliefs Held in Common by Catholics, Protestants, and Jews', which majored on their shared monotheism and on the moral and democratic implications of their fundamental brotherhood.[155] Emblematic of the NCCJ's success in this regard was the growing appeal of its Brotherhood Week, which had commenced in 1934 as Brotherhood Day, and which had been aligned with George Washington's birthday in 1935 in order to link 'the ideal of brotherhood to that of good Americanism'.[156] Although this week of celebratory, tri-faith meetings and activities had been marked more modestly in 1941, 'After Pearl Harbor, Brotherhood Week became a national event.'[157] Brotherhood Week 1942 saw meetings and media coverage increase by 50 per cent, and in 1943 President Roosevelt acted as its honorary chairman, reminding Americans 'that all men are children of one Father and brothers in the human family'.[158] Consequently, their new Judeo-Christian identity was rapidly internalised by many Americans and, in Matthew S. Hedstrom's words: 'The notion of a shared Judeo-Christian national identity met with such widespread acceptance that it quickly became a defining feature of American public life in the war and postwar years.'[159]

Despite its deeper theological anomalies,[160] part of the appeal of the new message of 'Judeo-Christianity' was that it meshed so well with the imperatives and idiom of American 'civil religion', especially when the crisis of war called so strongly for national unity. Although contested since 1967, when Robert Bellah popularised the term in a seminal essay,[161] American civil religion (or 'civic piety, religious nationalism, public religion, the common faith, and theistic humanism' as it has been alternatively labelled)[162] provides a divine justification for the ordering of American society and for the goals and conduct of the nation, representing the state's appropriation of national religiosity for its own purposes.[163] Appealing, in a historically Christian society, to biblical motifs (such as that of the Promised Land), theological themes (such as sacrificial death and redemption), and to a sense of ultimate dependence on divine providence, American civil religion has developed its own corpus of sacred texts (including the Declaration of Independence, the Constitution and the Gettysburg Address), its own saints (notably George Washington and Abraham Lincoln), its own rituals (such as congressional prayers and saluting the flag) and its own calendar feasts (for example, Memorial Day and Thanksgiving).[164] Aiming always to find a common religious basis for national life, the growing religious diversity of American society has ensured that the basis of American civil religion has progressed from 'evangelical consensus to Protestantism-in-general, to Christianity-in-general, to the Judeo-Christian tradition, and finally to deism-in-general'.[165] Furthermore, and in a constitutional context in which church and state are notionally separate, American civil religion has helped to reduce the scope for friction between a rigorist interpretation of constitutional norms and a believing society, underpinning a *'collaboration and cooperation'* model of disestablishment that conceives 'church and state as parallel institutions, institutionally independent of one another, but cooperating to accomplish shared goals'. Within such a context, congressional and military chaplaincy has been able to survive, and 'In God we trust' emblazoned on the nation's currency.[166]

It is easy to see how readily the 'Judeo-Christian' concept of national identity was harnessed and internalised by the formative forces of American civil religion in the era of World War II. One of the chief agencies in this process was, of course, the presidency itself, which had played a key role in shaping this national cultus, supplying much of its pantheon and many of its canonical texts. In the era of World War II, the presidency was filled by a particularly gifted archpriest in the form of the affable, communicative (and even suitably afflicted) Franklin Delano Roosevelt. A man of profound personal faith, Roosevelt's Christianity had been shaped in the elite but socially responsible environment of Groton, an Episcopalian boarding school founded by his friend and clerical mentor Endicott Peabody, whom he would fondly cite in his last inaugural address. A vestryman and senior warden at St James's Episcopal Church in Hyde Park, even holding the latter office throughout his presidency, Roosevelt was tellingly described by one of his sons as 'a frustrated clergyman at heart', being keen to lead religious services whenever the opportunity arose. In 1942, Winston Churchill even twitted him as a prospective Archbishop of Canterbury. Even so, Roosevelt's faith was tolerant, ethical and eminently practical, being very much that of the Christian gentleman so admired in the 'Anglo' patrician milieu in which he was raised, and one that would have been instantly recognisable among his aristocratic peers in Britain. In keeping with his background and education Roosevelt was thoroughly versed in the Bible, which informed much of his political rhetoric. He had a profound belief in providence and the power of prayer, and prized practical action and the imperatives of the Social Gospel over the dictates of doctrinal orthodoxy. He also defied some of the shibboleths of puritan, Protestant America by openly smoking, opposing Prohibition, taking a light view of the Sabbath, and appearing to indulge his children's divorces (his ongoing affair with Lucy Mercer was not public knowledge).[167]

Given his position, outlook and temperament, his exploitation of the radio, and an electoral base that embraced evangelical Southerners as well as Catholics and Jews, Roosevelt was ideally placed to champion the new, more inclusive form of 'Judeo-Christian' civil religion. Besides endorsing Brotherhood Week in 1943, he also ensured that the principal welfare organisations of America's three main religious traditions worked together for American service personnel under the umbrella of the United Services Organization.[168] As president, Roosevelt also sought to cultivate a broad range of clerical support; in 1935, for example, he issued a 'Letter to the Clergy of America' to 120,000 'representative clergymen', which sought their 'counsel and advice' on matters such as social security, public works and the state of local communities.[169] In terms of significant churchmen, Roosevelt was on first-name terms with Cardinal Mundelein of Chicago ('they called each other "Frank" and "George"') and in 1944 he penned a special Easter reverie on immortality as a favour to the influential *Christian Herald* and its editor, Daniel A. Poling.[170] Despite his own reputation in this respect, Roosevelt was even prepared to stress the importance of churchgoing, declaring in his eminently practical way that: 'Church work and church attendance mean the cultivation of the habit of feeling responsibility for others.'[171] Furthermore, in his trademark 'fireside chats' Roosevelt spoke regularly and non-specifically about prayer and the Almighty. In May 1940, for example, he assured nervous Americans that 'your prayers join with mine – that God will heal the wounds and the hearts of humanity.'[172] In his State of the Union address of January 1941, and while seeking to rally Americans for a possible war with Germany, Roosevelt named freedom of worship (more broadly understood as freedom of religion) as the second of the four freedoms that America sought to uphold, and nine months later issued a dramatic warning against the existential threat posed to religion by Nazi godlessness.[173] In sum, and as Andrew Preston has put it, 'Not since Abraham Lincoln had a president embodied civil religion so naturally', the twelve-year presidency of Franklin Delano Roosevelt effectively 'enshrining religious pluralism at the heart of the national faith.'[174]

Despite its mutations over time, the nation's civil religion both reflected and reinforced the religious influences and concerns that permeated American politics and society. In an article in *The Public Opinion Quarterly* in 1944, Madge M. McKinney challenged the notion that the 1928 presidential election was a sectarian aberration by analysing the religious affiliation of congressmen since 1935, finding that representatives and senators were far more likely to be succeeded by members of their own religion than of their own party: 'The conclusion: a candidate's religious background is more important to the success of his election than is the party which he represents.'[175] McKinney also revealed that: 'According to the best information obtainable, twenty states have elected no representative to either house of the last five Congresses other than those of the Protestant faith.' In addition to the predictable roster of Southern states, these included rural north-eastern states such as Maine, New Hampshire and Vermont. Although Utah was conspicuous in returning only Latter Day Saints, other Protestant denominations were so strong elsewhere that, in the 78th Congress, six of Alabama's nine representatives and both of its senators were Methodists.[176] In the wake of World War II, the Columbia philosopher Herbert Wallace Schneider reflected how religion seemed to infiltrate every corner of public life, regardless of the constitutional separation between church and state:

> Religion is a pervasive institution. It gets mixed up with education, medicine, politics, business, art – there is nothing free from its grasp and grasping. All efforts to fence off certain areas of life from which the churches must 'keep out' have been as futile as similar efforts to curtail government or science. Anything can be done religiously, and nothing is safe from ecclesiastical concern. Gone are the days when the salvation of the soul was a distinct and separate business … religion like government, now, more than in our recent past, affects or seeks to affect the whole of life … it is pervasive, reaching all classes and affecting all our interests and arts.[177]

Harry F. Ward, emeritus professor of Christian ethics at Union Theological Seminary concurred, noting in 1948 how religion lay behind some of the most contentious issues in American politics, such as the continuing presence of Myron Taylor at the Vatican, the subsidy (however indirect) of Catholic parochial schools, and the major political influence wielded by certain religious groups, most notably the Catholic clergy. Furthermore, the abiding influence of the Social Gospel Movement and the precepts of Catholic social teaching also meant that the churches had much to say on social and economic issues.[178]

Undoubtedly, religion continued to affect the lives and outlooks of tens of millions of notionally 'unchurched' Americans.[179] Often governed by narrow membership criteria when compared to Catholics and Jews,[180] Protestant church membership figures tended to disguise the fact that generations of intense and varied evangelistic effort had shaped a society in which the great majority of non-church members formed a great constituency of what FCC luminary H. Paul Douglass dubbed 'popular Protestantism'. As Douglass put it in 1938: 'Popular Protestantism corresponds substantially to the total American population of Protestant antecedents which is not already in the churches.' This often ambient 'popular Protestantism' was key to understanding the nature of American society, producing high levels of church weddings and funerals among 'non-church Protestants', driving 'ritual observances in courts and legislatures' and modulating the ethos and regimen of the nation's public schools.[181] By 1933, and with the sanction of state authorities and school boards, a system of 'released time' for religious instruction was operating in forty-five states; twelve states had sanctioned the reading of the Bible in public schools, eleven on a daily basis; and 'more than half the states in the union' gave 'high school credit for Bible study taken in church schools'.[182] Seven years later, and in defending the legitimacy of religious (though not 'sectarian') influences on the nation's public schools, Luther A. Weigle, dean of Yale's divinity school, could point out that: 'The reading of the Bible in the public schools is now required by statute in eleven states, specifically permitted by law in five states, and generally construed as lawful in twenty states which have no specific legislation on the subject.'[183] As Douglass explained:

> [T]he American people are steeped in an intensely religious tradition, which finds its way into the public schools, whenever it is not definitely prevented, in the form of prayer, hymn-singing, and Scripture-reading. And the virtues which the public schools attempt to inculcate are Christian virtues, conceived in conventional Protestant forms.[184]

Weigle agreed: 'The common religious faith of the American people, as distinguished from the sectarian forms in which it is organized, may rightfully be assumed and find appropriate expression in the life and work of the public schools.' [185]

Besides this generically Protestant influence on the public school system, Douglass stressed that 'virtually every non-church member acknowledges a certain attachment to some religious faith. This is well established both by official census questions and by representative house-to-house surveys.' Furthermore, 'nearly every one who is Protestant by antecedent also identifies himself as having some inner attachment to a particular sect or denomination.'[186] In explaining this situation, and besides mere 'antecedence', Douglass emphasised the penumbra of participants and outliers in normal congregational life:

> In a secondary sense membership is augmented by Sunday School pupils, persons enrolled in subsidiary societies and groups, and pledged financial supporters. Beyond these is the unidentified group 'under pastoral care', including the church's clients and dependents as well as sponsored groups such as the Boy Scouts and the various other clubs, which are in the church rather than of it.[187]

In view of this situation, Silcox and Fisher observed in 1934 that, 'To discover the potential constituency of any Protestant denomination, American church statisticians usually multiply the reported membership by 2.7', but even multipliers of 3.1 and 4.5 could be justified under certain conditions.[188] In fact, and despite a perceptible decline in church and Sunday school attendance, given the variety of many church programmes, the widespread use of church properties for fairly non-religious purposes, and large congregations at Christmas and Easter, Douglass claimed that American Protestants were crossing the thresholds of their churches more frequently than at any point in the past.[189]

As Douglass saw it, the great bulk of the nation's 'unchurched' represented 'a

Protestant community existing on the level of inherited traditions', one that was marked by 'limited institutionalization' but whose beliefs were not substantially different from those Protestants who were church members: 'The main difference is not located in the realm of faith, but relates merely to a more or less definite and fixed expression in institutional form.'[190] In terms of personal faith, and as far as both groups were concerned: 'The ethical aspects of religion appear, on the whole, to survive better than its theological formulations.'[191] Citing Douglass's study a decade later, William W. Sweet, professor of the history of American Christianity at the University of Chicago, said of the beliefs and attitudes of America's 'popular Protestants':

> [T]hey were exposed to some kind of religious influence in their childhood, have little real religious knowledge, but do have a kind of inarticulate religious faith; in a general way they believe in God and immortality, and in time of extreme emergencies they take to prayer; but they have no notion of the vital concepts of Christianity. Often these people are critical of the church – perhaps as a defense mechanism to uphold their failure to support it in any material way. They nevertheless call upon the clergy to perform weddings and conduct funerals, and many of them are careful to have their children christened ... unchurched Protestants are as a whole conservative, have more sympathy for fundamentalism than modernism, and are not slow to express their disapproval of what they would term 'new-fangled ideas' which tend to discredit their inherited prejudices. Often, too, anti-Catholic feeling is strong among them.[192]

In surveying the often hidden strengths of American Protestantism, Douglass could hardly ignore its sectional dimension, writing that: 'From the viewpoint of the country as a whole, modernity is very unequally distributed. Regionalism dominates the religious climate, and the "Bible Belt" is more than an ungracious figure of speech.'[193] However, the poor, largely rural and overwhelmingly evangelical South, still home to almost one-third of Americans in 1940, was the cause of great perplexity to Northern, liberal churchmen – a perplexity that the Scopes trial, Jim Crow, and historic sectional schisms among Methodists, Baptists and Presbyterians did nothing to remedy. As the historian John B. Boles wrote: 'In religion, as in other matters, the South has, at times, seemed to be another world from the nation as a whole.'[194] In analysing the correlation of religion and class in mid-century America, Yale academic Liston Pope complained that the Southern data served only to skew a national picture that was otherwise crystal clear:

> The South is overwhelmingly Protestant, and the ratio of church membership to population is higher there than in any other region.... The South is also notoriously poor in comparison with other regions, and has propor-

tionately smaller middle and upper classes. Gross inclusion of its figures in national studies therefore results in considerable distortion of the picture for other regions of the country.[195]

However, this was but a minor illustration of the persistent problematisation of the Protestant South, a common phenomenon among outsiders by the interwar years. Although Southerners (white as well as black) were 'active churchgoers', generations of 'an imagined divide' between Northerners and Southerners stretching back to the antebellum period had created a situation wherein: 'Northern cultural modernists configured their progressive beliefs as the polar opposite of southern evangelical Protestantism in order to draw a clear line between two American "worlds."'[196] As Colleen McDannell has pointed out, by the 1930s such was 'the "problem" of southern Protestantism' (its perceived deficiencies including wilful ignorance, emotional excess, moral hypocrisy and social inertia) that 'when the Atlanta reporter Margaret Mitchell decided to write a Civil War novel about a South filled with honor, character, strength, and beauty, she made her heroine a Catholic', thus presenting the beguiling picture of 'a romantic and heroic South without the Gospel.'[197]

Other salient features of American religious life were the predominance of women as active participants and the centrality of the home in religious nurture.[198] According to the findings of the 1936 Census of Religious Bodies, there were, on average, 'five women members for each four men', a pattern that held true in both rural and urban congregations.[199] Although membership did not necessarily equate with churchgoing, of the nation's twenty-six largest denominations all reported a greater proportion of female members than male. However, the ratio varied considerably between denominations. Among Mormons, the balance was almost equal and, among those with an inclusive view of membership, the disparity could be relatively slight, the Catholics reporting more than ninety male members for every hundred female, a pattern that was broadly true of several Lutheran bodies.[200] However, the situation was different in more gathered, mainstream denominations. For example, among Northern Presbyterians, Baptists and Methodists there were just under seventy male members for every hundred female members (in contrast, the comparative figure for their Southern counterparts was over seventy). Significantly, male membership of black churches lagged even further behind, with black Baptists having just over sixty male members per hundred female, and three Methodist denominations counting sixty or fewer.[201] However, it must be emphasised that the incidence of church membership among African American women was especially high, being estimated in 1933 at '73 percent of all colored women living in the United States', whereas membership among white women was 62 per cent. Moreover, there was a pronounced upward trend in church membership among African American men, rising from 39 per cent in 1906 to 46 per cent by 1926.[202]

The clear female ascendancy in the formal membership of America's churches had much to do with the comparative freedom that church participation could bestow upon women, especially in terms of their own organisations and institutions.[203] While the Protestant churches had served as a springboard for the Women's Christian Temperance Union, 'nuns were the backbone of Catholic institutions' (staffing Catholic elementary schools for 'a mere pittance' of 'often no more than $25 a month *per sister*' in the 1930s) and women were the main supporters and representatives of the Protestant missionary effort overseas.[204] Even at a local level, the dominance of women could be striking. As observed of African American women in Chicago's South Side in 1942: 'There is practically no associational life among lower class men, while lower class women of the respectable type find their most satisfying associational contacts in church clubs.'[205]

However, the predominance of women was also a function of traditional gender roles within the family, with mothers acting as principals in what was aptly described as 'the first school of religious training.'[206] Apart from ensuring a measure of religious instruction and devotion, to say nothing of attendance at public worship, the centrality of the family in this respect was instanced in the friction that religion could cause inside the family circle. In 1937, a revealing study of 'interfaith marriages' showed that 'far more of the conflicts were based on religious than on nonreligious factors, and were usually centred in the religious upbringing of the children.' Significantly, these problems were almost as common in 'cases where both husband and wife claimed to be indifferent to religion' as they were 'where either or both classed themselves as moderately religious or even devout.'[207] Quite apart from the rancour that religious difference could cause in mixed marriages (the wisdom of which was conventionally doubted, and which remained a minority phenomenon)[208] the family in general seemed to be failing in its essential duty of religious nurture. As early as 1933, a presidential Research Committee on Social Trends remarked that 'Religious observances within the home are said to be declining,'[209] an authoritative study indicating that only '1 in 8 white American born school children' participated in family prayers, that only one-fifth of rural white children and one-tenth of city children were exposed to family Bible-reading, and that 'Grace at meals was the practice in 30 percent of the samples from the large city and in 38 percent from the rural areas.'[210] As far as Ray E. Baber, professor of sociology at Pomona College, Claremont, could tell in 1948, domestic piety was still on the wane: 'Today the custom of family worship, formerly common in Christian homes, is comparatively rare, and even saying grace at meals, though still rather widespread, is declining. These are but two indications, within the family, of the broad process of secularization that has been so evident in recent years.'[211] Furthermore, so Baber went on, 'Formal religious instruction of the young, a function for which the home was responsible to a considerable extent in earlier days, is now delegated almost entirely to religious organizations', with the result that Protestant children, reliant on the vagaries of

Sunday school education, were largely 'illiterate in religion.'[212] The only hope, as Baber saw it in the immediate aftermath of World War II, was a renewal of the natural alliance between church and family, one that would see parents lead by example and lend their support to the church as one of 'the various character-building institutions and organizations in their community.'[213]

If the family seemed to be faltering as a natural ally of the churches, the situation in the media gave further cause for concern. Alighting upon a pattern discerned by the presidential Research Committee on Social Trends five years earlier,[214] in 1938 H. Paul Douglass registered an increasingly secular drift in the content of mainstream periodicals, especially of the more highbrow kind, lamenting that: 'The sensational periodicals … are the best supporters of conventional religion. A magazine's orthodoxy is about in proportion to its unworthiness to exist at all!'[215] Not that public interest in religion had lessened, necessarily. As Douglass went on:

> There appears to be more mention of God in periodical literature than formerly – but more skepticism about Him. A less personal conception of Deity prevails. Interest in life after death appears to have declined … Attitude toward 'open-minded' religion, which approves of science as an ally to the religious quest, has become more frequent, along with decreased liking for creed, dogma, and authority. Even in the intellectual magazines religion of this liberal type is approved in two-thirds of the references.[216]

Furthermore, in the 1930s the religious press appeared to be fighting a losing battle with the economic Depression and more secular interests. According to the Census of Manufacturers, in 1929 1,436 denominational periodicals had an aggregate circulation of 41,629,000; ten years later, this list of titles had shrunk by nearly one-quarter, and their circulation by almost a million.[217] Significantly, market share was also in decline, as the fate of the *Christian Herald*, 'the most widely circulated Protestant news and general interest magazine of the early twentieth century,'[218] served to illustrate. Alfred McClung Lee, professor of sociology at Wayne University, Detroit, observed in 1948 that:

> The interdenominational *Christian Herald* (monthly, 324,000), once one of the country's prominent magazines and advertising mediums, ranked thirty-third among all United States publications in circulation in 1915, but it sank to forty-third in 1925 and seventy-first in 1940. It is not so much that it has failed to grow but that it has not grown nearly so fast as the huge secular publications.[219]

By 1948, Lee could estimate that 'rather than reaching three-fourths of America's reading public as it did a century ago, the church press's impact – in terms of copies published – is now probably somewhere near one-tenth that of the secular daily press.'[220]

In Lee's view at least, the decline of the church press helped to prompt the churches' scramble for access to other media, as well as designs on the nation's public schools: 'This decreased proportion of printed impact is one reason church spokesmen try to penetrate more effectively the great mass audiences of the secular press and radio, motion pictures and public schools.'[221] While a raft of public relations departments, information departments and news agencies (such as the NCCJ's Religious News Service and the International Council of Religious Education's Department of Public Relations) kept the secular press supplied with a regular diet of religious news items,[222] in the 1930s the 'new evangelising tool'[223] of religious broadcasting seemed the most potent weapon in the churches' media arsenal. By 1935, Americans owned eighteen million radio sets, a number that had risen to forty-four million by 1939, representing 'coverage of 86 percent of all American households'.[224] Naturally, this growth gave rise to religious radio stars of national stature, such as the 'radio menace' Charles E. Coughlin, whose *Golden Ho*ur commanded 'the biggest radio audience in the country' by 1932, and, less controversially, Fulton J. Sheen, 'the embodiment of Christian proclamation', who starred on NBC's *Catholic Hour* from 1930.[225] Although there were seven Catholic radio stations by 1933, plus 'broadcasts of Catholic programs over commercial stations in many dioceses',[226] it was America's fundamentalists who appear to have made the most effective use of radio in the interwar period, 'one of the paradoxes of fundamentalism [being] that this militantly antimodernist movement eagerly assimilated the latest techniques of mass communication ... in order to propagate their old-time faith'.[227] As early as 1923, barely three years after the advent of regular radio broadcasting in the United States, fundamentalist radio stations were operating in New York and Los Angeles.[228] Elsewhere, the mushroom growth of local radio stations gave fundamentalists the opportunity to purchase air time and the scope to develop more attractive styles of religious programming. Despite the regulatory activities of the Federal Radio Commission from 1927, and their marginalisation by NBC and CBS (which opted to give free air time to Catholics, Jews and mainline Protestants for more irenic broadcasts) fundamentalists' exploitation of the airwaves continued throughout the 1930s, their greatest success being Charles E. Fuller's *Old Fashioned Revival Hour.* Through the shared programming of the Mutual Broadcasting System, by 1939 this folksy presentation of the undiluted gospel was being carried by 152 stations to an audience of as many as twenty million.[229]

Nevertheless, the impact of religious broadcasting on the nation at large should not be overstated; in 1938, James M. Gillis, a Catholic priest and broadcaster, stressed that effective preaching was still very much an interactive ministry. Furthermore, the sensibilities of those controlling 'the great radio systems' rendered their religious broadcasting distinctly anodyne ('You are a good fellow, and I am a good fellow and all the world is a good fellow') and that the listener could, in any case, be simply 'lolling half-dressed on a couch, his attention diverted by the family chit-chat or the Sunday supplement'. Consequently, Gillis maintained that 'broadcasting a sermon in most cases lessens its effect by half'.[230] In 1930, a trade survey conducted on behalf of NBC illustrated the patchy appeal of the message in this medium:

> Various classes of families were asked to state their preferences for the different types of programs; and 48 percent of the farmer families, 36 percent of the town families, 35 percent of those in small cities and 27 percent of those in large cities mentioned the religious services among their first five choices. The religious services ranked third in popularity among farmer families, but in towns they held seventh place, in small cities sixth place, and in large cities eighth place.[231]

Clearly, the interwar years were unsettled times for American religion. Mainline Protestantism stood embattled on several fronts, and a sectarian spirit was abroad among white and black Protestants alike, a spirit that thrived in the deprivation and dislocation of the Depression years. Although American Catholics were growing in number, they were mainly confined to their urban citadels and to the margins of American society, as underlined by the experience of Al Smith in 1928. Ethnically, religiously and politically divided, American Jewry was exposed to strong secularising tendencies from the inside, as well as to the widespread hostility of gentile society. While the Roosevelt administration and the growing Goodwill Movement represented steps towards a new, tri-faith America, the bedrock Protestantism of American society remained, albeit in a suitably passive form. Nevertheless, the place of religion in the American family, and in wider American culture, seemed in decline, a decline that could not simply be arrested by the exploitation of new media such as the radio. As early as 1933, President Hoover's Research Committee on Social Trends acknowledged that the past two decades had seen 'great religious uncertainty, a period in which old standards and attitudes have been very considerably modified'.[232] Viewing the interwar years as a whole, Colleen McDannell has been inclined to see them in more pessimistic terms:

> The fragmentation of Protestantism and Judaism in the early twentieth century both diversified religious observance and opened up a space for quiet absence from religious practices. Some Americans did not merely switch churches; they stopped going to church entirely. While it had always been acceptable for men of certain classes, especially young men, not to be involved in a religious organization, by the twenties many more Americans could count themselves among the unchurched. The rise of mass enter-

tainment, the legitimization of leisure activities on Sunday, the establishment of an anticlerical Marxian socialism, the popularization of Freud, and the public acceptance of agnostic intellectuals all contributed to the social acceptance of skipping church on Sunday or forgoing prayers on Sabbath. Americans may have still said that they were Methodist or Presbyterian, but this said more about their parents than about themselves.[233]

However varied minority fortunes may have been, by the late 1930s the general outlook seemed unambiguous. In a poll undertaken for *Fortune* magazine in January 1937, 49.9 per cent of respondents – by far the largest category – thought that religion was 'losing influence in the life of the nation'.[234] When asked by AIPO pollsters in February 1939 whether they went to church more or less often than their parents, 50 per cent of Americans answered less.[235] And the trend continued; national church attendance fell to a low of 37 per cent in November 1940, down four percentage points in less than two years.[236] Nor did the new and vaunted power of religious broadcasting stem the decline. In February 1939 only 31 per cent of Americans claimed to have listened 'to any church services on the radio last Sunday'; presumably, most of these were churchgoers anyway, as only 5 per cent of non-attenders even mentioned the radio as their main Sunday diversion.[237]

Then, on 7 December 1941, came the Japanese attack on Pearl Harbor, and, four days later, declarations of war by Germany and Italy. As we shall see in Chapter One, the outbreak of World War II in Europe in September 1939, and the growing threat of Hitler's Germany, especially after the fall of France in June 1940, fuelled impassioned debate between Christian pacifists and Christian realists in the United States, a controversy that compounded the many problems of the Protestant mainline. As Ray H. Abrams, one of the most influential pacifist writers of the interwar period, conceded in 1948: 'the churches and the clergy were hopelessly divided in their attitudes toward the war in Europe ... Clergymen had a perfect field day in writing letters and engaging in endless discussions over finespun theological questions about religion and war.'[238] With the pacifist, non-interventionist position associated with *The Christian Century* and its long-time editor Charles Clayton Morrison, the depth of the schism became clear when Reinhold Niebuhr, a Morrison protégé and thoroughly disillusioned liberal, decamped to found a rival periodical, the interventionist *Christianity and Crisis*, in February 1941.[239] However, the shock of Pearl Harbor abruptly ended 'the great debate' and largely dispelled the pacifist and isolationist doubts of America and its churches. Charles F. Zummach, a Northern Baptist minister, reflected:

Over night the whole temper of our people changed. Never did a people, or a nation, rally with such swiftness and such determination to the challenge and responsibility that confronted them. Our young men volunteered by the thousands; others were called to the colors by their draft boards. Pictures and stories of chaplains and young men from our churches began to appear in our denominational periodicals.[240]

For all the strength and resolve of pre-war pacifism, Congress voted to declare war against Japan on 8 December 1941 with only a single dissenting vote, that of representative Jeanette Rankin of Montana. In contrast, six senators and fifty representatives, including Rankin, had voted against war with Germany in April 1917.[241] Hansel H. Tower, a Methodist minister and navy chaplain, mused that: 'This is one of the paradoxes of American life. In many instances the same people and organizations who hold pacifist meetings in peace, wave flags and make fighting speeches in war' – a fact that did not escape the critical attention of his marine flock.[242] Despite the 'remarkable strength' of the interwar peace movement and the wider grounds afforded for conscientious objection in World War II,[243] the process of conscription produced only 100,000 or so conscientious objectors – a mere 'third of one per cent of those registered for the draft', and barely a higher proportion than in World War I.[244] Overall, very few draftees from the mainline churches chose to undertake Civilian Public Service,[245] let alone join the 6,500 'absolutists' who ended up in prison, three-quarters of them Jehovah's Witnesses who claimed ministerial exemption from the draft. In fact, such was the combative mood of the times that even a majority of Quaker, Mennonite and Church of the Brethren draftees – all adherents of the so-called 'Historic Peace Churches' – opted to serve in the armed forces.[246]

If the outbreak of war exposed the transience of a national mood, then it also served to re-energise American religious life. There was, in fact, a curious symmetry to the nation's war, beginning and ending on the Christian Sabbath in Hawaii and Japan. The stunning news of Pearl Harbor carried an extra sting as it shattered the tranquillity of an ordinary Sunday, breaking across America as millions went about their Sunday observance.[247] As Iona Connolly, a future Women's Army Auxiliary Corps (WAAC) from Chadron, Nebraska, remembered:

> On the morning of December 7, 1941, I was teaching Sunday school to a class of girls at the Congregational church. We came home from church, turned on the radio, and heard the news of the attack on Pearl Harbor. It was shocking. In fact, it was just about as unbelievable as the tragic attack on America on September 11, 2001.[248]

Further east, the news came as an even greater blow to Charles Edward Lunn, pastor of the First Baptist Church of Coatesville, Pennsylvania, as he contemplated that morning's sermon:

What could I say? I had advocated peace and had said that there could be no more wars. I was faced now with war's stern reality. I listened to the reports on the radio right up to church time. I could find no answer within myself so I went to my study and turned in prayer for strength and help.[249]

Nevertheless, it was on another Lord's Day, at least in Japan, that the aggressor was finally brought to book with the signing of Japan's instrument of surrender in Tokyo Bay on 2 September 1945.[250]

Together, personal conviction, the churches' general support for the war, and America's civil religion helped to ensure that the national war effort was infused with a sense of righteous purpose and dependency on God, a sense that demanded a corresponding degree of personal rectitude. As Paul Fussell complained: 'Given the wartime requirements of elevated morality, it was not hard (for Americans, at least) to understand the war as virtually a religious operation ... Wartime was a moment when everyone felt obliged to instruct others in ethics.'[251] However, this moral and religious earnestness fed much more than sermonising platitudes. Significantly, and despite the huge dislocation and mass migrations generated by the war (almost one-quarter of American civilians relocated to another county, and eight million Americans 'moved permanently to another state'),[252] World War II saw an end to an almost stagnant pattern of overall church growth. According to the biennial *Yearbook of American Churches*, in the decade 1930–40 the growth in total church membership – a constant of American religious life since at least 1890[253] – barely kept pace with that of the population at large, standing at 7.86 per cent as opposed to 7.2 per cent.[254] However, and whereas the population had grown by 9.1 per cent since 1930, by 1941–42 it was estimated that total church membership had risen by a much greater rate, 12.9 per cent. Furthermore, and with a church membership of 67,327,719 out of an estimated population of 133,952,672, by then 'The total reported for church membership was 50.3 per cent of the total population ... the highest proportion ever reported.'[255] By 1943–44, this proportion had risen still further to 52.5 per cent.[256] Analysing pre and post-war patterns of religious affiliation for the *Annals of the American Academy of Political and Social Science* in 1948, Liston Pope concluded that 'all the major religious bodies in the United States now draw a far higher percentage of their members from the lower class than they did before World War II'.[257] While this hinted at a broad pattern of newly affluent Americans returning to the churches under the stimulus of war, Catholicism continued its steady growth. In 1943, the weekly forces' magazine *Yank* reported that: 'The Catholic census for the United States, Alaska and Hawaii has increased 389,005, according to the official Catholic directory.... Of the 97 American Dioceses, 39 are unchanged, with a slight increase in 27 and substantial gain in 51, including 86,905 converts.'[258] Nonetheless, it was clear that even mainline Protestantism was recovering well. In 1944, for example, the Protestant Episcopal Church could report a gain of more than 11,000 communicants in only twelve months.[259] Likewise, the Presbyterian Church (USA) reported 'The largest annual net membership increase during nearly a quarter of a century, and the largest total membership during the 238 years of organized Presbyterianism in this country', with 93,560 new 'church members received during the year on profession of their Christian faith'.[260] Similarly, the Congregational-Christian Churches had an infusion of 20,000 new members in 1944, producing 'the largest net gain in 20 years'.[261] Despite this mainline revival, fundamentalism had lost none of its growing appeal, with Charles E. Fuller's *Old Fashioned Revival Hour* being carried by 456 radio stations in 1942 and enjoying 'the largest audience in national network radio'.[262] In addition to Fuller's continuing success, 1943–44 saw the advent of the Youth for Christ Movement, whose slick presentation of the old-time gospel in the trappings of the contemporary entertainment industry issued in hundreds of rallies across the United States and represented 'the first sign that the revival of revivalism, which had been percolating deep within the fundamentalist movement, was finally breaking out into public view'.[263]

Furthermore, and despite the disruptions and displacements of war, church-going was very much in vogue on the home front. In an illustration of tri-faith solidarity, and of the kind of admonition that so irked Paul Fussell, in 1944 the Jewish entertainer and radio star Eddie Cantor counselled his audience:

> Every single one of us needs refuge of one kind or another, and I know of no better place to go than the church. You know, the church must be a very strong and righteous thing – for it has survived every enemy it ever had.... And the book which embodies the principles of the church – the Bible – is still at the top of the best-seller list. We are extremely fortunate to live in a country where we can worship as we please, when we please. Let's make the most of that blessing. Go to church, whatever your race or creed. You'll meet old friends and make new ones.... The greatest calamity that can befall a people is the loss of religion. Don't let it happen here. **Go to church**.[264]

Significantly, busy civilian corporations and war plants were keen to be seen to be getting their priorities right. Following the lead of the military, by 1943 civilian chaplains had been engaged by Lockheed, in the Kaiser shipyards, and by several other companies, a pattern that was thought to herald 'a new trend in industrial relations'.[265] By the end of 1944, and at the Kaiser shipyard at Swan Island, Portland, Sunday religious services could be held for eleven thousand employees 'without interfering with production'.[266] These obligations were also met at the very heart of the nation's war effort. Easter 1943, for example, saw Washington DC awash with public piety:

> Holy Week and Easter Sunday received more attention than they have been given in a long time, if ever before, in the national capital. Religious services

for 30,000 workers in the giant Pentagon Building were held throughout the week, conducted by chaplains of the various faiths. And Easter services were held this year for the first time on the steps of the United States capitol; Capt. Robert D. Workman, chief of Navy chaplains, preached.[267]

In September 1944, Jewish, Episcopalian and Lutheran panellists on Chicago-based WGN's Northwestern University Reviewing Stand all agreed that 'church attendance has greatly increased since the war began', but were uncertain about its long-term significance.[268] However, in Cleveland, Ohio, a joint press survey found that the lax and indifferent were very much in a minority by 1945:

> 70.5 per cent of Clevelanders are church members; 92.5 per cent believe the churches are doing a good job in the betterment of the community; 42.5 per cent of the persons questioned attend church regularly; 32.5 per cent occasionally, 14 per cent hardly ever, and 11 per cent not at all.[269]

However, it was not simply a matter of showing up to church or synagogue, for many other indicators also pointed to a deepening of personal religiosity. For example, 1943 was a bumper year for the American Bible Society, it being announced that: 'Distribution of Scriptures by the American Bible Society ... reached a peak of 9,773,651, the highest number in its history. A total of 7,091,430 copies were circulated in the United States, also a record figure. Total distribution was 32 per cent above the previous record set in 1931.'[270] In 1946, an industry-sponsored survey *People and Books: A Study of Reading and Book-Buying Habits* announced that the Bible easily topped the list of titles read by 'active readers, those who read a book within the past month'. Furthermore, its compilers added that:

> Because of the unique place of the Bible among books, the findings of this study are open to question. For example, many people read parts of the Bible in responsive readings in their churches on Sundays. Since this has become a routine occurrence, it may or may not come to mind when people are asked what book they have read last. People who read a verse or a chapter of the Bible as a daily routine may also, when asked about the last book read, fail to include the Bible. Nevertheless, as an indication of the conscious reading of the Bible as a book, the findings of this study have considerable significance.[271]

The public appetite for religious literature was also reflected in a resurgence of the Protestant church press, with calculations based on the *Directory of Newspapers and Periodicals* showing that the circulation of Protestant newspapers and magazines surged from 5.9 million in 1940 to 8.4 million in 1944.[272] Sales of religious books enjoyed an even greater boom, their figures exceeding 'the astounding growth in overall book sales'.[273] Despite the distributive efforts of the ABS and similar agencies, 'Booksellers had trouble keeping Bibles in stock',[274] while Lloyd C. Douglas's novel *The Robe* (1942), whose hero – the Roman tribune Marcellus – wins Christ's garment at the foot of the cross, topped the national bestseller list for eleven months, selling nearly 1.5 million copies in less than two years and becoming one of the greatest successes in American publishing history.[275] As late as 1946, *The Robe* was the fourth most widely read book in America.[276] Coupled with the success of other religious novels such as Franz Werfel's *The Song of Bernadette* (1941), about the nineteenth-century Catholic visionary Bernadette Soubirous, and Sholem Asch's *The Apostle* (1943),[277] a retelling of the life of St Paul (both of which were, significantly, written by Jews), it seemed that the popularity of religious books alone was evidence of a sea change in the nation's religious life. As early as May 1943, a report in the FCC-sponsored forces' magazine *The Link* ran:

> According to the book-sellers' trade journal, *Publishers' Weekly*, religious books are in such demand that publishers are unable to keep up. Denominational book houses report increases from 31 to 110 per cent over a year ago. And in the general publishing field the story is the same. A survey has further revealed that by far the greatest sales are to laymen. The publishers cautiously admit this may be the sign of a 'great revival of religion'.[278]

Hollywood, of course, was also driving and exploiting the changing religious mood. Although the biblical epic was in abeyance, there was plenty of stirring piety on offer at the cinema, both before and after Pearl Harbor. While the exploits of piously belligerent Irish-Americans were celebrated in *The Fighting 69th* (1940), the triumphs of another religious subculture – that of the Protestant South – were acclaimed in *Sergeant York* (1941), this time with the added bonus of a former pacifist seeing the light. While Hollywood did its bit for preparedness before the shock of Pearl Harbor, thereafter it provided Americans with a string of reassuring, Oscar-winning stories of the triumph of steadfast, simple faith in the face of adversity – a unifying trope that lay at the heart of *Mrs. Miniver* (1942), *The Song of Bernadette* (1943), *Going My Way* (1944) and *The Bells of St. Mary's* (1945). Elsewhere, religion was accentuated in more conventional war films such as *Guadalcanal Diary* (1943), *The Fighting Sullivans* (1944) and *God is My Co-Pilot* (1945) – which, despite its title, was based on a book that was actually 'not especially religious'.[279] Even in *Casablanca* (1942), the parting words of Ilsa and Rick were the heartfelt commendation 'God bless you'.[280] Such was the importance of the religious motif in certain films that the government's Office of War Information, charged in part with promoting public understanding of American war aims,[281] pressed Paramount Pictures to include more religious references in *So Proudly We Hail* (1943), a film that depicted the ordeal of army nurses in the fall of the Philippines.[282] Once again, and surveying the situation in March 1944, *The Link* could only marvel at what was unfolding: 'Religion will be getting quite a play on the screen in 1944 if Hollywood carries out its present plans. Every major studio has announced at least one religious picture for the year, and MGM has scheduled four.' With original films such as *The Keys of the Kingdom* in the offing, and even a couple of biblical remakes in prospect, 'Hollywood admits there is a "religious cycle" in the making in filmdom.'[283]

Having dwelt upon the religious milieu from which the subjects of this study were drawn, it is now time to make some pertinent points about the military context in which they operated, and in particular the recruitment, configuration and morale of the US armed forces in World War II. Despite recent measures to increase the size of the army in the interests of hemispheric defence,[284] when war broke out in Europe in September 1939 America's regular army numbered only 190,000 men, an army that was scattered across the continental United States, its territories and possessions and which ranked seventeenth in the world after that of Romania.[285] A reflection of the nation's economic fortunes, its isolationism and its ingrained suspicion of standing armies, this small and poorly equipped force was backed by 200,000 National Guardsmen, the heirs of America's celebrated militia tradition, and around 100,000 barely trained officers of the Organized Reserves.[286] A week after Germany's invasion of Poland, Roosevelt's declaration of a state of limited national emergency paved the way for further enlargement of the regular army and the National Guard, as well as an increase in the size of the navy and the partial mobilisation of its reservists.[287] However, events in Europe, and especially the sudden and dramatic fall of France in June 1940, called for a higher state of readiness. In July, Congress sanctioned a $4 billion naval construction programme aimed at creating a 'two-ocean navy' and, in August, it passed a joint resolution that authorised Roosevelt to call the National Guard and army reservists to active duty for a period of twelve months, a measure that was accompanied by further mobilisation of navy reservists.[288] More controversially, that September the army's chronic shortage of manpower was addressed by the passage of the Selective Training and Service Act. Representing America's first peacetime draft, this allowed the conscription of 900,000 single men for a year's service in the Western hemisphere or in American territories elsewhere. Bitterly opposed in 1940, the draft – and their period of service – was extended in August 1941 by the margin of a single vote in the House of Representatives.[289]

America's entry into the war in December 1941, and the soaring manpower requirements of its armed forces, ensured the survival and expansion of the draft. Ultimately, 61.2 per cent of more than sixteen million armed forces personnel would serve as draftees, the centrality of the draft being confirmed when voluntary enlistments were largely suspended in December 1942.[290] Because the navy, the coast guard and the marines (all operating under the Navy Department) could rely on the voluntary system up to this point, the navy even coining the slogan 'Choose While You Can',[291] the army's reliance on conscripts was especially evident. Whereas almost 40 per cent of the navy's wartime recruits were volunteers,[292] in 1945 around 85 per cent of American soldiers were draftees, a figure that highlights the fact that it was the figure of the more or less unwilling draftee who 'determined [the army's] characteristics and above all its temper'.[293] Implemented by a network of 6,443 local draft boards and 500 appeals boards (the former sending a variable monthly quota of registrants chosen by lot to the armed forces)[294] the system of Selective Service tightened as the war went on. Ultimately, around fifty million men aged between 18 and 64 would register for the draft, but only those aged between 18 and 38 were ever called up. Furthermore – and although exemptions and deferments applied on the grounds of occupation, family circumstances and personal health – medical standards were gradually lowered and certain privileges whittled away, until married men, fathers, illiterates and even criminals were caught in the dragnet of the draft.[295] Despite the friction caused by its mechanics (friction that ranged from resentment at the policies of local boards to the large number of draftees bundled off to induction centres, but who then had to be rejected on medical grounds)[296] the draft succeeded in generating armed forces of unprecedented size. In December 1941 the army, including the Air Corps, mustered 1,657,000, the navy 383,000, the coast guard 28,000 and the marines 75,000; by May 1945, when the army reached its maximum strength, it numbered 8,291,000 and, by August, the navy had grown to 3,408,000, the coast guard to 170,000 and the marines to 486,000.[297]

However, the strategic and operational goals, organisational complexity and logistical requirements of armed forces deployed across much of the world meant that surprisingly few Americans experienced any prolonged fighting. As Allan R. Millett has stressed, America's war effort involved 'projecting military forces across two oceans and thousands of miles into four major theaters of war', namely Europe, the Mediterranean, the South-West Pacific and the Central Pacific.[298] The expeditionary nature of this effort in regions that were already ravaged by war, or simply incapable of sustaining the American military presence, meant that a colossal effort had to be devoted to constructing or developing thousands of overseas bases as well as simply supplying forces in theatre. Furthermore, meeting the material demands of America's machine-heavy armed forces, to say nothing of sustaining their vast consumption of munitions, required a logistical effort of staggering proportions: 'For example, the army estimated that it had to ship 4.5 tons of matériel for each soldier deployed overseas and 1 ton a month thereafter to support him.' The challenge faced by the navy was no less formidable, especially as 'Navy warships, depending on their size, could consume between 200 and 1,000 gallons of oil a day in normal cruising', a situation that in the Pacific demanded the creation of 'mobile supply and floating bases', complete with their own docks and repair ships, and the operations of a vast 'fleet train' of ancillary vessels such as tankers, store ships, ammunition ships and smaller aircraft carriers laden with replacement aircraft.[299] According to one telling calculation, 'the American [army] division and all the troops required to support it in the Second World War numbered 67,201 soldiers, or about a 1:4 ratio between active combatants and support troops.'[300] In the Pacific, the disparity was greater still, it being estimated that the services of eighteen men were required in order to support an ordinary rifleman on the front line.[301] Significantly, such were the logistical nightmares of the far-flung war against Japan, which was 'in many ways a battle against distance,'[302] that, despite the number of personnel allotted to support roles in the army and the navy, heavy use had to be made of indigenous labour, and: 'Throughout the entire war period in the Pacific, there was a shortage of engineer units and, indeed, of service and technical units of all types.'[303]

If the nature of America's war depressed the proportion of front-line personnel in its armed forces, the very definition of combat was open to question. According to the rather overblown claim of the US Navy, 'An estimated 3,639,615 (87%) of Navy Personnel served overseas and in all probability were exposed to combat.'[304] However, combat was a surprisingly subjective concept, and these optimistic figures are not borne out by a 1945 survey of army veterans returning from overseas, which found that only 39 per cent of officers and 37 per cent of enlisted men ever imagined themselves as having been in combat.[305] Consequently, the definition of a combat soldier –which, in earlier wars, would have seemed more of a tautology – was mutable and disputed. In the early stages of the war, it was generally assumed that 'anyone who had been under enemy fire, including long-range shelling and bombing, had been in combat'; however, by war's end, the definition of a combat soldier had been refined considerably, its many gradations meaning that 'full combat credit' could only be safely accorded to front-line infantrymen, tank crews, combat medics and combat engineers.[306] As Gerald F. Linderman has emphasised, prolonged combat was very much a minority experience throughout America's armed forces:

> From a population of 132 million, the military drew into service 16.3 million persons; fewer than 1 million, probably no more than 800,000, took any part in extended combat. In numerous theaters, fighting men composed 10 percent, or less, of the full military complement. Infantrymen, constituting 14 percent of American troops overseas, suffered 70 percent of the casualties.[307]

By the winter of 1944–45, and as a result of the fighting in North-West Europe, it had become painfully clear that, despite its enormous size and elaborate replacement system, the army simply did not have enough infantrymen available. Indeed, flawed casualty forecasts and attrition rates that exceeded 100 and even 200 per cent in many infantry divisions – figures that actually disguised much higher turnovers in their respective rifle companies – required the wholesale transfer and hasty retraining of men from other branches of the service, notably 'quartermaster soldiers and other support troops'.[308] For Orval Eugene Faubus, an infantry officer who castigated the army's naïve faith in the power of its tanks, artillery and aircraft,[309] the ordeal of the ordinary infantryman was uniquely terrible, writing in October 1944:

> Today I could not help but notice, as I have noticed before, the tired, strained faces of the troops as they streamed out from their shell ridden assembly to a mission of battle and death. And I thought that if, in future years, a veteran should say that he was in the war, or relatives should say that they had men in the war, one should find out in what capacity they served. If they served in the [Quartermaster Corps], the Air Corps, the Engineers, the artillery, or any other branch besides the Infantry, give them full credit for what they did. But if you find that a man marched and fought with the Infantry, take off your hat, say him a blessing, and a prayer that he might have a home in heaven for he has already had his share of hell.[310]

Nevertheless, there were comparable experiences in other parts of America's armed forces, perhaps most notably among the marines and the bomber crews of the Army Air Forces (AAF), as the Air Corps became in 1941.[311] Given their speciality in the hazardous ways of amphibious warfare, and the sheer tenacity of Japanese resistance in the Pacific, combat losses among marine units could be extremely high. Nearly six thousand marines died in the capture of Iwo Jima in February–March 1945, for example, with the total casualties amounting to one-third of the marines involved.[312] As Allan R. Millett has emphasised, 'the Marine Corps bled as never before ... That being a Marine in World War II was dangerous is obvious: With less than 5 percent of the American armed forces, the Corps suffered nearly 10 percent of all American battlefield casualties.'[313] However, it was among the 'commuter combatants' of America's bomber crews that casualty levels most closely approximated to those of the infantry.[314] Agents – and, indeed, victims – of the unrealistic confidence placed in the power and precision of the strategic bomber by pre-war enthusiasts at the Air Corps Tactical School in the interwar years,[315] aerial carnage marked the initial stages of America's daylight bombing campaign against Germany and occupied Europe (flying was, in fact, a dangerous enough business without enemy involvement as fifteen thousand American airmen were accidentally killed in World War II 'at training bases in the States and abroad').[316] Symbolised by the operations of the Eighth Air Force, which forayed out of airfields in southern and eastern England, casualties among the Eighth's bomber crews were horrendous. According to Gerald Astor's figures:

A total of 350,000 airmen served with the Eighth Air Force in England, and of this number, 26,000 were killed, or 7.42 percent. Compared to the percentages of the other military branches – U.S. Marines, 3.29 percent, the U.S. Army, 2.25 percent and the Navy .41 percent – the Air Corps sustained the heaviest losses. More airmen with the Eighth Air Force lost their lives than in the entire Marine Corps ... Strictly measuring the mortality rate for the 210,000 *air crewmen* [my italics] the casualty figure soars to 12.38 percent and in addition, 21,000 from the Eighth Air Force wound up in POW camps.[317]

Although some of these computations may be open to question, it is significant that American aircrew, who were all volunteers, often felt sympathy for the cannon fodder in the infantry, who were usually not.[318] However, the deep-penetration raids carried out by the Eighth Air Force on targets such as Ploesti, Regensburg and Schweinfurt in the summer and autumn of 1943 as part of the developing Combined Bomber Offensive, raids that incurred casualty rates of 20 and even 30 per cent, had a telling effect on aircrew morale.[319] In order to sustain their hopes, 1943 saw the introduction of fixed tours of duty for aircrew in the Eighth Air Force, the number of missions to be flown being raised from twenty-five as conditions notionally improved in the summer of 1944.[320] There were also other compensations and safeguards. While civilian fascination with aviation ensured that pilots were lionised as 'leather-jacketed, bescarfed, brave, rollicking hero-adventurers', all aircrew were closely monitored by their flight surgeons for battle fatigue, received a 'Flight Pay' bonus of 50 per cent, and were fourteen times more likely to win medals than were ground combat troops.[321] Still, the hazards of high-altitude combat flying over Hitler's Fortress Europe were always formidable. In addition to enemy flak and fighters, and a lack of immediate medical care for the wounded, the dangers posed by the elements, mechanical failure and simple pilot error ensured that as late as April 1944 'Hap' Arnold, the commander of the AAF, could warn that the prospect of death loomed large for his bomber crews and that 85 per cent of those in the Eighth Air Force would never complete their twenty-five sortie tour of duty.[322]

By most estimates, the navy appears to have escaped most lightly in overall terms, with nearly 63,000 fatalities amounting to roughly 1.5 per cent of those who served.[323] However, here again the dangers of combat at sea cannot be underestimated. Significantly, the proportion of the navy's dead far exceeded that of its wounded, the opposite pattern to that which obtained in the army and the marines.[324] In addition to thousands of naval aviators lost in accidents or at sea,[325] what this betrayed was the catastrophic levels of loss that could be incurred when a submarine or a surface ship foundered. Significantly, 'About 22 per cent of U.S. submariners who made war patrols in World War II failed to return – the highest casualty rate for any branch of service.'[326] In terms of surface ships, nearly 80 per cent of the fifteen hundred crew of the battleship *Arizona* were killed when its forward magazine exploded at Pearl Harbor on 7 December 1941 and, when the light cruiser *Juneau* blew up off Guadalcanal in November 1942, all but ten of its crew of seven hundred were lost, including five brothers of the vaunted 'Fighting Sullivans'. Finally, 70 per cent of the one thousand crew of the heavy cruiser *Indianapolis* perished after it was torpedoed on 30 July 1945, 'the last major warship lost in World War II'.[327] Besides these salutary examples, the ordinary effects of heavy naval ordnance on human flesh – to say nothing of bombs or *kamikaze* strikes – were fearsomely apparent to those who served at sea. As James J. Fahey of the light cruiser *Montpelier* wrote in September 1943:

> Some new men from the States have been assigned to our ship. I was talking to one of them, who was on the cruiser *San Francisco* when it was ripped to shambles by Jap battleships in the Solomons, and he said that after the battle you could walk around the ship and pick up arms, legs, etc. The dead were everywhere.[328]

For those who were potentially trapped below decks (whether to drown, suffocate or incinerate) naval combat was an unnerving experience. As Fahey, who felt himself lucky to be crewing an anti-aircraft gun, averred:

> The fellows down below the waterline never knew when a torpedo would come in on them and drown them like a bunch of rats. We should give plenty of credit to the men who are locked in and cannot see what is going on. They are under a great strain and cannot defend themselves.[329]

Recalling the threat of kamikaze attacks while stationed off Okinawa on the destroyer *Van Valkenburgh* in 1945, Laverne C. Etshman vividly described the miscellaneous, interconnected fears of naval warfare in the Pacific:

> [T]here were a lot of ways that a destroyer person [could die] – you could be hit by the ship or the plane itself. It could land on you or near you and blow you up. If the ship sinks and you happen to be in a locked place as most of our sailors were … fellows that were putting up ammunition or the guys who were running the ship down in the engine rooms … when the ships would sink they would go down with the ship which is a horrible way to go because you're alive, you're entombed in the ship, and you know you're not going to get out. It's just a matter of going down, down, down, and dying as you're going. That's kind of scary. Also I used to worry about being in the ocean, wondering who down there was waiting to nibble on my feet. That was scary too.[330]

In overall terms, therefore, the burden of fighting was unevenly borne by a relatively small minority of America's fighting men in units – or ships – that suffered a disproportionate share of the nation's casualties. Significantly, medical advances since World War I (such as improved casualty evacuation, and the use of penicillin, sulpha-drugs and blood transfusions)[331] greatly curtailed the general risk of dying from disease or from accidents, thereby underlining the particular vulnerability of the front-line combatant. As Allan R. Millett has observed, 'The medical services ... turned a corner in their battle against disease: for the first time the armed forces lost fewer dead (113,842) to disease and accidents than to the enemy (291,557)'.[332] In the army, three times as many soldiers died as a result of battle than from 'nonbattle causes' in the years 1942–45.[333] In overall terms, the result was a remarkably low incidence of mortality – annual death rates in the army amounted to only 12.09 per thousand, slightly over one-third of the mortality rate of the army in World War I, and one that reflected an enormous cut in mortality due to disease (16.47 per thousand per year in World War I, 0.59 in World War II).[334] In terms of the armed forces as a whole, 8.6 per thousand were killed in action, 3.0 died from other causes, and 17.7 received non-fatal wounds.[335] In other words, and despite the terrible sufferings of a few, and the dread expectation that they could also be thrown into the maw of battle, the vast majority of American service men and women emerged from World War II without experiencing any major traumas other than the emotional problems attendant on temporary dislocation, adjustment to military life and enforced separation from loved ones. Apart from the thanks of a grateful nation, their reward came in the form of the Servicemen's Readjustment Act of June 1944, more colloquially known as the 'GI Bill of Rights', or the 'GI Bill', which entitled America's veterans to a raft of benefits and privileges, including grants for education and vocational training; low-interest loans for business, farming and home-buying; and enhanced unemployment benefits. Passed unanimously by Congress, and described as 'the most comprehensive piece of social welfare legislation the United States has ever known', in the long term the various provisions of the GI Bill 'underwrote both prosperity and upward mobility in the postwar era' and helped to create 'one of the most prosperous, advantaged generations in American history'.[336]

While the GI Bill made the exit from military life as painless as possible for the veteran, from the outset the armed forces sought to make the transition to military life as smooth as possible for the recruit. If they served at sea at all, conditions on the navy's newer and larger vessels were fairly comfortable even for ordinary sailors, ample food being complemented by tiered bunks, rather than hammocks, and well-stocked canteens that served candy, soda and ice cream.[337] Anxious for some decades to present a more attractive and wholesome image to the American public, the navy actually prided itself on its ice-cream-making facilities, the availability and popularity of this confection being emblematic of the new value it placed on 'clean living and good fare'.[338] As far as the army was concerned, conditions were largely dictated by the pragmatic and enlightened outlook of its chief of staff, George C. Marshall. Due to his experience of World War I, his familiarity with the army's reserve forces, and his experience with the New Deal's Civilian Conservation Corps,[339] Marshall had a shrewd understanding of the character of America's non-professional soldiers. He was also acutely aware of the likelihood of political and public relations problems arising from this 'army of democracy', being ever conscious of 'the importance of little things to morale' and ruefully recalling that 'you had to feel that all of your soldiers were readers of *Time* magazine'.[340] Still, and as Marshall understood, a great deal was being asked of his overwhelmingly draftee army, men who were drawn from a highly individualistic, democratic and even anti-military society whose homes were not in imminent danger from their enemies. Prior to Pearl Harbor, America's draftees had to endure the manifold trials of enforced and possibly pointless peacetime soldiering; afterwards, most became indefinite exiles from their own country, while fully aware of the new-found prosperity of civilian society and conscious that wartime exigencies meant that there was very little prospect of returning home unless they were wounded.[341]

As they were usually called upon to serve and die in obscure and far-flung corners of the world, America's conscripts rarely fought in what seemed to them a clear defence of hearth and home – and thus Marshall fully accepted the need to inform and to motivate. While this issued, among other initiatives, in the famous *Why We Fight* film series,[342] what has been aptly described as Marshall's 'constant interest in winning the confidence of the citizen soldier'[343] also translated into an ongoing bid to monitor their attitudes and to provide for their every reasonable comfort. That this was a thankless task was reflected in the fact that, as late as December 1944, American high-school students still expressed a clear preference for the navy or the AAF over the army's ground forces, with the infantry being ranked as the least popular branch of all.[344] As a result of Marshall's solicitude, pollsters ranged far and wide in the US Army in World War II, their findings being cascaded down to regimental level through the army bulletin *What the Soldier Thinks*, which was first issued in December 1943 'at the direction of the Chief of Staff'.[345] Marshall's concern was more tangibly reflected in the material standards of ordinary service life, the chief of staff being of the view that 'the way to placate citizen soldiers and their politicians was by the best possible material conditions', a policy reflected in the comparatively high rates of army pay, the quality and quantity of army rations and the 'oases of abundance' that were America's overseas bases in a war-torn world.[346] A keen supporter of the welfare work of the Red Cross and the USO,[347] in 1942 Marshall also backed the reappearance of the World War I army newspaper *Stars and Stripes* and the launch of the new army magazine *Yank*, publications that enjoyed a good deal of editorial freedom.[348] Additionally, Marshall went to some lengths to ensure a culture of liberality in the distribution of medals and to enhance promotion prospects for meritorious service.[349] Finally, with the liberation of France, and at no small risk politically, Marshall even ensured that local breweries were appropriated for the critical task of making the American soldier that much happier.[350] Marshall's approach, of course, helps to contextualise the lavish religious provision that was made for the American soldier, while it also placed greater strains on the army's logistics.

There was one group, however, for whom prejudice thrived in the midst of plenty – and that was the African Americans. Although other racial minorities – such as Hispanics, Japanese, Filipinos, Chinese and Native Americans – served in the US military,[351] none were as conspicuous or as segregated as they were. Significantly, although the Selective Training and Service Act stated that there would be no discrimination on racial grounds in the selection and training of draftees, in October 1940 the War Department announced that, although African Americans would be drafted in the proper proportion and would be admitted to all branches of the army: 'The policy of the War Department is not to intermingle colored and white enlisted personnel in the same regimental organizations.' Furthermore, in 1941 George C. Marshall confirmed to Secretary of War Henry L. Stimson that 'the War Department cannot ignore the social relationships between negroes and whites which have been established by the American people through custom and habit'.[352] Indeed, discrimination was rife in the very administration of the draft; significantly, 'African Americans sat on only 250 of the 6,442 draft boards and on only three in southern states', namely Virginia, North Carolina and Kentucky.[353] Given the disproportionate levels of poverty and functional illiteracy among African Americans, rejection rates for African American draftees on the grounds of health and education were correspondingly high; conversely, deferments on the grounds of occupation were conspicuously low.[354] Throughout the war, the army indulged some of the worst manifestations of popular and institutional prejudice; supplies of blood plasma were segregated according to the racial origins of their donors, African American soldiers were far more likely to be executed for rape than their white counterparts, and, while there were 'few, if any' black officers posted to white units, care was often taken to ensure that in African American units 'no Negro was allowed to hold a rank higher than that held by the lowest-ranking white officer'. The quality of leadership was not enhanced by the common conceit that Southern white officers had a special capacity to command African American troops.[355] Besides all of this, 'white stereotyping of the Negro as timid, untrainable, and useful only for manual labor' meant that the great majority of African American GIs were allotted to service rather than to combat roles.[356]

In the words of Stephen E. Ambrose: 'The world's greatest democracy fought the world's greatest racist with a segregated Army. It was worse than that: the Army and society conspired to degrade African Americans in every way possible',[357] and nowhere was this more apparent than in the Jim Crow South. Adding to the other unfavourable dynamics of life for the African American GI was the fact that most of the army's vast new training camps were located in the Deep South, a policy justified by the fact that its climate allowed for lighter construction work and all-year-round training. However, and as Marshall later admitted, for many African Americans this was simply a recipe for trouble:

> I completely overlooked ... the tragic part of having these Northern Negroes in a Southern community. We couldn't change the bus arrangement, we couldn't change any of the things of that nature, and they found themselves very much circumscribed – to them outrageously so – because they were in there to train to fight for their country and put their lives ostensibly on the line, and they were being denied ... things that the white troops accepted as a matter of course.[358]

Marshall omitted to mention the accompanying threat of violence, and even lynching.[359] In the wider context of growing civil rights agitation and African American assertiveness in the United States, symbolised by A. Philip Randolph's March on Washington Movement and by the 'Double V' campaign inaugurated by the *Pittsburgh Courier* against 'our enslavers at home and those abroad who would enslave us',[360] the predicament of African American GIs resulted in a 'harvest of disorder' at home and abroad. Occasionally, such fracas could degenerate into fatal shoot-outs, as at Phoenix, Arizona, in November 1942, and Camp Stuart, Georgia, in June 1943.[361]

Nevertheless, there were distinct signs of improvement for African Americans in the armed forces over the course of the war. In general terms, and as Neil A. Wynn has argued: 'Some found the experience totally disillusioning; for others it was more positive. Despite everything, many gained an education, a skill, an experience of life beyond the United States, and often, quite simply, a degree of self-respect.'[362] On the eve of the draft the representation of African Americans in the armed forces had been disproportionately low. In 1940, they made up only 2 per cent of the army, they were barred from the Air Corps, and the number of African American officers could be counted on the fingers of one hand. Although the percentage of African Americans in the navy was of a similar order, all of its black sailors were enlisted men and most were rated as mess attendants, essentially 'seagoing bellhops' in a service whose technical requirements were deemed to be beyond them. The marines simply remained an unabashedly all-white corps.[363] However, this exclusivity began to unravel under the combined pressures of military necessity and domestic politics.[364] In December 1941, African Americans comprised nearly 6 per cent of the army, including nearly five hundred officers; by September 1945, they amounted to almost 9 per cent of the army and almost six thousand of its officers, both male and female.[365] Besides the distinction earned in North-West Europe by ground units such as the 761st Tank Battalion and 614th Tank Destroyer Battalion, five thousand African American service troops volunteered to fight as infantrymen at the height of the Battle of the Bulge, their performance in segregated, white-led rifle platoons being described by Marshall as 'a very splendid show'.[366] In the air, further advances were made by the demonstrable success of the experimental 332nd Fighter Group in Italy, squadrons that served under the leadership of Colonel Benjamin O. Davis, son of the only black general in the US Army.[367]

In the navy, where the proportion of African Americans had risen to over 5 per cent by the end of the war, [368] a similar pattern of uneven progress can be seen.[369] After steward's mate 'Dorie' Miller of the battleship *West Virginia* emerged as a hero of Pearl Harbor, in April 1942 it was announced by the Secretary of the Navy, Frank Knox, that African Americans would be admitted to all branches of the navy. This decision was eventually followed by the commissioning of its first black officers – the so-called 'Golden Thirteen' – in February 1944, and by experiments with all-black crews. By August, and following a precedent set by the US Coast Guard, which had commissioned an African American officer in April 1943, integrated crews were even serving on a small number of auxiliary ships.[370] As Secretary of the Navy from May 1944, James V. Forrestal, who was sympathetic to the cause of civil rights, lent some momentum to this process. Assisted by his links with the Urban League, 'a moderate civil rights organization', Forrestal made considerable progress 'toward dismantling the whites-only navy', desegregating some of its training schools and opening its female auxiliary, the Women Accepted for Volunteer Emergency Services (WAVES), to African American volunteers. However, the vast majority of African American sailors were unaffected by these developments, continuing to serve as mess attendants and as stevedores and construction workers.[371] As in the army, there were some dramatic clashes with authority, notably the Port Chicago 'mutiny' of August 1944 (occasioned by the dangerous conditions faced by African American ammunition loaders at Mare Island Navy Yard, California) and on Guam the following December, when African American sailors became embroiled in an armed feud with abusive marines.[372] Indeed, the Marine Corps proved 'the service most resistant to African American involvement', being essentially a white preserve until April 1942; twelve months earlier, its commandant, Major General Thomas Holcomb, had even declared that he would take 5,000 whites in preference to 250,000 African Americans.[373] Bound by navy policy, the marines reluctantly enlisted African American volunteers from June 1942, but African American volunteers and draftees were kept in segregated defence battalions and support companies for the remainder of the war; significantly, the first African American marine officer was not commissioned until November 1945, two months after the war had ended.[374]

Large and lavishly supplied, if internally wracked by the profound racial divisions of American society, America's mainly draftee armed forces overcame the logistical and, indeed, psychological problems of fighting a faraway war against Germany, Italy and Japan. Although their operational performance was by no means flawless, as their early defeats and 400,000 dead testify, in Allan R. Millet's judgement: 'The United States defeated Japan virtually by itself and became the second most important contributor [after the Soviet Union] to the defeat of Nazi Germany.'[375] In aggregate terms, America's armed forces were the largest in the world by the end of the war,[376] as well as being the best supplied and the most powerfully armed. Whereas the US Army, including the Air Corps, compared with the armies of Belgium and even Romania in 1939, by the summer of 1945 it had played the greater part in the defeat of Germany in Western Europe and, in the Pacific, was capable of delivering nuclear destruction across oceanic distances. However, and given the very nature of American society, the story of the US armed forces was spiritual as well as material, and the following chapters demonstrate how war affected the religious beliefs, behaviour and perceptions of more than sixteen million young Americans of the vaunted 'greatest generation'. Through studies of military chaplaincy, American military culture, the religious profile and character of service personnel, the ordeal of combat and wartime faith, contact with the wider world, and the moral costs of war, this volume will illustrate how, in religious terms, World War II affected those uniformed Americans who were to become the most dynamic element in post-war American society. In doing so, it will show how World War II was a catalyst for religious change, and how much the post-war revival of American religion owed to the lessons and vicissitudes of the war years.

Chapter One

Chaplains and Chaplaincy

Introduction

DESPITE the long history of American military chaplaincy, World War II marked its emergence as the paramount provider of religious and pastoral care for the US Army and the US Navy. Prior to this, army chaplains in particular had faced strong and persistent competition from comparatively well-resourced civilian agencies, most notably the Young Men's Christian Association (YMCA). Even if this competition could be ostensibly supportive and well-intentioned, only on the Western Front during the last year of World War I was a working system hammered out that placed chaplains at the centre of religious provision for the American soldier. Although in place for only a few months, the model of chaplaincy that emerged in France in 1918 was bequeathed to the post-war army, helping to ensure that army chaplains enjoyed an unchallenged pre-eminence in the religious care of the GI in World War II. In broader terms, American military chaplaincy stood as a powerful vindication of the unity of America's growing 'Judeo-Christian' identity, a working model of religious cooperation that seemed to transcend the raw divisions of American religious life in the service of a higher religious and national cause. However, the success of military chaplaincy was more than symbolic, for the combined efforts of twelve thousand commissioned army and navy chaplains also overrode strong pre-war objections to military chaplaincy in many American churches; kept constitutional challenges to chaplaincy in abeyance; made an incalculable contribution to the welfare and morale of more than sixteen million service men and women, and, finally, greatly enhanced the image of chaplaincy – and, by extension, that of the clergy – among Americans at large. This chapter examines the origins, causes and effects of this manifold wartime achievement, showing its underlying realities, its uneven quality and its long-term implications for religion in post-war American society.

Military chaplaincy prior to World War II

US military chaplaincy was well established by the 1940s, but its organisation in World War II was of relatively recent origin. Dozens of clergymen had served in the wars of the colonial era, and more than two hundred had served the patriot cause as army chaplains in the Revolutionary War (not always happily; one chaplain of the Continental Army had committed suicide after despairing of his life's 'disappointments').[1] Other chaplains had served in the Continental Navy, on ships of the various state navies and aboard privateers.[2] In 1791 the first chaplain was engaged to serve the fledgling republic's regular army, but the fortunes of regular army chaplaincy waxed and waned until a system of post chaplaincies was created in 1838, even disappearing for a time in the early 1800s.[3] The development of navy chaplaincy mirrored the nation's evolving naval strength; the first navy chaplain was appointed in 1799 and, after decades of gradual increase, in 1842 Congress fixed their number at twenty-four.[4] However, the rather uncertain situation of military chaplaincy before the Civil War was not due solely to the republic's modest military ambitions or to the tight constraints of public funding. Ironically, the first chaplain to the US national army was appointed in 1791, the year in which the Bill of Rights was ratified. Consequently, the tension between the 'Establishment Clause' and the 'Free Exercise Clause' of the First Amendment has inhered in American military chaplaincy throughout its history, the terms of the First Amendment presenting not so much an insurmountable 'wall of separation between Church & State',[5] as an open flank that has proved vulnerable to exploitation by opponents of military chaplaincy, especially in the aftermath of controversial foreign wars.

Challenged in the wake of the Vietnam War in the lengthy case of *Katcoff v. Marsh*,[6] the first major attempt to abolish military chaplaincy for constitutional reasons occurred after the Mexican War of 1846–48, whose outcome led to the annexation of vast swathes of Mexican territory and a consequent increase in the number of the army's post chaplains from twenty to thirty.[7] The ensuing decade saw a wave of public petitions to Congress, which called for the abolition of all government chaplaincies, congressional and military alike, critics protesting their illegality under the First Amendment, their exorbitant cost, and the prohibition of religious tests for national office that was enshrined in Article Six of the Constitution. For good measure, they also impugned the motives and calibre of the individuals who were drawn to such appointments.[8] Nevertheless, the judiciary committees of both houses proved staunch in their defence of these chaplaincies, facing down a motley alliance that included freethinkers, 'Protestant sectarians' and political opponents of President Polk and his controversial war with Mexico.[9] In March 1859 the House Judiciary Committee summarised its position on military chaplaincy:

> The spirit of Christianity has ever had a tendency to mitigate the rigors of war, if as yet it has not been entirely able to prevent it; to lend to acts of charity and kindness; and to humanize the heart. It was true philanthropy, therefore, to introduce this mitigating influence where, of all other places, its fruits were to be more beneficially realized, namely into the Army and Navy, and to abolish it, in this Christian age of the world, would seem

like retrograding rather than advancing civilization. While much good and no perceptible evil has resulted from the practice; while no constitutional prohibition exists in relation to it, and no tendency to a 'religious establishment' is discernible under it; while diversity of truth is tolerated as freely as the constitutional requirement, in the minister, as well as in those for whom he officiates; and while the expense is so small as not to be felt by any one, your committee do not think it necessary to interfere with the office of chaplain, as it exists at present, in the Army and Navy.[10]

If protests rumbled on into the Civil War,[11] that bloodiest of all American wars effectively 'rescued the chaplaincy from possible extinction as an American military tradition', its attendant carnage and trauma naturally doing 'much to commend the retention of this office'.[12] Calling on their state militias, in which regimental chaplaincy had survived since the American Revolution, both the Union and the Confederacy were served by hundreds of military chaplains (as many as four thousand, according to one estimate).[13] At the end of the Civil War, the army's system of post chaplains was militarised. From 1867, these chaplains were presidential appointees rather than locally contracted clergy, being commissioned officers who received pay and perquisites accordingly.[14] The next half century saw moves towards greater professionalisation, moves that were reflected in the formation of an Army Chaplains' Alliance in 1891 and that were encouraged by the example set by the autonomous Chaplains' Department in the British Army.[15] While the later nineteenth century saw advances in its bureaucracy and a growing body of professional literature on chaplaincy work,[16] the wake of the Spanish–American War witnessed the creation of army examining boards for would-be chaplains, the adoption of a regimental chaplaincy system and the introduction of promotion based on merit.[17] At the same time, the process of reform benefited from the civilian churches' growing interest in the field of military chaplaincy, an interest typical of this age of progressivism and the social gospel, an interest that was expressed by their new assertiveness in the appointments process and in the rise of denominational endorsing committees.[18] Further leverage was provided by the advent of the Federal Council of Churches of Christ in America in 1908 and in the creation of its Washington Committee on Army and Navy Chaplains five years later, a body that served as an important point of contact between the armed forces and mainstream Anglophone Protestantism in particular.[19] In 1914, the Association of Chaplains of the Military and Naval Forces of the United States, launched two years earlier, joined forces with the FCC to form the Association for the Promotion of the Moral and Religious Welfare of Our Soldiers and Sailors. Rebranded the Religious Welfare League for the Army and Navy in 1915, it was merged with the Washington Committee on Army and Navy Chaplains in March 1917 to form the FCC's General Committee on Army and Navy Chaplains.[20] However, the experience of World War I was to reveal that the higher management of military chaplaincy far outstripped its performance on the ground.

The massive expansion of the US Army during World War I was accompanied by a dramatic rise in the number of its chaplains, its August 1914 cadre of sixty-seven regular army chaplains being greatly reinforced by an influx of temporary chaplains from civilian life.[21] Notwithstanding the preparations made by the National Defense Act of 1916, the improvisation of an army in which four million were to serve between April 1917 and November 1918 (most of them as draftees, and half of them with the American Expeditionary Force (AEF) in France) placed huge demands on national resources and stretched the organisational powers of the army to the limit.[22] Predictably, not all went well; among other things, the AEF's initiation into modern warfare in continental Europe revealed grave deficiencies in its command, training, logistics and equipment.[23] All of these wider failings were also reflected in its chaplaincy arrangements. Chaplains' affairs were largely managed by the Adjutant General's Department, which with the assistance of endorsing bodies and the army's own examining boards, recruited and assigned 2,217 temporary chaplains between April 1917 and November 1918. These men were recruited with due reference to the religious composition of the army and reinforced the 146 regular and National Guard chaplains on duty when the United States entered the war.[24] Despite pre-war calls for the creation of an autonomous corps of chaplains with its own hierarchy,[25] chaplains remained answerable to local commanding officers and had no higher organisation or direction. Until a chaplains' school was opened at Fort Monroe, Virginia, in March 1918, they received no formal training for their military role and, in terms of specialist equipment, could expect no more from the War Department than a chaplain's flag and, perhaps, the use of an assembly tent.[26] Furthermore, and despite their numerical increase, their numbers were still judged to have been 'entirely inadequate' given the needs of the time.[27] According to the terms of the National Defense Act of 1916, every infantry, cavalry and artillery regiment was to have its own chaplain and a ratio of one chaplain per 1,200 soldiers was established for the remainder of the army.[28] However, due to wholesale reorganisation following America's declaration of war, the size of the army's infantry regiments soon mushroomed to three times their pre-war size, but it was not until May 1918 (and as a result of pressure from General Pershing and the civilian churches) that further legislation applied the ratio of one chaplain to 1,200 soldiers to the whole of the US Army.[29]

The consequences of this situation were painful and predictable – a chaos born of good intentions reigned. Short of guidance, experience, resources and numbers, the uncoordinated efforts of individual army chaplains were eclipsed at home and abroad by those of civilian organisations such as the YMCA, the Knights of Columbus, the Red Cross, the Salvation Army and the Jewish Welfare Board (JWB), all of whom could draw on a comparative wealth of useful resources and relevant expertise. Indeed, the American YMCA had a tradition of military work that stretched back to that of the United States Christian Commission during the Civil War. With the apparent exception of the JWB, these organisations even deployed their own civilian chaplains.[30] To complete the humiliation, the multiplication of 'training areas', army schools, testing grounds and transit camps spawned the proliferation of 'camp pastors' in the United States – civilian clergymen engaged by their own denominations, and even by commanding officers, to attend to their occupants.[31] While the occasional excesses of the camp pastor phenomenon were eventually curbed through joint action by the War Department and the General War-Time Commission of the FCC,[32] only in France was an effective degree of cohesion and control finally achieved in chaplaincy matters. With the guidance of senior British officers and chaplains (in itself part of a much wider process whereby the novice AEF learned from its allies)[33] in March 1918 a conference was convened at Pershing's behest to thrash out the organisation of chaplaincy in the AEF. Chaired by Bishop Charles H. Brent, the Protestant Episcopal Church's missionary bishop of the Philippine Islands and a personal friend of Pershing's,[34] the conference involved key army chaplains as well as civilian representatives of the American churches and the welfare agencies then present in France. Noting the inadequate definition of a chaplain's role in army regulations, and the many distractions this entailed, it was decided that all religious activities in the AEF should be coordinated from a chaplains' office at general headquarters (GHQ). This was established in April and consisted of an executive board of three chaplains, namely Brent (its chairman), Francis B. Doherty (a regular army chaplain and a Catholic) and Paul D. Moody (a National Guard chaplain, a Congregationalist and son of the well-known evangelist Dwight L. Moody). Brent, who had represented the YMCA in France hitherto, was commissioned as a major in the Adjutant General's Department and, though never officially an army chaplain, was known as senior general headquarters chaplain or, more colloquially, as chief of chaplains (his principal lieutenants, Doherty and Moody, were known as senior chaplains). Under this dispensation, a greater degree of organisation and purpose was gradually attained; chaplains' affairs were managed collectively from GHQ and a new hierarchy of chaplains was brought into being for the AEF's bases, divisions, corps and armies.[35] A further innovation was the creation of a supplementary chaplains' school in France in June 1918, it being thought that the stateside school (run by regular chaplains and now located at Camp Taylor in Kentucky) was inadequate to the task of preparing its students for modern war. As Moody recalled, the original school was 'almost entirely manned by chaplains whose experience was largely limited to tours of duty in the Philippines or long experience in the somnolent atmosphere of peacetime posts ... many who came to us in France were woefully unprepared for what they faced'.[36] Whereas the school at Camp Taylor dwelt on more rarefied subjects such as equitation and international law, the school at Neuilly-sur-Suize (later Louplande) in France, which doubled as a chaplains' holding depot, was grimly practical, its curriculum including gas drill as well as identification and burial of the dead.[37]

Despite the shadow cast by a controversial decision to abandon rank insignia for chaplains, a move urged on the War Department by Brent and Pershing that culminated in a virtual mutiny among the faculty of the chaplains' school at Camp Taylor in September 1918,[38] few could doubt the progress and promise of AEF chaplaincy in the closing months of the war. As the citation for Brent's Distinguished Service Medal put it, his labours had resulted in 'a schematic system of religious effort in the AEF',[39] a scheme that, so Moody claimed, represented 'the first time in the history of the American Army that any attempt was made to organize the work of the chaplains'.[40] Such was the extent of integration achieved that Jewish army chaplains worked 'in the closest co-operation with the field representatives' of the JWB, a body that also 'supplied each Chaplain with an automobile and typewriter, and a special fund of 500 francs per month to be expended as he saw fit in behalf of the uniformed men'.[41] Although their earlier freedom had been curtailed by the reorganisation of 1918, even the civilian welfare organisations that had joined the AEF in France seem to have been satisfied by its outcome. In fact, the YMCA concluded at the end of the war that its work 'properly belonged to the Army and that in any future war it should be carried on by military men'.[42]

Widely regarded as an effective organisation that served as a working example of interdenominational and even inter-religious cooperation, late-war AEF chaplaincy provided the template for the future of army chaplaincy. After some debate that centred on questions of supervision in specifically religious matters, the National Defense Act of June 1920 created the office of Chief of Chaplains among its many and far-reaching changes to the organisation of the US Army. As a presidential nominee subject to approval by the Senate, the chief of chaplains was to be selected from among chaplains holding the rank of major or above; he was to serve for a term of four years 'with the rank, pay and allowances of colonel' and was charged with much of the work hitherto undertaken by the Adjutant General's Department – namely investigating the qualifications of chaplain candidates and conducting the 'general coordination and supervision of the work of the chaplains' on behalf of the adjutant general.[43] A greater sense of chaplains' identity and cohesion was reinforced in April 1925 with the creation of a new association of serving and former chaplains, namely the Chaplain Association of the Army of the United States, by the appearance of its journal, *The Army Chaplain*, and by the growing use of the term 'Corps of Chaplains', although this title had no real legal basis.[44] As chief of staff, Pershing continued to show a familiar interest in army chaplaincy, speaking at a conference on moral and religious work in the army held in Washington DC in June 1923. Convened by the Secretary of War, and tasked with considering the future 'religious and moral training' of the regular army, the National Guard, and 'young men in the citizens' and reserve officers' training camps',[45] Pershing expanded on the role of the army chaplain in the shaping of good citizens before this gathering of 'distinguished clergymen, educators, laymen, line officers, and chaplains:'[46]

> The definite responsibility for matters of a religious and moral nature within a command devolves upon the commanding officers as completely as do strictly military matters. The chaplain is a religious specialist on the staff of the commanding officer and is charged with the details of this work. He must minister, so far as practicable, to the needs of the entire personnel of the command to which he is assigned, either through his own personal services or through the cooperative effort of others. He is enjoined to enlist the active aid and cooperation of such military and civilian assistants, both lay and clerical, as the needs of the command may require.[47]

Still, regular chaplains remained disgruntled over the loss of rank insignia that Pershing and Brent had engineered in World War I. Hence, in 1926, two years after Pershing's retirement and with Brent having revised his opinions on the matter, the chief of chaplains led a successful campaign for the restoration of these contested distinctions.[48] It was, therefore, with a heightened sense of identity, organisation and purpose that the regular chaplains of the US Army pursued their ministries in the widely scattered posts of the United States, its territories and overseas dependencies in the interwar years. Although the first chief of chaplains, the Congregationalist John T. Axton, managed to limit the activities of chaplains to those 'required of them by law, or pertaining to their profession as clergymen, except when there exists an exigency of the service',[49] this important qualifier – plus the sheer range of the civilian clergy's legitimate activities – ensured that chaplains undertook a host of marginal and even extraneous duties. In other words, chaplains very much remained 'the morale officers of their day', as they had been in the pre-war army.[50] Besides their responsibility to conduct or to provide religious services, in Axton's report for the year 1921–22 he noted that:

> [Chaplains] have ministered in hospitals and guard houses, cared for recruits in their perplexities and for the man about to be discharged who wished help in becoming re-established in civil life, they have visited families, maintained community contacts, and have officially performed many extra- professional duties, serving as exchange officers, athletic officers, counsel for the defense in courts-martial and supervisors and instructors in the schools for enlisted men.[51]

While Axton was strongly averse to chaplains acting 'as post exchange officers or as counsels for the defense in courts-martial', roles that appear to have been abandoned during the 1920s,[52] chaplains remained burdened with the running of Sunday schools and other religious organisations, with pastoral visiting and with promoting the moral welfare of soldiers and their families through educational, cultural and sporting activities.[53]

A new (and, in the longer term, quite useful) addition to the routine work of regular army chaplains in the interwar years was their ministry to the annual, month-long Citizens' Military Training Camps (CMTC). A legacy of an officer-training scheme hatched by the pre-war 'Preparedness' movement, the camps received a new lease of life under the National Defense Act of 1920. Intended to generate a pool of reserve officers by means of consecutive summer camps and a final examination, more than 400,000 men aged between seventeen and twenty-four passed through the CMTC before the scheme was terminated in 1940. However, most of them seem to have been animated by the prospect of outdoor holidays at government expense, as only a tiny minority ever earned a reserve commission. Still, if the scheme failed to achieve its intended goals it did hone the practical skills of the army's fledgling Corps of Chaplains. Given its scale and longevity, it provided many regular and, indeed, reserve chaplains with an opportunity to practise their pastoral techniques among young men who were essentially civilians, to develop more appealing styles of worship (as at West Point, compulsory church attendance was the norm for the putative officers of the CMTC), and to focus on the related challenges of counselling and character-building.[54]

The development of chaplaincy in the US Navy followed a very different trajectory. Despite the dramatic emergence of the United States as a global naval power at the turn of the twentieth century, the size of the navy's Corps of Chaplains, as it was already commonly known,[55] lagged far behind the growth of the wider service. Pegged at an establishment of twenty-four in 1842,[56] in 1909, when the navy briefly became the second largest in the world,[57] it turned to the Army and Navy Department of the YMCA to supply secretaries to serve ships without a chaplain.[58] In 1910, Alfred Harding, the Protestant Episcopal Bishop of Washington, complained to the Secretary of the Navy that the ratio of chaplains to sailors then stood at 1:2,251.[59] Such a ratio, and the needs of the navy ashore as well as at sea, meant that no fewer than twenty-nine of its major warships were without chaplains by January 1913.[60] At the height of the Progressive Era, the dearth of chaplains in America's increasingly prestigious navy acquired the aura of a national scandal and prompted one of the first interventions in military affairs by the newly created FCC.[61] Representing more than thirty Protestant denominations, the FCC joined forces with Protestant Episcopal and Catholic churchmen in lobbying Congress for a new quota system for naval chaplains (eventually fixed at one per 1,250 personnel) and for the creation of a new class of 'acting' (or probationary) chaplain, both of which were created by the Naval Appropriation Act of June 1914.[62]

A timely success, as events proved, for it helped to meet the greatly increased demands of World War I. Between April 1917 and November 1918 the number of naval personnel (including the US Coast Guard and the Marine Corps) grew more than fivefold to over 500,000 men and women, making it the largest navy in the world in human terms by the end of the war.[63] In keeping with the new quota system, and aided by the appointment of temporary chaplains and temporary acting chaplains, the forty navy chaplains on duty in April 1917 increased to 199 by November 1918.[64] However, and in contrast with many army chaplains, the navy's role in the war (which mainly consisted of escort duty, mine-laying and ferrying troops to France)[65] meant that its chaplains had a relatively unexciting war that added little to the long-term evolution of navy chaplaincy. Although a handful of navy chaplains served with the Marine Corps in France, only one died while on duty, a stateside victim of influenza; the corresponding figure for the army was twenty-three, including eleven killed in action.[66] In organisational terms, the most significant development was the appointment of the navy's first chief of chaplains, John B. Frazier, in November 1917. Although this had been in prospect for some years, as chaplains lobbied for parity with other specialists in managing their own affairs within the wider Navy Department,[67] this remained an unofficial post until November 1944, when the office of Chief of Naval Chaplains was sanctioned by law. Moreover, Frazier's appointment over the heads of more senior colleagues was largely due to his friendship with the Secretary of the Navy, Josephus Daniels, a fellow Southern Methodist, and to the Secretary's urgent need for help in the appointment and management of navy chaplains (Daniels had begun the war by interviewing candidates in person).[68] Although the duties of the position were vague and its tenure uncertain, it being understood that secretaries could hire and fire at will,[69] the position of Chief of Chaplains survived the departure of Daniels and the removal of Frazier in November 1921.[70] By the time of Pearl Harbor, Frazier had been succeeded by five more chiefs of chaplains (or, more formally, heads of the Chaplains Division of the Bureau of Navigation, renamed the Bureau of Naval Personnel in 1942),[71] including two Episcopalians, a Congregationalist and a Catholic, the mantle having fallen most recently on the shoulders of Robert DuBois Workman, a Presbyterian (USA) minister and former marine, who was appointed in 1937.[72]

The navy's interwar chiefs of chaplains, from their vantage point in the capital, oversaw a system of chaplaincy that in many respects resembled that of the army: subject to rotation, navy chaplains led public worship, ran recreational activities and undertook various jobs at the behest of their commanding officers on board ship, in naval installations, and with marine units at home and abroad. William Wilcox Edel, for example, a Northern Methodist who had joined the corps as an acting chaplain in 1917, served in Samoa, China and the United States and at sea on cruisers, battleships and seaplane tenders. In the course of a varied interwar career he served as the superintendent of education in Samoa, managed rest camps for the crew of the battleship *Maryland*, ran men's organisations ('The Century of Cornelius' among the 6th Marines at Tientsin and the 'Chancelmen' on the seaplane tender *Wright*) and acted as a locum for civilian churches ranging from the First Presbyterian Church at Pensacola, Florida, to the Protestant Episcopal Cathedral at San Mateo, California. He also raised funds for the building of a chapel at the Naval Air Station at Lakehurst, New Jersey, 'the only Navy chapel ever built by public subscription', and helped in relief operations following natural disasters in Samoa and Maryland.[73] A more typical form of relief and philanthropic work was to be found, however, in serving the Navy Relief Society, a semi-official navy charity that gave financial assistance to distressed sailors and their dependants and for which chaplains often acted as local secretaries and fundraisers.[74] Whether such miscellaneous duties were useful or not was a matter of opinion; while Edel clearly thrived on the variety of his ministry, at least one of his colleagues, the Catholic chaplain Frederick William Meehling, viewed interwar navy chaplaincy as rudderless, reflecting that: 'In my day I don't believe they knew what to do with us.'[75]

Despite the organisational development of army and navy chaplaincy, the pacifist mood of the interwar years was not conducive to a warm and general appreciation of military chaplaincy; indeed, it has even been claimed that the army's Corps of Chaplains faced the very real threat of being 'strangled in its cradle'.[76] Clearly, the very existence of military chaplains became more controversial during the 1920s and into the 1930s. Traumatised by the experience of World War I, in the decade following the Treaty of Versailles the mainline Protestant churches did much to shape and articulate the national reaction to the recent bloodletting, to the extent that in the 1920s pacifism essentially became 'the "party line" of liberal Protestantism'.[77] Consequently, the principal Protestant churches issued a spate of anti-war resolutions and pronouncements, promoted peace organisations such as the Fellowship of Reconciliation and the World Alliance for International Friendship through the Churches, and even pledged themselves to support conscientious objectors in the event of another war. They were also supportive of the League of Nations and its internationalism, even though the United States was not a member; they applauded the Washington Conference of 1921–22, which their activities had helped to instigate, and they cheered the wider, war-renouncing Kellogg–Briand Pact of 1928.[78] Nor, as their remorse became increasingly coloured by their dread of future conflict, did they hesitate to point a recriminatory finger at themselves for their outspoken support of the last war. Warming to this theme, the eminent liberal theologian Harry Emerson Fosdick, then of Park Avenue Baptist Church, New York, and one of America's most celebrated preachers, publicly renounced war and repented of his support for World War I in January 1928, declaring in *The Christian Century*: 'I do not propose to bless war again, or support it, or expect from it any valuable thing.'[79] That kind of support was later lambasted by the sociologist Ray H. Abrams in his 1933 book *Preachers Present Arms*, an excoriating (if rather misleading) compilation of churchmen's pronouncements on World War I that was republished by

The Christian Century in 1939, and which Daniel A. Poling acknowledged to be a check on similar rhetoric in World War II.[80]

In this heady atmosphere of regret, fear and self-reproach, it was perhaps inevitable that: 'The most vocal enemies and opponents of [military] chaplaincy in this period were not atheists and free thinkers, but fellow churchmen.'[81] Leading the case for the prosecution was *The Christian Century*, arguably the most influential magazine among liberal American Protestants. Although the Conference on Moral and Religious Work in the Army had been held only the previous year, in 1924 it called for a general withdrawal from what it termed 'the Chaplaincy Business', urging the FCC to end its endorsement of candidates for military chaplaincy on the grounds that: 'It is no more the business of the Christian church to train and furnish military chaplains than it is to train and furnish machine gunners and bayoneteers.'[82] As pacifism became ever more embedded in the mainline Protestant churches – who could embrace it with the same fervour they embraced Prohibition – pressure on military chaplaincy intensified. In a notorious sermon preached in Washington in April 1930 to a congregation that included the army's third chief of chaplains, the Baptist Julian E. Yates, the 'nationally prominent' Disciples of Christ minister Peter Ainslie pronounced that: 'There is no more justification for being a chaplain in the Army or Navy, than there is for being a chaplain in a speakeasy.'[83] While these words were condemned by the *New York Herald Tribune* as 'a blatantly outrageous slander',[84] *The Christian Century* doggedly maintained its hostility towards military chaplaincy. In January 1935 it renewed its call for an end to endorsement by the FCC, declaring that: 'We look with shame upon the blind servility with which the Christian church gave itself to the government of the United States in 1917 and 1918'. It urged its readers to consider 'whether the Christian church expresses the mind of Christ when it recruits its ministers for the military status of the chaplaincy.'[85]

If it is remarkable that a further constitutional challenge to military chaplaincy did not issue from an interwar milieu in which the overthrow of war had become 'an obsession among the mainline churches',[86] throughout the 1930s they expressed their hostility in other ways. In 1931, a questionnaire circulated to more than half of all the clergy in the United States by Kirby Page, a prominent pacifist, sometime Disciples of Christ minister and editor of the Fellowship of Reconciliation's journal *The World Tomorrow*,[87] revealed that 62 per cent of nearly 20,000 respondents thought that the churches should renounce war forthwith, that 80 per cent were in favour of unilateral arms reductions, and that only 45 per cent would offer their services as military chaplains in the event of a future war.[88] The tireless Page conducted a further poll of similar proportions in 1934, eliciting another 20,000 replies. This time, 67 per cent of these clerical respondents agreed that the churches should declare their opposition to future wars in advance, 62 per cent said that they would never participate as armed combatants, and another overwhelming majority voiced their support for arms reductions.

In many denominational circles, the signals were the same. By the late 1930s, a raft of denominational polls had revealed strong pacifist tendencies among Northern Baptists, the Disciples of Christ, and Congregationalists.[89] Some major denominations even registered their unhappiness with military chaplaincy *en bloc*. In 1934, the Newark Conference of the Methodist Episcopal Church, whose clergy had shown strong support for Page three years earlier,[90] called upon its bishops to cease supplying military chaplains. In October 1936, the International Convention of the Disciples of Christ voted to end Disciples' involvement in the FCC's General Committee on Army and Navy Chaplains and called upon the FCC 'to sever its connection with the war system by dissolving its Chaplaincy Commission'. That same year, the General Synod of the Evangelical and Reformed Church also decided to withdraw from the General Committee.[91] Fondly touted in critical circles by this time was a civilianised alternative to military chaplaincy (or, as the Disciples of Christ envisaged it, 'a non-military ministry of religion to men in the armed services at the churches' own expense and under their own authority, without involving the church of Christ in any alliance whatsoever with the state or the military system').[92] Such an alternative had, in fact, been mooted by the FCC since 1924, and growing support for the idea led its Department of Research and Education to canvass regular, reserve and retired military chaplains on the subject. Unsurprisingly, its questionnaire found that this group of respondents had a high level of 'service consciousness', that they were wedded to the rank system and that they firmly rejected the idea of civilians ministering to the armed services.[93] After extensive enquiries, and with the threat of war looming large in Europe, in December 1938 the FCC finally came to the conclusion that a civilianised chaplaincy system was unviable and advised its constituents to maintain their links with the existing system.[94]

This conclusion underlined the fact that, however vocal and determined pacifist critics of military chaplaincy were, they occasioned far more clamour than substantial change. While the employment and income that various types of military chaplaincy could offer to the clergy probably helped to blunt their onslaught in the hard years of the Depression, beyond the historic peace churches interwar pacifism enjoyed its greatest influence in relatively liberal and traditionally Anglophone denominations, notably 'the Disciples, Methodist (North), Presbyterian (USA), Congregational-Christian, and Baptist (North) denominations'.[95] Significantly, Page's 1931 poll had shown that the attitudes of the Episcopalian clergy were mixed, with only 650 declaring themselves unwilling to support any future war or serve as a combatant; furthermore, it did not consult the clergy of more conservative denominations, notably Southern Methodists, Southern Baptists, Lutherans and Catholics. In fact, and as one newspaper observed, the poll seemed to imply that chaplains were at hand should the need arise.[96] Furthermore, at a time when some major denominations were cutting their links with military chaplaincy, others were forging theirs; in 1936, the National Baptist

Convention of America, one of the largest black denominations in the United States, and the Lutheran Church (Missouri Synod), one of America's biggest and most conservative Lutheran bodies, joined the General Committee on Army and Navy Chaplains.[97] If the appeal of pacifism was therefore patchy in the final analysis, in the late 1930s, and as international horizons darkened, it began to lose some of its adherents, notably among proponents of neo-orthodoxy (or the 'theology of crisis') who rejected the liberal optimism on which it was so often predicated. Closely identified with these was Reinhold Niebuhr of Union Theological Seminary, 'the most influential public theologian of the 1930s and 1940s',[98] whose 'Christian realism' and growing hostility towards Nazism had, by 1940, led him to desert the ranks of the Fellowship of Reconciliation for those of America's interventionists, much to the chagrin of his former associates.[99]

Despite the unfavourable light in which military chaplaincy was widely viewed in the interwar years, hundreds of American clergy remained involved or connected with this ministry. National Guard chaplains, selected by their states without the need for ecclesiastical endorsement and largely independent of the Office of the Chief of Chaplains, continued to serve National Guard units at their annual camps and thus enjoyed the benefits of comparatively 'regular and systematic experience with troops'.[100] In keeping with the National Defense Act of 1920 and the policy of preparedness it enshrined, a separate body of reserve chaplains was also maintained. The interwar Officers' Reserve Corps, a mixture of World War I veterans, graduates of the Reserve Officer Training Corps and direct appointees,[101] had its own 'Chaplains' Section' comprising men who had 'few duties other than keeping themselves available for service in an emergency and giving some service in summer training camps'.[102] In 1931, there were 1,215 reserve chaplains as opposed to 120 regulars; in addition, 170 of the nation's 209 National Guard chaplains also held appointments in the reserve.[103] However, its denominational profile was not representative of the nation at large. Whereas Episcopalians and Presbyterians were over-represented, each comprising 15 per cent of the total, Catholics – with another 15 per cent share – were considerably under-represented.[104] Nor, indeed, was training satisfactory, a chronic lack of government funding and the demands of their own civilian ministries ensuring that the principal means of instruction was through extension courses run by the Chaplain School from 1924, courses that covered such topics as 'Practical Duties of Chaplains', 'Military Sanitation and First Aid', 'Welfare and Recreation', and 'Office Organization and Administration'.[105] If further instruction and more practical training was available to some, through short courses run by regular chaplains at certain army posts and by virtue of annual training camps,[106] most practical experience of ministering to large bodies of young men in camp conditions seems to have been acquired through work with the Civilian Conservation Corps (CCC).

The CCC was one of the earliest and most successful public works projects of the New Deal, very much expressing its quasi-warlike mobilisation of the nation against the crisis of the Depression.[107] Launched in 1933, before its demise nine years later it had employed more than three million young men aged between seventeen and twenty-five in conservation, construction and reforestation projects across the United States.[108] Although envisaged as a collaborative venture with civilian agencies such as the Department of Agriculture, the army's logistical capacity, leadership skills and administrative expertise assured its pre-eminent place in a scheme that represented 'the largest peacetime mobilization of men the United States had ever seen'.[109] If, as chief of staff, Douglas MacArthur denied any notion of the CCC being used as a military training ground,[110] it was understood from the outset that the army was responsible for saving its young volunteers from the moral as well as the material perils of unemployment and destitution. To meet the spiritual and moral needs of CCC camps, the chief of chaplains sent dozens of regular chaplains and mobilised hundreds of reservists, most of the latter serving for periods of at least a year. Given the number and distribution of its camps and the youth of their residents, the chaplain's ministry was often itinerant and usually involved recreational, educational and welfare activities in addition to providing religious services.[111] Although for the army as a whole the disruption caused by its involvement with the CCC 'probably more than erased any advantage' that may have accrued to it,[112] the Corps of Chaplains probably gained considerably from its participation, especially given the lack of practical training otherwise available to its reservists. Less than a year after the end of World War II, a survey of wartime chaplaincy maintained that chaplaincy to the CCC had transpired to be 'a proving ground for Army chaplain techniques', especially in terms of preaching and care of the sick.[113] A decade later, and writing as a veteran of World War II, Roy Honeywell insisted that through the CCC reserve chaplains had learned 'how to adapt themselves to an infinite variety of situations and to carry on their work without many aids which they would have considered indispensible in a civilian parish'. Furthermore, they had come 'to know a body of young men who were more representative of the youth of the country than any group in any home church'. All in all, Honeywell concluded, the benefits of their involvement with the CCC were such that they may even have 'outweighed ... the formal training program of the Army when they were called to cope with the perplexing exigencies of war'.[114]

Navy chaplains, however, were largely insulated from involvement with the CCC. They were also comparatively few. This was not simply due to funding constraints or to the mood of the times, for the number of reserve officers in the interwar navy appears to have been 'kept to a bare minimum' to safeguard the career interests of their regular colleagues.[115] In 1925, the number of reserve chaplains available to the navy was a mere thirteen.[116] Despite the considerable growth of the Chaplain Corps of the United States Naval Reserve in subsequent years, by 8 September 1939, when President Roosevelt declared a state of national emergency, it mustered a modest sixty-three.[117] Always outnumbered by their regular counterparts (who totalled ninety-four in September 1939),[118] the navy's reserve chaplains subsisted on a training diet of the odd week of active duty (often unpaid), the occasional summer cruise, monthly or twice-monthly lectures (in certain naval districts only), and correspondence courses on naval regulations and related subjects.[119] If a leavening of World War I veterans, both army and navy,[120] helped to offset this lack of systematic training, as with their army counterparts the denominational profile of the navy's reserve chaplains bore little resemblance to that of the nation at large. For example, of the eighty-six chaplains who served with the Naval Reserve between 1925 and 1939, forty-four were Episcopalians but only nine were Catholics.[121] Inevitably, the current strength of pacifist sentiment helped to limit the representation of some major churches. James Vernon Claypool (a Methodist, former marine and the navy's most senior reserve chaplain in 1939) remembered that in the mid-1920s he was 'a little out of step with the world', and that his decision to become a reserve chaplain caused consternation among his 'pacifist clerical brethren', who freely 'chided me because I was a chaplain in the naval reserve'.[122]

Direction and recruitment

Given the state of wider religious and political debate on the question of war, and the fact that ministers of religion were – much to the embarrassment of some – exempt from the draft,[123] the issue of how to respond to the unfolding war in Europe was something that greatly exercised America's younger clergy, especially between the passage of the Selective Training and Service Act in September 1940 and the bombing of Pearl Harbor. As the armed forces grew, military chaplaincy became ever more dependent on wartime volunteers of a suitable age, which eventually settled at under fifty-five for the army and under forty-five for the navy.[124] The scale of mobilisation and the demands of the quota system (one chaplain per 1,200 personnel in the army – though this rose to an unofficial target of 1:1,000 – and 1:1,250 personnel in the navy)[125] meant that an unprecedented number of clergymen were required. At the time of Pearl Harbor, 1,478 army chaplains were already on duty, all of them regular, reserve or National Guard officers; by the time of the Japanese surrender, this total had reached 8,141. Of these, 5,620 were Protestants, 2,278 were Catholics and 243 were Jews. Among the Protestants, there were even three Quaker chaplains.[126] However, even these figures masked the true scale of wartime requirements, for no fewer than 9,117 clergymen had in fact served in the army's Corps of Chaplains since September 1939.[127] To aid recruitment, from 1943 the War Department permitted qualified ministers to transfer to the Corps of Chaplains from other parts of the army, and not all of its chaplains were even American citizens. Such were the needs of the time that, by the end of 1943, clergymen of 'a cobelligerent or friendly country' were also allowed to serve.[128] Though smaller in absolute terms, the growth of the navy's Chaplain Corps was even more dramatic. On 7 December 1941, 192 regular and reserve navy chaplains were on duty; by August 1945, when the navy's Chaplain Corps reached its maximum wartime strength, this number had soared to 2,811. However, 2,934 navy chaplains served over the course of the war, among them 2,074 Protestants, 817 Catholics and 43 Jews.[129]

Despite the strain on clerical manpower, which even led to newspaper calls for the drafting of clergymen for chaplaincy service as 'the only answer',[130] a conspicuous source of potential chaplains that was not tapped were the female ministers of the United States, one of whom had been recommended (unsuccessfully) for a chaplaincy as early as the Civil War.[131] According to the Bureau of the Census, in 1939 there were 3,308 female ministers, comprising nearly 2.5 per cent of the national total.[132] Nevertheless, despite the inroads women had made into the ordained ministry prior to World War II,[133] to say nothing of the wartime creation of female auxiliary forces such as the Women's Army Auxiliary Corps and the navy's WAVES, American military chaplaincy was to remain an all-male preserve until the 1970s.[134] While this situation reflected the conservatism of the mainline churches in particular,[135] and the delicate nature of interdenominational relations in the two chaplain corps, it also reflected the reluctance of female personnel to accept the ministry of ordained women. On the formation of the WAAC in 1942, an 'informal inquiry' was undertaken as to the possibility of female chaplains serving at WAAC training camps, but the prevailing lack of enthusiasm meant that calls for their appointment went unheeded.[136] Also disregarded were calls for the appointment of non-Christian or non-Jewish chaplains. In 1943, the commander of the Japanese-American 100th Infantry Battalion, which was composed of men 'whose families were overwhelmingly Buddhist', filed a request with the Office of the Chief of Chaplains for the appointment of a Buddhist chaplain.[137] Despite objections that there were also 'a great many Christians among them, particularly of the Methodist and Baptist persuasion',[138] the Office of the Chief of Chaplains initiated discussions with the Buddhist Mission of North America, the only Buddhist group that had been included in the 1936 Census of Religious Bodies. When it transpired that the Buddhist Mission had no candidates who were 'physically qualified for the chaplaincy', the search for a Buddhist chaplain was simply abandoned.[139] (It was, in fact, not until 1987 that a Buddhist endorsing agency was recognised by the US Army, this being 'the first faith group outside the Judeo-Christian tradition to be recognized as an endorsing agency for [American] military chaplains').[140] Requests for a Baha'i chaplain also came to naught, this time on the grounds that America's Baha'is were insufficiently numerous to warrant a chaplain of their own.[141]

Despite these exclusions, the challenges facing the Office of the Chief of Chaplains were formidable enough. In addition to the 1,500 or so regular, reserve and National Guard chaplains on duty in December 1941, it was the task of William R. Arnold to turn almost eight thousand civilian clergymen from more than seventy denominations into army chaplains.[142] Although the fifth chief of chaplains, Arnold was the first Catholic to hold this office and, while his appointment in September 1937 finally recognised the claims of the largest denominational group in the Corps of Chaplains, it also reflected the Roosevelt administration's 'unprecedented recognition' and accommodation of American Catholics in general.[143] While Arnold's position and allegiance to Rome led to murmurings in Protestant circles throughout the war, he proved a lucky choice in the longer term. Arnold was reappointed for an unprecedented second term in 1941, when he was promoted to brigadier general, and he was raised to the rank of major general in November 1944.[144] Significantly, the army's approval was matched by that of the Vatican; at the behest of Pius XI, Arnold became a monsignor in August 1938 and his successor, Pius XII, made him a domestic prelate in 1941.[145] Furthermore, Arnold was a good choice in the age of the radio, the newsreel and the photo journalist. Tall, slim and dapper, with a good head of hair and a trenchant turn of phrase, the photogenic Arnold could also claim the newsworthy distinction that, as a civilian priest, he had served as a missionary in Peru and had even acted as a chaplain to a travelling circus, occasionally moonlighting as a clown.[146]

Though well favoured in Rome, Arnold also proved adept at handling the denominational intricacies and delicacies of the Corps of Chaplains, a very significant achievement given the constitutionally sensitive nature of his position and the deep-rooted anti-Catholic fears and prejudices of many American Protestants. In April 1941, Bishop R. Bland Mitchell of the Protestant Episcopal Church joked that: 'If Chaplain Arnold had been in charge of things a few centuries ago there would have been no Reformation!' Likewise, in 1943 a Southern Baptist magazine said of Arnold that: 'No man could be fairer or more impartial in his dealings with men representing various religious bodies.'[147] Nor was this simply toeing the line for the sake of good public relations. The pre-war, globe-trotting evangelist James Edwin Orr, a Northern Irish-born fundamentalist who served as a Northern Baptist AAF chaplain in the Pacific, later declared that: 'General Arnold, a Roman Catholic Monsignor, bent over double backwards in an effort to be fair to those of a different faith. I never heard a single charge to the contrary, and I have seen printed testimony from the most ardent fundamentalists to that effect.'[148] Significantly, late in 1944 Charles B. Burlingham, a New York attorney and mutual friend of President Roosevelt and Secretary of War Henry L. Stimson, aired some concerns about the Corps of Chaplains, one of them being the undue 'influence of the Roman Catholic church'. Although Catholic chaplains did not hold a disproportionate share of 'the administrative posts in the Corps', Burlingham insisted that they seemed to hold most of the 'top positions', including chief of chaplains, director of personnel, theatre chaplain in the ETO and commandant of the Chaplain School. He also alleged that Arnold had been slow to take action against the circulation of Catholic literature 'attacking the Protestant faith.'[149] Marshall duly referred the matter to Major General S.G. Henry, the army's assistant chief of staff for personnel, for investigation.[150] A short time later, in January 1945, Henry reported that Burlingham's charges of confessional cronyism were wholly unfounded. As they were staff appointments, many supervisory chaplains were selected not by Arnold but by 'the commanding general involved' and, whenever Arnold was called upon to make a recommendation, he was obliged to balance candidates' experience and suitability against their 'denominational affiliation'. Far from finding that the yoke of Rome lay heavily on the Corps of Chaplains, Henry concluded that:

> In the light of my limited investigation I am of the opinion that no denomination has been favored in providing personnel for key positions in the Chaplains Corps. I was unable to find any evidence of dissatisfaction by any denominational group in the assignment policies used by the Chief of Chaplains and I am also of the opinion that Chaplain Arnold has done an outstanding job in the skilful handling of this problem.[151]

Still, sections of Protestant opinion remained determinedly unconvinced. Persuaded that Catholic unity and organisation gave Catholicism an unfair edge in the management of chaplains' affairs,[152] Protestants could react sharply to any hint of denigration. Orr, for example, stated that the tendency of 'Hollywood producers of newsreels' to focus on Catholic subjects was perceived as an 'astounding disregard of fairness' by his Protestant colleagues, who formed by far the largest part of the army's Corps of Chaplains.[153] Protests were less muted in the autumn of 1945, when Brigadier General Harry H. Vaughan, the military aide to President Truman and himself a Presbyterian, made some unguarded remarks about superior Catholic organisation and personnel when addressing a Presbyterian women's meeting in Alexandria, Virginia.[154] Such was the chorus of protest from the FCC's General Commission on Army and Navy Chaplains, which demanded a repudiation, and *The Christian Century*, which warned of the threat of 'wholesale mudslinging' aimed at Protestant chaplains, redolent of the treatment of the YMCA after World War I,[155] that Truman himself was forced to intervene on behalf of his friend and fellow Missourian. That December, the president wrote to the General Commission distancing himself from Vaughan's comments and explaining that Vaughan had been speaking in a purely private capacity, not forgetting to mention that his aide was also 'a loyal churchman and a Sunday school teacher'. In an acid editorial, *The Christian Century* responded that:

> [T]he point is that, as the highest military official in the White House, [Vaughan] asserted that Protestant chaplains could not compare in quality with Catholics and that frequently Protestant chaplains were simply men seeking a three-year vacation. The fact that General Vaughan is a loyal

ruling elder in the church where he made his speech does not explain, cancel out or lessen the offensiveness of the speech.[156]

Six months later, *The Christian Century* published a comprehensive critique of army chaplaincy by the erstwhile Reformed Presbyterian chaplain Renwick C. Kennedy, which, among other things, insisted on the hidden reality of inter-confessional relations in the wartime Corps of Chaplains. While certain Protestants, such as Missouri Synod Lutherans and Southern Baptists, could prove awkward in terms of their 'narrow denominationalism':

> Catholics were the worst offenders in the matter of intolerant, denominational exclusiveness. There can be no doubt of this. There were some fine-spirited men among them, but not too many if interdenominational cooperation is one of the norms ... there was not a good spirit of fellowship or brotherhood within the corps itself. The major division of Protestants and Catholics was necessary but fatal. There were open clashes and constant undercover antagonisms. There were unethical, unchristian rivalries ...[157]

Whatever the truth of Kennedy's remarks about relations in the lower echelons of the Corps, things could have been much worse without Arnold's skilful performance as Chief of Chaplains. Significantly, Arnold was very much a capable and well-connected manager rather than a battle-worn veteran. An army career had not even been his personal choice, having been nominated for a chaplaincy by his bishop, without any consultation beforehand. Prior to World War II, Arnold had not seen a single campaign, and his career had followed the rather sleepy trajectory of a regular army chaplain in peacetime. Commissioned in 1913, he had spent World War I in the quieter surroundings of the Philippines and, in the interwar years, he had served as an instructor at the army's Chaplain School at Camp Taylor and at Fort Leavenworth. There then followed a further spell in the Philippines, a stint with the CCC in Texas, and his appointment as Chief of Chaplains in 1937.[158] If Arnold's career lacked drama, it nevertheless accrued important connections in the small, interwar regular army. He was familiar with Eisenhower from their days in the Philippines, Fort Leavenworth and Washington DC; with his namesake, Henry ('Hap') Arnold, a golf partner at Fort Leavenworth, with whom he swapped jokes about their common Swiss origins and divergent religious affiliations ('Hap' Arnold was a Baptist); and, most importantly of all, from their days as senior staff officers in Washington, Arnold knew the chief of staff and military manager *par excellence*, George C. Marshall. As the army's consummate staff officer, it was a telling reflection of Arnold's ability that Marshall thought so highly of him, and especially of his capacity 'to administer a tremendous organization in a businesslike manner'.[159] Addressing a conference of supervisory chaplains at the Pentagon in April 1945, Marshall averred that:

The work accomplished under Chaplain Arnold's direction and guidance represents a masterly achievement. What I am particularly impressed with is the way the standards of efficiency have been raised. To be perfectly frank, in the long past that had been the weakest point in the conduct of religious activities in the army. I always felt it came from this state of mind: If you had a poor colonel, you could get rid of him; if you had an ineffective chaplain, you accepted that fact as your cross to bear without thought of remedial action as in the case of an officer of the line.[160]

Indeed, Arnold stood so highly in Marshall's esteem that he was instructed to see him once a month, and whenever he had anything that he felt the chief of staff 'should know about'. Arnold was also asked to remember Marshall in his prayers and was included in meetings of the General Staff.[161] On his retirement as chief of chaplains, Arnold was awarded the Distinguished Service Medal for his 'eight year tour as chief of chaplains'[162] and was promptly reassigned to the Inspector General's Department as Marshall's 'personal representative … regarding all matters pertaining to the religious activities or responsibilities of the army'. Significantly, by giving Arnold this commission to 'travel and determine for me what is occurring in the Chaplains Corps all over the world', Marshall betrayed his anxiety about Arnold's successor, Luther D. Miller, formerly the senior chaplain of Sixth Army in the Pacific (and an Episcopalian, despite his Christian name) whom the chief of staff felt did not possess 'the necessary administrative knowledge to the extent that Chaplain Arnold does'.[163]

In addition to Arnold's prudence and administrative efficiency, what impressed Marshall was the authority and strength of character that he seemed to radiate. According to Marshall, who was inclined to such qualities by dint of his Episcopalian faith and professional calling, they even seemed characteristic of Catholic priests in general, a perception that may have been helped by Hollywood's flattering representations of the Catholic clergy. Pre-empting Vaughan, but writing confidentially to Henry L. Stimson in December 1944, Marshall went so far as to state that:

There has been no question in my mind from the start that we labor under the serious disadvantage of mediocrity in the senior ranks of the Chaplain service. It has not been an easy thing to handle and could not be met in quite the same drastic fashion I followed with troop commands…. While I have not the data to support this statement I rather imagine [Arnold] has used Catholic chaplains sometimes in key positions because of his inability to get the right man in the Protestant ranks. In my opinion, and speaking very frankly, the great weakness in the matter has been that of the Protestant churches in the selection of their ministry. The Catholic system provides a much higher average of leadership, judging by my own experiences, and the Protestant churches are too kindhearted in their admission of lame ducks. On a number of occasions in the past I have had to lean on Catholic chaplains for strong support in what I was trying to do. This same condition has proved to be the case in this war.[164]

However unfair or tendentious this verdict may have been, a critical example of Arnold stamping his authority on religious work in the army came when Marshall raised the suggestion that Paul D. Moody, who was now head of the General Commission on Army and Navy Chaplains, reprise Brent's leading role from World War I. Arnold's dry but succinct rejoinder, 'General, you have a chaplain organization', put paid to a reversion to the organisational anomalies of World War I and underlined Arnold's determination to keep religious work in the army firmly in the hands of its chaplains.[165] Accordingly, the Corps of Chaplains resisted the encroachments of civilians to the extent that even those senior churchmen seeking to act as visitors to the army had to be cleared by the Office of the Chief of Chaplains.[166] Furthermore, in 1941, a pact with the newly minted United Service Organizations (USO) recognised that chaplains were responsible for 'all religious activities' within the boundaries of army camps, thus averting the chaotic free-for-all that had marginalised army chaplains in the early months of World War I.[167]

In contrast with Arnold's impressive performance, the management of the navy's chaplains by Robert DuBois Workman was simply workmanlike. Appointed chief of chaplains in 1937 by the then Secretary of the Navy, Claude Swanson, Workman was a former marine sergeant, a minister of the Presbyterian Church (USA) and had been a regular navy chaplain since 1915.[168] Besides his uncertain tenure, Workman was also handicapped by the lack of clarity as to what his role actually entailed, his original duties including ministering to the Navy Department and presiding at navy funerals in Arlington National Cemetery.[169] Lacking the statutory guarantees and clarity of the National Defense Act of 1920, Workman had little more than precedent to go by. Essentially, his role was understood to involve examining chaplain candidates, advising the chief of the Bureau of Navigation on chaplains' assignments, corresponding with chaplains on duty, overseeing reservists, and guiding the chief of the Bureau of Navigation and the Secretary of the Navy in matters relating to navy chaplaincy and its policies.[170] From this uncertain footing Workman developed a knack of following where the army had led. As the historian of wartime navy chaplaincy admitted, the formalization of Workman's office by Congress, and his promotion to Rear Admiral in March 1945, seemed to establish a vital parity of esteem with the army.[171] In fact, it was still some way behind, for this was simply a concession granted after the signal failure of the General Commission on Army and Navy Chaplains to secure an independent 'Chaplains Bureau' in keeping with army precedent.[172]

Whatever the shape of their higher administration, finding enough army and navy chaplains proved an abiding challenge. Given the pastoral demands of the home front, a widespread suspicion of church–state entanglements, the strength of pacifist feeling prior to the war, and the often precarious nature of a minister's livelihood, the decision to apply for a chaplain's commission in either service was rarely taken lightly. William C. Taggart, then pastor of the Lamar Avenue Baptist Church in Wichita Falls, Texas – and convinced that 'A minister belonged with the men being prepared for the inevitable war' – chose to join the army as a chaplain after the draft was introduced in 1940. For Taggart, the overarching moral issues were very clear; as he saw it, due to 'the pagan menace' running amok in Europe, 'millions throughout the world were being starved, crippled, left homeless, and slaughtered'. Worse still: 'At the point of the bayonet the Bible was being replaced by *Mein Kampf.*'[173] Significantly, members of Taggart's own congregation deplored his decision and, before he left for the army, ostentatiously shunned his services because their minister was 'participating in war'. If this were not enough, Taggart also had to take into account the historic position of the Southern Baptist Convention, which was inherently wary of 'taking pay from the Government for preaching the Gospel'.[174]

Nor, it should be stressed, was this pay insignificant, a fact that could also be turned against those who became chaplains prior to Pearl Harbor. When commissioned as a first lieutenant, even the most junior army chaplain could expect to earn $167 per month, plus various allowances, and promotion to captain increased this monthly pay to $200.[175] Although the base pay of naval officers had not risen since 1908, it was still, by the standards of the Depression era, a handsome $2,000 per annum for a freshly minted lieutenant chaplain, who could receive up to $1,158 per annum in additional allowances if he had dependants.[176] In contrast, 24.4 per cent of all clergymen in the United States were paid a salary of less than $600 per annum in 1939, and 51 per cent enjoyed a salary of less than $1,200; in fact, in 1939 only 17.5 per cent earned an annual salary in excess of $2,000.[177] Furthermore, such were the depredations of the Depression that the number of unemployed ministers in the United States was, by some estimates, placed as high as thirty thousand.[178] These and other considerations lay heavily on the mind of Charles Edward Lunn, pastor of the First Baptist Church in Coatesville, Pennsylvania, before joining the army's Corps of Chaplains. Unlike Taggart, Lunn, a pre-war pacifist, did not even consider becoming an army chaplain prior to Pearl Harbor. Furthermore, his motives for joining included embarrassment at being exempted from the draft, a sense of the pastoral and missionary opportunity presented by the war, and even a mistrust of the quality and motivations of those who had already elected to become chaplains. In Lunn's words:

> Some of the pastors who were volunteering as chaplains were men who were dissatisfied with their pastorates, who wanted to move to another church, but a move was difficult for one reason or another. To go into the Chaplaincy was a way of escape – and a way to be patriotic also. Others

were so poorly paid that a first lieutenant's salary was a pretty big inducement to enlist. What about the better men? The men in the larger churches?
Not too many of them were going, so far as I knew.[179]

Critically, the chief disincentive for Lunn was financial. Married on the cusp of the
Depression, an ordeal that had led many ministers to be released or to abandon
their calling,[180] the Lunns had had their fill of 'poverty, anxiety, and hardship'.[181]
Now settled in a stable pastorate, joining the Corps of Chaplains presented the
prospects of resignation, giving up 'home and church', and suffering 'a big cut'
in income.[182] As things turned out, Lunn's congregation, like thousands across
the country, proved more accommodating than expected. Lunn was granted a
leave of absence and a committee was formed that 'hired a supply-preacher for
Sundays' and engaged his wife, an educationalist, 'to direct the whole program
of the church' in his absence.[183]

Similar latitude was shown to Russell Cartwright Stroup of the Southern-
based Presbyterian Church (US). Minister of the First Presbyterian Church in
Lynchburg, Virginia, Stroup had moved there from California during the Depression and, though a bachelor, his dependants included his elderly mother and
a disabled sibling. Commissioned into the Corps of Chaplains in August 1942,
even after an absence of two years Stroup's congregation refused to countenance
his resignation and engaged a retired minister to serve in his stead.[184] If such
arrangements were facilitated by the growing prosperity of the home front, which
also helped to reduce or eliminate church mortgages and to free funds for later
church building,[185] they were also eased by continuing contact between chaplains
and their home congregations. Stroup, for example, was in regular correspondence with his Lynchburg flock and preached to them in uniform on his return
from the Pacific in 1945.[186] Potential problems were also smoothed by official
recognition of the sacrifices involved. In 1943, a scheme was launched by the
army's Corps of Chaplains whereby: 'In recognition of the patriotic sacrifices
made by civilian churches of all faiths in giving the services of their pastors to
the Country, a Certificate of Award was designed, printed, signed by the Chief
of Chaplains, and forwarded to local congregations'.[187] Because many chaplains
had served two or more congregations, nine thousand of these certificates were
issued in 1943 alone and 'in many cases a chaplain was furnished to assist in the
ceremonies promoted by the churches receiving this recognition'.[188] The navy's
Chaplain Corps joined the scheme in 1944, with churches and institutions being
congratulated for giving the services of a named individual 'that he might serve
God and Country as a Chaplain in the armed forces of the United States'. In
the case of navy chaplains, certificates were accompanied by an effusive letter
of thanks from the Secretary of the Navy, expressing the navy's gratitude for
spiritual assistance rendered by whomever 'during the present world crisis'.[189]

As this charm offensive illustrates, because all military chaplains were volunteers, both chaplain corps had to be attuned and attentive to civilian sensitivities in order to ensure an adequate flow of recruits. While both made congregations feel valued and, as we shall see, kept the churches mindful of military chaplaincy and its needs through a constant stream of circulars, news stories and press conferences,[190] other expedients were also adopted. This was particularly true of the navy, where the problem of an insufficient chaplains' reserve was compounded by the elitist and inflexible nature of its entry requirements. Unlike the army's Corps of Chaplains, which proved more prepared to accommodate the divergent training regimes of different religious traditions and to recognise the value of pastoral experience, its navy counterpart required that navy chaplains possess a Bachelor of Divinity (BD) in addition to an ordinary bachelor's degree, a requirement that had been in place since before World War I and that militated against Orthodox rabbis and the ministers of many Christian denominations.[191] Significantly, this insistence on a full college and seminary education reflected not only common ecclesiastical assumptions about the greater effectiveness of an educated ministry but also a general prejudice against non-graduate officers that prevailed in the US Navy throughout the war, a prejudice that was as much social as professional in origin.[192] Clifford M. Drury of the Presbyterian Church (USA) – himself an academic, the historian of the navy's Chaplain Corps and a wartime navy chaplain[193] – sniffed that: 'Many who applied [for the Corps] did not have the full seminary training required; some had little or no college training; and a few did not even have a high-school diploma.'[194] However, while Drury insisted that an unyielding adherence to pre-war standards conduced to a 'wholesome prestige in civilian circles' and 'proficiency and morale within the Corps',[195] at no point in the war did the navy's Chaplain Corps recruit to its full establishment; indeed, as late as April 1945 it was still 20 per cent under strength.[196] Furthermore, its quest to ensure that the right kind of clergymen graced the wardrooms of the navy also led it into choppy constitutional waters. Given the shortfall in suitable candidates, Workman lobbied for the inclusion of future chaplains in the navy's V-12 Program, a scheme whereby college students of specific disciplines were classed as apprentice seamen and sponsored in their studies prior to their entry into the service, as officers, upon graduation.[197] However, government subsidy for, and navy interference in, theological training at institutions as renowned as Yale Divinity School and Union Theological Seminary, New York City, provoked strong protests, not least because of its apparent violation of the First Amendment. As the ever-critical *Christian Century* complained sarcastically in March 1943: 'Something new was added to American church life last week … the United States Navy stepping in to control the education of boys as Christian ministers, with their training for that holy calling fixed by the Navy's judgment as to what will produce officer material!'[198]

If the navy's Chaplain Corps had problems reconciling its needs with its aspirations, certain denominations – apart from the historic peace churches –

proved aloof, under-represented or less than fully cooperative. For example, the Lutheran Joint Synod of Wisconsin and Other States, a conservative Midwestern denomination of nearly 250,000 members in 1936, refused to allow its ministers to become chaplains on the grounds that they would be under government control – when the spiritual care of its members was entirely its own preserve.[199] Furthermore, and although the decade prior to the 1936 Census of Religious Bodies had seen a proliferation of sectarian groups, the Office of the Chief of Chaplains was reliant on the previous census of 1926 in determining denominational quotas for the whole of the army, a system that continued to co-opt the notionally unchurched while favouring the Protestant mainline.[200] Perhaps more seriously, both the army and the navy experienced a chronic shortage of Catholic chaplains. Citing the needs of the home front, many dioceses and religious orders were reluctant to release their priests, leading Arnold to lament that: 'Now we have a most efficient organization and the fullest and most generous cooperation from the Government, but a sad shortage of priests.'[201] Consequently, the army's Catholic chaplains were 50 per cent under establishment by 1943 and, despite some improvement thereafter, remained under establishment for the rest of the war.[202] This problem was compounded by the fact that the quota for Catholic chaplains was deemed to be too low in any case, given the official reliance on outdated figures from the census of 1926. In addition to faulty accounting, the sacramental needs of combat units meant that Catholic chaplains were usually overstretched. According to a post-war report, 'The Army Chaplain in the European Theater', five rather than four Catholic chaplains were needed to ensure 'adequate coverage' of an infantry division, and four as opposed to three for an armoured division.[203]

Money was also a problem. Although members of Catholic religious orders felt themselves to be overpaid as chaplains 'in view of their vows of poverty', many secular priests had long-standing financial commitments – educational and other – to relatives who were ineligible for dependants' allowances.[204] Understandably, these concerns weighed more heavily on married Protestant clergymen, with the shadow of the Depression and the spectre of post-war unemployment preventing many from coming forward. With more than half of the nation's male ministers aged over forty-five in 1939, their median age being '45.8 years',[205] recruiters found that they were obliged to concentrate on a generation of churchmen that was still very much traumatised by their experiences of the Depression. While seeking recruits in the Fourth Naval District (namely Pennsylvania, Delaware and New Jersey) a navy chaplain was told by one minister that, 'I am afraid the war will end soon and I would be out of a job' and, by another, that 'If I lose this church I will never get one as good.'[206]

Another major problem lay in the shortage of black chaplains, though here the causes varied somewhat between the two services. In the navy, the academic requirements of the Chaplain Corps, and probably its further insistence on weeding out applicants with suspect political sympathies,[207] served as a racial as much as a social filter, for in the 1930s, and even among 'the urban black clergy', only around 11 per cent had both a college degree and a seminary training. In rural areas, matters were worse still, for here 'only 2 per cent were college graduates; and almost none had seminary training'.[208] As a result, only two black ministers – one African Methodist Episcopal, the other Presbyterian Church (USA) – ever served as navy chaplains during World War II.[209] Given that Arnold was prepared to be flexible on the subject of educational requirements,[210] with eligibility being determined by one of three different criteria from June 1942, it having proved impossible to recruit enough chaplains from a pool of 'only 30,000 men in the Protestant ministry' who had the requisite 'four years of college and three years of theological study',[211] an observer duly noted in 1944 that the army's Corps of Chaplains now included 'many types of Negro preachers from the old shouting, camp-meeting type to the modern young chaplain, the product of some of the best-recognized divinity schools of this country'.[212] However, even the army was unable to secure a sufficient supply of black chaplains, notwithstanding a well-established tradition of black army chaplaincy. Black chaplains had served in the Union armies in the Civil War, and another sixty or so in World War I.[213] African Americans were also among the corps' interwar reservists and a steady trickle of black chaplains had been commissioned to serve the coloured regiments of the regular army since 1884.[214] In fact, this policy had meant that the Corps of Chaplains was the only component of the regular army in which there had been a steady presence of black officers and, as late as 1935, no fewer than three of its four black officers were chaplains.[215]

However, black ministers clearly faced greater disincentives to volunteer than did their white counterparts and a chronic shortage was the natural result. Besides the professional and financial risks common to both, black clergymen were confronted with the demands of the civil rights cause on the home front and by the daunting and invidious challenges posed by discrimination and segregation in both the armed services and society at large. While it fell to few white chaplains to have to calm fully armed, would-be rioters – as was the job of the chaplain of the 364th Infantry Regiment (Colored) at camp Van Dorn, Mississippi, in 1943[216] – it was widely recognised that the lot of the black chaplain was a difficult one. Assigned to black units in a still segregated army: 'The officers of most colored units were white and not infrequently the chaplain would be the only negro officer'.[217] Besides the social isolation this could entail, Protestant services were usually segregated (this was not generally the case with Catholic services, which, however, few black soldiers attended)[218] and some black chaplains even complained of having their sermons dictated by overbearing white officers.[219] To add to these indignities, and however indifferent army officialdom may have been to denominational niceties, Protestant chaplains could be categorised as 'Protestant (white)' or 'Protestant (negro)'.[220] Among their own flocks, black chaplains were also expected to play the necessary but invidious role of advocate and promoter of their soldiers' rights, with Chaplain Charles Dubra, who worked to improve recreational facilities for black soldiers in Australia, being dubbed a 'One-Man NAACP' by *The Baltimore Afro-American*.[221] In a candid and sympathetic depiction of the lot of the black chaplain, Wayne L. Hunter, a senior Presbyterian chaplain in the Pacific,[222] wrote in 1944:

> Generally the lot of the colored chaplain is more delicate than that of the white chaplain, and a greater demand is made on his tact and understanding. The colored men feel that their chaplain is their champion, and some of them feel that this should be his position, right or wrong. The fact that some of the Commanding Officers suspect that this feeling exists, does not make the chaplains' position any easier. Also there are some evidences of discrimination on the part of some officers which requires tact and keen judgement on the part of the chaplain. The fact that a higher percentage of our colored chaplains have found themselves in 'hot water', and also break under the physical and nervous strain cannot be misconstrued to mean that they are men of inferior quality but that a greater strain has been placed on them.[223]

Perhaps the most famous and controversial black chaplain of World War II was Luther M. Fuller, an African Methodist Episcopal minister who was widely credited with staging a 'one-man fight ... to obtain better conditions for soldiers in the South Pacific', and this after making waves by insisting on being served in a segregated dining car of a southern railway train.[224] Arraigned before an army reclassification board for these later efforts in 1943, a procedure that risked the penalty of being discharged,[225] the catalyst for Fuller's stand in the Pacific had been the shoddy treatment meted out to an African American coast artillery unit by its (Southern) white officers. After preaching a sermon that protested these conditions in September 1942, Fuller feared that he might be lynched by the perpetrators, and was put under an unofficial armed guard for his own safety before being shipped back to the United States.[226] On his return, Fuller produced signed letters of complaint, some of which he had transcribed, which were referred to the National Association for the Advancement of Colored People (NAACP).[227] Ultimately, Fuller was 'placed on the inactive list by the War Department ... as a result of his efforts to correct the mistreatment of colored soldiers', but not before he had been commended by his new commanding officer at Fort Dix, New Jersey, for his zeal as 'a vigorous, industrious and energetic worker [who] did his utmost in efforts to improve [his soldiers'] welfare'. Speaking on behalf of the Commission on Chaplains of the National Baptist Convention, Inc., W.H. Jernagin strongly condemned the army's decision to retire Fuller, protesting to the Secretary of War and the chief of chaplains that the case had 'lowered the morale of the entire colored population' and had served to hamper his own efforts to recruit additional chaplains.[228] Still, Fuller's stand seems to have had an effect; his former commanding officer in the Pacific was removed and eight new warrant officers were appointed, developments that seem to have improved the situation, especially as the new commanding officer was respected and admired 'for his wisdom, justice and knowledge of regulations'.[229]

Ironically, a later history of Army Air Forces (AAF) chaplaincy betrayed the sort of institutional problems that black chaplains faced, its author huffing that: 'There were several cases of negro chaplains agitating negro troops with the refrain of "discrimination" and "segregation".'[230] Another case of such 'insubordination' seems to have occurred at Camp San Luis Obispo, California, in 1943. According to one of the neighbourhood's 'few liberal citizens', who protested the case to the Office of the Chief of Chaplains, black personnel were treated so badly at the camp that, when a black chaplain intervened to ensure that his men were accorded 'equal rights', he was in turn 'persecuted', 'framed with false accusations' and ended up in confinement 'with his clothes taken away'.[231] In the Jim Crow South, of course, chaplains were confronted with the problems and frictions of still more blatant segregation. On one occasion in February 1944, two black chaplains who were taking the train to an AME church conference in Birmingham, Alabama, were roused from their seats by a white conductor before being arrested, threatened and insulted by white MPs, by whom they were 'greatly humiliated and belittled' regardless of their rank and status.[232] However, and in keeping with entrenched expectations in the army, black chaplains were still relied upon to use their influence upon black soldiers to avert potential violence, especially in the volatile climate of the South. On New Year's Eve 1943, Chaplain James C. Calvin defused a potentially bloody race riot on a train travelling from New Orleans to Atlanta after a white porter became involved in a scuffle with black soldiers and sailors in 'the colored coach'. With confrontation looming between white passengers and black GIs, two of whom were toting machine guns, Calvin was able to persuade the GIs to stand down and to explain the incident to the satisfaction of a white MP, who was understandably grateful for his firm intervention.[233]

Although black chaplains were supplied by other denominations (notably the Catholics, the Methodists and the Protestant Episcopal Church)[234] such underlying problems helped to ensure that most black churches failed to meet their official quota of chaplains, the well-established and relatively centralised African Methodist Episcopal Church proving an exception to this rule.[235] In January 1943, Arnold estimated that the black churches had supplied just over one-quarter of their allotted 445 chaplains.[236] However, and despite strenuous efforts in the intervening period, this proportion had slipped to under one-quarter by the end of the war, with the black Baptist churches (whose adherents among black GIs were thought to be five times more numerous than those of all the other churches combined) having supplied only eighty-four chaplains out of an allocation of

612.[237] In practical terms, this chronic deficiency meant that in October 1944 only thirty-one black chaplains were available to minister in the Communications Zone of the European Theater of Operations (ETO), where large numbers of black troops were employed in service units that were often small and widely scattered.[238] The problem was even worse in the Pacific, however, where geographical factors were even more challenging and where there was always a 'high percentage of negro troops' serving in 'truck companies, port battalions, quartermaster units and engineer battalions'.[239] The gravity of this shortage led to a number of expedients. First, black chaplains who failed to pass the course at the Chaplain School were 'given certificates of attendance and ordered to duty', a solution that incurred some criticism given the bureaucratic nature of chaplaincy work and the 'excellent or superior' standards set by many of their black colleagues (it is noteworthy that Chaplain Fuller was 'holder of seven college degrees, including a master of arts in music, religious education, and the liberal arts').[240] Second, in breach of established tradition (and occasionally even despite the wishes of the troops involved), white chaplains could be assigned to largely black units.[241] Third, religious leadership could be devolved, even abdicated, to laymen, such as at Milne Bay in New Guinea where, in the case of 'a colored port battalion', a 'layman who was in the battalion and who had had preaching experience was selected to look after [its] spiritual welfare'.[242] Fourth and finally, more capable black chaplains could find themselves in incongruous positions. For example, in New Guinea towards the end of the war the senior chaplain of the 93rd Infantry Division (one of only two black infantry divisions, and 98 per cent Protestant in composition) was John W. Bowman, a Catholic priest of the Society of the Divine Word and the 'only colored Catholic chaplain in the Southwest Pacific'.[243]

Critical to the process of securing chaplains from whatever source was the cooperation of ecclesiastical endorsing bodies. Regularly informed of denominational requirements based on quotas that had last been approved by a Secretary of War in 1928,[244] these bodies were charged with interviewing, selecting and endorsing candidates. This task appears to have been discharged quite rigorously, as hundreds of applicants for the army's Corps of Chaplains failed to clear this initial hurdle.[245] The three main endorsing bodies were the FCC-sponsored General Commission on Army and Navy Chaplains, a more independent successor of the FCC's General Committee, which represented around forty Protestant denominations; the Military Ordinariate, which had overseen Catholic military chaplaincy since November 1917 and which was headed by Archbishop Francis J. Spellman of New York; and, from January 1942, the Committee on Army and Navy Religious Activities (CANRA) of the Jewish Welfare Board, which proved remarkably successful in overcoming the 'historic and often bitter differences' between Orthodox, Conservative and Reform Judaism.[246] While some denominations and groupings, such as the Protestant Episcopal Church,

Southern Baptists and Lutherans, preferred to deal with the two chiefs of chaplains directly, the demand for chaplains and the cumbersome processes of the General Commission meant that in practice much of its work was devolved to denominational endorsing committees such as the Methodist Commission on Chaplains, a body for whom procurement was 'top priority' and that interviewed candidates 'wherever a sufficient number of the Commission members could be assembled for that purpose'.[247] A similar situation obtained in Jewish affairs, with CANRA being supported by the vigorous recruiting efforts mounted by America's main rabbinical associations, namely the Reform Central Conference of American Rabbis, the Conservative Rabbinical Assembly of America, and the Orthodox Rabbinical Council of America.[248] The problems of endorsement were not simply administrative, however. In September 1942, the deep theological cleavages within American Protestantism were once again exposed when the navy's chief of chaplains was visited by a delegation representing the newly formed American Council of Christian Churches,[249] a militantly fundamentalist body that claimed the right, quickly conceded, to represent its members in chaplaincy matters and complained that the General Commission had 'practically gained a monopoly on the quota of appointments allotted to the religious groups called Protestant Evangelicals'.[250] Following endorsement, the next hurdle to be cleared by any candidate was a medical examination and, in the case of the navy, screening by Naval Intelligence in the form of a personal interview. The latter precaution was intended to eliminate subversive influences and to guarantee shipboard discipline; in the event, it appears to have taken a steady toll of candidates with more radical political views, who were liable to be treated as potential agitators. As one Jewish source complained, the navy's screening system inevitably led 'to the rejection of certain outstanding rabbis who had been active in liberal causes'.[251]

The training of military chaplains

Those candidates who were successful were commissioned directly into the army or navy in the same manner as other professionals such as doctors and dentists.[252] As Israel Yost, a pastor of the United Lutheran Church from Bethlehem, Pennsylvania, recalled, a month after his medical examination in Philadelphia in December 1942 a letter arrived confirming his appointment and, 'with it was a form of the oath of office, which, when executed and returned to the War Department, signified my acceptance of the position as chaplain, first lieutenant, in the Army of the United States "for the duration of the war and six months thereafter unless sooner terminated"'.[253] However, it took more than paperwork to make a chaplain. Because of the civilian habits, background and outlook of the overwhelming majority of their chaplains, training (or 'indoctrination', as the navy Chaplain Corps preferred to call it) was a major concern of both services throughout the war. Novice army chaplains who served prior to Pearl Harbor benefited from the publication in April 1941 of War Department Technical Manual TM 16–205 entitled *The Chaplain*, essentially a revision of earlier chaplains' manuals dating back to 1912, and also from ad hoc post and divisional chaplains' schools.[254] However, in the wake of Pearl Harbor, the Corps of Chaplains responded to the needs of the hour by reactivating its Chaplain School at Fort Benjamin Harrison, Indiana, in February 1942 (its earlier school, then based at Fort Leavenworth, Kansas, had closed its doors to resident students in 1928, chaplains for the regular army being trained thereafter through 'a period of close association with a senior chaplain of long experience').[255] Owing to a shortage of space, the revived Chaplain School transferred from Fort Benjamin Harrison to the hallowed precincts of Harvard six months later, where it stayed for two years before moving to Fort Devens, Massachusetts, in August 1944. At Fort Devens, it was able to focus more heavily on battlefield training, including 'amphibious landing training, across the waters of a little lake' and 'on the infiltration course, crawling under barbed wire, under live ammunition'.[256] However, the unexpected severity of the ensuing north-eastern winter impinged on this training and, with an assault on Japan in prospect, the school was relocated to the warmer climes of Fort Oglethorpe, Georgia, in July 1945.[257]

Despite its peregrinations, by the end of 1945 the army's Chaplain School had produced 8,183 graduates, its faculty developing a robust curriculum that, 'since all students [were] presumed to come to the school well-grounded in their own faith', [258] placed a firm emphasis on the 'Practical Duties of the Chaplain'.[259] Intended for regular, reserve and National Guard chaplains who had already seen active duty, as much as for freshly commissioned students who came straight from civilian life,[260] by 1944 its five-week programme covered military law, military etiquette, military administration, counselling, morale-building, army organisation and 'the conduct of religious services, pastoral duties, and community contacts'. These subjects were accompanied by instruction in first aid, sanitation, field craft, map-reading, graves registration and chemical warfare, and by a vigorous routine of calisthenics, close order drill and route marches.[261] Although students attended 'the daily prescribed devotions of their own faiths',[262] the emphasis was otherwise very much on integration and mutual cooperation. There was no colour bar and the elimination of religious prejudice was an avowed aim of the school – as its commandant, William D. Cleary, was at pains to emphasise: 'Men of the different religious denominations are bunked together so far as possible. This practice is designed to promote tolerance and understanding and to break down bigotry, which will thrive only in the mud of ignorance'.[263] The overriding goal, however, was to instil a due sense of military discipline among students who were usually very much accustomed to thinking and acting for themselves. As Cleary explained the situation:

One of the great problems in training students who will be chaplains is the almost complete lack of formal discipline to which many of the students were subjected in the course of their work in civil life. It is this primary need for and value of discipline that must be explained to the student. His most difficult adjustment is to the rigid requirements of discipline in the Army, for, being a soldier, albeit without arms, he is subject to the same rules of discipline which govern our fighting men.[264]

The training received at the Chaplain School was augmented in various ways. These included further training at local chaplains' schools;[265] training and manoeuvres with the chaplain's assigned unit, which could even involve new-fangled parachute training for airborne chaplains; the publication of a new edition of TM 16–205 in 1944; regular 'technical circulars' from the Office of the Chief of Chaplains (on applied subjects such as 'The Chaplain at the Reception Centre' and 'The Chaplain in the Hospital'); local chaplains' conferences; and, later in the war, special courses for supervising chaplains and those selected for the AAF.[266] While chaplains who served in the ETO complained of the neglect of in-theatre training, in the Mediterranean Theatre of Operations the lessons of hard fighting up the Italian peninsula brought home to the senior chaplain of Fifth Army the importance of combat psychology, an appreciation that led to several chaplains' conferences being held on that subject in Florence in December 1944.[267] Despite the obvious need for such supplements and the fact that by no means every successful army chaplain passed through the Chaplain School (Edward K. Rogers, a United Lutheran chaplain who served with the 1st Infantry Division in North Africa, Sicily and North-West Europe, was among those who never darkened its doors and survived)[268] the basic training received at the Chaplain School was generally judged to have been worthwhile. According to an official evaluation made in 1944:

Opinion was unanimous that the training of the Chaplain School was invaluable to men with no previous military training or experience. Many chaplains with previous training and with long experience in the Regular Army or other components declared that the course served to refresh their memories of many matters and to acquaint them with new directives and policies. Others emphasized the helpful methods of work which they gained at the School.[269]

As in so many other matters, the navy's Chaplain Corps had a greater distance to travel in the development of its training programme. The system that had prevailed prior to 1942 at least had the virtue of simplicity: new chaplains were 'usually sent to one of the larger naval installations where they served with an older chaplain for several months before being given independent duty'. However, this apprentice system, as Clifford M. Drury conceded, 'lacked both completeness and uniformity'.[270] Frederick William Meehling, a Catholic, described his own mentor at Norfolk Naval Operating Base, Virginia, as 'good-natured, harmless [and] lazy'. He was also a rather bigoted Southern Methodist, once joking to a sailor about the reserved sacrament, kept in a small YMCA chapel on the base: '[The Catholics] think they have a body down there. My opinion is that if they have one, they ought to take it out and bury it'.[271] One of the experienced chaplains tasked with mentoring novice chaplains in the 1930s was William Wilcox Edel, who was then based in San Francisco as district chaplain of the Twelfth Naval District. As Edel remembered:

> A newly-appointed Navy chaplain was ordered to me for instruction, and the day after he reported, I took him to a Navy funeral.... As we rode back to my office, he asked, 'What did you say to the widow? It seemed so comforting from where I stood'. I answered, 'I merely made a sympathetic murmur'.[272]

This complacency in training matters disappeared abruptly in the wake of Pearl Harbor, with the apprentice system being jettisoned in favour of a new chaplains' school that opened at Norfolk Naval Operating Base in February 1942.[273] However, with limited space available and college campuses emptying across America, in little more than a year the school was transferred to the prestigious College of William and Mary at nearby Williamsburg, where it stayed for the rest of the war.[274] Like its army counterpart, the eight-week course at the navy chaplains' school was strongly practical in emphasis, it being presupposed that 'each chaplain came fully prepared professionally, according to the standards of his church'.[275] Students were taught how to 'rig for church' and how to lead services at sea; they were also briefed about the work of religious and secular welfare agencies and about the marriage laws of different states. They also became conversant with navy regulations, organisation, customs and etiquette. Looking forward to the day of battle (in the event, a minority experience), they learned about the chaplain's duty station while in action and trained in 'the techniques of abandoning a sinking ship and swimming through burning oil'. Their outdoor training also included drill, a two-week assignment to an experienced naval chaplain (an echo of the old apprenticeship system) and a weekly field-trip to naval installations or to marine and coast guard units.[276] The course concluded with each student going before an examining board that recommended either graduation, a remedial spell at the school or resignation.[277] Although each day commenced with separate devotions, as at the army chaplain school great emphasis was placed on promoting religious tolerance and harmony, in this case under the slogan of 'Cooperation without Compromise'. Accordingly, students were instructed in how to attend the wounded and dying of other faiths, a duty that might involve reciting unfamiliar prayers if an appropriate chaplain was not available.[278] Again, however, the main priority was to turn civilian clergymen, and mostly landlubbers at that, into navy officers through an unremitting stress on acting and thinking in 'the navy way'. As Drury duly noted:

> As far as possible naval terminology was used at the School. One came aboard. The walls of a building became bulkheads; the toilets, heads; the stairways, ladders; the floor was a deck; where the duty chaplains stood watch was the quarter-deck; the hours of the day ran from 1 to 24; time was counted by the clanging of the bell; and orders were responded to with an 'Aye, aye, Sir'.[279]

Inevitably, these adjustments were not always made easily. One former student, John Harold Craven, who had served as a marine before entering the Southern Baptist ministry,[280] remembered that:

> [W]e lived in barracks the first three weeks and slept in double deck bunks. That was an interesting experience for some of those ministers who were 40 or 45 years of age and had been living in a parsonage for years. It was quite a cultural shock to be thrown into a barracks with about a hundred other fellows, sleeping in an upper or lower bunk and having to make up your own bed. Lights went out at 10:00 P.M. and some of these men just were not ready for this, so you would find some of them sitting in the head reading magazines or books when the lights were out in the barracks.[281]

However, and if the success of 'indoctrination' at the navy chaplains' school can be measured by the disciplinary record of its graduates, then it was clearly quite significant. While almost three thousand men served in the Chaplain Corps during World War II, only one was ever court-martialled, in his case for making insufficient effort to reach his unit during a battle ashore. While a handful of others were asked to resign for the good of the service, the headline figures suggest that the induction of this relatively small and highly select body of men into 'the navy way' was remarkably successful.[282]

Organization and ethos

Once trained, the organisational complexity and far-flung deployments of the army and navy involved a tremendous variety of assignments and experiences. One post-war report on army chaplains in the ETO listed no fewer than forty different 'chaplain categories', three-quarters of which related to their assignments and ranged from 'Medical clearing company and field hospital chaplains' to 'Chaplains assigned to prisons and disciplinary training centers'.[283] As William D. Cleary emphasised in his wartime essay 'The Ministry of the Chaplain': 'There is an almost unbelievable variety in the type of assignment possible in time of war', it being 'impossible to describe the work of any one man and say, "This is a typical chaplain"'.[284] Navy chaplains could be assigned to a variety of naval bases and stations at home and overseas; to larger combat or transport ships; to flotillas of smaller vessels such as torpedo boats or landing craft; to a variety of marine units or construction battalions (the famous 'Seabees'); to the US Coast Guard, navy hospitals, and to various types of staff and headquarters work.[285] By the same token, the threefold division of the army into the Army Ground Forces (AGF), the Army Air Forces (AAF) and Army Service Forces (ASF) (initially known as the Services of Supply) in March 1942 underlined the wartime dynamic towards greater diversity and specialisation, a dynamic that was often driven as much by intra-service politics as by the impact of military technology and the demands of modern war.[286] Still, variety was the keynote even within each subdivision of the wartime army. Fundamentally, service with the AGF involved ministering to the army's combat formations and training infrastructure, the former embracing an array of troop types that included infantry, armoured, airborne, artillery, mountain and combat engineer units. In contrast, service with the ASF (of which the Corps of Chaplains actually formed a part) basically involved ministering to the army's support elements, which in addition to a host of posts and installations comprised an enormous medley of medical, quartermaster, ordnance, signal, transportation and engineer units.[287] Even in the AAF there was a great variety of assignments, its chaplains serving a plethora of bases and airfields and a multiplicity of training, bomber, fighter, transportation, engineer and other service units.[288]

Unsurprisingly, the range, scale and complexity of wartime operations demanded new administrative structures and the creation of new hierarchies of chaplains. In Washington, the navy's chief of chaplains ran an office that comprised a staff of just six on 7 December 1941. By the end of August 1945, this staff numbered thirty-seven, and their office was now subdivided into sections that dealt with recruitment, assignments, the V-12 Program, public relations and even the history of the corps.[289] Much responsibility was also devolved to district chaplains in the United States and to fleet, area and force chaplains overseas, the latter often having more chaplains at their disposal than had been serving in the corps at the time of Pearl Harbor.[290] The administrative revolution was no less pronounced in the army. By the end of 1943, and besides more minor components, the Chief of Chaplains' Office comprised a Personnel Division, a Planning and Training Division, a Technical Information Division and an Army Air Forces Liaison Division. Furthermore, key divisions were themselves subdivided; various branches of the Personnel Division, for example, dealt with recruitment, assignment, efficiency, records and promotions.[291] By the end of the war, the staff at the Chief of Chaplains' Office numbered 150, including twenty-five chaplains, whereas in 1939 it had numbered fewer than ten.[292] As in the navy, given the workload involved the army's chief of chaplains had to devolve much administration onto lower tiers of senior chaplains. These included service command chaplains in the United States (who were central to recruitment and public relations) and department (or theatre) chaplains overseas,[293] while beneath them were further strata of supervising chaplains at army, corps, division and regimental level in the AGF and at ports, districts and major hospitals in the ASF.[294]

The AAF, which represented the largest and most powerful air force in the world by 1945, absorbed around one-quarter of all army chaplains by the end of 1944.[295] Here, serious complications arose from the overarching politics of air power and from 'Hap' Arnold's pursuit of ultimate independence, a corollary of which was the assertion by the AAF of 'complete control of its attached ASF units'.[296] One consequence of these wider developments was the establishment of an Air Chaplain Division at the headquarters of the AAF in 1942,[297] a step that meant that the chief of chaplains' oversight of AAF chaplaincy was effectively shared with a newly minted 'air chaplain', namely Charles Irving Carpenter, a Methodist minister and erstwhile sports celebrity who had a record of successful work with the pre-war Air Corps. However, the direction of service politics meant that the autonomy of AAF chaplaincy grew inexorably. Eventually, this embraced a separate and distinct hierarchy of AAF chaplains, the selection of graduates of the Chaplains' School for permanent duty with the AAF, the creation of a supporting 'Air Chaplain Transition Course' at San Antonio, Texas, and the opening of a separate office for the air chaplain at the newly built Pentagon in June 1943.[298] These moves towards independence undoubtedly placed Arnold in a tricky position in relation to his namesake; when the chief of chaplains remarked that 'It looks as though some day you're going to have your own Corps of Chaplains', 'Hap' Arnold simply replied, 'That's what I want.'[299]

As we have seen, and for all the wartime rhetoric of religious harmony, another invidious problem lay in ensuring a fair representation of Protestants, Catholics and Jews among those senior positions that were in the chief of chaplains' gift. When wartime expansion demanded the appointment of the army's first deputy chief of chaplains in 1942, Arnold wisely selected George Foreman Rixey, another long-serving regular who, as a Methodist, represented the country's largest Protestant denomination.[300] Significantly, in 1945 it was confirmed from the ETO that 'the Chief of Chaplains has endeavoured to distribute field grade [i.e. supervising] positions in approximate proportion to the relative representation of the major faith groups in the Chaplains Corps, that is 25% to 35% to Roman Catholic chaplains and 65% to 75% to Protestant chaplains'. The report went on to emphasise that: 'In the European Theater (ground and service forces) the denominational distribution of field grades followed very closely the proportion of the major faith groups in the Corps.'[301]

Whatever their denomination, supervising chaplains faced daunting problems of their own. While senior chaplains in the Pacific had to contend with the vast size of this theatre of war and with the priority accorded to the war in Europe,[302] the needs of combat units always took priority over those of support units.[303] Furthermore, the number of chaplains in their charge fluctuated wildly with the expansion and contraction of corps and armies according to strategic and operational needs. For example, the fifty-seven chaplains assigned to Sixth Army on its activation in the United States in January 1943 had grown to four hundred by July 1944, by which time it was heavily engaged in New Guinea, but the total fell to three hundred by May 1945 after the critical stages of the Philippines campaign had passed.[304] Similarly, two months after the activation of Fifth Army in North Africa in February 1943, Patrick J. Ryan, the 'Fifth Army Chaplain', had fifty-six chaplains at his disposal; with the invasion of the Italian mainland that September, this figure climbed to 119, peaked at 222 early in 1944 and fell to 180 by the end of the war.[305] Naturally, such numbers caused problems in their own right. George R. Metcalf, a Protestant Episcopal priest and Normandy veteran, who was appointed assistant army chaplain to George S. Patton's Third Army in November 1944, compared his work to that of a suffragan bishop in a larger diocese.[306] Having been the rector of a parish in upstate New York three years earlier, by the spring of 1945 he saw his job as being 'to keep peace' among three hundred or so other chaplains. In a letter written to his mother that Easter, Metcalf recounted an array of current challenges that included juggling chaplains' assignments, meeting the demands of commanding officers, receiving an endless stream of visitors, and ensuring the delivery of Passover supplies to Third Army's widely scattered Jewish soldiers.[307]

Metcalf's last problem underscores the fact that the prime constitutional justification for military chaplaincy was the 'Free Exercise Clause' of the First Amendment, the implications of which were spelled out by William D. Cleary:

> [E]very man and woman in the Armed Forces has the right to the full exercise of his or her religion. A Roman Catholic has the right to attend Mass on every Sunday and Holy Day of Obligation. A Protestant has the right to the ministrations of a Protestant minister and to receive Holy Communion. Members of Protestant denominations that require their members to receive Communion only at the hands of their own clergy have a right to have their faith and practice respected. Jewish men and women have the right to attend the services of their faith, including especially the observance of the High Holy Days.[308]

However, it was impossible to expect that every soldier or sailor would have immediate access to a chaplain of their own faith or denomination, an ideal situation known as 'triple coverage',[309] irrespective of how carefully assignments were managed. In view of this situation, and as revised in 1924, army regulations required that chaplains should 'serve as friends, counselors, and guides, without discrimination, to all members of the command to which they are assigned, regardless of creed or sect, and will strive to promote morality, religion, and good order therein'.[310] In pursuit of this goal, it was envisaged that an army chaplain would 'make every effort to bring in other clergy to meet the distinctly religious needs of men to whom he is not competent to minister'.[311] When such help was not available, chaplains were expected to support laymen in holding religious services of their own and to obtain devotional material for them. Only as 'a last resort' was an army chaplain permitted, as Cleary put it, to 'conduct a general service of such a nature as to help all men to a deeper faith in the God who is the common Father of us all'. Furthermore, but again only *in extremis*, it was accepted that, whenever a chaplain of the same denomination was not available, 'any chaplain of any denomination' could read 'the appropriate prayers of the man's own faith' to a dying soldier.[312] How this could be done was illustrated in some 'suggestions' formulated by chaplains of the V Corps who went to Europe in January 1942,[313] and which were subsequently adopted as far afield as the Pacific:

> Procedure by a non-Catholic Chaplain when finding a Catholic man. Learn the man's first name if possible and say, '(John), I am not a Priest, but I have talked with Father (Kelly) and he asked me to say that since he cannot possibly be here I should read for you this prayer called 'The Act of Contrition'. Will you either say with me (or repeat after me) the following 'Oh my God I am heartily sorry for having offended Thee [etc] ...'. Father (Kelly) said for me to assure you that if you really and truly mean this prayer that you have just prayed, that you are assured Absolution from all your sins and of Eternal and Everlasting Life. He asked me to give you this Rosary which he has blessed for you to keep and to assure you that he grants you his blessing.[314]

True to its slogan 'Cooperation without Compromise', the same approach was also instilled at the navy's Chaplains' School.[315] Consequently, the war years abounded in somewhat beguiling tales of interdenominational and interfaith cooperation, whether of Protestant and Jewish chaplains leading each other's services, of a Lutheran chaplain organising a rosary service for Catholic sailors, or of a Baptist chaplain from Kentucky leading a Rosh Hashanah service for Jewish servicemen on New Georgia in 1943.[316] However, and besides the personal prejudice and foot-dragging identified by Renwick C. Kennedy in 1946, there were clear limits to this kind of cooperation. As Cleary listed them:

> A Roman Catholic chaplain cannot administer Holy Communion to a Protestant soldier. A Protestant chaplain cannot hear the confession of a Roman Catholic and grant him Absolution nor can he say Mass. A Jewish chaplain cannot perform the sacramental rites of the Christian church. Neither a Protestant nor a Catholic chaplain can minister fully to a Jewish serviceman.[317]

However, in actual fact the problems went deeper than this, for while the chaplains of Protestant 'non-liturgical denominations' (such as the Baptists, Methodists, Presbyterians and Disciples of Christ) were seen as 'more or less interchangeable' by the army (as, indeed, they often were in civilian life) it was found in the ETO that members of Protestantism's 'liturgical denominations' (basically Episcopalians and Lutherans) expected to receive the sacraments 'exclusively at the hands of clergymen of their own communion'.[318] Furthermore, wartime ecumenism plainly clashed with the tenets of Cleary's own church, canon law forbidding Catholics from participating in the worship of other denominations. Thus, from New Year 1944 a general service was more narrowly defined in the navy as a service that only Catholic chaplains could conduct for Protestant personnel, and only when no Protestant clergyman was available.[319] Beneath the wartime rhetoric of America's 'interfaith warfare against Japan and Germany',[320] such was the abiding complexity and sensitivity of these issues that they even ensnared the legendary war correspondent Ernie Pyle, whose reluctance to write about the religious life of GIs has been ascribed to the furore that one of his early columns had provoked, a column in which Pyle had quoted a Baptist chaplain who claimed that he was authorised to give the last rites to Catholic soldiers.[321]

Chaplains and morale

Besides fulfilling the 'free exercise' requirements of the First Amendment, the role of the chaplain illustrated the vital connection that was widely thought to exist between good military morale and the influence of religion. Although this connection had been made in Western Christian societies since the age of Constantine, and had been strengthened for Americans by the experience of the Revolutionary and Civil Wars,[322] for advocates of the reform of US Army chaplaincy in the aftermath of World War I the connection had been vindicated yet again by the experience of the AEF in France. One post-war pamphlet written in support of reform commenced with the claim:

> It was *morale* that won the war – however much other things may have contributed to fire the shot into the ranks of the enemy. And the finest morale has its foundations in religion. The American Army won largely because it was engaged in a great crusade – a fight for democracy, a fight for the very men against whom it was fighting [and] chaplains in the army had much to do with the creation of this kind of morale.[323]

Critically, such views enjoyed the powerful endorsement of Pershing himself. In September 1919, in his final report as commander-in-chief of the AEF to Newton D. Baker, the Secretary of War, Pershing pronounced that: 'Chaplains, as never before, became the moral and spiritual leaders of their organizations, and established a high standard of active usefulness in religious work that made for patriotism, discipline and unselfish devotion to duty.'[324] Pershing returned to this theme four years later at the Washington Conference on Moral and Religious Work in the Army, saying of the work of his former chaplains: 'Their usefulness in the maintenance of morale through religious counsel and example has now become a matter of history and can be accepted as having demonstrated, if need be, the wisdom of the religious appeal to the soldier.'[325]

In the wake of World War I, the morale-boosting role of the chaplain came to be increasingly identified with the uninhibited performance of his religious functions. Hence, and as the 1923 Conference on Moral and Religious Work in the Army emphasised, the duties of the chaplain clearly transcended those of a unit's morale officer, a lesser role that had often been his portion. As the conference agreed:

> The purposes of our Government in appointing chaplains and the place of religion in the Army have been misunderstood, because frequently a chaplain has been used simply to promote what is known as morale. The chaplain does promote true morale in the best possible way – by religious sanction. But morale which looks upon a man only as an efficient fighting machine means militarism in the ascendant, a denial of the soul, and an undoing of the man himself. Against such a process the spirit of America protests. The chaplain has a high and holy office. He is the servant of the religious needs of the men. When he is asked to promote morale first and religion afterwards, he is asked to be false to his mission.[326]

If the interwar years saw some disengagement from the more secular activities previously associated with chaplaincy work in the US Army, a fundamental tension remained and the chaplain was by no means absolved from other responsibilities in the promotion of morale. As the April 1941 edition of the technical manual *The Chaplain*, which bore the imprimatur of the War Department, put it:

> It is the chaplain's highest function to stimulate or inspire men through the medium of religion to an idealism which finds its fruition in loyalty, courage, and contentment, the very essence of good morale. It is the principal business of the chaplain to help build that character which makes best soldiers, best citizens, and best men. He may accomplish this through the religious motive or he may attempt to develop the spirit of loyalty and patriotism, pride in the service, team play, a sense of honor, unselfishness, and contentment by direct appeal. He is, to the degree in which he accomplishes this end, a most important factor in maintaining what is commonly called morale both in peace and war. *He should neglect no opportunity* [my italics] to help both officers and men to maintain a cheerful and courageous spirit, with unshaken faith in the high cause which they serve, through both the monotony of peace and the trying ordeals of war.[327]

Nonetheless, the religious dimension of the chaplain's morale-building role was recognised as being paramount. In November 1941, and on the very brink of war, Assistant Adjutant General, Brigadier General James A. Ulio wrote: 'The chaplain exercises an indispensable function in building military morale, for religion as a strengthening and stabilizing influence on the character of the individual can hardly be overestimated.'[328]

Under the impact of war, the implications of this unresolved tension quickly became apparent. A wartime article in the Catholic weekly *America* mused that:

> Both the Army and the Navy regard chaplains as important in maintaining morale. That means, to be truly successful, that they should be composed of almost equal parts of Billy Rose, Dorothy Dix, Florence Nightingale, Gene Tunney, Sumner Welles, and St. Paul. It would help considerably if, at one time or other, the chaplain had run a loan office, a department store, a missing persons detective agency, a library, a surveying office and, in many cases, a restaurant.[329]

This article also sketched a picture of 'Father Jim', a typical navy chaplain, who was both 'morale officer and entertainment officer' of his ship. Consequently:

> [E]very night his piano and orchestra entertained the ship's company. Every night there was an improvised show, from smart comedy teams to a Tennessee fiddler. Every morning he became news commentator, relaying the news received by wire the night before.[330]

However, such varied activity was at least in keeping with the accepted ethos of navy chaplaincy before and during the war. As William D. Cleary explained in 1945:

> The duties of a Navy chaplain differ somewhat from the Army chaplain in that he may be assigned certain miscellaneous duties in addition to the religious services, the visitation of the sick, conferences, and consultations. Additional tasks may include assisting in the educational, entertainment, and welfare program, and supervising ship and station libraries.[331]

If chaplains of the US Navy shouldered the 'collateral duties of the Navy chaplain' throughout the war, and thus served as librarians, newscasters, Navy Relief workers, and as the organisers of 'recreation parties, sightseeing tours, smokers, and other entertainment activities',[332] the official duties of the army chaplain narrowed significantly after Pearl Harbor. In this respect, the growing identification of the chaplain as a religious specialist first and foremost, which was already in evidence in the interwar years, was aided and accelerated by the expansion and activities of the army's Special Services. After World War I, and in light of 'certain serious deficiencies' in the performance of civilian welfare organisations, the army had formed its own morale branch, which, in the interwar years, and with the active participation of the chief of chaplains, 'accomplished much in the study of morale problems, and programs necessary to meet them'. In July 1940, and with the draft in prospect, a Morale Division was established in the Adjutant

General's Office. In 1941, this was placed under the chief of staff and renamed Morale Branch. A few weeks after Pearl Harbor, it was redesignated the Special Services Branch and was tasked with recommending and implementing policies conducive to good morale. Although now without the involvement of the chief of chaplains, the Special Services Branch was made responsible for the running of the army's post exchanges and its library and motion picture services.[333] Placed under the umbrella of the ASF in 1943, Special Services was subdivided that November and responsibility for 'the psychological approach to the mental attitude of troops' passed to Morale Services, rebranded the Information and Education Division in August 1944. This took charge of the army's newspapers and radio service, off-duty educational programme, orientation films and 'research work on troop attitudes'.[334] Despite its rather tortuous administrative history, the work of Special Services was certainly far-reaching and its sections were eventually organised 'at theatre, base section, air force, army, corps and divisional level'.[335] Primarily engaged in providing reading matter, mobile post exchanges, sporting events, USO concerts and other forms of entertainment for the troops, Special Services assumed many of the tasks associated with religious welfare organisations – and, indeed, with chaplains – during World War I.[336] Nevertheless, there were limitations to this situation. While its sections could never be everywhere at once, Special Services represented 'an emergency service of the Army' but one that 'lacked the prestige and experienced personnel of an established corps or technical service'. Consequently, its activities were not always supported, or even fully comprehended, by commanding officers.[337] Hence, and despite being present with American troops in Britain from 1942, after the end of the war in Europe an authoritative report on Special Services in the ETO found that: 'It is the general opinion of all consultants, that the special services organization in the European Theater was inadequate to efficiently carry out its mission.'[338]

Because of these inadequacies, and despite the notional narrowing of their remit, army chaplains could still be called upon to undertake work that was increasingly identified with Special Services, especially early in the war or when assigned to isolated units. Edward K. Rogers remembered that, in 1942 and while undergoing amphibious training in England, there would be 'trips ashore to buy what magazines and papers one could find'; later, and bound for Algeria and the Torch landings, Rogers busied himself 'distributing among the troops library books and games from the ship's stores'.[339] However, these were familiar chores in many far-flung corners of the world at this early stage of the war. Of the situation in Australia, it was reported that:

> In these early days the responsibility for soldier entertainment rested more heavily on the chaplain than it did later on when the Special Service and Information and Education sections and the American Red Cross began functioning effectively. The chaplains' monthly reports of those first few

months show that many of the chaplains were appointed as Special Service officers. The reports make constant reference to the arrangements which were made for movies, special shows, sight-seeing tours, recreation and entertainment.[340]

Chaplains assigned to those units that constructed the 1,500 mile Alcan Military Highway from Dawson Creek in British Columbia to Fairbanks in Alaska in 1942 were also called upon to provide entertainment for the troops.[341] Accordingly, Edward Gonzalez Carroll, a black Methodist chaplain and a graduate of Columbia University and Yale School of Divinity, established a library of five hundred books, formed a band and founded a music appreciation society that developed a particular taste for 'opera and the light classics' in the wastes of the Alaskan tundra. Furthermore, a religious film entitled *The Power of God* was shown in Carroll's tent so many times 'that the celluloid practically wore out'.[342]

Naturally, Special Services sections regarded the chaplain as an ally throughout the war; on the eve of D-Day, a guide to Special Services work in the ETO even spoke of the relationship between commanding officers, Special Services and chaplains as a 'trinity working for good morale. Together, they mould the fighting man. – They give him the "know how", the guts, the buoyant spirit, and the faith to win'.[343] However, and ironic as it may seem, a complicating factor was that some chaplains were reluctant to accept the steady curtailment of their role in terms of morale. Russell Cartwright Stroup, for example, took his wider responsibilities for morale very seriously throughout his wartime career. While in training with the 399th Infantry Regiment in the United States, Stroup practically lectured his commanding officer on what he could do to improve morale, writing to his family in May 1943:

> I had a long talk with the colonel on Saturday night about the morale of the regiment, which is not as good as it ought to be. I was quite frank and made some pointed suggestions to the colonel about what he should do. He has been trying to do what I suggested. I want him to get closer to the men – and in some way other than his usual role of critic. He has to criticize, and he has to discipline, but he should – as I told him – make a point to speak to the men on other occasions when he might praise.[344]

In 1944, and by then assigned to the 1st Infantry Regiment in the South-West Pacific, Stroup was positively put out when, upon the protest of a fellow chaplain, he was relieved of his 'secular duties' on board a transport en route for Australia; significantly, he chose to continue his work in the ship's mess regardless.[345] Frustrated though he was with such an approach to chaplaincy, Stroup remained a careful observer of troop morale. In November 1944, and with the 1st Infantry now in New Guinea, he expressed his dismay with GIs in general:

Last night I saw Noel Coward's movie *In Which We Serve*, an old film telling the story of a British destroyer, and telling it very well. But for the first time out here I saw most of the audience get up and leave. I've left several times when the show was some truly awful product, but this was good. Of course, it concerned the war, which they don't like to see, and it was filled with patriotic sentiment, which is anathema. This isn't just a lack of patriotic fervor: it's actual hatred of anything that suggests it. They fall for all sorts of cheap sentiment, except that one. I think that underneath they do have a feeling for their country, but they refuse to let on. Compared with every other army, we have done a poor job of indoctrination. This may be just as well, but personally I still have in me a good deal of the old screaming-eagle Americanism.[346]

Furthermore, in the often primitive conditions of the war in the Pacific, it could be unwise for chaplains to stand on the dignity of their clerical status. Following a tour of inspection in 1944, a senior Presbyterian chaplain, Wayne L. Hunter, even remarked that 'where chaplains were obstinate in this matter [a] poor relationship with the officers resulted'. As Hunter pointed out:

In a ... station hospital constructing its own installations, medical officers are quite likely to be filling in the capacity of engineers, and technicians are digging ditches or doing carpenter work. In these cases the chaplain has no patients and few men available to work with. Most officers feel that the chaplain should not stand apart on the basis of his professional qualifications, when their own professional qualifications are cast aside in the interest of expediency. Chaplains have taken on extra duties under such conditions, which are usually in related work such as censorship and providing for the general welfare of the men. One chaplain insisted on being malarial control officer in every new area which his organization entered, and did a very commendable job.[347]

In such circumstances, even Catholic chaplains could see their official duties as unduly circumscribed. In August 1944, Victor Laketek, a Benedictine monk and AAF chaplain stationed on the tiny island of Kanton in the Phoenix Islands, felt that his lot was far too quiet, complaining that:

The Navy chaplains are better off on islands such as this inasmuch as they have additional duties such as athletics, education, [and the] camp paper to fill up their time. We army chaplains are limited to Religious work & the special service officer handles the rest. Ordinarily this is a good idea – not to overload the chaplains with extraneous activities, but here I should appreciate some. There isn't a great deal of strictly Religious work here and the men are not very responsive.[348]

However, over the course of the war official policy moved inexorably in the opposite direction. Significantly, the 1941 edition of the technical manual *The Chaplain* had encouraged chaplains to pitch into 'Exceptional duties':

> A general rule which might reasonably be laid down for a chaplain with respect to all this class of duties is that he should hold himself in readiness to share in manly and sportsmanly fashion any and all [of] the duties of the commissioned personnel of the command where there exists a real scarcity of officers which would entail hardship upon his fellows by his nonparticipation. Such emergencies do occasionally arise and when they come a chaplain does not want to win the unenviable reputation of being a shirker when others are working overtime.[349]

Emphasising that 'A chaplain's value to a garrison or command is enhanced as his points of contact multiply', it positively urged chaplains to participate 'in the realm of organized social activity for enlisted men', in particular by organising dance clubs, 'Smokers, radio clubs, and other purely stag organizations [to] fill a place in whiling away the monotony that is liable to weigh upon men with few interests and limited diversional facilities'.[350] In stark contrast, and while grudgingly acknowledging the existence of an army regulation that permitted this sort of activity wherever there was 'a shortage of officers', the 1944 edition of the same manual stressed the need for cooperation with Special Services officers as 'the surest guarantee that neither will encroach upon the other's sphere of activity'. Furthermore, and while advising chaplains to 'give encouragement and aid to plans for the contentment and welfare of the men', it was explicit that purely secular recreation was the concern of others.[351] In December 1944, a further revision of army regulations governing the use of chaplains stated that: 'The chaplain is a member of the staff of the commanding officer and is his logical consultant in all matters pertaining to public religious observances in the command, and in matters involving morality, character building, and the spiritual phases of morale'. The cumulative effect of such changes enabled William D. Cleary to be even more emphatic about the proper role of the army chaplain by the end of the war:

> The Army chaplain is a member of the staff of the commanding officer of the unit to which he is assigned. He is the logical consultant of the commanding officer in all matters relating to religion, morals, and morale. Army regulations specifically direct that he shall not be required to perform secular duties which might interfere with his function as a minister of religion. For example, the Army chaplain will not be placed in charge of the sports or recreational activities of his unit. He will not be in charge of educational work or social service. He will not serve as Defense Counsel in a Court Martial or as War Bond Officer or Insurance Officer. All of these activities are necessary to the efficiency of the Army. They must be done

by someone; but they are not primarily religious and hence they will not be done by the chaplain. More than at any previous period in our Army's history, the War Department recognizes the unique function of the chaplain. The religious work which he is specifically appointed to accomplish cannot be done by any other officer in the Army. If the chaplain is not free to do it, it will not be done.[352]

The chaplain in combat

If the breadth of the army chaplain's remit was in contention during the war, the power of army and navy chaplains to rouse the spirits of their men with a prayer, a timely service or an apt and forceful sermon was widely understood. However, Jewish chaplain Morris N. Kertzer thought that the army could have made much greater use of its chaplains in enduing its soldiers with a sense of purpose, complaining that:

> [On] the whole the Chaplains Corps did little to stimulate understanding of what we were fighting for or against. Harping on the theme of loving our enemies, our Washington office lauded the efforts of chaplains who preached the doctrine of universal love. To my mind, there is nothing so frankly immoral as killing without hate. I cannot follow the moral gymnastics in the argument that we despised not our enemies, but only what they represented, as though a man and his principles could be divorced. If the average G.I. did not know why he was thrust five thousand miles from home to risk his life, we chaplains as a corps did little to offer him enlightenment.[353]

Nevertheless, and if the Office of the Chief of Chaplains was anxious not to create hostages to fortune, especially given long-term reactions to the alleged clerical hate-mongering of World War I, there were plenty of individual army chaplains who would have met with Kertzer's approval. Edward K. Rogers, for example, of the 1st Infantry Division, accepted an invitation in Tunisia in 1943 to 'give a talk to the troops on what is at stake in the war'. Delivered to several battalions whose soldiers 'were weary from the months in combat and a bit down in morale', his words seem to have had a tonic effect, 'for officers frequently mentioned that the boys wrote home in goodly numbers about what had been said'. Furthermore, and as Rogers recalled, 'For months soldiers would come up and tell me what these words had meant to them.'[354] Rogers put in a repeat performance prior to the cross-Channel invasion the following year, meeting with a similar response even though 'it was spoken from the mind and heart with only hastily written notes.'[355] Other chaplains were more spontaneous still, a Catholic chaplain during the siege of Bastogne using the opportunity of a Christmas Mass to advise his congregation 'Do not plan, for God's plan will prevail.... Those who are attacking you are the enemies of Christ.'[356]

As for the navy, Warren Wyeth Willard, a Northern Baptist chaplain serving with the 2nd Marine Regiment on Guadalcanal in 1942, received some striking affirmation from a marine who told him:

> Chaplain Willard ... your services are an inspiration to us. Corporal K.W. McClun and Private M.G. Baxter of my company attended the service you held behind the lines yesterday morning. After the worship was over, the corporal and the private formed their own two-man patrol and went out into Jap territory. They killed five Japs in the afternoon. Then they returned to us here.[357]

On larger ships it was common for Willard's colleagues to offer prayers before action, these being carried over their public address systems. Prior to the landings on Iwo Jima in February 1945, for example, and on the grounds that 'it has long been the custom among fighting men to ask God's blessing before engaging the enemy', the captain of the escort carrier *Bismarck Sea* invited its Episcopalian chaplain, Eugene Russell Shannon, to pray for all on board. With a hard fight in prospect, and faced with the fearsome threat of kamikaze attack, Shannon's prayer ran:

> Almighty God, the Supreme Ruler of the Universe, whose power no creature is able to resist, we humbly beseech Thee to behold us as seeking to serve for righteousness. As we stand this night on the threshold of another strike, grant to each in whatever task lies before him, courage, steadfastness, and complete devotion to duty ... May we have ears to hear the call to battle, eyes to see the enemy wherever he lurks, and skill to save our ship, our planes, and ourselves from the hand of evil; that finally we may glorify Thee, the Giver of all Victory, through Jesus Christ, our Lord ...

Despite these entreaties, the *Bismarck Sea* was sunk, and Shannon killed, by an air attack a few hours later.[358]

Although their own petitions were not always heard, the fliers of the AAF also drew comfort from similar preparation by their own chaplains, an early wartime innovation being the provision of 'pre-mission services' for bomber crews. Initially spontaneous and necessarily brief in character, they were introduced as a matter of policy throughout the Eighth Air Force in the autumn of 1942,[359] their proliferation and appeal being assured by a growing awareness of the novel and myriad horrors of aerial warfare in Europe and in the Pacific. These services were held in the short span of time between mission briefings and take-off, whether outside briefing rooms or with crews who were waiting to board their planes. For Protestants, they generally consisted of prayers, scripture readings and a benediction; Catholic devotions were similar, albeit with a greater sacramental emphasis on quick-fire confessions, Holy Communion and general absolutions.[360] Prior to their fateful flight to Hiroshima, even the crew of the B-29 bomber *Enola Gay* benefited from this pre-mission ministry, a fact that has given rise to the erroneous belief that their chaplain blessed the bomb that obliterated the city on 6 August 1945.[361] More usually, however, pre-mission services were poignant and picturesque vignettes that made great copy for religious publications. In *Action This Day: Letters from the Fighting Fronts*, Archbishop Spellman was keen to recount his one-off ministry to departing aircrew during his visit to Britain in the spring of 1943,[362] and two years later *The Priest Goes To War* rejoiced that '"Spiritual briefing sessions" before combat are common in the Air Force' and that some chaplains 'asked their men to sign a slip recording that they had received the Sacraments before going on a mission', a precaution that 'brought infinite consolation to many Catholic families'.[363] Nevertheless, senior AAF officers could be more ambivalent about these services and practice varied between bomber groups. In some cases, commanding officers called upon chaplains to offer prayers at the conclusion of each briefing; in others, they had to minister at designated spots.[364] In 1944, and apparently to avoid infractions of the First Amendment, Eighth Air Force chaplains were banned from holding services in briefing rooms where they might have captive audiences.[365] One base commander even questioned their value in terms of morale: 'Don't like my boys to be reminded that they are liable to need anything more than luck and guts to get home'.[366] Nevertheless, the prevailing readiness to participate was captured in the words of Chaplain William Taggart, who wrote of such services on Java in 1942:

> You'll stand under the wing of a B-17 and they'll gather around you as they take a last sip of coffee from the thermos or munch a piece of chocolate.... You hold the Bible in your hand and you quote a line or two from the Scriptures. They stop munching their chocolate; they put the cover on the thermos, and they listen. Then you utter a simple prayer, asking God to protect them and to look after their loved ones at home. And while you're praying the motors are being warmed up and are making so much noise that they can't hear your prayer. But it doesn't matter. They are thinking their own prayer.[367]

In the absence of a Jewish chaplain, Ralph Golubock, a Jewish pilot with the 44th Bombardment Group in England, alternated between Catholic and Protestant pre-mission services; until that is, before one mission, when he 'became agitated and finally pissed off'. The source of his indignation was simple: 'Why wasn't there a Jewish chaplain? Here I was going to lay my ass on the line and the Air Force didn't think it important enough to take care of my spiritual needs'.[368] In fact, so important were pre-mission services deemed to be that William R. Arnold claimed that they were among the chaplain's 'most effective religious services' and that a chaplain's absence on a mission day was demoralising for the fliers involved.[369]

Chaplains' services on the front line, and especially before battle, were no less welcome to the sorely tried combat soldiers of the AGF. Emphasising that the overriding duty of the army chaplain was to 'the men of his command who are on the fighting line', the 1941 edition of the technical manual *The Chaplain* advised that 'the chaplain should know of every impending engagement and should arrange so that every man who desires to do so may come to him for confession, or the sacraments, for a word of hope and cheer, and to leave with him a last message for loved ones at home'.[370] In light of these instructions, and in his published summary of the Corps of Chaplains' activities in 1943, Arnold reported that:

> Services before battle assume a new significance to both chaplain and men when they know that for some of those present it may be their last service. On the eve of battle the chaplain gives every man an opportunity for conference and spiritual consolation. He administers the sacraments of his own faith and makes available the sacraments of other religious groups.[371]

These duties were re-emphasised in the 1944 edition of the same manual,[372] usually being discharged with great diligence. In fact, the manner and frequency with which they were urged could prove irksome to the chaplains involved. During the bleak and trying autumn of 1944, Luke Bolin, a chaplain assigned to the 66th Armored Regiment of the 2nd Armored Division, wrote from the German border:

> My morale is low. I hold all the services I can for my men. I make them as dignified as possible and preach the best sermons I can. But the Div. Chaplain brought a letter. He apologetically said it wasn't for me; that he was simply passing it on to Protestant Chaplains! It burnt me up anyway. A chaplain, who probably lives in a nice heated trailer, who is never close enough to the front to be in danger, tells us to hold more dignified services, to hold at least 3 on Sunday and one each week day!! He sarcastically says that why we don't have a service every day is a dark mystery to him. It's no mystery to us and wouldn't be to him if he had a little more idea of what it means to be a combat chaplain. I told the Div. chaplain to tell him that I didn't in the least appreciate such B.S. and that if he had some conception of our problems he wouldn't put out such hash![373]

Nonetheless, combat soldiers usually proved highly responsive to the presence and services of a chaplain on the front line. As the celebrated GI cartoonist Bill Mauldin testified, 'I have a lot of respect for those chaplains who keep up the spirits of the combat guys. They often give the troops a pretty firm anchor to hang onto'.[374] Eben Cobb Brink, a Presbyterian (USA) chaplain who served with the 1st Armored Division throughout its baptism of fire in North Africa in 1942–43, provided just such an 'anchor' to the men of its vulnerable reconnaissance units:

> Often as he talked with the men, the chaplain discovered the desire in their hearts for the assurance of God, for some proof of the certainty of his reality, of his presence. A word of encouragement, a thought to cherish, a verse of Scripture to echo in their minds, a whispered prayer – something to hold to as they went forth to reconnoiter – and men faced more easily the unknown before them.[375]

This ministry was also vividly described by Audie Murphy, the most decorated American combat soldier of World War II, in *To Hell And Back*, his 1949 memoir of his service with the 15th Infantry Regiment in Italy and North-West Europe. Of an attack to enlarge the Anzio beachhead in 1944, Murphy recalled:

> On the third morning, a chaplain visits our company. In a tired voice, he prays for the strength of our arms and for the souls of the men who are to die. We do not consider his denomination. Helmets come off. Catholics, Jews, and Protestants bow their heads and finger their weapons. It is front-line religion: God and the Garand.[376]

Understandably, chaplains were in special demand on the eve of D-Day in June 1944, with one participant remembering that: 'Priests were in their heyday. I even saw Jews go and take communion.'[377] Charles W. Lusher, a Northern Baptist chaplain assigned to a Troop Carrier Group, wrote of his pre-invasion ministry to its aircrew and to soldiers of the 101st Airborne Division:

> I made my way from plane to plane. Inside the planes I went down the long line of paratroopers as they sat inside the ship. I tried to touch their hand and often a pat on the head. I missed one lad and he seriously said: 'Chaplain, lay your hand on my head.' I did it too and no one laughed. The grip of my crews and pilots were especially long and hard. To them I said, 'I can't run your ship, but I will pray.' Their response was an emotional, 'Thanks, Chaplain' or 'Thanks for coming.'[378]

The bloody and unrelenting nature of the subsequent fighting in the ETO ensured that this was no transitory phenomenon. William A. Kraft, a 21-year-old soldier of the 314th Infantry Regiment, and the only original member of his company to pass through the ETO unscathed, said of his experiences in France, Belgium, Holland and Germany: 'If we made an attack we'd have a church service anytime of the day or night, and the chaplain would be there. He knew some would not be there tomorrow.'[379] Similarly, Edward K. Rogers, who served as a regimental chaplain in the 1st Infantry Division, which suffered more than twenty thousand battle casualties in North Africa, Italy and the ETO,[380] noted the premium that his commanding officer had come to place on religious services by the autumn of 1944:

> After several weeks we were relieved in the woods area near Aachen to prepare for another mission.... It was one of those attacks which end in quick and glorious success or in miserable and costly failure. There was an element of tension among the battalion staff. The colonel said it would be good to have lots of church while we waited, which was just a way of saying there was hard work ahead of the troops.[381]

If the apotheosis of military chaplaincy was generally seen to lie in ministry to fighting ships and combat units, the structure of the US armed forces and the sheer disparity between the numbers of support and front-line personnel meant that combat was a minority experience for army and navy chaplains alike. While warships and combat units had the first call upon their services,[382] most spent the war in less dramatic situations that ranged from the humdrum to the outlandish. While the former included stationary hospitals and a plethora of quiet posts and support units at home and overseas, the latter embraced the varied ministry of army chaplains assigned to its Transportation Division (later Transportation Corps).[383] For much of the war, shipboard work on army transports approximated to that of navy chaplains, and troopship chaplains were among the last to relinquish their secular work to Special Services.[384] The far-flung work of the Transportation Corps also gave rise to the railway chaplain, a peripatetic figure who, ensconced in his chaplain's caboose, plied his trade along the stations of the trans-Iranian railway, which carried Lend-Lease supplies from the Persian Gulf to the Soviet Union.[385] The limited prospects of action were also affected by manpower policies. The navy's Chaplain Corps ran a rotation system that required the return to the US of 'all chaplains who completed an 18-month tour of duty at sea or at an overseas base'.[386] However, the army's Corps of Chaplains pursued a different policy of 'limited assignment'. As a post-war report from the ETO elucidated, prevailing wisdom held 'that forty is normally the maximum age up to which a chaplain may be given a combat assignment, and fifty the normal maximum age for mobile non-combat assignments. In the case of non-combat static installations, the only applicable criterion is the chaplain's ability to perform his day-by-day duties', a criterion that meant that chaplains over the age of fifty usually remained in the United States.[387] These constraints created a twofold problem. First, they served to demoralise older but more venturesome chaplains. As the technical manual *The Chaplain* acknowledged in 1944, they produced 'a sense of inferiority because they must stay behind and carry on routine work when others go to the danger zone and perform the more conspicuous kinds of service'.[388] Second, it kept younger chaplains tied to front-line units, causing: 'Numerous instances ... where chaplains who ought to have been relieved could not be replaced until they had reached the verge of complete collapse or had actually broken down, while physically capable limited assignment chaplains remained in the rear areas.'[389]

The pressure on those chaplains who did see combat was, of course, intense. In the army, the official establishment of chaplains per fighting division varied according to its type and, like divisional organisation in general, was subject to local circumstances and official adjustments over time. However, it was emblematic of the importance of the chaplain for infantrymen in particular that the official number of chaplains allotted to each infantry division rose from eleven in June 1941, to twelve in August 1942, and then to thirteen in July 1943. In fact most infantry divisions in the ETO had fifteen by the end of 1944. Simultaneously, and as the number of chaplains increased, the official strength of an infantry division actually shrank, from 15,245 in June 1941 to 14,037 in January 1945.[390] Regardless of the type of division in which they served, the chaplains of each division came under their own division chaplain and, while some were assigned to take care of organic medical, engineer, artillery and service units, their main responsibility lay with their infantry or armoured regiments, a common practice being to assign a chaplain to each of their battalions.[391] Inevitably, considerable cachet was attached to the role of the combat chaplain. As Thomas J. Donnelly, a Catholic chaplain who served with the 305th Infantry Regiment in the Pacific, reflected:

> For every man who carried a rifle into combat, perhaps twelve others were necessary to support him. In other words one out of many faced the enemy in battle. The proportion may be different but certainly, of the thousands of chaplains who did so much for God and country, only a small number underwent the same training, endured the same hardships, the same dangers, the same joys and sorrows, the same battles as the riflemen they accompanied into battle.[392]

It was, therefore, ironic that the most glaring omission in early chaplain training was the lack of specific guidance as to what to actually do on the battlefield, or how to survive upon it. If it was naturally assumed that the ultimate role of the army chaplain was ministering to soldiers in the midst of battle,[393] the 1941 edition of the technical manual *The Chaplain* had little to say in the way of specifics. Anticipating a rerun of World War I (despite the lessons of the German *blitzkrieg* in Europe) it discouraged chaplains from actually going 'over the top' in the attack, advising instead that they accompany troops on their 'march to the front', that they visit them while 'in the trenches', assist with collecting and treating the wounded in periods of action and, if possible, 'keep on hand hot coffee, hot soup, or other food to be used as a stimulant and nourishment for the men brought in cold and hungry and suffering from wounds or shock.'[394] Nor was the Chaplain School, while it remained at Harvard, in much of a position to remedy this serious practical deficiency. Although Israel Yost had trained at the Chaplain School in February 1943, he had no conception of his role in action after being assigned to the largely Nisei 100th Infantry Battalion in Italy later that year. As he remembered, what guidance he did receive was brief and ad hoc:

> No one had ever instructed me on my specific duties when the fighting began, not even with what part of the battalion I was to associate myself. The only advice given to me was that of an older padre tagging behind his men as they passed through our sector ... 'Well, you have three choices ... You can stay at the motor pool with the vehicles. Or you can attach yourself to the commanding officer's staff. Or you can stick close to the medics at the battalion aid station.'[395]

It was not until 1944 that this deficiency in basic training was essentially remedied. If the relocation of the Chaplain School to Fort Devens was designed to help with the practicalities of battlefield training, that year's edition of *The Chaplain* manual proved much more forthcoming. On the basis of recent and relevant experience, and once again accentuating the spiritual role of the chaplain, it stated:

> When the ground forces go into action, their chaplain should be with them. This may mean that he will move from one platoon to another or will minister to the wounded in exposed positions but never that he will place himself in unnecessary danger. He must be careful that his movements do not disclose hidden positions to the enemy nor draw his fire. If casualties are numerous, he will serve best at the forward aid station ... While he will do everything in his power to relieve and increase the physical comfort of the men, he will bear in mind that this is not his primary function. He will do his utmost to comfort the suffering and give the consolations of religion to the dying. Many of the wounded may wish him to care for valued possessions which might be lost in transit to a hospital or to send them to their families in case of death. He will carry out such requests faithfully. The chaplain who shares the peril of battle with his men, showing kindness that never fails and a sincere concern for their welfare, will gain a place in their confidence which will reinforce powerfully all his efforts to give moral and religious instruction and inspiration.[396]

This model of chaplaincy was vividly related by the chaplain of a battalion of combat engineers that landed amidst the chaos of Omaha Beach on 6 June 1944. Reproduced in a circular letter issued from the Office of the Chief of Chaplains that September, his description ran:

> I landed from [a Landing Craft, Infantry] in ten feet of water and had to swim fifty yards before I touched bottom, and we waded through a hail of

death to the shore. I was with my Combat Engineer Battalion that hit the coast at H-Hour plus thirty minutes. I spent the first hours ministering to the wounded while we were pinned down on the dune line until enemy resistance was further liquidated and a way opened to move off the beach to higher ground. Eighty-eights fell in our midst while digging in, killing and wounding men next to us. Work with the wounded and dying at the first aid stations, clearing stations, and evacuation points during the first few days has more than repaid for every sacrifice I have made and the toil of months of preparation for this task.[397]

Although navy chaplains ministered to navy construction battalions (or 'Seabees') working ashore in Europe and the Pacific,[398] the role of navy chaplains assigned to the Marine Corps more closely resembled that of army chaplains serving with the AGF. Given the amphibious role and elite status of the marines, ministry to marine units was usually the preserve of younger and fitter navy chaplains, few being beyond their mid-thirties at the end of the war.[399] Robert D. Workman, himself a former marine, was keen to stress that marine chaplaincy was only for a select minority, assuring the *Marine Corps Gazette* in 1943 that:

An effort has been made to send those men who are physically, mentally, and temperamentally prepared to go along with the hard-hitting marines no matter where orders and duties may take them. Many of these chaplains have asked for duty with the marines but not all who requested such honor were given it.[400]

Moreover, all navy chaplains were fully informed of the distinctive role and status of the Marine Corps:

In training all the chaplains coming into the Navy, provision has been made by which these neophytes may learn the history of the Marine Corps, its distinctive customs and traditions, and its complex organization which makes it ready to fight on land or sea or in the air. Experienced chaplains who have had cruises with marines in years past lecture the new chaplains on the ways and manners of the Marine Corps and indicate the reasons for its reputation as an unbeatable fighting organization. In addition, some student chaplains are sent to large marine bases for their field work, where they see and have a part in the work of the chaplains attached to marine units.[401]

Like army chaplains assigned to combat units, when in action marine chaplains assisted medical corpsmen (who were also provided by the navy), ministered to the wounded and dying and, through visiting front-line positions, raised the spirits of their occupants.[402] However, and despite Workman's ungrammatical boast that 'every combat unit of the marines in the field have been provided with chaplains',[403] the provision of chaplains for the Marine Corps fell short of that made for the AGF. When the reinforced 1st Marine Division, a force of some nineteen thousand men, landed in the Solomon Islands in August 1942 it was accompanied by only six navy chaplains.[404] Similarly, when Warren Wyeth Willard joined the 8th Marine Regiment in New Zealand in 1943, until the arrival of a Catholic colleague 'some months later' he was the sole 'spiritual leader of nearly three thousand men'.[405] Although the establishment of chaplains for a marine division was eventually fixed at sixteen, provision for its front-line units remained meagre, three-battalion infantry regiments and five-battalion artillery regiments having just two chaplains each.[406] The practical problems this could cause under normal circumstances were heightened by the impact of casualties when in action. Such were the ravages of climate and disease in the Solomons in 1942 that five of the six original marine chaplains were evacuated before the end of the Guadalcanal campaign in January 1943.[407] Likewise, the hazards of amphibious assaults in the Pacific were such that in 1944 more navy chaplains became combat casualties while serving with marine units ashore than on warships at sea.[408] On Tinian in July 1944 both chaplains of the 23rd Marine Regiment were 'wounded within a half hour of each other', leaving the whole regiment bereft of chaplaincy care in the midst of a major battle. John Harold Craven, another chaplain of the 4th Marine Division, whose hands were already full with the five battalions of his 14th Artillery Regiment,[409] had the urgency and cause of the situation impressed upon him:

> A little later in the morning I was walking by the [command post] of the 23rd Marines ... when [their colonel] called out, 'Hey, Chaplain, I don't have a chaplain now.' I said, 'Yes, I know.' In those days you just had one Catholic and one Protestant chaplain with a regiment, which is an impossible situation of course to really provide chaplaincy coverage. The idea of a chaplain for each battalion hadn't gotten to the Navy and the Marines. The Army had operated with that idea, but the Navy had the idea that all a regiment needed was a Catholic and a Protestant chaplain. I told him I knew that they both had been wounded and I was going to be nearby and I would help him all I could.[410]

Despite their high casualties, no more than 5 per cent of the navy's chaplains were serving with units of the Fleet Marine Force by the summer of 1945,[411] far more seeing action on board its larger warships. Indeed, it was one of their number, Howell Maurice Forgy, the Presbyterian (USA) chaplain of the heavy cruiser *New Orleans*, who inadvertently coined one of America's most famous wartime slogans, 'Praise the Lord and pass the ammunition', during the attack on Pearl Harbor, his words acquiring even greater resonance because Forgy had been 'somewhat of a pacifist before deciding to join the Navy in September, 1940'.[412] However firmly these 'seven immortal words of the Padre'[413] lodged themselves in the public imagination, and however distorted and misattributed they were,[414] their origins were simple enough. Because the *New Orleans* was berthed at Pearl Harbor undergoing repairs, its ammunition hoists were without power and its crew had to manhandle ammunition to its anti-aircraft guns by means of a human chain; as the crew tired, Forgy passed down the line of toiling sailors, hammering their 'wet, sticky backs' and shouting 'Praise the Lord and pass the ammunition.'[415] However, had the *New Orleans* been suffering casualties at that point Forgy would not have been at hand to utter these memorable words for, according to the rather archaic phraseology of navy regulations, at general quarters the chaplain was to report to a battle station designated by his commanding officer 'whereat he may attend the wounded.'[416] As sick bays were normally located below decks, often amidst a veritable 'honeycomb of sealed compartments,'[417] their occupancy could be more unnerving than otherwise for the wounded and medical staff alike, especially given the problem of abandoning ship should the need arise. James Vernon Claypool, who served as chaplain on board the new battleship *South Dakota* off Guadalcanal in the autumn of 1942, noted how its crew knew 'very well how the British *Prince of Wales* and the *Repulse* had been bombed and sunk off Singapore by Jap airmen', and wrote of the tension felt in its sick bay in anticipation of a repeat performance:

> My battle station was in the sick bay, where there was nothing one could do but wait. Waiting is the hardest kind of battle duty, all sailors agree. Soon, we knew, the stretchers would start carrying down wounded men. In the meantime, we waited … In the sick bay were medical and dental officers and enlisted men … We talked, but I think no one paid much attention to what was said. Our ears were cocked for that first sound of battle: gunfire and exploding bombs. Every few minutes there would be another announcement over the loud-speaker that an air attack was expected.[418]

Because the *South Dakota* was a new ship with a novice crew, most of whom had enlisted after Pearl Harbor,[419] it behoved Claypool to present a confident and unruffled demeanour throughout the sea battles that raged off Guadalcanal. As he confessed of one telling incident:

> About four a.m., when the rush of the injured coming to the sick bay slackened for a moment, I stopped beside a boy from Minnesota, one of the more seriously wounded. As I bent over his bed he looked at me and grinned.
> 'We won, didn't we?' he murmured.
> 'Yes, we did, Johnny.'
> My reply was not based on any knowledge of the facts. I think I would have said the same thing to that boy if the ship had been foundering.[420]

Although usually confined to the sick bay while in action, the steadying presence of their chaplain could be mediated in other ways to the rest of a ship's crew. As it was standard procedure to narrate the course of a battle from the bridge to those fighting below decks, captains often gave this commentator's role to their chaplains, presumably on the understanding that their words would be trusted and their voice prove reassuring.[421] As Joseph T. O'Callahan, the Catholic chaplain of the aircraft carrier *Franklin* explained, 'The purpose of such news-casting is not to make a game out of war, but rather to bring the war directly to the thousand-odd men whose battle stations are below deck. By keeping them informed they become a closer part of a unified fighting team.'[422] However, and as O'Callahan went on to stress, this was a subordinate aspect of the combat ministry of a navy chaplain:

> A chaplain's job in battle is to soothe the wounded, minister to the dying, pray with and for the aviators about to fly into battle. It was always agreed that religious duties had priority. But when I was not in the professional role of a priest I would be an amateur newscaster.[423]

The tricky role of combat commentator was also that of Merritt Francis Williams, the Episcopalian chaplain of the aircraft carrier *Wasp*, which was sunk off Guadal-canal in September 1942:

> Chaplain Williams was one of a number of chaplains who frequently broad-casted over the ship's public address system informing those below decks, where the suspense was often difficult to bear, about events taking place topside and in the air. The Captain of the *Wasp* felt that this was good for morale. It was understood that Chaplain Williams had complete freedom to leave the bridge at any time to assist in ministering to any casualties or to carry on other duties of his office.[424]

If carrier chaplains like O'Callahan and Williams steadied the nerves of navy and marine fliers in their ready rooms before missions in the Pacific, a situation that O'Callahan likened to before 'a big football game, but terribly more impor-tant,'[425] chaplains of the AAF had a similar role to play in steadying the morale of air and ground crew at operating bases. Of the Pacific theatre it was reported that:

> Often, the chaplain would keep vigil with the men waiting for the return of a mission. Many bombing missions from the Thirteenth Air Force [which eventually hit targets as far afield as Malaya and the coast of China] were out for twelve to fifteen hours. The anxiety and suspense was great among ground crews and personnel left behind, and Chaplains took every means to relieve tense nerves and anxiety states.[426]

In 1945, and echoing instructions given to AAF chaplains in the 1944 edition of the technical manual *The Chaplain*, William D. Cleary wrote:

Consider any one of the hundreds of chaplains assigned to the Army Air Forces. Normally, he does not fly on a combat mission. But he does see the planes off, often after a brief prayer with the officers and men who are about to fly over enemy-held territory. Then, with the remainder of the ground crew and headquarters, he 'sweats it out,' waiting for the planes to come back. The time finally arrives when they are due, and one by one they come in. Some are riddled with flak. Some are carrying wounded and dead. Some do not come back at all. The chaplain meets the incoming planes. He ministers to the wounded. He writes letters of condolence to the families of the dead. And then, at the evening mess, he sits down at a table where there are vacant places. There will be young officers there who, a few hours before, saw their friends go down in flaming planes. Yet the life of the squadron must go on, and the chaplain must do what he can to bring the stability and the courage and the faith which makes men able to bear the strain, day after day, month after month, for twenty, thirty, forty, or fifty missions.[427]

Despite the sentiments of 'Praise the Lord and pass the ammunition', what redounded to the credit of the nation's military chaplains was the fact that they remained, technically at least, non-combatants; in other words, and as Chaplain Forgy was at pains to stress, 'a chaplain cannot fire a gun or take material part in a battle'.[428] As various Christian traditions had different perspectives on the propriety of their clergy bearing arms, military policy was fundamentally guided by the terms of the Geneva Convention, to which the United States had subscribed since 1882, under which 'Chaplains, Medical Officers, and certain other military personnel' were classified as non-combatants.[429] During World War I, and despite rampant Germanophobia in the United States, the terms of the convention had been almost universally honoured, with as few as two reported cases of chaplains acting as combatants.[430] In World War II the army's Judge Advocate General reinforced the prohibition on the chaplains' use of arms against the enemy and forbade their participation in combat flying missions and small arms-training.[431] Nevertheless, grey areas remained and official policy was widely flouted. An early case in point was that of William C. Taggart who, while he accepted (grudgingly) the army's ban on combat flying, organised the anti-aircraft defences of a Dutch freighter on the evacuation of Java.[432] Other AAF chaplains were inclined to go further, however. Gerald Beck, a Catholic chaplain of the Eighth Air Force, was known to have flown on bombing missions. Like several of his colleagues, Beck was even thought to have been awarded an Air Medal, a decoration that could only be awarded to combat personnel, which he carried discreetly in his pocket.[433] However, the AAF was less indulgent of a much more egregious case that occurred in the CBI in 1944. According to the *Los Angeles Times*, Catholic AAF chaplain James M. Gilloegly 'landed in the "clink"' after borrowing a plane that he used, with the help of a confederate, to drop 'a hand-made bomb' on a Japanese headquarters in Burma.[434]

A further problem was that, under certain circumstances, the carrying of arms was tolerated and even encouraged. As the Battle of the Bulge raged in the winter of 1944–45, such was the fear of infiltration by German paratroopers, and their possible use of captured American uniforms, that even army chaplains in the ETO were 'ordered to carry arms ... whenever we were away from close contact with our own troops'.[435] In the Pacific, the carrying of side arms was widely endorsed for protection against wild animals,[436] a category that quickly and ineluctably came to subsume the Japanese themselves. Very soon after Warren Wyeth Willard's arrival in the Solomons in August 1942, he abandoned the role of non-combatant. Noting the deliberate killing of medics by Japanese snipers, 'doctors and corpsmen took off their Geneva crosses and put them away. I had been working with the doctors, who had given me the Geneva insignia to wear. Mine came off too. We realized that we were fighting a cruel and merciless foe'.[437] In his personal armoury, Willard counted a Colt .45 pistol and two hand grenades, which he dubbed 'Mike' and 'Ike', reasoning that, 'You've got to help the Lord once in a while', and that: 'They would have come in handy if I had run up against any wild animals'.[438] With reference to 'Praise the Lord, and pass the ammunition', Willard freely admitted as a serving chaplain that: 'If passing ammunition hastens the day of peace on earth, then I'd be only too happy to toss in a few shells myself'.[439] Such attitudes were widely shared by marine chaplains regardless of their tradition; for example, Paul Bradley, the Catholic chaplain of the 5th Marine Regiment, briskly disposed of a Japanese assailant on Iwo Jima, shooting him in the leg, though he had 'aimed for his midsection'.[440] Sharing the same hazards in the Pacific, the practice of army chaplains seems to have been identical. According to Thomas J. Donnelly: 'In this theater of war, insignia of rank or Red Cross brassard were not worn because it had been learned that the wearers of such gear became prime targets for the enemy. Everyone carried arms because no one was immune to fighting, and, especially at night, the enemy tried to get through the lines, and he did not ask any questions.' In his regiment's foxholes on Guam in 1944, Donnelly took his turn on watch like everyone else, 'and sat crouched in the hole with a pistol in one hand, extra clips of ammunition by my side and a knife close to my other hand, the latter to be used in close combat'.[441] Later, on Leyte, the threat of Japanese infiltration meant that Donnelly carried a rifle on the hazardous trip between the front line and his regimental headquarters.[442] However, such behaviour was never officially sanctioned. In fact, in August 1945, and in instructions issued by General MacArthur to his whole command, it was reiterated that: 'Chaplains will not bear arms or engage in combat or otherwise commit an act injurious to the enemy. They may be cited [for decorations] only for service in non-combatant professional duties'.[443]

Nevertheless, the non-combatant status of the chaplain was to some extent academic in the face of ordnance that was blind to such distinctions. In March 1944, the army announced that, 'Only the air forces and the infantry have suffered a larger proportion of casualties among their officers than the Chaplain Corps',[444] news that was clearly aimed to reassure Americans as to the diligence and courage of army chaplains. Of the 158 army and 24 navy chaplains who died in World War II, 73 and 10 (respectively) were killed in action or died of wounds, the rest succumbing to accidents, disease or the hardships of captivity.[445] Among those killed in action, Arvil E. Teem, a Southern Baptist, was 'struck by enemy fire' just twelve hours after joining the 636th Tank Destroyer Battalion on the Cassino front in February 1944. A year later, chaplaincy to the 10th Mountain Division suffered a major blow when a single German booby trap killed two of its chaplains and seriously wounded a third.[446]

Despite these losses and their significance, it was far more common for chaplains to bury the dead than to actually join them. In fact, the status of chaplains as specialists who nurtured the religious component of sound morale was exemplified by their grim responsibility for ensuring that the dead received a decent burial. In the army at least, and in keeping with wider developments, this responsibility acquired a more specifically religious focus as the war went on. In the comparatively raw and poorly organised army units that went to North Africa and Australia in 1942, chaplains frequently doubled as graves registration officers.[447] This role was in keeping with the extensive guidance given on the subject in the 1941 edition of the technical manual *The Chaplain*, where three pages of instructions were devoted to the establishment of cemeteries, the composition of burial details, the identification of the dead, the disposal of personal effects, and the marking, recording and reporting of soldiers' graves.[448] However, this requirement could prove impossible to meet, a situation that faced Harry P. Abbott, a United Presbyterian chaplain with the 1st Armored Division, on the expansive battlefields of North Africa. Because Abbott's command lost around three-quarters of its tanks and half-tracks in its first two weeks of action in Tunisia,[449] these responsibilities presented an almost insupportable burden, causing Abbott and other chaplains to lose touch with their units and exposing them to the dangers of 'mine fields and booby traps' while 'recovering bodies from tanks put out of commission in the fights'.[450] Subsequently, the interment and identification of the dead was increasingly left to graves registration companies of the Quartermaster Corps; indeed, and on the basis of their experience in North Africa, chaplains were officially relieved of grave registration work in the ETO only a few days into the Normandy campaign.[451] While chaplains were still expected, if necessary, to take charge of burial procedures in forward areas, the declining importance of this role was reflected in the 1944 edition of the technical manual *The Chaplain*, which devoted only a paragraph to the subject.[452]

If the duty of army chaplains towards the dead increasingly became that of performing burial rites and memorial services,[453] navy chaplains continued to observe the time-honoured tradition of burial at sea for those who died on board ship. In fact, in 1944 the Navy Department even published a new guide for burial at sea for use by all three major faith groups.[454] Although without many of the practical difficulties encountered by chaplains serving as graves registration officers, interment at sea was not necessarily an easier affair. For example, James Vernon Claypool remembered how, off the Solomon Islands in November 1942, forty dead crewmen of the *South Dakota* had to be buried in the depths of a tropical storm. Besides the problem of rapid putrefaction, many of the bodies were so badly mutilated that identification proved difficult for Claypool and his two assistants, both fellow officers. Although two sailmakers were detailed to sew the bodies into canvas, such were the horrors of their task that one 'collapsed and had to be taken away' while the other persevered, only to return from a subsequent leave 'wrecked in body and mind', saying that 'he could not get out of his mind the memory of those burials'. [455] Claypool, it should be emphasised, supervised and endured the whole business. Likewise, Joseph T. O'Callahan played a prominent part in burying the dead of the carrier *Franklin*, many of whom had literally roasted to death below decks:

> Boys don't like to carry burned corpses pickaback up steep ladders. I think that I carried most of the corpses. It has been a source of several nightmares since, perhaps because on one trip I was so exhausted that I fell asleep a moment on a step of the ladder. It is disconcerting to awake and find oneself clasping and facing a burned corpse.... It was necessary to give the burial parties frequent recesses from their tiring and depressing task. It was necessary to watch them carefully lest young minds already subjected to a strain beyond that endured by most people throughout an entire lifetime might be strained to the breaking point.[456]

Such resilience was also necessary for marine chaplains, who had to bury large numbers of dead ashore, often in tropical heat, and while shouldering the duty of graves registration officer. Warren Wyeth Willard wrote of his work burying the dead on Gavutu in the Solomon Islands in August 1942:

> I had to hurry to find a site for the cemetery.... The sun grew hot in the skies above and scorched the earth beneath.... Some of the members of the working party fainted because of the heat or the sight of the bloody and stiffened bodies of their friends.... The working parties seemed to melt away ... I secured three assistants. These men made a map of the cemetery for me. They took the valuables from the clothing of the dead, and placed them in envelopes. These were sealed, and on each was written the owner's name. The identification tags were removed and placed in separate containers.[457]

Things were no better two years later in the Mariana Islands. In this case, and as Otto Herrmann, the Lutheran senior chaplain of the 2nd Marine Division,[458] reported:

> [T]he big problem … was getting our dead buried, hundreds of whom had been lying where they fell. For 7 days I was in charge of a burial detail and, to set them a good example, myself handled the stinking, fly-covered dead without gloves (they hadn't arrived) despite the danger of gangrene poisoning, and held up my end of the stretcher as we piled the dead into amphibious tractors or trucks, and brought them to the division cemetery.[459]

Chaplains as counsellors

If, in practical and in spiritual terms, chaplains helped to provide a semblance of dignity in death as well as a measure of support in combat, then they also offered vital assistance to America's soldiers, airmen, sailors and marines in the myriad trials and tribulations of service life. Significantly, the phrase 'Tell it to the chaplain' became idiomatic during World War II,[460] 'a cynically polite way to tell a complaining buddy to shut up'.[461] Thanks to the bureaucratised nature of contemporary military chaplaincy, the number of occasions on which individuals did 'Tell it to the chaplain' can actually be measured in statistical terms. By 1942, army chaplains were conducting an average of fifty-three personal interviews per day and, in 1943, research conducted by the army's Special Services Branch confirmed that 'next to the commanding officer a far greater proportion of men went to see the chaplain than any other officer', a pattern that was confirmed in the post-war study *The American Soldier* (1949).[462] If the latter report found that Catholics were rather more disposed to seek out the chaplain than were Protestants,[463] recourse to the chaplain grew more pronounced among all personnel when serving overseas. Clyde E. Kimball, a Methodist chaplain assigned to the 5th Engineer Combat Regiment in Iceland, wrote with some surprise in March 1943 how even the twin attractions of a beer ration and an open post exchange failed to prevent a queue from forming for his evening office hours: 'In spite of their first PX night in [a] new camp, and [a] five cans of beer ration, a line was waiting to present their "tear slips" to the chaplain.'[464] At the end of the war in Europe, army sources estimated that, in the United States, '12% of the men consult the chaplain at one time or another in the course of a one-year period. This ratio increased by about 25% overseas.'[465] According to Arnold's figures, in a single month, May 1944, and with the Western Allies poised for the cross-Channel invasion, there were nearly a million contacts of this kind.[466] This burden was familiar to navy chaplains as well. For example, at the Naval Training Center at Sampson, New York, which at the height of the war had a capacity for thirty thousand recruits and an establishment of twenty-six chaplains, 161,000 personal interviews were conducted between October 1942 and July 1945.[467]

Although some visits to the chaplain were little more than courtesy calls, most involved at least an element of pastoral counselling. In this respect – and as few were trained psychiatrists – chaplains were expected to conduct these interviews very much as they would in civilian life. As William D. Cleary wrote:

> Whatever the problem may be, the chaplain will listen sympathetically and with understanding. Frequently he will refer the soldier or sailor to an agency better equipped to deal with the situation than the chaplain himself. Occasionally he will be able to present the case for consideration by the proper military authorities. Always, he will try to be a true counselor and friend. Always, he will remember that he is not primarily a social worker or a psychiatrist but a minister of religion and that his particular function is to bring to bear the resources and the techniques of religion.[468]

The vaunted role of the chaplain as a friend to all reflected his status as a minister of religion and his privileged position within the military. As Cleary explained:

> The chaplain stands in a unique relationship to the enlisted personnel of the Armed Forces. He is the only commissioned officer whom the soldier or sailor can approach directly without seeking the permission of his first sergeant or a division officer. The chaplain does not exercise command. He, therefore, is not responsible for the administration of discipline, and the soldier or sailor with a 'gripe' or a personal problem will talk far more freely with the chaplain than with any other officer.[469]

Significantly, recruits were encouraged to identify the chaplain as a friend and ally from the outset. As Cleary elaborated:

> The chaplain is also charged with a special responsibility to recruits. Every group of recruits coming into an Army or Navy Reception Center is addressed by a chaplain. He explains to them the religious program of the Armed Forces. He tells them that he is available for personal conferences. He speaks to them of the moral and religious implications of discipline and of the problems they will face, as many of them are away from home for the first time. He encourages them to write home regularly because he knows that there are no more powerful influences for good in a man's life than frequent contact with the loved ones he has left behind. In a word, the chaplain does everything he can to help the recruit make a rapid and normal adjustment to the new situation in which he finds himself.[470]

In overall terms, it seems that chaplains as a body had little difficulty in gaining the acceptance to which they aspired. On the basis of his own service in the United States, Clifford M. Drury, who in his counselling work simply mixed 'common sense' with his 'Biblical and theological convictions', remarked that: 'I found men coming to see me in the chaplaincy who would never come to me in a civilian church. There was more of an expectancy. If they had a problem, they would go see the chaplain. And I didn't find that in a parish.'[471] While its insistence on church attendance throughout recruit training probably helped to establish the position of navy chaplains among navy recruits,[472] the army achieved similar results through less direct means. In 1941, it was already part of army regulations that new recruits be addressed or even interviewed by their chaplains on 'matters pertaining to morals and character'. As that year's edition of the technical manual *The Chaplain* elaborated:

> The relations of the men to the chaplain especially are very important. The advice he gives them is prized because the chaplain is both an officer and a pastor. These informal talks will help the recruit to adjust himself to a life quite different from that in which he has been born and reared. The change is so radical that he needs an anchor to windward somewhere. The chaplain should be that anchor.[473]

By 1944, this role had been refined and even enlarged. That year's edition of *The Chaplain* not only recommended an 'appropriate chapel service in the evening' as 'a fitting climax for the men's first day in camp' but also outlined a more foundational role for chaplains at the army's reception centres:

> Most inductees have had no previous military experience. First impressions are very important, and the wise chaplain will seek to have a large share in creating [a] favorable impression of Army life for the men entering the service. If he can meet new arrivals at the train with a pleasant greeting, it will help many a timid soldier through a moment of strangeness, if not of anxiety. Some will fear their inoculations and shrink from other unfamiliar experiences, but a word of encouragement from the chaplain may be a great help.[474]

The help of the chaplain was certainly required, as the needs and problems of service personnel were multifarious to say the very least. Of a typical office day in January 1943, Clyde E. Kimball wrote:

> Three interviews that illustrate the variety: a man hoping for Officers' Candidate School, wanted advice and textbooks to study French, geometry and algebra. A wild-eyed fellow told of persecution by [a] 1st Sgt who threatened to shoot him in the back. A Staff Sgt ten years in the army, hopes he won't be sent home in a cadre to train a new regiment; it was too hard to leave his wife before.[475]

In William D. Cleary's 1945 essay 'The Ministry of the Chaplain', he put the situation thus: 'Men come to chaplains with every conceivable kind of problem. It may be that there is a special reason why a soldier or sailor wants a pass or a furlough.' Furthermore, 'It may be that there is trouble at home – financial trouble, or illness, or a difficulty in personal relationships between the man and his wife.' Again, for many and various reasons, 'It may be that he is unhappy in the Army or Navy.' And finally:

> The problem may be one that is distinctly moral and religious – the fear of death; scruples about the whole sorry business of engaging in war; remorse for a wrong that has been done; a loss of faith, due to any one of a score of causes; or a groping for faith on the part of a man whose background is for all practical purposes pagan.[476]

The appeal of the chaplain as a confidant was heightened by a code of confidentiality that, in the army at least, was respected even by its own system of justice. In 1944, and in confirmation of what was already accepted as 'unwritten doctrine', a War Department circular stated that, unless this right was expressly waived by the defendant, in disciplinary proceedings no personal information could be divulged by a chaplain that had been disclosed to him in his capacity as a clergyman.[477] However, this relationship of trust came under considerable pressure in both services in the case of practising homosexuals who, from January 1943, were not only liable to face criminal proceedings but to be discharged as undesirables (so-called 'blue discharges') if their activities became known to the military authorities.[478] How far military chaplains were complicit in the intensified campaign against homosexuals is debatable for, while the confidentiality of their own pastoral dealings remained sacrosanct, referrals to psychiatrists, the preferred method even of those chaplains who were relatively sympathetic, ran the risk of exposure and punishment.[479] Hence, the record of chaplains in relation to the nine thousand or so army and navy personnel who were the recipients of 'blue discharges' on the grounds of their sexuality is a mixed one.[480] As Allan Bérubé concluded: 'By working hand in hand with psychiatrists who were required to report their homosexual patients, chaplains unwittingly – or intentionally when they were hostile to homosexuals – helped military officers detect and discharge gay men and women who would otherwise have remained hidden in the ranks.'[481]

Despite the enormous variety of personal problems presented to chaplains, the largest proportion appears to have been domestic or familial in origin, followed, in descending order, by military, religious and moral difficulties (significantly, one navy chaplain reported that only 10 per cent of more than 118,000 interviews conducted at the Naval Training Station, Great Lakes, Illinois, in 1944 were 'on matters essentially religious').[482] Furthermore, certain factors could conspire to create unusually troubled times and units. Thomas J. Donnelly noted how all too many draftees were sent to the army in the aftermath of Pearl Harbor 'who should never have left home. Once they were in it took a lot of time and effort to get them out.'[483] Likewise, the mood was not happy at Milne Bay in New Guinea towards the end of the war: 'a feeling of being out of the main channel of the war effort seemed to cause a sense of despondency and monotony' among many of the remaining personnel, a situation that caused a corresponding increase in the number of 'personal interviews' held by chaplains.[484] For the same reasons, one AAF chaplain registered a prevailing unhappiness in many stateside service units:

> The soldiers here are far removed from the excitement and dangers of the combat zone and are frequently unhappy about being assigned to routine, monotonous tasks no matter how important these tasks may be.... It is difficult for them to feel the close-knit companionship and devotion to duty that come to a unit sharing common dangers which involve life and death. Many of our men are physically disqualified for overseas service and must fight down an insidious feeling of inferiority which is heightened when they come in contact with men who have returned from combat.[485]

While Charles Edward Lunn claimed to rejoice at his usefulness in ministering to 'lonely and sinful men',[486] it took some time for him to glean much satisfaction from his relentless counselling of AAF personnel, at first complaining how army inoculations had signally failed to immunise his flock against "'griping", gambling, liquor, girls, and worry'.[487] In his ministry to units in the United States and England, Lunn faced the full gamut of soldiers' problems, ranging from overbearing officers and poor 'chow' through to troublesome wives and bigamous marriages.[488] Naturally, and for the sake of morale at home, it behoved Lunn and his fellow chaplains to rejoice in sharing the burdens of those in service. In an article entitled 'I Am a Navy Chaplain', which was first published in the *Lutheran Standard*, Emil Frederick Redman said of his counselling work at the Naval Training Station, Great Lakes: 'Without a doubt, a chaplain's most satisfying work is done when he has those heart-to-heart talks with America's finest manhood.' [489] The reality, of course, could be rather different. Although chaplains could call on the practical assistance of other officers and agencies,[490] their situation as the recipients of multitudinous tales of woe (some of which were distinctly minor or even frivolous) became the subject of some doubtful service humour. On Guadalcanal, for example, Warren Wyeth Willard encountered the so-called 'Sympathy Chit', 'an imaginary pass to the chaplain's office' which was issued by their officers to troubled marines.[491] While cartoonists lampooned the unenviable lot of the navy chaplain as a friend and counsellor to all,[492] some army chaplains reversed the joke by distributing cards that entitled the bearer to so many cries on the chaplain's shoulder, by carrying towels for that purpose, and even by pinning pictures of movie stars to notice boards with the caption 'Unless the girl you want to marry is as good looking as this, don't see me'.[493] A self-reported offender in this regard was a Methodist chaplain, Rupert L. McCanon, who, while serving in Hawaii with the 40th Infantry Division, had 'T-S cards' (an abbreviation he understood as something much less polite than Kimball's 'Tear Slip') printed in four colours, 'white for privates, blue for sergeants, green for lieutenants, and gold for generals', the conceit being that troubled soldiers could 'hilariously' work their way 'up through the T-S ranks from privates to generals' after filling each card with the punches required.[494] In fact, the distribution of such tickets became so widespread that the joke had to be censured by senior army chaplains, who judged it 'unbecoming' and inherently counterproductive.[495] This view was shared by other chaplains, whose objections to their abiding use punctuated the correspondence pages of *The Chaplain* magazine towards the end of the war.[496] In any event, hard-pressed chaplains could find other means to deter the unduly importunate, with Thomas James Donnelly recalling how, at Fort Jackson, South Carolina, he used to escape from his office and seek refuge in an adjoining furnace room whenever he heard the telltale footsteps of a particularly fretful soldier.[497]

However, and regardless of the attendant ploys and gallows humour, the business of counselling the often badly disorientated members of a vast citizen army and navy was serious enough. John S. Garrenton, a Southern Baptist chaplain with the AAF in India, remembered one case especially because, after the soldier concerned had spent a good deal of time pining after his home and young family in Indiana, he returned to his quarters and shot himself.[498] With his characteristic acuity, Jewish chaplain Morris N. Kertzer summarised the significance of the chaplain's role in this respect. Subjected, like most of his colleagues, to an endless cavalcade of troubled soldiers, some aggressive, others embarrassingly grateful, and from problems ranging from 'the ridiculous and the tragic' to 'the sordid and the eloquently beautiful', Kertzer came to the apt conclusion that the chaplain was 'the emotional safety valve in the military establishment'. Moreover, he was surprised by the confidence that was normally evinced in the chaplain's ability to help:

> The young men who came into my office assumed I could offer expert medical advice, untangle complex legal puzzles, don the role of banker for substantial sums of money, persuade a faltering wife to learn the meaning of true love. When I look back upon the variety of problems which I was called upon to solve, I am amazed at the sublime faith which some G.I.s had in the Chaplain Corps, assuming us to be invested with encyclopedic [sic] omniscience and semi-divine omnipotence.[499]

Chaplains and the home front

Given the strong and intimate bonds between the services and the home front, chaplains – in their multifaceted role of soldier and sailor support – certainly helped to reinforce civilian morale in the United States. Critically, the importance of public relations, and in particular of publicising the benefits of chaplaincy work to the civilian population, was fully understood by William R. Arnold from the very advent of the draft. In September 1940, and at the invitation of the Secretary of War, Henry L. Stimson, Arnold outlined some basic requirements for chaplaincy work in the new draftee army, publicity ranking alongside the procurement and training of chaplains, the provision of chapels, and cooperation with the churches and the military authorities.[500] By 1943, the Office of the Chief of Chaplains had its own Technical Information Division, whose task was to transmit 'information in accordance with established War Department policies to the public through the press, publications, radio, motion pictures, and directly'.[501] In fulfilling this role, and in that year alone, more than a hundred manuscripts relating to army chaplaincy – 'ranging in size from a few lines to reams of paper' – were scrutinised by the Office of the Chief of Chaplains; press conferences were organised in Washington DC and New York City; chaplains returning from active theatres of war were interviewed by the Bureau of Public Relations; advice and participants were supplied to radio producers and scriptwriters; photographs of chaplaincy work were collected and distributed at the request of 'church groups'; and suitable excerpts from the chief of chaplains' monthly circular letters were 'distributed on request to certain church editors, church leaders, and other interested personnel'.[502]

That year, 1943, was also notable in other respects. A 'Chaplain Exhibit' was organised in conjunction with the Third War Loan Drive, forming part of the 'Back the Attack' army show held on the monument grounds in Washington that September. The exhibit, staffed by chaplains and enlisted personnel, included an assembly tent complete with chapel facade and featured a 'Hall of Heroes' (of those chaplains who had died or been captured); a comprehensive display of religious artefacts; lectures on the work of the Corps of Chaplains; daily services for Protestants, Catholics and Jews; and twice-daily organ recitals. Elsewhere on the monument grounds, twice-daily parades in the arena featured a chaplain's jeep sporting 'a Christian and a Jewish flag', which at the close of the day's proceedings became the focus for a solemn act of worship:

> At 2200 there was a Chaplain spot in the arena show at which time the altar was put upon the hood of the jeep and dressed with candlesticks and flowers. During this time the arena was darkened except for the spotlight on the jeep and simulated altar. The spot opened with church call and closed with taps. It was a most impressive close to the night arena performance.[503]

Indeed, so impressive was this slot deemed to be that it was even used in an afternoon show 'by special direction of Secretary of War Stimson' and also 'when a special show was given for the Members of Congress'.[504] With attendance at the 'Back the Attack' show exceeding 1.6 million and visitors to the 'Chaplain Exhibit' estimated at more than 500,000, plans were soon hatched for a 'chaplain booth' to be included in a 'department store exhibit sponsored by the Army Service Forces'.[505] In January 1944, three identical department store exhibits replete with chaplain booths were opened in Boston, Chicago and San Francisco. Featuring carefully chosen artefacts and photographs, housed in a lighted display case, and accompanied by a brief lecture, Arnold informed Marshall that 'the three exhibits will be seen by 80 million people'.[506] Accepting these ambitious figures, Marshall replied:

> I think you have done a good job in presenting to the people on the home front a picture of the vast activities of your office. I am sure that few of them realize the extent to which the Army goes in providing spiritual guidance and opportunities for worship for its men. It should be helpful to you as well as to the entire Army that more of the families of soldiers know about the work of the men of the Corps of Chaplains.[507]

Marshall's conviction was expressed, albeit in a rather tawdry manner, by a corps chaplain in Italy. According to the war correspondent Eric Sevareid, this senior chaplain 'kept a neat file of clippings about himself and always had a new story of his exploits for the reporters'.[508] In any event, the work of army chaplains also featured in books, newsreels, films and radio programmes. In December 1942, Pathé News arrived at the Chaplain School in Harvard to shoot a film entitled *The Army Chaplain*.[509] The following year, the subject received a more imaginative, though still sympathetic treatment, in the form of *For God and Country*, which starred Ronald Reagan as the fictive Catholic chaplain Michael O'Keefe and portrayed his salutary friendship with his Protestant and Jewish colleagues, his interaction with his men, and his heroic death in action while ministering to them on a Pacific island.[510] Produced by the Signal Corps and shot at MGM Studios, the film was primarily aimed at army personnel with the goal of promoting 'a better understanding of the chaplain's place, work, and accomplishments in the Army'.[511] In 1944 it was also released to the general public on a not-for-profit basis, copies being sent on request and showings being followed by voluntary collections 'to defray expenses'.[512] Furthermore, this image of cheerful and benign oversight was relayed to a wider public and, for a much longer period, in the form of the fictitious and denominationally elusive figure of *Chaplain Jim, USA*. Although, as in the pre-war years, enterprising army chaplains continued to feature on local radio stations (one chaplain directed a programme entitled *The Diary of a Chaplain's Clerk* for KFBC of Cheyenne, Wyoming, while another produced *Faith of Our Fighters* for WIBX of Utica, New York),[513] none approached the coverage of *Chaplain Jim, USA*. Broadcast by the Blue Network every Sunday across the forty-eight states as 'a public patriotic service', each episode began with the announcement: 'Once again the Blue Network presents *Chaplain Jim, USA*: the story of the problems – spiritual, moral and emotional – of your men in the army'. Aimed at 'millions of mothers, wives and sweethearts of "the men who wear the khaki of the United States Army"', the programme was inspired by the goal of 'realistically interpreting the chaplaincy for a nationwide public'. In this it appears to have been conspicuously successful, eliciting thousands of letters and phone calls, some expressing their appreciation of the programme, others raising problems of their own. By July 1944 *Chaplain Jim, USA* was being carried by 'approximately 50 stations' nationwide, had notched up more than two hundred episodes, and was still enjoying a 'very favorable reception'. True to form, the programme had the full support of the Office of the Chief of Chaplains; not only did Arnold preside at its launch but its Technical Information Division kept its scriptwriters supplied with copies of chaplains' reports, thus ensuring that 'most of the subject matter' was based on 'actual experiences'.[514] Another national radio success was the dramatisation of William C. Taggart's heavily publicised memoir *My Fighting Congregation* (1943) as part of the patriotic, long-running NBC radio show *Cavalcade of America*. Transmitted less than a week after D-Day, Arnold was once again invited to participate in the broadcast.[515]

A final coup for the army's chief of chaplains lay in the composition of an 'Official Chaplains' March' entitled *Soldiers of God*. With music by Ben Machan and words by the songwriter Hy Zaret (then a serving soldier, but later celebrated for his lyrics for *Unchained Melody*),[516] *Soldiers of God* was commissioned, published and promoted by the Office of the Chief of Chaplains. In January 1944, Arnold sent Marshall an autographed copy of the sheet music, hoping that 'it will rank with such band arrangements as the Marine Hymn, the Artillery Song, etc.' and confiding that it would be 'officially introduced to the public in the very near future'.[517] First broadcast in February 1944 as part of NBC's *Army Hour*,[518] it was also aired that Easter as part of Bing Crosby's immensely popular *Kraft Music Hall* show on the same network. Introducing the march, Crosby seemed to express the emergent religious mindset of Americans on the home front. It was, he reflected, a fitting time of year to pay tribute to the clergy of all faiths who had proved themselves the friends and guardians – temporal and spiritual – of the millions of soldiers in the US army. It was, he announced mistakenly, time to perform for the first time the new march of the Corps of Chaplains.[519]

Although Crosby sang only the first part of the march, its lyrics showed very clearly how the Corps of Chaplains saw its role in the present conflict:

> Faithful to God, we're serving
> On the battlefield today.
> Embracing the cause of Righteousness,
> We're marching on our way.
> Soldiers of God, we serve Him faithfully,
> And march in His name

Thru thunder and flame
Wherever the 'call' may be
Trusting in God, His strength we lean upon,
As into the fight,
The legions of Light,
The Soldiers of God, march on.
We are there, as the Chaplains of the nation,
Ev'rywhere with our fighting congregation,
Serving the Lord,
And serving the cause of humanity.
Onward we go till victory is won,
For Justice and Right,
The Legions of Light,
The soldiers of God march on![520]

As an official military march, it is hard to gauge the impact of *Soldiers of God* on the American public; nevertheless, its words echoed the title of William C. Taggart's earlier memoir, and the chief of chaplains thought it memorable enough to give the title of the march to his record of chaplains' activities in World War II (a record he wanted to 'share with the parents, wives, friends and relatives of servicemen'), which he co-authored with Christopher Cross and published at the end of the war.[521]

While the army's Corps of Chaplains set an impressive example in terms of public relations, the navy's Chaplain Corps was slower off the mark, probably because the navy only faced the full impact of the draft, together with its pastoral imperatives, from the end of 1942. In fact, prior to November 1942, when a publicity officer was recruited for the Special Services Section of the Chaplains Division, the Navy Department of Public Relations had not regularly engaged with America's religious press. However, from 1943, John Fortson, a former publicist for the FCC and a United Press reporter, was able to make up some lost ground by compiling a mailing list of three hundred religious publishers, periodicals and commentators whose members regularly received news items on navy chaplains.[522] From 1944, the Chaplains Division also benefited from the professional services of Ensign Esther Johnson, a WAVES officer and former journalist with 'public relations experience'.[523] However, it was not until the last months of the war that this growing public relations campaign seems to have hit its stride. Thanks to the support of the Secretary of the Navy, James V. Forrestal, the climax of Workman's tour of the Pacific in 1945 was a briefing of church leaders by the chief of chaplains in Washington, a gathering that also viewed the premiere of a seventeen-minute information film entitled *Navy Chaplain*. A co-production of Pathé News and the Special Services Section, this was designed to promote recruitment for the Chaplain Corps; however, and as Drury tactfully put it: 'The cessation of hostilities in August meant that the greatest use of the film was not realized.'[524]

In view of this situation, perhaps the greatest public relations asset possessed by the navy's Chaplain Corps in the war years was the celebrated Great Lakes Bluejacket Choir. Although chaplains had fostered choral singing in the pre-war navy (under the direction of William Wilcox Edel, the choir of the aircraft tender *Wright* had even found radio stardom in the early 1930s),[525] the wartime expansion of the navy and the advent of vast new training facilities gave much wider scope to established tradition. As its senior chaplain, Edel presided over the World Communion Service broadcast from the Naval Training Station, Sampson, in October 1944. Another coast-to-coast spectacular, the service was accompanied by Sampson's massed choirs, an ensemble that numbered no fewer than six hundred sailors and eight WAVES.[526] However, choral singing was pursued with even greater enthusiasm at the Naval Training Station, Great Lakes. Founded by the evangelical Lutheran chaplain Hjalmar Frithjof Hanson in 1941, the choir at Great Lakes grew from a membership of twenty to 'more than one thousand' by 1945,[527] largely through systematic recruiting among new arrivals. While one in six recruits auditioned for the choir, for a time whole training companies at Great Lakes consisted solely of choir members, thus greatly facilitating rehearsals.[528] If John Edward Johnson, a Presbyterian (USA) chaplain at Great Lakes, wrote how 'It was an inspiration never to be forgotten to hear one of the choir companies suddenly burst into four-part harmony as it marched along,'[529] the choir's impact on civilian society was no less striking. According to its director, by April 1944 more than fifteen thousand men had passed through it; it had given more than 265 radio broadcasts, had a weekly radio audience of more than fifty million, and had sung at more than 150 'bond rallies, patriotic programs and church concerts' to audiences totalling nearly a million. It was, so Hanson averred, a particularly 'thrilling experience' to hear throughout parades in Chicago and Milwaukee '500 recruits marching through the "Loop" singing "Onward Christian Soldiers" and "We've a story to tell to the Nation".'[530]

If the wartime work of military chaplains was represented to the American public by a variety of media, a much more direct form of interaction lay in the vast amount of personal correspondence that flowed between chaplains and civilians on the home front. Indeed, this was so ubiquitous that one chaplain remarked in June 1945: 'More than likely, [a] loved one will never receive a letter from anyone else other than the man, unless it is the chaplain.'[531] Prior to the outbreak of war, the 1941 edition of the technical manual *The Chaplain* had stressed the importance of writing home on behalf of individual soldiers, 'especially when sick or in trouble', reminding its readers that individual morale rested on personal happiness and that a happy soldier was of much greater 'value to the Government'.[532] Such correspondence was, however, more generally encouraged from the early months of the war by Arnold himself, who wrote for one magazine in 1942:

> A great deal of the chaplain's attention is occupied with mail. Where he can assist his men with difficult letters, he does so. Where he can be of service to parents inquiring about the welfare of their sons, he is more than glad to. When a soldier is sick, it is the chaplain who writes his letters home. And right here, let me urge the fathers and mothers of sons in service to join in the bond between the soldier and his chaplain. Write to your son's chaplain and tell him about your boy. Simply address the letter to 'The Chaplain' and post it to the same address you use for your son's mail.[533]

For Robert D. Workman, the navy chaplain also represented an obvious and critical link between the armed forces and civilian life, claiming on his return from an extensive overseas tour in 1944:

> Our chaplains ... become a link between the men and home. And by 'home' I mean all the things that are so precious in the connotations of that word – the bundle of American traditions that has developed in it: the American way of life that flourished in it, the American dream that was dreamed in it, the faith that permeated it. Linking home with the men and linking the men with home, this is an invaluable contribution made by the chaplain.[534]

The 'excellent effect' of chaplains' correspondence 'on both civilian and soldier morale' was emphasised after the end of the war in Europe.[535] Among the epistolary heroes of the Corps of Chaplains in the ETO was a hospital chaplain who, despite 'the expressed desire of the War Department that mail should be held to an absolute minimum', sent over four thousand letters in six months to the relatives, fiancées and friends of those under his care.[536] Similarly, the chaplain of a group headquarters contrived to take a photograph of 'every officer and enlisted man' in his unit, snaps that he then sent 'home for Mother's Day with an appropriate note on the back of each picture'.[537] However, such earnest efforts could occasionally backfire. Given that they were often bearers of bad tidings, chaplains were advised to avoid using official army envelopes and to write 'Good News' below their return address.[538] Furthermore, and as *Yank* reported in 1943 in an article entitled 'Wrong Address':

> Chaplains complain that cards they send to soldiers' parents informing them of their son's arrival in camp sometimes rebound unexpectedly. One soldier listed his wife under 'parents' and the irate lady wrote back, 'Sir, I'll have you understand I am not Private Blank's mother, I've been married to him now for almost a year.' Then there was the wife who hadn't heard from her husband in several years. She received her card and wrote, 'Thank you very much for telling me the b—d's location. I'm coming down.[539]

In fact, correspondence with the home front could assume a combative aspect from the outset. In April 1943, Cylde E. Kimball wrote to his wife from Iceland:

> Saw a man whose long-awaited mail brought him a request for divorce. Have just written the girl to tell her off. She has either cheated, was afraid to tell him before he left that she no longer loved him, or is afraid to wait and face him. He is risking his life; the least she could do is cheer him up.[540]

Stung by similar tales of marital infidelity, Gilbert Johnstone, a Northern Baptist chaplain serving with the AAF in New Guinea, wrote a scathing letter to the press on the topic of 'Cheating War Wives'.[541] Published on the front page of the *Chicago Daily News*, his letter triggered a national debate, prompting 'a flurry of pro-and-con argument by judges, social workers, clergymen – and service wives'.[542]

However, the most difficult form of correspondence was that which took place with the next of kin of deceased personnel. Apart from its inherently emotive nature, chaplains had to guard against offending the sensitivities of the bereaved and of falling foul of military censors. The pre-war expectation that army chaplains would write to next of kin was expressed in the technical manual *The Chaplain* in 1941,[543] but after three years of war the situation had become less straight-forward. In 1944, chaplains were alerted to 'considerations of military security' that stood to 'forbid or restrict this practice', and were warned that any private communication had to be accurate and that it must follow an official notifica-tion of death.[544] Nevertheless, it was reported from the ETO in 1945 that, while letters of condolence were 'a mandatory responsibility of commanding officers', the great majority of chaplains found that this duty fell to them.[545] The situation was the same in the Pacific, where by the end of the war army chaplains were expected to provide letters of condolence in triplicate, with each letter giving 'an outline of the circumstances surrounding death ... grave location, informa-tion about the burial service, and other information of personal or sentimental nature which may be of <u>comfort </u>to the family'.[546] Nor was it a case of simply writing these letters, difficult as they were. Failure to write for whatever reason led to complaints to senior chaplains; problems could arise if the bereaved took exception to the faith of the chaplain concerned, and letters of condolence elic-ited innumerable and often unanswerable questions 'from desperate relatives and friends seeking information concerning the death of their soldiers'.[547]

Navy chaplains laboured under the same burden of expectation in terms of personal correspondence and letters of condolence.[548] For example, Walter A. Mahler, who was assigned to the Marine Corps Recruit Depot, San Diego, from 1942 to 1944, remembered that as a part of his routine 'I used to send out a little card saying, "Your Marine went to Mass today. I know you'll be glad to know that even though he's away from home, he has not forgotten his God."'[549] However, a significant variation on the letter of condolence was the so-called 'casualty call' to bereaved families. This arose out of the pre-war charitable work of the Navy Relief Society, whose branch secretaries were often chaplains, and from an *ex officio* pre-war requirement that they visit the dependants of sick, distressed or deceased sailors who lived in the vicinity of their ships.[550] Although impossible to implement across the length and breadth of the United States, from May 1944 these sympathy calls were made a matter of policy whenever practicable. In the First Naval District alone (consisting of Massachusetts, Maine, New Hampshire, Vermont and Rhode Island) chaplains made no fewer than 2,370 calls on families of dead or missing sailors, marines and coast guardsmen between June 1944 and August 1945. Although hardly welcome, subsequent correspondence seemed to indicate that their efforts were widely appreciated by the families concerned.[551] A variation on this ministry of consolation was the scene in the Biltmore Hotel, Los Angeles, on 5 August 1945, when Joseph T. O'Callahan met with the next of kin of those who had died on the *Franklin*. 'Yours boys,' he told them, 'died suddenly.... There was no suffering.... They had died instantly as the intense heat seared their lungs and swept on. The vast majority of the 1000 who were killed died in the first four or five minutes.'[552]

Clearly, military chaplains did a great deal to justify a positive public image of military chaplaincy. However, what also contributed to that image was the heroic stature with which chaplains were endowed by the wider wartime media. This was the product of much more than the efforts of public relations specialists in the two corps of chaplains. Through the exploits of clergymen such as William Emerson in the Revolutionary War, and William Corby in the Civil War,[553] the nation's conflicts had already produced a storied tradition of the fighting parson and military chaplain (the two not being synonymous), which was a colorful theme in American civil religion. As President Roosevelt enthused to Walter H. Gray, the suffragan bishop of the Episcopalian diocese of Connecticut:

The history of the church in this country is an essential part of our history as a nation. In all previous national crises men of religion have stood beside their fellow men and stood in the front ranks; the preacher was with the pioneers who rolled back the frontier; he was with the men who carried guns at Lexington and Gettysburg and Chateau-Thierry.[554]

Indeed, and despite the currency of interwar pacifism, the cult of Francis P. Duffy, the most famous American chaplain of World War I, was robust enough to be marked by a statue in Times Square in 1937 and celebrated three years later in the film *The Fighting 69th*. This common predisposition to see military chaplains in a heroic light was illustrated in a wartime biography of Stephen J. Meany, formerly business manager of the Catholic weekly *America* and Duffy's successor as regimental chaplain to New York City's famous 'Fighting Irish'.[555] Once again federalised as the 165th Infantry Regiment in October 1941, the National Guardsmen of the 69th New York saw their first action of World War II on Makin Atoll in the Gilbert Islands in 1943.[556] Here, and although Japanese resistance proved lighter than on nearby Tarawa, Meany was wounded by a Japanese bullet and swiftly evacuated.[557] Although his brief role in this four-day battle was anticlimactic in comparison to Duffy's extensive career in France a generation earlier, it was reported that Meany had been saved by 'his miraculous medal of the Virgin Mary' and, in *Father Meany and 'The Fighting 69th'* (1944), the renowned writer and sports illustrator Burris Jenkins recounted how the stricken Meany had given absolution to a mortally wounded soldier. Jenkins also reflected on how Meany matched up to the illustrious Duffy: 'Of course he'd heard of Father Duffy and worshipped his memory as had every other American boy. But without the slightest presumption of trying to follow such mighty footsteps – nor has he even now.'[558]

Significantly, Burris Jenkins was the son of a pastor from Kansas City, but even those whom Arnold regarded as wholly 'disinterested newspaper writers' saluted the courage and commitment of army chaplains.[559] In February 1944, and from Fifth Army Headquarters in Italy,[560] H.R. Knickerbocker of the *Chicago Sun* wrote: 'It may surprise many Americans to learn that their Army Chaplain Corps has won more distinctions in proportion to its numbers than any other branch of service, including the air forces.'[561] Citing the case of the 34th Infantry Division, a National Guard division from the Midwest that had seen hard fighting in North Africa as well as in Italy, Knickerbocker paid fulsome tribute to a war record that he claimed 'should make the clergy of America proud and should comfort the mothers of America'. From a divisional establishment of fifteen chaplains, two had been killed, four wounded and two captured. Furthermore, the chaplains in question had earned eleven decorations, including the Legion of Merit Medal (a non-combat award, given twice); a Distinguished Service Cross (the army's second highest award for bravery on the battlefield); four Silver Stars (a lesser award for gallantry in combat); and four Purple Hearts (awarded to all those wounded or killed through enemy action). Omitting to mention that one chaplain, Albert J. Hoffmann, had accounted for three of these awards, Knickerbocker enquired rhetorically, 'What other unit in the Army can rival this record of the chaplains?'[562] The same question was raised less publicly by Major General Jens A. Doe, the commanding officer of the 41st Infantry Division, after its capture of Biak Island, off the north-west coast of New Guinea, later that year. In a letter of commendation on the operation dated September 1944, Doe recognised that: 'the Chaplain Corps, by percentage, received a higher number of decorations than any other individual group. In faithfully experiencing the many adversities, they sustained more casualties by percentage than any other group.'[563] By the end of 1943, and according to Arnold's figures, eighty-one army chaplains, or 3 per cent of those serving in operational theatres, had already been decorated.[564] Among them was Albert J. Hoffmann, a Catholic chaplain of the 34th Infantry Division who lost his leg to a mine on the Volturno River in November 1943 and who had the distinction of being one of the war's most decorated army chaplains.[565] Inevitably, Hoffmann became something of a celebrity on his return to the United States, where he went on to minister to fellow amputees at the Percy James Hospital, Battle Creek, Michigan. Supremely newsworthy, Hoffmann's story was reported in *Time, Newsweek, Life* and the *Saturday Evening Post*, and it was even recounted in a number of comic strips.[566] By the summer of 1945, and after two further years of war, no fewer than 1,281 army chaplains had been decorated, representing roughly one in seven of all who served in World War II.[567]

If the navy's awards were fewer in both absolute and relative terms, they were not to be outshone in the renown of their star chaplains. As the new commandant of the Marine Corps, and a celebrity in his own right after the Guadalcanal campaign, Lieutenant General Alexander A. Vandegrift waxed lyrical about the chaplains who had served with his 1st Marine Division in the Solomons,[568] telling readers of the Methodist magazine *World Outlook*:

> Besides the rites, sacraments, and services, they were asked by the men to help solve their problems and inner doubts. The chaplains were splendid men and were held in high regard. They were everywhere at once. They went wherever the other marines went, often in the front line of attack. They carried the wounded and cared for them. They helped the surgeons. Some marines owe their lives to them.[569]

Despite such plaudits from a national hero and winner of the Medal of Honor, navy chaplains had already made a significant impression on the public consciousness. When the Japanese struck at Pearl Harbor in the early morning of Sunday 7 December 1941, chaplains of the Pacific Fleet were rigging for church,[570] and the deaths of two of their number helped to symbolise the dastardly and even sacrilegious nature of the Japanese attack. Indeed, prior to the deaths of chaplains Aloysius H. Schmitt, Catholic, and Thomas L. Kirkpatrick, Presbyterian (USA), on board the battleships *Oklahoma* and *Arizona* respectively, the last and only US Navy chaplain to be killed in action at sea had died at the Civil War battle of Hampton Roads in 1862.[571] While the christening of two destroyer escorts in their memory in 1943 says much about the nation's exalted sense of resolve after Pearl Harbor,[572] a lighter note was, quite literally, struck by the popular songwriter Frank J. Loesser in 1942. Invoking Howell M. Forgy's words on board the *New Orleans*, Loesser's song 'Praise the Lord and Pass the Ammunition' conjured the vivid scene of a chaplain forsaking his Sunday service at Pearl Harbor in order to fire an anti-aircraft gun at the Japanese, a fiction that was originally reported in *Time* magazine. Although the hero of this fable was then identified by 'publishers, radio stations and the "gentlemen of the press"' as William A. Maguire, then senior chaplain of the Pacific Fleet, who had since returned to the United States and was selling war bonds on behalf of the Navy Department, the denials of Maguire and various other churchmen did nothing to dent its popularity. Indeed, and even though a detailed refutation was issued by the navy, Maguire still appeared on the cover of *Life* magazine on the strength of the original story.[573] Whatever the factual confusion, Loesser's 'Praise the Lord and Pass the Ammunition' was one of the most successful songs of World War II. By the end of the war it had sold a million copies of sheet music and twice that number of records;[574] in fact, by the autumn of 1943 a discernible reaction had set in, its endless and increasingly flippant renditions provoking 'the ire of churchmen the country over', and prompting *Variety* magazine, 'the bible of the show world', to criticise their apparent lack of patriotism.[575]

There was, however, nothing fictional about the combat decorations awarded to navy chaplains in the course of the war; these included at least forty-six Purple Hearts, eight Silver Stars, a Navy Cross and, uniquely for chaplains of either service at this point, a Medal of Honor.[576] The latter was awarded early in 1946 to the Catholic chaplain Joseph T. O'Callahan after the pulverising attack on the aircraft carrier *Franklin* off the Japanese home islands ten months earlier. With more than one thousand of its crew killed or wounded, and its flight deck torn into a scorched and twisted jumble of wreckage, the unfortunate *Franklin* was the most heavily damaged American aircraft carrier to stay afloat in the course of the war.[577] In fact, it was only due to exceptional damage control work that the *Franklin* managed to stay afloat, and it was a reflection of the versatility of the navy chaplain that O'Callahan played a leading role in these efforts. From late 1942, the navy had placed an intense emphasis on firefighting skills and damage control techniques and what seems to have differentiated O'Callahan's work from that of his Methodist colleague, Grimes W. Gatlin, who won a Silver Star on the *Franklin*, was his outstanding contribution in this respect.[578] In view of the ship's crippling officer casualties, O'Callahan filled a command vacuum on board the blazing carrier, his efforts to ensure the emptying of a turret magazine even arousing the ironic quip, 'Here it is, Padre. Praise the Lord and *dump* the ammunition.'[579] According to O' Callahan's citation, he not only 'ministered to the wounded and dying' but 'organized and led fire-fighting crews into the blazing inferno on the flight-deck; he directed the jettisoning of live ammunition and the flooding of the magazine [and] he manned a hose to cool hot, armed bombs rolling dangerously on the listing deck'.[580] O'Callahan's exploits certainly seem to have matched up to what the American public were coming to expect from Hollywood's celluloid clergy and, as another navy chaplain drily put it, 'O'Callahan was the one-man band.'[581]

For all of O'Callahan's heroics, no single chaplain acquired the renown of the four army chaplains who drowned along with nearly seven hundred others on board the army transport *Dorchester* in February 1943. Torpedoed by a U-boat off Greenland, the *Dorchester* went down in just twenty minutes; however, in sworn affidavits, a number of survivors spoke of how, after trying to calm those on board, these chaplains gave away their lifebelts and joined their hands in prayer before 'the stricken Ship made her final plunge'.[582] The inspiring story of 'The Four Chaplains' soon became the stuff of legend. Representing all three of America's major faith traditions, including the first Jewish chaplain to be lost in action,[583] their example stood as the supreme example of the much-vaunted 'Judeo-Christian' solidarity of wartime America.[584] Among the four chaplains was Clark V. Poling, a minister of the Reformed Church in America and son of Dr Daniel A. Poling, incumbent of the Grace Baptist Temple in Philadelphia, president of the World's Christian Endeavor Union, editor of the *Christian Herald,* and a strong wartime advocate of Roosevelt's foreign policy.[585] As a bereaved father and eminent churchman, Daniel Poling simply but eloquently spelled out the significance of their example: 'Four men in three faiths, joined in friendship and sharing in a holy mission, in death were not divided. Lost in action, they were found of God'.[586] Certainly, the story of 'The Four Chaplains' struck a deep chord on the American home front, their renown resulting in a host of local monuments and memorials.[587] In December 1944 each was posthumously awarded a Distinguished Service Cross and four years later, as a result of a special congressional dispensation that allowed their depiction less than a decade after their deaths, 115 million copies of a three-cent postage stamp were printed bearing their portraits, an image of the *Dorchester,* and the legend 'These IMMORTAL CHAPLAINS ... INTERFAITH IN ACTION'.[588] The national cult of 'The Four Chaplains' flourished into the Cold War period. In February 1951, and against the background of common sacrifices being made anew on the battlefields of Korea, President Truman, who had earlier described their example as 'the greatest sermon that ever was preached', dedicated an interfaith chapel to the memory of the four chaplains at Philadelphia's Grace Baptist Temple, a chapel that incorporated Catholic, Jewish and Protestant altars and which was installed at a cost of $300,000 donated by adherents of all three faiths.[589] A decade later, a posthumous Special Medal for Heroism, a unique decoration on a par with the Medal of Honor, was approved by Congress and awarded by President Kennedy (who, in a telling reflection of the limits of ecumenical and interfaith relations prior to the Second Vatican Council, absented himself from a fundraising banquet for the interfaith chapel in 1950).[590] As late as 1998, Congress passed a resolution that 3 February should be observed by the nation as 'Four Chaplains Day', a resolution that has also been passed by several state legislatures.[591]

In combination, sustained and varied outreach to the home front, coordinated and multifaceted public relations campaigns, favourable and sometimes lavish coverage in the American media, and the real inspiration of national heroes such as O'Callahan, Hoffmann and 'The Four Chaplains' meant that America's military chaplains had transcended their purely military functions by 1945; indeed, by the end of the war, and as the lyrics of *Soldiers of God* implied, American military chaplaincy had become a chaplaincy to the nation at large. Indicative of their newfound favour with the American public was the freedom and confidence with which prominent chaplains held forth to civilian audiences on the nature of the war. Significantly, an AIPO poll conducted in November 1941 had shown that a majority of Americans had disapproved of 'the question of American participation in the war' being aired from the pulpit.[592] Partly to assuage anxieties of this kind in relation to chaplains and the draftee army, in September 1941 the Jewish chaplain and Reform rabbi Aryeh Lev published a book entitled *What Chaplains Preach*. Here, Lev assured his readers of the essential similarity of the role of the chaplain to that of the civilian pastor, presented a sample of more than sixty chaplains' sermons and sermon outlines, and pointedly insisted:

> What should the chaplain preach? He should preach religion! The chaplain is his own judge as to just what that is and how it should be preached. No one can tell him what to say and what not to say ... No instructions to chaplains are contemplated with a view towards conformity, indoctrination or propaganda. Every chaplain takes an oath of allegiance to the Constitution of the United States when he receives his commission, and as long as he fulfills that pledge he is at perfect liberty to preach that which his religious training has taught him to say.[593]

If *What Chaplains Preach* was intended to allay suspicions of clerical drumbanging, it is striking that both chiefs of chaplains and their subordinates assumed this role with a vengeance after the shock of Pearl Harbor. In 1942, and in a magazine article on army chaplaincy, Arnold struck an apocalyptic note when he wrote that:

> This war is a different war ... The enemy is armed with all the clever devices of Lucifer himself, and his ugly aim is not the mere capture of land or material possessions, but the utter destruction of that spiritual wealth upon which the nations of democracy are founded ... On the present vast battlefield where our armies of light struggle with those of darkness, the spiritual arm of the service must be a living, challenging, and conquering arm ... Though the foe's material armament be equal to ours, we, nevertheless, are stronger in spirit and in the humanity of our motive. This, in addition to our faith, is certain victory. 'Behold the eyes of the Lord are on them that fear him: and on them that hope in his mercy. Our soul waiteth for the Lord: he is our help and protector. For in him our heart shall rejoice and in his holy name we have trusted [Psalm 33:18, 20–21].

Arnold reprised this theme the following year by declaring that: 'We are engaged in a great struggle to determine whether the religious principles of our own Nation can exist in the world of today.'[594] His counterpart, Robert D. Workman, was just as comfortable with the role of the wartime prophet. In an address given at the Hotel Roosevelt in New York City in May 1944 Workman insisted that, amidst the turbulence of war:

[The chaplain] interprets to the confused and inarticulate thinker the meaning of this din and shambles. He helps to direct the hearts and the minds of the men to an understanding of the purpose for which all this is done, to the pattern of life which must emerge out of their sacrifices. He makes them aware of the future, which must bring a lasting peace based on justice, common decency, and liberty for all.[595]

This role, however, could prove double-edged, as was the case with the intended dedication of the 5th Marine Division cemetery on Iwo Jima in May 1945. When Protestant and Catholic chaplains objected to a plan for Roland B. Gittelsohn, a Jewish navy chaplain, to offer prayers over the graves of hundreds of largely Christian marines, the division chaplain relented and Gittelsohn delivered his intended address at a smaller, Jewish ceremony. Nevertheless, Gittelsohn's text was copied by sympathetic colleagues and widely circulated on the island and in the United States, being printed in full by *The Chaplain*.[596] Here, and in a bold and radical statement of his own liberal politics, Gittelsohn invoked the vaunted theme of the United States' interfaith efforts to realise a better world and even linked them to the vexed and volatile question of civil rights:

We dedicate ourselves, first, to live together in peace the way they fought and are buried in this war.... Here lie officers and men, Negroes and whites, rich men and poor – together. Here are Protestants, Catholics, and Jews – together. Here no man prefers another because of his faith or despises him because of his color. Here there are no quotas of how many from each group are admitted or allowed. Among these men there is no discrimination, no prejudice, no hatred. Theirs is the highest and purest democracy.... Any man among us, the living, who fails to understand that will thereby betray those who lie here dead. Whoever of us lifts his hand in hate against a brother, or thinks himself superior to those who happen to be in the minority, makes of this ceremony and of the bloody sacrifice it commemorates, an empty, hollow mockery.... Thus, then as our solemn sacred duty, do we, the living, now dedicate ourselves – to the right of Protestants, Catholics, and Jews, of white men and Negroes alike, to enjoy the democracy for which all of them have here paid the price.[597]

However Gittelsohn's comments may have been received by his fellow citizens, such was the moral capital of military chaplaincy by this stage of the war that American army chaplains played a very public role in chastising German civilians for the horrors perpetrated by the Third Reich. After the liberation of Wöbbelin labour camp in May 1945, local Germans were compelled to inspect its horrors and were then obliged to bury its victims. The inscription for the cemetery markers was composed by the division chaplain of the 8th Infantry Division, the United Presbyterian Albert G. Wildman, who wrote:

Here lie the bodies of [number] victims of Nazi atrocity from Poland, Russia, Greece, Czechoslovakia, Belgium, Holland, and Germany, who died of starvation and brutality in the Wobbelin Concentration Camp. Buried [date] under the supervision of the 8th Infantry Division, U.S. Army, by whom the surviving prisoners of the camp were liberated.

God is our Refuge and Strength.[598]

In the nearby town of Ludwigslust, German civilians and POWs buried two hundred bodies in the town square, 'with services performed by American Army Chaplains of all religious faiths,'[599] and received a stinging rebuke from the Division Chaplain of the 82nd Airborne Division, the Episcopalian George B. Wood. Despite the enormity of the occasion, Wood chose his words carefully, although this did not diminish the impact of what he said. All too conscious of the pronounced anti-Christian, as well as anti-Semitic, tendencies of the Nazi regime, Wood reminded his German audience that they were now gathered in a public place for a religious ceremony. He stressed that the purpose of the assembly was to give a decent burial to those who had been murdered by Germany's armed forces at the behest of the German government. Those who were about to be interred represented only a small proportion of several thousand inmates who had suffered at a concentration camp only a few miles away. Their living conditions had been indescribable, worse than those of animals, and more than a thousand had starved to death in the past few weeks. Those whom they had gathered to bury had been stacked several corpses high in a single building, or had been retrieved from the human wreckage of the camp. However, Wood was emphatic that the blame for this situation lay with his listeners. Ultimately, they had lived in comfortable indifference only a few miles away, and had elected and tolerated the very government that was responsible. In contrast to their callousness, Wood stressed that it was the policy of the US army to make sure that all victims of the war – regardless of their status – were at least accorded a decent burial according to their religious allegiance. Furthermore, he announced that Eisenhower had decreed that the victims of Nazi atrocities would be buried in public, and their graveyards accorded the same respect as military cemeteries. The ceremony that would take place would be led by Catholic, Protestant, and Jewish chaplains of the 82nd Airborne Division; crosses would mark the graves of the deceased, and a permanent memorial would be erected to honour their memory. The prayers they would offer would not only be prayers of committal, but earnest entreaties that humanity would never again sink to such depths.[600]

Perceptions and judgements

On Sunday 19 August 1945, and in keeping with his recent proclamation of that Sabbath as a special day of prayer, President Harry S. Truman hosted a service of thanksgiving for the defeat of Japan, and the victorious conclusion of World

War II, in the East Room of the White House. Leading the service for the new president were the current chiefs of chaplains, Luther D. Miller for the army, who had replaced Arnold in April, and William N. Thomas, a Methodist, who had succeeded Workman in July.[601] Despite the change in personnel, the place of the two chiefs at this gathering was entirely fitting; since the outbreak of war in Europe, more than twelve thousand men had served as chaplains in the United States Army and Navy, a figure that represented an estimated 9 per cent of the country's Catholic priests, almost the same proportion of its Protestant clergy, and an even higher percentage of American rabbis, half of whom had volunteered their services as chaplains in this 'American Jewish war', as Deborah Dash Moore has styled it.[602] Throughout this period, the primary thrust of military chaplaincy had been the support of the nation's soldiers, sailors, airmen and marines, the ministry of military chaplains ensuring, at the very least, that the constitutional right of service personnel to freely exercise their religion had been protected under the terms of the First Amendment (unless, that is, they were Buddhist). While this was considered to be highly beneficial to military morale, especially given the armed forces' overwhelming reliance on wartime volunteers and draftees from a god-fearing if not uniformly churchgoing society, their presence had also helped these civilians-in-arms to face the stresses of combat and, more generally, cope with the numerous vicissitudes of service life. In fulfilling this role, and with the assistance of a well-oiled public relations machine, especially in the army's Corps of Chaplains, in the course of what was regarded as a manifestly just war by the great majority of Americans, military chaplains ceased to be treated as objects of suspicion, as they often were in the interwar years, and were instead represented as the indispensable friends and guardians of millions of absent sons, husbands and fathers. A case in point was the judgement of Daniel A. Poling, who toured the Pacific theatre as 'a special envoy of the President' in the summer of 1944. Representing the FCC (and, more ironically, the Christian Peace Union and the World Alliance for International Friendship through the Churches),[603] Poling returned from his Pacific sojourn to pronounce in the *Christian Herald*, 'Thank God for the Army and Navy chaplains in this the world's blackest spiritual hour!'; to report to the War Department that its chaplains were engaged in 'one of the greatest services of all times'; and to reassure concerned civilians that they 'need have no fear that loved ones will forget their God.'[604]

Unquestionably, the organisation of military chaplaincy had been far superior to that of World War I, and Arnold was no doubt right when he claimed that 'the spiritual branch of Army service today has been brought to the highest and most efficient point in its long history.'[605] From a command perspective, military chaplaincy seems to have given ample cause for support and satisfaction. Significantly, the post-war report entitled 'The Army Chaplain in the European Theater' divulged that:

93% of the chaplains interviewed for this study had been made to feel that the services which they had rendered were regarded and valued as materially helpful in promoting military efficiency, while the number of those who had been made to feel that their services were without value (1%), or who felt that the military authorities were indifferent to the value of chaplains (6%), is strikingly small.[606]

Fulsome praise was forthcoming from the highest levels of command. With reference to the ETO, General of the Army Dwight D. Eisenhower averred that: 'The work of the Army chaplain has been of inestimable value to American forces.... Their selflessness and unfailing devotion to the spiritual and material welfare of millions of Americans have won for them the admiration, respect, and affection of all commanders.'[607] Likewise, Lieutenant General Lucian K. Truscott, who commanded the Fifth Army in Italy in the latter months of the war, confirmed that:

> [The chaplains'] outstanding efforts in bringing the benefits of religion to the front lines as well as to the rear areas, their ministrations to the wounded and dying, and above all their personal conduct as men of God, living with the Fifth Army men as one of them, courageous and inspirational, through all the manifold hardships of the campaign, effectively contributed to the high morale prevalent among all units. To have served with them is an honor and a privilege and evokes praise of a job well done.[608]

Equally, Fleet Admiral Chester W. Nimitz, America's senior naval commander in the Pacific theatre throughout the war against Japan, testified to his regard for navy chaplains before the General Commission on Army and Navy Chaplains in May 1946:

> My own esteem for the chaplains is not so much based upon deeds of valor as it is appreciation for their routine accomplishments. No one will ever know how many young men were deferred from acts of desperation by a heart-to-heart talk with the 'Padre'.... By his patient, sympathetic labors with the men, day in, day out, and through many a night, every chaplain I know contributed immeasurably to the moral courage of our fighting men.[609]

Ironically, glowing affirmations were even forthcoming from former enemies; while under American interrogation, Bishop Franz Dohrmann, the senior Protestant chaplain of the German Army and a conservative nationalist by temperament, seemed to be 'very familiar with the objectives and personnel of the United States Army Corps of Chaplains and could not praise it too highly.'[610]

All, however, was not quite as it seemed. For example, and while it could work remarkably smoothly, the vaunted all-faiths ministry of the two corps of chaplains was fraught with unresolved tensions as, indeed, was the balance of secular and spiritual duties expected of the army chaplain. Furthermore, while some homosexual service personnel may have had cause to rue the day they told it to the chaplain, military chaplaincy also reflected American society's painful ambivalence over civil rights. On the credit side, black officers were nowhere better represented in the regular army than in its Corps of Chaplains, the army's Chaplain School was never segregated, and honest and earnest attempts seem to have been made to recruit sufficient chaplains from America's black churches in order to serve its black soldiers. Nevertheless, and as this suggests, in other respects army chaplaincy conformed to the segregated norms of army life and, in so doing, placed its black chaplains in a difficult and invidious position with respect to military authority. Moreover, and despite its own shortcomings, it should be stressed that the army's Corps of Chaplains almost stood as a model of progressive practice in comparison to that of its navy counterpart, an organisation that effectively resisted efforts to ensure that black clergymen were adequately represented within its ranks.

While the public perception and official depiction of chaplains were over-whelmingly positive, the views of chaplains themselves and the underlying impressions of service personnel could be more ambivalent. Significantly, and as victory hove into view in the summer of 1945, *The Chaplain* proved less reluc-tant to air the reservations and objections held by some of its readers. In July, for example, Bernhardt G. Hoffman, a Lutheran chaplain of the Missouri Synod, complained about the constant media portrayal of the chaplain as 'A Good Joe', arguing that, in the deluge of stories to this effect, 'the Chaplain Corps is belittled in the eyes of the public and will have a difficult time in justifying its [post-war] existence.'[611] Similar sentiments were expressed the following month, when the Methodist chaplain Raymond E. Musser sketched ten different types of chaplain, among them 'the "card-punching" type', who 'walks around wise-cracking loud-voiced about soldiers' sins, back-slapping through the mess, hen-cackling down the hospital wards', and 'the "officers' chaplain" type' who 'shudders at the very thought of eating with the [enlisted men] at the chow before church.'[612] In the same issue, but this time under an assumed name, a third chaplain complained vehemently about the '"boot-licking"' of career-minded chaplains, of those jumped-up civilian nonentities who, as military chaplains, were 'more at home with regulations than with the Scriptures', and of the pernicious 'racket' of rank that only served to engender 'unnecessary confusion and corruption'. He also decried the flagrant violation of the First Amendment represented by Amer-ican military chaplaincy in its present form, demanding: 'Who can deny that the historic relationship of church and state has been abrogated by the practical functioning of the Chaplain Corps?'[613] Perhaps the most comprehensive critique of military chaplaincy came from the pen of Renwick C. Kennedy in June 1946. A stern, self-appointed auditor of army chaplaincy (and, as we shall see, of the moral conduct of the American soldier in Europe), Kennedy drew on personal experience to answer the question 'How Good Were the Army Chaplains?' for the benefit of *The Christian Century*. According to Kennedy, chaplains 'had a reasonably square deal from the army', with a recognition even among the 'coarse and irreligious' that the chaplain 'represented [what] was needed, particularly under battle conditions'. Chaplains were, moreover, generally freer to do as they wished, better equipped, and less burdened than they had been in civilian life. In overall terms, but speaking of Protestant ministers in particular, Kennedy maintained that, 'Most of them were decent, kind, friendly Christian men' who did 'a good job under hard circumstances'. Nevertheless, and as we have noted, they could be riven with sectarian intrigues; they were hampered by their officers' rank ('enlisted men seldom like officers'); Catholics had 'too large a control ... for a minority religious group in the United States' (to the extent that 'Protestant chaplains felt that they were in the hands of Rome'); and, finally, without the backing of a monolithic church and its agencies, 'Protestant chaplains were on their own', and 'It was largely a matter of each chaplain for himself.'[614]

How widespread such disgruntlement was among military chaplains is impossible to tell; nevertheless, it was clearly present despite an unprecedented degree of training and indoctrination, and the existence of highly developed public relations machinery that assiduously placed the work of chaplains in the best possible light. It was, significantly, a telling cause of complaint among chaplains after the end of the war in Europe that the deft management of public relations so characteristic of the Office of the Chief of Chaplains in Washington had been lacking overseas. As a result, in the ETO the army's daily newspaper *Stars and Stripes* and weekly magazine *Yank* had given little coverage to chaplaincy work or to religious matters in general; controversial letters on religious subjects, some concerning chaplains, had gone unpublished and what did appear placed an undue emphasis 'upon the spectacular as compared to the significant' – a feature on 'religious snake charmers' being a case in point. Given the inherent dangers of leaving 'religious news coverage' to 'secular newsmen unqualified to judge or select in matters of religion', it was recommended that a Technical Information Branch be established in the office of each theatre chaplain 'with an experienced religious journalist as cheif [sic]'. The purpose of the branch would be:

> [T]o provide information about chaplains and religion in the Army to soldier publications like <u>Stars and Stripes</u> and <u>Yank</u>, to act as consultant to the staffs of such publications on all matters pertaining to religious news coverage, to coordinate and oversee religious news releases, to serve as a clearing point for all written material of a religious nature, and to encourage fuller religious expression by chaplains and laymen alike.[615]

However, despite some dissension among chaplains over their wartime record, and even without the benefits of positive and extensive coverage of their work in widely read soldier publications, the army's rank and file held a largely positive opinion of their chaplains. A 1945 survey of 2,985 officers and enlisted men from five theatres of war who passed through the AAF's Redistribution Center at Santa Ana, California, found that those who reacted favourably to their chaplains were in a healthy majority, ranging from 76 per cent among Catholics to 66 per cent among Jews and 60 per cent among Protestants. Those who had 'no comment' represented 16, 24 and 34 per cent respectively, while those whose reaction was definitely 'unfavorable' represented only 8, 10 and 6 per cent. Favourable verdicts included statements such as 'chaplains are doing a grand job', 'the chaplain served as a substitute for parents', and 'his prayers at briefing and at the take-off were greatly appreciated'. While it was to be expected that Protestants and Jews, whose own chaplains represented a spectrum of traditions and opinion, should have been more equivocal than Catholics in their verdicts on the chaplains they encountered, what was remarkable was that the most frequent comment among those deemed to be unfavourable in their reactions was the double-edged assertion that 'there were not enough chaplains'. Other adverse comments were predictable enough, including: 'Partial to men of their own religious denomination', 'Good fellow but too shallow', and 'Too much idealizing and not enough sound preaching'.[616] Significantly, and in a manner that suggests remarkably little difference between aircrew and ground crew in the way chaplains were perceived, the nature of these findings had been anticipated by nearly a hundred interviews conducted in 1944 among 'successful combat crew men returning to the Zone of Interior [i.e. the continental United States] for a 30-day period of rest and recuperation'. Although it was widely recognised that AAF flight surgeons also played a vital, quasi-pastoral role in relation to American aircrew,[617] Major Douglas D. Bond, the director of psychiatry of the Eighth Air Force, told its senior chaplain:

> [O]ne of the questions asked was related to the work of chaplains on the field with combat crews. Although 44 said that they had no close contact with the chaplain, 54 stated that they knew their chaplains well and felt that they had been a very decided addition to the group. Twelve of these men felt that the chaplain had been of very critical help in allowing them to go on, and several of these men spent anywhere from ten minutes to an hour, before each mission, with him. Although these figures may not look very impressive, it was our very definite impression, and I might add somewhat to our surprise, that the work of the chaplains on operational fields was of very definite and concrete benefit in allowing men to continue in the face of rather severe difficulty.[618]

Local surveys in the wider army also furnished detailed evidence as to how soldiers reacted to their chaplains. 'After VE-Day', the regimental chaplain of the 41st Armored Infantry Regiment, which had seen action in North Africa and Sicily as well as in North-West Europe, received thirty-nine replies to a 'religious questionnaire' that he had circulated among its officers and enlisted men. Although it was conceded that 'informal questionnaires of this type' tended 'to be answered by the more religious personnel in an organization', it was clear from other surveys that it was this very group that often proved most outspoken in their criticism. In the case of the soldiers of the 41st Armored Infantry, 'twenty-eight responded that the [chaplaincy] provisions had been adequate, eight declared that they had been inadequate, and three were non-committal'. Among the more positive comments were those of a Catholic Private first class (Pfc), who insisted that, 'Army chaplains set a better example for me to look up to than civilian priests in the church back home.'[619] Once more, however, the frustrations and disappointed expectations of more pious soldiers tended to colour complaints; a Protestant first lieutenant insisted that: 'individual chaplains should urge church attendance more actively. Most chaplains appear content with a meager congregation. Something more by way of church advertising should be added.' Similarly, a Protestant second lieutenant felt that chaplains should give an even higher priority to front-line units because: 'Men on the front need the chaplain more and he can be of greater help there … I heard many of my men say that when a man is dying a word or two from the chaplain might help more there than all he can do in the rear.'[620] In the ETO at least, a wider and more representative perspective could also be gleaned from censorship reports drawn up at theatre headquarters. Based on scrutiny of soldiers' correspondence, reports for the period February to August 1945 noted favourable references to chaplains on twenty-three occasions and unfavourable references on only twelve; there were also thirty neutral references that were classified as 'miscellaneous comment'. Among the positive verdicts, comments included an infantryman's assurance that, 'A chaplain is a soldier's best friend. We have a very fine one with our outfit', and an artillery officer's report that, 'Last night we had Jewish services … only another man and myself were able to attend … the Chaplain preached just as though we had 50 men there. It really was nice …' Significantly, criticism once again seemed to emanate mostly from those who wanted to see more of chaplains or who were unhappy with their theology and/or styles of worship. Among the latter was a fundamentalist Technician 5th Grade (Tec 5) who complained that:

[I]n all the time I've been with Chaplain *** he has never given an invitation. He has never been able to account for any new conversions. He is a bit modernistic in his theology and definitely is not evangelistic in his preaching. Still in all he is very sincere conscientious and a hard worker. He has the will but lacks the message.[621]

A striking exception to this general rule was the complaint of a lieutenant in the Corps of Engineers, whose racist fulminations underscored the often difficult position of the army's black chaplains:

Last Thursday night was the first anniversary of the battalion, and so the boys had a dance at the colored Red Cross, which all officers were ordered to attend by the battalion commander. It was a pretty disgusting affair for us to have to swallow, watching these men dancing with the lowest of class of whores in all of England (white), and the chaplain taking his white 'girl friend' around introducing her to the officers. This was more than we could take, so we lit out and crashed some college staff dance.[622]

However, and in the army at least, it is clear that the overall verdict on chaplains was a positive one; if more religious soldiers tended to predominate among their critics, this situation reflected personal religious zeal and existing tensions in American religion rather than the general failings of chaplaincy itself. What this favourable verdict signified for American religious life in the longer term is harder to establish. It is clear, however, that during the war the churches were hoping that the prevailing and discernible sense of goodwill towards chaplains in the army and navy would pay healthy dividends in the post-war years. Writing in 1945, William D. Cleary concluded his essay 'The Ministry of the Chaplain' by arguing that:

It seems clear that the devotion of the chaplains in the Army and Navy is not only bringing the ministry of religion to millions of men and women in the Armed Forces today, but that it is laying the foundation for the work of all the churches in the post-war world. The fact that the church cared enough to send priests and ministers and rabbis from the security of their civilian posts into the loneliness and hazards of battle will not be lost upon returning soldiers and sailors. They will recall that the chaplains were not compelled to enter the service. They came freely because of their desire to serve, and that service will not be altogether forgotten.[623]

In retrospect, it seems that these hopes did not prove illusory and that the favourable experience and perception of wartime chaplaincy on the part of millions of Americans, civilians and service personnel alike, left a significant legacy to the post-war United States.[624] In terms of the army, the influence and reputation of wartime chaplaincy provided a foundation for the development of its post-war 'Character Guidance' programme, which survived (however controversially) into the Vietnam era.[625] Moreover, their service as chaplains gave thousands of younger American clergymen further professional training and varied pastoral experience from which their churches stood to benefit in the longer term, especially given the greater emphasis on pastoral counselling in the ministry of the post-war churches.[626] The manifold specialisms of military chaplaincy also no doubt contributed to the trend towards greater specialisation in the post-war ministry.[627] Their service also entitled former chaplains, in common with millions of other veterans, to the considerable benefits of the 1944 GI Bill.

By the end of the war, and unless excluded by a dishonourable discharge, every chaplain with at least ninety days' service was entitled to 'one year of retraining or education' at government expense; depending on length of service and other circumstances, this could rise to four years of further education together with a subsistence allowance of $50 per month for married men and $75 for those with dependants. Significantly, chaplains were urged to make use of these opportunities in the interests of their future civilian ministries.[628] The wartime accomplishments of military chaplaincy also helped to widen and consolidate the role of the clergy in veterans' affairs at a federal level. Prompted by 'the splendid record of achievement written by Army and Navy chaplains' during World War II,[629] the overhaul of the Veterans Administration (VA) towards the end of the war included the creation of its own Chaplaincy Service 'along lines similar to that of the Army and Navy'. Under the direction of its first chief, the former Episcopalian army chaplain Crawford William Brown, this gave preference 'to men who had served as chaplains in the Army or Navy' and went on to employ scores of former military chaplains on a full-time and part-time basis as VA facilities expanded (a development that, incidentally, stoked the fears of *The Christian Century* about the post-war 'growth of a state clergy').[630] Finally, the wartime work of America's military chaplains also fed into the religious revival of the post-war years. Although Robert D. Putnam and David E. Campbell have credited 'this GI generation' and their wives with leading 'the surge to church in the late 1940s and 1950s', and for remaining 'the bedrock of American religious institutions' ever since,[631] they have ascribed this rediscovery of religion and 'traditional values' to post-war prosperity, the onset of the Cold War and the after-effects of foxhole religion.[632] Chapter Four will show that foxhole religion (a fleeting and minority experience, as we shall see) was probably of much less significance in promoting religion among GIs than were the concerted, lavishly supported, and all but ubiquitous efforts of an unprecedented number of army and navy chaplains between 1939 and 1945.

Conclusion

In many respects, World War II proved to be a triumph for American military chaplaincy and, by extension, for America's clergy. Serving as the organisational bedrock of religious life in the armed forces, America's army and navy chaplains ministered without the undue interference of civilian religious agencies and largely avoided the frustrations and embarrassments of World War I. Recruited in their thousands, for many Protestant denominations their ministry represented a tacit abandonment, if not repudiation, of the prevailing pacifism of the interwar years. Despite their diverse religious, confessional and denominational origins, and the inevitable friction this could generate, the public impression (at least) of army and navy chaplains was one of salutary, interfaith cooperation in a higher national cause. Furthermore, the competent, even canny, management of army and navy chaplains ensured that military chaplaincy rose to the urgent challenge of the times. Broadly speaking, and in the midst of a foreign war of unrivalled magnitude, the American armed forces benefited from a sufficient supply of trained and well-adjusted younger clergymen who proved indispensable in supporting the morale of millions of citizen soldiers, sailors and marines, many of whom were deemed to be without any prior church connection. This was achieved through a mixture of religious ministration and pastoral counselling, through the performance of secular duties ranging from librarian to graves registration officer, and through a front-line presence that resulted in an impressive tally of newsworthy decorations, including an unprecedented Medal of Honor. Assiduously cultivated, especially in the army's Corps of Chaplains, by publicity machines that exploited all available media to promote the reputation of military chaplains, their efforts and achievements helped to fashion among Americans at large a highly favourable impression of the clergyman in uniform, one that helped to forestall constitutional challenges to military chaplaincy per se, and that complemented the positive image that seems to have prevailed among armed forces personnel. Certainly, the indications are that the experiences and reputation of military chaplains in World War II stood the American churches in good stead, morally and materially, in subsequent years. However, this record of accomplishment was not without blemish. The carefully crafted image of military chaplaincy concealed multidirectional tensions and animosities between Christian and Jewish, Catholic and Protestant, liberal and conservative, liturgical and non-liturgical churchmen – tensions that inevitably broke to the surface from time to time. The prevailing image also ignored and obscured the plight of African American chaplains in the nation's segregated armed forces, chaplains who were pitifully few in the navy, and who were often placed in an invidious and even impossible position in the army. Nevertheless, American military chaplaincy clearly weathered the formidable challenges of World War II, a function not simply of its inherent strengths but also of a wider institutional culture that privileged the role of religion, and which forms the subject of the next chapter.

Chapter Two

Religion and American Military Culture

Introduction

A s we have seen, a greatly enhanced form of military chaplaincy formed the centrepiece of religious provision for American service men and women in World War II. However, and although it seems hard to dispute Doris L. Bergen's assertion that 'World War II marked the high point of the status of military chaplains in the United States',[1] it must be borne in mind that religious support went much further than formal military chaplaincy. This chapter will show that the American armed forces were, like American society in general, culturally and historically predisposed to support religion, and that this orientation had never been as emphatic as in the years of World War II. It will also demonstrate how chaplaincy was resourced and reinforced by unprecedented levels of material assistance, likewise provided by government, and how the sympathetic orientation of the armed forces also gave full rein to a massive and complementary civilian effort in support of their spiritual wellbeing. Overall, it will show how the underlying religiosity of America's armed forces, although sometimes well hidden, acted as the dominant factor in accounting for positive religious change among American veterans, a change that will be explored more fully in Chapter Four.

Religion and regulations

Religious life in America's armed forces was ultimately regulated by the Constitution and by the Bill of Rights. Article Six of the Constitution states that 'no religious Test shall ever be required as a Qualification to any Office or public Trust under the United States'; furthermore, and according to the First Amendment, 'Congress shall make no law respecting an establishment of religion, or prohibiting the free exercise thereof.' Nonetheless, and in common with many other areas of American public life, religious values suffused American military culture. In their respective oaths of enlistment and oaths of office, enlisted and commissioned personnel routinely invoked the help of the Almighty.[2] Furthermore, the free exercise clause of the First Amendment sanctioned military chaplaincy, and its many corollaries, while the historic Articles of War and Articles for the Government of the United States Navy (which remained in force until 1950) were derived from British models that predated the American Revolution and that were informed by a profound sense of religious obligation and Christian morality.[3] However, given the unambiguous terms of Article Six of the Constitution, the army and navy treated issues of religious affiliation with circumspection. On induction, recruits were asked their religious preference,[4] which was noted on their individual service records, and they also had the option of having it stamped on their identification tags (or 'dog tags', as they were widely known, implying that its wearer 'does not think and has need of a tender')[5] using either one of three initials – 'P' (Protestant), 'C' (Catholic) and 'H' (Hebrew). These identification tags were worn at all times.[6] Significantly, contemporaries noted that very few identification tags did not carry an indication of religious preference, and many of those that did not were not worn by atheists or agnostics. Some Christians, such as the much-decorated Audie Murphy, whose dog tags (and YMCA New Testament) are displayed in the Smithsonian Museum of American History,[7] simply eschewed a religious label, however general. The crude, three-fold categorisation also meant problems for the army's Nisei units, with the *New York Times* reporting that 50 per cent of the Japanese-American 100th Infantry Battalion were atheists – a basic misreading of their chaplain's practice of listing 'men who were neither Protestant nor Catholic under the category "No denomination".[8] In any case, 'No denomination' carried no weight in relation to the army's burial procedures. The practice of marking all American military graves with a religious marker was enshrined in the policies of the military and of the American Battle Monuments Commission, which was established by Congress in 1923. As David Max Eichhorn, a senior Jewish chaplain, elaborated to a chaplain colleague in 1945: '[T]he appropriate Army regulation is very clear: Anyone whose records indicate that he had no religious preference, and particularly one whose nearest of kin ... is Christian, is to be given a Christian burial and a cross to mark his grave.'[9]

Although an individual's service records were held at unit level, and could be made available to chaplains, in deference to constitutional sensitivities and the need to ensure religious harmony, any activity that smacked of a public religious census was discouraged. Consequently, while senior chaplains could form a rough idea of the religious profiles of major commands, official figures for religious adherence were not released by the US Army.[10] While the navy's Bureau of Navigation also 'kept no statistics on the religions of enlisted men',[11] the position of the army was emphasised on the eve of Pearl Harbor, with the Adjutant General, Major General C.S. Adams, stating on 5 December 1941:

> The [War] Department has no statistics for dissemination on the subject. Religious affiliations and denominational preference are approximately the same in the Army as in civilian life. The current strength of the Army is a fair cross-section of American life in all its phases, including religion.[12]

However prudent, this statement overlooked the under-representation of smaller, pacifist churches and also proved frustrating to Jewish-Americans, who were keen to vindicate their commitment to the war in the face of anti-Semitic slurs.[13] Indeed, considerable efforts were made to ascertain the true extent of Jewish representation in the armed forces through a host of local surveys. In brief, these investigations found that 'upward of 500,000 men and women of Jewish faith served in the various branches of the armed forces'. Of these, approximately 80 per cent served in the Army, '17 per cent in the Navy, 2 per cent in the Marine Corps and 1 per cent in the Coast Guard'. To further confound anti-Semites, it was noted with satisfaction that 12 per cent of those in the army served as infantrymen, 6 per cent in other branches of the AGF, and 30 per cent served in the AAF, one-quarter of whom were aviators. Through such methods, it was duly ascertained that the draft had secured a proportionate representation of American Jewry in the armed forces.[14] On the other hand, however, the deliberate dearth of authoritative figures could lead to some wildly speculative and partisan estimates as to the religious composition of America's armed forces. In 1942, for example, and harking back to World War I, the *National Catholic Almanac* claimed that: 'The Catholic population of the United States in 1917 was 17% of the total population, and yet so great were the number of Catholic enlistments in all arms, that 30% of the Army, 40% of the Navy, and 50% of the Marine Corps were Catholic.' The figures it gave for Catholic war dead, amounting to under 17 per cent of the total, scarcely served to substantiate such claims.[15]

Although opaque in other respects, religious labelling – and dog tags in particular – posed very real problems for certain groups. Israel Yost, the Lutheran chaplain of the 100th Battalion, discovered this in the course of a conversation with a Buddhist GI whom he had assumed to be a Christian. In this case, the sergeant's '"one gripe" against the U.S. Army' was that 'when I entered the army they wouldn't put a "B" on my dog tags … I can't see why the military did not give me the right to believe what I want.'[16] Likewise, America's Eastern Orthodox churches felt the failure to create a separate Orthodox category (under the proposed code of 'EO') to be 'a grave injustice'; in practical terms, this meant that Orthodox GIs were arbitrarily 'tagged' as either Catholics or Protestants.[17] Not surprisingly, Protestants could baulk at the sheer breadth of the 'P' categorisation, which embraced 'a wide diversity in practice and outlook'[18] ranging from Mormons, Seventh-Day Adventists and Christian Scientists to co-opted Eastern Orthodox and the 'highest' of Lutherans and Episcopalians – basically, all Christians who repudiated 'the authority of the see of Rome'.[19] Moreover, navy chaplains at the Marine Corps training station at Parris Island complained that even the term 'Protestant' was unfamiliar to some, especially those reared in 'the narrowness and aloofness of certain denominations', or in churches in which 'a conception of the worldwide Church' was lacking: 'Strange as it may seem to many in our enlightened land, religious illiteracy is widespread among our citizenry. Many recruits, affiliated with prominent denominations in Protestantism ask sincerely, "Am I a Protestant or to which group am I supposed to go?'"[20] In the army, specific denominational affiliations were not even noted on service records until 1942. Consequently, it proved difficult for Lutheran and Episcopalian chaplains to gather their co-religionists for communion services.[21] Further obstacles to receiving the sacraments were posed for members of these 'liturgical Protestant denominations' if they fell sick or became battle casualties; once again, hospital records simply employed the 'Protestant' classification and dog tags were of little use in signalling specific religious needs. Consequently, there was widespread recourse to unofficial identifiers such as 'Episcopal war crosses and Lutheran identification discs'.[22] Reflecting on these experiences, an immediate post-war report on chaplains' activities in the ETO recommended that:

> In view of the canonical requirement that Episcopalians and Lutherans receive the Sacraments exclusively at the hands of clergymen of their own respective communions, some differentiation should be made between these denominations and other denominations classified as Protestant, and their denominational preference should be entered upon identification tags and hospital admission and dispositions sheets, as is already done in the case of the Service Record.[23]

However, dog tags posed a much graver problem for Jews. In the first place, their 'H' designation could invite attention in an overwhelmingly gentile and often anti-Semitic environment. When a batch of 150 recruits were canvassed by a training sergeant for their religious affiliations, Herbert Walters, a lawyer from Brooklyn, felt distinctly awkward when he alone rose to identify himself as Jewish, thus becoming a figure of lasting curiosity to his comrades.[24] While their 'Hebrew' designation could be taken to imply a racial as well as religious categorisation,[25] it also subsumed a wide variety of Jewish beliefs and traditions. Apart from differences between Reform, Conservative and Orthodox Jews, the latter were divided between Ashkenazim and Sephardim, and Jewish chaplains were presented with a real challenge in preaching a message that would be acceptable to mixed congregations.[26] Furthermore, there was a huge imbalance between the main divisions of Judaism. Of the Jewish GIs he met in Europe, Chaplain Morris N. Kertzer, a Conservative rabbi from Iowa, wrote that Orthodox Jews consistently formed by far the largest component of army congregations, greatly outnumbering conservative Jews, and eclipsing the small minority from a Reform background.[27] However, these proportions were reversed among Jewish army chaplains; of the 311 who served, 147 were Reform, 96 were Conservative, but only 86 were Orthodox.[28] If the 'H' indented on their dog tags underlined the minority status of Jewish personnel while failing to differentiate between their traditions, a potentially lethal problem lay in the fact that it was specific enough to invite unwanted attention if captured by the Germans. Significantly, even Jewish chaplains baulked at being too readily identified to the enemy. Chaplain Max B. Wall of the 9th Infantry Division, when presented with his predecessor's jeep, was appalled to find that it was adorned with a Star of David – 'I'm going to be identified as a Jew automatically wherever I go. And the first German who sees me is going to [shoot at me].'[29] According to Kertzer this fear of being speedily, and possibly fatally, identified was common:

> The most frequent question asked of a Jewish chaplain in the battle zone was: 'How will the Nazis treat me if I am captured?' Should the soldier throw away his dog tags before going out on a night patrol? Should he deny his religion point-blank if taken prisoner? The problem was further complicated by the army custom of sending [German Jewish] refugees on night-raiding patrols because of their fluency in German.[30]

Some Jewish soldiers and airmen discarded their dog tags when threatened with capture, and were even ordered to do so by their officers.[31] However, Kertzer's inquiries found that '*as a general rule, the German army did not discriminate between Jews and Christians among their American prisoners*'.[32] Nevertheless, examples of German brutality towards Jewish POWs were sufficiently common for their fears to be justified. As Kertzer averred, it was impossible to assure Jewish GIs that they would be safe if captured; while they had little to fear from the average German soldier, there was always a chance that they might fall into the clutches of the SS.[33]

While, however broadly, the army was careful to record the religious affiliations of its soldiers, in the spirit of the free exercise clause of the First Amendment, army regulations also made clear that it was the duty of commanding officers to support their chaplains, to render 'every practicable aid' in the provision of religious services and to ensure that soldiers could attend them if they wished.[34] Even in the ETO, in the midst of the army's largest and bloodiest campaign of World War II,[35] this obligation appears to have been largely fulfilled, with a post-war report confirming that: 'Except amid the exigencies of combat, the conduct of divine service on Sunday by Christian chaplains was normal. Conflicts between Sunday services on the one hand and the training program or recreational projects on the other were exceedingly rare, and were almost invariably adjusted by consultation with the staff officer concerned.'[36] Circumstances permitting, and in keeping with peacetime practice, when a unit was in the field the location of the chaplain's tent (or billet) and 'the place of divine worship' was signalled by raising the chaplain's flag, normally a blue pennant with a white Latin cross.[37] The extent to which the obligations of the First Amendment were honoured by the army can be illustrated by the pains that were taken to provide appropriate foodstuffs for Jewish religious festivals, despite the shortages caused by the war and the additional pressure this placed on the army's logistics. For an otherwise meagre Passover Seder service held in the Anzio beachhead in 1944, Air Transport Command flew in wine from Algiers; in 1945, a much larger service held in Marseilles was supplied with several hundred eggs salvaged from a cargo vessel that had sunk in the harbour.[38]

The same obligations also applied in the navy, where commanding officers were required to ensure that 'divine service' was performed on Sundays wherever chaplains were attached and 'whenever the weather or other circumstances allow it to be done'.[39] These prescriptions of the Articles for the Government of the Navy, which dated back to 1800, had been reinforced and clarified as late as 1919 when the Secretary of the Navy, Josephus Daniels, issued a general order which stated that 'in no instance shall secular work be allowed to interfere with the holding of divine services', that ships' bands 'shall always be made available for use at divine service' and that, whenever a chaplain was not available to preside, commanding officers should arrange for the services of another naval chaplain or 'invite competent clergymen from ashore to come aboard and conduct religious services'.[40] During World War II, navy regulations still 'earnestly recommended' that all officers and sailors 'diligently' attend divine service and warned that: 'Any irreverent or unbecoming behaviour during divine service will be punished as a court-martial may direct'.[41] In a circular letter of 1944 addressed to all ships and stations, another Secretary of the Navy, Frank Knox, stressed the abiding importance of public worship, and urged commanding officers to 'encourage more than one service whenever all the men are not able to attend at any one time'. Knox also stated that, under wartime conditions, 'officers and men should be permitted to attend divine services in working uniforms when otherwise they would not be able to attend'.[42] Sanctioned by the formidable weight of custom and regulation, throughout World War II the navy maintained its established traditions of rigging for church on the Sabbath, sounding the church call, and hoisting the church pennant. This pennant (again, normally blue and emblazoned with a white Latin cross) indicated that divine service was being held and was, significantly, the only pennant or flag that could be flown above the national ensign. Although this practice was criticised by some ultra-patriots in the 1920s, the tradition acquired statutory force in the very different mood of the war years; indeed, and in a singular twist of fate (or act of providence) Congress sanctioned the practice just before the navy's stunning victory at Midway in June 1942.[43]

The navy tradition thus strongly upheld a churchgoing culture, a point that was not lost on religious commentators. In the middle of World War II, Chaplain Emil F. Redman, who had joined the navy in 1937, stated that: 'In my five and one-half years' experience in the Naval service, conditions under which divine services were cancelled happened only three times. All three instances occurred in the South Seas – once during a hurricane, and the other times when unprecedented rain inundated the entire compound at which I was stationed.' In addition to their regularity, Redman also testified to the 'greatest cooperation' that was given to chaplains in the provision of services at sea and to the 'excellent' response from officers and men, 'as many as one-third of all available personnel' attending on a purely voluntary basis.[44] Significantly, at the end of the war Captain Harold E. Stassen, a Northern Baptist, former Republican governor of Minnesota, and the president of the International Council of Religious Education, expressed his complete satisfaction at the religious opportunities that the wartime navy had provided:

> [A]s to the conduct of services and the attendance by the men, I consider that on the whole it was very good. All of the large ships had Chaplains on board and many of them two Chaplains, one Protestant and one Catholic. On these ships, services were regularly conducted on Sunday, unless actual combat conditions prevented it. Whenever the fleet was in port, church parties from the smaller ships would join the large ships for their services ... Thus it was a very familiar sound on any of the major ships of the fleet on Sunday to hear over the loud speaking system the following: 'The smoking lamp is out. Knock off all card playing and all unnecessary noise. Divine services will now be held.' This would be followed by the church call on the bugle. Then from all parts of the ship the men would assemble at the designated place for the services.[45]

Ostensibly, and despite their support for public religious observance, neither service actually *required* attendance from their personnel. Although the army's Articles of War, which dated back to the revolutionary era, had treated church attendance as compulsory and had prescribed stiff penalties for irreverent behaviour,[46] constitutional concerns and problems arising from the growing religious diversity of the army combined to make the relevant articles unenforceable. In 1912, the Judge Advocate General ruled that a commanding officer had 'no authority under the Fifty-Second Article of War to require soldiers to march to church and to participate in divine worship as part of a military formation'; in 1916, the problematic articles were dispensed with altogether.[47] However, and although technically resolved even before the United States entered World War I, the issue of compulsion remained a problem throughout World War II. In part, this was because church attendance was still enforced in influential sections of the US military. Because it could be justified under the principle of *in loco parentis*, and as it was deemed to enhance the professional understanding of trainee officers, enforced church attendance was the norm in the service academies of West Point and Annapolis, as it was in the interwar CMTC.[48] Furthermore, army regulations gave a hostage to fortune by stressing that: 'Ultimate responsibility for matters of religious and moral nature within a command devolves upon the commanding officer as completely as does that for strictly military matters ... without trespassing upon the ecclesiastical field, commanding officers are obligated to exercise active supervision over chaplains and their activities.'[49]

As a result of this situation, there was no shortage of enforced religious practice in the US Army in World War II. Evidently, and as in World War I, some commanding officers felt entitled to require attendance when occasion or military necessity demanded.[50] In August 1940, for example, the *Chicago Tribune* reported how ten thousand Illinois National Guardsmen had been assembled in a 'church formation' to hear a sermon on democracy and religion from their senior chaplain at Camp McCoy, Wisconsin.[51] However, this was no aberration. When Chaplain Clyde E. Kimball arrived in Iceland in 1942 he was nonplussed to find that the soldiers of the 5th Engineer Combat Regiment had been subjected to an organised regime of compulsory church attendance, 'with two companies sponsoring the service each Sunday.'[52] In 1945, with Christmas looming and the war now safely over, Chaplain K.W. Schalk warned readers of *The Chaplain* of the 'post and division formations' that had plagued Christmas and Easter throughout the war years. At Easter 1942 Schalk had been in a stateside camp where the commanding officer had caused a furore by ordering that 'every available Protestant enlisted man and officer' be present at an Easter Sunday sunrise service, with all other Protestant services being cancelled 'to assure a maximum attendance'. The following year, Schalk was assigned to an armoured division whose commander habitually ordered all of its soldiers to attend Easter and Christmas services 'regardless of religious conviction and church affiliation'. While Schalk saw such orders as infringements of the 'freedom of worship' for which the nation had fought, he had been struck by the readiness with which other chaplains had complied with these dictates, notwithstanding the resentment they provoked among officers and enlisted men.[53]

If the main Christian festivals furnished a good excuse for 'obligatory attendance under the apparent cloak of a military ceremony',[54] the prospect of action also served as a spur to mandatory religion. Although there can be no doubt as to the spontaneity of many of the prayers offered before D-Day, according to Chaplain Edward K. Rogers of the 1st Infantry Division instructions were issued that 'a short order of religious worship be held on every [landing] craft after we put to sea. The order was no doubt carried out on many of the craft under the leadership of chaplains, officers or enlisted men.'[55] Before sailing for their baptism of fire on Guam a month later, Colonel Vincent P. Tanzola ordered that the Catholics of the 305th Infantry Regiment be assembled in order to hear their chaplain, Thomas J. Donnelly. Conceding that this order did not sit comfortably with 'military regulations', Donnelly remembered:

> I selected a day and nineteen times I gave the same talk to the Catholic men of each company.... The men were unaware of what was coming and I really let go at them ... I told them that they were going into combat and bluntly added that some would not come back ... I concluded by telling them that I had asked six other chaplains to help me hear confessions on the next day. The desired result was obtained ... and I was satisfied that the Regiment

was ready for combat militarily and spiritually. I felt that everything had been done to prepare these men for combat before the Regiment sailed.[56]

Given their combat role, their ethos and the attitudes of their commanding officers, there was particularly strong support for churchgoing in airborne units, and not least in the 101st Airborne Division. Writing in the 1950s, Chaplain Francis L. Sampson of its 501st Parachute Infantry Regiment confessed that its chaplains had been embarrassed by the assistance they had received from a forceful sergeant known as 'Jumpy' Valent:

> He was a natural soldier and highly respected by all his men. But the chaplains always had to watch him, for at church call he would call out every man and threaten him (in language not usually associated with church services) if he didn't go to chapel. We always liked cooperation in getting men to services, but not quite so extreme as Valent offered. 'These so-and-so characters need some religion', he would say. Jumpy is a first sergeant now, still in the airborne in Germany, and still has to be watched by the chaplains for coercing men to church.[57]

Memorial and thanksgiving services offered other pretexts for compulsory services, while shrinking the scope for dissent. After its return to England from Normandy in the late summer of 1944, the 506th Parachute Infantry Regiment of the 101st Airborne was paraded for an obligatory Sunday morning memorial service in the grounds of Littlecote House in Wiltshire. The service included a sermon, an address by Major General Maxwell D. Taylor, the reading of the 506th's regimental prayer (composed by one of its lieutenants) and a recitation of the names of the regiment's dead and missing. At the conclusion of the service, two thousand survivors, suitably attired in their Class A uniforms, marched off to the accompaniment of 'Onward Christian Soldiers'. The fact that Sunday mornings were conventionally regarded as free time counted for nothing.[58] In Italy the following year, carefully choreographed thanksgiving services were held throughout Fifth Army to mark the end of the war in Europe. At Fifth Army headquarters, for example, two thousand service men and women were paraded to hear the 'petitions and expressions of thanks appropriate to the occasion'. These were offered by the three headquarters chaplains and were accompanied by the reflections and admonitions of their commanding general, Lieutenant General Lucian K. Truscott. With reference to this service, a sympathetic writer claimed that: 'Beautifully and with impressive simplicity it had somehow put a formal finish on the marvelous [sic], God-given success.'[59]

There were, of course, indirect ways of ensuring that GIs did not neglect public worship. Chaplain Morris N. Kertzer, for example, was appalled to find that the impressive attendance he encountered at a detention training camp had very little to do with the laudable piety of its unfortunate inmates. Faced with a complete absence of absentees, Kertzer's enquiries soon established that this had nothing to do with the inherent appeal of his services either. To his mortification and indignation, Kertzer discovered that religious services at least offered a modicum of shelter, and therefore a rare opportunity to escape from the painful effects of a scorching sun. Otherwise forced to linger outside in blistering heat, the pathetic plight of his wretched congregants induced Kertzer to lodge a strong protest, and he returned to the camp to find their situation much improved.[60]

In a less punitive environment, and in order to expose his air force flock to eternal verities, Chaplain Brunson C. Wallace found a useful tool in the form of the loudspeaker. As he reported to *The Chaplain*:

> Several months ago, feeling the need of emphasis upon prayer more than just on Sunday, and knowing that just a small percentage of men would be reached in daily prayer groups, I commenced a six o'clock 'Moments of Meditation' each evening over our public address system which could be heard throughout the group. It was carried out something like this: Attention was called to the meditation by playing familiar religious music ... Then with this same music in the background, I presented a thought for the evening, closing with a prayer. The whole thing lasted not quite five minutes ... I was a little dubious as to how this undertaking would be received, but later found out that most of the men looked forward to it, and greatly treasured these moments.[61]

Needless to say, such methods did not go unprotested. In the London edition of *Stars and Stripes* in November 1944, an anonymous paratrooper held forth about 'being compelled to attend church services'. In response, a sympathetic chaplain pointed to other infringements of religious freedom, especially in military hospitals:

> Personally, I can go your browned-off trooper one better. I've known of baser forms of compulsion, for example, when wounded men, tied down by casts and clamps and pulleys, are compelled to listen to a chaplain pray and sing hymns and preach a faith not shared by all the patients present. Real religion gains nothing from such bad-mannered zeal.[62]

The following week, a member of the WAC maintained that only those who had marched to the venue in formation had been admitted to a special Thanksgiving Day service held in Westminster Abbey. Likewise, in 1945 a Tec 5 complained to a *Washington Post* correspondent about how the commanding officer of the 677th Engineer Light Equipment Company had *required* attendance at Catholic and Protestant services.[63] For its part, and rather disingenuously in view of the evidence, the Corps of Chaplains insisted on its strict adherence to official army policy: 'Few instances of compulsory attendance at chapel or of required participation in church formations were reported [in the ETO]. In all such cases an explanation of the traditional policy of the American Army served to prevent a repetition of the incident.'[64]

As far as the navy was concerned, church attendance when ashore had always been treated as a voluntary matter and it had officially abandoned compulsion on board ship as early as 1862, when Congress passed 'An Act for the better Government of the Navy of the United States'; thereafter, it was the duty of the chaplain to attract a congregation, and that of the captain to help him. Once again, this was a pragmatic response to the growing religious diversity of the service and was thought to be more consistent with the constitutional principle of freedom of religion.[65] However, and as in the army, compulsion survived in certain quarters and in various forms. While cadets at the Naval Academy at Annapolis enjoyed the choice of which denomination's services to attend from 1859, attendance itself remained mandatory; moreover, the academy observed a tradition of morning prayers in the mess hall before breakfast.[66] Remarkably, during World War II obligatory church attendance seems to have been accepted with good grace – and even enthusiasm – by a new generation of cadets at Annapolis, or so William Drury claimed. Fondly recalling Sunday services at the Academy's newly enlarged chapel, Drury wrote:

> Although [it] could seat 2,500, it was still far too small to accommodate all who desired to attend [and] one of the four [cadet] battalions had to be excused each month from church attendance.... It was a most inspiring sight on a Sunday morning at the Academy during the war to see so many young men march to church in their immaculate uniforms under flying colours. Rarely was there an empty pew. Visitors were impressed with the beauty and solemnity of the service. There was always absolute silence when the colours were advanced or retired. The music of the great organ, the singing of the midshipman choir, and the participation of the large congregation all combined to give a unique quality to the worship service which could never be forgotten.[67]

The ethos of Annapolis spilled over into the navy's improvised officer training facilities. Samuel Hynes, for example, ruefully recalled the regime of his pre-flight school, located on the Athens campus of the University of Georgia:

> I suppose it must all have been modelled on the customs of the Naval Academy at Annapolis, and perhaps it worked there; but it seemed extravagant and a little comical.... We never walked anywhere, we marched – to meals, to classes, to church on Sunday (where we sang the hymn about God protecting those in peril on the sea), even to the movies.[68]

Furthermore, what the navy thought to be good for its officer cadets was also deemed beneficial for its trainee seamen, for whom compulsion had likewise become the norm by the end of the nineteenth century.[69] Hence, navy tradition served to ensure that for most of World War II compulsory church attendance was the rule for hundreds of thousands of recruits at its training centres at Great Lakes, then 'the largest naval training station in the world',[70] San Diego, Sampson, Bainbridge, Newport and Norfolk. In fact, only at Farragut was church attendance apparently treated as voluntary.[71] According to Chaplain Emil F. Redman, writing for the readers of the *Lutheran Standard*:

> At a training station, conditions are highly favorable for participation in church services.... It is a part of the training program. All men not on duty, on leave, or on the sick list go to church. This practice is adhered to wholeheartedly and without the slightest deviation. Attendance at the training station to which I am now attached runs into many thousands each Sunday.[72]

Chaplain Frederick William Meehling, a Catholic contemporary of Redman's at Great Lakes and another regular navy chaplain, was equally open about the practice, recalling that: 'everybody went to church. If they didn't go to church, they had to do something else. And the something else was usually less desirable than going to church was. So they were marched up and the drill halls were full of men.'[73]

Naturally, defenders of compulsory worship downplayed the degree of objection they encountered and were quick to insist on its pastoral and even missionary value. According to Redman, not only was the response among recruits generally enthusiastic but it also helped the churches to reclaim those who had gone astray:

> My observation, especially on my present duty, has been that the men not only enjoy the services but, because the word of God is preached and the services are properly organized, they also find them spiritually satisfying and stimulating. Despite the fact that about 50 per cent of the men under training have perhaps not been to church for months and even years, if at all, we find a most hearty response.... The relatively unchurched join in most heartily after a few Sundays.[74]

Likewise, John E. Johnson, a Presbyterian (USA) chaplain, claimed that when the National Preaching Mission of the FCC visited Great Lakes in October 1944 it discovered by means of personal interviews that one in five recruits had not been interested in attending church – that is, until they joined the navy.[75] Also, Johnson maintained that:

> While it is true that the average recruit would not make the slightest effort to attend church individually and of his own accord, it is also true that if the rest of his company, or most of his company, falls in for church, he will fall in, too. If divine service is in the plan of the day, he will take it as a matter of course, and may even become interested in it.[76]

Involuntary church attendance did not cease after training, for 'the navy way' ensured that de facto compulsion (or, at the very least, unavoidable co-option) thrived elsewhere, no doubt helped by the fact that irreverent or disruptive behaviour could result in a court martial. Clearly, there was an element of collusion when Chaplain Hansel H. Tower appropriated a large working party for a Sunday service on British Samoa in 1942. Preferring worship to work on the Sabbath, there was no opposition to the proposal that he hold an impromptu service:

> 'Hurry up, before they march us off,' said one.... The marines were singing 'Holy! Holy! Holy! Lord God Almighty, early in the morning our song shall rise to Thee' when the non-commissioned officer in charge of the working party arrived. He shrugged his shoulders impatiently, looked around at the newly religious who were fairly bursting with song, took a hymn book from a private and joined in the hymn. It is a court martial offence to disturb a church service.[77]

However, there was much less choice involved in the practice of broadcasting prayers over public address systems. Writing to *The Chaplain* in 1945, Chaplain Harold G. Sanders, a Southern Baptist attached to a navy construction battalion in New Guinea, reported that:

> [C]haplains at his advanced base hold a nightly 'lights out' prayer period over the P.A. system at the Receiving Barracks. The chaplains rotate in providing the service – either a prayer, or music from the organ, a solo etc. – and agree that it is one of the best received services they render.[78]

This practice was especially common on larger warships, with navy chaplains offering prayers, often on a daily basis, with the consent and encouragement of their captains.[79] On board the battleship *Wisconsin*, for example, morning and evening prayers were offered alternately by its Lutheran and Catholic chaplains. According to the former, Chaplain Raymond C. Hohenstein: 'I never heard any complaints. If there was a statement at all about the prayers as well as the services, it was in appreciation for what we had to offer.'[80] Although MacArthur concluded the Japanese surrender on board the battleship *Missouri* with a prayer on Sunday 2 September 1945, the whole surrender ceremony had been preceded by the ship's own devotions, which were normally broadcast every evening.[81] In the words of the ship's Methodist chaplain, Roland W. Faulk: 'The Captain decided that it would be more appropriate on this day to have the prayer as a prelude to the surrender ceremonies. The prayer was broadcast throughout the ship as the crew, officers and men, visitors and correspondents bowed reverently.'[82]

Nor was the Marine Corps immune from the effects of this alliance between chaplains and commanding officers. Following his assignment to the 14th Artillery Regiment at Camp Pendleton in 1943, Chaplain John Harold Craven, a

Southern Baptist, found that he had a free hand to interview all of its Protestant personnel:

> The first thing I started doing was interviewing every man in the regiment and getting an information card on every man. They were sent to me in groups as I had arranged with the battery commanders ... I started a file with the name, address, family background, religious affiliation, and interests and concerns, so that by the time we were ready to leave the West Coast and go into combat I had a file that was pretty complete on every man. The Catholic chaplain arranged to see the Catholic men, and I saw all the others. This information was a tremendous help later on, and we continued this policy, but there was nothing said in any regulations. I had never even heard of this ... we arranged that every man who reported to the regiment had to come and see the chaplain.[83]

In fact, this scheme echoed a similar initiative in the 8th Marines before the landings on Tarawa in November 1943. As Chaplain Warren Wyeth Willard recalled:

> I arranged with the combat team commander [Major Lawrence C. Hays] to interview the men, one by one. A sergeant from each company saw to it that the marines came promptly up to my quarters, so that an accurate check could be made of their religious affiliation and the records of next of kin be completed.[84]

However, this was far from being simply a clerical exercise, for as Willard went on:

> I earnestly appealed to the marines of my own faith and to those professing none. As I talked to them, I seemed to see myself before the judgment seat of God, rendering an account of how I had spent my time on board ship. From the pages of the Gideon New Testament I endeavoured to outline clearly and concisely God's plan of salvation.[85]

Willard's powers of persuasion were exercised in another way en route for Tarawa, when he prevailed upon his transport's commander to permit daily services to the accompaniment of the church call. Typically, these were far from being the anodyne rites of a tame civil religion: 'I would start off with the popular gospel choruses, which the marines loved so dearly. And then would follow a Biblical expository message, which was concluded with the invitation.'[86]

Significantly, the navy's willingness to disregard the implicit constitutional right *not* to participate in religious services does not seem to have prodded Frank Knox into action. However, his successor as Secretary of the Navy, James V. Forrestal, seems to have brought a very personal interest to the matter. A deeply lapsed Catholic who spent much of his life rebelling against the strict religiosity of his mother,[87] Forrestal confronted the issue in a communication dated 23 November 1944 that was addressed to all ships and stations. Here, Forrestal rebuked commanding officers for ignoring objections against compulsory services, stressing that 'military necessity does not require disregard of the basic constitutional guarantees inherent in our Democracy, which permit complete freedom of conscience and religious worship for all citizens'. Forrestal then went on to direct that: 'In recognition of the illegality of establishing religious requirements for service in the Navy, the widest possible latitude in religious matters, forms of worship, and beliefs shall be allowed during chapel services, and those who do not wish to participate in such services shall be excused therefrom.'[88] While this had the effect of ending compulsory attendance at the navy's training centres, with church attendance falling by 30 to 40 per cent at Sampson alone,[89] his ruling did nothing to change the regime at Annapolis or to check the practice of shipboard prayers on many of the navy's most famous capital ships.

Role models

Whatever Forrestal's position, it was significant that the lessons and heroes of American history seemed to provide ample vindication of the military value of religion. Despite the elusive quality of his own faith, George Washington served as America's prototypical Christian warrior. Immortalised in art and in literature as kneeling in prayer in the snow at Valley Forge, as commander of the Continental Army Washington worked closely with his chaplains, required his soldiers' attendance at divine service, and constantly sought to promote virtue and suppress vice. In personal terms, and despite the vagaries of the Revolutionary War, his underpinning faith in providence never faltered.[90] In the form of the Continental Navy's John Barry, 'The Father of the American Navy', the struggle for independence also left posterity with a seafaring model of pious bellicosity, albeit a Catholic one.[91] Of course, the Civil War greatly enlarged the American pantheon of Christian warriors – most notably in the figures of Robert E. Lee and 'Stonewall' Jackson but also in the form of lesser commanders such as the Protestant Episcopal bishop and Confederate general, Leonidas Polk.[92] If the moral pretensions of 'Lost Cause' mythology increased the disparity between the Confederate and Union rosters of soldier saints,[93] Union generals were not unmindful of the need to promote religion. As commander of the army of the Potomac, George B. McClellan promoted Sunday observance and underwent a religious conversion;[94] the colourful Union general Dan Sickles, for his part, introduced two new chaplains to his troops as representatives of the 'great commander', and even offered to detail soldiers for baptism.[95]

World War I did much to strengthen the perceived connection between personal piety and professional competence. General John Pershing, a staunch supporter of chaplaincy in the AEF, as we have seen, responded to a mother concerned about the moral and religious state of the army: 'We who are in authority recognize it as a trust to return to wives and mothers at home husbands and sons who are not only all that they were before they came to France, but something bigger and finer.'[96] At the request of the American Bible Society, Pershing also penned an introduction to its new army edition of the New Testament:

> To the American soldier:
> Aroused against a nation waging war in violation of all Christian principles, our people are fighting in the cause of liberty. Hardship will be your lot, but trust in God will give you comfort; temptation will befall you, but the teachings of our Savior will give you strength. Let your valor as a soldier and your conduct as a man be an inspiration to your comrades and an honor to your country.[97]

The Marine Corps was no less insistent on the vital link between religion and military virtue. Speaking to an audience of three thousand civilians at the invitation of the Trinity Men's Bible Class of West Brighton, Staten Island, Major General John A. Lejeune pronounced on Armistice Day 1928 that:

> Patriotism and religion are closely akin. Both flow from the noblest aspirations of the human heart. A marked feature of both is unselfish love for our fellowmen. The basis of both is the spirit of self-sacrifice. On the one hand, a grasping, rapacious, dishonorable, cowardly man can be neither patriotic nor religious. On the other hand, a generous, unselfish, honourable, courageous man is far along the path which leads to true religion and true patriotism.... Such, in the main, were the men who served in the American Army, Navy and Marine Corps during the World War.[98]

While Pershing's message to the American soldier was repeated for the benefit of GIs in World War II,[99] Christian doughboys also served as role models a generation later. Camp Kilmer, New Jersey, a key staging area for troops embarking for Europe, was named in honour of Joyce Kilmer, a convert to Catholicism and a celebrated 'poet, essayist, and literary critic' who was killed in France in July 1918.[100] Featured alongside Pat O'Brien's Fr Duffy and James Cagney's (fictional) Jerry Plunkett in the 1940 film *The Fighting 69th*, Kilmer's enduring celebrity was such that the Episcopalian chaplain Reuben Metcalf wrote to his wife in September 1942:

> Lord, thou hast suffered more for me
> Than all the hosts on land or sea
> So let me render back again
> This millionth of Thy gift. Amen.

Isn't it nice that so lovely a poem should have been written by a man whose name is commemorated in a camp which is the last dwelling place in this country for so many who go overseas? So I told the men last Sunday.[101]

However, the figure of Joyce Kilmer was dwarfed by that of Sergeant Alvin C. York. The most celebrated doughboy of World War I, York was a sharpshooting Tennessee backwoodsman who had undergone two conversions prior to his departure for France. The first, in 1915, led to his joining the Church of Christ in Christian Union, a small fundamentalist and pacifist church, while the second, as a draftee early in 1918, involved his conversion from conscientious objector to a willing American soldier.[102] Serving as an infantryman in the Meuse-Argonne in October 1918, in a single legendary incident York 'personally shot and killed 25 German soldiers, captured 132 more, and put 35 enemy machine guns out of action'.[103] Awarded the Medal of Honor for this spectacular feat of arms, he returned from World War I as one of America's most decorated war heroes. In the difficult interwar years, York devoted himself to the improvement of education in his home state, a cause that involved the foundation of The Alvin C. York Bible School.[104] A vocal interventionist by 1941, in that year an Oscar-winning biopic –*Sergeant York* – was released, with Gary Cooper in the title role. Such was the appeal of this war film, even among those who were poised to see the real thing, that in March 1943 *Yank* magazine reported that it was the third most popular film in American army camps.[105] As *Yank* also reported, the outbreak of war had made York the head of his local draft board and a star public speaker 'all over the country – to soldiers in camp, to War Bond rallies, to any crowd where patriotism is the theme'.[106] Furthermore, when York's old 82nd Division was reactivated in 1942 and given a new airborne role, its commanders (Omar N. Bradley and Matthew B. Ridgway) invited the old war horse to address its soldiers. Hence, and before its recruits had even learned to march:

Amidst bands and a full division parade, York told the 82d and a nation-wide radio audience how he single-handedly destroyed 35 machine guns, killed 25 German soldiers, and captured 132 men, disabling an entire enemy battalion.[107]

In Ridgway's words:

The old sergeant did a fine job. A quiet, simple, unpretentious man, he made a forthright speech that was highly effective.... He created in the minds of farm boys and clerks, youngsters of every station and class, the conviction than an aggressive soldier, well trained and well armed, can fight his way out of any situation.[108]

Nor did York mince his words in his advice to the readers of *Yank*:

This country's always been fair and square – fought its wars accordin' to the rules, but these here people we're a-fightin' now just don't have no honor. They're mean and they're dirty. And I'm a-tellin' our boys we've got to be just as mean an' just as dirty as they are.[109]

York's status as 'a national hero whose name was synonymous with patriotism, piety, and marksmanship' clearly had an effect.[110] In one telling incident, and after landing at night in Algeria in November 1942, a frightened soldier of Darby's Rangers was faced with the dilemma of whether to fire on some figures who were approaching his position: 'I heard a scuffling noise coming up the road. I said, "Lord, what is that?" And I thought to myself, *What would Sergeant York do?* I decided that Sergeant York would let the enemy soldiers all get by first, then shoot them.'[111]

The vaunted example of Sergeant York underlines the fact that, by the outbreak of World War II, the US armed forces were culturally, historically and professionally predisposed to promote religion. Furthermore, it was still believed that there was a strong religious quality to sound military leadership. As Matthew B. Ridgway maintained, leadership rested on character, an asset that he defined as 'self discipline, loyalty, readiness to accept responsibility and willingness to admit mistakes. It stands for selflessness, modesty, humility, willingness to sacrifice when necessary and, in my opinion, for faith in God.'[112] Nor was this simply a soldier's conceit, for in a highly esteemed address that was given to the officers of several combat divisions while training in the US, the eminent Presbyterian preacher and broadcaster Dr John S. Bonnell insisted on the importance of religious faith as a key accessory to sound leadership. With his background in psychology, and speaking with the added authority of a battlefield veteran of World War I, Bonnell assured his audiences that:

Through training, discipline, obedience, alertness, belief in the justice of the cause for which you are fighting, the development of the qualities of leadership in yourself and of a spirit of trust in those who lead you, combined with an unshakable faith in that Divine Power which rules the destinies of men – you will be enabled always to prove your fitness in the day when every man is tested.[113]

In addition to sound leadership, good morale was also seen as having a strong religious component. This was very much to the fore in Chaplain Harry P. Abbott's memoir of the North African campaign, the US army's first major contest against the Wehrmacht:

Men overseas, those who have had a taste of the 'real thing,' do not need to be persuaded to attend church. Even on the front line men demand the privilege of divine services, and many high ranking officers of the Army realize that, through this source, men are fortified to face the enemy and sometimes death with a smile on their faces, and without such fortification they might fail.[114]

Abbott's opinion was echoed by Brigadier General Paul M. Robinett, his former commander in North Africa. Regarded as 'a capable tactician who knew the art of war',[115] Robinett argued that political abstractions could not in themselves sustain his novice soldiers:

> For Americans the principles set forth in the Declaration of Independence, and in the Bill of Rights to the Constitution have furnished the inspirational guide whenever the country has been threatened, and will continue to do so as long as these principles are practiced among us; but the American, like any other good soldier, needs a higher faith to sustain him in battle – faith in the God of his fathers, however understood.[116]

Such convictions remained constant throughout the war. Chaplain Francis L. Sampson, from his own experience as a chaplain with the 101st Airborne Division, was emphatic in affirming the fundamental importance of religion in the making of a good soldier:

> It is impossible to foretell with one hundred per cent accuracy what any one man will do under the tension and stress of fire. There are too many undetermined factors and considerations to which the prophet has no access. Chief among these considerations, of course, is the free will. But it stands to reason that the habit of self-control and self-discipline must be already strongly entrenched in a man's character if he is expected to make the honourable choice between duty and self-preservation.[117]

Developing this argument to its logical conclusion, Sampson went on:

> [R]eligion is the indispensable support of those qualities of heart and mind so necessary for a good soldier. Good soldiers are necessary for a strong army. A strong army is necessary for the preservation of those God-given and inalienable rights which can be lost through weakness. It necessarily follows then that our American rights are dependent upon the strength of our religion.[118]

From a different arm of service, and a very different theological position, the Northern Baptist navy chaplain Warren Wyeth Willard was no less convinced of the correlation between personal faith and military proficiency. According to Willard, those marines who 'took Christianity seriously' were more inclined to throw themselves into their training, 'with all the zeal and energy which spring from faith in God'.[119] Not only this, but:

The out-and-out Christians in the Marine Corps obeyed orders without grumbling. They gave their officers no trouble over drunkenness, stealing, tardiness, sleeping on watch, or any of the other common faults of men in the service. Military authorities had learned long ago that the better Christians they were, the better fighters the marines made. The fact that the greatest individual soldier in World War I, Sergeant Alvin York, was an outstanding Christian speaks well for the faith in its relationship to military duty.[120]

Religion and command

'The military elite has been drawn from an old-family, Anglo-Saxon, Protestant, rural, upper middle-class professional background. This social setting has operated as the equivalent of the European aristocracy in supplying the cadre of [America's] military leaders.'[121] So wrote the sociologist Morris Janowitz in 1960, resting his conclusions on a detailed sample of 761 'Army, Navy, and Air Force general officers' from the period 1910 to 1950, and on a study of 465 army generals from the period 1898 to 1940 conducted by the historian C.S. Brown.[122] Significantly, Janowitz remarked upon the difficulty in obtaining specific information about the backgrounds of military officers, especially with respect to their religion, questions that were 'resented as impolite' in professional terms and sensitive in the context of American democracy.[123] Nevertheless, Janowitz was able to establish that the milieu from which professional army and navy officers were recruited (a milieu that had a strong Southern bias)[124] produced a professional officer corps that was overwhelmingly and disproportionately Protestant. In 1935, 88 per cent of the US Army's generals were Protestants and only 12 per cent were Catholics and, by 1950, this disparity had widened to 89 per cent and 11 per cent respectively.[125] According to Brown, the ratio of Protestant to Catholic generals in the period between the Spanish–American War and World War II was greater still, being in the order of 91 per cent to 9 per cent.[126] Significantly, Jewish generals were notable for their extreme rarity and, in this respect, the fate of Major General Maurice Rose, who died while leading the 3rd Armored Division in Germany, seems instructive. Born into a rabbinical family, and fluent in Yiddish as a child, Rose was commissioned from the ranks in 1917, after which he identified himself as 'Methodist, Episcopalian, or generically Protestant'.[127] Rose married a Protestant, raised his children as Protestants, and, at the time of his death, no religious preference was recorded on his dog tags or on his service record.[128] Killed while being taken prisoner in March 1945, his personal faith became a major bone of contention after his death. At the time, and at the insistence of 'a Jewish sergeant who conducted the Jewish services for the division', Chaplain David Max Eichhorn 'recited Kaddish' over Rose's grave, even though it had been marked with a cross. A few weeks later, a delegation of Jewish chaplains insisted that the cross be replaced with a Star of David and, when the body was reinterred in a permanent military cemetery, a Jewish chaplain escorted it.[129] Although the death of Rose was even depicted as an anti-Semitic atrocity, as he was a rabbi's son, the controversy over his religion rumbled on and, in 1949, a cross was reinstated after an official hearing confirmed the general's conversion to (Protestant) Christianity.[130]

If America's senior military leadership was very largely Protestant, the inculcation of a professional regard for religion was very much part of officer formation at the service academies of West Point and Annapolis, the nurseries of the army's and the navy's senior commanders. All cadets at West Point (opened in 1802) and midshipmen at Annapolis (opened in 1845) were required to attend chapel, this being justified with reference to the professional knowledge and understanding it would bestow.[131] Although this requirement was frequently a source of complaint, there can be little doubt of the historic and even growing importance that was placed on religious life at the service academies in the decades prior to World War II. At West Point, and as a result of a gift made to the American Tract Society, it was customary for each new cadet to receive a Bible with his name embossed upon the cover.[132] The first chaplain to West Point was appointed during the War of 1812 and its first purpose-built chapel was built in 1836. Sixty years later, and following a report by the Board of Visitors (prior to which the chaplain had also served as professor of geography, history and ethics) Congress moved to allow the superintendent of the academy to engage civilian clergymen to act as chaplains for terms of four years.[133] In 1900, two years after Congress had enacted a bill to allow denominational churches to be built at West Point,[134] a Catholic chapel was opened and a new, much larger, Cadet Chapel was dedicated in 1910. In 1944, a fourth church, the 'Post Chapel', was built for a different purpose, namely 'to accommodate the religious needs of Protestant soldiers and their families'.[135] Accompanied by Sunday inspections, marching in formation to the church of their choice, and the frequent absence of faculty members, compulsory chapel was widely resented as an onerous chore by trainee officers of both services, and the practice was widely deplored as inimical to future churchgoing habits.[136] Still, and despite their previous attitudes to compulsory chapel, graduates of West Point seem to have harboured a remarkable affection for their obligatory Sunday haunts. For example, when the new Cadet Chapel was built in 1910, and its predecessor risked demolition, a subscription was raised to have it rebuilt in another location.[137] After World War I, it was agreed by West Point's Association of Graduates that each class should donate two stained-glass windows to adorn the Cadet Chapel; each class from 1860 to 1976 (with the sole exceptions of those of 1861, 1863 and 1864) gave a pair of windows that depicted either scenes from the Bible or the lives of the early saints of the church.[138]

Apart from being a notable expression of *esprit de corps*, this long-term project served to underline the fact that the keynote faith of West Point was Episcopalian. Not only was the new Cadet Chapel deliberately modelled on 'the old Gothic cathedrals and chapels of England'[139] but all eight cadet chaplains from 1896 to 1941 were Episcopalians;[140] in fact, what its critics described as a 'calculated and unwarranted discrimination against other denominations' continued until 1959.[141] If, as Janowitz argued, Episcopalianism 'dominated organized military religion' in the first half of the twentieth century, nowhere was that dominance as emphatic as at West Point.[142] Besides their churchmanship, what also served as a unifying theme in the ministries of cadet chaplains at this time was their emphasis on the values of muscular Christianity, an approach that helped to promote the burgeoning culture of athleticism that took hold in the service academies from the 1890s.[143] Furthermore, in the aftermath of World War I, an effort was made by Chaplain Clayton E. Wheat to Christianise the secular strictures of West Point's honour code, with its historic emphasis on the necessity of plain and honest dealing among cadets. This took the form of a new 'Cadet Prayer', which ran:

> O God, our Father.... Strengthen and increase our admiration for honest dealing and clean thinking, and suffer not our hatred of hypocrisy and pretence ever to diminish. Encourage us in our endeavour to live above the common level of life. Make us choose the harder right instead of the easier wrong, and never to be content with a half truth when the whole can be won ... Help us, in our work and in our play, to keep ourselves physically strong, mentally awake and morally straight, that we may the better maintain the honor of the Corps untarnished and unsullied, and acquit ourselves like men in our effort to realize the ideals of West Point in doing our duty to Thee and to our Country ...[144]

Nor, and despite the qualms of so many Americans in the build-up to war, did the chaplain of West Point shrink from the prospect of a fight. In June 1939, H. Fairfield Butt admonished the graduating class in the Cadet Chapel:

> In the four short years you have been at West Point you have seen world opinion change from extreme supine pacificism to preparedness. We have seen the theft of Ethiopia, the rape of China and the assault on what was Austria and Czechoslovakia. We have seen that passive acquiescence does not stop a bully ... Democracy cannot long prevail without freedom of worship and the incentive of religion. Every powerful machine needs a governor. Let God be the governor in your life.[145]

Naturally, there was a subtle pressure to conform to the genteel yet muscular Episcopalianism promoted by the academy. According to Brown's findings, almost half of the army's generals from 1898 to 1940 were Episcopalians, and Janowitz put the proportion at an impressive 40 per cent as late as 1950. Furthermore, and as Janowitz concluded: 'There is good evidence that a substantial minority adopted the Episcopalian faith, rather than having been born into it.'[146] At West Point, and in its milder form, this pressure involved Protestant cadets from a host of different backgrounds (such as Eisenhower, whose Anabaptist parents had joined the Jehovah's Witnesses, and 'Hap' Arnold, who had been intended for the Baptist ministry)[147] sitting through 'an Episcopal service no matter what other denomination they might actually profess.'[148] In more severe cases, it might require the concealment – or even renunciation – of prior religious loyalties, with Jews being particularly vulnerable to academy norms and anti-Semitic prejudice. For example, in 1923 a visiting rabbi was told that Jewish cadets attended Protestant services as they did not wish to attract unwanted attention by forming a group of their own; in 1937, another rabbi discovered that Jewish cadets were still being essentially subjected to compulsory chapel.[149] Significantly, while at West Point Eisenhower was dubbed 'the terrible Swedish Jew', a moniker that was recorded in the yearbook of his class of 1915.[150] For Mark Clark, who entered West Point two years earlier and whose mother was of Romanian Jewish extraction, it was imperative to deflect any hint of hostility or suspicion by having himself baptised an Episcopalian in the Cadet Chapel.[151] As one biographer put it: 'This dispelled trifling or troublesome ambiguities, for military men were far more comfortable when they could firmly categorize people and things. [Clark] perceived, whether vaguely or clearly, the structure of American society and the advantage of being a Protestant with an Anglo-Saxon name.'[152]

For Catholics at West Point there was not such pressure to conform, but their status as de facto outsiders could operate to their disadvantage. In its formative years West Point had not seen many Catholics and, when Julius P. Garesche, a North Carolinian of French extraction, entered the academy in 1837 he was its only Catholic cadet.[153] At the consecration of the Catholic chapel in 1900, George Deshon, an academy graduate and now the superior of the Paulist Fathers, 'spoke of his own cadet days [in the early 1840s] when Gen. Grant and himself were room mates'. There were, he said, 'few professed Catholics at West Point in those days.... Only one officer crossed the river to Cold Spring, where a little Catholic church stood in what was almost a wilderness. That solitary officer represented West Point's Catholic population.'[154] While change certainly occurred in the intervening decades, it is significant that the Catholic chapel made clear concessions to the cultural norms of West Point by being built as a facsimile of an English medieval parish church.[155] Furthermore, even the congressional appointment system, which should in theory have provided a more representative body of cadets, worked against America's largely poor and immigrant Catholic population. As Janowitz has put it, 'congressmen, because of personal contacts, associations, and interests, tended to select from among the more privileged strata.'[156] In this respect, the appointment of Jacob L. Devers, who entered West Point in 1905, is illustrative of the sort of advantages that most Catholics did not enjoy; in Devers's case, his congressman was the superintendent of his Sunday school and, like his father, was a freemason.[157] In view of the strong undercurrents of anti-Catholicism in contemporary American society, exposure to the culture of West Point in the early decades of the twentieth century may even have induced a few Catholic officers to adjust their loyalties over time. This may have been the case with the hugely ambitious James M. Gavin, who entered the academy in 1925 after a troubled upbringing at the hands of working-class Irish Catholic foster parents.[158] Given the regime at West Point, it was also possible to infer that an individual's Catholicism could serve as a professional handicap. There were no Catholics among the five World War II generals (Marshall, MacArthur, Eisenhower, Arnold and Bradley, all of whom were West Pointers except Marshall) awarded the five-star rank of General of the Army between 1944 and 1950.[159] Although at least two Catholic West Pointers became corps commanders in World War II – namely Joseph Lawton Collins and Geoffrey Keyes – the fate of the Collins family seems to illustrate the uncertain footing of Catholic career officers in this period. Whereas Joseph Lawton Collins became chief of staff in 1947, and even married the daughter of a future chief of chaplains in 1921, his elder brother and fellow West Pointer, Major General James Lawton Collins, appears to have abandoned his Catholicism in mid-career.[160] Significantly, two of the more famous Catholic generals of World War II, William Joseph Donovan, director of the Office of Strategic Services, and Terry de la Mesa Allen, the colourful commander of the 1st and 104th Infantry Divisions, were not graduates of West Point.[161] Not only had the academy proved uncongenial to Allen but his controversial sacking as commander of the 1st Infantry Division in August 1943 led him to the conclusion that he 'had lost his command because he was not a member of the club (not an academy graduate) and because of prejudice against Roman Catholics'.[162]

Against this awkward background, the toxic sporting rivalry that arose between West Point and the University of Notre Dame in the early decades of the twentieth century did nothing to ease relations between the academy and American Catholicism. In view of this rivalry, which may well have been fuelled by resentment of America's 'Anglo-' elite among Catholics in general,[163] interwar football fixtures between the 'army' and Notre Dame teams were usually played at neutral venues in New York City. Such was their quasi-sectarian character that: 'Nuns lit candles for the [Notre Dame] team, and New Yorkers scrambled for the tickets that allowed them to cheer the Irish and to boo the Black Knights from West Point'.[164] This antagonism even persisted into the war years. As Francis L. Sampson, a Catholic chaplain with the 101st Airborne Division recalled, 'The beating Notre Dame took from the Army' in 1944 was nothing compared to the 'shellacking' he received from 'the West Pointers' once news of the game came through. Had the scores been reversed, Sampson believed, 'it would have been censored out of our news channels'.[165] After the war, long-running tensions over the Army versus Notre Dame fixture reached such a pitch that it was, at last, suspended. As General Maxwell Taylor, the academy's new superintendent, emphasised in a telling memorandum to Eisenhower in 1946: 'In the eyes of a large portion of the public it pits West Point against the Catholic Church ... Our coaches and players are now being flooded with threatening and often scurrilous letters and postcards. Some are jokes, others are not.'[166]

If West Point was strongly identified as another bastion of America's white, Anglo-Saxon Protestant establishment, then the same could also be alleged of the US Naval Academy at Annapolis. However, the influence of Annapolis was much more pervasive in the US Navy; whereas West Point trained only a privileged minority of army officers, until World War II almost all of the navy's officers were graduates of the Naval Academy.[167] Like their counterparts at West Point, midshipmen at Annapolis were nominees of their senators or representatives and were subject to a regime of compulsory chapel, usually in an Episcopalian form.[168] For the navy especially, this regime had a strong rationale; in the absence of chaplains, naval officers were expected to lead public worship and preside over burials at sea, orders of service being published to assist officers in these duties throughout World War II.[169] One of them, produced in 1944 by the chaplains of Norfolk Navy Yard, was entitled *A Charted Course for the Religious Life of a United States Ship at Sea With No Chaplain on Board*. This provided a digest of essential information on available resources, a comprehensive guide to the religious needs of Protestant, Catholic and Jewish sailors, and three different orders of service for burials at sea. Furthermore, its introduction reminded skippers and executive officers that 'they must fulfill their responsibility to their men and God by providing the opportunity for each man to worship God according to the dictates of his faith and his conscience'.[170] More specifically, it stated that: 'The Executive Officer, as the ship's personnel officer, should, when conditions permit, set aside a part of each Sunday for Divine worship. He, or the officers or enlisted men whom he appoints, may conduct Divine Services as suggested herewith.'[171]

The Episcopalian bias of the Naval Academy reflected the strength of the Protestant Episcopal Church in the US Navy in the early nineteenth century; in fact, until 1860 it was still widely believed that shipboard services *had* to be conducted according to the letter and rubrics of the Episcopal prayer book.[172] During the nineteenth century, as many as 40 per cent of the navy's chaplains and 40 per cent of its officers were Episcopalians, and navy officers were wont to compare their calling and its trappings with those of the Episcopalian clergy.[173] The first two decades of the twentieth century saw only moderate change. In these years, 28 per cent of Annapolis midshipmen were registered as Episcopalians, 16.5 per cent as Methodists and 15.5 per cent as Presbyterians. The dominance of mainline Anglophone Protestants was underlined by the fact that only 12.5 per cent of midshipmen were Catholics, 3 per cent Lutheran and 1.3 per cent Jewish.[174] By 1950, the proportion of admirals professing to be Episcopalians was still a striking 42 per cent,[175] a figure that may well reflect the same long-term tendency to conform that Janowitz discerned among army generals. If the Episcopal Church and its services provided a congenially hierarchical, decorous and ceremonial form of Protestant Christianity for army and navy officers, it also had the virtue of being socially acceptable and quintessentially Anglo-Saxon. Furthermore, for the navy it provided traditional forms of service that they could readily use at sea in the absence of a chaplain.[176]

As at West Point, a focus on religious formation remained strong at the Naval Academy throughout the Progressive Era and interwar years. In fact, the navy seems to have made greater attempts than ever to demonstrate its inherent Christianity. While its ships were still 'christened' as tradition dictated (a practice that, as we have seen, stuck in the craw of *The Christian Century*) its battleships continued to be launched to the accompaniment of a pre-Civil War 'Prayer for the Navy'. Similarly, under its governing articles, commanding officers were still obliged 'to guard against and suppress all dissolute and immoral practices', while 'profane swearing' remained a court-martial offence.[177] By the outbreak of World War II a new and distinctive 'Mariner's Cross' (a Latin cross superimposed on a compass rose) had been popularised by navy chaplain William W. Edel and William Whiting's 'Eternal Father, Strong to Save' had been adopted as the 'Navy Hymn'.[178] The Naval Academy's chapel, rebuilt and extended on two previous occasions, was enlarged yet again as war clouds gathered in 1940.[179] By this time, the academy's Methodist chaplain, William N. Thomas, had composed a counter-part to West Point's 'Cadet Prayer'. Written in 1938, 'The Prayer of a Midshipman' (or 'Midshipmen's Prayer') ran:

> Almighty Father, whose way is in the sea and whose paths are in the great waters, whose command is over all and whose love never faileth.... Keep me true to my best self, guarding me against dishonesty in purpose and in deed, and helping me so to live that I can stand unashamed and unafraid before my shipmates, my loved ones, and Thee.... Give me the will to do the work of a man and to accept my share of responsibilities with a strong heart and a cheerful mind. Make me considerate of those intrusted to my leadership and faithful to the duties my country has intrusted to me. Let my uniform remind me daily of the traditions of the Service of which I am a part.... If ever I am inclined to doubt, steady my faith; if I am tempted, make me strong to resist; if I should miss the mark, give me courage to try again ...[180]

Like the 'Cadet Prayer', 'The Prayer of a Midshipman' was heavily publicised during World War II, being featured, for example, in the widely circulated *Song and Service Book for Ship and Field* (1942), the Protestant serviceman's magazine *The Link* (1943) and the high-profile and interfaith *Soldiers' and Sailors' Prayer Book* (1944).[181]

Given the professional formation of many army and most navy officers, all were expected to set a healthy moral and even religious example to their subordinates.

In fact, Article 1 of the Articles for the Government of the Navy commenced by admonishing that: 'The commanders of all fleets, squadrons, naval stations, and vessels belonging to the Navy are required to show in themselves a good example of virtue, honor, patriotism, and subordination.'[182] Even in World War II, and notwithstanding the vast expansion of the officer corps of both services, this expectation still held. In the experience of James V. Claypool, chaplain of the battleship *South Dakota*, church attendance among senior naval officers was the norm. It was 'instilled into midshipmen at Annapolis and other officer training schools' and, he maintained, such conformity characterised those who were 'lifted to the top'. In fact, so Claypool claimed: 'In the Navy, we take along religion as we take along ammunition.' However, this culture had the tendency to create some anomalies, namely 'high Navy officers' who were 'sincerely devout, though not necessarily pious, men'.[183] Significantly, such habits and conventions were widely respected on the lower decks. According to Claypool, the sincere if starchy religiosity of Thomas Leigh Gatch, the first commander of the *South Dakota*, was one of the reasons for the affection in which 'the Old Man' was held by its largely novice crew.[184] In a similar vein James J. Fahey of the light cruiser *Montpelier*, and throughout his diary of his war in the Pacific, registered his approval of the religious example set by its commanders. Of his fellow Catholic, Captain Tobin, Fahey wrote:

> *Thursday, December 2, 1943:* Today at 1 P.M. we lost a great man – Captain Tobin. He left for the beach by PT boat.... He has been Captain of this ship since July ... He never missed a church service and always went to communion. He was proud of his religion, his country and the Navy. They sent the right man when they sent Captain Tobin to command the *Montpelier*.[185]

Such praise was not just reserved for Fahey's co-religionists, however:

> *Sunday, April 1, 1945:* Today is Easter Sunday ... Protestant sunrise services were held on nearby Grande Island.... At 9 AM Catholic Mass was held topside. Many of the churchgoers received Communion. Captain Gorry was present. He never misses Mass on Sunday. Every one of our Captains, both Protestant and Catholic, were devoted church members. They set an example for the rest of the crew ... The chaplains of both faiths get along together famously. One would think that they belonged to the same faith. This is the type of 'team play' everyone on the *Montpelier* appreciates. We are proud of all of them.[186]

The same expectations could also obtain in the army. Chaplain Karl A. Wuest, for example, was sharply critical of those 'absentee commanders' who failed to attend religious services, especially when 'soldiers, by attending, showed that they felt there could be no other more pressing obligations than the obligations to God'. As Wuest reasoned:

> If the commander was to be their leader in the field, he must likewise be their leader in God's field.... Some soldiers made pointed remarks about such conduct.... To them it sometimes appeared, as the godless proclaim, that religion was to satisfy the masses, the rulers of the masses being enlightened to such degree that they were beyond the pale of God's law.[187]

Worse still, according to Wuest, was the language of some who were placed in positions of authority:

> To me, and to the intelligence of many soldiers, it was disgusting to hear leaders, in all ranks, express themselves in profanity and smutty remarks. Leaders, rightly to bear the name of leaders, should have a dignity and an adequate vocabulary to express themselves intelligently to their subordinates.... And more, how poorly would such individuals fare outside the caste system?[188]

Such objections were not, it should be stressed, the preserve of chaplains. For example, in December 1944, a soldier complained to *The Link* magazine: 'Something else I've noticed is the lack of officers attending religious services. I noticed only one officer at chapel this morning. I believe much good could be accomplished if the officers would devote more time and attention to religious activities and encourage their men to do the same.'[189] The following year, another wrote:

> I have been shocked many times in the past two years to hear that word 'God-damn' used to such a great extent.... I have found officers to be nearly as bad as the enlisted men. The ones who don't swear and tell vulgar jokes to their classes are far in the minority.[190]

On one occasion, Chaplain Israel Yost was moved to act on objections raised by former combat veterans to the 'profanity' used by a junior officer during their return voyage to the United States. After complaining to a senior officer, the latter duly 'called in the foul-mouthed lieutenant, verbally reprimanded him, and warned him not to act in such a manner again.'[191]

Conversely, and as in the navy, a certain prestige accrued to those army officers who set the right example. In April 1943 *The Link* applauded the example of Brigadier General F.B. Prickett of the newly activated 75th Infantry Division. A West Pointer who trained and then led the 75th in the ETO,[192] Prickett had a very clear idea of the role that religion was to play. Prickett's 'Directive on Religion', a memorandum sent to all his unit commanders, began by invoking the Four Freedoms and by emphasising that: 'Religion is basic in American life and fundamental to our survival as a strong people.' Accordingly, he pronounced that: 'In this division a religious life will be considered the normal life for all personnel … Our ambition is to have everyone in at least one church service each week.' While conceding that, 'There will be no compulsory church attendance', the promotion of religion was deemed to be a responsibility of all in command: 'Experience shows that the success or failure of a religious program has a direct relation to the attitude and practice of officers and non-commissioned officers … to attend religious services is part of an officer's *leadership* [italics in original].' Prickett then went on to 'commend the practice of all personnel carrying a Prayer Book or a Testament', as it could prove 'very valuable when one is isolated from the chaplain, in peril, or in sudden need of spiritual help'. Conscious of the many ways in which his aspirations could be thwarted, Prickett also warned that:

> In view of our positive religious emphasis, ridicule or disrespect of a man's religious habits, devotions or church attendance, will not be tolerated. Personal epithets or disparaging comments will not be permitted. It is the duty of officers and non-commissioned officers to prevent ridicule or disrespect in barracks or elsewhere.[193]

Prickett also declared that he was 'holding the chaplains of this division to very high standards', that he expected them to train with the men, to allow 'adequate time for professional preparation', and to devote 'long and intense hours [to] counselling men who come to the chapel offices, particularly in the evenings'. He concluded his directive with an agenda for sacred music: 'Choirs are desirable in each chapel. This necessitates time for rehearsals. Commanding officers should provide opportunity for interested men to attend rehearsals with minimum interruption in training.'[194]

If such thoroughness was unusual, Prickett's sentiments and aspirations were by no means exceptional. Major General Thompson Lawrence was equally emphatic about the pressing need for religion among those most likely to see action. Another West Point graduate, Lawrence commanded another draftee formation, the 99th Infantry Division, before taking charge of an Infantry Replacement Training Center at Camp Roberts, California, in 1943.[195] According to Lawrence, the very nature of the foe had brought home the fundamental need for religious faith:

> I consider religion absolutely essential to civilized man; without it there is no basis for civilized procedure and man would degenerate into a mere beast. Witness the conduct of our enemies, particularly the Japanese, which bring forcibly to our attention the result of a lack of true religion.

In order to prevent the American soldier from becoming 'a bestial killing machine as exemplified by the Japanese', it was 'incumbent upon all of us in the Army to initiate, renew, or continue our religious faith – that ardent belief in the Supreme Being', which served as an all-important restraint. However, that faith had to be lived, which brought Lawrence to the subject of churchgoing:

Attendance at church is possibly only a minor manifestation of one's religion, but it is an absolutely essential manifestation; it is a public declaration of our sincere belief in the hereafter and that we intend by all our actions to prove that we are deserving of our allotted place in future life.

On the subject of hope in the hereafter, and its value to a combat soldier, Lawrence pronounced that:

It is my desire that every man under my command give this matter of religion in his daily life the most careful and sincere thought, and that the religious preference stamped on his identification tags shall represent a true conviction on his part. On the battlefield, with the possibility of death at any moment, the assurance of a life to come is the only true comfort. It has been said that there are no atheists in foxholes; as we prepare ourselves to take our place in this great struggle, we must renew our allegiance to God.[196]

Nor was this a gospel preached and practised by West Pointers alone. Brigadier General Claudius M. Easley, who was commissioned from Texas A&M after serving in the National Guard, was killed on Okinawa in June 1945 while serving as assistant commander of the draftee 96th Infantry Division.[197] In Easley's widely touted opinion: 'The best soldier in my estimation is not just one who calls himself an American, but who can also call himself a soldier of Jesus Christ. Americanism and Christianity must prevail.'[198] The conduct of the officers of the 88th Infantry Division ('the first selective service division to go overseas [and] also the first to go into combat')[199] once again illustrates the importance attached to religion and to religious example in draftee divisions. Early in 1944, and with most of its fighting before it, a Sunday service had to be held in a small stable near the front line in Italy. Although the congregation numbered fewer than twenty, these included 'the Division Commander, Major General John E. Sloan [in fact, a graduate of Annapolis], the Assistant Division Commander, Brigadier General Paul W. Kendall, and the Regimental Commander [of the 349th Infantry], Colonel Joseph B. Crawford.'[200] Inspired by their presence, the presiding chaplain confidently announced that: 'Where leaders of a Division humbly trust in God and meet in stables with men from the ranks to worship Almighty God, victory will come.'[201]

The promotion of religion was not simply intended for the combat troops of the AGF, however. Among the senior generals most noted for their piety was the 'officiously religious' John Clifford Hodges Lee, head of the Services of Supply (or Army Service Forces) in the ETO from 1942 to 1945.[202] Mischievously known from his initials as 'Jesus Christ Himself',[203] Lee was a staunch Episcopalian and president of the wartime European chapter of the Brotherhood of St Andrew, lending this Episcopalian men's organisation his 'energetic support'.[204] However, the huge number of personnel in the army's great miscellany of service units also stood to benefit from Lee's religious interests. Speaking at a staff conference in April 1942, Lee stated that: 'The regulations of the American Army place upon each Commander the responsibility for the religious and moral conditions within his command. His responsibility in this is as great as his responsibility in other matters of a military nature.' What Lee described as 'the care and development of the whole soldier – body and soul' was of prime importance. The nation's 'future citizens' were in the keeping of army commanders and there was a serious risk in service life of learning 'to disregard spiritual values and moral obligations'. Because of this, he reasoned: 'The value of religious experience in self-control and in self-sacrifice must be wisely fostered and carefully retained.' Hence, Lee stressed that:

> It is my wish that each Commander will encourage and will provide opportunity in his command for Divine Worship and Service. His personal leadership and his own attendance at these religious services is expected, in order that he may be fully conversant with the moral and religious training that is being given to the members of his command.[205]

Nor was this an idle exhortation, for in February 1943 a strongly worded order was issued from Lee's headquarters in England deploring the fact 'that on occasion men have been prevented from attending Sabbath religious services by duty requirements'. Emphasising that, 'It is the policy of this headquarters to encourage attendance at religious services', the order stated that – except in 'extreme emergencies' – 'no member of the command who desires to attend Sabbath services will be placed on duty interfering with such attendance'. Requests to attend services on other occasions were to be treated sympathetically and: 'Wherever possible, inspections, formations, etc., will not be scheduled so as to interfere with Sabbath services.'[206]

It was, however, in the army's newly formed airborne units that the emphasis on religious training reached its apogee. We have already noted how Matthew B. Ridgway enlisted Alvin C. York to serve as a model of militant piety to the novice soldiers of his 82nd Airborne Division. A good example of the idiosyncratic religiosity of many of America's senior military commanders, Ridgway combined a chequered marital history with a profound personal faith that was characterised by a love of scripture and an abiding trust in providence and the power of prayer.[207] In many ways a typical product of West Point, Ridgway claimed descent from the nobility of the Anglo-Saxon kingdom of Mercia, he was 'Edwardian and upper middle class in upbringing, speech and style', and his family 'consisted of mostly affluent Episcopalian New York City professionals'.[208] As a cadet, Ridgway embraced the academy's religious culture, acting as a Sunday school superintendent and playing a prominent role in its YMCA.[209] Throughout World War II he carried a military prayer book and, prior to particularly dangerous operations, drew solace from God's assurances to Joshua and from Christ's heroic resignation in the Garden of Gethsemane. Ridgway's trust in divine protection was brave to the point of recklessness, even standing to urinate in full view of the enemy and prompting one staff officer to explain that: 'He firmly believes that God will not permit him to be hit before Germany is totally defeated.'[210] As for the 101st Airborne Division, which was formed from the 82nd in August 1942, this was initially entrusted to Major General William C. Lee, America's leading pioneer of airborne warfare.[211] Chaplain Francis L. Sampson of the 501st Parachute Infantry Regiment wrote of a lecture that Lee gave to inaugurate its 'intensive training program' in England:

> This talk was the finest Christian analysis I have ever heard of the purpose of an army, of the dignity of the soldier's profession, and of the high standard of deportment and of personal integrity rightly expected of every man who had been given the opportunity of wearing his country's uniform.... To [Lee] soldiering was not just a career – it was a vocation, a total dedication like the priesthood. He told us what lay ahead, and that sacrifice and obedience to an heroic degree would be required of us. Enlisted men and officers alike were profoundly moved.[212]

Given the understandable concern of airborne commanders to steel their troops for their exceptionally dangerous combat role, religious oratory appears to have been something of a speciality among them. James M. Gavin, who replaced Ridgway as commander of the 82nd Airborne in August 1944,[213] was a prime example, despite his extramarital affairs, shaky Catholicism and tolerance of a regimental brothel in Sicily.[214] Another firm believer in providence and a diligent student of military rhetoric, Gavin had long believed that, 'Pre-battle talks to the troops' generally began with the assertion that, 'Our cause is a holy one.'[215] Accordingly, he reminded the soldiers of the 505th Parachute Infantry Regiment prior to D Day that, when they landed in France, their only friend would be the Almighty.[216] In a similar vein, and in a parting address to his battalion of the 506th Parachute Infantry Regiment on the eve of the Normandy invasion, Lieutenant Colonel Robert Wolverton intoned:

> Although I am not a religious man, I would like all of you to kneel with me in prayer – and do not look down with a bowed head, but look up, so that you can see God and ask His blessing and help in what we are about to do.[217]

Undoubtedly, America's commanders fully appreciated the reputational dividends of conforming to popular and professional expectations in this regard. Apart from General Nathan F. Twining (who endured nearly a week adrift in the Pacific while commander of the Thirteenth Air Force in 1943, and lived to testify to the power of prayer)[218] the notable exceptions to this rule seem to have been the army's leading airmen, the obvious irony of sermonising bomber barons no doubt having much to do with their silence. Still, given the wartime demands of cultural mobilisation, and the opportunities presented to them by the radio, the newsreel and the popular press, the dutiful gestures and pious pronouncements of many senior commanders were broadcast to military and civilian audiences alike. As commander of the Fifth Army in Italy, Lieutenant General Mark Clark became notorious for his 'compulsive self-promotion', even to the point of being censured by Marshall and Eisenhower.[219] Aided and abetted by his wife in the United States and by a Fifth Army public relations staff that numbered over fifty,[220] the Mark Clark publicity machine did not neglect to major on his religious virtues. Speaking at a large Masonic gathering in Indianapolis, Maurine Clark described her husband as 'an awfully good man, a rather religious man'.[221] In 1944, Clark duly contributed to a flagship volume of prayers entitled *Soldiers' and Sailors' Prayer Book*, 'a non-sectarian collection of the finest prayers of the Protestant, Catholic and Jewish faiths', which was published by the major New York publisher, Alfred A. Knopf.[222] Pocket-sized, and priced at $1.00, it combined traditional prayers and contemporary prayers, claimed to be 'like no other in existence' for the inspiration it could bring, and its contributors consisted of figures 'now distinguished in the service of our country'.[223] In addition to Clark's prayer for 'On the Eve of Battle', he added a personal note: 'It is a pleasure to contribute to the Soldiers' and Sailors' Prayer Book. I am convinced that a soldier can find strength through prayer. All my life I have found prayer stimulating and comforting, particularly during critical periods'.[224] Naturally, Clark milked the fall of the Eternal City in June 1944 for all it was worth. Not only did he ignore a British suggestion that the Poles be admitted to the American spearhead ('as a tribute to their valor at Monte Cassino and in acknowledgment of their Roman Catholicism') but Clark was the principal worshipper at the Fifth Army's 'Solemn High Mass of Thanksgiving' held in the basilica of Santa Maria degli Angeli on the Sunday after Rome's liberation.[225] However, Clark could not avoid the Italian campaign becoming a 'forgotten front', and the inevitable waning of his own profile, as a result of the cross-Channel invasion.[226] Still, he made enough personal capital from his sojourn in Italy, and from his rapport with Pope Pius XII, that he was nominated by President Truman to be America's prospective ambassador to the Vatican in 1951, a nomination that was eventually thwarted.[227] However, Clark was by no means alone in courting this kind of celebrity during the Italian campaign. One of the most famous anecdotes concerning Terry de la Mesa Allen, for example, arose out of a 1944 broadcast by a *Collier's* war correspondent, Quentin Reynolds, concerning the battle for Troina in Sicily. According to Reynolds:

> Terry Allen, in the midst of giving orders, asked to be excused. He walked away in the thin, gray dusk, and his officers waited. After a while, two

correspondents followed.... They found him about a hundred yards away, kneeling in prayer. The correspondents asked General Allen if he was praying for the success of the operation. 'No', Terry Allen said, 'I'm praying that tonight there will be no unnecessary casualties; I'm praying that tonight no man's life will be wasted.'[228]

Allen was, in fact, another contributor to the *Soldiers' and Sailors' Prayer Book*, his prayer 'May I Fulfill My Duty' asking also that his fallen comrades be given 'rest and peace and the rewards thou hast reserved for the brave.'[229]

In March 1945, an AIPO poll sought to identify whom Americans considered 'the greatest United States army general in the war': 43 per cent thought MacArthur, 31 per cent Eisenhower, 17 per cent plumped for Patton and only 1 per cent went for Marshall (the same percentage, incidentally, which gave mistaken answers such as Montgomery and Halsey). Clark, ironically, failed to register among those polled.[230] However, he was not on the wrong track in religious terms. Significantly, one facet of MacArthur's popularity was his flair for public expressions of piety throughout the war. Another Episcopalian,[231] and helped by his World War I connections with Fr Duffy and Joyce Kilmer (they were his subordinates in the famous 42nd 'Rainbow' Division) ,[232] this star student and former superintendent of West Point was utterly at ease in the mantle of the all-American holy warrior. Despite his awkward status as a remarried divorcee,[233] the complex but publicity-obsessed MacArthur made good use of his attachment to the Bible, of his prayerful confidence in the Almighty and of a rather dilettante interest in moral theology. Extravagantly lauded in a rash of publications in 1942–44, in which his religious faith did not go unremarked,[234] there was plenty of substance to MacArthur's reputation for piety, despite being otherwise dubbed 'a paragon of pretension.'[235] According to Dr William L. Stidger of Boston University's School of Theology, a religious pundit who claimed to be wary of the tendency of generals and statesmen to 'drag in God's name',[236] MacArthur was religious 'in a simple, natural way',[237] one that quite properly appealed to 'the average American.'[238] Citing the personal testimony of the exiled President Quezon of the Philippines, Stidger endorsed the general's reputation as a praying and Bible-reading soldier – 'a God's Book man', as Quezon quaintly put it.[239] This confirmed the image projected by MacArthur himself, who once claimed that: 'However tired I may be, I never go to bed without reading a portion of the Bible. The Bible stimulates that faith needed in times like these.'[240] Such was MacArthur's reputation for prayer that one wartime story portrayed the future general at a planning exercise earlier in his career, at which, on being asked how he would defend an untenable position, the young MacArthur replied, 'Sir, there are two things I'd do. First, I would get down on my knees and pray. And after that I'd go out and fight!'[241] More intimately, MacArthur's emphasis on prayer applied to the responsibilities of fatherhood as much as to the burden of command. During the war years MacArthur composed his famous 'Father's Prayer', and also claimed that he wanted his son to remember him not for his military reputation 'but in the home repeating with him our simple, daily prayer, "Our Father, who art in heaven"'.[242]

Despite the often saccharine details, there was a consecrated nature to MacArthur's war. In a 1943 order of the day issued after the Allied victory in Papua, MacArthur stressed that: 'To God Almighty I give thanks for that guidance which has brought us to this success in our great crusade. His is the honor, the power and the glory forever. Amen.'[243] More controversially, and upon landing on Leyte in October 1944, he delivered his famous address, which ran: 'People of the Philippines: I have returned. By the grace of Almighty God, our forces stand again on Philippine soil.... The hour of your redemption is here.... Rally to me.... The guidance of Divine God points the way. Follow in His Name to the Holy Grail of righteous victory.'[244] If this speech proved unpalatable to some (including one journalist who claimed that the credit was due to the ordinary soldier rather than to God, a jibe that MacArthur felt showed the 'baseness' to which 'some men had fallen'),[245] MacArthur was unperturbed and went on to issue a general order requesting thanksgiving services for the liberation of Manila in February 1945.[246]

MacArthur's performance at the ceremony marking the surrender of Japan that September was much more restrained and uncontroversial, earning the approbation even of *The Christian Century* and concluding with the words: 'Let us pray that Peace be now restored to the world, and that God will preserve it always.'[247] Nonetheless, in a subsequent broadcast to the American people he restated his abiding conviction that divine will lay behind the successful completion of a 'holy mission' – 'I thank a merciful God that he has given us the faith, the courage and the power from which to mould victory.'[248] He also returned to a theological problem that he had first addressed as chief of staff, when he had responded furiously to the notorious poll of the American clergy by Kirby Page on the legitimacy of war. On that occasion, MacArthur had protested that:

> The refusal to defend priceless principles at any cost is un-Christian. I need only turn to Luke and Matthew, of the Holy Bible, to sustain my contention that religion and patriotism have always gone hand in hand.... 'When a strong man armed keepeth his palace, his goods are in peace,' wrote St. Luke. And from the Sermon on the Mount, 'Think not that I come to send peace on earth. I came not to send peace but a sword,' St. Matthew.[249]

In the wake of another world war, and with the advent of the atomic bomb, MacArthur was not content with the mere bandying of scriptural texts, reminding the American people in their hour of victory that the solution to humanity's problems was essentially moral and spiritual:

We have had our last chance. If we do not now devise some greater and more equitable system, Armageddon will be at our door. The problem basically is theological and involves a spiritual recrudescence and improvement of human character that will synchronize with our almost matchless advance in science, art, literature and all material and cultural developments of the past two thousand years. It must be of the spirit if we are to save the flesh.[250]

Faced with such formidable competition from many quarters, it is understandable that Eisenhower felt himself to be at a disadvantage, on one occasion swearing, 'Damn it, I *am* a religious man.'[251] William L. Stidger, in contrast to his treatment of MacArthur, and in attempting to profile Eisenhower's religion in 1943, could only equivocate that: 'Nobody is saying that General Eisenhower is a chaplain, nor that he holds a devotional service every morning in his tent ... But what I do claim is that the "big shot" General has his intimate reverences, and that he knows when he is up against it.'[252] The only president to be baptised in office,[253] as the Allies' supreme commander in North Africa and Europe during World War II Eisenhower had no formal church affiliation and was obliged to compete with the pious posturing of publicity-mongering subordinates such as Patton, Clark and Montgomery.[254] Another disadvantage was that he was also known for his colourful language. When Archbishop Spellman visited Eisenhower's headquarters in North Africa in 1943, a staff officer was concerned that the general was 'careful to avoid his usual adjectives.'[255] (And with good reason; some months later, and of the near fiasco at Salerno, Eisenhower remonstrated with one subordinate, 'For God's sake, Mike, how did you manage to get your troops so fucked up?')[256] While his friend George S. Patton intimated that he and Eisenhower were 'under the protection of some supreme being or fate', and that Eisenhower's initials – 'D.D.' – stood for 'Divine Destiny', Eisenhower was actually named after his father, David, and the renowned nineteenth-century evangelist Dwight L. Moody.[257] Typically, Eisenhower's own perspective and pronouncements on divine involvement were more circumspect than Patton's. According to his son, John Eisenhower, his father waged war much as he played bridge or poker – trusting that 'the Almighty would provide him with a decent set of cards ... He appeared not to share the metaphysical feeling that God owed him anything specific, such as good weather on a given day.'[258]

Still, it is clear that Eisenhower had no doubt as to the sanctity of the Allied cause, that he attached great importance to prayer, and that his stock as a religious commander rose steadily as the war went on. Towards the end of the North African campaign, Eisenhower wrote that, 'I do have the feeling of a crusader in this war';[259] after another year of war, these feelings had intensified:

Daily as it progressed there grew within me the conviction that as never before in a war between many nations the forces that stood for human good and men's rights were this time confronted by a completely evil conspiracy with which no compromise could be tolerated. Because only by the utter destruction of the Axis was a decent world possible, the war became for me a crusade in the traditional sense of that often misused word.[260]

In March 1944, *The Link* magazine published Eisenhower's revealing thoughts on 'The Allied Soldier and Religion':

The Allied soldier sees himself as a defender of those great precepts of humanitarianism preached by Christ and exemplified in the way of life for which all true democracies stand. He sees this conflict as a war between these great principles and the forces of human greed and selfishness and love of power today typified in Nazism, Fascism and Shintoism.... The Allied soldier is not often articulate in his profession of Christianity; but he is risking his life to uphold principles that are implicit alike in Democracy and Christianity: principles of justice, liberty and right among men of all stations, everywhere.[261]

While there these was more than a dash of the autobiographical in these statements, Eisenhower returned to the crusading theme in his celebrated D-Day message to the 'Soldiers, Sailors and Airmen of the Allied Expeditionary Force', in which he pointed to the 'great crusade' that lay before them and urged, 'let us all beseech the blessings of Almighty God upon this great and noble undertaking.'[262]

While Eisenhower's religious reputation could only gain from such pronouncements, his trust in the efficacy of prayer and his advocacy of scripture also gave weight to his religious credentials. Eisenhower's unfeigned confidence in prayer stemmed from his youth, when only the prayers of his family had seemed to prevent the loss of his left leg due to blood poisoning.[263] Even before his D-Day message, his reliance on prayer had been signalled to the American public by reports of how he had prayed for the invasion fleet prior to the landings on Sicily in July 1943. As Stidger put it, after saluting the huge armada as it left Malta, Eisenhower had 'bowed his head in a short silent prayer.'[264] According to one correspondent, the general had turned to a staff officer to say: 'There comes a time when you have done all that you can possibly do, when you have used your brains, your training, and your technical skill, when the die is cast, and events are in the hands of God – and there you have to leave them.'[265] By the end of the following year, Eisenhower was in sufficient standing as a praying general that *The Link* was able to carry his portrait on its back cover together with the text of his 'Favorite Prayer.'[266] This, significantly, had been solicited for the *Soldiers' and Sailors' Prayer Book*. Originally heard recited by a company commander 'on a wet, cold night, just before starting a march to the front line', the prayer acknowledged the supreme moral issues at stake in the war, a readiness to sacrifice one's life if need be, and asked God for the strength to 'rise above all terror of the enemy' and to die 'in the humble pride of the good soldier and in the certainty of Your infinite mercy'.[267]

In addition to hosting a stream of high-profile churchmen at his headquarters, Eisenhower's stature was also boosted by his widely publicised commendation of National Bible Week, a venture that had begun in 1941 under the auspices of the Laymen's National Committee.[268] Intimately acquainted with the contents of the Good Book by virtue of his own upbringing,[269] Eisenhower's timely and enthusiastic endorsement ran:

> It is truly gratifying to know that the peoples of the United States are setting aside a week to honor the Book which is our 'daily bread,' the 'Word of God'. While the utterances of God as recorded in the Bible are ever the need of mankind, it is in war – and particularly in the present war, with its issues of humanity and morality – that their essential presence is felt. On this front, I am happy to report, this thought is foremost among our men. Our objective is total victory – not only victory by arms, but victory also for America's ideals. And, with the help of God in this fight for right which help our men are ever and devotedly seeking, this victory is assured.[270]

By the end of the war, some defining features of Eisenhower's presidential faith were already clearly apparent – namely its elision of Christianity and American political values, its emphasis on the necessity of prayer, and its stress on the importance of Bible-reading.[271] However much this faith was derided in later years on account of its 'formlessness' and lack of doctrinal rigour,[272] there can be no doubt of its appeal during the war and its immediate aftermath. In fact, in 1946, Eisenhower received the prestigious Churchman Award for 'the promotion of good will and better understanding among all peoples,' among its previous recipients being Franklin and Eleanor Roosevelt, Wendell Wilkie, Henry A. Wallace and Chiang Kai-shek.[273]

While Eisenhower had to earn his reputation as a pious soldier over time, none of America's top-rated generals were quite as controversial as George S. Patton. In religious terms, Patton was a melange of contradictions. The Methodist bishop William Barrow Pugh, after visiting Patton, noted in 1943 that: 'Gen. Patton is an extremely self-opinionated man and I imagine he thinks he's right all the time … The general's conversation included quotations from the Bible and many good army "cuss" words'.[274] A High Church Episcopalian,[275] Patton 'had a great admiration for the Catholic Church' and often attended Mass while overseas.[276] However, this was combined with a conviction that God was 'quite impartial as to the form in which he is approached'.[277] Patton's personal belief system encompassed a belief in prophecy, reincarnation, telepathy, ghosts, destiny, an elaborate conception of luck, and more than a dash of anti-Semitism.[278] His formidable knowledge of the Bible stood alongside a view of salvation by death in battle that was 'almost Japanese or Mohammedan' in character.[279] Nevertheless, and from the beginning of his combat operations in World War II, Patton proved a forceful propagandist for the God of Battles and indulged in religious rhetoric of an extremely belligerent kind. While en route to Morocco in November 1942, Patton's message to his troops proclaimed: 'The eyes of the world are watching us; the heart of America beats for us; God is with us. On our victory depends the freedom or slavery of the human race. We shall surely win.'[280] Consequently, and following the success of the American landings, Patton averred in an official communiqué that, 'the great success attending the hazardous operation carried out on sea and on land by the Western Task Force could only have been possible through the intervention of Divine Providence manifested in many ways.'[281] In March 1943, and by now in Tunisia, Patton reminded his troops of the critical advantage they enjoyed over the Germans – 'in the place of his blood-glutted Woten, we have with us the God of Our Fathers Known of Old.'[282] Likewise, and according to Patton, the American push through Avranches in August 1944 was only made possible 'by the driving power of the General Officers ... by the superlative ability of the Staff of the Third Army to improvise under pressure, and by the help of God.'[283] Patton's God of Battles was by no means an impersonal deity, however, and the general's sense of divine oversight and protection endured throughout the war. According to his nephew, Patton was convinced that: 'It is my destiny to lead the biggest army ever assembled under one flag and to smash the Germans with it. And so God isn't going to let me be killed before I do.'[284] Consequently, and on his triumphant return to the United States in 1945, Patton declared that his first priority was 'to go to the little chapel in San Gabriel, California, and bow my head in prayer and gratitude to God for what He has done for me.'[285]

And Patton certainly prayed, and believed in the power of prayer. According to Omar Bradley, before his attack on Gafsa in Tunisia in March 1943, Patton told his staff and commanders: "Gentlemen, tomorrow we attack. If we are not victorious, let no one come back alive." With that, George excused himself and retired to his room to pray.'[286] Three months later, Patton wrote in his diary, 'I pray daily to do my duty, retain my self-confidence, and accomplish my destiny. No one can live under the awful responsibility I have without Divine help. Frequently I feel that I don't rate it.'[287] In the winter of 1944–45, Patton had the luxury of a 'private chapel' at his headquarters in Luxembourg where, at his request, 'Morning Prayer services' were held once a week according to the Episcopalian rite.'[288] A year earlier, and on the strength of his reputation for piety, Patton had also been approached for a contribution to the vaunted *Soldiers' and Sailors' Prayer Book*. His resulting 'Soldier's Prayer' was a characteristic blend of reverence, bellicosity and doubtful theology:

> God of our Fathers, who by land and sea has ever led us on to victory, please continue Your inspiring guidance in this the greatest of our conflicts....

Strengthen my soul so that the weakening instinct of self-preservation, which besets all of us in battle, shall not blind me to my duty to my own manhood, to the glory of my calling, and to my responsibility to my fellow soldiers.... If it be my lot to die, let me do so with courage and honor in a manner which will bring the greatest harm to the enemy ...[289]

However, Patton's outstanding coup in this respect came in December 1944. With the advance of his Third Army stalled by the elements in Lorraine, he sought the help of his senior chaplains in producing a prayer for 'fair weather'.[290] Consequently, the Third Army chaplain, James O'Neill, a Catholic, and his assistant, George R. Metcalf, an Episcopalian, agreed 'independently to find or adapt a suitable prayer and then compare notes'. The result was a prayer cobbled together from a Catholic prayer for victory and five different collects from the 1928 American Book of Common Prayer:[291]

Almighty and most Merciful Father, we humbly beseech Thee, of Thy great goodness, to restrain these immoderate rains with which we have had to contend. Grant us fair weather for Battle. Graciously hearken to us as soldiers who call upon Thee that, armed with Thy power, we may advance from victory to victory, and crush the oppression and wickedness of our enemies, and establish Thy justice among men and nations. Amen.[292]

Having met with Patton's approval, the prayer was printed on a card that bore a personal Christmas greeting from the general to the troops of Third Army, a greeting that concluded, 'May God's blessing rest upon each of you on this Christmas Day'.[293] According to Daniel A. Poling, who was visiting Third Army at the time, 'That prayer and greeting had the ring of Joshua and David at their militant best' and, even more remarkably, the weather improved dramatically after the card appeared. As Poling put it, 'ordinary mortals might no longer believe that God started rains in answer to prayer, but ... along the Rhine I had found some two hundred and fifty thousand soldiers who firmly believed that He stopped the rains in answer to their prayers'.[294] In fact, such was the remarkable turn of events that O'Neill became 'the only U.S. Army chaplain ever decorated with the Bronze Star for writing a prayer'.[295]

Significantly, Patton's reputation as a coarse and even violent bully ensured that this incident met with reservations and even scepticism in some church circles. As Metcalf admitted: 'According to some accounts the Commanding General demanded with curses a prayer that would "do the job". Others picture unwilling chaplains reluctantly producing a military prayer contrary to their convictions'.[296] Patton's career had been overshadowed by his slapping and abuse of soldiers suffering from battle exhaustion in Sicily (behaviour that Pugh claimed had 'disturbed' some chaplains),[297] and also by his moral responsibility for the massacre of Italian prisoners of war at Biscari, but it was his brazen and unrelenting profanity that vexed churchmen most. On reaching the Rhine, for example, Patton wired back to Paris, 'Have just pissed in Rhine, for God's sake send gasoline.'[298] Similarly, and to the African American soldiers of the 761st Tank Battalion: 'I don't care what color you are, so long as you go up there and kill those Kraut sonsabitches.'[299] According to Bradley, Patton's language derived from the argot of the pre-war regular army, in which he had come to the conclusion that, 'profanity was the most convincing medium of communication with his troops'. In this charitable interpretation, Patton had simply failed to make the adjustments required in dealing with an army of citizen soldiers.[300] This was disingenuous, however, for Patton was, for example, fond of female company yet sufficiently careful of his public reputation to ensure that women were kept away from his headquarters.[301] In fact, Patton revelled in this notorious character trait. In some pre-war 'godfatherly advice' dispensed to his eleven-year-old nephew, Patton counselled, 'Never be obscene or use profanity in conversation unless the obscenity is so splendid or the profanity so outstanding that people will be so interested they will forget to be shocked.'[302]

This was not the case for many churchmen, however. As Poling recalled, Patton's conduct was more tiresome than interesting:

> I had met Lieutenant General George S. Patton, Jr., in Algiers in 1943, and had been impressed by the sincerity of his religious practices even as I had been depressed by the childishness of some of his other actions. To me, there was something almost psychopathic about General Patton's frenzies, and even now I cannot understand the man to my own satisfaction. I know that he was entirely sincere in his belief in God and that he loved the Lord. And yet General Patton was easily the most profane man I have ever known, in or out of the Army – and I grew up in the rugged West where 'men were men' and had appropriate vocabularies.[303]

Patton was a particular *bête noire* for *The Christian Century*, the paper opposing his permanent promotion to general, condemning his fascistic appreciation of the Anglo-American alliance, and deploring a post-war speech to a class of Sunday school children in which he hailed them as 'the soldiers of the next war'.[304] However, Patton was also a source of embarrassment to senior members of his own Protestant Episcopal Church. After Patton had sworn during a radio broadcast, a bishop even wrote to George C. Marshall, protesting: 'Can't something be done to stop this? Children listen to him.'[305] For some evangelicals, however, Patton's alarming idiosyncrasies were simply evidence of his need for salvation, an opinion that Patton did not share. In 1943, Patton wrote to a Donald M. Taylor of Peoria, Illinois:

> In spite of the efforts of the newspapers to paint me as a most profane and ungodly man, I am probably just as religious as you are. I am a Commu-

nicant of the Episcopal Church and attend services every Sunday ... I have received several letters from people making an earnest effort to save my soul, which, personally, I do not believe is in any great danger.[306]

Three weeks later, and to his wife, Beatrice:

I had a letter ... from a preacher.... He hoped I thought about Jesus and reminded that I would die and go to hell if I did not.... I wrote him that I was amazed at his temerity in writing me such a letter when I was a far better Christian than he was.[307]

Although it was claimed that Patton 'appreciated and desired the services of chaplains to a much greater degree than most Army commanders',[308] his relations with his Protestant chaplains were in fact quite strained. While he had an admiration for Catholic priests (apparently 'because they were so militant in their faith')[309] Patton may not have forgiven mainline Protestants for their pacifist proclivities in the interwar period, or for the personal criticism he incurred during the war years. Nevertheless, there was plenty for chaplains of all denominations to take exception to. In September 1943, Catholic chaplain Lawrence E. Deery of the 16th Infantry Regiment reported to the chief of chaplains that the general had excelled himself in a recent address to the 1st Infantry Division in Sicily. During his speech, Patton had stated that: 'On this island there are two things to avoid, a mosquito bite and the clap, the worse of the two is the mosquito bite.' Moreover, 'He accused every man and woman on the island of incest. "Every woman on the island has syphilis, if they are not born with it, then the men catch it off their sisters and give it to their wives".' As Deery pointed out:

Outside of the insult to men's intelligence, there is a good number of men in the First Division that were either born in Sicily or whose parents came from Sicily, and these men approached the Chaplain to voice their resentment at such remarks. They are still wondering why such a man is able to rise to the position of Army commander.

After discussion of Patton's attitudes and remarks at a chaplains' conference, Deery insisted that: 'Since it is the obligation of the Chaplains to promote the spiritual and moral welfare of the men in their charge, we feel that our work is in vain, when the commanding General will give his blessing to those things that are condemned by Divine law.'[310]

Not above slapping his soldiers, Patton was quite happy to belittle and berate his chaplains. As for those who were tempted to preach on sin, death and judgement, Patton complained:

There are too many of these weepers and wailers who can just barely stand up like men, and then prate about 'Those of ye who will this day die', and so on, to some poor bastards who are already scared half to death as it is.

What they need to be given is courage, and told that with God's protection and their own effort, they will live to sire litters of children – no, as a matter of fact, one litter apiece should be enough. It looks better.[311]

During one training exercise in North Africa, Patton bellowed at a hapless officer to get his men off the beach. When the officer protested that he was a chaplain, Patton retorted, 'I don't give a damn if you are Jesus Christ himself, get these men the hell off the beach[!]'[312] From Sicily in September 1943, Patton wrote scathingly:

> I had all the non-Catholic chaplains in the other day and gave them hell for having uninteresting services.... I told them that I was going to relieve any preacher who talked more than ten minutes on any subject. I will probably get slapped down by the Church union ...[313]

Patton was as good as his word. On one occasion, a senior chaplain arrived at the Communications Zone headquarters in Paris bearing a terse note from Patton: 'This man can neither preach nor pray. We don't want him.'[314] Handpicked in November 1944 for the 'difficult job of acting as General Patton's *personal* chaplain', Metcalf went to Third Army headquarters with some apprehension, conscious that his predecessor – '*a very good one*' – had been fired on account of being 'a bit wishy-washy in chapel'.[315] Although Patton had requested an Episcopalian in this instance,[316] and seemed happy enough with the O'Neill–Metcalf collaboration, Patton's persistent bullying naturally caused resentment. One account of the 'Prayer for Fair Weather' (typical of those that Metcalf disputed) had Patton brushing aside O'Neill's initial reservations about praying 'for clear weather to kill fellow men' with the words, 'Chaplain, are you teaching me theology or are you the Chaplain of the Third Army? I want a prayer.'[317] Significantly, Poling noted that not everyone was impressed by the prayer and its supposed effects and that the doubters 'seemed to be among the officers, especially a few chaplains'.[318]

However, it is ironic that – for all the celebrity of MacArthur's faith, the growing stature of Eisenhower in this respect, and the controversy that surrounded Patton – no general had more direct influence on the religious life of the army than George C. Marshall. As chief of staff from 1939, and a man of a comparatively aloof and retiring temperament, Marshall's wartime fame would never approach that of MacArthur, Eisenhower or Patton. Nevertheless, the strength of Marshall's faith did attract some media comment. In the wake of the North African campaign, when Montgomery's stock was high, Stidger was pleased to liken Marshall to Montgomery, Britain's leading general, as Marshall was likewise 'a sincerely and deeply religious man'.[319] The following year, a prayer that Marshall offered at an Easter sunrise service in Arlington National Cemetery was republished in *The Link*. [320] Above all, his role in shaping the American army – in religious as in other matters – was unrivalled.[321] A devout Episcopalian who had

1 President Franklin D. Roosevelt chats with Chaplain Crawford W. Brown, a fellow Episcopalian, at Camp Joseph T. Robinson, Arkansas, April 1943. Courtesy National Archives, photo no. 80-118(488).

2 President Harry S. Truman with four recipients of the Medal of Honor, January 1946. Joseph T. O'Callahan of the ill-fated aircraft carrier *Franklin*, the first chaplain to receive this award, is on the right of the group. National Park Service, Abbie Rowe, Courtesy of Harry S. Truman Library, 73-2155.

3 The crew of the USS *South Dakota* at a memorial service led by their Episcopalian chaplain, Newell Dwight Lindner, July 1944. Note the triptych placed beneath the guns of the gun turret. Courtesy National Archives, photo no. 80-G-238322.

4 A first aid station on Iwo Jima, February 1945. United Presbyterian navy chaplain John Henry Galbreath (kneeling, right centre) assists with a badly burned marine. Naval History and Heritage Command, photo no. 80-G-435702 Iwo Jima Operation, 1945.

5 Rouen, August 1945. Chaplain William T. Green presides at the marriage of Pfc Florence A. Collins of the WAC's 6888th Postal Directory Battalion and Corporal William A. Johnson of the 1696th Labor Supervision Company. This happy scene belies the difficult lot of the black chaplain in a segregated army. Courtesy National Archives, photo no. 111-SC-210939.

6 April 1945. A burial service led by American army chaplains for Jewish victims of an SS massacre near Neunberg, Germany. Courtesy National Archives, photo no. 111-SC-266662.

7 Illustrating its privileged role in America's armed forces, an army poster advertises the benefits of religion for the GI. RG 247 Records of the Office of the Chief of Chaplains. Records of Administration and Management General Records. Records Relating to the History of the Chaplains of the United States Army, 1941–58. Box 9. Courtesy National Archives.

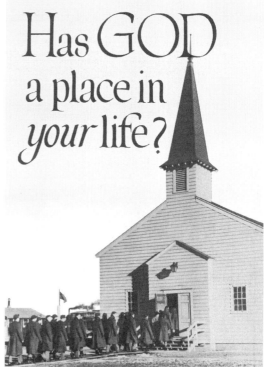

8 A poster on a similar theme encourages the use of the army's new and abundant 'mobilisation-type' chapels. RG 247 Records of the Office of the Chief of Chaplains. Records of Administration and Management General Records. Records Relating to the History of the Chaplains of the United States Army, 1941–58. Box 9. Courtesy National Archives.

9 Tripoli, Libya, April 1943. Francis J. Spellman, Archbishop of New York and Apostolic Vicar for the US Armed Forces, inspects the war-torn remnants of a Catholic chapel. Library of Congress, Farm Security Administration/Office of War Information, LC-DIG-fsa-8d31213.

10 Australia, July 1943. Another distinguished ecclesiastical tourist, Bishop John Andrew Gregg of the African Methodist Episcopal Church, with African American soldiers of the 630th Ordnance Company. Courtesy National Archives, photo no. 111-SC-180917.

11 The reassuringly salubrious and well-appointed interior of a model USO centre in San Francisco, December 1941. Library of Congress, Farm Security Administration/Office of War Information, LC-DIG-fsa-8c33738.

12 Invoking the model of the Holy Family, an army poster stresses the centrality of the family in American national life. RG 247 Records of the Office of the Chief of Chaplains. Records of Administration and Management General Records. Records Relating to the History of the Chaplains of the United States Army, 1941–58. Box 9. Courtesy National Archives.

IS THE FOUNDATION OF THE
★ ★ ★ NATION

For your country's sake today—

For your own sake tomorrow

GO TO THE NEAREST RECRUITING STATION
OF THE ARMED SERVICE OF YOUR CHOICE

13 As the experience of the Women's Army Corps illustrates, and notwithstanding the confidence of this 1944 recruiting poster, ingrained religious norms were to prove problematic for women's participation in America's armed forces. Courtesy National Archives, photo no. 44-PA-820.

14 France, 1944. Combat medics assist a wounded soldier. The considerable kudos of the combat medic certainly worked to the advantage of the religiously-inspired conscientious objectors who served in their ranks. Courtesy National Archives, photo no. 208-YE-22.

15 Memorial Day, May 1943. A Congregational minister leads prayers for the war dead in Ashland, Maine. Besides the theological pragmatism which this scene suggests, the prayers of civilians in general reassured a great many in America's armed forces. Library of Congress, Farm Security Administration/Office of War Information, LC-USW3-030702-C.

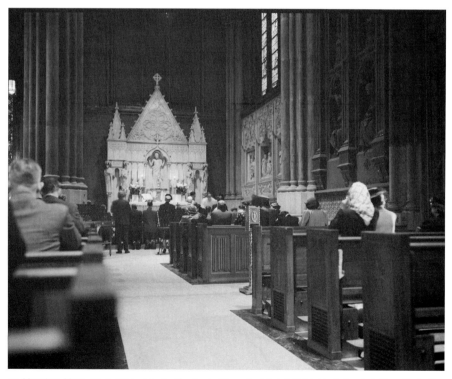

16 Morning Mass on 6 June 1944 in the Lady Chapel of Saint Patrick's Cathedral, New York. The Normandy invasion unfolded to the accompaniment of a barrage of intercessory prayer on the home front. Library of Congress, Farm Security Administration/Office of War Information, LC-DIG-fsa-8d36306.

been steeped in the catechism at Sunday school,[322] as a youth Marshall had dutifully pumped the organ at St Peter's Episcopal Church, Uniontown, Pennsylvania, and had been 'profoundly' influenced by its somewhat liberal incumbent, Dr John R. Wightman.[323] A teetotaller in his younger days Marshall, unlike Patton, professed to be 'ashamed' of the bad language he fell into during the war years but, even as chief of staff, he remained regular in his church attendance.[324]

Professionally as well as personally, Marshall placed great store on the value of religion and its agents. He was convinced, for example, that the American YMCA had emerged from its useful army work in World War I with a poor reputation that was wholly undeserved.[325] Furthermore, and in keeping with his overarching policy of nurturing morale by ensuring that all the reasonable requirements of American soldiers were met in full ('We are going to take care of the troops first, last, and all the time'),[326] Marshall was careful to ensure that their religious needs were amply catered for. In a national radio broadcast of 29 November 1940, Marshall assured the American public that:

> A subject of outstanding importance and one to which we have given extensive consideration is the moral and spiritual welfare of the young soldier. Our Corps of Chaplains, with one chaplain for every 1,200 men, is well organized and will be adequately equipped to provide religious services and training for all denominations similar to those found in the average city parish ... There should be no fear that any young man will suffer spiritual loss during the period of his military service, and, on the contrary, we hope that the young soldier will return to his home with a keener understanding of the sacred ideals for which our churches stand.[327]

Later, Supreme Court Justice Frank Murphy assured Stidger that Marshall was as 'deeply concerned with the moral and spiritual welfare of the men ... as he is to see that they are well equipped with arms, food and clothes.'[328]

Nevertheless, and conscious as he was of the need to sustain the spirits of somewhat unruly draftees who were often serving thousands of miles from home,[329] Marshall expected the army's chaplains to play their part. Convinced that, 'A good chaplain does not require a church; a poor one will empty a cathedral', before the North African campaign Marshall issued an order 'charging commanders with the same responsibility for the conduct of the chaplain' as they had for training matters. As Marshall remembered: 'We were not interested in the denominational matters or religious procedures, but intensely interested in the effectiveness of the chaplain. Was he carrying his weight or was he more or less innocuous?'[330] In view of these strictures, the 'agonizingly pathetic performance' of an army chaplain at a Memorial Day service in Tunisia in 1943 left an abiding and galling impression upon the chief of staff.[331] Ascribing the martial qualities of the Japanese to their religious beliefs,[332] throughout World War II Marshall hoped that religion would serve a similar purpose in the US

Army. In June 1941, and in a detailed address given at Trinity College, Hartford, Connecticut, Marshall insisted that war remained a contest of morale, essentially a struggle of the spirit, despite the vast material resources on which the US Army could ultimately draw:

> It is true that war is fought with physical weapons of flame and steel but it is not the mere possession of these weapons, or the use of them, that wins the struggle. They are indispensable but in the final analysis it is the human spirit that achieves the ultimate decision ... the determining factor in war is something invisible and intangible, something wholly spiritual ... the men in this Army we are building for the defense of a Christian nation and Christian values, will fight, if they have to fight, with more than their bodies and their hands and their material weapons. They will fight with their souls.... The War Department is seeing to it that this Christian army is not asked to live on rations alone. It has enlisted the aid of chaplains by the hundreds and is building chapels by the hundreds (555 to be exact) to give the Army the spiritual food we want it to have.[333]

Reprising this theme after war broke out, Marshall told 'a group of friends in Washington' that:

> It is not enough to fight. It is the spirit which we bring to the fight that decides the issue.... It is the morale – and I mean spiritual morale – which wins the victory in the ultimate, and that type of morale can only come out of the religious nature of a soldier who knows God and who has the spirit of religious fervor in his soul. I count heavily on that type of man and on that kind of Army.[334]

Together with a portrait of Marshall, and surmounting a V for victory, a version of this statement was featured on the cover of *The Link* magazine in August 1944.[335]

Standing in the shadows of such leviathans as MacArthur, Eisenhower, Patton and Marshall, the navy's senior commanders made much less of an impact in religious terms. If this was a reflection of its smaller size, it was also a function of its outlook and of the inferiority of its public relations machinery. Affected by the mindset of Admiral Ernest J. King, the commander-in-chief of the US Fleet and chief of naval operations, King 'loathed the press, spurned the Congress, and was indifferent to public opinion.'[336] A 'poor public speaker,'[337] King briefed only selected newsmen and drove the Office of War Information to despair that: 'The top navy brass ... wanted to issue no statements at all until the one declaring victory.'[338] In institutional terms, public discussion of religious matters was inhibited by the navy's unwritten rule, which was intended to preserve harmony in the close confines of a warship – that religion was a forbidden topic of conversation in the officers' mess.[339] All of this was not helped by the personality and reputation of King himself, as the admiral served as an unfortunate example of one of Claypool's 'devout, though not necessarily pious' naval officers. Although of Scottish extraction, King was an Episcopalian and could quote the Bible and the Book of Common Prayer with equal facility.[340] Like Eisenhower and Patton, he also supplied his favourite prayer to the compilers of the *Soldiers' and Sailors' Prayer Book* of 1944.[341] However, and unlike these generals, King's marital transgressions were public, shameless and habitual, while his foul temper seldom abated. In addition to his many affairs, according to one biographer: 'Women avoided sitting near him at dinner parties because his hands were too often beneath the table.'[342] As to the admiral's temper, one of his five daughters quipped that: 'He is the most even-tempered man in the Navy. He is always in a rage.'[343] Noted for his drinking, in spite of Prohibition and navy regulations,[344] King was hardly a champion of tri-faith America. Publicly accused by a Catholic priest of attending a Klan meeting in the 1920s, which he denied, King went on to ban one of his daughters from participating in a Catholic wedding on the grounds that: 'You'll be blessed with holy water and come back smelling of incense.'[345]

If America's top sailor was widely disliked and hardly credible as a model of martial piety, his supporting cast of prominent fighting admirals was also weak in this respect. The Commander-in-Chief Pacific Ocean Areas, Chester W. Nimitz, was less well known than many of his subordinates, partly because of his aversion to publicity but also because 'he was not an attractive subject for journalism because there was nothing particularly striking about his appearance, his conduct, or his manner of expressing himself.'[346] A lapsed Lutheran who shared the religious liberalism of his Unitarian, Massachusetts-born wife, Nimitz was lax in his religious observance. Although he was prepared to acknowledge that, 'It was God's mercy that our fleet was in Pearl Harbor on 7 December 1941,'[347] and was therefore largely salvageable, he felt acutely uncomfortable in the role of a champion of religion. In 1949, for example, it was only with great difficulty that he was persuaded to participate in a national radio broadcast on behalf of the American Bible Society. By his own admission, he was not very familiar with the Bible, had rarely entered a church since leaving the US Naval Academy, and was not sure whether he had even been baptised. Having refused to foist any religious views on his own children, Nimitz maintained that: 'I tried to frame my talk in such a way that I could not be accused of being a hypocrite.'[348] Among the fleet commanders under Nimitz in the Pacific there were none who bore comparison with the likes of MacArthur or Eisenhower. For example, Raymond A. Spruance, the victor of Midway and eventually the commander of Fifth Fleet, avoided publicity and was barely known to the sailors of his own command.[349] Nor was the colourful William F. ('Bull') Halsey, commander of Third Fleet (as Fifth Fleet was known when under his command), in a position to solve the navy's communication problems. As a sympathetic biographer admitted, Halsey was in no sense a born communicator – his 'speeches, private correspondence, and reports reveal that he often thought in clichés and that his vocabulary was narrow'.[350] His public pronouncements were, moreover, chiefly noted for their crude hate-mongering. Halsey's best-known slogan was 'Kill Japs, Kill Japs, Kill more Japs', which at least corresponded with his famous pledge that, after the war, 'Japanese will be spoken only in Hell.'[351]

There were, however, more eloquent (if less interesting) naval officers who could be presented as model Christian laymen. Vice Admiral Frederick Joseph Horne, for example, was 'an outstanding administrator' who loathed King but nevertheless spent most of the war as his vice chief of naval operations. While overseeing the navy's 'shipbuilding and shore establishment', Horne found time to contribute no fewer than three prayers to the *Soldiers' and Sailors' Prayer Book*.[352] Likewise, Rear Admiral Randall Jacobs, who became chief of the Bureau of Navigation (or, from 1942, the Bureau of Naval Personnel), was also enthusiastic about the cause of religion in the wartime navy. Representing the Secretary of the Navy at the inauguration of the Service Men's Christian League in Washington in November 1942,[353] Jacobs announced to the gathering:

> I can assure you that the sight of men kneeling beside their hammocks aboard ship to pray is an inspiring one.... I recall one account of an incident in the battle of the Solomon Islands where a young marine crouched in a dugout with the survivors of his company huddled in a close group, as shells and bombs screamed and fell about them, and led his fellows in prayer. It isn't always in such dramatic circumstances as these that men turn to their Maker. On a recent Sunday at the Great Lakes Naval Training Station, 52,000 officers and blue-jackets attended religious services of one form or another.[354]

A more junior, fighting sailor who earned distinction in the Solomons was Thomas Leigh Gatch, commander of the battleship *South Dakota*, who was wounded at the Battle of Santa Cruz in October 1942. Described by his chaplain, James V. Claypool, as 'an officer, a gentleman, and a Christian, in the best sense of all those words',[355] as commander of the *South Dakota* Gatch read the lessons at Claypool's Sunday services (thus emulating established practice in the Royal Navy) and 'encouraged all officers and men to attend.'[356] Portrayed in glowing terms in Claypool's descriptions of life at sea, as the navy's Judge Advocate General from September 1943, Gatch's prayer before the Battle of Santa Cruz was duly included in the *Soldiers' and Sailors' Prayer Book* of 1944: 'God grant that the woman that bore me suffered to suckle a man. Amen.'[357] For American Catholics, similar inspiration could be found in the life (and death) of Rear Admiral Daniel J. Callaghan, who was killed in action off Guadalcanal in November 1942 and buried at sea. A former naval aide to President Roosevelt, Callaghan was awarded a posthumous Medal of Honor for his conduct in engaging a larger Japanese force.[358] At a requiem mass for Callaghan, Archbishop Spellman pondered and theologised on the weight of Callaghan's example:

> The message of Admiral Callaghan's life, the message of every martyr's life, is a plea to us to live righteously and die rightly. It is a plea for us to love God as he loved Him, to serve his country as he did.... It is striking experience in the history of the Church that we have as canonized saints more soldiers than from any other profession, and this is reasonable, for the definition of sanctity is bravery supernaturalized.[359]

The Marine Corps also produced a fair crop of Christian commanders. Chaplain Warren Wyeth Willard, a veteran of the fighting on Guadalcanal in 1942, was forthright about the character of marine commanders in this regard: 'I ... noted that the two ranking marine generals in the Solomon Islands campaign, Major General Vandegrift and Brigadier General Rupertus [of the 1st Marine Division], along with Major General John Marston, of San Diego, California, commanding officer of our [2nd Marine Division], were all devout, Christian-spirited men.' This was crucial, so Willard insisted, because: 'Generally speaking, Christian soldiers are more reliable and courageous in combat than those who have not the knowledge of God.'[360] Though not mentioned by Willard, Major General Charles Barrett, the original commander of the 3rd Marine Division, was cut from the same cloth. As Chaplain Hansel H. Tower noted, at the dedication of a Protestant chapel on British Samoa in 1942 Barrett had stated that:

> We are glad a place has been erected in which men may worship God. A man's religion is the most important thing in his life and so it is fitting that one of the first buildings we erect is a chapel. It has been my policy for many years to attempt no important move without feeling that I have the approval of Almighty God.[361]

According to Tower, the assembled marines and sailors were 'deeply impressed by the words of this great and good man who had quietly given testimony to his religious convictions.'[362]

Although not a general until his retirement in 1946, a more famous (if highly controversial) Christian marine officer was Evans F. Carlson, the commander of the renowned Second Marine Raider Battalion and a former confidant of President Roosevelt.[363] The son of a New England Congregationalist minister, Carlson's unusual pre-war career had involved service as an enlisted man and as an officer in both the marines and the army. [364] Propelled to wartime fame by dint of his Raiders' exploits on Makin Atoll and Guadalcanal in 1942,[365] Carlson's much-vaunted egalitarianism (embodied in his famous motto 'Gung Ho!', or 'Work Together!') reflected his Congregationalist background and his admiration for the Chinese communist guerrillas of the Eighth Route Army, whom he had observed during the late 1930s.[366] Deeply impressed by their 'spiritual strength', Carlson promoted the ethos and practice of equality between officers and men and placed a huge emphasis on the importance of 'ethical indoctrination', a process of moral and political education whereby every one of his Raiders was brought to realise the importance of their individual and collective efforts.[367] Likened to John Brown by dint of his Yankee radicalism and ruthlessness,[368] Carlson made no apologies for his remarkable and rather uncomfortable synthesis of Christian and communist values, on one occasion telling a gathering of Methodist churchmen:

> Those Chinese of the Eighth Route Army ... were not professing Christians but they were practising Christian doctrine.... I have seen the doctrines of brotherly love work.... In the words of Christ: 'If you love only those who love you, what credit is that to you.... If you help only those who help you, what merit is that to you?[369]

Aided by a publicity machine that had served the Marine Corps well during the interwar period, especially by stressing its toughness and selectivity,[370] the corps was keen to burnish its religious credentials during World War II. In 1944 a 'Prayer for the United States Marine Corps', written by a regular navy chaplain, M.M. Witherspoon, duly appeared in the *Soldiers' and Sailors' Prayer Book.*[371] However, this goal was largely achieved through the career and example of Alexander A. Vandegrift, the foremost hero of Guadalcanal and a recipient of the Medal of Honor, who became commandant of the Marine Corps in January 1944. With a more conventional background than Carlson's, Vandegrift's very much lent itself to his wartime apotheosis as a Christian warrior. A native of Charlottesville, Virginia, as a boy Vandegrift had been deeply influenced by his paternal grandfather, a Baptist deacon and veteran of the Civil War, who prayed fervently to 'the God of Abraham, Isaac, Jacob, Robert E. Lee and Stonewall Jackson.'[372] As a Marine Corps general and, by his own estimation, 'a good Presbyterian,'[373] World War II gave him ample scope to emulate his childhood heroes. Vandegrift's message of August 1942 to the beleaguered soldiers of his 1st Marine Division, 'God favors the bold and strong of heart', resonated with the American public and was consequently 'published throughout the nation.'[374] On his return from the Solomons, Vandegrift also proved a powerful witness to the spiritual health of his marines on Guadalcanal. In one radio broadcast, for example, he stressed that: 'Religion out there was simple, but it was real. When people get down to bedrock, they begin to know what counts. Food, water, sleep are necessities, not luxuries. So is faith in God.'[375] He also maintained that religion had played the same sustaining role among his marines as it had among their revolutionary forebears 'at Trenton and Valley Forge', their experience amply vindicating the sentiments of 'In God We Trust.'[376] As a national hero and commandant of the Marine Corps, Vandegrift was another high-profile patron of the *Soldiers' and Sailors' Prayer Book,* offering a collect from *The Book of Common Prayer,* which gave thanks for 'deliverance from those great and apparent dangers wherewith we were compassed'.[377]

Chaplains' assistants

If chaplains were greatly assisted by the professional culture of the American military, and by prevailing concepts of command and leadership, they also derived more immediate help from a new, wartime breed of chaplain's assistant. As a body, the work of these men and women has tended to be underestimated, a situation that has not been helped by Kurt Vonnegut's depiction of the hapless Billy Pilgrim in his semi-autobiographical novel *Slaughterhouse Five*. According to Vonnegut, a life-long freethinker who later became president of the American Humanist Association, the chaplain's assistant cut a pathetic figure in the US army. Nothing but an object of scorn to his comrades, he was incapable of inflicting harm on the enemy or of providing support for his fellow soldiers. As essentially a clergyman's flunkey, the chaplain's assistant could expect no recognition or advancement from the army as an institution, and the effete form of religion he seemed to embody was positively distasteful to most of his comrades.[378]

Moving beyond these literary conjurations, an army chaplain – according to pre-war regulations, and subject to the agreement of his commanding officer – was allowed the services of an enlisted man to assist with his administrative and religious duties.[379] Treated as part of the army's 'clerk-typist' specialty, under the impact of mobilisation and war the role of these chaplains' assistants became more established, defined and wide-ranging, with George C. Marshall anxious to ensure the quality of 'the chaplain's immediate helper'.[380] By 1945, and as a result of War Department policy, chaplains' assistants usually held the enhanced rank of Technician 5th Grade (which equated to corporal) and had acquired the additional functions of chaplains' drivers and chaplains' bodyguards. It was also expected that they would play a prominent role in public worship.[381] However, the selection and training of chaplains' assistants remained local matters, assistants being chosen from the available pool of clerk-typists. For example, Chaplain Thomas J. Donnelly recalled how their first assistants were chosen by the three chaplains of the 305th Infantry Regiment:

> We, like all chaplains, had been advised to be most careful in our selection of an assistant. We were told to pick men of good character with the ability to type and, if possible, with the ability to play the organ.... The [Southern] Baptist chaplain selected a very likeable lad, a Scotch-Irish Presbyterian. A good young man, he could play the organ, and after a few beers at the Post Exchange, he would return to the chapel and play anything from Tin Pan Alley to Chopin. He became known as the Deacon.... The [Congregational-

Christian] selected a man who was a German-Jewish refugee. He had seen much persecution in Germany and was happy to be in the American Army. He, also, was very talented, and because of his faith, became known as the Rabbi.[382]

After observing his own flock for more than a month, Donnelly chose an Irish-born soldier named Kieran Patrick Fennelly, who soon became known as 'the Bishop'. Although not an organist, or even much of a typist, Fennelly's prime recommendation was his personal character. Educated, tactful and popular within the regiment, Donnelly averred that whether in a slit trench or in the chaplain's office Fennelly proved to be 'of great help to me in many, many ways'.[383]

From the chaplain's perspective, the support of a competent assistant could prove invaluable for a variety of reasons. Stressing their comparatively high moral and intellectual calibre, in March 1944 Garland E. Hopkins, a Methodist air force chaplain, claimed that 'an assistant's greatest value is in keeping the office and work of the chaplain going even when he is not present'.[384] Another chaplain, Robert S. McCarty, perceived the value of the chaplain's assistant as lying in the fact that he was 'the "contact" man between the chaplain and the battalion, letting the chaplain know what the men are doing and thinking'.[385] In the ETO, this was thought to be especially useful in the case of white chaplains assigned to African American units, an African American assistant being in a position to 'provide better liaison between the chaplain and the colored personnel of the unit'.[386] A good assistant could also prove vital in the enhancement of public worship. As a 'liturgical' Protestant who was obliged to hold services in offices, recreation halls and mess halls, to say nothing of outside venues, Chaplain Roy L. Yund of the United Lutheran Church valued the redeeming musical talents of a like-minded assistant. Writing for the *Ansgar Lutheran*, Yund reported that: 'I have been fortunate in having as my assistant Technical Sergeant George B. Arnold, Jr., a member of the American Guild of Organists, a former church organist and director of church music. He is an Episcopalian from Kingston, New York'.[387] Furthermore, and though not part of their official brief, some chaplains' assistants could lead worship in their own right. In part, this was because this was a natural niche for ministers who were ineligible for a chaplain's commission. William Galceran, for example, a Methodist minister from Mississippi, was turned down for an army chaplaincy on three occasions because he had only passed a four-year correspondence programme in theology from Emory University. Consequently, Galceran waived his exemption from the draft and enlisted 'as a buck private with the hope that some day he would become an assistant to a chaplain'. In time, and owing to the transfer and illness of the Protestant chaplains at Camp Barkeley, Texas, Galceran found himself responsible for the worship and pastoral care of five thousand trainee medics.[388] Similarly, in January 1943, Pfc. Jubie B. Bragg, Jr, a licensed minister and chaplain's assistant with the African

American 374th Engineer Battalion, wrote directly to Eleanor Roosevelt about a scheme to enhance the morale of African American soldiers. Not yet ordained, and thus ineligible to become a chaplain, Bragg proposed that he be commissioned and, as 'a Colored Commissioned Officer', be given a special mission of raising morale in African American service units, and in particular those that were too small 'to have a chaplain assigned'.[389] A further example of personal initiative on the part of a chaplain's assistant was that of Pfc. Joe Feigenbaum of the 7th Infantry Regiment who, it was noted by Chaplain Morris N. Kertzer, had effectively 'served as substitute Jewish chaplain' for the whole of the 3rd Infantry Division prior to his own arrival at Anzio.[390]

Some chaplains clearly formed a close bond with their assistants. Southern Baptist chaplain Wallace M. Hale of the 88th Infantry Division described his assistant, Sergeant Arthur P. Van Iderstine, as 'a talented, efficient friend and associate ... Although fifty years have passed, I miss that magic we had together'.[391] On the basis of his early combat experience in North Africa, Chaplain Harry P. Abbott also learned to appreciate the usefulness of a chaplain's assistant on the battlefield:

> The chaplain's assistant is a very valuable man for he is, in time of war, driver, personal bodyguard, secretary, organist, orderly, and anything else his many duties may require. Sometimes he even lightens the load for the chaplain for he is usually respected equally as much.... The work however, was not always pleasant, which comprised driving at night, hearing snipers' bullets whiz by in the dark, driving in the mud and rain and sleet, in the blackout, over mountains, sometimes near enemy territory ...[392]

Abbott's assistant also accompanied him in visiting field hospitals, a grim task in which he understandably faltered. As Abbott wrote:

> The chaplain and his assistant, T-5 Henry Whipple, move about from bed to bed with a word of cheer, a bit of news from the front, passing out chewing gum, candy, and writing paper to all (including the enemy.) It is indeed a ghastly experience to see men with an eye out, an arm off, a leg severed, a body horribly burned, or a hole in the throat or head.... One day as I was making my usual rounds of the hospital, I glanced around and saw my assistant sitting square in the middle of the floor in one of the wards. I said to him, 'Corporal Whipple, what is the matter?' and he replied, 'I just can't take it.' I could readily understand, as it was difficult for me.[393]

Despite this lapse on Whipple's part, other chaplains' assistants distinguished themselves in combat and, in Fifth Army alone, several were killed, wounded or decorated for their services to the wounded.[394]

The usefulness of chaplains' assistants was not lost on the wider army. Given their musical talents in particular, their potential for raising morale was significant. In June 1943, *Yank* reported how a chaplain's assistant helped to entertain the patients at a military hospital in Tunisia:

> Everywhere you go you bump into guys who are doing something that is similar to the kind of work they used to do in pre-khaki days. Pfc. John Morton of New York City is a case in point. John used to be the assistant organist at St. Bartholomew's Church on Park Avenue in New York City. Now he's the chaplain's assistant to an evacuation hospital. Every night he goes from ward to ward playing request numbers ranging from 'Star Dust' to 'St. Louis Blues', on a small field organ. He even holds jam sessions, with patients and visiting ambulance drivers filling in on other instruments.[395]

In a variation on this theme, Kenneth A. Connelly, a chaplain's assistant in the 333rd Infantry Regiment, threw himself into welfare work in general. Detailed to help the chaplain of his transport en route to Europe in September 1944, Connelly enthused:

> I was appointed assistant to the Troop Transport Chaplain for the duration of our crossing of the Atlantic and it was a marvellous job. The Ship's Chaplain supervises all the entertainment, movies, games, the library, variety shows, athletics, the publication of a daily news-sheet, the ship's broadcasting studio, etc. It was fun assisting him and kept me too busy to worry.[396]

Connelly's keenness and commitment survived the 333rd's torrid experience of the ETO, its commanding officer testifying that:

> Corporal Kenneth A. Connelly ... distinguished himself by meritorious service in connection with military operations against the enemy in Germany and Belgium ... Corporal Connelly has been unsparing in his devotion to duty. While under enemy observation and fire, and while working with the men of his unit during breaks from combat, his highly commendable performance has proved to be a definite morale factor in the regiment. His keen interest in the men, his visitations upon them, his service for them, and his cheerfulness at all times have served to inspire all who come in contact with him. His wonderful disposition, willing spirit, and performance of duty have been in keeping with the finest military traditions, reflecting much credit upon himself and making outstanding his service to our God and to our country.[397]

While there were many examples of chaplains' assistants who were vital reinforcements of chaplaincy work in the army, their situation was complicated by a number of factors. Although the AAF established a special, two-week training programme for its chaplains' assistants at San Antonio in 1944, training was otherwise localised and patchy.[398] There were also problems in finding qualified candidates for the appointment. When, as a novice chaplain, Karl Wuest unwisely advertised for a new assistant he was confronted with a queue of 'chow-line proportions', his first applicant being 'all for a place in some office'.[399] Because of this shortage, and their not uncommon proficiency as secretaries and musicians, many WACs were assigned to this role and AAF chaplains even had to resort to civilian employees.[400] Furthermore, and as they were selected from among the more capable enlisted men and women, not every chaplain's assistant was content to have his or her prospects of promotion limited to that of a non-commissioned officer (NCO). Hence, and while it was known that some assistants forsook promotion in order to fulfil this role, it was also accepted that: 'In other instances, qualified assistants were attracted elsewhere by the opportunity for advancement, and often were ultimately promoted in their new positions to the second and first grades'.[401] Retention was also complicated by transfers, as when a chaplain was reassigned it was not axiomatic that his assistant would go with him.[402] Consequently, towards the end of the war in the Pacific, 'it became a common practice for a chaplain to request that his assistant be allowed to accompany him on each change of station to avoid the problem of finding a new man and of having to train him'.[403] Finally, there was the danger that wholly unsuitable candidates might be pushed into this role for, as Jorgensen admitted: 'In a few instances the chapel was the dumping place for misfits who couldn't get along elsewhere'.[404]

Speaking at a chaplain's conference in Iceland in October 1943, Chaplain Clyde E. Kimball insisted that 'a chaplain's assistant can multiply or destroy the influence of the chaplain'; a few weeks later, his own assistant was court-martialled and received 'six months at hard labor' for an unspecified offence.[405] Significantly, Allan Bérubé has argued that the role of chaplain's assistant was a '"gay" job', claiming that: 'These enlisted men ... were "gentlemen's gentlemen" – clerks with musical training who aided the chaplain and helped to maintain the morale and welfare of the men ... The civilian counterparts to this job were the church organist, the choir director and the music teacher'.[406] While this might explain the source of Kimball's chagrin, it is a reductionist view of the wide range of men and women who served the US Army in this capacity in World War II. For one thing, their role was by no means as genteel as Bérubé asserted, for amidst the manifold rigours of the Pacific War: 'In addition to their regular duties they were carpenters, stone-masons and landscape engineers'.[407] Besides the element of would-be chaplains among them, it also seems that some felt a degree of unease about the war. Among the chaplains' assistants who served in the Pacific was the Hollywood star and conscientious objector Lew Ayres who, it was reported, 'turned down a staff-sergeant's rating in the Medical Corps to become a chaplain's assistant with a Tec 5 rating'.[408] When Daniel A. Poling encountered Ayres in New Guinea in 1944, he was serving as the assistant to a divisional chaplain and aspiring to be a minister. In the course of their 'intimate' conversation, the star of *All Quiet on the Western Front* (1930) (undeniably the most influential anti-war film of its time) and former husband of Ginger Rogers told Poling that: 'My principles have not changed but it was a question of what to do with my principles. Now I'm trying to help men.'[409] Although the chaplain's assistant was not a non-combatant per se, it seems likely that the role was congenial to religious men who were inclined towards pacifism – as was the case with Hale's assistant, Arthur P. Van Iderstine.[410] Another example was Charles E. Wilson, an alumnus of Wheaton College, who before he was drafted in 1944 had wrestled for years with the moral implications of killing. Having unsuccessfully sought a chaplain's commission while in basic training, Wilson saw action with the 10th Armored Infantry Battalion of the 4th Armored Division during the Battle of the Bulge. However, he remained troubled by the thought of killing other Christians and, after applying to become a chaplain's assistant, he was transferred to the 46th Medical Battalion of his old division. As Wilson remembered:

> My intent was not to escape danger, I knew too little of positional safety, nor the degree of threat to personal security any position might have in front line duty. My intent was to serve in a spiritually caring capacity in the best place possible in line with my vocational goals.[411]

Because chaplains' assistants were absorbed and reabsorbed into the wider specialty of 'clerk-typist', it is hard to state how many men and women served in this role in the US Army of World War II.[412] Nevertheless, their numbers ran into the thousands and they certainly acted as a significant boost to the work of the Corps of Chaplains, even persuading some that they should become a part of the corps itself. Significantly, a post-war report from the ETO was strongly in favour of strengthening their role, recommending that chaplains' assistants be recognised as a separate specialty, that they be selected from those with the right character and competences, that they should receive specialised training in the United States, that they should be distinguished according to their religious tradition, that they should hold the rank of Technician Third Grade, and that they should be transferred with the chaplains to whom they were assigned.[413]

If the army's chaplains' assistants usually proved their worth in World War II, the use and acceptance of their equivalents in the navy was more circumscribed. Like the army, the pre-war navy had acknowledged the need to provide some help for its chaplains, and yeomen (that is, ratings with clerical duties)[414] could be assigned for this purpose. However, neither musical ability nor an interest in chaplaincy work were thought to be prerequisites.[415] Beyond that, there was the problem of chaplains having to cope with the patently ill-adjusted. Reflecting on his experiences in the pre-war navy, Chaplain Frederick William Meehling even stated that: 'I only had one decent yeoman … the yeomen we had were those somebody couldn't use. The poor guys either couldn't see well or they were misfitted; they were problem children or something like that.'[416] Because of these problems, and after the creation of the new wartime rate of specialist, in 1942 senior navy chaplains successfully lobbied the Bureau of Naval Personnel for the additional rating of 'specialist (W)', the 'W' standing for welfare, in effect a chaplain's assistant. According to a contemporary circular that listed the qualifications for these new chaplains' assistants, candidates were to have demonstrable musical ability and, preferably, a college education. Furthermore, it was stressed that the role of the specialist (W) was not to lead services but to ensure that the chaplain's office ran smoothly:

> The specialist is assigned to the chaplain, to serve with and under the chaplain, and it is to the best interests of the Navy, therefore, that he be the type of individual who can fit into an office organization. Ability to use the typewriter, serve as a stenographer, adapt himself to office work and routine, possess a pleasing, gracious personality which will enable him to meet and serve people in an intelligent, understanding manner, will greatly enhance an applicant's suitability for this rating.[417] To support these new assistants, a Chief Specialist (W) was appointed to the Chaplains Division in Washington and successful applicants were even sent for an eight-week training course at the navy chaplains' school at Williamsburg, where they studied alongside trainee chaplains.[418]

In an article published in *The Link* in November 1944, Robert D. Workman, who had been instrumental in the creation of the new rate, waxed lyrical on the value of the naval chaplain's assistant:

> Yes, every Specialist (W) has a real job to do. He is the chaplain's right arm, taking over when the chaplain is out of the office, handling interviews, passing out literature and advice, giving information on scores of matters, helping men fill in complicated papers, answering questions concerning insurance, allotments, leave, liberty, how to advance in rates, and so on.[419]

Given their other, musical responsibilities (which included providing music for services, training and leading navy choirs, and organising glee clubs) Workman could only lament that: 'Our only regret is that we do not have more of them!'[420] However, the commitment of the navy to this new position remained limited. Unlike the US Coast Guard, the Bureau of Naval Personnel refused to allow chaplains' assistants to serve at sea and, out of nearly 1,500 applicants, only 509 ever served, including 38 WAVES. In practical terms, this meant that the vast majority of navy chaplains served without the help of a chaplain's assistant and, at the end of the war, the rate of specialist (W) was promptly scrapped by the Navy Department.[421]

The experience of the Marine Corps, in marked contrast, resembled that of the army. Navy chaplains to marine units before the war had also been entitled to the help of a clerk and, in pastoral terms, their role was considered significant.

As Chaplain Hansel H. Tower of the 7th Marines explained: 'A chaplain's clerk is important. He arranges interviews and encourages the timid to talk to the chaplain … When a conference is in progress the clerk does not eavesdrop and does not allow anyone to interrupt.'[422] However, the wider responsibilities of this role required more than just tact and discretion and the chaplain was hard-pressed to find suitable candidates. As Tower explained:

> The average chaplain's clerk in the Marine Corps is not trained especially for his work. Sometimes the chaplain is allowed to look around and interview several men for the job. First of all they must be of good character. They must know something about the services of the church, letter writing, filing and library work … That is quite an array of qualifications for a private. Since all of the offices are on the lookout for just such men, it is not always easy for the chaplain to find one who qualifies.[423]

Having gone through several clerks himself, Tower illustrated the embarrassment that incompetence could cause:

> A Catholic chaplain, Father Donlon, told his inexperienced clerk that he would celebrate Mass at six-fifteen that evening and asked him to put a note on the bulletin board to that effect. When the chaplain returned he saw a garish sign on the bulletin board which read:
>
>
>
> TONIGHT! TONIGHT! TONIGHT!
> Big celebration at Mass – 6:15 P.M.
> Come One, Come All
> Don't Miss It![424]
>
>

While Tower admitted that most chaplains' clerks were more or less equal to their task,[425] the Marine Corps proved quicker than the navy to formalise the role of the chaplain's assistant, this role being established in February 1942. Rated as master technical sergeants, 140 marines (including thirty-five women of the Marine Corps Women's Reserve) served as chaplains' assistants in the course of the war. Although only nineteen were trained at the chaplains' school, the majority served overseas, some saw action in the Pacific and two were awarded the Purple Heart. At the end of the war, the corps was sufficiently satisfied with the experiment to announce its intention of retaining the classification of chaplain's assistant for enlisted men.[426]

Military chapels

Highly symbolic of the new and heightened emphasis on the spiritual support of the American serviceman and woman was the massive, government-sponsored church-building effort that characterised the war years. The regular army had placed little value on chapel-building prior to World War II. After the Civil War, Congress had required commanding officers to set aside accommodation for educational and religious purposes on army posts, and a smattering of purpose-built chapels had duly appeared.[427] However, provision remained haphazard and even the crisis of World War I failed to act as a stimulus to the construction of chapels on permanent posts, chaplains making do with mess halls and with huts provided by civilian welfare agencies such as the YMCA.[428] With the slashing of military expenditure in the interwar years, the prospects of Congress voting funds for chapel-building receded still further. In 1927, Chief of Chaplains, John T. Axton, wrote to Chaplain Charles F. Graeser at Scott Field, Illinois:

> Of course we wish the government would make provision for chapels at all permanent posts but I see no prospect of this being accomplished any time soon and therefore we are encouraging the communities near our posts in the belief that they have a definite responsibility to aid in providing houses of worship for soldiers.[429]

Reduced to passing the hat round, even when chaplains were able to raise funds independently the War Department could be perversely obstructive. In 1928 when Chaplain Benjamin Tarskey arrived at France Field, Canal Zone, he was expected to hold his services in an aircraft hangar that also served as a gym and a cinema, the whole setting being dominated by a 'boxing-ring and gymnasium paraphernalia'. However, having begun to raise funds for a temporary chapel with the permission of his commanding officer, the Secretary of War scuppered the project by ruling that: 'The War Department expects Congress to provide appropriations for all necessary Army construction, and it is not considered desirable to accept private contributions for such purposes. Therefore, the request for authority to erect a chapel under the conditions stated ... is not favourably considered.'[430]

Ironically, it took the Great Depression and the New Deal to inject some momentum into meeting the army's chronic need for chapels. On its creation in 1935, it was not envisaged that the Works Progress Administration (WPA) should aid national defence but its administrator, Harry Hopkins, did seek out military construction projects that would provide work for the unemployed. Consequently, WPA funds financed the construction of barracks, runways and a handful of new army chapels.[431] Still, and even with the help of the New Deal, by 1939 only seventeen permanent chapels had been built on army posts.[432] Furthermore, a survey of chapel accommodation undertaken in 1939 under the aegis of the chief of chaplains underlined chronic deficiencies. According to the Office of the Quartermaster General, by 1940 the army maintained fifty-four post chapels, many being such in name only. At Portland Harbor, Maine, for example, the garrison of nearly two thousand were expected to worship in the post theatre.[433] Even at Fort Riley, Kansas, home to the prestigious Cavalry

School and the location of two nineteenth-century chapels,[434] things were not well. According to the findings of three inspectors: 'The Protestant Chapel is in poor interior condition. When the outside temperature falls below 20° F., the interior temperature cannot be raised above 60° F. The walls require paint, the aisle carpets should be replaced, and many pews are broken and insecure.'[435]

However, the political corollaries of partial mobilisation and the coming of the draft transformed an intractable case of neglect into an urgent priority. With the passage of the Selective Training and Service Act, the chief of chaplains pressed for the inclusion of chapels in the construction of the army's new training camps, advising that smaller, regimental-type chapels be built in preference to larger, less convenient structures.[436] Spurred on by the Office of the Chief of Chaplains, and rightly keen to assuage public concern as to the religious provision that the army was making for its reluctant warriors, the War Department's massive 'Chapel Building Program' was officially launched in 1941. Funded by an appropriation of nearly $13 million voted by Congress in a bill signed by the president on 17 March, on 20 March the War Department's Bureau of Public Relations issued a press release announcing that '604 CHAPELS WILL BE BUILT THROUGHOUT THE ARMY AT A COST OF $12,816,880.' The release was suitably candid about the current state of provision – only 17 out of 160 army posts had dedicated chapels and less than $1 million had been spent on them since 1918:

> Under such conditions the chaplains of the Army have been handicapped in providing for the spiritual needs of the soldiers. Men from well organized parishes found themselves praying on Sunday in the same room in which they danced the night before – that was the recreation hall, and they frequently had to sweep out the place to prepare it for devotions.

The provision of the new chapels (545 for ground troops and 59 for the Air Corps) was essential, it was claimed, for the spiritual wellbeing of the army and, by implication, in helping to maintain 'the present high morale of the troops.' The chapels, each of which could seat four hundred soldiers, would incorporate offices for the chaplains and would be equipped with an electric organ, their facilities enabling chaplains 'to develop a full program, stressing religious activities and also providing a centre for cultural and pastoral activities.' In sum, the release claimed that:

> In this program is reflected the Army's concern for the moral welfare and spiritual training of the trainee and its recognition of the spiritual qualities of true military character. It is part of the Army's determination to fulfil its duty to God as well as to country.... Like the church or chapel in the home community, the Army chapel will be a focal point of influence. In camp it will provide the soldiers, their relatives and their friends with a comforting

point of orientation relating the military environment of the soldier to that of his civilian status.[437]

In subsequent months, the 'Chapel Building Program' continued to the accompaniment of blaring publicity. On 1 May 1941, a further press release from the War Department announced that groundbreaking ceremonies for the first of the new chapels would be held at Arlington Cantonment, Virginia, the following Sunday. The cantonment's commanding officer would preside, chaplains of the army's three major religious traditions would be present, and an officer of the Quartermaster Corps would offer some fitting reflections on 'The First Chapel'. Their audience would consist of the 12th Infantry Regiment, which would be drawn up 'in hollow square formation while the band plays'. Further details were also provided about the chapels themselves. Depending on their location, they would be built either by civilian contractors under the supervision of the Quartermaster Corps or by the Corps of Engineers. Either way:

> The chapels will be 95 feet, 7 inches long and 37 feet wide. They will be constructed to conform with other camp buildings. Actual construction in all camps is expected to be under way within a month ... Present plans call for these chapels to be built entirely of wood, of substantial construction, but they are not intended to be of a permanent nature.[438]

The culmination of this public relations campaign came at the end of July, with the official opening of the flagship chapel at Arlington. With characteristic adroitness, the chief of chaplains had advised Marshall some weeks earlier:

> The first of our new chapels will be completed about the middle of July at Arlington Cantonment. We are planning a short ceremony to commemorate the occasion at eleven o'clock on the morning of Sunday, July 27th. The Bureau of Public Relations has made arrangements for the ceremony to be broadcast.[439]

Arnold then went on to observe:

> Since it is due to your interest in the spiritual and moral welfare of the men in our army that this project has been brought to fruition the occasion would be incomplete without your presence. I would be very happy if you could be present to accept the chapel from the Quartermaster General with such remarks as you may desire to make.[440]

In response to the general's misgivings about usurping the role of the chief of chaplains in accepting the chapel, Arnold replied smoothly:

> With sincere respect for your suggestion that I rather than you should accept the chapel and do the speaking, I am still convinced that the enlarged religious program for the Army will receive more momentum from your

words and actions than from mine.... News and movie photographers and broadcasters will be there to give the program wide publicity.[441]

The carefully choreographed 'initiatory ceremony' duly took place on the scheduled date, albeit at a slightly later time – apparently to facilitate a coast-to-coast broadcast of the proceedings by CBS. Under a cloudless sky, and in the presence of journalists, photographers, a cluster of Pathé news cameramen and the 703rd Military Police Battalion,[442] Arnold delivered an introductory address in which he announced that:

> The opening of this chapel today for Divine Worship is the first of many similar ceremonies that will take place throughout the Army during the next three months.... The erection of these chapels marks the beginning of a complete and effective mobilization of the spiritual power of our Army. The President of the United States, the Congress, church authorities, the religious people of the nation, and the officers and men of the Army have felt and expressed the need of religious virtue and fervour in our military service. There is a vital significance in the statement that 'battles are won by military power but wars are won by spiritual power.'[443]

Duly acclaimed by the chief of chaplains for their respective parts in this vital process, the quartermaster general, Major General Edmund B. Gregory, presented the chapel to the chief of staff with the reflection that:

> The Quartermaster Corps ordinarily devotes itself to caring for the material needs of the soldier. We feed him and clothe him, and we house and transport him, but no matter how well a man is fed or clothed or trained, he cannot be a soldier unless he has within him a sincere belief in the way of living of the nation which he represents. Nothing will contribute more to that belief than the opportunity for every man to worship as he chooses.[444]

Marshall, for his part, and following a list of prompts provided by Arnold, declared that:

> I do not believe any army in the history of the world has ever been created with as much care for the moral and spiritual guidance of its soldiers as this great emergency army of the Western Hemisphere. There is complete religious freedom, along with unusual opportunity for actual participation in religious worship.... These little chapels, one for each regiment, will make a tremendous return to the good citizenship of this country, a return out of all proportion to their cost or to their size and number.... We are determined to have a clean army, morally and physically, and these chapels are very important contributions to that end.[445]

In the final address, Arnold placed the present 'Chapel Building Program' squarely in the context of American history and civil religion:

> What our forefathers believed and declared and did when they founded this nation, succeeding generations must believe and reaffirm and do if they want this nation to survive.... Lincoln in his generation saw this country threatened with self-destruction, the worst of all dangers. He brought us through to safety because he took his stand with Washington and Jefferson. He turned to God, reaffirmed the primacy of the Creator and the obligation of His creatures to adhere at any cost to the eternal order of creation.... Now it's the turn of our generation to give this nation a new birth of freedom that it may not perish from the earth. To this end we must reaffirm our belief in God, our dependence on His Providence, our loyalty to His law.... Only those who understand and seek God will have the faith, the courage, and the spirit of sacrifice to defeat our foes ... we build this house of prayer to the Living God near the monument of Washington, Jefferson, and Lincoln, and nearer still to the monument on yonder hill where lies the entombed body of a glorious but nameless hero [the Tomb of the Unknown Soldier].[446]

After the cutting of the ribbon and an inspection of the chapel to the strains of an organ recital, the brief ceremony drew to a close. Well satisfied with the day's events, and with the publicity they had garnered, Arnold wrote promptly to the program manager at the Washington office of CBS, congratulating him on 'the excellent radio coverage' the ceremony had received and on the company's 'outstanding' recognition of the importance of 'the first of 600 chapels which will bring religious ministration to the million and a half soldiers at present in the United States Army'.[447] However, the further expansion of the army after Pearl Harbor meant that these six hundred chapels proved to be but the first tranche of a much greater chapel-building programme. In time, some major army camps acquired an impressive number of their own, with no fewer than twenty-eight being constructed at Camp Shelby, Mississippi. In some locations, chapels were sited so close to each other that their congregations could disturb each other's singing.[448] By VJ Day no fewer than 1,532 army chapels were in use in the United States, three-quarters being of the 'mobilisation type' constructed at Arlington. The remainder were either permanent structures, hybrid 'chapel-theatres', or a smaller 'theatre-of-operations' type that also proved suitable for minor posts in the United States. According to figures supplied by the chief of engineers in 1946, World War II resulted in an expenditure of nearly $32 million on structures that were solely intended for use as army chapels.[449]

This unprecedented crop of new chapels, it must be stressed, symbolised more than just the determination of the War Department to meet the religious needs of its citizen soldiers. The design of its 'mobilisation-type' chapels as produced by the Quartermaster Corps was deliberately based on America's vernacular church architecture – on 'the small country churches which dot the countryside of America', and on 'the typical small church found in every community'.[450] Thus, in a very real way, these prominent structures were intended to serve as reassuring symbols of home. This point was not lost on army chaplains, especially as almost half of all Americans in 1940 still lived in rural areas or in towns with populations of less than ten thousand.[451] According to Chaplain Karl A. Wuest, a Catholic, these army chapels successfully conveyed an impression of reassuring normality:

> The classical painting that depicts a small village of homes in the shadow of a church spire finds its counterpart in the Army camp. There too, the spire of the chapel is surrounded by the barrack –homes of the soldiers. To the weary of heart, to the passer-by, to men of all faiths, to any and all, the doors of the chapel are forever open to receive them into the House of God.[452]

Inspired by these surroundings, Floyd S. Smith, a Disciples of Christ chaplain, composed a hymn for his congregation to sing at Fort Benning, Georgia:

> There's a chapel on the hill by the beacon,
> No lovelier place on the base;
> No spot is so dear to my knowledge
> As the little white church on the hill ...
> How sweet on a clear Sunday morning
> To list to the church bugle call;
> Its tones so sweetly are calling,
> O come to the chapel on the hill.[453]

However, additional significance lay in the fact that these army chapels were also intended to serve as practical symbols of religious freedom and interfaith cooperation. A major practical question at the planning stage was whether to apportion these chapels on a denominational basis, with 70 per cent being Protestant, 25 per cent Catholic and 5 per cent Jewish.[454] The decision that they should be interfaith involved a fair amount of compromise; a proposal from Senator T.B. Bilbo of Mississippi that they include baptisteries had to be rejected, and Catholics were obliged to use an office for the reservation of the sacrament. Chapels were allotted numbers rather than names and, when services were not being held, the interior was to be as neutral as possible, with the fittings, features and ornaments of specific traditions being carefully covered or removed.[455] As announced in the War Department press release of March 1941: 'A feature of the chapels will be an altar that can be moved back on a track ... the altar fits into a recess at the rear of the chapel, so that the front of the altar becomes an architectural element of the wainscoting.' For Jewish worship, an Ark was also incorporated above the altar to hold the Scroll of the Law.[456] However bland and restrictive to some, the very inclusiveness of these army chapels was hailed by others as uniquely American. Speaking at Arlington in July 1941, the quartermaster general averred that:

> The most significant feature of every chapel ... is an altar which is designed so that it can be moved and adapted to the services of any denomination. There is nothing in construction that could stamp it as so distinctively American as this altar, because only in a free country could you find a church built to be used for worship by Catholic, Protestant and Jew alike.[457]

These chapels were also presented as clear and tangible expressions of freedom of religion, one of the much-vaunted Four Freedoms that Americans sought to uphold, a theme that was well to the fore at opening ceremonies. Speaking at the opening of four new chapels at Camp Davis, North Carolina, and warning of the global scourge of 'selfish pagans, now wounded unto death by the sting of vanity and the force representing the Four Freedoms',[458] Chaplain Edward J. Mattson averred that:

> This ceremony is a vivid illustration of what it means to live in a country which guarantees freedom and encourages brotherhood, so that Catholic, Jew and Protestant can unite in a conviction that one may pray as he pleases.... These chapels symbolize freedom of worship. But they symbolize more. They also symbolize freedom from want, for charity is taught within; freedom from fear, for neighbourliness is promoted within their walls; freedom of speech, for in them is taught the Golden Rule, which implies a respect for conscience and man's right to express himself according to conscience.[459]

Although guilty of over-interpreting the Atlantic Charter of August 1941 (which did not, in fact, explicitly mention freedom of religion),[460] Lieutenant General George H. Brett, commander of the Caribbean Defence Command, also linked these chapels to the Four Freedoms in his speech at the opening of a new chapel at Fort Clayton in the Canal Zone:

> This chapel symbolizes the unity of purpose behind the war effort of the United Nations. If our world were ruled by Axis tyrants instead of by free men, a group like this, assembled for the purpose of dedicating a house of common worship, would be unthinkable. Before we could begin our devotions in any public place, we would be scattered and pursued by the vengeful Gestapo ... Much has been said concerning the four great Freedoms enunciated by the Atlantic Charter. All four of them find expression here today. We have Freedom of Religion. That is evidenced by the very nature of this gathering. We have Freedom of Speech. And here, under the protection of American justice, we are free from the dread scourges of Want and Fear.[461]

The navy also lacked suitable chapel accommodation in the interwar years. According to Chaplain William W. Edel, who strove consistently 'to secure chapels for the Naval stations' at which he served,[462] in the late 1920s the only purpose-built chapels at naval stations were the chapel at the US Naval Academy at Annapolis and the 'small wooden chapel at the Mare Island Navy Yard near San Francisco'.[463] Other than this, there were a number of 'abandoned wooden buildings which enterprising chaplains had converted into usable chapels, but these were few and inadequate'.[464] In one example of improvisation, in 1928 the chaplain of the 4th Marines in Shanghai appropriated a local theatre, with summer services being held in 'the beautiful, artistic Italian Gardens of the Majestic Hotel'.[465] Significantly, the so-called 'Cathedral of the Air', which was built at Edel's initiative at Lakehurst Naval Air Station, New Jersey, in the early 1930s, was funded entirely through public donations and was presented to the navy by the American Legion.[466] However, the ravages of the Depression ensured that this ambitious 'Norman Gothic stone building' was given to the navy unfurnished.[467] As the threat of war gathered, a greater willingness to fund navy chapels became apparent. In 1939–40, the chapel of the Naval Academy was enlarged and, thanks to a recent fire and some strenuous lobbying by Edel, Congress appropriated $150,000 for the building of a new chapel complex at Norfolk, the first appropriation of its kind since $5,000 had been voted to build the chapel at Mare Island in 1900.[468] However, it was not until Congress voted nearly $13 million for the building of army chapels in March 1941 that the momentum began to gather. That July, Workman wrote to the chief of the Bureau of Navigation describing the state of the navy's chapels. In addition to the twenty-five bases, stations and hospitals where accommodation was either wholly inadequate or non-existent, Workman listed another eleven where improvements to chapel provision were badly needed (these included the Naval Air Station at Lakehurst, whose vaunted 'Cathedral of the Air' was still lacking 'Altar, pulpit, lectern, chancel furniture, pews, kneeling benches, and an electric organ').[469]

According to those who championed the cause of an independent 'Chaplains Bureau' for the navy, the subordination of navy chaplaincy was a major obstacle to securing a 'full program' of chapel-building 'comparable to that of the army'.[470] Unlike the army, 'Congress made no all-inclusive appropriation for naval chapels'; instead, these were constructed or improved under the public works appropriations for specific installations.[471] Still, the cumulative results were impressive enough, especially after the outbreak of war. In 1942, almost $1.3 million was voted for the building or enlargement of eighteen chapels. A similar figure was voted for an additional thirty chapel-building projects in 1943 and, in 1944, nearly $1.6 million was voted for a further twenty-seven. In 1945, eight more were authorised to the tune of $872,000.[472] However, even these figures did not reflect the real extent of new provision. Some chapels were purchased or leased by the navy as its installations multiplied or expanded, a few were improvised from Quonset or

Dallas huts, and others were simply adapted from existing structures.[473] Consequently, whereas Workman had listed seventeen navy chapels in use in the continental United States in July 1941, a survey conducted in 1947 counted 111.[474]
Significantly, and because church attendance was mandatory for its trainees for
much of the war, the vast new drill halls at Sampson Naval Training Station,
which could accommodate Sunday congregations of several thousand, were fitted
with integral chapels.[475] According to Edel, the senior chaplain at Sampson:

> The drill hall chapels consisted of a chancel and altar in a niche about
> 20 feet wide, 8 feet high, and going back into the wall about 5 feet. Two
> large panelled doors, one swinging from each side, concealed the chancel
> containing altar, lectern, and altar railing, during the week. When the doors
> were opened and seating was arranged, they made good wartime places of
> worship. This too was an innovation and provided place and equipment for
> worship in each of the drill halls.[476]

Whatever form they took, there was no doubt as to congressional willingness
to fund navy chapels in 'continental shore establishments'. As the chief of the
Bureau of Naval Personnel remarked in May 1944, this easily overrode budgetary
concerns: 'Congress has invariably approved this Bureau's chapel program, and in
one recent instance has increased the public works authorization by an amount
equal to the chapel program which had been eliminated by the Bureau of the
Budget.'[477]

Moreover, new chapels also proliferated in the navy's pre-war, overseas naval
districts. In the Caribbean (the Tenth District), seven new chapels had appeared
by 1947; in the Hawaiian Islands (the Fourteenth District), twenty; in the Canal
Zone (the Fifteenth District), three; and, in Alaska (the Seventeenth District), a
further seven. Only in the Japanese-occupied Philippines (the former Sixteenth
District) had the war halted the building of new chapels at public expense.[478]

Where navy practice also differed from that of the army was in the provision of denominational chapels. In January 1943, for example, two new chapels
were dedicated for the use of marines at Camp Lejeune, North Carolina; one,
the St Francis Xavier Chapel, was solely for Catholic use, while the other was
shared by Protestants and Jews. Similarly, six months later a Quonset hut was
dedicated as a synagogue at Camp Perry, Virginia.[479] Nevertheless, the navy was
fully aware of the practical benefits and propaganda value of interfaith provision.
In November 1942 an elaborate new chapel was dedicated at the Naval Training
Station at San Diego. Furnished with stained-glass windows and a baptistery,
it came 'completely equipped for all major faiths including needed vestments,
prayer books, and other ecclesiastical appointments'.[480] Meanwhile, at Sampson,
and developing a technique employed elsewhere, Edel found a local solution to
the needs of Protestants, Catholics and Jews by installing a three-sided revolving
altar in the chancels of two large chapels built in 1943.[481]

Religious broadcasting

Regardless of the many variations and subtleties of chapel design, if an American soldier or sailor still had difficulty in getting to chapel or to synagogue, especially when serving overseas, then the armed forces could fulfil their constitutional obligations by bringing chapel to him or to her in the form of broadcast services. In Dutch Guiana, for example, an enterprising chaplain fulfilled his obligation to provide Sunday services for widely scattered installations by securing a Sunday morning slot on the government-owned AVROS radio station.[482] Partly because of the vast distances involved, religious broadcasting was a harder proposition in the Pacific; nevertheless, in 1944 'a series of Sunday religious services' was broadcast from 'the local radio station' at Milne Bay in New Guinea. While 'nearly all bases' on the world's second largest island soon emulated this initiative, some stations went one better by carrying 'a short religious message' on a daily basis.[483] By the end of the war, broadcasting facilities in the liberated Philippines were such that eminent visitors such as Archbishop Francis J. Spellman and Dr W.H. Jernagin were able to relay their greetings to a vastly extended audience via a network of army radio stations.[484]

Nevertheless, the extent to which chaplains capitalised on this new medium varied from theatre to theatre. In North Africa, and after a long period of piecemeal religious broadcasting over local 'American Expeditionary Stations', a standard theatre-wide programme was introduced in August 1944 entitled *The Mediterranean Church of the Air*. A co-production of the Chaplain and Morale Services sections of the Services of Supply headquarters in this theatre, this venture sought to ensure a consistent standard of religious broadcasts over local radio stations. Oversight rested with a supervising chaplain, and chaplains of the army's three major faith traditions were chosen to deliver an appropriate share of the broadcasts (Protestants 50 per cent, Catholics 42 per cent and Jews 8 per cent). Significantly, care was taken to ensure that African American chaplains were represented in the Protestant quota, especially in those areas where black troops were numerous. The duties of the supervising chaplain included liaising with local station managers and censoring chaplains' scripts, ensuring that they contained 'nothing objectionable or prejudicial' and that they conformed to 'army policy on religious matters'. While recordings of the programme's theme music were sent to all participating stations, announcements were standardised and its sequence fixed to the second.[485] This enhanced model of religious broadcasting was duly adopted in Italy. Whereas a senior Fifth Army chaplain had pioneered a thirty-minute Sunday programme known as *Fifth Army Vespers*, this was eventually superseded by *The Mediterranean Church of the Air*, broadcast by a single 'mobile radio station' to which 'chaplains reported according to a rotating assignment'.[486]

In contrast to these developments in the Mediterranean, arrangements in the

ETO remained fairly loose and ad hoc throughout the war. From October 1943 the transmitters of the American Forces Network (AFN) – three months after it began its broadcasts to US troops in Britain – carried a Sunday programme named *Radio Chapel*. Produced and hosted by John J. Weaver, a London-based army chaplain, *Radio Chapel* consisted of a 'sermon … three hymns and a prayer' and was enlivened by regular guest preachers (often 'an eminent English clergyman') and by recordings of choral music. In time, the programme was supplemented by *Music for Sunday*, another half-hour programme that was supported by the Los Angeles-based Armed Forces Radio Service, which provided recordings of sacred music by 'outstanding artists'.[487] Significantly, and as the cross-Channel invasion loomed, the volume of religious broadcasting increased sharply:

> During Lent [1944] a daily four-to-seven-minute meditation immediately preceded the news summary at 1800 hours. Jewish services were broadcast on the High Holy days in the spring and in the fall, and a special Roman Catholic program was presented during Holy Week. From 29 November 1943 to 6 June 1944, the American Forces Network carried religious meditations once a day at various hours. In addition, for nine months preceding 6 June 1944, spot announcements encouraging Sabbath and Sunday chapel attendance were carried on Friday and Saturday evenings. Both 'Radio Chapel' and the daily Lenten devotions were 'must' programs, which all stations were required to carry.[488]

After D-Day, the substantial religious output of the AFN was reinforced by help from the British Broadcasting Corporation (BBC), which cooperated with Weaver in the production of twenty religious broadcasts as part of a collaborative Allied Expeditionary Force Programme (AEFP).[489] This was especially useful as attempts to make use of 'whatever chaplains happened to be available' for local broadcasts – on 'mobile transmitters accompanying the field armies' – proved singularly unsuccessful.[490] However, the question of religious broadcasting, and alternate AFN/BBC Sunday services on the AEFP, proved a bone of contention. In the opinion of Dr J.W. Welch, an Anglican clergyman and the BBC's director of religious broadcasting, *Radio Chapel* was nothing more than a medley of 'fruity American harmonies' and pep talks on 'popular psychological lines' – in short, 'sugary rubbish' that was hardly fitting for men going into battle. Hence, Welch insisted that the BBC was distanced as much as possible from American religious broadcasts.[491] If *Radio Chapel* cut little ice with the authorities at the BBC, most American chaplains seem to have been remarkably ignorant of religious broadcasting by the AFN. According to a post-war report on chaplains in the ETO:

> With more adequate publicity, the broadcasts would have been able to carry out even more effectively a very valuable function in supplementing the direct ministrations and services of individual chaplains, particularly

to isolated units.... Experience indicates it would have been desirable to have had a chaplain, assisted by enlisted assistants of appropriate grades with radio experience, assigned on a full-time basis to the American Forces Network to coordinate and produce religious programs and to act in general as director of religious broadcasting.[492]

Spiritual sundries

Courtesy of the American government, the lavish provision of chapels and a new emphasis on religious broadcasting to the forces was complemented by a munificent supply of other materials. The Chief of Chaplains' Religious Fund, disposing of $40 per chaplain per year, helped to provide the army's vaunted new chapels with altar and chancel furnishings including crosses, candelabra, communion sets, pulpit Bibles and Kiddush cups.[493] By the beginning of 1944 the War Department had also authorised 'a chaplain's outfit' for all chaplains ministering to troops on manoeuvres, in combat zones or in occupied territories. Issued by the Quartermaster Corps, this comprised a field desk, a chaplain's flag, a portable organ and 150 *Song and Service* books complete with their own special chest. Chaplains were also entitled to a portable typewriter and, if assigned to 'a tactical unit', a jeep and a trailer as well. By this stage of the war, and if not already furnished by their own denominations, chaplains could procure portable altars and communion sets from the chief of chaplains.[494] A variety of religious consumables was also provided by the army. One innovation from 1943 was the leaflet *Hymns From Home*, of which five million copies were printed. An attractive leaflet that included 'the words of 13 most used hymns',[495] these were supplied to chaplains in packs of fifty and were even distributed with cartons of field rations by the Quartermaster Corps.[496] However, in this case supply seems to have outstripped demand; Catholic chaplains rarely used them and, when received with their rations, 'the men merely scanned the folders and threw them away'.[497] Although Protestants found *Hymns From Home* more useful, a Lutheran chaplain complained that 'none of the hymns [such as 'Church in the Wildwood' and 'Battle Hymn of the Republic'] were strictly Christian and nowhere was the name of Jesus used ... we ought to have three types of sheets: one for Protestants, another for Roman Catholics, and a third for Jews'.[498]

A more popular and pressing demand was for communion supplies, an issue that posed particular problems in the South-West Pacific. According to a 1944 survey of religious behaviour in the First Cavalry Division, which had by then seen extensive action in the Admiralty Islands, consumption of sacramental bread and wine rose by as much as 400 per cent during periods of combat and their immediate aftermath.[499] Hence, by March 1945, and with the liberation of the Philippines well under way, the demand for communion wafers in the

US Army in the South-West Pacific exceeded that of the Catholic population of Australia.[500] A few months earlier, and with the Sixth Army poised to invade Leyte, a careful inventory had established that the chaplains' supplies then held at Hollandia, New Guinea, were totally inadequate for operational needs. Consequently, Hollandia's senior chaplain had to make 'special arrangements for 15,000 pounds of sacramental elements to be brought from Australia by air, and three C-47's were allocated for this purpose'.[501] However, it was not simply an issue of obtaining sufficient quantities of communion supplies, as storage posed a further difficulty; in the climatic conditions of the South-West Pacific, 'Communion wafers would often get mouldy and stick together'.[502] The procurement and storage of communion supplies was also complicated by the pilfering of communion wine across the supply chain, a problem that became so acute that chaplains had to accompany shipments to their destinations.[503] However, even outside the Pacific theatre the logistical problem of maintaining the sacramental life of the army could prove a major challenge. In September 1943, it was reported in *Yank* that: 'Two million paper cups have been purchased for [Protestant] chaplains on transports and overseas posts ... The use of paper cups will prevent loss and breakage and will help in the administration of the elements in the Holy Communion service'.[504] Similarly, in the Normandy bridgehead in the summer of 1944 the pressures of supply and demand meant that a senior army chaplain had to resort to some desperate measures:

> [T]he Senior Advance Section Chaplain is reported to have secured through the mayor of Isigny and the Civil Affairs Officer at Carentan, 'after much wrangling', enough wine locally for the chaplains' immediate needs. The nuns at Bayeux undertook the making of wafers. 'Flour was obtained by saying Mass for some quartermaster bakery company and then inveigling a couple of sacks of flour out of the company commander'.[505]

If anything, supplying the ritual needs of Jewish soldiers was an even greater headache. In the Pacific, the Jewish Welfare Board's initial policy of shipping material to its agent in Australia, rather than entrusting it to the army's normal channels of supply, meant that a great deal was wasted, being simply abandoned and left to spoil on Australian quaysides.[506] Furthermore, given the enormous length of supply lines in the Pacific, shipments of wine for Seder services were no less vulnerable to thieves than were shipments of communion wine. According to the Jewish chaplain at Milne Bay in 1944, 15 per cent of his Seder wine was pilfered in transit.[507] Naturally, things were simpler in the ETO. In 1945, Chaplain Arthur Brodey, the Jewish chaplain attached to Supply Headquarters, oversaw the distribution of '30 tons of supplies' for Seder services to Jewish GIs of the First and Ninth Armies, the Ninth Air Force and the Communications Zone – 'The Seder supplies filled more than five freight cars and consisted of 28,000 pounds of matzoh, hundreds of bottles of French wine, prayer books and festival foods.'[508] This example serves to illustrate that, despite moments of shortage, it was the sheer abundance of American supplies that stood out, in this as in so much else. The inferences that were drawn from this plenitude by foreign observers even grew irksome to Chaplain Morris N. Kertzer, who complained that:

> Chaplains of Allied nations made heavy demands upon our religious supplies, usually remarking 'You Americans have everything.' It was true that no other army permitted its men such a plethora of religious equipment, literature, and provisions for special feasts, but I suspect our brothers-in-arms attributed this not to a true concern for the spiritual welfare of our men, but merely to an overabundance of worldly goods.[509]

Before Pearl Harbor, navy chaplains had found that the navy and their parent churches were equally unhelpful in supplying them with the equipment necessary for their ministries. Like other naval officers, chaplains were required to purchase their own uniforms but they were also implicitly expected to 'buy all of their religious supplies', including 'a cross, candlesticks, communion set, communion elements and altar cloths as minimal equipment'. Other items (such as sheet music, flower vases, portable organs, typewriters, portable communion sets and religious literature) was sporadically available through denominational channels.[510] As for the Navy Department, when Chaplain Hansel H. Tower joined the 7th Marines in Cuba early in 1941, he discovered that his official entitlement consisted of a church flag – an item that his quartermaster did not have.[511] Tower's attempts to improvise a pulpit only ended in embarrassment when Tower, a Methodist, found himself giving a sermon from an old beer crate while 'an awed congregation looked on and marvelled'.[512] Such acute and chronic shortages helped to ensure that $5,700 was voted for the purchase of ecclesiastical equipment in the naval appropriations for 1942 – the first time this had ever happened in the history of the navy. If this was quickly spent in the purchase of small numbers of brass altar pieces, communion sets and missal stands, by the fiscal year 1945 appropriations for ecclesiastical equipment had soared to $175,000. By this stage of the war, public funds were also being used to furnish navy chaplains with other items such as portable organs, field altars and typewriters.[513]

In a culture shaped so profoundly by the Bible, this unprecedented governmental attempt to ensure the spiritual sustenance of the armed services would have been incomplete, to say the least, without an ample supply of scripture. The idea of supplying the Bible to the nation's defenders at public expense was not necessarily new. In 1783, Washington had been approached by Dr John Rodgers, a Presbyterian clergyman from New York, about presenting a copy of the new Aitken Bible – the 'Bible of the Revolution' – to soldiers of the Continental Army. Although the general proved supportive, with the Revolutionary War now over and his army disbanding, he did not think it was a practical suggestion and the project was dropped.[514] Thereafter, a typical blend of constitutional sensitivity, official indifference and public parsimony helped to prevent the idea from being implemented by either the War or the Navy Departments. In any case, there was no lack of civilian suppliers. The nineteenth century witnessed a proliferation of Bible societies in the United States and a consequent boom in the publication and distribution of Bibles and scripture portions; by the end of the century, the American Bible Society (ABS) alone had published and distributed more than four billion items since its formation in 1816.[515] Naturally, in years of war servicemen had been the prime objects of such distributions. During the Civil War, the ABS distributed nearly six million items, half of them to Union soldiers via the Christian Commission.[516] In the Confederacy, where stocks of Bibles and printing materials were comparatively scarce, the Confederate States Bible Society made determined attempts to run British-supplied Bibles through the Union blockade.[517] Although the Spanish–American War saw the ABS supply seventy-five thousand volumes to the army and navy, which were distributed through service chaplains and the YMCA,[518] this effort was eclipsed by that of World War I. Rising to the task of providing for a vast and polyglot national army, the ABS published millions of Bibles and scripture portions in languages ranging from Armenian to Yiddish, its total distributions amounting to roughly seven million items.[519] The favoured format for these wartime items of scripture was 'the vest-pocket size New Testament'. Bound in khaki or navy blue, a large number of copies incorporated the text of a letter of commendation written by President Wilson in July 1917, in which he averred that: 'When you have read the Bible you will know that it is the Word of God, because you will have found it the key to your own heart, your own happiness, and your own duty.'[520]

Seen in this long-term context, and given other movements in this direction, it seems inevitable that, by 1941, the tradition of supplying scripture to America's soldiers and sailors should have become a responsibility of government. If other purveyors found it difficult to meet the scale of the army's demands with the coming of the draft, a useful pretext for this unprecedented step was a heartfelt letter written to the president only days after it came into effect:

> President Roosevelt:
> I was recently reading how that King George of England gives a New Testament to every man who dons the uniform, with a testimony of his faith written in each one. Now I truly believe God will honor such faith and I believe that England as long as she honors God thus, will never be conquered.
> I think it would be timely if our president would do likewise and place a Testament in the hands of conscripted men. Perhaps many would give their lives to Christ and the prayers of faith would save our country from war. It would be a God-honouring thing to do and all Christians would support

you 100% and you would reap eternal reward. I'm a great believer in prayer and in God and hope you are too.

Sincerely in Him,

Mrs. Evelyn Kohlstedt

Ayrshire, Iowa[521]

Strongly endorsed by the chief of chaplains, Kohlstedt's idea was quickly put into effect. On 6 March 1941, only days before the president signed the bill that supplied the army with six hundred new chapels, Roosevelt signed his foreword to what became known as the 'Army Testament':

> To the Members of the Army:
>
> As Commander-in-Chief I take pleasure in commending the reading of the Bible to all who serve in the armed forces of the United States. Throughout the centuries men of many faiths and diverse origins have found in the Sacred Book words of wisdom, counsel, and inspiration. It is a fountain of strength and now, as always, an aid in attaining the highest aspirations of the human soul.
>
> Very sincerely yours,
>
> Franklin D. Roosevelt[522]

On 20 July, and in a press release carried in Sunday papers across America, the War Department formally announced its new policy of providing an 'Army Testament' to all soldiers who desired one.[523] To emphasise the point, each khaki-bound Testament was emblazoned with the inscription 'Presented by the Army of the United States'. Furthermore, and in an NBC *Army Hour* broadcast of May 1942, Arnold presented a suitable Army Testament to three GIs who represented the army's major faith traditions.[524] In June, Arnold sent Marshall a copy of 'each of the three Testaments' and the chief of staff responded by expressing his satisfaction 'that sufficient funds were authorised to make possible the distribution of these Testaments to all soldiers'.[525] By the end of 1943 more than five million copies had been distributed by army chaplains, a number that had climbed to eight million by VJ day.[526] The number of copies actually published was in the region of eleven million.[527]

However, the hasty production and distribution of Army Testaments revealed some underlying tensions in American religious life. First, constitutional considerations meant that they were never issued as official items of army kit or otherwise forced upon individuals. As a report from the Office of the Chief of Chaplains emphasised, restraint and respect for religious freedom was of the essence: 'The portions of Scripture are never distributed by chaplains in a haphazard or purposeless manner. They are discriminately given to interested readers and are kept available for all Army personnel upon request on the basis of one portion to each individual.'[528] Second, their preparation and publishing history reflected the pains that were taken to uphold the balance of the army's Judeo-Christian alliance. In terms of the Protestant New Testament, controversy was minimised by the decision to use the King James Version without annotation. As there was obviously no Jewish equivalent of the New Testament, a selection of readings from the Jewish scriptures was published and issued instead.[529] However, the Catholic New Testament posed much greater problems, with the original edition of daily readings from the New Testament raising objections on the basis of some anti-Semitic annotations (including, for Apocalypse 2:9, 'The Jews are the *synagogue of Satan*. The true synagogue is the Christian church'). Consequently, this had to be withdrawn until a revised version became available, the classic Douai translation of the Gospels being published in its stead.[530]

If the publication and distribution of millions of Army Testaments to individual soldiers was not sufficient, the war years witnessed some further refinements of army policy. In particular, the sensational and much-publicised account of the role played by a pocket New Testament in keeping Captain Eddie Rickenbacker and his fellow survivors of a ditched B-17 alive as they drifted in the Pacific in 1942 led to an almost obsessive interest in stocking lifeboats and life rafts with the word of God as an essential item of equipment. In 1943, it was arranged that every lifeboat on army transports would be supplied with a copy of all three Army Testaments, suitably 'packaged in a waterproof container'. Furthermore, and at the request of 'Hap' Arnold of the AAF, the chief of chaplains also prepared 'three special religious booklets (Protestant, Catholic, and Jewish) for emergency use ... in Air Corps multiman life rafts'. These were part of the enhanced equipment of these rafts and comprised Protestant and Catholic versions of the Gospel of St Matthew and a selection of psalms. Printed on water-resistant paper and protected by 'a metal foil waterproof container', they accompanied such essentials as a whistle, a compass, a mast and a sail. Produced in great quantities, seventy-four thousand surplus copies remained at the end of the war.[531]

As Mrs Kohlstedt had anticipated, these sedulous efforts to supply the Word of God to the army were widely applauded on the home front. Helpfully, 1943 (a year in which almost 1.25 million Army Testaments were published at the request of the chief of chaplains)[532] marked the tercentenary of the publication of Edmund Calamy's *Souldiers Pocket Bible*, an occasion that stirred for many Anglophone Protestants memories of the English Civil War, Cromwell's Ironsides and the Puritan militancy of their forebears. While this theme was popularised through publications and exhibitions on the home front,[533] not everyone was impressed. The War Department's decision to distribute Army Testaments was even denounced in an Italian broadcast from Rome in 1942, which scoffed that:

> We have new proof of American hypocrisy. Their War Department has decided to distribute Bibles to all American soldiers. There will be three editions of this Bible – one for Protestants, one for Catholics, one for Jews.

This foolish attempt to confer dignity on their war is very hypocritical, and it is doomed to failure because it is only the Negroes who read the Bible in the U.S.[534]

In the United States, and faced with what could be considered as yet another infringement of the First Amendment, one secularist society was sufficiently enraged about the Army Testaments to threaten legal action.[535] At the other end of the spectrum, and in response to the changes made to the first Catholic edition of the Army Testament, Elizabeth Dilling, the well-known anti-Semite and self-styled director of the Patriotic Research Bureau, held that Christian scripture was being compromised and hurled anathemas at all involved.[536] For another, more measured, critic of the president it seemed that only Franklin Delano Roosevelt would have the gall to add to Holy Writ. As *The Chaplain* reported in February 1945:

Recently the War Department had 5,883,000 Bibles printed at a cost of $932,000. Each one contains a letter from the President commending the reading of the Bible by the army. This has greatly annoyed Representative Bennett of Missouri, who says that the Bible needs no endorsement from any candidate for public office. To back up his position he quotes Revelation 22:18: 'If any man shall add unto these things, God shall add unto him the plagues that are written in this book.'[537]

Less publicly, though more importantly, a post-war chaplains' report from the ETO disclosed some fundamental flaws in the conception and execution of the Army Testaments initiative. Significantly, it revealed that these scripture portions were more welcome to Protestants than to Catholics or Jews; the latter tended to prefer prayer books, with Catholics (who, according to the 1946 survey *People and Books*, had the largest share of 'non-readers' in any case)[538] prizing missals above all. Furthermore, it revealed why millions of scripture portions seem to have been destroyed or discarded over the course of the war. In terms of the Protestant New Testament, it stressed how it could have been 'made more readable by using modern paragraphing and punctuation, with the verses indicated either in the margin or by exponential figures in the text'. It also conceded that: 'Soldiers almost invariably preferred the Gideon edition, with Psalms, or the American Bible Society edition; both were smaller in size than the government edition, and the typefaces were far clearer and more legible.' Finally, it emphasised that the inferior production standards of the Army Testaments had rendered them unsuitable for prolonged use in the field: 'Chaplains are agreed that the present editions are too large in size, that the print is too small and that the binding is neither adequately flexible nor sufficiently durable.'[539]

Unlike the War Department, the Navy Department never took responsibility for issuing scripture to sailors or marines. In part, this was because there was less pressure to do so; after all, the navy did not have to worry about handling draftees until the end of 1942. The danger of duplication of effort was also evident as the American Bible Society and the Gideons International had been very active in the navy prior to Pearl Harbor. The venerable ABS had been involved in naval work since 1820 and, in 1940–41, it supplied around forty thousand Bibles, New Testaments and scripture portions to the navy.[540] Inspired by their secretary in Honolulu, the Gideons commenced their navy work in 1940 with the goal of supplying 'a white leather Testament to every Navy and marine man'. Again, the prime medium of distribution was the navy chaplain, and such was the instant popularity of their attractive new edition that the Gideons placed an order for half a million copies in the spring of 1941, a special khaki-covered version also being produced for the marines.[541] According to a contemporary advertisement, which urged its readers to 'ARM THEM WITH THE GOSPEL, TOO!', a dollar would buy four service Testaments for the forces and a million copies a year would be needed 'during the present great mobilization'.[542] Although unfunded by government appropriations,[543] the Gideons' editions of the New Testament proved superior to the Army Testaments in many respects. Backed by Workman, they included a message of recommendation by the president which, dated 25 January 1941, was later recycled for use in the Army Testaments. However, they also incorporated the psalms, a selection of hymns, and some suggestions for Bible study.[544] By the end of 1945 the Gideons had supplied more than three million copies of their navy edition of the New Testament, representing almost one-third of the 9.5 million New Testaments that they supplied to the armed forces in the course of the war. These massive donations to the navy were augmented by those of the ABS, which provided a further 1.9 million Bibles, Testaments and scripture portions between 1942 and 1945.[545] As a result of the Rickenbacker phenomenon, the ABS also took responsibility for supplying New Testaments in waterproof containers for the navy's life rafts, eventually providing over fifty-six thousand units.[546] Reviewing the combined efforts of the United War Emergency Bible Program of the American and Massachusetts Bible Societies in March 1945, one navy chaplain noted that their efforts alone had involved 'the raising of $3,000,000 over regular expenses' in the space of only three years.[547] Not only this, but in the course of these prodigious efforts the society had even run short of paper, a 1943 appeal for an extra four hundred tons realising only seventy-one.[548]

Civilian visitors

In supplying chapels and scripture (to say nothing of chaplains and their personal equipment) the American military was clearly guided and driven by the need to allay the religious and moral concerns of civilian society. In tandem with a prevailing concern for the morale of service personnel, this public relations imperative informed its willingness to accommodate and even encourage extensive overseas tours by a variety of high-profile religious visitors representing various endorsing bodies and all three faith traditions.[549] Among Protestant dignitaries, none could match the wartime record of Daniel A. Poling, who represented a valuable link between the armed forces and the home front by virtue of his presidency of the World's Christian Endeavor Union, his editorship of the interdenominational *Christian Herald*, and his 'all-out support' for Roosevelt's foreign policy.[550] A veteran of YMCA work in France in World War I, and a reservist in the army's Corps of Chaplains since 1920, Poling was commissioned by Roosevelt to undertake a goodwill tour of Britain in the spring of 1941 as an antidote to British disenchantment 'with the pacifist and neutralist attitudes' of many American churches and their leaders .[551] In 1943, Poling embarked on a ten-week, morale-boosting tour of the European and North African theatres in the combined capacity of 'an accredited war correspondent', a special representative of the government and as an emissary of the Service Men's Christian League.[552] In a journey of twenty-two thousand miles 'by air and rail and jeep', Poling 'talked and prayed with thousands', held numerous meetings with GIs in 'advanced positions and behind the lines', gave a radio broadcast from Algiers and conferred with Eisenhower on three separate occasions.[553] On his return to the US, Poling was emphatic about the sound moral and spiritual health of the American soldier and of the unprecedented challenge posed to the church in meeting 'the spiritual needs of her sons in the service'.[554] These conclusions were given added weight by the fact that his son, Chaplain Clark V. Poling, had been reported 'lost in action' on the *Dorchester* during the course of his marathon tour.[555] Despite his personal loss, by the end of the year Poling had completed a second tour of American forces overseas, although his widely-reported conclusions after this visit were less sanguine. In fact, Poling's verdict was now reversed: there was a distinct alienation from the churches that did not bode well for the future.[556]

In 1944 Poling resumed his travels by visiting the South-West Pacific, again representing several religious organisations including the FCC, the World's Christian Endeavor Union, and the World Alliance for International Friendship through the Churches. Prompted by an invitation from the Australian churches, Roosevelt was once again keen to give his blessing. In May 1944 the president wrote to Poling in order to stress the importance of cementing Australian–American relations in this fashion and casting Poling as the nation's 'spiritual ambassador of good will'.[557] During his weeks in the Pacific, Poling addressed numerous gatherings of soldiers and sailors and graced the dedication ceremonies of several military chapels. As usual, he was given every facility; at MacArthur's request he was escorted to 'the island fronts' by senior army and navy chaplains and was flown five thousand miles to permit visits to twelve different islands.[558] On his return home, Poling saluted the work of chaplains in this vast theatre of war and claimed to be struck by the prevailing levels of church attendance in the South-West Pacific, levels that he claimed exceeded those of 'all other theatres' on account of the ubiquity of the Japanese.[559] However, Poling again found cause to chastise the home churches, this time on account of their general failure to keep in touch with service personnel.[560] Early in 1945, he embarked on a final, six-week trip to 'the fighting fronts of Europe', this time with the blessing of the chief of chaplains and acting as an accredited war correspondent.[561] However, by this stage the patience of his hosts was wearing thin. George Reuben Metcalf, then assistant army chaplain to the Third Army, wrote to his mother just days before the end of the war in Europe:

> I drove Dr. Poling around the Bastogne battlefield. He is primarily a newspaper man, who is also a clergyman. I had an awful job keeping him from picking up booby-traps and such and he practically carried a whole glider home with him ... he was here in February.[562]

Still, Metcalf seems to have hidden his misgivings fairly well for, in one of his newspaper columns, Poling reported that:

> I had a never-to-be-forgotten day with Chaplain Metcalf when we visited scenes of desperate fighting around and within the 'Bulge'. Among other experiences that he related, he told of how again and again men who had received even a minimum of religious education in their churches and synagogues at home had something with which to meet the battle ordeal that other men did not have.... That should send America back to the Church and to Sunday school classes again; should put a prayer of gratitude upon our lips and fill our hearts with humility and our minds with a new purpose ...[563]

Quite apart from the incidental dangers of souvenir hunting, it must be stressed that these visits were not without risk to those involved, especially given their reliance on aerial transport. Again at Roosevelt's request, and while Poling was engaged in his 1943 tour, Bishop Adna Wright Leonard commenced his own wide-ranging 'tour of inspection' of American troops and Protestant chaplains in Europe and North Africa.[564] Formerly the Methodist bishop of the Washington Area, as chairman of the General Commission on Army and Navy Chaplains, of the National Council of the Service Men's Christian League and of the Methodist Commission on Chaplains, Leonard was triply qualified for his appointed role – and his tour duly commenced in April. Following his arrival in Britain he conducted an open-air service in Hyde Park on Easter Sunday and, after a number of meetings, retreats and inspections in the British Isles, he boarded a plane for Iceland where he died in an air crash on 3 May. Significantly, the roster of Leonard's fellow victims underlines the importance attached to his visit. Besides the two army chaplains assigned to escort him, piloting the aircraft was none other than General Frank M. Andrews, then commander of all American forces in the ETO, whose ill-placed confidence in his ability to fly in all weathers was mainly responsible for the accident.[565] If Leonard was the most senior American ecclesiastic to become a casualty of World War II, his fate did not deter other visitors. Undaunted, Dr William Barrow Pugh, a Presbyterian and Leonard's successor as chairman of the General Commission and of the Service Men's Christian League, swiftly resumed Leonard's itinerary, visiting Britain and North Africa in the summer of 1943 and touring the China–Burma–India theatre in 1944.[566] Again, Pugh was clearly well-qualified for this kind of mission, having served as a chaplain in World War I and being deeply involved in the USO and the wartime work of the Presbyterian Church (USA).[567]

For American Catholics, the war's star tourist was Francis J. Spellman, the diminutive Archbishop of New York who was appointed as military vicar for the United States in December 1939.[568] No doubt because of his frustrated ambition to become a chaplain in World War I,[569] Spellman took to this role with remarkable gusto. Abetted by a new auxiliary bishop of the army and navy (namely John F. O'Hara, formerly the president of Notre Dame University)[570] in the summer of 1942 Spellman embarked on an eighteen-thousand-mile tour of ninety-two military stations in Alaska and the south-west United States.[571] As with Poling and Leonard, Spellman's overseas travels were sponsored by Roosevelt and they began in February 1943, his first tour of twenty-four weeks and forty-six thousand miles embracing 'Europe, Asia, Africa, and South America'.[572] In the course of this sojourn Spellman met Eisenhower, Churchill, de Gaulle, Franco and Eamon de Valera and, even though an enemy alien, was able to visit the Vatican by taking a flight to Italy from neutral Spain.[573] Because his mission was accompanied by so much speculation as to its diplomatic significance,[574] the archbishop's account of his peregrinations took the form of a number of personal letters addressed to his father that dwelt largely on innocuous meetings with the powerful and influential.[575] These were first serialised in *Collier's* and then, in a revised form, published as a book under the title *Action This Day*, a title that Spellman derived from a slip of Churchill's stationery.[576] The archbishop's many encounters with America's soldiers, sailors and airmen led him, despite their subordinate role in his account, to compare them to 'crusaders of old' who had 'gone into battle for the country they love, and for the cause in which they believe'.[577]

Although unable to visit India, China or the Pacific on his original tour,[578] in 1944 Spellman returned to the Mediterranean and to the ETO, once again with Roosevelt's blessing. Here he stumbled across King George VI in Italy and again met with Eisenhower and Pope Pius XII.[579] Significantly, and while visiting Fifth Army headquarters in Italy, he donned 'a GI uniform for his trips around the front' and, as Mark Clark remembered, 'got a big laugh when we would make him stand inspection beside the table before he could eat'.[580] Hosted by J.C.H. Lee in Normandy, and by generals Bradley, Hodges and Patton in north-eastern France, once again Spellman's journeys aroused much speculation as to their purpose; but *No Greater Love*, Spellman's account of this visit, placed a much stronger emphasis on his dealings with ordinary soldiers and sailors, whom he had now elevated to the status of martyrs or prospective martyrs. Significantly, Spellman derived his title from John 15:13 and *No Greater Love* conjured a succession of dramatic hospital visits and field masses for American personnel in Italy, France and inside the German border.[581] In a passage that both reassured and challenged the Catholic faithful at home, Spellman wrote:

> *No one* could witness the devotion of these lads without becoming better. If only their loved ones could kneel in a chapel at twilight and watch them as they tell their beads, or tread wearily the way of the cross! If only they could see their boys as I daily have seen them in the greatest picture of this world's worst war, kneeling in prayer, earnestly asking His guidance and protection! In mud and sand, in heat and cold, in sleet and rain, in many lands, on many battle fronts, I have seen this precious picture of our boys reflected in the cup of my chalice, and I long to print this picture on the hearts and memories of those at home as it is imprinted on mine. Then would they drain themselves of selfishness and bigotry, and emulate our boys in selfless devotion to God and country, so to be worthy of that reflection and of the blood that soaks the earth from end to end![582]

Spellman's third and final major tour of World War II, this time of the Pacific theatre, was anticlimactic by comparison, taking place in 1945 under the shadow of the recent surrender of Japan.[583] Still, Spellman embarked with the usual letters of introduction (this time from President Truman) and arrived at Pearl Harbor to celebrate a number of masses of thanksgiving and to be feted on board the battleship *New York*.[584] From Pearl Harbor Spellman flew to the Marianas and from thence to Iwo Jima and the Philippines, his VJ day Mass of thanksgiving (with 'more than five thousand men and women of the Armed Forces' in attendance) being broadcast from Manila to the United States by short-wave radio.[585] Unable to visit units and bases in northern Luzon, Spellman then made a series of brief visits to Okinawa, Korea and Japan before returning to the US (via China, India, the Middle East and Europe) for the consecration of William R. Arnold as Auxiliary Bishop of the Army and Navy.[586] As if underlining the constant dangers of aerial travel, on the lengthy return leg of this tour Spellman's plane was feared lost over central China and he began his transatlantic flight from the Azores 'in weather that was not considered safe' for a certain distinguished general.[587] However, and although Spellman's published accounts of these tours made light of these risks and much of religious tolerance, inter-Allied cooperation and his links with Roosevelt, it would appear that Spellman allowed his mask to slip while staying up late with Patton at Third Army headquarters in 1944. According to Spellman, who was already beginning to feel an encroaching mistrust of Roosevelt's foreign policy,[588] the general was 'frank and outspoken even on first acquaintance, and frankness is a most engaging quality'.[589] However, and with the candour that Spellman so admired, Patton perceived that his visitor was 'a very clever little Irishman' who was congenially 'anti-Roosevelt, anti-CIO, anti-Negro, Jew, and English', in other words 'quite a man'.[590]

A fourth ecclesiastical figure to tour the battlefronts at Roosevelt's behest in 1943 was Bishop John A. Gregg of the African Methodist Episcopal Church, a veteran of the Spanish–American War who was already known as 'the flying Bishop' on account of his early enthusiasm for air travel.[591] Accompanied by Chaplain J.A. DeVeaux, formerly the division chaplain of the 93rd Infantry Division and the army's senior African American chaplain,[592] Gregg travelled as a representative of the Fraternal Council of Negro Churches, a body that represented '40,000 churches and six million members', and with the crucial support of the president, George C. Marshall and Eleanor Roosevelt.[593] Punctuated by a brief return to the United States in the autumn of 1943 and concluded by a personal visit to South Africa early the following year, Gregg's 'Missionary Journey' took him nearly seventy thousand miles 'by air alone, besides some 12 or 15 thousand miles by train and automobile'.[594] At the conclusion of his odyssey, Gregg had covered the South and South-West Pacific, Britain, North Africa, Italy, the Middle East, India and West Africa. The bishop's wide-ranging visits and verbal message of goodwill from home were no doubt especially important for black GIs, given the lack of black chaplains, the comparative religiosity of African American troops, their many grievances in a segregated army and the high levels of functional illiteracy among them. Furthermore, and though he disowned any idea that he was engaged in a tour of inspection, Gregg was careful to raise any complaints that reached his ears with local commanding officers, usually at their invitation.[595] Courteously received by MacArthur, Nimitz and J.C.H. Lee, who even gave the bishop the use of his sumptuous personal train while en route from Scotland to London,[596] Gregg described his approach to black GIs 'outside of the few religious services held on Sundays' in the following terms:

> I told them I was sent out under orders of President Roosevelt and General Marshall of the War Department, as a representative of the Fraternal Council of Negro Churches [and] General W.H. [sic] Arnold, Chief of Chaplains. I would then check as to their home cities, states and their church membership. I informed them that I bore messages of cheer and good will from those dignitaries, as well as from their fathers, mothers, wives, brothers, sisters and sweethearts at home. Knowing America very well, I was able to mention some persons or streets, or some special interest in almost every place mentioned, which brought visions of home to them in those far away lands.[597]

According to Gregg, his methods invariably met with a warm response: 'On many occasions I have shaken hands until it seemed that my arms would drop off, as they surged forward for our autographs, or to slip into our hands, an address of the home folk asking that we urge them to write more often.'[598] This positive image was confirmed by an Australian war correspondent, Frederick Rainsford Peterson, who wrote of the bishop in New Guinea: 'This is no "kid glove" tour that the Bishop is taking. He is getting in where the men are. He has been seen clambering up on to the top of revetments and chatting to negro workers on their bulldozers.'[599] Inevitably, the question of the war and its relationship to the burning issue of civil rights was never far away and, as Gregg insisted:

> [A]lmost without exception, those men showed themselves to be real soldiers, saying they would stick it out in spite of homesickness and hardships, to win for their loved ones enjoyment of the Four Freedoms and the assurance of a better day, tomorrow. That same spirit I found among our forces wherever I went, around the world, for Negro soldiers are everywhere and they are doing a commendable work of which we may justly be proud. It is comforting to believe that such sacrificing services cannot go unrewarded; and the law of compensation, assures that though hindered and hampered, their service will yet be paid off in good dividends.[600]

Despite the delicacy of his mission, the verdict among senior chaplains was that Gregg had made his intended 'contribution towards welding into a greater solidarity and unity the efforts and aspirations of the Negro citizenry with those of the rest of the nation.'[601] In February 1944, Edward L. Trett, the senior chaplain in the China–Burma–India theatre, reported to Arnold:

> The Bishop and Chaplain DeVeaux conducted themselves with splendid dignity and decorum upon all occasions ... they visited all of the colored troops in major units and several of the units of company size or even smaller. The Bishop had served in all parts of the States and always was able to put his finger on a few spots familiar to some men in each assembly.... He demonstrated splendid friendliness and a fine sense of humor.... They both pointed out that colored people in the Army and in civilian life in the United States now have the best opportunity ever afforded them to integrate themselves favourably in the national life of the country and in the country's industries; to acquire financial competence and recognition upon which to base a heightened self-respect.... These visitors had no personal axes to grind, no chip on their shoulders, and no desire to serve as rabble rousers. They addressed themselves to the task of inspiring the men to be good citizens, understand the causes for which we serve and fight, and to do an outstanding fine job in their individual service.[602]

A 1946 report on army chaplaincy in the Pacific held a similar view. This confirmed the importance of tours by 'clergymen and church representatives from the United States'[603] as a means of informing and inspiring the home and fighting fronts and stated that: 'The decision of the President to send Bishop

John Andrew Gregg on a good will mission among negro troops in the Pacific was a wise one. The men were proud of this outstanding religious leader among their people.'[604]

With these successful precedents set, the war's first 'Jewish Presidential Religious Mission' was undertaken in 1943–44 by Barnett R. Brickner, a prominent Reform rabbi from Cleveland, Ohio, and the chairman of the Jewish Welfare Board's Committee on Army and Navy Religious Activities (CANRA).[605] Such a visit was timely for another reason, as in October 1943 Moritz Gottlieb, a special commissioner for the Jewish Welfare Board (JWB), had been dispatched to the South-West Pacific in order to sort out the administrative mess that had resulted from the JWB's decision to appoint and fund a local rabbi as its agent in Australia.[606] In yet another gruelling tour, this time of forty-five thousand air miles in the company of the senior Jewish chaplain Aryeh Lev, Brickner visited Britain, Italy, the Middle East and the China–Burma–India theatre.[607] Although he was keen to accentuate the positive in public ('Our fighting men are definitely more tolerant, racially and religiously, than people at home', Brickner told the *Boston Globe*),[608] behind the scenes he was much less sanguine, and much of his tour was concerned with identifying and addressing the religious needs of Jewish personnel in consultation with commanding officers.[609] For example, after his tour of Britain, and at the behest of J.C.H. Lee, Brickner submitted a report in February 1944 that recommended more Jewish chaplains be 'requisitioned', that Jewish chaplains be assured 'proper transportation', and which complained about the lack of Jewish chaplains at senior levels:

> This is the only Theater in which a Jewish Chaplain is not represented on the staff of a higher echelon so as to act as coordinator and advisor on Jewish matters. Jewish Chaplains in such echelons can do the regular administrative functions as well as any other chaplain, and at the same time conduct religious services for Jewish men in their area.[610]

According to Roy J. Honeywell, the original plans for these overseas visits involved only 'representatives of the three major faiths and of the Negro churches', but greater resources and the success of the overseas visits of Poling, Pugh, Spellman, Gregg and Brickner in 1943–44 bred 'a more liberal policy', which ensured that a steady stream of high-profile ecclesiastics visited the armed forces overseas, even after the end of hostilities.[611] In the autumn of 1944, for example, the Jewish Welfare Board sent another mission to the Pacific at the request of the War Department, during which Rabbi Philip S. Bernstein (another chairman of CANRA, who was again accompanied by Chaplain Lev) was able to express the gratitude felt by American Jews towards their Australian co-religionists 'for their magnificent efforts on behalf of the American troops' and, more importantly, to address problems of Jewish chaplains' numbers and coverage that were even more acute than in the ETO.[612] A subsequent visitor to the South-West Pacific in the autumn of 1945 was Dr W.H. Jernagin, a senior Baptist churchman and the president of the Fraternal Council of Negro Churches in America who, as a younger minister, had preached to black troops in France during World War I.[613] While Jernagin 'formulated a number of specific suggestions which he proposed to make to the War Department', and discussed the problems of black troops in a meeting with MacArthur,[614] his meetings with more than twenty thousand African American soldiers were distinctly evangelistic in tone. His visit to the 93rd Infantry Division in the Philippines, for example, resulted in 243 conversions while, at a crowded meeting for African American troops in the Manila area, '316 came to the platform to shake Dr. Jernagin's hand and signify their desire to live more completely for God'.[615] All of these experiences convinced Jernagin that, 'the Gospel of Jesus Christ is the greatest need of men in all and any situation' and that this had been 'evidenced by the hunger and eagerness of the men in the Armed Forces who heard and accepted the Gospel'. Nevertheless, his tour produced some pointed criticisms as well. In purely religious terms: 'It was regrettable to note that the Negro Churches failed to supply Chaplains in sufficient numbers to meet the need, and this deficiency had to be supplied by men of other races not always sympathetic to the needs of the Negro troops to which they had been assigned.' Conversations with chaplains had proved that 'some Commanding Officers were not interested in the religious welfare of their command' while, despite some 'unusually efficient white Chaplains', it was abundantly clear 'that Negro Chaplains are more effective with Negro troops'.[616] As a result of an incident on Guam, Jernagin even called for the transfer of the white chaplain of the 1868th Engineer Aviation Battalion, who had favoured the withdrawal of all twenty thousand African American troops on the island after two of their number had been killed near a Chamorro settlement 'supposedly attempting rape'. As Jernagin put it: 'I feel that a man with his spirit is not suitable to serve Negro troops or able to represent the spirit of Christ in his ministry to them.'[617]

Although the origins, emphases and findings of Jernagin's mission were different from that of Gregg's (Jernagin travelled at the request of the General Commission on Army and Navy Chaplains rather than that of President Truman), in the short term his tour was still judged by senior chaplains to have been a success and, in particular, as having been 'of great value in boosting the morale of the colored troops'.[618] Significantly, chaplains in the ETO came to a similar conclusion about the numerous visits they had received and facilitated, not only from Poling, Spellman, Gregg and Brickner but also from Henry K. Sherrill and Henry W. Hobson, Protestant Episcopal bishops who also represented the General Commission on Army and Navy Chaplains, and Bishop G. Bromley Oxnam, who represented the Methodist Church.[619] According to a post-war report on army chaplaincy in the ETO, the purpose of these visits had been:

[T]o establish personal liaison between the chaplains and their respective denominations, to express to the church-affiliated personnel of the theater the interest of the civilian churches on the home front, and to report both to the President and to their respective religious bodies on the state of religion and morals in the army.[620]

While the report conceded that these visits had probably been most successful in terms of public relations, with visitors taking back to the United States 'a very considerable quantity of reassuring information about the work of chaplains and the state of morals and religion in the Army', in terms of their direct 'benefit to the service' a sample of chaplains found that only 9 per cent felt they had no value, 10 per cent had no opinion and 39 per cent 'felt that the tours had some value', while 31 per cent 'regarded them as exceedingly valuable'.[621] Given the great preponderance of favourable wartime opinion, such visits continued to be a feature of service life in the immediate post-war period, with *The Chaplain* announcing a slew of impending ecclesiastical visitors in September 1945:

By invitation of the Secretary of War and the Secretary of the Navy, the following church leaders, chosen by the General Commission on Army and Navy Chaplains, will visit various theatres of operations: Bishop Edwin F. Lee, director of the General Commission will tour the South-West Pacific; Dr. Dan T. Caldwell, director of the Defense Service Council of the Presbyterian Church, U.S., will go to the India–Burma Theater; and Dr. Alfred C. Carpenter, superintendent of camp work for the Home Mission Board of the Southern Baptist Convention, will visit the China Area. Dr. William Barrow Pugh, stated clerk of the Presbyterian Church, U.S.A., and former chairman of the General Commission ... is now en route to the Pacific Ocean Area.[622]

Auxiliary chaplains

The usefulness of civilian clergymen in direct support of military chaplaincy was not confined to the visitations of high-level ecclesiastics, however. Despite William Arnold's determination to resist the encroachment of civilians and to maintain the ascendancy of army chaplains in army ministry, practical factors could conspire to frustrate this goal. If GIs were free, when circumstances allowed, to worship where they pleased, in some cases the use of recognised civilian clergymen was unavoidable. In the China–Burma–India theatre, for example, which was 'low in shipping priority and at the far end of the "world's longest supply route"',[623] there could be no option but to harness whatever clergy were locally available. As one account of chaplaincy in this theatre conceded:

In sparsely-settled areas in India, several American missionaries – stationed there before the war – have been added as contract chaplains. They wear the American uniform without insignia, but their help in taking care of the religious needs of men thousands of miles from home is welcomed and praised by the hard-working 'regular chaplains'.[624]

If the celebrated William T. Cummings – of 'no atheists in a foxhole' fame – was a Maryknoll missionary who played an equivalent role in the defence of the Philippines,[625] during the Allied defence of Burma in 1942 the hard-pressed airmen of the American Volunteer Group were served by an American clergyman, Paul Frillman, who was formerly a Lutheran missionary to China.[626]

If a Catholic army chaplain acknowledged in 1944 that, 'For over a year the Catholics of the [AAF in Central Africa] were cared for only by missionaries',[627] a chronic shortage of Catholic chaplains throughout the war ensured that this expedient was not confined to overseas mission territories; in fact, 'The Catholics made more use of civilian clergy to supplement the work of chaplains than almost any other church'.[628] In October 1942, Bishop John F. O'Hara noted that the Military Ordinariate was already reliant on 'more than three hundred auxiliary chaplains, to supply for non-existent commissioned chaplains'. Formally recommended and duly recognised by the chief of chaplains, these civilian priests (who were either infirm or otherwise prevented from joining the armed forces) ministered to service personnel on a part-time basis and usually without remuneration.[629] Catholic reliance on part-time chaplaincy grew in the course of the war; by the end of the conflict the army had been served by more than 2,000 priests acting in an auxiliary capacity in addition to nearly 3,300 commissioned Catholic chaplains.[630] However, the extent of such dependence was not without parallel in other traditions; in 1942, for example, a number of civilian rabbis 'volunteered to serve in various camps during the summer months, foregoing their vacations'.[631] If the number of civilian clergymen sent from America to the ETO to 'supplement the ministrations of chaplains' was very small, a JWB representative was always in theatre; Mormon and Seventh-Day Adventist field representatives 'worked very closely with the chaplains' in England; and, following the liberation of Paris, a handful of Episcopalian, Methodist and Baptist clergymen established themselves in the French capital.[632] Still, and notwithstanding their significant role in carrying the pastoral burden of the war, it was not until the end of 1945 that the War Department formally recognised the office of the paid auxiliary chaplain. As *The Chaplain* put it: 'The employment, from appropriated funds, of civilian clergymen as auxiliary chaplains has been authorized by the War Department, subject to certain conditions. Serving under commissioned Army chaplains, their duties will be of a purely religious nature and none will be employed on a full-time basis'.[633] Whatever else, and as William Arnold always intended, there had been no return to the encroachments of the 'camp pastor' and the pastoral free-for-all of World War I.

Religious welfare agencies

The dominance of the military chaplain was also maintained in relation to the challenge posed by the United Service Organizations (USO). Whereas many religious welfare agencies had operated in competition with chaplains and with each other in World War I, such wastefulness and tension was largely averted by the results of a meeting that was held in New York City shortly after the passing of the Selective Training and Service Act. Convened by Frank Weil of the Jewish Welfare Board, this meeting produced a formal alliance between six of America's leading welfare agencies – namely the YMCA, the YWCA, the Salvation Army, the National Catholic Community Service, the Jewish Welfare Board and the more secular National Travelers Aid Association. Initially dubbed the United Service Organizations for National Defense, the relationship between the USO and the military was thrashed out at a conference in Washington in January 1941.[634] Significantly, in an NBC broadcast only a few weeks earlier, Marshall had issued a summons to national organisations and communities across the country to join with the War Department and 'assist these young men to lead clean, sound lives while they wear the uniform of their country'.[635] Chaired by President Roosevelt and attended by both Marshall and Nimitz, at this founding meeting it was agreed that the affiliates of the USO should provide recreation for service personnel in civilian areas, that their centres should do this under a common name, and that the government would provide premises where needed.[636] Formally incorporated in February 1941, USO centres proliferated thereafter. Although the first of 332 government-built centres was not opened until the end of November 1941,[637] the delay proving a source of embarrassment and frustration for Roosevelt and the Secretary of War,[638] by March 1942, 570 centres were active in 257 communities across forty-three states. Opened at a rate of more than four per day throughout 1943, at their wartime peak in March 1944 more than three thousand USO centres were in operation, their efforts supported over the course of the war by more than a million civilian volunteers and by public donations totalling more than $200 million.[639] After Pearl Harbor, the USO extended its operations to include work in military hospitals, the provision of mobile units for isolated posts, and to meet the needs of migrant defence workers. Although the size and character of individual centres could vary according to local requirements, the demands of segregation, and the agencies responsible for them, USO centres for service personnel typically provided food, non-alcoholic drinks, a recreation lounge and personal assistance in the form of cleaning, sewing and information. A particular attraction of their wholesome, homelike atmosphere was their supporting army of approved hostesses – local volunteers who provided female conversation, company and dance partners, and who could be briefed in their work by military chaplains.[640] As its first honorary chairman, President Roosevelt was especially pleased by the unity of national and religious effort symbolised by the USO, crowing in 1942 that: 'This is more than we were able to do during the last war. All agencies under one tent. This is a fine job!'[641]

If somewhat eclipsed by the secular functions of its centres, and by the fame of its much-lauded Camp Shows division, a major facet of USO activity was its religious work. In fact, in its constitution and by-laws the USO saw itself as serving 'the religious, spiritual, welfare, and educational needs' of the armed forces – in that order.[642] According to the 1944 edition of *The Chaplain*, a clear division of labour existed between the army chaplain and the USO in this respect: 'the United Service Organizations set up their program in 1941 in communities adjacent to the camps and in the centers where service personnel were likely to congregate in considerable numbers, and the chaplains were made responsible for all religious activities in the camps.'[643] While many USO centres were located on church premises (the National Catholic Community Center Building in New York, for example, was home to a USO centre that eventually served 'well over two million men'),[644] civilian clergymen were also on hand at USO centres in order to help service men and women with their personal problems. Not only that, but as an article entitled 'Religion and the USO' explained: 'Besides the person-to-person contacts with ministers provided by many USO centers as part of their service to service men, regular services and vesper meetings are held, and in some there are Bible classes as well.' Significantly, William R. Arnold even conceded that: 'There are many civilian clergymen who for one reason or another cannot become Army chaplains. I try to show them that they have equal opportunities to serve the Army through [the] USO.'[645]

Undoubtedly, this aspect of the USO's work was a major component of its public appeal. In Julia M.H. Carson's lightly fictionalised survey of USO work, *Home Away from Home: The Story of the USO* (1946), the official historian of the USO was at pains to emphasise the religious value of its activities. Religious work was, she claimed, 'part of the total USO fabric', and included close liaison with military chaplains, the distribution of religious literature and, courtesy of its camp shows entertainers, even hymn-singing and similar support for religious services.[646] However, proselytising was eschewed on USO premises, their prime religious purpose being 'to insure American servicemen and women the fullest possible opportunity to worship in accordance with their individual beliefs.'[647] Inevitably, and as in military chaplaincy, this insistence on inclusivity created problems of its own. While religious zealots of all persuasions could dismiss the religion of the USO as shallow and tepid, even when centres were run by a single religious agency (as opposed to a multi-agency endeavour or a 'community conducted' enterprise) their exterior signage carried only the logo of the USO and their religious iconography – whether 'the star of David, or a Crucifix, or a picture of Christ' – was confined to their office spaces.[648] Nevertheless, within these self-imposed limits, the efforts of the USO were remarkable. As

USO centres operated only in the United States and in 'non-combat zones in the Atlantic and Pacific areas', with the addition of the Philippines after their liberation,[649] in 1943 the USO began the mass distribution of devotional kits to service personnel 'at ports of embarkation'.[650] Produced by the YMCA and the Salvation Army, the USO's *Kit of Religious Materials for a Protestant Service Man* came in a special envelope and comprised 'pocket-size books of devotional readings, stimulating essays on the technique of maintaining Christian faith, and favourite hymns' together with 'a bright little volume entitled, *A Spiritual Almanac for Service Men*', which was published by the Christian Commission for Camp and Defense Communities.[651] Eventually, the USO even placed an order for a million miniaturised copies of *The Link* magazine.[652] Given its modus operandi, there were equivalent devotional kits for Catholics and Jews, while the USO also 'made available for Catholic servicemen some two million rosaries and for Jewish military personnel such basic items as prayer books, mezuzahs, and phonographic recordings of Jewish liturgical music'.[653] According to one report, as early as May 1943 the religious efforts of the USO were already making an impression on the armed forces:

> Distribution of religious material to service men at USO centers in the U.S. has shown a recent increase of 46 per cent. Thus the service organization is keeping pace with the mounting interest in religion which has been noted everywhere by observers. According to the USO, in one month alone, a total of 294,455 service men received religious literature which is given out only upon request. The USO also reports 3,107 religious sessions held in one month in U.S. clubhouses, attended by 315,363 men. Overseas, a like proportion attended USO services.[654]

In 1944, religious activities on USO premises attracted a total attendance of 4.7 million and, in the three-year period 1943–45, the USO distributed twenty-seven million religious items.[655]

However, the religious efforts of the USO were not without complications of another kind. As we shall see in Chapter Six, the contents of its camp shows proved to be a recurring source of friction with army chaplains. If it was not sufficient embarrassment for a religious organisation to be identified as a purveyor of smut to the military, in the sexually charged atmosphere of wartime the wholesale mingling of the sexes (however closely supervised) in USO centres was another hostage to fortune. As early as February 1942, the cover of the *Saturday Evening Post* carried Norman Rockwell's tribute to the USO – a delighted GI sandwiched between a pair of mature and glamorous hostesses.[656] Significantly, attractive hostesses did become the objects of male interest and fantasy. Decades after the war, Samuel Hynes, a Marine Corps pilot, still remembered the friendly, nineteen-year old receptionist at a USO in Laguna Beach, albeit in largely sexual terms.[657] Similarly, while in training at Camp Swift, Texas, John T. Bassett of the

10th Mountain Division developed a secret infatuation with a married hostess.[658] While this was hardly the purpose for which hostesses were enlisted, the USO's large-scale recruitment of respectable young women for dances at USO centres was open to question as it 'inherently bore some resemblance to procurement of girls for less honorable activity'.[659] Indeed, some Protestant churches still viewed dancing to be sinful and, given 'the sexual implications and physically liberating qualities of dance', the Salvation Army in particular sought to promote other recreations in its own USO venues.[660] Finally, and even taking into account the USO's policy of not holding religious meetings 'where other facilities – such as churches, town halls and so forth – were available',[661] there can be little doubt that its religious programme was a minority interest, accounting for only 5 per cent of attendances in the United States in 1944 and only 1.9 per cent overseas (in marked contrast, dances accounted for 42.9 per cent and 28.9 per cent respectively).[662]

The massive, government-sponsored efforts of the USO were also heavily supplemented by a host of denominational initiatives at a national and local level. At their wartime peak, for example, 107 Christian Science study rooms were open in various military stations. Emblematic of a benign breach of the rules against providing civilian groups with military accommodation, one Christian Science source deduced that: 'The fact that one was allowed at all within the limits of a camp was proof of the favorable recognition Christian Science activities had already gained there through their practical results'.[663] To augment these 'sanctuaries' for service personnel, Christian Science 'Service Centers' also sprang up in cities and towns across the United States, the British Isles and as far afield as 'North Africa, the Middle East, India, and Burma'.[664] With characteristic diligence, a vast quantity of Christian Science literature was distributed by the Camp Welfare Office of The Mother Church in Boston:

> Copies of [*The Christian Science Monitor*] were made available to servicemen in the United States through gift subscriptions to chaplains of all denominations, camp libraries, hospital wards, day-rooms, officers' clubs, USO clubs, Masonic service centers, Red Cross buildings, Salvation Army rooms and similar places. All Army and Navy posts, Marine bases, Coast Guard units, and ports of embarkation were included in this distribution. In many cases, the *Sentinel* and *Journal* were also accepted.... Hundreds of ships received subscriptions to the periodicals. When the ship's chaplain consented, sets of Mrs. Eddy's writings, with her biography and a Bible, were placed in the library.[665]

On a more personal level, it was reported that, 'Vest-pocket copies of the Bible and Science and Health, called service sets ... were given to every man or woman in the armed forces requesting them'; in total, fifty thousand were distributed at a cost of $250,000.[666]

Despite this competition, American Lutherans seem to have set the standard in denominational work, being applauded by *The Chaplain* magazine in October 1944 for leading 'the procession in the efficiency with which they have carried the influence of their churches to their sons and daughters in uniform'.[667] That month, *The Link* magazine marvelled at the resourcefulness of the Missouri Synod alone in keeping 'in touch with its service men, assigned all over the globe':

> Appreciative service men and women tell church leaders that they follow their members, wherever they are, 'with all the thoroughness of the FBI'. There are more than 100,000 names on the master list. A thousand letters and cards come in each day at the synod office on LaSalle Street, Chicago. Many of these represent 'one more change of address'. Forty-five full-time workers and an equal force of part-timers equip the newly enrolled Lutheran service man with prayer-book, Lutheran identification tag, and a list of 727 key pastors in [the United States] and ten other countries. Each month a news leaflet, *At Ease*, follows the uniformed men and women to their places of service, and there are also monthly bulletins to aid and inspire daily personal worship.[668]

Together with the Service Commission of the National Lutheran Council (which represented no fewer than eight Lutheran bodies), the Army and Navy Commission of the Missouri Synod also devoted a large part of its resources to the creation of eighty-four Lutheran Service Centres at home and abroad.[669] While some were part-time centres maintained by local parishes, the majority were full-time facilities staffed by a pair of dedicated 'service pastors' (representing both parties to this Lutheran partnership) and, where necessary, by an additional 'hostess-secretary'. Similar to USO centres in terms of their homelike character and their reliance on a supporting body of volunteer hostesses, the religious emphasis in Lutheran Service Centres was much more pronounced:

> The typical Service Center contained a lounge, reading and writing rooms, game room, rest rooms, canteen – and the chapel, which was considered the 'heart' of the Center. In the chapel the service pastor conducted general and private worship services, performed weddings and baptisms, administered Holy Communion, led Bible discussions, and otherwise carried out the spiritual ministrations which he was called upon to perform.[670]

As a vital facet of Lutheran ministry to the armed forces, hundreds of thousands of pastoral interviews took place in these centres and they also served as distribution points for millions of Lutheran publications.[671] Nevertheless, even in such a denominational setting the devotional side of their work struggled to play more than a marginal role. Between 1941 and their termination in 1949, a total of 12,255,204 attendances were recorded at Lutheran Service Centers; however, only 624,989 attendances at worship and fewer than 60,000 communicants were registered.[672] This disparity was conspicuous even in the showcase Lutheran Service Centre that was the King George Hotel in San Francisco. Hosting nearly 1.5 million visitors over a period of five years, its patrons represented no fewer than forty-nine denominations, with the number of Lutherans and Catholics roughly equal. Furthermore, though it exercised a 'ministry of supply', and served as 'a supply station for port of embarkation chaplains', fewer than eighty thousand pamphlets, prayer books, testaments and Bibles were taken by its visitors.[673]

There was, however, almost no limit to the number or ingenuity of those pious civilians who sought to give spiritual and moral succour to the armed forces. According to the Church Peace Union, by March 1945 no fewer than sixty-six church agencies were directly 'engaged in furnishing religious supplies to chaplains'.[674] Mindful of the pandemics of vice and homesickness afflicting service personnel, by 1943 a host of 'Mothers by Proxy' had appeared 'in towns from coast to coast', their homes thrown open in emulation of a scheme pioneered by a Lutheran minister in Monroe, North Carolina.[675] Local churches often ran special hospitality,[676] prayer,[677] and correspondence programmes,[678] while some local draft boards were thoughtful enough to hand a Bible to each departing draftee.[679] In a similar vein, the First Presbyterian Church of Greensboro, North Carolina, sent a copy of Lloyd Douglas's bestselling novel *The Robe* (also an Armed Services Edition) to each of its members in the armed forces, and: 'With each copy went a special message from the author, who was so pleased with the project that he contributed $100'.[680] Finally, and in a multimedia age where recorded messages were commonly sent by service personnel to loved ones at home, churches could reciprocate by sending recordings of familiar Sunday services to their members in the forces.[681]

The religious military press

Despite the heavy use of newer media, the war years also witnessed a massive and vigorous resurgence of what Kurt O. Berends usefully dubbed 'the religious military press'.[682] Given the disruption and displacement of the war years, and the place of reading as an individual activity, religious books and magazines had an inherent capacity 'to minister across the miles', being 'perfectly suited for a transient population disrupted by war'.[683] Consequently, and as Chaplain Ellwood C. Nance observed in 1944 in *Faith of Our Fighters*:

> With few exceptions every denomination in America is spending large sums of money on special publications for men in service.... At the Army Chaplain School library there are approximately five hundred different sample copies of religious tracts, magazines, and other publications which are available to chaplains and the servicemen. The quality of subject matter in many of these is excellent.[684]

From a chaplaincy perspective, this verdict was borne out by a post-war report from the ETO that noted how little religious rancour had been caused despite the enormous range and diversity of suppliers:

> It speaks well both for the churches and for the chaplains that with all the tracts and publications that were distributed exceedingly little offense was given or taken. 83% of the chaplains declared that they were aware of no instances in their experience where offensive literature was distributed, while in the remaining 17% the instances recalled were isolated and exceptional. In several of these latter cases the offenders were not chaplains but overly zealous lay missionaries of their respective faiths. 4% reported instances where objectionable tracts had been received but not distributed.[685]

The originators of this literature ranged from the Chaplains' Association of the Army of the United States to private individuals. At its national convention in May 1940, the former approved a new *Song and Service Book for Ship and Field*, which comprised orders for Protestant, Catholic and Jewish services and a selection of more than 160 hymns.[686] Bound in red and navy blue for the army and navy respectively, this semi-official volume was endorsed by both chiefs of chaplains and, when its original publisher, A.S. Barnes & Co. of New York, proved unable to meet demand in 1942, its production was transferred to the Government Printing Office in Washington.[687] A firm favourite among American Protestants was the khaki-coloured, vinyl-bound *Strength for Service to God and Country* (1942), a compilation of suggestions for daily scripture reading and devotions edited by Norman E. Nygaard, a veteran of World War I and a civilian Presbyterian (USA) chaplain to 'the Lockheed Overseas Corporation, a civilian unit of airplane mechanics and engineers attached to the United States Army.'[688] Featuring contributions by Daniel A. Poling and other eminent churchmen, *Strength for Service to God and Country* was the 'single best-selling inspirational book of the war' with sales easily exceeding a million.[689] In denominational terms, Catholic publications included *My Military Missal*, *Letters to Service Women*, Fulton Sheen's *Shield of Faith* and *Contact*, the latter a series of devotional pamphlets whose monthly circulation rose from five hundred to forty thousand in 1943–44.[690] No less mindful of the edifying power of religious literature, in 1944 the Commission on Evangelism of the Methodist Church allotted $50,000 to the task of supplying extra copies of the Methodist devotional magazine *The Upper Room* (whose circulation then stood at three million) to the armed forces.[691] Nevertheless, such publications represented only a minuscule proportion of the titles available. Besides the inevitable swathe of denominational prayer books there were, for example, the interfaith *Soldiers' and Sailors' Prayer Book* of 1944, to which so many of America's top commanders contributed; Willard L. Sperry's *Prayers for Private Devotions in War-Time* (given 'to each of the successive groups of Chaplains going through the Unites States Army Chaplain School at Harvard');[692] Daniel A. Lord's *A Salute to the Men In Service* (a booklet written for the National Catholic Community Service that urged its readers to 'Fight bravely and live splendidly');[693] G.A. Cleveland Shrigley's *Prayers for Women Who Serve* (prepared for the YWCA and likewise distributed through the wider network of the USO)[694] and Alva J. Brasted's *Az You Were!* (an A to Z, illustrated guide to Christian manners and patriotic virtue written by a former army chief of chaplains).[695] If, in 1943, Harry Emerson Fosdick's *On Being a Real Person* met with an eager reception among some military readers after its selection as an Armed Services Edition by the Council of Books in Wartime,[696] from the opposite end of the theological spectrum the fundamentalist Moody Bible Institute offered its own unambiguous view of the Christian life through pamphlets such as *It Happened This Way!*, a letter from a converted soldier that began:

> Dear Mom and Dad:
> I'm saved!
> Last night, after days of anxious searching for the way of salvation, I found it! I just simply accepted Jesus as my Saviour and entrusted my whole life and self to Him. Praise His blessed name!
> This is how it happened …[697]

For their part, the parents of Sergeant George Bowler Tullidge III, who was killed in action in Normandy on 8 June 1944 while serving with the 507th Parachute Infantry Regiment, sought to promote a spirit of piety and virtue among his comrades by publishing his religious reflections on a number of 'poems, excerpts, and Bible verses' in a pamphlet entitled *A Paratrooper's Faith*, trusting 'that other boys who read it may receive an inspiration and help from these thoughts of great minds and souls of the past and present'.[698]

If all of this was emblematic of the remarkable zeal and ingenuity of the faithful, this welter of diverse and well-intentioned efforts could, on occasion, backfire. Ernie Pyle wrote of an incident in North Africa:

> One fellow I know got two letters – one a notification that a friend had subscribed to the Reader's Digest for him, which he already knew, and the other a mimeographed letter which his wife had sent him, about some church festival. He had received no personal letter from her in weeks. The recipient used very unchurchly language when he told about it.[699]

Similarly, Russell Baldwin, a medic with the engineers of the 551st Heavy Pontoon Battalion, received just one present at Christmas 1944 – 'a box of chocolates from the East Shore Methodist Church' in Euclid, Ohio. However, the gift rather dampened his spirits as 'they were so mouldy we couldn't eat them. They'd been in transit a long time, I guess'.[700] Besides placing an undue strain on military postal systems, the indiscriminate goodwill of pious civilians could even antagonise some of its recipients. In January 1944, *Yank* published a joint letter from eight sergeants stationed in Britain who complained that 40 per cent of the mail they received consisted of unsolicited cards:

> Victory cards, soldier cards, aviation cards, birthday cards, 'Cheer up buddy' cards, 'We miss you' cards, 'My Son, My Son' cards, 'God have mercy on you' cards and so on, ad nauseam.... I haven't the heart to attach any specimens. I know you, too, have been subject to this barrage of waste paper.[701]

More troubling still to the military authorities was the fear that the activities of minor religious agencies could be used as a cover for espionage. In June 1942, the German-American editor of the *Human Relations Brief* approached the Office of the Chief of Chaplains for a complete mailing list of army chaplains in the United States in order to 'aid us in our effort to be of service to our Lord and to our country'. In response, he was reminded that 'the giving out of lists of camps and chaplains is strictly forbidden as one of the necessary safeguards of military information'.[702]

Chaplains were, of course, the main conduits of this enormous outpouring of religious largesse. By March 1946, the National Catholic Community Service had obtained and distributed more than 42.5 million 'items of religious material', including nearly 4.5 million rosaries, about the same number of miraculous medals, nearly 900,000 'holy cards', and almost 25 million missals, prayer books, leaflets and booklets. Of these, 20 per cent had been distributed via the USO, but 71 per cent had passed through the hands of chaplains – mostly overseas (29 per cent) or at ports of embarkation (23 per cent).[703] By 1942, the American Bible Society was working flat out to keep chaplains supplied with scripture; in that year well over 2.5 million New Testaments 'were ordered by the Society for free distribution to chaplains' and, on certain days, 'there were nine thousand or more copies issued, boxed, and shipped direct to the chaplains as soon as they were bound'.[704] Some distribution methods could be unorthodox. On British Samoa in 1942, Hansel H. Tower was obliged to drop consignments of literature (including Bibles, Testaments and a range of religious magazines) to isolated outposts by plane, becoming 'a fairly accurate bombardier' in the process.[705] However, Warren Wyeth Willard, another marine chaplain, relied on more conventional means of distribution. Having taken delivery of '2400 copies of Gideon New Testaments the night before we said farewell to the West Coast',[706] the Guadalcanal campaign afforded plenty of opportunities for him to press them into needy hands. On one occasion, the recipients were a bedraggled group of rescued American sailors: 'The survivors had lost all their possessions on board the sunken ships. Sea bags, books, money, clothing, all were gone. The men had to start from scratch again. I was overjoyed at the opportunity of presenting each man with a Gideon New Testament', Willard wrote brightly.[707] In October 1942, after the balance of his Testaments had arrived at Tulagi, Willard cautioned potential recipients:

Consecrated men back in the United States ... have invested their money in these books in order that you might have them free of cost. Sailors and marines have risked their lives to transport them to you. No one is obliged to accept the gift. Only those who feel conscience-free to have a New Testament, and really want to study it, may have a copy, because the Word of God is precious on these islands, and I think that I am the only fortunate chaplain to have a stock of them at present.[708]

Early shortages of scripture and other devotional material proved only temporary, however. The diary of Clyde E. Kimball, a Methodist army chaplain who served in Iceland, England and North-West Europe from 1942 until his death in December 1944, reflects the variety of religious items supplied to the army, and the efforts taken by its chaplains to ensure their distribution and subsequent use. For example, at a remote radar installation in Iceland in October 1942, Kimball doled out '20 New Testaments, 15 R.C. Prayer books, 35 medals, 10 rosaries, etc.' to a congregation of only twenty-four.[709] The following February, and at a service that was astutely timed to take place between two cinema shows at a larger camp, Kimball distributed five hundred Gideon New Testaments, each of which bore his autograph.[710] While these Testaments served the triple function of souvenirs, devotional aids and certificates of church attendance, by the time Kimball reached Luxembourg in the autumn of 1944, the resources available to him also included tracts, triptychs, magazines, religious films, sound recordings and 'gospel stationery'.[711] As in so many other areas of supply, by the end of the war superabundance seems to have been the norm – a situation that was reflected in the regular 'At Your Service' column of *The Chaplain* magazine. In August 1945, for example, it carried a notice that:

The following items are made available to chaplains: 1,000 envelopes and 2,000 sheets of Scripture Text stationery with choices of insignias of any branch of the armed services; Scripture Text pencils up to 300 per chaplain, and shipments of selections of 50 beautifully illustrated tracts ... The above items will be sent immediately without cost upon request to John Ferguson, 8998 N. Martindale Avenue, Detroit 4, Michigan.[712]

That same month, Chaplain Cornelius Van Schouwen of the Christian Reformed Church wrote from his Railway Operating Battalion in Germany:

I received 25 *Banners*, 12 copies of the *Free Methodists*, 13 *Evangelical Messengers*, seven *Christian Digests* and eight *Christ's Ambassadors Herald*. I also received 200 tracts from the *Young Calvinists*, 500 copies of *The Hope of the World*, 500 copies of *The Church Prepares for Peace*, and 500 copies of *God's Mysterious Way* ... I have been utterly surprised again and again in receiving so much Christian literature from a great variety of sources, even from institutions outside of the CRC, throughout my tour of duty in

Europe. I simply do not have the time to thank all these people and sources individually and I express my appreciation now. All of it was made available to the soldiers I served.[713]

Such was the deluge of religious literature that the ordering, storage and distribution of religious reading matter formed the subject of an entire article in *The Chaplain* magazine in April 1945. Entitled 'Litter – Or Literature?', Chaplain Ira S. Fritz advised his colleagues how to avoid accumulating large stockpiles of unwanted publications, mainly by ordering judiciously selected items in reasonable amounts and by refining their distribution methods. In respect of the latter, a 'tract-of-the-week' was recommended, as was preaching occasional sermons on 'the privilege and duty of all Christians to spread God's Word by means of printed page'.[714]

Chaplains and civilians

Chaplains were as much the objects as the instruments of civilian munificence. On entering the service, the JWB's Committee on Army and Navy Religious Activities (CANRA) furnished each Jewish chaplain with a library of religious books for his personal use and presented him with his rank insignia.[715] Recognising that Jewish chaplains were often faced with extra costs in ministering to their scattered flocks, CANRA also supplied interest-free loans for the purchase of automobiles and a special monthly allowance to every Jewish chaplain.[716] Indeed, certain civilian organisations were formed solely to meet the varied needs of chaplains, among them the California-based Chaplains Service Corps, of whom it was said that: 'All that a Navy chaplain had to do was to make known a need and, if within the range of human possibility, it was met.'[717] In the course of the war, the Chaplains Service Corps proved to be a fruitful source of items such as records and record players, books, games, musical instruments, and even pet dogs.[718]

For army chaplains, the supply of portable altar sets early in the war proved a prime example of how an obvious and expensive need was met by civilian agencies. In October 1942, the *Boston Herald* reassured its readers that the liturgical needs of Catholic chaplains were already well provided for:

> Catholic priests ... have equipment weighing about 70 pounds. The routine of training hardens them so that they can carry this load if necessary.... The equipment, furnished by the Catholic Chaplains' Aid Association, includes a marble altar stone consecrated by a bishop, a small chalice, a crucifix, candlesticks, vestments, and linens.[719]

However, Israel Yost noted that by 1943 similar provision had also been made by many Protestant churches:

Most denominations provide their chaplains with a portable altar set; mine from the Lutheran church resembled a small suitcase with space for a small cross on a stand, two candlesticks, containers for bread and wine, a chalice, a paten, a cassock and surplice, and a small supply of New Testaments and religious tracts.[720]

CANRA was no less active in catering to Jewish needs, supplying a portable ark to each Jewish chaplain who went overseas: 'In this suitcase ark which the chaplain or his assistant could carry, were to be found not only the Torah, but also the other basic requirements for a Jewish religious service in the field.'[721] Non-Jewish chaplains were also targeted by CANRA, which periodically dispatched kits of Jewish religious supplies to units and installations that were thought to be in need of them. In 1943, for example, a Baptist army chaplain stationed in the western Solomon Islands was notified of all Jewish religious holidays and informed that CANRA was sending 'a tallith (prayer shawl), shofar (ram's horn) and other necessary paraphernalia to each division headquarters that did not have a Jewish Chaplain.'[722]

In the case of the navy, from 1941 the provision of altar sets by civilian groups was complemented by the extended loan of triptychs (i.e. three-panelled altar paintings) that were intended 'to help create religious atmosphere in what were often drab surroundings' aboard warships and in navy libraries, theatres and mess halls.[723] The triptych used on the *South Dakota*, for example, featured a sailor and a marine kneeling before the risen Christ and was usually placed under 'the sixteen-inch guns of the battleship' during communion services.[724] The task of supplying these sizeable works of art, which usually measured around three feet by five feet, was undertaken by the New York-based Citizens Committee for the Army and Navy, Inc., whose earlier welfare work had been superseded by the advent of the USO. The first of these triptychs was sent to the battleship *North Carolina* before it was commissioned in May 1941. By December 1945, the navy had taken delivery of more than three hundred, most of them original works of art painted by individual artists at a cost that ranged from $300 to $400 each.[725] In time, the Citizens Committee for the Army and Navy, Inc. extended its beneficence to the army. Army triptychs were usually 'Painted on individual commission by outstanding American artists' and could measure up to five feet by eight feet.[726] Taking delivery of one example in Iceland in 1943, a somewhat bemused Clyde E. Kimball wrote that: 'A number of families sponsored these as gifts ... It is an original design, intended to appeal both to Catholics and Protestants. This was the gift of "The King Family," Dayton, Ohio.'[727]

Civilian agencies were also keen to add their own advice to the pool of published knowledge available to chaplains, notably in the form of the army's manuals and circular letters. In February 1943, CANRA commenced publication of *The Jewish Chaplain*, a periodical whose rather formal tone and content was eventually supplemented by a lighter, more 'gossipy' publication entitled *The Schmoose Sheet*. In addition to news items, this included information on recent Jewish publications and on post-war employment.[728] In time, the General Commission on Army and Navy Chaplains followed suit with an illustrated monthly magazine entitled *The Chaplain* – a self-styled 'Trade Journal for Protestant Chaplains'[729] – which appeared from October 1944 and was 'sent by first class mail to all Protestant chaplains in the Army and Navy'.[730] As ever, the Lutherans were quick to anticipate the needs of their chaplains and a *Service Manual for Lutheran Chaplains Serving with the Forces of the United States* appeared as early as 1942. Edited by a veteran chaplain of World War I and published by the Army and Navy Commission of the Missouri Synod, this 'endeavored to anticipate every need of the chaplains in performing their arduous duties', its compilers including 'in one handy volume not only the customary forms used in the Lutheran church, but added prayers for special occasions, and material for bed-side ministry'.[731] Similarly, and with its own massive stake in ministry to the military, the American Bible Society hoped to maximise its returns by publishing a brochure entitled *The Chaplain and His Use of the Bible*, which described 'many tested methods, applying not only to the distribution of the Scriptures, but to all other religious literature as well'.[732]

Religious organisations for service personnel

Besides a plethora of civilian organisations that catered for the religious needs of the armed forces, there were others that recruited among the military or were formed for them. Among the former were broadly based civilian organisations such as the pan-Protestant Christian Endeavor Movement, as well as denominational groups such as the Luther League and the Episcopalian, quasi-military Brotherhood of St. Andrew, which at one point had around two thousand members in the ETO alone.[733] The largest of these, however, was the Holy Name Society, which had been founded in the US in 1909 as a Catholic men's society whose purpose was: 'To beget due love and reverence for the Holy Name of God and Jesus Christ; and to suppress blasphemy, perjury, oaths … profanity, unlawful swearing and improper language; and as far as members can, to prevent those vices in others.' Organised into diocesan unions, and with a reported membership of 2.5 million by 1942,[734] the Holy Name Society seems to have flourished among GIs in the United States. In September 1942, it was estimated that one-quarter of all Catholics in the armed forces 'were Holy Name members' and, according to another: 'More than 200 Army installations had Holy Name Societies, often organized in connection with a local church, which scheduled fellowship meetings, breakfasts after early Sunday masses and visits with local Holy Name groups.'[735] However, under the very different conditions of overseas service such tight organisation was prone to unravel and in 1945 it was noted that: 'The

Holy Name Societies [in the ETO] were almost all informally organized local groups; in exceptional cases they were duly chartered unit chapters of the Holy Name Society organized prior to the coming of the organization to the theater.'[736] In fact, chaplains in the ETO noted severe problems in sustaining 'Pious Societies for Service Men' regardless of their purpose or denominational affiliation:

> 71% of the chaplains reported that, due to the mobility of combat troops and the turn-over of personnel in more static installations, it had been impossible for them successfully to organize or to maintain soldier religious organizations. In the remaining cases, 63% of the organizations were Roman Catholic Holy Name societies, 21% were local chapters of the (Protestant) Service Men's Christian League and the rest were either merely local groups or chapters of the Brotherhood of St. Andrew or similar organizations.[737]

The Brotherhood of St. Andrew, which was credited with 'a slight degree of success among the American troops in the European Theater', managed to form chapters in London, Cheltenham and Paris as well as in larger tactical units such as the 84th, 95th and 99th Infantry Divisions. Still, it was indicative of the practical problems it faced that attendance at meetings of its London chapter averaged a mere eighteen even though its meetings were open to men of all faiths.[738]

Inevitably, there were earnest attempts to create organisations that were more attuned to the specific needs and circumstances of service personnel. The Christian Endeavor movement – given its ecumenical character and its stress on youthful, lay participation and leadership in its religious activities[739] – seemed to provide a model that was eminently adaptable to military conditions. Consequently, in 1942 a collaboration of the Federal Council of Churches of Christ in America, the General Commission on Army and Navy Chaplains, the International Council of Religious Education, and the World's Christian Endeavor Union led to the creation of the Service Men's Christian League (SMCL).[740] Inaugurated at a high-profile Armistice Day dinner at the Mayflower Hotel in Washington DC, the SMCL was hailed as 'a powerful weapon for the blitzing of evil and for the building of the kingdom of God on earth',[741] its stated purposes being:

1. To offer to the chaplains of the armed forces a programme for men on active duty, which may be used at their discretion.
2. To provide a means of Christian fellowship, devotion, evangelism and education for the purposes of fortifying the serviceman's Christian life.
3. To assist the man in service in maintaining his church affiliation and to prepare him for Christian citizenship in his community, nation and world when he returns to civil life.
4. To provide for the chaplains and the men in the armed services such help – devotional, evangelistic, educational, and organisational – as may

be required to enable the Service Men's Christian League to fulfil its ministry for Christ.[742]

To its advocates, the SMCL was a counterpart of the 'young adult movement in civilian life' and, for some, even 'the Church of the Armed Forces'.[743] Organised into local units by supportive chaplains, at the heart of its activities were 'group meetings, with programs of worship and individual participation'.[744] However, flexibility was of the essence – the league's 'interdenominational approach and elastic organization' being intended 'to fit any and all needs'.[745] If the league was portrayed as 'a fellowship of Protestant men in the service, united to sustain each other in the Christian way of life and to bring others to accept Jesus Christ as Savior', allowance was made from the outset for the creation of a complementary Service Women's Christian League (SWCL).[746] In any case, league programmes varied from unit to unit and they were broad enough to appeal to many service women (regardless of the SWCL) as well as some Catholics.[747] In addition to their devotional gatherings, and depending on capacity and circumstance, unit activities could range from the building of jungle chapels to providing Christmas parties for hungry French and Italian children.[748] Indicative of the league's flexibility was the fact that in 1944, and as part of its local programme, Eleanor Roosevelt addressed an 'SM/WCL' unit in Washington that was composed entirely of WAVES.[749] Although Lutherans and Southern Baptists remained aloof, it was claimed that the churches that backed the league through its sponsoring agencies represented 'approximately 90 percent of the nation's Protestant church membership'.[750] Likewise, and less than a year after its launch, league sources claimed that its membership represented a true 'cross section of the Protestant life of America'.[751] The league's expansive profile was certainly matched by the rate of its growth. The first league unit was established in December 1942 at the US Naval Training Station, Newport, Rhode Island.[752] By April 1943, fifty-four units were active 'in 21 states and overseas'.[753] That November, it was claimed that hundreds of units were now in existence and that a precise estimate was impossible given that 'experience has indicated that the units formally reported to headquarters are but a small proportion of those actually organized'.[754]

Significantly, what helped to drive this exponential growth was the wholesale conversion of many existing groups into league units:

> Thus Bible classes became S.M.C.L. units – as did prayer meetings, bull sessions, literary clubs, post-war planning classes and what-have-you. World's Christian Endeavor, one of the sponsoring agencies, which already had units operating in the service, threw its full weight and experience behind the program, its leaders urging all existing C.E. units to merge with the new all-Protestant League.[755]

However, a further factor that drove its expansion was the nature and scale of the resources behind it. The first chairman and vice-chairman of the SMCL were, respectively, Bishop Adna Wright Leonard and Daniel A. Poling.[756] Besides its eminent leadership, league activities were informed and guided by an illustrated monthly magazine, namely *The Link*. Intended to bind together what were often very disparate units, among its regular features *The Link* supplied news, schemes of Bible reading and subject materials for group discussion. When *The Link* first appeared at the beginning of 1943, it had a print run of 100,000 copies per month; by June, monthly demand had soared to more than twice that figure.[757] Available free of charge to chaplains and service personnel,[758] this accounted for only part of its popularity. According to a review by *Yank* in February 1943, *The Link* was 'a slick little pocket-size mag' that contained: 'None of the old hoke too often handed out in Sunday school, but straight-from-the-shoulder stuff for Christian soldiers, with a few thoughts on Christian living.'[759] Driven by ever-increasing demand, 4.2 million copies of *The Link* were printed between May 1944 and April 1945 and, six months later, its monthly readership had reached an estimated 1.7 million.[760] In the considered opinion of chaplains who had passed through the ETO, *The Link* was 'avidly read', widely utilised for the purposes of devotion and instruction, and, as 'a well edited, well printed, and appealingly written magazine, published at an annual cost of over $200,000', it represented the crowning achievement of the SMCL.[761]

Despite the success of *The Link* and the existence of covenant cards, membership cards and membership insignia,[762] the sheer flexibility of its modus operandi meant that it was hard to estimate the true size, character and influence of the league. However, among its core adherents there was enough enthusiasm for the organisation to stir calls for it to become the basis of a post-war Christian veterans' organisation.[763] Sympathetic sources certainly liked to claim that league units took root wherever American personnel were to be found – on the battlefields of Tunisia, for example, or on the Alcan Highway in Alaska and among marines in the Solomons.[764] However, others were more sceptical of the resilience and ubiquity of the league. Veteran chaplains in the ETO were inclined to play down the success of the SMCL for the same reasons that had hampered other soldiers' organisations. In their view: 'In spite of considerable effort, relatively little in the way of even transitory organizations in the European Theater was achieved by the Service Men's Christian League'.[765] In fact, and as early as July 1943, the problems of maintaining league activities amidst regular turnovers of personnel had been highlighted in *The Link* itself, with First Lieutenant Joseph R. Cross noting how the league unit at his replacement training centre was regularly 'depleted as the cycle of training [was] completed'.[766]

Not surprisingly, more conservative evangelicals ('a vast, varied, and interactive aggregation' that included fundamentalists, Missouri Synod Lutherans, Southern Baptists and Pentecostals)[767] were often less than enthusiastic about the league. If its liberal and ecumenical tendencies could be off-putting, the prospect of working in collaboration with heterodox, Catholic or Jewish chaplains (who were often the de facto sponsors of local league units)[768] served as a further deterrent. If Ivan M. Gould, the league's general secretary, sought to allay conservative fears by insisting that 'the fundamental basis of the League is evangelistic'[769] even some of its conservative supporters had their reservations. Towards the end of 1944, a chaplain's assistant wrote to *The Link*:

> Give us more gospel messages explaining the Plan of Salvation.... Such articles as those on World Peace, Social Welfare, A Better World are fine, but the good old-fashioned gospel message beats them all and should have primary place ... we in turn are doing our best to bring those that know not our Christ into His fold.[770]

In the same issue, another correspondent confessed that:

> I have been greatly enjoying THE LINK as it comes to us month by month, but I agree ... that some of the Topic Talks lead one to believe that all men, saved or unsaved, are 'sons of God,' that 'all men are essentially good,' and that man naturally grows better, which is scripturally untrue.... God's great plan of redemption for man is through the atoning death of His only begotten Son, and believers on Him become sons of God and joint heirs with Christ.[771]

In January 1945, and from his hospital bed, a Private Ralph Cushing even made a strident appeal for a return to evangelical orthodoxy. Yet again, this was largely triggered by the prevailing sentiments of *The Link*:

> I feel that there is one danger which must be studiously avoided. That is the danger of just recognizing anyone's conception of religion so long as it is sincere.... We must get back to preaching that there is a heaven to gain and a hell to shun; that God is a just God, a loving God, but also a God of wrath to workers of unrighteousness.... We must also face reality again in old-fashioned prayer meetings where the Christian will get power, renew family altars and read and study the Bible more.[772]

In view of the effort that was invested in the league, it was ironic that conservative evangelicals, with their evangelistic imperatives and much greater sense of independence from army and navy chaplains, thrived amidst the turbulence of war as they had done in the years of the Depression. In the navy, for example, the war provided ideal conditions for the growth of the Navigators, a fundamentalist movement founded by Dawson Trotman that began its work among sailors in 1933. Reliant on a system of personal mentoring, and benefiting from a navy policy that allowed experienced sailors to choose a ship on which to serve on re-enlistment, by the outbreak of war the Navigators already had a modest but significant following on the lower decks; the battleship *West Virginia*, for example, which was sunk at Pearl Harbor, was a hotbed of Navigator activity. Inevitably, and amidst the massive expansion and personnel movements of the war years, the Navigators were able to extend their influence dramatically. By 1943, more than one thousand ships and installations harboured at least one member of the movement – men such as Jack Armstrong, a machinist's mate who was converted on the *West Virginia* and who ran a Bible class on the light cruiser *Atlanta* before his death in the Solomon Islands in November 1942.[773]

This combination of personal influence and the conservative gospel also appears to have made inroads in the army. Army chaplains reviewing their experiences in the ETO (and in stark contrast to their verdict on the SMCL) observed that:

> Statistics are not available, but there is a great deal of evidence that throughout the theater members of the more zealous fundamentalist denominations gathered together in informal fellowship groups, normally, but not necessarily, under the sponsorship of the unit chaplain, for the promotion of the religious life of the participants. Usually built about one or two individuals with a capacity for leadership, the life of such organizations was generally determined by the presence of the founder-leaders. Wise chaplains recognized the fact that these informal organizations met a definite need in the religious life and experience of the participants, and by intelligent guidance they frequently were able to use them as a lever to promote the more formal types of religious observance in the unit.[774]

By the end of 1945, the new Youth for Christ movement had also gained a foothold in the army, with chaplains and soldiers leading large evangelistic rallies in the United States and in the Pacific.[775] For example, that September in Manila, Dr Alfred A. Carpenter of the General Commission on Army and Navy Chaplains found that a 'GI Gospel Hour' was being held by enlisted men every Saturday evening in a funeral home; the same group also held a well-frequented 'Youth for Christ' meeting on Sunday evenings, which was usually attended by 'several hundred' personnel.[776]

In a comparable fashion, the Catholic guilds that were specifically for service personnel seem to have fared better than the Holy Name societies. The war generated at least two of these, those of St Genevieve for Catholic WACs and Our Lady's Knights of the Skies for Catholic airmen. The former emerged out of a study circle formed at Fort Des Moines, Iowa, in autumn 1942 and Oveta Culp Hobby, the extremely diligent director of the Women's Army Corps, though a Protestant was involved in the design of a guild medal.[777] The confraternity of Our Lady's Knights of the Skies, on the other hand, was the brainchild of William J. Clasby, a Catholic chaplain stationed at Santa Ana Army Air Base, a vast new training camp that also doubled as an overseas replacement depot for the AAF. These situational factors appear to have lent themselves to the appeal of the confraternity, which numbered fourteen thousand members by autumn 1942 and eventually reached a wartime peak of 100,000.[778] While all members were pledged to support the confraternity's 'principles of citizenship and faith', their devotional commitments were essentially personal, members being required to recite a decade of the rosary every day and receive Holy Communion once a week when possible. In terms of practical and spiritual support, members received regular circulars, an insignia was devised that depicted 'a kneeling cadet upon whom the Blessed Virgin is conferring knighthood', and every week a Holy Hour was held for the confraternity by its founder in the base chapel at Santa Ana.[779] Clearly, there were those who derived great consolation from their membership of Our Lady's Knights of the Skies, and a heartfelt letter to Clasby (apparently one of many thousands) read:

> I've been overseas now for about eight months, stationed in India and flying a very hazardous route over the Himalayas to China. I have lost many of my friends during this time and have had a few close shaves myself ... I think, therefore, that Our Lady's Knights of the Skies is a marvellous idea as it is a constant reminder to perform an Act of Perfect Contrition before even going into the air. My prayers always include at least one decade [of the rosary] and we here always go to Confession and Communion as often as it is possible. [780]

Conclusion

Under the sanction of the free exercise clause of the First Amendment, it would appear that the American military developed something that resembled 'an establishment of religion'; moreover, and in the burial policies relating to service personnel, something akin to a 'religious Test' obtained. Although in train before 1940, the peacetime draft and the war years saw the culmination of this process. By World War II, religion was part of the irreducible identity of the American soldier, sailor or marine. Even if a broad religious allegiance was not carried on identity tags or on service records, it embraced all of the fallen. Helping to underpin this process was an abiding professional conviction of the military value of religion, especially in relation to sound discipline and good morale, a conviction born of age-old military tradition and of the perceived lessons of America's previous wars, especially the Revolutionary War, the Civil War and World War I. A sense of the utility of religion, and a spirit of religious conformity, was fostered among the professional officer corps by the service academies of West Point and Annapolis, where the privileged place of religion – and even mandatory religious practice – helped to drive these lessons home. Always conscious of the professional and public ideal of the godly commander, the statements, gestures and example of America's most celebrated commanders in World War II illustrates how much they strove to live up to expectations, exploiting new media to further their personal reputations in the process.

If American military culture was inherently sympathetic to the claims of religion, the politics of the peacetime draft helped to privilege its position still further. In keeping with its provision for their other needs, the War Department ensured that its draftees were amply supplied with chapels of their own, as they were with chaplains by the hundred; in time, and especially after the outbreak of war, this would be augmented by the advent of the chaplain's assistant, by the unprecedented supply of scripture at government expense, by the mushroom growth of military religious broadcasting, and by an open-handed provision of religious necessities of all kinds, including supplementary civilian chaplains. Although not as bountiful as the army in this respect, the navy did not lag too far behind, making huge improvements on its chapel provision and providing its growing number of chaplains with a wealth of new resources that had been denied them hitherto. In addition to all of this were the massive and myriad contributions of civilian religious agencies, contributions that the military were generally at pains to facilitate. If the extensive tours of high-profile churchmen to various theatres of war were emblematic of the close working relationship between the civilian churches and the military, the USO stood as a national embodiment of such concerted effort. Other religious bodies and publishers made their own contributions, whether in the form of hospitality and correspondence programmes, support for chaplains, or in a growing mountain of scripture portions and religious publications aimed at soldiers and sailors. Furthermore, civilian models and expertise were harnessed to strengthen religious life in the military, especially in the form of new religious organisations for service personnel, notably the Protestants' Service Men's Christian League and the Catholic confraternity of Our Lady's Knights of the Skies.

In sum, and whether or not they were ever exposed to combat and the vagaries of 'foxhole religion', America's service men and women were embraced for greater or lesser periods of time by military organisations that treated religion as normative, and which increasingly resourced its representatives to the hilt. Lacking the glamour of combat, or the drama of the battlefield conversion, this was the most common, most defining religious experience of America's soldiers and sailors. As we shall see, for a minority this exposure would be augmented and fortified by the experience of combat, or by other factors incidental to military life. Nonetheless, this institutional emphasis on religion was the unifying factor that, as we shall see more fully in Chapter Four, proved instrumental in shaping the wartime (and post-war) religious attitudes and behaviour of America's service men and women.

Chapter Three

The Faithful in Arms

Introduction

I̅N̅ the previous chapters, we have seen how religious life in America's armed forces in World War II was shaped and influenced by their chaplaincy systems, by their commanders, traditions and institutional cultures, by political imperatives surrounding the draft, and by a plethora of concerned civilian organisations. We now turn to the sixteen million men and women who served during the war, the overwhelming majority of whom were not military professionals and whose wartime religious outlook and experience owed at least as much to their civilian backgrounds as to the conditions of service life. Consequently, this chapter shows how key features of civilian religious life were reflected in the military, sometimes to a degree that belied the image of the US Army in particular as an all-American melting pot. Hence, this chapter will draw attention to such constant factors as the relative religiosity of Catholics, of African Americans and of women, the fundamental importance of home and family to American religious life, and the effects of inducting large numbers of the religiously committed into the army and navy. The chapter also examines how devotional tastes and religious traits – notably hymn-singing, scripture-reading and self-reliance – translated into military life and even flourished under wartime conditions. Finally, it illustrates the limits to which the military environment could influence civilian habits and preconceptions, showing that the insistent military rhetoric of religious tolerance was often much more in evidence than its reality, and that the cross-currents of religious conflict posed a persistent problem throughout the war years.

Civilian imprints

Despite the efforts of the chaplaincy services, the American armed forces in the interwar years had not been widely recognised for their piety and clean-living.[1] While soldiering in particular, with its oppressive emphasis on conformity and subordination, was widely regarded as 'a fundamentally un-American activity',[2] the mores of army life were hardly those of respectable society. Paydays at army posts were often marked by binges of gambling and drinking (the latter unchecked by Prohibition), and by the descent of droves of prostitutes. As if to highlight the army as a staging post to hell, at Clark Field an illicit gambling racket was even run by an erstwhile Franciscan who was known to his clients as 'Padre'.[3] If the misery of the Depression drove even men from middle-class backgrounds to enlist, this did little to allay the anti-army animus that prevailed among many civilians, for whom the regular army resembled a penal institution filled with the dregs of society.[4] Despite its occasional dangers, foreign service did nothing to enhance the reputation of the army's enlisted men, and the notorious fleshpots of the Philippines, China, Hawaii and Panama only sharpened their appetite for 'cheap liquor and cheaper women', as George C. Marshall coldly put it.[5] Even after the outbreak of war, newly minted chaplains had mixed feelings about being assigned to regular army units. Edward K. Rogers, despite having impressed members of the 1st Infantry Division with his skills on a firing range at Fort Benning, was distinctly perplexed by what he subsequently found:

> The religious situation of the regiment did not give one room for joy. Few came to church in those days.... I have often wondered if being a regular army outfit, made up of many men who had been away from homes for a long time and separated from whatever church life they had known, did not play a part. At any rate, it was no source of joy to have only twenty-five or thirty at Sunday services in those early days. Perhaps I was wasting my time in the army.... The language and habits of the men did not help me any either.[6]

The marines seemed no better, at least to navy chaplains. Sharing some of the same notorious postings with the army, during the interwar years the Marine Corps also cultivated an image of tough and unbiddable self-reliance.[7] As a result, some navy chaplains were distinctly leery of the marines and Frederick William Meehling, when he was moved from the battleship *Colorado* to the Marine Barracks at Quantico in 1937, was frankly aghast at the prospect of his new posting:

> When I received that news, I died a thousand deaths. I said, 'What did I do to deserve to be sent to the Marines?'.... When I had them on the battleship, I wasn't quite their chaplain. I was the chaplain for the sailors there.... I don't think the whole three years that I was in the COLORADO I had half a dozen marines to go to church on Sunday. So I felt that I was sort of being punished for some reason or other. So I wrote to everybody short of the pope and the president to see if I couldn't have my orders changed.[8]

In contrast to the army and the marines, the US Navy had been cultivating an image of respectability since the turn of the century. Reliant on a flow of steady and intelligent recruits to perform a gamut of technical roles, ranging from electrician to aviation machinist's mate,[9] navy wisdom held 'that its best men came from small towns in mid-America' rather than from the sweepings of the nation's cities and waterfronts.[10] As the historian Frederick S. Harrod put it:

[M]any in the navy believed that the ideal sailor was native-born, young, educated, white, from a small town or rural area, and from what the navy considered a 'good family'. The [Navy Department] thought that such a person would be most able to learn the skills a modern navy needed, would most probably stay for the full term of enlistment, and would reflect most favourably on the service.[11]

During the Depression, the navy could afford to be very choosy with its recruits. Despite a (temporary) pay cut that affected all federal employees in 1933, during the 1930s desertion plummeted, re-enlistment soared and, in 1935, the navy rejected almost 90 per cent of its would-be recruits.[12] By 1939, Robert D. Workman could report to the National Council of the YMCA that the proportion of high-school graduates among the navy's enlisted men had climbed from 18 to 42 per cent within a decade, that their 'intelligence quotient' had risen from 85 to 103, and that more than one-third of them had earned good conduct medals. Furthermore, the nation's sailors were reassuringly older as a body and were thus more likely to be steady husbands and fathers.[13] In 1941, the *Christian Herald* joined this chorus of reassurance, citing a YMCA secretary who insisted that: 'United States sailors are today the finest and cleanest bunch of service men in the world. They're selected carefully, and they're kept clean.'[14]

As one of the principal architects of the new navy, in an address given in 1914 at a Methodist Episcopal church in Washington, Secretary of the Navy, Josephus Daniels, had declared that: 'I am the father of more than 50,000 young men … and there is nothing more upon my heart than to see them men of strong Christian character, living clean lives for home and kindred and country.'[15] A champion of the cause of education, who sought to make 'every ship a school' for its bluejackets, on moral grounds Daniels staunchly refused to allow the recruitment of felons during World War I and forbade the distribution of prophylactic packets among sailors going on liberty.[16] Although his educational scheme faltered in World War I, and his tough stand on prophylaxis was abandoned by his successors in the 1920s,[17] Daniels's enduring moral legacy to the navy of World War II was his General Order 99 of June 1914, which stated that: 'The use or introduction for drinking purposes of alcoholic liquors on board any naval vessel, or within any navy yard or station, is strictly prohibited, and commanding officers will be held directly responsible for the enforcement of this order.'[18] Still, and despite such efforts, the navy was never in serious danger of becoming a nautical Sunday school. As one sailor recalled of the crew of the transport ship *Antares*, while at Pearl Harbor in 1940: 'Most of the guys would head for shore and find themselves the prostitutes and the bar and that scene.'[19] Furthermore, and despite signs that the navy's relations with civilian communities had improved in recent decades,[20] as late as World War II Chaplain Hansel H. Tower could complain of establishments that still boasted signs such as 'Sailors, Soldiers, Marines and dogs not allowed.'[21]

Although it had been a long-term goal to make the navy more representative of the nation as a whole (or, more precisely, of white America) in World War II this objective was largely achieved through the eventual, inexorable operation of the draft. In religious terms, the draft meant that the armed forces increasingly replicated the religious contours of civilian society. From the point of view of the evangelist, this in itself represented a continued call to action. As army chaplain Alvin O. Carlson warned: 'Servicemen are a cross-section of humanity, and if the test of Christianity is membership in a church, then ours is **not** a Christian nation.' According to Carlson's arithmetic – and even making 'a liberal allowance for the small sects' – just over half of all Americans had 'no church affiliation' and, among those who did, there were plenty of 'men and women who go to church perhaps once a year – at Easter or at Christmas'.[22] Although the navy felt the effects of the draft much later than the army, by 1944 Ellwood C. Nance could assert that, 'the faith of our fighting men is essentially the same in both the Army and the Navy'.[23] This growing correlation between civilian and service life led to the duplication – and even accentuation – of religious patterns, tendencies and characteristics in the armed forces that were already apparent in civilian society, such as the greater degree of religious practice of Catholics over Protestants, blacks over whites, and women over men. Furthermore, and in the melting pot of army and navy life, religious belief and practice in the armed forces also underlined important regional variations, subtle generational differences, and the religious centrality of family and home.

In 1944, and according to one Catholic commentator, 'fifty per cent of the American Army goes to Church [and] Catholics hold the lead for regular attendance'.[24] Two years later, and reflecting on this claim in *Let's Talk It Over*, a volume of Catholic apologetics, navy chaplain Jerome P. Holland asserted that:

> Without passing judgement on the validity of the reasons usually given ... it is simply stated that a large number of non-Catholic Americans do not go to church. On the other hand, frankly admitting that there are some nominal Catholics who never put a foot in the church and who think as the Non-Catholic Mind does, it is true that, by and large, Catholics do go to church regularly.[25]

Arguing that Catholics were neither unduly superstitious nor endowed 'with some kind of mysterious insight not given to the rest of the American people',[26] Holland ascribed their churchgoing habits to clear and consistent instruction in 'fundamental and universal truths' that was imparted from the pulpit, in the home, in the Catholic school 'and finally by every method and agency of Catholic teaching'.[27] Ultimately, however, Holland claimed that it was the sacramental mystery of the Real Presence that drew Catholics to their churches:

The Catholic Church is not a meetinghouse. It alone claims that God dwells within its walls in the tabernacle.... With malice toward none, and charity toward all, with a decent sympathy and respect for sincere, good people who worship God as they deem best, according to the light of their consciences, this is the answer to the crowded Catholic churches and to the empty pews in the churches which the people who think with the Non-Catholic Mind might attend but do not.[28]

For many Protestant observers, however much they may have disagreed with Holland's sentiments they could not dispute his mathematics, and they could even put a more negative spin upon the statistics. Writing in *The Link* in October 1945, army chaplain Raymond R. Miller stated that:

Cold figures bear witness to the fact that Catholics are at least ten times as diligent in their attendance at divine services as are Protestants. In visits to the sanctuary for private worship the ratio is more nearly one hundred to one in favour of the Catholics. While it may be true that attendance at worship or visits to designated spots for worship are not the only tests of piety, they are nevertheless good indices with ample Scriptural and ecclesiastical sanction and authority.[29]

If, in its broadest terms, church attendance among Protestants was unimpressive, African Americans stood as a conspicuous exception to this general rule. Another reflection of the situation in civilian society, even in the regular army a much greater role had been played by religion in black units than in white. According to Tommie Baugh, who served in the African American 24th Infantry Regiment from 1920 to 1940, its chaplain held considerable sway in the regiment and: 'You almost had to attend church because the Chaplain was always on you.'[30] While a study undertaken by the Army War College in 1936 confirmed the comparative religiosity of African American soldiers,[31] white units serving overseas suffered from higher rates of venereal disease than their black counterparts and the incidence of alcoholism was also lower in black units.[32] Given the right circumstances, and the enduring status of the minister in African American life, this situation could be replicated in World War II. For example, Chaplain James R.C. Pinn (a graduate of Howard University, a former concert pianist, CCC chaplain and minister of Shiloh Baptist Church in Newport, Rhode Island) exerted enormous influence on the 41st Engineer General Service Regiment (Colored) during its posting to Liberia in 1942–43. According to Pinn: 'The men of my regiment, the Forty-first Engineers, were always typified by a deeply religious life – and they showed it by their songs.' Unlike other units, who seemed 'addicted to songs of the "swing" variety', the 41st 'preferred the old "spirituals"' and became widely known as '"The Singing Forty-first"'. On its three-week voyage to West Africa, the favoured repertoire was '"What Would I Do Without the Lord" ...

"Give Me that Old-Time Religion" ... "The Old Ark's a 'Moverin'" and 'When the Saints Go Marching In'. Faced with submarine alerts, there was a constant demand for Bibles and Testaments, 'Bible reading increased', and 'Two Bible-discussion groups were formed', both conducted by the men themselves. Nor did this situation abate as the 41st carved out a new military base from the African jungle for, as Pinn stated proudly: 'My regiment has always had a 90 per cent church attendance record, and this continued throughout my stay in Africa'.[33] On his part, and while recalling religious life in the 761st Tank Battalion, the celebrated 'Black Panthers',[34] Mark Henderson wrote that while the battalion had no chaplain and 'the occasion to worship in an organized service was rare', religious convictions were nonetheless 'expressed in private prayer or group prayer', typically 'before meals, or in memory of a fallen comrade'.[35] Even whites not noted for their sympathy with African Americans could be impressed by their piety. Orval Eugene Faubus, later the governor of Arkansas during the 1957 desegregation crisis at Little Rock Central High School, was struck by a scene in Germany in March 1945 while serving alongside the 761st:

> While I stood briefly in a church, now being used as a shelter by our troops, a GI was playing the chapel organ and a Negro soldier was singing with deep feeling an old familiar religious hymn. Strange assemblage and a strange scene for such a place. Other battle-stained GIs listened with weary, strained faces turned toward the singer and the player.[36]

For white Protestant chaplains, who were usually accustomed to much less fervour,[37] ministry to African American troops could be an edifying experience. In February 1944, Clyde E. Kimball, a Methodist chaplain assigned to the 1128th Engineer Combat Group in England, marvelled that: 'The new company is colored, and what a difference in response! About everyone came to church and how they did sing! I gave them four Bibles, two Testaments, forty *Upper Rooms*, and 150 other religious tracts or papers. And I have the names of twenty-seven men who want Bibles'.[38] Subsequently, Kimball littered his diary with inspirational accounts of the religious enthusiasm of African American troops; for example, in mid-May he wrote:

> Today I held three good services. At a colored camp, I had a theater hut nearly full. One sergeant played the piano and another sergeant my organ, and a quartet sang spirituals. A man was baptized and professed his desire to join the church. At another service a sergeant and two of his men did the same thing. Made me mighty happy.[39]

Likewise, and as Herbert E. Rieke, a Christian Scientist, reported from an airfield in Italy in December 1943:

I hold a service for the colored men on the field on Sunday afternoon and Wednesday afternoon at 3.30 … About 90 per cent of them attend regularly. I was wondering one day whether they were getting what I was saying and so I asked one of the men if he'd mind reviewing the last chapter I had presented. He gave it accurately. Now I do this frequently to make certain that they are all carrying along with it. I certainly love to work with colored people. They are so willing to believe.[40]

While such condescension may help to explain why black troops were not always happy to have even sympathetic white chaplains, the benefits of allowing black GIs to find their own religious leadership were highlighted in *The Chaplain* magazine in September 1946. According to Chester L. Miller, a Methodist chaplain from Detroit, at an AAF Special Training Unit at Lincoln, Nebraska, he found himself ministering to GIs in need of remedial education and to 'the Air Corps misfits and washouts generally'. However, his approach to African American personnel paid dividends and, at the same time, did something to bridge the fault lines of rank and race:

We had a high of 3500 men at one time, 450 of whom were Negroes. Among the Negroes I had two men who were ordained, even though quite illiterate, ministers. But, I had them conduct services because in that situation they were more qualified than a seminary trained man. I always supervised and attended and would speak a few words at each service. We had a very high attendance among the Negroes and few among the whites.

Hospitalised for a period, Miller remembered that:

One Sunday afternoon, during visiting hours, in walked these two colored private soldiers … I was in an officers' ward and most of them had visitors at the time … I was very amused at the 'stares' and questioning looks we got from all over the ward. But, I kept that to myself for my heart was warmed because of the spirit and desire which prompted those two colored men to walk a mile and a half each way to see their chaplain friend.[41]

Such was the army's ingrained conviction of the religious susceptibility of black GIs that religion continued to be a means of promoting discipline and acquiescence among a constituency that had ample cause to feel aggrieved at its treatment. In the winter of 1944–45, and because of an apparently successful week-long programme of revivalist meetings held in response to 'a serious morale problem' that had arisen 'in a camp where a large body of Negro troops were stationed', the chief of chaplains urged the staging of revivals in other stateside camps with large numbers of black GIs. To take place with the support of post commanders and with the participation of local black churches, Arnold advised his senior chaplains that this initiative had the backing of George C. Marshall himself, who, it was claimed, agreed 'that such action successfully accomplished will provide a means of promoting the moral and spiritual welfare of the army'.[42] While many camps complied with Arnold's wishes over the following months (at Camp Lee, Virginia, for example, the programme was accompanied by a pamphlet written by an African American chaplain, David L. Brewer, which spelt out the 'Characteristics of the Ideal Soldier'),[43] some post chaplains were openly uncooperative. From Fort Sam Houston, Texas, for example, J. Stuart Pearce wrote:

> In reply to your letter regarding the holding of a revival meeting for the colored troops stationed here, this is to advise you that there is no peculiar morale problem among our colored troops.... Being a 'Presbyterian' of the 'Southern' persuasion and having served my church for a number of years as Superintendent of Home Missions and Evangelism it goes without saying that I am thoroughly in favor of 'Revival Meetings' of the right kind for men of all colors and if conditions here indicated any special need for such a meeting I should be glad to arrange for it. There is no such need apparent at present.[44]

In contrast, the scheme offended the liberal principles of Chaplain Abbot Peterson at Camp Edwards, Massachusetts:

> In our religious services we have never segregated blacks and whites. Negro troops have been welcomed to our services and have attended without causing the slightest friction. In fact, they have contributed materially to the conduct of worship by providing us with excellent choirs from time to time.[45]

The creation and expansion of a wartime lexicon of women's auxiliary forces (namely the WAAC/WAC, the WAVES, the SPARS, the WAFS, the WASPs and the MCWR) ensured that another characteristic of American religious life was apparent in the armed forces, namely the gendered nature of public religious observance. In fact, and in a socially conservative society, the vaunted religiosity of America's women soldiers proved a crucial means of countering the lurid and imaginative slurs that were cast on their reputation after the WAAC was established, not without controversy, by an act of Congress in May 1942.[46] Growing to a wartime peak of 99,288 in April 1945,[47] the WAAC (or WAC after its redesignation in July 1943)[48] was dogged by its public image, a problem encapsulated by the multiple adverse meanings that could be read into its early slogan, 'Release a Man for Combat'.[49] Amid widely credited stories that the WAAC was a haven for prostitutes, lesbians and nymphomaniacs,[50] *The Link* addressed the furore head-on in August 1943, a few weeks after 'Capitol Stuff', a nationally syndicated newspaper column, had alleged that:

> Contraceptives and prophylactic equipment will be furnished to members
> of the WAAC, according to a super-secret agreement reached by high-
> ranking officers of the War Department and the WAAC Chieftain [Oveta
> Culp Hobby].... It was a victory for the New Deal ladies ... Mrs. Roosevelt
> wants all the young ladies to have the same overseas rights as their brothers
> and fathers.[51]

While *The Link* condemned 'Smearing the WAACs' as a typical blast of toxic,
anti-administration bile from the Robert R. McCormick press,[52] it also published
the salutary testimonials of chaplains at two WAAC training centres in order
to confound the pernicious 'Axis-inspired gossip concerning the WAACS going
on in some sensational newspaper quarters'. According to Chaplain Ralph W.
Graham, at Fort Des Moines, Iowa, Sunday and even midweek services were
'always filled', their chapel was thronged throughout the day by WAACs seeking
an opportunity for 'meditation and prayer', and the chaplain's office was inundated by 'a constant stream' of visitors seeking 'pastoral counsel'. Chaplain Frederick W. Hagan at Fort Oglethorpe, Georgia, was equally forthcoming about the
joys of ministering to the WAAC: 'In all my 17 years in the Army I've never seen
anything like the interest shown by these fine young women. Crowds at Sunday
morning services are usually so large that some WAACS have to stand outside
and wait for the next service – of which there are seven on Sundays.' Another
chaplain added the picturesque detail that it was sometimes necessary to enlist
the aid of the military police 'to direct WAAC traffic as one congregation comes
out and another is preparing to go in'. Nor was this piety simply for show as, at
Fort Oglethorpe, Testaments and Bibles were widely distributed 'and many a foot
locker holds a small library of religious books'.[53] To this evidence was added the
findings of an interdenominational delegation of churchmen who visited Fort
Des Moines before 'Capitol Stuff' dropped its bombshell. According to their testimony, which was duly released to the press, parents could rest assured 'about
the moral and spiritual welfare of their daughters', the WAAC being a 'sacrificial contribution which American women are making' and an organisation that
would 'strengthen their character'.[54]

Not everyone was convinced, of course. Bishop James Cassidy of Fall River was
opposed to the WAAC from the outset, claiming that it contravened Catholic
teaching.[55] Even before 'Capitol Stuff' had done its worst, a radio evangelist in
Arkansas took up the cudgels against the WAAC at the instigation of a disturbed
army nurse who claimed that recruits were inspected naked by male medical
officers, who showed them pornography as part of the process.[56] Likewise,
after rumours of streetwalking WAACs had gripped a 'Midwestern city', some
local clergymen were investigated by the FBI for inciting WAACs to desert.[57]
Significantly, and as part of a delegation that comprised 'the leaders of twenty-
eight national women's organizations' that visited Fort Des Moines and Camp

Crowder, Missouri, in August 1943, Mrs Samuel McCrea Cavert, wife of a leading figure in the FCC, was disappointed to learn that few home churches kept in touch with their female soldiers and that churches in neighbouring communities failed to provide 'social centers and hospitality for our women in the services'.[58] Nonetheless, the consensus was that religious life in the WAAC was, by army standards, remarkably vibrant. According to WAAC Captain Louise E. Goeden:

> Chaplains find that Wacs are a distinct aid in the post's religious activities. Just as the women in civilian life support church affairs and take part in the religious program, so do they after they have donned the khaki of Uncle Sam's Army. They attend services as a matter of course – and chaplains will testify that they do it in proportionately larger numbers than do the men – and also take part in such activities as singing in the choir and decorating the church for special occasions. Besides this, they furnish an example to the men and are often an encouragement for them to attend services.[59]

Goeden also cited the verdict of two chaplains who believed that the WAAC helped to rescue those women who had faltered in their faith:

> 'Many women who had ceased to attend services at their home parishes, or who attended irregularly, appear Sunday after Sunday at the fort for Holy Communion.' 'Many of the women of the corps are much more religious and faithful in the discharge of their obligations than they were in civilian life.'[60]

Oveta Culp Hobby, the director of the WAAC, was acutely aware of the need to protect and enhance its image in order to safeguard its role and survival. As one history of the corps has stressed: 'A volunteer force, the WAAC had to appeal to small town and middle-class America to recruit the skilled clerical workers, teachers, stenographers, and telephone operators needed by the Army.'[61] Besides releasing statements such as Goeden's through the War Department's Bureau of Public Relations, in which she had previously served as head of its Women's Interest Section,[62] Hobby, although a Protestant, took an active interest in the promotion of the cult of St Genevieve among Catholic WAACs. Originating in a Catholic WAAC study group at Fort Des Moines, the idea of having a patron saint for the corps held an obvious appeal, especially in the fevered months of 1943.[63] Under the circumstances, the virginal St Genevieve, who in the fifth century had helped save Paris from the pagan Huns, was an inspired choice. By June 1943, Hobby was writing to the chief of chaplains, stressing the support the scheme had received from the Catholic hierarchy and requesting guidance as to how a medallion of the saint might be approved for the use of the corps.[64] The chief of chaplains also worked behind the scenes to promote WAAC recruitment, advising the corps on a section entitled 'THE CHURCH ON THE POST PROVIDES RELIGIOUS GUIDANCE' in a WAAC recruitment brochure.[65]

With the WAAC acting as a lightning rod for opposition to female service in the military, the WAVES, founded by an act of Congress in July 1942 and reaching their peak strength of eighty-six thousand in August 1945,[66] attracted less attention and salacious rumour-mongering. Consequently, this enabled a more balanced appraisal to take place of the religious habits and inclinations of the nation's female bluejackets. Fresh from a posting to the heavy cruiser *Minneapolis* in the Pacific, Methodist chaplain Robert F. McComas was assigned to the Naval Communications Annex and WAVE Quarters 'D' in Washington in September 1944, where he found himself responsible for more than five thousand WAVES.[67] In a candid, post-war description of his work, McComas conceded the debilitating effects of separation, ill-adjustment and gruelling work schedules on his charges:[68]

> This routine, combined with the exacting but often monotonous nature of the work, plus the fact that the war seemed to be dragging on forever, had a telling effect upon the personnel. Some of them became exceedingly depressed and cracked under the strain, while others let down morally. Long sick-call lines and numerous captain's masts made personnel officers and chaplains aware of the seriousness of the situation.

As McComas's counselling work reached crisis proportions, he responded by mounting a religious programme that was 'broad in its scope and diversified in its appeal'. This programme was accompanied by a religious survey of the whole station based on a random sample of one-twentieth of its Protestant personnel, churchgoing and non-churchgoing alike. To ensure even greater rigour, 'answers were written out in the presence of an interviewing officer to insure [sic] the individual's best possible unaided effort'.[69]

While many WAVES seemed to find 'a fortress in religion', the results of this survey were salutary, showing how a high level of religious practice could readily co-exist with a remarkable degree of religious ignorance. Only 15 of the 169 WAVES who cooperated with McComas did not regard themselves as churchgoers. Just under half of the rest (68) attended weekly, 39 attended monthly, while 47 attended less than once a month. However, and when questioned on the particulars of their faith, and despite an average of 'seven to eight years in Sunday school', the answers received 'revealed an abysmal ignorance'; only one-third had 'at least some idea' of what a sacrament was and, when asked to place ten books of the Bible in the Old or the New Testament, the average score was 5.34 – a result that could have been achieved through simple guesswork. Despite this scriptural illiteracy, there was an underlying support for ecumenism, for, while it was felt that there should be 'enough denominations to enable everyone to find a church in which he can feel at home', the sample agreed that 'the Protestant churches as a group should stress more the important things they have in common rather than the less important things which separate them'.[70] In overall terms, McComas was left with the conclusion that his WAVES had vindicated the religious reputation of American womanhood; however, he also insisted that the Protestant churches were failing to provide this key constituency with proper religious instruction:

> [Women] have long had the reputation of being good church-goers. They are attending better today than ever before. Here they are not present merely to show off their new hats, because they all wear the same kind. They are not attending to impress anyone with their essential goodness or to please their parents. They come to worship because they feel a need for it. They are spiritually hungry. They want the church to recognize that need and to give them a decent spiritual meal.[71]

Nevertheless, navy chaplain George W. Wickersham was much more sceptical of the Marine Corps Women's Reserve, in which nearly eighteen thousand women were serving by June 1945.[72] Combining the innate conservatism of the corps with his less than progressive view that 'military life places a woman in the wrong psychological position for her womanly purposes',[73] Wickersham dismissed the Women's Reserve as 'a gosh-awful mess', and claimed to be less than impressed by the 'W.R.'s' who crossed his path at Parris Island in 1944:

> Most of our women grew either melancholy or wild. In general they seemed to divide themselves into three main groups: those who kept their virtue but were unhappy, those who purchased temporary relief at the cost of their virtue and those who were camp-followers anyway. And when night fell in the ladies' barracks, be assured that the latter two groups made it no easier for the former.[74]

Less controversial than the wartime auxiliaries were the pre-war Army Nurse Corps and Navy Nurse Corps, established in 1901 and 1908 respectively.[75] Smaller than the main female auxiliaries, fewer than sixty thousand women served in the Army Nurse Corps during World War II, while the Navy Nurse Corps reached its peak of just over eleven thousand in 1945.[76] Performing a much more traditional female role than the wartime auxiliaries, and with their reputation enhanced by their early heroics at Pearl Harbor and in the defence of the Philippines, America's military nurses were in less need of having their religious credentials defended before the bar of public opinion. Nevertheless, anecdotal evidence from former members of the Army Nurse Corps suggests that, in this respect also, they too maintained the best traditions of American womanhood. Grace M. Emory Stewart, who served in Britain with the 79th General Hospital and the 312th Station Hospital, remembered that: 'Not much was said but we all attended Chapel regularly as possible'.[77] For her part, Gloria Sangermano, a nurse from Pittsburgh, Pennsylvania, who spent the last months of the war on a dermatology ward in India, reflected a typical mix of religious reticence and understated conviction: 'We didn't get into it much – but I served as godmother for someone who converted to Catholicism while overseas.'[78]

If the gendered nature of American religious life was reflected in its armed forces, then so were some of its other salient characteristics. While much has been made of military service as a vast melting pot of all sorts and conditions, the vagaries of military requirements, culture and organisation could also serve to underline the ethnic, regional and segregated character of American religion. Given the concentration of America's Jewish population in the urban, industrial areas of the north-east and Midwest, and their higher-than-average anti-Nazi animus, nearly one-third of Jewish GIs served in the AAF (a branch of the army that never reached one-quarter of its total strength), and a disproportionate number of these served as aircrew.[79] Conversely, and with almost blanket exemptions for agricultural workers in place from November 1942,[80] over time the operation of the draft probably served to depress the proportion of Protestants in the armed forces. In 1942, the *National Catholic Almanac* estimated that Catholics, who were also chiefly concentrated in the urban and industrial centres of the north-east and Midwest, comprised approximately 17 per cent of the population (22,293,101 out of 131,669,275).[81] However, in June 1943 *The Link* alleged that: 'A recent tabulation of religious preferences compiled by the United States Army shows that 59 per cent of all soldiers are Protestant. Thirty-one per cent listed their preference as Catholic, two per cent as Jewish and eight per cent as having no preference.'[82] In the navy and the marines, whose institutional racism ran deeper than that of the army,[83] a dogged reluctance to admit African Americans added another ingredient to this religious imbalance. Although the navy's resistance was progressively worn down, the marines proved more obdurate. Before Pearl Harbor, there were no black marines; by the end of the war, fewer than twenty thousand had served in the Marine Corps. Of these, all had been classified as reservists and none had been commissioned.[84] As Allan R. Millett put it: 'From General Holcomb down to the ranks, there was considerable unhappiness about making the Corps anything but a club for white men.'[85] Consequently, by 1944, and according to the Catholic writer Dorothy Fremont Grant, 'the consensus among our Army and Navy Chaplains is that 38% of the Army is Catholic, at least 50% of the Navy, and more than 50% of the Marine Corps', quipping that 'Catholics take to water, from Baptism on.'[86]

Even allowing for a fair degree of exaggeration, the disproportionate number of Catholics in the US armed forces appears to have been a wartime fact. However, this favourable balance accentuated problems raised by the cultural and ethnic cleavages within American Catholicism, divisions that were reflected in its many 'national' parishes. Evidently, Catholic chaplains, with their ethnically mixed flocks, had to negotiate these differences with care. For example, and despite the occasion, and his Irish ancestry, Chaplain Joseph T. O'Callahan recalled that the diversity of the Catholics on board the aircraft carrier *Franklin* precluded a Mass in honour of St Patrick on 17 March 1945:

[A]t midafternoon, about the time when 'New York's Finest' were leading the parade down Fifth Avenue toward the reviewing stand at the Cathedral of St. Patrick, some twelve hundred boys gathered in the fo'c'sle of the *Franklin*. It was not a St. Patrick's Day celebration ... For some it was their heavenly patron's feast; others had for patron St. George or St. Boniface, Sts. Cyril and Methodius, Santiago or the patron saint of any of half a dozen other nationalities. But whatever their ancestry they were Americans. The heavenly patroness of America is our Blessed Lady, and on this Saturday a Mass in her honor was to be said.[87]

If the ethnic heterogeneity of American Catholicism remained apparent, then so too did the broader outlines of the nation's religious geography. Despite the mechanics of the draft, and the inevitable posting and reposting of millions of personnel, military service did not entirely efface the signs and influence of the nation's regional and sectional cultures. This was especially true in the army's National Guard units, the military embodiments of American localism. The 1st Battalion of the 116th Infantry Regiment, for instance, was recruited from the Virginian towns of Lynchburg, Harrisonburg, Roanoke and Bedford.[88] Likewise, the 35th Infantry Division, which could boast the decidedly homespun President Truman as one of its World War I veterans, was originally composed of National Guardsmen from Kansas, Missouri and Nebraska, and the fortunes of its Nebraskan 134th Infantry Regiment were keenly followed throughout the war by a specially assigned correspondent from Omaha's *World-Herald* newspaper.[89] If such localism could have severe consequences for some communities, as the Virginian town of Bedford discovered to its cost on D-Day,[90] even on a moral level the implications of such regionalism were apparent. As Ernie Pyle noted while a patient at a field hospital in Italy:

The Forty-fifth Division was originally made up largely of men from Oklahoma and West Texas. I didn't realize how different certain parts of our country are from others until I saw those men set off in a frame, as it were, in a strange, faraway place. The men of Oklahoma are drawling and soft-spoken. They are not smart alecks. Something of the purity of the soil seems to be in them. Even their cussing is simpler and more profound than the torrential obscenities of Eastern city men. An Oklahoman of the plains is straight and direct. He is slow to criticize and hard to anger, but once he is convinced of the wrong of something, brother, watch out.[91]

This regional distinctiveness had implications for the religious composition of National Guard units and, numerous though Catholics may have been in overall terms, Catholic chaplains could still find themselves in units where Catholics were notable by their absence. Such was the lot, for example, of Aquinas T. Colgan, a Carmelite from Chicago, who served (and died) in the Pacific with the

31st ('Dixie') Infantry Division, an 'overwhelmingly Protestant' National Guard formation initially composed of National Guardsmen from Louisiana, Mississippi, Alabama and Florida.[92]

However, such regional traits and imprints were by no means confined to the National Guard. Arriving at a replacement depot in France in 1944, Max B. Wall, a Jewish chaplain and a resident of New York City, was assigned to the 9th Infantry Division – originally a regular formation – because he could speak Yiddish and the division had a high proportion of 'Jewish boys from the New York area'.[93] Even the draftee army harboured units that had a discernibly local or regional cast, with inevitable repercussions for their religious composition. Reassigned in December 1943 from the 399th Infantry Regiment to the 1112th Engineer Combat Group, neither of which had yet seen action, Chaplain Russell Cartwright Stroup was immediately struck by the considerable differences between these units. Not only was the latter mainly composed of Midwesterners, but it was also older, better educated and more Protestant.[94] The same was also true of the mountain warfare specialists of the crack 10th Mountain Division, a division that sought to attract the 'skiers, mountain climbers, forest rangers, and park and wildlife-service men' of America,[95] none of whom were especially numerous among the urban working classes of the north-east and Midwest. In consequence, and according to one of its members, who reported to *The Link* from Camp Hale, Colorado, in 1944, the religious tone of the division was distinctly Protestant, although modulated by undercurrents of reticence and scepticism:

> Religion is a vital factor in the lives of most soldiers, even though they don't admit it. Up here, where most of the men are of German, Danish, Finnish, Swedish and Norwegian descent, the majority are Protestant, and we have some lively religious discussions.... Since this is a volunteer group, many of the men are college-trained, and, as is usual in college, many of them pose as cynics so far as religion is concerned.[96]

However, even run-of-the-mill draftee infantry divisions could have a distinct regional and religious stamp. The religious implications of the often crude administrative processes of forming these divisions were clear to Thomas J. Donnelly, a Catholic chaplain from New York City. As part of the original cadre for the 77th Infantry Division at Fort Jackson, South Carolina, Donnelly found that most of his original comrades, officers and 'non-coms' alike, were 'dyed-in-the-wool southerners', and that: 'Some of them, upon seeing a Catholic priest for the first time in their lives, stared in curiosity. They looked as though they were trying to make sure I did not have the devil's tail and horns'.[97] This situation was transformed, however, by the arrival of trainloads of draftees from the north-east. Assigned to the 305th Infantry Regiment, Donnelly soon became responsible for more than seventeen hundred Catholics, more than half of its soldiers.[98] Similarly, after activation at Camp Gruber, Oklahoma, in July 1942, the first contingent of draftees for the 88th Infantry Division consisted of men 'drawn mainly from New England, New York, New Jersey, and Delaware' and, as there was 'an unusual concentration of technical and administrative talent' among them, they were largely used to fill out 'the enlisted ranks of the division's logistical superstructure'; in contrast, the second tranche of the 88th's so-called 'enlisted fillers' were drawn from 'a wide area of the Midwest and Southwest' and these rustic 'Okies', as they were disparagingly known, were mainly assigned to the division's 'less technical slots'.[99] Given that the 88th was not regularly tapped to provide drafts of replacements for other units, this regional configuration endured within the division until its departure overseas in December 1943.[100]

The case of the 88th also helps to illustrate the importance of the army's personnel policies in shaping the character (religious and otherwise) of its components. At its reception centres, and in addition to medical inspection and the other rituals of induction, inductees were subjected to an aptitude/ intelligence test known as the Army General Classification Test (AGCT) and to a brief interview with a classification specialist. On the basis of the results, inductees were given their army assignments, which were (ideally) as closely related to their civilian skills and occupations as possible.[101] However, many civilian skills did not readily map onto army requirements. No official qualification existed for assignment as a rifleman, for instance, and, as Major General Lewis B. Hershey, the director of Selective Service, never tired of quipping: 'I haven't seen a draft questionnaire yet in which the guy said he shot people for a living.'[102] Controversial during the war, the army's personnel policies have been criticised ever since. While discriminating against African Americans (who, on the grounds of their colour, inferior schooling and limited employment opportunities in civilian life, largely became 'the Army's hewers of wood and drawers of water'),[103] and being informed by a host of other 'hereditarian and elitist assumptions',[104] some military historians have claimed that these policies fundamentally undermined the army's effectiveness. Martin van Creveld, for example, argued that they discriminated against 'the young, the not-so-bright or the socially disadvantaged', producing a dysfunctional army in which those inductees who scored lowest in the AGCT were routinely assigned to the combat arms while the Army Service Forces (who administered the system) took the pick of the crop. That is, however, if members of this fortunate elite were not otherwise siphoned off into the AAF, officer candidate schools, or the college-based Army Special Training Program.[105] Developing van Creveld's critique, Theodore Wilson has shown that the overall effect of these personnel policies was to cast a disproportionate burden of infantry combat onto the shoulders of America's disadvantaged whites, those most likely to be designated 'rifleman' or, in bureaucratic jargon, 'Specification Serial Number' 745. As Wilson concluded:

In sum, the stereotypical squad portrayed in all those 1940s and 1950s war films – young, uneducated 'hicks, micks and spics' leavened by a crusty careerist and an older, well-educated idealist, 'doc' or 'prof' – was not far off the mark. The system ensured that those with less education, little or no pre-war vocational experience – the depression dropouts, the slum kids, the backwoods boys from Appalachia and the Deep South – ended up as '745s', riflemen. It appears that the personnel gurus planned it that way. Their intentions, of course, were noble – to ensure the proper assignment of those qualified to do the army's *important* work such as flying airplanes, fixing tanks and classifying inductees.[106]

This searing indictment aside, Wilson's conclusion may well help to account for the well-attested predilection of the infantry for 'foxhole religion', as the army's own personnel policies seem to have conspired to push GIs from America's evangelical, Catholic and Jewish heartlands furthest into harm's way.

Nevertheless, and for training purposes in particular, administrative and logistical factors dictated that regionalism and its religious corollaries could even impact upon the AAF, the navy and the marines. At Santa Ana Army Air Base, Norman Wesley Achen, an Arizonan, was hardly pitched into an all-American (or even all south-western) melting pot; in fact, he found himself among 239 Texan cadets and in a hellhole of Texan chauvinism.[107] More congenial was James J. Fahey's experience of Great Lakes Naval Training Station, Illinois, to which he travelled along with a 'very large' group of fellow recruits 'from the New England states'.[108] On his first assignment to Sampson Naval Training Center, New York, Chaplain John Harold Craven, a Missourian, noted that its recruits came 'from all over the Northeastern part of the country, from Boston, New York City, and Syracuse'.[109] Norman H. Boike, for his part, and after enlisting in the marines just after Pearl Harbor, remembered taking a train all the way from Detroit to Parris Island, South Carolina, and collecting batches of other recruits from the South and Midwest en route, including 'a huge group of fellows from Kentucky and Tennessee', but 'amazingly none from Ohio'.[110] Even after training, pure chance could conspire to ensure local concentrations of regional, cultural and religious groups in the navy and in the marines. When James J. Fahey was assigned to the new light cruiser *Montpelier* in November 1942 he wrote that, in contrast to his early days as a navy recruit, 'Most of the fellows are rebels from the South', even though the crew as a whole came 'from about every State in the Union'.[111]

In addition to the regional implications of logistical convenience and administrative accident, Samuel Hynes, a self-described 'yokel' from Minneapolis, noted some social and cultural factors that distinguished US Navy from Marine Corps fliers:

The Marines are administratively attached to the Navy, but no Marine likes to admit it, and the Navy is generally regarded (by Marines, that is) as a softer, more gentlemanly, less belligerent service. Of my flight school friends it was certainly true that the well-bred ones tended to take Navy commissions; and those like myself who felt provincial, or common, or under-bred, chose the Marine Corps, where those qualities wouldn't show. The Marines that I knew, both the officers and the enlisted men, seemed to be mainly southerners and mid-westerners – country boys, red-necks, and yokels. I don't think I ever met a Marine from New York or San Francisco, or a rich one.[112]

Naturally, such configurations could carry religious implications. In the Russell Islands, for example, a Catholic army chaplain felt obliged to take a navy Seabee battalion under his wing. Composed of skilled workmen and craftsmen, this had been 'recruited from the Atlantic Seaboard states ranging from Maine to Pennsylvania' and was 'predominantly Catholic'.[113] By the same token, and before his death in the Pacific early in 1944, the war correspondent Raymond Clapper noted the skewed religious configuration of the crew of an unspecified aircraft carrier. Although a cross-section of Catholics, Jews, Mormons, Christian Scientists and other Protestants, for no obvious reason Catholics comprised 60 per cent of its crew of three thousand, their numbers helping to sustain a Catholic chaplain, a daily Mass, and devotional services every evening.[114]

Regardless of denomination, colour, gender or locality, and sometimes to the consternation of their commanders, an overweening attachment to home was characteristic of American service personnel throughout the war. As one army chaplain remarked in July 1944:

Those of us who have dealt with men in the Armed Forces on overseas assignments have been constantly amazed at the power of the average man to idealize the home town and his home folks. No matter where he is – even in Hawaii, 'the Paradise of the Pacific' – he has considered his being there nothing but an imposition. Podunk is heaven, compared to 'the pineapple island'.[115]

If rather unwarlike, this 'idealization of the absent'[116] was nevertheless considered to be critical to service morale. Consequently, America's military machine, to say nothing of civilian organisations such as the Red Cross and the USO, devoted vast resources to the maintenance of home links, emblematic of which was the provision of telephone exchanges at stateside camps, the introduction of V mail, the development of service broadcasting, and the ubiquity of Coca-Cola at a nickel a bottle.[117] As Lee Kennett has aptly observed of America's accidental warriors:

The G.I. was in a very real sense suspended between two ways of life and held in that state of suspension as long as he wore a uniform. Physically he left civilian life, but mentally he never joined the Army; he was in the service but not of it. He spent part of his time thinking about what was for him the present – that is, his Army existence – and fully as much time thinking about his past – and what he hoped would be his future – in the civilian world.[118]

However, if this hankering for home was a natural consequence of the fact that 'home and family assume a rosy glow of perfection from a muddy foxhole or drafty tent on the other side of the world',[119] it also reflected the profound and enduring influence of domestic ideology in American society and culture.

Significantly, this 'idealization of the absent' had strongly religious undertones, for the ideal American home – whether blessed by the presence of the family Bible, or by an image of the Sacred Heart – was a place where faith was nurtured.[120] Maintained by an epitome of pious femininity and suffused with religious and moral values, it was celebrated by Catholics in the cult of the Holy Family and was the harmonious hub of a vibrant, if private, devotional life, especially in the form of family prayers and, for Protestants, Bible-reading.[121] Whether positive or negative, for most Americans the influence of their home backgrounds on their religious practice was formative and fundamental. As AAF chaplain Thomas H. Clare remarked: 'The men who go to church in the army, are the men who used to go to church in civilian life. As usual, the Catholics are the best churchgoers, with the Protestants next, and the Jews last – perhaps because of the limited facilities available to them.'[122] On leaving the army after the war, Chaplain Francis L. Sampson noted that the war had taught him above all else the importance of a proper home and religious upbringing:

The one factor that did follow the men wherever they went, the one thing that stood by them during the darkest hours and gave them the help and courage they needed was the discipline and training they had received at home. These were the imperishable assets that did not disintegrate under the fire of temptation or the fire of enemy bullets. Yes, I reflected as I was leaving the Army, Christian home training is the greatest endowment parents can give to their children. Of course I had always believed this but had never had it so graphically illustrated in civilian life.[123]

Making a different point on the same theme, and while addressing the state of religion in the services in 1946, William N. Thomas, the new chief of navy chaplains, deflected criticism of his colleagues by insisting that: 'Blame for lack of religion among GIs must be placed where it belongs – in the home, the community, and the Church.'[124] According to his predecessor, Robert D. Workman, the supreme value of *The Link* magazine lay not in the intellectual stimulus provided by its comparatively highbrow content, but in the fact that 'it makes former ideals, influences and associations recoverable'.[125] The importance of the golden thread of religion in connecting home and service life was even underlined by secular pundits, an article 'Mental Health in Military Life' in the *Marine Corps Gazette* of November 1945 explaining that religious observances were of value to the fighting man partly because: 'As a continuation of his accustomed civilian practices, they constitute a strong connecting tie with home and all that home signifies.'[126]

Clearly, and despite the much-lamented crisis in family life caused by the upheavals of the war years, a religious upbringing was one of those aspects of home life that provided an inspiration and moral compass for a great many service men and women. Brought up on a farm near Elberon, Iowa, Howard Heaton, who served in North-West Europe with the 17th Airborne Division, remembered that his family were regular churchgoers. Not only this, but: 'We gave thanks for every meal. When I was younger, we prayed before I went to bed. We read the Bible together in the evenings, and we prayed together … We believed in hard work, respect for other people, and the need to look out for your fellowman.'[127] Very much a product of his background, in the midst of war Heaton found both solace and meaning in the faith he had imbibed in childhood:

> From the minute I flew into France, I always figured the good Lord had His hand in everything and would take care of me … Due to a lot of things, I am convinced that the only reason I survived was because God had a plan for me. I'm not sure exactly what that plan was. Maybe it was just to survive and lead a normal life.[128]

In the very different milieu of pre-war Manhattan, similar values also prevailed in the childhood home of Charles Dryden, a pilot in the African American 99th Pursuit Squadron:

> Mom was the gentlest, most devout, loving mother anywhere, ever.… Together Mom and Dad emphasized four things in my rearing: love and serve God, obey your parents, be loyal to your family, and get a good education.… My parents were such devout Christians that they passed this on.… From my youngest days, we always attended Sunday school, and I had the guidance of my parents, my aunts, and other relatives, who were my role models.[129]

No less than Heaton, and though sorely tested by the entrenched racism of American society, Dryden averred that his faith proved a constant support: 'That kind of upbringing impacted all my life and made it less difficult for me to live with and cope with the meanness and mean-spiritedness I encountered … it has been a fairly easy journey for me through life with that kind of faith.'[130]

The importance and place of religion in the ideal home was registered in many ways. The ultimate female icon among wartime GIs seems to have been Mrs Miniver, the indomitable, churchgoing, British middle-class housewife played by Greer Garson in the eponymous Hollywood movie of 1942.[131] Described by one army chaplain, Eben Cobb Brink, as a 'soul-stirring story of today's quiet faith and heroism', such was the film's appeal that, when it was screened prior to embarkation for North Africa, he was flooded with requests for editions of the New Testament that included the Psalms, the keynote text of the film being Psalm 91 ('He that dwelleth in the secret place of the most High shall abide under the shadow of the Almighty. I will say of the Lord, He is my refuge and my fortress: my God; in him will I trust ...').[132] In the religious press, one of the most widely publicised letters of the war was penned by an army nurse. Written on the Sabbath from a field hospital in North Africa, and reflecting on the indelible imprint and significance of her family's churchgoing habits, it was published in *The Christian Family* before being given star billing in *The Link* in September 1943, and then republished by Chaplain Ellwood C. Nance in his 1944 compilation *Faith of Our Fighters*:

> Your church attendance wasn't just a gesture lightly made, nor a duty grimly performed. It was vital and real, the open avowal of your most cherished convictions, backed up by your daily conduct. Family worship, grace at meals, the individual prayers you taught us children to say, the unfailing sympathy and courtesy you showed to us and to each other – it was all summed up when we sat together, a unit, in the family pew on Sunday morning.[133]

Nor was hers an isolated reaction, for she observed with reference to her patients:

> And you'd be surprised (or maybe you wouldn't, being the sort of people you are) at how many of them draw their courage from the same place I do – from recollections of their families at private prayer and public worship, from the clear knowledge (like mine) that, despite the apparent triumph of so much they have been taught is evil and the apparent defeat of so much they have been taught is good, their parents maintain a serene and unwavering faith in a God of love and mercy, and express that faith openly before a desperate and doubting world.[134]

That religious faith and practice in the services was closely linked to an enduring attachment to home was clear to Joseph W. James, a Southern Baptist chaplain who served with the 3rd Bombardment Group in New Guinea, and who found his Sunday evening services thronged with airmen:

> Deep in the jungle, near the bank of a running stream, the men would gather on Sunday evenings to sing the songs and hymns they had learned in their churches back home. They would sing 'Rock of Ages', 'Lead Kindly Light', 'The Old Rugged Cross', 'The Church in the Wildwood', 'Tell Me the Old, Old Story', and 'Blessed Assurance'. Then they would look off into the distance and Chaplain James would know that they were seeing their families and friends with whom they used to sing these songs.[135]

Nor was this merely pious fancy. In a letter to two college friends in the summer of 1944, Corporal William Kiessel wrote of how thoughts of home were to the fore during pre-invasion services, Protestant, Catholic and Jewish alike:

> At all these sacred gatherings there is a sincerity and informality that makes for a better and greater fellowship and gives a deeper sense of the intangible value of friends, home, and the eternal verities of life ... In those services we all wish we'd lived better, been more complimentary and less critical, written home more lovingly and more often...[136]

Again, and in a letter written to *The Link* from New Guinea in 1944, an army officer testified to the efficacy of church worship, and of hymnody in particular, in bridging time and space:

> I felt the familiar homelike glow of worship as we sang 'The Church in the Wildwood' and 'Onward Christian Soldiers' and 'Faith of Our Fathers'.... I could close my eyes as my lips spilled forth a song and be anywhere in the world I wanted to be. I could be on the third row of the church back home, sitting with the whole family.... It was there in that little chapel that I realized all over again, in a different way, the length and width and depth of a man's religion. I realized again the endlessness of its power to soothe and comfort, reaching down out here into hearts that are sick with the miles that stand between them and their loved ones ...[137]

Furthermore, religion was integral to the idealised vision of home that service members wished to realise after the war. For example, and while reflecting in his diary on the manifold discomforts of serving on a warship in the tropics, James J. Fahey wrote in July 1944:

> It is just the little things in life that you look forward to.... When you had them you thought nothing of them, you took them for granted. Now you look forward to meeting your family and friends, being able to go to the corner store and get the morning paper, and read your favourite topics, or visit the drug-store for a big ice cream soda, looking at the buildings and going to the Parish Church, and the local theater.[138]

Inevitably, these ever-present feelings of nostalgia peaked at certain times of the year – notably Easter, Mother's Day, Thanksgiving and Christmas – to say nothing of the Jewish festivals of Rosh Hashana, Yom Kippur, Hanukah and Passover.[139] However, for Christians, Christmas served as the supreme focus of the wartime longing for an idealised home life. As one Catholic source averred: 'The spell of Christmas is universal among our service men.'[140] Reflected in the massive appeal of Irving Berlin's 'White Christmas', first performed by Bing Crosby at Christmas 1941, successive wartime Christmases underlined the ubiquitous absorption with home. While the regulars of the pre-war navy had made much of Christmas, marking the season with illuminations, concerts, and parties for orphaned children, Robert D. Workman observed that wartime and the advent of a citizens' navy had only helped to intensify 'the Christmas spirit'. Christmas 1943 saw sailors, marines and coast guard personnel flock to church 'in unprecedented numbers', and he anticipated more of the same at Christmas 1944:

> Marines may decorate cocoanut Christmas trees with scraps of colored paper; men in submarines may have a folding Christmas tree only twelve inches tall on the mess table; and our men on treeless, windswept islands in the Aleutians may have to build their own tree in order to achieve an appropriate atmosphere.... But wherever these men are, there will be no lack of remembrance. There will be traditional 'Merry Christmas' greetings; thoughts will be of home and loved ones; in their hearts will be the humble gratitude of men giving thanks for God's most precious gift – the gift of His Beloved Son.[141]

By the same token, and according to army chaplain Eugene L. Daniel, Christmas 1943 and 1944 were especially trying times for his fellow American POWs languishing in German captivity.[142] However, these were difficult times for the US Army in general. As a history of Fifth Army's chaplains put it, in war-blighted Italy, Christmas 1943 was scarcely a time of good cheer:

> The mood of men living under the pressure of war, in mud and cold that defied description, with victory seemingly nowhere in sight, was not conducive to the celebration of a feast of peace. For many of the chaplains it was a matter of going from little group to little group, with or without the chaplain's folding organ, and singing a carol or two. It meant reading the Christmas story, often with the briefest comments.[143]

In Britain, where preparations for the cross-Channel invasion were gathering pace, and where American troop numbers were more than five times what they had been in December 1942,[144] Ambassador John G. Winant composed a seasonal message of goodwill to 750,000 GIs at the invitation of *Stars and Stripes*. Reflecting on the imminent invasion, and the theme of sacrifice implicit in 'the story of the Child in the Manger', Winant's message concluded:

> Christmas for us will always be a day of homecoming, and we are far from home, but we know the worth of kindly comradeship, and we are stationed in a friendly country. We are grateful that we have a chance to protect the homes where we first caught a glimpse of Christmas Day, and where stockings still hang over the firesides and children laugh and play because none dare invade our land, while we march forward with our face toward the enemy.[145]

A year later, with the Battle of the Bulge hanging in the balance, and for a great many GIs the only Christmas they would spend in or near the front line, the celebration of Christmas 1944 acquired an even keener edge. As Stephen E. Ambrose observed, in the midst of a wintry and forested landscape that was reminiscent of a Christmas card, 'Loneliness was their most shared emotion. Christmas meant family.... Family and home meant life.'[146] At the headquarters of the Third Battalion of the 134th Infantry Regiment, then in rest in the French city of Metz, the nexus of feast, family and faith furnished material for a sobering sermon by its chaplain, who pointed out:

> In the midst of war we are celebrating in peace and happiness the birth of a babe nearly two thousand years ago. It is a wonderful thing that one man could bring such joy into the world when others bring such misery. In our homes back in the States tonight the greatest joy obtained by men is being reached because a man named Jesus lived in a country called Palestine. Around us tonight the most terrible destruction and pessimism hovers because that man was forgotten.[147]

Others chose to see the situation in more ironic terms. George S. Patton joked on Christmas Day 1944, 'Noel, noel, what a night to give the Nazis hell', and wrote in his diary, 'A clear cold Christmas, lovely weather for killing Germans, which seems a bit queer, seeing Whose birthday it is.'[148]

William B. Hanford, an artillery observer with the 103rd Infantry Division, remembered how, on Christmas Eve 1944: 'We came into the village of Farbersville, just as an air burst exploded over the main street. I thought about the Star of Bethlehem and how different this was from the biblical eve that was probably being celebrated back home.'[149] Nevertheless, it was an indication of the potent grip that Christmas had over the American imagination that, after spending Christmas night in a ruined barn, there was a distinctly festive air at Hanford's battery the following morning; gifts from home were unwrapped and a truck arrived to take its Catholics to Mass. A festive dinner was consumed on their return, after which a chaplain and his assistant made a welcome if unexpected appearance:

> Hymnbooks were passed out, and everyone sang. Even Len Harris, who was Jewish, sang. With the temperature zero, Len could hardly be expected to wait outside until the service was over, and he was good-natured about it, saying, 'My rabbi wouldn't mind. I haven't had much chance to sing lately, and they were nice songs.'[150]

Kenneth A. Connelly, a chaplain's assistant in the 84th Infantry Division, was impressed by the fundamentally domestic and civilian appeal of such services, writing in a letter on New Year's Day 1945:

> This has been a week of church services ... and everything considered, it has been successful. We even took our field organ out into the snowy

woods and lured a congregation out of their fox-holes with blasts of 'O Come All Ye Faithful.' And those cold and homesick G.I.'s, with little but terror for a Christmas gift sang the everlasting carols that you, no doubt, were singing at Prospect Church. And in the heart of each of them was the memory and the hope of a family; a redeeming thought that gave them the grace and strength to act like the heroes they are.[151]

While Jewish GIs could join in Christian celebrations with good grace, ordinarily their respective religious festivals 'confirmed among Jews a sense of their own separateness.'[152] According to established army custom, it was expected that Jewish soldiers would cede their weekend passes and other privileges to their Christian comrades at Christmas and Easter. Although this was done on a reciprocal basis, with Jewish soldiers getting furloughs for Passover, Yom Kippur and Rosh Hashana,[153] their relative numbers meant that the burden of this custom weighed more heavily on Jew than on gentile. Consequently, at Christmas in particular it was quite possible to find whole army posts fed, guarded and even waited on by their Jewish personnel.[154] However, and as with their Christian equivalents, the great religious festivals exerted a strong emotional appeal for otherwise non-observant Jews; in fact, 'three-day-a-year' Jews (those who attended synagogue on the two days of Rosh Hashana and then on Yom Kippur) were a highly discernible category among American Jews of the war generation.[155] They were even recognisable to Christian chaplains, whose duty it was to make provision for them when necessary. As Thomas H. Clare, an Evangelical and Reformed chaplain in India, remarked:

> The best times, of course, are the great religious festivals and holidays which come in the Jewish calendar, particularly Pesach (Passover) and Rosh Hashana. The Jewish boy may evince no interest in religious services for months, but as soon as a favorite Jewish holiday draws near he begins to feel a sort of psychic nostalgia which should be satisfied.[156]

Describing a Hanukah celebration at Dijon in 1944, Chaplain Morris N. Kertzer noted how 400 Jewish GIs were trucked in from the length and breadth of Burgundy, how stalwart volunteers – some of them WACs – made 2,000 potato pancakes, and how an ambulance was on standby to ensure deliveries of these pancakes to wounded Jewish soldiers at a nearby general hospital. [157] Reflecting on the pronounced wartime enthusiasm for their festivals among Jewish GIs, Kertzer wrote in 1947:

> The intense interest in festivals and holidays alone, among Jewish men overseas, may well alter religious custom in the American synagogue for years to come. Enthusiasm for such observance may carry even the most minor holidays into positions of prominence on the Jewish calendar. At the same time, there is likely to be strong G.I. influence in the ritual and manner of

observance, originating both in military custom, and in the soldiers' exposure to the ritual of the North African, European and British Jews.[158]

Nevertheless, symptoms of underlying and abiding attachment to the religious expressions of home life were by no means confined to group activities
such as the celebration of festivals, hymn-singing and wistful talk of the future.
On an individual level, personal habits of Bible-reading also helped to ease the
pangs of separation, so much so that in 1944 the American Bible Society sponsored 'a great Nation-wide Bible Reading' lasting from Thanksgiving through to
Christmas. As explained to the service readership of *The Link*, this ambitious
scheme of daily Bible-reading had been formulated because so many of them had
'written home asking ... families and friends to join [them] in reading the Book
together'. On these grounds, therefore, it was argued that 'a home front emphasis
on Bible reading is an essential part of keeping faith with you men on the fighting
fronts'.[159] In the event, daily passages read by Orson Welles were carried by radio
from coast-to-coast and it was estimated that 'more citizens of the U.S.A.' were
reading the Bible in those weeks than at any point in the nation's history. Such
was the success of the venture that it was repeated 'on a world-wide basis' in 1945,
with the roster of thirty-four daily readings being chosen by service personnel.[160]

However, the religious dimensions of military and civilian life were not always
easily reconciled. As we have seen, the contemporary systems of army and navy
chaplaincy made little allowance for the denominational or devotional preferences of Protestant or Jewish personnel. Furthermore, service men and women
often evinced a marked preference to worship in civilian churches. As Chaplain
Thomas J. Donnelly recalled, while the 77th Infantry Division was in training at
Fort Jackson, South Carolina:

> After a few weeks, there was some loosening up in the restrictions and
> many would take advantage of the free time by visiting and attending
> churches in the surrounding areas. This was good because it gave everyone
> the opportunity to spend some time with civilians. Above all, it got them
> away from the harsh realities of their daily military life and brought them
> back to the way it was in their home towns and parishes.[161]

Unfortunately, such was the extent of opting out that in November 1944 *The
Link* carried an admonitory article by Chaplain G.E. Hopkins, a Methodist AAF
chaplain, who deplored excessive individualism and extolled the many virtues of
the homogenised Protestantism of the military:

> It has been rather disappointing to me to find so many Christians in the
> armed forces who seemingly feel no responsibility toward the chaplain or the
> chapel. They are interested in churches near the post, or they have decided
> to worship privately, using devotional books and religious pamphlets. They
> are good men, and sincere, but they are overlooking a grave responsibility

which the Christian Church imposes upon its members; the responsibility of being our brothers' brother. It is not enough that we continue to live the Christian life; it is not enough that we personally go to church somewhere.... The government has spent millions of dollars to provide chapels, chapel properties and chaplains. The chaplain is your pastor; you are a member of his parish.... There is nothing sectarian about either the chapel or the chaplain. There is no Methodist nor Baptist nor Episcopalian. There is only Protestant.... Never in civilian life were you able to lift religion above the petty lines of creeds and sects as you can in the service.[162]

The leaven in the loaf

Whatever their nature or cause, these responses were deeply rooted in the essential vitality of American religious life, being reflections of a society in which belief in God was all but universal. This vitality was also reflected in the fact that there was a large element of recognisably religious men and women diffused throughout the nation's armed forces, a natural corollary of a society in which church membership approached 50 per cent of the population. Inevitably, the faith and courage of some proved an inspiration to their co-religionists and to Americans more widely. For example, one early hero of the war was Captain Richard E. Fleming, a Marine Corps pilot posthumously awarded the Medal of Honor for his exploits at Midway in June 1942.[163] A graduate of Saint Thomas Military Academy, Minnesota, Fleming was a devout Catholic and daily Mass-goer who had received Holy Communion on the day of his death.[164] As a sibling averred, and Archbishop Spellman was keen to reiterate: 'The greatest gift which a man can receive is that of a happy death; and that blessing, even in the midst of shock and shell, was given to Dick a hundredfold.'[165] Among those celebrated by evangelical Protestants were Bill Tollberg and Johnnie Hutchins, winners of the Navy Cross and Medal of Honor respectively, who also gave their names to destroyer escorts as a result of their self-sacrificial feats in the Pacific War.[166]

On 26 July 1943 the London edition of *Stars and Stripes* reported on a hero of a very different kind in a story entitled 'Former Mormon Missionary Returns Here as Fort Pilot'. This concerned First Lieutenant Robert G. Hodson, of Provo, Utah, who in 1938 was 'a volunteer Mormon missionary' to England and was there again as a B-17 pilot. Although Hodson was reluctant to 'talk much about Mormonism around the station', he declared that he knew of nothing 'more important to the survival of religion than the defeat of the Nazis', and said that his faith gave him 'confidence for his job and a belief that he has just a little better chance of getting through the war.'[167] As the military historian Max Hastings recognised in his study of the apocalyptic struggle for Germany: 'God meant a lot to many men of that generation, especially Midwestern Americans.'[168] However, this important acknowledgement understates the ubiquity of this constituency throughout the American armed forces, one that was neither confined to Europe nor to natives of the Midwest. Adding substance to the claims of General Alexander A. Vandegrift, Chaplain Warren Wyeth Willard found plenty of religious marines among his flock on Guadalcanal, whom he described as 'the most intriguing group of men I had ever met'.[169] Among them was an explosives expert, namely 'Private Emory B. Ashurst, of Chicamuxen, Maryland'. A man who revelled in his work, Ashurst 'loved to toy with machine guns and other weapons', and yet 'combined with his fearlessness and zest for adventure was a radiant faith. He was always present for divine services. He was always willing to aid his chaplain in any task he could perform'.[170] Such incongruities could be more poignant, however. In Europe, Lester Atwell noted his company commander, formerly a professor of philosophy in the rarefied atmosphere of a Catholic college, lying dead in the snow of the Ardennes.[171] Similarly, John T. Bassett, serving in Italy with the 10th Mountain Division, remembered an older comrade whose presence seemed at odds with the horrors and obscenities of war: 'Fuller was a quiet, gentle sort who lived for his family. War was monstrous to him. It could have destroyed him, but he went through each day operating on faith. He simply believed that God would not separate him from his wife and children'.[172] The admiration that such individuals could evoke was captured in a letter written in May 1945 by Richard Kennard, a marine lieutenant on Okinawa, to his parents:

> As the weeks go by I have grown to be very fond of my enlisted friend Jack Adamson, raised on a farm in north Wisconsin. He is a perfect Christian and in my eyes the most ideal American boy I have ever known. I have lived very close to him and so know just what I am saying. Jack is the cleanest, most meticulous lad I have ever seen. He is completely unselfish, and always thinks about his buddies in the gun section first. He has worked ever since he could walk. He doesn't smoke, drink, or swear. You know a good Christian will always have many friends and yet be little appreciated because there are so few people today who understand what it is like.
>
> (Kennard even asked that, in the event of his death, whatever money he had should go to Adamson.)[173]

Among the broad diffusion of committed laymen were some who exercised a ministry of their own. One of the most senior examples was that of Brigadier General Carl B. McDaniel, deputy commander of the Seventh Air Force, who 'took an active interest in the religious life of his Command' and undertook duties as one of several 'auxiliary chaplains' on Okinawa in autumn 1945.[174] Given how thinly spread their chaplains were, this was particularly true of Jewish laymen. As Morris N. Kertzer wrote, 'In an armored division in which I served, a young Jewish sergeant filled in as substitute Jewish chaplain in my absence, conducting regular Sabbath services for the men', adding that 'he had thousands of counterparts all over the world, enlisted men and officers, who conducted as many services as did the Jewish chaplains.[175] However, this was also common among Protestants. On the destroyer Ralph Talbot, for example, a strapping erstwhile seminarian known as 'Parson' led services, distributed Bibles, buried the dead, and had a near-miraculous escape when a Japanese shell burst only three feet from him.[176] Similarly, an army chaplain's assistant attached to a general hospital told *The Link* how, in the absence of a chaplain, a Sunday service had been saved by one of its patients, an officer who had 'almost entered the ministry before the war broke out' and who had decided to 'enter seminary' on his discharge.[177] A more conspicuous element among the keen Protestant laity were the products and students of dozens of fundamentalist Bible schools. For these men and women, military service was a heaven-sent opportunity to implement evangelistic methods honed in civilian life, and their apparent success was the cause of much satisfaction in fundamentalist circles. For example, in January 1945 the following advertisement for Chicago's Moody Bible Institute appeared in the *Christian Herald*:

> Hundreds of young men and women, going from Institute classrooms into their country's service, are accomplishing great things for God. They're using their training in active soul-winning.... One sailor held a weekly Bible class, the attendance growing from 5 to 180 in two months ... a marine won twelve of his fellow marines to Christ ... an Army nurse writes of witnessing to American air casualties in an English hospital ... a soldier was wakened at midnight by a fellow soldier under conviction, who knew where to come to learn the way of salvation.... All of these are Moody-trained witnesses. Letters from every front tell of similar experiences. Isn't it worthwhile to co-operate in providing the tuition-free training which enables these young Christians to witness so effectively?[178]

Significantly, such zealots were not only of interest to the religious press and, as in the case of Robert G. Hodson, even found their way into *Stars and Stripes*. In October 1943 its London edition carried a story entitled 'Army Sergeant Goes to Town In Pulpit of an English Church', its subject being the ministry of Master Sergeant Don Robertson, a Northern Baptist from Little Falls, New Jersey, and his electrifying effect upon a sleepy 'congregation of English folk'. As reported: 'The talk wasn't delivered in the sonorous cadence the British are accustomed to in their religious diet, and it made such an impression that the sergeant was asked to return the following Sunday with another message.' In fact, it transpired that Robertson had given 'more than a dozen such sermons' in English churches, and nor was this hot-gospeller in the least intimidated by his comrades. Besides 'presiding at countless Army services', Robertson 'spent most of his spare time inculcating a fuller religious spirit among his fellow GIs. To the delight of overworked chaplains, he organized choir and prayer groups and made sure they were carried through.' Furthermore:

Robbie's method of developing interest in church activities is simple and direct. He usually picks the mess hall when searching for recruits. 'Hey, you snake in the grass,' he bellows when he spots a GI peacefully munching on a piece of spam, 'how about laying off the pubs tonight and coming down to the prayer meeting?'[179]

While the devout were naturally to be found acting as chaplains' assistants, for reasons of temperament and conviction they were also well represented in the Medical Corps. This was again a natural corollary of the draft. According to the terms of the Selective Training and Service Act of 1940, and providing their claim was accepted by their local draft boards, those men who 'by reason of religious training and belief [were] conscientiously opposed to participation in war in any form' could be assigned to non-combatant military service or to 'work of national importance under civilian direction'.[180] Due to the strength of interwar pacifism in the Protestant churches, the growth of the Jehovah's Witnesses and Seventh-Day Adventists, and the more accommodating terms of the 1940 act, in World War II the draft yielded a somewhat larger crop of conscientious objectors than in World War I, when the right of conscientious objection was limited to Quakers, Mennonites and Brethren, 'the Historic Peace Churches'.[181] However, the highly devolved nature of the Selective Service system meant that no national enumeration of conscientious objectors was possible, and estimates of their numbers varied considerably.[182] However, in 1952 they were reliably estimated at approximately 100,000, with between a quarter and a half of them eventually serving as non-combatants in the armed forces.[183] Although objectors could, at first, find themselves serving in any non-combatant role, from January 1943 the Medical Corps was the only branch of the army to which they could be assigned.[184] Here, they were usually 'indistinguishable from noncombatant nonobjectors as to types of work performed',[185] and their constituency could be further blurred by the impulse to take up arms – one that was widely felt by combat medics – and by the ongoing transfer of individuals to and from combatant roles.[186] If, for example, some combat medics succumbed to the urge to shoot back, Ralph 'Preacher' Davis, a hero of the Rangers' assault on Pointe-du-Hoc on D-Day, applied for a transfer to the Medical Corps on religious grounds as late as September 1944.[187] Anticipating the course of events, and holding that the Sixth Commandment did 'not bar co-operation with the military machine so long as the individual was not required to participate in direct killing', the Seventh-Day Adventists purposefully 'organized and trained [their] young men to be stretcher-bearers and Medical Corps assistants' before the United States even entered the war, and as many as twelve thousand duly served in the army as non-combatants.[188] Although the proportion of conscientious objectors in the Medical Corps should not be exaggerated, especially as it grew in size from 130,000 to 670,000 between December 1941 and March 1945,[189] the kudos of the combat medic served to enhance the stature of the conscientious objector in uniform. The classic case in point was that of Pfc Desmond Doss, a Seventh-Day Adventist from Virginia, who earned a Medal of Honor (the first conscientious objector to do so) and the status of a comic-book hero for his service with the 77th Infantry Division on Okinawa, where he rescued and treated dozens of wounded Americans under fire.[190]

Whether declared conscientious objectors or not, pious medics often took a religious lead at a local level. Even Paul Fussell, a second lieutenant in the 410th Infantry Regiment in North-West Europe, although insisting that he was 'not at all religious' admitted to having 'prayed once or twice in the war, largely with my medic, who always carried a Bible.'[191] For his part, Lester Atwell, who spent much time with the aid men and litter bearers of the 345th Infantry Regiment,[192] was keenly aware of their strong religious constituency. Once, while sharing a room with four litter bearers from an attached medical battalion, the evening closed with an unexpected invitation: 'Before we say goodnight, I think we all ought to say our prayers. How about it?'[193] However, such tendencies were not always harmless. Early in 1945, and in the prolonged absence of a Protestant chaplain, other medics (including a few conscientious objectors and a medical technician known as 'Preacher') took to holding meetings of their own; noisy, sectarian and ultimately acrimonious, their gatherings did little for the cohesion or harmony of Atwell's unit.[194]

Despite the massive growth of army and navy chaplaincy and their own exemption from the draft, even the clergy were present among the wider army and navy. During AAF chaplain William C. Taggart's abortive voyage to the Philippines with the 19th Bombardment Group in December 1941, he shared his cabin with Lieutenant James Tull, another Southern Baptist minister who had been called up for the Air Corps as 'a reserve line officer.'[195] Similarly, and while stationed in Iceland in 1942, Chaplain Clyde E. Kimball came across a fellow Methodist minister from South Dakota who was serving as an infantry officer.[196] In fact, this phenomenon was common enough for a *Yank* correspondent to report from Australia in February 1943: 'Three combat officers hereabouts were preachers back home. If a full-fledged chaplain isn't around, these officers pinch hit.'[197] In fact, for some clergymen, service as an enlisted man offered the only real prospect for a military ministry. One case, which drew some publicity in September 1942, was that of Private Thomas Dodney, an Episcopalian priest, veteran of World War I, and a university professor, who volunteered for the army on the grounds that: 'This is war; one doesn't ask for jobs, does one?'[198] Nor was this simply an army phenomenon. On Guadalcanal in 1942, Warren Wyeth Willard found that one of his navy corpsmen, Pharmacist's Mate James H. Peterson from Western Springs, Illinois, was 'an ordained Episcopalian clergyman' who not only assisted Willard with his services but 'administered communion to the natives.'[199]

Hymnody and scripture

The warp and weft of American religious life was no less apparent in the devotional tastes and material culture of American service personnel. Described by Mark Noll as 'gauges of popular spirituality',[200] and implicitly recognised as such by contemporaries, religious pundits were eager to identify and assess popular trends in hymnody, for example. As early as its second issue in March 1943, and in a feature entitled 'Service Men's Favorite Hymns', *The Link* published the results of polls taken in ten stateside army camps. Significantly, only one hymn topped the poll in more than one location, the denizens of Fort Bragg, North Carolina and Camp Roberts, California, favouring 'The Old Rugged Cross'. However, 'Rock of Ages' won out at Fort Warren, Wyoming, and elsewhere tastes ranged from 'Abide with Me' (at Camp Shelby, Mississippi), to 'When the Roll Is Called Up Yonder' (at Fort Jackson, South Carolina). Significantly, the article concluded with a summons to its readers to undertake polls of their own,[201] and it seems that two years of further observation and reflection served to refine – not to say sharpen – the study of hymnody and its significance in the armed forces. In the February 1945 issue of *The Chaplain* magazine, Chaplain Marvin E. Maris expanded on the tonic value of hymn-singing in the Pacific theatre, calling it 'the most effective antidote for the blues' in an island existence where life was 'boring and monotonous rather than adventurous and thrilling'. According to Maris, tastes differed noticeably along sectional lines for, although 'the old hymns of the Christian tradition' were generally favoured, Southerners had a marked predilection for 'the gospel hymns', which a Southern quartet sang 'with genuine impressiveness'.[202] This sectional pattern was also discerned by Stanley R. Plummer, a navy chaplain's assistant, who wrote in May 1945:

> I have noted with interest that men coming to this station from all sections of the United States bring with them thoughts and ideas about music peculiar to those sections.... In many cases it is possible to estimate a man's religious background by the type of music he prefers. Invariably the men from the Southern states choose the gospel and revival type of hymn such as 'When the Trumpet of the Lord Shall Sound', while from the Northerners come requests for such hymns as 'A Mighty Fortress Is Our God'.[203]

However, these differences were far more palatable to Protestant chaplains than the shock results of a survey released in April 1945. Announcing that 'Faith of Our Fathers', written by the English Catholic convert Frederick William Faber, was now the GI's favourite hymn, an article in *The Chaplain* magazine explained that: 'Last autumn the Office of the Chief [of] Chaplains, U.S. Army, took a sort of Gallup Poll on the popularity of hymns among some 850 chaplains of the service commands. Protestant chaplains put at the top, "Faith of Our Fathers," written by Frederick William Faber, a Catholic'. An awkward choice given that it dwelt on the sufferings of Catholic martyrs in the Reformation era, a positive and even jocular spin was placed on the result, the article going on to explain its surprising appeal. 'The vote', it maintained, 'indicated more than a choice in hymnology. It indicated also a refusal to be turned aside from the best in Christian song because of prejudice. Their feeling about it was somewhat like that of Lincoln in regard to "the Southerners' national anthem."' If Abraham Lincoln could appropriate 'Dixie', then it stood to reason that Protestants could surely embrace 'Faith of Our Fathers':

> Why did so many chaplains express a choice of 'Faith of Our fathers'? Perhaps it is because of the tune, 'St. Catherine's', adapted by James Walton, but more likely because it is familiar to and loved by so many service men. At evening in farmhouses, at camp-meetings, in schoolhouses, in country churches, at dedications, at commencements they have sung that hymn and it has left a trail of memories.[204]

The choice of 'Faith of Our Fathers' was also encouraging insofar as it seemed to reflect the GI's elusive fervour for the Allied cause: '"Faith of Our Fathers" also owes its popularity to the fact that it epitomizes what men in uniform are now striving for. Again the faith must pass through the ordeal of 'dungeon, fire and sword".[205]

Given that trends in hymnody were regarded as of barometers of popular piety, the claims of this poll met with surprise and indignation nonetheless. Much chagrined, Andrew G. Solla wrote to *The Chaplain*: 'I am very sorry that I find myself in complete disagreement with my fellow chaplains, who voted for 'Faith of Our Fathers' as the most popular hymn. They were carried away by its rather easy tune. Not understanding the hidden significance of it'. According to Solla, his colleagues were missing the point and forgetting their history: 'Faith of Our Fathers' was full of mendacious Catholic propaganda (what about the Protestant victims of Mary Tudor, or of the St Bartholomew's Day Massacre?), drenched in Mariolatory, and nothing more than a paean of praise 'to the old tyrannical institution into which [Faber] had betaken himself'. As Solla concluded: 'If the dear brethren who put it at the top of the list want to follow Faber's footsteps, let them praise, and sing "Faith of Our Fathers." But as for me I want none of it'.[206] However, the controversial primacy of 'Faith of Our Fathers' should not obscure other significant trends. Towards the end of the war, the Army and Navy Commission of the Missouri Synod found that the tastes of its service personnel were reassuringly conservative and Lutheran. Heading the field in its own '"best-loved" hymn contest' was Luther's 'A Mighty Fortress Is Our God', followed by 'Rock of Ages', 'Abide With Me', 'What a Friend We Have in Jesus' and 'Beautiful Savior'.[207] Furthermore, the appeal of the 'revival type' hymn remained clear. John M. Whallon, a navy chaplain and self-confessed 'stuffy Presbyterian, eastern seaboard type', speaking of his experiences on board a Landing Ship, Tank (LST) wrote of how the chance acquisition of an old piano had led him to a new realisation of the emotional power of 'Gospel Songs':

> [T]hese songs have a vital place in our church program for the young people.... No word I have yet spoken has brought the gospel message to our men as forcibly as the singing of these old songs. How many times, after long days of being under attack, have we gathered round the old piano which we rebuilt, and sung ourselves back into a spirit of bright cheer![208]

Such observation and debate seems to underline the wisdom of the War Department in taking such pains to ensure the availability of hymnals and hymn sheets to army personnel. However, the same is also true of its efforts to ensure access to Holy Scripture. Regardless of its form or provenance, what was remarkable about the Bible in the armed forces was its sheer ubiquity. Surveying the debris on Omaha Beach in June 1944, Ernie Pyle was struck by the number of Bibles among the 'human litter' that had once belonged to fallen GIs.[209] Contemplating the situation towards the end of 1943, one pundit reflected:

> Almost every man in uniform now has a Bible or a New Testament. It is his. It was given to him by his folks or by his church. Or, if he left home without one, his chaplain has probably given him one. It's his own book. When the war is over, and he turns in his gun and his parachute and his blanket and his bombsight and all the rest of the things that the Government has lent him, he'll keep this little Book. Years from now he'll show it to his children as one of his most precious keepsakes.[210]

Throughout his service with the 1st Marine Division, Eugene B. Sledge carried a small Gideon New Testament in his breast pocket, in which he kept the notes that would inform the most acclaimed American memoir of the Pacific war.[211] In Sledge's words, although drenched by sweat 'during the early days', once protected by a small rubber bag taken from a Japanese corpse, 'The little Bible went all the way through Okinawa's rains and mud with me, snug in its captured cover.'[212] Even an unread Bible could be the subject of strong personal attachment. While visiting a guardhouse in Northern Ireland, Eben Cobb Brink was confronted with a 'victim of the draft' who 'did not seem to care for Army discipline, decency, clean entertainment, or good companionship'. Nevertheless, he had kept 'the Bible that his mother had given him when first he left home' and, when fanned, this spark of filial piety proved the basis for his redemption.[213] Likewise, and while fretting over the reticence of GIs in religious matters, and on their penchant for profanity, Chaplain Rolla M. Varndell conceded that: 'New Testaments are very prevalent in the army – and they are read. Of the many associates I have had I know of only one who didn't have a New Testament or seem to want one.'[214] Audie Murphy, the most decorated American soldier of World War II, embodied some of these anomalies, as his personal artefacts (now on display at the Smithsonian Museum of American History) serve to show; although he was disinclined to have a religious allegiance indented on his identification tags, he was clearly unwilling to go without a YMCA New Testament.[215]

In civilian terms, Protestant America at least was very much a Bible-conscious (if not Bible-reading) society, and the pressures and anxieties of war seem to have made this characteristic even more pronounced. As already noted, National Bible Week was launched to promote Bible-reading in 1941 and, at the same time, the centrality of the Bible to American Protestant culture encouraged and sanctioned the War Department's distribution of scripture to its new draftee army. According to an AIPO poll conducted in February 1939, 40 per cent of those polled claimed to have read at least a portion of the Bible during the previous month and 5 per cent of the whole said that it was a daily resort. During the war years, AIPO probed these habits by asking in successive polls in November 1942, 1943 and 1944 whether individuals had 'read the Bible at home within the last year'. Those who answered in the affirmative were, respectively, in a majority of 59, 64 and 62 per cent. More notably, those in the 21–29 year age group who said they had read the Bible in private at least once in the previous twelve months increased from 48 per cent in November 1942 to 57 per cent in November 1943, by far the largest increase among the three age groups. Significantly, and while the reading of scripture continued to play little or no part in the lives of a substantial minority of American adults, the proportion of those who claimed to read it every day had doubled since 1939 – standing at 11, 13 and 10 per cent in the three successive polls.[216] Less surprisingly, further evidence garnered by the AIPO at the request of the American Bible Society showed that 'about twice as many women as men read the Bible daily', and that 'residents of small and farm communities read it more often than do residents of cities'.[217] To add to this gender and urban/rural divide, there was also the inevitable sectional differences – the Protestant South produced the highest proportion of Bible readers, while the lowest yields came from the Catholic strongholds of New England and 'the Middle Atlantic States'.[218]

How far were these patterns replicated in the US armed forces? Among American POWs in the Philippines, it would seem that the pages of pocket New Testaments could serve as useful substitutes for cigarette papers.[219] Despite this aberration, it seems very clear that the Bible was widely read and studied by service personnel. As we have seen, this partly inspired the American Bible Society's 'great Nation-wide Bible Reading' and its global successor in 1944 and 1945. More locally, in January 1943 Chaplain Clyde E. Kimball registered the need for a Bible class because his flock were so anxious to discuss the Good Book;[220] in fact, this need became more urgent given the currency of outlandish, and presumably fundamentalist, exegesis. As Kimball complained, 'I am surprised how often someone quotes some passage in the Bible to me and asks, "Doesn't that prove that the war will end on such and such a date?" They think, if I "believe" the Bible, that I'll agree with them.'[221] However, it did not take the bleak conditions of an

Icelandic winter to nurture this kind of interest. In the Pacific in 1941, Chaplain William C. Taggart noted how scripture-reading surged after news of Pearl Harbor reached his troopship: 'I saw Bibles on bunks which had been buried at the bottom of bags since the beginning of our voyage ... Several of the men asked me to bring them pocket-size Testaments when I came to their bays again. Two of the men wanted to know if they could join our Bible-study class.'[222] Significantly, Taggart saw this as emblematic of the national cause and the four freedoms:

> Free men at war remained free. There was no man-made master to tell us what to think; no Gestapo here to report our opinions ... We had questions and asked them unafraid. We were free men of many faiths at war against a common enemy, discussing freely our doubts and exchanging opinions and looking to our Bible for guidance. And through free, independent thinking we saw in the Scriptures the will of God.[223]

Nor did interest abate as the war went on. In an echo of Taggart's experiences in the Pacific, Chaplain Harry B. Abbott wrote of the 1st Armored Division in North Africa a year later:

> As I have walked about the bivouacs of various units, and as I have accompanied officers on their tours of inspections, I have been pleased to see so many men with New Testaments among their possessions; and many times I have seen them passing away the dull moments by intense study, or discussions of their bible and religion. Often their only companions were prayer-books, a religious tract, a New Testament, a Catholic Missal, or a Jewish Old Testament, sent to them from home or given them by their pastor, priest, rabbi, or chaplain. Somehow, through the exercising of their religious prerogatives, they seem to become more sober and more mature in their thinking and acting.[224]

As late as April 1945, *The Chaplain* magazine carried a letter from Ernest Lee Carter, a Methodist navy chaplain, concerning the runaway success of his Bible classes:

> Service men are not neglecting their religious interest even in the jungle land of New Guinea.... During the seven sessions in which we studied the Sermon on the Mount the average attendance was 1,519 although it rained during three of the sessions. Recently the average attendance has increased to 1,824 and the highest attendance at a single session was 2,284.[225]

Inevitably, these patterns were partly dictated by the fact that Bible-reading habits, or at least a sense of their value, were imported from civilian life. As the poignant inscription in a Bible retrieved at Cherbourg from the body of Staff Sergeant Alton C. Bright from Tennessee read, 'To Alton C. Bright from Mother. Read it and be good.'[226] However, given the religiously mixed constituency of the army and navy, varying levels of literacy, and the lack of privacy in barrack rooms and below decks, frequent Bible-reading as a private devotion remained a minority pursuit. For example, only one of twenty-nine veterans of the 32nd Infantry Division, originally a National Guard division from Michigan and Wisconsin, referred to the Bible in relation to reading habits and religious convictions encountered while in the army.[227] Inevitably, officers enjoyed an advantage over enlisted men in this respect, several telling Chaplain Israel Yost of the Japanese-American 100th Infantry Battalion that 'they carried New Testaments and read the scriptures fairly regularly'.[228] However, it must be borne in mind that scripture was issued by the War Department not so much to encourage daily devotions as to be an aid in times of crisis and, in that respect, the more occasional recourse to scripture to be found among service personnel was again very much in keeping with national and civilian norms. As one GI recalled of a well-attested incident at Faïd Pass in Tunisia in January 1943:

> We were under artillery fire, and a church assembly was out of the question. But, being quite a determined man, our chaplain solved this by sending a message, together with several Testaments, to the various foxholes. The message requested us to read several verses in the Testament, then pass the note and the book on to the next foxhole. This we did, and the result was an immediate brightening of our outlook.[229]

A navy chaplain, from his experience with the marines in the South-West Pacific, confirmed the common recourse to scripture at such times:

> Please never believe anyone who may say that the men take the Bibles and Testaments only to put away and not to read or study. This is far from the truth. The Testament is a wonder-worker in a foxhole when an air raid is on, and the bombs come close to your place of safety.[230]

This was not mere piety-mongering, moreover. Of the doomed American defenders of the Philippines in 1942, Melville Jacoby, a correspondent for *Time* magazine, averred that: 'The sight of a soldier sitting by a machine gun reading a Bible is not uncommon in Bataan or Corregidor.' He also confirmed that there had been a run on New Testaments since the news of Pearl Harbor.[231] Furthermore, and however low-key their reading of scripture may have been at other times, an Australian soldier who served alongside the Midwesterners of the 32nd Division on New Guinea was struck 'that so many American soldiers carried and read Bibles' during the fighting around Buna.[232] As the Bible was clearly a common refuge *in extremis*, what applied to infantrymen in their foxholes also applied to other categories of service personnel. Prior to the battle of Kula Gulf in July 1943, the radio officer of the light cruiser *Helena* went down to his room where, in solitude, he read 'the Twenty-third and Ninety-first Psalms over and over'. Afterwards, and to his surprise, 'When I went on deck, I saw men thumbing worn pages of the little Bibles that many of them carry. Toughened old seadogs, veterans of many a battle and many a crap game, were unashamedly praying. Some listened with solemn concentration while others read aloud.'[233] Percy M. Hickcox, a Methodist chaplain who served with the 81st Infantry Division in the Pacific, was also struck by the keenness with which scripture was devoured by patients in the division's field hospitals:

> [W]ith a dearth of reading material among our hundreds of patients most of them held closely to their religious literature.... I marvelled upon the rows of men in tent after tent reading their copies of the New Testament. In garrison days I used to announce my arrival in the wards, and a man here and there would take the New Testament and literature which I carried. Among these combat wounded my assistant and I would go loaded down with the Scriptures. There were no announcements of our visit but man after man would ask, 'Chaplain you have just what I've been wanting. Can I have one of those books?'[234]

Among airmen, Lieutenant Charles L. McClure, a survivor of the April 1942 Doolittle raid on Tokyo, recalled that, while sheltering from the Japanese in a Chinese hospital, group Bible-reading every Sunday acted as a potent boost to morale:

> On one occasion, I remember, I was feeling utterly miserable when the meeting started. After a few passages had been read from Psalms I actually felt that I would be able to get up from my bed and walk. It was, for a time, the best medicine I could have taken.[235]

In January 1945, *The Chaplain* magazine recounted how, prior to a night-time mission in the South-West Pacific, a pilot read aloud the story of the road to Emmaus to twenty-five others, ending with the words, 'If I should come down tonight, I should like to feel those thoughts were my last.'[236] More dramatic still was the story of Staff Sergeant Howard G. Collett of the Air Corps, who was killed in action over the Pacific in October 1943 and posthumously awarded the Distinguished Service Cross:

> It is an inspiring story of faith and courage.... [Collett] was a gunner in a bomber that was knocked out during an attack on Celebes.... Machine guns of Jap fighters had either killed or wounded every member of the doomed ship's crew as it fell to the sea. Collett was gravely hurt, but he read aloud from his pocket Bible over the plane's intercommunication system until he sank beneath the waves.... There were no heroics in that simple act of faith. The gunner wasn't thinking of medals, but only of helping his comrades in their plunge into eternity.... Death was leaping at them.... The gunner read from his Bible. There, in the silent waters off Celebes, a ghostly Cross must surely bless his grave.[237]

As at Faïd Pass, reassuring words of scripture were often dispensed by chaplains if combat loomed. According to Warren Wyeth Willard, a keen advocate of the importance of scripture to his marine flock on Guadalcanal: 'It is well known that the Word of God has no equal as a morale builder for battle. The knowledge that only flesh is mortal gives men confidence and courage.' For Willard, the essence of reassurance was to be found in Romans 8:35–39: 'Who shall separate us from the love of Christ? Shall tribulation, or distress, or persecution, or famine, or nakedness, or peril, or sword …?'[238] Another apt text was derived from Joshua 1:9: 'Be strong and of a good courage; be not afraid, neither be thou dismayed: for the LORD thy God *is* with thee whithersoever thou goest.' These words were used as the basis for at least three wartime sermons by Chaplain Russell Cartwright Stroup.[239] On the last occasion, and looking ahead to the landings on Luzon, Stroup remarked: 'It's a good text [for the 1st Infantry Regiment]. It demands something of us and expects something of God. I like the picture of a man in the might of his own manhood, sustained as he must be by the unfailing power of God – an undefeatable combination.'[240] Faced with the carnage of the Normandy battlefields, another infantry chaplain, Alvin O. Carlson of the 134th Infantry Regiment, favoured the words of St Paul in 1 Corinthians 16:13, 'quit you like men, be strong.'[241] These he used as the basis of a sermon given prior to the American breakout from Normandy, a sermon that Carlson peppered with other Pauline texts such as Ephesians 6:10 ('be strong in the Lord, and in the power of his might'), and Ephesians 6:11 ('Put on the whole armour of God, that ye may be able to stand against the wiles of the devil').[242] That such texts resonated with many Protestant GIs seems clear. It was no accident, for example, that, as his battalion was being overrun at Salerno in 1943, a hapless sergeant of the largely Texan 36th Infantry Division was scooped from his foxhole by the Germans while reading the 23rd Psalm ('The LORD *is* my shepherd; I shall not want …').[243] Another Southerner who found comfort in a more obscure passage of scripture was Oklahoma-born John Oliver Brixey of the 11th Infantry Regiment, who remembered:

> I think the big memorable experience … was the night that our unit attacked Frankfurt … and we had to cross the Mainz [sic] … and it was night, and the artillery was coming in, with mortar fire and rifle fire, and as we attacked the city … we, the squad that I was in or the platoon that I was in, entered this town, and we entered this particular building, and when it came my turn to cross that river, I remembered something from scripture and I probably didn't realize it, but it's in Proverbs 3:6, and it says, 'In all thy ways acknowledge Him and He will direct thy paths'. I didn't know that scripture at that time, but I do remember saying this when I picked up my M-1 … 'OK Lord, here we go', and as I went across that river, and fell at

the base of the foundation of that building, my sergeant, Sergeant DeBerry, said, 'Brixey, that's a good move, keep your head down.'[244]

However, the archetypal example of the fortifying power of scripture, and a powerful wartime stimulus to the distribution of religious literature among service personnel, was the case of the World War I fighter ace and Medal of Honor recipient, Captain Eddie Rickenbacker, and the six other survivors of a B-17 that ditched into the Pacific, south-west of the Hawaiian Islands in October 1942. For a generation that had witnessed the prolonged and fruitless search for Amelia Earhart, and the disappearance of several other prominent aviators in the interwar years, the death of Rickenbacker in the vastness of the Pacific seemed a foregone conclusion.[245] Nevertheless, and after braving the elements, thirst, starvation, sharks and the Japanese for more than three weeks while drifting thousands of miles in their flimsy life rafts, the dispersed survivors were finally rescued by US Navy floatplanes from the vicinity of the Ellice Islands. Key to their survival was the forceful leadership of Rickenbacker himself,[246] who had been touring the Pacific on 'a world-wide mission to inspect United States air combat groups' at the behest of the Secretary of War.[247] However, and by common consent, the decisive and overarching factors were providential oversight and the sustenance that had been provided by 'a little khaki covered New Testament' carried by the plane's flight engineer, the youthful Jonny Bartek.[248] A gift of the First Baptist Church of Freehold, New Jersey, the volume was accompanied by a small, Presbyterian *Devotional Guide for Service Men* and came 'enclosed in a waterproof case with a zipper to seal it.'[249] Sufficient to withstand more than three weeks at sea, according to Rickenbacker's account of their ordeal, *Seven Came Through*:

> Watching [Bartek] read it, the thought came to me that we might all profit by his example.... With the New Testament as an inspiration, we held morning and evening prayers. The rafts were pulled together, making a rough triangle. Then, each in turn, one of us would read a passage. None of us, I must confess, showed himself to be very familiar with them, but thumbing the book we found a number that one way or another bespoke our needs. The Twenty-third Psalm was, of course, a favorite. I have always been stirred by it, but out on the Pacific I found a beauty in it that I had never appreciated.[250]

Their story was, of course, a wartime sensation. On Bartek's return to the United States he presented his battered and salt-stained New Testament to the American Bible Society, embarked upon 'a speaking tour of defense plants throughout the country' and dictated his own account of their experiences, which was published in 1943 as *Life Out There* – in which he duly announced his intention of becoming a minister.[251] A third survivor, Lieutenant James C. Whittaker, an agnostic who had found God in his life raft, also embarked upon a national speaking tour in which he addressed 'armies of airplane workers, steel workers, and ship builders' about his ordeal and his new-found faith.[252] Whittaker also published an account of their experiences, *We Thought We Heard the Angels Sing*, which ran through thirteen printings between its publication in March 1943 and May 1945.

The pioneer spirit

Besides the centrality of scripture, the experience of Rickenbacker and his fellow survivors illustrates another salient feature of American religious life, namely its inherent and vital capacity for self-organisation in a society without an established church. Given the nature of the war, and despite an unprecedented supply of chaplains, chapels and other religious resources, in countless situations GIs, bluejackets and marines were ultimately required to make their own religious provision. This was especially true, as already noted, of Jewish personnel. When the Fifth Army landed at Salerno in September 1943, it had only one Jewish chaplain, Aaron Paperman, and the first service for its Jewish soldiers 'within the limits of [Hitler's] anti-Jewish empire' was led by an enlisted man.[253] If the situation was bad enough in Europe, in the vast expanses of the Pacific theatre Jewish and Christian chaplains were even more reliant on the organisation and activities of Jewish laymen;[254] consequently, they performed functions that ranged from the burial of the dead to the leading of High Holy Day services.[255] For other small minorities, the need for self-sufficiency also applied. In this respect, John Harold Craven, a navy chaplain and a Southern Baptist, recalled an especially vigorous Mormon subculture on board a troop transport in the Pacific:

> I remember coming back from Iwo Jima we had a lot of men in [the] ship's company that were Mormons ... there was one fellow that played the banjo – Mormon priest – and he really put on a good entertainment. They would have their services, and they wanted me to attend their services, and they came into our Bible class. I found out more about Mormon doctrine during that trip than at any time in seminary. They would gather around me and really throw me a lot of questions and I asked them questions, and we had some good dialogue.[256]

After being badly wounded and blinded in Normandy, another Mormon, Second Lieutenant H. Smith Shumway of the 18th Infantry Regiment, had to rely on his own resources. In the absence of any Mormon elders, and prior to a major operation, Shumway blessed and anointed himself with mineral oil, a ritual that gave him a vital measure of inner peace.[257]

However, the vagaries of war and of service life meant that no religious tradition was immune from such demands. There were, for example, few Catholics among the men of the Japanese-American 100th Infantry Battalion in 1943.

Consequently, its chaplain, Israel Yost, noted that: 'At times a sergeant led a few Roman Catholics in the praying of the rosary in my tent when conditions prevented transporting these worshipers to a chaplain-priest's Mass nearby.'[258] While convening for the rosary was a fairly common practice among Catholic personnel,[259] the presence of keen members of Catholic organisations contributed to other Catholic activity. When doing his rounds in Alaska, for example, Chaplain John J. Reedy stumbled across an unlikely meeting of the Legion of Mary where 'the topic of discussion of the men in the rough clothes the climate requires, as they sat around a stove, with a statue of Our Lady on a near-by table, was fallen-away Catholics and what progress the Legion was making in getting them back'.[260] As we have seen, for mainline Protestants part of the rationale for the creation of the Service Men's Christian League was to harness and exploit this ubiquitous impulse. Writing from Italy in 1944, an artillery corporal told *The Link* how the men of his battery had held fourteen services of their own in the absence of their chaplain:

> We have a choir and the attendance has jumped from 12 to 50. Our membership is made up of Catholics, Protestants and Jews. We hold services each week, in and out of combat. I don't know whether our activities are unique or not, but it is at least one attempt to bring divine help when it is most needed. I find that more and more boys are turning to God for help and comfort. If we have a particularly tough time with Jerry shelling, the church attendance jumps – and a certain percentage of new ones always stick.[261]

A further article published in *The Link* in 1945 told of how 'fifteen shaved-head recruits' formed an impromptu Christian fellowship in their hut shortly after their arrival at 'a navy boot camp'. With the encouragement of their hut captain – 'a Christian gentleman in every respect' – its members quickly progressed from spontaneous hymn-singing to group scripture-reading and collective worship.[262]

As the organ of the SMCL, *The Link* strongly encouraged this American capacity for sturdy self-reliance. In November 1943, and in response to an anxious enquiry from an army signaller as to how to cope without a chaplain, the magazine advised:

> First of all, you must learn to minister to yourself. You should face the time when every man must be his own chaplain. Your equipment is your Bible, your prayer life and your firm faith. THE LINK is constantly stressing the need for personal spiritual development.... As a Christian soldier you have a responsibility. Find a few buddies, invite them to join you at a definite hour and *for the definite purpose* of worship and religious discussion. *Prepare* for that meeting and ask others to take some part ... you can recall or find somewhere the words of some familiar hymns. Work it out in your own way.... This is the way the Christian Church began and grew.... Men everywhere in the service are valiantly carrying on in lieu of chaplains.[263]

In 1944, and responding to an enquirer who was organising and leading Sunday services but running short of inspiration, *The Link* produced a lengthy and detailed list of recommendations. Besides advice about physical environment and where to obtain resources such as hymn sheets, hymnals and orders of service, it also urged a broad, participatory and democratic approach:

> I would also make some of the men responsible for the various parts of the service. Try letting one of them give the 'sermon' or lead the discussion, offer prayer, etc. The more of your group you have participating, the better response you will have.... A period of prayer, silent or spoken or both; a song service if you have the proper leadership; an instrumental number by a member of the group, if available; a brief thought-starting talk by the leader or someone chosen by him, and a quiet period of dedication at the close of the service – and there it is.... One final suggestion: get yourself a committee, three to five men, who will meet regularly with you for prayerful planning of the service. And every chaplain would join me in saying, 'God bless you, and keep it up!'[264]

Naturally, SMCL units could stand as guarantors of public worship, even when chaplains were notionally available. In a vaunted 'Letter of the Month', Howard W. Bacon, the Methodist chaplain of a fighter group based in India, wrote in *The Link*:

> Because of the terrain, weather conditions, and transportation difficulties, it is not always possible for the Group Chaplain to reach each one of the units in our group as regularly as desired. With this realization in mind, some of the men in one of the Squadrons asked permission to start a branch of the SMCL so that they could have regular Christian fellowship during the week and at times when it would be impossible for me to hold a service for them.... I was happy to sponsor such an organisation and to offer assistance in every way possible.[265]

Likewise, and in an article entitled 'You Don't Need a Chaplain', in November 1944 *The Link* hailed the work of Ensign Stanly R. Tebbetts in making provision for Christian fellowship and worship 'at a base in the Pacific where there is no Protestant chaplain'. In civilian life the Boys' Work Secretary of the Boston YMCA, Tebbetts forged ahead in raising a unit of the league among men with 'a real interest in vital religion' and a wish to have more than just 'a Sunday morning service'. The lesson was clear, or so *The Link* averred: 'where there isn't a chaplain, the religious program does not have to languish. The SMCL fits that situation perfectly.'[266]

Others, however, defined themselves against the league. If impelled by the same underlying need for prayer and fellowship, fundamentalists were also moved to organise by an absence of chaplains who were plainly of their ilk.

For example, only five chaplains of the Independent Fundamental Churches of America, a federation formed in Illinois in 1930, ever served in the US Navy, and none of these were commissioned until 1944.[267] This constituency was also moved by its strong suspicion of 'interfaith' chaplaincy and of its mainline Protestant exponents. Understandably averse to submitting their activities to the direction of Catholic and Jewish chaplains, there was also the much more insidious modernist, liturgical and even crypto-Catholic tendencies of their Protestant colleagues to contend with; at the Marine Corps training station at Parris Island, for example, Protestant navy chaplains revelled in the 'ecumenicity' of their work and in exposing tens of thousands of marine recruits to 'the liturgical treasures of the Church'.[268] In theological terms, the reciprocal hostility of more liberal chaplains could be open and visceral. In 1944, for example, Russell Cartwright Stroup, who pointedly eschewed 'evangelistic sermons' in his army ministry,[269] wrote an article for the magazine *Presbyterian Outlook* entitled 'Fear in the Shadows'. Here, he fiercely denounced more conservative colleagues who were tempted to preach hellfire and damnation to combat troops:

> In the valley of the shadow of death there are chaplains, God forgive them, preaching the 'gospel' of fear. Fortunately, they are few; but some there are, as in the churches back home, who raise the grim spectre of death and fan the fires of hell, hoping to compel the men to seek the Father who has assured us that in that dark valley we need not be afraid. Some shivering little souls may be won that way, but real men – and most men out here in the South Pacific are that – instinctively turn with disgust from such a perversion of the saving gospel of Jesus Christ whose perfect love casts out all fear.[270]

Such was the sympathetic response that this piece evoked in mainline circles that Stroup noted:

> A Methodist chaplain from one of the Air Corps groups called on me yesterday because he had seen my article.... The editor, Aubrey Brown, wrote me that he had supplied several thousand reprints to Methodist, Episcopal, and Presbyterian denominations to be distributed to their chaplains, and this nice person had just received this.[271]

Republished by *The Chaplain* magazine in December 1944 (and, significantly, eliciting only a single mild objection some months later)[272] Stroup had not quite finished savaging the fundamentalist opposition, writing home in November 1944:

> I have been enjoying myself by writing a very fierce [anti-fundamentalist] article on 'The Gospel Gestapo' – a delicious title.... Everyone seems afraid to tackle those babies or to bring their activities into the open. I get a lot of fun doing it, even though what I write might never be published.[273]

However, as a Presbyterian and an adoptive Southerner, Stroup was also wary of liturgical innovation, writing another piece for the *Presbyterian Outlook* on the dangers of ritualism. As Stroup remarked: 'the very persons who wouldn't agree with the other article might like that one. Most of the conservative members of the churches in the south are opposed to excessive ritual. It is the progressives who favor it. So that article might serve as a counterirritant.'[274] Still, it was the progressives who seemed to set the tone for Protestant chaplaincy, despite recognition of the fact that 'among the Protestants, the strongly evangelical find it difficult to enjoy liturgical worship, and vice versa.'[275] There may, in fact, have been a growing divergence between the style of worship favoured by most Protestant chaplains and that which was gaining ground in civilian society. For example, in 1945 it was acknowledged at a meeting of the New Jersey Synod of the Presbyterian Church (USA) that the American people preferred 'a warmer gospel, even if it be not so philosophically co-ordinated.'[276] Nevertheless, this preference seems to have been at odds with what was urged upon Protestant army and navy chaplains. Besides the much-vaunted use of triptychs in the army and navy, *The Chaplain* magazine championed a mildly liturgical approach to public worship, its first three issues carrying a series by Dr Albert W. Palmer, president of Chicago Theological Seminary, on 'Creating the ATMOSPHERE for Worship.'[277] The first article encouraged the use of 'tables, crosses, candlesticks, curtains and bouquets of flowers' and concluded:

> One more symbol must not be forgotten, and that is silence. Too often our Protestant services seem to be too largely engaged in urging people to say something, sing something, listen to something. Beyond all this a service of worship should have in it spaces of silence, opportunity for meditation, an invitation to personal unspoken prayer.[278]

In terms of music, Palmer favoured the use of 'well beloved hymn tunes or parts of sacred oratorios or great musical settings for the mass like those by Palestrina, Mozart or Gounod.'[279] As for the role of the minister, and the form and content of his public prayers, Palmer maintained:

> 'While you cannot preach about the social gospel every Sunday, you can pray about it!' Therefore, with all your soul be an intercessor for peace, for racial and economic justice, for the city of love and beauty, for a civilization of brotherly man, for childhood ... Of course there is a place for liturgical and responsive prayers.... But in the supreme moment the congregation will be lifted higher by one who makes his prayer, pours out his soul to God in spontaneous adoration.[280]

Although Palmer was hardly clamouring for bells and smells, there were clearly some unsettling Catholic tendencies abroad in the eclectic world of mainline Protestantism and its chaplain representatives. Moreover, in the course of their training and military careers the latter were far more likely to have had direct exposure to Catholic influences than would have been the case among their civilian counterparts. We have already noted how, and to the chagrin of some, 'Faith of Our Fathers' became a favourite army hymn during the course of the war. Stroup, for his part, and despite his professed wariness of ritual and his willingness to convert a Catholic soldier, read and admired *Blessed Are the Meek*, a bestselling life ⸌f St Francis of Assisi, and found comfort in Cardinal Newman's hymn 'Lead, Kindly Light'.[281] More remarkably, Alva J. Brasted, a Northern Baptist and the army's former chief of chaplains, in his 1944 book of Christian manners cited Ignatius Loyola's tutelage of Francis Xavier as a prime example of Christian conversion, and even described the latter as 'one of the greatest Christians of history'.[282] If the early Jesuits stood high in Brasted's esteem, then the AAF chaplain Charles E. Lunn, another Northern Baptist, concluded his 1947 memoirs with the unusual reflection: 'To trust implicitly in the purposes of God is like a thread running through a rosary. Such faith gives the smallest bead a place, a meaning, a value. Without it, life's happenings are as scattered beads on the cathedral floor!'[283]

Inevitably, and as chaplains were all too aware, only some of the myriad Protestant devotional groups that coalesced, at least for a time, in the armed forces were inclined to seek their help or become league affiliates. Besides more local and ephemeral groups, we have already noted the prolific growth of the Navigators among American sailors, part of what *The Link* described in 1944 as 'one of the most significant trends for religion in the Navy: namely, the spontaneous and enthusiastic interest in small prayer and devotional groups'.[284] Towards the end of the war, the 'GI Gospel Hour' that took root in the Philippines and in Japan seems to have been an outgrowth of the fledgling Youth for Christ movement in the United States, with its penchant for lively music and the old-time gospel.[285] *Religion in the Ranks*, a Northern Baptist publication, noted how, following the liberation of Tacloban in the Philippines, 'a group of Christian soldiers' organised 'G.I. Gospel Hour' meetings in the city's only Protestant church. As an army nurse, Lieutenant Alice V. Schmidt, enthused: 'The singing set the rafters ringing and many accepted Christ as their personal Savior, truly, a bit of heaven here on earth.' However, and because it reached out to Filipinos as well as Americans, this venture implicitly set at defiance 'the dominating religious power in the Philippine Islands'.[286] As we have seen from Lester Atwell's experience, such evangelical gatherings could be problematic for other reasons and, following a tour of inspection in the spring of 1944, a senior army chaplain advised that:

> It is important that services conducted by laymen be under the supervision of a chaplain, although not necessarily of a chaplain belonging to that group. An example of the lack of such supervision was found in [Milne

Bay] where a group of enlisted men were holding Pentecostal services that were causing some disturbance in the area.

At Milne Bay, action was taken and the service was 'maintained in different form and conducted by various chaplains and [served] a very constructive purpose.'[287] However, and as the same chaplain emphasised, delicate and diplomatic handling of such cases was essential:

> While it is my feeling that services for such groups should be encouraged by chaplains, I also feel that it would be easy to encourage excessive demands on the part of these groups if this encouragement is not done tactfully. There are a large number of representatives of these small 'off color' groups which consider themselves 'separate and distinct' and it is an impossibility to give each the representation it feels it rightly deserves.[288]

According to one sailor, by the end of the war the split between Protestants in the navy was more or less even between modernists and evangelicals.[289] Hence, and in order to cater for different and often antagonistic Protestant constituencies, some chaplains could feel the need to be all things to all men. Consequently, George W. Wickersham, a Low Church Episcopalian navy chaplain, reorganised his Bible classes for the 8th Marines in 1945. After one participant 'stamped out of the Quonset hut declaring that he would be better off reading his Bible in his tent than listening to us tear it apart', Wickersham inaugurated a regimental Bible class and a 'Christian League', in the hope that 'my fundamentalist friends would attend the first, and my more analytical ones, the second.'[290]

Besides these corollaries of the profound theological divide within American Protestantism, the grim realities of segregation and the lack of black chaplains often meant that African Americans had little choice but to organise their own devotions. In the case of the navy, where African American chaplains were scarcer even than independent fundamentalists, Clifford M. Drury grudgingly conceded that: 'Negro naval personnel sometimes conducted their own religious services.'[291] However, this was no doubt understating the situation for such services were, for example, a regular feature of religious life at Norfolk Naval Training Station. As *The Norfolk Seabag* reported on 21 April 1945, every Sunday there was an early morning service for African American sailors. Held in one of the station's training units, it had been requested by the men themselves and was sponsored by the station's chaplain, who provided a pulpit, an altar, a triptych, cross and candlesticks. The service was well attended and was led by a cook, James Smith, who had been ordained a Baptist minister the previous year. According to the same report, characteristic of the service was the singing of spirituals, the use of a Sunday school manual, and the freedom of the congregation to comment on the lesson of the day.[292] As for the army, in February 1944 Private Bert B. Babero complained to Truman K. Gibson, a prominent black attorney and an aide to the

Secretary of War, that a lack of religious provision was symptomatic of the many indignities and inconveniences that African Americans had to endure at Camp Barkeley, Texas:

> Camp Barkeley is one of the largest army camps in Texas and the only Medical Replacement Training Center in the south.... None of our commissioned officers are Colored.... Up until a few weeks ago, we could attend only one theater out of five on the post ... on the local buses we are compelled to sit in the back, [and threatened] by the drivers if we refuse ... Our living quarters are terrible being formerly C.C.C. barracks, located just in from of the camp cess pool.... We have one service club.... It is poorly equipped.... We don't have a library, a chapel or a chaplain. We conduct our own services in one of the poorly constructed class rooms.[293]

However, the inherent vitality of African American religious life ensured that, as at Norfolk Naval Training Station, enlisted men were usually on hand to lead and organise services. As a report from the Pacific emphasised, white chaplains responsible for African American units 'usually had one or more volunteer "assistants"' to help them. Bertram L. Smith, an Episcopalian chaplain who relied heavily on this kind of support, observed that:

> Many of these men were ordained before coming into the military service: many have been 'called to preach' after entering.... Every Colored unit, with one exception, of this Command has one or more preachers. They conduct Sunday and Weekday Services, an undertaking rarely found in white units. On weekdays, these Services are held after work hours. The services are dignified, devotional, and moving.[294]

Smith even spoke of attending an evening service held in a mess hall during 'a ten-day revival'. On this occasion, three preachers spoke and: 'The preaching was fervent and good, the singing was excellent, the devotional element was real and deep.'[295] Representative of these African American soldier-preachers was Corporal D.C. Morton of the 923rd Air Base Security Battalion, a part-time student at Morehouse Theological School in Atlanta when he was drafted. Ordained by his pastor before being inducted, while in training Morton 'assisted at the weekly church services and evening prayer meetings' and, during his battalion's first overseas posting, led weekly Bible classes. Later, and when it proved impossible for a chaplain to hold a regular service or for large numbers of men to go elsewhere, Morton became the battalion's de facto pastor, leading Sunday evening services 'in the enlisted mess', which were attended 'by a considerable body of men'. Not surprisingly, and especially in view of the army's conviction that religion was critical to the morale and discipline of African American soldiers, Morton's superiors in the 923rd were 'in whole hearted accord' with his work and 'felt he should be given special recognition in view of his devotion to the religious welfare of his fellow men'; eventually, Morton received an official letter of commendation for his ministry.[296]

Regardless of the munificent support it enjoyed from the state and elsewhere, a further indication of how religious habits and patterns from civilian life infused the nation's armed forces lies in the financial and practical support that it was given by its intended beneficiaries; remarkably, the combined weight of government and civilian efforts did not turn American soldiers, sailors and marines into passive recipients of religious aid. In this respect also, self-esteem, church tradition, and the inherent voluntarism and self-sufficiency of American religious life remained very much in evidence. As army chaplain Percy M. Hickcox testified:

> The soldier does not take his religion purely as a G-I issue. He is eager to support his chapel. Regular chapel offerings are not generally taken, but he is not content to accept a religion which costs him nothing. We have brought up our young people to view giving as an act of worship and consecration. Often a plate is left at the door for voluntary offerings to be used to add further to the furnishings of the house of worship, to buy flowers, or the like. I have collected money left on the communion rail by worshippers who would not accept this sacrament without making this financial donation.[297]

Managing such non-appropriated funds even became one of the many bureaucratic chores of the army chaplain, and it required careful supervision by the Office of the Chief of Chaplains. Needless to say, the sums accrued in the so-called 'Chaplain's Fund' could be considerable. In the African American 92nd Infantry Division, for example, the money held in half a dozen of these funds amounted to almost $1,400 in July 1945.[298]

Civilian churches also gained from the freewill offerings of service personnel. As we will see in Chapter Five, in certain parts of the world these donations often flowed directly to missionary work. As for the situation in the United States, Hickcox noted how one church that had willingly accommodated 'military congregations' was able to build 'a social hall and religious education unit' on the proceeds.[299] It was also common to send money home to one's church, especially for members of denominations that prized independency. Lieutenant Waverly Wray of the 82nd Airborne Division, a Southern Baptist from Batesville, Mississippi, and very much in the mould of Alvin York, gave half his pay in order to help build a local church.[300] William C. Taggart remembered that, among the personal effects of an Alabamian fighter pilot killed at Buna, was an envelope containing a donation for 'the Forest Lake Baptist Church in Tuscaloosa'.[301] Nor, given the new-found plenty of the war years, was it only officers who could afford such generosity. One Sergeant Zoschke, a member of the Northern Baptist 'Mt. Zion Church near Junction, Kansas' gave '$20.00 per month to his church from his pay'.[302] Similarly, and as *The Chaplain* magazine reported in February 1945:

When a service man came to CHAPLAIN M. PRUGH of the Sixth Division Artillery to request baptism in keeping with his newly found faith in Christ, he seemed anxious that all arrears should be met. Even before the plans for the administration of the Sacrament were completed, the man took out his wallet and said: 'Here, Chaplain, is $50. I want you to send it to the treasurer of my mother's church back in Texas. I have never given a cent to the church, and I want to make up for lost time.'[303]

However, the most vivid and dramatic manifestation of this religious conditioning was the building or improvisation of a host of temporary chapels in almost every theatre of war. This remarkable phenomenon was the subject of an illustrated feature in *The Chaplain* magazine in November 1944, which estimated that the chapels built so far already numbered in the hundreds.[304] Significantly, this was a grass-roots phenomenon and was not dictated by army or navy policy. Despite the concerted church-building effort for its camps in the United States and overseas territories, as far as the War Department was concerned chapel-building was not its concern elsewhere. In the Pacific, for example, it was noted that:

In the long march from Australia to Tokyo the invariable situation was a scarcity of material and labor during the development of a new base or camp. Mess halls, barracks and necessary operational buildings naturally had first priority, and very often it required unusual initiative and ingenuity on the part of the chaplain to provide a place for worship. Too much appreciation cannot be expressed for the cooperation of Commanding Officers who made material available in spite of scarcity and to the men of the units who volunteered their labor after long hours of regular duty.[305]

In a similar vein, the Navy Department made no provision for chapels whatsoever in its official inventories of the materials required for the building and supply of foreign bases.[306] Necessarily the results of local initiatives and ingenuity, these chapels varied enormously in type and design according to the availability of skills and resources. At the Naval Operating Base at Argentia, Newfoundland, for example, a chapel was constructed in the winter of 1944–45 out of materials listed as 'salvage'. Its furniture was manufactured at Argentia's sawmill and carpentry shop while its fittings were purchased with a $5,000 gift from the officers' club. A local welfare fund found the money for the organ.[307] Other chapels were even constructed with the help of local labour, as in the case of a 'stone-block chapel' at an advanced airfield in Italy and a large memorial chapel on Guadalcanal, which was built of thatch by four thousand islanders and furnished with 'a native-carved mother-of-pearl inlaid altar'.[308]

As for the motives of their originators and builders, one army chaplain was reminded of the ancient precedent of the Israelites, and of their desire to build a suitable temple to mark the end of their wanderings.[309] While the ubiquitous desire to cultivate home associations no doubt played a part, the erection of a chapel could also be as much an expression of esprit de corps as it was of popular piety: 'There is a tradition with the Marine Corps in this war', so one navy chaplain averred, 'that wherever an outfit goes, as soon as mess tents and other immediate necessities are taken care of, up goes the chapel.' Everyone was expected to play their part in its construction.[310] Furthermore, in describing a makeshift chapel in North-West Europe, *The Chaplain* magazine insisted that this chapel-building impulse was also a fundamental expression of the national psyche:

> The first permanent United States Army chapel in France in World War II was established [on] D-Day plus seven by CHAPLAIN THEODORE P. BORNHOEFT only five days after his arrival in France. Services in the little canvas church are reminiscent of pioneer days when the forefathers of these soldiers took their guns to church too ...[311]

The rhetoric of the frontier resurfaced the following month when *The Chaplain* sought to locate this phenomenon more precisely in a broader historical and cultural context. Ignoring the recreational dimension of these projects, and the possible stimulus of the church-building programmes being effected by the War and the Navy Departments, *The Chaplain* insisted that this creative urge was innate in the American serviceman: 'Americans take pride in news of beach-heads established and of the speedy erection of places of worship. It is well to remember that such procedure follows the true pattern of our founders.' Invoking the example of the Pilgrim Fathers and of other bands of seventeenth-century settlers, it went on to claim that: 'These pastors and their spiritual flocks were the prototypes of all chaplains and their supporters who, amid danger and sacrifice, have established beachheads on distant shores. The Cross, the Book and the Chapel have been given their indispensable places. It is the American way.'[312] However florid and partial, there does appear to have been an element of truth in the claim that this generation of Americans was naturally inclined to consecrate new landscapes with places of worship. A more sober post-war report from the Pacific observed that the church-building bug had not been apparent among GIs in Australia, its symptoms emerging only when GIs encountered the vast and seemingly unchurched wastes of the Pacific region:

> While the troops were stationed in Australia they did not seem to give so much thought to the erection of unit chapels but were satisfied to use the mess halls and day rooms. Civilian churches were readily accessible. However, as soon as they moved into the islands, they began showing a specific interest in having their own houses of worship. It may be that the desire for a chapel was due to the fact that there were no established churches but that does not afford a full explanation. It seemed also to be an

expression of a desire to have in the area a tangible symbol of their religious faith from which they derived comfort.[313]

Despite a slower start among air units, the same disposition was also evident on the mainland of Asia.[314] Surveying the whole of the China–Burma–India theatre, its senior chaplain, Edward L. Trett, remarked that: 'In the most unexpected places chapels seem to arise. They're built of bamboo and are not the type that would win the annual award of the Society of Architecture, but into their erection and beautification go as much pride and devotion as ever was put into ancient cathedrals.'[315]

The effects of this 'American way' were even apparent in Europe. Although, in continental terms, Europe had the world's greatest concentration of churches, traditional settlement patterns, the ravages of war and the confessional divide between Catholics and Protestants meant that the need for chapels was often felt, perhaps especially by the latter. In the winter of 1943–44, and from 'Somewhere in Sicily', an informant wrote to *The Link* magazine:

> We have fixed up a chapel in a room about 40 ft. x 60 ft. We picked up an altar from a small abandoned chapel near by, and constructed a low railing around it. We also secured a piano and 132 folding chairs from a near-by town. We are using two white parachutes (slightly damaged) for decorations. Half of one is used as an altar cover. The other half, as well as the second, is spread out over the ceiling.... A Catholic priest, who is learning to speak English, comes out from a near-by town and conducts mass on Sunday at 9:00. Our Protestant services are at 10:00. One of the few Jewish chaplains on the Island comes round to hold services about once every three weeks.[316]

In the Italian campaign, and especially in the prolonged fighting up the spine of the Apennines, large caves were found to be easily convertible into relatively safe front-line chapels.[317] In Italy and in France, where these were scarce at the best of times, a particular effort was made to repair and even rebuild Protestant churches. In Florence, for example, a mission church belonging to the Southern Baptist Convention was renovated in the winter of 1944–45;[318] similarly, a shell-blasted Protestant church in one French village was rebuilt through the combined efforts of an army chaplain, the local mayor, impressed prisoners of war and sundry 'Christian soldiers' (who, as a result, found themselves 'housed in worshipful surroundings and singing the Lord's song in a strange land').[319]

Still, a lack of available churches was an infinitely greater problem in the Pacific, where church-building inevitably took place on a much larger scale. Daniel A. Poling was just one distinguished tourist who noted 'literally hundreds of Chapels built of native materials' during his travels in the South-West Pacific while, according to *The Chaplain* magazine, by the end of 1944 American-built chapels dotted the landscape 'from the Aleutians to the South Pacific'.[320] In the words of one senior chaplain who toured the South-West Pacific earlier that year, a slew of local initiatives had proved highly effective in supplying places of worship:

> I was very much impressed by the number of chapels. Every chaplain seems to have a chapel of some kind where installations have been built, and chapels seem to be included in plans for all installations.... As installations are developed the chapels improve. The common chapel is of native style construction with floor and benches, with the altar with cross and candlesticks in the foreground.... A great deal of initiative and ingenuity has been shown on the part of chaplains in building their chapels and a great deal of cooperation on the part of the commanding generals and officers.[321]

Due to the course and momentum of the American advance from 1943, some chaplains had to plan and build a succession of temporary chapels, and navy personnel alone built sixty-two chapels on Okinawa after its capture in June 1945.[322]

While some island chapels might be built only of driftwood, coconut logs and palm leaves,[323] others were considerable architectural and artistic achievements, however basic their materials. A chaplain of the 40th Infantry Division wrote from New Britain in November 1944:

> General Brush, our Division Commander ... turned up at one of my Sunday morning church services. Fortunately we had just completed our new chapel. The altar and *reredos* were made of peeled mahogany saplings. The candlesticks, altar cross and communion rail were built of tropic cedar and lightly stained with a blow torch. A swell screen was constructed of banyan roots. 'Holy, holy, holy' is lettered in bamboo across the *reredos* above the altar. Banana palms and ferns bank altar, *reredos* and communion rail, and cocoanut palms landscape the exterior. The sides and front of the building are latticed with more peeled tropic cedars, the whole surmounted by a cross.[324]

However, the Pacific theatre's chapel-builders par excellence were the navy's specialised and all-volunteer construction battalions, or 'Seabees'.[325] As Lieutenant Esther Johnson enthused in an article for *The Chaplain*:

> Chaplains with Seabees frequently find their entire congregations made up of draftsmen, carpenters, cabinet makers, lathe operators, metal-smiths, moulders, silversmiths, sail-makers, jewellers, electricians, plumbers, textile weavers, stone cutters, brick layers, masons, and architects.... These skilled artists, artisans and artificers have produced stained-glass windows from an Aussie raincoat and jungle twigs, ornate lamp fixtures from tomato cans,

organ pipes from bamboo poles, chancel canopies from parachutes, elaborate religious themes in oil paints, flower vases from shell cases, mosaics from bits of glass, tin and rocks ...[326]

Emblematic of Seabee accomplishment was a chapel of the 96th Seabees in the Philippines.[327] Dedicated in June 1945, their chaplain wrote:

> It is made largely of scrap material, but is a little gem, painted white on the outside with a cargo light, high in a big mahogany tree, flooding the building and grounds with light. The cupola contains a bell, cast from an acetylene drum. The personnel of the battalion is obviously proud of their chapel, which stands as a symbol of cooperation in the finer things. Officers and men attended in such numbers that every seat was crowded, and there was scarcely standing room.[328]

This technical ingenuity was also apparent in the army's Service and Air Forces. In Le Mans in the summer of 1944, the 757th Railway Shop Battalion built 'the first [Railway Operating Battalion] Rolling Chapel', along with other necessities such as dental and medical cars. Converted from a 'forty-foot, all steel French baggage car', as the 'Church on Wheels' for the Protestants of the 729th Railway Operating Battalion it could be found in as many as seventeen different locations at different times: 'The chapel on wheels with its big white cross on either side would be hitched to an engine and off the Chaplain would go, bringing the church to his men. When he came to a station, the chapel would be sidetracked and services held.'[329] In New Guinea, a fighter group overcame the problem of its dispersion by converting a larger aircraft into 'an air-borne chapel, complete with altar'.[330]

The limits of tolerance

As we have seen, in stressing the premium that the army placed on religious tolerance Chaplain G.E. Hopkins emphasised one of the defining features of religion in the American military. Indeed, Deborah Dash Moore has gone so far as to argue that the inclusive and conciliatory concept of the 'Judeo-Christian tradition' was 'largely a creation of the American military in World War II'.[331] Emblematic of the military's promotion of harmonious cooperation, which was as much a military imperative as a religious virtue, were the chaplaincy systems of the army and navy ('Where a Catholic Chaplain can teach Protestant Chaplains how to conduct Jewish services in the absence of a Jewish Chaplain', as one Jewish chaplain pithily put it).[332] Much wartime rhetoric and propaganda, addressed to a society whose religious divisions were often raw and blatant, focused on the nation's chaplains as models of interfaith amity; clergy who, though loyal to their own traditions, were the vanguard of what would become the Judeo-Christian civil religion of post-war America.[333] As early as December 1942, for example, the National Conference of Christians and Jews honoured William R. Arnold with a special citation that read:

> Brigadier General William R. Arnold
>
> FAITHFUL PRIEST, Chief of Chaplains of the United States Army, has impressively emphasized the importance of religion in a democracy and of adequate service for the spiritual needs of the men in the United States Army. He has kindled in the entire Corps of Chaplains respect for the convictions of citizens of every religious faith in our country.
>
> The Chaplains' Corps has developed morale among the men, based on the discipline of high religion, and promoted cooperation on the part of those of all faiths without compromise on the part of any. This is essential to unity of purpose and action in the armed forces as it is essential to national unity in the nation at large.[334]

Such themes were well to the fore in official, or semi-official, publications on army chaplaincy in particular. *Soldiers of God*, a book co-written by William R. Arnold and Christopher Cross, who doubled as assistant director of publicity of the Mutual Broadcasting Company, New York,[335] purported to be the 'True Story of the U.S. Army Chaplains'. Published in 1945, it was dedicated 'TO THE CHAPLAINS OF ALL FAITHS WHO HAVE GIVEN THEIR LIVES IN THE SERVICE OF GOD AND COUNTRY'. Here, readers are regaled with stories of mutual respect and pious interdependence. In the wilds of Alaska, for example, Protestant and Catholic chaplains pitched in to ensure that Rosh Hashana was celebrated in appropriate fashion:

> Lieut. Stanley Dickens, the Special Services Officer, read the appropriate verses from the prayer book furnished by the National Jewish Welfare Board. The ceremonial wine was contributed by Chaplain Robert Biassioli, a Catholic. It came from his supply of wine he used for Mass. The sermon was delivered by Base Chaplain Walter C. Lundbergh, a Protestant.

'Those who participated', its authors proclaimed, 'will long remember that it was the cooperation of a Protestant and Catholic clergyman that made it possible for them to usher in their New Year in the traditional Jewish manner.'[336] Seized by a similar spirit, it was likewise claimed that a Southern Baptist chaplain was responsible for the rebuilding of a devastated church in Normandy: 'Chaplain Izard is a Baptist. The church of St. Laurent Sur Mer is Catholic. The men who helped to rebuild the church are of all denominations – Protestants, Catholics and Jews.'[337] As a reformed bigot, Chaplain Karl A. Wuest, a Catholic, claimed an almost Damascene conversion to military norms on meeting his regiment's Protestant chaplain:

In civilian life I had had no dealings with the ministers of other beliefs. I had seen no point in making their acquaintance, for they could work their side of the street while I worked mine. We had not a shred in common. I could get along best by ignoring them, for their teachings were opposed to mine.... I had, as it were, a mighty large chip on my shoulder. Now, with that handclasp, the chip fell away with a mighty pleasing thud.[338]

Such were the heights of mutual sympathy and esteem that Arnold and Cross (or, perhaps more accurately, Cross and Arnold) even wrote of the comforts offered by 'Universal religion'. While their language seems oddly reminiscent of theosophy, their concept of 'universal religion' was worlds away from the arcane deductions of the theosophist cognoscenti, basically representing an aggregate of America's three great religious traditions, an aggregate that the pressure of war made increasingly tangible.[339] Although the dedication of military cemeteries furnished a powerful platform on which to parade the religious unity of wartime America[340] (hence, in part, the scandal over Chaplain Gittelsohn's experiences on Iwo Jima), an emotional backdrop of crosses and stars of David was not essential for such occasions. In a vivid scene from the war in the South-West Pacific, an interfaith burial service was even conducted from the air. In the summer of 1945, a transport aircraft went down in the remote mountains of New Guinea, killing twenty-one people on board. Hence, and as Roy J. Honeywell described it:

> A few days later Catholic and Protestant chaplains flew to the scene. Though landing was impossible, crosses and a Star of David were dropped, to be placed by the Filipino paratroopers who were to dig the graves. While the plane circled above the spot, the chaplains recited the funeral rituals of their faiths. As there were no Jewish chaplains within a thousand miles, one of them read the burial service of that faith in honor of the Jewish girl among the victims.[341]

Naturally, and with amenable clergy of all three traditions showing the way, military service could be presented as an antidote for religious prejudice of all kinds – an impression that has lingered, with the historian Kevin M. Schultz arguing that, with 'the tri-faith arrangement its standard operating procedure', military life succeeded in bringing 'members of the various faiths closer together'.[342] In 1944, and conscious of the simmering religious and racial tensions in those neighbourhoods that had experienced 'mushroom growth' as a result of the war, the Christian Institute for American Democracy of New York City embarked upon an advertising campaign aimed at promoting religious tolerance among Americans on the home front, invoking the theme of tri-faith unity in the American military. With the support of newspapers, advertising firms, churches, the USO and even shipyards and labour unions, its campaign was fronted by a billboard poster depicting three GIs advancing through a belt of barbed wire under the caption:

FIGHTING SIDE BY SIDE
PROTESTANT
CATHOLIC
JEW
So that Every Person may Worship God in his own way!

Accompanying the poster campaign were twenty-two versions of 'full-page newspaper ads stressing the need for unity among Catholics, Protestants and Jews
in the face of Nazi propaganda to disrupt friendly relations'. These were carried
in at least 250 different newspapers, their message being: 'Americans, be just ..!
Recognize your neighbors' rights as equal to your own. Defend those rights. Protestants, Catholics and Jews die together in the war for the same cause. Let no one
divide *us*. Keep America free from racial and religious persecution.'[343] Significantly, Robert D. Workman sat on 'the national committee for this campaign'[344]
and, not least through the ongoing activities of the National Conference of Christians and Jews, its sentiments were actively impressed upon service personnel.
Galvanised by the religious and ideological configuration of the war, and under
the umbrella of the NCCJ's Commission on Programs in Army Camps, Naval and
Air Bases, from mid-1942 its 'Tolerance Trios' plied their way through stateside
camps and installations, visiting nearly eight hundred by the end of the war,
and addressing as many as nine million service personnel.[345] With their travel
facilitated by the military, mass rallies promoting 'interfaith understanding' were
held at military posts from Alaska to the Canal Zone, such as that which took
place in May 1944 at Gulfport, Mississippi, which was attended by more than ten
thousand sailors.[346] Reinforcing the message of its Tolerance Trios was a glut of
supporting publications aimed at service personnel, with eight million copies of
NCCJ pamphlets being distributed via army and navy chaplains, to which could
be added five million tri-faith prayer cards, and 250 copies of a film entitled *The
World We Want to Live In*, which the NCCJ supplied to the Signal Corps after
well-received screenings by its own representatives.[347] Summarising the NCCJ's
achievements, Kevin M. Schultz has claimed that:

> By the end of the war, nearly every American soldier had touched a piece
> of NCCJ literature, watched an NCCJ film, or gone to an NCCJ Camp
> program meeting … Tolerance between the three faiths became sacrosanct,
> and the NCCJ, along with the federal government, had made the tri-faith
> arrangement America's standard operating procedure.[348]

In view of these efforts – of the example set by their chaplains and the common
experience of serving alongside those of other faiths – it was widely claimed that
America's armed forces served as national (and, indeed, global) models of religious tolerance. As a Jewish navy chaplain, Charles E. Shulman declared that:
'The larger spirit of common sharing and common destiny under one flag which

protects the rights of Catholic, Protestant, and Jew alike is one of the bright notes in the present dark age.'[349] A Methodist colleague, Chaplain Hansel H. Tower, confirmed that: 'The armed forces are meeting the problem of serving all religions in an admirable manner. There is a surprisingly small amount of friction between the faiths in the Army and Navy.'[350] Tower was particularly struck by the design of the navy's interfaith chapels, complete with their revolving altars, which he was convinced could serve as the model for a new breed of civilian, interfaith community churches: 'The limitations to the idea lie only in the intolerance and smallness of people who should be big and brotherly', he claimed.[351] Nor was this tolerance simply a matter of official policy and clerical broadmindedness. Chaplain Harry P. Abbott insisted that: 'Veterans have learned in the army that men of all denominations and religions can live and work together, and worship in their own ways without compromising their principles, ideals, or training.'[352] Fresh from his Pacific sojourns as a representative of the Jewish Welfare Board, Moritz M. Gottlieb claimed of Jewish GIs:

> [T]heir new faith, which is not of one religion above another, or one race above another, is a stronger and more virile religion than that carried away by most men before they went away to fight.... Our soldiers have stopped thinking of their companions as white or black, Christian or Jew, Irish or Italian. Men are judged solely on the basis of character, on their courage, humility, and willingness to sacrifice for the common good.[353]

According to Arnold and Cross, this sense of commonality was by no means confined to American Jews, who clearly stood as the prime beneficiaries of this new spirit of religious amity and collaboration:

> The Protestant decides that the Catholic boy he ignored before 'isn't such a bad egg after all.' The Jew and the Catholic learn that they can get along. Primitive conditions increase the spirit of friendliness and tolerance. Men of all faiths learn that their existence depends on cooperation. Bigotry seems to vanish in foxholes.[354]

There was, no doubt, plenty of substance to these claims. For example, Chaplain Morris N. Kertzer remembered that many of the treats provided for the children invited to his Hanukah celebrations at Dijon in 1944 were donated by Christian GIs:

> I announced that sixty of the packages had been prepared by a group of Christian soldiers from the American Army who had volunteered to give up their own rations, and had, moreover, spent an evening preparing the packages. At this announcement, the expression on the children's faces was one of wonder and awe. After four years of flight, hiding from an enemy they could not understand, living in a shadow terrifying to their childish

imaginations, it was incomprehensible to them that anyone in the world should sacrifice these precious candies for them.[355]

In addition to these personal manifestations of goodwill, Kertzer recognised that the army itself made a diligent attempt to inculcate religious tolerance through a variety of media as part of its training regime; indeed, the highest compliment that he heard paid to the US army was a complaint by a bigoted colleague that it was too prone to coddle its minorities.[356] Despite this aberration, Kertzer's experience of Christian chaplains had been overwhelmingly positive:

> [I]n the main, army life had a tremendous effect on most chaplains. A southern Methodist preacher, who had never seen a Jew out on the Texas range, who first heard of Catholics when his mother spoke of the bogeyman, shared a tent or a foxhole with a rabbi and a priest.... These were experiences that leave permanent marks on our thinking, and what is more important, on our preaching. It is easy to denounce another faith if one does not have a precious friend who adheres to it.[357]

In any case, and as Kertzer also emphasised, the army's institutionalised culture of religious tolerance could be enforced by the sanctions of army discipline:

> *The United States Army officially and unequivocally stood against any form of prejudice, racial or religious.* Any proven act of religious intolerance was dealt with severely. The bigot might have his private views, but they dare not be expressed or overtly translated into an act of discrimination. I have seen men from the southern states lean over backward to avoid the charge of race discrimination. I have seen men lose their rank because of an anti-Semitic remark.[358]

In sum, and even with the benefit of hindsight, Kertzer claimed to be extremely impressed by what he had experienced in the army. Such was the contrast with civilian norms and expectations that it had even occasioned a change in the content of Jewish chaplains' sermons: 'Pride in our spiritual heritage and its challenge to our army lives were the dominant motifs in our messages. Too much had already been said to the troops about dislike of the Jew, and they welcomed the clean air of creative, constructive Jewish thinking.'[359]

Still, and however edifying and pervasive this ethos of inclusivity and cooperation may have seemed, it was impossible to paper over the cracks of America's deep religious divisions. No doubt many saw the need for religious tolerance more in terms of patriotic necessity than as a positive virtue and, as navy chaplain John Harold Craven conceded, 'The level of patriotism of that time' did much to mitigate 'interchurch relationships'.[360] Significantly, a widely held reticence on religious matters no doubt helped to defuse latent religious tensions. If one navy veteran claimed that, 'I don't have to sit on the front row to believe in Jesus

Christ',361 army chaplain Harry P. Abbott noted that, while the typical GI was religious, 'he does not wear his religion on his coat sleeve'. Far from being 'mere Sunday religion', it was 'a deep sincere, unselfish, practical religion', dominated by the precept of the Golden Rule.362 Also at work were fears of inadequacy, hypocrisy and even ridicule. Such was the marines' reluctance to openly discuss religion that Chaplain Hansel H. Tower found that some were hesitant to even commit their thoughts to paper: 'Some said that they would be glad to do so, but after thinking the matter over for a few days several of them confessed that they could not put what they truly felt about religion into words.'363 Even one who did remarked that:

> The average man in the service is very shy or hesitant about letting his buddies know that he worships God. His prayers are silent and often his heart longs for an outlet in public worship, yet he feels that should he state firmly and openly his faith in God, his buddies would laugh at him and he would lose face among them.364

One army chaplain agreed that, 'The great majority of soldiers are religious, yet are somewhat afraid to admit it', the main reason for their reticence being 'a certain feeling they'll be ridiculed or "not be one of the gang"'.365

However, this reticence was also a precaution against the hidden shoals of religious difference, a wariness that arose from an eminently practical and sensible concern to avoid sowing discord among one's immediate comrades. Besides the vaunted (and, indeed, much mythologised) bonds of comradeship that obtained among front-line infantrymen,366 the need for small group cooperation and cohesion was almost a sine qua non throughout the armed forces, and avoidable conflicts were not to be indulged. As an artillery chaplain, Chaplain Karl A. Wuest noted that:

> Soldiers from all parts of the country, with different temperament, with diversity of religion, with different likes and dislikes, must become one in the team of manning the artillery piece. Whatever their differences, these must be foregone in the accomplishment of the task at hand. The life of each depended on the dexterity and cooperation of the others.367

Significantly, and despite the simmering antipathy of the two protagonists, the only explicitly religious argument recalled by Audie Murphy in his memoir *To Hell and Back* occurred between a Catholic New Englander (Emmet J. Kerrigan) and an Appalachian backwoodsman (Snuffy Jones), and only while the latter was in his cups:

> When he has become thoroughly drunk, [Snuffy] is hit by religious fervor. In a tearful and wailing voice, he confesses his unworthiness to live, and rants of the mercy of God. In dead earnestness, he turns upon Kerrigan,

begging him to repent and give up his sinful ways. Kerrigan tolerates the advice for a while before planting a very solid boot in the seat of Snuffy's pants.

Undaunted, the earnest if drunken Snuffy continued, now invoking all the vivid torments of Hell. Kerrigan's response was not what he sought, however: "'I repent that I've waited so long to do this," says Kerrigan grimly as he taps him on the jaw with his fist. Snuffy folds up.'[368]

It was no doubt to avoid incidents such as this, and their possible repercussions, that so many World War II veterans who participated in the US Army Military History Institute's Veterans Survey were quick to stress their comrades' silence on religious matters. To the question, 'How and to what extent were religious convictions expressed in your unit?', the standard answer (if given) was to invoke the availability of chaplains, the provision of services, and/or the silence of others. For example, and as former Staff Sergeant Newman W. Phillips stressed, among the men of Company L of the 126th Infantry Regiment this was, 'For the most part a very private matter';[369] likewise, and as Clinton Rodefer, a flight engineer with the 449th Bombardment Group, put the matter: 'TO EACH HIS OWN, NO COMMENTS.'[370]

If it was easy to misconstrue the various signals of conflict avoidance for a more wholehearted tolerance, religious tensions in the armed forces continued to reflect tensions in domestic religious life – tensions between Christians and Jews, Protestants and Catholics, and within and between America's Protestant churches, to name but a few of America's religious fault lines. Significantly, and despite the admiration they evoked from optimistic commentators, even the armed forces' interfaith chapels could become scenes of inter-confessional wrangling. When Chaplain Francis Leonard Garrett, a Methodist, arrived at the Naval Air Station, Alameda, in the summer of 1944, he was perturbed to find that its senior chaplain, a Catholic, had inaugurated perpetual exposition of the Blessed Sacrament, in effect hijacking the chapel for Catholic use throughout the week.[371] Another navy chaplain, Frederick William Meehling, who came to regard World War II navy chaplaincy as a cutting-edge venture in ecumenism,[372] remembered the problems posed by a Protestant chaplain who used the occasion of Easter Sunday to attack the Catholic Church from the pulpit of a chapel at Quantico, Virginia; in this instance, it was a senior officer, a Protestant, who took offence: 'If there's any fight between religions, Protestants and Catholics, let them decide that between Oxnam and Spellman up there in Washington, the higher echelon, not down here.'[373] Nevertheless, religious jibes were not uncommon in the Marine Corps, where Catholics could be known by the old pejorative of 'mackerel-snappers'.[374] For his part, Chaplain Francis L. Sampson of the 101st Airborne Division noted that the preferred terms for Catholics used by his regimental commanding officer were 'fish-eaters' and 'left-footers'.[375] Even

John Harold Craven, a Southern Baptist, was perplexed to hear the views of a marine colonel concerning a Mass held in connection with the dedication of a Marine Corps cemetery on Saipan: '"The Protestant service I could understand", he said, "but during the Catholic service the man just turned his back to us and said some words I didn't understand, mixed himself a drink and drank it all, but didn't offer any to anybody!"'[376] Such wisecracks could even lead to fisticuffs; Lawrence Lynch, for example, one of the most flamboyant Catholic army chaplains in the Pacific theatre, and who was not above lecturing his assistant on the merits of religious tolerance, came to blows with a fellow officer in a mess hall on New Caledonia after the latter had mocked the sacrament of confession.[377] Francis L. Sampson, who was reputed to have partaken in a similar brawl,[378] wrote of a Catholic colleague, Ignatius P. Maternowski of the 508th Parachute Infantry Regiment, who was killed on D-Day: 'On more than one occasion he had volunteered to put the gloves on with officers who interfered with his work, tried to wise-crack about the Church, or made smart remarks about confession.'[379] Sampson also remembered how minor differences between Protestants and Catholics could surface in the most hazardous and unlikely circumstances. Quite literally caught in the crossfire in the early hours of the Normandy landings, Sampson recalled how he tried to calm the wounded paratroopers he was attending in a makeshift aid station:

> As the shelling continued, I had the men take turns in leading the others in the Lord's Prayer. Of all the times and places for a religious argument! When one of the men finished with '... for Thine is the Kingdom, and the Power, and the Glory, now and forever', one of the Catholic men said that it didn't belong there. The Protestant men insisted that it did. The other Catholic men joined in to insist it didn't belong.[380]

Grateful for the distraction, Sampson 'told them each to say it in whatever way he had learned it'. In fact, Sampson recalled that this intrusion of normality even acted as a tonic: 'Scared as I was, this argument struck me [as] so funny at the time that I almost became hysterical.'[381]

If most Christians could at least bicker over the precise wording of a prayer they held in common, the Japanese-Americans of the 100th Battalion and 442nd Infantry Regiment, a tiny religious and ethnic minority, were pejoratively known as 'buddhaheads'.[382] While this unflattering and somewhat misleading sobriquet came to be owned as a badge of pride, the unpleasant undertones of a much older interfaith rivalry were to be found throughout the armed forces. With reference to his experiences in the 19th Infantry Regiment, which served in the Pacific with the 24th Infantry Division, Sergeant Roger Kenneth Heller, a pre-war college student and a Lutheran, remembered that anti-Semitism was endemic in a regiment that was '2/3 Roman Catholic'.[383] Deeply ironic in this respect was the experience of Tec 5 Julian Richard Jacobs, who wrote of his experiences in the 34th Infantry Division:

> I was called a kike, S.O.B. Jew, a Hebe etc. just because of my name. And down South I was religiously looked down on. I always called this double discrimination because I was not Jewish. I'm a French Canadian Roman Catholic. Ignorance abounded in the army. It's tough to face Jewish discrimination when your [sic] not even Jewish ... You get angry and feel like exploding at the person.[384]

Despite his own positive experiences of the army, Morris N. Kertzer was under no illusions as to the ubiquity of anti-Semitic sentiment, however unspoken. According to Kertzer, low-level anti-Semitism was rife, and no Jewish GI suffered from the delusion that the US army could dispel a living, centuries-old legacy of hate and suspicion. In terms of its manifestations, Kertzer listed the higher thresholds for promotion that Jewish GIs seemed to face, and even higher thresholds for bravery when it came to the distribution of battlefield awards. As for the mundane matter of postings, it often seemed that otherwise well-qualified Jews were deliberately thwarted when seeking transfers, especially to medical or to legal duties.[385]

Significantly, and while Jewish GIs were liable to turn up in force for festival celebrations, they could feel much less enthusiastic about the visit of a Jewish chaplain:

> When I met a group of men for the first time, I entertained no extravagant illusions that they were thrilled and excited about my visit.... Once in a while the men would receive me resentfully, wishing I would stay away from their battalion and not remind the others that they were Jewish.[386]

This was hardly surprising, for anti-Semitic slurs and low-level harassment were commonplace among a generation that had experienced the interwar high-watermark of American anti-Semitism. Edward Martinez, who served as an armourer with the 73rd Bombardment Wing in the Pacific, was well aware of the wartime dynamics and inequalities of the American melting pot. As the only Mexican American in a unit that was dominated by German and Italian Americans, his own derisive moniker was 'Bandit'; worse, however, was the plight of a Jewish GI who never even made it to the Pacific:

> We didn't have any Jews in our outfit. We had one in the States. I knew he was Jewish because everybody used to call him Jewish names and he didn't care for how we used to cuss him up a little bit. He was an American, like us. He was in the service, the only Jew. He didn't go overseas with us, not with our outfit.[387]

Furthermore, and for all the claims of religious tolerance in the armed forces, the career of Chaplain Thomas H. Clare shows how little this mood had affected the men of the 341st Bombardment Group. On one occasion, and while travelling in India in a truck convoy, an Irish American complained of another driver:

'These – Kikes sure get in my hair.'
'I think he's Polish,' I said.
'Same difference. All they got in Poland is Kikes. That's why Hitler went after 'em. Ever see a Polack which wasn't a Kike?' he asked, turning to me.
'I came! I saw! I grabbed! That's them in three words.'[388]

Even among its officers, the suspicion of being Jewish was problem enough. Of the group's chief of operations, an officer named Stromberg, Clare wrote:

Strom wasn't Jewish; but he felt that his name suggested that he was; and so he was quite touchy on the point. He threatened to knock my block off one day over this matter.... 'Chaplain, he said, 'on every post I've been, the boys have kidded me about this Jewish business. I'm sick of it. Why,' he broke into a laugh, 'someone even called up my mother once and asked her if she had time to serve at some kind of an affair in the synagogue.' [389]

On yet another occasion, Clare had to calm a young Jewish private, who raged:

I got too much pride to let a gang of stupid morons like those guys push me around. The first chance I get to lay my hands on a Tommy gun I'll blast the whole – bunch off the map. That sergeant, too. They'll kill me, but I'll have the satisfaction of taking them with me.... I'm no Kike or Jewish bastard like these guys call me ... I'm as good as the next guy. And when I go I'm taking that sergeant with me. He can't call me what he did and get away with it.[390]

While Clare's illustrations, all of which concern AAF ground crew, may imply that it was those least likely to be exposed to the binding pressures of combat who were most likely to retain their civilian prejudices, anti-Semitism was also to be found among medical units, combat soldiers, senior commanders and – it seems – even among chaplains. Muriel Engelman of the Army Nurse Corps, who served in England and North-West Europe, was one of two Jewesses among the hundred or so nurses of the 16th General Hospital. Even in this comparatively civilised environment, where half of the 'physicians and dentists' were Jewish, there were murmurings among her Christian colleagues: 'I didn't see any overt anti-Semitism. Of course, my maiden name was Phillips, so every so often somebody would make a little remark because they didn't know that I was Jewish with a name like Phillips. And if I said something, "Oh well, you don't look it."'[391] Nor was anti-Semitism at a discount in units slated for combat. One of the murkier themes in the history of 'E' Company of the 506th Parachute Infantry Regiment, Stephen E. Ambrose's fabled 'Band of Brothers', was its relationship with its first commanding officer, Herbert Sobel. Widely reviled as a martinet, it is clear that being Jewish did not help his popularity: 'Behind his back the men cursed him, "f—ing Jew" being the most common epithet.'³⁹² However, some anti-Semites weren't so discreet. Sergeant Wilbert D. Goldsmith, who served in the 39th Infantry Regiment of the 9th Infantry Division in North Africa, Italy and North-West Europe, recalled that:

> In August 42 the Jewish High Holy days came early and having no Jewish chaplain [on] the Post, the Post chaplain saw to it that all the Jewish personal [sic] was invited to the Temples in near by [sic] Baltimore for services. My platoon leader upon being denied a weekend pass and was given [the] reason was steaming. When he called us out for inspection, he did it with an ethnic slur. I heard it and asked [him] to repeat it.

Goldsmith then asked him 'to step outside and to take off his shirt', for, as he said, 'One could not fight a non com with his stripes on.' After the ensuing fight was 'broken up by other noncoms and enlisted men', both parties were summoned by their company commander to explain the reasons for the fracas. According to Goldsmith:

> I informed him to ask my sergant [sic]. When asked he said it was just a misunderstanding and as far as he was concerned, he would just as soon forget it with no hard feelings.... I knew that if I informed the Capt as to what had led up to the fight, he would have had to strip the sargent [sic] of his stripes.... Upon leaving the headquarters together, the sargent said to me, that I was a smart little boy. No I said I was a smart little Jewish Boy.³⁹³

Anti-Semitism, in fact, was a contributory factor in the undoing of one of the army's most capable and controversial generals, namely George S. Patton. While even the voluble Patton was careful not to disport his anti-Semitic prejudice during the war, one senior Jewish chaplain suspected that it explained why no Jewish chaplain was assigned to Patton's Third Army headquarters in the summer of 1944.³⁹⁴ Whatever else, his prejudice certainly coloured his views with respect to the government of post-war Germany, views that led in September 1945 to his dismissal as military governor of Bavaria and his removal from the command of Third Army.³⁹⁵ If Patton seems to have been sincere in his conviction that de-Nazification methods were Gestapo-like and 'utterly un-American', and that Germany needed to be 'rebuilt as a buffer against the real danger, which is Bolshevism from Russia,'³⁹⁶ there can be little doubt that anti-Semitic perspectives coloured his unsympathetic response to the claims of Jewish Displaced Persons over those of German civilians: 'I do not see why Jews should be treated any better or any worse than Catholics, Protestants, Mohammedans, or Mormons', he wrote.³⁹⁷ While Patton evinced salutary rage at the discovery of Germany's concentration camps (as one Jewish GI remembered, at Ohrdruf he had screamed: 'See what these sons of bitches did, see what these bastards did. I don't want you to take a prisoner …'),[398] his zeal for collective punishment waned over the summer of 1945. Furthermore, he was affected by a concurrent reaction to the seemingly alien, Eastern European survivors of the Holocaust. As Martin Blumenson has emphasised, Patton's anti-Semitism was an expression not only of his low regard for non-Anglo-Saxon peoples but also of his inveterate snobbery. In fact, he 'shared whatever endemic anti-Semitism existed in America, in the U.S. Army, and among the rich and fashionable during the early and middle years of the twentieth century'. In earlier days, Patton had even 'listened with interest and sympathy' to a brother-in-law 'who believed passionately in the reality of the long-discredited Protocols of Zion'.[399] Faced with the shattered remnants of impoverished Eastern European Jewry, in private Patton gave full vent to a growing anti-Semitic animus. On 21 September, he noted in his diary:

> General Louis Craig came in to see me this morning to explain how he had arranged for taking care of the Jews.... He said the conditions and filth were unspeakable. In one room he found ten people, six men and four women, occupying four double beds. Either the Displaced Persons never had any sense of decency or else they lost it all during their period of internment by the Germans. My personal opinion is that no people could have sunk to the level of degradation these have reached in the short space of four years.[400]

Two days after being notified of his sacking by Eisenhower, an unrepentant Patton wrote:

> [C]onsiderable remains to be done [at the Displaced Persons' Camps], primarily because the Jewish type of DP is, in the majority of cases, a sub-human species without any of the cultural or social refinements of our time … it is an unfortunate fact that the people at home who are so vociferous in their demands for the betterment of the Displaced Jews have no conception of the low mental, moral, and physical standards of the objects of their solicitude …[401]

The following day: 'Of course I know the expression "Lost tribes of Israel" applied to the tribes which disappeared – not to the tribe of Judah from which the current sons of bitches are descended. However, it is my personal opinion that this too is a lost tribe – lost to all decency.'[402]

While Patton's bile was directed at non-American Jews, some of the incidents in interfaith relations that William R. Arnold chose not to publicise were the occasional complaints made by American Jews against Christian army chaplains. One of these was made by a Jewish woman from Paso Robles, California, in September 1945 and involved a problem that she claimed 'concerns me and my family personally, and, in my opinion, the Jewish people generally'. According to her version of events, a chaplain at nearby Camp Roberts had forbidden his daughter from associating with hers at a local public school and had voiced his disapproval of their friendship to their teachers, their schoolmates and to her. Although he claimed that this was on behavioural grounds, she suspected that other motives were at work, motives that were wholly inconsistent with his status as an army chaplain. The chaplain was, she claimed, 'Lutheran and of German descent' and therefore, 'His background probably influenced him in his thinking.' If this was the case, she argued, the incident should 'disqualify him as a Chaplain in the U.S. Army where he is supposed to minister to all men, regardless of race, creed, or color'.[403] Because she called for the chaplain (who was not, in fact, a Lutheran) to be 'investigated',[404] he was duly called upon to give his side of the story. This he did, claiming that his concern was simply that of any parent, and insisting that: 'It is incidental that the other girl is of Jewish parentage – I would act similarly in any case, regardless of race, religion, or color.' Furthermore, he was swift to defend his interfaith credentials:

> As regards my personal attitude toward people of Jewish faith, I believe my record as a Chaplain will speak for itself. The relations that I have with Jewish personnel and the cooperation I have always given to Jewish Chaplains will be attested by them. This is not a question of 'race prejudice' at all, but exists only in the mind of the one who brought the complaint in the first place.[405]

While this personal dispute appears to have petered out, it does at least illustrate the extent to which army chaplains had become identified in the public mind as unimpeachable purveyors of interfaith tolerance and cooperation.

Less open to question were the opinions and actions of a second chaplain, who in July 1944 wrote to Rabbi Joachim Prinz of Newark, New Jersey, after Prinz had spoken at Camp Barkeley, Texas. Reflecting on Prinz's words on the need for Jews to live with the same dignity as other nations, he retorted that 'the Jew cares very little about dignity, if he can, by losing it, make a dime ... the Jew grovels till his Bank Roll is fat and then by the economies of Capitalism takes advantage of his fellow-men. The result is an accumulation of wrath that ends in his suffering.' As for the need for expropriated property in Europe to be returned to its Jewish owners, the chaplain snorted that, 'the Jews took advantage of an impoverished Germany after World War I and bought every thing they could put hands on.... The judgment of myself and others here is that this type of robbery and stolen goods need not be returned when recaptured.' Weighing the evidence as he saw it, he concluded his hate-flecked diatribe by stating:

> My one hope for your people is the Christianization of them. Until that happens, I fear they will always turn their genius into channels for material gain, blinded to anything higher and powerless to obtain the higher. Their material gain will in turn become their bitterness and cause of their persecution.[406]

Although Prinz dignified this letter with a closely argued reply, and noted in mitigation that the chaplain belonged to a 'Southern Protestant group that has always impressed me as being particularly poorly educated',[407] the Jewish Welfare Board understandably questioned how he could function as an army chaplain. In a letter to the chief of chaplains, Rabbi Philip S. Bernstein warned:

> This letter from Chaplain [‒‒‒] is very disturbing. It indicates a deep seated prejudice against the Jews and an attitude toward their faith which would make it very difficult for Chaplain [‒‒‒] to render services to the Jews in the armed forces of the United States in accordance with the policies of the Office of the Chief of Chaplains. How can a chaplain who believes that the only hope for the Jew is to get them to turn away from their own faith be expected to help Jews adequately to maintain their own faith?[408]

Although no specific course of action was demanded, it was implicit that the JWB regarded the chaplain's letter as sufficient grounds for his removal from the Corps. However, as no action was taken, his name has been withheld.

Evidently, there was no lack of Christian anti-Semites in the US armed forces during World War II, though those in authority often chose not to be too open about the fact. When conversing with an inmate of a psychiatric ward in India, Richard Beard, an army psychologist, quickly learned of his patient's paranoia, Christian faith and anti-Semitic proclivities: 'At the outset, he had asked me if I were a Jew. He condemned the Jews for keeping him in the hospital, charged that I was allied with them. Of course, he could name no Jews.'[409] Beard went on to make another observation: 'It is interesting to note that the most devoted follower of the church whom it has been my misfortune to have on the ward turned out to be the most vicious personality whom I have encountered.'[410] However, and in sharp contrast with the inference drawn by Beard, a post-war investigation of anti-Semitic prejudice among army veterans living in Chicago demonstrated that it was those GIs with *most* religion who were *least* susceptible to anti-Semitic sentiments, perhaps an indication that the official, religiously tolerant ethos of service chaplaincy and service life did rub off on those who were most exposed to its moderating influences. Conducted by the University of Chicago and sponsored by the American Jewish Committee, the study was based on open-ended interviews conducted with 150 Christian, white, veteran enlisted men.[411] Remarkably, it found that there was no correlation between anti-Semitism and confessional background, be it Catholic, Protestant or mixed.[412] However, when correlated with their answers as to the importance of religion in the army, and working on the assumption that 'the subjects were obviously projecting their own feelings … and not basing their answers on carefully observed behaviour in others',[413] it was established that: '[The fifty-two] veterans who answered the central question by stressing the acceptance and importance of religion in the army were *significantly more tolerant* than the rest of the sample.'[414] In contrast, those whose opinions were more ambiguous were more likely to be anti-Semitic, leading to the conclusion that, 'while permanent religious attitudes correlated positively with tolerance, vascillation [sic] on this score was accompanied by a higher degree of anti-Semitism.'[415] Also remarkable was the fact that: 'Throughout the interviews when reasons for the dislike of Jews were mentioned, references to religion were almost totally absent.'[416]

Despite the inevitable salience of inter-confessional and interfaith feuding, the often painful fractures within American Protestantism were also felt in the armed forces. Besides the continuing friction between progressives on the one hand, and evangelicals and fundamentalists on the other, the Protestant Episcopal Church continued to suffer from the divergences of practice and mutual antagonisms of its 'High' and 'Low' church parties. As a senior navy chaplain complained to George W. Wickersham, High Church Episcopalians could really muddy the confessional waters:

> Now, if I send a Roman Catholic and an Episcopalian who isn't low [to a small base], I will soon get a call from the Commanding Officer inquiring as to the whereabouts of his Protestant chaplain. Why, only yesterday [one commanding officer] berated me over the phone for sending him two Catholic chaplains![417]

Remarkably, and despite the wider drama of progressive versus fundamentalist, the fiercest row to unfold in the pages of *The Link* during the war took place between 'High Church' and 'Low Church' Episcopalians. In response to Chaplain Hopkins's enthusiastic endorsement of the generic quality of army Protestantism, in January 1945 Corporal John S. Dugger, a chaplain's assistant, made a firm reassertion of Episcopalian exceptionalism:

> I have worked in the Chaplains Department [sic] for nearly two years, and I have yet to see Episcopalian men worshiping in general worship services conducted by other 'Protestant' chaplains when there is an Episcopalian chaplain on the post or an Episcopalian priest in a near-by civilian community. In many cases, civilian priests are hired to say the Mass for Episcopalian men.[418]

Dugger followed this by claiming that:

> I am only one of many, who, in the absence of an Episcopalian chaplain, attend Roman Catholic masses. I find, too, that this practice is commonly advocated by civilian parish priests. So, let's have men like Chaplain Hopkins do a little research before publishing statements of that kind, which, I am sure, are quite distressing to the parents of Episcopalian men in service.[419]

This Anglo-Catholic challenge to the Protestant consensus unleashed a welter of mainline fury. According to the editor: 'Nothing we have printed recently has brought down such a storm of indignation from our readers ... The result was an avalanche of mail; one agreeing with the corporal, and all the rest jumping down his throat with both feet.'[420] From the navy, Seaman First Class Thomas M. Laird protested:

> I have been a member of the Episcopal Church during my entire life-time and I have never heard it suggested that I attend a Roman Catholic service in preference to one of another Protestant denomination.... That any parents of service men should find it 'distressing' that their sons do not attend a Roman Catholic mass in preference to worshiping with other Protestant boys is beyond my understanding.... Is Cpl. Dugger aware that the name of the church which he so strongly upholds is the Protestant Episcopal Church and that it has been and still is considering organic union with the Presbyterian Church?[421]

While Dugger's sole supporter agreed that 'the [Episcopal] church uses the word "Protestant" in the strict sense of "non-Roman," and not in the popularly accepted sense',[422] Paul S. Sanders, a Methodist navy chaplain, was quick to identify and dismiss the provenance of such claims:

> I should like to make two guesses: (1) that Cpl. Dugger has been reared in an Anglo-Catholic parish (probably in the Diocese of New York or Long Island or Eau Claire) which parishes and dioceses are not representative of the Episcopal Church as a whole; (2) that Cpl. Dugger has never read the Episcopal weekly *The Churchman*, which recently advocated that parishes not in accord with the Anglo-Catholic bias of their diocesan authorities, refuse to contribute to diocesan mission funds.[423]

A third salvo from the navy, by Specialist Second Class Donald W. Pempin, likewise stressed the minority status of Dugger's opinions:

> CORPORAL DUGGER is obviously a 'high churchman', which is certainly his privilege. However, may I remind him that 90 per cent or better of the constituency of his church consider themselves far from what we term 'high churchmen'.... I have worked in the chaplain's department [sic] for 28 months and have known many Episcopalian men who gladly supported the Protestant Chaplain, whatever his denomination.[424]

The fundamentalist challenge was, of course, potentially much more destabilising than Episcopalian fractiousness. As in civilian society, to progressive Protestants its growth was evident throughout the war and across the armed forces. Indeed, and as the conflict in Europe ended, there were clear signs of nervousness in this respect. Speaking at the New Jersey Synod of the Presbyterian Church

(USA), the words of Dr. Thurlow Fraser reflected the growing anxieties and self-doubt of many liberal churchmen. According to Fraser:

> One of the reasons why churches are dissolving congregations a little more than twice as fast as they are being organized is our lack of passion in presenting the gospel. The American people are emotional folk. They like their idealism, their patriotism, and their religion served hot. A lot of us Presbyterian ministers have the emotion educated out of us. Somewhere in the long course of preparation for the ministry our passion has grown cold. The people, unattracted by cool logic, turn from us to those who give them a warmer gospel, even if it be not so philosophically co-ordinated.[425]

Expressing full agreement with Fraser, the Baptist *Watchman-Examiner* added:

> Church statistics indicate that the fastest growing sects in this country are those which place no rigid insulation around their emotions. These churches are multiplying, and their adherents are constantly winning large numbers of converts. It is the best sport of the highbrow to decry this type of emotional Christianity, but we do not find that the highbrow is very successful in winning souls to Christ. If a wrong condition may be cured by its antidote, then the excessive emotionalism on the part of some sects may yet serve to melt the icicles hanging from the chandeliers in some of our 'cultured' churches.[426]

The ongoing strife between progressives and fundamentalists had its reverberations in the armed forces. While progressive chaplains such as Stroup railed against 'The Gospel Gestapo',[427] a conservative evangelical message could also alienate more liberal laymen. For example, and writing in April 1944, Ken Petengill fumed to his Catholic girlfriend about his recent experiences in a Southern church:

> We had met two more of the boys and they suggested we go to the Baptist church and see what was going on. So I tagged along and joined lustily in singing hymns. Then it happened – a fatherly graduate of Mississippi University started a long prayer. He built it up and built it up and finally asked all those who had been saved to raise their hands, then all those who were sinners, but wanted to be saved to raise their hands. Honestly, I thought I'd get sick – That only added to my distrust and dislike of the Church as an institution. He was sincere, undoubtedly, but it's not for me.[428]

Fundamentalists, of course, were completely unapologetic. James Edwin Orr, relieved at the number of fellow evangelicals he had encountered in the army's Corps of Chaplains, and having witnessed the tensions between conservatives and progressives at the Chaplain School at Harvard, declared: 'I have little more than pity and contempt for a minister of a denomination who flouts the teachings of his Church and makes a mock of its doctrine. I respected the faithful Roman Catholic and Hebrew Chaplains, but not the false prophets in my own camp.'[429] En route to Australia, Arthur F. Glasser, one of the few navy chaplains to be recruited from a separatist fundamentalist denomination,[430] found himself at loggerheads with a liberal colleague after he had led a service for two hundred Seabees. 'He had attended the service', Glasser recalled wearily, 'but had not liked the preaching. He frankly told me that he did not think I had preached the "heart" of the Christian message.' The feeling was, of course, mutual, and their antipathy barely concealed, as is made clear by Glasser:

> When I heard him preach I reacted against his message with much the same vigor he had manifested. He was a 'liberal' or 'modernist', and I was an 'evangelical' or 'fundamentalist'. Our messages were poles apart. This difference we both strongly sensed and candidly discussed. Despite the antagonism of our messages we managed to maintain a measure of outward composure and friendliness, and talked theology by the hour.... We regarded each other 'in error' and in need of drastic change. In ourselves we vividly embodied the two irreconcilable and actively antagonistic segments of Protestantism today.[431]

If this problem was contained by recruitment requirements and by an institutional ethos which worked against the recruitment and retention of more conservative Protestant chaplains, these factors did not spare the armed forces from embarrassment. In 1944, a media storm erupted over the chequered career of Laurel Garnett Gatlin, a Southern Baptist chaplain who had served as a pastor in Benton, Kentucky, before joining the navy in 1942.[432] Significantly, an official biography of navy chaplains, published in 1948, noted that Gatlin had been relieved from active duty at Norfolk Naval Operating Base in Virginia in June 1944 and, after a month, had been reinstated as a chaplain in the Third Naval District covering New York, New Jersey and Connecticut.[433] In actual fact, and as *The Chaplain* magazine noted, Gatlin had been at the centre of a very public and deeply divisive row over his fundamentalist methods and theology which the official history of the navy's Chaplain Corps, published only six years later, pointedly refused to even mention.[434] Despite the Corps' blushes and selective amnesia, the nature and course of the Gatlin case clearly underlined the growing influence and assertiveness of fundamentalists in military matters in the latter stages of the war.

Conclusion

The American serviceman and woman remained a civilian at heart, and this was as true of religious matters as it was of anything else. In military organisations that consciously sought to promote religion, religious provision made by the War and the Navy Departments, and the religious values they sought to instil, interacted with attitudes and behaviour imported from civilian life. In the armed forces, Catholics, women, African Americans and Southerners seemed more religiously observant and susceptible than the general run of white Protestant males, as they were in civilian society. Furthermore, the proliferation of religious groups (such as SMCL units) at a local level reflected a historic capacity for self-organisation, to say nothing of religious fractiousness, and ensured that few could claim to be bereft of religious provision even when, as in the case of Jews and African Americans, suitable chaplains were frequently unavailable. The synergies between military provision and civilian habits were also apparent in the church-building boom that accompanied American forces overseas, one that stood as a dramatic counterpart of that sustained by federal funds much closer to home. Likewise, the unprecedented provision of chapels and religious aids – all free of charge to service personnel – did not dissuade them from seeking to give to their home churches or even to their chaplains. Still, the situation was not entirely harmonious, and the complementarity between civilian and military circumstances was far from complete. Such was their enduringly civilian mindset that military personnel often preferred civilian over military churches when they were accessible. Furthermore, given the almost limitless diversity and fragmentation of American religious life, and the limits of what the military could offer in terms of support, Protestants in particular risked being disappointed by what the military could offer. Such disappointment, which could issue in self-conscious separation, reflected a further element over which the military had little control, namely the depth of the tensions and antagonisms that were inherent in civilian religious life. Although the wartime rhetoric of toleration gained in urgency and in traction, and was to become a staple of American military culture in the war years, it had limited appeal in what was still a deeply fractured religious culture. Ultimately, not even the binding force of Axis bombs and bullets could exorcise the tensions that were inherent in contemporary American religion. However, they could trigger a remarkable resort to prayer and to other means of supernatural support, themes that form the subject of the next chapter.

Chapter Four

Foxhole Religion and Wartime Faith

Introduction

I N previous chapters we have examined chaplaincy provision, the institutional strength of religion in America's armed forces, and the interplay of civilian religious tendencies and habits with the tenor and circumstances of military life. In this chapter, we look more closely at the effects of the threat, experience and aftermath of combat on religious belief and behaviour. Inevitably, we focus on the much-vaunted phenomenon of 'foxhole religion', locating it in the context of a national wartime culture of prayer and of other, more service-specific stimulants to religious belief and practice. We also examine how the perils of World War II fuelled a range of discourses and practices that were, at the very least, of doubtful orthodoxy, and we weigh their significance for more orthodox forms of religion. The chapter will go on to show how lengthening casualty lists, and the prospect of the war reaching its denouement in a cataclysmic invasion of the Japanese home islands, helped focus attention on the afterlife in 1944 and 1945, and we consider what common perceptions of death, judgement and the afterlife meant for the broader development of American religion. The chapter ends with a survey of the nature and direction of religious change in the American armed forces in World War II, assessing its manifestations and its implications for post-war religious life.

Foxhole religion

To a very great extent the intensity of religion in the military seemed contingent on the proximity or experience of danger. In April 1943 *The Christian Science Monitor* reported that Roy E. Bishop, an experienced, pre-war Methodist navy chaplain, had noticed that: 'Ever since the outbreak of war in the Pacific the attendance at religious services and the interest in spiritual matters [had] shown a tremendous increase.' At Bishop's own base on Samoa:

> [A] fair estimate of the men attending services … was now 75 or 80 per cent compared to the old peacetime figure in the services of about 25 per cent. And, giving point to the pilot's expression of 'coming in on the wing and a prayer,' [Bishop] said the fliers seemed to be the staunchest churchgoers of all.[1]

With an even longer perspective, Methodist army chaplain Percy M. Hickcox later wrote from the Pacific:

> At the beginning of my fifth year of service as a chaplain in this present conflict, I am ready to admit that the religion of our soldier is one which is largely determined by crisis. It is the elementary urge of men to turn to God in time of danger just as they turn to their chaplains in time of trouble.[2]

Chaplain's assistant Kenneth A. Connelly concurred, writing from Belgium in January 1945:

> About ninety-five out of every hundred men in our outfit have either been to some service or in to see the Chaplain since we left the States. Worship and Communion really mean something here, where the sound of rifle fire means death instead of range practice. Every battle boosts attendance for men want the assurance and hope of their Christian faith when they face death.[3]

By the same token, however, it seemed that there was no shortage of indifferentists in positions of relative safety. One Catholic army chaplain confessed to great difficulty in generating any religious enthusiasm in a 'Coast Defense outfit' that was widely dispersed along the West Coast; in fact, it seemed that: 'The spirit of Catholicism … was dead, and all it needed was decent burial.'[4] Charles Edward Lunn, a Northern Baptist chaplain newly assigned to Robins Field, Georgia, a post that majored in aircraft repair and mechanics' training, felt his spirits sink at the sight of his first congregation:

> We were supposed to be immune from typhoid, typhus, yellow fever, cholera, tetanus, and many other diseases. When I looked at the size of my first congregation of soldiers … I discovered that most of the men were already immune to religion! Sometimes I have wondered whether we were fighting for freedom of worship or freedom from worship.[5]

Nevertheless, it would be unwise to reduce varying degrees of religious enthusiasm to a neat home/ overseas dichotomy, for it could even be claimed that different theatres of war witnessed different levels of religiosity. According to a post-war survey of chaplains' work in the Pacific: 'Statistics will bear out the fact that attendance at Divine worship in the Pacific theater was comparable if not larger than attendance in other theatres [sic].'[6] While this may have been due to a lack of alternative diversions in comparison with the ETO, even those with a similar combat role could evince very different religious reactions. According to Philip Ardery, the experience of combat flying in Europe led to a 'resurgence of religion' among American bomber crew: 'Fellows who hadn't attended services in years found themselves going to Sunday services.'[7] However, and without the stimulus of walls of flak and swarms of enemy fighters, churchgoing among bomber crews in India seemed no better than in civilian life. As Chaplain Thomas H. Clare wrote:

> I've observed the personnel of my squadrons at close range. Night after night the combat men, enlisted men and officers, play poker recklessly and drink freely. Never have I met a more profane crowd, and I've been around a little. The officers think religion is something put out for the enlisted men; the combat enlisted men think it is strictly for the ground personnel.[8]

However, the situation was different again among aircrew of Transport Command in the China–Burma–India theatre (CBI), who routinely had to brave the crossing of the Himalayas in shipping supplies to China. Consequently, and according to their staff chaplain, John S. Garrenton, by the beginning of 1944 voluntary church attendance in this theatre was in the order of 75 per cent.[9]

These situational variations were by no means limited to airmen, for among ground troops and sailors the same local and nuanced patterns obtained. Chaplain Harry P. Abbott remembered how, during the campaign in North Africa, a hitherto unreceptive tank battalion of the 1st Armored Division requested extra services. As he recalled, 'when the chaplain arrived, all were assembled under the trees. Everyone was there.' Seeing an opportunity to remonstrate: 'The chaplain spoke and said, "Men, how does it happen we have such a large attendance today? Back at Fort Knox I had to urge some of you to go to church." One sergeant spoke up and said, "Chaplain, those German 88's are making believers out of us."'[10] The same fluctuations of religious enthusiasm were apparent on board the heavy cruiser *Tuscaloosa* in the course of a single voyage in the summer of 1942. Tasked with shipping medical supplies to the north Russian port of Murmansk, the *Tuscaloosa* had to run a gauntlet of German aircraft, surface ships and submarines while negotiating appalling weather and treacherous seas in the 'perpetual daylight of Arctic summer'.[11] Understandably this was seen by the ship's chaplain, Frederick William Meehling, as 'a suicide mission', and Meehling blessed the ship with holy water 'from stern to stem every night'. With attendance surging at his services, the *Tuscaloosa*'s captain agreed to hold 'a service of thanksgiving for the entire ship's company' should it return safely to Iceland, a pact that met with the fervent endorsement of all on board. Blessed by ideal weather conditions throughout its dangerous mission – including a providential fog that shrouded its movements off Murmansk – the *Tuscaloosa* returned unscathed. However, there was something distinctly scriptural about the aftermath of this near-miraculous mission. As Meehling put it:

> It was really funny about this thanksgiving service, you know. The percentage of attendance was about the same as in the scriptures at the time Our Lord healed the ten lepers. Only one, you remember, returned to give thanks.

And out of almost one thousand three hundred men on board, there were a hundred and twenty men present to publicly thank God for a safe return.[12]

Although widely assumed that combat personnel were more susceptible to religion than those in service units, it is wise not to place too much stress even on this distinction. The army and the navy's African American service units proved a clear exception to this general rule and, on occasion, the dangers faced by service personnel could be just as great. As Ernie Pyle wrote of the Anzio beachhead:

> At Anzio everybody was right in it together. From the rear to the front was less than half an hour's drive, and often the front was quieter than the rear.... The unromantic finance officer counting out his money in a requisitioned building was hardly more safe than the company commander ten miles ahead of him.[13]

That conditions in the Anzio beachhead served as a great religious leveller was, significantly, confirmed by Cecil P. Sansom, a Southern Baptist chaplain with the 38th Evacuation Hospital, who wrote:

> A security that holes and sandbags and embankments could not supply, was discovered by many for the first time in turning to the Rock of Ages. At no time in this chaplain's experience was the attendance so good, the interest so sustained in divine service, as during those gruesome, hectic days, when for every man and woman there [sic] each hour might be this [sic] last.[14]

Nevertheless, certain constituencies did display a greater susceptibility to religion because of their combat role. As we have seen, and given the particularly hazardous nature of airborne training and operations, there was a special attempt by airborne commanders to promote morale by religious means. In combination, their policy, the predicament of their troops, and a new and select band of airborne chaplains appear to have succeeded in evoking the desired response. Chaplain Francis L. Sampson witnessed an upward curve in religious practice as the 501st Parachute Infantry Regiment moved from training, through to manoeuvres, to its first combat jump over Normandy in June 1944.[15] As another airborne chaplain averred: 'I know that the majority of men who jump do ask for God to help them. Why, you can't help but ask as you throw yourself from an airplane and realize that if the chute does not open you will die suddenly and violently.'[16] As the WAAC embraced the virginal St Genevieve, the cult of St Michael the Archangel flourished in the fertile soil of America's fledgling airborne forces, assets that the army had not even possessed prior to the summer of 1940 and for whom the words of Revelation 12:7–8 seemed especially apt: 'And there was war in heaven: Michael and his angels fought against the dragon; and the dragon fought and his angels, And prevailed not.'[17] While the legendary image of a winged angel overthrowing Satan with his flaming sword was no doubt appealing to intrepid airborne generals such as Lee, Ridgway and Gavin, *The Link* magazine also harped on the religious calibre of the airborne soldier. In November 1943, it carried an article by 'parachuting padre' Lee Edwin Walker, who rejoiced that: 'There are few if any atheists when the static lines are hooked up and the open door is waiting for a fellow to go through!'[18] A year later, Chaplain Delbert A. Kuehl, another airborne chaplain and a Northern Baptist, confirmed that: 'After a year of almost continuous combat, fulfilling many a difficult mission, and at times fighting under almost impossible conditions, many of these "wild men from heaven" have learned to know Jesus Christ – and those who knew Him, to trust Him more.'[19] In December 1944, the magazine carried a letter on 'Airborne Religion', which described how a pan-Protestant 'Airborne Christian Church' had been established in a glider infantry regiment. Organised to ensure the provision of religious services whatever the operational situation, the church was guided by its regimental chaplain (a Southern Baptist) and by a regimental council; each company had its own soldier-preacher (or 'sky-pilot'), who was aided in turn by a 'co-pilot', a company council and a 'minister of propaganda' who handled its publicity.[20] In 1945, America's airborne troops drew the attention of the prolific William L. Stidger, who announced that, 'the boys I respect are these hard-boiled paratroopers with their pants tucked into their boots. No wonder they swagger. Any boy who has bailed out at 20,000 feet and swung his oscillating way down to earth holds my deepest admiration.'[21] Naturally, Stidger maintained that this courage owed much to their religion, citing tales of how prayer had helped a rookie paratrooper make his first descent and how a chaplain had helped another to make a combat jump over Italy.[22] In August 1945 *The Link* hailed a letter of the late Sergeant George Bowler Tullidge III, of the 507th Parachute Infantry Regiment, as 'One of the finest letters to come out of this war'. Addressed to his younger brother, it urged a steady habit of Bible-reading, the keeping of good company, and filial obedience to their mother and father.[23]

Inevitably, there was much in this picture that was overdrawn. En route to Normandy, for example, a war correspondent mistook paratroopers kneeling on the floor of their transport for pre-battle devotions when they were, in fact, simply allowing the benches to take the weight of their parachutes and other equipment.[24] However, evidence from secular sources indicates that there was much more than pious whimsy to this picture of airborne religiosity. Significantly, the prayer of the 506th Parachute Infantry Regiment was written by a combatant officer, Lieutenant James G. Morton, and ran:

> Almighty God, we kneel to Thee and ask to be the instrument of Thy fury in smiting the evil forces that have visited death, misery, and debasement on the people of the earth. We humbly face Thee with true penitence for all our sins for which we do most earnestly seek Thy forgiveness. Help us to dedicate ourselves completely to Thee. Be with us, God, when we leap

from our planes into the dread abyss and descend in parachutes into the midst of enemy fire. Give us iron will and stark courage as we spring from the harnesses of our parachutes to seize arms for battle. The legions of evil are many, Father. Grace our arms to meet and defeat them in Thy name and in the name of freedom and dignity of man. Keep us firm in our faith and resolution, and guide us that we may not dishonour our high mission or fail in our sacred duties. Let our enemies who have lived by the sword turn from their violence lest they perish by the sword. Help us to serve Thee gallantly and to be humble in victory. Amen.[25]

Significantly, Leo Claude Martin of the 501st Parachute Infantry Regiment averred that a 'company commander led his men in prayer before [the] Normandy jump', and that religious convictions clearly 'helped' performance.[26] Likewise, Richard E. O'Brien, of the same regiment, testified that: 'We had two great chaplains. Father Sampson later became Chief of Chaplains ... Great Men.' Furthermore, O'Brien held that religious convictions had helped performance in terms of: 'Personal leadership, Can do attitude, and a very close comradeship between troopers'.[27] A third veteran of the 501st, Michael Zelieskovies, concurred that, 'We had a priest (Father Sampson) who kept us spiritually fulfilled', adding in terms of religious convictions: 'They helped – knowing we were on the side of God.'[28]

If, as the case of the airborne forces most clearly shows, there was a sustainable correlation between religious faith and personal danger, it was a phenomenon that became the subject of an almost obsessive interest among Americans during World War II: 'I thank God I'm still alive. I prayed ... if you don't pray to God and you get into a war, you believe in him. I didn't see an atheist.' So spoke Joe Baldwin, a veteran of the 4th Infantry Division, whose bloody experience of the campaign in North-West Europe began at Utah Beach on 6 June 1944.[29] These words, of course, encapsulate the most famous commentary on soldiers' religion in World War II, namely that: 'There are no atheists in foxholes.' Ascribed to William T. Cummings, a Catholic priest and accidental army chaplain who took part in the defence of Bataan and 'died of exposure and starvation' on board a Japanese prison ship in 1945,[30] this adage became one of the most well-worn clichés of the war, and was even the subject of a drawing by the Pulitzer Prize-winning cartoonist Vaughn Shoemaker.[31] In a particularly vivid and comprehensive description of the phenomenon, Frederic P. Gehring, a Catholic navy chaplain, wrote of the religious effects of a Japanese naval bombardment on Guadalcanal:

The shells trailed dazzling paths of crimson as they rocketed out of their ships' cannons. Then they seemed to hang suspensefully in air before crashing down on us with terrifying impact.... Alongside me, head bowed, there were Catholic boys reciting their rosaries, Protestants murmuring prayers, and Jewish boys, with closed eyes, fingering the holy *mezuzahs* they wore around their necks. The adage that there are no atheists in foxholes was already familiar to me ... Even those who hadn't uttered a word of prayer or been inside a house of worship for years before the war, were looking now for a Divine hand to shield them.[32]

Commonly recited by veterans decades later,[33] Cummings's words could be invoked with utter conviction by those who saw combat at the time. As Sergeant Alvin McAnney wrote to his wife from Luxembourg in 1944:

They can laugh about foxhole religion but every front line soldier embraces a little religion and are [sic] not ashamed to pray. When you face death hourly and daily you can't help but believe in Divine Guidance. My faith in God has increased a thousand fold. He pulled me thru when nothing else could.[34]

Likewise, Pfc Albert Kishler wrote to a friend in December 1944:

The man who said that there are no atheists in foxholes had hit the nail on the head. When the sun goes down and darkness steals in, life to the infantrymen becomes nothing more than a gust of wind ... it's you and good old Mother Earth and God. And when the time comes that you leave that hole and charge across several hundred yards of enemy territory with machine guns burning, 88's and mortars thinning your numbers, God is never forgotten. To us, death is no distant unknown.[35]

The force of Cummings's maxim, and the assumptions and sentiments that underlay it, spawned variants more suited to others who faced comparable risks. In keeping with the title of a 1943 autobiography by the veteran army aviator Colonel Robert L. Scott, the conviction that 'God Is My Co-Pilot' was common among American airmen. Gordon Bennett Robertson, after making the potentially catastrophic mistake of dumping his B-29's bomb load on the runway *before* taking off on his fourth mission, wrote to his wife: 'Well, I know now that God is my co-pilot, and he gets on board before I take off.'[36] Chaplain William C. Taggart remembered a young fighter pilot who 'always used the term "we" when he talked about the action that shattered his shoulder with an explosive shell', an aviator who insisted that: 'I don't sit in the cockpit alone. I have a Person in the cockpit with me always who's on my side when I meet the Japs.'[37] For his part, Norman Wesley Achen, a pilot who was shot down over Germany in 1944, remembered surrendering his controls to God as his P-51 fighter crash-landed. Reflecting on this incident, his subsequent captivity and eventual escape, Achen testified: 'He's a good co-pilot. They, they don't come any better.'[38] Significantly, chaplains appealed directly to this wartime trope. In an article in *The Link* magazine, Methodist AAF chaplain Arthur B. Mercer advised its readers to 'Avoid Crack-Ups' by using their conscience as their compass, the Bible as their octant,

God's purpose as their radio beam and Christ as their co-pilot – one who 'can fly us on through – through even the Valley of the Shadow of Death – and make for us a happy landing'.[39]

The claims of Cummings's dictum struck a similar chord among mariners. John Kempton, who served as a radio technician on a submarine chaser, became a '"fox-hole" Christian' during a Japanese air attack, an experience that led him to attend church and to give much closer attention to his Gideon New Testament.[40] As Douglas E. Leach, who served on the destroyer *Elden*, put it: 'Somebody once remarked that there were no atheists in the foxholes, a considerable exaggeration, of course. But it was equally true that there were few atheists among those Americans who went down to the sea in ships.'[41] Certainly, for those sailors who saw action and survived, the presence of God could be no less immediate than in the proverbial foxhole. Reflecting on the wartime career of the light cruiser *Montpelier*, James J. Fahey wrote:

> The U.S.S. *Montpelier* set a record that will be hard to touch. It bombarded Jap-held strongholds 53 times. It participated in 26 invasions, 42 operations and 30 campaigns against the Japanese … Back in 1942 if someone told me that the U.S.S. *Montpelier* would come through all this, I would not have believed him. I am not saying this because I want to brag. I am saying it to show how the Good Lord always watched over us at all times. The U.S.S. *Montpelier* was also His flagship.[42]

Furthermore, the perils of the ocean itself, and the fear of being lost on millions of square miles of the Pacific or the Atlantic, cast a long shadow over those who regularly braved their immensity. In view of this, and of the apparently miraculous delivery of some who found themselves in that dread predicament,[43] 'life-raft religion' came to be identified as a separate subspecies of emergency religion, alongside that of the foxhole and belief in the divine co-pilot.[44]

Nevertheless, Cummings's well-worn words had become stale and contested even before the war had ended. On New Year's Day 1945, Kenneth Connelly wrote wearily:

> Last month we had 17 baptisms, all involving letters, reports, certificates, etc. Lots of boys are joining their home churches, too. The maxim – repeated *ad nauseum* [sic] – that there are no atheists in foxholes holds as true as any general statement, although a few of our boys are outdoing themselves in proving that it is not quite true.[45]

There were, of course, many grounds on which to challenge the veracity of the claim. In terms of the special religious stimulus provided by combat, public opinion polls, to say nothing of the vast majority of service personnel who expressed a religious preference, showed that there were precious few atheists in American society in general, although this point was seldom made by commentators. More commonly, there was the demonstrable fact that not every soldier, sailor, airman or marine turned to the Almighty in moments of danger. While, as we shall see, this could simply be a natural function of a particular combat role, sometimes it was due to sheer indifference, or plain hostility, towards religion. Lester Atwell, a practising Catholic whose milieu was that of the combat infantryman and combat medic, remarked that, 'Even in our own small group there were several Catholics in name only', and 'I often wondered how the comfortable expression grew up: "There are no atheists in the foxholes".'[46] Reflecting on the religiosity of US airmen in India, and those of the 341st Bombardment Group in particular, Chaplain Thomas H. Clare concluded that the picture was distinctly mixed: 'Do these boys think of religion when they get into tight spots? Some of them do; others do not.'[47] As an illustration, Clare cited the contrasting reactions of two crews whose aircraft had got into trouble. The pilot of one had told him:

> I was too darned busy in that plane to think about praying, but as we were coming down I did call Porter on the radio and say: 'Porter, this is it. If you want to do any praying, brother, do it now.' 'You pray,' he answered. 'I'm getting ready to jump.'

As for the other, an engine had stalled while crossing the Himalayas – 'the worst possible place in the world for that sort of thing to happen.' Consequently: 'At least three of the crew told me that they prayed plenty until that plane was safely down.'[48] On occasion, however, the situation could be much starker. In the Guadalcanal campaign, and in an incident that induced an uncharacteristic moment of self-doubt, navy chaplain Warren Wyeth Willard spoke to a marine who remained obdurate to the end:

> A wounded sergeant was brought in from Tanambogo. He had been shot through the abdomen. I could see by the cold sweat on his face that he was dying. I knelt beside him and spoke softly. 'Sergeant, I'm your chaplain. May I read to you from the Word of God? Or would you like to have me pray with you?'
>
> 'I never went much for that stuff back home,' he answered weakly, 'and I don't care for it now.'[49]

Whatever else, the symptoms and significance of 'foxhole religion' greatly divided religious commentators. For some, supplications for deliverance that were born of physical terror were practically worthless – the most abject type of 'gimme-prayer'.[50] Reflecting on its Jewish manifestation – 'Foxhole Tshuvah' – army chaplain Morris N. Kertzer concluded that, 'those who look upon the broader meaning of religion would agree with our prophets who considered faith based on fear as less than inadequate'.[51] Nevertheless, in 1943, and drawing on his experiences in World War I, Alva J. Brasted, a former chief of chaplains, published an article in which he compared the religion of doughboys in World

War I to that of GIs in World War II. In the process, Brasted invoked an incident
on board a troopship that had nearly foundered in a tropical storm, a calamity
that resulted in a torrent of prayer from those on board and in large services of
thanksgiving after the storm had abated. The lesson for Brasted was clear: 'In the
first World War, in this, and invariably when men are face to face with death they
look Godward – the help of religion is sought.'[52] However, in the very next issue
of the same journal, *Religious Education*, this claim met with a stinging rejoinder
from Dr J. Hutton Hynd of the rationalist and ultra-liberal Ethical Society of St
Louis. In the form of a letter, and the text of a Sunday morning address given on
a Missouri radio station, Hynd deplored the crude assumptions that informed
Brasted's stories, claiming that his article confirmed 'the view that religion ... is
a matter of calling for help in a predicament – a peculiarly popular yet pernicious view of religion in my opinion'. Stung by the saying 'there are no atheists in
foxholes' (which, he observed, was 'quoted far and wide, and with general assent
and relish')[53] Hynd harked back to his experiences as a Royal Air Force mechanic
in World War I, claiming to be all too familiar with the worthless vagaries of the
serviceman's faith:

> To the men ... any person who took 'religion' seriously was a mere goody-
> goody to be laughed at. But when danger threatened – prayer, Bible reading,
> mascots, etc. etc. This is NOT religion; it is more akin to crass superstition.
> Religion is a way of life. Religion does not give one safety; religion does not
> bring him home again. A religious service, chaplain and all, was wiped out
> by a Japanese bomb the other day. That's how it goes. I think the chaplains
> should make it clear to the men that religion is a matter of daily living –
> not a matter of calling upon the gods in a fox-hole. There is something
> wrong with religious education when such a notion of religion is accepted
> so generally and officially.[54]

Certainly, the dynamics of foxhole religion were not dissimilar from patterns
in civilian life. According to the findings of a nationwide survey published in
1947, 'provides help in times of stress' was the third most popular answer among
sixty-five given by 2,500 respondents to the question of why they were religious,
coming after 'gives meaning to life' and 'motivates human kindness'.[55] As one
pundit drily remarked of his fellow Americans, 'the vast majority take religion
for granted as a ready help in time of trouble, not as something requiring a
daily regimen'.[56] Others, nevertheless, were inclined to treat such manifestations
as signs of religious awakening, even as proofs of Proverbs 9:10: 'The fear of
the LORD is the beginning of wisdom.' Significantly, the evangelical and conver-
sionist heritage of American Protestantism disposed many to sympathise with
the oft-quoted maxim of the seventeenth-century Puritan divine, John Flavel,
who famously counselled that: 'Man's extremity is God's opportunity.'[57] As one
army chaplain opined: 'I say that it is better for a man to be exposed to the way

of salvation in an hour of crisis than to fail to have any knowledge of it at all. One never knows when the salvation of his God will break through upon his needy soul.'[58] The difference between transatlantic perspectives on this phenomenon had been illustrated in the wake of World War I, when committees of British and American churchmen published parallel reports on the religious condition of their respective armies. For the former, who were largely concerned with remodelling English and Scottish Christianity in the post-war era, the importance of 'funk religion' (so called) could be either too readily dismissed or too easily exaggerated; in essence, it simply reflected the resilience of an elemental belief in, 'an Unseen Power, inaccessible to the senses, which is yet mightier than high explosives, which knows all and which hears prayer.'[59] For Americans, however, the existence of 'the emergency religion of the trenches' was much more encouraging:

> It is not unreasonable to expect that some few men have returned with the vivid memory of times when the entire dependence of man on a power greater than man, the need and possibility of the companionship of God, and the care of One who knoweth even the sparrows when they fall, was keenly felt. The experiences may have been bound up with much that is crude and on the level with 'natural' religion [but] 'An idea is not necessarily false because it is primitive. To discover for one's self whatever truth there is in the simpler phases of religion may be the best way to revitalize more adequate forms more conventionally held.'[60]

Naturally, the debate resumed with a vengeance against the dramatic backdrop of another world war. Reflecting on the 'Lessons of Guadalcanal' in the *Marine Corps Gazette* of August 1943, Captain Gerald H. Shea assured his readers that: 'as on Bataan there are no atheists on Guadalcanal. Religion plays a large part in men's lives during war everywhere; many a man wears his cross or Saint Christopher medal right along with his dog tags.'[61] However, fundamentalist navy chaplain Arthur F. Glasser begged to differ; according to him, the very nature and dynamics of foxhole religion meant it was inimical to the growth of faith. Conscious of their broken promises, the numerous backsliders it produced were too ashamed to be receptive to the gospel thereafter. After interviewing veterans of Guadalcanal, Glasser pronounced that:

> A prayer for help from physical danger is far different from the pattern of true prayer laid down in the Bible.... This true prayer of repentance and faith is apparently what God rarely heard on Guadalcanal. Through ignorance the men merely prayed for physical protection, fully confident that if God would hear their prayers and help them, they would never fail in their devotion to Him. But they found that their experiences alone were insufficient to preserve their spiritual life. Even the most vivid memories soon

faded and they then fell into sin. Skepticism and disillusionment resulted. Praying now seemed hypocritical.[62]

Rather than condemning foxhole religion as a scandal for 'the cause of Christ',[63] Roy B. Anderson, another navy chaplain, was disposed to see both sides of the argument, writing of a Seabee battalion in the Pacific:

> Many of our men have passed through the very 'shadow of death' and know what it is to fear for one's safety. The foxhole experience has been talked about so much that the expression has become threadbare. Some ask whether or not there is such a thing as battle experience making a Christian out of a man. Too many who have had a foxhole experience have long since forgotten the resolutions or good intentions that they made at the time.

Nevertheless, so Anderson went on, the experience of Japanese air raids did lead to a spike in church attendance among his Seabees and: 'As superficial as some of these experiences might have been, today some men are Christians because a bomb or shell landed too close for comfort.'[64]

Inevitably, the same range of opinion was present in the army. In *Invasion Diary*, the war correspondent Richard Tregaskis's account of the war in Italy, he recounted a 'supposedly authentic' story concerning a foul-mouthed GI who had loudly called upon God to save his life during a barrage, prompting a jibe from an adjacent foxhole, 'Hey, Joe, why don't you knock off that cryin' for help, and talk to somebody you know?'[65] Although *The Link* seemed disposed to take a more favourable line on the phenomenon of foxhole religion, as we shall see, in keeping with the breath of its readership it was prepared to publish the views of dissenters. Among them was W.J. Miller, who wrote from an infantry training camp in 1944. While he considered the magazine 'a wonderful voice of militant religion', he had grave doubts about the sentiments behind 'There are no atheists in fox-holes'. As Miller reasoned:

> Finding God is man's most important work, but there is a dead-line on it, and we shouldn't be encouraged to wait until then... God will help us when we call on Him in a tight spot, but how many of *us* would not be hurt if we were asked to send presents, but weren't invited to the party?[66]

Edward K. Rogers, a much-decorated United Lutheran chaplain who served with the formidably experienced 1st Infantry Division, found it difficult to come to a firm view on the subject. After hard fighting at Long Stop Hill in Tunisia, he found that 'a great host of men came to church' – and that: 'Many had never bothered to do so before and many such were quite faithful thereafter.'[67] Later, in Normandy, he confessed to difficulties in controlling the size of his congregations at impromptu field services:

The first Sunday ashore we were able to have a number of services and the men came in goodly numbers. After that it was almost impossible to hold a service because of artillery and mortar fire and what few we had were limited in attendance to about fifteen men. It was impossible to keep the number under control for each time one opened his eyes after a prayer or looked up from reading a few more had joined the circle. It was an old familiar story of men wanting to worship in combat.[68]

As for the perseverance of those he baptised, often as a result of such experiences, the high turnover of manpower experienced by infantry regiments made it hard to judge: 'I will say that most of the men whom I have instructed and baptized have been very sincere about their faith. Seventy-five percent of them have left us one way or another during the past two years so I can't speak of their present religious life.'[69] Overall, however, Rogers came to the conclusion that, '"combat religion" is soon forgotten by some men.... Often it does a lot of good, perhaps more often it rolls off like water off a duck's back.'[70]

Despite this clear lack of consensus, and ever conscious of the need to promote the public image of army chaplains and their work, the Office of the Chief of Chaplains did its best to maximise the significance of these often fleeting symptoms of faith. In his introduction to the 1945 volume *Soldiers of God*, William R. Arnold artfully declared: '[T]his is not a book to glorify "foxhole religion." The purpose of *Soldiers of God* is not to select a few dramatic conversions to faith and point to these as proof of a religious upsurge.' Nevertheless, he reasoned:

We all know that many men who never before were devoted to God have found faith under fire. That is one of the results of war, neither to be accepted as necessarily representative of the experiences of all servicemen, nor to be condemned as hypocritical or transitory. There are those who do not see the relationship of religion to their day-by-day living until they face a crisis, a fact true in peace as well as war.[71]

In essence, his argument reprised the leitmotif of Chaplain Ellwood C. Nance's earlier and widely-read *Faith of Our Fighters* (1944),[72] in which chaplains lined up to insist on the value, veracity and longevity of the kind of faith to be found in a foxhole. It was left, however, to De Loss I. Marken, a Disciples of Christ chaplain and the Division Chaplain of the 34th Infantry Division,[73] to summarise the thrust of the book: 'These boys learn to know God. You know you don't need colored windows and a pipe organ to worship God. There's no better place in the world to learn to know God than a foxhole.'[74] This wisdom was accepted, in a more qualified form, by the historian Daniel B. Jorgensen:

While the statement became popular in the war that 'there are no atheists in foxholes'.... There was a new awareness on the part of all servicemen and women of the resources which religion had to offer, and there was a new sensitivity to the cogency and relevancy of religious teachings to the peculiar environment of which they were a part.[75]

Despite uncertain and dissenting voices, the prevailing view among army chaplains seems to have been that combat (however broadly defined) did serve to act as a positive stimulant to personal faith. Eben Cobb Brink, a Presbyterian (USA) chaplain, testified from his early experiences with the 1st Armored Division in North Africa that: 'The battlefield offers, to those who are able to listen amidst the turmoil of conflict, a stirring study of men's souls.'[76] The sincerity and potential of faith awakened on the battlefield was affirmed at length in 1945 by Chaplain Alvin O. Carlson's *He Is Able: Faith Overcomes Fear in a Foxhole*. Here, Carlson, a Presbyterian, focused on the authenticity of many battlefield conversions, their deep-rooted origins in camp, at home, at church and at Sunday school, and the obligation of the church to sustain converted veterans in their Christian lives on their return to civilian society.[77] Nor did *The Link* magazine fail to deliver a favourable verdict on the intrinsic value of 'foxhole religion' and its variants. From the vantage point of Boston University's School of Theology, William L. Stidger rejoiced in these wartime developments in a 1944 article entitled 'When the Chips Are Down':

> Men don't kid when the chips are down. Nor do nations. We are all dead in earnest and there is no bluffing, no camouflage, no bunk … That's why American soldiers who never did much praying before are praying now, and are doing so without apology or shame. From all over the world dispatches tell of officers and men who get in tight places praying because they have no other place to go, for the chips are down all over this globe just now, and men know it when they face death.[78]

If they recognised its value, some chaplains were also aware of the need to cultivate 'foxhole religion'. Significantly, the very first issue of *The Chaplain* magazine raised the need for further discussion of 'the after-results of religion that grows so luxuriantly in foxholes'. In particular, Chaplain Albert W. Shumaker was keen to discover, 'What happens to it when the men leave the frontlines and are no longer in need of any divine miracles to save their skins?', prompting the magazine to inquire, 'Is there anyone present who can outline the best procedures for a chaplain's foxhole follow-up?'[79] Chaplain F.H. Woyke, a Northern Baptist who served with the 279th Station Hospital in Europe, as part of his ministry sought to factor the effects of foxhole religion into his programme of preaching:

> With many in the audience unconverted, evangelistic sermons have been frequent. For those who had just recently turned to God in foxholes, I included sermons on the meaning and development of the Christian life. At

one time I preached a series of 'foxhole sermons' on texts which the men had circled as they read their Bibles in combat.[80]

Similarly, in March 1945 *The Chaplain* carried a letter from Chaplain W.P. Smith, a Methodist, describing a pastoral programme conceived by another Northern Baptist to ensure that 'religious experiences in the foxholes are lasting':

Chaplain William F. Shearin, senior chaplain in a general hospital in North Africa, is doing one of the finest jobs I have ever seen of helping these men who return from the front evaluate their religious experiences. He has some kind of religious meeting several nights each week. These meetings are well attended and the men enter into the discussions and activities with enthusiasm. Here they have the opportunity to think through their religious experiences at the front and to tell others about them.... If a program similar to Chaplain Shearin's could be carried out at all our general hospitals where the wounded men come back from the front, a great deal would be accomplished toward helping these men who turned to God in the 'foxhole' keep close to him all the rest of their lives.[81]

Foxhole religion was dissected as well as cultivated, however. It was, for example, the subject of lengthy discussion by a panel of civilian churchmen in September 1944. Taking part in Northwestern University Reviewing Stand, broadcast by Chicago-based WGN, the panel agreed that foxhole religion was not 'a very high grade expression of faith'. However, this conclusion masked a range of personal opinion: Rabbi Maurice Pekarsky understood it as 'a religion of crisis'; Charles W. Kegley, a Lutheran pastor and chairman of the university's board of religion, dismissed it as 'scared stiff religion'; and John Huess, an Episcopalian, shrugged that it 'may be the beginning' of a 'higher kind' of faith.[82] In April 1945, *The Link* published an essay entitled 'Foxhole Religion', in which Chaplain Oscar A. Withee took a close, if rather impressionistic, look at the subject. According to him, and 'depending upon the man concerned', foxhole religion followed three general trajectories. First, there was the devout believer who prayed for moral support and that God's will be done; he would live, or die, in a fitting state of Christian resignation. Second, there was the soldier who prayed 'for simple bodily deliverance'; he kept 'his foxhole religion as a handy life-preserver for emergencies' but was essentially indifferent to religion. In the safety of home in particular, his combat experience was liable to wane and be forgotten 'and there is no practice of any Christian virtues or contribution to the things God is interested in'. Third, however, there was the GI who also prayed 'to be delivered bodily' but whose experience prompted him 'to further look into the part prayer plays in life and for what purpose God may have spared him. He senses an obligation and seeks to fulfil it as a useful Christian citizen.'[83] After the capture of Iwo Jima, navy chaplain John H. Galbreath quizzed veterans of the 5th

Marine Division about their thoughts as they lay in their foxholes under Japanese fire. Apparently, 'all acknowledged that they implored divine protection' and one said that he thought of his pew in his home church, findings that *The Chaplain* magazine thought 'should interest future students.'[84] More systematic, however, was a survey undertaken by Wayne L. Hunter, a senior army chaplain in the Pacific, of the religious behaviour of the 1st Cavalry Division from July 1943 to June 1944. During this period the division moved to Australia, where it trained prior to serving in New Guinea, and then served in the Admiralty Islands, where it saw combat from February to April 1944. Very significantly for those who stressed the importance of nurturing foxhole faith, Hunter identified May 1944, the immediate post-combat month, as the peak period in terms of communions, confessions and general church attendance, easily exceeding those of the Christmas, Easter and even pre-combat periods. Consequently, Hunter deduced that 'men are as ready to express thanks as they are to ask for favors'; indeed, and as Hunter concluded, 'the increase during the month of May can be accounted for only by a change of attitude on the part of those who experienced combat.'[85] These patterns were perceived more generally, however, notwithstanding Meehling's disheartening experiences on the *Tuscaloosa* in 1942. In February 1943, for example, and fresh from operations in the Atlantic, navy chaplain Prescott B. Wintersteen told a conference of Unitarian chaplains in Boston that:

> If [sailors] know they are close to battle, the attendance is good. The best attendance is after battle. They are mighty glad they got through. If they did not think before they had reasons to be grateful, they know then they have. We had one service after a battle when every possible person who could go was there.[86]

Similarly, in April 1944 Charles I. Carpenter, the army's 'air chaplain', told the University Religious Conference that, 'recent battle area reports show church attendance increases at the end of a mission or a campaign rather than being greater before the action.'[87]

However much debate was had, or ink was spilt, over the merits and demerits of foxhole religion, its sheer salience helped to obscure other religious stimuli that could be present in service life. Army chaplain Clyde E. Kimball discovered in 1943 that the severity and boredom of the Icelandic winter served as a strong inducement to church attendance at isolated posts.[88] Likewise, and as navy chaplain Hansel H. Tower pondered, the source of the quickened interest in religion among his marines in British Samoa in 1942 had nothing to do with the proximity of the Japanese. In fact, in its isolation and tranquillity, their lot seemed akin to being on retreat:

> Many of these men, who began a serious consideration of religion, had not thought of themselves as being religious at home. They had not read

the Bible or gone to church regularly. Their new interest in religion had not been precipitated by fear or trouble; for they were not in any great danger ... Their interest seemed to arise from the fact that they were separated from the many activities that had formerly filled their lives and had crowded out religious consideration ... One young man said, 'You know, Padre, I think I was religious all along, but I never took time before to find it out.' [89]

J.R. Mclean, an army lieutenant, found that the same situation obtained in New Guinea:

It is not the whispering of flying shrapnel fragments that tells us there is an almighty God.... Rather, on clear nights when there's a hint of breeze, when nature smells pure and clean, when crickets, katydids, and frogs pour their choral concert into the dark, when stars wink, when the moon smiles, and light, silvery clouds rest in the sky, when the illusion of peace surrounds us, we acknowledge a kindly, beneficent, and almighty God.[90]

For airmen also, the experience of another element – in all its beauty and danger – had the same effect. As one flyer wrote to his family:

It seems a fellow just gets to realize that God is there – all around us – because such beauty and vastness could not otherwise be understood. You can't argue with a sunset that is so immense and beautiful that it makes a whole Fortress grow speechless. We get so we sort of understand God and feel he is real – because there is such overwhelming evidence all around us.[91]

Another milieu in which religion could thrive was captivity, although this remained very much a minority experience. Of more than sixteen million Americans who served in the armed forces in World War II, less than 1 per cent found themselves in Axis prison camps or as internees of neutral powers such as Switzerland or Sweden. Furthermore, their experiences varied considerably according to who captured them and when, and even according to the rank they held. Of the ninety-four thousand GIs who went into captivity in the European Theater of Operations (ETO) and Mediterranean Theater of Operations (MTO), more than one-third were aviators and most were captured in 1944, notably during the Battle of the Bulge.[92] Conditions for American POWs in Europe were certainly hard enough. Besides the deprivation and isolation that captivity entailed, ordinary enlisted men were eligible for forced labour under the terms of the Geneva Convention.[93] Furthermore, and as the Third Reich slowly collapsed from the winter of 1944–45, living conditions deteriorated and prisoners were subjected to the heightened danger of air attack and, if held in the East, to long forced marches out of the path of the advancing Soviets. Nevertheless, and despite its many hardships, German captivity was enviable in comparison to Japanese, with even the treatment of Jewish-American *Kriegies* being broadly consistent with the norms of the Geneva Convention (at one POW camp, German guards even advised an American chaplain 'to warn Jewish soldiers not to reveal their religion').[94] According to post-war figures compiled by the Office of the Adjutant General, almost 99 per cent of GIs survived their captivity in Europe, whereas the survival rate in the Pacific was less than 60 per cent.[95] Not only were most of the twenty-eight thousand or so American POWs in the Pacific usually captured much earlier in the war, but Japanese observance of the Geneva Convention was fitful and capricious at best, and conditions for Allied POWs basically amounted to 'a saga of systematic deprivation and brutality, overlaid upon the hazards of war'.[96] Bad though conditions in Europe could be, on average American prisoners of the Japanese endured a captivity that was three times longer than that of their counterparts in Europe. Furthermore, nothing that Americans suffered in German or Italian hands compared to such horrors as the Bataan Death March, Japan's 'Hell Ships', or the endemic sadism, starvation and disease of its POW camps.[97]

Nevertheless, and in keeping with a classic spiritual trope in Christianity and Judaism, the experience of captivity – with all its hardships, uncertainties and opportunities for enforced reflection – could evoke a strong religious response among American prisoners. Helped by the work of the YMCA, 'the recognized agency for getting religious materials, recreational equipment, and educational materials to prison camps in Germany', on arrival early in 1944 Chaplain Eugene L. Daniel created a successful 'church program' for the American flying officers incarcerated in Stalag Luft III at Sagan in Silesia. The programme at Sagan majored on choral music and Bible study, with a Sunday morning service as its centrepiece, and 'before long there was a fine group of faithful churchmen who supported the program and tried to set a good Christian example'.[98] Francis L. Sampson had a comparable experience among the enlisted men in Stalag II-A at Neubrandenburg early in 1945. By then home to more than five thousand Americans, within weeks a chapel had been constructed in the American compound, complete with altar, crucifix and improvised hangings and candles. According to Sampson, 'Each day most of the Catholics attended Mass' and 'A soldier who had been in a Lutheran seminary also conducted Protestant services with dignity on Sundays.' In fact: 'Religion was a constant subject of conversation, and many men with little or no religion in their background sought instructions.'[99] Undoubtedly, a variety of factors were at work to elicit such a response. In some cases, religion provided a familiar prop amidst the shock and disorientation of capture. For example, on Christmas Eve 1944, and only days after being taken prisoner with most of the 106th Infantry Division, Chaplain Paul Cavanaugh was enjoined to lead an impromptu carol service for his fellow prisoners in Stalag IX-B at Bad Orb.[100] However, the elimination of competing attractions also played a role.

Eugene L. Daniel, shortly after his arrival at an Italian POW camp at Capua early in 1943, had almost 100 per cent attendance at his service in the American compound, simply because: 'There was nowhere else to go.' Nevertheless, he also noticed that: 'Never before had I received such rapt attention while I was preaching. They were hanging on my words, hoping to hear something that would help them through their ordeal.'[101]

Some prisoners emerged from captivity with a real sense of having embraced a religious opportunity. Writing to his parents in April 1945, newly liberated Pfc James F. Norton announced:

> I always considered myself a good Christian until I was captured, and then I learned what a fool I had been and what it really means to have faith and the power of prayer. I prayed day and nite, and these prayers were heard with the result that today I can really call myself a good Catholic and firm believer in the will of God.[102]

As far as the Corps of Chaplains was concerned, the ministrations of its nineteen members who were captured in the ETO (no fewer than twelve between 16 and 21 December 1944)[103] seemed to be highly successful. Despite a lack of resources, and even recourse to writing 'sermonettes on scraps of paper', which were then wrapped around rocks and lobbed over the wire at one location when permission for services was withheld, their efforts were deemed to have made a critical difference to the experience of American POWs. As a post-war report put it:

> In spite of these limitations, the religious work of the chaplains was astonishingly extensive and well received.... Chaplain Raymond S. Hall declares in his report to the Chief of Chaplains: 'I believe the work of the chaplains did more than anything else to help the men meet prison life and to overcome it.'[104]

Some religious consolation could even be garnered amidst the torments of Japanese captivity. For example, with captured American chaplains unevenly distributed throughout the Japanese empire, and the Japanese authorities seemingly indifferent to the situation, American prisoners joined in the daily prayers that were led for nearly three years by seven Allied chaplains (only one of whom was American) at Zentsuji prison camp in Japan.[105] Here, Allied POWs built their own chapel, improvised a camp hymn book, and were even visited by a Japanese Catholic bishop.[106] At Cabanatuan, the largest prison camp in the Philippines, a committee of Protestant chaplains organised an interdenominational prisoners' church that recruited a large membership; furthermore, lay chaplains were trained to accompany drafts of prisoners as they were shipped to other camps.[107] Elsewhere, the continuing ministry of Chaplain William T. Cummings was widely admired, notably by Sidney Stewart, a Protestant Oklahoman whose faith endured largely due to his words and example.[108] Stewart also stressed how local circumstances could turn religious practice into an act of resistance, as at Davao penal colony on Mindanao in 1944:

> It's true that the Japanese do not allow us to have church services here in the prison. But we are able to defeat them. The various chaplains hold little meetings at night when it is dark. And there are prayer meetings early every morning before the men go out to work. So even though they suppress an open church service, the Japanese have made us more defiant and stronger in our belief. Even those who might not have attended the services at all do so now, because they feel that they are taking something from the Japanese.[109]

For Stewart, Japanese behaviour represented 'the brutality of ignorance and superstition', the conduct of a culture unredeemed by Christianity and 'modern civilisation'.[110] For Glenn Frazier, a survivor of the Bataan Death March, the sentiments of the 23rd Psalm even acquired a new meaning because of their utter negation by his captors:

> Yea though I walked 106 miles through the valley and in the shadow of death.... I knew the Lord was my shepherd. They forbid me to lay down in green pastures for six days and seven nights. I was marched by running water but was forbidden a drink. The Japanese prepared their tables before me but I was forbidden food. They maketh me march without mercy. But only God could restoreth my soul ...[111]

Prayer

Although the 'foxhole religion' phenomenon tended to obscure other, equally powerful circumstantial stimulants to faith, it at least underlined the fundamental value that was attached to prayer by the overwhelming majority of Americans. Recalling a night trapped at an aid station in Normandy under intense German fire, Chaplain Francis L. Sampson noted how only prayer seemed to account for the unlikely survival of its occupants: 'How we survived that night I shall never know, except that the calm, fervent prayers of those wounded men didn't leave God any choice in the matter but to answer them.'[112] In contrast, and in a poignant description of a busy ward at a tented field hospital in Sicily, Ernie Pyle wrote of his frustration at the fruitless prayers that were offered over a mortally wounded soldier:

> The wounded man was still semiconscious. The chaplain knelt down beside him and two wardboys squatted nearby. The chaplain said, 'John, I'm going to say a prayer for you.'
>   Somehow this stark announcement hit me like a hammer. He didn't say, 'I'm going to pray for you to get well', he just said he was going to

say a prayer, and it was obvious to me that he meant the final prayer. It was though he had said, 'Brother, you may not know it, but your goose is cooked.' Anyhow, he voiced the prayer, and the weak, gasping man tried vainly to repeat the words after him. When he had finished, the chaplain added, 'John, you're doing fine, you're doing fine.' Then he rose and dashed off on some other call, and the wardboys went about their duties.[113]

However, Pyle's troubled reactions are perhaps less remarkable than the conduct of the participants in the scene he had witnessed. Besides the presence of the chaplain, which was plainly taken for granted, there was the effort of the stricken soldier to say a final prayer and the reverential, momentary presence of two hard-pressed medics. In other words, what even these observations seemed to capture is the great and unselfconscious importance that was attached to prayer by American soldiers and sailors, especially (although my no means uniquely) at times of mortal danger.

As products of a society that was overwhelmingly composed of believers, if not avid churchgoers, this general recourse to prayer is not in the least surprising. However, it may well have been reinforced by the outlook of the American home front, an outlook that was strongly influenced by the much-trumpeted story of Rickenbacker and his companions and by wartime publications such as *The Great Answer*. Written by the well-known author Margaret Lee Runbeck, published by the Boston publisher Houghton Mifflin, and rated among the 'Twelve Best Books of 1944' by Daniel A. Poling,[114] *The Great Answer* regaled its readership with stories of providential answers to prayer from the fighting fronts. Significantly, much of its material was furnished by the two chiefs of chaplains and the whole exercise was actually intended to boost the sale of war bonds – 'In you lies the power to answer some of the prayers uttered in this war', as Runbeck reminded her readers.[115] Writing in 1945 of this fervid mood on the home front, navy chaplain Hansel H. Tower complained that such faith in the power of prayer was distinctly problematic:

A sort of life raft, fire bucket attitude toward religion sprang up here at home while I was away. Increasing numbers of people have been thinking and talking about a revival of religion that is to come because men in fox holes, crashing planes and on life rafts had prayed and were saved ... This proven effectiveness of prayer, they insisted, would demonstrate conclusively to the world that God hears and answers prayer. Many chaplains have shared in this shallow, short-sighted concept of religion.[116]

This problem was also appreciated by army chaplain Alvin O. Carlson, who cautioned his readers about the case of a flier whose life raft had been found drifting in the Pacific a long time after his death. As the evidence of his diary revealed, the deceased had prayed and hoped for deliverance no less fervently than the members of Rickenbacker's party.[117] Others also drew attention to the problem of those countless, anguished prayers that were not answered. Charles F. Zummach, of the First Baptist Church, Trenton, Illinois, anticipated that, after the war:

> We will hear and read a great deal about the results of prayer in times of danger. One will be able to substantiate any argument either for or against such prayers by the stories related by returned Service Men. To many it has brought a new sense of our dependency upon God and a strengthening of faith in a prayer-answering God. To others it has brought much mental confusion. Such books as 'God Was My Co-Pilot', and 'We Thought We Heard the Angels Sing', have created confusion in the minds of many. Or take the much publicized account of Eddie Rickenbacker's deliverance, which so many deem providential. We immediately ask: 'Where was God when other young fliers prayed for help, who have never been heard of again?' They too prayed for aid, no doubt.... Was God playing favourites in hearing the prayers of some and turning a deaf ear to the pleadings of others? Should our faith be based on the results of such praying?[118]

In 1944, and in a bid to identify more useful proofs of the existence and workings of God, *The Link* published an essay by the tireless William L. Stidger entitled 'Finding God Without A Raft', which insisted that, 'The truth of the matter is that for every man who has a deep and revolutionary experience as the result of some unusual manifestation of Providence, there are many who find God in less "miraculous" ways', including the example of a spouse and even the gallant conduct of an enemy.[119]

However, and given the fundamental religiosity of American society, the real efficacy of prayer did not lie in its perceived success so much as in the fact that it had an intrinsic value in terms of personal and collective morale. Because of this, the presence of a chaplain was especially comforting before and during action. On the aircraft carrier *Franklin*, Chaplain Joseph T. O'Callahan told departing pilots: 'O.K. fellows, it doesn't take long to say a sincere prayer. Now I'll take over that part of the job; from now on you concentrate on your specialty.'[120] The presence of a chaplain in such situations could easily overcome earlier suspicions or animosities. Harold Lindstrom, a nervous private with the 75th Infantry Division, found that his initial hostility towards his own chaplain dissipated during the Battle of the Bulge: 'things were different. I was ready to listen. I was afraid of the future and was looking for all the help I could get.'[121] George R. Metcalf, then a chaplain with the 29th Infantry Division in Normandy, remarked upon the same reaction in July 1944, writing to his wife:

> At the Aid Station I am combination surgeon and priest and comforter of shock patients. Occasionally a small group of men passing in some shel-

tered spot, stop for a chat and we have a prayer together. It is all very grim business and we are often very scared, but the gratitude of the wounded and the cheer the men seem to feel to have the Chaplain about is moving.[122]

The value of a chaplain's prayers on the front line was also impressed upon George C. Farmer, a Disciples of Christ chaplain with the 95th Infantry Division, who remembered that, at Metz in the autumn of 1944, he visited some hard-pressed GIs who were pinned down in an underground bunker. On this occasion, the words of John Flavel seemed particularly apt:

> Before I left each room I asked if they would like to join me in prayer, and every man in chorus voice answered 'Yes, sir.' The men as a unit, without any suggestion from me, got on their knees and I felt a great responsibility upon me.... It was a great challenge to me to try to turn their extremity into God's opportunity.[123]

Such was the value of a chaplain's presence in such circumstances that most GIs seem to have been indifferent to confessional considerations. Many Protestants, for example, proved ready and even eager to receive the sacraments from a Catholic priest, regardless of the strictures of Catholic canon law. Francis L. Sampson recalled that: 'Many non-Catholic men came to confession at the front, and not infrequently I discovered that they received Communion from me without my realizing who they were.'[124] In the ready rooms of the *Franklin*, Chaplain Joseph T. O'Callahan found that a touch of repartee overcame the awkwardness of pressing his ministry on a religiously mixed body of pilots: 'I'm getting around to all the ready rooms to say a short prayer and give general absolution. This absolution is for the Catholic boys but we'll let you non-Catholics in on it – guaranteed not to hurt!'[125] According to O'Callahan, his approach seemed to work, for: 'No matter what the faith of these boys ... all join with their Catholic shipmates in an appreciation of the importance of this moment of prayer.' [126] This was equally obvious prior to other battles in other parts of the world. Recounting the moments before an attack in northern Italy in April 1945, John T. Bassett of the 10th Mountain Division wrote:

> We ate our last hot meal on the hillside and watched the company chaplain perform Mass on the hood of his jeep for some Catholic soldiers. Several non-Catholic GIs walked down to the outer fringe of the kneeling soldiers and also knelt down, removed their helmets and clasped their hands together against their chests.[127]

Russell Baldwin, a combat medic with the 551st Heavy Pontoon Bridge Battalion in North-West Europe, even remembered how such spontaneous, front-line ecumenism almost cost him his life:

We went to church services whenever we got chance. I was Protestant but there was a church service the priest was going to hold on the hood of a jeep ... and before we actually arrived a shell came in and he was no longer a priest – he was gone. Killed before we got to the service. Another couple of minutes, maybe, and I'd have been ...[128]

The presence of a chaplain was but a bonus, however, because prayer was a common denominator for servicemen in action. In August 1944 *What the Soldier Thinks*, the army's monthly digest of GI attitudes, offered some counsel to airmen on the subject of 'Getting Through A Rugged Flight Mission'. Based on the opinions of aviators who had returned to the United States after seeing action, and who flew without the support of chaplains during their combat missions, it urged its readers to: 'Think helpful thoughts that will banish fear.' Predictably, these thoughts included thoughts of 'religion and God' – an example being: 'Trust God and right will be the victor, for there is no 2nd place in war.'[129] According to Philip Ardery, an experienced pilot and the commander of a bomber squadron in the air war against Germany, religion certainly proved its worth in the skies above North Africa and Europe:

> I have heard many times that religion 'is the opium of the people,' but I saw its force among men who fought some of the greatest air battles the world has ever known. It did not serve to reconcile them to their shortcomings, their failures, or their unanswerable needs. It seemed to me that the religion given them by their chaplains, Protestant, Catholic, and Jewish alike, was no sanctuary for a pilot who quit combat. *It was the strength of a pilot who might have had to quit without it* [my italics].[130]

Significantly, flying officers could use prayer as more than just a personal means of controlling fear. As Ardery also recalled:

> My religion didn't take me to [Sunday] services with regularity, but I went occasionally, not only for myself but to let the men in my squadron know I didn't consider attendance a sign of weakness. I felt if they saw me there it might help some of them to go who wanted to but were kept from going out of embarrassment.[131]

Some bomber pilots went further. Lieutenant Robert Bluford of the 466th Bombardment Group, a pre-war ministerial student, led the prayers of his crew next to their B-24 (aptly named 'Parson's Chariot') prior to each of their seventeen missions.[132] Moreover, William H. Schaefer, who flew thirty-five missions with the 306th Bombardment Group, told the crewmen of his B-17 prior to a mission on D-Day:

> 'Look, I don't care what kind of religion you have, or if you have none. That makes no difference to me. But you've got to know how to pray. And I want

you praying for people on the ground as well as for the crews. And for all of us. Especially those on the ground.' Not a one of them batted an eye. They knew damn well I meant it.[133]

Prayer served the same purpose among ground troops and mariners. According to Bud DeVere, a marine veteran of the Guadalcanal campaign: 'I did my share of praying in the foxhole. Or on top of the ground when I got caught without one. We all did.'[134] In North-West Europe, Lester Atwell's instinctive response to enemy shelling was to recite an Act of Contrition, and that of a Protestant comrade to sing 'Onward Christian Soldiers'.[135] In terms of fear control at sea, the importance of prayer was underlined during the fiery ordeal of the carrier *Franklin* in March 1945. Deep in the bowels of the blazing vessel, one of the ship's medical officers took charge of several hundred men trapped in the enlisted men's after mess:

> Fear gripped one, then another; voices that began in whispers ended in something like screams. But Jim Fuelling squelched the incipient panic: 'Quiet, men, quiet ...! We're trapped here for a time, but don't lose your heads. Don't squander your energy. We haven't much oxygen; don't waste it. Breathe quietly. Sit on the deck, say a prayer, let's all say a prayer' ... And Doc Fuelling continued his conquest of panic; he continued to lead the boys in prayer.[136]

The importance of prayer, and its steadying effects, was fully appreciated by the chain of command. It was reflected, for example, in the award of a Bronze Star to Joseph P. Reichling, chaplain of the 894th Tank Destroyer Battalion, at Anzio. After calmly donning his steel helmet, Reichling refused to abandon an open-air, Easter Sunday Mass even though his congregation was spotted and scattered by German shellfire.[137] According to the April 1944 edition of *What the Soldier Thinks*:

> The judgment that *'there are no atheists in foxholes'* is close to the truth, if one is to examine the statements of officers and men on the power of prayer to help banish fear.... Prayer is more likely to be a help to enlisted men than to officers, but even among officers, a majority from [Europe and the Pacific] say that it helped them a lot when the going was tough. *Almost two out of three* enlisted men say the same and less than one man in five says the thought of prayer never occurred to him. Among officers, one in four says he never thought of it.[138]

Although officers were less prone to pray than enlisted men, the next edition of *What the Soldier Thinks* directly addressed the subject of 'How Officers Combat Fear Among Their Men'. Based on evidence gathered from three seasoned army divisions, prayer was duly listed among 'Seven Ways of Combating Fear'. Some of these ways were distinctly practical – such as 'Leading by example', and 'Taking all possible pre-battle and battle precautions' – but tested methods of harnessing the power of religion and prayer included reading scripture 'in plain view of everyone' and holding 'short prayer meetings with those who desired to attend'.[139] Significantly, by December 1944 George S. Patton was especially anxious to promote a habit of prayer in his Third Army – and it was not simply a question of changing the weather. At Patton's behest, Third Army's Chaplain James O'Neill wrote a message that was circulated 'to every unit in the Third Army' which ran:

> Our glorious march from the Normandy Beach across France to where we stand, before and beyond the Siegfried Line, with the wreckage of the German Army behind us should convince the most skeptical soldier that God has ridden with our banner.... As chaplains it is our business to pray. We preach its importance. We urge its practice. But the time is now to intensify our faith in prayer, not alone with ourselves, but with every believing man, Protestant, Catholic, Jew, or Christian in the ranks of the Third United States Army [and] we must urge, instruct, and indoctrinate every fighting man to pray as well as fight ... Urge all of your men to pray, not alone in church, but everywhere. Pray when driving. Pray when fighting. Pray alone. Pray with others. Pray by night and pray by day. Pray for the cessation of immoderate rains, for good weather for Battle. Pray for the defeat of our wicked enemy whose banner is injustice and whose good is oppression. Pray for victory. Pray for our Army, and Pray for Peace.... This Army needs the assurance and the faith that God is with us. With prayer, we cannot fail.[140]

Among front-line soldiers, such was the near consensus on the importance and ubiquity of prayer that some derided the tenor and approach of more secular, social-scientific studies of the behaviour of men in combat. These included *Fear in Battle*, a study by two Yale anthropologists, Dr John Dollard and Dr Donald Horton, which was published under the aegis of *The Infantry Journal* in 1944. Based on the experiences of '300 veterans of the Abraham Lincoln Brigade', which had fought for the Republicans in the Spanish Civil War, this study signally failed to mention the importance of religion as a coping mechanism, perhaps unsurprisingly given its subjects (many of whom were secular Jews)[141] and the politico-religious alignments of that conflict.[142] Protesting to the editors of *The Infantry Journal* in June 1944, an incredulous correspondent wrote from Camp Stewart, Georgia, that such studies 'cannot be accepted as standards of fear study and fear control for use by the U.S. Army':

> Religion, so vital to a large part of our fighting men, must be figured in any discussion of fear in combat.... Any study of fear and its control must

include the testimony of the reactions and emotions of those for whom religion is so necessary. If this testimony is left out, the report is incomplete.[143]

Significantly, *The American Soldier*, a compendious post-war study by the Social Science Research Council, completely vindicated this criticism. Elaborating on some of the surveys that had informed *What the Soldier Thinks*, and sifting the evidence of others, it concluded that, 'the fact that such an overwhelming majority of combat men said that prayer helped them a lot certainly means that they almost universally had recourse to prayer and probably found relief, distraction, or consolation in the process'.[144] This conclusion was primarily based on surveys carried out among the enlisted men of four infantry divisions in the Pacific in March and April 1944, and in four more infantry divisions in Italy in April 1945. In both theatres, prayer was shown to be the most common source of support for the combat infantryman 'when the going was tough', being cited by 70 per cent of enlisted men in the Pacific and 83 per cent of those in Italy.[145] On the basis of complementary surveys conducted among the junior officers of two veteran infantry divisions in the Pacific and two in the ETO in April 1944, the proportions for junior officers were shown to be 62 per cent and 57 per cent respectively.[146] Critically, prayer tended to be of greatest support among those who had *most* exposure to combat; in the Italian survey of April 1945, no less than 84 per cent of privates and Pfcs and 88 per cent of non-commissioned officers who had seen more than nine months of combat agreed that prayer had 'helped a lot'.[147] Furthermore, and according to close analysis of the respondents in the Pacific and in Italy, 'a definite relationship between stress and reliance on prayer' was established, it being found that prayer was most important to those who had suffered from exceptional levels of stress, such as being subjected to 'friendly' artillery or air attack, seeing close friends killed or wounded, and to those, such as new replacements, who had fewer coping mechanisms to fall back on.[148] This conclusion was, moreover, borne out by a reanalysis of some of this data more than sixty years later.[149]

There were, inevitably, those for whom prayer did not serve as a significant or sustaining force when in action. However, and as these wartime surveys suggest, this could reflect combat roles and responsibilities as much as any affinities with the veterans of the Abraham Lincoln Brigade, with infantry officers naturally having less opportunity to pray than the men they directed and commanded. According to Elisha Atkins, a Marine Corps veteran, Harvard graduate and contributor to the 1945 volume *Religion of Soldier and Sailor*:

There is a widespread notion that a prayerful attitude accompanies a man like a guardian angel throughout the various phases of combat and does not desert him once the crisis is over. From my own observation, the facts are not so. Battle is a preeminently practical affair, and all of a man's physical and mental resources are concentrated on the one most immediate, most natural and tangible mode of salvation available to him – action.[150]

Another marine officer, Richard Bruce Watkins, placed the perspective of the front-line officer in context when he wrote that officers and NCOs actually benefitted from the burden of command, having no time to dwell on their personal situation when in action. This was in contrast to the ordinary marine, who was simply left to fret about whatever command would come next, and what it might imply.[151]

Philip Ardery remembered that the chaotic conditions of aerial combat offered scant opportunity for prayer; however, this placed an extra premium on proper preparation for combat missions: 'In my case religion made me say short prayers before going to sleep at night, and sometimes during a fleeting instant at the height of combat. I think this undoubtedly made me a better combat officer. It comforted me so that I could sleep before missions.'[152] Gordon Bennett Robertson, a B-29 pilot in the Pacific, recalled that the straight and level approach required on the bomb run itself gave vulnerable and uncomfortable bomber crews ample opportunity for prayer and reflection:

> As Father Cummings, a U.S. Army chaplain on Bataan had said early in 1942, 'There are no atheists in foxholes.' Well, perhaps there are no atheists on the bomb run either. This was the moment of greatest anxiety for many crew members and resulted in a lot of believers and nonbelievers alike trying to make a deal with God: 'Please, God, see me through this safely, and I promise to work for a better world when I get home' or 'I promise to go to church every Sunday' or similar vow or assurance. I was talking to Him more than praying or trying to make a deal: 'O.K. now Boss, let's go through here just like the last time and get home in one piece.'[153]

Also symptomatic of a common and profound belief in prayer was the value attached to the prayers of others. Lester Atwell was importuned for a prayer by an agitated litter bearer who had been sent to collect wounded in the dark on the Belgian–German border: 'Say a prayer we'll be all right' as he felt 'it's going to be my unlucky night.'[154] After the war, one of Atwell's comrades recalled how he and another soldier had spent several hours praying with a mortally wounded GI in the rubble of a farmhouse near Olzheim, confessional differences notwithstanding.[155] The role of prayer as an expression of comradeship was no less apparent to Orval Eugene Faubus who, as a liaison officer in the 320th Infantry Regiment in North-West Europe, very much 'felt and prayed' for his comrades on the front line.[156] The significance of this aspect of camaraderie was underlined by the example of Sergeant John Basilone of the Marine Corps, who was propelled to fame by winning the Medal of Honor on Guadalcanal in October 1942. During his much-publicised return to his hometown of Raritan,

New Jersey, Basilone attended a High Mass that was offered, at his request, 'for his buddies on Guadalcanal'. After the service, he told waiting reporters that he had prayed for all in the armed forces and, in particular, for a comrade who had not returned from the Solomons.[157] This theme of praying for his fallen comrades was very much part of Basilone's personal contribution to the 1944 *Soldiers' and Sailors' Prayer Book*, in which he said that, 'I pray each night for my comrades who paid the Supreme Sacrifice and I know they are triumphant inhabitants of heaven – white flowers of a blameless life.' [158] As we shall be seeing, this was by no means a solely Catholic practice or isolated assumption.

If the prayers of comrades were deemed to be both fitting and efficacious, great importance was also attached to the prayers of those at home and, in particular, to those of female relatives. Typical of this syndrome was Sergeant John J. Koehler, a Marine Raider and veteran of Guadalcanal, for as *Newsday* reported in November 1943:

> Other warriors of this war may credit rabbits' feet or other favorite fetishes for the fact that they have walked with death and still live to tell about it. But Koehler KNOWS what is his buckler and his shield.... He gives full credit to the prayers of his twin sister, Sr. Ave Marie, a Dominican nun in Corpus Christi Convent, Mineola.[159]

Captain John Woolnough, a bomber pilot serving with the Eighth Air Force, on the threshold of completing his combat tour of thirty missions wrote to his sister in October 1944:

> I want to thank you especially for your kindness towards me and above that, your prayers for me and my crew. I am indeed a sinner, but I do believe in God and His power and goodness. I've seen God answer my prayers, and calm my nerves, and give me rest. Always before any mission I pray to God for strength and guidance.... I've said nothing about this to anyone. Now I feel free to tell it, as I have 29 missions behind me and only one to go. I have faith God will go with me in the last one as He has in the past.[160]

Given the place of domestic ideology in American religious culture, the prayers of a pious mother were invested with particular meaning and power. Like Koehler, John Giarratano, who served in England with an ordnance company of the AAF, eschewed lucky charms but claimed that the prayers of his mother 'had a lot to do with comin home'.[161] Looking back decades later on his time on Iwo Jima, a navy corpsman, Stanley Dabrowski, insisted that he owed his survival to the prayers of his mother.[162] This reliance on a mother's prayers was also clear to chaplains. Percy M. Hickcox, for example, noted a common refrain among the wounded of the 81st Infantry Division: 'Chaplain, pray to God to forgive my sins, will you please? I was raised in a Christian home, and I have a good Christian mother who is praying now for me.'[163] Similarly, Alvin O. Carlson quoted a remarkable poem – 'My Mother's Prayer' – that had been written by Corporal Walt Cecil, a regular contributor of religious verse to *The Link* magazine.[164] Invoking the scene of a GI in the midst of battle, Cecil played on the striking contrast, and significant interplay, between the fearsome realities of battle and the equally real petitions offered by a distant mother for her soldier son. Penetrating even the din of battle, and the terrible roar of artillery fire, the GI hears the quiet but insistent prayers of his mother for his safety, and is eventually vouchsafed a vision of loving, domestic maternal piety. Entering his mind despite the scenes around him, the GI sees his mother kneeling in prayer, her tearful petitions marking her fitting devotion to God and to her absent son. Far from adding to his distress, the subject of the poem feels inspired and reassured by the scene, the poem concluding with the stirring words:

> I lift my weary head up high,
> And I feel my Father's care;
> For I know that he is always nigh
> Because of my mother's prayer.
>
> So fight I on in fearless way,
> And flaunt my enemies' lair;
> I remember that on each new day
> My mother breathes a prayer.[165]

Quite apart from the special prayers of their families, throughout the war years the armed forces and their personnel were also the subjects of a sustained, national outpouring of prayer that took myriad forms. In terms of local initiatives, in May 1943 *The Link* reported that:

> When a brand-new bomber from the U.S. was delivered to him in North Africa, Pilot Capt. Wm. R. Pritchard was surprised to see this message scribbled on its side: 'God bless the crew of this plane. I will say a prayer for your safe return.' After that bomber had successfully completed 19 perilous missions without a single member of the crew being wounded, Capt. Pritchard was impressed. 'We (the crew) think there's something to that little prayer,' he said. 'After all, if it was just luck, the law of averages would have ruled us out long ago. There have been all too many times when something above and beyond our armored protection and skill has pulled us through.'[166]

In the Catholic diocese of Peoria, Illinois, 1942 commenced with the inauguration of a new 'Prayer Front' that consisted of 'an unending chain of rosaries and a Daily Mass crusade'; in the words of Bishop Schlarman, 'The Western Front, the Home Front, the Atlantic Front, are all depending on the Prayer Front.'[167] As for the very different case of Madison County, Tennessee, Orval Eugene Faubus wrote:

In the few church buildings in the county, and in the many school houses which served also as places of worship, there resounded often the voices of the ministers and the people praying for the safety and wellbeing of their sons who had gone away to war, and for the restoration of peace to the world. Perhaps no member of my group will ever forget the voice of the countrywoman unashamedly lifted in prayer as we boarded the buses for our departure. The memory followed me all the days afterward and lingers with me still.[168]

From Ohio in December 1944, Reva Beard wrote to her husband, then serving as an army psychologist in India, that in their home town of Findlay: 'The women have a prayer meeting every Thursday afternoon in someone's home and some of them always have letters from their sons to read.'[169] Likewise, in Alexandria, Virginia, a United Nations chapel was dedicated at the historic Protestant Episcopal Church of Christ Church in 1943, this being 'set aside for all who desire to pray for loved ones in the service'.[170]

On a national level, the North Atlantic Wing Prayer Squadron was formed in December 1943 by a Northern Baptist air force chaplain, William V. Morgan. His initial aim was simply to make 'the personnel of the North Atlantic Wing prayer-minded' by persuading them to sign a card that pledged them to pray each day 'for world-wide spiritual revival, for those in command of our armed forces, for chaplains, for comrades in service, and for loved ones'. However, the movement quickly acquired a large civilian following, striking a chord among the relatives of AAF personnel and civilian employees in the United States. Benefiting from the intrinsic appeal of its objectives, its interdenominational ethos, and the snappy design of its membership cards (these were adorned with 'a little blue P-38' and were small enough to be stuck onto household mirrors and aircraft cockpits) membership of the Prayer Squadron rose to over ten thousand by the end of 1944.[171] If one of its more remarkable affiliates was a group of ten-year-old children who met in a garage, the parochial and Sunday school children of America were widely enlisted as warriors in this national spiritual offensive. On 3 July 1944, for example, *Stars and Stripes* carried a photograph of the children of a Catholic parochial school in New York City 'offering victory prayers for Allied troops battling in France'.[172] More famous, however, was the case of a boys' Sunday school class at Capitol View Methodist Church, Atlanta, which began praying for individual Allied leaders in March 1942. Commencing with MacArthur, by March 1945 the class had a list of 143 'Allied war leaders' whom it prayed for every Sunday – a roster that included Marshall, Eisenhower, Patton, Clark, Nimitz, Halsey and Vandegrift, as well as figures such as Montgomery and Marshal Tito. Remarkably, the class received in turn more than sixty letters of appreciation, and was even visited by Montgomery's brother, a British Army chaplain, when he accompanied a hospital ship to Charleston, South Carolina, in November 1944.[173]

Certainly, America's service men and women were left in no doubt that they were among the prime beneficiaries of the fervent prayers of a believing nation, and this awareness had an effect. As Patton observed to Third Army's Chaplain James O'Neill in December 1944:

> Chaplain, I am a strong believer in Prayer.... God has His part, or margin in everything.... That's where prayer comes in. Up to now, in the Third Army, God has been very good to us. We have never retreated; we have suffered no defeats, no famine, no epidemics. This is because a lot of people back home are praying for us. We were lucky in Africa, in Sicily, and in Italy. Simply because people prayed.[174]

Similarly, marine Major General Roy S. Geiger wrote from Guam to the boys of Capitol View Methodist Church testifying that: 'It is comforting and inspiring ... to know that we are never forgotten in your prayers.'[175] According to Chaplain Harry P. Abbott, the knowledge of being prayed for had a tangible effect upon the inexperienced troops who took part in the Torch landings in November 1942:

> Many of them brought letters from their pastors and loved ones and read extracts stating that they were being remembered in prayer back home. This seemed to make the men feel more courageous and more determined in their desire to get the war over as soon as possible and return to their normal pursuits of life and happiness, for which they were fighting.[176]

Citing the United Brethren newspaper the *Religious Telescope* as his source, Abbott also highlighted the case of a marine who, having realised the importance of prayer on Guadalcanal, had donated $150 for the purpose of teaching boys and girls 'how to pray'. These examples led him to the conviction (later vindicated, as we have seen, by the pundits of the Social Science Research Council) that, 'most soldiers genuinely believe in prayer as a means of communication with God and as an outlet for their fears by casting their burden upon him and asking his divine protection upon them'.[177]

It is only in light of this general belief in the efficacy of prayer, and in the reassurance bestowed by the prayers of others, that one can fully appreciate Patton's 'Prayer for Fair Weather' (to say nothing of its perceived success) and the phrasing of Eisenhower's celebrated Order of the Day on D-Day itself. In the latter case, Eisenhower assured 'each individual of the Allied Expeditionary Force' that, 'You are about to embark upon the great crusade' and that, 'The hopes and prayers of liberty-loving people everywhere march with you'.[178] For those Americans under Eisenhower's command, this reassurance was clearly well founded, for in the July 1944 edition of *The Link*, the magazine described the spiritual preparations that had been made throughout the United States in support of the cross-Channel invasion:

By the time this reaches you, D-Day will probably be a matter of history. But as we go to press, widespread preparations are being made by church and civic leaders throughout the country for special spiritual obser- vances.... Plans include the tolling of church bells summoning the people to worship, the sounding of police and fire sirens, the blowing of bugle calls announcing a call to prayer, the conducting of downtown and residential mass meetings. It is arranged in many cities for all traffic to come to a stop, work benches to stand idle and all business to suspend for a period wherein all people will be asked to pray silently. Radio stations and motion picture houses also will present prayers by transcription and trailer.... All in all, the invasion will probably inspire the greatest wave of mass intercession in history.[179]

And so it seemed to prove. Reporting on reactions in Bedford, Virginia, a Mrs George Parker wrote: 'Church bells and chimes, but no whistles, have announced the beginning of the invasion. A feeling of awe and extreme quiet is prevailing.... Churches have been open ... with sad-faced worshippers going in and out constantly.' That afternoon, the service of intercession held in Bedford's Presbyterian church – a service focused on 'the one theme of supplication to God for guidance and divine aid in the struggle in which the United Nations are engaged'[180] – was packed to overflowing. As Parker reported: 'A crowded house, extreme quiet, and rapt attention marked the simple, deeply spiritual service. So many young people in the congregation.'[181]

Providence, fatalism and luck

Despite the vaunted power of prayer, and the relative safety enjoyed by a large proportion of American service personnel during World War II, life remained precarious for all too many of the nation's servicemen. The twists of fate that could spell the difference between life and death were often strange, even perverse. Ernie Pyle, for example, noted what happened to an American spotter plane at Anzio in 1944:

One of the worst strokes of Fate I ever heard about happened to a Cub there on the Fifth Army beachhead. A 'Long Tom' was the unwitting instru- ment. This certain gun fired only one shell that entire day – but that one shell, with all the sky to travel in, made a direct hit on one of our Cubs in the air and blew it to bits. It was one of those incredible one-in-ten-billion possibilities, but it happened.[182]

Similarly, Chaplain Thomas H. Clare beheld the freakish demise of a fighter pilot in India. Returning safely from a mission over Burma, a circling vulture collided with his cockpit, causing his plane to hit the runway 'with a sickening crash and burst into flames ... he was burned to death before we could get him out.'[183] However, ground troops were no more immune from the remorseless scythe of the grim reaper, even away from the battlefield. In Tunisia, Chaplain Harry P. Abbott was staggered by the number and variety of fatal motor accidents:

> One lad stuck his head out of the cab of the truck in which he was riding, to see better in the darkness, only to have his head come into contact with a steel pole. He was killed instantly. Two others drove over an embankment in the dark, failing to negotiate a curve. They, too, were buried. A cook slept too close to the exhaust of his truck and, as another ran the motor to charge the battery, the fumes overcame the cook, and he too died. Others drove off a bridge – and on goes a never-ending story.[184]

Given the vagaries of fate there was a confusion of narratives concerning the ultimate arbiter of personal survival. As a group, perhaps only convinced Christian Scientists could view physical dangers with equanimity for, in the cosmology of Mary Baker Eddy, only the spiritual world was real – and matter, with all its travails, illusory.[185] Hence, and as a wartime study of attitudes towards fear and death put it:

> Christian Scientists, like many other religious denominations, glorify war services; but they also deny the 'reality' of war and of death. Some, at least, believe that they or God can control for the better the situations of persons in the armed forces by 'spiritual work,' though the 'scientist' be remote from the scene in terms of 'mortal mind.'[186]

Possibly because the perversity of fate raised uncomfortable questions about the sovereignty of a benign and loving God, the more secular concept of luck held sway for a great many others. Luck was seen as a capricious, manipulable yet finite quantity – cast as inherently female in terms of its waywardness and spite-fulness.[187] Audie Murphy, whose survival was undoubtedly remarkable, recalled his calculations on entering Germany:

> The road across Germany is a long one; and each mile of it must be bought with somebody's blood. Why not mine? My luck has been extraordinary, but there is an end even to the extraordinary. So until the last shot is fired, I will go on living day to day, making no postwar plans.[188]

By 1944 it was even common for bomber groups to award '"Lucky Bastard" certificates to fortunate crew members after the completion of their thirtieth mission.'[189] However, and like Audie Murphy, the B-17 pilot John Muirhead saw luck as a largely malevolent force. For Muirhead, luck was 'that insolent, wayward bitch ... who ruled our lives with her gambols and all the bloody things that amused her. She moved from plane to plane, and those she chose not to destroy, she visited in her way, leaving vile reminders of her malice.'[190]

The wartime navy had a veritable roster of reputedly lucky and unlucky ships; first among the former was the aircraft carrier *Enterprise*, dubbed the 'the Lucky *Enterprise*', which survived (if not unscathed) virtually all of the major carrier battles of the Pacific war.[191] As one of its crew pointed out: 'Most of the time when the *Enterprise* was hit they did not have a flight deck full of gassed up planes ... we were lucky, but we also had a highly trained crew.'[192] However, the tendency to personify the causes that lay behind unforeseen and potentially lethal accident and injury was especially marked among aviators, who were perhaps most vulnerable to the dangers posed by the elements and by defective, man-made machinery. The war years, for example, saw the appearance of the gremlin. Described as 'those imaginary pixies of the air who play all kinds of tricks on fliers', the gremlin appears to have been a Royal Air Force (RAF) creation that represented a modern, aeronautical evolution of traditional British fairy lore, in which 'elves, goblins and fairies were frequently thought of as highly malevo-lent'.[193] However, and like the image of the divine co-pilot, the figure of the wily and malignant gremlin was readily appropriated by religious writers. In March 1944, for example, *The Link* warned its readers to 'Watch Out for the Gremlins!' – in this case the spiritual perils of indecision, procrastination, laziness, insub-ordination, fear, irreligion and immorality.[194] More firmly rooted in scripture, and in traditional maritime lore, was the Jonah figure. In December 1942, *Yank* profiled the career of Sergeant Ralph T. Morris of the AAF, a North Carolinian and former salesman then serving in Australia who had been 'in 14 crack-ups of one sort or another'. Clearly an optimist, Morris claimed that, 'If anything, I'm lucky. I haven't even been scratched.' Nevertheless, he conceded that, 'the pilots around here have gotten the idea that I am a jinx and they always prepare for the worst whenever I climb into one of their ships. But can I help it?'[195]

Many indiscriminately elided the discourse of luck with that of providence. One GI ascribed survival of an enemy barrage to 'God's protective armour plus sheer good luck'.[196] Likewise, and after jumping into Normandy with the 505th Parachute Infantry Regiment, James M. Gavin wrote to his daughter on 12 June 1944: 'I feel that Providence has bestowed upon me more than my share of favour and that I am fortunate to still be here, and the more experience that I have, the more I realize how lucky I am to have survived three combat jumps.'[197] Cath-olic navy chaplain Joseph Gallagher, asked how he had survived a devastating mortar blast on Saipan, answered, 'I was so very, very lucky. It's just the hand of God.'[198] For James J. Fahey, luck and the Almighty could both play a role in determining the fortunes of war. On 13 November 1943, Fahey wrote in his diary about the torpedoing of USS *Denver* off the Solomons: 'Today, being the 13th, proved to be a very unlucky day for the light cruiser *Denver*. She is number [CL] 58. Adding the five and eight together, the answer – 13.... The *Montpelier* was also hit by a torpedo ... a dud. Unlike the *Denver*'s, our luck was still holding.'[199] On

12 August 1945, however, and after surviving another torpedo attack at Okinawa, Fahey reflected:

> The Good Lord was watching over us again tonight. All the close calls we had since 1942 were more than just luck. Any one of them could have put us out of action. The Hand of the Good Lord prevented them from happening. As I said before, there is someone on this ship that He likes extra special.[200]

Faced with the fact of his own survival, Gordon Bennett Robertson could only admit his confusion as to its ultimate source:

> I must acknowledge that we were blessed with an inordinate amount of luck. There were so many times ... when we were in the right place at the right time – or had just left the wrong place.... My father told me once that my mother, who had passed away in 1938, was looking after me. The chaplain had a different idea of who was looking after me, but I had some questions about his candidate – not that he might not be right, but I couldn't figure out how He made His selections. What was there about me that was worth saving? We lost 485 B-29s in total in the Pacific and almost half of the 29th Bomb Group – weren't all those guys just like me?[201]

In terms of the beliefs heightened or created by the war, perhaps more problematic than luck from an orthodox point of view was fatalism; as an Episcopalian clergyman explained: 'Fatalism ... denies the providence of God. It is not religion. Its indications are not good.'[202] As defined by Samuel Stouffer and his fellow social scientists in 1949: 'Fatalism ... allays anxiety by holding that there is in fact a single inevitable future course of events so worry is pointless.... There is no point in anxiety if you are only going to be hit when the shell has your number on it.'[203] Pernicious because it diminished the importance of prayer, denied the role of free will and savoured of despair, it could yet be mistaken for Christian resignation. There were, however, further difficulties with this outlook. Practically speaking, fatalism could foster an unhealthy 'belief in personal invulnerability';[204] as Gordon Bennett Robertson observed, 'it could lead to carelessness in the belief that if your number wasn't "up", you could survive anything.'[205] According to one chaplain, it could even engender a 'pagan fanaticism' similar to that of the enemy.[206] For another contributor to *The Link*, fatalism was simply disempowering – 'man has never accomplished anything by that attitude – neither cured a disease nor built a bridge nor reaped a harvest.'[207] Chaplain Oscar A. Withee, a Northern Baptist, was still more emphatic: 'Fatalism is Silly,' he declared in August 1945, stressing instead the centrality of human agency, the distinction between faith in God and fatalism, and arguing that 'It is hardly conceivable that a man dash across No-Man's-Land shouting, "I'll not die until my time comes." He does not throw caution and his best judgment to the winds in assaulting a machine-gun nest ... "Banzai" is not in the Christian philosophy.'[208]

Despite these concerns, there can be no doubt as to the importance of fatalism as a personal coping mechanism, especially among infantrymen and aviators. Although, somewhat surprisingly, the war produced little or no 'quantitative data on the incidence of ... fatalistic points of view among combat troops',[209] it was argued in 1949 that the army's policy of replacing losses 'by individuals rather than by units', and 'of keeping divisions in action for extended periods', served to promote a widespread feeling of hopelessness – 'men easily concluded that there would be no end to the strain until they "broke" or were hit'.[210] In this vein, Ernie Pyle wrote of a highly decorated infantry sergeant in Italy:

> The years rolled over him and the war became his only world, and battle his only profession. He armored himself with a philosophy of accepting whatever might happen.... 'I'm mighty sick of it all,' he said quietly, 'but there ain't no use to complain. I just figure it this way, that I've been given a job to do and I've got to do it. And if I don't live through it, there's nothing I can do about it.[211]

According to a survey published in *What the Soldier Thinks* in 1944, fatalistic thoughts such as, 'Just one bullet has your name on it', and, 'Don't worry ever about getting knocked down.... Always remember, "Some days you win; some days you lose"', had also proved helpful for airmen in 'Getting Through a Rugged Flight Mission'.[212]

Despite these variations of belief and outlook, it should be emphasised that a significant proportion of service personnel clearly acknowledged the sovereign role of the Almighty in determining the course of their war. When stationed in Iceland, Chaplain Clyde E. Kimball salvaged a 'lucky' horseshoe as a souvenir; ironically, it had been fastened to a building that had been demolished by a German bomb.[213] Similarly, at an aid station in Lorraine in 1944, a wounded GI accosted Chaplain Benedict A. Henderson: 'I guess you did some real praying today because a mortar hit my rifle, broke the stock and twisted the barrel, but the mortar turned out to be a dud. That wasn't just luck. Nobody could tell me it was'.[214] The Hollywood actor and B-24 pilot James Stewart, comforted by a copy of the 91st Psalm his father had given him and paternal advice to surrender his fear to God, was convinced that: 'no matter what might happen, I knew that He would be with me. In this world or the next'.[215] In view of what they believed to be the proven power of prayer, some veterans eschewed the concept of luck altogether. Joseph Towell, who served in a chemical mortar company in France and Germany, 'Just prayed. Stayed in touch wit[h] God'.[216] For John W. Dewey, serving with the 86th Mountain Infantry Regiment in northern Italy, a case of divine intervention seemed apparent after he survived the shelling of an observation post on the Gothic Line: 'At twilight, we returned to our foxhole to check where the last shell had landed. I found it buried in the ground, not five feet from my observation post and directly in line with the very peephole I had been using.

It was as though God had interceded, and a silent prayer of thanks acknowledged my appreciation.'[217] During the air attacks on Nichols Field in the Philippines in 1942, Johnny Walker, a Pentecostal soldier from Little Rock, Arkansas, was saved from death by a summons like that of Samuel. Having heard his name called three times, Walker left his bunk to join a soldier who was digging a foxhole outside:

> 'What do you want?' I asked.
> My buddy looked up, confused. 'I didn't call you,' he said.
> Just then, there was a tremendous explosion ... the bomb had landed on the spot where my bunk had been. The bunk, which was about thirty feet away, had disappeared. So had a water buffalo that had been standing about twenty feet away.[218]

No less vivid was the experience of J.S. Adams of the 37th Engineer Combat Battalion, who was involved in clearing mines from Omaha Beach just after D-Day:

> [O]ne day as I was walking down there, to get on my dozer ... [it] just seemed like somebody grabbed me by the shoulder and stopped me. And when I stopped and I moved my foot aside, there's a mine about an inch and a half from being stepped on, and now God was watching over us ... you can't imagine it until you have something like that happen.[219]

There were, of course, problems with such interpretations. In adversity, an extreme sense of God's presence (or otherwise) could easily tip into despair. Hawaiian-born Pfc Johann Carl Friedrich Kasten, who was elected to liaise with the German authorities at Stalag IX-B after being captured during the Battle of the Bulge, found that the shock of capture and captivity was too much for some of his fellow POWs:

> One morning the two Chaplin's [sic] came to me with a problem ... one of our men told them he had been forsaken by God and wanted to die. I explained to the Chaplin's [sic] that it was a church problem – theirs, as I am an Atheist. They insisted that I had to accompany them to see this man. When I appeared beside his bunk his response was as before, 'I have been forsaken by God and I want to die'. I took from his wallet a picture of his family which I held up to his face and harshly told him, 'You're [sic] family is expecting you back and if you haven't the guts to live for yourself you have to live for them.' [H]is only reply was as before 'I have been forsaken by God and I want to die'. Two days later he died as well as two others for the same reason.[220]

Moreover, and as Gordon Bennett Robertson appreciated, there were always those who were, inexplicably, not so favoured with divine protection. Nonetheless, Russell Baldwin of the 551st Heavy Pontoon Bridge Battalion, declared:

I believe in miracles 'cause they happened to me and I believe in miracles because I saw so many happen. There, on the banks of the Moselle River, I was talking with three men … shells were coming in, ground bursts, and of course when you get a ground burst whoever's under that gets it. Don't ask me why, but a shell, we heard it coming, we all hit the dirt [and] somebody operating that gun changed it to an aerial burst and an aerial burst is up here – those in the 'doughnut' get it…. All three of them were blown to kingdom come [and] I'm still here. That's the kind of miracle I'm talking about.[221]

If some understood its theological difficulties, this providential understanding of fate seems to have been widely promoted by army and navy chaplains; after all, alternative interpretations that hinged on luck or fatalism could be less congenial, survivors were usually grateful, and the less fortunate were scarcely in a position to quibble. Israel Yost, who believed emphatically that his own safety lay in the hands of God while serving in Italy,[222] remembered that: 'On Saturday, January 29 [1944], I held brief services for all the companies [of the 100th Battalion] … I preached directly about why God spares some of us: it is for our conversion to his way or to do his work.'[223] In 1942, and just before landing in the Solomon Islands, Warren Wyeth Willard reminded a group of anxious marines of the promise of Psalm 34:7, 'The angel of the Lord encampeth round about them that fear him, and delivereth them.' Significantly, he claimed: 'During the next few days hundreds of our marines fell in battle. But so far as I know, not one of those men who filed into my room that night to pray fell either wounded or dead.'[224] Despite the perils of serving with the 1st Infantry Division in North Africa, Italy and Europe, Edward K. Rogers claimed that: 'I never did hear of a church service being shot up. God has something to do with that, I'm sure.'[225] Similarly, and despite the Anzio beachhead being exposed to sustained and heavy shelling over a period of months, a chaplains' publication rejoiced that: 'There is no record of casualties sustained by men attending church at any time at Anzio.'[226] The end of hostilities, of course, offered plenty of scope for chaplains to drive the lesson home. Writing from Tokyo Bay at the end of August 1945, Samuel Hill Ray, who was then serving as a Catholic chaplain on the seaplane tender *Hamlin*, informed his family that:

God has been very good to our ship. One day, when things are settled, with the consent of the Captain already given, I am going to offer a public prayer of thanks for all hands over the whole ship. I believe all men will be glad to do this. They often say how wonderfully our ship has been protected.[227]

A further illustration of this confusion of the religious and the secular, the orthodox and the heterodox lay in the bewildering array of talismans, or semi-talismans, carried by service personnel, and the rituals and taboos they observed.

Ironically, in 1918, in a famous lecture delivered at Munich University, Max Weber had confidently propounded the driving force of scientific and technological progress in the 'process of intellectualization', a process that had spelt the 'disenchantment of the world'. As Weber put it: 'One need no longer have recourse to magical means in order to master or implore the spirits, as did the savage for whom such mysterious powers existed. Technical means and calculations perform the service. This above all is what intellectualization means.'[228] While such postulations were doubtful enough against the backdrop of World War I, in World War II the armed representatives of the most technologically advanced and machine-minded society on earth embraced these 'magical means' with conspicuous fervour. W. Edgar Gregory, a former army chaplain, averred that:

> There was tremendous dependence upon amulets and charms. Men loaded themselves down with every type of religious charm they could find, some even carrying a number of Catholic medals in their pockets. Many men carried pocket Testaments and prayer books as protective devices. Probably only a few of those who carried pocket New Testaments ever read them. There was a naïve belief among them that the presence of a New Testament somehow warded off evil. The one thing I did not see – though I have no doubt it happened – was a Christian soldier wearing a Jewish *mezuzah*.[229]

This picture was subsequently corroborated by Stouffer and his colleagues, who observed:

> Many magical or semimagical practices have been reported among combat men. Men might carry protective amulets or good-luck charms, some of which had a religious symbolism and some of which did not: a cross, a Bible, a rabbit's foot, a medal. They might carry out prebattle preparations in a fixed, 'ritual' order. They might jealously keep articles of clothing or equipment which were associated with some past experience of escape from danger. They might scrupulously avoid actions regarded as unlucky (some with implicit rational grounds): 'three on a match', or saying 'My number is about up.'[230]

American aviators seem to have been especially reluctant to trust in 'technical means and calculations' for their survival, despite being near the apex of industrial and technological achievement. Indeed, and as James Muirhead remembered, among bomber crews the courting of Lady Luck was unrelenting:

> We did everything we could to please her: we showed her trinkets, crucifixes, St. Christopher medals, the foot of a rabbit, vials of holy water, small pieces of paper with prayers written on them, lucky coins, sacred photo-

graphs in gold lockets, a pair of loaded dice, a pressed flower from a girl, a picture of a child in an embossed leather case, and many other beloved charms. But we never really knew what she thought of such things.[231]

In addition to confounding the maxims of Max Weber, this phenomenon provided an ample fund of colourful anecdotes for war correspondents. In Tunisia, Ernie Pyle happened upon a military policeman from Indiana whom he noted was, 'the only soldier I ever saw who dug round foxholes instead of rectangular ones. He said that literally it was so it would be harder for strafing bullets to get at him, but figuratively so the devil couldn't get him cornered.'[232] Later, in Italy, Pyle underlined the diversity and commercialisation of the wartime talisman phenomenon, the local guides at Pompeii offering 'to sell us obscene little good-luck emblems in silver or bronze, and books of "feelthy" photographs.'[233] Among army aviators, Pyle met a transport pilot who duly knocked on wood after saying that he had never been shot at,[234] and a flight commander who refused to have seven planes under his command, as each time his flight had been allotted an extra plane it 'lost a plane the following day.'[235] Having observed the importance of talismans for American fliers in England, and the consternation that the loss of an amulet could provoke,[236] John Steinbeck discussed this phenomenon at length in a dispatch entitled 'Magic Pieces', which he wrote from Italy in November 1943. According to Steinbeck's analysis, the importance of personal amulets grew over time, they came in a multitude of different forms, were seldom spoken about, and were widely seen as endowing their owners with a limited amount of protection, their powers being drawn on only 'sparingly'. Significantly, and despite the wartime boom in the talisman trade, commercial items rarely had the appeal of more personal, 'associational' items; for many who owned talismans, they were as much an expression of 'loneliness and littleness' as they were of fear.[237]

Addressing this issue in December 1942, *Yank* carried a cartoon of a paratrooper being harangued by a sergeant while packing his parachute: 'Throw that horseshoe and rabbit's foot and four-leaf clovers outta your chute – and your girl's picture too!'[238] Despite its perceived folly and eccentricities, the possession of talismans clearly made sense to many; as Paul Fussell wrote from the jaundiced perspective of a disenchanted veteran: 'In the midst of calmly committed mass murder, reliance on amulets will seem about the most reasonable thing around.'[239] Despite his reliance on the words of the psalmist, and his dependence upon God, even James Stewart was careful to wear the same necktie when flying, 'an old superstition that remained with him for the rest of his life.'[240] However, other service personnel of a pious disposition firmly rejected the use of talismans; as army veteran Carl W. Hardwick put it, he 'Just prayed. That's the best luck there is.'[241] However, and no doubt for the reasons explained by Steinbeck, the lure of the talisman proved compelling. Illustrative of Steinbeck's point that their ownership was 'by no means limited to ignorant or superstitious men',[242] James M. Gavin felt the benefits of a five-leafed clover that he received from his daughter in 1944, just before he took command of the 82nd Airborne Division,[243] and even Eisenhower carried a purse of lucky coins, the contents of which 'he rubbed before crucial operations'.[244]

According to James McPherson, talismans had been rare among the overwhelmingly Protestant soldiers of the Union and Confederate armies.[245] If so, the extensive use of talismans in World War II was symptomatic of the dramatic diversification of the American religious landscape since the Civil War, and also vindicates Sally M. Promey's point that: 'Despite frequent assertions to the contrary, Protestants as well as Catholics make, buy, and otherwise consume material objects for their affinities with properties that might be labeled "magical".'[246] The range of religious artefacts that could be appropriated as amulets was vast, facilitated by the sheer quantity in which they were made and supplied to the armed forces. Jewish servicemen often fastened a mezuzah or a Magen David to the chains of their identification tags, with Chaplain Morris N. Kertzer noting the popularity of mezuzoth for use 'as a charm and an amulet' among Jewish inductees at Fort Dix.[247] Such was the insatiable demand for rosaries among Catholics that the Catholic writer Dorothy Fremont Grant reported that: 'Realizing the difficulty of supplying rosaries made of the customary materials, the Holy See has permitted the use of those made wholly of string, save for the cross. Crocheted knots serve for the "beads".'[248] In addition to rosaries and scapulars, a great variety of miraculous medals and other items were also carried. Lester Atwell described one soldier who wore 'a Franciscan rosary around his neck and a bunch of religious medals on a safety pin pulling a hole in every undershirt he owned'.[249] Salvatore Tocco, who served in a reconnaissance unit of the 4th Armored Division in North-West Europe, carried a cross in his pack throughout his army days. A gift from his mother, in later years it hung in his car.[250] However, such paraphernalia also included St Christopher medals, small crosses that were usefully inscribed with blood types and serial numbers, and also the aptly shaped 'key of heaven', bearing the text 'What does it profit a man to gain the whole world if he lose his own soul'? (Mark 8:36)[251]

There was, of course, a very fine, sometimes shifting, and even indistinguishable dividing line between devotional artefacts and talismans. However, the sheer amount of cross-appropriation (no pun intended) suggests a high incidence of the latter, with a clear case of syncretism being apparent in the miniature buddhas used as talismans by American submariners. As the *Washington Post* reported in March 1945:

> Buddhas are apparently the fetish of torpedomen. Its [sic] an old custom for the wife or sweetheart of a submarine captain to present two figures of the Oriental diety [sic], one for each of the torpedo rooms. The purpose?

Just before firing, the torpedoman in charge will quietly rub the protruding stomach of the little figures. They say it brings luck.[252]

Again, a veteran marine officer remarked in 1945 that: 'There is a well-substantiated story that some of the marines getting ready to make landings on the island of Bougainville in the Solomons prepared themselves by hanging both a cross and the tablets of the law about their necks. Here is Pascal's wager with a vengeance!'[253] More common, however, was the tendency for Protestants and even Jews to appropriate Catholic artefacts, a practice that was encouraged by gift-giving and by the religious geography of the European and Mediterranean theatres of war. William Greene, who hailed from the mountains of North Carolina, one of the most Protestant states in the Union in the 1930s,[254] confessed that, as a junior naval officer in the Pacific, he owned 'a religious medallion', a gift that he used to hold in his hand while saying 'a little prayer', fearful that if he did not do this every day 'something would go wrong'.[255] If Eisenhower was the recipient of 'a beautiful rosary' blessed and sent to him by Pope Pius XII in 1945,[256] a Catholic chaplain told of a Jewish tail gunner on a battered B-17 in the Pacific who, though he refrained from saying the rosary with two crewmates, nevertheless 'pulled a miraculous medal [of the Virgin Mary] from his blouse and held it tight'.[257] Even Thomas H. Clare, a chaplain of the impeccably Protestant Evangelical and Reformed Church, accepted the gift of a Sacred Heart medallion at a Catholic orphanage in India. Although he laughed that he had 'buried lots of men who had these medals around their necks, and they were just as dead as any other corpses', he later confessed: 'I've still got the medal attached to my dogtags and I intend to keep it there, and not only as a souvenir.'[258] However, and as Steinbeck observed in November 1943, St Christopher medals held the most appeal for non-Catholics: 'St. Christopher medals are carried by Catholics and non-Catholics alike and in many cases are not considered as religious symbols at all, but as simply lucky pieces.'[259] Nevertheless, Chaplain Joseph T. O'Callahan construed this popularity as a sign of creeping Catholicism, claiming that: 'My Navy life has taught me that there are very many non-Catholics, particularly aviators, who have a devotion to St. Christopher.'[260] Even such a well-known Protestant luminary as Daniel A. Poling accepted the loan of a St Christopher medal from its GI owner for a dangerous flight over the Himalayas in 1943. Far from being embarrassed, Poling wrote that: 'When I reached Kunming safely, I sent the medal back with my thanks and the earnest assurance that it had been effective, even as his faith had blessed me.'[261]

However, for other Protestants the talismanic use of Catholic artefacts was yet another cause for concern. Although *The Link* acknowledged that, 'Religious medallions carried by fliers are recognized and serve as a pass key to aid' among the natives of the South Pacific,[262] one of the concerns surrounding the Service Men's Christian League's own insignia (for most of the war, owing to a shortage of metals, a plastic disc bearing a cross and the legend 'United in Christian Fellowship')[263] was that it was open to misuse. Intended to be 'worn with the "dog tag" or carried as a pocket piece',[264] Ivan M. Gould, the general secretary of SMCL, urged caution in its distribution: 'These symbols are not supposed to be scattered around promiscuously. That is why we are selling them at ten cents each. We are suggesting that chaplains order them in quantity and then distribute them to the members of the unit at a League meeting'.[265] Concerned Protestants were even more leery of investing portions of scripture with talismanic powers. As Steinbeck had it, rather than carrying them in their breast pockets, 'those soldiers who carry Testaments, as many do, carry them in their pants pockets, and they are never considered as lucky pieces'.[266] Herbert W. Wicher, a Presbyterian army chaplain in Italy, made much the same point when he wrote:

> One Sunday I was making the rounds of a field hospital … when almost half of the men reached into their pockets and pulled out battle-battered New Testaments to show them to me. Most of them had lost their razors and tooth brushes in combat, but they still had their Testaments. They don't carry them as a sort of magic charm. They are always coming to me with questions about passages that puzzle them.[267]

However, even here the dividing line between faith and fetish was far from clear, especially in view of the many stories that circulated of bullet and shrapnel-stopping New Testaments. According to Paul Fussell, and especially when carried in a breast pocket, the New Testament 'became one of the war's most common amulets, and to its mystical efficacy were imputed numerous miracles of salvation'.[268] In Italy in 1944, Chaplain Charlie Webb, a Southern Baptist, was called to the bedside of a wounded soldier of the Japanese-American 100th Infantry Battalion: 'When the chaplain approached his bed, the soldier reached beneath it and drew out a New Testament, which had one end blown away. He then drew aside his pajamas to show the chaplain the slight wound in his side. "This testament saved my life", he said gratefully'.[269] Similar stories were carried by the secular military press, with *Stars and Stripes* reporting on 28 December 1944: 'Pfc Lercy B. Cutsail, of Frederick, Md., now at 129th General Hospital, was hit in the arm by a shell fragment during the battle for Aachen, but another fragment lodged in the New Testament he was carrying in his left shirt pocket, just over his heart'.[270] Mindful of the assurance given in Psalm 34:7, some evangelical chaplains were quite happy to affirm providential protection for those who carried and read the Word of God. Alvin O. Carlson cited the testimony of a soldier of the 134th Infantry Regiment who wrote, 'I thank God for the Gideon Testament that I carried just over my heart, for it saved my life. I also thank God for the power of that Word in my soul that has given me eternal life in Christ'. According to Carlson: 'A piece of shrapnel from a heavy German shell was found in this soldier's Testament, causing the medical officer to declare that the little book had saved his life.'[271] Warren Wyeth Willard, from his experiences in the Guadalcanal campaign, was no less convinced:

> Gideon New Testaments and those millions circulated by the American Bible Society were never meant to be charms. Men went into battle with their New Testaments buttoned in their front shirt pockets because they trusted God's Word. However, they often did stop bullets. Three men of my regiment were saved by New Testaments from wounds or death. One marine was hit in the chest by a Jap 25-caliber bullet, which pierced his Testament, only to stop at the back cover. Another lad's Testament was smashed pretty thoroughly by shrapnel from a Jap shell. I looked at the Gideon New Testament of the third man, Private O.E. Spicer, of Tivoli, Texas. The shell fragment had gone partly through.... 'You have been spared from wounds and death by the grace of God,' I told him. 'I hope you'll live only to serve him.'[272]

Another questionable use of scripture included the practice of sticking texts into aircraft cockpits. One aviator claimed never to have really 'registered' the 23rd Psalm that adorned his instrument panel until he ditched into the Mediterranean.[273] Similarly, Herbert H. Rieke, a Christian Scientist chaplain serving with the AAF in Europe, naïvely rejoiced in the fact that his proposal to paste biblical texts into their cockpits was warmly received by the pilots under his care – 'They were happy and appreciative of the idea', he enthused, and, 'One pilot insisted that I paste the passage directly on his gun sight.'[274] However, the cause célèbre in this respect was the case of the metal-bound scriptures that found their way onto the American domestic market during the war years. Sometimes marketed as 'Shields of Faith', and inscribed with a suitable message ('May the Lord be with you', or 'May this keep you from harm'), these were supposed to be worn over the heart in a left breast pocket, and Steinbeck described the product as 'a gruesome little piece of expediency which has faith in neither the metal nor the Testament but hopes that a combination may work'.[275] Despite such disdain, and his insistence that he had 'never seen one carried', these were common enough to be factored into the equipment allowance of the assault troops who led the invasion of Sicily.[276] Furthermore, Chaplain Clyde E. Kimball, an avid collector of Bibles, was happy to receive a specimen as an anniversary present from his wife in June 1944.[277] However, many shades of orthodox opinion were outraged by the shamelessness of this gimmick. In April 1945, *The Link* carried a letter from a SMCL member and erstwhile ministerial candidate, Corporal Richard L. Hixson, who ranted:

> In my mind modern thieves have taken place of the ones Christ ran out of the temple.... Last Christmas two sincere, sympathetic, but unreasoning people sent me New Testaments of the heart shield type; for my birthday

I received another. A dollar ninety-five cents was marked as the price of this Testament which has a piece of tin on it. We who believe in the saving power of Jesus Christ don't believe He needs the help of these commercializers to save us from our enemies. These deceivers would have us believe we have a weak God who needs material assistance, and these hypocrites who would use God's Word for their own selfish ends should again be exposed and 'driven out of the temple'.[278]

By this time, an American publisher had already been 'indicted and found guilty of fraud in advertising bullet-proof New Testaments for men in the armed forces'.[279] However, and amidst some excited rumours about their efficacy (a Lutheran marine, for example, claimed that one specimen had turned a sniper's bullet on Tarawa)[280] it fell to the Ordnance Department to demonstrate the practical dangers of metal-covered Testaments by showing 'that the ragged pieces of these plates when shattered by a bullet would be apt to cause a worse injury than the bullet itself'.[281]

Finally, mere flesh and blood could be enlisted in the often desperate and even magical struggle for self-preservation.[282] Chaplains themselves, despite – or even because of – their status, could serve as talismans. Reflecting on the irony and causes of this, Gregory wrote:

> Many men felt that wherever there was 'a man of God' nothing could be too bad. Although the percentage of chaplain casualties was as high as that for any other corps (with the possible exceptions of the infantry and Air Forces) the men still persisted in believing that there was a certain degree of security in having a chaplain around. The chaplains themselves strengthened or weakened this irrational feeling by their behaviour. Chaplains had to take unusual chances – and school themselves to show no fear – because the men expected it of them. American soldiers in battle were themselves willing to take unnecessary risk to see that their buddies received proper burial and expected their chaplains to be as daring.[283]

Again, examples of such dependence were legion; as an air mechanic told Ernie Pyle about one air raid in North Africa: 'As soon as those bombs started dropping I started hunting a chaplain. Boy, I needed some morale-building'.[284] Similarly, Philip Ardery wrote of Chaplain Gerald Beck of the 389th Bomb Group:

> He slept in various tents with the enlisted men, and later when we had barracks he slept in their barracks. They would carry his cot and bedding from one sleeping place to the next, each group anxiously awaiting his time to visit them. The superstition was that a crew would not be shot down as long as he was sleeping in their quarters.[285]

Another chaplain, Benedict A. Henderson, told of how he passed among GIs of the 319th Infantry Regiment prior to an attack in eastern France: 'As I came abreast of each man he turned to me and silently put out his hand and touched me. Not a man said a word. But each one nodded and smiled and gave my arm a little squeeze.'[286] A transport squadron in North Africa even harnessed the power of Christian Science in order to perform the quasi-exorcism of supposedly jinxed aeroplanes. After accompanying an unlucky crew on a successful supply drop to partisans in southern France, Herbert Rieke wrote that: 'The operation officer then asked me to go with other planes upon which he claimed there was a "jinx". Each time there was a successful mission. We never lost a man or a ship on any of those trips while I was with the organization.'[287] Moreover, and when a chaplain was not available, other friends of the Almighty could suffice. During a chapel conversation with a group of battle-scarred combat veterans, Chaplain Lawrence D. Graves was told:

> There was a Roman Catholic fellow and myself in our patrol. He didn't cuss and neither did I. We seemed to have a lot in common. I noticed the guys always bunched up close to us when they were in danger. I couldn't figure it out. Then it came to me. We showed respect for God. That's why the group wanted to be near us.[288]

The Afterlife

The imperative of self-preservation, and its many corollaries, plainly led to much confusion and many departures from orthodox norms. However, the same was also true of attitudes towards death and the afterlife. For American Jews, this was scarcely a problem for, as one Jewish commentator explained in 1948, there was no systematic doctrine of the afterlife to begin with in Judaism, 'the consensus of belief [being] that even the wicked, after a process of purification, come into the presence of God.'[289] Things were very different for most American Christians, however. By World War II, the broad and diffuse influence of liberal thought in the mainline Protestant churches over several generations had greatly eroded old theological certainties over judgement, heaven and hell.[290] After careful study of the nation's soldiers in World War I, it had been observed by the producers of the 1920, FCC-sponsored report, *Religion Among American Men as Revealed by a Study of Conditions in the Army* that: 'A *vague belief in immortality was ... general* among men as they came out of civilian life into the army.' However, the report warned, 'Whether or not their belief can be called "Christian" is a debatable point', for it was by no means apparent how this near-universal belief meshed with the hope of the Resurrection. Instead, it appeared 'for the most part an undefined faith that death is not the end, that there is more life ahead', one that derived 'almost no color from previous education, Catholic, Protestant, or agnostic'. In fact, it seemed 'to have little of moral judgment involved in it, as conditioning the fact or the character of the future life'. Although scarcely forbidding, at the same time this nebulous conception of the hereafter was hardly a motivating force, being simply one of those 'comforting thoughts upon which men fell back in times of stress'.[291] There were, of course, progressive theologians on hand to help fill in the gaps. In his classic (or notorious) 1924 statement of liberal theology, *The Faith of Modernism*, Shailer Matthews, perhaps its archpriest in the interwar years, spoke not in terms of divine judgement, heaven and hell but of 'an advance through death of those possessed of Christ-like attitudes to a complete and joyous individuality'.[292] Moreover, when Depression-hit Americans were polled on the subject of the afterlife in 1936, it scarcely mattered to many, with 36 per cent denying its existence.[293] By 1944, however, public attitudes had been transformed by the war. When asked, 'Do you believe there is a life after death?', 76 per cent of respondents said yes, 11 per cent were undecided and only 13 per cent replied in the negative. Significantly, the gender gap was remarkably narrow, with only 13 per cent of men and 10 per cent of women denying its existence.[294]

As in the mass bloodletting of the American Civil War and the First World War,[295] the issue of the afterlife proved to be of major interest to American servicemen. However, this interest was not constant and appears to have grown dramatically in 1944–45. Initially, and as America's armed forces readied themselves for the great strategic counterblows in Europe and the Pacific, casualties were relatively light. In February 1943, and due to the Battle of the Atlantic, *Yank* reported that casualties among America's merchant seamen were 'nearly four times that of the current rate of casualties suffered by the armed forces'.[296] That July, *Yank* placed the estimated totals of America's wartime casualties to date (nearly ninety-one thousand, with just over fifteen thousand dead) in their broader context: they paled in comparison with those of the British, let alone the Soviets; the Australians had suffered far more casualties than the Americans in New Guinea, as had the British in Tunisia. In fact, so *Yank* calculated, the number of Americans killed in Tunisia was considerably fewer 'than the number of lives lost through automobile accidents in California during 1941'.[297] However, this situation was transformed in the course of 1943. In only thirty-eight days of fighting in Sicily, American losses approached nine thousand, the Combined Bomber Offensive intensified the bloodbath in the skies above Europe (with monthly loss rates among Eighth Air Force bomber crews nearing 40 per cent by October), and the American public was shocked by the number and the images of marines killed in the taking of 'Bloody Tarawa' that November.[298] Including the AAF, the army's battle casualties alone soared from 40,000 in 1942, to 74,000 in 1943, to 521,000 in 1944.[299] Hence, by the beginning of 1945 there were no illusions about the ordeal through which so many Americans would have to pass in order to prevail in Europe and the Pacific, and sober expectation was not disappointed. In the event, the Battle of the Bulge in the winter of 1944–45 resulted in more than eighty thousand, the capture of Okinawa in a further fifty thousand.[300] More than half of all American casualties in the war in the Pacific were sustained in the twelve months before the atom bombs were dropped.[301] In June 1945, *The Christian Century* solemnly announced that the nation's casualties exceeded a million.[302]

Whereas one social scientist remarked upon 'a "healthy" absence of thoughts of death' among troops training in the US in 1943,[303] later experience and the prospect of a very costly invasion of Japan after the defeat of Germany pushed thoughts of the afterlife very much to the fore. As early as June 1944, and given the exceptionally high casualties among front-line marines, one of their chaplains testified to their commensurate interest in the question 'What happens when you die?'[304] At the end of 1945, Evangelical and Reformed chaplain George A. Creitz, who served with the 22nd Marines on Okinawa, reflected that: 'You always have the men's undivided attention when you preach fundamentals to them. Once when I preached on the subject of immortality, requests for the sermon were 2000 per cent higher than for any previous sermon I ever preached to the 22nd Regiment.'[305] This ultimate question made an indelible impression on Robert Leckie of the 1st Marines who, invoking the Gospel of St John and Shakespeare's *Midsummer Night's Dream*, wrote of the Japanese corpses he saw rotting on New Britain in 1944:

> The mystery of the universe had once inhabited these lolling lumps.... Does this force, this mystery, I mean this soul – does this spill out on the ground along with the blood? No. It is somewhere, I know it. For this red-and-yellow lump I look down upon this instant was once a man, and the thing that energized him, the Word that gave 'to airy nothing a local habitation and a name', the Word from a higher Word – this cannot have been oblit-erated by a quarter-inch of heated metal.[306]

The Chaplain magazine showed a heightened interest in these questions as the war entered its final year, publishing a 'Thought-Starter' on 'Life After Death' in February 1945. Written by Halford E. Luccock, professor of homiletics at Yale Divinity School, its author observed that, while the afterlife proved to be of 'continuing interest' to American servicemen, this was not so true in civilian society. The critical difference was, of course, the proximity of death itself. Borrowing heavily from psychology, Luccock argued that the war had produced among servicemen a full appreciation of 'the fine flower of human personality' and the conviction that, in a universe 'which treasures forever every bit of matter', this – 'its highest and greatest product' – could never be snuffed out. In any case, so Luccock went on, the very fatherhood of God ensured that 'his children have a permanent place in his care, and are not thrown away like a squeezed orange when the accident of death occurs'.[307] As Easter 1945 approached, these arguments were reinforced by an essay entitled 'The Other Side of Death' by the

Episcopalian clergyman Frederick Ward Kates. Here, the arguments of Bishop Charles Henry Brent, writing during the previous world war, were reiterated for the present generation. 'It is our duty to look at the unfearful side of death', Brent had insisted. Acting on this precept, and invoking Teddy Roosevelt's maxim that, 'Only those are fit to live who do not fear to die', Kates insisted that: 'Death holds no terrors for the clean and brave and true of heart. Death only terrifies him who is afraid to live.'[308] The same issue of *The Chaplain* also included strong affirmations of immortality by Harry Emerson Fosdick and the late Charles E. Jefferson. According to Jefferson, the famous Congregational pastor of New York's Broadway Tabernacle Church: 'If God is our Father, he would not deceive us for a few years and then allow us to drop into nothingness. If we are his children and share his life, we must, of course, live with him forever.'[309]

While chaplains were plied with these arguments and reflections, *The Link* engaged with its own, wider, lay readership. Reflecting what had clearly become a common concern, in May 1945 it published a letter from Corporal Joe G. Moore to his pastor at the First Baptist Church, Bethlehem, Pennsylvania. Convalescing at a hospital in England after being wounded in action, Moore had written:

> As the artillery bursts blossom across a field of cabbage, an orchard, or a pasture one has a totally helpless feeling.... When Death comes knocking at the door the question of Eternity stands forth in all its clarity.... 'What next?' assumes its true immensity.... The realization that one well placed pellet can destroy forever all that has been one's joy through a short life-time, is not a comfortable one for those who have considered nothing of the Eternity that must be faced without war's embellishments.[310]

Significantly, Moore was silent about his own hopes and expectations in this regard, and nor did *The Link* offer much in the way of particulars. In March 1944, it published the poem 'Gone From My Sight' by the late Presbyterian clergyman and writer Henry Van Dyke, a heartening reflection on death that likened the departing soul to a ship disappearing to a known destination over the horizon.[311] In October 1944 this was followed by a reverie by the British Congregationalist, and one-time incumbent of Fifth Avenue Presbyterian Church in New York, J.H. Jowett, who argued that death was but a gatekeeper and the present life merely part of a larger existential sea.[312]

Whether such metaphorical ruminations were sufficient for the climactic and threatening months of America's bloodiest foreign war is doubtful for, in April 1945, *The Link* went on to publish a more thorough exposition of the subject. Written by Georgia Harkness, a prominent Methodist and professor of applied theology at Garrett Biblical Institute, 'If a Man Die ...' examined the question of immortality 'from the viewpoints of science, philosophy and religion'. In sum, she argued that only religion could provide the answer, and that the answer lay in Christ. However, her perspectives remained distinctly liberal, reasoning that:

It is irrational to suppose that a God of fatherly love and sustaining power, who has made man in His own image and who loves all men as His children, could let men's lives be abruptly cut off without hope. A God who would let the millions of helpless victims of this present war be snuffed out utterly would not be the God of Jesus. Without the perspective of immortality there is no answer to the problem of unmerited pain.[313]

With hell and eternal punishment long banished to the periphery, Harkness reasoned that: 'Regarding the precise nature of the life eternal we must be content to trust God's goodness, for He has not revealed to us the whole mystery. Certain it is that immortality cannot mean mere endless duration, but a deathless quality of life.'[314] Significantly, her contribution was supplemented by some thoughts of the late George W. Truett, a Southern Baptist minister and theologian, who, armed with Revelation 22:3, was much less reticent on the question of 'What Will We Do in Heaven?':

Heaven means more than a place of rest. It is not some Buddhist Nirvana where activity ceases and where personality is obliterated. Heaven is to be an active place.... 'His servants shall serve Him.' What that service is to be we do not know, but it is enough for us to know that it will all be under the infinite arrangement of Him whose wisdom and power and love are perfect. [315]

Such sentiments and speculation influenced and rationalised the hazy, optimistic and domestic conceptions of the hereafter that were 'powerfully implanted' in America as a result of the massive mortality of the Civil War.[316] Indeed, their currency even found a distant echo in the third verse of the famous 'Marines' Hymn', which appeared in its modern form in 1919:

> If the Army and the Navy
> Ever look on Heaven's scenes;
> They will find the streets are guarded
> By United States Marines.[317]

The day before his death in October 1942, Lieutenant William G. Farrow, who was tried and executed for his part in the Doolittle Raid six months earlier, wrote to his mother reassuring her that, in ultimate terms, all would be well. His faith was secure, they would meet again in a better place, and all was in God's hands. He also asked her to read 'Thanatopsis' by William Cullen Bryant, a poem which captured what he felt about his situation.[318] If Bryant's meditation on death said nothing of judgement, let alone hell, these were also conspicuously absent from the 1943 film *A Guy Named Joe*, which featured a deceased war hero, played by Spencer Tracy, returning to earth to serve as the guardian angel to a rookie pilot.[319] For John Muirhead (who, as a bomber pilot, thought a good deal about death and the afterlife), eternal bliss had little to do with traditional tropes that most Americans had long since rejected as 'too cold and boring':[320]

> I wondered what death would be like. Dante said in heaven we would sit around all day adoring God. I wouldn't care for that. If there were a heaven, and I could have it as I wanted it, it would be the same as here, only without the sadness, without the pain. There would be dogs, of course, and I would have a red house on a beautiful river. I would learn to play the cello. Not far away, on a field near the river, there would be a perfectly groomed baseball diamond …[321]

Orval Eugene Faubus's views on death and the hereafter evinced a common and unselfconscious eclecticism. To the widow of a sergeant who had died in France in 1944, Faubus wrote in an almost classical vein: 'He is already across the dark river, which we all must cross, and has entered into the portals of that country which waits for the good and the brave.'[322] Similarly, Gilbert Omens of Chicago, who died serving as a Spitfire pilot with the RAF, wrote in a last letter: 'Mother, when this war is over and the boys come back, stand up and cheer them, because I will be there flying over their heads with the rest of the squadron of the dead. We never die; the things we have done will live forever.'[323] After the end of the war in Europe, General Lucian K. Truscott of the Fifth Army wrote of the prospect of 'a soldier's Valhalla, where the tales of valor and deeds of mercy rest with the immortals'.[324] However, MacArthur was more assertive of Christian hope and tradition. In April 1942, and with reference to the mothers of the fallen defenders of Bataan, he averred: 'I can only say that the sacrifice and halo of Jesus of Nazareth has descended upon their Sons, and that God will take them unto himself'.[325]

Given the range and complexity of their theological milieu, and the intense pastoral demands of the war, this chaotic array of beliefs and perspectives was widely indulged by Protestant churchmen and chaplains. Counselling a mortally wounded GI in a general hospital near Bastogne, Daniel A. Poling advised:

> You must have learned in school … that nothing in nature is ever anni-hilated. Forms change and patterns of life, but life itself goes on…. Only 'things' are left behind…. Although I do not know the country to which I travel, I shall have friends awaiting for me there who do know it and I shall not be lonely.[326]

Likewise, and in the words of Chaplain Harry P. Abbott, death was 'the Great Beyond', a fatally wounded soldier in North Africa embarking 'on that far journey to his eternal home'.[327] Though a United Brethren chaplain, Abbott condoned prayers for the dead, penning the clumsy lines:

> Poppies, poppies, when we see them,
> Let us breathe a prayer,

> That wherever our dead be over there,
> That God will watch over them.[328]

Prayers for the dead were, in fact, very common among Protestants, from President Roosevelt downwards. Although not known as a High Church Episcopalian, in his fireside chat of 24 December 1943 Roosevelt prayed: 'we ask that God receive and cherish those who have given their lives, and that He keep them in honor and in the grateful memory of their countrymen forever.'[329] Likewise, his prayer for the nation's servicemen on D-Day included the petition: 'Some will never return. Embrace these, Father, and receive them, Thy heroic servants, into Thy kingdom.'[330] For his part, Orval Eugene Faubus betrayed almost Catholic predilections when he wrote to Arkansas's *Madison County Record* in 1944: 'My prayer is that God will grant all the fallen the peace in the next world that was to them here denied.'[331] Significantly, and while in India, Chaplain Thomas H. Clare was practically compelled to hold a special memorial service after a delegation of enlisted men demanded: 'Why don' we have mass for ev' man that goes down? Tell us, Chaplain, huh?' Despite Clare's Evangelical and Reformed background, the ensuing service 'went off very well', although :'The hymns and the prayers were for the dead; my address was for the living.'[332] Memorial Day offered an obvious opportunity for this trend to manifest itself. In a model sermon that was later published in *The Chaplain*, in 1945 Chaplain Eldon W. Borell, an Episcopalian, asked his congregation on the island of Espiritu Santo:

> But have they really died? Or is it that they merely have passed through a gate, as it were, and are continuing their lives unseen by us who remain behind in this earthly tabernacle? We know the Christian answer.... Our prayers ascend for the souls of these our comrades lying on distant battlefields beneath Crosses and Stars of David. May light perpetual shine upon them and may their souls rest in peace.[333]

In terms of its fundamentals, Catholic theology remained more clear-cut. Recalling his solemn duty of writing letters of condolence to the bereaved, Chaplain Karl A. Wuest drew comfort from the traditional Catholic practice of praying for the dead: 'It was especially at such times that I was glad for the recipient's faith in God. For their element of help was not lacking to the departed souls.'[334] However, if the fundamentals of Catholic theology held firm, it was widely assumed that the gates of heaven had swung open to admit the souls of the nation's war dead. As we have seen, John Basilone spoke of his fallen comrades as 'triumphant inhabitants of heaven – white flowers of a blameless life,'[335] but such a positive image of the fallen was by no means confined to laymen fresh from the front line, and nor indeed to Catholics. A wartime propaganda painting by *Saturday Evening Post* cover artist John Falter depicted a fallen GI, arms outstretched and wearing a crown of barbed wire, over the title 'BY HIS DEEDS ... MEASURE YOURS.'[336]

Likewise, and even in the pages of *The Christian Century*, the Congregationalist theologian and hymn-writer John Wright Buckham could claim in 1945 that the nation's fallen were, like Christ, partakers in the redemption of the world:

> For all who suffer undeservedly because of the sin of others, through devoting themselves to a noble cause share with Christ in this agelong redeeming service.... The undeserved suffering and death of these young people unites them with Christ and gives them a part with him in saving the world.[337]

Catholics, however, were usually happy to settle for mere martyrdom. To Wuest, the soldiers he buried in the Italian mud – and for whose souls he routinely offered Mass – were 'martyrs of man's barbarianism'.[338] More importantly, they were also martyrs in the eyes of Francis Spellman, who described the nation's servicemen as 'our country's finest and fittest, blighted by the curse of Cain, blessed with the spirit of eternal martyrdom'.[339] To the archbishop, the sacrifice of the war dead was intrinsically meritorious, and thus they lived 'enshrined in loving hearts and in God's glory'.[340] In 1944, Spellman even turned the Christ-like sufferings of the GI into 'a short, fervent meditation penned for the consolation of parents who had lost their sons in the war', which he entitled *The Risen Soldier*.[341] For Spellman, the blood-soaked sands of Omaha Beach were comparable to Golgotha, for there, 'like the Captain of their souls, these men died that we might live!'[342] Such was Spellman's exalted view of the fallen that he quoted with approval the sentiments of an apparently non-Catholic GI, who had comforted the mother of a comrade with the words:

> Men like Jim never die. They always remain with us in the good they have done. And I'd like you to believe what I told my own mother about my brother – Jim will always be watching over you from up there saying, 'Please don't weep in vain. I came to earth to get here. What more happiness could we ask?'[343]

Significantly, such were the needs of the time that many evangelicals were no less strident in emphasising the depths of divine mercy. In Cabanatuan, Robert P. Taylor, a Southern Baptist chaplain, reassured a dying POW who was sceptical of the validity of deathbed conversions that: 'God's response to our need is not based on our timing but on his great love for us'.[344] Chaplain Alvin O. Carlson of the 134th Infantry Regiment, in light of his positive verdict on foxhole religion and on the sincerity of battlefield conversions, proclaimed that salvation was freely vouchsafed to those who gave their lives 'and who accepted our Lord and Saviour Jesus Christ'.[345] Likewise, Chaplain Warren Wyeth Willard, who boldly preached 'the unadulterated gospel of Jesus Christ' to marines and sailors in the Pacific, [346] urged his marine congregations in particular to heed its saving call:

Amid scenes of desolation on Tanambogo, and in full view of the cemetery at Gavutu, I lifted up Jesus Christ as the only begotten Son of God,
the Light of the world, the only and sufficient Saviour of all mankind. I
felt led to invite those whose hearts had been touched by the Holy Spirit
to surrender their lives unconditionally to Him. Ahead, I could see other
battles, more casualties, and a larger cemetery. I pleaded with the men to
prepare here and now for the life to come. At the service on Tanambogo
thirty-seven officers and men signified their willingness to give their hearts
to Christ. On Gavutu ... forty-two officers and men surrendered their lives
to Him who alone demanded their first allegiance.[347]

According to Willard, his relentless 'Questing for Souls' worked to the eternal
benefit of those who responded, many of whom were subsequently killed.
Reviewing a single week's work in August 1942, he wrote:

I pleaded with our marines to make their peace with God through the
acceptance of Jesus Christ His son. Exactly 130 officers and men, some with
tears streaming down their faces, surrendered their lives to Jesus Christ....
Weeks later, over on Guadalcanal, many of these new-won converts laid
down their lives on the battlefield. But they died in the Christian faith.
Therefore, those dead now live, and will live forevermore in the presence
of the glory of God.[348]

Loss and gain

Given its myriad nuances and complexities, the condition and trajectory of religion in the American armed forces during World War II gave rise to a host
of varied, and often conflicting, judgements and opinions. It could scarcely be
otherwise given the uneven pattern and tempo of military operations on a global
scale, the size of the armed forces, the variety of roles they embraced and the
sheer diversity of American religious life. However, optimists saw the condition
of religion among America's service personnel as both cause and effect of a wider
revival of religion in American society; their 'rediscovery of God'[349] was part
of a national, wartime phenomenon of rejuvenated faith and religious purpose
after the uncertain and crisis-ridden years of the interwar period. Given more
than sixteen million subjects and a global religious laboratory, it was, of course,
easy to seize upon corroborative evidence for or against this view. For example,
many evangelicals drew strength from a host of localised revivals. If Warren
Wyeth Willard rejoiced at a bumper harvest of souls in the Solomon Islands in
1942,[350] like-minded chaplains advertised similar successes in *The Chaplain*.[351]
Among them was Harold G. Sanders, another navy chaplain and a Southern
Baptist, who by the end of 1944 had sent around ten thousand V mails 'to families and churches announcing the attendance and religious decision of men in

the service.'[352] In total, navy chaplains reported 52,372 baptisms during the war years. While some were baptised into paedo-baptist churches, or into smaller denominations, such as the Disciples of Christ, which also practised believer's baptism, the figures imply that the navy's 335 Baptist chaplains enjoyed a flourishing wartime ministry.[353] At Parris Island, for example, more than one-third of the 1,300 marine recruits and permanent personnel who were baptised between January 1945 and June 1946 joined Baptist churches, their numbers exceeding those of the Methodists and Presbyterians combined.[354] Furthermore, the fluidity of service life and the vagaries of individual choice ensured that the numbers of decisions for Christ far outstripped those of actual baptisms; according to Willard, while the latter could be numbered by the dozen, the former were to be counted by the hundred.[355] Whatever the ratios, dramatic battlefield baptisms made colourful copy for the secular and the religious press. As *The Link* editorialised in July 1944:

> Headlined on the front pages of newspapers throughout the United States the other day was a report that heartened us no end. It was a story, written by an alert Associated Press legman, of the baptism of thirty veteran infantrymen in the cold surf of the Anzio beachhead in Italy.[356]

According to Leroy W. Raley, the Southern Baptist chaplain who immersed twenty-four of these soldiers (the rest were merely 'sprinkled with sea water' by a Methodist colleague) all had felt 'the need of a greater ideal when they go back to face death'.[357] It was, so *The Link* declared, part of a 'spiritual history over which the Church will be proud to ponder in decades to come'.[358]

There was, however, always room for doubt. Other evangelicals professed to be unimpressed, if not disheartened, by the spiritual poverty of their fellow servicemen. En route to the South Pacific in February 1943, the fundamentalist Arthur F. Glasser was deeply worried by the spiritual inertia of his brother officers, who in aggregate represented 'the average college-bred American on his way to war':

> Young, alert, personable – these were the doctors, dentists, construction engineers, deck and supply officers, aviators, and Marine raiders who had been unceremoniously called from their sheltered environments of campus and laboratory to work and fight in the most sordid, bestial war of history.... Here were educated Americans; yet few, if any, had experienced more than the most casual contact with the Christian church. Perhaps for sentimental or traditional reasons they tolerated or respected that institution, but down deep in their hearts they were half-way consenting that the church was really out-of-date.[359]

Glasser was no happier with the spiritual condition of the marines with whom he bivouacked on New Caledonia:

I learned how to huddle with them in their dark tents, with senses dulled by the endless drumming of the rain on the canvas, a true partner in their common woe. I was face to face with the common lot of the nameless foot-soldier of World War II. Like Ezekiel of old, 'I sat where they sat,' and my heart went out to these pitiable sheep in their loneliness and discouragement. I coveted them for the Lord, for so few appeared to rejoice in the consolations of the gospel.[360]

Concern was also voiced from the opposite end of the Protestant spectrum. Half-way through the war, Dr William Barrow Pugh was still not convinced of its salutary effects on servicemen's religion, warning: 'There has been no such thing as a religious revival. We must be realistic in these things.'[361] Consequently, in the summer of 1945 Clarence W. Hall, the editor of *The Chaplain* magazine, set off to the Pacific as an accredited war correspondent with the avowed purpose of seeing for himself, 'just what the average GI is thinking about religion and what part religion plays in his daily life under combat condition.'[362] As for Willard S. Smith, the Northern Baptist chaplain of an army ordnance battalion in France, by 1945 stories of combat soldiers turning to religion were hardly representative of the army as a whole:

To help understand the situation, we need always to remember that the *average* soldier, the American GI, is not only the muddy, tired, fighting doughboy who has been at the front ... he is the MP directing traffic at Cherbourg, the quartermaster soldier checking supplies at a hundred depots, the driver rolling the GMCs across to wherever there are men who need food, ammunition, gasoline ... the mail clerks at the APOs, the ward orderly in the hospital, the baker, the welder, the typist, the electrician ... why do the folks at home expect men doing these jobs to develop a particular interest in religion?[363]

In consequence, he argued, the situation was little different from civilian life:

I see no marked increase in religious interest among men of the Army. Attendance at chapel here in France is about the same as it was back in the States – just average. Men who went to church at home attend chapel service in the Army. And those who seldom went to church at home seldom go now.[364]

Even Catholic opinion remained divided on the question, a situation that was acknowledged by the Catholic weekly *America*. Whereas a senior navy chaplain claimed that, in the Southwest Pacific, 95 per cent of Catholics were keen Mass attenders, and 40 per cent weekly communicants, an army chaplain in the same theatre of war expressed his complete scepticism as to the vitality of Catholicism in the services. Dismissing the fervid accounts of crusading piety that seemed to fill Catholic publications, he was adamant that the piety of Catholic soldiers not only left a good deal to be desired but raised very serious questions about the post-war prospects of the civilian church.[365] Speaking at a Catholic convention in New York in August 1941, Chaplain George J. Zentgraf had pulled no punches at the low religious calibre of his flock at Camp Pendleton, Virginia:

> Father Zentgraf said he had found among the Catholics hundreds who had forgotten their religion and never had made their first communion or been confirmed. Many of these, he said, had attended 'non-sectarian schools, some city college or something, where they learned nothing but paganism and where Communist ideas were taught on the sly.'

Worse still, unruly draftees had sabotaged his ministry, 'and the Holy Name Society was smashed by the selectees with their communistic disregard for authority.'[366] After the outbreak of war, and keen to establish the facts, a Catholic army chaplain profiled 164 Catholics admitted to a base hospital over a twelve-day period, and his findings gave no great cause for rejoicing in heaven:

> Of these, he discovered sixteen with bad marriages; eight, nominally Catholic, would have absolutely nothing to do with the priest; twenty-six had been away from the Sacraments from one and a half to eighteen years; four had not made their first Communion. In other words, out of 164 men whom the Army had received from civilian life, fifty-four had major impediments to the practice of normal Catholicism – he did not even try to summarize the minor deficiencies.[367]

Faced with an accumulation of often conflicting evidence, even Dorothy Fremont Grant – normally bullish in her treatment of Catholic affairs – accepted in 1944 that: 'Our Chaplains have discovered about one third of the Catholic men under arms do not practice their Faith: they are not 100 per cent apostles by any means.'[368] This was certainly an understatement.

Nevertheless, a highly susceptible American public was subjected to a constant flow of reassurance as to the spiritual health of the defenders of the nation, a wartime narrative of burgeoning faith that came to dominate public perception. Richard Tregaskis, for example, commenced *Guadalcanal Diary*, his famous 1943 narrative of the campaign, with a description of well-attended Sunday services en route to the Solomon Islands, adding how church attendance surged as the landings drew near.[369] By this time even the secular press was often emphatic about the reality of a religious revival. In December 1942, for example, Chaplain Edward J. Burns wrote in the *New York Times* of 'a tremendous revival of faith in the hearts and souls of hundreds upon hundreds of thousands of soldiers who, perhaps, in the careless years of uncertain peace, had become just a little bit rusty in the true meaning and understanding of spiritual belief.'[370] A few days later, the *Los Angeles Times* announced that, 'religious response among naval personnel is far greater in the second World War than its predecessor of 25 years ago.'[371] In March 1943 the *Washington Post* summarised the general situation by declaring that:

> From every part of the world where Americans face the realities of war, reports come in to show that they turn to reassurance in religious faith ... Religious conviction – reaffirmed or newly found – is reported all the way through the ranks from ordinary privates and seamen up to the gold braid at the top.[372]

With a religious revival stirring on the home front, dramatic manifestations of muscular, battlefield faith proved distinctly newsworthy. In an article republished in *The Link*, Sergeant David Dempsey, a Marine Corps combat correspondent, described a Protestant service held behind American lines on Saipan:

> Many of the marines hold small paper hymnbooks with one hand [and] instinctively clutch the stock of their rifles with the other.... Even the tempo of the command post slows down for this half-hour of devotion. The quiet of the sickbay is even quieter as a doctor and several corpsmen disappear to attend the service.... The chaplain is a young man of 24. He knows that many of his listeners have undergone an almost evangelical conversion since going into battle, that they have seen the reality of death on one hand and the miracle of salvation on the other.... He tells them that it is almost always a great, personal, near-tragic event that converts men to steadfast faith in God, that they should not feel ashamed because they have not come to know God as intimately before. The test will come when the fighting is over and the personal danger is gone. He pleads with them to begin now to give their lives a truly Christian pattern. Not much older than most of them, he and his words carry conviction.[373]

In terms of the religious press, the wartime missives of Chaplain Eben Cobb Brink, as originally published in the Presbyterian magazine *Today*, were intentionally written 'to share with others the discovery of a deeper understanding of the presence of God in a man's life'. As Brink put it in a 1944 anthology: 'If it eases the loneliness of heavy hearts or encourages those who face serious problems, if it brings nearer to the reader the abiding presence of our Heavenly Father, it has justified its writing and the sharing of the experiences upon which it is based.'[374] Sometimes this sharing of good tidings from the front was couched quite carefully, however. Writing in 1943, and after more than a year of war, AAF chaplain William C. Taggart acknowledged that profanity, drinking and gambling had persisted among the officers and men of the 19th Bombardment Group, and that their levels of churchgoing were somewhat disappointing. Nevertheless, he insisted that in overall terms the situation was encouraging; after all, his congregation came from every corner of the United States, and a good many of them had only been to church as children. Moreover, there had been some conversions, and those who had sought divine help in action had done so out of the best of religious and even patriotic motives. According to Taggart, those who found comfort in their faith when in action were not simply cowardly or weak-willed opportunists, clinging to whatever was available. On the contrary, they were firmly convinced that they were fighting on the side of the Almighty, and it was this, along with their personal faith, that gave them the courage and resilience to persevere against the odds.[375]

In 1944 *Faith of Our Fighters* – well received even by *The Christian Century*, which described it as 'the best all-round book on the chaplaincy' published to date[376] – showcased many edifying vignettes of religious life in the armed forces. For example, Sergeant James E. Hague, another Marine Corps combat correspondent, described 'Sunday Mass on Bougainville' as follows:

> Just as at home, a few marines stand a short distance from the chapel tent, smoking a last cigarette before going in to Mass.... There, one of them has thrown away the half-smoked cigarette and dropped to his knees on the fringe of the tent. He takes a rosary from around his neck. He wears it constantly. He kisses the crucifix and begins to tell his beads.... Nearly every one of these Catholic marines has some mark of his faith on his person – a miraculous medal, a cross, a scapular, a rosary. Most are reading their pre-Mass prayers from sweat-soiled, rain-crumpled prayer books.[377]

Likewise, and though conceding that 'the average son of Israel is not *perfect* in all religious matters', Nance quoted the words of Frank L. Weil, the president of the Jewish Welfare Board, in trumpeting 'The Fervent Faith of Our Hebrew Warriors':

> These youthful fighters are God-fearing men, participating in religious services and anxious for religious guidance. They will be among the leaders who will build the American future and who will uphold the democratic traditions of ancient Judaism. It is they who will help make it possible for us to look to the future with a spirit of optimism and courage.[378]

Given such coverage, it was but a short step to casting the armed forces as national nurseries of religion, with service life liable to reveal and revive even the most vestigial faith. By the end of the war, navy chaplains at the vast Marine Corps training station at Parris Island, South Carolina, had partly realised this vision by developing 'a religious program ... so unique, effective, and far-reaching' that it came to 'national attention'.[379] So close was its connection with the wider training regime that James Allen Knight, a Methodist chaplain who had gone to Parris Island in 1946, reported that: 'The religious program is part of the overall program of the Post. It is integrated with the program of recruit training with such precision that chaplains interview recruits at the time they are being classified.'[380] This vaunted scheme hinged on constant exposure to the station's chaplains, on a vigorous programme of religious instruction and chapel activities, and 'on co-operation and friendly relations with the Drill Instructors', critically important figures whom the chaplains wisely chose to cultivate. The results of this programme were more than usually impressive – it raised a large crop of new and enthusiastic members of the home churches and, though chapel attendance was voluntary, recruits packed the chapels at Parris Island 'for almost every service of divine worship'.[381] Taking a wider view, in a wartime essay entitled 'Catholic Servicemen and their Chaplains', the civilian Jesuit Stephen B. Earley insisted that: 'The practice of religion in the Armed Forces immeasurably surpasses that in civilian life.'[382] Chaplain Merle M. Grove of the Disciples of Christ, reflecting on his own 'experience with a combat infantry regiment in France', and on the evident appeal of 'the grand old gospel hymns' for his congregations, agreed that: 'We have found that the army is not a place to forget one's religion, but a place to develop it.'[383] For his part, Chaplain Eben Cobb Brink made the important – if mundane – observation that religion in the military was unhindered by questions of finance and had the advantage of not *having* to be paid for by its beneficiaries. As one GI had confided: 'Back home I lost interest in the Church because it was always raising money and doing so many things that didn't make any difference to me. Chapel over here is just worship, and one feels he gets near to God.'[384] However, Chaplain Alvin O. Carlson saw the general situation more positively, writing in 1945:

> It is true that not all men in the armed forces are yielding to Him and His Son Jesus Christ, but a great number are responding. Perhaps the frontiers of Sicily, the South Pacific islands, Normandy, Brittany, the Siegfried Line and Berlin will become the training places of Christian soldiers who will understand and heed the apostle's words, 'Thou therefore endure hardness, as a good soldier of Jesus Christ.' [2 Timothy 2:3][385]

Jewish commentators were no less optimistic about the religious value of service life, or less hopeful of its future implications. According to Moritz Gottlieb, the faith of its members in uniform was a lesson for American Jewry. On his return from 'a 32,000-mile inspection tour of the Pacific battle fronts' in 1943,[386] Gottlieb sighed that: 'I have been back only a few days, and I find it difficult to orient myself once more to the American way of life. *I regret to say that the whole synagogue and church picture as I see it here has no vitality compared with what I saw over there.*'[387] He also foresaw that:

> When we have won the war, what a joy to the hearts of mother, father, sister, brother, and all those who had to stay home, to find their men returning from war with a greater sense of spiritual and religious values, than the

average had before going away to war. Yes, that will be one of the great, if not *the greatest and most lasting values* that can come from this war.[388]

Another much-travelled representative of the Jewish Welfare Board, Rabbi Barnett R. Brickner, was also deeply impressed by the picture he formed from his peregrinations, being convinced that, 'men on all fronts are developing a very real religious interest, and not just those in foxholes and bomber fields'. Apparently, 'chaplains of all faiths the world over reported to him that 30 per cent of available men at any given post attend religious services', raising the question '"What city church or synagogue could say as much?"'[389]

Significantly, more dispassionate observers of the state of religion in the armed forces tended to agree with Brickner. Even after the Secretary of the Navy intervened to end compulsory church attendance for ordinary navy recruits, it was still noted that large numbers of navy trainees paraded for church, if only in response to peer pressure or, in certain cases, for its sheer novelty value.[390] According to an article in *Yank* in February 1943, religious practice in the army was healthier than in civilian life: 'Church-going may have seemed sissy back home but down here [in Australia] it's different. In fact, the chaplains claim the Army average is better than the civilian. The average soldier worships at least once a month – a lot of boys oftener.'[391] Furthermore, it did not go unnoticed that churchgoing was conspicuously high by the standards of other nations. Even before Pearl Harbor, the willingness of Catholic sailors to attend Mass evoked the envious admiration of the Bishop of Ponce, Puerto Rico. As Chaplain Frederick William Meehling remembered:

> I must have had a hundred of them, all in whites. And I remember what [the bishop] said. He got up in church and he said, 'You young men don't know what a good work you're doing. Down here, where men don't usually go to church, it's good to see this fine group of men intelligently attend mass.' He was so impressed that he said, 'You don't have to fast during Lent.'[392]

Later, the Bishop of Auckland was so impressed by the conduct of Catholic GIs in New Zealand that he wrote effusively to the National Catholic Welfare Conference: 'great numbers amongst the officers, especially of the medical staff, and the men are a shining example to clergy and laity of all that is good; we are impressed by their spirit of prayer and reverence, and their sacramental life.'[393] In continental Europe, where Mass attendance was often highly gendered and even deeply politicised, the sight of Catholic GIs flocking voluntarily to Mass prompted no less surprise and admiration. According to William R. Arnold and Christopher Cross:

> The French civilians and French priests constantly expressed their astonishment at the number of American soldiers who attended church. The

greatest lesson the French people could learn from the war, two French priests told Chaplain [Benedict A.] Henderson, was from the example our soldiers set when they filled the churches.[394]

The role of the Catholic GI as an ambassador for the faith was also a prominent theme in the memoirs of Chaplain Francis L. Sampson of the 101st Airborne Division: 'Every French priest I met commented upon it with wonder and admiration', he wrote. Having Americans nearby was not only edifying but lucrative; bivouacked in a village near Cherbourg, $300 was taken in two successive collections for the local *curé* – 'more than his congregation had been able to contribute in a whole year'.[395] Later, from observations of American POWs in Stalag II-A, a French priest praised the Americans as 'the world's greatest lovers of the Eucharist'.[396]

Protestant and Jewish GIs made a similar impression on their respective co-religionists in Europe. As the historian Graham Smith has demonstrated, 'during the war one of the most popular activities associated with the black Americans was the singing of Negro spirituals in British churches'.[397] However, the broader appeal of religious services to Americans also prompted comment among civilians. As a chaplains' report from the ETO put it:

> The policy of voluntary attendance was frequently vindicated by the astonishment expressed by Britons and Europeans observing the proportionately large number of worshipers at American military services. Thus Chaplain (Captain) Gerhard J.C. Gericke, writes: 'People are surprised at the amount of religion displayed by Americans.... Speaking about one of my services, where I have an attendance of around 100–150 every Sunday, they marvel at the way the boys drift in from all corners. And then the shocked statement: "Who of the age of twenty goes to services [in France]?"'[398]

Jewish GIs, who were experiencing a general revival of their own religious identity and practices, prompted a similar reaction among European Jewry. According to Morris N. Kertzer, those Jewish civilians who had attended army services had been astonished by the size and keenness of the congregations, and by the open demeanour of Jewish army chaplains. So much so, that Kertzer was disposed to believe that a vivid and lasting example had been set.[399]

Anticipating the wider, long-term effects of wartime religious life in the armed forces, Floyd E. Ammerman, an experienced chaplain's assistant, was confident that, 'when we are all returned home we will find the church attendance much larger than pre-Pearl Harbor'.[400] With an eye to the religious balance sheet of 1941–45, Chaplain Harry P. Abbott was also optimistic, pronouncing that:

> [M]any veterans who never before were religious will become religious. It is also my observation that men who were religious before they went into the army, for the most part, will be religious on their return, and that those

who were totally indifferent to all phases of religious activities are in the great minority and will continue to be so.[401]

Kertzer was equally emphatic about the 'positive, constructive pattern of Jewish living which grew up during this war', writing in 1947:

> Thousands of young men and women who had never seen the inside of a synagogue attended services faithfully. Large segments of our youth who would have been lost to Judaism found the way back while they were oceans away from family and temple. If a chaplain canvassed his congregation of one hundred men on the minor festival of *Purim*, he would learn that less than a score would have attended the synagogue at home during the Feast of Esther. Whatever the motives of the men, whether they sought companionship or felt closer to home when they heard the tale of Mordecai and Haman, they came in great numbers. The other minor festival, *Chanukah*, loomed equally large on their calendar; they sent cards home to their loved ones, ate potato pancakes after service and sang 'Rock of Ages.'[402]

Significantly, these prognoses were not unduly optimistic. Whatever else, encouraging and widespread signs of GI religiosity persisted well beyond the end of hostilities, perhaps helping to illustrate how religious practice could be stronger *after*, rather than before, the experience of combat. Returning to the United States at the end of May 1945, Chaplain Francis L. Sampson was impressed by the high levels of Mass attendance on board his troopship, and by its underlying cause:

> The whole boat seemed intoxicated with the joy of going home. I celebrated Mass every day, and the attendance was very good. Apparently most of the men were mighty grateful to the Power that brought them through. I doubt if many will ever forget their experiences or the Providence that made it possible for them to return to their families.[403]

As twelve hundred veterans awaited their separation at Fort Sheridan, Illinois, Sampson was also impressed to find that one Sunday: 'The chapel was packed for three Masses.'[404] However, his experiences were very much part of a broader phenomenon. According to a study of its Corps of Chaplains from July 1945 to September 1946: 'As victory approached, in the spring of 1945, many chaplains and visiting denominational leaders reported a rise in religious interest throughout the Army.'[405] Significantly, this increased into the summer. For example, from the 55th General Hospital in England, 'Chaplin [sic] Ernest G. Nelson ... reported intense activity in the religious and social ministry to servicemen. He reported that he had given out thousands of tracts, New Testaments, portions thereof, and Bibles.' Furthermore, 'Chaplain John W. Kennedy, in the European theater, reported that some of the chaplains in his division were holding as high [sic] as

18 services as week, in addition to interviews and calls.'[406] This phenomenon was also in evidence on the other side of the world, where the occupation of Japan revealed that: 'Attendance at religious services did not seem to wane with the cessation of hostilities. If anything there was in many instances, a sizable increase in the number who came to worship.'[407]

Various chaplains' surveys undertaken shortly after VE day add substance to this picture of a heightening of religious belief among army veterans in the ETO. For example, a 'religious questionnaire' circulated among the men of the 41st Armored Infantry Regiment, part of the 2nd Armored Division (the self-styled 'Hell on Wheels'), produced thirty-nine replies that pointed to some broad trajectories: 'Twenty-three of the respondents stated that they had become more religious as a result of their war experiences', while 'Six declared that they had become less religious and ten that their attitude toward religion had not been changed.'[408] On a more ambitious scale, Chaplain Ben L. Rose of the Presbyterian Church in the United States distributed four hundred questionnaires among the men of the 113th Cavalry Group (Mechanized), a unit that had also seen much action in North-West Europe in the preceding year.[409] Of 128 respondents, 'Ninety-six declared they were church members, 28 stated they were not, and four did not answer.' While this might suggest an over-representation of the religiously committed, of the 128 who stated an affiliation or otherwise: 'Forty-three (34%) declared that they attended divine service more frequently in the Army than in civilian life, 44 (35%) stated that the frequency of their attendance was unchanged, and 39 (31%) reported that they were attending less frequently.' Nevertheless, and among the sample as a whole, the war seemed to strengthen their churchgoing aspirations as:

> To the question, 'When you return to civilian life, do you think you will attend church more regularly, less regularly, or about the same as you did before you entered the army?', 65 (53%) answered 'more regularly', 56 (46%) replied 'about as often as before', and only one replied 'less regularly.'

Hence, it was deduced that, at the very least, 'As far as the results of this survey go … service in the European Theater will have a constructive effect upon the church-going habits of those who were church-members before their military service.'[410]

Another survey, this time conducted by chaplains among 2,985 'returnees passing through the AAF Redistribution Station at Santa Ana, California', produced some striking results. Embracing both officers and enlisted men, and veterans of five different theatres of war, when asked 'whether or not Army life has been helpful or a hindrance to attendance at religious services', 50 per cent of Catholics, 31 per cent of Jews, 35 per cent of Protestants and 40 per cent of those with 'no preference' answered that army life had been helpful in this regard. Nevertheless, the exigencies of service life had taken their toll, with those who deemed it a hindrance amounting to a substantial proportion of all four groups (25 per cent, 22 per cent, 33 per cent and 15 per cent respectively, with the balance stating that there had been 'no change' to their situation). While it is understandable that almost as many Protestants felt disadvantaged as advantaged in attending their preferred type of worship, the fact that the unaffiliated felt by a large margin that they had been helped rather than hindered in this regard was due to the fact that, 'these persons were thrown into more intimate relationships with the Chaplains than they had had with civilian clergy before entering the Army'.[411] Of the Catholics, Protestants and Jews who found that army life had helped their religious attendance, three main reasons were given. Forty per cent, 57 per cent and 42 per cent of Catholics, Protestants and Jews respectively said that services were simply 'more convenient'; 33, 30 and 30 per cent said that they were more 'directed to personal needs', with only 13, 13 and 7 per cent speaking of the 'sobering effect of combat experience'. Other factors included the influence of friends, a positive relationship with the chaplain, the greater importance attached to religion in army life, and the lack of an alternative means of spending one's time.[412] Significantly, of the Catholics, Jews and Protestants who had claimed that army life hindered their attendance at religious services, only a very few were prepared to state that they had simply no interest in them, amounting to only 14, 9 and 11 per cent respectively of Catholics, Jews and Protestants in this category.[413]

While the Santa Ana survey clearly exposed the positive effects of the religious influences that were inherent in service life, and thus points to the fact that religious life was not unaffected by what Michael S. Sherry described as 'the story of America's militarization' from the 1930s,[414] perhaps its most striking findings concerned the extent to which religious attitudes had changed as a result of overseas service, and also the direction of this change. First and foremost, a majority of Catholics, Jews, Protestants and those with 'no preference' stated that there had been no change, though this preponderance varied within each category, comprising 47, 54, 46 and 51 per cent respectively. However, 45 per cent of Catholics, 41 per cent of Jews, 39 per cent of Protestants and 32 per cent of the unaffiliated stated that their religious attitudes had changed and, in all four categories, the direction of this change was overwhelmingly positive, applying to 98 per cent of Catholics, 91 per cent of Jews, 99 per cent of Protestants and a startling 100 per cent of the unaffiliated.[415] When probed on the causes for this positive change, four main reasons were given, although (frustratingly) only the responses of Catholics, Jews and Protestants were actually recorded. Significantly, the principal reason was the same across the board, namely that: 'army life brought [a] new appreciation and understand[ing] of religion'. This answer was given by 54 per cent of Catholics, 54 per cent of Jews, but only 39 per cent of Protestants. There was also a notable discrepancy in how far members of these three groups thought that 'army life emphasized a need for the church', this being felt by 26 per cent of Catholics and 25 per cent of Jews, but only 7 per cent of Protestants. In a further mark of Protestant individualism, only Protestants (18 per cent of them, in fact) stated that 'in [the] combat zone one feels closer to God'. In terms of personal religious experience, 7 per cent of Catholics, 11 per cent of Protestants and 17 per cent of Jews asserted that 'danger brings a sense of reality to religion', the larger proportion of Jews possibly reflecting their particular sense of vulnerability in the war against Germany. Other, miscellaneous reasons that were given for positive religious change included 'revitalized prayers; confirmed belief in God; new tolerance toward others [sic] religious beliefs [and] a heightened interest in religion but no sectarianism'.[416] In explaining these patterns, Carpenter's successor as 'air chaplain', Gynther Storaasli,[417] placed a particular onus on the greater sense of the collective in Catholicism and Judaism. According to Storaasli:

> [T]he Catholic and Jewish personnel to a very much larger extent than the Protestant felt the increased need for the church. A possible explanation for this is that the Catholic and Jewish personnel more closely identify relations to the church with relations to God than do the Protestants.[418]

Essentially, therefore, this AAF survey underlined the fundamental resilience of faith, the largely positive trajectory of religious change, and the relatively minor importance of the combat experience as a catalyst for change in comparison with other, more institutional factors. Significantly, these findings were subsequently and substantially confirmed by those of civilian social scientists. For example, in autumn 1946 an article appeared in *The Public Opinion Quarterly* entitled '"The" Veteran – A Myth'. Written by Leo P. Crespi and G. Schofield Shapleigh (the former an assistant professor of psychology at Princeton, the latter a Princeton graduate), the article challenged the undifferentiated and sensationalised treatment of America's veterans by addressing 'some of the more important generalizations about the veteran's psychology',[419] specifically those concerning family relationships, independence, religion, sex and morals, alcohol, boredom and racial tolerance. Their means was a survey of 199 veterans then enrolled as Princeton students. There were, naturally, certain problems with this sample group. Historically, Princeton was a bastion of American Presbyterianism, whose renowned seminary had become a battleground between fundamentalism and modernism in the interwar years, the former having the worst of the fight.[420] Of the students concerned, all were aged between nineteen and twenty-nine, all had 'been at Princeton for varying periods prior to their military experiences', former officers and combat veterans were over-represented, and all of the respondents were white, the question on racial tolerance turning on whether African Americans should be admitted to the university ('long a moot point among Princeton students').[421] Nevertheless, the religious experiences of this sample of America's WASP elite tallied with those of other veterans. Of the group as a whole, when

384 of Uncle Sam

asked whether their religious faith had been affected by the war, 53.3 per cent said that it had 'not changed', 25.1 per cent said that it had 'increased', 18.6 per cent that it had 'decreased', and 3 per cent offered 'no opinion'. However, when the sample was divided according to age group (19–22, or eighty-eight members of the sample, and 23–29, the remaining 111), and between 'combat veterans' and those 'without combat experience'(representing 117 and 82 respectively), the pattern changed dramatically. The subcategory most likely to have felt a decrease in faith were non-combat veterans aged between nineteen and twenty-two, 26.8 per cent of whom reported to this effect, whereas those who reported an increase amounted to a comparatively meagre 12.2 per cent. In stark contrast, 41.4 per cent of combat veterans aged between twenty-three and twenty-nine reported an increase in their faith, while those in this subcategory who reported a decrease represented only 8.6 per cent. While demonstrating that, 'Among the older veterans there is a clear indication that combat causes increases in religious faith to far outshadow decreases',[422] as a result of their further investigations into 'sex and morals' Crespi and Shapleigh also came to the significant conclusion that combat veterans as a category were much more likely to have 'become less liberal in their moral attitudes'.[423]

These trends and findings were greatly amplified by the voluminous study of attitudes and behaviour in the US Army which was published in 1949 as *The American Soldier*. Based on wartime surveys conducted by the Research Branch of the Information and Education Division of the War Department,[424] and published by Princeton University Press under the aegis of the Social Science Research Council, this comprehensive survey reviewed issues ranging from job assignment and job satisfaction to attitudes towards the points system for redeployment and discharge. Inevitably, religious practice and attitudes came within its purview, and its first volume, subtitled *Adjustment During Army Life*, investigated the prior, civilian church attendance of wartime GIs. Significantly, and despite the abiding cultural equation of Christian and martial virtues, it concluded that former churchgoing habits had a 'negligible' impact on the ability of GIs to adapt to army life.[425] However, and on the basis of figures compiled in the winter of 1943–44,[426] it did indicate the extent to which GIs were, at the very least, anxious to identify themselves as churchgoers. According to these figures, only 16 per cent stated that they 'almost never' went to church, the rest ranging from 'several times a year' (16 per cent), through to 'once a month' (11 per cent), 'two or three times a month' (18 per cent), and 'once or twice a week' (39 per cent).[427] Furthermore, it indicated that more frequent attendance was largely associated with younger soldiers, those who attended church at least two or three times per month representing 45 per cent of those aged thirty and over; 51 per cent of those aged twenty-five to twenty-nine; 58 per cent of those aged twenty to twenty-four; and 71 per cent of those under twenty.[428] While this might suggest that the significant proportion of younger Princeton men who reported a loss of faith might have been starting from a much higher rate of practice, the second volume of *The American Soldier*, subtitled *Combat and Its Aftermath*, demonstrated how a felt loss of religion obtained among combat and non-combat veterans alike. In December 1945, a survey of enlisted men in the continental United States showed that 30 per cent of 'men with combat experience' and 35 per cent of 'men without combat experience' felt that their time in the army had made them 'less religious'; in contrast, 29 per cent and 23 per cent respectively felt the reverse.[429] Once again, however, these figures served to highlight the bifurcation of religious faith and religious behaviour for, when asked whether their army career had increased or decreased their 'faith in God', 79 per cent of combat veterans and 54 per cent of non-combat veterans stated that it had increased their faith, while only 19 per cent and 17 per cent said it had decreased.[430]

The American Soldier also underlined the huge importance of personal prayer, which, it acknowledged, had very much 'become a matter for popular bromides'.[431] As we have discussed, it showed that among combat veterans prayer had been the most important of 'possible sources of support in combat', exceeding even the comforts and demands of comradeship and 'the loyalty code'.[432] Among combat officers, on whom rested the burden of command, and for whom a concern not to let 'the other men down' loomed larger as a source of support, 'prayer was still said to help a lot by larger proportions than found it helpful to think of "what we were fighting for," "hatred for the enemy," or of "having to finish the job in order to get home again".[433] Prayer had, in short, proved to be the psychological mainstay of the American infantryman in World War II and, unlike other sources of psychological sustenance (such as 'thinking of the meaning of what we are fighting for', and 'thinking that you had to finish the job in order to get home again') the importance of prayer did not diminish over time; on the contrary: 'If there was any difference between men of different lengths of combat experience, it was in the direction of the old-timers' being more likely to say they were helped a lot by prayer.[434] While this dependence on prayer had no discernible correlation with a soldier's educational background,[435] in addition to more experienced combat soldiers, prayer was especially important to those who had been subjected to greater degrees of combat stress.[436] Significantly, the compilers of *The American Soldier* made no judgement as to the qualitative value of prayer offered under these circumstances, stating only that: 'What the act of prayer implied probably varied greatly from one man to another, depending among other things on his previous religious beliefs.[437] They also acknowledged there was 'practically no data available to throw light on the interesting question of the relationship between prayer in battle and formal religion'.[438] Nevertheless, and in the light of a clear growth in personal faith, they acknowledged that there was 'some evidence of a lasting effect of the battlefield experience upon religious attitudes'.[439] Certainly, this appears to have been the inference drawn by the American press upon the publication of *The American Soldier* in 1949. As a United Press article put it in a syndicated story that was splashed in a slew of 'provincial papers':

> PRAYER HELPED KEEP TROOPS GOING, VETS REVEAL IN SURVEY
> Prayer helped more than anything else to keep American GI's fighting when the going was tough during World War II … Second only to prayer as a source of support in combat was the thought 'that you couldn't let the other men down.'[440]

Besides these broader trends, a further indicator of the spiritual health of the armed forces was the number of vocations to the ministry and priesthood they produced. Given the hard years of the Depression, the gender dynamics and missionary imperatives of American religious life, by the end of the war it seemed as though the armed forces were poised to deliver a crop of seasoned, muscular men of God into the hands of America's churches. Fortified by the benefits of the GI Bill, these would reinforce and reinvigorate the ranks of the nation's clergy and help to consolidate and exploit the religious gains of the war. As Ralph Douglas Hyslop, of the Congregational-Christian Board of Home Missions predicted early in 1945:

> The entrance into the Christian ministry of numbers of men who have served in the armed forces of the country should result in an impressive strengthening of our whole ministry. Like the Chaplains who will return to churches after the war, these men will have few if any illusions about war itself but will have greater knowledge than most of us of the nature and capacity of the human spirit under tension. They will be older than the usual candidate for ordination, when they complete their training. The necessity of adjusting to civilian life after life in the armed forces will have matured them and prepared them for later adjustments which are often difficult for the young minister. We ought to expect, in the next twenty-five years as in the last, that some of the strongest ministers will be men who have seen action.[441]

In the later stages of the war, identifying and mentoring this new generation of clergymen was of growing concern to army and navy chaplains. For example, in August 1944 Chaplain Clyde E. Kimball was confronted with a somewhat problematic call to the ministry, noting in his diary that: 'I talked with a boy tonight who has little education but wants to be a minister. He decided so on the beach on D Day.'[442] In Hawaii that autumn, and as the 4th Marine Division prepared for Iwo Jima, Chaplain John Harold Craven found himself in charge of 'fourteen men who were going to study for the ministry'. Eventually, they requested 'some classes in theology', which Craven provided twice a week after his Bible study.[443] A more ambitious effort was mounted by a Congregational-Christian

AAF chaplain, Wade L. Carter, who organised in his heavy bombardment group 'a gospel team' from those who were interested in the ministry. The role of its members was to lead Carter's evening services and their improvised training consisted of courses in 'Old and New Testament, logic, sermon preparation and public speaking'.[444] Despite these local initiatives and responses, in general terms it took some time for chaplains' efforts to attain any semblance of coherence. In fact, it was only late in 1944 that William R. Arnold's monthly circular letter included 'a form on which the names and military addresses of aspiring postulants were to be reported'. Even then, less than 10 per cent of army chaplains in the ETO made use of it, preferring to provide 'personal educational assistance' in the form of courses, 'theological books' and 'periodic conferences', or to detail 'such aspirants as enlisted assistants to chaplains of their own faith, under whom the opportunity to try their vocation would be more easily available than in the ranks'.[445]

Early in 1945, however, the General Commission on Army and Navy Chaplains began to take a lead. That April, an article in *The Chaplain* magazine urged its readers to take a more proactive approach to 'Recruiting for the Ministry', reminding them that: 'Tomorrow's church leadership is largely in your hands'.[446] Nor did it hesitate to sound the tocsin, warning of the urgent need to 'Man the Church' in the post-war years:

> There will probably be far too many technicians after the war, and far too few workers-with-people, including church leaders. The ministry's median age is 45.8, older than any other major professional group except veterinarians …! Young men aren't coming along to replace our older ministers, and many thousands of churches slump below the level of self-support because they are pastorless. Dozens close yearly because they lack able leadership. At the same time, missions candidates for postwar days are far too few to match either the needs or the financial resources already available. Has church begun to mean something to an able young service man? Then show him that he can help man it, vigorously, to keep it strong and expanding.[447]

While *The Chaplain* appealed to its readers, in the summer of 1945 its sister magazine, *The Link*, carried a two-part feature by Chaplain Willard S. Smith entitled 'The Ministry as a Life-Work'. Here, Smith discussed the nature and practicalities of a ministerial calling, advising against undue haste and stressing the need for proper discernment. He also emphasised the need to like people ('*all* people'), to be able to relate appropriately to men and to women, and to embody 'a glow that is friendliness and compassion and the love of the Master in one'.[448] Finally, he discussed the sheer variety of ministerial work both at home and abroad, the various ways of making ends meet as a minister, and the massive importance of having an understanding wife.[449]

These appeals were backed, significantly, by a concerted attempt to identify and harness prospective candidates for the ministry. Commencing in January 1945, the Office of the General Commission, which appears to have instigated Arnold's earlier circular, began to write to chaplains directly, requesting details of interested parties that could be forwarded to their respective denominations. By mid-April, 'one thousand names had been received from 580 chaplains', the result representing a 'fine show of Protestant unity' and, in the words of a senior Presbyterian, 'the most encouraging thing for the ministry in the last ten years'.[450] These individuals came from the army and the navy, they included a conspicuously large number of sergeants and corporals, two WACs (who wished to undertake missionary work), 'and one man of Jewish faith'. There were, nevertheless, only twenty African Americans among them.[451] Still, by August the number of names had risen to 2,000, climbing to 3,789 by October (a dividend, no doubt, of the end of the war in the Pacific) and to 4,750 by June 1946.[452] Even allowing for the accumulation of candidates in the armed forces over the war years, this total represented a significant augmentation of America's younger Protestant clergy, of whom fewer than 65,000 were under the age of forty-five in 1939.[453]

However, senior army chaplains appear to have been piqued by the results of a scheme that had gone so well without them. From the ETO it was churlishly alleged that 'a preponderant majority were members of denominations which do not make exacting demands in terms of educational and religious background upon candidates for their ministries'.[454] Similarly, of the 4,750 names that had been received by June 1946, another source sniffed that: 'It was found that for many of these both entire college and seminary courses would be required.'[455] However, the commission itself was justifiably pleased by the results. Far from representing a ragbag of fringe denominations, of the names received by October 1945 two-thirds were those of Methodist, Baptist, Presbyterian, Lutheran and Episcopalian laymen.[456] Moreover, the scheme represented a triumph of ecumenical endeavour, being hailed as 'the most constructive united effort Protestantism has thus far initiated in enlistment for the ministry'. In fact, its success served as a catalyst for a new FCC Commission on the Ministry, which corresponded with service candidates and liaised with nearly two hundred seminaries on their behalf.[457] This was clearly an important task for, in their apparent concern to pour cold water on the General Commission's recruitment scheme, it was also claimed by senior chaplains in the ETO that recent levels of seminary enrolment hardly reflected this vaunted surge of interest in the post-war ministry.[458] However, this body of prospective candidates did not stand fully qualified and on the cusp of seminary training, as many recognised, but occupied a broad spectrum of educational attainment, and one that did not neatly conform to 'the customary routine of a ministerial education', namely: 'Grammar school, high school, college, seminary'.[459]

Although this ministerial dividend could only be realised in the longer term, census figures indicate that between 1940 and 1950 the number of priests, ministers and rabbis in the United States increased from approximately 133,000 to 161,000.[460] Furthermore, and according to Mark Noll, by 1950: 'Protestant and Jewish seminaries were enrolling twice their prewar numbers, and Catholic institutions also experienced substantial increases.'[461] Among those ordained in 1949 was Paul Moore, a former marine officer and future Episcopalian Bishop of New York.[462] According to Moore, his decision to enter the priesthood arose directly from an experience on the Matanikau River on Guadalcanal:

> I remember when I was leaning over trying to bring one of my men to safety seeing bullet marks in the sand around my feet and thinking, you know, if I get out of this, maybe it means I should do something special. There was a feeling – I don't know if it's very good theology, whether it's superstition or what, but certainly I felt that I had been extremely fortunate, and that I was, in a sense, living on borrowed time, and this was another good reason to give my life to the Lord, and it seemed that being a priest was the way.[463]

However, disentangling the war experience from other, antecedent factors was often more difficult. There were those for whom the war had interrupted existing plans, or for whom training for the ministry or priesthood was a logical extension of civilian trajectories. In December 1945, *The Chaplain* reported:

> The Methodist Commission on Chaplains reports that more than 500 candidates for the Methodist ministry have been reported to them. Of this number, 296 have been leaders, officers, or have taken part in the Youth Fellowship groups in their home churches. Some decided to enter the ministry after joining the armed forces.[464]

It was clearly not the case, therefore, that foxholes made clergy in quite the same way that they were deemed to make Christians.

Still, service candidates were definitely thought to be worth having. While many universities, and even seminaries, made concessions for returning veterans in terms of their curricula and entrance requirements,[465] the GI Bill could only offer limited assistance towards a course of ministerial training that could last for up to eight years beyond high school. For instance, service men and women under the age of twenty-six, and provided they had served for more than six months, qualified 'for the payment of tuition, fees, textbooks and other expenses' for only a year at an institution of their choice, besides receiving '$50 a month for subsistence and $75 per month for married men.'[466] Consequently, more affluent and prestigious seminaries were willing to lend special assistance to former GIs, with New York's Union Theological Seminary inaugurating in 1945 a '$60,000 program to provide scholarships for returning servicemen interested in training for the ministry.'[467] In May 1946, and placing the success of the General Commission's recruitment campaign in the wider context of the armed forces' demobilisation policies, the director of the FCC's Commission on the Ministry emphasised the higher significance of the whole venture. According to Dr. John Oliver Nelson, the ultimate strength of the ministerial calling had ensured that the whole initiative had succeeded because the higher intentions of those involved were 'unaffected even in combat'.[468]

If gauging the motives, numbers and impact of the veteran-turned-clergyman on America's Protestant churches is inherently difficult, the situation is not much clearer with respect to the Catholic Church. The decades prior to World War II had seen a dramatic increase in the number of Catholic priests in the United States and, between 1880 and 1930, the number of its secular and regular priests increased fivefold.[469] Not only is it hard to disaggregate war-related vocations from this pronounced longer-term trend but, in the dioceses of the north-east, the pace of growth actually slackened between 1930 and 1960.[470] Still, it seems that the military experience of millions of young Catholic men did nothing to arrest, still less reverse, a dynamic of growth in the American priesthood that was to culminate in a record number of almost fifty-four thousand priests by 1960.[471] Indeed, it seems clear that returning servicemen played a major role in the unprecedented post-war expansion of America's contemplative monasteries, especially after the publication of Thomas Merton's *The Seven Storey Mountain* in 1948.[472]

Besides those called to the ministry, rabbinate and priesthood, there was also a heavy onus on the churches to cultivate veterans in general, and especially those whose faith had been found, or reawakened, while in the services. This point was naturally pressed by serving chaplains; as Eben Cobb Brink put it: 'Our problem is, not that men shall find faith on a battlefield, but that they shall not lose that faith which they have found.'[473] Warming to his theme, he urged that:

> The Church of Christ must not fail these boys of ours when they come home again. They must be able to hear from its pulpit the stirring story of God's love for all mankind; they must learn from its Sacraments the meaning of fellowship offered to man by the Saviour; they must share its program and its services, knowing that the Church of Christ can justify its existence only when these programs and services reach out into every community to touch the hearts and lives of all men.[474]

Harry P. Abbott saw the situation in even starker terms, declaring that: 'The churches now have the greatest challenge they have faced in their history.'[475] Consequently, he sketched a rehabilitation programme that local churches could follow, one that included the formation of veterans' groups, the appointment of veterans to positions of responsibility within the church community, and even the establishment of 'Sunday-school classes for veterans, their wives and sweethearts, with a recreational program ... including banquets, dramatics, and games of the proper type, that the church can and will become the social center for the returning veteran' in lieu of the USO and 'similar organizations'.[476] As long as veterans were properly handled, so Abbott averred: 'I have no qualms for the future as far as the church is concerned, or the spiritual life of America; providing the churches meet the challenge that is set before them.'[477]

Nor was this perceived hankering after the churches merely pious supposition. As revealed in *The American Soldier*, when in April 1945 nearly four thousand GIs in the ETO were asked to indicate which organisations they were active in before the war, and which organisations they intended to be active in on their return, the church led the field in both cases by a very considerable margin. Although it no doubt strained the definition of the term that 62 per cent of non-high-school graduates and 72 per cent of high-school graduates claimed to be 'active' in their churches before the war, 72 and 78 per cent of them respectively wished to be active on their return. Moreover, and as one commentator put it: 'Whether the men were as fully integrated ... as they wanted to believe is less important than the fact that they wanted to believe it and that they expected to be even more active after the war than before the war.'[478] Significantly, the lessons of the war in this respect were being studied and digested as it was still being fought, a process assisted by a constant and sizeable flow of discharged servicemen back into civilian life.[479] In June 1944, *The Link* surveyed some of the religious projects that were already in place for the benefit of the returning veteran. A Methodist church in Oregon, Illinois, for example, had formed a 'Post-War Planning Committee' on the understanding that, 'confetti, parades and welcoming speeches will not be enough for returning service people'. The Congregational-Christian Church, meanwhile, had mounted a national effort to form 'study commissions' across the country, each being charged with examining 'one special problem church people will confront' with the coming of victory. Furthermore, and anticipating a welter of mental health problems, the Federal Council of Churches had organised 'some sixty seminars to train chaplains, civilian pastors and U.S.O. workers, physicians and nurses and Red Cross people in the art of counselling'.[480]

Among the religious benefits accruing from the war, many were also tempted to perceive a palpable increase in mutual forbearance among the principal faith traditions. In 1944, Chaplain Ellwood C. Nance maintained that the war had, above all else, underlined the need for religious toleration and cooperation:

> [W]hile we are appraising the faith of our fighters ... in the Army and the Navy, it is the usual thing to respect each other's faith, to co-operate with each other in obtaining the common blessings of religion in the life of each unit and military community. An exclusive sectarian appeal will receive a poor response from the majority of our servicemen.[481]

From the rehabilitation subcommittee of the War Services Committee of the Disciples of Christ, Ewart H. Wyle, a former chaplain who had been discharged on health grounds in 1943, expanded on this view. Reconverting American soldiers into American civilians would, he stressed, be a prolonged business.[482]

There were, however, 'five methods of approach' by which churches could smooth the transition from serviceman or servicewoman to civilian. Above all, there was a need to model the forces' spirit of religious tolerance, for: 'Be assured that if we insist upon worshipping at the altars of nonessentials, intolerant bickerings, and quarrels, we shall worship without these men who found something big in God and in his church.'[483] In addition, church programmes had to be expansive, varied and vibrant, for: 'No longer can the church confine itself to a program of preaching, praying, and singing.' The need to allow veterans to share responsibilities was also emphasised, as was their capacity to take the lead in the 'difficult' aspects of local church programmes, especially 'scouting, athletic activities, teaching posts, and missionary efforts'. Finally, churches should share the veteran's profound appreciation of peace, so that they were prepared to 'embrace all mankind in a Christian and God-fearing brotherhood.'[484]

Book-length studies of this issue pursued these themes. Published in 1945 and hailed as 'the first manuscript of book proportion on this specific subject',[485] *The Church and the Returning Soldier* by Dr Roy A. Burkhart, the pastor of a dynamic 'community church' in Columbus, Ohio, ranged over a number of critical issues. Underlining the importance of the churches in the context of small-town and rural America, from which more than 40 per cent of soldiers came, Burkhart stressed the long-term dangers of an anti-civilian animus among GIs, and the importance of the churches as counterweights to potentially divisive and self-serving veterans' organisations.[486] He also showed how churches, when grounded in their wartime efforts to support their service personnel, could legitimately reclaim their returning veterans while providing a new kind of ministry that catered for their physical and psychological needs. Conscious of the efforts and the resources this would require, Burkhart called for a new kind of ministerial training and for a more managed and professional church programme, one that was best provided by 'community-centred', ecumenical churches like his own.[487] Published later in 1945, and widening his focus to include civilian war workers as well as service personnel, J. Gordon Chamberlin addressed the 'whole range of problems related to demobilization' in his book *The Church and Demobilization*. As a member of the Methodist Church's Department of Christian Education of Adults, Chamberlin warned of the need to be sensitive to infinite variations in the outlook and experience of individual veterans. Nevertheless, he agreed that the churches should seek to mitigate the post-war employment situation, that vigorous wartime programmes mounted by individual churches should give them considerable purchase over their returnees, that civilian ministers needed to hone their counselling skills, and that church work with veterans should be pursued along the same lines as that with 'young adults'. Whatever else, the churches should strive for the reintegration of veterans, not the creation of a distinctive veterans' subculture. However, on a national level Chamberlin advised that the churches should foster links with veterans' organisations, if only to be on hand to lift 'the quality of memorial services for those who gave their lives, so that these services will not become maudlin but will be instead worthy remembrances of the cause for which so many died'.[488] According to the December 1945 issue of *The Chaplain*, Chamberlin's book represented 'a very able treatise that will give any local pastor or committee just the kind of briefing they need if they are to be awakened to their opportunities'.[489] By this time, however, this type of preparation was often well advanced; in December 1945 *The Chaplain* reported that the FCC had created a new Commission on the Church's Ministry to Returning Service Men and Women. Under Burkhart's chairmanship, this partly superseded its now defunct Christian Commission for Camp and Defense Communities.[490]

The end of 1945 also saw the publication of a pamphlet entitled *Going Home*, which according to *The Chaplain* magazine was available 'free' and 'in quantity'. Written by a former Methodist navy chaplain, J.L. Ellenwood, it included a foreword by Harold E. Stassen (Minnesota's 'Christian statesman' turned navy officer)[491] and was published jointly by the SMCL, the YMCA and the Salvation Army, copies being 'distributed personally by the chaplain and from literature racks in separation centers, chapels, and other strategic spots'. Its purpose was to remind the veteran that, 'while you are looking for a job and taking part in the veterans' group, you should not forget the church on the corner [which] should be your church'.[492] However, the role of the chaplain at separation centres went well beyond the distribution of literature. Indeed, and to balance the prominence of the chaplain in the navy's reception process, the assignment of 'civil readjustment' chaplains to the navy's separation centres was authorised early in 1945, their duties being to 'address groups of dischargees and be available for personal interviews when such were desired'. By VJ day, at least one Catholic and one Protestant chaplain were attached to each of these centres and, at its peak, around 150 navy chaplains were engaged in this work. At certain locations, it was estimated that well over 50 per cent of dischargees availed themselves of the opportunity of a last interview with the chaplain, many leaving with letters of introduction to their prospective civilian pastors.[493] Reviewing the chaplain's contribution at one of these centres, a naval officer, William Luitje, remarked that chaplains dealt with problems that 'ranged all the way from gripes to honest-to-goodness moral questions'.[494] However, and in addition to a host of marital problems, Luitje also observed that: 'There were many religious questions. Some men had found new interests as far as religion was concerned and they wondered how they would be received in the home to which they were going.'[495] In terms of their message, Luitje noted that:

> The Chaplains were in charge of the Discharge Ceremony talks. These talks featured the lessons that the men had learned unconsciously as a result of their experience in the navy. As for example, loyalty, self-discipline, the will to win, a world view, tolerance in religion and the idea that 'A man's

a man for a' that.' Their responsibilities as citizens and their pride in their service were pointed out to them ... In short the talk was as inspirational as possible in giving the men something to think about as they went into civilian life again.[496]

In contrast, the equivalent work of army chaplains appears to have been much less defined. Assigned to the army's separation centres, it was noted that:

The official duties connected with separation centers were perhaps less important than those seemingly unofficial duties which the chaplains took upon themselves in reestablishing contact between the men being separated and the civilian churches. Many chaplains ... made it a practice to notify home pastors, especially those of their own denomination, of the names of the men about to be separated and the probable dates of discharge.[497]

In terms of veterans' organisations, the overriding emphasis on the reintegration of veterans into wider church communities and structures helped to scotch any hopes that the SMCL would emerge as a Christian veterans' organisation at the end of the war.[498] According to *The Link*, this hope was born out of a reaction to the rightist politics and even loutish behaviour associated with the American Legion and the Veterans of Foreign Wars.[499] An added stimulus was that a Catholic veterans' organisation already existed, the Catholic War Veterans of the United States of America (CWV) having been created by a former Catholic army chaplain in Astoria, New York, in 1935. Armed at its foundation with the blessing of Pope Pius XI, the CWV was to be at the forefront of Catholic anti-communist agitation in the post-war years.[500] Nevertheless, in December 1945 *The Chaplain* reported that the nation's largest Protestant denomination, the recently reunited Methodist Church, was very much against the formation of a Protestant equivalent:

Church-related veterans' organizations should not be fostered or encouraged, in the opinion of the Committee for Veterans Affairs of the Methodist Church.... Instead, churches are advised by the committee to help veterans become part of the usual activities and programs of the church on an equal footing with others. Veterans are urged, however, to join and participate in the general veterans' organizations.[501]

Conclusion

The experience of America's bloodiest foreign war naturally helped to promote the currency of William T. Cummings's claim that 'there are no atheists in foxholes'. However tendentious and strongly contested, this dictum was current well before Americans felt the full impact of spiralling casualties in 1944 and 1945. There were, of course, other situations that were likely to stimulate a religious response, captivity being a conspicuous example, but none was more widely felt or anticipated than the experience of combat. The defining expectation of military life, even for conscientious objectors in uniform, the threat of combat loomed larger as victory approached, with shortages of front-line manpower helping to ensure that support troops were fed into combat roles and veterans of the ETO earmarked for what was feared would be an apocalyptic invasion of Japan. Inevitably, the experience and the threat of danger served as a major religious stimulant in a society that was overwhelmingly composed of religious believers, however untutored in their faith or irregular in their going to church or synagogue. In this context, the simple act of personal prayer played a critical role for those exposed to combat, its importance possibly heightened by the accentuated prayerfulness of the American home front, which continued to supply a steady stream of recruits for the armed forces throughout the war.

Even in the most technologically advanced armed forces in the world, the myriad imponderables of war (especially for aviators) encouraged a strong reliance on prayer and fostered the use of talismans, a widespread sense of fatalism and a pronounced belief in luck. However, such phenomena could not be easily disaggregated from the world of more orthodox religion, as the wearing of rosaries and the carrying of metal-clad Bibles serves to illustrate. Besides helping to confute Max Weber's vaunted equation of industrial and technological progress with the 'disenchantment of the world', the growing loss of life in Europe and the Pacific also focused attention on the afterlife, an interest that steadily grew in the armed forces as the war reached its climax in the summer of 1945. Against this background, eventual victory in Europe and the abrupt end of the war in the Pacific gave a new and inexpressibly welcome lease of life to millions of young Americans, a fact that helps to account for the favourable patterns of religious change detected by a slew of contemporary surveys. Spared – seemingly providentially – from the ordeal of further conflict, determined to realise their idealised visions of home, and perceptibly influenced by the religious provision of service life, millions of veterans returned to churches that were prepared to receive them, and were ready to benefit from their commitment, their veterans' privileges and their post-war prosperity.

Chapter Five

Global Encounters

Introduction

I<small>N</small> November 1943, a Lutheran American army chaplain, Israel Yost, baptised seven Japanese-American soldiers in a ceremony in southern Italy. As Yost remembered:

> This was a unique event: it took place in an Italian Roman Catholic church converted for the time into an American aid station; the pastor was a German American and the new believers were Japanese Americans; one of the witnesses, Sergeant Akinaka, was a member of the Church of Latter Day Saints (Mormon); the other witness, Doc Kometani, told the converts that this was the most important decision they had ever made.... That evening two of the medics sang Hawaiian songs to guitar accompaniment; they included two hymns in Hawaiian, 'Leaning on the Everlasting Arms' and 'Jesus, Savior, Pilot Me'.[1]

This almost surreal vignette captures in vivid tones the often surprising corollaries of the wartime encounter between a wider world of faith and America's ethnic and religious melting pot. Citizens of a country that was highly regionalised and economically self-sufficient, David Reynolds has remarked that: 'There was, revealingly, no national newspaper and most Americans had spent little time beyond their home state, let alone visited New York or Washington, D.C.'[2] Insular and isolationist attitudes had been reinforced in interwar America by the outlook of first- and second-generation immigrants from Europe, who had typically sought to leave the troubles of the Old World behind them. World War II, however, forced many of them to return, albeit temporarily, and created an American military diaspora of vast proportions. In overall terms, about 73 per cent of American servicemen served overseas between 1941 and 1945, with the average sojourn lasting sixteen months.[3] As one veteran and academic commentator wrote in 1946:

> During World War II and the subsequent military occupation, American soldiers were dispersed to every corner of the globe. Perhaps eight million [sic] were at one time or another engaged in foreign service. No continent, few countries, and few islands failed to receive at least some military or naval representatives of the United States.[4]

Whether serving in Europe, the Mediterranean, Asia or the Pacific, these peregrinations often had a religious dimension. A few GIs, for example, went as Christian or as Jewish pilgrims to the Holy Land, and a great many more to early Christian sites in North Africa and Italy.[5] After its liberation, Rome in particular proved to be a massive draw and Americans (seemingly regardless of denomination) flocked to papal audiences – which had been denied to the Germans.[6] In fact, their unusual decorum on these occasions prompted misgivings on the part of Pius XII, who confided to Mark Clark that: 'I think your American soldiers do not like me … they do not utter a sound. They do not say one word.' In response, Clark assured the troubled pontiff that American soldiers were 'less demonstrative and that their background prompted them to maintain a reverent silence in the presence of the head of the Roman Catholic Church'.[7] However, such questions of etiquette were but a minor detail of the American encounter with the religious beliefs and practices of so much of the contemporary world. As this chapter will show, Americans were strongly inclined to understand their enemies and their allies in religious terms, their reactions to certain societies and cultures being heavily influenced by a sense of religious commonality, or difference. Furthermore, these reactions often had far-reaching implications for the post-war world, helping to cement the 'special relationship' between Britain and the United States, to advance the rechristianisation of much of Germany, and to fuel the post-war boom of the international missionary movement.

The war against Nazi Germany

As products of pre-war and wartime American society, America's GIs, marines and bluejackets were bombarded by images and portrayals of their Axis foes that were heavily coloured by religious themes and concerns. For example, in his 1942 booklet *A Salute to the Men in Service*, Daniel A. Lord, the influential Jesuit writer and champion of public morality, spelled out the deeper meaning of their struggle against the Axis powers, a war that he saw as a struggle of radically conflicting ideas. On the one hand, there were the convictions held by Americans, chief of which was that 'God is the Creator of our country and the guarantor of the freedoms of our Constitution'. From this flowed others – that the individual had inalienable rights; that justice should be accorded to all; that minorities should be protected; that the home was sacrosanct; 'that Christ's law of love is to be expressed in charity toward one's fellow men, and in care of the sick and the weak, and in protection of the defenseless'. All of this the Axis held in utter disdain, and so 'made war on God, the Creator and guarantor of our liberties'.[8] If 'Mussolini and his black-bloused thugs' had failed to convince Italians, Hitler and Hirohito had met with more success, at least temporarily: 'Hitler set himself up above God. The Mikado turns out to be god on earth. The Nazis kicked Christianity and Judaism, from which Christianity sprang, into the concentration camps, and substituted the beer-swilling gods of Valhalla.'[9] From the poisonous fountains of pagan apostasy and heathen idolatry flowed other evils, notably the Nazi concentration camps, 'the rape of Nanking' and the awful threat of Hitler's New Order in Europe and the Pacific. In this New Order, dominated by self-styled races of 'supermen', political and religious dissent would be crushed, minorities enslaved (or worse) and, in the case of the Nazis at least, women degraded to objects for 'the creation of new soldiers or new robots for the leader'.[10] The faults of America's British and Soviet allies were but minor flaws by comparison, and the alignments of the war could hardly be clearer:

> Christ has been banished from Germany; he was never welcome in Japan … There they are, side by side, their ideas and ours…. We want the old glorious ideas to continue and the fine basic ideals to flourish. And we'd die rather than have the slavery of the Nazi and the pagan cruelty of the Jap sweep across the world and take dominance over our country. We are fighting for the glorious ideals and ideas of a Christian America. We have no intention of letting a pagan tyranny and brutality take us by the throat and squeeze from us the principles that Christ gave us and our Founding Fathers put into heroic practice.[11]

Ever since Hitler took power in Germany in 1933, American fundamentalists had speculated on his significance for the end times.[12] More commonly, anti-Nazis in the United States had widely recognised the pagan, anti-Christian character of the Nazi regime, its celebrity pre-war victims ranging from the famous Protestant churchman Martin Niemöller to the 'musical Catholic family of Baron Georg von Trapp'.[13] Indeed, so anti-religious was Nazism deemed to be that its persecution of the Jews was seen more in this context than as a corollary of its vicious, pseudo-scientific anti-Semitism.[14] Such was the strength and credibility of the Nazi threat to religion that it offered the best ground on which Roosevelt could rally support for his administration's pro-Allied posture in the face of isolationist, pacifist and even pro-Axis sentiment. Besides presenting Hitler's onslaught against the Jews as a function of Nazi irreligion, the administration's religious propaganda stressed the plight of persecuted German churchmen and the danger that the Nazi world view posed to the religious values and fundamental cohesion of American society.[15] Accordingly, and as Roosevelt sought to secure Lend-Lease aid for Britain in January 1941, the president named freedom of worship as one of the 'four essential human freedoms' that the United States sought to uphold, claiming nine months later in a Navy Day address that Hitler planned to replace the Bible with *Mein Kampf,* and to abolish all of the world's religions in favour of an 'International Nazi Church'.[16] In a speech to the Free World Association in May 1942, Vice President Henry A. Wallace acclaimed the Bible as the source of human freedom and vowed that Americans would 'drive the ancient Teutonic gods back cowering into their caves', warning that: 'The

Götterdämmerung has come for Odin and his crew.' Hitler and his minions were, according to Wallace, the very agents of Satan, whose 'religion of darkness' was characterised by its odious racial conceits.[17] In 1943, a particularly lurid poster published by the Office of War Information amplified these sentiments, picturing a Nazi dagger plunged through a Bible over the caption 'THIS IS THE ENEMY'.[18] In the light of these perceptions and depictions of Nazism, the liberation of Rome in June 1944 held particular significance for the president, and not only because it was the first Axis capital to fall:

> [W]e ... see in Rome [Roosevelt intoned] the great symbol of Christianity, which has reached into almost every part of the world. There are other shrines and other churches in many places, but the churches and shrines of Rome are visible symbols of the faith and determination of the early saints and martyrs that Christianity should live and become universal ...[19]

Despite the 'cautious patriotism' modelled by some American churchmen at this time,[20] Lord's fulminations show that others were more than prepared to echo these views. For example, 1943 saw the release of *The War Against God*, an anthology compiled by the author and folklorist Carl Carmer and published by the New York publisher Henry Holt. As a concerned layman, and in the democratic spirit inherent in Christianity, Carmer sought to demonstrate that Hitler and his cronies were 'engaged in a deliberate attempt to annihilate the Christian religion'.[21] On the basis of the evidence he adduced, and of the examples of Christian resolve he applauded, Carmer proclaimed that: 'Now we may sing "Onward, Christian Soldiers" honestly, knowing that every soldier of the armies of the United Nations fights on the side of the Christ, his motto no longer "For God and country," but "For God and a brave new world".[22] However, and despite the force of this rhetoric, it was nevertheless recognised that the fragile ties of a common Christianity still held between Americans and ordinary Germans. In 1943, Stewart W. Herman published *It's Your Souls We Want* with Harper Brothers, another major New York publisher. Based on his experiences as the United Lutheran pastor to the interdenominational American Church in Berlin from 1936 to 1941,[23] the purpose of Herman's book was, 'to provide a factual basis and a few of the most essential insights' concerning the critical question of whether the German people would ultimately put their faith in Christ or in Hitler.[24] Dedicated to the 'Confessional' (or Confessing) Church, Herman's book reflected a common awareness that, however much German Christianity had been threatened by Nazi persecution, the self-sacrificial stand of resolute churchmen – both Protestant and Catholic – had ensured that the light of true Christianity had not been extinguished, a fact that offered hope for the post-war redemption of the German people.[25]

Despite, and even because of, the GI's perceived lack of ideological commitment to the war, determined attempts were made to identify his (or her) struggle with the cause of religion, among others. As William R. Arnold put it for the *Washington Post*: 'We are at war with pagans, atheists and Satan himself ... the forces of Christ and humanity have never lost a war and can never lose one.'[26] This assurance was shared, and echoed, in many other quarters. One of the most famous propaganda posters of 1942 featured Joe Louis, the African American world heavyweight boxing champion, wielding a bayonet under the caption, 'Pvt. Joe Louis says – "We're going to do our part ... and we'll win because we're on God's side"', sentiments he had aired just before enlisting.[27] At Christmas 1943, the editor of the *Marine Corps Gazette* even struck a militant note in relation to the babe of Bethlehem, arguing that:

> Christmas means peace. But not 'peace at any price', not a peace of compromise, or of injustice, or of timidity. If that had been the kind of peace that Christianity stood for, it never would have emerged from Palestine. It would have died with its Founder, and you and I, unless we were students of obscure incidents of ancient history, would never have heard of it. But Christianity was militant; its followers literally conquered the world, and they must be militant if they are to do so again.[28]

Likewise, from a Memorial Day service held in a large military cemetery in Italy in 1944, the American war correspondent Eric Sevareid reported how a senior chaplain 'announced over the loud speaker that the men who lay dead before us had died in the cause of "true religion"'.[29] According to Kevin M. Schultz, the message of religious unity and tolerance so assiduously preached and published by the National Conference of Christians and Jews throughout the war must have had an effect: 'Justifying the fight in cosmic terms, giving the very real possibility of death some meaning, and advancing a religious justification for national goals like tolerance and unity must have been compelling during a vicious war.'[30] Even Hollywood played its part. The first of seven 'orientation' films in the *Why We Fight* series, which was produced by the Information and Education Division of the War Department with the assistance of the director Frank Capra,[31] sought to underline the religious dimensions of America's war. Released in 1942 and entitled *Prelude to War*, the film stressed the Nazis' attack on religion and presented their persecution of the Jews in this context.[32] It was, in fact, indicative of how ingrained these convictions had become that an investigation of the reception of this film among army trainees detected no significant shift in existing attitudes – '75% of the men believed at the outset that Hitler would "close all our churches" if he could conquer America', and 82 per cent already believed that he 'would "persecute and torture Jews and other minority groups"'.[33] Furthermore, and despite a discernible ignorance of 'the "Four Freedoms" concept of war aims' among army recruits as late as the summer of 1943 (only 13 per cent could name more than two),[34] the Victory Medal, awarded to all who served in the armed forces between 7 December 1941 and 31 December 1946,[35] was point-

edly inscribed with the whole quartet – 'FREEDOM FROM FEAR AND WANT
... FREEDOM OF SPEECH AND RELIGION'.

The Link magazine also tried hard to urge upon its readership the religious
meaning and necessity of war against Nazi Germany. In April 1943, and echoing
the *United Presbyterian*, it published the text of 'the profession of faith prepared
for the replacement of Christianity by the Nazis, as written by Rudolph Hess'.
In it, the Nazi faithful prayed for victory in 'the great struggle between German
humanity and all the races of the earth' and professed adherence to *Mein Kampf*
and its commandments, and to the führer 'unto eternity'.[36] In 1944, it reported
on the Nazi wedding ceremony, deploring its neo-pagan, National Socialist flum-
mery and fuming:

> ADOLF HITLER has dreamed up a lot of *ersatz* things for the benefit of his
> 'master race'. But none more strikingly demonstrates his fanatical desire to
> banish all 'foolish Christian customs', as he bombastically describes them,
> than the Nazi wedding ceremony ... By such paganistic hocus-pocus do
> marriage-minded Nazis become man and wife.[37]

The Link also stressed that the self-appointed champions of the so-called master
race were not content to merely frolic around sacred fires, mystical shrubs or
beneath pictures of the führer, for theirs was a persecuting zeal. Consequently,
it dwelt on the Nazi assault on the churches, reviewed publications such as
Herman's *It's Your Souls We Want*,[38] and reported on Nazi infractions of religious
freedom, such as the ban on religious services in German prisons, which applied
'even in the case of prisoners awaiting execution'.[39] *The Link* was also happy to
echo the clarion words of Jan Christian Smuts, South Africa's prime minister,
minister of defence and commander-in-chief:

> This at the bottom is a war of spirit ... [Hitler] has sought strength in the
> ancient and discarded forest gods of the Teuton. His faith is a reversion
> of the pagan past and a denial of the spiritual forces which have carried
> us forward in the Christian advance that constitutes the essence of Euro-
> pean civilization.... He has trampled underfoot the great faith which has
> nourished the West. He has trampled on the Cross and substituted for it a
> crooked cross – a fit symbol for the new devil worship which he has tried to
> impose on his country and the world. Nietzsche's superman is substituted
> for the Man of Nazareth as the new leader of the human race.... Behind
> all the issues of this war lies a deeper question now posed to the world.
> Which do you choose – the free spirit of man and the moral idealism that
> has shaped the values and ideas of our civilization, or this horrid substitute,
> this foul obsession now resuscitated from the underworld of the past?[40]

In keeping with wider perspectives, the resistance of German churchmen and
of the churches in Nazi-occupied Europe was seen as a beacon in the night. In

its second issue of March 1943, *The Link* magazine proclaimed 'LET NO MAN THINK that Christianity has lost its ancient readiness to suffer martyrdom rather than surrender to the pagans who would banish it.'[41] This verdict was based on the impression that church resistance was growing in Germany and that, as in the United States, Protestants and Catholics had formed a united front against the menace of Nazi apostasy:

> Evidence accumulates that Hitler is bent on the destruction of traditional Christianity in Germany. The effect of this blanket assault has been to consolidate all religious forces in at least a passive resistance to National Socialist ideals ... There is undoubtedly an interfaith solidarity in Germany today never before witnessed. Among loyal Christians of all faiths the persecution of the church has been a means of rallying support to the cause of religion generally.[42]

In March 1944, the magazine was tempted to conclude that the worst was now over, and that collective church resistance had succeeded in turning the Nazi tide:

> The year 1943 will probably go down in history as the period which witnessed the breakup of National Socialism as a spiritual menace. One of the chief factors in the Nazi failure was their inability to crush the churches. Religious groups gained considerably in influence during the past year, according to available evidence, and emerged as a body likely to play an important part in the reconstruction of Europe after the war.[43]

Among the symptoms of Nazi defeat was the success of 'a great evangelism campaign' by the Dutch Reformed Church and its publication of a defiant 'Wartime Confession of Faith' that denounced anti-Semitism as 'one of the most stubborn and deadly forms of rebellion against God'. Also encouraging was 'the growth of German church resistance during the year', manifested by the abandonment of 'a tradition which has caused them to remain isolated from public affairs.'[44] Just how far some German churchmen had moved in that direction was signalled in January 1945, when *The Link* reported that: 'A number of active church laymen were executed in Germany after the July attempt on Hitler's life.' According to the general secretary of the World Council of Churches, such 'aggressive action' was yet another positive sign that the Christian church was on the march.[45]

Given the needs of the hour and the parameters of this highly dualistic narrative, *The Link* simply turned a blind eye to the complicity of the so-called 'German Christians' in the attempted Nazification of German Protestantism, and overlooked the conduct of those German Catholics who likewise found Nazism congenial.[46] Indeed, it took a Jewish chaplain to hazard the view that: 'Were it not for the miserable failure of their churches, the fanatical voice of Hitler might have fallen on deaf ears.'[47] However, *The Link* could and did find room to reproach the Confessing Church for the qualified nature of its opposition to Hitler. In May 1943, and noting that 90 per cent of its pastors were now thought to be serving in the Wehrmacht, it reported the words of a Swiss churchman, Dr Arthur Frey, who criticised the Confessing Church for its quietist approach to wider German politics:

> Frey praises the church for persistently fighting Nazi doctrines, but insists that the policy of Confessional [sic] leaders in confining themselves to opposing Nazi doctrines only within the church, and not carrying their opposition with equal vigor into politics, is responsible for the 'misery and weakness' of the German Confessional Church today.[48]

In short, the limited stand of a few was not sufficient to outweigh the sins of the many, a view that subtly condoned the massive destruction that was visited on Germany and its people by the Anglo-Americans from 1943 onwards. Indeed, in March 1944, and with the Combined Bomber Offensive making headway against the German war effort, *The Link* claimed that the unleashing of Allied fury was accepted as condign punishment by German civilians, many of whom were turning to the churches for solace and succour:

> Chain letters asserting that the bombing of Germany by the Allies is 'a punishment from God' are being widely distributed in Berlin.... Being circulated surreptitiously, the letters quote passages from the Bible to prove that the bombings are not due primarily to British and American air squadrons, but are a means through which God is severely punishing the German people.... Several German newspapers have warned that it is a political offense to print or circulate such letters.... The reaction of many German people to repeated bombardments has been to turn increasingly toward religion for comfort, and churches in various parts of the country are reported crowded with visitors.[49]

Naturally, the position of *The Link* was shared by its younger stablemate, *The Chaplain* magazine. In December 1944, for example, it portrayed Hitler's view of the war as 'a great battle for humanity's liberation from the curse of Mount Sinai', and claimed that his followers had revelled in defying every one of the Ten Commandments: 'Every sin condemned has been glorified as a service to the dictator and the Master Race – killing, lying, adultery, covetousness, every one of the ten, even to the second – making an idol out of a mortal and putting him into the place of God.'[50] Likewise, and taking as its text Ephesians 6:12 ('We wrestle against principalities, against powers, against the rulers of the darkness of this world'), in May 1945 *The Chaplain* published an essay by Edward L.R. Elson, a Presbyterian (USA) army chaplain, which compared present times with those of St Paul. Not only was totalitarianism 'the dominant political doctrine of St. Paul's day', but Nazism stood as 'a paganism as blatant and ruthless as anything the early Christians beheld'. Given Hitler's 'demonic conception of a nation', it was the bounden duty of all Americans 'to preserve our heritage and our life as a covenant nation'.[51] As for the German people, the justice of their fate seemed as undeniable as it was inexorable. Reporting an interview between an Associated Press correspondent and a German army chaplain, *The Chaplain* emphasised the latter's plight within the German military and, most of all, his admission that, 'God's punishment on us is terrible but deserved, as far as the nation as such is concerned. Hitler once promised that in ten years he'd make Germany a place nobody would again recognize. How terribly prophetic have these words proven!'[52] A year after the end of the war in Europe, and quoting from *Theology Today*, *The Chaplain* rejoiced in the shattering of Nietzschean hubris and in the utter vindication of the authority and power of the Christian God:

> 'GOD IS DEAD', wrote Friedrich Nietzsche in the second half of the nine-teenth century … God died and Superman was born. But what happened? God's death in the minds of men brought moral disintegration, cultural anarchy, cold cynicism, the dissolution of international law, and, finally, a world catastrophe … In these last years Superman, the Man-God, has fought the God-man and every influence that came from Nazareth by all the means in his power. Master races have tried to establish new orders in which the life of mankind would be repatterned after their own image. Today, in consequence, the nations writhe in the fierce flame of God's judg-ment, and 'the inhabitants of the world' have a supreme opportunity to learn righteousness.[53]

These views and assumptions were, significantly, shared in the wider army. Clearly, they sustained the typology of the Allied war effort as a crusade – a concept that, as we have seen, was warmly embraced and trumpeted by Eisen-hower. In March 1943 George S. Patton, while steeling his II Corps for its attack on Gafsa in Tunisia, urged its chastened and inexperienced GIs that, although their German adversary was 'a war-trained veteran', his defeat was a foregone conclusion if only for religious reasons: 'We are brave. We are better-equipped, better fed, and in the place of his blood-glutted Woten, we have with us the God of Our Fathers Known of Old'.[54] Nor was the army newspaper *Stars and Stripes* any more equivocal in its commentary on the overarching significance of the war: 'Gone With Their Gods Are the Godless', its *Warweek* supplement rejoiced on 12 May 1945:

> 'GOTTERDAMMERUNG' … means 'twilight of the gods'. Applied to Hitler and Mussolini it might better be translated 'twilight of the false gods'.… Everywhere, free men know now that the thing which produced Hitler – which produced beautiful optical instruments, broad speed highways, jobs for Germans as well as the piles of stinking corpses at Belsen and Dachau,

Buchenwald and Ohrdruf – was a kind of perverted religion ... 'I believe in god the Fuehrer,' was the sacrilegious statement which Josef Kramer, Nazi commandant at Belsen, made in an interview with a Warweek reporter.... If the world takes the wrong course it will be because we let it happen, because we will have left a chance for the false gods to appear again.[55]

In case GIs had any scruples about the devastation visited on Germany, *Stars and Stripes* was also ready with compelling confirmations of the remorseless justice of Allied conduct. On 21 March 1945, for example, it reported the return of a Catholic bishop to the ruins of Cologne:

The Most Rev. Wilhelm Stockums, Senior Auxiliary Bishop of Cologne, had been hunted since last June by the Gestapo for telling his congregation that he 'prayed to God' for Allied bombers to 'reduce' his church – the beautiful, world-famed Dom Cathedral – to 'dust' before permitting 'the pagan master of this land' to convert it into a Nazi monument.... Last week the Bishop celebrated a solemn requiem mass for U.S. troops a few hours after he had been discovered in his hiding place –an old folks' home – by Capt. Peter Wiktor, an 8th Division Catholic chaplain from Detroit.... The mass was celebrated for 'fallen heroes of the American Army' as well as for the deliverance from Nazi bondage of millions of German Catholics.[56]

Furthermore, it could call upon the testimony of first-generation German refugees serving in the US Army. As one of their number, a son of the novelist Thomas Mann, wrote in *Warweek*: 'They Saw Hitler as ... Their Messiah' and, consequently:

The complete defeat and extinction of the Hitler regime is a vital necessity, not only for my new homeland, the United States of America, but also for the whole world and, in particular, for my former country, Germany. The Germans who still fail to see this will have to be taught a terrible, lasting lesson.[57]

If service personnel had problems in memorising the four freedoms, the extent to which they internalised the prevailing religious narrative of the war against Germany should not be underestimated. Long before their dreadful discoveries at Dachau, Ohrdruf, Nordhausen and Buchenwald in the spring of 1945, there was ample evidence of Nazi depravity. As early as April 1943, a marine aviator seethed from the Pacific: 'Trust in God. Trust in Him to bring this barbarism to a finale.... Feel sorry for the demagogues ... for surely their souls ... shall know no rest and they shall burn in eternity.'[58] A few months later, and outraged by the Vatican's apparent preference for a negotiated peace, Captain Curtis C. Davis, of the 324th Fighter Group, wrote to his mother from Italy:

This is a war for keeps; and we will not rest satisfied until starvation and butchery have been visited upon German soil. There can be no parleying with the Devil. There is no such thing as a conditional victory; for then neither side is the conqueror, and the issue is still undecided. It is an all-or-nothing question and I for one trust that many a head will fall.[59]

In December 1944, and accompanied as it was by the ruthless execution of dozens of Belgian civilians, the massacre of eighty-six American prisoners by the Waffen SS at Malmédy 'sent an electric shock through the U.S. Army';[60] however, this simply reprised conduct that had been encountered in Normandy six months earlier. In that instance, SS troops had executed more than twenty American prisoners, mostly wounded paratroopers, captured in the village church of Graignes. Among other victims of this lesser known massacre were their teenaged French nurses and two French priests, Abbé le Blastier and Fr Charles Lebarbarchon, whom the Germans 'found guilty of aiding the enemy'.[61] Moreover, the conduct of the Germans at Graignes was consistent with what was widely thought to be an utter disregard for the sacred. As Albert J. Hoffmann's chaplain's assistant wrote in November 1943:

Father [Hoffmann] tells me he always thought the stories about German atrocities were 'baloney' but since the invasion of Italy he knows better. He was with the first of us who entered a small Italian town and he went right to the Church. There he found the tabernacle broken open and filled with rubbish. The chalice was broken and the candlesticks, too. The Stations of the Cross were thrown over onto the floor and the vestments were torn and scattered all over. What the Germans do not take with them, they destroy.[62]

In keeping with wider assumptions, non-Jewish GIs largely understood the persecution of the Jews as religiously motivated. It was in the spirit of Judeo-Christian solidarity, therefore, that many rallied to protect their fellow, Jewish, POWs.[63] At Stalag II-A, for example, Chaplain Francis L. Sampson and Sergeant Harley Lucas, 'the American "Man of Confidence"', protested the separation of most 'Jewish-American prisoners from the rest of us', concerned about 'possible reprisals against them as the war drew to a close'.[64] More dramatic was the experience of Pfc Johann Carl Friedrich Kasten, a Honolulu-born GI of German extraction who was captured in the Ardennes and later appointed 'Man of Confidence' at Stalag IX-B at Bad Orb. Although a professed atheist, when summoned by the camp authorities to produce 'the names of all the Jews in the American camp', Kasten simply replied: 'We are all Americans, we don't differentiate by religion.' Badly beaten for this show of defiance, he was further punished by being sent to a slave labour camp at Berga after warning his fellow POWs not to cooperate in the imminent round-up (in the event, their frustrated German captors were reduced to walking down the assembled lines of American prisoners, hauling out those

who simply 'looked Jewish').[65] Furthermore, and despite the brutal and pernicious nature of Nazi ideology, Christian GIs required little persuading of their
underlying religious affinity with the Germans they fought. This was illustrated
by their reaction to the motto *Gott mit Uns*, which was traditionally engraved on
German army belt buckles, and to the *balkankreuz*, the stylised cross still emblazoned on German aeroplanes and armoured vehicles.[66] While the rules of war
were generally observed, if only through a sense of enlightened self-interest,[67] the
ubiquity of Americans of German extraction (the majority of whom were Catholic or Lutheran, and the most conspicuous of whom was Eisenhower himself)
also emphasised the limits of German otherness. Given this ethnic and cultural
proximity, and further sustained by influential propaganda tropes that stressed
Christian survival in Germany, there was a very strong awareness of Christians in
the Wehrmacht. Among the clergy in particular, this could border on an instinctive sympathy. In 1943, Edward K. Rogers, a United Lutheran army chaplain, had
an illuminating conversation with a captured German army chaplain in Tunisia:

> This priest had found it necessary to go secretly to the chapel to say mass.
> Little opportunity was given to chaplains to minister to the soldiers. They
> are not assigned to line troops, as we assign our padres, but have to stay
> some twenty miles back of the front. There is, as a result, little opportunity
> to minister to the dying and dead in the lines. It occurred to us that perhaps
> the German Army just kept chaplains 'on the books'.[68]

Much later, in northern France, Rogers inadvertently captured a German infantry
officer who turned out to be a Lutheran pastor, prompting a further revelation:
'In Germany the clergy are drafted for service as soldiers. He had been called into
the service when the war began and then sent to officers' school. He had fought
in France in 1940 and for two years in Russia where he had been wounded.'[69]

For another United Lutheran chaplain, Israel Yost, the religious state of
German prisoners was a matter of compelling interest. In May 1944, he prayed
in German with a badly wounded prisoner who had identified himself as '*evan-
gelische*'; two months later, he wrote to his wife:

> Recently speaking to several prisoners [in German] I asked, 'Are you
> Catholic or Evangelical (that is, Lutheran)?' One answered 'Neither.' Said I,
> 'You are Nazi then?' 'Yes.' Another answered, 'I was Lutheran.' I countered,
> 'Why can't you say, "I am Lutheran"?' His reply was, 'I believe in God,' and
> the implication was that that was all he believed in. The others spoke up
> either for Catholicism or Lutheranism.[70]

Visiting captured German wounded in a hospital in Troyes in 1944, Chaplain
Alvin O. Carlson was spared a similar, depressing interview with one of the Nazi,
anti-Christian 'believers in God' – or *Gottgläubige*.[71] Instead, he was introduced
to a Lutheran pastor, and relative of Martin Niemöller, whose father 'had been

killed because of his stand against Nazism' and who was now serving as an NCO. Fatally wounded, the pastor was suitably penitent over Germany's culpability for the present war:

> I want you to understand that I don't condemn your nation. We are responsible for all this. Germany has sinned against God, and we are paying for it now.... I can't live long, but you will. Please remember this ... that not all people in Germany have yielded to Nazism. Keep on preaching the Gospel of the Bible, and men will some day help Germany to go the right way.[72]

In another ward of the same hospital, Carlson met a German layman, a colonel and the grandson of a pastor, with a very similar message:

> He asked me to pray with him and for him, that he might become renewed in his faith in God. He also gave me his medals and a leather case which I now have in my possession. He told me that he was sure that if Germany would return to the faith of Martin Luther, she would never make another attempt to conquer the world.[73]

The wartime odyssey of Catholic chaplain Francis L. Sampson, who had the rare distinction of falling into German hands on more than one occasion, was punctuated with signs of the survival of Catholicism amidst the weeds and tares sown by the National Socialist state. Saved from summary execution in Normandy by a German paratrooper NCO who 'snapped to attention, saluted, made a slight bow' and showed Sampson a miraculous medal,[74] Sampson later ministered to wounded German prisoners at an American field hospital:

> About sixty per cent of these Germans were Catholic, and they always made the Sign of the Cross when I took out the stole. They made acts of contrition and received Viaticum reverently as well-instructed and good Catholics. These, I later learned, were mostly from Bavaria. Many of them were in their early teens; some had not even begun to shave.[75]

Later, and having been captured once again at Bastogne in December 1944, he fell in with three German soldiers who all turned out to be Catholics and treated him 'with great respect'. Significantly, 'They wondered at a priest being in the army and said that although they had heard that their division had one chaplain (there are eighteen chaplains to a division in the American Army) none of them had seen him in two years of service.'[76] During his subsequent captivity, a German guard assisted with the creation of a camp chapel and others, who were regular communicants, chose not to reveal that a forbidden radio had been hidden in its pulpit.[77] In fact, the mildly seditious quality of a devout German Catholic, despite his own criticism of the German churches, even impressed itself on a Jewish chaplain, Morris N. Kertzer, who recalled his 'first face-to-face meeting with the Nazi' in a field hospital at Anzio:

The medical officer who stood nearby looked at the Nazi, then at my rabbinical insignia. He smiled and whispered, 'Tell him who you are and let's see what he says.' I leaned down again and asked the soldier a few questions. He was forty, father of two children, a resident of Bavaria ... 'Do you see this insignia?' I asked. 'It means that I am a rabbi, a Jewish minister who takes care of Jewish soldiers.' He looked up at me and remarked, 'I'm a Catholic. We both worship the same God. To the devil with Hitler.'[78]

Building on the pre-war celebrity of Martin Niemöller (who was widely invoked as an inspirational figure because of, rather than in spite of, his background as a World War I U-boat commander),[79] American servicemen were persistently reminded that there were fellow Christians serving in the Wehrmacht. The German fighter ace Werner Mölders (who, because of his staunch Catholicism and opposition to euthanasia, proved a problematic war hero from a Nazi point of view) was even held up as a religious role model, it being claimed that printed copies of his testimony of faith were often found 'among the personal effects of German soldiers on the fighting fronts to-day.'[80] Long before American airmen and ground troops closed in earnest with their German adversaries, the war at sea had underlined these commonalities between German and American Christians. In August 1942, *Yank* reported the burial of twenty-nine German submariners at Hampton, Virginia, 'the first enemy dead to be buried on American soil since the start of the war.' Interred with Christian rites, a Catholic priest and a Protestant minister both read a burial service over the graves, as: 'No one knew the faith of these men.'[81] However, when faced with a live congregation such gestures, with all their implied co-option, could backfire. When the *U-233* was sunk in the North Atlantic in July 1944, it was left to Sheridan Bell, a Methodist navy chaplain, to preside at the committal of its former captain from the flight deck of the escort carrier *Card*. Establishing that the deceased had been 'a member of the German Lutheran Church', Bell decided to drape the body with 'our church pennant which is the white pennant ... with the blue cross upon it'. With the survivors and most of the ship's company in attendance, he then 'read as a service a beautiful prayer for our enemies which is in one of our Navy handbooks', tempering this with a somewhat pointed scriptural text, namely Psalms 19:9: 'The judgments of the Lord are true and righteous altogether.' However, just as the body was committed to the deep, and before Bell 'could step back to the microphone and continue the committal service, the entire company of survivors whipped out the Nazi salute and in perfect cadence gave a farewell cry to their Commanding Officer'. As Bell remembered: 'Immediately following this outburst, which took us by surprise, I stepped up to the mike and was able to finish the committal service with its statement of the resurrection and the hope of the Christian faith.' [82]

Enduring religious commonalities with the Germans even informed the army's propaganda activities. While the Office of Strategic Services forged and circulated

Das Neue Deutschland, a newspaper that featured a column by one 'Fr Schiller', which urged surrender upon German soldiers in Italy,[83] the army also appealed to the enemy's finer instincts. In one of the most remarkable and widely reported incidents of the Italian campaign, on Easter Sunday 1944 a service was broadcast for the benefit of those Germans in their sector by the chaplains of the 349th Infantry Regiment, part of the newly arrived, and all-draftee, 88th Infantry Division.[84] Triggered by the idea of using loudspeakers to broadcast Protestant and Catholic services to GIs on the front line near Castelforte, the concept evolved to include their German adversaries as well, as: 'Since the Christian Religion is for all races and nations, for enemies as well as friends, it was finally determined to hold a short German service for the enemy soldiers at the very start.'[85] Preceded by the laying of miles of cable, the enlistment of an army nurse to sing Handel's 'I Know That My Redeemer Liveth', and the use of pack mules to bring up 'the organ and other equipment', the venture commenced with an address by Lutheran chaplain Oscar H. Reinboth, of the Missouri Synod. After reading the Easter Gospel in German, Reinboth continued: 'Should not all Christendom be jubilant this day? Should not all people rejoice – now that Christ died and rose again for all men – for Germans and Americans alike – therefore, I wish you also today in [the] name of my soldiers a Happy Easter.'[86] Whatever the feelings of the Germans may have been across 'the four hundred yards of devastated no-man's land', the ensuing American services were uninterrupted by enemy fire and, according to a United Press correspondent (one of a pack of photographers and war correspondents gathered to witness the scene), GIs even emerged from their foxholes to participate more directly in these Easter devotions.[87] The influential newsman David Lawrence drew out the deeper meaning of this episode – which he termed 'The big news of the week-end' – for his civilian readership:

> There was something courageous and sincere about that simple statement of faith, in the midst of an atmosphere of bloodshed and conflict…. When an American chaplain reminds the soldiers of an enemy country that Easter services are for them as well as for Americans, he is only saying that in the abstract sense the American people have no hate for another people as such, and that in his opinion Christianity offers a connecting link between peoples of like belief.[88]

Significantly, as Allied forces closed in on Germany, the US Army employed religion more directly as an instrument of psychological warfare. On a 'strategic level', leaflets containing German churchmen's statements of war guilt were dropped over Germany,[89] and , in local cases 'where interrogations of German prisoners-of-war indicated that an opposing force was homogeneously religious', the Psychological Warfare Division played on the anti-Christian character of the Third Reich and especially on 'the failure of the German army to provide adequate opportunity for religious worship and the anti-clerical attitude of National Socialism.'⁹⁰ Appeals made through loudspeakers 'in the effort to break down morale and induce surrender' included the following, which was employed by the Psychological Warfare Detachment of the 12th Army Group: 'Your leaders won't let you practice your religion. If you surrender, you will find in the American prisoner-of-war compound not only food, shelter, and medical care, but also a chaplain, and you can go to church services.' The same message was also relayed through 'a number of locally distributed leaflets.'⁹¹ Similarly: 'With the liberation of Luxembourg, the radio station in the capital, the most powerful on the Continent, was used to broadcast the Sunday High Mass from Luxembourg Cathedral in order to feed nostalgia and discontent among German Roman Catholic troops.'⁹² While these methods would have had little effect on Nazi zealots, it is worth remembering that, as the defence of the Reich became ever more reliant on the children of the Hitler Youth and on the older men of the Volkssturm, for the latter in particular, who had not been exposed to Nazi indoctrination in their formative years, such appeals probably had some resonance. Furthermore, it should be noted that the axis of the American advance passed largely through the traditionally Catholic heartlands of western and southern Germany,⁹³ areas that had been unsettled for some years by the anti-clerical and anti-Christian direction of Nazi rule and in particular by its sundry violations of the 1933 Concordat.⁹⁴ As a post-war survey of army chaplaincy conceded, 'the accidents of war caused a much larger percentage of Germans from Catholic regions to become prisoners than would be expected from the general religious distribution throughout the Reich.'⁹⁵ In fact, the conclusion drawn by its chaplains after the end of hostilities was that the US Army could have made more of the obvious potential to sow religious discord among its opponents, noting that:

> An unsuccessful effort was made in September 1944 by the Psychological Warfare Detachment of the 12th Army Group to secure the services of a Lutheran chaplain whose background and qualifications fitted him both for this aspect of the detachment's work and particularly also for the interrogation of influential enemy Churchmen. In future operations, such a need should be anticipated by adding to the staff of the psychological warfare organization at army level from the outset a chaplain of each major denomination likely to be encountered among the enemy.⁹⁶

After years of exposure to an impression of German apostasy, and fearing fanatical, Nazi-inspired popular resistance on entering Germany, the realities of contact with German civilians could prove perplexing. As early as 1943, when Chaplain Eugene L. Daniel arrived in Austria as a POW he was surprised to hear the familiar sound of church bells: 'To hear church bells as the first intelligible sound when we came to Germany was a surprise to me. I had been under the impression that most of the churches in Germany had been closed by the Nazis.'⁹⁷ In the course of his subsequent stay, Daniel was introduced to a discreetly anti-Nazi Lutheran pastor in Freising and was even shown round Munich by a friendly guard.[98] Later, and amidst the ruins of Catholic Cologne in March 1945, 'delirious civilians handed out beer and wine in a welcome that the soldiers could only describe as "terrific".[99] In contrast, at the village of Steinach in April, resistance to the advance of the 3rd Infantry Division included 'nuns who held up tanks by kneeling in the streets with upraised crucifixes'.[100] For GIs of the 90th Infantry Division, their advance through Germany provided the opportunity for an early visit to a renowned mystic and putative saint, namely the 'village stigmatic called Therese Neumann, who had allegedly cured local people of many illnesses. She also made cryptic utterances in Latin, Greek and what appeared to be biblical Aramaic, while her diet seemed to consist solely of communion wafers'.[101] On 22 April 1945, the visitors to her partially demolished home in Konnersreuth in Bavaria, which had been captured by the Americans only the day before, included chaplains, ordinary GIs and a correspondent and interpreter from the 90th's divisional newspaper.[102] Five months later, a chaplain's assistant from the 190th Field Artillery Group informed readers of the *Los Angeles Times* that he had seen Neumann on three occasions, and also that the stigmatic had successfully repelled an attempt by 'S.S. men' to arrest her.[103] In addition to illustrating the enormity of the Nazis' dechristianisation agenda, the Catholic landscape of much of southern and western Germany, and the general piety of the civilian population, confounded and confused earlier stereotypes. Writing in *The Chaplain* magazine towards the end of 1945, the Congregational-Christian Air Force chaplain Lawrence D. Graves averred that: 'Many soldiers have been astonished at the prevalence of religion and the observance of the practice of worship throughout Germany'.[104] As Peter Schrijvers has put it: 'Some GIs simply suspected the Germans of hypocrisy; others were at a loss and could only decide that "Germans have strange minds about religion as everything else".[105]

In fact, in preparation for the defeat and occupation of Germany a good deal of thought had been given to questions of religious policy. In 1944 a compendious civil affairs handbook on the Christian churches in Germany was prepared by the Research and Analysis Branch of the Office of Strategic Services (OSS), a source that was intended to convey 'the basic factual information needed for planning and policy making'.[106] For example, while the handbook described at length, 'The Nazi attack upon the Christian churches in Germany',[107] and especially the vicissitudes of the Confessing Church and the onslaught against Catholic organisations and education, it also noted that, as late as 1939, 94.5 per cent of the population of the Reich were at least nominal church members, 54.2 per cent being Protestants and 40.3 per cent Catholics.[108] Although high-level statements were made on this subject before and after this date, most notably at Potsdam,[109] for practical purposes the army's early religious policy in occupied Germany was defined in February 1945 by the civil affairs (or G-5) Division of the Supreme Headquarters Allied Expeditionary Force, being explained and contextualised in a publication entitled *Military Government Germany Technical Manual for Education and Religious Affairs*. Aimed at Allied officers responsible for these formative aspects of German life, its six chapters on religion discussed the organisation of Germany's major religious groups, the history of the religious press, the question of ecclesiastical property and the role of religious organisations in social work.[110] Keen to stress the importance of the task entrusted to them, Lieutenant General Sir A.E. Grasett, the British chief of G-5, warned that, 'The work to be attempted should be regarded as a crusade,'[111] its guiding principles being the removal of 'clergy guilty of undesirable political activity' and the enforcement of freedom of worship (even for adherents of the German Christian movement) as long as this freedom was 'not used as a cloak for objectionable political or military activity.'[112] While Kenneth Connelly noted how the former led to the arrest of a friendly church organist (and, it transpired, leading local Nazi) who had lent him the key to a picturesque village chapel,[113] the latter involved the full emancipation of former dissidents such as Martin Niemöller and the Jesuit Rupert Mayer, both of whom returned to their ministries under American protection.[114] Furthermore, Orval E. Faubus observed how their new-found religious freedom was welcomed with enthusiasm by civilians near Hanover. In this case, they celebrated with a parade, religious services, and with the dispatch of a civic delegation to the unsuspecting headquarters of the 320th Infantry Regiment:

> There was much bowing and formality on the part of our visitors as they made known the purpose of their call. We received them courteously but without much formality. They said the religious affair was the first of its kind in many years as Hitler had not permitted such ceremonies. We stated that as Americans we were glad to see religious freedom restored to them and to their country.[115]

However, this encouragement of religion soon evolved as a facet of the nascent stand-off against communism in Germany. As Orval E. Faubus also noted, when his regiment's Catholic chaplain returned to the United States, he carried with him a message from senior German churchmen to President Truman. Significantly, the crux of this message was that, 'the President had better move with dispatch to assume firm control in the American zone or the Communists would take over all of Germany and move into other countries further west.'[116]

In addition to exposing the new ideological fault lines in occupied Germany, this incident also underlined the place of the army chaplain as an important point of contact for the German churches, organisations that a post-war survey recognised as 'in many regions the only effective institution[s] through which the occupation powers could reorganize local communities,' as well as being 'one of the most important channels for the reorientation of the German mind.'[117] However, major problems were posed for chaplains by Eisenhower's non-fraternisation policy, introduced in September 1944. As it applied to chaplains, this forbade 'shaking hands with clergymen in connection with official visits' and required the strict segregation of mixed congregations in civilian places of worship.[118] While the war was still in progress, and as GIs 'enjoyed the right to commandeer the houses of enemy civilians as they saw fit,'[119] it could even result in the eviction of German clergymen by their American counterparts. As Charles E. Wilson, a chaplain's assistant in the 4th Armored Division, wrote of one such incident in March 1945: 'Today we occupy the best home in town, the home of the town priest.... Father O'Donnell tactfully requested the priest to move out. We moved in. No questions asked. No answers given. We pay no rent. We are conquerors here.'[120] Widely criticised by American chaplains in a shattered and vanquished Germany as 'undesirable', 'ineffective' and even 'unchristian',[121] their infractions of the non-fraternisation policy (common enough among GIs at large)[122] could have serious repercussions. In one incident, a chaplain was arrested and threatened with court martial for 'collaborating with the enemy', a case that led to a strident complaint to the War Department from a women's relief association in the United States.[123] In another incident, a Jewish chaplain, George Vida, was arrested for delivering food to a family of German Jews in Frankfurt.[124] However, the gradual relaxation of the non-fraternisation policy, first in relation to German children in June 1945, and then in relation to German adults 'on the streets and in public places' in July,[125] helped to pave the way for freer interaction. The Seventh Army, in an attempt to assist the work of de-Nazification in its area, and even before the policy of non-fraternisation was all but scrapped that October,[126] in September 1945 directed its chaplains to engage in activities with German youth.[127] Consequently, and in the area of a single American division, by the summer of 1946 tens of thousands of German youths had participated in sports activities, cinema shows and Christmas parties organised by American chaplains.[128]

However, Germany was not to be simply left to work out its own salvation under American tutelage, but was to be actively reclaimed for Christ; as Bishop Henry Knox Sherrill of the General Commission averred after a visit to the country late in 1945, 'the only nostrum for the recovery of Germany will be the application of the principles of the Gospel.'[129] By this time, at hand to assist in this process was a considerable body of would-be missionaries whose ambitions and optimism partly rested on signs of German receptivity, which had been detectable throughout the war. According to Chaplain Eben Cobb Brink, a clear indication had come as early as the Axis surrender in Tunisia in May 1943. Parking his chaplain's car – flying its chaplain's flag – in front of a column of German prisoners, Brink was approached by one of their number:

> He had recognized the flag – and because he loved the Saviour he had stopped to speak to the first Christian chaplain he had seen for a long time. One thing he wanted before he went back to the road to join the long column of his countrymen trudging on to the prison enclosures: to ask the

Americans to preach Christ to the men they were taking captive, to ask if there would be chaplains in the prison camps. 'We must have God with us when someday we go back to the fatherland, and you Americans must show him to us again, for we have lost him.'[130]

After leading a penitent and mortally wounded German airman to Christ, Chaplain Alvin O. Carlson was also convinced of the need for a post-war missionary offensive 'to the lands and peoples ravaged by war': 'We must seek the truth of God's Word and pray for spiritual guidance during the coming days of reconstruction. Ours is a glorious opportunity. *We must not fail.*'[131]

Understandably, for Lutherans especially there appears to have been a particular poignancy, as well as urgency, in rescuing their spiritual homeland from Nazi apostasy. In September 1945, *The Chaplain* magazine reported how a Lutheran chaplain from Florida, Arthur M. Weber, was now in temporary charge of an area that included Wittenberg, 'where Martin Luther began the Protestant Reformation';[132] four months later, it related how another Lutheran chaplain, Goodwin T. Olson, had visited Göttingen and had viewed what it thought to be 'the only complete Gutenberg Bible in existence', an artefact that predated the Reformation and was in much better shape than much of Germany.[133] Whatever the underlying symbolism of this encounter, the enthusiasm among American Protestants for the redemption of Germany – the soiled and upturned cradle of the Reformation – was widespread. Writing from Camp Claiborne, Louisiana, in January 1944, chaplain's assistant Kenneth A. Connelly declared:

Strange though it may seem, I have a burning desire to go to (or remain in) Germany after the war and discover just what happened within that mysterious, fanatical country while the outside world was locked out. I don't know what kind of a missionary I would make or what form my work could possibly take but I'd like to go into the camp of the enemy and 'talk it over.' After the war, after the slaughter ceases and a truce is declared, then something can be done. Then the real soldiers, the constructive thinkers and Christian doers, must come into action. I should like to join that army.[134]

This missionary impulse had also taken hold of American Baptists. According to the very first issue of *The Chaplain* magazine, by the autumn of 1944 the nation's Baptists were already mobilising for post-war action in new and war-ravaged mission fields:

Baptists, with over a million youths in the armed forces, are planning to send missionary recruits close on their trails into enemy-relinquished lands. 'We believe,' writes one of their editors, 'that nothing will more effectively detach men and women from the hatred generated in them by the war than the comprehension of the gospel of Christ.'[135]

In 1946, F.H. Woyke, a Northern Baptist army chaplain with the 279th Station Hospital in Germany, reported to fellow Baptists on some encouraging portents of post-war work in Germany. Although German Baptists were few, less than 0.1 per cent of the population in 1939,[136] and their infrastructure lay in ruins, Berlin's Baptists appeared to be a resilient sort and were 'carrying on as best they can.'[137] Furthermore, the venerable American Bible Society was on hand to help with the missionary effort in the immediate post-war months and, in September 1945, *The Chaplain* reported that, 'The largest single order for the Scriptures – 350,000 copies – ever received in the 129 years of the American Bible Society' had been 'recently shipped to Europe.'[138]

Although army chaplains were not responsible for religious affairs in occupied Germany, they did have much greater control over the hundreds of thousands of German POWs captured by the Americans during the course of the war. Among the high-profile duties undertaken by certain chaplains after the end of the war in Europe was their ministry to Nazi war criminals, and most notably to Hermann Göring.[139] Although one of the supreme figures in the Nazi movement and the Nazi regime, Göring had been widely considered as a 'prominent and sincere Protestant', having married his second wife in a Lutheran ceremony in 1935, and having their daughter Edda baptised as a Lutheran.[140] Indeed, and from the heights of his position in the party, Göring had openly scoffed at Nazi neo-paganism, while his credentials as a Lutheran layman had been sufficiently strong for him to have been considered as an ideal secular head of the Reich Church by some prominent figures within it.[141] Consequently, some cautious optimism was entertained of the spiritual, if not bodily, reclamation of the reichsmarschall, *The Chaplain* announcing in January 1946 that, 'CHAPLAIN Carl Eggers reports that he spent a short time discussing the Scriptures with Herman [sic] Goering who seemed to have studied the Bible extensively', adding that: 'The chaplain is the former pastor of the Hope Lutheran Church, Tonasket, Washington.'[142] However, in Göring's case such hopes turned out to be illusory, the reichsmarschall proving to be a capricious and contradictory captive under the ministry of Eggers's successor and fellow Missouri Synod chaplain, Henry F. Gerecke.[143]

Despite the notoriety of these prisoners, an ordinary POW's freedom to worship was guaranteed under the terms of Article 16 of the 1929 Geneva Convention Relative to the Treatment of Prisoners of War,[144] an obligation taken very seriously by the War Department. Raised by civilian churchmen: 'Even before any prisoners were taken, the matter of their spiritual care was the subject of discussion between church organizations and the Office of the Chief of Chaplains.'[145] Asked to permit the FCC and YMCA to assume responsibility for 'the spiritual welfare and recreation of prisoners of war interned within the United States', the Secretary of War instead insisted 'that the religious ministrations were to be under Army chaplains.'[146] Accordingly, the provost marshal general was 'authorized to designate certain buildings at prisoner-of-war-camps as separate places of worship,'[147] and 'Prisoner-of-War enclosure chaplains' were recognised as one of the forty specialist categories of army chaplain.[148] However, there were considerable variations in the degree, organisation and nature of the care provided. For those 425,000 Germans and Italians captured in Europe and shipped across the Atlantic to work in the United States,[149] theirs was a relatively privileged and even comfortable lot in spiritual as in temporal terms.[150] In contrast, arrangements for German POWs in continental Europe in 1944–45 were swamped by the scale of Germany's defeat. As a post-war report explained:

> While the chaplains assigned to the prisoner-of-war overhead detachments assumed pastoral care for the prisoners of war, there was no coordinated overall policy for ministrations to such prisoners, and a wide difference was noted between the ministries provided in England, where conditions were relatively static, and on the Continent. At first, the unexpected magnitude of the problem led to a considerable amount of confusion. Assignments of chaplains to prisoner-of-war enclosures were not always made on the basis of particular fitness for the work, but on current chaplain availability.... Conferences of prisoner-of-war chaplains were infrequent. On the Continent, amid the movement of battle and the rapid processing of prisoners-of-war to the rear areas, ministrations were of necessity sketchy and only emergency pastoral ministrations with infrequent regular religious services were provided.[151]

As the steady flow of German prisoners became an inundation in the spring of 1945, the chaplains of the reconstituted 106th Infantry Division, together with numerous hospital chaplains, were diverted into the work of ministering to POWs.[152] Nevertheless, even under these circumstances there was scope for energetic chaplains to make their mark. Responsible for tens of thousands of German POWs in Italy at the end of the war, Wallace M. Hale, the Southern Baptist division chaplain of the 88th Infantry Division, duly embarked upon a vigorous programme of rechristianisation:

> Undertaking to destroy the so-called 'Nazi Religion', a by-product of National Socialism, Chaplain Wallace M. Hale set about to bring a rebirth of Christian religion to the German prisoners under 88th control. Chaplain Hale organized and directed his assistant chaplains, representing several faiths, in screening former German chaplains and ministers from the ranks of the PWs. Religious essentials of equipment were borrowed or improvised and when the screening was completed, a Chaplains Corps was set up and functioning in the remnants of the German Army for the first time since 1942 when the Nazis virtually had abolished the office.[153]

According to Hale, under these conditions church attendance reached 70 per cent among POWs,[154] although a lack of alternative recreations certainly helped (as the 88th's assistant division commander put the situation: 'They're out there, and if they want to play tiddlywinks it's OK … If they don't, that's okay too').[155]

Although the strategy of making use of German clergymen to minister to their fellow prisoners had been in place in the ETO since January 1945,[156] given the circumstances that prevailed in the intervening period it was not until August that it could be put on a proper footing. Nevertheless, from this point on, and under the oversight of a senior American chaplain based in Paris, the goal was to recruit a Protestant and a Catholic chaplain for every two thousand POWs. As American chaplains returned home to be discharged, these German chaplains could even assume responsibility for their American captors. 'An interesting outgrowth of this situation', so Roy J. Honeywell noted, 'was a number of arrangements by camp commanders for German chaplains to say Mass and hear confessions for American troops in places where there was a shortage of American chaplains.'[157] However, and even if the role of American army chaplains in this aspect of the rechristianisation of Germany soon became one of supervision, this was still a task that demanded considerable ingenuity and industry. As the ETO's theatre chaplain pointed out as early as August 1944, it was often very difficult to establish the credentials of captured clergymen as 'identifying papers … prayer books, bibles and Mass kits' were usually confiscated en route to POW compounds. Even when they had been screened and approved, there was very little equipment –and in particular 'German Bibles and Scriptures' – to furnish them with.[158] Furthermore, an element of training was desirable and: 'In England, a school for prisoner-of-war clergy was established with courses in democracy, religion, and homiletics, but the end of the war came before a parallel program was generally introduced on the Continent.'[159] Nevertheless, by October 1946 no fewer than 474 German clergymen, both Protestant and Catholic, had been engaged by the Americans to minister to German POWs in the ETO alone.[160]

In the United States, the religious work of army chaplains with Axis POWs took place in scores of base and branch camps, under the authority of the chief of chaplains and backed by agencies such as the YMCA, the American Bible Society and the World Council of Churches.[161] Individual denominations also played an active role. Given the shortage of Catholic chaplains in the army, Catholic ministry to POWs necessarily devolved upon civilian auxiliary chaplains.[162] Furthermore, in September 1943, and on the assumption that around 45 per cent of German prisoners were 'of Lutheran heritage', the Emergency Planning Council of the Lutheran Missouri Synod offered help with the vetting of prisoners who claimed to be Lutheran clergymen, the supply of 'approved hymnals, devotional literature and German Bibles', the ministrations of civilian clergy and, lastly, with 'the general welfare of prisoners of war' as defined by the military authorities.[163] In time, such work bore fruit in the opening of a 'Little POW Seminary' for the benefit of German prisoners at Fort Lewis, Washington,[164] and in the baptism of a German POW in the baptistery of a Baptist church in Oklahoma.[165] However, and despite these reassuring signs, the rechristianisation programme got off to a rocky start. After the first sizeable tranche of German prisoners, captured in Tunisia, arrived in the United States in 1943, there were clear signs of active resistance. That September, Chaplain Harry C. Fraser wrote a memorandum to the chief of chaplains citing some widespread problems; in addition to the need for German-speaking Catholic and Lutheran chaplains, there were also the difficulties posed by an element of hard-core Nazis. According to Fraser:

> Separation seems inevitably called for where sentiment varies from indifference and war-weariness to violent Nazism. In some camps this anti-christian attitude has made services well nigh impossible. Boycott of services is practiced, if not enforced by local 'kangaroo courts' of Nazi indoctrinated persons. Grim looking individuals scrutinize, for future consideration, prisoners who do attend service. This is not so true where the lower grades of enlisted prisoners are segregated and where humane hospitalization, or where kindness and consideration, has made its impression on the impressionable.[166]

At the same time, it was also reported by Bishop John F. O'Hara that, while 'Reports from practically all the prison camps are laudatory and optimistic', a 'handful' of German prisoners at Camp Blanding, Florida, had 'proved recalcitrant', telling a visiting priest not to return.[167]

As in Europe, a heavy reliance was also placed on the ministry of captured clergymen to their fellow POWs; as a Catholic source explained: 'The use of these priests as chaplains has greatly facilitated matters, and has lessened considerably the demand on commissioned chaplains for this work.'[168] However, in this respect things also got off to a shaky start. In November 1943, O'Hara petitioned the chief of chaplains for 'the transfer of Father Langer from Camp Mexia, Texas; Father Langer is violently anti-Nazi', O'Hara explained, 'and the Nazis there make it hard for him'.[169] At the same time, the Office of the Chief of Chaplains was weighing a complaint against a Protestant clergyman, Lieutenant Rudolph Letz, who was interned at Trinidad, Colorado. An effective pastor, who got on well with the American chaplain in charge, Letz nevertheless continued to mention Hitler in his services, praying openly 'that God would protect him'.[170] However, by the end of the war matters had improved considerably, 'largely through the increased use of prisoner clergy and through the greater availability of civilian clergy to assist the chaplains'. Doubtless, the outcome of the war also helped to mute Nazi opposition. By the middle of 1945, it would appear that around a hundred American army chaplains, assisted by 'some 300 German auxiliary chaplains', were serving German POWs in the continental United States.[171]

Naturally, this ongoing mission among former members of the Wehrmacht on both sides of the Atlantic did not escape the attention of the American religious press. In 1946, the experience of Paul Gebauer, a Southern Baptist chaplain and former missionary to Cameroon, was recounted in a Baptist celebration of wartime faith entitled *Religion in the Ranks*. In a camp for seven thousand German POWs, Gebauer had befriended a German pastor from East Prussia who, after a little gingering up, led 'one hundred and fifty-six SS men' to Christ within a week.[172] By this time, however, the religious responsiveness of German POWs had been reported to a service readership for three years by *The Link* and, more latterly, by *The Chaplain* as well. Given the position of its American military readership in relation to its subjects, this coverage was initially ambivalent. In November 1943, *The Link* reported without comment the words of the American newspaper correspondent Jay Allen, who had been in German custody after the fall of France:

> Jay Allen was on the dais of the Overseas Press Club. He listened to a speech by Inez Robb, the newspaper woman. Mrs. Robb recently had returned from a tour of the prisoners-of-war camps in America. She told of the bronzed Nazi prisoners, of their camp jobs, and then said, significantly, that most of the prisoners attend religious meetings ... 'I know about Nazis and their religion,' Allen spoke up. Two years ago he was in a Nazi jail in Paris after he had been arrested trying to cross the border. 'In that jail the religious meetings were long and well attended. The Nazi jailors [sic] showed how devout was their faith by torturing the prisoners only AFTER the religious sessions were over.'[173]

However, there was a perceptible softening of attitudes in 1944. In June, *The Link* published a letter from Sergeant Hiram D. Lucas, a surgical assistant at Camp Livingston, Louisiana, recounting the dilemma he experienced over how he should treat two Germans under his care:

> Yes, I had two Nazis at my command – they were completely in my hands – with guards and bayonets all around. Should I treat these patients with contempt and revenge, withholding the anesthetic so that their operation might be one of suffering, of pain and torture? Or should I treat them Christianly and humanely and take their case just as I would that of an American soldier?[174]

In the event, Lucas opted to 'treat them with Christian principles', reasoning that:

> These were husbands, these were sons, perhaps fathers. I did my best for them, for their families' sake. I hope that my unbiased and unprejudiced attitude toward the German people collectively –the women and the children – will be that of every American who has to deal with or care for their welfare.[175]

However, his anxiety for their wellbeing did not end with their physical condition, for Lucas had much deeper concerns: 'Let us help them to become Christians.

We can start even before the war is over to care for and treat our prisoners of war as Christ would have us do.'[176] *The Link* humanised the image of German prisoners in the same issue by announcing that it had a readership among them, the chaplain of a POW camp in New Mexico having gained 'the full approval of the commanding officer' for his distribution of the magazine.[177]

By 1945, this work of rechristianisation had ceased to be controversial, even among service personnel. In March, an article by Roswell P. Barnes, associate general secretary of the FCC, was carried by *The Link*, which described what the YMCA, the World Council of Churches and other Protestant agencies were doing for POWs throughout the world. Here, it explained that their work in the United States overwhelmingly concerned German POWs; that a Swedish clergyman monitored the supply of 'equipment and materials'; that much was being done by prisoners themselves, and that American army chaplains and civilian clergymen were primarily involved 'where there are no pastors among the prisoners'.[178] Admittedly, in Europe things could be a bit more rough and ready, as *The Chaplain* reported in March 1945:

> One Sunday evening in France, CHAPLAIN STANLEY E. ANDERSON stood before a congregation of German prisoners. They long had been stuffed with *Mein Kampf* and nurtured on the so-called glory of the gods of Nordic paganism. The chaplain saw that they needed a change of diet, but neither he nor they possessed a single copy of the New Testament, the Bible or of devotional literature in German. This is how he met the shortage of spiritual rations for these gospel-starved Nazis: 'Therefore I typed many copies of John 3:16 in German which I gave to them ["For God so loved the world, that he gave his only begotten Son, that whosoever believeth in him should not perish, but have everlasting life"].'[179]

Indeed, and as far as *The Link* and *The Chaplain* were concerned, the wider work of rechristianisation progressed and seemed to thrive throughout and beyond the last year of the war. Two additional clergymen arrived in New York from Sweden in March 1945; appointed by the Lutheran primate of Sweden, both were former army chaplains and came to help in the religious work that was taking place in 'more than 500 camps' across the United States and Canada.[180] That November, and from Europe, *The Chaplain* reported on the 'tremendous' attendance 'of Nazi prisoners at religious services held by clergymen taken from the prisoners' ranks'.[181] Among the German pastors released and repatriated in 1946 were those who, at their own request, had been treated to a series of lectures on 'Church Life in America' at Dermott, Arkansas,[182] and, even at the end of that year, the 'special theological school established in a POW camp near Mansfield, England', was still in operation, home to one hundred German prisoners-of-war studying for the ministry.[183]

The war against Japan

The religious dimensions of America's struggle were equally apparent in the war against Japan. Although the Pacific War has been heavily represented as a racial conflict,[184] the religious differences between Japanese and Americans were no less apparent than the racial. Significantly, even John W. Dower's seminal book *War Without Mercy: Race and Power in the Pacific War* (1986) repeatedly uses terms such as 'Manichaean', 'holy war' and 'mark of the beast' in order to convey the apocalyptic quality (for both sides) of the struggle between the Japanese and the Anglo-Americans.[185] Alone among the major belligerent powers in World War II, the Empire of Japan was neither historically or primarily a Christian polity, its core religion being the 'ancient faith' of Shinto, 'or the "Way of the Gods"'.[186] While the overwhelming majority of Japanese adhered to an ancient blend of Shinto and Buddhist beliefs and practices, even down to the honouring of both Shinto and Buddhist deities in Japanese households,[187] the political imperatives of the Meiji Restoration prompted the rise of a new and pervasive form of 'State Shinto'. Built on an ancient foundation of 'Popular Shinto', and helping in its turn to generate new forms of 'Sect Shinto', 'State Shinto' was vigorously propagated by Japan's school system, by the organs and bureaucracy of civil government, and by the Japanese armed forces. In essence, and against an unsettling backdrop of rapid reform and modernisation, State Shinto proclaimed the divine origins and nature of the emperor and of the Japanese people through a 'mythohistory' that aimed to promote 'the psychic solidarity of the Yamato race'.[188] According to the American Japanist and anthropologist John F. Embree,[189] whose book *The Japanese Nation: A Social Survey* was published in a special 'overseas edition' for the use of the armed forces in 1945, the principal goals of State Shinto were 'to secure support for the state, create national solidarity, and give strength and stability to the nation in the face of political and social change'.[190] The problems of this situation for Japan's tiny Christian minority were implicit in the terms of the Meiji Constitution of 1889. Although freedom of religion was guaranteed to all 'Japanese subjects' in Article 28, this was only 'within limits not prejudicial to peace and order, and not antagonistic to their duties as subjects', while Article 3 also stressed that: 'The Emperor is sacred and inviolable'.[191] In practice, state officialdom acted upon the legal conceit that State Shinto was not a religion, and therefore required observance of its 'rituals of patriotism in the form of bowing at shrines, and respect for the Emperor' on the part of all of the emperor's subjects, a demand that Embree noted 'caused constant conflict with Christian mission schools'.[192] As Japanese politics swung further towards the right in the 1930s, and Japan began to acquire the character of a rogue state due to its brutal adventurism in China, both nationalist ideologues and government policy became more assertive of the demands of State Shinto, and more wary of the foreign influences in Japanese church life. Consequently, in Stewart W. Herman's survey of developments in Nazi Germany he compared the perverted 'messianism' of the Third Reich with that of Japan's rampant ultra-nationalists:

> Absolute Shintoism ... carries with it not only loyalty to the emperor as a ruler, but faith in him as the Son of Heaven.... In this form, at least for the radical imperialists of Japan, Shintoism is seen as a doctrine of salvation for the whole world, whereby all the nations of the earth will be brought back to harmony and prosperity under the divine sovereignty of the Tenno [i.e. emperor].[193]

While Christian intransigents – notably Seventh-Day Adventists and Pente-costals – were liable to be imprisoned for their open refusal 'to participate in Shrine worship', and for their impertinent insistence 'that all persons, including the Emperor, were subject to a last judgment',[194] the Japanese churches as a whole felt a tightening squeeze during the 1930s. Bowing to renewed pressure on this question, in 1936 both the Vatican and the National Christian Council permitted participation in the shrine ceremonies of State Shinto, 'based on the Government's declaration that they were civil only'.[195] From 1939, and like many Shinto and Buddhist sects, the Christian churches also felt the effects of the Religious Organizations Law. By promulgating new terms for the formal recognition of religious bodies, this required the amalgamation of smaller Christian groups and helped to pave the way for a new, pan-Protestant Church of Christ in Japan, an unhappy union consummated in 1941.[196] Lastly, in 1940, Protestant churches were required to sever their links with overseas bodies, regardless of the financial costs, while the Vatican was prevailed upon to commence the appointment of native Japanese bishops.[197] All of this, it should be stressed, did not go unno-ticed in the United States. Although not the prime focus of America's overseas missionary efforts, hopes for the evangelisation of Japan had never dissipated. As a former missionary to Japan noted in 1945, with the opening of the country to European influences, and after two decades of Protestant missionary work, the success of the Gospel had once seemed assured. As one contemporary had written in 1876, it even appeared inevitable that 'The doctrine of the divine descent of the Mikado' would eventually be cast aside. However, the currents of Japanese politics in the inter-war years had swept such hopes away, leaving American observers to rue those indications of Japan's underlying character they had so long chosen to ignore. Reflecting on his own missionary days in Japan before the war, W.A. McIlwaine even claimed that the popularity of liberal theology had sapped the virility of Japanese Protestantism, helping its general capitulation to the demands of State Shinto.[198]

Regardless of continuing support for the missions in Japan, and the arrival of American missionaries until the outbreak of war,[199] it was the *lack* of commit-ment to the evangelisation of Japan that Christian pundits were prone to bewail after Pearl Harbor. Despite its disproportionate impact on Japanese health care and education,[200] the fruits of three generations of relatively unhindered missionary work in Japan, to say nothing of the legacy of the Catholic missions of the sixteenth century, amounted to only 350,000 souls in 1940, or 'less than half of 1 per cent of the total population of the country'.[201] Consequently, in March 1945, and as the war in the Pacific entered its last and bloodiest stages, Dr Halford Luccock reminded readers of *The Chaplain* of the prescience of John R. Mott, who in 1901 had said of Japan: 'If in the next few years we can send 10,000 missionaries to Japan, we may win that land for Jesus Christ. But if not, forty years from now we shall have to send 100,000 bayonets' (in the event, a massive underestimate).[202]

Although the enduring celebrity of the Presbyterian churchman Dr Toyohiko Kagawa helped to remind readers of *The Link* of the limited stock of Christian virtue that survived in Japan (with this Christian 'superstar' even apologising to Chinese Christians for the excesses of the Japanese military),[203] more generally *The Link* was keen to emphasise the anti-Christian character of Japan's war in Asia and the Pacific. In March 1943, for example, it published a concise but comprehensive report on the impact of Japanese warmongering on the global missionary enterprise. Citing 'recent reports from Stockholm', it claimed that, in their determination to eliminate 'all western religious influence in the occupied areas', Japanese forces had interned even German missionaries – not that this would worry their Nazi confederates. Furthermore, it reported the tragic fate of Christian missions in the Far East. As summarised by the *International Review of Missions*:

> The great majority of the foreign missionaries in the occupied areas, as well as in Japan itself, have had to leave their posts. Many of the small number who remain are under arrest. The extensive educational work of colleges and schools, much of it of a high quality, has been taken over by the Japanese authorities.[204]

Invoking the United Nations Information Office in New York, it concluded by stressing the general and unprecedented scale of the devastation wrought on Asia's missionary infrastructure by the Japanese:

> [23] per cent of Christian medical work in China has been 'interrupted', and an estimated $1,500,000 of damage caused to plants and equipment.... Many mission buildings, churches and hospitals were also damaged or destroyed in China, Manila and other war areas. While this destruction is believed to have resulted from indiscriminate bombing, rather than from deliberate intent to wipe out missions, it has taken a great toll of missionary property.[205]

Things had deteriorated further by March 1944, when *The Link* reported on the pathetic remnants of Protestant missionary work in Japan:

> There are thirty-nine Protestant missionaries still in Japan, some of them in internment camps and some of them relatively free to carry on their ministries, according to the Foreign Missions Council of North America ... Of this total, ten are Germans, seven are Fins [sic], six or [sic] British, one is Canadian, and fifteen are Americans. The Germans and Finns are free, for Japan is not at war with their nations.[206]

The following month, it published an extract from an article in *Collier's* magazine. Entitled "'Christianity Must Go,' says Japan', and written by Robert Bellaire, a journalist with extensive experience of pre-war Japan, the extract comprised the words of a Japanese official and propagandist in occupied China, who had told Bellaire that Christianity – as a religion of hope, deliverance, and judgement – had to be extirpated in China in order for Japan to consolidate its Asian conquests.[207] Bellaire was already well known for his views on Japan's intentions for Christianity in the Far East, having been cited by Carl Carmer in his 1943 exposé *The War Against God*: 'JAPAN IS AT WAR WITH CHRISTIANITY', Bellaire had declared, 'the Japanese have been quietly stabbing Christianity in the back ever since that religion was first introduced into Japan. One of the major objectives of the Japanese in this present war is to wipe Christianity from the face of the earth.'[208]

The Chaplain magazine, suitably primed and no less convinced than *The Link*, freely expounded the religious dimensions of the conflict. In November 1944 it reported that, 'At the time of the banishing from Japan of all Caucasian missionaries', an elderly deportee encountered a Japanese censor busily working his way through a stack of Bibles, blotting out the words 'King of kings and Lord of lords' (1 Timothy 6:15 and Revelation 19:16) on the grounds that, 'it would not do for Japanese people to be told there was any one above the Emperor.'[209] Naturally, it rejoiced in the defeat and humiliation of this same, vaunted god-emperor, while also heaping scorn on the Japanese proclivity for ancestor worship, a practice rooted in Buddhism rather than Shinto:[210]

> In September [1945] the newspapers carried a strange and interesting story of the ceremonial visits of the emperor of Japan to three shrines for the purpose of making a report to his ancestor about the end of the war. The first thought of everyone on reading that was that it was bad news for the Honourable Ancestors![211]

Though *The Chaplain* registered Reinhold Niebuhr's unease with the use of the atom bomb, and his warnings against racial pride and national hubris on the surrender of Japan, it also echoed his words in *Christianity and Crisis* (his own magazine) that, 'We were indeed the executors of God's judgment' in the use of the bomb.[212] *The Chaplain* was also quick to report the early spiritual fruits of victory, noting the first Christian broadcast from Tokyo since 1941 (courtesy of the American military), the unique potential of Kagawa's 'Christian-democratic' contribution towards the reconstruction of his country, and the growing interest in Christianity among ordinary Japanese.[213]

The religious dimensions and significance of the war against Japan were also evident on the ground, and not least in the almost total lack of a religious – and potentially moderating – point of contact between the antagonists. Various incidents that occurred on different sides of the world on 1 April 1945, Easter Sunday, help to illustrate this point. As GIs continued their advance into Germany, it became clear that the celebration of Easter was still common to Americans and Germans alike. Sergeant Lindy Sawyers returned a looted Easter cake to a German family and, like many other soldiers in the 99th Infantry Division, attended a service in a local church. Before a mixed congregation of GIs and German civilians, two other soldiers of the 99th played the violin and piano for three hours. As Private Joe Bombach recalled: 'The Germans loved it. I thought it was one of the most memorable happenings we had. It brought us all together for a day.' Elsewhere in the American sector, German civilians distributed decorated Easter eggs to bemused GIs.[214] Things were very different as American soldiers and marines landed on the island of Okinawa, soon to become the scene of the bloodiest operation of America's Pacific war. With the initial landings unopposed, a party of wary marines fired into a cavern from which voices had been heard – three Okinawan civilians were killed and the sole survivor, a three-year-old boy, was retrieved. As Lieutenant Chris Donner wrote: 'They brought him back to us and Monahan washed the blood off the boy, who had ceased to cry. My team carried him on their shoulders all the rest of the afternoon … So this was Easter Sunday warfare. It sickened me.'[215]

In contrast to the situation in Europe, in the Pacific a raw and visceral hatred characterised attitudes towards the enemy. With too few Japanese Americans to confound national stereotypes or easy generalisations, in 1943 a survey conducted among soldiers in training at Camp Adair, Oregon, showed that enthusiasm at the prospect of killing a Japanese soldier was much, much greater than that for killing a German, in the order of 7:1 even among poorly motivated soldiers whose combat performance was later judged to be 'below average'.[216] In July 1944, *What the Soldier Thinks* reported that surveys conducted among 'thousands of combat veterans who have met the Axis enemy on the battlefields of the world' showed that: 'Vindictiveness against the Japs is greater than vindictiveness against the Germans. This is true among American soldiers everywhere.'[217] Although the same proportion (13 per cent) of European and Pacific veterans reported having actually seen battlefield atrocities committed by the enemy, 42 per cent of infantry veterans in the Pacific and 58 per cent of those in Europe were in favour of wiping out 'the whole Japanese nation' after victory had been achieved; the proportions favouring the same fate for the Germans being 22 and 24 per cent respectively. Nor was contact with the vanquished likely to soften such vengeful attitudes towards the Japanese, with twice as many infantrymen from the Pacific claiming that 'contact with enemy prisoners made them feel "all the more like killing them"'.[218]

Such attitudes were present even among religiously committed and morally earnest GIs. As Chief of Staff, George C. Marshall insisted that 'Military power wins battles, but spiritual power wins wars'. However, *The Link* seemed concerned that this power could take an ugly turn, and warned against the moral dangers of hate, a feeling normally evoked by the Japanese. In December 1943 it endorsed the view that 'The Christian believes in justice but he deprecates hate. He will have no part in the propaganda that Americans must learn to hate their enemies more before they can secure decisive victory. He refuses to hate the enemy soldier in uniform, the soldier's wife and the soldier's children'.[219] Still, one erstwhile pacifist, Kermit Stewart, was surprised by how easily he had adjusted to killing Japanese – whom he effortlessly put on a par with Nazis, rather than Germans. Serving as a lieutenant in the Philippines with the 43rd Infantry Division, Stewart wrote:

> I sometimes reflect with amazement on my role in this war. I used to be a music teacher – I was a pacifist – talked about the infinite value of the human personality – how barbaric it was to kill a man because he was in another color uniform. But here I am.... One day a Jap who had been bypassed nearly killed one of my sergeants. He was in a hole in a river bank. I, and some of my boys, covered the sergeant (he got the honor) while he crept up and threw two grenades into the hole. Then the men dragged out the Jap, and poured a whole magazine of tommy-gun into him. After that it's my job to search the body for documents. And it doesn't bother me! Do you wonder that I say I'm sometimes amazed at myself? I'm more of a pacifist than I ever was, but as long as there are vermin like Japs and Nazis, they have to be exterminated – and it is hellish work.[220]

While this bitter animus against the Japanese can be readily ascribed to a potent mixture of racism and a thirst for revenge,[221] it is worth pausing to consider the fundamental nature of Japanese transgressions. Unlike German atrocities, the scale of which only became fully apparent to Americans with the liberation of the concentration camps towards the end of the war in Europe, Japanese depravity had been manifest as early as the Rape of Nanking in December 1937, an atrocity that was captured and conveyed in photographs and motion pictures by the American Episcopalian missionary John Magee.[222] Furthermore, and however murderous the Malmédy massacre of December 1944, this was at least a departure from what had come to be expected of German conduct towards American POWs, being put in the shade by Japanese atrocities against American and Filipino prisoners in incidents such as the Bataan Death March of April 1942 and the Palawan massacre of December 1944. However, these episodes were not merely breaches of international law but were profoundly offensive to Christian, or Judeo-Christian, moral norms that were tightly woven into the fabric of American life and culture. Although Japan had not ratified the 1929 Geneva Convention Relative to the Treatment of Prisoners of War, of more fundamental importance was the fact that the non-Christian Japanese did not inhabit the same moral universe as Americans. The author Willard Price, widely regarded as a wartime expert on Japan (genuine Japanists were few and far between), warned that the Imperial Rescript to Soldiers stated that 'Inferiors should regard the orders of their superiors as coming directly from us'; consequently, it followed that, 'Since the Heavenly Emperor is a God, the Japanese army under His Majesty also is just and righteous.'[223] This moral cleavage was also stressed by a 1944 article in the *Marine Corps Gazette* entitled 'False Gods – False Ideals'. Written by Otto D. Tolischus, a former internee and Japan correspondent for the *New York Times*, it explained that:

> As a moral and ethical system, Shinto has only one command – to follow the 'Way of the Gods.' This way is illustrated by the actions of the gods themselves.... In fact, the concepts of abstract good or bad do not arise. There is no conflict between good and evil, not between God and man, nor between man and nature. There is no moral law, no original sin, no fall of man, no hell. As one Japanese put it, only bad people like the Chinese need a moral law; the Japanese, being gods, need only look into their hearts to know what to do. And whatever their hearts prompt them to do is good.[224]

The same message was rammed home in the 1945 *Guide to Japan*, which warned American service personnel that neither Shinto nor Buddhism had a recognisable moral code, the latter also being without a concept of sin.[225] Consequently, and as the historian Michael Burleigh has written: 'Although Japanese soldiers had a sense of right and wrong, there was no transcendental moral code to offset the absolute dictates of officers, who in turn were the unquestioning servants of the Emperor. If they said kill, you killed.'[226] By the 1930s, and as Tolischus elaborated,[227] the systematic promotion of State Shinto, not least in and by the Japanese military, had created a situation whereby:

> To die in battle for the Emperor was to die a holy death.... Each officer cadet had to learn by heart in the first three days of his training the 27,000 sacred words of the Emperor on the duties of a soldier. The suicide charge on the battlefield, the refusal to surrender, the stark fear of dishonour were instilled in all Japanese.[228]

Disturbed and repelled in equal measure by these values and conduct, Americans were in turn galvanised by their own religious and moral system, one in which Christian forgiveness was now inevitably at a discount. As the devoutly Catholic sailor James J. Fahey wrote in his diary in February 1945 after rehearsing the details of the Palawan massacre:

> These men were Japanese prisoners since 1942 and spent all that time under the cruel treatment of the Japs until the end. Some of the prisoners escaped and were picked up by our subs. It is going to be a pleasure to bombard this island and blow its defenders to bits. It's too bad the poor prisoners cannot be here to see it happen.[229]

With the benefit of hindsight, the former B-29 pilot Gordon Bennett Robertson had no regrets about his role as an agent of American retribution:

> We fought an enemy who was completely and absolutely uncivilized, unprincipled, cruel, inhuman, and sadistic. They brazenly, contemptuously, and boldly demonstrated all these attributes during their fourteen-year-long attempt to conquer East Asia and the Pacific Rim.[230]

Significantly, and in his lengthy enumeration of Japanese atrocities, he was careful to emphasise the sufferings of the only largely Christian country in Asia: 'Later, as we recaptured the Philippines, as a final act of barbarism, they destroyed the churches, convents, schools, and universities and slaughtered 100,000 Filipinos.'[231]

The moral and religious tone of America's war in the Pacific was set as early as 7 December 1941. Whereas the first American service personnel to die at German hands had perished in remote and controversial convoy escort duties in the North Atlantic, the Japanese attack on Pearl Harbor was not only undertaken without a prior declaration of war but occurred on a Sunday morning as army and navy chaplains prepared for their usual church services.[232] Significantly, nearly four years later this factor was noted by Major Charles W. Sweeney as he wrestled with his conscience about the dropping of the second atomic bomb.[233] As a survivor of the Pearl Harbor attack recalled: 'My barrack bunkmate and I were arguing about which Sunday Mass we should attend – the eight A.M. or the ten A.M ... The Japanese planes hit at about seven-fifty-five, and we never got there. I still have the bullet that came through my locker.'[234] Likewise, Richard M. Becker of the transport ship *Antares* was unable to reconcile the 'whole chaotic situation' with 'a beautiful Sunday morning and church time', being bitter about the timing of the Pearl Harbor attack decades later: 'And what the hell [the Japanese] did was say, "Hey, Sunday morning them suckers will all be going to church. Let's just get over there and come on them on a Sunday morning, and they won't be expecting."'[235] As we have noted, it was not only the sanctity of the Christian Sabbath that was shattered, but chaplains were killed and places of worship targeted during the attack. The Japanese willingness to exploit the religious sensibilities of their American foes continued throughout the war.

According to Robert Leckie of the 1st Marine Division, on Guadalcanal the Japanese routinely bombed American positions on Sunday morning, a stratagem that was 'nourished on the great success of Sunday morning at Pearl Harbor'.[236] Even the Marine Corps magazine *The Leatherneck* warned that: 'Pearl Harbor proved it is not always wise to worship on a schedule known to the enemy'.[237] Beyond all of this, and as one marine officer emphasised, the typical Japanese soldier 'would as soon kill a chaplain administering the last rites to the dying as he would an active enemy'.[238]

In *Close-Up of the Jap Fighting Man*, originally delivered as a lecture at Fort Leavenworth's Command and General Staff School in October 1942, the Japan expert Lieutenant Colonel Warren J. Clear quoted the ominous words of General Hayashi: 'The sword is our "steel bible"'.[239] He also warned of how the innate cruelty of the Japanese had found an historic outlet in the treatment of Christian missionaries and their Japanese converts:

> The pages of history show no more terrible brutality, the fiendish refinements of cruelty visited on the victims being almost beyond belief. Christians were buried alive, torn asunder by oxen, thrown from cliffs onto the rocks below, tied in pairs in huge rice bags which were pyramided and then set on fire. Japanese official records of the times reveal tortures too revolting to be described. The sadism that is latent in every Japanese male had to be satisfied. It is little less vicious today among the yellow fighting-men. We ought to keep these matters in mind.[240]

There was, indeed, an abiding animus against Christianity in Japanese popular culture, one that resurfaced in wartime propaganda. As John Dower has pointed out, contact with Catholic missionaries in the sixteenth century gave rise to the ridiculous, if essentially demonic, figure of the Christian padre.[241] Consequently, anti-Christian (and even anti-Semitic) tropes were common in Japanese propaganda in World War II, with Japanese cartoonists liable to portray Roosevelt and Churchill in this contemptible guise. Elsewhere, Christian prayers were spoofed, the Christian cross depicted as a dagger, and the Pietà parodied with a new and risible cast of a prostrate Churchill, grieving Roosevelt and mournful Chiang Kai-shek.[242]

Given this background, it is highly significant that much of the Pacific war unfolded in what, for Western Christians, represented a vast mission field of relatively recent standing. Amidst the islands of the Pacific, and as at Buna on the coast of Papua, for example,[243] mission stations could be counted among the few tangible signs of European influence and were often significant military locations and objectives. In this arena, Japanese mistreatment of missions and missionary personnel, a multinational and religiously diverse breed still very much revered by many American Christians, gave an added religious edge to the war, as it did on the mainland of Asia. On their occupation of Mindanao, for example, Japanese soldiers plundered their way through the Jesuit community at Sumilao; according to William R. Arnold and Christopher Cross, they not only ignored a sign written by a superior officer 'forbidding entry or looting' but 'behaved like wild animals. They took all the cooking equipment, all the food stores, and killed all the pigs and turkeys.'[244] Later, a disgusted marine noted how, at a native church in the Solomon Islands, the occupying Japanese had used Church of England hymnbooks as toilet paper.[245] However, this was small beer compared to what took place – or was thought to have taken place – elsewhere in the Solomon Islands. Despite the initial moderation of Japanese conduct towards Christian missionaries when they first moved into the archipelago, and the desire of Catholic missionaries in particular to remain neutral and at their posts,[246] the activities of Allied coast watchers (originally recruited by the Royal Australian Navy from Europeans who had settled in New Guinea, the Solomons and the New Hebrides) implicated those who had not already been interned or evacuated in the intelligence war.[247] Ultimately, this led to the arrest and mistreatment of Catholic missionaries on Bougainville, the brutal execution of four of their number on Guadalcanal, and the extraction by the US Navy of twenty-nine civilians, including sixteen Catholic missionaries and four American nuns, from Bougainville in January 1943.[248] According to a brief history of American chaplaincy on Guadalcanal, the two Marist priests and two Marist nuns who died on Guadalcanal were 'all bayonetted [sic] through the throat.'[249] Stories of their sufferings grew in the telling; as James J. Fahey noted on board the light cruiser *Montpelier* in February 1943:

> One of the crew from [a] PT boat told us that they picked up 5 nurses at Guadalcanal who had escaped from the Japs. Some of them were almost insane after what they had been through while being held.... He said the Japs also raped the nuns and then killed them, some had their heads cut off.[250]

Likewise, in April 1945, Admiral William F. Halsey told one reporter: 'Most of the Japanese atrocity stories you hear about are not exaggerations.... It is no rumour that nuns in the Solomons were subjected to 48 hours of continuous rape and then had their throats cut by the Japs.'[251]

There can be no doubt as to the grim reality of Japanese atrocities against European missionaries and Christian clergy during the course of the Pacific war, and not least in America's pre-war Pacific possessions. Among the other details of a lengthy naval career, Chaplain Frederick William Meehling remembered the fate of a native Chamorro priest on Guam – captured by the Japanese only four days after Pearl Harbor – whom Meehling had known as a seminarian: '[H]e was kind of the first martyr of Guam ... he told them, "Wait until the Americans are back. They'll put you in your place." They got so tired they finally beheaded him.'[252] Chaplain Thomas J. Donnelly, one of the liberators of the island in July

1944, confirmed this story, and noted the general mistreatment of the Chamorros' religion:

> Their lot had been difficult under the Japs. They were nearly all Catholics but were impeded in the exercise of their religion.... The missionaries had been taken off the Island and only two native priests were left. These two were hampered in their work and one was put to death.... Their churches were used as arsenals and commissaries ...[253]

In the vast archipelago of the Philippines, America's greatest Pacific gain from the Spanish–American War of 1898, similar incidents occurred on a much larger scale. According to Fr Edward Haggerty, whose community at Sumilao on Mindanao suffered from the depredations of the Japanese in 1942, two French Canadian priests were tortured, murdered and thrown into a river by the Japanese after emerging from hiding on the assurance of not being harmed. Other foreign priests who also turned themselves in on the promise of being allowed to continue their ministries were 'promptly clapped into [a] concentration camp'. In fact, so Haggerty claimed: 'If all the priests had believed the Jap promises, Mindanao would have been left for three years almost entirely without priests.'[254] Moreover, the final months of Japan's occupation of the Philippines were marked by further excesses against the ever-suspect European clergy who were still at large. In December 1944, three Irish priests were arrested and tortured in Manila by the *kempeitai*, Japan's feared military police; in the subsequent battle for the city, they were rearrested and simply vanished. Meanwhile, amidst the orgy of violence perpetrated by the Japanese defenders of Manila, twelve German teaching brothers were also killed in the chapel of the city's De La Salle College.[255]

Although there was no coordinated effort to uproot Christianity across Japan's Greater East Asia Co-Prosperity Sphere (initial Japanese policy in the Philippines, for example, sought 'not to molest the church when it was represented by Filipinos'),[256] because Japanese excesses could be very easily construed as the policy of a heathen, persecuting and anti-Christian power, the spirit of the four freedoms – and a good measure of Christian triumphalism – was all too evident in the vaunted liberation of native Christians and the restitution and repair of missionary property by American forces. As Robert D. Workman said of the American advance in the Pacific in a Christmas message of 1944:

> The Chaplain sees it from his vantage point – the religious. He sees each island stepping-stone as a new forward area for the worship of Almighty God, as a push whereby Divine Services can be conducted; as the breaking of infidel fetters imposed by a treacherous enemy upon God-loving people.[257]

Of the fighting on Guadalcanal, and mindful of widespread American mistrust of British imperial rule here and elsewhere, navy chaplain Warren Wyeth Willard wrote:

Regarding our own treatment of the natives, all praises be to the good Lord above! On August 7 [1942], and the days thereafter, when rivers of Japanese blood flowed freely, to our best knowledge, marines did not wound or kill a single native.... And very definitely, with a few possible exceptions, the natives were not pro-Japanese.... Their native villages had been needlessly pillaged. Their beautiful native-built churches had been used for barracks by the Japanese.... British rule at its worst would have been far better than Japanese rule at its best.[258]

He also rejoiced at the return of plundered missionary property to its rightful owners, and specifically his return of a silver chalice – 'found in Jap loot on the island of Gavutu' – to an Anglican missionary on Florida Island.[259] This theme was also taken up by *The Chaplain* magazine. In December 1944, it reported on the desecration of a mission church at Hollandia by the Japanese, a building that had previously served 'as a symbol of Western civilization and religion' to the natives of Dutch New Guinea. Happily, this had now been restored to its proper use by an army chaplain, the Southern Baptist Ernest D. Elliott, and was now 'crowded to the doors by communicants of all faiths'.[260] By the same token, of course, any religious legacy of Japanese occupation had to be effaced. Accordingly, in September 1943 the *Chicago Tribune* reported that the senior navy chaplain in the Aleutians was busily making plans for the erection of a new chapel on the island of Kiska, newly 'recovered American soil', which would supplant 'a Japanese Shinto shrine' on the present site.[261]

The alignment of the American war effort with the cause of Christianity in Asia and the Pacific was accentuated by the fact that even German missionary clergy were vulnerable to Japanese atrocities and, in mainland China, German missions were even frequented by American intelligence officers.[262] Furthermore, Christian missionaries could participate quite directly in pro-Allied activities and operations, a development that disturbed *The Christian Century* in view of its possible implications for the post-war image of Western missionaries in Asia.[263] On this score, Japanese suspicions of missionary collusion with Allied coast watchers were by no means unfounded, for missionaries from Allied nations did perform this role in the Solomon Islands and elsewhere.[264] Given the prevailing ignorance of Japanese language and culture in pre-war America, missionaries also served as a valuable source of expertise on an alien and enigmatic enemy. The senior Japanese language officer of the 1st Marine Division, throughout its months on Guadalcanal in 1942, was a fairly elderly former missionary to Japan who came equipped with forty years' knowledge of the country.[265] With the return to the United States of interned missionaries via the SS *Gripsholm*, a Swedish vessel chartered by the State Department for the repatriation of Allied civilians in exchange for Japanese diplomats,[266] other missionaries were duly pumped for information. In October 1942, for example, L.W. Moore, a Presby-

terian clergyman who had spent almost nine years in Japan, warned OSS inter-
viewers (including J.F. Embree) that Japanese Christians were 'not sympathetic
towards the United Nations', that Japanese morale remained high and that: 'Ridi-
culing the Emperor or bombing his palace would only increase their enmity.'[267]
In August 1945, *The Chaplain* reported that another former missionary and *Gripsholm* passenger, Frank L. Fesperman, was now assigned as a chaplain to Camp
Hood, Texas, where he was teaching Japanese to 'American soldiers who desire to
chatter in that tongue after their expected arrival in Tokyo.'[268] Besides the provision of much-needed intelligence and linguistic expertise, other missionaries
gave succour to pro-Allied resistance movements, notably on Mindanao, where
fugitive Dutch, Canadian, American and even Irish missionaries served as de
facto 'Guerrilla Padres' in a Filipino insurgency against the 'superstitions, slavery,
emperor-cult [and] boastful paganism' of the Japanese.[269] In China, American
servicemen received help of all kinds from resident missionaries, with Lieutenant
General Albert C. Wedemeyer, commander of US forces in China and Chiang
Kai-shek's Allied chief of staff in the last year of the war, stating that:

> United States Forces in China have been assisted in many ways by mission-
> aries of all faiths and denominations. Sick or wounded men in remote and
> inaccessible areas have received their unselfish ministrations. The weary,
> the heartsick, and the discouraged have often been comforted by their
> cheerfulness and their steadfast devotion.[270]

In keeping with this view of a Christian confrontation with a heathen and
diabolical foe, and mindful of the religious freedom granted to POWs under
Article 16 of the Geneva Convention, much could also be made of the sporadic
persecution of Christianity among American POWs taken by the Japanese. In
this case, the ordeal of an estimated thirty-seven army and navy chaplains taken
prisoner in the Philippines (and liberated, in some cases, from Cabanatuan in
January 1945)[271] handed more ammunition to the army's chief of chaplains. As
Arnold and Cross thundered:

> The Chaplains who returned [from the Philippines] disclosed something
> more than a mere saga of great courage and perseverance. From them came
> additional proof that the Japanese soldiers are brutal torturers and wanton
> murderers. The Chaplain's story is one of defiance against those who
> wanted to stamp out Christianity.... Although often so weak from hunger
> they could scarcely stand, they always found the strength for God's word,
> sometimes secretly because the Japanese considered Chaplains dangerous
> propagandists, since they trained their own clergy as such.[272]

In reality, Japanese policy towards captive chaplains and their ministrations
varied considerably according to time and local circumstances, ranging from

complete prohibition to considerable latitude, with only the prior censorship of sermons being a predictable feature of their approach.[273]

However overstated Arnold's claims may have been, by this stage of the war, and having confronted excesses ranging from vivisection to cannibalism and the *kamikaze*, Americans fighting the Japanese needed no convincing of the depravity and folly of Japanese religious beliefs. Desperate suicidal charges, a familiar denouement of ground fighting in the Pacific, were accompanied with the cry of '*Tenno heika banzai*', or 'His Majesty the Emperor, May he live forever'.[274] Consequently, marine Major General William H. Rupertus concluded that the Japanese commander on Guadalcanal had been positively hindered 'by troops crazy to die for the Emperor's sake'.[275] Likewise, it was perceived that the norms and imperatives of Shinto placed a lethal constraint on individual initiative. According to one appraisal of the Japanese soldier: 'Their Shinto religion makes for excellent discipline which results in letter-perfect obedience to orders, but it militates against individuals taking tactical advantage of situations, or even of using their common sense'.[276] Later in the war, and having witnessed American airmen machine-gunned in their parachutes as they bailed out over Japan, Gordon Bennett Robertson felt nothing but hatred for 'those goddamned, uncivilized, barbaric, sadistic, subhuman, infidel Jap bastards'.[277] As for the navy, James J. Fahey learned of the lethal religious imperatives of the enemy first by rumour, and then by experience. Speaking to American wounded evacuated from Guadalcanal in July 1943, Fahey was told that, 'the Japs are as tough and fierce as they come; the Jap is not afraid to die, it is an honor to die for the Emperor, he is their God'.[278] That November, the crew of the *Montpelier* had more immediate experience of this pathology:

> This afternoon, while we were south of Bougainville ... we came across a raft with four live Japs in it.... As the destroyer *Spence* came close to the raft, the Japs opened up with a machine gun at the destroyer. The Jap officer then put the gun in each man's mouth and fired, blowing out the back of each man's skull. One of the Japs did not want to die for the Emperor and put up a struggle. The others held him down. The officer was the last to die. He also blew his brains out.[279]

A year later, in Leyte Gulf, and now confronted with the terrifying phenomenon of the *kamikaze*, Fahey wrote simply: 'You do not discourage the Japs, they never give up, you have to kill them. It is an honor to die for the Emperor'.[280] If Fahey was nonplussed to hear Japanese radio broadcasts describe these assailants as 'Sacred',[281] Lieutenant Ben Bradlee, a destroyer officer, gave succinct expression to the cultural and religious chasm that separated Americans from their Japanese adversaries, not least on the subject of a purifying death: 'I could not imagine waking up some morning at 5 a.m., going to some church to pray, and knowing that in a few hours I would crash my plane into a ship on purpose'.[282]

According to Otto D. Tolischus, 'The Way of the Gods' had locked the Japa-nese into a world of profound ignorance, 'the average Japanese' living 'in a world that is pre-Hellenic, prerational, and prescientific – a world not of cause and effect, but of miracles and magic, peopled with myriads of gods and spirits who are as real to him as physical existence'.[283] Given the primitivism of Japanese religious beliefs and their apparently self-defeating corollaries, significant effort was devoted by influential components of the American military to the study and exploitation of the practical weaknesses of the Japanese religious imagina-tion. For example, amidst the numerous research reports prepared and published by the Allied Translator and Interpreter Section (ATIS) of MacArthur's South-West Pacific headquarters were many that dealt, directly or indirectly, with Japa-nese religious beliefs and their military implications. In April 1944, for example, ATIS published a report on 'Self-Immolation as a Factor in Japanese Military Psychology', highlighting the contribution of Shinto to 'the Japanese concept that death in battle is a privilege' and stressing the compelling significance of the Yasukuni Shrine:

> The YASUKUNI Shrine in TOKYO is the national pantheon where the spirits of all who die for the Emperor are deified and enshrined.... The soldier will join the ranks of the mighty and potent dead at the YASUKUNI Shrine to continue the struggle for JAPAN by other and even more effec-tive means than physical combat. The Japanese belief inherent in Shinto thought, that the spirit is more powerful than a living man, is behind many of their references to spiritual strength.[284]

Again, in February 1945 ATIS turned its attention to 'Superstitions as a Present Factor in Japanese Military Psychology', justifying its interest on the basis of the looming invasion of Japan's home soil and the fact that: 'Indoctrinated with the belief that they are fighting a "Holy War" [and] fulfilling a "divine" mission, Japa-nese soldiers believe that supernatural forces exert a powerful influence over the outcome of battles.'[285] After an extensive survey of Japanese cosmology – including astrology and beliefs surrounding fire, charms, the weather, and various flora and fauna – the report concluded that: 'Their fatalistic attitude appears to be a potential source of weakness ... In the face of mounting disasters, superstitions now dormant or casual may re-assert their power over the Japanese and provide a more fertile soil for suggestion.'[286]

By October 1945, it was obvious to ATIS that Japan's religious hubris had proved entirely counterproductive. Summarising the supposed sources of Japa-nese superiority and the implications of *Yamato damashii*,[287] a further report published that month stated that:

> The Japanese doctrine of spiritual superiority has its roots in the teaching of National Shinto; that the heaven-descended Emperor is the highest-ranking

god on earth; that the Japanese partake of certain god-like qualities which set them above all non-divinely descended races and nations; that the end, the design to further the glory and might of the Japanese Empire, justifies any means toward that end.

Consequently, it stressed that:

The Japanese are taught to regard this war as a Holy War, with the armed forces and the people as the instruments of the Divine will, those members of the Japanese race now in the flesh are aided and strengthened by the spiritual power of those who have crossed over to 'death's other kingdom'.

Hence, the sources of their spiritual strength were manifold:

Thus, they believe that their spiritual authority is due to the unbounded spiritual power of the whole natural order: the deities who created the 'sacred soil' of Japan; the Imperial ancestors, the family ancestors, the local deities, and also the spirits of all those who have given their lives for the Emperor.[288]

Given such assumptions, the dawning realisation of complete defeat had proved disorientating and demoralising for many in the Japanese military: no amount of indoctrination, even when combined with wilful myopia, could compensate for their country's material inferiority. Furthermore, confusion and demoralisation had resulted 'when fact denies faith'. Human weakness had 'repeatedly caused Japanese soldiers to fall short of the superhuman demands' made upon them, and 'The cult of the "Japanese Spirit"' had led to a wholly 'unnecessary wastage' of manpower through inadequate medical care, a contempt for basic safety devices such as the parachute, and premature suicides on the battlefield.[289]

For many Americans it was possible to add that Japan had placed its hopes on false gods in any case. The submariner Peter Bocko felt no qualms about sending Japanese shipping and sailors to the bottom; as far as he was concerned, it was: 'Exhilarating. This is what we wanted. Japanese did the wrong thing. They were going to join, join whoevers ... their God, old Hiro[hito] ... sat back in his palace there, way up in Tokyo Bay.'[290] Sy Kahn, a secular Jew from Manhattan who was serving with the 244th Port Company in the South-West Pacific,[291] was no less willing to pour scorn on the religious delusions of the Japanese, writing of a group of bedraggled Japanese prisoners at Cape Gloucester, New Britain: 'So these pitiful prisoners were the vaunted "Sons of Heaven", the supermen who were going to exterminate the white race.'[292] For others, the course of the Pacific war seemed to illustrate the palpable intervention of the Judeo-Christian God of Battles. Typically, Warren Wyeth Willard ascribed the success of the marine landings on Guadalcanal in August 1942 to a classic display of divine favour:

During three days preceding August 7, when we first attacked, it would have been difficult for enemy planes to detect our approach. On August 6, the weather was very foggy. Our ships, moving forward like dark shadows, and just as silently, stole into the Solomon Islands area without the Japs knowing we were coming. The Almighty had sent the clouds and the rain. At various times and in diverse places He has entered the affairs of men. He was present with us in the battle of the Solomons.[293]

If, as Admiral Nimitz asserted, providence had disposed that the attack on Pearl Harbor had at least allowed American warships to be salvaged, other incidents also begged a providential interpretation. Speaking of the inexplicable withdrawal of Vice Admiral Takeo Kurita's warships at the Battle of Leyte Gulf in October 1944, Rear Admiral Thomas Sprague attributed the consequent survival of his escort carriers to the 'definite partiality of Almighty God'.[294] At home, even *The Christian Century* – and despite its aversion to bombing in principle[295] – seemed happy with the military and religious chastisement of the Japanese, noting that the firebombing of Tokyo on 9 March 1945 (dubbed, ironically, 'Operation Meetinghouse'): 'blasted large cracks in the myth by which a weak and offensive little man had become a conquering god'.[296] However, by 1944 the fundamentalist American Council of Christian Churches was already urging the bombing of Shinto shrines in order 'to shatter the Japanese belief "in the protective power of the divine emperor and his ancestors"', recommending the Yasukuni Shrine and the Great Shrine at Ise for particular attention. It was, in the arch view of *The Christian Century*, simply a case of 'a few theological arguments in the shape of two-ton block-busters dropped on the right holy places'.[297] Nevertheless, such advice went unheeded, with the city of Kyoto, 'Japan's historic, cultural, and religious center', being spared by the Secretary of War for what seem to have been cultural and strategic reasons.[298]

There was, of course, some sympathy for Japanese Christians who, while sharing a common faith, were less likely to prefer self-immolation when serving in Japan's armed forces. On Tulagi in 1942, Willard visited a Japanese prisoner who claimed to be a Christian and for whom this otherwise combative chaplain professed to have 'only the greatest sympathy'.[299] At Easter 1943, Earl Van Best, a Methodist navy chaplain, administered communion to a lone Japanese Christian in a POW compound 'somewhere in the Pacific', and to the accompaniment of a sailors' quartet singing 'Nearer, My God, to Thee'.[300] Later, and with the support of the senior chaplain of the Pacific Fleet,[301] a marine band performed an Easter concert for the inmates of the same stockade – the programme including Easter hymns, some light music and a fair amount of yodelling. If a somewhat strained display of Christian goodwill, the concert was implicitly evangelistic, one of its organisers reflecting that: 'It would be wonderful to be able to win these people over to our way of life, to our way of thinking, to our way of worshipping. It's not an impossible ideal!'[302] It was not. In the summer of 1944, a Japanese Catholic priest was captured by a surprised marine on Guam and, in a highly exceptional display of religious commonality, later said Mass for his captors 'on the Jap side' of his POW enclosure.[303] Later, on an Okinawan beach, a failed *kamikaze* surrendered to the surprised senior chaplain of Tenth Army, Roy N. Hillyer. According to Hillyer's version of events:

> For two years ... he had been in a prison camp for refusing to fight America. Then one day he had been told that he must either go into the Emperor's dwindling air force to be trained as a pilot or be shot. This was his first mission, and, true to a vow he had made not to 'commit murder against my fellow Christians,' he had found a way to lag behind the others and then jettison his plane, running the risk of either being shot down or of exploding his bomb when crash-landing on the water.[304]

Another would-be prisoner was not so lucky; on seeing Hillyer, he reached into his tunic and was instantly shot and killed by the chaplain's escort. Instead of a grenade, however, they found that he was reaching for a Japanese New Testament, on which had been written the words: 'Read this daily, my son, for in it are the things eternal.'[305]

Still, wartime sympathy for Japan's Christian minority was a finite quantity. As some influential American commentators maintained, as a group they were much too tainted by their accommodations with the imperial regime, acceding to the demands of state Shinto and serving in the Japanese armed forces regardless of their conduct.[306] Robert Bellaire even accused 'the Christian church in Japan' of being 'a nest of spies and a haven for the undercover operations of the Tokyo militarists.'[307] In any event, and despite calls for the bombing of Shinto shrines, the concentration of Christians 'in larger urban areas' ensured that Christian places of worship suffered disproportionately from the effects of American bombing.[308] According to William P. Woodard, by the end of the war '1,374 (1%) Shinto shrines, 4,609 (6%) Buddhist temples, 2,540 (15%) Sectarian Shinto churches, and 446 (23%) Christian churches had been destroyed.'[309] The ultimate example of this apparent indifference to the fate of Christian Japanese over non-Christians was, of course, the atomic destruction of Nagasaki, then home to 70 per cent of Japan's Catholic population.[310] Although the secondary target for the B-29s of the 509th Composite Group on 9 August 1945,[311] in this instance the plutonium bomb was used against the historic heart of Japanese Catholicism, detonating close to the city's Catholic cathedral, and effectively decimating the country's Catholic population. However, and in a manner comparable to the bombing of Rome, the destruction of Nagasaki appears to have disturbed remarkably few American service personnel – even Catholics. In 1983, a survey of surviving Catholic chaplains indicated that almost two-thirds of them supported the use of the atom bomb at the time, whereas less than one-sixth had opposed it, figures that throw into question the assertion that Catholic priests 'were almost uniformly opposed to the atomic bombing of Japan'.[312] Furthermore, and in a telling display of contemporary insouciance, the Jesuit navy chaplain Samuel H. Ray wrote from Tokyo on 29 August 1945:

> My dear Mother, Sisters and Brother.... At Sunday Mass I am going to tell the Catholic men all about the Catholic Martyrs of Japan. We have twelve feasts during the year commemorating Jesuit Martyrs of Japan. Most of them are Japanese natives who had become Catholic and would not renounce their faith. Most of them were killed in the 17th century in the area of the ill-fated Nagasaki. This was, as you know, the second city to be crushed by the awful atomic bomb.[313]

Italy

Among the major Axis powers, and despite the 'new wave of millenarian speculation' triggered in fundamentalist circles by the rise of Mussolini in the 1920s,[314] the military and religious threat posed by fascist Italy ranked a very poor and distant third. As *The Leatherneck* magazine scoffed in March 1943, 'ITALIAN SOLDIERS WOULD RATHER SING THAN FIGHT FOR IL DUCE'.[315] The secular, modernist and anti-clerical rhetoric of many fascist ideologues, and the fascist obsession with the trappings and glories of pagan Rome, meant that there was occasional friction between the Catholic church and Italian fascism. However, there was scarcely any suggestion that, in themselves, the belligerent character and quasi-religious ideology of fascist Italy amounted to any major threat to the religious life of the United States. Indeed, patching-up relations between the Vatican and the post-Unification Italian state represented a crowning achievement for Mussolini's regime, and it was by virtue of the terms of the Lateran Treaty of 1929 that the military vicar of the United States, Archbishop Francis Spellman, was able to visit the Vatican in 1943 despite the state of war between Italy and the US.[316] As the Concordat of 1929 also guaranteed the Catholic Church considerable freedom within the fascist state, the rank odour of religious persecution never surrounded Mussolini's Italy as it did Hitler's Germany or Hirohito's Japan, even though Mussolini's regime committed atrocities against the Ethiopian Coptic Church after the Italian invasion of 1935, embraced an anti-Semitic agenda from 1938, and turned on the Salvation Army the following year.[317] With the Catholic Church still entrenched in Italian society, the Italian armed forces amply supplied with chaplains of their own, and the cult of St Catherine of Siena firmly embedded among Italian servicemen,[318] there was never any attempt at the kind of religious reclamation that characterised the American approach towards German POWs. Following the Badoglio Armistice of September 1943, many Italian prisoners were recruited by the US Army into pro-Allied engineer units and eventually returned to their homeland while the war was in progress.[319] For those who remained, there was even scope to capitalise upon the religious interest of their American captors. In the summer of 1944, for example, William R. Arnold even backed the request of an Italian POW chaplain for permission to go on retreat. When this was turned down, he wrote to a US army chaplain at Camp Sutton, North Carolina:

> Our request for the release of Father Cortesi came back this morning disapproved. There was a sympathetic attitude towards the request, but under present circumstances it was not deemed advisable to make exceptions of this character to the normal restrictions imposed on prisoners of war…. Tell the good Father to make the best of the situation in the knowledge that God's grace can accomplish its wonders under the most adverse circumstances. Assure him of a fervent remembrance in my own prayers and Masses.[320]

While, as in the German case, the sting of anti-Italian feeling was inevitably drawn by the presence of hundreds of thousands of Italian Americans in the American armed forces, not all of them took to their estranged cousins while serving in Italy. As one Italian American complained to Ernie Pyle:

> I look at it this way – they've been poor for a long time and it wasn't us that made them poor. They started this fight and they've killed plenty of our soldiers, and now they're whipped they expect us to take care of them. That kind of talk gives me a pain. I tell them to go to hell. I don't like 'em.[321]

Furthermore, an encounter with the chilling ornamentation of a tribunal room in 'the old Fascist Building at Salerno' in 1944 persuaded navy chaplain Paschal E. Kerwin and Admiral Bertram Rodgers, both Catholics, to undertake an act of ritual cleansing. As Kerwin wrote:

> A huge judgment table of wood carved with the fasces design stood at one end of the room, and over it, engraved in gold letters in the red marble wall, was the famous Fascist oath to Mussolini. I remember standing there one day contemplating using it for a chapel and the wooden table for an altar. The Admiral stood beside me and asked me to translate the oath in which people swore by God and their blood to defend Fascism and the cause of Mussolini. It was really blasphemous. When the Admiral heard its meaning, he immediately ordered a sailor to get black paint and cover the gold lettering. Then I told him I would say Mass on the Fascist table the next morning. He attended. This was an event I shall never forget. As I looked up during Mass I could barely see the outline of the oath, and I prayed God that no one would ever have to subscribe to such a thing again. From then on the Fascist tribunal room became our church.[322]

More usually, however, it was the idiosyncratic piety of Italian civilians that impressed itself upon Americans. Ernie Pyle remarked on the ubiquitous pattern of domestic decor in southern Italy, a pattern that comprised portraits of grand-parents, photographs of family weddings, 'and always a number of pictures of Christ and various religious scenes and mottoes … invariably the faded pictures on the walls were of the same sort'.[323] Nevertheless, and in an odd echo of the 'Italian question' that had so exercised America's Catholic hierarchy around the turn of the twentieth century, the temper of southern Italian Catholicism in particular struck an uncomfortable chord with many Catholic GIs. As Eric Sevareid wrote:

> Soldiers sometimes discuss their religious beliefs among themselves; observers such as correspondents are rarely included in this talk. But I had a distinct feeling that some of the devout Catholic soldiers I knew, for whom the Vatican was the whole center and meaning of Rome, were bolstered in their feeling about their Church by the splendor and majesty of the Papacy. I thought of two Catholics who in southern Italy had confessed to me that they were shaken by the sight of shabby, unshaven priests begging cigarettes on the curb and even offering to take the men to prostitutes.[324]

Even Jewish chaplains could discern the qualitative difference between Italian and American Catholicism, with the vagaries of the former even affecting Italian Judaism. As Morris N. Kertzer explained: 'Italian Jewry … had for centuries been outside the mainstream of Jewish life. Its religious forms seemed almost alien to us, being modelled after the Catholic ritual.'[325] And as for Catholicism, Kertzer claimed that Catholic soldiers who had been raised in the United States had been shocked by their experience of its Italian manifestation. The heart of the Catholic world had failed to inspire them, and it seemed clear to Kertzer at least that Italian religion in general was mired in rank superstition, with Italian Catholics and Jews equally obsessed with its form rather than its substance.[326]

Despite the vagaries of Italian Catholicism, especially in Sicily and southern Italy, there was sufficient sense of a shared faith for Catholic (and, presumably, even non-Catholic) GIs to show their support for the straitened Catholic Church. In Sicily, GIs collected more than $500 to support an impoverished Benedictine convent, and then employed its nuns as laundresses for $100 per week.[327] Similarly, after driving the Germans from the town of Capaccio in southern Italy, a contribution of twenty-five thousand lire was raised for the restoration of an ancient church tower that had been damaged during the fighting.[328] As the war moved northwards, and in a palpable symbol of reconciliation, Christmas 1943 saw Chaplain Gabriel Waraksa of the 54th Medical Battalion celebrate Mass for Catholic GIs and Italian civilians 'in a blacked-out tent' close to the front line:

If the war belied the Christmas message of peace, yet the meeting of Christian people from two nations – strangers meeting with homefolks, who the year before had been enemy peoples to one another – bore testimony to growth in good will among men. Some of the soldiers' candy that went as gifts to the hungry children, played its part in making the atmosphere more Christmas like.[329]

What surprised many was the openness of ordinary Italians even to representatives of the Protestant churches. At Maknassy Pass in Tunisia in 1943, Harry P. Abbott's chaplain's insignia swiftly put Italian prisoners at their ease, with some even offering to assist the United Brethren minister 'in digging graves for both enemy and Americans'.[330] In March 1944, *The Link* published a piece by Everett D. Penrod, a Nazarene air force chaplain, which told of his salutary encounter with an Italian cleaning woman. On being told that Penrod and his chaplain companion were both Protestant ministers, the woman was shown a Bible, an object that she treated with unaccustomed awe, gazing at it 'from a distance' and speaking 'only in a whisper'. As a result of this reaction, so Penrod claimed: 'She made me feel that this was indeed the sacred Word of God, and I felt more reverent toward my Bible than ever before in my life.'[331] Even the Catholic clergy seemed fairly receptive, with Chaplain Israel Yost, a United Lutheran, recalling that he had 'a long talk with a local priest' in September 1943 which 'set up a pattern' for others. As 'the first Protestant minister' the priest had ever met, Yost told him that: 'I believe in the Trinity; I respect the Virgin Mary but I do not pray to her; I pray to the Father through Jesus; I do not believe in the pope.'[332] Later, before the Gustav Line in January 1944, Yost wrote to his wife: 'The Italian folks nearby have been asking me for a Mass; I explain I am Protestant. Every night a group of them gathers in a nearby house to say the rosary. We can hear the melodic, chanting-like mumble and the solo voice of the one who recites the leader's part – impressive.[333]

Nevertheless, Protestant chaplains usually preferred the company of Italian Protestants, who, in the case of the Waldensians in particular, seemed to provide a model of heroic perseverance while also being less tarred with the fascist brush. Fresh from recounting the edifying reaction of Penrod's cleaner to the sight of Holy Writ, *The Link* magazine announced that the Waldensians had remained true to their dissenting traditions:

> News coming out of Sicily since the Allied occupation of that island indicates that all through the regime of Mussolini the ancient Waldensian Church of Italy and Sicily retained its democratic and Protestant beliefs. The synod, meeting annually in the Piedmontese Alps, continued to send messages of loyalty to the King [Victor Emmanuel III] and ignored Il Duce. Of the eighty Waldensian pastors, it is reported, only three were Fascists.[334]

However, offshoots of Anglophone Protestantism were no less admired. While in Brescia in the early summer of 1945, Israel Yost made sure to visit 'the Waldensian pastor and the Salvation Army'.[335] The latter, though proscribed in Italy in 1939,[336] underwent a renaissance with the collapse of Mussolini's regime and the slow advance of the Allied armies up the Italian peninsula. In March 1945, for example, *The Chaplain* magazine reported its remarkable revival in Florence, from where Chaplain Harold Barry, himself a Salvationist, reported that, 'many Yanks have been attracted to the Red Shield canteen of The Salvation Army ... where a five-piece orchestra is heard and where 7,500 cookies and pastries are baked and served daily'.[337] In Florence, the arrival of the Americans in 1944 revived the fortunes of its Baptist church, 'part of the mission program of the Southern Baptist Convention', while breathing much-needed life into 'the beautiful American Episcopal Church' as well.[338] In the former case, the presence of numerous if temporary reinforcements guaranteed the repair of its roof, a decent celebration of Christmas and a donation of 'over $1200 for the continuance of the Gospel work in this great city'.[339] Suitably heartened by the recent revival of the Protestant cause in Italy, a revival that was inextricably linked to the victory of Allied arms, in September 1945 *The Chaplain* magazine declared that the Protestant churches were now poised to play an important role in post-war Italy:

> The Rev. Robert W. Anthony of New York City reported upon his return from Italy that 500,000 Protestants will unite for the reconstruction of their country. They have formed a provisional National Protestant Committee which includes Waldensians, Baptists, the Pentecostal churches, Seventh Day Adventist, Brethren, Methodists and English Wesleyans and The Salvation Army.[340]

Britain and the British

Despite ingrained suspicions of British imperialism and the British class system, to say nothing of constitutional differences and the huge number of Americans of non-British descent, the British had the closest religious affinities with wartime Americans. This was not simply a function of a common language, although that obviously helped. By the outbreak of World War II, the historic links between British and Anglophone American Protestantism remained as strong as ever. Besides the ties of denomination and tradition that could see distinguished British clergymen transplanted into prestigious American pulpits (if not vice versa), the missionary, ecumenical and peace movements furnished other arenas for wider interaction between British and American Protestants. Among evangelicals, and no less than George Whitefield and Moody and Sankey before them, international evangelists such as British-born 'Gypsy' Smith enjoyed a truly transatlantic appeal. Nor, despite the slackening pace of immigration into the United States, should the impact of British-born Americans be underestimated in national church life. For example, Edmund P. Easterbrook, who was appointed the US Army's second chief of chaplains by President Coolidge in 1928, was a Methodist who had been born and raised in Torquay.[341] Similarly, the distinguished Presbyterian minister Dr Peter Marshall, who was appointed chaplain of the US Senate in January 1947, had arrived in the United States from his native Scotland barely twenty years earlier.[342] Finally, it is important to recognise the vital influence of the worldwide Anglican Communion, especially upon America's Anglophone elite, in advancing and underpinning a sense of shared religious identity. As we have seen, in the first decade of the twentieth century, the new cadet chapel at West Point was built in deliberate imitation of an English cathedral and Episcopalians dominated the senior ranks of the US Army and the US Navy until long after World War II. At the very highest levels of national leadership Franklin Delano Roosevelt and Winston Churchill, though very different in their personal faith and churchgoing habits, were both products of an Episcopalian/ Anglican public-school education in which the values of muscular Christianity were very much to the fore. As a result of their education and upbringing, in their wartime rhetoric both drew freely and extensively on an acquired repertoire of religious language and imagery, which had a powerful resonance on both sides of the Atlantic. Significantly, their famous meeting at Placentia Bay in August 1941, at which they signed the Atlantic Charter, was accompanied by an open-air Anglican service and by the singing of 'Onward Christian Soldiers'.[343]

However stage-managed, the scenes at Placentia Bay were emblematic of a much deeper and more widely felt sense of religious commonality. Between the fall of France in June 1940 and Pearl Harbor in December 1941, the ordeal of a kindred Christian nation (reported on the radio by Edward R. Murrow of CBS, and symbolised in the destruction of its historic churches and cathedrals by brutal and indiscriminate Nazi air attack) gave powerful moral leverage to American interventionists,[344] easing the flow of controversial Lend-Lease aid to Britain. Appropriately enough, a solemn guarantee of that assistance was delivered in the language of the King James Bible by Roosevelt's special envoy to Britain, Harry Hopkins. Speaking at a dinner in Glasgow early in 1941, in a simple but eloquent manner that prompted an emotional response from Churchill, Hopkins quoted from Ruth 1:16, 'whither thou goest, I will go; and where thou lodgest, I will lodge: thy people shall be my people, and thy God my God'. According to Britain's Canadian-born minister of aircraft production, Lord Beaverbrook, this biblical pledge mattered more than all the armaments that Britain had received up to that point.[345] Consequently, even by the time GIs began to arrive in force in Britain in 1942, Americans were identifying the British as a plucky Christian people with whom they had a strong spiritual affinity. As *The Leatherneck* tellingly observed when reviewing the strategic situation that April, 'to lick Hitler,

St. George must slay the Nazi dragon in its own lair.[346] Hollywood did much to foster these perceptions, most notably through the image of the British home front conjured in William Wyler's *Mrs. Miniver* (1942), a critical and commercial triumph and 'Hollywood's most famous pro-British film.'[347] As one American officer wrote home in July 1942: 'I am glad that I have a little bit of English blood in me ... And after seeing and hearing these English people, knowing what they have gone through, I am sure you would feel the same.'[348] Significantly, a providential interpretation of the Dunkirk evacuation of May–June 1940 – arguably the nadir of Britain's war effort – had considerable traction among Americans. In a sermon preached at New York Avenue Presbyterian Church in Washington DC in September 1940, Scottish-born Peter Marshall spoke of the evacuation as having 'the magical quality of a great Biblical story'; Dunkirk was a 'miracle', he claimed, which had been wrought through the common endeavour of ordinary people, by 'the little men with the help of God.'[349] This image was stoked by another Briton, Royal Navy chaplain John T.C. Laughton, 'at the Protestant Episcopal Church of the Incarnation' in May 1942. According to the *New York Times*, in a stirring sermon Laughton compared the mood in Britain after Dunkirk to that of the disciples at Pentecost: '"God, without Whose help Dunkerque would never have been possible, will give us the strength we need." And He had done that.'[350] No less fervent was Margaret Lee Runbeck's appraisal in *The Great Answer* (1944), where she asserted that the beaches of Dunkirk were to the British as the Red Sea was to the Israelites, and that henceforth, 'the name of Dunkirk will stand to common people as a synonym of God-with-us, as a talisman for anyone to hold on to in severe extremity.'[351]

If such providential glosses on the course of the war provoked conflicting opinions in *The Link*,[352] there was much greater consensus on the robust faith of Britain's wartime leadership, and notably that of its redoubtable, half-American prime minister, Winston Churchill. According to Archbishop Francis Spellman, during their meeting in March 1943, 'The subject of religion came up', and consequently:

> Mr. Churchill said that he is a man of faith. He believes that Almighty God has saved England in several critical situations. Notably, he remarked the failure of the Germans to follow up their success at Dunkirk, the calm sea which prevailed for the first day in many weeks at the time of the invasion of North Africa, and several other occurrences of like moment.[353]

Churchill's religious credentials were also endorsed by *The Link*, which published part of a radio address given by Churchill only three days before he met Spellman:

> Religion has been the rock in the life and character of the British people, upon which they have built their hopes and cast their cares. I rejoice to learn of enormous progress that is being made among all religious bodies

in freeing themselves from sectarian jealousies and feuds, while preserving fervently the tenets of their own faith.[354]

Another British politician to make a very favourable impression upon the American public was Lord Halifax, a staunch Anglo-Catholic and Britain's ambassador to the United States from 1941 to 1946, whose more conventional Christian faith also served to recommend him to an American audience. The departing ambassador's lengthy reflections on the implications of the war for Christendom, and on the demands of peace, were published in *The Link* in 1946, as was an encomium from the *New York Times*, which described Halifax as:

> [A]s sincere a friend of us and of our way of life as Britain ever sent to our country to represent her interests here.... He has shown us that the typical Englishman is not too dissimilar from the typical American, holding the same fears, the same high hopes, basically the same loyalties to the same principles and standards.[355]

Although the status of King George VI as the Supreme Governor of the established Church of England was inimical to an array of American constitutional norms and values, the pious domestic image of the wartime house of Windsor also met with an enthusiastic response. In June 1943, *The Link* reported with approval the words of Queen Elizabeth on the need for 'a revival of religion' and on the religious role of women in the home. Speaking in an 'Empire-wide broadcast', the Queen had insisted that: 'Our homes must be the place where it should start. It is the creative and dynamic power of Christianity which can help us to carry the moral responsibilities which history is placing on our shoulders.'[356] A story even circulated in the US about the remarkable survival of the Windsors' family Bible. As reported in *The Chaplain*:

> When the Royal Chapel at Buckingham Palace was bombed, some beautiful and valuable things were destroyed.... But among the treasures which escaped was the King's family Bible – on the flyleaves of which are recorded the royal births, marriages and deaths for several generations.... The secretary who found the Bible among the ruins wrote to a friend saying: 'We took it as an omen of what is going to survive when this war is finally over.[357]

Most remarkable, however, was the encounter between Queen Elizabeth and the American chaplain DeLoss I. Marken when she and King George visited the 34th Infantry Division in Northern Ireland in 1942. As Chaplain Eugene L. Daniel remembered:

> The Queen was perfectly charming. At a tea later in the day, the Queen allowed Chaplain Marken to take pictures of her, if he would first give her 'time to powder her face.' Marken, who was a very folksy man, rejoined the group after the picture taking. To everyone's amazement he put his arm

around the Queen's shoulder and said: 'I certainly want to thank you for letting me take your picture. You are the nicest queen I know and if we ever decide to have a queen in America, I am going to vote for you.' The Queen replied: 'Oh you palavering Yankees!' The visit of the royal couple was a tremendous morale booster and one that none of us will ever forget.[358]

Despite the many points of friction that could develop between Britons and Americans in Britain – friction that could arise, for example, from the use of an unfamiliar (British) currency, from disparities of pay between British and American servicemen, and from the US Army's treatment of African American GIs – perhaps the most striking feature of this friendly occupation was that it was so amicable in general terms. According to David Reynolds, 'On the eve of D-Day there were at least 1,650,000 members of the United States armed forces in the British Isles' and, as US Army surveys showed, in the ETO a consistent proportion of almost three-quarters of Americans held at least a moderately favourable opinion of 'the English people'; in fact, a survey conducted in Berlin in August 1945 suggested that the popularity of the British had enjoyed a post-war surge after first-hand experience of the hitherto romanticised Russians.[359] Naturally, a common religious culture made a major contribution to the largely positive interaction between GIs and British civilians, as well as being an implicit dimension of the nascent 'special relationship' between Britain and the United States. In April 1943, readers of *The Link* were reminded that one London church that had braved the Blitz had been 'largely built by Americans', its steeple being adorned by a representation of the Stars and Stripes.[360] Again, and in much the same way that GIs cast a curious and critical eye over the character, equipment, command and performance of their British allies,[361] some Americans took a deep interest in the religious traditions, character and innovations of the British armed forces. In North Africa in 1943, the considerable ego of Francis Spellman was flattered by an invitation to distribute shamrock to soldiers of the Irish Guards, a St Patrick's Day ritual in this traditionally Catholic regiment.[362] On his return to England, Spellman's appointments included a conference with 'Bishop Dey, Military Vicar of the British Army, Father Coughlin, principal Catholic Chaplain in the British Army, and Father O'Neil, Chief Chaplain of the Canadian forces'.[363] Even for a Protestant publication such as *The Link*, the visit to the Vatican of the British Army's 38th (Irish) Brigade in 1944 was obviously newsworthy, with the magazine reporting that the pontiff had been regaled 'with ancient Irish religious music *played on bagpipes*'.[364] However, and at least according to Sherwood Eddy, there were some Protestant parallels, with *The Chaplain* recounting Eddy's tale of one 'courageous old missionary who won so many young officers to Christ in their youth that one or two of the British regiments later commanded by them in India were known as "The Hallelujah Rangers" or "God Almighty's Own"'.[365] Of particular interest to *The Link* and *The Chaplain* magazines were the attempts of British chaplains to recruit for the post-war ministry. In March 1944, *The Link* noted that: 'A hundred or more soldiers in the British army have expressed their wish to become clergymen. Some are already being prepared *for the ministry by their chaplains*.'[366] In time, this initiative (which, by the end of the war, had identified 'several thousand ministerial candidates') helped to inspire a similar recruitment drive by American churches and army chaplains.[367] As for the RAF, in August 1944 one GI enthused at length in *The Link* about its new, residential 'Moral Leadership' courses, which he had heard about 'from two fellows of the RAF' at a church meeting in England. Run by RAF chaplains, aimed at 'character-building', and fully supported by RAF officialdom, Private Herbert G. Nabb claimed that:

> I wish that I could weave into this letter something of the inspiration and enthusiasm of the two young people who told us about it.... What has been done here in England with such success could be done at home. I know there is a tremendous need for such training. Though our forces are provided with the best of battle equipment, their spiritual and moral welfare is sadly neglected.... Why could not our forces have something similar to this course the RAF has begun? I pray that the idea will fall into the hands of those who are capable of promoting it.[368]

Another, very significant, RAF innovation was reported by *The Chaplain* in 1946, namely that: 'CHAPLAIN ELSIE CHAMBERLAIN, formerly minister of Christ Church, Friern Barnet, Middlesex, England, has been appointed chaplain for the Royal Air Force, the first woman to hold that post in any of Britain's services.'[369]

Having a two-year edge on their American counterparts, Britain's armed forces also provided some ready-made religious role models for World War II. In December 1944, Dr John Sutherland Bonnell, the Canadian-born incumbent of New York's Fifth Avenue Presbyterian Church and author of *Britons Under Fire*, based on his trip to a beleaguered Britain in 1941,[370] wrote in *The Chaplain* of the simple faith of a British bomb disposal officer working at the height of the London Blitz. Engaged in his supremely dangerous task, this 'young second lieutenant' had admitted to finding comfort in the words of the fourth verse of the 23rd Psalm, 'Yea, though I walk through the valley of the shadow of death ...'. However, he was careful to add that this did not mean that he did not expect a fuse to go off, but that, 'somehow when I repeat these words to myself, I feel as though it doesn't make any difference what will happen. I am made strong by the assurance that God is with me.' Bonnell's gloss was emphatic: 'Lay hold of this message now, repeat it to yourself each night before you go to sleep on your army cot, or in your bunk in a ship at sea. Then, when the hour of crisis comes, it will keep you steadfast in any emergency.'[371] In terms of Christian commanders – the new Joshuas and Gideons of the Allied war effort – the very first issue of *The Link* invoked the example of Major General Robert Sturges and his invasion of Vichy-held Madagascar in 1942: 'Every detail of its planning and execution was prayed over.'[372] Furthermore, and rather ironically given his later reputation in the United States, in 1943 Montgomery was also held up by American commentators as the quintessence of a victorious Christian warrior. Flamboyant, egotistical, the son of a bishop and a dab hand with scripture, on the basis of his victories in North Africa Montgomery's example was clearly one to emulate. Air Force Brigadier General Auby C. Strickland, writing to his son on the occasion of his thirteenth birthday, counselled: 'If you have a firm footing in your relationship with God, you need never worry about anything.... Our great General Montgomery loves and believes in God. That is his great weapon.'[373] Similarly, *The Link* reported rather tartly in April 1943:

> BERNARD MONTGOMERY, the British general who was first to overwhelm a German army in this war, is the son of a bishop and the grandson of a man who wrote a life of Christ. The man who, at this writing, was chasing Rommel across the desert, is a stern disciplinarian. It should interest the critics of the so-called 'bluenoses' that General Montgomery does not drink.[374]

Predictably enough, William L. Stidger also lent his voice to this chorus of approval, publishing a piece on Montgomery in *The Link* in July 1943. Entitled 'That Guy Prays!' – and writing in honour of 'a preacher's kid who made good in a manner quite disconcerting to Herr Hitler' – Stidger noted how Montgomery's reputation as a praying, Bible-reading, non-smoking, teetotalling general (in fact, as an essentially 'Cromwellian figure') had seized the imaginations of Americans from park benches on Boston Common to the US Supreme Court in Washington DC. Echoing the words of Supreme Court Justice Frank L. Murphy, Stidger proclaimed that: 'We are fortunate in having two great generals, Marshall and Montgomery, who are deeply and sincerely religious men, men who believe in the principles on which our two nations were founded.'[375]

While it would be true to say that Montgomery's exalted reputation did not survive the strains and stresses of coalition warfare – to say nothing of the postwar battle of memoirs – another British general, Lieutenant General Sir William Dobbie, enjoyed more lasting appeal in the United States. Unusually for an officer of his rank and generation, Dobbie was a high-profile evangelical and a member of the Plymouth Brethren, who had been governor of the critical island fortress of Malta throughout much of its protracted siege of June 1940 to May 1943.[376] There was, in fact, much about the World War II siege of Malta that lent itself to religious commentary; as in 1565, when facing the Ottoman Turks, its beleaguered Christian defenders were hard pressed by the seemingly overwhelming forces of a cruel and infidel foe bent on overrunning Europe. At the start of the siege in June 1940, only three obsolescent fighter planes – dubbed 'Faith', 'Hope' and 'Charity' – had been available to defend the island and, of these, only 'Faith' had survived.[377] Dobbie himself very much saw the island's ordeal as a series of providential escapes and interventions and, after his replacement in May 1942, he set about sharing these convictions with the world.[378] Addresses given by Dobbie were duly published by *The Link* in March 1944 and in May 1945. The first spoke of the general's conversion and faith in Christ,[379] the latter of the serenity that his faith had given him during the siege of the island: 'Reliance on God meant everything to me, and I believe to many of the people of Malta, too.'[380] Undoubtedly, the general's militant faith and salutary message resonated with many Americans, *The Chaplain* reporting in March 1945 that Dobbie and his wife were now 'conducting evangelistic services in America.'[381] As a result of their tour, 'millions' of copies of Dobbie's profession of faith were produced and his autobiography, *A Very Present Help*, whose title was derived from the 46th Psalm, quickly secured an American publisher.[382]

It was indicative of the enduring religious ties between the two nations that the activities and pronouncements of British churchmen were frequently addressed in *The Link*. The enthronement of Dr N.V. Gorton as the new Bishop of Coventry, an ancient cathedral city that had been practically martyred by Luftwaffe bombing in November 1940, was described in a clipped but inspiring style in May 1943:

> The processional cross of Coventry was made from three large nails salvaged from the wreckage, and the bishop's episcopal throne consisted of an oak seat placed upon blocks of fallen masonry. The British Broadcasting Corporation called it 'the strangest enthronement ceremony a bishop ever had.' The bishop pledged that the cathedral shall rise again.[383]

Likewise, in June 1944, *The Link* enthused over an eight-point programme for the future of liberated Europe devised by 'Anglican and Free Church leaders in Britain'. Based on the Atlantic Charter, their requirements included, 'Relief measures to feed the starving, fight disease [and] promote health', the restoration of 'the rule of law, national and international', the realisation of religious freedom and, in overall terms, represented a programme that could be readily embraced by 'young people, both in Europe and America.'[384] For the benefit of its more clerical readership, snippets of wisdom from the leading lights of British liberal Protestantism, notably Archbishop William Temple and Leslie Weatherhead, garnished the pages of *The Chaplain*,[385] which also majored on the transatlantic movements of prominent British churchmen.[386]

Significantly, the War and Navy Department's *Instructions for American Forces in Britain*, published in 1942, saw no reason to include any religious advice to its readers, other than to warn them about the strictness with which Sunday was observed, and against traipsing around historic churches while services were in progress.[387] With the great majority of GIs based in England (as opposed to Scotland, Wales or Northern Ireland),[388] for GIs of Protestant, Anglo-Saxon stock service in the British Isles could be a homecoming in more ways than one. After his arrival from Iceland in December 1943, Methodist army chaplain Clyde E. Kimball noted that, despite the ubiquity of fog and the blackout,[389] England was decidedly "'civilized'", with its 'trees and grass and English-speaking people' constantly bringing to mind his own north-eastern corner of the United States.[390] With the coming of spring, Kimball set off on a lengthy journey to visit 'the ancestral home of the Kimballs', an East Anglian village that his Puritan forebears had left three centuries earlier.[391] However, his spiritual heritage as a Methodist also led him to sites of Methodist interest,[392] taking him to London to see Leslie Weatherhead's City Temple, which was sadly lying in ruins.[393] Kimball's constant quest for antiquarian Bibles also led him round the bookshops of the capital, and eventually to the British Library, in the hope that he had chanced upon 'a first edition of the King James Bible', then worth around $1,000.[394] In terms of England's deeper Christian past, in February 1944 Kimball was awed by the ruins of a medieval abbey, 'a sacred and wonderful spot', where, in its 'ancient atmosphere of worship', he felt drawn to prayer.[395] A week later, a visit to an eleventh-century cathedral evoked a similar response, though here Kimball was perturbed to find signs of recent vandalism.[396] In terms of contact with the Christian present, as chaplain of the 1128th Engineer Combat Group Kimball socialised with a local vicar who had been present as an army chaplain at Dunkirk,[397] and on Empire Youth Sunday 1944 preached in an Anglican parish church, albeit as 'a representative of the rebellious black sheep of the Empire'.[398]

Kimball's experiences were by no means unusual for American chaplains. In April 1943, for example, Chaplain James L. Blakeney 'gave the first sermon by an American in ancient King's Chapel of the Savoy, telling a large congregation that Britain and the United States had a mission "to bring enlightenment to the whole world"'.[399] However, for Episcopalians their English sojourns were even more of a spiritual homecoming, as the experiences of George Reuben Metcalf help to illustrate. A staunch Anglophile and assigned to the 29th Infantry Division (or 'England's Own', as it was known, due to the length of its stay in the country),[400] other members of the 29th may have rued their inactivity but, for Metcalf, the division's twenty-month stay in England was an unprecedented opportunity to network with other members of the Anglican Communion, and with other Anglo-Catholics in particular. Consequently, he hobnobbed with the denizens of the cathedral close at Salisbury, writing cheerfully that in England there were 'always new clergy to meet and new cathedrals to visit'.[401] After his return from Normandy, and now on 'limited assignment', Metcalf was an ideal candidate to act as the US Army's Protestant chaplain for metropolitan London, a charge that he welcomed as 'the plum post for a chaplain of my persuasion in the British Isles'.[402] In this capacity he reprised his social whirl, breakfasting with 'England's leading liturgist', while dealing constantly with the Bishop of London and Dean of Westminster.[403] With other American chaplains, Metcalf attended the Convoca-

17 In the cellar of the Race Institute in Frankfurt in July 1945, Jewish chaplain Samuel Blinder inspects one of the many Torahs looted by the Nazis from across occupied Europe. Courtesy National Archives, photo no. 111-SC-209154.

ALL SOLDIERS OF GOD

18 In sharp contrast, an army poster celebrates the strong 'tri-faith' identity of America's armed forces throughout World War II. RG 247 Records of the Office of the Chief of Chaplains. Records of Administration and Management General Records. Records Relating to the History of the Chaplains of the United States Army, 1941-58. Box 9. Courtesy National Archives.

19 Foxhole religion? Prior to the invasion of Normandy, Catholic chaplain Edward J. Waters blesses a mixed congregation of soldiers and sailors at Weymouth, June 1944. Courtesy National Archives, photo no. 111-SC-190504.

20 On the other side of the world, Presbyterian (US) navy chaplain Rufus W. Oakey presides at a service for marines during the fighting for the island of Peleliu, September 1944. Courtesy National Archives, photo no. 127-N-95743.

21 Burial at sea for two sailors of the escort carrier *Liscomb Bay*, which was sunk by a Japanese submarine off the Gilbert Islands, November 1943. Given their predicament, losses among the crews of ships lost in action could be catastrophic. Courtesy National Archives, photo no. 26-G-3182.

22 An American corpse on a Normandy beach, June 1944. American casualties soared during the latter part of the war – a disquieting fact that was not lost on American servicemen. Courtesy National Archives, photo no. 26-G-2397.

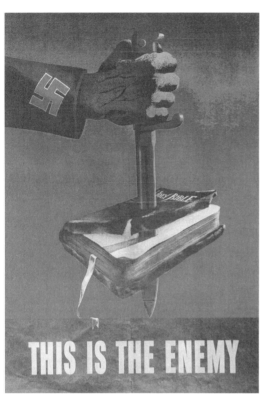

THIS IS THE ENEMY

23 Office of War Information poster, 1943. The Nazi persecution of religion proved to be a powerful propaganda theme before and after America's entry into the war. Courtesy Northwestern University Library, https://images.northwestern.edu/multiresimages/inu:dil-fa69d030-5193-42ed-85e1-cc22f70857f0. Accessed 29 January 2015.

24 Chaplains could be a moderating influence in behaviour towards individual Germans. Here, in France in July 1944, Southern Baptist chaplain John G. Burkhalter of the 1st Infantry Division seeks to identify a dead German soldier. Signal Corps photo no. 191879-S. Courtesy of US Army Heritage & Education Center.

25 Guam, 15 August 1945. Acknowledging the divinity of Emperor Hirohito with reverently bowed heads, Japanese prisoners of war listen to his announcement of Japan's surrender. Courtesy National Archives, photo no. 80-G-490320.

26 A more fearsome indication of the religious chasm that separated the United States from Japan. The aircraft carrier *Bunker Hill* burns off Okinawa on 11 May 1945 following a successful *kamikaze* attack. Courtesy National Archives, photo no. 80-G-274266.

27 Christendom united during United Nations week at Oswego, New York, June 1943. From left to right, Polish, French, Yugoslavian, Belgian, Greek and Norwegian worshippers attend chapel at Fort Ontario. Library of Congress, Farm Security Administration/Office of War Information, LC-USW3-032435-D.

28 Another telling image of inter-Allied religious solidarity. Thanksgiving Day, 1944, and men of the USAAF hear Ward J. Fellows, a Congregational-Christian chaplain, deliver a sermon in Cransley parish church, Northamptonshire. The (Anglican) vicar of Cransley is seated to the rear of the pulpit. Courtesy of the Imperial War Museum, catalogue no. D 22929.

29 Major Charles W. Sweeney, a devout Roman Catholic who grappled beforehand with the moral implications of his mission, receives the Air Medal after the bombing of Nagasaki in August 1945. Courtesy of the Air Force Historical Research Agency, Maxwell Air Force Base, Alabama.

30 Nagasaki after the dropping of the atom bomb. The ruins of the city's Roman Catholic cathedral are clearly visible. Courtesy National Archives, photo no. 77-AEC-52-4459.

31 The general moral health of the nation's defenders was a constant source of concern for religious commentators. Here an army poster reflects their anxieties by warning against the moral implications of gambling. RG 247 Records of the Office of the Chief of Chaplains. Records of Administration and Management General Records. Records Relating to the History of the Chaplains of the United States Army, 1941–58. Box 9. Courtesy National Archives.

32 Invoking an idealised vision of home and family life, another poster appeals to the enlightened self-interest of its army readership. RG 247 Records of the Office of the Chief of Chaplains. Records of Administration and Management General Records. Records Relating to the History of the Chaplains of the United States Army, 1941–58. Box 9. Courtesy National Archives.

tion of Canterbury in October 1944, noting that this was 'the first time visitors have attended such a session,'[404] and a few weeks later sat in the choir stalls in Westminster Abbey during the memorial service for Archbishop Temple – his neighbours being the US Navy's Admiral Stark and the RAF's notorious 'Bomber' Harris.[405] In fact, it was symptomatic of the enhanced and intimate dealings between Anglican and Episcopalian churchmen that Bishop Henry W. Hobson of southern Ohio, then visiting the ETO on behalf of the General Commission on Army and Navy Chaplains, was reputed to be 'the last person, other than relatives' to speak with Archbishop Temple before his untimely death.[406] Furthermore, American chaplains turned up in force for the enthronement of Temple's successor, Archbishop Fisher. As *The Chaplain* reported in August 1945:

> American Protestantism was more widely represented at the recent enthronement of the ARCHBISHOP OF CANTERBURY than at any previous ceremony in history. This was possible because of the presence in Europe of so many American clergymen serving as chaplains. CHAPLAIN FRANK H. LASH and CHAPLAIN JOHN J. WEAVER were selected as personal chaplains to the Archbishop – the first time that Americans have been so honoured.[407]

By dint of their wartime circumstances, even Episcopalian chaplains outside the charmed circles of the capital could enjoy access to the luminaries of the Church of England. In April 1944, for example, Temple presided at a devotional day held for more than sixty Episcopalian chaplains serving with American units in England.[408] Instigated by Chaplain Walter P. Plumley, then based in rural Lancashire, it was described in the following terms in a circular letter from the Office of the Chief of Chaplains:

> ALLIED RELIGIOUS COOPERATION: The Archbishop of Canterbury recently conducted a 'Quiet Day of Spiritual Re-Armament' for the chaplains of the _ Command in St. Martin's Church, Trafalgar Square, London. Three devotional services were given by the Archbishop in a conference which began at 11:30. 'These services, interspersed with luncheon and tea for the group, were most inspirational in character. It was uniformly felt that the chaplains in attendance returned to their respective units better fitted for the work which is theirs to perform.' (Chaplain's Monthly Report.)[409]

However, and if taken to formidable lengths by Episcopalians, the chaplains of other, historically Anglophone Protestant churches also proved keen to get back to their roots and to network with their British co-religionists. As the photographic history *Chaplains of the Methodist Church in World War II* (1948) acknowledged in a section entitled 'Honoring Our Founders': 'During World War II many Chaplains had opportunity to visit Wesley's Tomb [at Wesley's Chapel, London] and there dedicate themselves anew to the spirit of Him whom Wesley proclaimed'.[410] Early in 1944, Chaplain Charles Edward Lunn, a Northern Baptist, joined with two hundred British ministers at the quarterly meeting of the London Baptist Association, where he met one pastor who had had 'two churches blown out from under him' and was now renting a chapel from the Congregational-ists.[411] Baptist chaplains also gathered with the Baptist Union of Great Britain and Ireland in April 1944 and one of their number, Chaplain F.H. Woyke, even found a welcome in the hillsides from the leaders of the Welsh-speaking Baptist Union of Wales.[412] Greatly 'thrilled by the harmonious and inspired singing of the Welsh hymns', it was impressed upon Woyke that, 'so many of our common American names are of Welsh rather than of English origin, among them: Thomas, Lewis, Jones, Davies, Evans, Bevan [and] Hughes'.[413]

If American Catholics and Jews were less tied to England by history or senti-ment, and had more limited access to their co-religionists, especially in the rural areas of southern England where most GIs were concentrated in the build-up to D-Day, this contact was by no means entirely absent. Chaplain Henry F. Ford, a personal friend of Cardinal Hinsley, preached in Westminster Cathedral and Chaplain Francis L. Sampson (despite his Irish ancestry) developed a warm affection for the British, whom he described as an 'amazing breed'.[414] In part, Sampson's opinion rested on a positive experience of fellow Catholics in and around the Berkshire town of Newbury, where he concelebrated Mass with an elderly English priest who relished preaching to Sampson's paratroopers, or '"our gawllant Amerrrican allies" as he called us'.[415] While stationed near Newbury, Sampson also nurtured strong links between his flock in the 501st Parachute Infantry Regiment and local Catholic institutions, notably an orphanage at Cold Ash, whose children his soldiers visited and wrote to, and a Benedictine boarding school, which became the venue for mutually incomprehensible games of cricket and baseball.[416] On the monastic front, a photograph of a GI retreat to Prinknash Abbey near Gloucester even graced the pages of *Yank* in December 1943.[417]

Although a Lutheran, whose access to English co-religionists was negligable, army chaplain Edward K. Rogers was deeply impressed by the attractions of England, admiring its venerable cathedrals and village churches, 'which have told the story of faith for eight hundred years'.[418] In particular, Rogers acknowledged that:

> The cathedrals and abbeys are a lesson in patience and purpose. Through the centuries, not just years, they were built. The changing styles of archi-tecture tell how those structures grew to the glory of God through the centuries. It is good that most of them have come through the war, and it is sad that many others in Britain and elsewhere have suffered so much from bombs and shells. They can be replaced, but not in a way that will tell the story of the past.[419]

Chaplain's assistant Kenneth A. Connelly was also impressed by the natural and man-made features of the English landscape. For Connelly, arriving in autumn 1944, England was reminiscent of the environs of Seattle – minus 'a few mountain peaks' – and the richness of its secular and religious heritage led him to write that: 'The English countryside still breathes the romance of a millenium [sic], the thatched roofs still abound, congregations lift their voices in the shadows of pillars nine centuries old, and there would be little incongruity in meeting King Arthur on one of the narrow, winding roads.'[420] Once again, however, England's medieval cathedrals were especially noteworthy:

> I have stood in awe in the stone forests of cathedrals and wondered that any historians could have been foolish enough to call the Middle Ages dark. That contemporary shrine and highest expression of American religion, Radio City, which houses the radio, movies, and thirty-six chorus girls most resplendently, seems a tawdry, simple, empty spectacle after one has seen something like Salisbury Cathedral.[421]

Nor, it must be stressed, was it only chaplains or chaplains' assistants who felt the warm embrace of England's Christian heritage. Ben Smith, an air gunner with the 303rd Bombardment Group based at Molesworth, Cambridgeshire, recalled that:

> The villagers near the air bases quickly adopted the American fliers as their own. The Yanks visited in their homes, shops and churches and became a part of village life.... I loved this verdant country. Somehow, I had the feeling that I had been here in another life.... Near our base there was an old Saxon church, St Swithin's. It was a thousand years old and still being used for worship. There were many such churches scattered throughout this part of England.... This was the country of John Bunyan, the great Puritan preacher. He had preached in all of the glades and hamlets hereabouts and had written his great allegory *Pilgrim's Progress* in Bedford Gaol only a few miles away.[422]

According to Presbyterian army chaplain Eben Cobb Brink: 'It was naturally in the great, old churches of England that men came closer to God.'[423] However, at the same time it was recognised that the damage to Britain's ecclesiastical infrastructure had been enormous. In March 1945, for example, *The Chaplain* reported that an estimated 2,500 buildings belonging to British Methodists alone had been 'damaged or destroyed by bombing in Great Britain', three hundred of these being recent victims of Hitler's V-weapons.[424] Nevertheless, and while touring London in 1944, Chaplain Charles Edward Lunn, a Northern Baptist, was impressed by the quiet resilience of church life in the beleaguered capital: 'Yonder was a church whose roof was blown off, and every stained glass window broken. A large sign was fastened to the building. It read: "This church though blitzed is still in use".'[425] Kenneth Connelly, another visitor to London in 1944, was struck by the contrasting fate of the capital's historic churches, by 'a London where chapels thirteen centuries old have been blown to fine dust ... a London that has whole acres of rubble around fantastically surviving St. Paul's'.[426] In fact, St Paul's Cathedral, an icon of Britain's survival of the Blitz, was the subject of recurring comment. Writing to his bishop from England, Chaplain Walter P. Plumley said: 'St. Paul's appears to be one of the miracles of this war, as she stands defiant to Hitler's evil, surrounded by blocks of desolation'.[427] Chaplain Eben Cobb Brink was still more emphatic about the marvel that was St Paul's Cathedral, stating that: 'As one leaves [its] quiet atmosphere and walks out to the scene of destruction, one takes new courage. Here is living proof of the Master's promise! "I will build my church; and the gates of hell shall not prevail against it [Matthew 16:18]".' This image of English churches and cathedrals surviving amidst the wreckage of war seared itself onto the American consciousness, their significance as symbols of the antiquity and fortitude of Christianity – to say nothing of the good fortune of the United States – being clear to all. In December 1942, *Yank* carried a photograph of the towers of St Paul's Cathedral on its inside cover, along with the caption: 'Christmas in Britain – 1940[.] *We who came much later should never forget it*'.[428] Eighteen months later, *The Link* published a poem that echoed a connected theme. Entitled 'American Soldier Abroad', its concluding verse ran:

> Here where my eyes behold havoc and ruin
> I shall remember my own cherished land,
> Its churches the symbol, the sign and the token
> That God and His Kingdom forever shall stand.[429]

Emblematic of the worst sufferings of British Christianity in World War II, Coventry Cathedral also had a hold on the American imagination, with a Mother's Day service being held in its shattered precincts in May 1945.[430] Likewise, and while convalescing in the English Midlands in 1945, George Wilson, an officer in the 22nd Infantry Regiment, was part of a group that visited the ruins of the city, remembering – if a little hazily – that:

> Most interesting of all was our trip to the very old city of Coventry, the site of the immortal King Arthur and his legendary Round Table. Less than one hundred yards from the King Arthur collection was a church dating back to A.D. 500 that had been hit by German bombs. About seventy-five percent of the church was in ruins, but the local people had pledged to rebuild it.[431]

In addition to Britain's hallowed Christian history and its built religious landscape, a more human factor was also at work. According to Edward K. Rogers, a return to England was a welcome prospect for the men of the 1st Infantry Division after their experiences in North Africa and Sicily. England was, he said, 'the place where we would rather go if America was out of the question', a place where GIs could converse with the locals, where they would be received as friends and as guests, and where there was no shortage of places to visit. In short: 'The American soldier gets a break in Britain ... he is lucky to be in Britain if he must be away from the U.S.A.'[432] However, a key element in this reception was the positive interaction between the British churches and American service personnel. As early as 1942, *The Manchester Guardian* reported on arrangements that were being made by Britain's churches to welcome these wartime guests, especially given that 'many Americans are traditionally devout churchgoers':

> The American chaplains here are arranging locally for men wishing to attend church to go to local services; the usual camp services are held for the men who cannot get away and at units far from a town. British clergymen of all denominations are cooperating in the scheme, and church members are inviting American boys to their homes and to church outings. Many of the men come from small towns where the activities of the church members supply the main social life, and it is here perhaps that they will find England most like home.[433]

Of all the dates in the calendar, Thanksgiving was the occasion that helped to underline a common faith, a shared heritage and mutual goodwill, especially as in 1942 and 1943 Thanksgiving Day was also designated a special day of prayer by President Roosevelt.[434] In 1942, and in a remarkable display of Anglo-American solidarity, Thanksgiving services were held in churches across Britain.[435] In London, Westminster Abbey played host to a Protestant Thanksgiving service, it being the first time in the abbey's history that a service was led by a 'Nonconformist' (in this case, a US army chaplain), and 'the first time that a foreign flag was draped on the high altar'; in effect, the Dean of Westminster, who delivered the benediction, relinquished his control in 'a concession which has never before been made in the history of the Abbey'.[436] In the shires, the Salvation Army played host for a Thanksgiving service and tea in the Yorkshire city of Hull and, in the Gloucestershire market town of Tewkesbury, GIs participated in a Mass for Thanksgiving at St Joseph's Catholic Church. Here, local clergy concelebrated with an American army chaplain, a GI choir led the singing, and the Mass was preceded by a procession flanked by 'a bodyguard of members of the American forces'.[437] A pattern having been established, it was repeated in successive years. In Tiverton, Devon, for example, Thanksgiving was marked in 1944 at the town's Congregational Church. As the local press reported:

> In celebration of American Thanksgiving Day an inspiring and memorable service was held at Tiverton Congregational Church on Sunday. Transatlantic friendship was symbolised by the Union Jack and 'Old Glory' around the pulpit, and the Rev. S.R. Laver had the assistance of Major W.C. Rindsland, who read the lesson, and Chaplain Edward Dyer, who offered prayer.[438]

In London, further Thanksgiving services were held in Westminster Abbey in 1943, 1944 and 1945, with Westminster Cathedral and the West London

Synagogue hosting Catholic and Jewish services as well.[439] In 1945, and before a congregation of '3,000 American soldiers, sailors, and airmen', the Archbishop of Canterbury offered his thanks for the ultimate victory of 'Our common cause', which 'held us together in an equal partnership of close-knit effort, suffering, and sacrifice'.[440]

Anglo-American religious unity was marked in many other ways. In 1943: 'An Anglo-American Christian Fellowship was established ... for the purpose of linking individuals, Sunday Schools, churches, schools, and even cities of the two nations together through the exchange of letters and speakers'.[441] In Britain, combined religious services were held for British and American personnel, the first taking place in October 1942 when men of the Royal Corps of Signals and of the Eighth Air Force assembled for a 'joint Anglo-American parade service' somewhere 'in the Home Counties'.[442] It was also expressed in the mutual celebration and observance of national occasions besides Thanksgiving. In 1942, Eisenhower set a precedent by directing that 'American Army Forces' based in the British Isles should participate in Britain's national day of prayer on 3 September, 'as far as military necessity will permit'.[443] Twelve months later, military and ecclesiastical dignitaries again 'took part in the American observance of the National Day of Prayer and Dedication, marking the fourth anniversary of Britain's entry into the war'.[444] Significantly, a few weeks earlier Chaplain George R. Metcalf and sixty GIs of the 29th Infantry Division had marked Independence Day ('miscalled Thanksgiving by some Britishers!') by participating in a joint service held in a twelfth-century parish church. According to the division of labour, the rector led the service while Metcalf took 'some prayers, the sermon and the blessing'. As Metcalf said of the service, the mood went much deeper than superficial bonhomie:

> Many were there and most of the parish and the local Home Guard and some of our boys from another station. We sang 'God Save the King' followed by 'America' (same tune of course), talked to our men about what the Fourth means to us, about our country, its geography, story and national convictions, all as they appear in the sight of God – this, after explaining to our British friends that as they had taken us into their church so we wanted them to be present as we talked of home, present as close friends at a family table, thus returning hospitality, in a sense ... the English expressed deep appreciation, and our men were much moved, so I guess the Holy Spirit got in a good bit of work.[445]

For Chaplain Eben Cobb Brink, contact with Britain and its churches served to make the fundamental alignments of the war clearer still, namely 'a united Christendom arrayed against the forces of evil'.[446] This certainly seemed to be the case on 6 June 1944, when news of the cross-Channel invasion triggered an earnest and very public recourse to prayer on the part of Britons and Americans alike. Led by King George VI and President Roosevelt, the assault on the beaches of occupied Europe was accompanied by what appears to have been an Allied bombardment of the throne of grace. While civilians flocked to pray and attend impromptu services in churches across Britain, New Yorkers gathered for 'a mass prayer meeting at Madison Square Garden' and 'prayers were offered during the day in the various states in accordance with D-Day proclamations issued by the governors'.[447]

In a much less dramatic way, this unity also found expression in the expansion of the Service Men's Christian League beyond the ranks of the American armed forces. In Canada, one branch of the SMCL scored a signal success by recruiting Simon Eden, the eldest son of the British foreign secretary, who was then serving in the RAF.[448] Similarly, in 1944 a Private C. Carlile wrote effusively to *The Link*:

> I thought it might interest you to know that THE LINK is not only helping the doughboys, but is also helping some of us British 'Tommies'. In our particular sector, somewhere in Italy, we are really getting together – to our mutual advantage.... The first SMCL service I went to, under American auspices, brought me, in addition to many more things, a copy of THE LINK.... To me it was a moral and spiritual banquet.[449]

This religious commonality with the British was even impressed on the readers of *Yank*. From the Libyan town of Tobruk, retaken by Montgomery's Eighth Army after El Alamein, Sergeant George Aarons, a staff correspondent, wrote towards the end of 1942:

> The town square was dominated by a church, resembling a New England Methodist church ... British soldiers in town ... stopped in the church, each one removing his cap as he entered. We followed them in and saw warm sun shining from a hole on the left side.... There were no furnishings except a bench on which the Tommies sat. A British major praying suddenly brought to my mind that today was Sunday.... A sign near the altar read: 'There was much destruction here, so please don't lend your help.' ... We looked for signs of Germans using the church but couldn't find any. The absence of wooden furnishings however indicated that the Nazis had stripped it for firewood.[450]

In chaplaincy terms, it was inevitable that common faith and a common language should have practical corollaries. The war saw some high-level gatherings of Allied chaplains and, in its aftermath, Canon Frederick Llewelyn Hughes, the chaplain-general of the British Army, was presented with a portable altar by the Army and Navy Commission of the Protestant Episcopal Church: "'In remembrance of the happy relationship between American and British Chaplains'".[451] Unlike a certain colleague in the 34th Infantry Division, Chaplain Harry P. Abbott was content to simply offer grace when King George VI, Queen Elizabeth and US ambassador John Winant visited the 1st Armored Division in Northern Ireland in 1942.[452] Later, and on a troopship bound for North Africa, Abbott took part in an inter-Allied Holy Communion service, one that was not only the largest but also 'the most solemn memorable Communion Service' he ever expected to hold.[453] En route to Iceland in 1942, Methodist Chaplain Clyde E. Kimball distributed New Testaments to British sailors, finding that: 'One wanted to pay (others also) and when I refused brought me cigarettes and matches to give to some "broke" American soldier.'[454] On arrival in Iceland, he became acquainted with the British YMCA and visited facilities run by other, more minor, British religious organisations, finding the local Sandes Home to be: 'Much smaller than our Red Crosses, or USO's, but homey.'[455] Significantly, and at the request of two senior RAF chaplains, Kimball was also tasked with looking after some RAF personnel, whose attendance at church proved surprisingly good; at one camp, he had an attendance of thirty out of thirty-eight, leading him to wonder: 'Can any civilian church do so well?'[456] At Sabbath morning services in the confines of the Anzio beachhead in 1944, Chaplain Morris N. Kertzer found himself ministering to Jewish GIs and Tommies alike in his improvised synagogue, noting that, in contrast to the Americans, there were: 'Few indeed among them, London or Highlander, who did not know the words by memory.'[457] Conversely, such was the shortage of American chaplains in German POW camps prior to D-Day that their care largely devolved upon their British counterparts. As Chaplain Eugene L. Daniel, for some time the only Protestant American chaplain in German captivity, remembered, British chaplains even predominated at Stalag VII-A's memorial service for President Roosevelt in April 1945.[458] However, perhaps the most notable example of shared chaplaincy was the ministry of Albert E. Basil, a British commando chaplain who, owing to a general shortage of American chaplains at that time, served with the US Army's 1st Ranger Battalion in Algeria and Tunisia. A Catholic priest, Basil was technically a member of the Royal Army Chaplains' Department. Nevertheless, and though a self-described 'stowaway' who continued to wear his British commando beret, aided by his innate courage and knowledge of Italian, Basil went on to earn a Silver Star – and the genuine regard of his American flock – for his conduct in the North African campaign.[459]

Owing to the scale and requirements of the American migration to Britain, civilian churches also had to make organisational and pastoral adjustments. Because of the size and number of US Army Air Forces (USAAF) bases in East Anglia especially,[460] ancient rural churches found themselves within their perimeters. At New Year 1944, for example, Chaplain Charles Edward Lunn, then senior chaplain of the IX Air Support Command, addressed 'a church full of eager young men', the venue being 'a little parish church, which is over nine hundred years old, and which happens to be located on our station'.[461] Given this shortage of space, which was no great problem in the United States, more drastic still was the fate of certain churches on a stretch of the north Devon coast, which late in 1943 was designated an amphibious training area in preparation for Operation Overlord. In the event, whole communities had to be evacuated from the area, as well as the irreplaceable contents of their churches – items that included 'candlesticks, pulpits, and even fragile chancel screens'[462] However, it was much more usual for Americans to arrive as guests rather than bailiffs, a common wartime courtesy being that of inviting American chaplains to preach in local places of worship. In October 1943, Chaplain Charles Edward Lunn informed his congregation at the First Baptist Church of Coatesville, Pennsylvania, that: 'I have had the opportunity of preaching in several Baptist Churches here in England. The people are very hospitable and kind'[463] Likewise, and while stationed in northern England, AAF chaplain Walter P. Plumley was often invited to grace the pulpits of Anglican churches in Lancashire, his papers including a keepsake that advertised the fact that 'REV. W.P. PLUMBLEY [sic] (Chaplain U.S.A. Forces.)' would be preaching at Rivington parish church at 3 p.m. on Sunday 20 June 1943.[464] On the strength of several such preaching engagements, and clearly capable of drawing a crowd, Plumley reported to his bishop in the United States: 'The Church of England in this section of England is very vigorous. The Churches are having capacity congregations in the morning and amazing congregations in the evening. I preached at one evening service when over 900 were present'[465]

Nor were many British Protestants unduly bothered about the denominations of their guests. In February 1945 *The Chaplain* reported how a certain 'hospitable rector' had invited three American chaplains to officiate at a joint service in his parish church. Although it was said that no Nonconformist service had ever been held within its walls, his parishioners duly 'joined some thousand American worshipers in uniform', sang 'America The Beautiful' and 'My Country 'Tis of Thee', and 'listened to a sermon by a Quaker chaplain and devotions by CHAPLAIN G.J. DARSIE, Disciples of Christ, and CHAPLAIN W.M. ETHRIDGE, Baptist'. As Paul E. Parker, the Quaker chaplain concerned, observed: 'Thus history viewed new scenes upon old paths ... as men of many faiths and two nations merged their voices in thanksgiving to Almighty God'[466] On other occasions, churches were lent to American chaplains for their own services, but the ecumenical sentiment was often the same. According to Eben Cobb Brink, a Presbyterian, on the occasion of such services:

> It was a new experience for many [GIs] to see their chaplain standing in the high pulpit of a sanctuary so kindly offered to the use of the Americans by a local congregation – a congregation which a few months before would have been shocked at the thought of a minister from another denomination preaching in their pulpit. Strange things the war has done![467]

As a further variation on this theme, on Christmas Eve 1943 an Anglican church in Cheltenham, Gloucestershire, was made available to an American chaplain for a Christmas service. Although it took the form of an Episcopalian sung Eucharist,

Holy Communion was open to all, prompting its incumbent, Canon J.B. Good-liffe, to reflect that the packed church was: 'a moving sight, and deeply reverent. It was good to see a General communicating beside a black soldier ... we had a vision of what must be the Christmas of To-morrow – when distinctions of class, colour, and nationality are merged in the unity of the Spirit of God.'[468]

In any event, their usual freedom of choice in matters of worship meant that GIs were keen to attend civilian churches when serving overseas, and especially in England. Inevitably, for the combat fliers of the Army Air Forces, or the combat soldiers of the Army Ground Forces, England was a staging post to the wider war, a way station on their collective *via dolorosa*. Chaplain Eben Cobb Brink of the 1st Armored Division registered the effects of their arrival in England among the men of his battalion prior to their voyage to North Africa: 'At no time in the history of the battalion had church attendance been greater than it was during those weeks in Britain. Men who knew that terrific things lay not many weeks ahead thought more seriously of God and their need of him.'[469] Chaplain Harry P. Abbott, of the same division, agreed that, 'wherever we were, whether in Ireland, England, Africa, or any other place ... many of our men sought out churches, wherever the opportunity offered, that they might attend them,' Abbott trusting that 'these civilian contacts will no doubt have their influence on them in the future.'[470] In the winter of 1942–43, a discernible drift to the 'local churches' among American officers billeted in the Lancashire town of Bury helped to assuage officialdom's fears that the risky and traditionally unpopular practice of billeting might sour relations between the US Army and British civilians.[471] The prospect of an American descent on local churches was even signalled to the inhabitants of Somerset in August 1942, when the *Somerset County Herald* gave notice that: 'American soldiers in Britain will attend ordinary church services instead of services in camp.'[472] This preference for a civilian milieu remained a persistent trait among GIs in Britain. As one Red Cross worker admitted: 'Yes, our soldiers do appreciate some contact with the churches. In my various clubs I always placed a list of churches with addresses, hours of service, etc. Many ministers have told me of the interesting and sometimes sad visits they received from our boys.'[473] Indeed, some chaplains thought it wise to simply embrace this preference, *The Chaplain* acknowledging in August 1945 that: 'The habit of visiting historic congregations for Sunday morning worship has grown in favor with American servicemen. CHAPLAIN HOWARD M. WILSON conducted a number of these "worship tours." These tours consisted of examination of relics and points of interest in and around ancient English churches.'[474]

In view of the relative affluence of these churchgoers, and the conspicuous generosity of their contributions to church collections, for struggling congregations in Britain GIs could represent a vital infusion of numbers and resources. On one occasion, a clergyman in Stoke-on-Trent, Staffordshire, showed a Red Cross worker a note left in his church by an anonymous GI: 'It had no signature, but merely said, "For the Poor," and enclosed were seven pounds ($28.00).'[475] However, and because they also helped to enliven the worship, GI choirs proved to be doubly welcome, the Episcopalian chaplain Robert F. Pfeiffer writing to *The Chaplain* in 1944:

> During the past twelve weeks I have taken a male quartet and visited as many churches here in England, preaching and singing. It is a fine way to establish a bond of Christian brotherhood – and a natural and painless one! We have preached and sung to varying church groups – Salvation Army, Church of England, Methodist and Congregational. We are usually entertained after the services, and so we have gotten to know English people and they us. Requests for return engagements are coming in fast. What better bond of unity can we have in Christ than our common great hymns?[476]

However, American chaplains were also grateful for the hospitable reception extended to visiting GIs by British churchgoers, and especially for the wholesome influence this could entail. According to Edward K. Rogers, 'one of the finest places for a soldier to make friends is in a church', especially given the benefits of being drawn into the domestic circles of 'the highest type' of hosts.[477] On the return of the 1st Infantry Division to England, Rogers was relieved to find that: 'The churches welcomed the men and they attended in good numbers. Chaplains were invited to preach. Americans began to appear in the choirs in some cases and to take part in meetings during the week.'[478] In this respect, the experience of USAAF Station 522, a depot based in Smethwick, on the edge of Birmingham, is no doubt illustrative. Manned by successive supply companies, and visited every Sunday by either a Protestant or a Catholic chaplain,[479] its denizens ineluctably found their way to local churches, adding a new ingredient to local church life. Bearwood Baptist Church ran special social evenings for GIs and, on Mothering Sunday 1944, held a service that was led by a senior American chaplain. At St Gregory's Catholic church, to which truckloads of GIs were regularly transported, Americans served on the altar and enlivened the proceedings of its Sunday evening youth club, bringing biros, nylons, chewing gum and records, as well as their Protestant friends.[480]

Although British civilians were positively encouraged to extend hospitality to American service men and women, with the American Red Cross establishing a Home Hospitality Division in 1943 to promote such interaction,[481] one of the key benefits of church-based hospitality was that it drew GIs into the orbit of churchgoing women. As Rogers remarked, the return of the 1st Infantry Division to England was followed by a spate of reunions with British friends and correspondents, and: 'Soon there were a number of marriages of the men and their young ladies, whom they met about eighteen months previously.'[482] The civilising and even saving effects of contacts with respectable women were also obvious to Charles Edward Lunn, who advised one young officer who seemed inclined to stray:

> I accept all the invitations I get to go out to dinner in the British homes. There are nearly always women present. Just to talk with them and have fellowship with them in a family setting helps tremendously. I also go to civilian churches when I get the opportunity. There a fellow always gets a chance to come into contact with the opposite sex in a wholesome way. In these ways you get an opportunity to have fellowship with many women without getting serious with any one of them.[483]

Because of their welfare role, chaplains were often involved in the thorny question of GI marriages to British women, a phenomenon that both the American military and the British authorities were keen to discourage. Technically, and in order to get married in the ETO without being court-martialled, GIs were obliged to give a period of notice and to seek the permission of their commanding officer, whose duty it was to ensure that the marriage would not 'bring discredit' upon the service. As part of the policy of obstruction pursued by the US military, chaplains were enlisted to dissuade soldiers contemplating marriage and to vet prospective brides.[484] However, this involvement meant that having a church-going background was at least a positive recommendation, and there is plenty of evidence that many of Britain's thirty-five thousand or so GI brides were very far from being the loose or flighty opportunists they were widely perceived to be.[485] For example, their meetings at Bearwood Baptist Church led to the marriage of Sergeant John Blazek and Margaret Green. After Blazek had made his intentions known, Green's home was visited by a deputation of three American officers, including Chaplain Robert S. Trenbath.[486] Clearly, the history of the happy couple met with their approval, with a later photograph of the wedding party showing Blazek's commanding officer poised uncomfortably on the edge of the group.[487] Significantly, John M. Eggen, an Evangelical Lutheran chaplain who spent most of his army career plying the North Atlantic as a transport chaplain, was impressed by the apparent piety of the 'four shiploads of British wives' he brought to New York at the end of the war. The experience, he said, had led him to 'change radically my former estimate of this class of women'. Far from being 'mere adventuresses', 'gold-diggers', and 'street pick-ups', they appeared to be determined 'home-makers', with a prudent and thrifty disposition born of the wartime situation in England. As for religion, Eggen estimated that around 40 per cent of these British war brides would 'brave seasickness or the restlessness of the children in their arms to attend the various Sunday church services' on board. Beyond that, and in general religious terms:

> How often have I wished that the average parishioner in the average American church took these matters as seriously as do these British wives. It may

be that the horrors and suffering and uncertainty of the British during this war have had the effect of bringing these young women closer to God, or it may be attributed to the church-consciousness which is instilled into the people in a state-church country. To me, however, these war brides displayed a greater interest in spiritual matters than would be found in a similar cross section of America's womanhood.[488]

Clearly, Eggen's opinions were coloured by an American perception of the strength of Christianity in wartime Britain that many British pundits, haunted by an abiding fear of secularisation and chastened by signs of decline in the interwar years,[489] would simply not have shared. In its customary fashion, *The Christian Century* sought to douse this rosy image of Britain, pointing out the relatively low levels of church membership among the British people and their soaring levels of illegitimacy and divorce.[490] Nor were the ubiquitous links between the churches and GIs immune to abuse. For example, before leaving the vicinity of Kidderminster, in Worcestershire, the soldiers of the 357th Infantry Regiment had a whip-round for a local clergyman as 'a gesture of gratitude' for letting them use his church. Amounting to £15 11s 9d, these contributions were in addition to a similar sum that the same vicar had also 'conned' from them. After the presentation, however, a tipsy officer informed one of its chaplains that, 'the Vicar had blown the entire fund on drinks for everyone at the *Eagle and Serpent*'.[491] Nevertheless, and despite such aberrations, the bonds of affection still held. In addition to the countless Christmas and Thanksgiving parties thrown by indulgent GIs for British children, which were often facilitated by their chaplains,[492] another focus of American largesse was the revived adoption scheme for war orphans run by the newspaper *Stars and Stripes*. Originating in World War I, which had seen doughboys 'adopt' nearly 3,500 French children at a cost of five hundred francs per child,[493] the scheme was resurrected for the benefit of British war orphans by a relaunched *Stars and Stripes* in September 1942.[494] Within eighteen months, the Stars and Stripes War Orphan Fund had raised more than £45,000 ($180,000).[495] Such was the success of the scheme that the initial target of £50,000 was eventually raised to £100,000, its object being to ensure that, for a period of five years, individual war orphans would be provided with 'the extra things of life' that they would have received 'had they not lost their parents'. Part of the appeal of the scheme was that particular orphans could be adopted by individual units, and lionised when they visited.[496] Once again, chaplains were often heavily involved in these proceedings, with Charles Edward Lunn liaising with the American Red Cross in order to identify a suitable 'niece' for his unit.[497] Edward K. Rogers remembered that his regiment raised almost £600, sponsoring five children and leaving 'a small balance to assist with their education'.[498]

The intimate connection between the British churches and the American military was also reflected in a process of spontaneous memorialisation that began long before the war in Europe had ended. For example, having marked Thanksgiving Day 1942 with a children's party and a service at St Lawrence Church in Chorley, Lancashire, Chaplain Walter P. Plumley organised the formal presentation of an American flag to the same parish church in February 1943. Significantly, the building had a historic connection with the Pilgrim Fathers, Chorley being the ancestral home of their military adviser, Captain Myles Standish, the flag being hung above the church's 'Standish Pew'. In the words of the presentation ceremony, the rector solemnly accepted the gift 'as a symbol of the friendship and comradeship in arms which unites our two peoples, and may those who look up at it in the years to come strive to do what in them lies to foster that brotherhood in happier days than these'.[499] This gift was by no means unique, however. A year later, and more than two hundred miles away, a 'very large congregation' of Britons and Americans assembled in the parish church of Cullompton, Devon, to dedicate the American flag that had been presented at Thanksgiving 1943. According to *The Western Times*:

> The Vicar expressed thanks to the visitors who had made the service possible, and mentioned that the rood screen was being used as a place to speak from for the first time since the Reformation 400 years ago. It was a memorable occasion, and in due course a tablet will be placed in the church commemorating the event and those who took part in it.[500]

However, windows, organs, fonts and even entire chapels were also installed as American memorials in British churches. In January 1945, the *Christian Herald* featured a stained-glass window dedicated to the memory of the fallen of the 96th Bombardment Group, which already graced St Andrew's Church, Quidenham, in Norfolk.[501] The following month, *The Chaplain* noted that two stained-glass windows dedicated to the memory of the 401st Bombardment Group – windows that were then illuminating the temporary chapel of 'a Flying Fortress Base in England' – would eventually be 'installed in a nearby church', where they would continue to serve 'as a memorial to the lost men of the Bombardment Group' and 'as a link to perpetuate Anglo-American goodwill'.[502] Later that year, American naval aviators at Dunkeswell in Somerset presented its parish church with a new organ and plaque in memory of nearly two hundred officers and enlisted men 'who had lost their lives during the war'. Addressing the congregation, the Bishop of Exeter spoke of two nations 'unexpectedly brought together' by the conflict, and of its American victims who were 'now laid in the friendly earth' of England.[503] At Kirkbean, in the Scottish Lowlands, Americans chose to honour a different kind of hero, namely John Paul Jones, the intrepid patriot sea captain of the Revolutionary War. Here, in 1945, a baptismal font was presented to the parish church on behalf of 'officers and men of the U.S. Navy stationed in Great Britain'.[504] American memorial chapels were mainly to be found in the parish churches of East Anglia, 'dedicated to the memory of the fallen who were stationed at American heavy bomber bases in those parts'.[505] Nevertheless, and in view of the fame and symbolism of St Paul's Cathedral, it was appropriate that the principal religious memorial to the American presence in Britain was the creation of 'a Chapel in St. Paul's Cathedral in memory of American soldiers who gave their lives while based in Great Britain'.[506] Promoted by the American and British-Commonwealth Association, which had been founded in 1941, and announced in the British press in November 1945, the scheme had the support of King George VI, Eisenhower, John Winant, and the dean and chapter of the cathedral itself. Funded by the British public, and 'situated at the east end of St. Paul's, beyond the High Altar', the purpose of the chapel was to house a Roll of Honour and so 'commemorate these valiant American dead and enshrine for ever the underlying moral unities which link our two peoples together'.[507] Inevitably delayed by the urgent needs of post-war reconstruction, the chapel project was the work of years, and it was not until 1951 that building work actually commenced, the chapel being dedicated in 1958.[508]

Australia and New Zealand

Although lacking the established churches and ancient church fabrics of the mother country, the American experience in Britain found more than a distant echo in Australia, where a wartime peak of 120,000 GIs were stationed by September 1943.[509] Chaplain William C. Taggart, on arrival in Australia after Pearl Harbor and through his contact with an unflappable chaplain of the Royal Australian Air Force (RAAF), quickly perceived the importance of their shared faith as an asset in the Allied struggle against the oncoming Japanese: 'Our enemy had only the machinery of war in which to have faith. And when that was smashed, what was left? We had the "weapon" that no amount of bombardment could break down. Through adversity, through bitter defeat, our faith in Him only grew stronger'.[510] Ordinary GIs, however, found the usual consolation in relatively familiar, civilian church settings. As an American chaplain testified:

> On any occasion if one visited a local church in any Australian city he would find a large percentage of the audience to consist of American troops. After they became acquainted, the 'Yanks' found their places in church choirs and Sunday School classes where they were given a gracious welcome to use their experience and talents.[511]

At Easter 1944, their turnout for services in the headquarters city of Brisbane prompted one Australian schoolgirl to ponder: 'Why is it that the Americans – comparative strangers – are such devout churchgoers even in a land not their own?'[512]

As in Britain, and besides swelling civilian congregations, Americans were noted for the generosity with which they passed the collection plate, and one

Australian Methodist minister even hailed them as 'a kind of Godsend'.[513] The fastidiousness of Sunday observance and patterns of church hospitality were also very much the same, with GI choirs (especially those composed of African Americans) being widely welcomed, GIs invited to the homes of reliable churchgoers, and American chaplains deluged with invitations to preach.[514] In fact, there was even 'a danger that the men would be over-entertained because of the concentrated efforts on the part of the Australian people to show their appreciation'.[515] American servicemen married well over fifteen thousand Australian women,[516] and once again their chaplains were heavily involved in vetting procedures, with one chaplain conducting no fewer than 4,500 investigations.[517] In Australia, there was also a sufficient variety of religious affiliation to suit everyone's tastes. If a preaching American bluejacket was billed in Brisbane as 'a young man with a wonderful message',[518] fundamentalist navy chaplain Arthur F. Glasser was able to find plenty of evangelical company in Melbourne, visiting the offices of the Scripture Gift Mission and China Inland Mission, and locating 'an active church' in the suburbs whose minister was a secretary of the Unevangelized Fields Mission.[519] Broadly speaking, the churches also helped to ensure that the reception accorded to African American GIs in bullishly 'white Australia' was generally better than in the United States. Clarence Toomer, who served in a quartermaster unit in Australia, averred that: 'You hear all kinds of stories about Australians not liking blacks, but the citizens were cordial. They received us with open arms. The people in Melbourne had Sunday teas in their homes and churches and would invite the black troops, and we went.'[520]

In a telling illustration of the prevailing goodwill and racial tolerance shown towards black GIs by white Australians,[521] in New Guinea Chaplain Charles H. Dubra ministered not only to other African Americans in the 96th Engineer General Service Regiment but also 'held many services for Australian troops in isolated posts'.[522] Given the problems that faced Americans and Australians alike in the South-West Pacific, there was a good deal of cooperation of this kind. Such was the shortage of American army chaplains during the early stages of the American build-up in Australia, it even seemed as if the pastoral care of American troops might pass entirely to Australians, and a request for the help of seventy Australian chaplains was duly 'initiated'.[523] Although this embarrassment was averted, necessity as well as civility dictated that, in the vastness of Australia and the South-West Pacific, American chaplains had plenty of interaction with Australian chaplains and their flocks, especially by means of joint religious services.[524] In New Britain in 1944, for example, Australian Christians of the RAAF attended Chaplain Glasser's 'Third Bible Church of Cape Gloucester', and even lent their squadron's piano to enliven its worship.[525] The building of Australian–American chapels was by no means unknown,[526] and one church, namely the pre-war mission church of St John-on-the-Hill at Port Moresby, acquired an iconic significance for Australians and Americans who served in the New Guinea campaign. As one history of this vibrant church and recreational centre related, 'it became for hundreds – nay, thousands – of green-clad men, Australians and Americans, something that spelt home, something exalted, something that exemplified the fellowship which war service can inspire'.[527] Uniquely among the chaplains of Allied nations, Australian chaplains also showed a tangible interest in *The Chaplain* magazine. Visiting Borneo in 1945, its editor, Clarence W. Hall, wrote that: 'I met and conversed at length with two of the [senior] chaplains to the Australian Army.... Both were familiar with this journal, and expressed eagerness to receive it regularly'.[528] In 1946, *The Chaplain* even published an article by an Australian chaplain, Arthur E. Bottrell, on the subject of 'Christian Fellowship', in which Bottrell wondered what its fate might be as: 'The time has now come when the blood-soaked earth, upon which this wartime fellowship flourished, has dried out'.[529]

Much less frequented than Australia, with a peak American presence of around twenty thousand between 1942 and 1944,[530] New Zealand offered similar benefits. Navy chaplain Warren Wyeth Willard, following his departure from the Solomon Islands, was engaged in a hectic round of speaking engagements at New Zealand churches, attracting the patronage of the prime minister's wife and even donning a cassock and surplice to preach to the congregation at Wellington Cathedral. As Willard put it, 'I enjoyed the fullest freedom, with all men encouraging me'.[531] While local businessmen built and staffed an 'Everyman's Hut' for the men of the Eighth Marines (its name indicating its link with Toc H, the Empire-wide Christian service organisation)[532] Wellington's Jewish community also proved highly supportive of Jewish leathernecks, with the latter finding 'a real friend and helper in Rabbi Katz, spiritual leader of the synagogue in Wellington'.[533] Arthur F. Glasser also found New Zealand congenial in 1943. In Auckland he tracked down supporters of the China Inland Mission, finding their company so inspiring that he described New Zealand as 'just tops – the "Mountain top" of Christian fellowship'. Indeed, his instinctive affection for 'conservative New Zealand' prompted renewed spasms of loathing for the modernist threat, for 'Pagan thought disguised as "liberalism" was being introduced by professor, preacher, and layman alike into the thinking of young Christians the world over', a 'deadly menace which had contributed much to the downward drift of the age into atheistic materialism and war'.[534] Still, putative agents of this danger also found common ground in this corner of the Antipodes, with American Methodist chaplains, including the urbane and influential William Wilcox Edel, participating in ecumenical and denominational conferences in New Zealand in 1945 and 1946.[535]

China and the Soviet Union

However much wartime Americans may have felt and experienced a strong religious affinity with white Anglophone nations, it is somewhat ironic that none
of these possessed a leader as sainted as China's Chiang Kai-shek, leader of the
Nationalist Party and a Christian convert whose reputation for piety was sedu-
lously promoted by his consort, the equally acclaimed and media-savvy Madame
Chiang. Long before Pearl Harbor, many American Christians had developed
a strong emotional attachment to China, whose political and religious development seemed to point the way to the emergence of a vast new capitalist,
Christian – and primarily Protestant – republic in Asia.[536] Encouraged by their
consciousness of long-standing missionary endeavour, by Pearl Buck's 1931 best-
selling novel (and subsequent Hollywood blockbuster) *The Good Earth*, and by
the keen and beneficent interest of Henry R. Luce and his formidable media
empire, Americans were widely convinced of their natural affinity with China
and its people.[537] Inevitably, this sympathy grew as China became the victim of
Japanese aggression, China's ordeal from 1937 prompting the rise of United China
Relief, a coalition of relief agencies – many of them Christian – that played on
China's receptivity to Christianity in its fundraising efforts.[538] The importance
of China's Christian potential was also emphasised by Frank Capra in his film
The Battle of China (1944), part of his *Why We Fight* collaboration with the War
Department, which dwelt on footage of a native Chinese church and stressed
the similarities between Confucian and Christian teachings.[539] If Luce, as a son
of Presbyterian missionaries to China,[540] and Congressman Walter H. Judd, a
former medical missionary who had laboured in the same Asian vineyard,[541]
were in the vanguard of 'Christian Sinophiles' in promoting the interests and
image of Nationalist China among Americans at large,[542] *The Link* carried the
same message to its military readership. Despite a late-war souring of relations
with Nationalist China, as late as 1946 it could still regurgitate the view that:

> OF ALL the peoples of Asia, the Chinese are most like Americans. Those
> who know both peoples often remark at the likenesses. One of the reasons,
> perhaps, is that we both live in countries where there is plenty of space and
> a great variety of climate and food. We are alike, too, because we both love
> independence and individual freedom.[543]

However, *The Link*'s most consistent message in this respect was that the
Chinese were led by a pious and progressive Methodist couple whose lives were
models of Christian devotion, fortitude and forgiveness. In September 1943 it
published a praise piece by William L. Stidger, which he based on an interview
with an American missionary in Madame Chiang's retinue. This portrayed the
generalissimo memorising the Psalms, revealed his favourite hymns and scripture
texts ('O God, Our Help in Ages Past' and the 23rd Psalm, respectively, topped

the lists), and assured its readers that: 'Every religious word, prayer and hymn Chiang Kai-shek utters is as sincere as sunlight ... If any great statesman on earth has a religion that really is *real*, it is Chiang Kai-shek!'[544] *The Link* returned to the compelling subject of Chiang's favourite hymn in November 1944, this time citing 'Rock of Ages',[545] while it advertised his daily devotions once again in January 1945 with an account by a Canadian missionary of how the generalissimo had conducted his evening prayers during a Japanese air raid on Chungking, Chiang praying not only for himself but for those who were being bombed – and even for the Japanese.[546] Chiang Kai-shek's thoughts on world peace and fellowship – namely following 'The way of the Cross' – were duly published in *The Chaplain* magazine in October 1944.[547] As for Madame Chiang, *The Link* portrayed her as a willing party to her husband's domestic devotions,[548] as a strong advocate of forgiveness in building the post-war world,[549] and as one who had come to appreciate the value of her mother's Christian example.[550] Nevertheless, and despite the swathes of copy devoted to the luminous Christian witness of China's leading couple, not all Americans succumbed to its aura. General Joseph W. Stilwell, who as Chiang Kai-shek's chief of staff was deeply contemptuous of the couple he reviled as 'Peanut' and 'Mme. Bitch',[551] and whose return to the United States in November 1944 marked a new low in relations with Nationalist China, was as dismissive of Chiang's piety as he was of his wider abilities. For example, as early as August 1942 Stilwell seethed, 'Chow at Huang Shan [the Generalissimo's summer residence] ... Chiang K'ai-Shek was late. He had been doing his evening prayers, which are not to be interrupted by anything. This is a new angle. Anyway, *he* takes it seriously, whether it's sincere or not,' adding facetiously: 'Maybe he is fortifying his intuition by communing with his Maker.'[552]

Until the end of the war in Europe, significant and direct contact with the United States' other major ally, the Soviet Union, was even more limited, being mainly confined to maintaining the flow of Lend-Lease supplies through Iran. Furthermore, perceptions of the religious condition of the Soviet Union were initially coloured by a strong awareness of Stalin's savage persecution of religion prior to the German invasion of June 1941. Before the United States entered the war, the reputation of the murderous, tyrannical and atheistic Soviet Union posed real problems for Roosevelt as he sought to extend Lend-Lease assistance to the beleaguered workers' and peasants' paradise. Although American Catholics were, as a group, most averse to aiding the Soviet Union, even a majority of American Jews were reluctant to provide this help on the same basis that it had been given to Britain. In the event, Lend-Lease for the Soviet Union was only approved in Congress in October after pressure was exerted on Pope Pius XII to soften the Vatican's uncompromising anti-communist line, and after American pressure in Moscow had accelerated the concessions to religious freedom that had already been precipitated by the Axis onslaught.[553] Despite this success, and the acclamation of the Soviet war effort that accompanied the course of America's war against Germany, the essential nature of the Soviet regime still jarred with religious Americans. In 1945, *The Chaplain* magazine reported the slightly absurd – though richly ironic – story of two high-ranking American businessmen at a banquet in Moscow. Regaled with Russian songs by their Stalinist hosts, they responded to an invitation to reciprocate by singing 'Jesus Wants Me for a Sunbeam'.[554] In August 1945, the magazine tackled the emergent problem of post-war relations with the Soviet Union in an article entitled 'Troublesome Russia'. Sponsored by the Carnegie Endowment for International Peace, this acknowledged the immensity of the Soviet Union's wartime sacrifice – and the need to avoid provocations – but accepted that 'the vast majority of Americans do not like Communism' and that the wartime alliance had been basically one of convenience. It also said of Stalin:

> Of course Commissar Joseph Stalin is irritating, remaining remote and cunning like Odin in the halls of Valhalla. Americans complain of the way he refused newsmen and military guests to view his armies in action, delayed reports on Lend-Lease for the U.S.S.R., prefers to deal with German war criminals in his own way, and of the unique manner in which he interprets the agreement at Yalta concerning Poland.[555]

However, even Stalin's worst American critics could scarcely dispute the fact that the Orthodox Church – for better or for worse – had been a major beneficiary of the Great Patriotic War. At the end of 1945 *The Chaplain* reported: 'Patriarch Alexei, supreme head of the Russian Orthodox Church, has announced that all major problems of church–state relationships in the Soviet Union have been satisfactorily solved. He indicated, in an exclusive interview, that Premier Josef Stalin is taking a personal interest in the work of the Russian Orthodox Church.'[556]

If few other than Roosevelt were prepared to give Stalin credit for being a former seminarian,[557] or, indeed, for possessing the belief in God that Stalin eventually claimed,[558] Americans were more enthusiastic about the enduring faith of the Russian people, now free to express itself amidst a struggle to the death with Nazi Germany. Accordingly, *The Link* peppered its pages of foreign news with reassuring – if rather naïve – stories of religious revival among Soviet citizens. In March 1943, for example, and giving 'the New York office of the World Council of Churches' as its source, it cited a survey that had found that the great majority of Russians had 'not lost the faith of their fathers'. However, this survey had been conducted among Soviet POWs by Orthodox exiles in Czechoslovakia, a White Russian agenda being suggested by its aim of aiding 'the future work of the Orthodox Church.'[559] Equally uncomprehending was its report in March 1944 that 'Nazi-controlled Baltic countries are experiencing a great religious awakening' – with packed churches, devotions in the streets and a distinct shortage of atheists.[560] If editors of *The Link* were clearly unfamiliar with the national, ideological and religious fissures within the Soviet empire, a story published in

June 1944 to the effect that Soviet POWs in Rumania had built a church that had been consecrated by the Metropolitan of Transylvania should have at least raised suspicions. However, if they existed, they were clearly overridden in the desire to offer 'another proof that all Russian youth did not lose their faith despite the efforts of the Society of the Godless'.[561] If *The Link* spent a surprising amount of time publicising the wrong wartime revival among Stalin's subjects, at least other stories were more on target – such as the non-enforcement of earlier restrictions on religion, the extent of enduring attachment to the Orthodox Church, the scale of the faithful's donations to the Soviet war effort, and the opening of an Orthodox seminary in Moscow.[562] Even Protestants felt the benefits, with Russian Baptists joining 'openly' in a World Day of Prayer with their co-religionists in February 1943, and Baptists and evangelicals participating in 'an all-Soviet meeting in Moscow' in the summer of 1945.[563] Regardless of the overall accuracy of *The Link*'s coverage of religious developments in the Soviet Union, it seems clear that it was anxious to reassure its readers in America's armed forces that they were basically engaged in the same Christian struggle against a common Nazi enemy as were their remote Soviet allies.

France and liberated Europe

More familiar to American service personnel, though much less approved of than the British, were the French. In fact, and on the basis of a survey conducted in August 1945, over a year after D-Day, it would seem that the French were less popular among GIs in the ETO than were the Germans, with 50 per cent of respondents having a 'rather unfavorable' or 'very unfavorable' opinion of them (the figure for the Germans was only 45 per cent).[564] Significantly, growing resentment against the French in the aftermath of the war in Europe eventually led to the publication of a special army booklet entitled *112 Gripes About the French*,[565] which sought to tackle such classic complaints as: 'The French welcomed us at first; now they want us to get out' (no. 16); 'The French have no guts; they're decadent' (no. 33); and ' Why isn't there decent plumbing in French houses? The toilet facilities are disgraceful!' (no. 42).[566] In seeking to account for such abiding Francophobia, commentators identified the success of army information and orientation programmes in promoting a better image of the British and the Soviets, and also discerned the pernicious legacy of World War I.[567] Still, they had to concede that: 'France as a symbol was weak, defeated, inadequate, and, in spite of all rational explanations of her defeat, anything but admirable. With these considerations in mind, it is not hard to see why, if negative hostile attitudes toward "Allies" emerged, the French would be the most likely target'.[568]

Besides the adverse impact of 'the alleged sharpness of the French in business dealings and their alleged uncleanliness', which stood in stark contrast to 'unexpected German deference and friendliness, as well as German cleanliness',[569] there was much less of the palliative of a shared religion. The inevitable War Department *Pocket Guide to France* (1944) had sought to play up the country's spiritual heritage and its moral and religious credentials, claiming that, 'the same spirit that built [its] matchless cathedrals exists in France today'. Not only were greater and lesser churches 'crowded on Sundays and Saints' Days', but the parish clergy lived very close to their flocks; it was, so it was claimed, therefore 'easy to imagine how the French feel about the pagan ideologies of the Nazis'.[570] Experience, however, seemed to prove otherwise. France, with its aggressively secular republican traditions, proved to be nominally Catholic for the most part, and was further divided from most Americans by a different language. It was also without a tradition of recent, large-scale emigration to the US that helped to lubricate relations with many other Europeans. Finally, and despite the claims of the War Department and the heroic defiance of many lesser clergy, there was no high-profile equivalent of a Niemöller or von Galen to redeem the craven conduct of the French Catholic hierarchy. After the fall of France in June 1940, Catholic bishops had largely thrown in their lot with the Vichy regime, and in August 1944 the Archbishop of Paris, Cardinal Suhard, even suffered the indignity of being excluded from his own cathedral for the service of thanksgiving for the liberation of the city.[571] Soon afterwards, and when Archbishop Spellman visited Paris: 'General de Gaulle asked the Archbishop of New York to celebrate a special Mass for the GIs in Notre Dame without any reference to His Eminence of Paris'.[572] While Protestant Americans mixed freely with France's small but largely uncompromised Protestant population,[573] even Catholic chaplains could have reservations about the tawdry condition of the eldest daughter of the Church. If Chaplain Francis L. Sampson admired the conspicuous piety of the Norman peasantry,[574] and warmed to the spiritual qualities of the French parish clergy,[575] he was dismayed by what he saw as Gallic fickleness and hypocrisy, recalling that:

> On the way to Cherbourg we passed through a town where the Free French were having a riotous time shaving the heads of women collaborators and marching them through the streets. A French priest who had spent considerable time in a German concentration camp told me that the very ones leading the demonstration had themselves been very friendly and helpful to the Germans. In Paris and other large French cities, our forces were cheered and wined and dined by the 'patriotic' populace. But our men who had been captured by the Germans and marched through to prison camps a couple of months before had been spat upon, kicked, and hooted at by people in these same cities.[576]

For his part, the Episcopalian chaplain and Anglophile George Reuben Metcalf was simply dismissive of the French, writing in January 1945: 'I am coming to believe that there are shutters over the soul of France. It seems to be such a polite Godless country: you feel it in the social atmosphere. There is selfishness in the air'.[577]

There was, of course, contact with other, 'liberated' European nations – with the Belgians, the Dutch, the Austrians, and the Czechs. The Dutch, for example, were generally well regarded, at least in their homeland. While sanitation again played a role,[578] there was no Dutch equivalent of Vichy and GIs could not mistake the enduring importance of religion in Dutch society, still largely 'pillarised' along confessional lines. As in England, and even Iceland before that,[579] Methodist chaplain Clyde E. Kimball could mix easily with his civilian counterparts, explore Holland's Protestant heritage, and participate in services for civilian congregations. After preaching at one Protestant church, Kimball was especially gratified to be presented with 'a beautiful Dutch Bible, 300 years old'.[580] From the moment he descended into Holland in September 1944, Chaplain Francis L. Sampson was equally impressed by Dutch Catholicism. At the small town of Heezwik: 'One of the soldiers told them that I was a priest, and you can't imagine the excitement. Southern Holland is solidly Catholic, and what Catholics!' After being entertained by the parish priest, Sampson emerged from the presbytery to be met by 'a whole monastery of Norbertines ... I had to shake everyone's hand'.[581] Following his capture at Bastogne that December, Sampson's ministry to Allied POWs in the various national compounds of Stalag II-A in Germany also helped to underline the resilience and unity of Christendom, and of the Catholic Church in particular.[582]

Religious internationalism and missionary horizons

Regardless of direct experience of overseas conditions, Christian service personnel were also affected by the growing spirit of internationalism abroad in American society. As the contents of *The Link* reflected, the nature of the New World Order and the role of Christianity in the post-war era were subjects of abiding concern to its service readership, as they were to their churches back home.[583] In May 1943, for example, *The Link* announced that: 'America's leading statesmen are increasingly turning to the Church for the creation of that kind of public opinion that will help us win the peace. The President has said the government "is counting on the leadership of our clergymen" to facilitate a program of discussions on the postwar world".[584] To fuel this debate, and in order to counter Axis propaganda claims that 'American fighting men were short on war ideals', in 1943 *The Link* ran an essay competition on the theme of 'What I Am Fighting For', offering a cash prize and the chance of publication in *The Link* and the *Saturday Evening Post*.[585] Although most of the prizewinners focused on the defence of American homes and values,[586] Pfc. Elbert D. Scott pronounced from Scott Field, Illinois: '[W]e will attempt to build a new civilization – not one founded on greed and fear, but one that is founded on liberty and justice, one in which the human spirit is looked upon as the noble thing it is, a civilization based on the philosophy of Christ.'[587] In addition to this essay competition, *The Link* called upon SMCL units to 'Plan Your Post-War World Now!'[588] Emblematic of this growing Christian 'One World' consciousness was the apparent success of the World Communion Sundays (or World Wide Communion Days) held in 1943 and 1944.[589] Endorsed by the Federal Council of Churches since 1940, and held throughout the US on the first Sunday in October, these were intended to stir, in a strife-torn world, 'a fresh sense of world fellowship in Christ with all who name themselves Christian, whatever their race or creed.'[590] Although it was a vain aspiration that 'every Christian service man and woman' would be able to participate,[591] on both occasions the cavernous Farragut Unit Drill Hall at the Naval Training Center, Sampson, New York, was the scene of an impressive and reassuring display of ecumenism and Christian internationalism. Although navy trainees were still obliged to attend Sunday services, they could not be ordered to partake in Holy Communion. Nevertheless, in 1943 around 7,000 out of a congregation of 7,500 received Holy Communion, and in 1944 the number of communicants climbed to 8,000 out of a congregation of 8,400.[592] Presided over by Sampson's senior chaplain, William Wilcox Edel, both services were the subjects of radio broadcasts and a variety of civilian clergymen were on hand to assist the navy chaplains involved, including in 1944 Dr William Barrow Pugh of the General Commission on Army and Navy Chaplains. In that year, this Eucharistic jamboree was carried 'from coast to coast', it commenced 'with the church call sounded by eight buglers', and was described as 'one of the largest Communion services ever held under one roof'.[593]

However much their experience and sense of the wider world may have strengthened a feeling of shared religious identity among Christian service personnel, this development was still more in evidence among their Jewish comrades. As Chaplain David Max Eichhorn wrote to his wife from France in October 1944:

> The more they see and hear about what has happened to the Jewish communities of Europe, the more Zionistic they become ... I don't know how long it will last but, for the time at least, our men are more intensely and proudly Jewish than I have ever known a similar group to be in the States.[594]

And fellow Jews were to be found in unlikely places. In Berlin in 1945, visiting Chaplain George Vida held a service that was attended by American, British, French and even Soviet soldiers, the international mix being further enriched by 'a sprinkling of civilians'.[595] Likewise, in the Asia-Pacific theatre, significant Jewish communities were to be found as far afield as Australia, New Zealand and Shanghai.[596] However, in the war against Germany, and from the moment Jewish GIs set foot in North Africa in November 1942, there was a powerful sense that they came not only as liberators but as the rescuers of their co-religionists.

Naturally, and as the ultimate embodiments of their deliverance, Jewish chaplains were the focus of particular attention on the part of North African and European Jews. As Chaplain Morris N. Kertzer testified:

> Our insignia, the Star of David resting upon the Ten Commandments, was the symbol of liberation to the Jews of Rome, as it was all through Europe and North Africa. Every chaplain had the uncomfortable role of a messiah, being the living symbol of liberation to a people whose hearts overflowed with gratitude ... 'Look, Sarah, our *Mogen David*' ... 'Come here, Papa, the Ten Commandments'.... Throughout the war, in French, Italian, Yiddish and Arabic, these were the words our chaplains heard. The little symbol given us by the United States Army was the sign of hope to the battered remnant of the House of Israel. 'Somewhere in the world, we are respected,' was what the insignia said to them. 'Somewhere in the world, our Ten Command- ments, dashed down again and again, still live'.[597]

Still, this quasi-messianic role was not without its problems for Jewish chap- lains, the urgency of its demands among displaced persons (DPs) leading to considerable friction with the American military hierarchy, especially after VE day. Besides its tendency to usurp the primary (i.e. military) obligations of Jewish chaplains, their relief work was often undertaken in breach of military regula- tions (involving, for example, fraternisation with German Jews and the unsanc- tioned use of military resources) and it also complicated Allied policy towards DPs, a policy that was initially geared towards their repatriation.[598] Ultimately, in August 1945, and triggered by a highly critical report conducted by Earl G. Harrison at the request of President Truman, the situation of Jewish DPs led to the appointment of Chaplain Judah Nadich as a special advisor to Eisenhower on Jewish affairs. In this capacity, Nadich assisted the creation of separate camps for Jewish DPs who would not return to their country of origin and helped to coordinate the activities of Allied military government, the United Nations and Jewish relief agencies.[599] Even then, of course, some of the activities of Jewish chaplains remained highly illicit, in particular their collusion with Zionist groups in shipping thousands of illegal Jewish settlers to Palestine in defiance of the ailing British mandate and its immigration quotas.[600] As part of the *Berihah* (Flight) organisation, and in addition to moving would-be emigrants, American chaplains were also involved in the shipment of supplies and even weapons to Palestine.[601] As Kertzer cheerfully admitted, his colleagues were perfectly aware of the dangers they were courting, and knew all too well the draconian sanctions of American military justice. Nevertheless and despite the threat of discovery, their illicit collaboration with Zionist organisations went on unabated.[602]

Although Jewish chaplains encountered Lithuanian Jews among former pris- oners of the Soviets in Teheran in 1943,[603] the first experience of Jewish chap- lains in their wartime role as deliverers of their people came in North Africa. If

North Africa's Jews had not been subject to deportations under Vichy, Italian or Nazi aegis, their position had grown more precarious as the war unfolded. According to the Lutheran army chaplain Edward K. Rogers, at the time of their liberation in May 1943 the Jewish population of Tunis numbered some sixty thousand, or one-fifth of the population. Under Vichy administration, Jewish civil servants had been dismissed, Jewish businesses closed and, it was rumoured, arm bands readied for distribution. With the assumption of German military control the situation grew worse; synagogues were closed or appropriated, Jewish property ransacked or confiscated, women abused, and some Jews were even executed. Elsewhere, Tunisian Jews had been 'miserably treated by the Italians', who had mistreated Jewish women and encouraged local Arabs to loot Jewish property. Not surprisingly, and when Rogers arrived with a Jewish chaplain at a large synagogue in Tunis, they met with a rapturous welcome, being 'whisked off through several streets to the home of the Grand Rabbi of Tunisia', where they were feted for several hours before receiving a very public send-off.[604] A year later, these scenes were repeated in Rome, where deportations to the Nazi death camps had already commenced.[605] Here, Jewish chaplains Morris N. Kertzer and Aaron Paperman arrived soon after the fall of the city, just as Allied troops were stumbling ashore on the distant beaches of Normandy.[606] Finding 'the synagogue of the Chief Rabbi of Rome' on the edge of the Eternal City's medieval ghetto,[607] they met with a delirious reception from their fellow Jews: 'When the Jewish refugees in the neighbourhood saw the Tablet Insignia worn by Chaplain Paperman and his companion, Chaplain Kertzer, they kissed the insignia and made a great celebration in the streets as they passed along.'[608] On the following Friday, the same synagogue – 'the first large synagogue in liberated Europe' – held a *Shehechiyonu* service for four thousand Roman Jews. Though led by the chief rabbi, inter-Allied Jewish solidarity was symbolised by Kertzer's presence and by that of Chaplain Urbach of the British-sponsored 'Palestine Forces'. The service was also the scene of a poignant reunion between a returning GI and his mother – 'a mother brought back from the land of the dead by an army of liberation which included her own son.'[609] That July, and under the aegis of the American Jewish Committee, a service was broadcast by NBC from Rome's 'Temple Israelitico', the very first Jewish service to be broadcast from 'an allied liberated area.'[610]

Similar, if more muted, scenes were repeated as Kertzer and his fellow Jewish chaplains made their way across North-West Europe in the months after D-Day, where they were often called upon to lead services for pockets of Jewish survivors and occasionally felt 'the thrill of restoring a House of God.'[611] After Rheims was taken at the end of August 1944, for example, Chaplain Charles Edward Lunn helped a Jewish colleague reclaim a small synagogue in the city 'which had suffered much damage during the German occupation'. Although it was filled by Jewish GIs for its first service, there were a dozen civilians present – all that remained of the city's Jewish community after years of occupation, flight and deportation.[612] In September, Chaplain David Max Eichhorn restored synagogues at Verdun and at Lunéville, the former with the help of German POWs specially detailed for the purpose.[613] At the end of November, and on the Sabbath that followed the fall of the fortress city of Metz, the Jewish chaplain of the 5th Infantry Division rededicated the city's synagogue with the help of civilian labour; during the German occupation it had functioned as an army brothel.[614] A year later, in Frankfurt, Chaplain George Vida had the satisfaction of supervising a detail of 'former S.S. men' as they cleaned one of the city's synagogues for a rededication service. In the event, two thousand people attended, mostly GIs but including 'about 500 civilians from the German-Jewish population'.[615] Speaking at a field service near Aachen in October 1944, and in words that were carried to the United States by NBC, Chaplain Sidney M. Lefkowitz underlined the deeper significance of this ongoing work of restoration:

> Here we humbly announce to the universe the good tidings that the light of religious freedom has pierced through the black darkness of Nazi persecution…. That freedom of conscience again exists in a land which sought to deny men that right; that an eternal faith has lived through and will outlive the fanatical power which sought to destroy it.[616]

Although Chaplain Kertzer was wont to be critical of the religious ignorance and laxity of his flock (comparing it, for example, with the Zionist 'missionary zeal of the Palestinian soldiers in Italy who would start a Hebrew school and a youth club within forty-eight hours after [a] town was taken')[617] he acknowledged that renewed contact with his ravaged European roots helped to rouse the religious consciousness of the average Jewish GI. Indeed, he saw this phenomenon as a distinct advantage for the Jewish chaplain in the ETO as, in the Pacific, Jewish personnel were often 'thousands of miles from the mainstream of Jewish life [and] there was little to stimulate an interest in their heritage'.[618] In fact, Kertzer anticipated that the Jewish GI's experience in Europe would have a major effect upon American Jewry in the aftermath of the war, for 'the impact of what he experienced will certainly affect his thinking and his attitudes as a Jew during the next decade'.[619] Furthermore, the interaction of the Jewish GI with his fellow Jews in Europe was no less significant when not overtly religious:

> The Jewish soldier with even a mild interest in his origins invariably sought out his own people in the communities of Europe. Almost unaware that the U.S. insignia on his uniform was a symbol of liberation to the remaining remnant of European Jewry, he would explore the ghettos, acquaint himself with their merchants, discover the synagogues and sometimes, when in an especially nostalgic mood, make a futile search for a good Jewish delicatessen…. Within but a few days after the fall of a city, it was an easy

matter to gather from the soldiers themselves the general state of the Jewish community, its approximate size, the condition of its synagogue and the fate of its rabbi.[620]

By such interest and interaction, so Kertzer maintained: 'Many a community was reborn only through the enthusiasm and activity of these soldiers.'[621] This '"Jewish" curiosity', as Kertzer described it, had the additional benefit of being a healthy distraction that lowered crime and VD rates among Jewish GIs, helping to bring them into the wholesome orbit of Jewish family life while serving overseas.[622] While some European and North African Jewesses duly became GI brides, a common language –Yiddish- also helped to cement relations between GIs and surviving Jews of eastern European stock. As Kertzer put it, Yiddish served as a vital lingua franca, and a WAC in his congregation even drew crowds because her Yiddish was inflected with a familiar and unmistakeably Galician brogue.[623]

Like their Christian counterparts, Jewish GIs responded generously to the needs of their co-religionists, and especially to the survivors of the Holocaust. As Chaplain Eichhorn wrote from the vicinity of Lunéville in November 1944:

> The soldiers in the past two weeks have given me over $800 to help [twenty-two elderly women] and other Jewish refugees who needed help. God bless the American Army and the American Jewish soldiers. There is no other Army like it in the world. I had to plead with the men not to give me as much as they wanted to give. Many of them wanted to empty their pockets and give me all they had.[624]

With chaplains such as Eichhorn very much in the vanguard of Jewish relief efforts among displaced persons in liberated Europe[625] (especially, so Kertzer claimed, given the procedural myopia of Jewish relief organisations and the inflexibility of US army bureaucracy),[626] Jewish service personnel proved to be a vital source of first-hand assistance in addressing the needs of the time. In sum:

> Jewish G.I.'s throughout the world contributed tens of thousands of dollars to Jewish relief and rehabilitation. At the holiday seasons and on many other occasions the Jewish chaplains would make appeals which would meet with a generous response, and they sent CANRA the funds to transmit to the Joint Distribution Committee and the United Palestine Appeal. CANRA encouraged these appeals and publicized them.[627]

As Kertzer marvelled, and with tart allusion to the contrasts with civilian life:

> What refreshing confidence our congregants had in our financial sagacity and in our honesty in the handling of funds! Occasionally, a chaplain overseas would suggest the need for money to help the afflicted among the civilian population of the area. The men gave without question, eager to

help if they could, trusting the chaplain's judgment of the need. Some chaplains raised and disbursed thousands of dollars.[628]

However, this assistance was not only financial. In one case, a Jewish soldier from a signal battalion took it upon himself to manage the correspondence of hundreds of survivors of a trainload of human freight that his unit had liberated in Germany.[629] More widespread, though technically all but impossible (especially in France, where the mechanisms of post-war adoption were clogged by 'endless red tape') was the reflexive impulse to adopt a Jewish orphan. As Kertzer remembered, Jewish GIs would often speak of taking orphans back to the States, and of surprising their wives. [630] Under the leadership of Chaplain Herbert Eskin, Jewish GIs of the 100th Infantry Division adopted a more buccaneering approach in the vicinity of Stuttgart, raiding local villages at night to commandeer much-needed foodstuffs at gunpoint.[631]

According to Kertzer and Eichhorn, contact with Europe and its Jews ensured that the vast majority of Jewish GIs returned to America as convinced Zionists.[632] However, an instinct for rescue, restoration and resettlement, plus support for 'a Jewish commonwealth in Palestine', were not the only effects of exposure to overseas Jewry. As Kertzer emphasised, Jewish GIs were perceptibly influenced, both positively and negatively, by the forms of Judaism they came across in Europe and North Africa. In terms of positive influence, Kertzer warned that it was not only their appetite for the Jewish festivals that had been whetted overseas, for:

> The returning warrior will surely be impatient of provincialism. He has learned that there are few norms for orthodoxy, that customs which his congregation deem inflexible and unalterable are foreign to other Jews who likewise call themselves orthodox. In wishing to adopt some of the ceremonies which impressed him overseas, he may, for example, seek to introduce the custom of decorating the Temple in white, and having both cantor and rabbi dressed in white robes, on the Sabbath of Consolation following the Fast of *Ab*. Moved by the beauty of the Sephardic ritual, the reverence for the *Torah*, the formal recognition of the rabbi as he enters the synagogue, the veteran may influence his congregation to adopt similar customs.... Like the famed Jewish travelers, Eldad the Danite and Benjamin of Tudela, the serviceman has become acquainted with exotic forms of Judaism that will create in him a tolerance for variety and a willingness to seek new modes of religious expression.[633]

Nevertheless, there was as at least as much to decry as to emulate. As we have noted, Kertzer himself claimed to be taken aback by the quasi-Catholic rituals of Italian Jewry, and by the example of an elderly Jewess whom he caught 'peddling crucifixes' and other paraphernalia outside St Peter's Basilica in Rome.[634] In Dijon, the laxity of local Jews was manifest; their cantor, for example, promptly reached for a cigarette when leaving the synagogue and ran a stall in the local marketplace on the Sabbath.[635] At Marseilles, the ancient Jewish community was hopelessly stratified along social and ethnic lines, and Catholic accretions were also detectable in its worship.[636] In Kertzer's estimation, the quality of the rabbinate in France, Italy and North Africa was decidedly poor. Even those who served eminent synagogues were notable by their mediocrity. If transplanted to the United States, Kertzer maintained, they would have been entirely out of their depth. It was not just that they were poor scholars, but they preached badly and completely lacked the common touch.[637] As for some Western European Jews, they had tried too hard (and, ultimately, in vain) to assimilate:

> The evident coolness of French and Belgian Jews towards their American coreligionists can be explained partially by the difficulties of language. They were also far from Jewish tradition and, therefore, did not share the East European love of hospitality. The West European Jew feared too close association with us would invite the charge of 'alien' and cast suspicion on his national loyalty.[638]

In Kertzer's not unbiased opinion, the little that recommended Jewish life in France was entirely the product of Zionist influence.[639] However, if Jews were going to remain in Europe despite the lessons of the recent past, he was adamant that a huge missionary effort was required of American Jewry in order to avoid the ultimate triumph of Nazi ambitions through a protracted process of 'self-extermination' realised through conversion, intermarriage and simple falling away.[640] Professedly inspired by the new missionary impulse that was abroad in post-war American Protestantism, Kertzer argued that:

> We are not a missionary folk, even among our own people, but if ever we could use missions, the time is now.... Our rabbinical schools could make a worthwhile contribution to the revitalization of Europe.... We should have a cultural mission fund of a half-million dollars to train men and women for service in the European Jewish community.... For every great academy of learning destroyed, at least one consecrated rabbi must take its place; for every hundred scholars consigned to the Auschwitz furnace, at least one teacher must be sent to don the mantle. It is futile comfort to announce that the Jews have outlived Adolf Hitler. But his will indeed be the last word if Judaism does not long outlast him.[641]

In this regard, Kertzer was clearly preaching to the choir, for his convictions were already widely shared by American Jews, and not only in relation to Europe. In 1946, a CANRA report stated that:

> [S]ome chaplains reported the need for long range help to older civilian communities in certain countries. For example, in Iran, India, North Africa,

and Latin America there were Jewish communities which were losing their youth. There was a mission, it was felt, for American rabbis with modern training in synagogue and center activities to come to these countries and rewin the young, not only through their own programs but also by training native Jews as leaders. Meetings were convened of seminary presidents, representatives of rabbinic bodies and CANRA-JWB to formulate a program for such overseas religious assistance. As this report is being written, the Committee is recommending the sending of four rabbis for such purposes to the countries where the chaplains have indicated the greatest need.[642]

An important corollary of the growing spirit of internationalism in American Christianity during the war was the dramatic revival of interest in the overseas missionary enterprise and so, as Gerald L. Sittser has put it: 'The war became a catalyst for the renewal of American missionary work.'[643] According to navy chaplain Warren Wyeth Willard, the affliction of a second global war in two generations was the strongest possible summons to greater missionary effort, especially of the conservative evangelical kind:

> [I]n order to make this warlike world a habitation of peace, after the war is over we must proclaim the gospel of Christ in all the world. Surely, as nations return to a normal routine, our churches back in the homeland should send missionaries everywhere to preach Christ, and teach that a man must be born again if he is to enter the Kingdom of God.[644]

Such logic had considerable purchase on the home front, made all the more compelling by masses of first-hand testimony from the armed forces to the inestimable value of Christian missions. As one Baptist publication averred in 1946, 'the war has had its recompense for many of our young people' for, though wrenched from hearth and home:

> It has broadened their outlook, deepened their understanding of human problems on a worldwide scale, and afforded them the opportunity to observe the results of foreign mission work in many lands and among strange and uncivilized peoples. They were able to note the contrast between pagan religions and Christianity as we know it, and the differences between Christian and non-Christian natives.[645]

Long before war's end, *The Link* rejoiced in this growing mission-mindedness, congratulating its military readership in November 1944 on their part in boosting the cause of overseas missions: 'If you who will be wearing the overseas ribbons have your way, apparently, there will be a new forward movement in foreign missions.' An early sign of this rekindled interest in the Great Commission was the fact that in 1943, and 'for the first time in seventeen years', the tally of 'new missionaries appointed by the Presbyterians exceeded the number lost through death, retirement and resignation.[646] By early 1944, ambitious post-war plans were well on the way to being realised. At the fiftieth annual convention of the Foreign Missions Conference of North America, the coordinating body for the great preponderance of Protestant missionary societies,[647] Dr William Axling, a Northern Baptist, told an assembly of '600 mission leaders' from more than sixty denominations and 120 boards and agencies that: 'The Protestant foreign mission enterprise of the future must present to the world a united front, manned by a unified personnel, and backed by the pooled spiritual and material resources of the Church of Christ.'[648] While the missionary mainstream duly strategised, *The Link* also noted that a 'large number of Adventist youth' were enrolled on language courses ranging from Arabic through to 'Malayan', and that at Wheaton College, Illinois, the flagship of fundamentalist higher education: 'Courses in the Russian and Chinese languages are attracting sizable enrollments.'[649] For its part, the fundamentalist Christian and Missionary Alliance was developing its aeronautical capabilities in 'isolated missionary fields', hoping that, with a budget of $1 million per year, its 'Circuit-riders of the skies will add to their Bibles a pilot's license.'[650]

There was also a strong (and, it would prove, realistic) expectation that direct exposure to the mission fields would render the armed forces a rich source of seasoned, post-war missionaries. In 1944, the '900 Presbyterian young people in various stages of preparation' for missionary work already included: 'A hundred appointments-in-waiting ... made to men and women in the armed services.' These, *The Link* explained, would 'proceed to their mission posts immediately after they are mustered out. Some of them will be evangelists, others teachers, still others doctors, and some agricultural advisers.'[651] In December 1944, *The Link* published a strongly worded 'MESSAGE TO THE STUDENT IN UNIFORM' from the Student Volunteer Movement (SVM). Warning of the possible disappointments and hazards of the post-war world (including 'unemployment, race and class conflict, and imperialism'), this message stressed the importance of actively working for peace, urging its readers to 'Get missions into your postwar planning':

> Some of you will have seen with your own eyes the ways in which the Church around the world has been creating this peace spirit, and thereby helping set up a better world. Many of you have already written that you plan to take training after you are discharged to fit yourselves as missionaries among the peoples of the lands or islands where you are now fighting. You will be glad to know that the sending agencies of the churches are looking to the armed forces as one of the sources of the thousands of overseas workers who will be needed for replacements and to open new work at the close of the war. There may be a place for you in the Church's program.[652]

This call from the SVM was repeated in August 1945, this time ending with a pointed appeal to the need for world peace: 'How are you going to make your life count so that your children won't have to do again what your father did and you are doing?'[653]

According to Robert T. Handy, flagging support for foreign missions had been one of the most telling symptoms of the 'American Religious Depression' of the interwar years, even predating the economic collapse of 1929.[654] Although fundamentalists, typically, remained immune to this crisis of confidence,[655] in 1932, and as the Depression was wreaking havoc with the finances of America's major missionary boards, an influential report was published entitled *Re-Thinking Missions: A Laymen's Inquiry After One Hundred Years*. Backed by seven denominations representing much of mainline Protestantism, completed with the cooperation of their missionary boards, and focusing on India, Burma, China and Japan, its recommendations amounted to a progressive manifesto on the future of missions. Among other things, these included working 'with greater faith in invisible success'; giving 'largely without any preaching'; cooperating with 'non-Christian agencies for social improvement'; adopting a non-confrontational stance towards other religions; and embracing complete unity of effort and organisation 'in place of the complex, costly and duplicative machinery which now exists'.[656] According to Henry P. Van Dusen of Union Theological Seminary, the exercise was a disaster, serving only 'to encourage misgivings' and 'to shake and even shatter the confidence of large numbers of people in the missionary enterprise as a whole'. Overall: 'It conveyed the impression that there were a few, probably a very few, individual instances of Christian work abroad which merited continuance; but that Missions by and large were of dubious value and validity, hardly justifying well-considered support'.[657] However, and writing from the very different perspective of 1945, Van Dusen rejoiced that:

> Today, another 'laymen's inquiry' is in process. It embraces *the whole world* [my italics]. It is fortuitous, not carefully organized. It is being conducted, not by college professors and scholars, but by hard-bitten soldiers, sailors, airmen and marines of the armed forces of the United Nations. So far as can be judged, the verdict they are returning is almost altogether favourable.... Instances of complete 'about face' from indifference, scepticism or derision to ardent enthusiasm pile up by the hundreds.[658]

Presenting the experiences and impressions of service personnel in a volume entitled *They Found the Church There*, Van Dusen claimed that the circumstances of a global war had served to reveal the essential oneness of 'the Christian world mission', its unique comprehensiveness in catering for body, mind and spirit, 'the role of native Christians in the extension of the Church', and the practical yet inestimable value of many isolated 'outposts of World Christianity'.[659] Recognising the negative aspects of American military encroachment, with its 'trail of disease and demoralization', and also the continuing evils of colonial exploitation, Van Dusen claimed that a massive debt was now owed to the 'native peoples' of the mission fields, a debt that demanded restitution of their 'bitter losses in property and equipment', new restraints upon 'commercial interests', and a wholehearted conversion to the missionary enterprise, for:

> The truth is that the missionary endeavours of the Christian Churches have never received a vindication so definitive and so unchallengeable as that which is coming to them today.... No enterprise in history aimed at the amelioration of humankind and the building of a fairer common life has ever received more decisive approbation.[660]

Evidence from India, where 350,000 American troops served,[661] seems to bear out the truth of these claims. Although British imperial rule was widely mistrusted by Americans, not even their pre-war (and somewhat ironic) fascination with the works of Rudyard Kipling could lessen the inevitable sense of racial, cultural and religious distance from the storied soldiers of British India, let alone the teeming and impoverished masses of the Indian population.[662] In fact, a reaction of utter incomprehension was fully anticipated by the War and Navy Departments' 1943 *Pocket Guide to India*, a booklet warning that: 'INDIA is a strange, colorful land, one that relatively few Americans have seen. Customs, dress, language, color, religious beliefs and political institutions will have little resemblance to anything you have known in America.'[663] The Indian people, it went on, were 'bewilderingly different in their language, religion and physical appearance' and, if 65 per cent of its population of nearly 400 million were Hindu and 25 per cent Muslim, another 40 million belonged to a subsidiary but equally baffling 'variety of religions and cults'.[664] While providing thumbnail descriptions of Hinduism, Islam '(is-LAHM)', Sikhism and Zoroastrianism, the best advice the guide could give its readers was to remain wary and respectful of native religious practices at all times:

> It's a good rule to keep away from both Moslem mosques and Hindu temples unless you are in the hands of a competent guide. The presence of unbelievers is resented. You might innocently offend their most sacred customs. For instance, you would be desecrating a mosque or a temple if you entered wearing shoes ... Always keep an attitude of respect and your unintentional offenses will be more readily forgiven. Never smile or joke among yourselves at peculiarities or strange customs that you observe. Your English may be understood. Even if not, your mocking attitude will be sensed and fiercely resented.[665]

Despite these cautions, a mixture of ignorance and disdain seems to have characterised GI reactions to India's non-Christian religions. In December 1942, as part of its 'Yanks at Home and Abroad' series, *Yank* reported on the experiences of two American sergeants who had secured a rare invitation to the celebration of a Hindu religious festival, namely Dussehra, by a battalion of Gurkhas. Jokingly entitled 'Gurkas [sic] Don't Shoot the Bull; They Behead It With One Blow', it reported how sacrificial bullocks were tethered to a post that seemed reminiscent of 'a totem pole', and that: 'Two guys were holding the buffalo from behind … and pointing it toward the west because it isn't kosher if he isn't facing that way when beheaded.'[666] While no explanation of the nature or purpose of the ceremony was attempted (the story focused instead on the surprise of its American spectators and on Gurkha prowess with the kukri), Ernie Pyle's jocular coverage of the religious complexities of the Indian Army was no more enlightening. Of a detachment of Hindu soldiers on board an LST on the Mediterranean, Pyle mused:

> The Indian soldiers base practically every action on their religion. They brought their own food, and it had to be cooked by certain of their own people. They made a sort of pancake out of flour that was full of weevils and worms. But it was sacred, and if an American cook tried to help out and touched the pan, the whole batch had to be thrown away. Even going to the toilet was a religious ritual with them. They carried special toilet-seat covers previously blessed by some proper person, and would no more think of using an unblessed toilet than you would think of committing murder.[667]

Unsurprisingly, and with a few rare exceptions,[668] there appears to have been general and abiding confusion about Indian religions. A week after *Yank*'s coverage of sergeants Dapero and Dolton's adventure with the Gurkhas at Dussehra, it published a photo feature entitled 'On Many Fronts With the Army Air Forces', which included a snap of an army and a Sikh mechanic over the fatuous caption, 'INDIA POWWOW. Ismar Singh, Moslem [sic] mechanic at a US Army airplane depot in India, gets some good tips on fixing an engine from Sgt. George Spohn, who's a long way from Camden, N.J.'[669] More than a year later, and in a survey of the Indian Army and its composition, *Yank* latched on to the high status of the soldier in the Hindu caste system, a status that, it explained, would 'make any American GI turn green with envy' as it meant that 'no fighting man, even the lowest ranking *sepoy* or buck private, may be called upon to pull KP, latrine duty or any similar fatigue detail'.[670] In terms of the religious military press, the religions of India and of the Indian Army proved to be of very marginal interest, with *The Link* reporting on the formation of a 'Christian battalion' in July 1945, a venture in which Protestant and Catholic leaders had apparently cooperated.[671]

However, more than just bemused ignorance of native religious beliefs obtained among GIs in India. Although *A Pocket Guide to India* stressed the sacredness of cows to Hindus – warning that: 'It is just as well to avoid harming any of these animals no matter where you are'[672] – volunteers for GALAHAD Force (or 'Merrill's Marauders') caused outrage by aiming potshots at cows and peasants alike as they traversed the country by train.[673] Similarly, Chaplain Thomas H.

Clare noted that such advice did nothing to constrain a passing craze for archery in the 341st Bombardment Group in north-east India:

> Some of the more enterprising chaps made crossbows which worked in trigger-fashion, but they soon gave that idea up: they had to walk too far to retrieve the arrows, and then, like as not, they'd find them sticking in somebody's cow, which is a serious business to a Hindu. You never saw so many cows as they had up there. Well, frames, anyway. You could hang your hat on the thigh bone of every single one of them.[674]

Although Clare avoided diatribes on idolatry, in addition to scoffing at sacred cows he was also dismissive of the caste system and of other aspects of Hindu belief and practice, admitting that: 'I find myself caught in the illogic of having sympathy for [Hindus] as individuals, but not as a group.'[675] Musing on his dealings with a Bengali contractor dubbed 'Benny the Brahmin', Clare came to the conclusion that: 'The caste system makes it nice for him. It provides him with a beautiful excuse to avoid real, sweaty work. His system was to charge me two rupees a man per day and pay a quarter of a rupee to each man – eight cents.'[676] However, if the caste system served as an excuse for congenital idleness, the temple of Kali at Calcutta was simply a theatre of the absurd:

> It is situated at one of the mouths of the Ganges, and to it the pilgrims flock by the thousand. First they bathe in the filthy water of the river, which is colorful with its mass of floating garbage, and then they repair to the Temple of Kali to pray. After they have discharged their duties in the temple, which consist mainly of wailing and howling at the statue of Kali, they visit the curio shops within the compound to buy trinkets and have their pockets picked by the best gang of professional dips in the world.[677]

Amidst India's alien, variegated and often violent religious landscape, Hindu funerary customs seem to have caused the greatest offence to American sensibilities. Wilbur Nickels, a US Navy signalman who arrived in Calcutta in June 1945, remembered that his first impression of India was the sight and smell of funeral pyres burning along the approaches to the city: 'Yeah, we saw where all the piers were set … where the people were put on these piers and were burned.… We saw about eight people that were being cremated, you know. Women there with black hair, and all that hair, it was a stench … unbearable almost.'[678] According to Clare, Hindu funeral practices had a discernible knack of reaffirming the Christianity, however nominal, of the GIs who witnessed them:

> There is a sense in which our boys may be said to be religious in a negative way. They are always glad that they are *not* anything but Christians. It is India more than anything that has brought this attitude out, and particularly the seeming heartlessness of Indian funerary customs. In India when

one dies, his body is hustled out with all speed and taken to the burning ghats. In Dacca we used to see the bodies hauled to the ghats slung on a pole and carried by two men who shouted, 'Gods! Gods!' as they hurried along.... As far as I was able to find out, the children rate nothing more than being thrown into the river. The practice in Agra was revolting. It made our boys heartily glad to be Christians.[679]

Despite some lingering doubts as to the motives and sincerity of native converts,[680] such reactions naturally translated into sympathy and support for Christian missionaries as the principal agents of moral and material improvement in the subcontinent. In the CBI at Christmas 1942, for example, more than $3,200 (or 10,000 rupees) was collected among the personnel of the Tenth Air Force, a sum later disbursed to Christian missionaries in northern India.[681] Interaction between missionaries and GIs in the CBI was endemic to the theatre,[682] and the latter were generally impressed. As army psychologist Richard Beard lectured his wife from the 142nd General Hospital in Calcutta in October 1945: 'According to the Chaplain, the only good colleges in India are the Christian Church schools.'[683] Fully convinced of the impotence of Hinduism and Islam in the face of the catastrophic and controversial Bengal famine of 1943–44, Thomas H. Clare joined forces with a Catholic convent in Dacca in seeking to alleviate its local effects through a food reclamation and distribution programme sponsored by the US Army.[684] As far as Clare was concerned, one of the deeper mysteries of the famine was that the Bengalis seemed to 'starve peacefully', making 'no effort to riot or to steal'. Ascribing this lassitude to the effects of their religion, Clare sighed that: 'The Hindu doctrine of Karma could well produce such a quiescence [sic]; but this would not account for the supineness of the Moslems, unless they, too, have a philosophy of fatalism, which is more than likely.'[685] Moreover, and in Clare's opinion at least, food supplies were gravely complicated by the activities of local profiteers, a situation that was aggravated by the bitter sectarian passions of contemporary India:

> Hundreds of such rascals were accused by the authorities and by public people, but only rarely was one punished. They were either Moslem or Hindu, and consequently there was much confusion as to how and by whom they were to be tried. The standard defense of the Hindu grafter was that he was being framed by the Moslems; the Moslems made the same charge against the Hindus. Thus were the authorities powerless to take action; for to do so might result in another flare-up of the communal strife which made the city a shambles from 1941 to 1943.[686]

Writing to *The Link* from India in December 1944, Corporal Kenneth E. Briggs mused on the faith of an Indian convert and on the potential of Christianity as a long-term solution to India's myriad woes, pointing out that: 'This man lives in a country full of Hinduism and Mohammedanism, a country full of sickness, disease and starvation, a country of endless strife; yet above this, he has the faith in the living God that will bring him to his knees in reverence.'[687] And, according to *The Link* at least, by July 1945 the evidence seemed to show that there was hope for the growth of Christianity in post-war India, especially given the impending merger of several Protestant bodies into the united Church of South India. According to the 1941 census, there were roughly 9,750,000 Christians in India, a 50 per cent increase since 1931, with most of these living in its southern provinces.[688]

While Hinduism failed to evoke a positive reaction among Americans in the CBI, the same was also true of Islam in general, another reaction that underlined the fact that 'tri-faith America' was by no means multifaith America. Islam was a religion that the US Army in particular had some experience of, not least because of its campaigns in the Philippines. During the interwar years several regiments of Philippine Scouts were absorbed into the regular army, including a number of Moros who served in their own companies and with their own imams, these units being increased in the months before Pearl Harbor.[689] Furthermore, and if the small, countercultural and home-grown Nation of Islam resisted any involvement in a white man's war that was patently not a jihad,[690] other members of America's tiny Muslim minority (chiefly immigrants from the Balkans and the Middle East) did serve in the armed forces, though their numbers and organisation were insufficient to secure any army or navy chaplains.[691] Nevertheless, in New Guinea in July 1943 Bishop John A. Gregg placed wreaths on the graves of a Christian, a Jewish and a Muslim GI, an observance that, in the bishop's words, 'emphasized the universality of this global conflict' as all three had 'made the supreme sacrifice for the Four Freedoms'.[692] Nevertheless, Islam still remained an exotic and unfamiliar faith, with Beau Geste a far more familiar figure to most Americans than the Prophet Mohammed. This fact helps to account for the blithe adoption of a mosque as the Fifth Army's insignia in 1943. As *Yank* elucidated:

> Here is the official insignia of the U.S. Fifth Army, the first American field army to be created in this war. It was activated in North Africa last January under Lt. Gen. Mark W. Clark. The device represents the land in which the army was created. The background is red, the mosque blue, and the 'A' and the '5' white.[693]

Inevitably, however, there was friction between American and Islamic norms. While stationed in Iceland in 1943, Chaplain Clyde E. Kimball had a salutary conversation with 'a young Arabian merchant seaman', who was in hospital recuperating from his 'third torpedoing':

> He speaks seven languages, but never went to school, so cannot read or write.... Says Mohammedans believe 'Aysu' (the way he pronounces 'Jesus')

is a good man who talked with God and now lives with him. Says Christians are wicked because they preach monogomy [sic] and go with many women, – preach temperance and get drunk.[694]

Such uncomplicated reflections were no doubt shared by many Muslims, especially as the khaki and olive drab migrations of the war years impacted heavily upon North Africa and the Middle East. However, and as in India, the War and Navy Departments' ubiquitous pocket guides were on hand to explain the religious beliefs and sensitivities of the locals. As the 1943 *Pocket Guide to North Africa* elaborated, 90 per cent of the region's seventeen million people were Muslim, and that linguistic and tribal divisions meant that: 'The one bond which touches nearly all … is the religion founded by Mohammed.'[695] At this point, the guide offered a quick summary of Islam: 'The people do not worship Mohammed as Christians worship Christ; they think of him as a prophet, like those of the Old Testament. The religion is called Islam (i-SLAM, meaning "submission to God") and the believers are called Moslems. Their Bible is the Koran.'[696] Later, and after dealing with dress, money and sundry points of etiquette, the guide embarked on a deeper exploration of Islam in North Africa, explaining that Mohammed 'preached against the same vices which are the targets of the average American evangelist', and also that Muslims were particularly short-tempered during the month of Ramadan.[697] It also warned very strongly about respecting mosques and shrines: 'The deep religious faith of Moslems is especially evident in their feeling about their places of worship – the mosques and the tombs of saints. *Keep away from mosques and the tombs of saints.* The Moslems will not tolerate Christians inside of them.'[698] The guide also left its readers in no doubt as to their inferior spiritual status in the eyes of their Muslim hosts: 'Like all firm believers they feel that the souls of those of other faiths will not be saved. It follows that non-believers are inferior people – if not in this world certainly in the next. Consequently Christians or Jews are considered inferior by every true Moslem.'[699] Significantly, the guide headed its 'List of Do's and Don'ts' with a series of religious admonitions:

> DON'T enter mosques.
> Smoke or spit somewhere else – never in front of a mosque.
> If you come near a mosque, look away and keep moving.
> Avoid shrines or tombs in the country.
> Discuss something else – *never* religion or women – with Moslems.
> Keep silent when Moslems are praying, and don't stare at them.
> Don't refer to the people as heathen; they are very religious.[700]

Very similar advice was dispensed in *A Pocket Guide to Iran* (where 'Thirty thousand US troops radically increased the carrying capacity of the Trans-Iranian Railway bearing Lend-Lease materials northwards'),[701] and in other army publications such as *A Short Guide to Iraq*, which also appeared in 1943.[702] The former explained that 'the Iranis' mainly belonged to 'the Shia sect of the Moslem religion', which, it shrugged, 'probably won't make much difference in your relations with the Iranis, but it might come in handy to know about it'.[703] However, and regardless of the difference between Sunni and Shia, the guide was emphatic that a particularly zealous and intolerant form of Islam thrived in Iran:

> UNTIL a few years ago, if a foreigner had attempted to enter a mosque (Moslem church) in Iran, he would probably have been beaten to death, and even today it is safest to keep strictly away from mosques unless you are invited there by a responsible person. At that time the Iranis were among the most fanatical of all Moslems, and the mullahs (priests) were the men who really ran the country.... At any rate, the Moslem religion is still a force all over the country so that you should know something about it in order to avoid making any bad breaks.[704]

For its part, *A Short Guide to Iraq* attempted to make a virtue of this kind of zeal, saying of the reception likely to be accorded to intrusive GIs at Iraqi mosques:

> This isn't preaching. You probably belong to a church at home, and you know how you would feel towards anyone who insulted or desecrated your church. The Moslems feel just the same way, perhaps even more strongly. In fact, their feeling about their religion is pretty much the same as ours towards our religion, although more intense. If anything, we should respect the Moslems the more for the intensity of their devotion.[705]

This advice served a definite and important purpose. Given the strategic significance of North Africa and the Middle East, and the pro-Axis activities of Hadj Amin el-Husseini, the exiled mufti of Jerusalem,[706] the inflammatory potential of clodhopping GIs gave serious cause for concern. As George S. Patton remembered, in his first meeting with Sultan Mohammed Ben Youssef of Morocco in November 1942, 'he informed me that, since we were in a Mohammedan country, he hoped the American soldier would show proper respect for Mohammedan institutions'. Patton promptly assured him that 'such an order had been issued in forceful language prior to our departure from the United States and would be enforced'.[707] However, in December 1942 *Yank* reported a slew of stories on misbehaving GIs that had already been aired on Axis radio. These included the claim that:

> The population of North Africa has to suffer much annoyance and disturbances by the American soldiers. The USA soldiers stalk women and try to tear down their veils, they try to visit the holy places of the Mohammedans, try to enter Arab houses by force and make themselves conspicuous by drunkenness and loud behaviour. It was, however, reported that the USA

soldiers had gotten detailed instructions how to behave, but it seems as if there were more illiterates in the USA than has been acknowledged officially.[708]

This was accompanied by claims that, in Oran, drunken American officers had become the targets of a 'sneering native Mohammedan population', with three having been thrown into a sewer, and that 'various mosques in Morocco and Algiers have had to hang up signs in English requesting the American soldiers not to disturb religious services and not to spit their chewing gum onto the floor'.[709]

Despite these concerns, and the advice directed at them, as in British India it proved difficult for GIs to summon much respect for local religious traditions. Once again, and notwithstanding a notional distaste for European imperialism, it seemed hard to empathise with colonised peoples who were not only poorer – and usually darker-skinned – but whose mores differed so wildly from those that obtained in the United States.[710] Furthermore, and if the Americans, like all infidels, were held in contempt by pious Muslims, Christian Americans generally reciprocated these feelings with interest. Although Patton read the Quran en route to North Africa ('a good book and interesting'),[711] and talked with the Sultan of Morocco about divine assistance for the Allied cause ('a one-hundred-per-cent hit'),[712] he came to the conclusion that Islam was nothing but a blight on North Africa. In his 'Notes on the Arab', dating from June 1943, Patton wrote:

> One cannot but ponder the question: What if the Arabs had been Christians? To me it seems certain that the fatalistic teachings of Mohammed and the utter degradation of women is the outstanding cause for the arrested development of the Arab. He is exactly as he was around the year 700, while we have kept on developing. Here, I think, is a text for some eloquent sermon on the virtues of Christianity.[713]

Some GIs simply sneered at Islamic practice. Passing an Arab prostrated towards Mecca as his dependants waited in a cart, one of Pyle's companions jibed, 'I guess he's making a deal for the whole family.'[714] According to Pyle, that was the only time he ever saw an Arab pray in public, the admonitions of the army's published guides proving as overstated in religious matters as in others.[715] Nevertheless, in Italy, a reputation for religious credulity clung to the feared Moroccan Goumiers of the French Expeditionary Corps. As the Catholic chaplain Karl A. Wuest remembered:

> The death penalty for them was beheading. And they didn't like it. For if heaven for them was to be a place of bodily pleasure and the dead were taken into heaven by the hair, as they believed, it didn't help much to have the head go up, without the body. Many more stories, of equally doubtful veracity, went the rounds.[716]

Ignoring Muslim sensitivities on this score, GIs proved as uninhibited in their support for Christianity in largely Muslim societies as they did in other parts of the world. As Archbishop Francis Spellman noted from 'Somewhere in North Africa' in March 1943: 'The American troops have been very helpful and generous with the missionaries. American gunfire damaged the Casablanca Cathedral and the contributions of American boys have paid for the repairs'.[717] In what seems to have been part of this process, a sailor wrote home to his parents enthusing that more than 4,500 bluejackets had crowded a Christmas midnight Mass in an unnamed North African cathedral, the collection amounting to $7,000, 'which was more money than had been collected in that cathedral for a whole year'.[718] The same largesse was shown by Protestant GIs in North Africa, Chaplain Edward K. Rogers noting how one medical officer, a battlefield convert, had donated $10 on his first visit to a French-speaking church, 'a lot of money to that congregation'.[719] In Tunisia, Rogers also encountered 'an English Methodist missionary who had spent thirty years working among the Berber people of the hill country'.[720] From him, Rogers learnt that: 'The Berbers were the descendants of the original natives and had retired to the hills when the Arabs conquered the country. Their religion was more animism than Mohammedanism, but they had been influenced by the latter'.[721] Significantly, the missionary was armed with 'a letter from military authorities requesting that he be given transportation when possible'.[722] After the Axis surrender in Tunisia in May 1943, some American chaplains were even prepared to indulge in some freelancing missionary work of their own, with one Catholic chaplain making a number of local converts, including 'a stunning young belly dancer'.[723] Equally, and despite the dire warnings of *A Pocket Guide to Iran*, in 1943 *The Link* magazine ran a 'Spotlight on Iran' by J. Christy Wilson, a faculty member of Princeton Theological Seminary who had been a missionary there for twenty years. Here, Wilson extolled the work of Presbyterian missionaries 'in this land of Daniel and Queen Esther and the Magi', stressing the far-reaching effects of their educational and medical work. According to Wilson, such was the influence of the former that 'individual conduct in Iran, among all classes and religions, is often judged by the ethical standards of Christ rather than by those of Mohammed'. Furthermore: 'Even in the fanatical shrine city of Meshed, up near the border of Afghanistan, there is a Christian hospital of which any American might well be proud.' Given the modest growth of 'a new evangelical Christian church', Wilson assured those of his readers who were heading to Iran that they would find there 'small congregations of Protestant Christians in the main cities and some villages of the country', and that 'in the Persian church you will find the same comfort and inspiration as in your church back home'. In particular, Iran's dauntless Christians were 'eager to meet a member of their faith from overseas, who realize that Christianity is a sound basis for friendship'.[724]

An awareness of being in well-worked mission fields was even stronger in the vast oceanic melting pot that was the Pacific, embracing native peoples as diverse as the pygmies of central New Guinea, who were still barely touched by European culture, and the Chamorros of the Marianas, who had been exposed to Western influences since the days of Magellan.[725] *The Link*, especially in its first year of publication, constantly reminded its readers of the complex missionary heritage of the Pacific and of their corresponding responsibilities. In April 1943 it published a survey of American missionary work by Dr Henry Smith Leiper, the American Secretary of the World Council of Churches. Entitled 'Christians in Unexpected Places!', Leiper deplored the fashionable, pre-war denigration of missionary work, especially by 'casual travelers who know nothing about the real story of Christian missions', and drew an outline of the American missionary effort for the benefit of the 'inquiring American military man, traveling the world at Uncle Sam's expense'. According to Leiper, from modest beginnings in the first decade of the nineteenth century, their nation's 'missionary program' had expanded to become 'one of the great overseas activities of Americans'. Partners in a great collaborative effort with Christians of other nations, by the late 1930s American and Canadian Protestants were donating 'about $48,000,000 a year towards this enterprise', while their missionary staff represented more than eleven thousand of the twenty-seven thousand or so 'non-Roman missionaries from the Christian agencies of all countries'. As a result, and through their missionary efforts, Americans had acquired a major stake in fifty-seven thousand mission schools, over one hundred colleges, and a thousand mission hospitals. Whatever the merits or demerits of missionary methods, Leiper insisted that American investment in the missionary enterprise had produced millions of converts and a vast fund of goodwill towards America, a fund whose dividends could be felt across the globe – and especially in its war zones.[726]

In June 1943, *The Link* also published an article by Raymond L. Archer, a former Methodist missionary who had escaped from Singapore just before its surrender. Characterising the American experience of overseas service as a vast and fruitful encounter with the mission fields, Archer declared that:

> Down in the South Pacific, up in Alaska, over in North Africa, or elsewhere, you are not only learning about geography from this war. You are learning about missions! You are seeing at first hand just how 'missionary lend-lease' is paying off. When you get home again, it is likely you will have a some-what broadened appreciation for the long program of the Church in foreign fields. And on 'Mission Sunday' you will perhaps have a quicker perception of the ultimate goal of that coin or bill you drop into the collection.[727]

Invoking the vast sweep of the Pacific and its numerous archipelagos, Archer proclaimed that: 'For more than a century it has attracted thousands of Europe's and America's best Christian youth, eager to extend the Gospel to new and unreached groups.' From the Pacific region had arisen 'some of the most thrilling stories in all missionary annals – stories of devoted men and women who have transformed whole tribes and peoples within a generation or two'. The ultimate example of such transformation was, of course, the conversion of whole tribes and cultures – notably in the Solomon Islands, Fiji and Sumatra – from cannibalism to Christianity, creating a situation whereby the helpless European visitor could expect unstinting hospitality rather than a place on the menu. In sum, so Archer assured his readers, because of this holy and heroic effort over a span of generations, 'in many cases you will feel that in spite of the war that rages through the South Pacific, "the place whereon thou standest is holy ground" [Exodus 3:5]'.[728]

At the very least, the role of the American serviceman or woman in this ongoing missionary effort was to set a good Christian example. In May 1943 *The Link* published a letter that gave the reactions of a GI to a radio broadcast on the subject of world Christianity. Supplied by the secretary of a Presbyterian missions board, the letter stated:

> I certainly didn't know the Christian churches were as strong as he said they are in some of the other countries.... He said that before the war one of the strongest of these churches ... was in the Netherlands East Indies, and that there were over a million Christians there.... It seems that a year and a half ago the Christians in Samoa got worked up over the bombing of London and actually took up a collection of ten thousand dollars for the relief of the churches in Britain![729]

Beyond these facts and figures, though, a single imperative shone through:

> [W]hat struck me was his saying that the churches never dreamed of sending out as many Christian missionaries to the ends of the earth as would be there right now if every Christian in the service would be just that: *a Christian in the service*. Not necessarily a Christian missionary, but a missionary Christian.[730]

Two months later, the magazine's treatment of the serviceman's role in fulfilling the Great Commission was even more direct. Another article, this time by Dr S. Arthur Devan, director of the General Commission on Army and Navy Chaplains, announced 'You're a Missionary Now!' and went on to illustrate 'the lasting religious influences which armies have had on native populations', citing examples that ranged from the benefits accrued by French Protestantism from occupying British soldiers after the Napoleonic Wars to the planting of Lutheranism in southern Russia by German military settlers in the eighteenth century.[731] Whatever else, Devan warned:

> Every chaplain and every Christian soldier or sailor or marine who during this war finds himself in a non-Christian country may be an Ambassador of Christ. Our religion, as well as our flag, will be credited or discredited

by the kind of contacts American men make with the people in far-way, non-Christian lands. We have a special responsibility for the impression we make, not only as Americans, but as Christians.[732]

However, this did not exhaust the potential for missionary activity, for:

You will also find opportunities of witnessing and preaching too, 'as love knows how'. American soldiers and sailors may come to these parts of the world not only as liberators, in the political and military sense, and benefactors in the economic sense, but thoughtful Christian contacts may make them missionaries too. New meaning will be given to military service if you keep this in mind.[733]

Clearly, such missionary concern and enthusiasm was whipped to new heights by Allied experience in the Solomons and New Guinea. Here, and in contrast to the heathen savagery of the enemy, Americans discovered that a common Christianity had created a strong and dramatic bond with native peoples who seemed, superficially at least, even more alien in cultural and racial terms than the Japanese. In New Guinea, thousands of Papuan porters, many of whom were recruited via the London Missionary Society,[734] proved crucial to the logistics of the campaign. In particular, they ferried sick and wounded Allied soldiers over precipitous mountain trails with such care and compassion that it earned them the epithet of the 'Fuzzy-Wuzzy Angels' – a poem with this title, written in honour of their 'Christ-like ministry', appearing in *The Link* in November 1943.[735] With Japanese brutality acting as a further spur to pro-Allied sentiment,[736] Christian Papuans also gained a reputation for rescuing and returning stranded Allied airmen and sailors, a significant development given the infamous cannibal traditions of this region.[737] As a Lutheran army chaplain, Arnold M. Maahs, testified on the basis of his own experiences in New Guinea:

[I]t is true that the Christian natives were our staunchest friends and helpers, and no one will ever know the many deeds of mercy and kindness which they performed during the war. Many an airman and many a wounded soldier owes his life to the Christian natives who sheltered him and brought him back to his own troops or carried him carefully and tenderly over miles of rough, slippery, muddy jungle trails.[738]

In the Solomon Islands, this pattern was replicated among the Christian Melanesian population, who provided much-needed labour and local intelligence for the Allies.[739] Once again, stories abounded of succour from natives wearing crucifixes, reading Bibles and humming 'Onward Christian Soldiers'.[740] In *Air Forces Magazine* it was even claimed that:

Scores of crash survivors in New Guinea, the Solomons and northern Australia owe their lives to native friendliness. Religious medallions carried by fliers are recognized and serve as a pass key to aid. In the Solomons, the term 'Tie Loto' means 'church people' and a flier using the word 'Loto' will be welcomed and treated as a friend.[741]

In perhaps the most notable rescue of the Solomon Islands campaign, the Marine Corps' leading fighter ace, Joe Foss, was plucked from the sea by friendly natives off Malaita Island, where he was sheltered by the clergy and converts of a Catholic mission.[742]

If Americans had every reason to be grateful for their potential or actual delivery from the jungle, shark-infested waters and from the Japanese, they were also forcefully impressed by the genuine piety of native Christians, a piety commented upon in *The Leatherneck* even in the interwar years.[743] In Melanesia in World War II, however, Christianity was understood – with some immediacy – to be a transforming faith that had saved many hapless Americans from what, in earlier times, would have been a much grislier fate.[744] As a late war recruitment appeal by the Student Volunteer Movement put it: 'Hundreds of you in the South Pacific area would have made the main course at a cannibal feast had not the missionary wrought changes. You can thank him that you were saved rather than eaten.'[745] Springing from these perceptions, a widely publicised wartime cartoon showed a sceptical GI reproving a Bible-reading Melanesian 'YOU MEAN TO SAY YOU BELIEVE **THAT**?', to which the native replied, gesturing towards a cooking pot, 'IF I DIDN'T – YOU'D BE IN **THAT**!'[746] However, it was not simply a question of Christianity triumphing over cannibalism. According to one American soldier in the Solomons, who was cited in a radio broadcast by Lieutenant General A.A. Vandegrift:

> This morning I came upon some natives building a grass hut. One black boy was perched on top of the center support singing the hymn, 'Jesus Christ Is Risen To-day,' in his own tongue. It was at first quite a shock to me. I called up to him and he came down from his perch and began to sing again. I joined him in English. How strange to hear this primitive boy and myself singing praises to our God! Truly the brotherhood of God knows no bounds![747]

Victory in the Solomon Islands presented a chance for Americans to observe the temper of Melanesian Christianity more closely. Marine Joe E. Ross, writing to his pastor in Houston, was especially moved by a chapel erected in an American cemetery by well-disposed islanders:

> It is just a little shrine built by one people to another because they know and worship the same living God.... Somehow it softens the fate of shipmates.... Maybe you can understand how that little symbol means so much more than the Statue of Liberty in New York harbour. This is a token of love from the hearts and hands of a trusting people.[748]

While helping to burnish and even romanticise the image of native Christianity, the hard campaign in the Solomons also promoted a greater regard for overseas missionaries. Chastened by the extent to which missionary work had been undervalued in the pre-war church, Ross confided:

> I have often thought since of the requests for funds for missions and the indifferent response usually encountered. It is really a good laugh on us that we didn't pay more attention to that work. Because of the work of a few men with limited funds at their disposal, American boys several thousand miles from the nearest Woolworth store have been received as friends and shown every courtesy a primitive people have to offer.[749]

Chaplain Arnold M. Maahs agreed, writing ruefully:

> Many people in America consider a missionary a queer, long-haired, wild-eyed individual, a super-enthusiast whose work is to be humoured by contributions of nickels and dimes. In New Guinea he is considered an intensely practical man, a man of position and influence, whose work is tremendously important among the native population.[750]

According to Warren Wyeth Willard, on Guadalcanal: 'The marines changed their minds about foreign missions and missionaries. Many a man told me that when he returned to civil life in the homeland, he would support the great foreign missionary enterprise with liberal contributions.'[751] Particularly esteemed in the Solomon Islands were Walter Baddeley, the Anglican Bishop of Melanesia, and Bishop Jean-Marie Aubin, the Vicar Apostolic of the Southern Solomon Islands. Evading capture by the Japanese, the indomitable Baddeley proved a generous host to American servicemen at 'the least pretentious espiscopal palace in the world', and had the distinction of being a much-decorated veteran of World War I, having commanded a British infantry battalion on the Western Front.[752] On one occasion, and having addressed 'a large gathering of American sailors on board one of their great ships', its captain rose, 'as a good Churchman', to recant his earlier views on foreign missions and to assure Baddeley that 'many other men' were doing likewise.[753] As for Aubin, Floyd W. Radike, an army officer and veteran of Guadalcanal, confessed being awed and humbled by the bishop's resourcefulness and resolve. Preceded by 'the disposal of beer bottles, pinups, and dirty clothes', after hosting Aubin for several days Radike remembered that: 'We all felt that we had been in the company of a great and holy man.'[754]

Although the American presence in the Pacific had the unforeseen effect of promoting some Melanesian cargo cults (including the politico-messianic 'John Frum Cult' in the New Hebrides, which was boosted by the arrival of black GIs who appeared to be on an equal footing with their white comrades),[755] a much more common aspect of the Pacific war was the moral and practical support given to Christian missionaries by American service personnel. Seemingly a helpless target of Japanese malice, and with its long-term efforts supremely vindicated by the fortunes of war, Christian missionary work was the object of a surge of practical goodwill, benefiting from the ample pay available to its new admirers, the time that often hung heavily on their hands, and the lavish resources that were available to the US Army and US Navy. Besides resolutions of future generosity, American servicemen were liberal with their immediate giving. After Bishop Baddeley preached to an American unit, his congregation promptly gave almost $200 towards his work. Likewise, GIs of the 25th Infantry Division alone 'contributed $2,500 toward the restoration of churches in the South Pacific';[756] to put this in context, in 1941 the whole of the Anglican diocese of Melanesia had subsisted on a budget of less than $5,000.[757] Catholics were equally forthcoming – those of one division donating more than $1,000 to the Solomon Islands missions, while a single collection from a mixed congregation of soldiers, sailors and marines on Guadalcanal realised $825. According to one estimate, by 1944 Catholic servicemen serving in this region had donated an average of $5 each to local Catholic missions, total donations being well in excess of $100,000.[758] In terms of support in kind, Floyd W. Radike recalled that: '[Bishop Aubin] was most anxious to get medicines for the natives. I passed this word to the headquarters through my resident radio station, and a day or two later the supply boat arrived with at least a half-dozen cases of medicine.'[759] As for the four Marist missionaries killed at the Ruavutu Mission on Guadalcanal, Roman Catholic Major General Joseph Lawton Collins, then commanding the 25th Infantry Division, ordered that their bodies be reinterred by an American chaplain – and that their mission chapel and buildings be repaired 'as much as possible.'[760]

This flow of beneficence was by no means limited to the campaign in the Solomons, or indeed to the years of the war. According to the fundamentalist AAF chaplain James Edwin Orr, the 'upsurge of missionary interest was a most gratifying feature' of his ministry in New Guinea in 1944, where spontaneous donations towards missionary work averaged $10 a head, with some of his flock giving as much as $50 'to make up for back time.'[761] Furthermore, James J. Fahey was to donate the whole of his royalties for his *Pacific War Diary* (1963) to the building of a Catholic church in southern India.[762] During the war, *The Link* urged enthusiasts for missionary work 'to give to the nearest mission directly so that you may see some of the results first-hand'; when this was not feasible, it advised sending contributions via their home churches, accompanied by a letter to 'stimulate giving' in their own congregations.[763] Many of these letters furnished edifying copy for the church press.[764] Inspired by 'Men and Missions Sunday', which was observed by American Protestants in November 1943, a Service Men's Christian League unit in Australia collected in excess of $200.[765] In the Gilbert Islands in 1944, members of the 4th Marine Air Wing raised the same amount to finance the education of native catechists at a London Missionary Society training institute.[766] The liberation of the Marianas and the Philippines prompted gallant efforts to rebuild their ecclesiastical and missionary infrastructure. On Saipan, at least one Chamorro chapel was rebuilt by American Catholics, their restoration work including the reconstruction of its crucifix and statuary.[767] On the island of Cebu in the Philippines, and at the instigation of Chaplain Thomas J. Donnelly, Catholics of the 77th Infantry Division rebuilt 'a dilapidated Church named in honor of the Blessed Trinity', commissioning native workers to provide appropriate fixtures and fittings. A local leper colony also received gifts of 'candy and cigarettes for the patients', a Catholic school and orphanage received coffee and foodstuffs ('generously supplied by a number of mess sergeants'), and a convoy of fifteen army trucks supplied materials for the construction of a new hall.[768]

Donnelly's role as a keen facilitator and promoter of local missionary and church work was far from unusual among American chaplains in the Pacific. The fundamentalist navy chaplain Arthur F. Glasser lent his support by ostentatiously kicking a native idol in front of his marines on New Britain,[769] but the approach of his chaplain colleagues was usually less belligerent. In New Guinea, for example, James Edwin Orr arranged for a large party of Christian natives to visit his fighter group's base, where they led a lively and colourful service in its theatre area.[770] In a similar vein, *The Chaplain* magazine reported in February 1945 that:

> CHAPLAIN KENNETH M. HAY has been conducting trips to mission villages in the Southwest Pacific. On one occasion 207 enlisted men visited a station where, prior to the arrival of missionaries fifty years before, cannibalism, inter-tribal warfare and a low state of morality existed. The visitors found citizens who under missionary training had become carpenters, boat-builders, cabinet-makers and masters of other crafts. There were schoolhouses and churches, and the industry and intelligence of the natives as observed by the American soldiers furnished an object-lesson in the physical and spiritual transforming power of Christianity.[771]

Given the displacement of European missionaries caught in the path of the Japanese advance in the Pacific, many chaplains also found themselves responsible for the care of native Christians until the return or reinforcement of their former pastors. As Chaplain Eldon W. Borell wrote from an unnamed missionary outpost in 'the South Pacific Area':

> Most of the natives of this island have been evangelized by Church of England missionaries. Each Sunday, in addition to services in my own unit, I celebrate an Anglican Eucharist in their lovely chapel. They regularly attend and enter into the spirit of the services with a devotion that is truly inspiring.[772]

In the Solomon Islands, and as part of the process of reconstructing the Ruavutu mission on Guadalcanal, 'with the aid of a native catechism' Chaplain Terrence P.

Finnegan spent three hours hearing the confessions of Catholic natives.[773] Likewise, when an American chaplain was detailed to act as a native pastor on Ulithi Atoll in the Caroline Islands, a Japanese possession before the war, 'it was the first Mass the people had had in seven years'.[774]

However, these incidents formed only fragments of a lengthy and varied litany of chaplains' support for missionary work in the Pacific, including frequent visits to mission stations near Milne Bay in New Guinea, the creation of a scholarship fund for Filipino candidates for the Episcopalian ministry (this in memory of an American chaplain who had died in Japanese captivity), and weekly conferences of Protestant chaplains with the local missionary clergy after the liberation of Manila.[775] As the 1946 *History of Chaplains' Activities in the Pacific* made clear, the war years were momentous ones for the future of Christian missions in the region:

> In most of the islands of the Southwest Pacific interesting contacts have taken place between our chaplains and soldiers and the Christian missionaries. Chapel congregations have often contained large numbers of native Christian worshippers. These contacts should add immensely to the understanding of the value of foreign missions by future laymen of the churches back home. Foreign missions, after all, is just another name for International Christianity.[776]

Given the extent of chaplains' wartime involvement in such missionary work, *The Chaplain* magazine could claim that: 'Thus are American chaplains the bearers of oil for the lamps of faith the world round'.[777] Nevertheless, the Pacific war had other, more subtle, effects on American missionary consciousness. In the opinion of the prominent African American churchman W.H. Jernagin, the scale of wartime experience of missions and missionaries in Melanesia called for a much more serious commitment to this mission field from the African American churches. In 1946, Jernagin wrote in *Christ at the Battlefront*:

> I was impressed with the fertile field open to Christian Missions on all of these islands, and I feel that the Negro Church must accept some of the responsibility to these people in the islands of the sea and not leave it entirely to the white group. There are reasons why our work might be limited, but when one considers that most of these are people of color, it is a fact that the Negro Church as a body has not accepted this as a part of its responsibility.[778]

Another effect of the scale of the contact with Christian missions throughout the Pacific war was the sidelining, for members of the American armed forces at least, of the missionary effort in China. Once described by Sherwood Eddy as 'the lodestar, the goal' of America's overseas missionary effort,[779] prior to World War II China had been American Christianity's pre-eminent mission field,[780] its conversion 'the missionary movement's ultimate prize'.[781] However, America's overarching strategy of treating the Pacific as the principal theatre of war against the Japanese (while supporting Nationalist China with airpower, supplies and military expertise) precluded the deployment of large numbers of service personnel to China itself, as did Stalin's promise at the Teheran Conference of entering the war against Japan after Germany had been defeated. As General Frank D. Merrill summed up the situation in 1944, 'all [US] plans for operations against the Japanese assume that China does nothing but contain some Japanese. We do not desire to get mixed up on the Continent with large U.S. forces'.[782] In comparison with the significant and widespread interaction of American service personnel with Christian work in so many, often small, Pacific islands, similar contact in the vastness of inland China was scattered and small-scale. In 1946, Presbyterian navy chaplain William Sanford La Sor recalled that, in the last months of the war, he was one of only two navy chaplains assigned to just two thousand naval personnel in the whole of China, a widely scattered charge whose members were engaged in various liaison, intelligence and meteorological duties. Significantly, La Sor had nothing to say about missionary work.[783] However, if interest in the China missions was diminished as a result of this imbalance, it did not wholly disappear. For those Americans exposed to China, its poverty, disease, corruption and perceived amorality seemed to underscore its need for gospel-driven progress (as did the apparently common phenomenon of coolies launching themselves in front of the rotating propeller blades of taxiing American aircraft, apparently in the belief that this was a good method of dispatching pursuing dragons).[784] Furthermore, chaplains could take a hand in stimulating interest in China's missionary future, with *The Chaplain* magazine dutifully publishing an occasional piece on this subject in 1945, including an all too familiar pronouncement by one Chinese Christian to the effect that, 'The door is wide open in China for the Christian message', and that: 'The call in China for Christian-based leadership in our national life is insistent and sincere'.[785] On the basis of the expectation that 'we are on our way to the Orient', at Easter 1944 Chaplain Arthur F. Glasser took donations from marines and Australians to the value of $1,300 for the China Inland Mission – a conservative missionary society that was 'interdenominational', 'international' and, most importantly for Glasser, unyieldingly 'biblical in its principles and in its practice'.[786] For his part, and while stationed at an American evacuation hospital at Myitkyina in Burma in 1944, army chaplain Thomas W.B. Magnan reacted as if the war had brought the Chinese mission field to him. Getting to work among patients brought in from Chinese Nationalist units under Stilwell's command, Magnan reported that:

> This group changes on the average of once a month with the result that some 50 Chinese soldiers are constantly going back into the line with a fairly good knowledge of the story of Christ, able to sing some Christian

hymns, and knowing how we pray and hold our services.... Seed thus sown may blossom out all over China some day.[787]

Still, and despite his own efforts and initiative in imparting the gospel, in a significant indication of the new primacy of the Pacific in missionary awareness in the armed forces Mangan went on to reflect that: 'Those of us who have served in the Far East, especially the islands of the Pacific, have eaten of the fruit thus planted by missionaries in the minds and hearts of natives.'[788]

Helping to subordinate interest in China, the experience of the Pacific war also underlined for many Americans the urgent need for the evangelisation of Japan. Navy chaplain Warren Wyarth Willard, after being taken to task in the Solomon Islands for burying a Japanese prisoner according to Christian rites, and therefore with due respect, had remonstrated: 'Regardless of what they would do to you, we have our Christian standards.... Let us not lapse back into paganism because others, like the Japs, have not been brought out of paganism and barbarism because of the indifference and neglect of the Christian Church.'[789] Similarly, the sight of bedraggled Japanese prisoners in the Philippines stirred the missionary conscience of an evangelical GI, who resolved to go to Japan after the war and bury himself 'in the heart of heathendom', believing that 'Christ hadn't failed them. *We* had.'[790] After the capture of Iwo Jima in March 1945, and in a gesture that was rich with symbolism, a new branch of the Service Men's Christian League, composed entirely of marines and navy corpsmen, resolved as its 'first project' to purchase more than one hundred 'New Testaments in Japanese and Korean to be distributed among prisoners of war'.[791] In fact, what could be achieved among the Japanese, once freed from the shackles of state Shinto, was already apparent in the steady stream of converts to Christianity among the army's Nisei units. Although, in the spirit of the Geneva Convention, a Buddhist priest was identified by American chaplains to conduct 'Shinto and Buddhist services' among fellow POWs at New Bilibid Prison in the Philippines in 1945,[792] for the duration of the war there were no Buddhist (let alone Shinto) chaplains for either the Japanese-American 100th Infantry Battalion or the 442nd Infantry Regiment. Furthermore, it is clear that the most experienced chaplain assigned to these units, namely Israel Yost, and despite his sense of fair play in other respects, regarded his role as a missionary opportunity. While Yost lobbied for the release of a Shinto priest, the stepfather of a Japanese-American GI who had been interned on Honolulu,[793] his wartime correspondence reveals that he also felt impelled to win the souls of his Nisei for Christ, writing to his wife in January 1944:

> Some good friends are gone – one was a Buddhist. It's worried me since that he died a Buddhist and not a Christian. I visited the men prior to a recent action; I knew many would not live through it. I asked many, 'Are

you all set to go?' hoping they would take the opportunity to speak of religion if they cared to. None did, but maybe they knew what I meant.[794]

Yost's memoirs and correspondence are littered with references to the instruction and baptism of Japanese-American converts.[795] Just prior to embarking for Anzio in March 1944, for example, Yost took the opportunity to instruct five Nisei catechumens and to baptise four others.[796] According to the *New York Times*, Yost was even the envy of his fellow chaplains in the 34th Infantry Division, of which the 100th Battalion was a part, simply because his unusual assignment meant that he had been given a golden opportunity for fruitful missionary work.[797] The war in the Pacific, however, gave other Americans ample opportunity to help to Christianise the Japanese. In terms of the Japanese diaspora, the security crackdown on Japanese organisations in Hawaii enabled navy chaplain John Harold Craven to commandeer part of the Buddhist temple on the island of Maui. After Craven secured the help of local missionaries, this duly became the First Baptist Church of Kahului, which attracted a congregation of English-speaking Japanese and whose original Sunday school teachers were Craven's marines.[798] In December 1945, *The Link* signalled that Japan had moved centre stage as a missionary objective by republishing an article from *Theology Today* on the prospects for the gospel in this hitherto unrewarding mission field. Here, Presbyterian army chaplain W.A. McIlwaine, 'a former missionary to Japan', judged the outlook to be fair providing that 'the message preached was not too meek or other-worldly, but 'a virile Gospel, stronger than all the strength and opposition in Japan'.[799]

Building on a momentum that had been gathering throughout the course of the Pacific war, contact with Japanese Christians and their leadership began immediately after the capitulation of Japan. Hastening ashore with some fellow chaplains after the formal surrender, Samuel H. Ray headed for the Jesuit community at Tokyo's Sophia University, where they were warmly welcomed by his mainly German confrères. As Ray remembered: 'When we brought fresh beef and butter and sugar and coffee and candy and cigarettes and canned soup and canned milk, we appeared like angels from heaven.'[800] Later, Ray inspected the devastated Catholic infrastructure of Yokohama, helped newly released internees, and supplied cases of badly needed medicines to the hospital of the Missionary Sisters of St Francis.[801] Though the northernmost island of Hokkaido was much less ravaged by war, Chaplain Thomas J. Donnelly of the occupying 77th Infantry Division also made a beeline for the local clergy, finding a Japanese Catholic priest in Asahikawa with whom he conversed in Latin.[802] In short, and as summarised by the *History of Chaplains' Activities in the Pacific*:

A new experience to the chaplains in the Eighth Army was the contact with civilian ministers and laymen of the Christian groups in Japan. Every effort was and is being made by the Chaplains to win the peace in Japan as outlined by General MacArthur through the exemplification of Christianity and democracy and of carrying on the work of keeping the officers and men of the Eighth Army up to the highest ideals of service for God and country.[803]

In December 1945, and after meeting with a deputation of senior American and Japanese churchmen, Chaplain Ivan L. Bennett, the senior American chaplain in Japan, used his position as a senior staff officer to secure shipping space for a massive consignment of Christian literature, a consignment that included 100,000 Bibles, 2.5 million New Testaments and 250,000 hymnals, all in Japanese.[804] Unsurprisingly, it was noted that: 'Christian leaders in Japan have shown deep appreciation for the attitude manifested toward them.'[805]

If meetings with Toyohiko Kagawa were highly prized by Protestant chaplains,[806] the warmth and spontaneity of more grass-roots contact was equally in evidence: 'When our troops reached Japan, they were once again given a genuine welcome by the Christians. A great many of their churches had been destroyed but wherever one was standing it was made available for use by the Americans.'[807] Examples of this included the loan of a Presbyterian church at Yokohama for use as a base chapel, free access to the Catholic cathedral and Episcopalian church in Kyoto, and the opening of a Methodist church in Kobe.[808] The occupiers reciprocated with their customary largesse. At Christmas 1945, 'The Chaplains at GHQ sponsored a Christmas service and party in cooperation with the Sunday School Board of the church of Christ in Japan', an event that involved two thousand Japanese children in a celebration at Hibiya Park Hall in Tokyo.[809] Furthermore, and while based in northern Honshu with the 81st Infantry Division from September 1945 to January 1946, the experiences of Methodist army chaplain Percy M. Hickcox underlined the extent to which chaplains and GIs could become involved in rebuilding and even enlarging Japanese church life in the early stages of the occupation. During his first trip to the city of Hirosaki – 'known as "the Holy City" because of the strength of its Christian Churches' – Hickcox visited its Episcopalian bishop, 'a large Methodist Church which before the war had a local membership of sixteen hundred', and a Catholic parish priest.[810] Significantly, his sense was that they were all united in the common cause of reshaping post-war Japan according to Christian and democratic principles:

> Had we come here as civilian clergymen we might have been received only as curious tourists. As chaplains in the uniform of the U.S. Army, we were fellow workers in an enterprise which represented the highest endeavour of our Christian homeland and which we alike looked upon as the hope of this stricken people and ultimately of the world.[811]

Nevertheless, this great enterprise was not just the concern of clergymen. Lauded as 'veritable angels from heaven' by a Japanese Methodist preacher,[812] ordinary veterans of the 81st were also keen to be involved. Early that December, and in the devastated port city of Aomori, a Sunday afternoon service was inaugurated in the precincts of a local Buddhist temple, a product of the joint efforts of the 81st's chaplains, a Japanese Methodist minister and enthusiastic GIs. As Hickcox wrote:

> Again we found our soldiers keenly interested in missionary work, and announcement to them that they could sing in our Temple Choir and otherwise help in Japanese Christian services for the city met with ready response from officers and men.... A large group of earnest Christian soldiers responded quickly to the challenge of this practical expression of religious enterprise.[813]

Boosted by a generous distribution of Christmas gifts, by the time the 81st left Japan towards the end of January, attendance at this service had soared from a small handful of civilians to nearly two thousand.[814] Nonetheless, and as Hickcox was keen to emphasise, the benefits of this venture were mutual:

> As chaplains we were convinced that one of the finest ways we could serve our men was to lead those who were so minded to express their faith in this practical manner. These missionary services had kindled a zeal for the spread of the gospel in the hearts of our men. They had actually participated in the gospel program at work in a foreign country, and in these several score of soldiers who voluntarily assisted us in this rewarding field was sowed seed which back at home will bear fruit in years to come.[815]

These efforts, it should be emphasised, were very much in line with key aspects of official religious policy during the first four months of the Allied occupation. Guided by the terms of the Potsdam Declaration of July, and by the United States Initial Post-Surrender Policy of September 1945,[816] MacArthur introduced freedom of religion in Japan by means of the Civil Liberties Directive in October, and went on to sever the links between the Japanese state and Shinto through the 'Shinto Directive' of December. Before the year was out, he had also expressed his support for the return of Christian missionaries 'to the maximum extent practicable'.[817] On New Year's Day 1946, Emperor Hirohito dramatically renounced any claim to divinity in his so-called 'Declaration of Humanity'.[818] Many American veterans of the Pacific war duly headed to Japan to spread the gospel in succeeding years.[819] Major outgrowths of the 'GI Gospel Hour' phenomenon included the creation of the Far Eastern Gospel Crusade in 1947 and the foundation of the Far Eastern Bible Institute and Seminary in 1948.[820]

Notable post-war missionaries to Japan included Jacob DeShazer, one of William G. Farrow's crewmates on the Doolittle Raid, who survived three and a half years of brutal captivity. In May 1944, DeShazer was provided with a Bible and, as he later put it, this enabled him to understand his desperate situation in an entirely different light. When contemplating his Japanese captors, and the many torments they inflicted on their prisoners, his reading and understanding of the Bible served to transform his previous, instinctive hatred for them into Christian love and compassion. Ultimately, what the Japanese lacked was any knowledge of Christ and of his teachings. All of their behaviour, he deduced, was simply a natural function of the lack of Christ in their lives.[821] DeShazer arrived in Japan in 1948, as a missionary of the fundamentalist Free Methodist Church. In time, his converts would include Mitsuo Fuchida, a Japanese navy pilot who had led the attack at Pearl Harbor.[822]

By the late 1940s, and given the transformation of the Japanese religious landscape, the outlook for Christianity seemed promising indeed. With the freedom and equality of religions guaranteed by the constitution of November 1946,[823] the advent of a post-war Protestant prime minister in 1947, and MacArthur's repeated pronouncements on the desirability of a Christian future for the country,[824] by 1949 Daniel Poling could rejoice at the progress Christianity was making in Japan, especially given the growing threat of godless communism. This advance, it should be emphasised, had been primed by the American military and was sponsored and overseen by an American general who, by his own admission, had 'asked for missionaries, and more missionaries.'[825] According to Poling:

> I visited [MacArthur] on his invitational orders to address our troops and American civilians at the Easter dawn service and to confer with his chaplains … I saw the constructive effects of religious activity. Roman Catholic missionaries had been giving Japanese communities instruction from almost the start of the occupation. Sherwood Eddy, Dr. Stanley E. Jones, Dr. John R. Mott, and other Protestant leaders had brought the message of Christ to tens of thousands of eager listeners. Within a short space of time some two hundred thousand Japanese had publicly declared themselves Christians … The Easter sunrise service held in Tokyo in 1949 was an impressive answer to Japan's Communists, and it was perhaps the greatest Christian demonstration in all Asian history up to that time … More than ten thousand Japanese and Americans gathered there. Three hundred Japanese youths in white silk vestments sang the 'Hallelujah Chorus.' As I preached my Resurrection message, [Job 14:14] 'If a Man Die, Shall He Live?', to this vast gathering, I could not but feel that Japan, at least, was destined to become a great positive force in the resistance to the Kremlin's designs on Asia.[826]

Conclusion

After years of an isolationism born of both long-term and short-term factors, World War II forced Americans to confront the challenges of a wider, more troubled world. To a considerable extent, they were fortified by a perception of their adversaries that was heavily conditioned by their own religious convictions and identity. Whether explicitly or implicitly, wartime Americans understood the war against Nazism as a battle against a barbaric and recrudescent paganism that persecuted Christianity and Judaism with equal zeal. At the same time, Germany itself – the cradle of Protestantism and the ancestral home of so many Americans – was seldom regarded as entirely estranged from its historic Christian faith. Continuing resistance from within the churches, embodied by figures such as Niemöller and von Galen, supported the view that Germans were reclaimable, as did contact with the growing number of German POWs captured by the Americans between 1942 and 1945. In the course of the war and in its aftermath, this sense of religious commonality involved the US Army and its Christian chaplains in extensive conversion and reclamation activities among hundreds of thousands of German POWs, efforts that appear to have met with notable success in Europe and in the United States. In contrast, there was an almost total absence of such affinities in the war against Japan, the only historically non-Christian power among the major belligerents. To Americans, the dreadful manifestations of a different and arcane moral universe, the risible and blasphemous deification of the emperor, and the perceived persecution of Christian missionary work gave a religious edge to a conflict that was already inflamed by the manner of Japan's attack on Pearl Harbor and by the racial and cultural chasm that separated the two belligerents. Significantly, whereas the antics and manoeuvrings of pro-Nazi churchmen were often conveniently ignored by American commentators, scant sympathy or understanding was shown to those Japanese Christians who had been forced to make accommodations to the pre-war imperial regime.

Conversely, a shared religious identity did much to warm and to lubricate relations with the British, lending a further dimension to the evolving 'special relationship' between Britain and the United States. If felt most keenly by Anglophone Protestants, a sometimes inflated regard for British religiosity, and for the enduring Christian heritage of the British Isles, was as much a consequence of the lengthy GI presence in Britain as was the hedonism and promiscuity that will be studied in the next chapter. Naturally, and in the context of the Pacific war, this situation was very much replicated in British-settled Australia and New Zealand. In terms of continental Europe, the relative piety of the Netherlands, for example, helped to foster a positive response to the Dutch, whereas the more secular traditions of French society contributed to an increasing contempt for the French. If American Christians were often invigorated by contact with their European co-religionists across the world, this was even truer of American Jews, their role as liberators of their fellow Jews proving a powerful stimulus to Jewish identity, especially for those who served in North Africa and Europe.

Ensconced in their Judeo-Christian identity, the reaction of American service personnel towards other religious cultures was more complex. Overall, a sense of condescension, puzzlement and disdain seems to have prevailed in reactions towards India, the Islamic world, and even to "'democractic', almost Christian, Western-world-loving China', as Paul Fussell described it.[827] Conversely, the war brought about a tremendous vindication of overseas missionary work, whose benefits and potential, especially in the Pacific region, were made tangible and immediate to many young Americans in contexts as different as China and New Guinea. In consequence, their experience served as a major boost to America's reinvigorated, post-war missionary movement, with veterans often at the leading edge of post-war missionary enterprise, and most notably of renewed missionary designs on Japan.

Chapter Six

Religion, War and Morality

Introduction

CHAPLAINS and other interested parties could find much to reassure them concerning the religious state of the American serviceman or woman. Atheists were rare (even non-existent in military cemeteries) and, quite apart from combat and other experiences, the American military environment seemed to promote a greater religious consciousness. Furthermore, and in contrast to the brutal example set by other armed forces, America's soldiers and sailors could be admirable exponents of the Golden Rule, and even of the Christian missionary impulse, among Allied, liberated and even enemy civilians. Nevertheless, and as the experience of World War I had recently shown, military service in the context of a global war was inherently hazardous from a moral point of view, the path of the American serviceman and woman being strewn with perils and pitfalls of enormous variety and Bunyanesque proportions. As a result, the moral conduct of a great many service personnel gave considerable cause for concern, often falling disturbingly short of contemporary civilian norms and standards. With this in view, and when assessing the effects of war on faith and morals, John W. Early, the Lutheran senior chaplain of the 79th Infantry Division, wrote after VE day:

> The moral and religious life of personnel serving in the European Theater has been impaired somewhat, because of the close association with all types of men, the increased opportunities for misuse of sex and alcoholic liquors, and the hatred and contempt that was encouraged for the rights of conquered individuals. Evidence of this is to be found in the number of rape cases reported or noted, the shipment of loot by all grades of personnel, the size of PTA accounts and money orders sent, the operations of Civil Affairs Groups in liberated and occupied countries, and the unchristian motivation of Psychological Warfare Division personnel.[1]

This chapter will consider the moral experience of military service, and consider its religious implications both in the shorter and the longer terms.

Morality and military service

Writing in *The Link* in March 1945, Congregational-Christian chaplain Lawrence D. Graves claimed that a certain proportion of service personnel had sought to place their consciences in a state of suspended animation for the duration of the war, claiming that:

> Soldiers have a tendency to rationalize their sub-normal behavior and say, 'This is on the house; we won't count this one.' Inwardly revolting against the inconveniences of war, they sometimes find a satisfactory solution in stopping the moral clock. In this non-moral vacuum which they have created for themselves, they set up a system of indulgence which will cover every wicked excursion and debauchery. They assume a toughness and an air of irresponsibility which does not naturally belong to them. They do things which would shock the folks back home, and they refrain from doing things which would have an opposite effect. They seem to pride themselves in appearing to be worse than they really are.[2]

However, and as Graves insisted, such delusions called to mind the warning of Matthew 16:26, 'For what is a man profited, if he shall gain the whole world, and lose his own soul?' As Graves went on:

> The soldier will someday be an ex-soldier, and he will then turn his talents to the serious business of civilian living. True, he will lay down his Garand and his steel bonnet, but for the life of him he won't be able to leave the record of his moral evil along with his Service Record. No general can exonerate and call off the consequences of sins committed.[3]

Besides the prospect of veterans returning under an intolerable (if unrecognised) burden of sin, there was also the danger posed to American society by suppressed patterns of habituated vice, or 'the beasts we held in check'. According to Graves, material victory could be compromised by the threat of spiritual failure on a massive scale: 'Won a war but lost his soul! What a shabby victory for us if there are many men like this! What a tragedy for them who return impaired and crippled by their own Samson-like defeats!'[4] Consequently, Graves summoned his readers to be steadfast in their own witness and example, urging that: 'our life as soldiers can become a piece of the great pattern of victorious living through Him that loved us and gave Himself for us! It's altogether up to us!'[5]

However, even the steady and religious could feel beleaguered in the conditions into which they were thrust. Coming from a society that had never been impressed by the moral standards of the regular army, for many new recruits the moral contaminants of service life during World War II were evident – even blatant – from the outset. Writing in 1944, the Presbyterian army chaplain Eben Cobb Brink conceded that in many cases civilian norms began to unravel in the army's training camps, and that: 'The moral and spiritual breakup of lives in the Army is all too sad a story, for some there are who cannot stand the strain.'[6] As an uprooted, self-described 'yokel' from Minneapolis, Samuel Hynes found that flight training as a Marine Corps pilot entailed 'an abrupt loss of privacy and family' and an unprecedented opportunity for hedonistic excess.[7] As the navy banned its officer cadets from marrying, a spate of backstreet abortions occurred among the girlfriends and secret wives of his fellow cadets.[8] Hynes himself discovered that the social dislocation and relaxed sexual mores of the American home front turned nights spent in Mobile, Alabama, 'into one montage of drunkenness, fumbling, and the loneliness of late streets'.[9] For many, this wartime confrontation with a wider and more fallen world was much less congenial than Hynes found it to be. After serving for almost two years, Howard Orr, an army pilot, still took exception to aspects of his environment, complaining to his father in January 1945 about the rampant 'sex, drinking, smoking, and dirty talk'.[10]

However, the moral turpitude of service life was not simply an aggregate of wayward personal choice, for the tone could be set by the army itself. Paul Fussell, who was then a potential officer, wrote of the army reception centre at Fort MacArthur, San Pedro:

> There, illusions were shattered from the very start when we were treated not at all as officer material but as ordinary drafted scum. We were lined up, insulted, shouted at, numbered, and hustled into a barracks building by contemptuous sergeants. Next day, conditions did not improve: we were put through a physical examination featuring scrutiny of one's anus ('Spread those cheeks!') with, sometimes, public critical commentary.... Here, we were serfs, or even lower than that.... Our inquiries about when we would head for [officer candidate school] triggered the most obscene sarcasm and abuse.[11]

For Russell Baldwin, a Methodist church member from Euclid, Ohio, basic training at Camp Livingston, Louisiana, also proved to be a revelation:

> [W]hat a conglomeration of humanity! You see, I came up in a very conservative family ... profanity I never heard, very little, and the ways of the world I knew very little about. Boy, I learned them overnight there ... we had everything from the profanity and the smoking to bragging about sex activity and we had homosexuals in the crowd ... you name it, we had 'em there.[12]

Within weeks, he found himself administering 'prophylactic care' to those who had been 'out with the women'. In his subsequent career as a combat medic, he had to deny drugs to a senior officer, who turned out to be 'a drug abuser', and came to the conclusion that certain homosexuals were tempted to appear for emergency prophylactic treatment late at night – 'they just wanted someone playing with them, I guess'.[13]

For many American civilians, the moral image of the army – so carefully cultivated by George C. Marshall – was also tainted by the admission of convicted felons into its ranks, to the number of around 100,000 by the end of the war.

Keen to promote the army's reputation, the War Department had originally sought to exclude felons from the draft, a policy that was often criticised as unjustly depriving patriotic petty criminals of the right to serve and, more widely, as penalising the law-abiding. From July 1941, the army accepted felons in 'meritorious' cases and, by 1944, this policy had evolved to the point that certain types of prisoners could be drafted in exchange for parole.[14] So controversial was this policy that *The Link* addressed the situation in September 1944, reminding its readers of the rehabilitative potential of military service and of the Christian imperative to forgive, while also noting that: 'Protest has come pouring in from parents (many of whom are devout church-members) regarding the admission of felons into the armed forces.'[15] If concerned parents objected to their drafted sons being forced to rub shoulders with convicted criminals, the chaplain's capacity to act as a moral policeman was also distinctly limited. According to Chaplain Morris N. Kertzer, chaplains were virtually impotent in that respect, writing after the war:

> I have been asked if chaplains considered themselves as the guardians of men's morals. If we saw ourselves in that role, what an unhappy lot was ours. Advocating that the soldiers' language be laundered, that drunkenness be discouraged, that an army-operated brothel be abolished was an invitation to unpopularity and transfer. The Commanding Officer's ideal chaplain was one who 'didn't get in his hair.' A resolute man of God who pursued his convictions to the bitter end discovered that he had the blessing but not the support of the Chaplains Office in Washington. Many a chaplain was crucified for his tenacity, finding that his efficiency rating, and, in turn, his usefulness, was determined in the end by his Commanding Officer.[16]

In fact, all too often chaplains could do little more than make eloquent complaints about the condition of their charges. Eben Cobb Brink acknowledged that:

> Armies are made up of all kinds of men. And were the [chaplain's] diary to be opened too wide, it would tell of men who held no high principles, who never had eyes to see God. It would tell of men who drank too much, and of lives ruined by drunkenness. It would tell of men whose characters were ruined, and who soiled the characters of others. It would tell of remorse, and tragedy, and of men who sought the chaplain only because trouble made it expedient to do so. It would tell of letters written by the chaplain, trying to straighten out the muddled affairs of sinful lives; and of pathetic letters received by the chaplain from those whose problems were the tragic results of sinfulness.[17]

As an AAF chaplain in England, Charles Edward Lunn wrote to his wife in August 1943:

The churches never reached the masses of humanity, and it seems that those it [sic] did reach were given the form of religion without its spirit. Thus men's souls are driven into evil habits like the red maple leaves before the autumn wind. I see wickedness and immorality on the part of our soldiers, both officers and enlisted men, that makes my inner soul shudder.... It is easier to die in battle, giving one's life for an ideal for loved ones and friends, than it is to face the almost insuperable task of living from day to day, striving to keep clean, pure and upright, overcoming the temptations that press in with more reality and relentlessness than the pursuing enemy on the battlefield.[18]

After a fruitless conversation about casual, wartime sex with a young fighter pilot, Lunn even felt tempted to resign his commission, despairing that he 'didn't have what it took to reach men who had given themselves over to immorality.'[19] For Chaplain George W. Zinz of the 45th Evacuation Hospital in North-West Europe, the situation was doubly painful as too many of his brethren seemed disposed to deny or excuse the sinfulness around them. Conscious of the endemic problems of gambling and cursing, and of rampant racketeering and a soaring 'venereal rate' after the liberation of Paris, Zinz protested that his natural anxiety was simply dismissed by fellow Christians:

'Chappie, you know war always brings about this condition. One must relax and get rid of this tormenting tension.' That is the answer I get for my effort to stem the onrushing tide. 'You are not looking at it with a liberal, an open mind. Close your eyes and blame it on the war,' others will say. It is difficult enough to try to give comfort and help to one who is dying after having fought for our ideals but to have to bear these remarks and attitudes of many, who have come from so-called Christian homes, is like bearing the load of another Cross.[20]

In the Pacific, even the indefatigable evangelist James Edwin Orr found prolonged exposure to service life debilitating, admitting that, after two years in the army and 'a year in the tropics,' by 1945 his 'enforced association with profanity, lewd conversation, and drunkenness' had led to a spiritual depression.[21]

Amidst wholesale vice and depravity, ordinary officers and enlisted men felt their isolation more keenly, these men of course lacking the professional and institutional cushioning of their chaplains. For example, towards the end of 1944 Corporal Latimer W. Garrett confided to his fellow 'Linkers':

The slow adjustment to a 'freak' life has been difficult.... Isolation and loneliness make for dullness of mind and tiredness of spirit.... Of the battalion, one per cent is an optimistic average of attendance at [SMCL] meetings. Approximately one out of every fifty men attend church services occasionally. The *morale* code is upheld, but have we still got a *moral* code? In the case of men out here, masturbation seems to be presumed, the third commandment is null and void, drunkenness is a goal to be reached, adultery and fornication are aims. Has our Christian background sufficed? Obviously, it has not.[22]

For men such as Garrett, restraint and self-control could make them marginal and ill-adjusted figures. Lester Atwell remembered an officer of the 345th Infantry Regiment, a victim of combat exhaustion, whose collapse was not simply due to the battlefields of North-West Europe – 'why hadn't he been better prepared?', Atwell pondered:

What had he expected of war? He seemed too to be bothered by the foul language, the cruel streak, the dishonesty in many of the men, and it appalled him to discover that America was made up in part of such. Yet he was an educated man, he was not young, he had taught in a college and had coached its football teams. I could not help thinking that his war had not been won on any playing fields.[23]

In a telling incident, Nathan Robbins, a navy officer on board an LST in the Pacific, felt duty bound to educate his cabin-mate on the facts of life, writing to his wife in December 1944: 'The room-mate, Ensign Liechty – Engineer for the ship, is a nice lad (25 years) and is a Mormon. He is quite naïve and innocent and I have started a sexual lecture to educate him – he is a virgin, so he says and the questions almost prove it.'[24] For Samuel Hynes and his fellow trainees, then embarked on a wartime spree of self-discovery, the one dissenter in their midst met with a wall of disdain if not outright persecution. As Hynes recollected, although not without a twinge of regret:

Obscenity was masculine; anyone who objected to it, or simply didn't use it, must therefore be feminine – a queer, a pansy. In a bunk just down from mine lived a gentle, Bible-reading Georgia boy named Newton.... He would wait until midnight to go to the toilet or take a shower, so that he could be alone there, and he would leave the room when the talk got too coarse. He must have hated us and the way we lived; but he wanted to belong, too, and so he kept coming back, and hanging around. We teased him, called him 'Newt the Fruit', and hinted, if he seemed to have made a friend, that unnatural acts took place in the shower after lights out. The mood was meant to be joking, and I think many of us felt some fondness for him, but his manner was outside the limits of our world, and so we had to keep him outside, too.... We didn't actually persecute poor Newton, but we despised him, and that is worse than persecution when you're nineteen, and want to belong.[25]

No doubt voicing the frustrations of many, Private John Caragazian, a former student at 'a college with a religious foundation', complained to *The Link* in October 1945:

> [W]hen I go to the chapel twice a week, I am laughed at; when I refuse to gamble I am abused; when I refuse to drink or smoke, I am referred to as a softie. That attitude, unfortunate as it is, is almost universal in regard to the men serving our country. Bars, pool rooms, indecent performances, places of immorality are far more preferred than the decent places such as the chapel, library and places with a Christian atmosphere. Religion as a whole is disregarded or as a whole considered as unnecessary.[26]

Such recurrent complaints caused consternation beyond military circles, for many religious commentators still perceived the classic link, under divine providence, between the moral and spiritual state of the armed forces and ultimate victory or defeat. A traditional theme in appeals to soldiers and sailors over the centuries, and one that was firmly anchored in the Bible (see, for example, Joshua 6–7), this trope was invoked by the Jesuit Daniel A. Lord, author of the Motion Picture Production Code of 1930,[27] in his beguilingly entitled *A Salute to the Men in Service* (1942). Here, and in a section headed 'The Treason of Mortal Sin', Lord rehearsed some ancient verities for the benefit of his readers: 'Don't let's be unpleasant and untruthful,' he began, 'but the plain fact is that God is on the side of the land that loves and serves Him.'[28] Central to that equation was the moral and religious state of the nation's armed forces. Conjuring the picture of a divine audit, Lord went on:

> 'Let's see,' we seem to hear Him say. 'Are these my soldiers? Are these my faithful sons?'
> Then He sees you.... He sees that you're really doing a grand job for Him. You are in the state of sanctifying grace. You are refusing to commit mortal sin.... He says, 'That's my fighting man right enough. I'll give victory to the side he is fighting for.'[29]

However:

> On the other hand, He may look down upon our Armies and Navy and cry out (let's suppose): 'Why, it's hard to tell these men from the Nazis and Japs. Their language, their treatment of women, their attitude toward drink, the things they read, the pictures they hang on their walls and pass from hand to hand, the stories they tell, the attitude they take toward theft.... What is there about any of them that marks them as my friends, my soldiers?'
> This is a pretty serious matter.
> The soldier who is leading a pure, fine, honorable, honest, clean life is the greatest asset we have for victory.
> God is going to be with him in battle.[30]

Framed more humorously, *Az You Were!*, Alva J. Brasted's cartoon book of manners, sought to convey the same message, promoting virtues that Brasted claimed 'should characterize every good soldier of both God and Country'.[31]

Although heard from civilian pulpits in Europe, with one Belgian priest seeing the Ardennes offensive of December 1944 as a divine punishment of American sinfulness,[32] the persistence of these perspectives in the United States helps to underline the fact that, despite the upheavals and challenges of the war years, a conservative moral consensus also held sway in American society. However much religious Americans may have differed, for example, over the acceptability of gambling or smoking, over what one could eat and when, or over how much liquor (if any) one could imbibe, there was broad and solid agreement over the basic sinfulness of theft, cursing, drunkenness or extramarital sex. For Robert Leckie of the 1st Marines, this was underlined in an odd encounter with a fellow marine in Melbourne: '"Trouble with these Australian girls," he complained, "is that they ain't go no morals. They're too easy. Catch an American girl giving herself away like they do. No siree, buddy – they've still got morals."' As a well-instructed Catholic, for Leckie this brought to mind Luke 18:9–14: 'The descendants of the Pharisee are legion. "O God. I give thee thanks that I am not as the rest of men … adulterers, as also is this Australian, as also is this American, as also is …"'[33] As Samuel Hynes agreed, in moral matters in particular:

> We were puritans; it didn't matter where we had come from, the whole country between the two coasts shared that tradition of severity, work, and repression. Certainly middle westerners and southerners were alike in taking sex and liquor as two forms of sinfulness, to be indulged in, usually at the same time, and to be punished for, but not to be taken lightly, and certainly not as a business deal with a whore.[34]

Significantly, intrusions of civilian norms could be felt even among Hynes's loose-living comrades. On Saipan, for example, where nurses and Red Cross girls were on hand, he noted that one pilot censored his otherwise ribald songs whenever 'there was a woman at the bar'. On another occasion, a married, would-be seducer recoiled from a Red Cross girl when she admitted to wearing a diaphragm, a revelation that left him washed-up 'with his libido and his guilt'.[35] Likewise, and despite the libidinous conduct of so many GIs in wartime Europe, in November 1944 Orval Eugene Faubus noted the shock and dismay that were occasioned by the capture of a letter addressed to the German 'Front Line Soldier' from the 'League of Lonely War Women':

> Cut out our badge on this letter. Display it visibly on your glass in every tea room, in every bar which is in the vicinity of a railway station; soon a member of our League of Lonely War Women will take charge of you, and the dreams you dreamt in the front lines and the longings of lonely nights

will find fulfilment.... It is you we want, not your money, therefore ask for our membership card at once. There are members everywhere, since we German women understand our duties towards our country and towards those who defend it.[36]

Faubus even sent a copy of the letter to his wife, branding it 'ample proof for all those who doubt the utter depravity of the German people under Nazism'.[37]

There was, of course, an enormous spectrum of moral problems ranging from the particular, or comparatively minor, to the general, and undeniably severe. In the former category were two issues tackled by *The Link* in 1944, namely whether dancing and Sunday moviegoing were at all permissible. The question of dancing, raised by an 'old-fashioned' reader from 'the Dakota plains', had been prompted by the perplexing realisation that, in the eastern United States, 'churches put on dances too'. In this case, *The Link* affirmed the wholesomeness of dancing, at least when properly supervised, while warning that 'it is wrong to dance where the music, the drinking, and the people are aiming the dance at the lower sexual appetites'. Ultimately, it left the question open to individual judgement.[38] A somewhat harder line, however, was taken towards the question of Sunday movies. Here, army chaplain Frederick W. Cropp acknowledged that the Sabbath could be observed differently by Christians but ventured his opinion that Sunday should be spent in 'worship, reading, resting, music, walks and conversations ... calling on the sick, and several other items which I haven't time for on other days'.[39] Needless to say, and even for those to whom such a regime may have appealed, this was often completely unrealistic. According to Lester Atwell, in the five months between his arrival in France and April 1945 only one Sunday was spent as a planned day of rest.[40] For Orval Eugene Faubus, only hospitalisation in March 1945 allowed him to be even conscious of the Sabbath after 'many, many weeks'.[41] Similarly, in the Pacific, it was not until 15 August 1945, after Japan had sued for peace, that MacArthur confirmed an order that: 'Military duty and labor during church hours will be reduced as circumstances may permit and athletic and recreational activities on Sunday will, if practicable, be so scheduled as not to interfere with attendance at services'.[42]

If the war inevitably played havoc with traditional routines of Sabbath day observance, other norms were also severely disrupted. For Christian Scientists, for example, it was a serious matter that they were 'whisked into hospitals' and subjected to inoculations and other 'medical treatment'.[43] Similarly, a special dispensation meant that Catholic personnel were not required to abstain from meat on Fridays, the church acknowledging that the soldier 'has to eat what is set before him'.[44] Their pre-Communion fast was likewise reduced to one hour for liquids and three hours for solids.[45] Such dietary problems were, of course, far more pressing for Jews. As Morris N. Kertzer explained, approximately 500,000 young American Jews had been unable to observe Judaism's strict dietary laws as a result of the war and of the many exigencies of service. However beneficial it may have proved in other respects, this service had constantly demanded considerable and even habitual adaptation to immediate circumstances, and all that implied for the life of an observant Jew. Although a great many service personnel were basically non-observant even as civilians, the fact remained that a great many in this core constituency had also been forced to make some key accommodations over a period of years, and with this in view it seemed that Orthodoxy may well have become a significant casualty of the war.[46]

Although 'kosher canned meats' were made available in Post Exchanges and via the JWB,[47] this did not make much of a difference. As a chaplains' report from the ETO put it:

> For Jewish men who were scrupulous as to their religious dietary require-
> ments, the Jewish Welfare Board provided canned kosher food to supple-
> ment the Army ration. The demand by and large was not great, although
> some felt the kosher food highly essential, and there were many isolated
> calls for it. In general, it was available when it was required, but there
> was considerable ignorance of the availability of this food among Christian
> chaplains.[48]

Segregation and civil rights

For many, including liberal whites as well as blacks, to say nothing of foreign opinion, one of the most obvious and disturbing aspects of American military life was its racial segregation. Chaplain's assistant Kenneth A. Connelly aired senti-ments that were increasingly common during the war years when he despaired from a 'Southern Training camp' in 1943:

> A black man with the mind of Einstein, the soul of St. Francis and the
> energy of Thomas Edison would be a very successful latrine attendant or
> bootblack. If Mr. Stalin should attack us someday on the very grounds on
> which we are now attacking Hitler – those of unjust racial persecution –
> he would have a strong point in his favor. There isn't too much difference
> between our treatment of the Negro and Hitler's treatment of the Jew. If
> the Negroes ever held the economic power in the south that the Jews held
> in Germany they would be drawn and quartered too, never fear.[49]

Nevertheless, and in a pattern that was true of other moral and political issues, a coherent or effective response simply failed to materialise among military chaplains. Despite the wartime ferment over civil rights, the army's Office of the Chief of Chaplains characteristically viewed considerations of efficiency as trumping those of racial justice. Consequently, and while facilitating the activities of African American churchmen and the recruitment and non-segregated training of African American army chaplains, it refused to associate the Corps of Chaplains with the contentious cause of officially promoting race relations. Significantly, when the Methodist army chaplain Garland E. Hopkins wrote to William R. Arnold in January 1944, suggesting that the corps promote 'a constructive program of interracial relations within the ranks of the army' in the same manner that it promoted the cause of interfaith relations, he was told that chaplains already had the opportunity to do considerable good in this field 'by sound advice, good example and friendly contacts'. Meanwhile, Garland was assured, the chief of chaplains was 'doing everything in his power to create a Christ-like attitude among service personnel so that we can all live together peacefully and enjoy the rights that belong to all citizens of our Democracy'.[50] A similar proposal from Chaplain Louis B. Alder was rebuffed in June 1945, Alder being told that: 'a basic concept of the Army limits its activity to the proper indoctrination of military personnel only. The responsibility for the proper indoctrination of the civilian population is definitely a responsibility of civilian individuals and agencies'.[51] When deemed necessary, the Office of the Chief of Chaplains was even prepared to smooth the ruffled feathers of Jim Crow, as in April 1945 when George F. Rixey, the acting chief of chaplains, wrote to a Methodist minister in Montgomery, Alabama, regretting the 'embarrassment' caused by the presence of African Americans at a recent chaplains' conference hosted by his church. (To be fair, the limits of Rixey's sympathy were betrayed in his specious assertion that: 'War Department policy recognizes officers and enlisted men according to their rank and special qualifications or duties but cannot make distinctions because of race or creed'.)[52]

In contrast, and at least amidst the relatively liberal, mainline Protestant circles of *The Link* and *The Chaplain*, there was evidence of growing support for racial justice and civil rights as the war progressed, with the cause of Japanese-Americans being embraced in the process. This trend very much mirrored developments in the mainline churches and in the associated religious press, with the Federal Council of Churches, which had inaugurated Race Relations Sunday in 1922, renewing its calls for 'Christian fellowship among the races'.[53] If *The Link* got off to a shaky start with wisecracks about the supposed indolence of African Americans,[54] in February 1944 it published a piece proclaiming that 'anyone who entertains a Jim Crow sentiment, or a Yellow Race hostility, or an anti-Semitic complex is false to the American ideal, and should be exported to the Old World, as unfit for the New, wherein *"all men are created equal"*'.[55] In the course of subsequent months it would publish a prayer for racial tolerance,[56] set an SMCL 'Topic Talk' on racial and religious bigotry,[57] echo the words of Harry Emerson Fosdick ('RACE PREJUDICE is as thorough a denial of the Christian God as atheism is')[58] and advertise individual pledges to further the cause of civil rights in the post-war world.[59] It also editorialised on the Nisei 'Japyanks' of the

100th Infantry Battalion (suspicions of whom were castigated as 'sorry examples of racial prejudice that makes us ashamed in our nobler moments'), condemned the policy of segregation in the armed forces (featuring 'An Open Letter From Mom', which stressed that 'Discrimination has been pretty bad in the services'), and published a poetic reflection on the equality of the races and 'the bitter road of prejudice'.[60] Predictably, its stable-mate *The Chaplain* adopted a similar line. In January 1945 it applauded the appointment of the FCC's first African American vice president (namely, Dr Benjamin E. Mays of Morehouse College, Atlanta) and, in February, it acclaimed the newly discovered racial tolerance of the navy's chaplain school, although without broaching the question of why it had taken so long for African Americans to be admitted in the first place.[61] As 1945 progressed, Chaplain Raymond E. Musser looked forward to the elimination of 'racial hatred' as part of a 'new and better world' and, in August 1945, the text of Chaplain Roland B. Gittelsohn's controversial Iwo Jima sermon was published in full.[62] To complement all of this, the work of African American chaplains was reported in glowing terms. In August 1945, for example, seven-foot-tall African Methodist Episcopal chaplain Robert H. Gross was acclaimed as 'a mighty man indeed in organizing recreational programs, choirs and in creating a drift to chapel services' among the men of the 385th Engineer Battalion, which was then in France, while the death of Northern Baptist chaplain Clarence W. Griggs on Okinawa – 'the first Negro chaplain to be killed in action' – was announced in the same issue, it being emphasised that the deceased 'was a graduate of Fisk University, Nashville, Tennessee, and of Union Theological Seminary, New York City'.[63]

In March 1946, another African American army chaplain, Charles E. Byrd, once again drew attention to the potential of the chaplain's role in 'educating the races toward better relationships', especially as the war had demonstrated that 'the judgment of the God of history' demanded 'the discarding of the doctrine of the "master race" in any form'.[64] If the Office of the Chief of Chaplains remained impervious to the policy imperatives of such insights, some individuals did act upon them, besides those African American chaplains who traditionally championed the interests of the black soldier. At the instigation of an African American GI, Lutheran chaplain Israel Yost scored a minor victory when he intervened to end segregation at a cinema in Camp Davis, North Carolina, concealing his identity until a recreation officer had admitted 'that he was keeping the colored men in their proper place'.[65] For Catholic chaplain Karl A. Wuest, his voyage to North Africa in the company of African American troops proved to be a revelation: 'They were jolly and courteous and accommodating and fun to be with, as I found out by going among them and spending long hours talking with them. They were serious, too, and religious, even though they didn't often let it come to the top'.[66] For these reasons, among others, Wuest was scathing in his post-war condemnation of segregation and of the slow implementation by the US military of President Truman's Executive Order 9981:

The Army, undemocratic in many regards, has, in recent years, belatedly adopted too few principles of nonsegregation among its troops. The ability of the soldier, not his color, should rightly determine his position in the military. The enemy didn't check first on the color of the skin before he let fly with both barrels. And, as defenders of their country, both white and Negro were sacrificed in the slaughter, to preserve freedom for those who would, in an unfreedomly manner, discriminate because of a color line.[67]

In this, Wuest was in accord with another German-American Catholic chaplain who served in Italy, the badly maimed and much-decorated Albert J. Hoffmann. In August 1944, and in the words of *The Baltimore Afro-American*, Hoffmann administered a 'smack at home-front race prejudice' at a gathering of the Catholic Order of Foresters in Chicago:

War with your sons is a grim reality [declared Hoffmann] and every one of them plays it to the utmost of his strength and courage. None of these boys make sany [sic] distinctions as to race, religion, politics or color. They are all American soldiers. They fight for each other and many of them die in the fighting.[68]

Northern Baptist chaplain Warren Wyeth Willard, also drawing on his capital – if not his celebrity – as a veteran of Guadalcanal, took special note of the navy's African American stewards in his memoir *The Leathernecks Come Through* (1944). Alluding to the shoddy treatment of African Americans by the US Navy, and recounting how he had helped to bathe a shipwrecked steward on Guadalcanal, Willard wrote:

I thought of how kindly the colored mess attendants had treated me while I was aboard the transport. Faithfully and without complaint, they had cooked the meals for the officers, made up the beds, cleaned the rooms, and in many other ways assisted us. Now it was my privilege to serve one of them.... Somehow I felt that I owed him a great debt.[69]

Later, Willard was gratified to hear a British colonial officer's egalitarian opinion of the Solomon islanders, especially 'because there were some people who still considered the coloured man had a different nature from that of his white brother'.[70] Finally, and musing on the deeper meaning of the gift of an inlaid cane by a Christian islander on Tulagi, Willard reflected that it stood as 'a symbol of the way men of different races and colours can work together as brothers. Just as the white mother-of-pearl shines forth from the background of the jet-black ebony, so white man and black man, each retaining his racial identity, can harmonize and blend in one great unity of all mankind'.[71]

The dilemma of killing

While segregation raised some pressing moral problems for blacks and liberal whites alike, of more general concern was the moral effect and legacy of military service and of combat in particular. For Russell Baldwin, arrival in France via Utah Beach shortly after D-Day served as an apt introduction to the physical and moral ordeal of the ETO, stepping abruptly into an environment where the air was foetid with the smell of engine oil, vomit and excrement, with all kinds of debris (including human body parts) floating in the water – 'a real nasty situation'.[72] As Ernie Pyle warned the American public:

> Our men can't make this change from normal civilians into warriors and remain the same people. Even if they were away from you this long under normal circumstances, the mere process of maturing would change them, and they would not come home just as you knew them. Add to that the abnormal world they have been plunged into, the new philosophies they have had to assume or perish inwardly, the horrors and delights and strange wonderful things they have experienced, and they are bound to be different people from those you sent away.... The stress of war puts old virtues in a changed light. We shall have to relearn a simple fundamental or two when things get back to normal ... what's wrong with a small case of 'requisitioning' when murder is the classic goal?[73]

The morally chaotic environment of the battlefield was not simply confined to the process of killing, however. Despite the much-romanticised comradeship of the front-line soldier, the perils of combat often revealed the sheer cravenness of the survival instinct. John T. Bassett, an infantryman of the 10th Mountain Division, admitted that survival on the front line could be a question of ignoring the appeals of a wounded comrade, or of trying to rob another of the cover of his foxhole.[74] In fact, the very exclusivity of the vaunted bonds of comradeship could take a heavy toll on those who stood outside the charmed circle, a factor that helped to account for the high casualty levels suffered by newly arrived (and, therefore, expendable) replacements.[75] As Audie Murphy freely confessed: 'Let the hill be strewn with corpses so long as I do not have to turn over the bodies and find the familiar face of a friend'.[76] As for killing itself, the technology available meant that this was usually done impersonally, and at a distance. As the American war correspondent Eric Sevareid wrote:

> One never saw masses of men assaulting the enemy.... One felt baffled at first by the unreality of it all. Unseen groups of men were fighting other men that they rarely saw. They located the enemy by the abstractions of mathematics, an imagined science; they reported the enemy through radio waves that no man could visualize; and they destroyed him most frequently with projectiles no eye could follow.[77]

In the words of Chaplain Harry P. Abbott of the 1st Armored Division: 'Only a small percentage of our soldiers, mostly in the infantry, pulled the trigger and saw a man crumple up.'[78] The remote nature of the slaughter in which so many Americans participated did not, of course, render it morally neutral. With this in mind, Abbott asserted that their talent for destruction had no adverse moral effect upon American gunners for, if the carnage they wrought was obvious, they wished it had not been necessary and 'derived satisfaction from the realization that they helped to protect [the infantry], and to hasten the climax of the war, thus saving men on both sides'.[79] Killing was, of course, a much more personal and visceral business for infantrymen, and its ghastly realities stoked understandable fears about the brutalisation and prospective behaviour of those who were accustomed – and even hardened – to the necessity of what was often face-to-face killing. Naturally, America's churches were all too conscious that these potentially corrupting demands had been made of their members as much as of any other servicemen. In December 1943, for example, *The Link* had published a telling feature entitled 'Foxhole Fodder',[80] which furnished a number of inspirational texts for the infantryman (the last of which was 'Be thou faithful unto death, and I will give thee a crown of life', Revelation 2:10) and concluded with the message:

> While you are away, we will be with you; in all your wanderings we will be thinking of you; in your time of loneliness and danger, we will be praying for you; when you march we will march with you; when you come back, we will welcome you home and the reunion will bring peace to our hearts.[81]

However, underlying anxieties about what to expect after the war, especially in relation to the future conduct of front-line veterans, clearly persisted. Significantly, here again the debate about the influence and effects of foxhole religion loomed large, with optimists taking comfort in the view that its beneficial impact on the individual would ultimately serve to counter the morally corrupting implications of front-line service. In 1945, a confident forecast was made by the Southern Baptist army chaplain Charles H. Ashcraft from the battlefields of the Southwest Pacific.[82] As *The Chaplain* magazine reported:

> The religious experience of the soldiers in foxholes will endure to guide the men through life, Ashcraft says, discounting the theory about GI religion being a 'fear' religion. 'Out where men in a few moments age years into maturity, mentally and physically, the corresponding maturity of their religious experience cannot be logically questioned.... A soldier lying out behind enemy lines wounded for twenty-four hours has plenty time for serious contemplation about religion. Those with such experiences do not easily depart from their decision.[83]

More than a year after the surrender of Japan, it seemed to some as though this confidence had been well-placed. Writing in *The Chaplain* magazine, William Hints, a Methodist minister from Wyoming and a veteran of World War I, proclaimed 'Thank God for the Tight Corners'. In his opinion, it was simply apparent that the 'most valuable discoveries' were to be made in dangerous situations. Furthermore, 'What we learn in extreme peril is a revelation of the nature and character of God and the order of things. Our findings stay with us as touchstones of experience, as events and incidents that remain as permanent references so long as we live.' There was nothing at all to fear from the battlefield backgrounds of returned veterans, for those 'who have actually participated in the actual events of life at its most strenuous activity, and death in its irrecoverable reality', had simply 'plumbed the depths and scaled the heights of experience'.[84]

Nevertheless, what impressed and unsettled Ernie Pyle on the basis of his experiences in North Africa was the speed with which so many American airmen seemed to forget the terms of the Sixth Commandment: 'When they first arrived, I frequently heard pilots say they didn't hate the Germans, but I didn't hear that for long. They lost too many friends, too many roommates. Soon it was killing that animated them.'[85] Especially revealing was the mood of some following a successful strafing mission:

> It was a great holiday from escorting bombers, a job they hated. Going out free-lancing to shoot up whatever they could see ... that was utopia.... That was what they had done that day. And they really had had a field day. They ran onto a German truck convoy and blew it to pieces. They laughed and got excited as they told about it. The trucks were all full of men, and 'they flew out like firecrackers.' Motorcyclists got hit and dived forty feet before they stopped skidding. Two Messerschmitt 109s made the mistake of coming after our planes. They never had a chance. After firing a couple of wild bursts they went down smoking, and one of them seemed to blow up.... The boys were full of laughter when they told about it.... And they were so casual about everything – not casual in a hard, knowing way, but they talked about their flights and killing and being killed exactly as they would discuss girls or their school lessons.[86]

Likewise, Pyle also discovered that the attitudes of American infantrymen hardened over the course of the Tunisian campaign:

> The most vivid change was the casual and workshop manner in which they talked about killing. They had made the psychological transition from their normal belief that taking human life was sinful, over to a new professional outlook where killing was a craft. No longer was there anything morally

wrong about killing. In fact, it was an admirable thing ... it hadn't been necessary for me to make that change along with them ... killing to me was still murder.[87]

In fact, the infantryman's appetite for killing the enemy, and so winning the war, seemed insatiable:

He wanted to kill individually or in vast numbers. He wanted to see the Germans overrun, mangled, butchered in the Tunisian trap. He spoke excitedly of seeing great heaps of dead, of our bombers sinking whole shiploads of fleeing men, of Germans by the thousands dying miserably in a final Tunisian holocaust of their own creation.... In that one respect the frontline soldier differed from all the rest of us ... we wanted terribly yet only academically for the war to be over. The front-line soldier wanted it to be terminated by the physical process of his destroying enough Germans to end it. He was truly at war. The rest of us, no matter how hard we worked, were not.[88]

Seasoned and blooded in North Africa (and long before the grisly revelations of Dachau and elsewhere could evoke an exculpatory gloss) American infantrymen in Italy and North-West Europe could display a ruthlessness that crossed the threshold of the murderous. In Italy, for example, a British intelligence officer found that American officers had issued orders that any German attempting to surrender should be beaten to death.[89] After the breaking of the Gustav Line in the spring of 1944, Eric Sevareid stumbled across a pair of GIs in a shattered Italian village, where nearby: 'A young German soldier lay sprawled just inside a sagging doorway, his hobnailed boots sticking into the street.' The scene prompted an admission that he had paid the ultimate penalty for lagging behind: 'Thus casually was deliberate murder announced by boys who a year before had taken no lives but those of squirrel or pheasant.'[90] According to Sevareid: 'As weeks went by and this experience was repeated many times, I ceased even to be surprised – only, I could never again bring myself to write or speak with indignation of the Germans' violations of the "rules of warfare".'[91] In view of this admission, it seems ironic that one factor that enraged GIs against German prisoners was their alleged exploitation of innate American decency. As Orval Eugene Faubus fumed from Normandy in July 1944:

Almost all of them hope to go the States. The bastards have been fighting to destroy our way of life, our kindness, our generosity, our willingness to forgive, and have criticized us for those qualities. Yet they are the first to take advantage of [American qualities] when they can be useful.... Like a heartless criminal who gives no mercy in the commission of his crimes but is the first to cry pitifully for mercy when he is caught.... The Germans have shown no mercy to those they have conquered. I hope the guilty scoundrels get none when they are finally finished.[92]

Such sentiments were certainly acted upon at Dachau in April 1945, where dozens of SS prisoners were summarily shot by furious GIs, or literally torn apart by their former prisoners.[93] As the Jewish chaplain David Max Eichhorn wrote revealingly:

> We cried tears of hate. Combat hardened soldiers, Gentile and Jew, black and white, cried tears of hate. Then we stood aside and watched while the inmates of the camp hunted down their former guards.... We stood aside and watched while these guards were beaten to death, beaten so badly that their bodies were ripped open and innards protruded.... These evil people, it seemed to us, were being treated exactly as they deserved to be treated. To such depths does human nature sink in the presence of human depravity.[94]

Although events at Dachau prompted Eisenhower to urge the prosecution of GIs responsible for these and similar acts, no prosecutions ensued.[95] In fact, and far from being exceptional, the shooting of German prisoners, or of Germans trying to surrender, was widespread among GIs in North-West Europe. According to Paul Fussell, 'We were very hard on snotty Nazi adolescents' and, as Lester Atwell confirmed, '"The boys ain't takin' any prisoners today" was a fairly common statement, and there was never any doubt as to its meaning.'[96] Furthermore, and even if they were captured alive, special forms of retribution were reserved for enemy snipers, who were feared and loathed in equal measure. Such retribution included digging their own graves, or being told to 'run for it' before being shot.[97] For Atwell's 87th Infantry Division, the climax of this spiral of retribution came at Tambach in south-west Germany, where a number of German prisoners were shot in cold blood after surrendering. Significantly, the ensuing prosecutions had to be aborted when the perpetrators threatened to show that the brutality of their actions was consistent with the conduct shown towards a captured German sniper by their own divisional commander.[98] Although the evidence is murky, and despite Eisenhower's posturing after Dachau, during the ground war against Germany and Italy it would seem that quite senior commanders actively discouraged the taking of prisoners; on D-Day, for example, there seems to have been a widespread understanding among the assaulting divisions that no prisoners were to be taken. Whether this was because of a lack of facilities for POWs, or to sharpen the edge of aggression, or both, is not clear.[99] However, at Cherbourg in June 1944, a touch of the Wild West was employed to encourage its German garrison to capitulate, a German corpse being strapped to a horse that was chased into the city with a message that read, 'All you sons-a-bitches are going to end up this way'.[100] German corpses could even be mutilated in order to obtain valuables. William B. Hanford, an artillery forward observer with the 103rd Infantry Division, remembered how one combat medic – 'Cajun Joe' – used his scalpel to acquire enough rings to buy a car after the war. As Hanford put it: 'Cajun Joe was a nice guy otherwise, but war was a crummy business, and the Articles of War took a beating from both sides.'[101]

Battered enough in North Africa and Europe, legal and moral conventions took an even greater hammering in the war against Japan. In 1943, such were the qualms of Secretary of the Navy Frank Knox that he felt compelled to take 'the advice of leading churchmen on the morality of killing enemy leaders' before agreeing to the aerial ambush of Admiral Yamamoto over the Solomon Islands that April.[102] However, such niceties were usually at a discount in the war against Japan. Here, a catalogue of Japanese transgressions and atrocities aroused a condign wrath that was widely inflamed by a virulent racism, a profound sense of cultural and religious superiority, and by the sulphurous pronouncements of senior American officers. Although few could ultimately rival the crude but memorable rhetoric of Admiral William F. ('Bull') Halsey (who after the capture of Peleliu in October 1944 congratulated his marines on their 'hill[-]blasting, cave[-]smashing extermination of 11,000 slant-eyed gophers'),[103] this was not through any lack of group effort. Corporal Curtis Allen Spach of the 5th Marine Regiment recalled that, before landing on Guadalcanal in August 1942: 'Each one of us received a letter from our commanding officer, the last sentence reading Good Luck, God Bless You and to hell with the Japs.'[104] Similarly, James J. Fahey wrote that, as the light cruiser *Montpelier* crossed the equator near Truk in March 1944, its captain announced that: 'I hope we kill a lot of those slant-eyed bastards who are polluting these waters.' [105] Even *Yank* lent a hand. In October 1943, for example, it sported the photograph of a large road sign on Guadalcanal that read:

KILL THE BASTARDS!
DOWN THIS ROAD MARCHED ONE OF THE REGIMENTS OF THE
UNITED STATES ARMY
KNIGHTS SERVING THE QUEEN OF BATTLES
TWENTY OF THEIR WOUNDED IN LITTERS WERE BAYONETED
SHOT AND CLUBBED BY THE YELOW BELLIES
KILL THE BASTARDS![106]

Two weeks later, it carried a photograph of a Japanese corpse over the wisecrack, 'You can't say there ain't no flies on Tojo. This Jap was knocked off at Rendova Island.'[107]

It would be pointless to rehearse too many details of the scale and variety of the violence visited upon their thoroughly dehumanised foes by American soldiers, marines and sailors during the course of the war in Asia and the Pacific, especially as they have been surveyed and catalogued elsewhere.[108] Suffice it to say that the war in the Pacific was largely characterised by what Peter Schrijvers has termed 'pervasive barbarization'.[109] This was an environment unconstrained by the rules of war, one in which Americans proved worryingly reluctant (from an intelligence, as well as a moral perspective)[110] to spare those few Japanese who were willing to surrender, and in which even the mutilation of Japanese corpses was commonplace. While, as in Europe, profit as well as revenge was a prime motivation for such desecration, common methods when fighting the Japanese extended to the extraction of gold teeth from the skulls of enemy dead or, in some cases, enemy wounded.[111] Furthermore, Japanese skulls and other body parts were widely harvested as trophies and, when suitably flensed or pickled, even sent home to families and girlfriends in the United States, an unsettling development that forced senior commanders – including Nimitz in 1942 and the Joint Chiefs of Staff in 1944 – to make explicit, if futile, attempts to suppress the practice.[112] As late as 1945, marines could be found boiling Japanese skulls in oil drums on Iwo Jima in the knowledge that each could fetch a price of $125, or parading a Japanese skull on a pole in order to intimidate Japanese-American civilians in Hawaii.[113]

Strongly condemned by the American churches, especially after the photograph of an autographed skull and a navy officer's girlfriend appeared as 'The Picture of the Week' in *Life* magazine in May 1944,[114] what seems significant about such trophy hunting was that it often took place with the tacit consent, or even approval, of otherwise pious and clean-living servicemen. When James J. Fahey spoke to trophy-laden marines fresh from the capture of Saipan in July 1944, it was merely a matter of note that: 'One Marine liked to pull the gold teeth from dead Japs, he had 17 of them. The last one he got on Saipan [and] while he was pulling the gold tooth the Jap was still moving his hands.'[115] Four months later, Fahey noted a similar acquisitiveness among his shipmates in the wake of an unsuccessful kamikaze attack on the *Montpelier*:

> The deck near my [gun] mount was covered with blood, guts, brains, tongues, scalps, hearts, arms etc. from the Jap pilots.... One of the fellows had a Jap scalp, it looked just like you skinned an animal.... One of the men on our mount got a Jap rib and cleaned it up, he said his sister wants part of a Jap body. One fellow from Texas had a knee bone and he was going to preserve it in alcohol from the sick bay.[116]

For his part, Eugene Sledge of the 5th Marines was only dissuaded from joining his comrades in the harvesting of gold teeth on Peleliu by a navy corpsman, who carefully appealed to his sense of hygiene above his sense of decency.[117]

Clearly, sheer hatred did much to prompt this cauterisation of the moral senses. Faced with tending to dirty and dishevelled Japanese prisoners on board the hospital ship *Relief*, navy corpsman John A. Carver felt nothing but disgust and loathing: 'They were belligerent little SBs, is what they were.' In fact, they were only welcome insofar as their corpses could be used for the odd practical joke.[118] For James Fahey, the shooting of helpless Japanese airmen in their parachutes was simply a reversion to the pre-Christian principle of an eye for an eye. 'The Japs were the first to do things like this', he declared, 'and we returned the favor.'[119] Nor was Fahey remotely disturbed by the bodies of numerous Japanese civilians floating in the sea around Saipan, even though they were plainly visible during church services. 'The water is full of them', he observed nonchalantly, 'the fish will eat good.'[120] Sledge, who kept his notes of the Pacific war in his copy of the New Testament,[121] remained very much a Southern Christian gentleman. Sledge prayed the Lord's Prayer and the 23rd Psalm before and during action and, in basic training, received maximum ratings for 'obedience' and 'sobriety'.[122] Nevertheless, the sight of three butchered marines on Peleliu not only confirmed his impressions of Japanese depravity but also mitigated the more heinous activities of his comrades. As Sledge remembered:

> One man had been decapitated. His head lay on his chest; his hands had been severed from his wrists and also lay on his chest near his chin. In disbelief I stared at the face as I realized that the Japanese had cut off the dead Marine's penis and stuffed it into his mouth. The corpse next to him had been treated similarly. The third had been butchered, chopped up like a carcass torn by some predatory animal.

Consequently, so Sledge continued:

> My emotions solidified into rage and a hatred for the Japanese beyond anything I ever had experienced. From that moment on I never felt the least pity or compassion for them no matter what the circumstances. My comrades would fieldstrip their packs and pockets for souvenirs and take gold teeth, but I never saw a Marine commit the kind of barbaric mutilation the Japanese committed if they had access to our dead.[123]

Despite this slide into barbarism in the Asia-Pacific war in particular, the invincibly civilian nature of the bulk of the US armed forces frequently surfaced in the form of misgivings about the morality of killing. In spite of the elation that Ernie Pyle had perceived among aviators fresh from strafing missions in North Africa, in Italy he noticed that they were not immune from self-doubt:

> One night I was gossiping in a tent with a bunch of dive-bomber pilots, and one of them sitting next to me said in a sudden off-hand way, 'I wonder what those Germans in that truck are doing tonight?'... He was referring to a truck he had strafed and blown up the afternoon before. Such things sometimes got under their skins. The pilots liked to go on a hunt, and it was thrilling to sweep down and shoot hell out of something, the same as it is to shoot a running deer, but they really didn't relish the idea of killing

people who weren't trying to kill them.... The pilot said to himself, 'Some of them aren't doing anything tonight,' and then the subject was changed.[124]

Audie Murphy, one of the US Army's most accomplished killers, carefully observed the inhibitions of others in this respect. On Sicily, he was surprised to be admonished by a lieutenant for shooting a pair of fleeing Italian officers:

> I later discover that such mental confusion is common among new men. In the training areas we talked toughly, thought toughly; and finally believed that we really were tough. But it is not easy to shed the idea that human life is sacred. The lieutenant has not yet accepted the fact that we have been put into the field to deal out death.[125]

Later, and as an officer in North-West Europe, Murphy encountered the same confusion from a replacement who had shot a German while on outpost duty:

> Barnes is shaking like a nude in a blizzard.
> 'G-g-goddam,' he stutters, 'I sh-shot somebody.'
> 'Shoot him again. He's still alive.'

After a sharp exchange, Murphy warned:

> 'Just be glad it's not yourself. Remember he's your enemy. And he'll likely die in a litle [sic] bit. Brace yourself.'
> 'Good g-g-god,' he says wonderingly, 'to think I was brought up in a Christian home.'
> 'All of us were. Don't get the idea that you've got a special case in this man's army.'
> 'I couldn't kill a chicken.'
> 'The chickens didn't try to kill you.'[126]

These dilemmas were equally familiar to John T. Bassett of the 10th Mountain Division. One of his comrades, 'a quiet homely Dutchman', persistently volunteered for 'steady KP' – namely 'cleaning out greasy pots with lukewarm muddy water' – because, as he told Bassett, 'at least I'm doing something useful, which is better than killing, which is not'.[127] Bassett himself ruminated that:

> We thought the Krauts were evil; but we were evil too. I was prepared to kill a man, or men for a crime or crimes he or they may not have committed. Should it be right for me to kill a middle-aged Kraut who loved his family and believed in God, not in Hitler, but who was drafted by the Third Reich to serve his country? I could not stop to think it out: the line dictated that I follow it obediently, and since I was a good soldier, I did so.[128]

Chaplains were, significantly, all too familiar with this inner moral turmoil, leading Chaplain Harry P. Abbott to conclude that:

> Our men do not like to kill, because of their education, their religious training, and lofty ideals; and no man, in his right sense, enjoys or relishes it.... I do not believe that our men in the European Theatre cherished hatred in their hearts, except in those cases where they have seen their own buddies killed at the hands of the enemy.... I have met some soldiers that seem to be indifferent toward human life. Theirs was only a grim determination to conquer the enemy regardless of the cost – they asked no quarter and gave none. They were consumed with a desire to even accounts by exterminating their enemys [sic]. But this type of man was the exception.[129]

Writing in a hospital in France in October 1944, Chaplain Alvin O. Carlson, another veteran of the ground war against Germany, characterised GIs as: 'young men with keen intellects, perfect physiques and enlarged vision – men who hated to kill more than to be killed. They had been taught in Sunday school and at their mothers' knees to love one another.'[130] Still, Abbott added the crucial qualification that his verdict applied only to Europe for, in the Pacific, the Japanese 'apparently had no sense of decency or respect for the Geneva convention rules, or for the rules of civilization and humanity.'[131]

Doubtlessly reinforced by the pacifist sensibilities that had gripped much of American Protestantism in the interwar years, the issue of killing proved to be among the most common dilemmas presented to chaplains by those who sought their counsel. En route for Algiers in November 1942, Presbyterian chaplain Eugene L. Daniel was aware of the 'natural revulsion for killing even an enemy' that was felt by the soldiers of the 168th Infantry Regiment:

> Few had an adequate idea about a 'Just War'.... Early in the night of the landings at Algiers, Colonel Bear asked me to go into the hold of the ship with him and speak to his men. I told them that our going into battle was much like the situation when a mad dog was loose in our neighborhood. Hitler and the other Axis leaders were like mad dogs loose in the world community and we had to stop them even if we had to kill in order to do so.[132]

Present among the Midwestern National Guardsmen of the 34th Infantry Division, these inhibitions were just as obvious among the draftees of the 88th Infantry Division while in training at Camp Gruber, Oklahoma. According to Wallace M. Hale, its assistant division chaplain, being trained to kill could prove profoundly unsettling:

> Suddenly, one of our better young men is drafted into the military or perhaps he volunteers. He's immediately told that his job is killing. The

killers he has known have been thugs in the news or in the artificial situation of the movies, but he is now being trained with a seriousness and lethality that shocks his innermost emotions and sensibilities.[133]

Based on his dealings with officers and enlisted men, Hale, a Southern Baptist, came to the conclusion that:

> Roman Catholics, at this particular time, could bring themselves to accept a 'just' war, but I found that most Protestants were basically pacifistic. They hated war. They felt that war was sinful. They honestly considered that their participation in war was against their religious principles and yet most of them went on to war, and did a good job.[134]

In an apt illustration of what Chaplain Lawrence D. Graves described as stopping the moral clock, an officer even told Hale: 'Chaplain, when the war is over, I am going to get myself straightened out with God, and then I am going to live a Christian life.... No man can fight a war and do what Christ taught him to do.'[135] Convinced that most soldiers killed 'with a gnawing feeling underneath that this thing should not have taken place', Hale concurred with S.L.A. Marshall's controversial post-war claim that most American soldiers in World War II were disinclined to fire their weapons – even in combat – due to the fact that 'an American ground soldier ... is what his home, his religion, his schooling, and the moral code and ideals of his society have made him'.[136]

However, American airmen also had problems in crossing this moral threshold. Norman Wesley Achen of the 334th Fighter Squadron, for example, was traumatised by the effects of his P-51's machine guns on the occupants of a German staff car in a strafing mission just after D-Day. As Achen stated: 'I didn't tell my family about this for 50 years, I couldn't talk about it. I have trouble now with it. That's the first time I'd ever killed anybody and it wasn't a nice looking thing ... I threw-up in my oxygen mask.' On landing in England, Achen sat in his flying suit under a shower. Later, 'the chaplain showed up and tried to get me to discuss this with him and I, I couldn't do that.... Finally, I asked the chaplain.... "Have you ever killed anybody?" And he said, "No." And I remember ... he said, "no, that's not my mission, when you get ready we'll talk".'[137] If fighter pilots could be tormented by the killing of enemy combatants, bomber crew, who were often charged with pulverising targets that were manifestly civilian, could feel such qualms all the more. Significantly, some troubled flyers did not approach their own chaplains over the matter, possibly because some were so forthright in their support of American bombing. For example, and in response to 'a group of American clergymen' who protested 'the obliteration bombing of German cities', Southern Baptist chaplain Tilford L. Junkins wrote to *Stars and Stripes* in March 1944 claiming that their 'pacifistic thinking' was 'not a cross-section of the thinking of the ministry', and that: 'We chaplains and many other ministers blush that men of our calling should be so complacent and unwise in their attitude.'[138] It may also be significant that the whole question was ignored as a counselling issue in a post-war history of AAF chaplaincy.[139] Nevertheless, Robert Rodenhouse, a B-29 pilot, felt deeply disturbed by the firebombing of Tokyo in March 1945, by far the most destructive air raid of the war. As he recalled, he chose to refer his dilemma to his pastor at home rather than to his chaplain. Coming from a strongly Christian background, Rodenhouse found it hard to comprehend why God would allow that kind of catastrophe to occur. Worse, he found it hard to understand why he had been chosen to play a part in it. Grappling with these questions, he eventually wrote to his pastor for guidance, and duly received the reply that this was a mystery known only to God. Still, and however troubling the situation, the sovereignty of the Almighty held firm. What He had willed had been realised.[140]

Likewise, it would seem that Major Charles W. Sweeney of the 509th Composite Group chose to share his doubts with a clergyman other than either of his unit's chaplains.[141] Having flown as a wingman to the *Enola Gay* during its bombing of Hiroshima, Sweeney was fully aware of the cataclysmic power of the atomic bomb when he was selected for the bombing of Nagasaki (or Kokura). Consequently, he felt obliged to confer with a priest prior to his second atomic mission. As Sweeney, an earnest and devout Catholic, remembered: 'My faith and belief in God were the core of who I was. Since I was a child I had found guidance in the teachings of Jesus and the Church. Jesus taught us to love. He turned the other cheek. Where would He draw the line?'[142] Seeking answers to this question, he sought out the Catholic chaplain of a neighbouring squadron on Tinian, the pair of them reviewing Japanese conduct in the light of just war theory and the teachings of St Thomas Aquinas. When their lengthy and searching conversation had ended, Sweeney left the chaplain feeling 'at peace with myself.'[143]

Significantly, as early as 1943 *The Link* magazine had initiated a wider debate on the burning subject 'Killing In Battle – Is it Murder?'[144] Although it was hardly likely to publish or endorse answers that were roundly in the affirmative, simply posing the question furnished a useful platform from which to contest and refute pacifist arguments. *The Link* debate (such as it was) commenced with a piece by the late Samuel Logan Brengle, a leading Salvationist, who in World War I had been aware that certain young men were departing for war without the blessing of their parents. As Brengle put it, and in a classic statement of just war theory:

> Society has not only the right but the duty to protect its members. Rulers fail of duty if they do not give such protection.... So a soldier, fighting not with any thought of personal vengeance but only in the interests of humanity and the sacred, inalienable rights of men, does not murder when he kills, but is God's minister and is doing an awful but a righteous service.[145]

Six months later, and from a social gospel perspective, AAF chaplain Lawrence D. Graves wondered why Christians seemed so fixated by the Sixth Commandment:

The prostitute and procuror, the bootlegger and the gangster, the ward heeler and the corrupt politician, the city slum dwellers and the vast army of itinerant starvelings – all grow from the vine we water and tend.... Not many bother to consider these running sores in our social life which are, all are willing to admit, disgusting and wrong.... What is the matter with the conscience of the soldier who shudders at the thought of battle but is willing to live, with no qualms whatever, amid offenses against other equally important commandments?[146]

For his part, Chaplain Raymond R. Miller preferred a more biblical approach, juxtaposing the Sixth Commandment with Exodus 21:12: 'He that smiteth a man, so that he die, shall be surely put to death.' As the role of executioner was thereby sanctioned in Holy Writ, Miller reasoned that:

When a lawless nation sets out to commit murder on a wholesale scale, it is just as necessary for a constituted power, dedicated to the preservation of law and order to arrest, to try and sentence the offender nation as it is in the case of individuals. This is the justification for war, and the justification for the individual who has a part in it.[147]

A year later, and prompted by the revision of the American Revised Version of the Bible in 1944, Northern Baptist Air Forces chaplain Albert N. Corpening entered the lists with a fourth and final argument that the Sixth Commandment had been mistranslated all along. Hostage to the limitations of the Latin Vulgate Bible, 'kill' should have been rendered as 'murder' in the King James Bible, as it was in other, more recent renditions of the Decalogue that were now available to service personnel. Hence, Corpening maintained that:

[I]t is my earnest hope that the revised American Revised Version and other future versions will come out in the open and help correct an error that has kept hundreds of thousands of Christians from performing their civic and other duties and has brought a sense of guilt upon thousands of others who did.[148]

However, chaplains were by no means limited by this daunting array of arguments. Confronted in Italy by a Nisei GI who was afflicted by his knowledge of the Sixth Commandment, Israel Yost insisted that as a chaplain he was as much and as immediately implicated in this moral dilemma as was the ordinary infantryman:

The army has me here so you do your work better. When I build up your morale, I'm guilty of whatever you do wrong because I help you do a better job of it.... I could have sat the war out at home. I didn't, because I look at this war not as a right thing to do, but as the lesser of two evil things. If we do not fight the Nazis they will kill off more and more innocent people and that would be wrong. So we are forced to kill off the Nazis, even though killing is wrong, to stop them from continuing to do a greater evil ... the next time you get upset about what you are doing, just remember I'm in this with you, too.[149]

In the Pacific, the approach of Warren Wyeth Willard to the scruples of a 'handsome young leatherneck' who feared that he would be 'confronted at the last bar of judgment with a charge of murder' was still more robust:

I told him that the problem had vexed many others. Then I reminded him that the Japs had embarked on a policy of murder, rapine, and enslavement to make themselves masters of the world, that God did not order us to sit supinely by while all we believed in and hoped for was swept away by ruffians. I told him that our missionaries and others had brought back from China confirmed stories which branded the Japanese ruling class as a gang of cut-throats.... Thoroughly convinced myself of the justness of our cause, I was able to persuade the young marine that what had happened in Canton might well happen in New York or San Francisco if our country were made up entirely of religious fanatics who condemn even self-defense. Too many of our people had been lulled into apathy by the misleading propaganda of some of our pacifists and their mistaken appeal to Biblical authority.... 'Get in there and fight, young man,' I exhorted him. 'Have no qualms of conscience about your not doing the right thing. And may God have mercy on the souls of all those back home who would rather see their country perish than rise up in defense of their churches, their homes, and their liberties.'[150]

Willard's outspoken enthusiasm for the cause no doubt informed the laconic manner in which he described the elimination of the determined Japanese defenders of the island of Tanambogo in the Solomon Islands, die-hards who were simply entombed in their caves by American explosives.[151] Nevertheless, overt manifestations of hatred and revenge – antithetical, at least in theory, to the just war tradition – were discouraged and often provoked a reaction from those who aimed to uphold its principles. Significantly, *The Link* consistently challenged the notion that Americans needed to cultivate that animus of hate that was so evident among their German and Japanese adversaries. At the end of 1943, for example, it reprinted a piece from the magazine *Church Management*, which argued that:

The Christian believes in justice but he deprecates hate. He will have no part in the propaganda that Americans must learn to hate their enemies more before they can secure decisive victory.... We question the assumption that the best soldiers are those who hate. *The best soldiers are those who believe that they have a divine commission to destroy a menace to society*. They are not sadists; they take no delight in killing; they accept the disagreeable task as the only way to secure freedom in the world. They disagree with the pacifists because the latter do not feel that the will of God will ever command them to a service as distasteful as this. The Christian soldier does not so limit the will of God.[152]

The following year, it cited the words of Henry St George Tucker, the presiding bishop of the Protestant Episcopal Church, who also condemned the assumption that the stoking of hatred and vengeance would help the nation to prevail: 'if the New Testament has any one lesson to teach, it is that the end never justifies the means, that it is never legitimate to use a bad motive to produce a good end, because good ends can never be produced by bad motives'.[153]

Significantly, chaplains on the ground often sought to model and promote a proper spirit of mercy and even charity towards the enemy. In Tunisia, Eben Cobb Brink was anxious to demonstrate to hordes of dazed Axis prisoners 'that there were no enmities under the flag of blue with its cross of white'.[154] Likewise, in a field hospital in Tunisia, Henry P. Abbott distributed comforts – 'writing paper, gum, and candy' – to American and German wounded without distinction.[155] In Abbott's words:

> To [the chaplain], when the enemy is dead, in the hospital, or a prisoner of war and in captivity, he is no longer considered in the broadest sense, 'enemy'.... The writer saw enemy prisoners weep sincerely when a few small kindnesses were shown. Some dying, appreciated a little kindness.... It is only through this manner that we can promote a spirit of brotherhood in a world in which war shall thrive no more. Even on the battlefield there are times when the Christ-like spirit prevails over the gods of war.[156]

On occasion, such solicitous behaviour could even incur the wrath of American commanders, whose priorities were naturally different. For example, Charles E. Wilson, a chaplain's assistant in the 4th Armored Division, remembered the baleful reaction of Lieutenant Colonel Creighton Abrams on discovering how German POWs had been ushered out of the elements and into the shelter of a nearby church by one well-meaning chaplain during the advance into Germany:

> Followed by an entourage of somber-faced officers, Abrams angrily pulled a much-chewed, unlit cigar from his moth [sic], and shouted with a resurrection voice of such irritated wrath, that every snoozing German soldier leaped [sic] to his feet and a strict attention.... Abrams roared: 'What in hell is going on here? Get these god-damn sons of bitches out of here right now. And get that damned Chaplain out of here before I shoot him on the spot!'[157]

Apparently, the cause of this outburst lay in the adverse implications for morale of the fact that, shortly after risking their own lives, Abrams's troops were still out in the mud, sleet and snow while their former adversaries were enjoying the comparative warmth and shelter of the church.[158]

On other occasions, however, such interventions worked in the chaplain's favour. Near Hanau in late March 1945, a battalion commander in the 90th Infantry Division was physically restrained by his chaplain from killing a member of the Hitler Youth who had just been captured. As Major John Cochran recalled:

> I asked him if there were more like him in the town. He gave me a stare and said, 'I'd rather die than tell you anything.' I told him to pray, because he was going to die. I hit him across the face with my thick, heavy belt. I was about to strike him again when I was grabbed from behind by Chaplain Kerns. He said, 'Don't!' Then he took that crying child away. The Chaplain had intervened not only to save a life but to prevent me from committing murder. Had it not been for the Chaplain, I would have.[159]

However, an even more significant intervention occurred in 1943, after GIs of the 180th Infantry Regiment massacred more than seventy Italian POWs in two incidents near the Sicilian town of Biscari. There the matter may well have rested, but for the discovery of these incidents by the Southern Baptist senior chaplain of the 45th Infantry Division, William E. King. Due largely to King's involvement, an officer and a sergeant were eventually court-martialled for their part in these atrocities, though their punishments were light in view of the fact that they could plead Patton's pre-invasion exhortations as mitigation, Patton having urged the inexperienced 45th to 'kill devastatingly' and become known as the 'Killer Division'.[160]

Even in the moral abyss that was the Pacific war, chaplains could strive hard to maintain a moral balance. Warren Wyeth Willard, despite his detestation of the Japanese, still expected his marines to observe the rules of war, recalling that before their descent on Guadalcanal:

> I preached the gospel of Christ, as usual. I also begged the men to be kind to the Japanese we might capture ... we have our own high standards of decency and civilization to live up to.... If in the past the Japs have stooped to lawlessness and cruelty, it behooves us not to follow in their steps. Let us imitate Him who was good, and not those who are evil.[161]

In the same spirit, and at the very end of the campaign, Catholic navy chaplain Frederic P. Gehring helped a starving and vermin-ridden Japanese soldier to surrender, ignoring advice to: 'Let him die there, Padre. Who needs him?'[162] Likewise, Chaplain Thomas J. Donnelly of the 77th Infantry Division would have no truck with some of the barbarities of the Pacific conflict, on one occasion ordering a young Filipino to bury a Japanese head; significantly, the errant Filipino claimed to be gathering heads on the instructions of Donnelly's commanding officer.[163]

One notable and consistent exemplar of just war precepts was Chaplain Russell

Cartwright Stroup who, after counselling a Jewish GI of the 399th Infantry Regiment on the problem of hating the Germans,[164] found himself transferred to the Pacific theatre. There, and in a series of assignments to front-line units, Stroup sought to implement the injunctions of Romans 12:20 ('Therefore if thine enemy hunger, feed him; if he thirst, give him drink') and to ensure that prisoners were taken and properly treated.[165] In fact, Stroup became acutely aware of what he termed 'jumpy trigger fingers', noting that: 'It is a fortunate Nipponese who can get near enough to give up.'[166] With their chaplain even prepared to give Japanese corpses a decent burial,[167] Stroup's example had an effect on certain soldiers of the 239th Engineer Construction Battalion in New Guinea. On one occasion, an ailing and bedraggled prisoner was ostentatiously presented to Stroup and was treated well thereafter.[168] In October 1944, and now with the 1st Infantry Regiment, Stroup wrote that: 'One of the most difficult things to do is to convince men, against the natural reactions of fighters, and the efforts of the army, that they should not corrupt their souls with hatred.'[169] Three months later, on Luzon, Stroup hinted that this message was by no means uncontroversial:

> All of us were mighty thankful when the [last] job was successfully accomplished and we were able to move out last night. We only took one prisoner, but I was able to minister to him. Against the orders of a misguided and, I think, now repentant ~~officer~~ *individual*, I gave the prisoner food and water, reminding the ~~commander~~ *others* that I had my orders from a Superior who had insisted that if my enemy hungers I should feed him and if he was thirsty I should give him drink.[170]

It was on the basis of this record and example in the Pacific that Stroup could write a conciliatory, post-war article for the *Presbyterian Outlook* (and, ultimately, for *The Link*),[171] 'On Hating Our Enemies', and on the need for reconciliation with Japan. Objecting to the 'mounting flood of vicious, hate-poisoned attacks on the Japanese, not as a nation but as men', Stroup reasoned that:

> [T]o become infected by the fatal malady of bigoted prejudice is to forfeit all we may hope to have gained from the sacrifices we have made. A permanent peace depends upon the spiritual unity of mankind bound together by the bonds of understanding. To hate the Japanese is not so much to hurt them as to harm ourselves and to defeat our hope for a future freed from the horror of war.[172]

Sacred structures

If the pressures of war put the sanctity of life at a considerable discount, it was inevitable that the sanctity of religious structures should go the same way. Although protected in theory by Article 56 of the 1899 Hague Convention on the Laws and Customs of War on Land,[173] by the explicit wishes of the Anglo-

American Combined Chiefs of Staff committee,[174] and by the natural sensitivities of god-fearing Americans, from 1942 to 1945 the air, ground and naval forces of the United States inflicted colossal damage on the religious infrastructure of continental Europe, to say nothing of the Pacific and Japan. On D-Day, for example, and because of the value of church towers as observation platforms, among the prime targets for the American naval bombardment at Omaha beach were the churches of Colleville and St Laurent.[175] Although the Methodist army chaplain Clyde E. Kimball wrote optimistically in July 1944 that, 'I am of the opinion that both sides are disposed to spare such things if practicable',[176] the ancient churches of Normandy suffered grievously throughout the campaign, after which nearly six hundred Norman towns and villages 'required complete reconstruction'.[177] As one GI ruefully noted of the destruction visited on the Norman town of Saint-Lô: 'We sure liberated the hell out of this place.'[178] By the latter months of the war in Europe, what was perceived as the increasingly cavalier treatment of church structures even evoked a protest from some army chaplains in the United States, *The Chaplain* magazine reporting in November 1944 that:

> Chaplains at Fort Custer, Mich., recently raised vigorous protest against the use of a mock church as a target by military police in training there – and made their protest stick. The structure was situated in 'Hitlerville', a village of shacks built to represent an enemy center, and was facetiously named 'St. Lucifer's Church'. Stormed the padres: 'We believe it borders on sacrilege to set up a house of worship as a target, and particularly to shoot up an altar. The American is taught from childhood to venerate churches.' [179]

This, at least, seems true enough. With the capture of Saipan in July 1944, one conscience-stricken marine sought the counsel of a Catholic navy chaplain, fearing he had committed sacrilege after killing a Japanese soldier in a former chapel.[180] In what may have been a connected incident, another navy chaplain, Frederick William Meehling, noted that: 'The Marines ... had destroyed a Catholic church and they had qualms of conscience about it. So they took up a collection of several hundred dollars.'[181] Nevertheless, on Saipan there was at least some comfort to be drawn from the fact that 'a cast metal figure of the crucified Christ on an eight-foot concrete cross' survived the fighting. According to the *Los Angeles Times*, this was pierced only by a fragment of shrapnel that 'penetrated the figure's side at almost the exact point where the New Testament says the Roman centurion's spear was thrust'.[182] From Europe, the scene of much greater devastation of this kind, a Bill Mauldin cartoon depicted his eponymous infantry heroes, Willie and Joe, sitting amidst a pile of rubble over the caption, '*It ain't right to go around leanin' on churches, Joe.*'[183] In contrast, and following the capture of Cologne in March 1945, some GIs attributed the remarkable survival of its cathedral, like that of St Paul's in London, to divine intervention.[184] For his

542

God and Uncle Sam

part, Orval Eugene Faubus was impressed by the 'religious symbols' that he saw 'everywhere in Europe', and lamented the destruction of a fine church at Pontpierre in Luxembourg:

> I shall never forget the beautiful church at Pontpierre. The glass, which had been shattered from the stained windows, crunched under my feet as I walked up the aisle. The beauty of the colored, stained glass windows, the intricate construction, the rich cloth and curtains by the altar and pulpit, the figures of the saints, all were most impressive. And I shall never forget the haggard-faced, unknown officer who knelt, praying, his muddy boots sticking back underneath one of the seats.[185]

However, such regrets could do little to stem this deluge of destruction and accompanying profanation. Captured during the Battle of the Bulge, Johann Carl Friedrich Kasten recalled without apology that, during their march into Germany, he and other American POWs were held in a local church and: 'That night I slept on the alter [sic], the only space left and as I have no religion I had no qualms.'[186] One GI who did have misgivings was Sergeant Alvin McAnney, who wrote to his wife in the autumn of 1944 from Luxembourg:

> We were pulled out for a couple of hours to see a show the other day. I saw Marlene Dietrich and her show in person a few miles back. They held it in a shell splattered Catholic Church. It's really a pity these beautiful old churches being devastated over here.[187]

Although a Catholic, Lester Atwell was not unduly unsettled by being billeted 'for several days in a small rural Catholic church', where: 'The pews had all been pushed in a heap up near one of the side altars.' On entering, Atwell confessed that 'I felt as though I should have removed my helmet', and was embarrassed to find himself smoking a cigarette, but he quickly got used to this surreal environment, even after the church began to double as a cinema, showing films such as Rita Hayworth's *Cover Girl* (1944) and Abbott and Costello's *Lost in a Harem* (1944).[188] Although a Catholic chaplain eventually put an end to these screenings, the air of unreality evoked by a ruined church landscape was no less immediate to the chaplain's assistant Kenneth A. Connelly, who wrote of Aachen in February 1945:

> Civilization in the conquered territory approximates perhaps that of the stone age. So far for breath-taking horror Aachen exceeds all. Chalk dust and twisted steel with a few reminders of past glory – principally the old cathedral (the oldest in Europe if I'm not mistaken). Charlemagne was crowned Emperor of the Holy Roman Empire there, I believe. Although it is far from untouched it still retains its grandeur. The spectacular golden mosaic on the dome of the cathedral is untouched and the skeletal

outline of a beautiful Gothic chapel remains. The windows, which occasional jagged segments of stained glass suggest were magnificent, are gone
forever.... The Bishop of Aachen seems to be in residence too for a hastily
contrived throne has been built for him in his devastated church. Such are
the contrasts, the common pictures that make one feel he is rather drunk
and not seeing things quite as they are.[189]

Among those directly commissioned to undertake the bombing of churches
and of sacred sites, reactions were mixed to say the least. In October 1943, and
upon being told they were about to bomb Munster, which had been identified
as a crucial railway junction for the munitions manufacturers of the Ruhr Valley,
murmurs of dissent were heard among the aircrew of the 95th Heavy Bombardment Group at Horham in Suffolk. Not only was the city and its cathedral identified with the Catholic bishop Clemens August Graf von Galen, who was known
as an outspoken critic of the Nazi regime,[190] but the raid was due to take place
on a Sunday and deliberately targeted the centre of the city, the aiming point
being the cathedral itself. As a former lead navigator, the aptly named Ellis B.
Scripture, remembered:

> I'd been raised in a strict Protestant home. My parents were God-orientated
> people and were quite active church members. I was shocked to learn that
> we were to bomb civilians as our primary target for the first time in the war
> and that our aiming point was to be the front steps of Munster Cathedral
> at noon on Sunday, just as mass was completed. (Later the field order was
> revised so that 'bombs away' was scheduled for 1500 hours ... this undoubt-
> edly saved many lives!) I was very reluctant to fly this mission; in fact I had
> a hard time realizing that we would have such a target.[191]

Although subsequently persuaded 'that war is not a gentleman's duel', some of
Scripture's reservations were shared by the pilot of another B-17, Captain Rodney
Snow:

> Reaction at the briefing really didn't register for awhile. What got to me
> was that it was a Sunday mission, and probably the only one I flew on the
> sabbath. Being of Scots-Irish descent and a regular Presbyterian did give
> me some deep reservations about the need for Sunday bombings.[192]

In contrast, none of these considerations had any purchase over Scripture's pilot,
Captain William Lindley, who recollected:

> About the only thing I can remember about the briefing was this was
> the first American mission where the target was the city itself and not
> an industrial complex. One of the purposes of the strike was to destroy a
> university in the city center. Apparently, it was being used as a center for
> developing hard-line Nazis.... Some of the crews at Horham had misgiv-

ings about using the city center for an aiming point.... Not me, I thought it was great.[193]

In the event, and although only minor damage was inflicted on Munster Cathedral, nearly seven hundred German civilians died in the raid of 10 October 1943.[194] However, and as in so many other cases, American sensitivities quickly hardened towards the task in hand. By early June 1944 *Stars and Stripes* could carry a front-page report entitled 'Cathedral At Rouen Burns', which matter-of-factly described the destruction of Rouen's impressive medieval cathedral as a result of American air raids the previous week:

> Fire swept the famous cathedral at Rouen, France, following the explosion of a delayed-action bomb or land mine.... According to the Germans, smoke was not seen until an hour after the explosion.... Fanned by a strong wind, the fire spread throughout the entire cathedral and the adjoining palace of the archbishop.[195]

By this point, the vulnerability of sacred buildings to aerial attack had already been underlined by the Italian campaign, which was famously likened by one German general to waging 'war in a museum'.[196] Despite the intense anxieties of the Vatican, which had been expressed to the State Department as early as December 1942, and the forceful representations of Archbishop Spellman, the antiquity and sanctity of the country's Catholic infrastructure furnished very limited immunity to Allied bombing. Prior to its capture by the Americans in October 1943, Allied aircraft 'had damaged forty churches in Naples alone'.[197] Although the inviolability of Rome was naturally a top priority for Pius XII, American bombers struck Rome's marshalling yards as early as July 1943, badly damaging the fourth-century Basilica of St Lawrence-Outside-the-Walls in the process. Before Rome fell to the Allies the following June, American bombers returned repeatedly to the Eternal City, and for good measure even managed to bomb the pope's summer palace at Castel Gandolfo.[198] However, the most infamous (and, as it transpired, unnecessary) bombing of this kind occurred with the destruction of the Benedictine abbey of Monte Cassino, the cradle of Western monasticism, by masses of American bombers in February 1944 – only a matter of days after Lieutenant General Mark Clark had 'issued strict instructions to his Fifth Army [and] in duplicate to the Allied air forces, that all attacks on papal or church property should be carefully avoided unless absolutely dictated by military necessity'.[199] Undertaken at the urging of the commander of the New Zealand Corps on the Cassino front, Lieutenant General Sir Bernard Freyberg, the bombing left the abbey in ruins, killed scores of Italian civilians sheltering in its precincts, and served to provide the Germans (who had scrupulously respected the neutrality of the site hitherto) with an almost impregnable defensive position.[200]

With respect to the aerial obliteration of Monte Cassino, it was telling that *Stars and Stripes* insisted that the Germans had transformed the abbey 'into a huge pillbox', and that 'between 50 and 100 Germans fled from the famous monastery' in the wake of the attack.[201] In actual fact, grave reservations about the operation had been entertained all along by Clark and by the Catholic commander of II Corps, Major General Geoffrey Keyes.[202] However, over the course of 1943 the commitment of American troops to the hazards of ground warfare in continental Europe seems to have caused something of a sea-change in American attitudes towards the bombing of sacred sites. According to an AIPO poll conducted in April 1943, 51 per cent of Americans opposed the bombing of Rome, with 67 per cent of Catholic and 52 per cent of Protestant respondents objecting to the idea.[203] However, less than a year later, in March 1944 – and when asked, 'If military leaders believe it will be necessary to bomb historic religious buildings and shrines in Europe, would you approve or disapprove of their bombing them?' – 74 per cent expressed their approval, including 75 per cent of Protestant and 63 per cent of Catholic respondents.[204] Although Archbishop Spellman sought to articulate Catholic opposition to the bombing of Rome in particular, how far he spoke for his flock in the armed forces is very much open to question. Although an Italian-American GI from the 34th Infantry Division later insisted that 'THE BOMBING OF MONTE CASINO [SIC] WAS WRONG',[205] from Cassino itself an artillery officer asserted that he had 'Catholic gunners in this battery and they've asked me for permission to fire on the monastery'.[206] As for the initial bombing of Rome in July 1943, such was the sensitivity of the mission that Catholic aircrew were given the opportunity to opt out; nonetheless, a Catholic chaplain cheered bombers departing from one airfield with the unequivocal endorsement, 'Give them hell!'[207]

Profanity, blasphemy and obscenity

In view of the scale of the carnage and destruction wrought in World War II, and the formidable moral problems that this raised, it would be easy to underestimate the continuing importance of more personal transgressions to the Puritan sensitivities of contemporary America – sensitivities that were, for example, reflected in the Motion Picture Production Code of 1930. In a war that transformed the American military into the most potent and effective killing machine in the history of the world, and whose members were often involved in both licensed and unlicensed atrocities, American chaplains joined battle with undiminished vigour against such perennial vices as profanity, obscenity, gambling, drunkenness and promiscuity, vices that the army's Articles of War and the Articles for the Government of the United States Navy had customarily sought to curb and to which, as *The Link* needlessly emphasised, 'the Christian is traditionally opposed'.[208] Notwithstanding America's cultural attachment to scripture, the vast consumption of service Bibles and New Testaments during the course of the war can in part be ascribed to their furtive use as a source of cigarette papers.[209] More obvious than such profanation, however, was the brazenness, ubiquity and even perverse creativity of verbal blasphemy and/or obscenity. Although army regulations forbade 'cursing and abusive language',[210] Paul Fussell remembered that his fellow inductees at Fort MacArthur were usually berated as 'shitheads, assholes, and dumb fucks'.[211] This prohibition was more brazenly flouted by General George S. Patton, who became the very embodiment of this unpleasant trait for the wartime generation. Similarly, and although the Articles for the Government of the United States Navy fulminated against those who were 'guilty of profane swearing, falsehood, drunkenness, gambling, fraud, theft, or any other scandalous conduct tending to the destruction of good morals'[212] – and the 1944 edition of *The Bluejacket's Manual* consequently warned that, 'The use of profane or filthy language is forbidden'[213] – the force of such injunctions was largely rhetorical. Having joined the marines in New York in January 1942, Robert Leckie was swiftly introduced to the colourful argot of the corps by the master gunnery sergeant who became his 'momentary shepherd': 'Those rich mellow blasphemous oaths that were to become so familiar to me flowed from his lips with the consummate ease of one who had spent a lifetime in vituperation.'[214] Nevertheless, it was only on the rifle range at Parris Island that Leckie came to appreciate its awful nakedness and fury:

> The rifle range also gave me my first full audition of the marine cursing facility. There had been slight samplings of it in the barracks, but never anything like the utter blasphemy and obscenity of the rifle range. There were noncommissioned officers there who could not put two sentences together without bridging them with a curse, an oath, an imprecation. To hear them made our flesh creep, made those with any depth of religious feeling flush with anger and wish to be at the weather-beaten throats of the blasphemers.[215]

Besides the habitual and unthinking violation of the Third Commandment, even general conversation throughout the armed forces was befouled by the compulsive use of a particular word. As Leckie put it:

> Always there was that four-letter ugly sound that men in uniform have expanded into the single substance of the linguistic world.... It described food, fatigue, metaphysics. It stood for everything and meant nothing ... one heard it from chaplains and captains, from Pfc.'s and Ph.D.'s – until, finally, one could only surmise that if a visitor unacquainted with English were to overhear our conversations he would, in the way of the Higher Criticism, demonstrate by measurement and numerical incidence that this little word must assuredly be the thing for which we were fighting.[216]

No less jaded by its prevalence, Ernie Pyle wrote from England in 1944: 'If I hear another fucking GI say "fucking" once more, I'll cut my fucking throat.'[217]

Illustrative of how dramatically service language could deviate from the norms of respectable civilian society was the fate of a signboard erected at Scott Field, Illinois, which proclaimed, 'THRU THESE GATES PASS THE BEST DAMNED RADIO OPERATORS IN THE WORLD'. Although comparatively mild, and located at a minor entrance to the installation, the sign gained national notoriety when it appeared, along with a batch of radio operators, in an issue of *National Geographic* in September 1943.[218] Following shrill protests from various churchmen, a letter of complaint from the chief of chaplains to his namesake, 'Hap' Arnold, and a feeble attempt to defend its contents on semantic grounds by Major General F.L. Martin (who was responsible for Scott Field), the sign was duly painted over – and so, sighed Chaplain Thomas M. Carter ruefully, ended 'the epic of the offending sign'.[219] However, such was the strength of these sensitivities that even Audie Murphy shuddered at the thought of telling the mother of a fallen comrade of his last words, words that were once again fairly tame and spoken *in extremis*:

> Briefly a picture trembles in my mind. It is that of a white-haired woman who stands before a cottage on a shady street in Savannah.
> 'I am his mother,' she says, 'What were his last words?'
> 'Said, "Think I'll walk over and twist his goddamned ears off."'
> 'Whose ears?'
> 'Those of a German who was trying to kill us.'
> 'My boy went to his God with a curse on his lips?'
> 'His God will understand.'[220]

Although John C. Burnham has argued that, 'World War II greatly accelerated the process of breaking down barriers against profane and obscene language,'[221] ingrained pre-war sensibilities were not entirely effaced by the conditions of service life, even in the heat of combat. As Chaplain Lawrence D. Graves briefed readers of *The Chaplain* magazine, a battle-hardened paratrooper had told him that a hearty curse was more resented in the midst of battle than it was in a church, for: 'There were mighty few ... who did not utter fervent prayers when the 88's and mortars got especially hot. Yes, sir, it hurt like anything when someone would spill out a nasty oath when death came tumbling out of the sky.'[222] Besides the providential and prudential reasoning that informed such a reaction, it is worth stressing that in such circumstances it was often difficult to tell an oath from a supplication. Marine First Lieutenant John Doyle confided in his father that, under the terror of Japanese bombing, 'Prayers and curses run intermingled off your lips';[223] furthermore, and while surveying the aftermath of a skirmish in Sicily, the reaction of one of Audie Murphy's comrades –'Jesus' – made it impossible for him to tell 'whether the word is meant as an oath or a prayer'.[224] In a remarkable illustration of the primacy of faith over works in this regard, Chaplain Warren Wyeth Willard was prepared to give his marines the benefit of the doubt, writing of their landing on Guadalcanal: 'There were plenty of oaths that day. But I knew that many of these men were Christians at heart, and that often profanity among them was more of a bad habit than deliberate sacrilege.'[225]

However, many of Willard's peers were not as complacent. Chaplain Hansel H. Tower noted that, even in stateside training before Pearl Harbor, the vocabulary of his marines left much to be desired. In addition to their '"biological talk," which plainly and vulgarly speaks of reproductive and excretory activities', Tower observed that ordinary conversation was laced with dubious language, and even 'discussions of religion were carried on with a sprinkling of profanity'. Furthermore, this idiom was rehearsed even in the presence of the chaplain: 'Occasionally someone would become conscious that his language was a bit over expressive and he would beg my pardon. The average chaplain hears so much profanity that he is rarely conscious of it until someone apologizes.'[226] As Tower concluded, and because of its detachment from the civilising influences of home, service life was intrinsically corrupting in this regard, lamenting that: 'There are some men who use excellent language at home, but who lapse into a degenerate form of speech when they enter the service. Officers are not always an exception.'[227] Army chaplain George W. Zinz was even more forthright, asserting that:

> Cursing and foul conversation are rampant. One is amazed at the finesse exercised in this lowest form of speech. Many think it even an accomplishment to add new curse words and degrading stories to their collection. Once again one shudders to think where it will end and wonders what has happened to the thinking processes of the mind.[228]

Just as remarkable as the ubiquity of foul and profane language was a broad and emphatic insistence that it needed to be checked. In May 1944, and after only six weeks in the army, an agitated private wrote to William R. Arnold from Camp Upton, New York: 'When I got here I was shocked by the language I heard all about me. The air is thick all the time with swear words, obcene [sic] and degrading language. Even non-commissioned officers sometimes use profane language in addressing the recruits.' This, he pointed out, was not only 'against Army regulations' but the Third Commandment applied in equal measure 'to the Jewish, Catholic, or Protestant soldier'.[229] In December 1943 an 'H.B.O.' had already written to *The Link* complaining that:

> I think there is more swearing in the service than in civilian life; at least, I notice it more. It is more violent than the use of 'hell' and 'damn.' Most offensive to me is the use of our Lord's name and the constant repetition of well-worn obscenities. What can be done about stemming the tide?[230]

In response, the magazine rehearsed some classic arguments against swearing –

it was symptomatic of 'ignorance', 'an inferiority complex', 'lack of control' and 'downright evil character'. Hence, 'the profanity tide' was to be countered by adhering to a strict standard of speech, by challenging blasphemers as 'though they had insulted your best friend', and by assisting 'the man who honestly wants to quit profanity by helping him search for and remove the causes', possibly with the aid of improving literature.[231] The letter of the unidentified 'H.B.O.' certainly struck a chord with a Catholic reader of *The Link*, Sergeant Francis M. Mulligan, who volunteered that: 'I have been in the army for four years and spent three years overseas. The author of "Bucking the Profanity Tide" says there is more swearing in the service than in civilian life. I agree. It seems the younger fellows especially cannot speak two words without using profanity.'[232] There was also a stream of complaints from civilian quarters. In October 1943, for example, an evangelical Lutheran minister from Texas challenged William R. Arnold over a newspaper profile of Eisenhower, whose 'cuss words couldn't be anything but American', while a Catholic priest from New Jersey reported the anxiety of 'a good Catholic mother' over 'the swearing of officers in forts, camps, etc. at their men'.[233] 'Do Service Men Have to Swear?', sighed John O. Cross in the pages of *The Christian Advocate*, adding that: 'Our boys with the armed forces meet profanity everywhere, and many come to believe that learning it is a part of the training routine.'[234] Worrying enough to decent Americans, *The Link* did not hesitate to emphasise the dire effects of such a bad example on other peoples. In February 1945 it claimed that a notice, billed as a stinging 'rebuke for representatives of "Christian America"', had appeared on a 'mess-hall bulletin board' on Guadalcanal. Purportedly written by a local chief, it ran:

> American soldiers are requested to please be a little more careful in their choice of language, particularly when natives are assisting them in their unloading of ships, trucks, and in erecting abodes. American missionaries spent many years among us and taught us the words we should not use. Every day, however, American soldiers use those words and the good work your missionaries did is being undermined by your careless profanity.[235]

Various strategies were adopted to counter this wartime bonanza of profanity and obscenity. Appealing to a dual sense of patriotism and providence, army chaplains repeatedly invoked the efforts of George Washington to deter the pernicious habit of swearing in the Continental Army, and in particular his general order on profanity issued at New York in July 1776:

> The General is sorry to be informed that the foolish and wicked practice of profane cursing and swearing, a vice heretofore little known in an American army, is growing into fashion. He hopes the officers will, by example as well as influence, endeavor to check it, and that both they and the men will reflect, that we can have little hope of the blessing of Heaven on our arms,

if we insult it by our impiety and folly. Added to this, it is a vice so mean and low, without any temptation, that every man of sense and character detests and despises it.[236]

If Eisenhower's poor example in this respect precluded a letter of a similar kind, as was favoured in certain quarters,[237] by May 1944, and along with 'a fine picture of General Washington', this much-favoured text had been turned into a poster that was widely circulated throughout the US Army.[238] In addition, *The Link* enlisted the help of the 'eminent Christian psychologist' and Canadian veteran of World War I, Dr John Sutherland Bonnell, who warned of the dangers of profanity in connection to prayer:

> Let it never be forgotten … that some day that soldier, sailor or airman may wish to take that sacred Name upon his lips in prayer in some hour of desperate emergency. If he has bandied it about in cheap conversation and in sordid discussions, it may well be that the very power of prayer and of realizing God's Holy Presence may be lost.[239]

As we have noted in Chapter Three, Holy Name societies, already well-established in Catholic parochial life, also flourished in the armed forces. For example, a new society launched by chaplains at Amarillo Army Air Field enlisted 1,250 members in a matter of weeks.[240] In fact, such was the perceived success of this organisation as a safeguard against profanity that a Presbyterian (USA) AAF chaplain, Moore R. Miller, formed 'a League of the Divine Name' for his own battalion, which he hoped would prove the beginning of a 'Protestant counterpart of the Holy Name Society'.[241]

Preaching, example and personal intervention were also harnessed to this wartime campaign against 'Cursing and the use of foul language', a plague that, as one chaplain earnestly pointed out, was 'hindering the war effort by driving God and His help away from our efforts'.[242] Although Chaplain Israel Yost's efforts to persuade a medic of the 100th Infantry Battalion to amend his language were rebuffed on the grounds that 'he was too old to change his ways',[243] Chaplain Samuel Hill Ray believed he had better success among the Catholics of the seaplane tender *Hamlin*, preaching a sharp 'Sermon on Your Language' in which he warned that, 'from the High School of Vulgarity to the College of Impurity, obscenity and profanity, the graduation is very easy'. Ray also condemned 'the flippant, frivolous, care-free manner' in which the names of God and Jesus Christ were bandied about, averring that: 'I sometimes wonder that the tongues of these men have not withered between their teeth'.[244] However, Ray was careful to temper his stern line in the pulpit with forbearance in other circumstances, stressing that: 'I never corrected the men in public. I never wanted to repel them. I wanted to win their confidence in such a way that they would come to me for advice and direction without fear of reprehension.' Apparently, this twin-track approach paid off, with one inebriated sailor even being 'spanked … until he could not sit down' by some indignant shipmates after he had used 'every combination of bad language' in Ray's presence.[245] Besides these more earnest efforts, humour was also enlisted as a means to expose the folly of 'obscene and vulgar language'.[246] In September 1943, *The Link* published 'Ten Reasons Why I Swear', a satirical piece that included quips such as 'It pleases Mother so much', 'It indicates how clearly my mind operates', and 'It makes me a very desirable personality among women and children and in respectable society'.[247] Other chaplains sought to discourage the vice by inaugurating charitable schemes such as 'The Chaplain's Cussing Fund', or 'Chappie's Cussin' Coins', whereby a small contribution was levied 'for each swear word or evil idea expressed by military personnel'.[248]

Sexual immorality

An equally alarming and intractable problem was the voracious and sometimes violent libido of the American serviceman. Significantly, and in their capacity as censors, officers could find the personal correspondence of their men disturbing in this respect. As a B-29 pilot in the Pacific, where sexual opportunities were rarer than in the United States or in Europe, Gordon Bennett Robertson was struck by the 'graphic' nature of the 'stern admonitions' to wives and girlfriends 'to behave themselves', and also by an attempt by a censoring officer to censure an unrepentant sergeant over the 'lengthy, minute, explicit, meticulous, specific, and exquisite detail' of a letter to his wife.[249] Although by no means a stranger to the sexual adventurism of the war years, even Marine Corps pilot Samuel Hynes remembered that censoring duties on Okinawa afforded an unsettling insight into the minds of his men:

> Sometimes their amorous feelings for their wives and sweethearts were expressed with a forthrightness that seemed pornographic to middle-class young men like us…. It was funny, and it was astonishing, that there were marriages in the world … in which sexual relations were apparently conducted with such violent and inventive enthusiasm.[250]

Like Robertson, Hynes recalled an unsuccessful attempt by another officer – 'a gentle, priest-like Catholic boy named Feeney' – to curb the aspirations and vocabulary of one correspondent:

> Lt. Feeney: 'Sergeant, you can't do this.'
> Sergeant: 'Do what, sir?'
> Lt. Feeney: 'Write a letter like this to your wife.'
> Sergeant: 'What about it, sir?'
> Lt. Feeney (nervously): 'Well, you say you're going to fuck her cross-eyed. That's no way to talk to your wife.'
> Sergeant: 'Why not? She's my fucking wife, ain't she? Sir?'[251]

In keeping with the general savagery of the war in the Pacific, it would appear that such violent sexual impulses were translated into the rape of thousands of Okinawan and Japanese women by victorious American marines and soldiers before and after the surrender of Japan.[252] While many of these rapes went unreported, rape was also a significant problem for the US Army in Europe, despite the fact that ninety-nine death sentences had been passed for this offence by August 1945, twenty-nine of which were carried out.[253] There were 121 GIs convicted of rape by American courts martial in Britain alone,[254] but the women of defeated or even liberated countries were more vulnerable still. Between July 1942 and October 1945, 64 per cent of complainants in rape cases in the ETO were German, 16 per cent were French and 13 per cent were British – figures that point to a dramatic increase of sexual violence in the months following D-Day.[255] As a post-war report on military offenders in the ETO elaborated:

> Rape became a large problem in the European Theater of Operations with the Continental invasion. Records at the office of the Theater Judge Advocate show a large increase in rape during August and September of 1944, when the Army broke into Continental France and in March and April of 1945, with the large scale invasion of Germany.[256]

However, amidst these destitute and/or defeated populations, the politically, militarily and economically privileged position of the GI fuelled further transgressions and other forms of sexual exploitation. In Germany, for example, the trauma and destitution of the civilian population interacted in a sordid and tragic fashion with 'the Ayran cult of blonde beauties within American culture', and with the beguiling conceit that the Third Reich had fashioned a generation of compliant German women who were 'immoral, dreamy eyed, Kinder, Kirche, Kueche, Nazi baby machines'.[257] Moreover, it was not only younger women who were caught in the sexual backwash of defeat. As Lester Atwell remembered, a pair of elderly and 'saintly'-looking German women in the Saxon town of Plauen gave themselves in a 'line-up' for fifteen or sixteen GIs in exchange for a chocolate bar or some tinned food from each.[258] At Plauen, and according to Atwell, large numbers of German women were encountered for the first time and 'licentiousness broke out on a tremendous scale':

> Countless girls and married women who under normal circumstances might have led provincial monogamous lives – here deprived of homes, sometimes bereaved of family, thrown out of employment, afraid of approaching starvation and surrounded by conquering troops – turned nymphomaniac or prostitute at every opportunity through the day or night in return for a chocolate bar, a C ration or a few cigarettes.[259]

All of this, it should be added, occurred despite the sanctions of the non-fraternisation policy, a situation that spawned the GI witticism: 'Copulation without conversation is not fraternization'.[260]

One of the consequences of this dire situation was a staggering rise in the incidence of venereal disease, with VD rates among GIs in Germany spiralling by 235 per cent between VE day and the end of 1945.[261] If the increased rate of 251 per 1,000 soldiers per year represented five times the average rate for the US Army for the whole of the war (namely 49 per 1,000),[262] there was little reason for complacency elsewhere. In Britain, for example, and partly due to the activities of the so-called 'Piccadilly Commandos' and hosts of lesser-known wartime prostitutes in the capital and elsewhere, in 1943 the VD rate among GIs was more than 50 per cent higher than among troops in the United States, standing respectively at 43 and 26 per 1,000 per annum.[263] After the liberation of Naples by the Fifth Army in October 1943, the city became a notorious hotbed of prostitution, with the threat of starvation forcing thousands of women onto the streets. By early 1944, VD patients were occupying up to 15 per cent of all American hospital beds in Italy;[264] that same year, the surgeon general of Fifth Army cited Italian medical sources, which estimated that 'half the "available" women in Italy had some form of venereal disease'.[265] If the problem of VD was in overall terms less acute in the Asia and the Pacific theatres than in the Mediterranean and the ETO,[266] with the liberation of the Philippines the incidence among troops on the islands of Luzon and Leyte soared to 100 cases per 1,000 per year.[267] As James J. Fahey wrote of Manila in May 1945:

> Over here the people have nothing, the Japs took everything away from them, and the Japs brought bad habits upon the girls. It's a shame the way the girls make money. It's the same all over the city. I never saw anything like it. Most of the girls are from 15 to 20. Little kids about nine years old are out drumming up business. They say about 70% of the females are diseased.[268]

Such were the excesses of their American liberators, that fundamentalist army chaplain James Edwin Orr feared for the prospects of missionary work in the post-war Philippines, blaming 'the presence of so many ungodly servicemen who, by their outrageous conduct in pursuit of liquor and women, destroyed the illusion held by Filipino Protestants that America was a Christian country'.[269] In post-surrender Japan, the temptations and exploitation engendered by defeat and desperation were no less severe, with bands of prostitutes being organised by local officials in order to safeguard public order and racial purity at the behest of the Home Ministry.[270]

The military implications of rampant prostitution were troubling enough. In the four-year period 1942–45, the US Army alone recorded 1,250,846 admissions for VD, the largest single category 'among the infectious and parasitic diseases'.[271] As 1943 drew to a close in Italy, 'a sample of four US infantry divisions showed more VD cases than battle casualties.'[272] As the very first issue of *The Chaplain* magazine despaired in October 1944:

> OUR HEAVIEST WAR losses, apparently, are not those on the field of battle. Writing in the *Woman's Home Companion*, Patricia Lochridge makes this statement: 'The casualties the navy will suffer this year from venereal disease are enough to man a fleet of twelve battleships, six carriers, twenty-four cruisers, and eighty destroyers. The army casualties are enough to form approximately twenty-six complete combat divisions.'[273]

Once again, circumstances in the military contrasted starkly with the situation in the United States. Such was national concern over VD during the 1930s that, by 1940, twenty out of forty-eight states required blood tests to be taken before marriage licenses could be issued, a number that had risen to thirty by 1944.[274] Furthermore, the Progressive Era had seen considerable energy devoted to eliminating white slavery and had witnessed major advances in the wider anti-prostitution cause; such was its success that, by World War II, prostitution was 'officially illegal almost everywhere'.[275] Even in New York, solicitation carried a prison sentence and, as in World War I, attempts to suppress the oldest profession were redoubled as the nation prepared for war. In addition to a raft of state and civic measures that led to the closure of hundreds of red-light districts and the apprehension and treatment of those suspected of carrying VD, the May Act of July 1941 resurrected World War I prohibitions by making all forms of prostitution illegal in the vicinity of military installations.[276] While this did not prevent military clients being driven to prostitutes further afield, the proliferation of 'brothels on wheels', or the activities of swarms of less conspicuous freelance prostitutes, from the perspective of 1945 one navy chaplain could still maintain that: 'The local police, military police and federal authorities have done an excellent job of cleaning out the areas around camps.'[277]

If social hygiene campaigners found much to applaud in the work of 'Blitzing the Brothels',[278] a cause that had an earnest supporter in the Secretary of War, Henry L. Stimson,[279] military chaplains were uncomfortably sandwiched between the norms of civilian life and the traditional, more pragmatic approach of the armed forces. For example, although the army had long sought to prevent infection through moral suasion and instructional films and lectures, its comprehensive, copper-bottomed solution to the problem of VD also embraced the provision of condoms and of prophylactic facilities and, when overseas, even the de facto regulation of local brothels – a practice that continued surreptitiously into World War II.[280] Ultimately, therefore, the army was disposed to treat venereal disease as a disciplinary rather than as a moral problem.[281] When Ernie Pyle stumbled across 'Casanova Park', a wired compound for VD patients at a hospital in North Africa, he was told by its commanding officer – 'a Regular Army man' – that: 'There's no damned excuse for a soldier getting caught nowadays unless he just doesn't care. When he gets a venereal he's no good to his country and somebody else has to do his work. So I want him to feel ashamed.'[282] By the same token, and typical of army policy in Italy, at the 23rd General Hospital near Naples hundreds of venereal patients lingered in a similar compound, stigmatised by hospital garb that bore the large red letters 'VD'.[283] Still, despite the army's initial reluctance and in order not to be seen as rewarding vice, from 1942 it began to induct and treat VD sufferers, accepting no fewer than 200,000, including a number of syphilitics.[284] As for the navy, the Bureau of Navigation had resolved as early as 1937 to stop treating venereal disease as 'an offense against discipline', becoming reliant on education and prophylaxis instead.[285] With the tacit consent of the civilian population, the Oahu brothels that served the naval base at Pearl Harbor were unofficially regulated for most of the war, and were reputed to represent an industry worth $10 million a year.[286] If the army and the navy unofficially connived in the provision of approved brothels, the positions of the army and the navy towards VD were effectively aligned in late 1944 when new legislation virtu-ally dispensed with the assumption of personal responsibility for infection and branded only the concealment of venereal disease a military offence, prompting *The Christian Century* to deride the new conceit of 'venereal infection incurred "in line of duty"'.[287]

Clearly, many chaplains chafed at the basic amorality of military policy. From the army's arrival in North Africa, its chaplains complained to Washington of the supervision of local brothels, in this case commandeered from the French.[288] Likewise, navy chaplain Samuel Hill Ray fumed from Tokyo only days after the Japanese surrender:

> All the chaplains have become upset over the cat-houses to which our sailors have been exposed. The Navy sent in doctors and prophylactics and corpsmen and allowed these syphilitic women to operate. The Navy claimed these conditions could not be helped and they had to protect the men from disease.... The chaplains, both Protestant and Catholic have protested and even written back to the States about these conditions, all of which has not helped the reputation of the Navy. I have done all I could to protect the kids of my ship.[289]

Towards the end of 1945, and in a good illustration of how the attitudes of tempo-rary chaplains could diverge from the more resigned, careerist and worldly-wise position of their regular colleagues in this regard, chaplains of the 2nd Marine Division rebelled 'when the Division started to open certain "approved houses" unofficially' in the vicinity of Nagasaki.[290] Despite sundry shenanigans, and some foot-dragging on the part of their superiors, their protest had the desired effect, at least temporarily, and contributed to a General Order on the 'REPRESSION OF PROSTITUTION' that was issued by the Secretary of the Navy, James V. Forrestal, in June 1946.[291] However, throughout this episode the reticence of more senior, regular navy chaplains contrasted sharply with the zeal of their essentially civilian subordinates. In fact, the senior Fleet Marine Force chaplain, Herbert Dumstrey, had even admonished Chaplain George W. Wickersham:

> You know, Wickersham … we make too much of the Decalogue. Now there's the commandment about the Sabbath, for instance, and yet you and I say nothing about the men playing ball on Sunday. There's the commandment about swearing, and yet we all know that the language in the Marine Corps is terrible. Then we turn around and make such a fuss over the Seventh Commandment. And at that, the Seventh Commandment does not say anything about fornication. It specifies adultery.[292]

Hearing this argument with incredulity, just as risible to Wickersham and his fellow rebels was the recent statement of the army's chief of chaplains to the Military Policy Committee of Congress:

> It is not mere chance … that the morals [of GIs] have been safeguarded and their characters strengthened. The results are due in no small measure to the policy and program of our army and navy which has always considered of primary importance the moral and spiritual welfare of the men committed to their care.[293]

The tensions between representation and reality in this respect were underlined by the famous case of the Methodist navy chaplain Dr Norbert G. Talbott, who resigned his commission in September 1943 after appearing before the pre-graduation examining board at the navy chaplains' school. Here, Talbott was 'asked certain questions designed to find out what he would do when faced with certain situations which involved a moral problem or a conscientious conviction'.[294] Although the situations were hypothetical and no transcript of his interview was made, Talbott afterwards alleged that he had been quizzed about being asked to 'arrange for a dance and provide beer for the men', to being ordered 'to give the men a talk on the necessity and use of preventive measures against venereal disease', and to being invited 'to attend a party during which liquor was served'.[295] In the event, Talbott's story became a *cause célèbre*, his story being published in January 1944 in the fundamentalist *Christian Beacon*, which was noted for its 'sensational and aggressive religious journalism',[296] and later by *Time* magazine and *The Christian Advocate*.[297] Resulting from the 'distortion of facts and false implications which were broadcast in such publicity',[298] numerous letters of protest were sent to the Secretary of the Navy, Frank Knox, while the head of the chaplains' school, Clinton A. Neyman, a Northern Baptist, was quizzed about the matter in March 1944 before the Senate Committee on Naval Affairs. According to Neyman's testimony, Talbott's story was unreliable, the situations he had conjured were implausible, and he had in fact resigned for other reasons. As Neyman contended, 'I have been in the navy almost twenty-six years. I still have to have presented to me, by any commanding officer that I have ever had, an order to conduct a dance, to procure any beer, to furnish any female companions, or to make any lectures on prophylaxis.'[299] Although *The Chaplain* magazine printed a lengthy rebuttal of Talbott's claims that November – 'The Facts in the Talbott Case' – which pointed out that he had never taken the matter to his endorsing authority or to the General Commission, it admitted that 'the clamorous little band of critics' he had energised had created a public relations crisis. Besides attacking 'the navy's Chief Chaplain', they had impugned the integrity of navy chaplains, hampered recruitment (when 'as never before in their lives young Americans in uniform need the protective, consoling, and saving service of ministers in uniform'), and had 'brought anxiety to many kinsmen of sailors, seabees, coast guardsmen and marines, and have shaken their faith in the character of the chaplains who serve them'.[300]

For those chaplains – apparently, the majority – who were prepared to live with the moral ambivalence of service life in this respect, their primary weapon in the fight against vice was the personal appeal to the better nature and sentiments of their flocks. Often, this was a direct if jarring accompaniment to the wisdom of the medical profession. As Israel Yost wrote of an occasion in France in October 1944: 'After the battalion surgeons had instructed some 650 men on proper prophylactic procedures against venereal disease, I presented a "sex morality lecture" emphasizing Christian principles concerning relations between men and women.'[301] Although it would be easy to present such talks as trite and sentimental,[302] surviving specimens indicate that they could be anything but. In a brief, hard-hitting talk given by Methodist chaplain Raymond E. Musser at Camp Campbell, Kentucky, and eventually published in *The Link*, Musser addressed three categories of GI: 'The Wills', 'The Won'ts' and 'The Mights'. Congratulating the 'Won'ts', Musser voiced his wish that they could be exempted from his talk, for:

> You have trained yourselves to be high-minded. A girl to you is a companion, a friend. Tired of associations with men only, you seek out the USO functions, the church and 'Y' social centers, and accept invitations into the homes of nice people with nice daughters. There is no 'wolfing.' You sensible soldiers have your own wives or sweethearts, and would no more think of sex indulgence or erotic petting than you would consent for your own women to do so back home.[303]

He was equally direct with another fixed category, namely 'The Wills':

> You 'wills' should be exempted, since nothing I might say would deter you from sex indulgence.... You salacious soldiers will take up on the street corner and in a strange house with any slut, no matter how uncouth or how shot through with venereal disease, just because she is a woman who

will give or sell her body to your desire for a few minutes. Such whoredom is outside the conception of the clean-minded male.[304]

Turning to 'The Mights', Musser warned them that:

> Since your induction you have heard appeals to keep your body well and clean, since a diseased body can neither give it nor take it; you have listened to medical officers' plain testimony that there is no sure cure for these dreadful, humiliating, health-shattering, infectious diseases that God put as a curse upon fornication.... Let no libertine kid you about your 'puritan' morals ... let no cynic convince you that there is anything sissy about goodness.... While the boy that sowed wild oats is struggling with divorce proceedings you will be living contentedly with your One-and-Only.[305]

Model talks such as this were duly compiled by the Office of the Chief of Chaplains and were also a recurrent feature of *The Chaplain* magazine.[306] Navy chaplains could be no less candid. In an article published in *The Link* in October 1945, Presbyterian (USA) chaplain John M. Whallon warned against the long-term dangers of unfaithfulness while acknowledging the temptations that assailed the sailor in home ports, even conceding that:

> In the short stride of several blocks recently, I received a dozen bids myself ... half of the solicitors were children who did not appear to be more than eight years old ... one, not more than four, was barely able to pronounce the familiar two-syllable invitation to come up and see his 'sister'.[307]

Despite these efforts there was a tangible impression of fighting a losing battle; in fact, even an article published in 1946 that sought to challenge public stereotypes of 'the veteran' had to concede that 'the thesis that war experience tends to liberalize morality' was 'too well supported from past wars to be denied', and that 'almost two-thirds' of a sample group of Princeton students reported that 'their attitudes towards sex and morals have become more liberal as a result of their wartime experiences'.[308] For his part, Chaplain Whallon was depressed to note that on one occasion only five out of a liberty party of fifty sailors had refused to accept an issue of prophylactics before going ashore, and one of these because he already had his. Though not all may have used them, Whallon was mortified by the realisation that '90% either had no convictions against their use or were unwilling to defend their convictions with so much as a gesture of refusal'.[309] A similar lack of success was apparent in the army. In 1945, a secret survey of the sexual behaviour of GIs indicated that 'only a tiny minority abstained from intercourse out of religious conviction'.[310] While it should be pointed out that the secular advice of instruction films and medical officers seems to have been equally ineffective,[311] the discouraging results of their labours appear to have caused ripples of dissension among chaplains themselves. In contrast to *The Christian Century*, for example, Methodist army chaplain Arthur B. Mercer concurred with the removal of penalties for the contraction of VD.[312] Among Catholics, of course, contraception was a particularly sensitive issue, especially as the armed forces were being inundated with them. According to John C. Burnham: 'At one point, fifty million condoms reached service personnel *each month* – often dispensed free or from machines.'[313] Consequently, in March 1945 John F. O'Hara, the auxiliary bishop of the army and navy, felt moved to confront George C. Marshall about the alleged delivery of 'three hundred tons of rubber contraceptives' to the army in New Guinea, as he had done two years earlier about the issue of 'prophylactic packets' to GIs overseas.[314] However, pre-war navy chaplain Frederick William Meehling took a more nuanced view of the distribution of condoms:

> I felt if a man wants to throw himself away and he's old enough to make up his mind what he wants to do, that's his business. I may not agree with him, but he has to make the decision. And if he wants to, he should be protected. They should be available if he wants to ask. But to stand on the quarterdeck and say, 'You can't go ashore unless you take two of these with you,' I'm dead against that. That's an invitation to dance. And that's the policy I've always had about those things.[315]

Significantly, one of the most rancorous wartime debates to occur in *The Chaplain* took place after Episcopalian army chaplain William A. Spurrier issued a lofty invitation to his colleagues in October 1944 to 'Lay That Prattle Down!' A recent graduate of Union Theological Seminary, where he had majored in ethics and theology,[316] the crux of Spurrier's argument was that 'the chaplains and the Church should not be so moralistic':

> I would suggest that we stop this goody-goody prattling and attack the problem positively. Let's tell the soldier in frank detail about the physical, psychological and spiritual components of sex- masturbation, intercourse, sex drives, satisfaction, sublimation, frustration and repression. Let's point out the advantages and disadvantages and what each one requires in the way of emotional reactions, desire and will.... If [the GI] wants to play around with the women, then don't rear up on our self-righteous horse and prattle about sin; tell him what the cost of such action is and ask him if he is willing to pay the price.[317]

However, such liberal and worldly-wise arguments met with a furious response in other quarters. According to Chaplain K.W. Schalk, Spurrier's article did not meet with the approval 'of five out of six chaplains in my immediate neighborhood', it lacked wisdom and was 'a direct insult to the men on duty overseas in combat.'[318] Northern Baptist chaplain Frank M. Arnold, responding in April 1945, was even more forthright:

I have read with surprise and disgust the article by Chaplain William A. Spurrier in the first issue of THE CHAPLAIN. The burden of the article may be summed up in one sentence: 'It is all right to sin, so long as you can avoid the consequences.' Surely this is the essence of paganism.... Extra-marital sex relations are wrong, not because they may cause physical, emotional or social difficulties, but because God has said, 'Thou shalt not.'[319]

If chaplains clearly felt the strain of this wartime environment, in at least one case the generally turgid and confusing moral atmosphere of war proved too much, resulting in an ignominious fall from grace. In this case, a Catholic AAF chaplain in England who had taken an ostentatious stand against the distribution of condoms and the availability of pornography was found to have contracted VD after an affair of his own, a revelation that led to his transfer to the United States and, subsequently, to the Philippines where the chastened padre eventually redeemed himself.[320]

As this case illustrates, the battle against pornography was closely allied to the campaign against promiscuity, for nothing advertised the libido of the serviceman more publicly than his insatiable appetite for pin-ups. As Ernie Pyle once remarked:

There was one pin-up gallery in a room occupied by six mechanics of my dive-bomber squadron. Tacked on the walls were three dozen of the most striking pin-ups I ever saw. Before long the squadron had to move and give up its nice quarters. I suggested that the pin-ups be left there and the room roped off by the Italian government as a monument to the American occupation. I'll bet the place, if given a few centuries' time, would become as historic as Pompeii.[321]

Given this conspicuous weakness for pornography, however mild by later standards, it was ironic that American commentators seized upon enemy tastes for the obscene. Given the fundamental amorality of Shintoism, one American journalist remarked that 'pornographic pictures' seemed 'part of the equipment' of the Japanese soldier.[322] Likewise, Warren Wyeth Willard expressed his disgust with these signs of Japanese decadence on Guadalcanal, sniffing that: 'Pornographic photographs seemed to be popular with the enemy soldiers, who even carried handkerchiefs upon which had been printed in colours lascivious pictures of an extremely perverted nature.'[323] However, and as the battle was raging against the emperor's pornographers on Guadalcanal, *Yank* was under fire for its insufficiently sexual content, an indignant 'GROUND CREW PRIVATE' protesting that 'the boys are interested in sex, and *Esquire* and a few other magazines give us sex and still get by the mail, so why can't YANK?'[324] Although the magazine was always a fruitful source of pin-ups, *Yank* obliged in September 1943 with a cartoon of two GIs in a harem being waited upon by a pair of lithesome, veiled and bare-chested servant girls, the accompanying caption reading 'PSST, HARRY – ARE YOU SURE THIS IS THE USO?' However, this aroused the ire of a Private G.W. Miller, who deplored the cartoon as 'most immoral and degrading' and called for a clean-up of the magazine.[325] A debate then ensued in 'Mail Call', *Yank's* correspondence column, in which the single letter from 'A CHRISTIAN SOLDIER' in support of Miller was swamped by a torrent of those against,[326] a group of 'fighting aerial gunners' making the telling point that: 'As yet, we haven't heard any complaints from the chaplains, because they are broadminded enough to enjoy the jokes.'[327]

However, many chaplains and concerned laymen were clearly not happy with the ready availability of such material. Whatever the indulgence shown towards *Yank*, in 1943 chaplains in the CBI mounted a sustained but unsuccessful effort to tone down the contents of *Roundup*, 'the United States soldiers' weekly in the China–Burma–India theater', whose front page was always 'ornamented with a large photo of a woman with beautiful, long, lovely legs, exquisite hips and noteworthy bosom'.[328] Later, in September, an editorial in *The Link* claimed that it was being enjoined to 'launch out on a vigorous crusade against the flood of dirty literature engulfing magazine stands these days'. Accordingly, it called upon its readers 'to hold the line for decency by refusing to read, and encouraging your pals to refuse to buy, those periodicals that are obviously tainted with dirt'.[329] On his part, the country's devoutly Catholic postmaster general, Frank C. Walker, exercised his powers of censorship in 1944 by cancelling the mail privileges of *Esquire* magazine, thus stemming the flow of especially prized pin-ups to the armed forces, a decision that had to be overturned in the US Court of Appeals.[330] While William R. Arnold expressed support for Walker, and kept his own well-thumbed dossier on pornography in army publications,[331] Francis L. Sampson was shocked by the pornographic art that adorned the former French army barracks at Mourmelon-le-Grand, occupied by the 101st Airborne Division in autumn 1944. According to Sampson, this was 'obscene beyond description' and had to be covered over. However, and as he ruefully admitted, 'most of the men were not as scrupulous on the subject as were Chaplain Engel and myself'.[332]

American servicemen, of course, were by no means lacking in such artistic talents, as the risqué adornments of countless aircraft, tanks and even ships testified.[333] According to a *Stars and Stripes* feature entitled 'Nudes, Names and Numbers',[334] by August 1943 'Typical examples of warbirds with personality' were Eighth Air Force B-17s such as *Impatient Virgin* and *Piccadilly Commando*, both of which sported 'informally undressed gals'.[335] If *Yank* paid its own homage to the 'The Vulgar Virgin' in May 1943,[336] John Muirhead recalled with affection the artwork featured on his own aircraft, a B-17 dubbed *Laura*:

> Her image stretched languorously along the forward fuselage from just above the chin turret to the leading edge of the wing. She peered at me over

her wineglass with a warm smile, accepting my homage to her splendid breasts that were bravely tipped by two spinning propellers. A grease stain marred the pink roundness of her shoulder, but did not to me diminish her charm nor my admiring lust. Neither did the intrusion of the riveted edge of an access panel on the perfect curve of her buttocks seem to me to be a distraction from her invitation.[337]

Significantly, there was little control over such naming or decoration. As *Stars and Stripes* chortled:

A pilot from Maine is apt to come out any rainy morning and find that his plane has been named TEXAS. Or the quiet teetotaler who quit divinity school to join the Air Force is apt to come out on the line and find a nude stretching from the plastic nose to the pilot's compartment because his tail gunner (who did not quit divinity school to join the Air Force) knew a guy in Site Six who used to be a commercial artist in St. Louis and could still draw a plenty sexy nude.[338]

Nevertheless, tastes could and did vary. Despite the extent of questionable art and nomenclature, army aviators were also prepared to have their aircraft blessed, given more exalted monikers, and even adorned with religious imagery. Among the more famous names were *Parson's Chariot*, *St Christopher*, *Queen of Heaven*, *Queen of Angels* and *Our Lady of the Skies*.[339] Another bomber, *Ave Maria*, sported a rather glamorous portrait of the Virgin Mary, Our Lady of Loretto being 'the official heavenly patroness of aviators'.[340] Even the salacious enthusiasm for pin-ups could be overestimated. Congratulating the readers of *The Link* in June 1944, Chaplain Raymond E. Musser wrote that:

[A] trip through the barracks or hospital would prove to any who doubt it that you men prefer your own girls. Many a regiment or ship has chosen by actual ballot some wife, sister or girl-friend of a man in the outfit or complement as its 'Sweetheart of '44'. Pin-ups are not too popular.... With men who know American maidens best, it's their own girls, ten to one![341]

In June 1945, *What The Soldier Thinks* revealed that, although its regular 'Pin-up Girl' had the endorsement of four out of five readers of *Yank* magazine – whose circulation then stood at over two million – it was exceeded in popularity by the cartoon figure of 'The Sad Sack', and even by its 'Combat Stories'.[342] Recalling the decorative preferences of the 100th Infantry Battalion in billets in Italy, Chaplain Israel Yost wrote that:

To decorate the 'rooms' of their 'homes', soldiers put pinup girls on the walls. To offset the type some of the medics had posted, I hung up my chaplain's flag above the couch I was sleeping on. In one company [command post] the captain had a very special pinup girl displayed: a little girl lying in bed under a quilt, holding her soldier-daddy's picture and smiling at it. A medic's pinup was also one of a kind: a ten-year-old-girl wearing a pink dress and with two pink ribbons in her hair, holding a white prayer book and standing framed in a church window.[343]

Playing on these diverse tastes, the churches furnished plenty of 'Christian kitsch' of their own. Popular among Protestants was Warner Sallman's 'Head of Christ', painted in 1941 and subsequently 'distributed by the hundreds of millions' throughout the United States and across the world.[344] Underlining the appeal of Sallman's depiction of Christ, which eventually acquired the status of 'an evangelical icon',[345] *The Link* reported in January 1945 that:

> One million reprints of 'The Universal Christ', a painting by Warner Sallman, have been distributed through USO clubs and chaplains to men and women in the armed forces, it was reported recently in New York by the YMCA Army and Navy Department.... The most widely distributed picture of Christ during the war years, it continues to be printed in large quantities to meet increasing demands for it by service men and women.[346]

Eventually, *The Link* complemented Sallman's work with its own series of 'Biblical Pin-Ups', beginning with 'Pharaoh's Daughter', the saviour of the infant Moses, in January 1946.[347] In fact, this treatment of biblical heroines may well have been triggered by the appeal of 'The Pinup Madonna', a sultry image of the Virgin Mary that had been produced by a Holy Ghost seminarian at the instigation of a Catholic army chaplain keen 'to offset the offensive pin-ups in his overseas camp'.[348]

There were, furthermore, sporadic and localised attempts to clean up. While collections of pornography stood to be confiscated as contraband,[349] 'A VERY DISILLUSIONED GI' complained to *Yank* in June 1943:

> You may as well discontinue printing pictures of your most beautiful pin-up girls. It seems that a certain person, taking over the command of a certain company in the London area, has forbidden any pictures to be hung on walls except those of your family or sweetheart. To add insult to injury, one of his boys had to take down the picture of the Commander-in-Chief. It is rather a strange thing, but the quotation under the picture starts with 'For God and Liberty'.[350]

Two months later, *Stars and Stripes* reported how an inspection at one airfield had resulted in a short-lived clamp down on the 'names on planes that couldn't be bantered around in mixed company. No more VULGAR VIRGINS, or T.S.'s.'[351] Consistent with the efforts of navy chaplain Samuel Hill Ray to combat foul language on board the *Hamlin*, he earned the moniker 'Anti-Pin-up Padre' after stopping pictures of nude Polynesian women from gracing the ship's calendar.[352] However, not all chaplains were disturbed by the pin-up phenomenon. As Thomas H. Clare shrugged:

Personally, I could never work up much sweat about pin-up girls. On the whole, they are beautiful. And they're certainly more wholesome than the vulgar obscenities which came out of France during the last war. To old Private G.I. the pin-up girl represents his conception of what the American girl is like. She is the ideal he has his heart set upon back home.[353]

However, such latitude was not normally shown to USO shows, performances that were often thought to flout accepted standards of decency and good taste in front of a more or less captive audience. As Daniel A. Poling remembered of a show put on for two thousand GIs in Kunming, at which 'Chinese were also present, as well as a number of women':

The first performer was a Broadway comedian who evidently believed that American men automatically turned in their characters when they put on their country's uniform. He told a string of dirty stories and concluded with an obscene song whose refrain, the only printable part as he sang it, was, 'I want a woman.' I wondered how the fellow, with such ad-libbing as this, had ever managed to get his credentials as an overseas entertainer.[354]

However, Poling noted that the tour of the offending artist was cancelled soon after this performance, the potential and mechanics of retaliatory action being explained to readers of *The Chaplain* in December 1944:

While serving a colored battalion on manoeuvres in central Oregon in the fall of 1943, the Special Services Division put on a stage show that had features which were disgusting and morally degrading. CHAPLAIN LEONARD DEMOOR, through his supervisory chaplain, put in a formal protest. He in turn took it to the commanding officer, General Patch, a hero of Guadalcanal and now General Patton's successor at the head of the Seventh Army ... Says Chaplain DeMoor: 'The general saw to it that the Special Services officer was censured, and that there would be no repetition of such an offense against the moral sensibilities of our men in the service.'[355]

The files of the Office of the Chief of Chaplains illustrate how common a problem this was, with numerous chaplains taking up the cudgels against the alleged smut merchants accredited by the USO. For example, and as part of Arnold's often testy wartime correspondence with Lawrence Philips, the executive vice president of USO Camp Shows, Inc., in 1943 Arnold addressed the complaints of Southern Baptist chaplain Oluf C. Jensen from a 'rain-soaked island' in the Pacific. Affronted by two acts in particular that were of 'the rawest bar-room type ... raw, lewd [and] suggestive', Jensen had written:

I cannot understand why the entertainers that come out here think that they have to dig in [the] gutter.... I am surprised that the USO Camp Shows would send shows out here that they don't first see and hear to know what type of entertainment they are sending.... Something ought to be done to provide the right kind of entertainment.... If there isn't a change, I'm going to write to my church organization, the Southern Baptist Convention and have them publish throughout the whole convention the type of entertainment that is provided by USO funds for their sons at the front.[356]

That December, Arnold paid the USO a backhanded compliment by remarking to Philips: 'Evidently you are laboring for decency to good effect. This office has received no letters of criticism for several weeks and the Monthly Reports received for November are not producing the usual nasty comments.'[357] As the DeMoor case serves to illustrate, such confidence was somewhat misplaced.

Gambling, drink, smoking and drugs

Besides the challenge of smut and pornography, another rampant problem was that of gambling, a pastime that was subject (notionally, at least) to strict regulation in civilian life, regulation that all but collapsed under service conditions. According to Ernie Pyle, such were the poker-playing skills of one artillery regiment that its men made $15,000 'from other outfits on the ship' simply in the course of their voyage from the United States to Britain.[358] However, gambling did not stop with poker. As Pyle also remarked from Italy:

> The boys bet on anything. While I was home in the United States, they said they had bet on whether I would go to the Italian front or to the Pacific theater. They made bets on when we would get to Rome, and when the war would be over, and a couple of them were betting on whether Schlitz beer was sometimes put in green bottles instead of brown.[359]

Emblematic of the wartime gambling craze was a series of articles published by *Yank* in 1943 that explored various dice and card tricks in intricate detail, although without offering any moral gloss of its own.[360]

In contrast to common attitudes towards swearing and obscenity, but like attitudes towards drink, reactions to gambling seemed to diverge along confessional lines, with Protestants being much more opposed than Catholics. In April 1943 *The Christian Century* reported that, 'To help build army morale, the war department has bought 750,000 pairs of dice', seething:

> Has the general staff no sense of responsibility concerning the kind of citizen it returns to the country when the soldier has completed his service? It is one thing to be a bit lenient in disciplining soldiers whose ideas of entertainment have been acquired in pool halls or the alleys of city slums. It is a different matter entirely for the war department to take its cue from alley loafers in its provision of entertainment for the men in service.[361]

Five months later, Methodist army chaplain Clyde E. Kimball noted that the attractions of gambling could lead to a neglect of religious duties, with a Sabbath payday in England causing many to forsake their Sunday devotions in favour of the resulting crap games.[362] Another army chaplain, the Northern Baptist George W. Zinz, lamented the generally corrupting effect of the prevailing gambling culture:

> Many a man comes into the Army to see dice thrown and cards dealt for the first time.... He is easy prey for the professional gambler who revels in his power. The element of chance always has intrigued the red-blooded American and surely exerts its every guile. Nevertheless, one is shocked at the increase of gambling and the willingness of non-gamblers of pre-war days to yield to this scourge.[363]

A good example of the latter was noted by Lester Atwell, who saw how one soldier-preacher capitulated to the temptations of blackjack on the heartfelt plea of a comrade who protested, 'Ah cain't towk religion *ohll* the time. Whyn't you ever want to play cards with me? Ah git *tired* of religion, an' it's not a sin to play cards, hones' it isn't.'[364] Nonetheless, and true to the puritan heritage of American Protestantism, *The Link* insisted on the inherent sinfulness of gambling. In November 1943, Chaplain Raymond R. Miller asked 'What's Wrong About Gambling?', answering his own question by asserting that: 'gambling is a complete waste of time and energy; *it produces nothing.* And because it produces nothing it comes under just condemnation of God and man.' Although Miller conceded that the Bible had little to say about gambling directly, the fact that it represented '*an attempt to gain ownership of that for which one has neither attempted any productive work nor offered anything in exchange*' made it tantamount to stealing.[365] Similarly, for Ben W. Sinderson, a Disciples of Christ AAF chaplain writing in April 1945, the wartime growth in gambling threatened to ruin the moral character of post-war America; moreover, it stood condemned by the scene of the crucifixion, for there Christ's crucifiers had indulged in a 'Crap Game At the Foot of the Cross.'[366]

Despite the aspiration of the US Navy to curb gambling through direct disciplinary procedures, perhaps the most effective constraint it imposed was the partial withholding of pay. As James J. Fahey remarked from the *Montpelier* in April 1945: 'On paydays we are allowed to draw only $10. If more money is needed, a very good reason has to be provided. Many on board are gambling and this curtails it somewhat.'[367] However, for chaplains opposed to the pastime a more direct approach could be adopted. Ministering to marines in Cuba prior to Pearl Harbor, Methodist navy chaplain Hansel H. Tower was mortified to find that, after he had lobbied for the men of a quarantine camp to be given their pay in full, its tents had been transformed into gambling dens:

> In both of them poker playing and crap shooting were in full swing ...
> When they saw me, the games stopped and a deep silence settled. A lecture
> was indicated and I gave it. When I had finished, the winners felt that they
> had been taking the last crust of bread from hungry wives and children.
> Some of them even went so far as to restore the money they had won.
> There was no more poker playing or crap shooting in the measles camp.[368]

Later, in Alaska, a Baptist army chaplain broke up a poker game by brightly
suggesting that he hold an impromptu service, a proposal that was welcomed
with relief by those who were losing.[369] However, Catholic chaplains, whose Irish
and Italian constituents were widely associated with illicit gambling in American
urban life,[370] could evince a very different response to the gambling problem. On
the island of Leyte in the Philippines, Chaplain Thomas J. Donnelly was intrigued
by the advice of a former bookie on how to 'beat the horses'.[371] Furthermore,
Philip Ardery noted that Chaplain Gerald Beck of the 389th Bombardment
Group was an accomplished gambler in his own right, recalling that:

> He had a very worldly side that caused some comment. He loved to gamble
> on cards or dice. He gave his winnings away, but he was nearly always a
> heavy winner. I saw him make six straight passes with the dice one night,
> and the game broke up – not because he had all the money, but because
> no one in the game had nerve enough to fade him.[372]

If Catholic chaplains did not share the anti-gambling zeal of many of their
Protestant colleagues, they could also prove to be a promising resource for the
inveterate gambler. On one occasion, Chaplain Francis L. Sampson was asked to
exchange a five-dollar bill on the grounds that 'a chaplain's money in a crap game
is better than a rabbit's foot and puts just the right "hex" on the dice'.[373]

An additional wartime scourge of America's armed forces was the demon
drink. Widely held, in military as in civilian life, to be the wellspring of other
vices, in 1945 a report on military offenders in the ETO emphatically concluded
that intoxication was 'the largest contributing factor to crime in the European
Theater of Operations', looming large in 'crimes of violence and involving the sex
motive'.[374] On a more personal note, Methodist navy chaplain Hansel H. Tower
testified that:

> It has been my experience that many of the civilians and service men who
> have come to me in serious trouble have had their trouble either directly
> brought on by the use of alcohol, or complicated by it. This is not a hasty
> statement and is made after carefully considering many cases.[375]

Although the Catholic Church had a comparatively liberal attitude towards
alcohol, the Jesuit writer Daniel A. Lord was typically direct concerning its ill
effects, warning in his 1942 *Salute to the Men in Service*:

No need here to go into a tirade on the 'evils of drink' …
You know that drink is prelude with a serviceman to fighting, obscenity, and general loose conduct.
You know where drinks are served, there is usually easy access to trouble.
You know when a man drinks with a girl what is most likely to follow …
If a drunk is obnoxious under all circumstances, a drunk in uniform is revolting.[376]

Despite the signal failure of the Eighteenth Amendment, as in World War I the demands of war seemed to favour the Prohibitionist cause. While America mobilised, Prohibitionists targeted the supply of liquor to American soldiers, with Senator Morris Sheppard of Texas, chairman of the Senate Committee on Military Affairs and champion of the Eighteenth Amendment, introducing a bill to allow the Secretaries of War and the Navy to create 'dry zones' in and around military camps.[377] As a hostile 'CAPTAIN BARLEYCORN' warned in the *Infantry Journal* in May 1941: 'History repeats. As in 1917, the first wedge in the prohibition campaign-to-come is to shut off alcohol from the soldier. Then what happens later is a matter of opportunity for the drys.'[378] The urgent need for national efficiency after the outbreak of war strengthened the Prohibitionists' hand, with the calamity of Pearl Harbor easily attributed to the Saturday-night drinking habits of the US military.[379] With the sale of hard liquor still banned under some local options and across the states of Oklahoma, Mississippi and Kansas,[380] a new enthusiasm for Prohibition was widely felt in American Protestantism, with the United Lutherans, the Disciples of Christ, Presbyterians and Baptists rallying to safeguard service personnel from the evils of drink.[381] In this, they received strong backing from *The Christian Century*, which consistently reported and editorialised on the scourge of alcohol in the armed forces. In April 1943, for example, it emphasised the human risks involved in shipping beer overseas, printing the letter of a Methodist minister from Oklahoma City who complained to President Roosevelt: 'Mr. President, millions of people are disturbed over this situation. Christian parents do not want the lives of their sons set in jeopardy to convoy alcoholic liquors across the seas.'[382] Indeed, and as *Yank* noted recurrently in its 'News From Home' feature, Prohibitionist confidence was running high by 1943. That February, it noted how: 'Miss Lilly Grace Matheson, secretary of the Women's Christian Temperance Union, said the return of prohibition is just a matter of time. "We shall soon find America dry again, perhaps within a year," the lady promised.'[383] In July, it publicised the prediction of Dr Howard Hyde Russell, 'co-founder of the 50-year old Anti-Saloon League', who claimed that: 'This country will be dry by 1950 – and I will live to see it.'[384] Two months later, it observed that, while beer was being consumed in unprecedented quantities: 'The United States Treasury Department disclosed that there were 12,000 fewer places to buy whisky than one year ago and 32,000 less than in

1937'. It also reported that 36 per cent of Americans were now in favour of rein-
troducing Prohibition.[385]

According to successive AIPO polls, wartime support for Prohibition peaked
in October 1944, when 39 per cent of Americans said that they would 'vote to
make the country dry', an increase of seven percentage points on the last peacetime poll of October 1940.[386] Nevertheless, the lessons of the recent past meant
that Prohibition gained little political traction, as the fate of Sheppard's 'dry
zone' bill after his sudden death in April 1941 serves to illustrate.[387] Significantly,
the mainstream religious military press fought shy of an all-out attack on the
demon drink, instead promoting temperance sentiment, figures and amenities.
In March 1943, for example, the 'Bible Bits' column of *The Link* invited its readers
to consider such passages as Isaiah 24:9, 'Strong drink shall be bitter to them that
drink it'.[388] The following month, it noted with sympathy *The Christian Advocate*'s call upon the president to show more support 'for sobriety in the interest
of the nation's war effort'[389] and upheld Bernard Law Montgomery, the victor of
El Alamein, as a paragon of temperance and military efficiency, stressing that: 'It
should interest the critics of the so-called "bluenoses" that General Montgomery
does not drink'.[390] As for *The Chaplain*, in October 1944 it invoked the wisdom of
the enemy, quoting a Japanese proverb that ran: 'First the man takes a drink; then
the drink takes a drink; then the drink take the man'.[391] On firmer ground, in May
1945 it cited the fervent but familiar testimony of Sergeant Alvin York, 'the soldier
who in World War I disarmed and brought 153 German prisoners into camp':

> I used to drink liquor; drank it for ten years; drank it until I broke the
> hearts of those who loved me and prayed for me. And then one night in
> 1914 I knelt at the altar in a little mountain church in East Tennessee, and
> confessed and repented of my sins. I arose from that altar a new man in
> Christ Jesus, and I broke with liquor forever.[392]

Significantly, Lieutenant James C. Whittaker was careful not to detract from the
semi-miraculous escape of Eddie Rickenbacker and his companions from the
wastes of the Pacific. Despite the many thousands of nautical miles they had
traversed in their life rafts, he assured his readers that, on arrival at Honolulu, 'we
set out to gratify a desire that had burned within us for many weeks. We wanted
strawberry malted milks!'[393]

By dint of General Order 99, issued by Secretary of the Navy, Josephus
Daniels in 1914, the ships and stations of the US Navy had, in theory at least,
been conquered for the cause of Prohibition. Consequently, and as *Yank* duly
reported, even King George VI – who was 'unaware that United States vessels
carry no liquor' – had to make do with soft drinks when he attempted to 'splice
the main brace' on an American warship in North Africa in 1943.[394] If US Navy
practice differed from the hallowed traditions of the Royal Navy in this regard, it
also dictated that celebrations on board the battleship *Missouri* after the Japanese

surrender in September 1945 had to be in keeping with navy regulations, with the Allied commanders marking the occasion with coffee and doughnuts.[395] However, navy conventions also differed from the regime in the US Army. Although the army was not a 'dry' institution, the consumption of alcohol was regulated nonetheless. According to guidelines set in 1901, only the sale of purportedly non-intoxicating 3.2 per cent beer (legal even in the days of Prohibition) was permitted on army premises, with officers enjoying the perk of a monthly ration of hard liquor as well.[396] While the mailing of hard liquor to soldiers was illegal, the wartime army sought to palliate its restrictions on alcohol by ensuring that its post exchanges were well stocked with 'cola drinks, ice cream, candy, cigarettes and other merchandise'.[397] Certainly, attempts were made to ensure that military regulations were at least seen to be observed. Samuel Hynes, for example, remembered that, while in training, a salty marine sergeant would insist that all bottles of whisky were appropriately wrapped.[398] Likewise, in 1943 the sale of hard liquor was banned in the army officers' clubs and messes; as *Yank* explained, this meant that officers 'could either drink beer and be happy or hike to nearby towns for the harder stuff'.[399] Nevertheless, loopholes remained. In the AAF, the practice arose of administering shots of whisky to returning aircrew after missions, whisky that at least one B-29 pilot thought superior to standard issue spirits.[400] Under similar circumstances, flight surgeons on the navy's aircraft carriers could make liberal distributions of 'medicinal liquor' to navy fliers.[401]

However, the nation's armed forces failed to prevent – or even significantly curtail – a wartime epidemic of excessive drinking. Even allowing for a degree of British hauteur and inter-Allied prejudice, it is remarkable that one British army officer should have written in North Africa: 'Though we are not angels, an army which is drunk all day is no good to be associated with'.[402] For many, however, drinking was undoubtedly fuelled by the enormous stresses of combat; as Captain Robert Morgan, pilot of the celebrated bomber *Memphis Belle*, admitted, whisky was 'the only antidote I had for all those exploding B-17s that haunted my dreams'.[403] Nevertheless, and given the place of combat as a minority experience, this drinking was more than simply compulsive, and had even less to do with the occasional lack of potable water.[404] As Gordon Bennett Robertson remembered, even among combat fliers considerable ingenuity could be devoted to heavy recreational drinking; great quantities of so-called 'kickapoo joy juice' were manufactured from rationed spirits and grapefruit juice, gallon jugs of the concoction being chilled by high-altitude flights in the unpressurised sections of B-29 bombers.[405] Moreover, the depth of American resources ensured that even the more innocuous army beer could be available in massive quantities. For example, on their arrival in Italy from the United States, the GIs of the 10th Mountain Division 'had beer coming out of their ears, but not too many complaints'.[406] In fact, the army even requisitioned overseas breweries – worked by civilians – to help ensure a steady supply of beer to its soldiers.[407]

In any event, for the GIs – comparatively well-paid, free from the legal and domestic constraints of home, and often let loose in shattered societies with a historic capacity for the manufacture of huge quantities of all kinds of unfamiliar alcohol – the impact of drink on discipline and health could be alarming. As army sources ruefully noted: 'raw Calvados in Normandy and new schnapps in the Saar Basin ... were upwards of 140 proof. Such liquor was successfully used by the troops as fluid for cigarette lighters.'[408] The whole of continental Europe, in Peter Schrijvers's memorable phrase, seemed to be 'the victim of a conspiracy of wets',[409] and the results were predictable. In one incident in Sicily in July 1943, an inebriated GI even shot and killed the Catholic chaplain of the 30th Infantry Regiment.[410] Nor did it help matters that captured stockpiles of booze were often among the spoils of war. After the fall of Cherbourg in June 1944, Lieutenant General Omar Bradley announced that 'every soldier in Normandy would eventually receive two bottles of wine and three of liquor'. Nevertheless, Cherbourg's American liberators promptly indulged in 'one big drunk' to the accompaniment of celebratory firing and explosions.[411] It was to prevent such excesses that the custody and distribution of such plunder was given to the Quartermaster Corps, whereas the issue of hard liquors 'such as cognacs and whiskies' was entrusted to the various components of the Medical Department.[412] Under this regime, and mindful of 'his promise to give them a party in celebration' of the occasion, in March 1945 Eisenhower authorised the issue of champagne and wine to the soldiers of every American division as they crossed the Rhine.[413] However, such liberality did nothing to check the plague of overindulgence or its consequences. To prevent drunken fatalities, all live ammunition was collected in Lester Atwell's battalion before the news of Germany's surrender could even be announced.[414] Furthermore, alcohol was an identifiable factor in more than one-third of all reported rapes in France and Germany and, according to army medical sources, in the months from October 1944 to June 1945 more GIs died in the ETO due to alcohol poisoning than to 'acute communicable disease'.[415]

While recovering bodies on the stricken carrier *Franklin*, Chaplain Joseph T. O'Callahan was relieved to find that the ship's doctor took a pragmatic view of the use of medicinal whisky.[416] However, in the wartime navy, and as in the years of Prohibition, tight restrictions on alcohol served to encourage racketeering, petty criminality and bootlegging. In January 1944, James J. Fahey noted how bottled beer was available to sailors on the island of Espiritu Santo, and how the ten-cent chits needed for their purchase could change hands for up to five dollars.[417] A year later, at Mindoro in the Philippines, whisky was available from nearby soldiers at $17 a pint.[418] Soon after, and while engaged in a working party unloading cases of beer from a supply ship, Fahey noticed how a considerable number of cases found their way to other vessels, and how: 'Some of the men broke into the beer and [felt] pretty good.' After completing their task, Fahey's shipmates were rewarded with still more beer.[419] John Kempton, who served in the Pacific, remembered a similar 'Army mistake of having sailors guard 100k cases of beer',[420] and how 'two-can beer parties were always a big hit' on his small submarine chaser. Furthermore, Kempton noted that 'hard liquor' could be bought from island airfields, pilots flying it in for huge profits, or obtained by other means. Besides 'jungle juice' – 'alcohol put into a coconut ... till it was ripe to drink' – one particular form of moonshine, 'Pink Lady', made a tolerable beverage when strained 'thru some homemade bread' and mixed with fruit juice. Alternatively: 'Other sources of "good" alcohol [were the] pharmacist mate, torpe-domen, quartermasters etc.'[421] Even in the 'wetter' US Army, traditional skills and wiles honed in the Prohibition era also meant that a great deal of effort went into subverting regulations. As noted in Chapter Three, supplies of communion wine were liable to be intercepted along the supply chain. Chaplain Francis L. Sampson was also vexed to discover a different scam when a Dutch priest informed him that he had been asked for communion wine on numerous occasions over the space of two days, each request purportedly coming from Sampson himself. As Sampson reflected, 'I began to wonder how many priests throughout Normandy and Holland (and probably England too) had been prevailed upon to part with their wine on the same pretext.'[422] Bootlegging also thrived among GIs in Europe, despite their easier access to better-quality alcohol. Ernie Pyle observed that, after Allied troops had drunk Naples dry, 'there was considerable bootlegging of very dangerous booze'; and Lester Atwell's companions, at least, enjoyed the delights of 'kickapoo juice' on the front line in Germany.[423]

However serious, it should not be assumed that the military's drinking problem was universal. As a post-war survey of 'veterans enrolled as students at Princeton University' demonstrated, the 57.2 per cent who reported 'an increased proneness to indulgence in alcoholic drinking as a consequence of their wartime experiences' represented 'a majority trend' rather than a wholesale descent into alcoholism.[424] As Gordon Bennett Robertson acknowledged, even aviators could refuse their post-mission shots of whisky and many of his fellow flyers 'drank little or not at all except at an infrequent party'.[425] One salutary success for the wartime 'drys' came in 1944, when America's top-scoring fighter ace, Major Richard I. Bong, declined 'a case of Scotch' from Eddie Rickenbacker after exceeding Rickenbacker's tally of kills from World War I. According to *The Christian Century*: 'He expressed a preference for soft drinks, and got them.'[426] Still, amidst a drinking culture that could wildly diverge from strict civilian standards, and which often showed signs of spiralling out of control, it was easy for military chaplains to feel compromised by their situation. On the basis of a survey of over six hundred GIs, in August 1943 Chaplain Edgar Ackerman sought to assure the readers of *The Christian Advocate* that 'The Drinking Problem in the Army' was greatly exaggerated.[427] Whether Ackerman's case – 'that it all balances out' – was convincing or not, the Office of the Chief of Chaplains was careful not to formally condone even the sale of 3.2 per cent beer in army exchanges, and was greatly perturbed when certain breweries tried to associate their products with chaplaincy work.[428] Israel Yost underlined the dilemma of the 'dry' chaplain when he wrote:

> When offered a taste of Vermouth wine, I took a sip and pronounced it terrible. It became my policy to always taste any new alcoholic beverage offered me, and then declare I did not like it. In this way I avoided being considered prissy and also let it be known that I was not a drinking man.[429]

However, and at the opposite end of the spectrum, it seems likely that certain chaplains broke the regulations themselves. While O'Callahan could be forgiven his medicinal tipple on the devastated *Franklin*, Frederick William Meehling acknowledged a drinking problem among Catholic chaplains in the pre-war navy; his predecessor on the *Colorado* was even dismissed from the service after falling off the gangplank while inebriated.[430]

Although the use of tobacco did not excite the same passions as the use and abuse of alcohol, on scriptural grounds (notably 1 Corinthians 6: 19–20, 'What? know ye not that your body is the temple of the Holy Ghost') smoking was still viewed with disapproval by more conservative Protestants, to say nothing of sectarian groups such as Mormons, Jehovah's Witnesses and Seventh-Day Adventists. In 1935, 62.1 per cent of American adults were non-smokers, a proportion that had fallen abruptly to 51 per cent a decade later, when almost three-quarters of American men were self-confessed smokers.[431] In the intervening years, non-smokers had certainly been put under enormous strain in the military context. While tobacco farmers were deemed essential workers in World War II, and were thus exempted from the draft, service life became essentially tobacco-dependent, with prodigious quantities of cigarettes being provided by civilian well-wishers, doled out by Red Cross workers and even distributed with field rations.[432] In this respect, the American military seems to have played an important part in forging 'a nation of smokers', absorbing as much as 30 per cent of wartime cigarette production.[433] However great the temptations of nicotine, wider drug abuse was also an identifiable problem, especially in Asia and the Pacific. In India, recreational drugs were so readily available that it was feared by Harry J. Anslinger, the commissioner of the Federal Bureau of Narcotics, that the number of America's drug addicts would soar after the war.[434] Although the military took a hard line against such drug abuse, and the problem never became epidemic even in the CBI,[435] addiction could be an inescapable consequence of military service. For example, the treatment of wounds, injuries and illness could have unhealthy side-effects, a case in point being that of Barney Ross, a former boxing star and decorated war hero, who became an addict after receiving a cocktail of drugs for malaria and shock in the Pacific.[436] In order to overcome fatigue, it is estimated that one in ten GIs took amphetamines during the course of the war, with as many as 180 million Benzedrine tablets being obtained from the British, despite official reservations about their use in the US Army. The long-term effects of their availability seems to have been reflected in statistics from 1947, which indicated that '25 per cent of all men in army stockades were heavy and chronic users'.[437]

Pilfering and plundering

A much bigger problem was a basic disregard for public and private property, one that belied Ernie Pyle's folksy patter praising the 'American doughboy's fundamental honesty' during the Sicilian campaign, when 'the various Army headquarters were flooded with Sicilians bearing penciled notes written on everything from toilet paper to the backs of envelopes saying, "I owe you for one mule taken for the U.S. Army".[438] Arguably, the endemic problem of wholesale theft was an inevitable corollary of the very nature of service life, an existence that afforded little sense of private ownership and was often lavishly supported by the impersonal agency of the state. As Samuel Hynes described the situation, even from an officer's perspective:

> Stealing was not, of course, called *stealing*; you called it *scrounging*, and nobody had any qualms about doing it. In a world where everything belonged to the government, nothing belonged to anybody, and we quickly lost our back-home sense of the inviolability of personal property. If an object was portable and no one was guarding it, it was as much yours as anybody else's.[439]

In combination with criminal elements and tendencies imported from civilian life, such attitudes inevitably served as powerful stimuli to pilfering, profiteering and black-market activity on an enormous scale, especially in Europe and North Africa. The city of Naples alone, 'site of the vast Army depots that constituted Peninsula Base Section', supported 'a whole illicit economy of vast proportions', with huge quantities of food, clothing, fuel and other military supplies finding their way into civilian hands.[440]

However, such depredations did not stop with stockpiled military property, for the blasted landscapes and dislocated societies of continental Europe also offered ample scope for straightforward looting. It is, indeed, one of the ironies of the American experience of World War II that troops supplied with so much should have taken so freely, and not only in Germany. As one American army chaplain later wrote:

> The U.S. soldier ... pillaged not only shot-up German towns, but French, Dutch and Belgian also. Often he was quartered in a private home, a public building, a chateau, a castle. He promptly mailed home the contents of the building – silver, china, pictures, linen, ornaments, anything not too large to go into a mail sack. He proved to be an adept at stealing, and strangely

enough did not seem to regard it as stealing. Officers and nurses were as guilty as enlisted men, perhaps worse. Their opportunities were often greater.[441]

Although their Soviet and British allies did the same – the former on a colossal and licensed scale – they at least had the partial excuse of shattered societies of their own to rebuild.[442] In fact, the British appear to have been shocked by the brazenness of American conduct, *The Christian Century* noting in May 1945 a report in the British press that American officers had systematically looted a German hotel, behaving 'like seventeenth century mercenaries' and disregarding the 'cynicism about the Allies and their intentions' that such conduct was likely to breed.[443] Although the source in question blamed *Stars and Stripes* for its 'violent propaganda', the naming of the British-led attack across the Rhine in March 1945 – Operation Plunder – at least spoke of a shared thirst for vengeance.[444]

As far as the Americans were concerned, there was certainly a strong element of retribution in the robbing of German civilians as well as POWs. Apart from the settling of more personal scores, and as a post-war report on military offenders in the ETO pointed out, the roots of such conduct could be seen in the army's own orientation programme, which cultivated 'hatred towards the Germans' and thus 'made it easy for the soldier to justify looting, assault, burglary, robbery and even rape'.[445] However, it must be re-emphasised that GIs succumbed to similar temptations even among liberated populations. In the words of a post-war report on the administration of military justice in the ETO:

> Pillaging and looting in conquered and liberated countries were offenses of frequent occurrence and constituted a special disciplinary problem. Offenses ranged from simple acquisition of a mattress for added comfort to armed and violent robberies.... In the opinion of some judge advocates, leniency and unwillingness to interfere on the part of some commanding officers contributed in important measure to the large number of instances of pillaging, looting and allied offenses.[446]

As this report hinted, the motives for this conduct were many – a desire for souvenirs, for trophies, for things that might prove useful as well as profitable.[447] However, it is hard to escape the impression that this wave of plundering, all of which was technically forbidden under one or other of the Articles of War,[448] was also fuelled by the collective trauma of the Great Depression and by the uncertain prospects for post-war prosperity, another symptom of the insecurity that led many GIs to send purloined items of army property – including rations – home to their families.[449]

All too often, this tendency to treat war-ravaged Europe as 'a giant flea market full of bargains'[450] took a turn towards the surreal, and even the sacrilegious. As Lester Atwell described the looting habits of his battalion in forward areas:

Usually, leaving a town, the infantrymen were loaded down with bottles of wine, books they could not read, clocks, statuettes, pictures. They'd carry them along, and then as the hike grew lengthy, they'd begin to drop them. For miles in the snow on the sides of the road, you'd see a trail of books, ornaments, carving sets and little clocks. In the next town, the looting would start up all over again. Generally, the officers were just as avid and as guilty as the men.[451]

This looting was often violent, uncontrolled and indiscriminate. As Atwell went on:

Advance housing parties made hay while waiting for the battalion to arrive; then the line-company boys poured through the houses, working excitedly in teams, ripping out drawers and scattering the contents on the floor, smashing locked chests with the butts of their rifles, overturning tables and bookcases. By law, men were allowed to take as souvenirs only captured German army equipment, but frequently, with a superior officer's connivance and signature, chests of silverware were sent home, silver dishes, banquet cloths, mother-of-pearl opera glasses, cameras, jewellery, ancient dress sabers – everything from paintings to thimbles – and this while we were still in Allied territory.[452]

In keeping with such scenes, in the wake of its capture in March 1945 Atwell remembered that the German city of Koblenz had 'the chaotic air of a drunken, end-of-the-world carnival.'[453] Even churches and church institutions could not escape this apocalyptic free-for-all. In Koblenz, Atwell and his companions made themselves at home in a hospital run by Dominican nuns, the mother superior's office affording 'vast relaxation' and a venue in which to sample abandoned foodstuffs and champagne.[454] However, and as Audie Murphy remembered, the sacrilegious treatment of ecclesiastical artefacts could stir unease, a heated argument erupting when one of his comrades tried to illuminate a cave on the banks of the Volturno river with what appeared to be an altar candle.[455] Similarly, in June 1944, near Omaha Beach, a pair of Alabamian engineers made an inauspicious start to the liberation of France by robbing the poor box of the parish church of St Laurent, much to the fury of its *curé*.[456] However, such problems clearly persisted and, in February 1945, 'cases of looting of churches in the European Theater' were being brought to the attention of George C. Marshall by the ever-vigilant Bishop John F. O'Hara, who protested that a Catholic mother had walked into St Patrick's Cathedral in New York carrying 'a chalice sent home by her son.'[457]

The problem of evil

Amidst the death, destruction and moral degradation of the bloodiest war in history, it was inevitable that some Americans in uniform should consider the problem of evil and question their faith accordingly. Although American aviators were seldom in a position where they could contemplate the effect of their missions at close hand, those caught up in the ground war were often confronted by the impact of the conflict upon the most innocent civilians. In this regard, the body of a little girl killed in an artillery duel in northern Italy proved overwhelming for John W. Dewey of the 86th Mountain Infantry Regiment:

> At the sight of her broken, lifeless figure, I was reminded of my seven-year-old sister. I cried until tears would not come anymore. I carefully picked the child up in my arms and carried her to the rear, where Graves Registration could locate her family and she could be given a decent burial.[458]

Faced with the brute realities of war, another soldier of the 10th Mountain Division, John T. Bassett, found that the sight of a crucifix in a ruined Italian cathedral stirred only symptoms of spiritual revolt at Easter 1945:

> Oh well, what the hell difference did it make anyway? So Jesus Christ was resurrected from his tomb and rose again briefly alive and then entered his Father's Kingdom. I had heard the story from the time of my childhood.... 'So, anyway, God, I know you are up there,' I said softly, 'and I know you see me and that you hear me, and I know you believe me: but I do not believe you really care about us. There have always been wars, and the Bible says there will always be wars. So, God, I ask you: do I really need to be forgiven?'[459]

For William B. Hanford, a forward artillery observer in the ETO, the theological implications of war seemed all too obvious: 'God could have nothing to do with this stupid war if he was a just God, I decided. And if he was not *just*, then why did all those religious folks worship him?'[460] Such protests could be more than simply personal, however. Sheltering from German air attack in an Icelandic ditch in October 1942, Methodist army chaplain Clyde E. Kimball was surprised to find himself berated by a frightened officer, '"You religious men are to blame for all this!", he claimed, '"Your religion has failed to compel people to be good!"' Kimball chose to construe this as: 'The remark of a quite naturally scared man who admitted he'd never been among those who tried to help religious work.'[461] Eugene Sledge was struck by the silent but eloquent reaction of a bedraggled marine to a 'muddy little communion service' amidst the misery of the Okinawan campaign of 1945:

> He watched the chaplain with an expression of skepticism that seemed to ask, 'What's the use of all that? Is it gonna keep them guys from gettin' hit?' That face was so weary but so expressive that I knew he, like all of us, couldn't help but have doubts about his God in the presence of constant shock and suffering. Why did it go on and on?[462]

Furthermore, and although various indicators seem to show that the experience of war generally strengthened personal faith, a slide into protest atheism was always a possibility. Schuyler Jackson, a former college student who served as a sergeant with the 502nd Parachute Infantry Regiment in the ETO, remembered that:

> I was never religious and I lost any feeling for it [in Normandy]. During a break I was sitting with a guy whose brother was a priest and his sister a nun. He was always talking up religion. He never cursed and his one sin was he chased women without a pause. He took his Bible out and told me, 'This is what saved us.' The words were no sooner out of his mouth [when] a treeburst shell snapped his neck. I've been an atheist since then.[463]

Likewise, Robert Koloski, a Catholic medic who was wounded at Monte Cassino, found that in the long term his faith cracked under the pressure of his wartime experiences:

> After the war ... I decided that Christianity had nothing going for it as far as I was concerned. Let's face it, the Germans had a belt buckle with *Gott Mit Uns* on it, so if He was with them, and also with us, what the heck was going on? I won't say I was irreligious in any sense during the war but certainly afterwards. I mean, it just doesn't make sense.[464]

Fully aware of these problems, *The Link* published explanatory articles on questions such as 'Why Doesn't God Stop War?', and 'Why Doesn't God Fight?' The first of these stressed human sinfulness as the basic cause of the war, while the second emphasised that the Allies did not have a monopoly of right on their side, and that divine love and mercy were often to be felt amidst pain and suffering.[465] In any case, and whatever the reception may have been to these ventures into theodicy, most veterans seem to have emerged out of the maelstrom of war more grateful for their own survival than perplexed by wider philosophical and theological issues. As John O. Brixey, who served with the 11th Infantry Regiment, said of his own experiences in the ETO:

> I learned in the throes of battle to appreciate life very deeply. And I learned that you didn't have it so bad when you looked about you and you saw men wounded without a leg or an arm, or a head, and you still had all parts of your body. You realize the blessing that you had for each moment, and you lived each moment to its end ... as I look back at the combat that I experienced, I would never want to change anything that happened. I can look back and see about eleven instances when I could have been killed [and] that has made me a more aware person of the sovereignty of God, and that He has created Good and that He has created evil. He is the creator of all things and we, as human beings, need to remember He is the only one that's big enough to be God.[466]

Besides, the liberation of the concentration camps undoubtedly served to give the war in Europe much greater moral clarity and purpose, with Allied propaganda announcing to their former inmates: 'Alleluia! The Lord is victorious, and the spirit of unrighteousness has been reduced to dust and ashes!'[467] As Eisenhower pronounced at Ohrdruf in April 1945: 'We are told that the American soldier does not know what he is fighting for. Now at least he will know what he is fighting against.'[468] Decades later, even Paul Fussell could agree that:

> As the war ignominiously petered out, the troops knew more about the enemy than they had known when, early on, they had sneered or giggled at the word *crusade*. They had seen and smelled the death camps, and now they were able to realize that all along they had been engaged in something more than a mere negative destruction of German military power. They had been fighting and suffering for something positive, the sacredness of life itself.... Hardly any boy infantryman started his career as a moralist, but after the camps, a moral attitude was rampant and there was no disagreement on the main point.... The boys' explosive little tour in France had been a crusade after all.[469]

At the sickening spectacles of Ohrdruf, Nordhausen, Dachau and Buchenwald, even those with strong grounds to question the moral pretensions of the United States could acknowledge its superiority over the Third Reich. As Staff Sergeant Willard Moore of the 3438th Quartermaster Truck Company, an African American GI, put it:

> I think the only man ever to call me an American, and say it like I was as good as any American he was likely to find, was a little Jewish man. We took our trucks to get them out of the concentration camps.... My eyes never saw a worse sight in my life than these people, dead and dying, and I may never understand how God could let any man do that kind of evil and ugliness to his fellow man.... I am ashamed to say I was afraid to touch him but he hugged me like nobody ever hugged me in my life.... I would like to think this man liked me for being a good Christian, but I think he loved me for being an American.[470]

In combination with sheer war weariness and a well-honed hatred of the Japanese, this growing conviction of the utter depravity of the Axis powers helped to condition responses in the services to the use of the atom bomb a few months later. Significantly, and although the use of the atom bomb was widely condemned by civilian churchmen, both Protestant and Catholic,[471] and was branded an 'inhuman and reckless act' by *The Christian Century*,[472] such sentiment seems to have been rarer among the public at large. One AIPO poll showed that, on 8 August 1945, 85 per cent of Americans approved of the use of the atom bomb against Japanese cities, with only 10 per cent expressing their disapproval.[473] A month later, a further survey by the National Opinion Research Center found that 67 per cent of Americans still favoured the atomic destruction of Japanese cities, with only 27 per cent preferring their use against uninhabited targets.[474] Although Admiral William D. Leahy, chief of staff to presidents Roosevelt and Truman, proved a notable exception to this rule,[475] support for the atom bomb seems to have been even stronger among the nation's armed forces.[476] A sample of twenty-six veterans who served in or with the 1st Marine Division, in capacities ranging from pharmacist's mate to pioneer sergeant, shows that relief and elation at the surrender of Japan was universal and that none of them had any qualms about the use of the bomb at the time;[477] furthermore, and despite the passage of decades, only two veterans were even inclined to qualify their original enthusiasm. In fact, a much greater source of regret was that it had not been used sooner and more widely. As Richard E. Milana trenchantly put it, 'to[o] bad we were not ready to drop a few on all German cities as well'.[478]

Such feelings were not only held by Pacific veterans who would have been in the vanguard of operations against the Japanese home islands, but were shared by those earmarked to join the invasion from the ETO. In Paul Fussell's trenchant essay 'Thank God for the Atom Bomb' (1981), he recalled the reaction to the news of the atom bomb among the men of the 45th Infantry Division, which was then at a staging area near Rheims awaiting transfer to the Pacific:

> When the atom bombs were dropped and news began to circulate that 'Operation Olympic' would not, after all, be necessary … for all the practiced phlegm of our tough façades we broke down and cried with relief and joy. We were going to live. We were going to grow to adulthood after all. The killing was all going to be over, and peace was actually going to be the state of things.[479]

As for gainsayers, Fussell seethed that: 'The future scholar-critic who writes *The History of Canting in the Twentieth Century* will find much to study and interpret in the utterances of those who dilate on the special wickedness of the A-bomb-droppers'.[480] Likewise, and fresh from the abundant perils of the European war, John O. Brixey was on a pre-Pacific furlough in the United States when news of Japan's surrender came through:

> The 11th Infantry Regiment, which I was in, [was] scheduled for the invasion of Japan, with other units. We had been given a thirty-day furlough, and I was sitting at home, on the farm, at Wewoka, Oklahoma … I felt great joy and great relief that the war had ended. And I realized that many people lost their lives in dropping that bomb, but I wouldn't change one thing from how that happened. Because I knew we were slated for the invasion of Japan, and I had a premonition that I was not coming back.[481]

Given the prevalence of such attitudes, and the pervasive, all-consuming desire to go home, even the response of critical chaplains was shaded with ambiguity. In Paris, for example, Episcopalian chaplain John U. Harris announced in the American pro-cathedral that, 'The atomic bomb infringes into the realm of God's prerogative', before conceding that its destructive force might yet serve as a spur for unity among Christians in the post-war world.[482] Likewise, attempts by *The Link* to stir debate on the atom bomb were muted and belated, commencing in January 1946 with an article and recommended 'Topic Talk' entitled 'The Atomic Bomb'. Here, navy chaplain Paul C. Allen, a Northern Baptist, posed the question: 'Should the formula be destroyed?' Ultimately, he was against this course of action, maintaining that, 'We cannot build walls against ideas' and urging instead the need for Christian stewardship of nuclear technology.[483] Given its different readership, *The Chaplain* began its ruminations as early as October 1945,[484] by the end of the year adopting a position of pragmatic acceptance.[485] Even for those chaplains who felt distinctly uneasy at the nuclear annihilation of Hiroshima and Nagasaki, the ambient mood seems to have been one of resignation. As Israel Yost reasoned, and despite his ministry to Japanese American soldiers throughout the Italian campaign: 'Everyone is praising the atom bomb; it makes me shudder! Of course it will save American lives, but what a thing to be set loose on the world! But all of war is inhumane, unreasonable, and unchristian.'[486] In a similar vein, and having celebrated the impending capitulation of Japan on Okinawa on 10 August 1945, a date he described as 'the happiest day of our lives',[487] James J. Fahey visited Hiroshima the following autumn. After touring the devastated city, he fell into conversation with a survivor who had lived in the United States and who protested that 'the bomb never should have been dropped on Hiroshima because it did not help the war effort'. A normally thorough and articulate diarist, Fahey made no record of his response.[488] For his part, and while recognising the manifold evils attendant on war, former navy lieutenant Jack DeKorne, who served in the Pacific on board the light cruiser *Atlanta*, had no regrets about the nature of Allied victory in World War II, or the part he played in it:

> There is no war that is good. No war is good for anybody, even the people who are victorious loose [sic] something.... 'War is hell'.... But if you look past that, I felt, and still do feel good about what we did.... If the other side had won ... this world would be a totally, totally different place. It would be different in how we would even be able to believe [in] or serve Christ.... Civil liberties would be totally changed. So I feel very good about World War 2 in spite of all the people who lost their life [sic] ... and the devastation that occurred because of it.[489]

Prodigal sons

Asked to consider the 'Effect of Service in the European Theater on the Moral and Religious Life of Army Personnel', American chaplains in the ETO found it impossible to reach a consensus; in fact, senior chaplains returned some very different verdicts:

> The opinions of chaplains on the effect of service in the European Theater on the religious and moral life of military personnel follows almost exactly a normal curve: 12% of the chaplains interviewed believe that such service helped greatly, 28% that it helped somewhat, 28% that it left the religious and moral life of personnel essentially unchanged, 20% that it impaired it somewhat, and 12% that it impaired it greatly.[490]

Among the optimists, Hamilton H. Kellogg, the Episcopalian senior chaplain of First Army, opined that: 'Service in the European Theater has helped somewhat: It has shown them that religion is a twenty four hours per day, seven day per week matter, not merely a Sunday affair.'[491] In contrast, Chaplain Richard A. Risser of the Presbyterian Church (USA), who served with the 9th Armored Division, wrote:

> I should say that service in the European Theater has somewhat impaired the moral and religious life of military personnel. The long separation from home and family finally becomes too much for some of the men, and they break morally. With others, this same separation deepens their spiritual life, but this does not happen too often. The presence of death in combat has helped still others to realize their own need, and thus deepened their religious life. But by and large, the long separation from home, combined with the ever present temptations which follow in the wake of large bodies of men, makes inroads on the moral and spiritual life of the troops.[492]

Significantly, chaplains in the continental United States, or 'Zone of the Interior', tended to be 'more pessimistic' in their assessments of the moral and religious impact of the war. However, when viewed in aggregate, the evidence led to some important inferences:

a. Service in the European Theater generally confirmed men in the religious and moral state in which they entered upon overseas duty.
b. Conversions and lapses tended to cancel each other out. This left the total situation practically unchanged, except for the generally negative effect of social factors implicit in overseas military service, such as separation from the sanctions of home, disruption of habitual religious practices, and the coarsening effect of living in an almost exclusively masculine world.

Furthermore, a marked bifurcation between faith and morals seemed to have emerged that would have been unsustainable in a civilian context:

c. Differentiating between religion and morals, there was an increased awareness of God born of peril and a greater moral obtuseness as a result of the multiplied destructiveness of mechanized and airborne war.[493]

Given the countless moral pitfalls that World War II and its aftermath had strewn in his path, it is hardly surprising that many religious commentators took a decidedly pessimistic view of the moral condition of the victorious GI. Significantly, a year after the end of the war in Europe, this seemed to have gone from bad to worse. Hence, after General Joseph T. McNarney became commander of American forces in the ETO at the end of 1945, a very public attempt was made to tighten discipline. As McNarney stated to a press conference in April 1946, the problem was reflected in the 'participation of personnel in black market activities, by drunkenness, and by the high rates of venereal disease, automobile accidents and absence without leave that prevailed in the command'.[494] However, among the most trenchant critics of the American soldier was a former army chaplain, Renwick C. Kennedy, who published a stinging critique of 'The Conqueror' in *The Christian Century* a week before McNarney's press conference:

> Taking him by & large, making all the allowances for him that you can, he is more than a little pathetic.... He is not very clear in his own mind about why he fought, nor about what his victory means. As a matter of fact, he is not much interested in such matters.... His interests are more primitive. They are chiefly three: (1) to find a German woman and sleep with her; (2) to buy or steal a bottle of cognac and get stinking drunk ... (3) to go home.[495]

Kennedy went on:

> There he stands in his bulging clothes, fat, overfed, lonely, a bit wistful, seeing little, understanding less – the Conqueror, with a chocolate bar in one pocket and a package of cigarettes in the other ... the chocolate bar and the cigarettes are about all that he, the Conqueror, has to give to the conquered.[496]

Weighing his merits and demerits, Kennedy maintained that:

> The average American in Europe was not a bad guy.... He fought bravely. He died by the thousands. He was generous to both Allied and enemy people with whatever he and the army had. Yet he was a failure as a propaganda agent for democracy, for the American way of life and for himself as an individual.[497]

A major problem in this regard was the sheer superciliousness of the American soldier:

> Unconsciously he assumed the master-race, superman idea. It is incredible how naïve and stupid he often was, though he never knew it: men judging

whole populations by the few harlots, drunks and black marketers they met.... They did not learn much ... they did not feel there was much to be learned.... It never occurred to them that many Englishmen, Frenchmen and Germans soon came to look upon them as uncouth barbarians.[498]

In sum, Kennedy concluded:

The conduct of the average soldier ... was at the least noisy and boisterous. At the worst it was criminal. The average was odious and disgusting.... The army did little to control the conduct of its soldiers.... But the individual soldier must bear most of the blame. He lacked the character and pride to make a good showing for himself, his army and his country.[499]

Such opinions, and the fears that they raised, were not confined to Chaplain Kennedy, a Reformed Presbyterian, but were felt across the religious spectrum. As early as August 1944, *The Link* published a timely prayer for right conduct in foreign lands, including such petitions as:

Make us messengers of Thy truth and bearers of Thy blessings. May we work as Thy helpers, bringing kindness and sympathy, courage and love to those who know loneliness, loss and defeat ... May our words and deeds be valiant examples of good will and brotherliness. May we do our full share to make a clean world and a good world.[500]

Not trusting to the power of prayer alone, or even to the sacred character of the Eternal City, in 1944 Archbishop Spellman had lobbied hard to ensure that the presence of Allied troops actually stationed in Rome was kept to a minimum, and that visiting troops were 'quartered outside the city in rest camps established for that purpose'.[501] Furthermore, and mindful of the nature and effects of Allied conduct on the ground, Spellman threw his weight behind the Italian civil authorities in order to ameliorate the numerous problems of liberation and Allied military government.[502] The conduct of GIs in Italy was not only an issue for Catholic churchmen, however. In January 1945 *The Link* published an anguished letter by Corporal Rolla M. Varndell, who deplored Allied behaviour in the war-torn peninsula and warned of its possible repercussions. As Varndell saw it: 'Instead of many of the soldiers acting as Christian gentlemen, worthy of the great nations whose uniforms they wore, they tried to show their superiority over a conquered people ... But who cared? They were only dagoes'.[503] Allied soldiers distinguished themselves by their reckless driving and their abuse of Italian wine and Italian women:

[Italians] drink regularly, but don't get drunken. The soldier, however, didn't know when to stop and in many cases became a spectacle, often causing fights and drunken brawls.... Self-respecting Italian girls, attending to their own business, were often accosted by spineless soldiers not able to control their passions. Disrespectful names were often hurled towards the Italian girls, and in many cases were understood by them.... But in the depth of this humiliation there remained a spark of pride ... unless the American and British peoples and soldiers redeem themselves by acting as Christian people should act, that flare will in time become a great conflagration.[504]

Even amidst the euphoria of liberation, identical fears of alienating the French were voiced by Orval Eugene Faubus. In Le Mans in August 1944 Faubus anticipated that: 'Our propensity to have things our own way, the oftentimes rude manners of some of our drinking GIs and officers, and the inclination of some of us to abuse their generosity, may somewhat cool their friendly attitude.'[505] In the restive and recalcitrant winter of 1945–46, and with the excitement of the liberation long passed, Faubus found himself posted to a camp near Rheims 'servicing transient troops being deployed home'. Here, he found that morale and discipline had all but collapsed: 'Everyone was bitching, including doctors and Red Cross personnel, even the chaplains.' Furthermore, the range and quality of Franco-American relations had suffered accordingly, with drunken parties – full of 'French prostitutes' – being thrown in the guardhouse.[506] By 1947, and as far as the Jewish chaplain Morris N. Kertzer could tell, through its sins of omission and commission at all levels the US Army had all but succeeded in alienating the very population it had largely liberated three years earlier:

Observers returning from France have pointed out that the French saw us at our worst. Tired, homesick men, living on the edge of physical annihilation, are not the best ambassadors of good will. But intelligent handling of the problem could have prevented the disastrous chasm that finally developed between us. Many military men did not see the value of good relations, of pleasing the French in any way. Despite instructions from the High Command, they persisted in the attitude that 'These Frogs should thank God we kicked the Nazis out and gave their country back to them. We weren't sent here to entertain them.' One found it hard to explain that we were fighting for victory and One World at the same time.[507]

In terms of explaining the complex and often paradoxical behaviour of frontline soldiers in particular, Audie Murphy pointed to the anomalies that were inherent in their situation, wryly reflecting that: 'In combat, we can destroy whole towns and be patted on the back for our efforts. But here in the rear, the theft of a chicken is a serious offense indeed.'[508] Likewise, and as noted at the beginning of this chapter, Chaplain Lawrence D. Graves remarked upon a tendency for the abnormal conditions of war and service life to gravely disrupt an individual's moral outlook, to lead many 'to think that they can reach out and stop the moral clock – sort of suspend all character development for the duration.'[509] Six months after Graves issued his warning in *The Link*, Chaplain Edgar

E. Ackerman warned how the combat soldier seemed particularly susceptible to moral failure:

> Temptation is great.… He has been in combat or moving about so rapidly in small villages that he has necessarily led a comparatively rugged exist-ence, away from all the normal relaxation and entertainment afforded by civilian life. Then suddenly he finds himself stationed in one of the larger cities. Here are good looking women, night clubs and all that goes with it; and so he goes 'overboard'.[510]

From a Jewish perspective, Chaplain Morris N. Kertzer agreed, asserting that moral decline was as much a facet of 'Foxhole Faith' as recourse to prayer:

> Most discussions of 'foxhole religion' center upon the soldier's relation to God. Little attention is paid to his moral code, which certainly underwent a severe trial in his European tour of duty. The hazards of war were not all at the battlefront. Our men were granted a kind of dispensation from the fourth [Sabbath-keeping], sixth [not killing], and eighth [not stealing] Commandments, and often let the seventh [not committing adultery] slip into the 'list of exceptions'. They attended chapel regularly, but their moral standards were far from puritanical … G.I. Joe tended to be careless in his morals, yet more pious in mood and general behaviour than he had been as a civilian.[511]

For chaplains, the dereliction of civilian moral norms was particularly evident when otherwise solid men succumbed to infidelity while overseas. In the same month that Chaplain Graves complained about the frequency of self-served moral dispensations, Chaplain Frederick W. Vogell rallied chaplains with the appeal 'Marital Infidelity – Hit It Hard!', averring that, while the sin was common enough in civilian life, 'in the armed forces it is of such proportions that one wonders where God's pure men are'. [512] In November 1945, and with the war over in Europe and in the Pacific, Chaplain Edgar E. Ackerman seemed to imply that the situation had worsened with the more sedentary nature of occupation duties, remarking that: 'Wherever troops have been stationed on foreign soil there has been a tendency among an alarming number to follow the practice of "shacking up". Particularly instructive was the case of a hitherto steadfast officer who had fallen in these circumstances:

> I heard of one young officer who had been overseas two years, who had been exceptionally model in his conduct and more than faithful to his wife. In the turn of events he was given an administrative position in one of the larger cities, and now he is living with some woman in quite open adultery. I don't know what inward, moral struggle took place before he 'fell', but his number is legion. We cannot always say of such that 'they never were any good', for by all the standards of normal peacetime living they were.[513]

From such evidence, it seems clear that, for a great many service personnel, their war experience was one in which loose living did not seem terminally incompatible with religious faith, where they negotiated a morally perilous landscape in which the sacred and the profane were often crazily intermingled. In Audie Murphy's 1949 memoir *To Hell and Back*, their predicament was captured in the figure of Snuffy Jones, a bibulous backwoodsman with a penchant for vivid and extempore hellfire preaching.[514] It was also reflected in Tex Ritter's 1948 hit 'The Deck of Cards', in which a GI, arrested for producing his playing cards in a North African church, cogently explains the rudiments of his faith by means of the Ace through to the Jack.[515] The wider context of personal faith enduring, despite a catalogue of moral hazards and lapses, seems to be illuminated by the case of the army's African American troops, who were widely regarded as a conspicuously religious element among GIs despite their unusually high rates of venereal disease.[516]

Although the war and its aftermath was marked by severe problems of readjustment and soaring divorce rates among veterans (as early as November 1944, 37 per cent of discharged veterans agreed that the war had changed them *only* for the worse, making them more nervous, irritable and self-centred),[517] it seems clear that the churches still had much to work with in the post-war years. As Chaplain Edgar E. Ackerman anticipated in November 1945: 'When we chaplains return to our civilian pastorates we must be prepared to become salvage companies in mending broken human relationships and morally broken-down personalities.'[518] Well before the end of the war, *The Link*, at least, was optimistic about the prospects for such reclamation. In June 1944 it published an account of how, after the presentation of a Purple Heart to the widow and child of a fallen pilot at Buckley Field, Colorado, soldiers had flocked to an army chapel to pray for 'a quiet and peaceful America', for 'all heroes and fathers who are fighting this war', and to 'go into battle on the side of God and righteousness'.[519]

Not that this would prove to be an easy process of rehabilitation in many cases. Russell Baldwin, a combat medic in the ETO, recalled that: 'I was blessed to come home a whole person – well, almost, 'cause I was pretty alcoholic. I needed help, I was unstable, very unstable.' However, and with the help of 'loving parents', 'good friends' and the medical profession, he eventually 'came through it real well', becoming a member of the Methodist Church and a YMCA worker with 'troubled youth'.[520] Likewise, Wayne Sisk, formerly of the now legendary E Company, 506th Parachute Infantry Regiment, wrote in 1991 of how a drunken and guilt-ridden return culminated in his ordination as a Freewill Baptist minister in 1949: 'My career after the war was trying to drink away the truckload of Krauts that I stopped in Holland and the die-hard Nazi that I went up into the Bavarian Alps and killed', he maintained. Then, however, came a moment of epiphany:

[M]y sister's little daughter, four-years-old, came into my bedroom (I was too unbearable to the rest of the family, either hung over or drunk) and she told me that Jesus loved me and she loved me and if I would repent God would forgive me.... That little girl got to me. I put her out of my room, told her to go to her Mommy. There and then I bowed my head on my Mother's old bed and repented and God forgave me for the war and all the other bad things I had done down through the years.... I haven't whipped but one man since and he needed it.[521]

Fifty-five years after the end of World War II, a questionnaire sent to 'a random national sample of 7,500 World War II veterans' by Brian and Craig S. Wansink revealed that 'religious behavior was high' among the 1,123 respondents. More than half a century after the war, 'approximately 69.1% were church members, attending church 3.1 times per month'.[522] Significantly, and in an interesting reflection of the enduring effects of 'foxhole religion', especially on those who were identified as most susceptible to it by the Social Science Research Council in 1949, the Wansinks' survey established that those veterans who had experienced 'heavy combat' and who viewed their military experience in negative terms were much more likely to attend church than those who saw their military experiences more positively.[523] In short, the Wansinks' findings suggest that the return-to-church sentiments expressed by thousands of GIs in the ETO in April 1945 were largely realised in the course of later life and that, for a combination of reasons, the religious milieu of the post-war United States seems to have been well-adapted to reabsorb them.

Although this lies outside the chronological scope of the present study, it is worth suggesting some reasons why this was so, besides the likely effects of post-war prosperity, a return to domesticity and the ordinary implications of the life cycle. First, these men were returning, however damaged and derailed, from what was generally regarded to have been a just war that had ended in victory over the forces of fascism, militarism and heathen darkness in Europe and in Asia. Second, such was the scale and duration of America's military mobilisation that they generally returned to churches to which their problems were familiar, a situation helped by the relatively recent experience of World War I and by the unprecedented number of former chaplains among their priests and ministers. Third, the parable and paradigm of the prodigal son – especially apt for this GI generation – was deeply embedded in America's Christian psyche, a cultural trope that sanctioned and encouraged a welcoming reception of the wayward on their chastened return to home and hearth. Fourth, another cultural factor was the historic and defining influence of Arminian soteriology over the greater part of Anglophone Protestantism, a fact which meant that, as in earlier generations, awakened and penitent veterans could readily seek divine mercy and salvation. Fifth, in the immediate post-war years this traditional invitation to individual repentance (in contrast to the collectivism of the social gospel, whose attractions were muted by the benefits that veterans received by virtue of the GI Bill) was extended and amplified by a new, attractive and conciliatory form of evangelicalism represented by the young Billy Graham, a force that by the late 1950s had openly chosen collaboration rather than confrontation with more liberal elements in the Protestant churches. Sixth, Roman Catholicism, another influential and expansive force in post-war American society and religion, and a church that counted former soldiers (such as St Francis of Assisi and St Ignatius Loyola) among some of its premier saints, was not only more assured of its place in national life because of the war but also offered forgiveness and reintegration to its returning prodigals through the theology and mechanisms of sacramental confession. Seventh, and lastly, Deborah Dash Moore has shown that the totality of the war experience served to strengthen American Jewish identity. Under the capacious umbrella of 'the Judeo-Christian tradition', Jewish GIs not only felt co-equal with their Christian comrades but also felt their common Jewish identity reinforced by the religious rights and privileges accorded to Protestants, Catholics and Jews alike by the American military.[524]

Conclusion

As noted in Chapter Three, the innate moral conservatism of American society meant that the moral norms and standards of military life were viewed with suspicion even in times of peace. However, in the context of the moral and physical dislocation of World War II, vast numbers of Americans were exposed to a greatly enlarged arena of moral temptation. There was, of course, much to be concerned about. Under these conditions, civilian religious patterns and norms were widely disrupted, ranging from Sunday observance to the maintenance of dietary laws and regulations. In institutional terms, liberal religious opinion could also be offended by the institutionalised racism of American military organisation. More generally, however, it was the prospect of killing that proved unsettling. Coming from a Christian (or Judaeo-Christian) society that normally deplored violence, and which had recoiled from the horrors of World War I, the prospect of killing proved both widely and deeply troubling for America's draftees and volunteers. While chaplains often had to confront this problem through an advocacy of just-war precepts, what is more striking in retrospect is the ease and rapidity with which these iron constraints were collectively cast aside in the cauldron of war – even with respect to enemy civilians. By 1945, and especially in the war against Japan, it was the enthusiasm and penchant for killing that chaplains found most worrying, and against which their example and arguments from the just-war tradition were often directed. Ultimately, the brute mathematics of killing led the great majority of veterans – not unreasonably, from their perspective – to contemplate atomic destruction with equanimity and even enthusiasm.

Besides the Sixth Commandment, other moral norms also became notable casualties of war. Despite the safeguards conferred by religious sensibility and international law, American military forces damaged or destroyed countless churches and sacred structures in Europe and in the Pacific, among them some of the most venerated sites in Christendom. In addition to stimulating an appetite for killing and destruction, the experience of wartime military service was morally corrosive in other respects. By common agreement, the language of the armed forces was generally shocking, being matched in its profanity only by its obscenity and creativity. While the colourful figure of George S. Patton provided a recurrent and uncomfortable reminder of this phenomenon, the myriad dislocations of war also presented an enlarged field of sexual opportunity. In this regard, and despite the recognition that was usually accorded to the claims of religion on the army and navy, the approach of the American military to prostitution and venereal disease was fundamentally pragmatic and even amoral, embracing as it did the distribution of contraceptives, prophylaxis kits, and even the furtive regulation of selected brothels. In sexual terms, a conspicuous appetite for pin-ups, and the indulgence that was usually shown to pornographic, or at least salacious, expressions of military art, again seemed to flaunt a prevailing disregard for civilian norms. However, this did not exhaust the prevailing catalogue of vice. In spite of various control mechanisms and standing regulations, drunkenness was widespread and gambling endemic, these problems complicated by the different positions of the churches towards alcohol and games of chance. Finally, in the military environment, and amidst the turmoil of war, the Eighth Commandment seems to have lost a good deal of its binding force – as the War and the Navy Departments, to say nothing of much of war-torn Europe, found to their cost.

In isolated cases, elements or all of the above could induce the loss of religious faith, especially for those incapable of finding an adequate theodicy. Nevertheless, and despite downbeat prognostications and evidence of lapse and backsliding on a massive scale, what is remarkable is how, in the longer term, the religious culture of the United States proved capable of sustaining the vast, collective aberration of war. Returning from what was overwhelmingly regarded as a just and necessary conflict (and, for the most part, with an increased sense of dependency on God, consciousness of personal guilt, and desire for religious fellowship), America's veterans returned to a religious culture that proved capable of absorbing them and which could extend to them, in a variety of different forms, a necessary sense of forgiveness, salvation and homecoming.

Conclusion

Tᴇɴ years after the end of World War II, the Jewish theologian and sociologist Will Herberg published *Protestant–Catholic–Jew*, a seminal study of religion in contemporary America. As Herberg saw it, and although there had been no federal census of religious bodies since 1936, there was every indication that organised religion was booming by the mid-1950s. 'That there has in recent years been an upswing of religion in the United States can hardly be doubted', he wrote, 'the evidence is diverse, converging, and unequivocal beyond all possibilities of error.'[1] With Protestantism, Catholicism and Judaism now functioning as 'equi-legitimate' expressions of American religion,[2] a prime indicator of national religious vitality was the pervasiveness of religious self-identification. When requested to state a religious preference, '95 per cent of the American people' *chose* to identify themselves as Protestants, Catholics or Jews; in other words, so Herberg explained, 'virtually the entire body of the American people, in every part of the country and in every section of society, regard themselves as belonging to some religious community.'[3] Nor did the irreligious – or simply reticent – pose any kind of threat to this strong religious consensus, for the dominant trend of religious belonging had 'led to the virtual disappearance of anti-religious prejudice'; as Herberg put it: 'The old-time "village atheist" is a thing of the past, a folk curiosity like the town crier.'[4]

However, the key indicator of what Herberg billed as 'The Contemporary Upswing in Religion' was the growing number of Americans who were now deemed to be church members. By 1953, they amounted to 59.5 per cent of the population, 'marking an all-time high in the nation's history.'[5] However, even this landmark statistic failed to do justice to the true vitality of American religiosity for, as Herberg stressed, 'considerably more Americans regard themselves as church members than the statistics of church affiliation would indicate'. Emphasising the lack of an obvious line of demarcation between church members and mere participants in church life, and taking into account the self-identification of the man or woman in the street, rather than formal church membership criteria or the adjudication of religious statisticians, Herberg declared that:

> About 70 to 75 per cent of the American people, it may be safely estimated, regard themselves as members of churches; another 20 or 25 per cent locate themselves in one or another religious community without a consciousness of actual church membership – they constitute a 'fringe of sympathetic

bystanders', so to speak. Only about five per cent of the American people consider themselves outside the religious fold altogether.[6]

While general church attendance was also rising, a natural concomitant of the upward trajectory in church membership figures, the rate of Sunday school enrolments was more than double that of national population growth. Furthermore, and 'particularly in the suburbs of the big cities', church-building projects were being funded on a massive scale; by 1953: 'The value of new "religious buildings"' was $474 million, more than six times their value in 1946. In fact, between the end of World War II and 1952, the Catholic Church alone had been opening new churches at an average rate of approximately four per week.[7]

There were, indeed, many other signs of the vigorous state of American religious life that went unremarked by Herberg. Hollywood, for example, released a string of biblically themed epics commencing with *Samson and Delilah* in 1949, reaching the peak of their success in 1956 with Cecil B. DeMille's *The Ten Commandments*, a remake of a 1923 film that eventually generated 'the fifth highest inflation-adjusted domestic receipts' of the twentieth century.[8] Then there was the new crop of post-war 'religious best-sellers', notably Joshua Loth Liebman's *Peace of Mind* (1946), Norman Vincent Peale's *A Guide to Confident Living* (1948) and *The Power of Positive Thinking* (1952), and Thomas Merton's *The Seven Storey Mountain* (1948).[9] Also, there was the new dynamism and formidable growth of the overseas missionary movement; whereas there had been around 12,000 American Protestant missionaries in 1935, by 1952 there were 18,500.[10] Last but by no means least, there was the dramatic resurgence of evangelical Protestantism on the national stage, a development marked by the advent of Billy Graham as the nation's foremost evangelist in the Los Angeles and Boston crusades of 1949–50.[11] Significantly, and notwithstanding Graham's patent charisma, the conspicuous power of his preaching, and the compelling nature of his message, his breakthrough occurred at a point when the stock of the clergy had attained new heights in American society. In 1942, polls had shown that Americans ranked 'religious leaders' after 'government leaders' and 'business leaders' in terms of 'doing the most good'; by 1947, religious leaders were already ahead in the public's esteem, with one-third of all Americans rating them as the greatest contributors to the nation's wellbeing. By 1953, this proportion had risen to 40 per cent, prompting the pollster Elmo Roper to state that: 'No other group – whether government, Congressional, business, or labor – came anywhere near matching the prestige and pulling power of the men who are the ministers of God.'[12] Furthermore, and if religious convictions had conditioned the pacifism, isolationism and even timidity of pre-war America, a bullish spirit of religious militancy infused post-war American foreign policy and the nation's sense of selfhood. As the American Institute of Public Opinion discovered less than a month before Pearl Harbor, 55 per cent of Americans felt that their clergy should not 'discuss from the pulpit the question of American participation in the war'. Of those who disagreed, by far the largest group thought that the message to be conveyed was that the 'United States stay out of the war'.[13] In stark contrast, and as America's confrontation with global communism developed into containment and the Cold War, evangelicals and Catholics in particular –the most aggressive and dynamic elements in American religious life – proved outspoken in their anti-communism, sometimes heedless of its implications in a nuclear age.[14] This spirit also suffused the broader realm of American civil religion for, as Herberg averred: 'Confronted with the demonic threat of Communist totalitarianism, we are driven to look beyond the routine ideas and attitudes that may have served in easier times ... in this latter conflict religion commends itself as our greatest resource and most powerful "'secret weapon"'.[15] Significantly, in 1954, the year before *Protestant–Catholic–Jew* was published, Congress added the phrase 'under God' to the Pledge of Allegiance and, the year after its appearance, it established 'In God We Trust' as the national motto.[16] Looking back on this 'panorama of piety', Robert S. Ellwood wrote:

> While of course one cannot gauge the profoundest depths of religious life through statistics, the overwhelming evidence is that religion in the United States in the 1950s was very much alive both spiritually and cultur-ally, perhaps as much or more than in any other modern society anywhere – for that matter, more than in many ancient or medieval societies.[17]

Significantly, Herberg identified post-war factors as driving this national religious revival. These were the desire for religious consolation in the awful shadow of nuclear war; the expansion, prosperity and conformism of America's 'new suburban middle-class society'; and the baby boom and heightened family consciousness of post-war America.[18] There was also, according to Herberg, a generational cause, a function of the dynamics of the American melting pot and of the supplanting of ethnicity by religion as 'the differentiating element [and] context of self-identification and social location' for 'the third generation' of immigrant families.[19] Nevertheless, and as Sydney E. Ahlstrom rightly surmised, 'the "post-war revival" began long before the fighting ceased'.[20] As we have seen, the years of World War II saw a significant upturn in national church member-ship figures, and this in spite of the wholesale disruption of peacetime routines and very high levels of mobility among Americans at large; indeed, and as David M. Kennedy has emphasised: 'Not since the great surge of pioneers across the Appalachian crest in the early years of the Republic had so many Americans been on the move'.[21] Related to this phenomenon was a renewed emphasis on the importance of churchgoing, a boom in the publication and consumption of religious literature, the marked popularity of religiously themed films, and the growing resurgence of evangelical Protestantism. However, if all of this was apparent from the civilian experience, further factors were at work among the one in nine Americans who donned military uniform and who, as veterans, were to have such a profound impact on post-war society. In *American Grace* (2010), a comprehensive study of American religious life since the 1960s, Robert D. Putnam and David E. Campbell confirmed the essential truth of Tom Brokaw's contention that piety was a distinguishing feature of the fabled 'greatest generation'. As Putnam and Campbell noted, 80 per cent of American men born in the 1920s 'served in the military in World War II', thereby becoming eligible for the many financial, educational and other benefits conferred upon veterans by the GI Bill. The effects for American religion were far-reaching. As Putnam and Campbell put it:

> It was this GI generation who as young husbands and fathers, together with their wives, led the surge to church in the late 1940s and 1950s [and] this cohort would remain unusually observant for the rest of their lives. Throughout all the shocks and aftershocks of the ensuing half century and even into the next millennium the GIs and their wives and widows would form the bedrock of American religious institutions.[22]

However, and like Will Herberg, Putnam and Campbell ascribed this religious enthusiasm among veterans to post-war factors, and perhaps to a distant echo of foxhole religion:

> The anxieties of World War II seem to have revived American interest in religion that had flagged in the 1920s and 1930s – 'no atheists in foxholes', it was said.... Postwar affluence, social mobility, and the onset of the Cold War and its attendant nuclear standoff encouraged a paradoxical mixture of optimism and anxiety and a renewed appreciation for traditional values, including both patriotism and religion. Most important, the returning veterans and their wives began producing what would soon be called the baby boom. Then, as now, getting married, settling down, and raising children were associated with more regular churchgoing ... The postwar boom in churchgoing was fueled above all by men who had survived the Great Depression as teenagers and World War II as grunts, and were now ready at last to settle into a normal life, with a steady job, a growing family, a new house and car, and respectable middle-class status. Churchgoing was an important emblem of that respectability.[23]

However, such explanations are inadequate in accounting for the religious habits of America's veterans, if only because so few were actually infantry 'grunts', or occupied a foxhole – or even a ship or an aircraft – under fire. In fact, a wide range of factors served to influence the pattern and temper of veterans' religion. As Chapter One has shown, America's armed forces were served by systems of military chaplaincy in the army and the navy that were, in terms of their aggregate size and the resources available to them, without precedent or parallel in the annals of warfare. In part an expression of George C. Marshall's determination to ensure the best possible conditions for the citizen soldiers of America's draftee army, the chaplains of the army and navy alike were comparatively well-trained, represented a broad cross-section of mainstream American religious life, and generally enjoyed the confidence of the men and women they served. Given that every soldier, sailor and marine, notionally at least, had their chaplain, this well-orchestrated and well-resourced chaplaincy system left large numbers of the previously 'unchurched' with a positive image of the younger American clergy. Given the nature of the war, with huge levels of military mobilisation and the country arrayed against the forces of heathen darkness and paganism, military chaplains easily assumed the role of chaplains to the nation at large. Significantly, and with many civilians being brought within their orbit by dint of their ministry to millions of citizen soldiers and sailors, even civilian society embraced the sympathetic image of the military chaplain, lauding their courage and example, especially in the case of the interfaith icons who were 'The Four Chaplains'. Although this positive image was partly manufactured and sustained by a highly effective public relations effort, there can be little doubt of the role played by literally thousands of army and navy chaplains in promoting a benign image of organised religion, not only on the battlefield but also in the vast burden of counselling and welfare work they undertook.

Still, such highly effective chaplaincy systems were the tip of a much larger iceberg, as Chapter Two has demonstrated. In common with so many of America's public institutions, and despite the notional constraints of the First Amendment, America's army and navy were heavily predisposed to accept and promote religious influences, for reasons that were both professional and pragmatic. While God was invoked in oaths of enlistment and oaths of office, army and navy recruits were expected to identify themselves according to a narrow range of religious descriptors, and the dead were interred according to religious rites. Nor was it unusual for soldiers, and especially sailors, to be corralled into acts of collective worship that were to all intents and purposes compulsory. Convinced of the moral and disciplinary value of religion by centuries of professional precedent, the elite of the nation's officer corps received a religious formation as part of their professional training at West Point and Annapolis. Steeped in a tradition of American military leadership that upheld such figures as George Washington, Robert E. Lee, and 'Stonewall' Jackson, senior army officers in particular were still expected to provide a religious lead and, over the course of the war, Americans were not disappointed by the religious gestures and pronouncements of MacArthur and Eisenhower, even as the vagaries of Patton's behaviour caused widespread concern. Rising to the needs of the hour, the War and Navy Departments erected hundreds of new chapels and supplied an array of further religious resources that ranged from millions of paper communion cups to thousands of chaplains' assistants. Furthermore, and most notably through the USO, the military cooperated closely with civilian religious agencies in providing respectable recreational opportunities for service personnel and even, in the case of the SMCL, helped to promote new religious organisations for them. Significant cooperation was also evidenced in the support and facilitation of wideranging, morale-raising tours of overseas theatres by a number of prominent church leaders. Instanced by the generally uninhibited flow of religious support to service personnel from a host of civilian agencies, and conspicuously advertised in hundreds of new military chapels and in the production of the 'Army Testament', ultimately the religious influences brought to bear on the American armed forces in World War II helped to generate a state-sanctioned, and even state-driven, revival of religion.

As Chapter Three has shown, these policies and measures interacted with some salient features and underlying strengths of religion in civilian society, from which draftees continued to be drawn long after the surrender of Japan. If troubled in many respects, religious life in the interwar period was very robust in others, and this pattern was reflected in the armed forces during World War II. As in civilian life, in general Catholics tended to be more religiously observant than Protestants, women more so than men, and African Americans were more susceptible to religion than were whites; in terms of sectional differences, white Protestant Southerners were usually distinguished by their conservative and evangelical tastes. Irrespective of race or creed, home influences loomed large in the religious formation and behaviour of individuals, and religion itself was strongly equated with the home environment, however idealised, to which most longed to return. However, official religious provision in the armed forces did not mesh easily with America's voluntary and inherently fractious religious culture. While small devotional groups proliferated in the armed forces, by no means all of these were organised or directed by chaplains, many being formed in implicit protest against their perceived inadequacies, be they confessional, theological or even racial and cultural. Less controversially, service personnel could find it hard to come to terms with a system of religious provision that made no financial demands upon them, and the self-reliant quality of American religion was evinced by the spontaneous erection of hundreds of temporary chapels in the Pacific in particular. A further illustration of the partial mismatch between civilian religiosity and military-sponsored religion lay in the abiding preference for civilian churches over military, and in the limited, though still appreciable, appeal of the tri-faith message of religious tolerance among military personnel drawn from a society that had long been plagued by inter-confessional and interfaith enmities.

Chapter Four dealt with the issue of 'foxhole religion', the most famous concept associated with GI religiosity in World War II, and one that was often charged with condescension and even disdain. Here it was argued that foxhole religion, or the emergency piety stirred by the anticipation or immediate experience of battle, has to be set in a much wider context of religious belief and behaviour in civilian as well as in military life. Whether viewed favourably as a manifestation of religious awakening and ultimate belief, or more negatively as an expression of craven selfishness, the religiosity that could be fostered by the extreme conditions of war was also to be found aboard warships, in military aircraft, on life rafts and in captivity. Moreover, the compulsion to pray in foxholes, or their aerial and nautical equivalents, was no different from that which moved so many civilians to pray in less dramatic times of hardship. In any case, and as the relatively small proportion of America's front-line soldiers and sailors implies, an excessive weight has been placed on the importance of this phenomenon, one that could well have arisen from a heightened belief in prayer on the American home front, from the fact that American civilians – unlike tens of millions in Europe and Asia – were spared the experience of front-line conditions, and from the fact that early Cold War American society clearly took solace in religion while under the threat of nuclear destruction. However, 'foxhole religion' was a transient phenomenon among many of its practitioners and was as much a concomitant of wartime fear and uncertainty as were the ephemeral talismans, fatalism and fascination with luck that were also conspicuous in the armed forces. More significant in the long run, it seems, was the growing interest in the afterlife that was evidenced in the last and bloodiest year of the war, a heightened interest that served as a significant prelude to the sudden termination of the war against Japan, and to a grateful return to a civilian future. As far as contemporary surveys show, the experience of combat generally increased personal faith, but combat remained very much a minority preserve, and a heightened belief in God (if not a holier existence) was a more general development in service life. Indeed, the wider, post-war draw of the churches seems to have been more a product of an overwhelming desire to return to the comforting norms of civilian life, and of the institutional emphasis placed on religion by the armed forces, than it was to the attentions of the enemy.

A further stimulus to post-war religiosity was provided through confrontation with the wider world, the subject of Chapter Five. Although easily eclipsed by the Manichaean vision of the Cold War, it must be emphasised that America's war against the main Axis powers – Nazi Germany and the Empire of Japan – was profoundly coloured by religious concerns and animosities. It was not merely that the two regimes were brutal, expansionist and anti-democratic. For many if not most Americans, Nazi Germany's ultimate sin was apostasy – the shocking reversion of the birthplace of Protestantism to a barbarous Nordic paganism from which naturally flowed the idolisation of Hitler and the persecution of Christianity and Judaism, its spiritual parent. Significantly, and with the example of continuing Christian resistance acting as a spur, the American crusade against Nazi Germany was accompanied by a process of religious reclamation and re-christianisation in which the US Army played a prominent part, especially in terms of the de-Nazification of hundreds of thousands of German

POWs. Within this context, contact with North African and European Jews, and with survivors of the Holocaust in particular, also served to strengthen and to further a reawakened sense of their religious identity among many Jewish GIs. In terms of the war against Japan in Asia and the Pacific, Americans grappled with obstinately heathen foes who literally deified their ruler, knew of no moral constraints to outrage, massacre or suicide, and who actively persecuted the cause of Christ, especially in their perceived onslaught against European missionaries. By the same token, a shared religion bound Americans more closely to their allies. Though a rather tenuous cord, if carefully spun, in the case of the Soviets and the Nationalist Chinese, long-standing religious commonalities and affinities with the British and Australians helped to cement their close wartime alliance, on an individual as well as a political level. Furthermore, and if exposure to Indian religions and to the Islamic world seemed only to confirm for many American service personnel the assumed superiority of Christianity in particular, for other Americans the war in the Pacific, and contact with Christian indigenes in particular, seemed to serve as a supreme vindication of missionary endeavour and as an urgent summons to post-war missionary action, especially given the critical need to Christianise a vanquished Japan.

However, and as Chapter Six elaborated, this global crusade – mounted in part on behalf of freedom of religion – generated a formidable litany of cruelty, vice and moral failure. Inevitable corollaries of war, perhaps, but ones that were experienced by millions of men and women who came from a society that was religious, puritanical and historically anti-military. If the segregated nature of America's armed forces partly undermined their credentials as champions of international decency, these were further weakened by the aptitude and even enthusiasm with which many young Americans embraced the tasks of killing and destroying – even to the point of killing civilians by the tens of thousands, murdering POWs (or taking no prisoners at all, as so often was the case in the Pacific) and laying waste hundreds of sacred structures that had been venerated for centuries. Even mutilation of the dead was not uncommon. Given the depth and extent of these aberrations from civilian norms, the atomic annihilation of Hiroshima and Nagasaki raised few eyebrows, let alone protests, among American service personnel. However, the experience and opportunities of a far-flung war challenged and eroded many other standards as well, standards that were underpinned by religious values and that ranged from taboos over drinking, gambling, smoking and even dancing, to respect for private property and decency in language, sexual conduct and in what was flaunted before the world. As civilians at heart, it is scarcely surprising that most service personnel appear to have felt that the experience of military service left them feeling less religious, as opposed to less believing, and with a desire to return to civilian normality. Seen in this context, and with material concerns allayed by a raft of veterans' benefits, widespread feelings of personal guilt were no doubt expiated in the religious revival of the post-war years.

What, then, is there left to say? Only that the experience of America's service men and women from 1941, or even 1939, to 1945 shows that the religious experience and legacy of World War II deserves much greater attention that it has received so far, not only in America but internationally. Inevitably, the greatest man-made catastrophe in history had very strong religious dimensions and repercussions, aspects of the war that have been overlooked in the implicit belief that World War II was, as Paul Fussell alleged, 'a notably secular affair'. Finally, and with respect to the wider question of the impact of war on religious faith, the example of 'the greatest generation' very much indicates that it depends on the war in question, and also on its aftermath. Still, and regardless of its long-term benefits for American religion, the experience of World War II was unquestionably a terrible way to find salvation.

Notes

Introduction

1 Brokaw, 1998, p. 55.

2 Rose, 2008, p. 3.

3 Brokaw, 1998, p. xx.

4 Adams, 1994, p. 2.

5 Fussell, 1996, pp. 167–68.

6 Fussell, 2005, p. 15.

7 Fussell, 1996, p. 173.

8 Fussell, 2005, pp. 34–35.

9 Fussell, 1989, p. 51.

10 Fussell,1996, pp. 22–23, 73.

11 Rose, 2008, p. 42.

12 Ibid, pp. 5, 7.

13 Spivey, 2009; Rabey, 2002; Carroll, 2007.

14 Honeywell, 1958; Gushwa, 1977; Crosby, 1994; Drury, 1948–50; Jorgensen, 1961; Dorsett, 2012; Barish, 1962; Bernstein, 1971; Grobman and Judah, 1993; Pellegrino, 2013; Wansink and Wansink, forthcoming.

15 Sittser, 1998, p. 357.

16 Virden, 2014, pp. 96–97.

17 Kevin L. Walters, 'Beyond the Battle: Religion and American Troops in World War II'. University of Kentucky. Ph.D Diss., 2013. At the time of going to press, this dissertation was under embargo until 5 December 2015.

18 See, for example, Kidd, 2010; Gribbin, 1973; Shattuck, 1987; Miller, Stout and Wilson, 1998; Rable, 2010; Piper, 1985; Schweitzer, 2003; Ebel 2009 and 2010; Gunn, 2009; Herzog, 2011.

19 Martin, Drury, 1980, pp. 56–57.

20 Chesterton, 1922, pp. 11–12.

21 Hutchison, 1989, p. 13; McDannell, 2004, pp. 16–17.

22 Hutchison, 1989, pp. 4–6; Coffman, 2013, pp. 3–4.

23 Hutchison, 1989, p. 5.

24 Coffman, 2013, p. 10.

25 Handy, 1976, pp. 384–85; Butler, Wacker and Balmer, 2008, p. 329; Gaustad, 1990, pp. 257–59, 261.

26 Carpenter, 1980, pp. 74–75.

27 Gaustad, 1990, pp. 261–63.

28 Carpenter, 1997, pp. 13–32.

29 Butler, 2011.

30 Silcox and Fisher, 1979, pp. 27–28.

31 Ahlstrom, 2004, pp. 920–21; Mead, 1951, pp. 64, 131.

32 Handy, 1960; Ahlstrom, 2004, p. 921.

33 Handy, 1960, p. 9.

34 Quoted in Handy, 1960, p. 9.

35 Greene, 2011, p. 602.

36 Ibid, p. 610.

37 Marsden, 1990, pp. 172–73.

38 Ahlstrom, 2004, pp. 921 and 925.

39 McDannell, 2006, pp. 241–44.

40 Sweet, 1948, p. 47.

41 Ibid.

42 Braden, 1944, p. 116.

43 Murphy, 1941, I, p. iii.

44 Braden, 1944, p. 112.

45 Braden, 1948, p. 57.

46 Ahlstrom, 2004, p. 920; Curtis, 2011.

47 Braden, 1948, p. 57; Mead, 1951, p. 145.

48 Braden, 1948, p. 57.

49 Ibid, pp. 57–59.

50 Ibid, p. 54.

51 Ibid, p. 60.

52 Sweet, 1948, p. 47; Murphy, 1941, II.1, p. 18.

53 Braden, 1944, p. 116.

54 Braden, 1948, pp. 59–60.

55 Ibid, p. 61.

56 Braden, 1944, p. 112; Mead, 1951, p. 124.

57 *The Christian Century*, 12 January 1944, pp. 45–47.

58 Ibid, 2 February 1944, p. 140; Braden, 1944, p. 122.

59 Braden, 1944, pp. 115–16; Murphy, 1941, I, Table 5, p. 51.

60 Murphy, 1941, I, Table 5, p. 51.

61 *The Christian Century*, 26 January 1944, p. 108.

62 Ibid.

63 Goldschmidt, 1944, p. 349.

64 Ibid, p. 350.

65 Ibid, p. 354.

66 Pope, 1948, p. 84.

67 Ibid, pp. 85, 88–89.

68 Ibid, p. 89.

69 Ibid, p. 89.

70 Murphy, 1941, I, p. 77.

71 McDanell, 2006, pp. 245–47.

72 Murphy, 1941, I, p. 83.

73 Sweet, 1948, p. 49.

74 Ibid, pp. 49–50.

75 Pope, 1948, pp. 90–91.

76 Quoted in Allitt, 2003, p. 45.

77 Daniel, 1942, pp. 358–60.

78 Ibid, p. 360.

79 McDannell, 2004, pp. 248–55.

80 Ibid, pp. 258–66.

81 Queen, Prothero and Shattuck, 2001, I, pp. 196–97; McDannell, 2006, p. 246.

82 Fischer, 1999, p. 467.

83 Ibid.

84 Murphy, 1941, I, p. 85.

85 Daniel, 1942, p. 360; McDannell, 2004, p. 199.

86 Allitt, 2003, p. 46.

87 Williams, 1999, p. 374.

88 Lincoln and Mamiya, 1990, pp. 209–210.

89 Marty, 1991, p. 121; Queen, Prothero and Shattuck, 2001, I, pp. 266–67; Holifield, 2007, pp. 226–27.

90 Lincoln and Mamiya, 1990, p. 209.

91 Ibid, pp. 210–11.

92 Burke Smith, 2008, p. 110.

93 *The National Catholic Almanac*, 1942, p. 619.

94 *Census of Religious Bodies, 1936. Bulletin No. 23, Roman Catholic Church*, p. 1.

95 Ibid, *Bulletin No. 27, Methodist Bodies*, p. 5.

96 *The National Catholic Almanac*, 1942, p. 633.

97 Bureau of the Census, 1976, Series A 6–8, p. 8.

98 Murphy, 1941, I, pp. 20, 43.

99 *Census of Religious Bodies, 1936. Bulletin No. 23, Roman Catholic Church*, p. 3.

100 Ibid, p. 27; Dolan, 2002, p. 152.

101 Morris, 1997, pp. 160–63; Marsden, 1990, pp. 191–92.

102 Queen, Prothero and Shattuck, 2001, II, pp. 472–73.

103 Cantril, 1943, p. 574; Pope, 1948, p. 85.

104 McDannell, 2006, p. 239; Morris, 1997, pp. 133–34; Dolan, 2002, pp. 133–34; Casino, 1987, pp. 67–68.

105 Pope, 1948, pp. 89–90.

106 *Census of Religious Bodies, 1936. Bulletin No. 72, Jewish Congregations*, p. 1.

107 Ibid.

108 Ibid, p. 3; Moore, 2004, p. 11.

109 *Census of Religious Bodies, 1936. Bulletin No. 72, Jewish Congregations*, pp. 1–2.

110 Bureau of the Census, 1976, Series A 6–8, p. 8.

111 Ahlstrom, 2004, p. 972.

112 Pope, 1948, p. 87.

113 Ahlstrom, 2004, p. 973.

114 Moore, 2004, pp. 4, 7.

115 Herberg, 1955, p. 191; Harrison, 1948, p. 31.

116 Schultz, 2011, loc. 398.

117 Ibid, loc. 568.

118 Silcox and Fisher, 1979, p. 109.

119 Schulz, 2011, loc. 434; Gaustad, 1990, pp. 238–39.

120 Nolan, 1987, pp. 298–99.

121 Renshaw, 1996, pp. 206–7.

122 Marty, 1991, p. 246; Morris, 1997, p. 159; Marsden, 1990, pp. 188–91; Reynolds, 2010, p. 334.

123 Silcox and Fisher, 1979, pp. 101–3.

124 Noll, 1992, p. 431.

125 McDannell, 2006, p. 248; Silcox and Fisher, 1979, p. 101.

126 Morris, 1997, p. 200.

127 Ibid, p. 197.

128 Ferraro and Burke Smith, 2008.

129 Cantril and Strunk, 1951, p. 95.

130 Schultz, 2011, loc. 422.

131 Schneider, 1952, p. 32; Preston, 2012, pp. 322–23.

132 Pope, 1948, p. 88.

133 Silcox and Fisher, 1979, p. 102.

134 Smith, 2006, pp. 207–8.

135 Schultz, 2011, loc. 414.

136 Morris, 1997, pp. 145–49; Marty, 1991, pp. 273–81; Preston, 2012, pp. 332–33.

137 Marty, 1991, p. 273.

138 Cantril and Strunk, 1951, p. 381.

139 Ibid.

140 Ibid, p. 383.

141 Ibid, pp. 383–84.

142 Schultz, 2011, loc. 385.

143 Ibid, loc. 544–62, 604–10.

144 Ibid, loc. 592.

145 Ibid, loc. 623–29.

146 Ibid, loc. 629.

147 Ibid, loc. 658.

148 Hedstrom, 2013, p. 148.

149 Schultz, 2011, loc. 783.
150 Hedstrom, 2013, p. 148.
151 Schutlz, 2011, loc. 813.
152 Ibid, loc. 843–49.
153 Silk, 1988, pp. 40–42; Schultz, 2011, loc. 1181; Hedstrom, 2013, p. 143; Moore, 1998, pp. 34–35.
154 Hedstrom, 2013, pp. 142–43.
155 Schultz, 2011, loc. 1234.
156 Ibid, loc. 1334.
157 Ibid.
158 Ibid, loc. 1340.
159 Hedstrom, 2013, p. 142.
160 Schultz, 2011, loc. 1199–1212.
161 Bellah, 1967; Hammond, Porterfield, Moseley and Sarna, 1994.
162 Smith, 2006, p. 15.
163 Ibid.
164 Ibid.
165 Quoted in Smith, 2006, p. 16.
166 Corbett and Corbett, 1999, pp. 21–23.
167 Smith, 2006, pp. 191–220; Preston, 2012, pp. 315–17; Meacham, 2005, pp. 17, 27–29, 119, 128, 148–49, 156–57; http://www.presidency.ucsb.edu/ws/index.php?pid=16607, accessed 4 July 2014.
168 Schultz, 2011, loc. 882–888.
169 http://www.presidency.ucsb.edu/ws/?pid=14939, accessed 4 July 2014; Smith, 2006, p. 199.
170 Morris, 1997, p. 148; Poling, 1959, pp. 209–10.
171 *The Link*, March 1943, p. 43.
172 http://www.presidency.ucsb.edu/ws/index.php?pid=15959, accessed 4 July 2014.
173 McDannell, 2004, pp. 143–45; Kennedy, 1999, pp. 469–70; Dallek, 1979, p. 291.
174 Preston, 2012, p. 315.
175 McKinney, 1944, pp. 111–12.
176 Ibid, pp. 112–13.
177 Schneider, 1952, pp. 58–59.
178 Ward, 1948, pp. 72–83.
179 Sweet, 1948, p. 50.
180 Murphy, 1941, I, p. 20.
181 Douglass, 1938, p. 508; Greenawalt, 2008, p. 104.
182 Fry and Jessup, 1933, p. 1036.
183 Weigle, 1940, p. 72.
184 Douglass, 1938, p. 508.
185 Weigle, 1940, p. 72.
186 Douglass, 1938, p. 507.
187 Douglass, 1938, p. 512.
188 Silcox and Fisher, 1979, p. 28.
189 Douglass, 1938, p. 513.
190 Ibid, pp. 506–7, 520.
191 Ibid, p. 522.
192 Sweet, 1948, p. 50.
193 Douglass, 1938, p. 517.
194 Mathews, Hill, Barton Schweiger and Boles, 1998, p. 166.
195 Pope, 1948, p. 85.
196 McDannell, 2004, pp. 80, 84.
197 Ibid, pp. 85, 88–89.
198 Hulsether, 2007, p. 90.
199 Murphy, 1941, I, p. 23.
200 Ibid, p. 23.
201 Ibid.
202 Fry and Jessup, 1933, p. 1021.
203 Brereton, 1989, pp. 146–47; Breckinridge, 1933, pp. 746, 748.
204 Hulsether, 2007, pp. 93–95; Silcox and Fisher, 1979, p. 173.
205 Daniel, 1942, p. 360.
206 Baber, 1948, p. 92.
207 Ibid, p. 94.
208 Ogburn, 1933, p. 662; Putnam and Campbell, 2010, Figure 5.4, p. 151.
209 Ogburn, 1933, p. 662.
210 Ibid, p. 674.
211 Baber, 1948, p. 98.
212 Ibid.
213 Ibid, pp. 99–100.
214 Fry and Jessup, 1933, pp. 1017–18.
215 Douglass, 1938, p. 517.
216 Ibid, pp. 517–18.
217 McClung Lee, 1948, p. 121.
218 Coffman, 2013, p. 69.
219 McClung Lee, 1948, pp. 124–25.
220 Ibid, p. 121.
221 Ibid, p. 121.
222 Ibid, pp. 126–28.
223 McDannell, 2006, p. 250.
224 Carpenter, 1997, p. 130.
225 Hangen, 2002, p. 33–34; Morris, 1997, p. 147; Noll, 1992, pp. 507–9.
226 Fry and Jessup, 1933, p. 1052.
227 Carpenter, 1997, p. 125.
228 Boyer, 2001, p. 646; Carpenter, 1997, p. 129.
229 Carpenter, 1997, pp. 130–31; Carpenter, 1980, p. 71; Hangen, 2002, pp. 86–91.
230 Gillis, 1938, pp. 74–76.

231 Fry and Jessup, 1933, pp. 1052–53.

232 Ibid, pp. 1018–19.

233 McDannell, 2004, p. 17.

234 Cantril and Strunk, 1951, p. 742.

235 Ibid, p. 700.

236 Ibid; Noll, 1992, p. 476.

237 Cantril and Strunk, 1951, p. 700.

238 Abrams, 1948, pp. 111, 113

239 Ibid, pp. 112–13; Coffman, 2013, pp. 112–14, 129–30.

240 Leuschner, 1946, p. 17.

241 Kennedy, 1999, p. 523, n. 5.

242 Tower, 1945, p. 96.

243 Abrams, 1948, p. 116; Corbett and Corbett, 1999, pp. 109–10, 186.

244 Sibley and Jacob, 1952, p. 84; Dear and Foot, 1995, p. 263; Wagner, Kennedy, Osborne and Reyburn, 2007, p. 902.

245 Sibley and Jacob, 1952, Table VII, p. 168.

246 Abrams, 1948, p. 116; Wagner, Osborne and Reyburn, 2007, p. 101; Gaustad, 1990, pp. 286–87; Sibley and Jacob, 1952, pp. 27, 85–86, 168.

247 Terkel, 1984, p. 25.

248 Rabey, 2002, p. 87.

249 Lunn, 1947, p. 5.

250 Fahey, 1992, p. 382.

251 Fussell, 1989, pp. 166, 168.

252 Jeffries, 2007, p. 41; Kennedy, 1999, pp. 747–48.

253 2001, *Yearbook of American and Canadian Churches Compilation of Statistical Pages 1916–2000*, 1945, p. 151.

254 Ibid, 1941, p. 137.

255 Ibid, 1943, p. 150.

256 Ibid, 1945, p. 151.

257 Pope, 1948, p. 86.

258 *Yank*, 23 May 1943, p. 15.

259 *The Link*, July 1944, p. 38.

260 Ibid, December 1944, p. 14.

261 *The Chaplain*, December 1945, p. 33.

262 Carpenter, 1980, p. 71; Carpenter, 1997, p. 139.

263 Carpenter, 1997, p. 161.

264 *The Link*, December 1944, p. 38.

265 Ibid, June 1943, p. 28.

266 Ibid, November 1944, p. 12.

267 Ibid, June 1943, p. 24.

268 *Chicago Tribune*, 4 September 1944, p. 21.

269 *The Chaplain*, December 1945, p. 33.

270 *The Link*, July 1944, p. 38.

271 Link and Hopf, 1946, pp. 68–70.

272 McClung Lee, 1948, p. 121.

273 Hedstrom, 2013, p. 118.

274 Ibid, p. 118.

275 *The Link*, July 1943, p. 62; Fussell, 1989, p. 236.

276 Link and Hopf, 1946, p. 68.

277 Hedstrom, 2013, p. 155.

278 *The Link*, May 1943, p. 35.

279 Morris, 1997, pp. 197–98; Smith, 2001, p. 199.

280 Smith, 2001, p. 199.

281 Wagner, Kennedy, Osborne and Reyburn, 2007, p. 797.

282 Smith, 2001, p. 199; Koppes and Black, 1987, pp. 99–104.

283 *The Link*, March 1944, p. 47.

284 http://www.history.army.mil/brochures/brief/overview.htm, p. 6, accessed 29 August 2014.

285 Spector, 2010, p. 80; Atkinson, 2002, p. 8.

286 Weigley, 1968, pp. 419–20, 428; Chambers, 1999, pp. 60–61.

287 http://www.history.army.mil/brochures/brief/overview.htm, pp. 6–7, accessed 29 August 2014; O'Connor, 1986, p. 175.

288 Weigley, 1968, p. 427; O'Connor, 1986, p. 175; Dear and Foot, 1995, p. 996.

289 Jeffries, 2007, p. 20; Klein, 2013, pp. 81–83, 213–14.

290 http://www.nationalww2museum.org/learn/education/for-students/ww2-history/ww2-by-the-numbers/us-military.html, accessed 22 July 2014; Millett, 2010, p. 52.

291 Kennett, 1997, pp. 8, 19.

292 http://www.history.navy.mil/library/online/ww2_statistics.htm, accessed 23 July 2014.

293 Kennett, 1997, p. 4.

294 Ibid, p. 9.

295 Jeffries, 2007, pp. 20–1; Kennett, 1997, pp. 16–19.

296 Millett, 2010, p. 52; Kennett, 1997, pp. 10–11, 16.

297 Dear and Foot, 1995, Table 4, p. 1192 and Table 7, p. 1198; Lada and Reister, 1975, p. 3.

298 Millett, 2010, p. 62.

299 Ibid, pp. 62, 74; Spector, *Eagle Against the Sun*, 2001, pp. 300, 423.

300 Millett, 2010, p. 60.

301 Ellis, 1990, p. 157.

302 Schrijvers, 2010, p. 101.

303 Ibid, pp. 89–93; Spector, *Eagle Against the Sun*, 2001, p. 299.

304 http://www.history.navy.mil/library/online/ww2_statistics.htm, accessed 23 July 2014.

305 Ellis, 1990, pp. 157–58.

306 Stouffer, 1949, II, pp. 62–64

307 Linderman, 1997, p. 1.

308 Doubler, 1994, p. 247; Ambrose, 1998, pp. 280–82; Gawne, 2006, p. 15; Atkinson, 2013, pp. 407–12.

309 Faubus, 1971, pp. 416–17.

310 Ibid, pp. 343–344.

311 Wells, 1995, p. 5.

312 Dear and Foot, 1995, pp. 603–4.

313 Millett, 1991, p. 439.

314 Reynolds, 1996, p. xxix; Linderman, 1997, p. 39.

315 Spector, 2010, pp. 83–84.

316 Miller, 2007, p. 166.

317 Astor, 1998, p. 486.

318 Miller, 2007, p. 164; Linderman, 1997, p. 38.

319 Linderman, 1997, p. 39.

320 Ibid, p. 37; Wells, 1995, pp. 102–6; Bowman, 2003, pp. 225–26.

321 Linderman, 1997, pp. 37–38; Bowman, 2003, p. 148.

322 Linderman, 1997, p. 39.

323 http://www.history.navy.mil/library/online/ww2_statistics.htm, accessed 23 July 2014.

324 http://www.nationalww2museum.org/learn/education/for-students/ww2-history/ww2-by-the-numbers/us-military.html, accessed 23 July 2014.

325 http://www.history.navy.mil/library/online/aviation_fatal.htm, accessed 23 July 2014.

326 Spector, *Eagle Against the Sun*, 2001, p. 487.

327 Ibid, pp. 5, 208; Costello, 1981, p. 587.

328 Fahey, 1992, p. 50.

329 Ibid, p. 20.

330 VHP, Laverne C. Etshman, online transcript.

331 Ellis, 1990, pp. 169–72.

332 Millett, 2010, p. 75.

333 Lada and Reister, 1975, p. 11.

334 Ibid.

335 http://www.nationalww2museum.org/learn/education/for-students/ww2-history/ww2-by-the-numbers/us-military.html, accessed 23 July 2014.

336 Jeffries, 1996, p. 158; Keene, 2001, p. 205.

337 Henry, 2002, 26–27.

338 Harrod, 1978, p. 148.

339 Coffman, 2004, pp. 191–92, 243; Pogue, 1973, p. 95.

340 Marshall, Pogue and Bland, 1991, pp. 473, 577.

341 Ibid, pp. 471–72, 481–82; Pogue, 1966, p. 105.

342 Pogue, 1966, p. 117.

343 Pogue, 1973, p. 94.

344 Ibid, p. 87.

345 *What the Soldier Thinks*, December 1943, n.p.

346 Reynolds, 1996, p. 81; Kennedy, 1999, p. 713.

347 Pogue, 1973, pp. 84–85.

348 Ibid, pp. 92–93; Marshall, Pogue and Bland, 1991, pp. 486–87.

349 Pogue, 1973, pp. 88–90.

350 Marshall, Pogue and Bland, 1991, p. 482.

351 http://www.nationalww2museum.org/learn/education/for-students/ww2-history/ww2-by-the-numbers/us-military.html, accessed 24 July 2014.

352 Wynn, 2010, pp. 27–29; Polenberg, 1972, pp. 123–24.

353 Wynn, 2010, p. 44; Kennedy, 1999, p. 633.

354 Jeffries, 1996, p. 107; Wynn, 2010, p. 44; Kennedy, 1999, pp. 771–72.

355 Polenberg, 1972, pp. 124–25; Wynn, 2010, pp. 52–53; Spector, *Eagle Against the Sun*, 2001, p. 387; Field and Bielakowski, 2008, p. 170.

356 Spector, 2001, *Eagle Against the Sun*, p. 389.

357 Ambrose, 1998, p. 345.

358 Pogue, 1973, pp. 98–99.

359 Wynn, 2010, p. 47.

360 Jeffries, 1996, pp. 109–10; Wynn, 2010, p. 40.

361 Wynn, 2010, p. 48.

362 Ibid, p. 61.

363 Chambers, 1999, p. 8; Wagner, Kennedy, Osborne and Reyburn, 2007, p. 294; Harrod, 1978, pp. 57–62; Spector, *At War at Sea*, 2001, pp. pp. 264–65

364 Hastie, 1942.

365 Dear and Foot, 1995, p. 7.

366 Pogue, 1973, p. 97.

367 Field and Bielakowski, 2008, pp. 162–66; Takaki, 2008, p. 353.

368 Wagner, Kennedy, Osborne and Reyburn, 2007, p. 294.

369 Reddick 1947 and 1949.

370 Field and Bielakowski, 2008, pp. 195–96, 213–14; Wynn, 2010, p. 61.

371 Spector, *At War at Sea*, 2001, p. 269.

372 Field and Bielakowski, 2008, pp. 202–5; Spector, 2001, *At War at Sea*, p. 269; Moore,

2006, pp. 201–3; Sutherland, 2004, I, pp. 208–9, 308–9.

373 Sutherland, 2004, I, p. 343.

374 Ibid; Field and Bielakowski, 2008, pp. 206–12.

375 Millett, 2010, p. 84.

376 Jessup, 2010, p. 266.

CHAPTER 1

Chaplains and Chaplaincy

1 Budd, 2002, pp. 9–10; Thompson, 1978, pp. 118–19; 223–26; Stephenson, 2008, pp. 83–84.

2 Drury, 1949, pp. 3–5.

3 Budd, 2002, pp. 10–12.

4 Ibid, p. 13.

5 Smith, 2006, p. 77.

6 Kaplan, 1986; Brinsfield, 1997, pp. 120–30.

7 Norton, 1977, p. 76.

8 Ibid, pp. 76–78; Honeywell, 1958, pp. 84–86; Klug, 1969, p. 77.

9 Klug, 1969, pp. 75–77; Norton, 1977, p. 78; Preston, 2012, pp. 150–52.

10 Klug, 1969, pp. 76–78.

11 Drury, 1949, p. 65.

12 Budd, 2002, p. 61; Armstrong, 1998, pp. ix–x.

13 Budd, 2002, pp. 10, 28, 30.

14 Ibid, pp. 64–5; Stover, 1977, p. 3.

15 Budd, 2002, pp. 82, 88; Stover, 1977, p. 76.

16 Budd, 2002, pp. 86–90.

17 Stover, 1977, pp. 147–52.

18 Budd, 2002, pp. 101–2.

19 Drury, 1949 pp. 144–45.

20 Budd, 2002, pp. 103–4; Stover, 1977, p. 208.

21 Thompson, 1946, p. 35.

22 Ayres, 1919.

23 Mead, 2000, pp. 94–98, 127–30, 171.

24 Honeywell, 1958, p. 171; Jorgensen 1961, pp. 16–17, 26–27.

25 Stover, 1977, pp. 157–58; Budd, 2002, p. 88.

26 Honeywell, 1958, pp. 174–75, 185.

27 Committee on the War and the Religious Outlook, 1920, p. 104.

28 Weigley, 1968, p. 348; Stover, 1977, p. 150.

29 Keene, 2001, p. 129; Stover, 1977, pp. 209–11; Thompson, 1946, p. 39.

30 Stover, 1977, pp. 212–14; International Committee of Young Men's Christian Association, 1920, p. 3; Moody, 1945, p. 14.

31 Ayres, 1919, pp. 28–29; Stover, 1977, pp. 212–13.

32 Stover, 1977, p. 213; Budd, 2002, pp. 125–27.

33 Jorgensen, 1961, pp. 17–18; Honeywell, 1958, pp. 181, 184, 199.

34 Thompson, 1946, p. 37.

35 Jorgensen, 1961, pp. 18–19; Stover, 1977, pp. 220–1; Thompson, 1946, p. 36.

36 Moody, 1945, p. 13.

37 Honeywell, 1958, pp. 175, 180–81; Stover, 1977, pp. 215–17.

38 Stover, 1977, pp. 204–6.

39 Ibid, p. 217.

40 Moody, 1945, p. 15.

41 Jewish Welfare Board, 1920, p. 42.

42 Thompson, 1946, p. 38.

43 Budd, 2002, p. 131; Thompson, 1946, p. 40; 1924, 'Army Regulations No. 60–5. Chaplains. General Provisions', par. 2; Stover, 1977, p. 223.

44 Gushwa, 1977, p. 32; Young, 1959, pp. 411–12; Honeywell, 1958, pp. 201–2.

45 1923, *Report of the Conference on Moral and Religious Work in the Army*, pp. 1–2.

46 Ibid, p. 1.

47 Ibid, p. 3.

48 Gushwa, 1977, pp. 28–31.

49 1924, 'Army Regulations No. 60–5. Chaplains. General Provisions', par. 5; Jorgensen, 1961, p. 63; 1941, *Technical Manual 16–205: The Chaplain*, p. 18.

50 Coffman, 2004, p. 117.

51 1922, *Report of the Chief of Chaplains*, p. 3.

52 Jorgensen, 1961, pp. 63–64.

53 Gushwa, 1977, pp. 23–6; Jorgensen, 1961, pp. 64–72.

54 Weigley, 1968, pp. 342–43, 399; Gushwa, 1977, pp. 35–38.

55 Drury, 149, p. 143.

56 Ibid, pp. 62 and 142.

57 Howarth, 1991, p. 288.

58 Drury, 1949, p. 140.

59 Ibid, p. 138.

60 Ibid, p. 139.

61 Ibid, pp. 141–42.

62 Ibid.

63 Ibid, pp. 162–63; Howarth, 1991, p. 324.

64 Drury, 1949, pp. 163, 168.

65 Howarth, 1991, pp. 309–10, 312.

66 Gilroy and Demy, 1983, p. 28; Drury, 1949, p. 173; Stover, 1977, p. 225 n. 9.

67 Drury, 1949, p. 143.

68 Edel, 1994, pp. 63–64; Drury, 1949, pp. 164–65.

69 Drury, 1949, pp. 213, 215.

70 Ibid, p. 213; http://www.history.navy.mil/library/guides/rosters/chaplain.htm, accessed 27 October 2011.

71 Drury, 1949, pp. 165, 213; Drury, 1950, p. 85.

72 Appelquist, 1969, pp. 128–30; Drury, 1949, p. 213; Drury, 1948, pp. 302–3.

73 Drury, 1949, pp. 82–83; Edel, 1994, pp. 79–150; Martin, 'Edel', pp. 19–59.

74 Drury, 1949, p. 232.

75 Martin, 'Meehling', p. 40.

76 Gushwa, 1977, p. 49.

77 DeBenedetti, 1980, p. 116.

78 Ibid, p. 112; Sittser, 1997, pp. 16–20; Smith, 2006, pp. 184–85.

79 Abrams, 1969, p. 235.

80 Poling, 1943, p. 10.

81 Gushwa, 1977, p. 27.

82 Ibid, p. 27; Poling, 1943, p. xi.

83 *New York Herald Tribune*, 16 April 1930, pp. 1, 6.

84 Gushwa, 1977, p. 54.

85 Klug, 1969, p. 81; Drury, 1949, p. 219.

86 Preston, 2012, p. 298.

87 DeBenedetti, 1980, pp. 122–3; Josephson, 1985, pp. 724–26; Chatfield, 1992, p. 62.

88 Jorgensen, 1961, pp. 58–59; Sittser, 1997, pp. 24–25.

89 Sittser, 1997, p. 25.

90 Abrams, 1969, p. 238.

91 Gushwa, 1977, p. 54; NARA, RG 247, Records of the Office of the Chief of Chaplains. Records of Administration and Management General Records. Records Relating to the History of the Chaplains of the United States Army, 1941–58, Box 3, 'Military History of the Second World War. The Corps of Chaplains', p. 5; Drury, 1949, pp. 220–21.

92 Drury, 1949, p. 221.

93 Ibid, pp. 220–21.

94 Jorgensen, 1961, p. 59.

95 Drury, 1949, p. 220.

96 Abrams, 1969, p. 238; Jorgensen, 1961, pp. 58–59.

97 Gushwa, 1977, p. 54; Mead, 1951, pp. 32, 120.

98 Noll, 2002, p. 148.

99 Preston, 2012, pp. 303–6; Handy, 1976, pp. 393–5; Noll, 1992, pp. 525–27; Queen, Prothero and Shattuck, 2001, II, pp. 514–16; DeBenedetti, 1980, p. 135.

100 NARA, RG 247, Box 3, 'Military History of the Second World War. The Corps of Chaplains', pp. 13–14.

101 Chambers, 1999, pp. 60–61.

102 NARA, RG 247, Box 3, 'Military History of the Second World War. The Corps of Chaplains', p. 13.

103 Honeywell, 1958, pp. 209–10.

104 Ibid, pp. 202–3.

105 USAHEC, Ole K. Davidson Papers, certificates of completion; Gushwa, 1977, pp. 20–21; Honeywell, 1958, pp. 207–9.

106 Gushwa, 1977, p. 21; Honeywell, 1958, p. 207.

107 DeBenedetti, 1980, pp. 124–25.

108 Kennedy, 1999, p. 155; Perret, 1991, p. 19; Gushwa, 1977, p. 59.

109 Gushwa, 1977, p. 60.

110 Ibid, p. 59.

111 Ibid, pp. 58–68; Jorgensen, 1961, pp. 52–53; Brasted, n.d.

112 Weigley, 1968, p. 402.

113 NARA, RG 247, Box 3, 'Military History of the Second World War. The Corps of Chaplains', p. 15.

114 Honeywell, 1958, p. 212.

115 Spector, *At War at Sea*, 2001, p. 261.

116 Drury, 1949, p. 207.

117 Drury, 1950, p. 1.

118 Ibid; Drury, 1949, pp. 201 and 210.

119 Drury, 1949, p. 211.

120 Ibid, pp. 210–11.

121 Ibid, p. 210.

122 Claypool, 1944, pp. 32–33.

123 *The Christian Century*, 16 May 1945, p. 596.

124 Honeywell, 1958, p. 223; Drury, 1950, p. 42.

125 1946, *History of Chaplains' Activities in the Pacific*, p. 312; Lee, 1966, p. 227; Nance, 1944, p. 97; Drury, 1950, p. 40.

126 Honeywell, 1958, p. 216; *The Chaplain*, February 1945, p. 45.

127 Gushwa, 1977, pp. 96, 99.

128 *The Link*, May 1943, p. 38; Honeywell, 1958, p. 223; Office of the Chief of Chaplains, 1944, p. 5.

129 Drury, 1950, pp. 1, 51.

130 *The Chaplain*, May 1945, p. 47.

131 Armstrong, 1998, p. 6.

132 *The Chaplain*, August 1945, p. 30.

133 Markkola, 2006, p. 560; Noll, 1992, pp. 512–13.

134 Brinsfield, 1997, p. 40; Gilroy and Demy, 1983, p. 35.

135 Holifield, 2007, p. 262.

136 Honeywell, 1958, p. 223.

137 Yost, 2006, p. 1.

138 *The Link*, May 1943, p. 19.

139 NARA, RG 247, Box 3, 'Military History of the Second World War. The Corps of Chaplains', pp. 135–36.

140 Brinsfield, 1997, p. 244.

141 NARA, RG 247, Box 3, 'Military History of the Second World War. The Corps of Chaplains', pp. 136–39.

142 Honeywell, 1958, pp. 215–17.

143 Smith, 2006, p. 204.

144 Ancell and Miller, 1996, p. 9.

145 Thompson, 1946, pp. 40–41.

146 *Washington Post*, 20 February 1943, p. B4.

147 Jorgensen, 1961, pp. 87–89.

148 Orr, 1948, p. 65.

149 Lester, 1992, Reel 33, Box 84, 0142 et seq., 'Brief', 18 December 1944.

150 Ancell and Miller, 1996, p. 144.

151 Lester, 1992, Reel 33, Box 84, 0176 et seq., 'Memorandum for the Eyes of General Marshall Only', 3 January 1945.

152 *The Christian Century*, 22 November 1944, pp. 1342–43.

153 Orr, 1948, p. 67.

154 Venzke, 1977, pp. 5–6.

155 *The Christian Century*, 7 November 1945, p. 1227.

156 Ibid, 26 December 1945, pp. 1435–36.

157 *The Christian Century*, 5 June 1946, pp. 716–17.

158 Ibid; Jorgensen, 1961, p. 87; Nance, 1944, p. 95.

159 Lester, 1992, Reel 33, Box 84, 0142 et seq., 'Memorandum for the Secretary of War: Subject: Army Chaplain Corps', 18 December 1944.

160 Ibid, Reel 7, Box 60, 0880 et seq., 'Remarks to conference of supervisory chaplains', 5 April 1945.

161 Jorgensen, 1961, p. 87.

162 *Christian Science Monitor*, 6 April 1945, p. 3.

163 Gushwa, 1977, p. 181; Lester, 1992, Reel 7, Box 60, 0880 et seq., 'Remarks to conference of supervisory chaplains'; Reel 33, Box 84, 0142 et seq., 'Memorandum for the Secretary of War: Subject: Army Chaplain Corps'.

164 Lester, 1992, Reel 33, Box 84, 0142 et seq., 'Memorandum for the Secretary of War: Subject: Army Chaplain Corps'.

165 Jorgensen, 1961, p. 89.

166 1946, *History of Chaplains' Activities in the Pacific*, p. 456; Gushwa, 1977, pp. 106–7.

167 1944, Technical Manual 16–205: The Chaplain, p. 9.

168 Appelquist, 1969, p. 128; Drury, 1949, pp. 213–14; Drury, 1948, pp. 302–3; *The Link*, October 1944, p. 6.

169 Drury, 1949, p. 215.

170 Drury, 1949, p. 215.

171 Drury, 1950, p. 91; *The Chaplain*, May 1945, p. 46.

172 Drury, 1950, pp. 90–91; *The Christian Century*, 12 January 1944, p. 37.

173 Taggart and Cross, 1943, pp. 2, 5; *New York Times*, 20 March 1943, p. 12.

174 Taggart and Cross, 1943, pp. 2–3, 20.

175 Gawne, 2006, p. 50.

176 Drury, 1950, pp. 298–99.

177 2001, *Yearbook of American and Canadian Churches Compilation of Statistical Pages 1916–2000*, 1945, p. 155.

178 Holifield, 2007, p. 227.

179 Lunn, 1947, pp. 8–10.

180 Handy, 1960, p. 9; Handy, 1976, p. 387; Rabey, 2002, p. 200.

181 Lunn, 1947, p. 8.

182 Ibid, p. 9.

183 Ibid, p. vii.

184 Stroup, 2000, pp. 1, 3, 5, 97.

185 *The Chaplain*, October 1944, p. 30; Allitt, 2003, pp. 33–34.

186 Stroup, 2000, pp. 149, 161–2,167, 203.

187 Office of the Chief of Chaplains, 1944, p. 61; *New York Times*, 25 July 1943, p. 21.

188 Office of the Chief of Chaplains, 1944, p. 61.

189 Drury, 1950, pp. 54–55.

190 Drury, 1950, p. 46; Office of the Chief of Chaplains, 1944, pp. 17–26.

191 Drury, 1949, p. 143; Drury, 1950, p. 43; Slomovitz, 1999, pp. 77–8; Bernstein, 1971, p. 8.

192 Holifield, 2007, pp. 231–32; Spector, *At War at Sea*, 2001, pp. 261–62.

193 Martin, Drury, 1980, p. xv.

194 Drury, 1950, p. 43.

195 Ibid.

196 Ibid, Appendix III, p. 312.

197 Spector, *At War at Sea*, 2001, p. 262; Methodist Church Commission on Chaplains, 1948, p. 164.

198 Drury, 1950, p. 69; *The Christian Century*, 10 March 1943, pp. 284–85.

199 Kaplan, 1986, p. 1222; Mead, 1951, p. 120; *Census of Religious Bodies, 1936. Bulletin No. 18. Lutherans*, pp. 78–84.

200 NARA, RG 247, Box 3, 'Military History of the Second World War. The Corps of Chaplains', p. 108.

201 Crosby, 1994, pp. 23, 136; NARA, RG 247. Chief of Chaplains. Office Management Division Decimal File 1920–45. Box 3. 000.3 Catholic Denomination Volume I. Arnold to Bishop of San Diego, 1 November 1941.

202 Gushwa, 1977, p. 100.

203 1945, 'Reports of the General Board. 68. The Army Chaplain in the European Theater', p. 7

204 NARA, RG 247, Box 3, 'Military History of the Second World War. The Corps of Chaplains', p. 102.

205 *The Chaplain*, August 1945, p. 30.

206 Drury, II, p. 48.

207 Bernstein, 1971, pp. 9–10.

208 Holifield, 2007, p. 230.

209 Drury, II, p. 53.

210 Honeywell, 1958, p. 222; *Christian Science Monitor*, 11 June 1942, p. 6.

211 *The Christian Century*, 30 September 1942, p. 1173.

212 Wilson, 1945, p. 33.

213 Norton, 1977, pp. 94–96; Office of the Chief of Chaplains, 1944, p. 2; Scott, 1919, p. 482.

214 Hastie, 1942, p. 58; Stover, 1977, p. 88.

215 Moore, 2006, p. 18; Field and Bielakowski, 2008, pp. 152–55.

216 Wynn, 2010, p. 48.

217 1946, *History of Chaplains' Activities in the Pacific*, p. 396.

218 Ibid, p. 108.

219 *The Baltimore Afro-American*, 2 June 1945, p. 3.

220 1946, *History of Chaplains' Activities in the Pacific*, pp. 93, 511.

221 Moore, 2006, p. 70; *The Baltimore Afro-American*, 18 March 1944, p. 15.

222 1946, *History of Chaplains' Activities in the Pacific*, p. 507.

223 Ibid, pp. 108–9.

224 *The Baltimore Afro-American*, 18 September 1943, p. 20; *Atlanta Daily World*, 24 September 1941, p. 1.

225 *The Baltimore Afro-American*, 10 July 1943, p. 2.

226 Ibid, 17 April 1943, p. 1.

227 Ibid, 10 April 1943, p. 20.

228 Ibid, 6 November 1943, p. 18.

229 Ibid, 17 April 1943.

230 Jorgensen, 1961, p. 128.

231 NARA, Record Group 247. Chief of Chaplains. Office Management Division Decimal File 1920–45. Box 199. 291.2 Race, Negro Volume I. J.S. Pogue to W.R. Arnold, 6 November 1943.

232 Ibid, 'Mal–treatment and arrest', 16 February 1944.

233 Ibid, 'A Special Report', 8 January 1944.

234 NARA, Record Group 247. Chief of Chaplains. Office Management Division Decimal File 1920–45. Box 199. 291. 2 Race– General. Luther D. Miller to R.W. Coleman, 17 October 1945.

235 Honeywell, 1958, p. 216.

236 NARA, Record Group 247. Chief of Chaplains. Office Management Division Decimal File 1920–45. Box 199. 291.2 Race, Negro Volume I. W.R. Arnold to L.H. King, 22 January 1943.

237 Gregg, 1945, p. 16; Honeywell, 1958, p. 215.

238 Gushwa, 1977, p. 100; Honeywell, 1958, p. 215; 1945, 'Reports of the General Board. 68. The Army Chaplain in the European Theater', p. 13; Field and Bielakowski, 2008, p. 187.

239 1946, *History of Chaplains' Activities in the Pacific*, p. 396.

240 CARLDL, 'History of Military Training: Chaplains Supplement', 1945, pp. 7–8; 1945, 'Reports of the General Board. 68. The Army Chaplain in the European Theater', pp. 2–3; *The Baltimore Afro-American*, 17 April 1943, p. 20.

241 Gushwa, 1977, p. 100; 1945, 'Reports of the General Board. 68. The Army Chaplain in the European Theater', pp. 2, 13.

242 1946, *History of Chaplains' Activities in the Pacific*, p. 188.

243 Crosby, 1994, pp. 61–63; *The Baltimore Afro-American*, 17 November 1945, p. 3.

244 Lester, 1992, Reel 33, Box 84, 0176 et seq., 'Memorandum for the Eyes of General Marshall Only'.

245 Gushwa, 1977, p. 97; Jorgensen, 1961, p. 91; Drury, 1950, pp. 45–46.

246 Barish, 1962, p. 12; Gushwa, 1977, pp. 97–98; Jorgensen, 1961, pp. 91–93; Bernstein, 1971, Preface.

247 Drury, 1950, p. 45; Jorgensen, 1961, pp. 92–93; Methodist Commission on Chaplains, 1948, p.164.

248 Bernstein, 1971, p. 8; Grobman, 1993, p. 3.

249 Carpenter, 1997, pp. 48–49.

250 Drury, 1950, p. 45.

251 Bernstein, 1971, pp. 9–10.

252 Forty, 2003, p. 14; Jorgensen, 1961, p. 146.

253 Yost, 2006, p. 33.

254 CARLDL, 'History of Military Training Chaplains: Chaplains Volume I– to December

1944; 1945, n.p.; 1944, *Technical Manual 16–205: The Chaplain*, p. 15.

255 Honeywell, 1958, p. 205; CARLDL, 'History of Military Training Chaplains: Chaplains Volume I – to December 1944; 1945, n.p.

256 Cleary, 1945, p. 71.

257 Gushwa, 1977, pp. 108–10; CARLDL, 'History of Military Training Chaplains: Chaplains Volume I – to December 1944; 1945, n.p.; CARLDL, 'History of Military Training. Chaplains Supplement – to June 1945 (Volume 2); 1945, p. 7.

258 Nance, 1944, p. 108.

259 Cleary, 1945, p. 70.

260 Office of the Chief of Chaplains, 1944, p. 30.

261 Nance, 1944, pp. 109–11; Office of the Chief of Chaplains, 1944, pp. 27–30.

262 Nance, 1944, p. 111.

263 Ibid, p. 107.

264 Ibid.

265 1944, *Technical Manual 16–205: The Chaplain*, p. 16.

266 *Chicago Tribune*, 21 April 1942, p. 3; Gushwa, 1977, pp. 111–13; pp. 113–19, 121; Honeywell, 1958, p. 352; 1945, 'Reports of the General Board. 68. The Army Chaplain in the European Theater; pp. 21–22.

267 1945, 'Reports of the General Board. 68. The Army Chaplain in the European Theater; pp. 21–2; 1945, *American Chaplains of the Fifth Army*, pp. 58–59.

268 Rogers, 1946.

269 CARLDL, 'History of Military Training Chaplains: Chaplains Volume I; 1945, n.p.

270 Drury, 1950, p. 56.

271 Martin, 'Meehling', pp. 29–30.

272 Edel, 1994, pp. 124–25.

273 Drury, 1950, pp. 56–57.

274 Ibid, pp. 57–60, 66.

275 Ibid, p. 63.

276 Ibid, pp. 62–65; Cleary, 1945, p. 71.

277 Drury, 1950, p. 66.

278 Ibid, pp. 59, 64.

279 Ibid, pp. 62–63.

280 *The Chaplain*, April 1945, p. 47.

281 Martin, 'Craven', p. 6.

282 Drury, 1950, p. 298.

283 1945, 'Reports of the General Board. 68. The Army Chaplain in the European Theater; Appendix 1, pp. 1–2.

284 Cleary, 1945, p. 72.

285 Drury, 1950, pp. 85–115, 196, 242–47.

286 Weigley, 1968, pp. 442–43.

287 Ibid, pp. 442–47; Office of the Chief of Chaplains, 1944, p. 3.

288 Jorgensen, 1961, pp. 105–11.

289 Drury, 1950, pp. 85–98.

290 Ibid, p. 106.

291 Office of the Chief of Chaplains, 1944, pp. 3–4.

292 Jorgensen, 1961, p. 89.

293 Office of the Chief of Chaplains, 1944, p. 61; 1944, *Technical Manual 16–205: The Chaplain*, pp. 77–78.

294 Office of the Chief of Chaplains, 1944, pp. 58–59; 1944, *Technical Manual 16–205: The Chaplain*, pp. 72–80.

295 Jorgensen, 1961, p. 101.

296 Craven, 1955, p. 375.

297 1944, *Technical Manual 16–205: The Chaplain*, p. 80.

298 Jorgensen, 1961, pp. 99–105, 120–21; Gushwa, 1977, p. 111; 1944, *Technical Manual 16–205: The Chaplain*, p. 75; 1946, *History of Chaplains' Activities in the Pacific*, p. 268.

299 Jorgensen, 1961, pp. 87, 99.

300 Ancell and Miller, 1996, p. 274; Jorgensen, 1961, p. 89.

301 1945, 'Reports of the General Board. 68. The Army Chaplain in the European Theater; p. 9.

302 1946, *History of Chaplains' Activities in the Pacific*, p. 310.

303 1945, 'Reports of the General Board. 68. The Army Chaplain in the European Theater; p. 3; 1946, *History of Chaplains' Activities in the Pacific*, p. 145, 263–64.

304 1946, *History of Chaplains' Activities in the Pacific*, pp. 254, 257; Gawne, 2006, p. 265.

305 1945, *American Chaplains of the Fifth Army*, pp. 10–11.

306 Metcalf, 1957, pp. 161, 170.

307 Ibid, pp. 203–5, 211–12, 236.

308 Cleary, 1945, p. 91.

309 1946, *History of Chaplains' Activities in the Pacific*, pp. 213, 224.

310 1924, 'Army Regulations No. 60–5. Chaplains. General Provisions; par. 5.

311 Cleary, 1945, p. 92.

312 Ibid, pp. 92–93.

313 Stanton, 2006, Chart 3, p. 6.

314 USAHEC, Ole K. Davidson Papers; 'My Days in the Service; 'Suggestions for Chaplains Procedure with men of other than their own Faith'.

315 Drury, 1950, p. 214.

316 Ibid, pp. 214, 221; Cross and Arnold, 1945, pp. 162–66; Nance, pp. 80–82.

317 Cleary, 1945, p. 90.

318 1945, 'Reports of the General Board. 68. The Army Chaplain in the European Theater', p. 8.

319 Drury, 1950, p. 214.

320 Nance, p. 72.

321 Pyle, 2001, p. xi.

322 1923, *Report of the Conference on Moral and Religious Work in the Army*, pp. 5–7.

323 1923, *Army Chaplains Need Special Organization*, p. 1.

324 1919, *Final Report of Gen. John J. Pershing Commander–in–Chief American Expeditionary Forces*, p. 93.

325 1923, *Report of the Conference on Moral and Religious Work in the Army*, p. 3.

326 Ibid, pp. 5–7.

327 1941, *Technical Manual 16–205: The Chaplain*, pp. 50–51.

328 Ancell and Miller, 1996, p. 328; Ulio, 1941, pp. 321–30.

329 Nance, 1944, p. 63.

330 Ibid, p. 59.

331 Cleary, 1945, p. 75; *The Marine Corps Gazette*, October 1943, p. 10.

332 Drury, 1950, pp. 249–51.

333 1945, 'Reports of the General Board. 113. Special Services Organization', pp. 1–2; Jorgensen, 1961, p. 210.

334 Ibid, p. 2.

335 Ibid, p. 4.

336 Gawne, 2006, p. 83.

337 1945, 'Reports of the General Board. 113. Special Services Organization', p. 3.

338 Ibid, pp. 2, 4.

339 Rogers, 1946, pp. 28, 30.

340 1946, *History of Chaplains' Activities in the Pacific*, p. 79.

341 Wagner, Kennedy, Osborne and Reyburn, 2007, pp. 170–71.

342 Methodist Commission on Chaplains, 1948, p. 42; *Yank*, 28 February 1943, p. 5.

343 1944, *ETOUSA Special and Morale Services Guide*, p. 7.

344 Stroup, 2000, pp. 17–18.

345 Ibid, pp. 116–17.

346 Ibid, pp. 157–58.

347 1946, *History of Chaplains' Activities in the Pacific*, pp. 105–6.

348 Flint, 2008, p. 863.

349 1941, *Technical Manual 16–205: The Chaplain*, p. 56.

350 Ibid, pp. 59–60.

351 1944, *Technical Manual 16–205: The Chaplain*, pp. 50–51.

352 Cleary, 1945, pp. 73–74.

353 Kertzer, 1947, p. 44.

354 Rogers, 1946, p. 64.

355 Ibid, p. 146.

356 Atkinson, 2013, p. 465.

357 Willard, 1944, pp. 149–50.

358 Drury, 1948, p. 249; Drury, 1950, pp. 198–99.

359 Jorgensen, 1961, p. 168.

360 Ibid, pp. 168–69.

361 Sweeney, 1997, p. 162; Crosby, 1994, p. 245; Bourke, 1999, pp. 268–69.

362 Spellman, 1943, pp. 88–89.

363 Society for the Propagation of the Faith, 1946, 'Blessings'.

364 1944, *Technical Manual 16–205: The Chaplain*, p. 64.

365 Jorgensen, 1961, p. 168.

366 Miller, 2007, p. 81.

367 Taggart and Cross, 1943, p. 117.

368 Astor, 1998, pp. 226–27.

369 Office of the Chief of Chaplains, 1944, p. 52; Jorgensen, 1961, p. 170.

370 1941, *Technical Manual 16–205: The Chaplain*, p. 65.

371 Office of the Chief of Chaplains, 1944, p. 50.

372 1944, *Technical Manual 16–205: The Chaplain*, p. 63.

373 Blaker, 1999, p. 273.

374 Mauldin, 1945, p. 103.

375 Brink, 1944, p. 50.

376 Murphy, 1949, p. 108.

377 Ambrose, 2002, between pp. 194 and 195.

378 VHP, Charles Luther Blount, online typescript of Charles Lusher's diary.

379 CARLDL, Sims, 1985, p. 1.

380 Office of the Adjutant General, Statistical and Accounting Branch, 1953, p. 80.

381 Rogers, 1946, p. 183.

382 Drury, 1950, pp. 106, 208.

383 Gawne, 2006, p. 75.

384 Office of the Chief of Chaplains, 1944, p. 48; Eggen, 1976, p. 58.

385 Office of the Chief of Chaplains, 1944, p. 54; Dear and Foot, 1995, pp. 874–75.

386 Drury, 1950, p. 42; Martin, 'Craven', p. 28.

387 1945, 'Reports of the General Board. 68. The Army Chaplain in the European Theater', pp. 3, 14.

388 1944, *Technical Manual 16–205: The Chaplain*, pp. 76–77.

389 1945, 'Reports of the General Board. 68. The Army Chaplain in the European Theater', pp. 3–4.

390 Forty, 2003, p. 69; 1945, 'Reports of the General Board. 68. The Army Chaplain in the European Theater', p. 18.

391 1945, 'Reports of the General Board. 68. The Army Chaplain in the European Theater', pp. 5–6; Donnelly, 1986, p. 33; Chandler and Collins, 1994, p. 148.

392 Donnelly, 1986, Introduction, n.p.

393 Office of the Chief of Chaplains, 1944. pp. 50–53.

394 1941, *Technical Manual 16–205: The Chaplain*, pp. 65–66.

395 Yost, 2006, pp. 11–12.

396 1944, *Technical Manual 16–205: The Chaplain*, p. 64.

397 1945, 'Reports of the General Board. 68. The Army Chaplain in the European Theater', p. 78.

398 Drury, 1950, pp. 193–94.

399 Martin, 'Craven', p. 13.

400 *The Marine Corps Gazette*, October 1943, p. 10.

401 Ibid, p. 11.

402 Willard, 1944, pp. 20, 76, 169–71; Martin, 'Craven', pp. 18–19; Drury, 1950, pp. 185–86, 198; Crosby, 1994, p. 74.

403 *Marine Corps Gazette*, October 1943, p. 10.

404 Wagner, Kennedy, Osborne and Reyburn, 2007, p. 522; Willard, 1944, p. 172.

405 Willard, 1944, p. 206.

406 Drury, 1950, p. 110; Martin, 'Craven', pp. 20, 23; Forty, 2006, p. 57.

407 Drury, 1950, p. 176; Willard, 1944, pp. 172–73.

408 Drury, 1950, p. 188.

409 Martin, 'Craven', p. 23.

410 Ibid, p. 20.

411 Drury, 1950, pp. 1, 110.

412 Drury, 1948, pp. 95–96; Forgy, 1944, p. 7; *Los Angeles Times*, 2 November 1942, p. 7.

413 Forgy, 1944, p. viii.

414 Ibid; Crosby, 1994, pp. 14–15.

415 Forgy, 1944, p. 11.

416 Drury, 1950, p. 12.

417 Claypool, 1944, p. 11.

418 Ibid, pp. 2–3.

419 Ibid, p. 2.

420 Ibid, pp. 14–15.

421 *The Chaplain*, December 1944, p. 46.

422 O'Callahan, 1956, p. 43.

423 Ibid, pp. 43–44.

424 Drury, 1950, p. 177; Drury, 1948, p. 297.

425 O'Callahan, 1956, p. 38.

426 Gawne, 2006, pp. 305–6; 1946, *History of Chaplains' Activities in the Pacific*, p. 280.

427 1944, *Technical Manual 16–205: The Chaplain*, p. 64; Cleary, 1945, p. 94.

428 Forgy, 1944, p. 10.

429 Chambers, 1999, p. 293; Methodist Commission on Chaplains, 1948, p. 98.

430 Budd, 2002, p. 152.

431 Jorgensen, 1961, p. 147.

432 Taggart and Cross, 1943, pp. 107, 111, 113–14, 129.

433 Freeman, 1991, p. 147; Bowman, 2003, p. 245; Jorgensen, 1961, p. 153.

434 *Los Angeles Times*, 1 May 1944, p. 5.

435 Yost, 2006, pp. 214–15.

436 Drury, 1950, p. 176.

437 Willard, 1944, p. 21.

438 Ibid, pp 139, 195.

439 Ibid, p. 193.

440 Crosby, 1994, p. 48; Drury, 1950, p. 159; Rabey, 2002, p. 7.

441 Donnelly, 1986, p. 73.

442 Ibid, pp. 96–97.

443 1946, *History of Chaplains' Activities in the Pacific*, p. 130.

444 *New York Times*, 24 March 1944, p. 2.

445 Office of the Adjutant General, Statistical and Accounting Branch, 1953, p. 112; Drury, 1950, p. 155.

446 1945, *American Chaplains of the Fifth Army*, pp. 39, 72–73; Cross and Arnold, 1945, p. 226.

447 1946, *History of Chaplains' Activities in the Pacific*, pp. 78; 150–51.

448 1941, *Technical Manual 16–205: The Chaplain*, pp. 66–69.

449 Atkinson, 2002, p. 234.

450 Abbott, 1946, pp. 41, 62.

451 Ibid, pp. 108–10; Gawne, 2006, p. 73; 1945, 'Reports of the General Board. 68. The Army Chaplain in the European Theater', p. 82.

452 1945, 'Reports of the General Board. 68. The Army Chaplain in the European Theater',

pp. 82–83; 1944, *Technical Manual 16–205: The Chaplain*, pp. 65–66.

453 1945, 'Reports of the General Board. 68. The Army Chaplain in the European Theater', pp. 54–55, 65–66, 82–83.

454 Drury, 1950, p. 223.

455 Claypool, 1944, pp. 20–24.

456 O'Callahan, 1956, pp. 122–23.

457 Willard, 1944, pp. 29–30.

458 Drury, 1948, p. 124.

459 Drury, 1950, p. 224.

460 Weinberg, 1945, p. 273.

461 Bérubé, 1990, p. 48.

462 Jorgensen, 1961, p. 196; Stouffer, 1949, I, p. 400.

463 Stouffer, 1949, I, p. 400.

464 Kimball, 1947, p. 64.

465 1945, 'Reports of the General Board. 68. The Army Chaplain in the European Theater', p. 51.

466 USAHEC, Walter P. Plumley Papers, Office of the Chief of Chaplains, Circular Letter No. 267, 1 August 1944.

467 Edel, 1994, p. 157; Drury, 1950, p. 249.

468 Cleary, 1945, pp. 86–87.

469 Ibid, p. 85.

470 Ibid, pp. 88–89.

471 Martin, 'Drury', p. 84.

472 Martin, 'Edel', p. 59; Martin, 'Meehling', p. 69.

473 1941, *Technical Manual 16–205: The Chaplain*, pp. 46–47.

474 1944, *Technical Manual 16–205: The Chaplain*, p. 55.

475 Kimball, 1947, p. 51.

476 Cleary, 1945, pp. 85–86.

477 1945, 'Reports of the General Board. 68. The Army Chaplain in the European Theater', p. 51.

478 Bérubé, 1990, pp. 137–41.

479 Ibid, pp. 164–65.

480 Ibid, p. 232.

481 Ibid, p. 165.

482 Jorgensen, 1961, pp. 196–97; Gushwa, 1977, pp. 133–34; Honeywell, 1958, p. 297; Drury, 1950, p. 249; Nance, 1944, p. 141.

483 Donnelly, 1986, p. 27.

484 1946, *History of Chaplains' Activities in the Pacific*, p. 188.

485 Cross and Arnold, 1945, p. 145.

486 Lunn, 1947, p. 132.

487 Ibid, p. 13.

488 Ibid, pp. 20–21, 80–89.

489 Nance, 1944, p. 141.

490 Jorgensen, 1961, p. 199; Donnelly, 1986, pp. 27–28.

491 Willard, 1944, p. 125.

492 Drury, 1950, p. 254.

493 Honeywell, 1958, pp. 295, 298.

494 McCanon, 1969, pp. 48–49.

495 Jorgensen, 1961, p. 232.

496 *The Chaplain*, June 1945, p. 6; September 1945, p. 42.

497 Donnelly, 1986, pp. 28–29.

498 Garrenton, 1957, pp. 96–99.

499 Kertzer, 1947, pp. 32–33

500 Jorgensen, 1961, p. 89.

501 Office of the Chief of Chaplains, 1944, p. 3.

502 Ibid, pp. 19–20.

503 Ibid, p. 26.

504 Ibid.

505 Ibid.

506 Lester, 1992, Reel 7, Box 60, 0851 et seq., Memorandum on 'Chaplain Exhibit' and 'Chaplain Booth Lecture', no date.

507 Ibid, Marshall to Arnold, 17 January 1944.

508 Sevareid, 1976, p. 402.

509 Gushwa, 1977, p. 109.

510 Ibid; Jorgensen, 1961, p. 218.

511 Office of the Chief of Chaplains, 1944, p. 67.

512 USAHEC, Walter P. Plumley Papers, Office of the Chief of Chaplains, Circular Letter No. 267, 1 August 1944.

513 Gushwa, 1977, pp. 77–78; Jorgensen, 1961, p. 219; USAHEC, Walter P. Plumley Papers, Office of the Chief of Chaplains, Circular Letter No. 267, 1 August 1944; *The Chaplain*, May 1945, p. 47.

514 Nance, 1944, pp. 160–66; USAHEC, Walter P. Plumley Papers, Office of the Chief of Chaplains, Circular Letter No. 267, 1 August 1944.

515 *New York Times*, 23 January 1944, p. BR 4; NARA, RG 247. Records of the Office of the Chief of Chaplains. Office Management Division Decimal File 1920–45. Box 217. 319.1 Reports– General File Volume 3/3. Undated memorandum.

516 Hy Zaret Obituary, *Independent*, 4 July 2007.

517 Lester, 1992, Reel 7, Box 60, 0851 et seq., 'The Chaplains' March' memorandum, 27 January 1944.

518 *New York Times*, 13 February 1944, p. 14.

519 https://www.youtube.com/

watch?v=mvWuJgxxM7Y, accessed 11 September 2014.

520 Cited in *New York Times*, 13 February 1944, p. 14.

521 Cross and Arnold, 1945, p. 16.

522 Drury, 1950, p. 96.

523 *The Link*, September 1944, p. 15.

524 Drury, 1950, p. 97.

525 Martin, 'Edel', p. 42.

526 Ibid, pp. 63–64.

527 Drury, 1948, p. 117; Johnson, 1945, p. 56.

528 Johnson, 1945, p. 56.

529 Drury, 1948, p. 139; Johnson, 1945, p. 56.

530 Drury, 1950, p. 236.

531 *The Chaplain*, June 1945, p. 21.

532 1941, *Technical Manual 16–205: The Chaplain*, pp. 49–50.

533 Nance, 1944, pp. 100–1.

534 Nance, 1944, pp. 116–17.

535 1945, 'Reports of the General Board. 68. The Army Chaplain in the European Theater', p. 56.

536 Ibid, pp. 56, 66 n. 24.

537 Ibid, p. 66 n. 24.

538 *The Chaplain*, June 1945, p. 22.

539 *Yank*, 31 January 1943, p. 17.

540 Kimball, 1947, p. 72.

541 Jorgensen, 1961, p. 196.

542 *The Chaplain*, November 1944, p. 47.

543 1941, *Technical Manual 16–205: The Chaplain*, p. 69.

544 1944, *Technical Manual 16–205: The Chaplain*, pp. 65–66.

545 1945, 'Reports of the General Board. 68. The Army Chaplain in the European Theater', p. 57; 1945, *American Chaplains of the Fifth Army*, p. 61.

546 1946, *History of Chaplains' Activities in the Pacific*, p. 126.

547 1945, 'Reports of the General Board. 68. The Army Chaplain in the European Theater', pp. 57, 67 n. 26–7; Rogers, 1946, p. 212.

548 Drury, 1950, pp. 26, 224; Crosby, 1994, p. 76.

549 Martin, 'Mahler', p. 24.

550 Drury, 1950, pp. 12, 104.

551 Ibid, pp. 104–6.

552 *Los Angeles Times*, 6 August 1945, p. A1.

553 Honeywell, 1958, pp. 49, 137.

554 Cross and Arnold, 1945, p. 187.

555 Jenkins, 1944, pp. 33, 45.

556 Stanton, 2006, p. 230.

557 Jenkins, 1944, p. 30.

558 *New York Times*, 28 November 1943, p. 64; Jenkins, 1944, p. 14.

559 Office of the Chief of Chaplains, 1944, p. 15.

560 Ibid, p. 14.

561 Nance, 1944, p. 151.

562 Ibid, p. 152; Gawne, 2006, pp. 216–19.

563 USAHEC, Ole K. Davidson Papers, letter of commendation, 3 September 1944.

564 Office of the Chief of Chaplains, 1944, p. 14.

565 1945, *American Chaplains of the Fifth Army*, pp. 22–23; Crosby, 1994, p. 106.

566 Crosby, 1994, pp. 103–5; Gushwa, 1977, p. 152; 1945, *American Chaplains of the Fifth Army*, p. 23.

567 1945, 'Reports of the General Board. 68. The Army Chaplain in the European Theater', p. 57.

568 Ancell and Miller, 1996, pp. 661–62.

569 Nance, 1944, pp. 241–42.

570 Martin, 1983, p. 20.

571 Drury, 1950, pp. 22, 207; Martin, 1983, p. 21.

572 http://www.history.navy.mil/danfs/index.html, accessed 28 October 2011; *The Link*, August 1943, p. 25.

573 Maguire, 1943, p. 3; Drury, 1948, p. 171; Crosby, 1994, pp. 14–16; Martin, 'Hohenstein', pp. 28–29.

574 Crosby, 1994, p. 15.

575 *The Line*, September 1943, pp. 63–64.

576 Drury, 1950, pp. 159–65.

577 Drury, 1950, p. 200; Spector, *Eagle Against the Sun*, 2001, p. 536.

578 Spector, *Eagle Against the Sun*, 2001, p. 537; Drury, 1950, pp. 200–1; Methodist Commission on Chaplains, 1948, pp. 20–21.

579 O'Callahan, 1956, pp. 85–86, 94, 105.

580 Drury, 1950, p. 201.

581 Martin, 'Mahler', p. 27. The USS *O'Callahan* was duly launched in 1965.

582 Cross and Arnold, 1945, pp. 167–72; Poling, 1944, pp. 135–36; Nance, 1944, pp. 155–59; Gushwa, 1977, pp. 128–29; Methodist Commission on Chaplains, 1948, p. 63.

583 Gushwa, 1977, p. 153.

584 Moore, 1998, p. 37.

585 Jorgensen, 1961, p. 93; Smith, 2006, p. 204.

586 Poling, 1944, p. 136.

587 Kurzman, 2004, p. 185.

588 Gushwa, 1977, p. 129; Methodist Commission on Chaplains, 1948, p. 63; Kurzman, 2004, p. 184; Holifield, 2007, p. 237.

589 Holifield, 2007, p. 237; *The Milwaukee Journal*, 4 February 1951, p. 1.

590 Poling, 1959, pp. 256–61; Gushwa, 1977, pp. 129–30.

591 Kurzman, 2004, p. 184.

592 Cantril and Strunk, 1951, p. 790; Gushwa, 1977, pp. 93–94.

593 Lev, 1941, p. 10.

594 Office of the Chief of Chaplains, 1944, Introduction.

595 Nance, 1944, p. 120; Drury, 1950, p. 87.

596 Slomovitz, 1999, pp. 98–101.

597 *The Chaplain*, August 1945, pp. 21–23; Moore, 1998, pp. 44–46; *The American Israelite*, 5 July 1945, p. 1.

598 Venzke, 1977, pp. 2, 11.

599 Ward and Burns, 2007, p. 398; CARLDL, 'After–Action Report 82nd Airborne Division May 1945', p. 9.

600 http://www.parafame.org/trustees.htm, accessed 26 July 2011; http://www.strike-hold504th.com/germany.php, accessed 14 July 2011.

601 *The Chaplain*, November 1945, p. 42; Drury, 1950, pp. 89, 212–14; Venzke, 1977, pp. 1–2.

602 Drury, 1950, pp. 51–2; Barish, 1962, p. 20; Grobman, 1993, p. 8; Moore, 1998, p. 33.

603 1946, *History of Chaplains' Activities in the Pacific*, p. 472.

604 Ibid, pp. 481, 483.

605 Nance, 1944, pp. 95–96.

606 1945, 'Reports of the General Board. 68. The Army Chaplain in the European Theater', p. 57.

607 Ibid.

608 1945, *American Chaplains of the Fifth Army*, Foreword.

609 Drury, 1950, p. 308.

610 Bergen, 2004, p. 174; 1945, 'Reports of the General Board. 68. The Army Chaplain in the European Theater', pp. 57, 67–68.

611 *The Chaplain*, July 1945, pp. 19–21.

612 Ibid, August 1945, pp. 14–16.

613 Ibid, pp. 31–32.

614 *The Christian Century*, 5 June 1946, pp. 716–17.

615 1945, 'Reports of the General Board. 68. The Army Chaplain in the European Theater', Appendix 27, pp. 67–69.

616 Ibid, Appendix 15, pp. 32, 35–36.

617 Wells, 1995, pp. 79–80; Stouffer, 1949, I, p. 400.

618 1945, 'Reports of the General Board. 68. The Army Chaplain in the European Theater', p. 68.

619 Ibid, Appendix 14, p. 31.

620 Ibid, p. 30.

621 Ibid, Appendix 16, pp. 38–42.

622 Ibid, p. 41.

623 Cleary, 1945, pp. 97–98.

624 Holifield, 2007, p. 237.

625 Loveland, 2000; Loveland, 2004; Venzke, 1977, pp. 39–46.

626 Gregory, 1947; Holifield, 2007, pp. 241–42.

627 Holifield, 2007, p. 249.

628 *The Chaplain*, July 1945, pp. 17–18.

629 *The Chaplain*, March 1946, p. 19.

630 Venzke, 1977, p. 49; McCanon, 1969, pp. 152–60; NARA, RG 247 Records of the Office of the Chief of Chaplains. Records of Administration and Management General Records. Records Relating to the History of the Chaplains of the United States Army, 1941–58. Box 3. 'The Corps of Chaplains 1 July 1945 to 30 September 1946', pp. 19–21; Holifield, 2007, p. 252; *The Christian Century*, 21 November 1945, p. 1277.

631 Putnam and Campbell, 2010, pp. 84–85.

632 Ibid, p. 83.

CHAPTER 2
Religion and American Military Culture

1 Eichhorn, 2004, p. 13.

2 http://www.history.army.mil/html/faq/oaths.html and http://usmilitary.about.com/od/joiningthemilitary/a/oathofenlist.htm, accessed 3 January 2013.

3 Chambers, 1999, p. 355; Donagan, 2011, pp. 141–56.

4 Nance, 1944, 103; Fahey, 1992, 4.

5 Elkin, 1946, p. 422.

6 Gawne, 2006, 104–5; Enjames, 2003, I, 255.

7 http://www.audiemurphy.com/places018.htm, accessed 2 September 2013.

8 *New York Times*, 3 February 1944, p. 9; Yost, 2006, pp. 128–29.

9 Eichhorn, 2004, p. 162.

10 Gawne, 2006, 111–12; *The Chaplain*, December 1944, 12; NARA Record Group 247. Chief of Chaplains. Office Management Division Decimal File 1920–45. Box 259. 333.1 Extracts from Reports of Inspectors. Volume II. Visit of Inspection to Camp Mackall, 3 April 1943, Inclosure No. 2; 1946, *History of Chaplains' Activities in the Pacific*, p. 507.

11 Harrod, 1978, p. 63.

12 Fredman and Falk, 1954, p. 104.

13 Ibid, pp. 103–4.

14 Ibid, p. 105.

15 *The National Catholic Almanac*, 1942, p. 566.

16 Yost, 2006, pp. 104–5.

17 NARA, RG 247 Records of the Office of the Chief of Chaplains. Records of Administration and Management General Records. Records Relating to the History of the Chaplains of the United States Army, 1941–58. Box 3. 'Military History of the Second World War. The Corps of Chaplains', pp. 124, 127.

18 Ibid, p. 111.

19 Silcox and Fisher, 1979, pp. 22–23.

20 *The Chaplain*, November 1946, p. 20.

21 1945, 'Reports of the General Board. 68. The Army Chaplain in the European Theater', pp. 44–45, n. 21–22.

22 Ibid, pp. 52, 72.

23 Ibid, p. 45.

24 Moore, 2004, pp. 65–66.

25 Moore, 1998, p. 47.

26 NARA, RG 247 Records of the Office of the Chief of Chaplains. Records of Administration and Management General Records. Records Relating to the History of the Chaplains of the United States Army, 1941–58. Box 3. 'Military History of the Second World War. The Corps of Chaplains', p. 121.

27 Kertzer, 1947, p. 28.

28 Grobman, 1993, p. 9.

29 Wall, 2004, p. 191.

30 Kertzer, 1947, p. 141.

31 Atkinson, 2002, p. 356; Kertzer, 1947, pp. 141, 144.

32 Kertzer, 1947, pp. 141–42.

33 Ibid, pp. 142–45.

34 Cleary, 1945, pp. 74–75.

35 Office of the Adjutant General, Statistical and Accounting Branch, 1953, p. 8.

36 1945, 'Reports of the General Board. 68. The Army Chaplain in the European Theater', p. 41.

37 1937, 'Army Regulations No. 60–5. Chaplains. General Provisions', par. 11; Gushwa, 1977, p. 38; 1945, 'Reports of the General Board. 68. The Army Chaplain in the European Theater', p. 43. By the beginning of 1945 public worship in the armed services could be marked by a customised chaplain's flag, a Chicago textile company providing no fewer than sixteen different designs. *The Chaplain*, February 1945, p. 48.

38 Kertzer, 1947, pp. 15–16, 30.

39 http://www.history.navy.mil/faqs/faq59-7. htm, accessed 12 September 2014, Article 2.

40 http://www.history.navy.mil/faqs/faq59-37. htm, accessed 12 September 2014; Cleary, 1945, pp. 75–76.

41 Nance, 1944, p. 135.

42 Drury, 1949, p. 210.

43 Drury, 1949, pp. 229–30; Drury, 1950, p. 123.

44 Nance, 1944, pp. 136–37.

45 Leuschner, 1946, pp. 115–16.

46 Norton, 1977, pp. 51–52.

47 1945, 'Reports of the General Board. 68. The Army Chaplain in the European Theater', p. 47; Honeywell, 1958, p. 168.

48 Gushwa, 1977, p. 79; Stover, 1977, pp. 239, 247.

49 1937, 'Army Regulations No. 60–5. Chaplains. General Provisions', par. 9.

50 Honeywell, 1958, pp. 186–87.

51 *Chicago Tribune*, 19 August 1940, p. 14.

52 Kimball, 1947, p. 38; Stanton, 2006, p. 536.

53 *The Chaplain*, December 1945, pp. 43–44.

54 Ibid, p. 44.

55 Rogers, 1946, p. 146.

56 Donnelly, 1986, pp. 68–69.

57 Sampson, 1958, p. 49.

58 Ambrose, 2001, pp. 118–19.

59 1945, *American Chaplains of the Fifth Army*, p. 82.

60 Kertzer, 1947, p. 39.

61 *The Chaplain*, April 1945, pp. 32–33.

62 1945, 'Reports of the General Board. 68. The Army Chaplain in the European Theater', pp. 47–48

63 Ibid, p. 48.

64 1945, 'Reports of the General Board. 68. The Army Chaplain in the European Theater', p. 41.

65 Drury, 1949, pp. 100–1.

66 Ibid, p. 73.

67 Drury, 1950, p. 211.

68 Hynes, 2005, pp. 31–32.

69 Drury, 1949, p. 128.

70 Fahey, 1992, p. 5.

71 Drury, 1950, p. 210.

72 Nance, 1944, p. 138.

73 Martin, 'Meehling', p. 69.

74 Nance, 1944, pp. 138–39.

75 Drury, 1950, p. 221.

76 Johnson, 1945, pp. 48–49.

77 Tower, 1945, p. 121.

78 *The Chaplain*, June 1945, pp. 40–41.

79 Drury, 1950, p. 211.

80 Martin, 1983, pp. 38–39; Drury, 1950, p. 211.

81 Drury, 1950, pp. 269–70.

82 *The Chaplain*, September 1946, p. 33.

83 Martin, Craven, 1980, p. 13.

84 Willard, 1944, p. 209.

85 Ibid.

86 Ibid.

87 Hoopes and Brinkley, 1992, pp. 13–15.

88 Drury, 1950, p. 210.

89 Ibid.

90 Smith, 2006, pp. 24–27; Preston, 2012, p. 86; Kidd, 2010, pp. 116–19.

91 See, for example, Wilson, 1914 and Griffin, 1908.

92 Rable, 2010, pp. 137–38.

93 Ibid, pp. 138 39; Miller, 2007, p. 205.

94 Rable, 2010, pp. 95–96; Miller, 2007, p. 203.

95 Rable, 2010, p. 112; Tsouras, 2005, p. 371.

96 Cross and Arnold, 1945, p. 137.

97 Perry, 2011, pp. 144–45.

98 *The Leatherneck*, December 1928, p. 12.

99 *The Link*, September 1944, p. 4.

100 Ebel, 2010, p. 89.

101 Metcalf, 1957, p. 20.

102 Lee, 1985, pp. 10–21.

103 Chambers, 1999, p. 839.

104 *Yank*, 20 December 1942, p. 14.

105 Ibid, 14 March 1943, p. 16.

106 Ibid, 20 December 1942, p. 14.

107 Soffer, 1998, pp. 36–37.

108 Ridgway and Martin, 1956, pp. 52–53.

109 *Yank*, 20 December 1942, p. 18.

110 Lee, 1985, p. 114.

111 Rabey, 2002, p. 218.

112 Cited in Rawson, 2011, p. 151.

113 *The Chaplain*, December 1944, p. 24.

114 Abbott, 1946, p. 6.

115 Atkinson, 2002, p. 222.

116 Abbott, 1946, p. 4.

117 Sampson, 1958, pp. 33–34.

118 Ibid, 1958, p. 34.

119 Willard, 1944, p. 34.

120 Ibid.

121 Janowitz, 1960, p. 100.

122 Ibid, p. 81.

123 Ibid, pp. 80, 97.

124 Ibid, pp. 87–89.

125 Ibid, Table 18, p. 98.

126 Ibid, p. 97.

127 Ancell and Miller, 1996, p. 281; Atkinson, 2013, p. 581.

128 Eichhorn, 2004, p. 161.

129 Ibid, p. 162.

130 Weigley, 1981, p. 675; Atkinson, 2013, p. 582.

131 Abercrombie, 1977, pp. 17 and 20, note 7; Loveland, 1996, p. 301.

132 Pappas, 1987, p. 154.

133 Ibid, p. 154; Stover, 1977, p. 241.

134 Pappas, 1987, p. 155; Stover, 1977, p. 242.

135 Pappas, 1987, p. 155.

136 Stover, 1977, pp. 239, 247.

137 Pappas, 1987, p. 155.

138 Ibid, p. 32.

139 Ibid, p. 18.

140 Stover, 1977, pp. 245–49.

141 Venzke, 1977, pp. 50–51.

142 Janowitz, 1960, p. 99.

143 Pope, 1995, pp. 439–40.

144 Bennett, 1942, p. 194.

145 *Los Angeles Times*, 12 June 1939, p. 10.

146 Janowitz, 1960, p. 98.

147 Smith, 2006, pp. 222–23; Coffey, 1982, p. 15.

148 Coffey, 1982, p. 18.

149 Coffman, 2004, pp. 237–38.

150 Smith, 2006, p. 235.

151 Atkinson, 2007, p. 183.

152 Blumenson, 1984, p. 17.

153 Janowitz, 1960, p. 98.

154 *New York Times*, 11 June 1900, p. 5.

155 Pappas, 1987, p. 155.

156 Janowitz, 1960, p. 89; Coffman, 2004, p. 144.

157 Coffman, 2004, p. 146.

158 Booth and Spencer, 1994, pp. 20–31.

159 Chambers, 1999, p. 589.

160 http://www.arlingtoncemetery.net/josephla.htm, accessed 13 February 2014; Ancell and Miller, 1996, pp. 60–61.

161 Ancell and Miller, 1996, pp. 5 and 87.

162 Astor, 2003, p. 226; Atkinson, 2007, pp. 99, 159–60.

163 Reynolds, 1996, pp. 22–23.

164 Taylor, 1989, p. 152.

165 Sampson, 1958, p. 95.

166 Taylor, 1989, p. 153.

167 Coffman, 2004, pp. 151, 235; Spector, *At War at Sea*, 2001, pp. 135, 137–38.

168 Spector, *At War at Sea*, 2001, p. 135;
Karsten, 2008, p. 74; Drury, 1949, p. 242.

169 Drury, 1950, pp. 275–77.

170 Hodgkins, 1944, p. 1.

171 Ibid.

172 Drury, 1949, pp. 68–69.

173 Karsten, 2008, pp. 25–26, 73.

174 Ibid, Table 3–1, p. 75.

175 Janowitz, 1960, Table 19, p. 99.

176 Drury, 1949, p. 243.

177 http://www.history.navy.mil/faqs/faq59-7.
htm, accessed 12 September 2014, Articles 1 and
8; Mygatt and Darlington, 1944, p. 15.

178 Martin, 'Edel', p. 53; *The Chaplain*,
September 1945, p. 41; Mygatt and Darlington,
1944, p. 69.

179 Drury, 1949, pp. 72, 127, 160, 242.

180 Drury, 1949, pp. 242–43; Martin, 'Fondren
Thomas', pp. 34–35.

181 Bennett, 1942, pp. 193–94; Drury, 1950, p.
4; Mygatt and Darlington, 1944, pp. 65, 67; *The
Link*, May 1943, inside cover.

182 http://www.history.navy.mil/faqs/faq59-7.
htm), accessed 12 September 2014, Article 1.

183 Claypool, 1944, pp. 73–74.

184 Ibid, pp. 2 and 53–60.

185 Fahey, 1992, p. 84.

186 Ibid, p. 302.

187 Wuest, 1953, p. 25.

188 Ibid.

189 *The Link*, December 1944, p. 50.

190 Ibid, July 1945, p. 37.

191 Yost, 2006, p. 259.

192 Ancell and Miller, 1996, pp. 263–64;
Stanton, 2006, pp. 141–42.

193 *The Link*, April 1944, p. 22.

194 Ibid, pp. 22–23.

195 Ancell and Miller, 1996, pp. 183–84.

196 *The Link*, October 1945, p. 65.

197 Ancell and Miller, 1996, pp. 93–94.

198 *The Chaplain*, July 1946, p. 49.

199 1945, *American Chaplains of the Fifth Army*,
pp. 40–41.

200 Ibid, pp. 22–23.

201 Ibid, p. 43.

202 Reynolds, 1996, p. 105; Ancell and Miller,
1996, p. 185.

203 Reynolds, 1996, p. 105.

204 1945, 'Reports of the General Board. 68.
The Army Chaplain in the European Theater',
pp. 59, 68.

205 Gregg, 1945, p. 218.

206 Ibid, p. 217.

207 Mitchell, 2002, pp. 12–18.

208 Ibid, pp. 3, 10; Soffer, 1998, p. 11.

209 Soffer, 1998, pp. 12–13.

210 Atkinson, 2007, p. 107; Mitchell, 2002, pp.
12–13, 15; Keegan, 1982, pp. 75–76.

211 Ancell and Miller, 1996, p. 186.

212 Sampson, 1958, pp. 43–44.

213 Ancell and Miller, 1996, p. 114.

214 Booth and Spencer, 1994, p. 64; Biggs, 1980,
pp. 44–45.

215 Gavin, 2007, p. 111; Booth and Spencer,
1994, pp. 60–61.

216 http://voices.yahoo.com/d-day-veterans-
landed-normandy-remember-two-363691.
html?cat=37, accessed 21 December 2012.

217 Keegan, 1982, p. 75.

218 Nance, 1944, p. 210.

219 Atkinson, 2007, p. 184.

220 Ibid.

221 Ibid, p. 376.

222 Mygatt and Darlington, title page.

223 *Christian Herald*, April 1944, p. 53.

224 Mygatt and Darlington, 1944, p. 23.

225 Atkinson, 2007, p. 565; 1945, *American
Chaplains of the Fifth Army*, pp. 46–47.

226 Clark, 2007, p. 5.

227 Ibid, pp. 256, 297–98; Ellis, 1969, p. 159;
Inboden, 2010, pp. 154–55.

228 Astor, 2003, p. 215.

229 Mygatt and Darlington, 1944, p. 91.

230 Cantril and Strunk, 1951, pp. 263–64.

231 Nance, 1944, p. 195.

232 MacArthur, 1964, p. 61

233 Ibid, pp. 83, 106–7.

234 James, 1975, II, pp. 417–18.

235 Atkinson, 2007, p. 49.

236 Nance, 1944, p. 192.

237 Ibid, p. 193.

238 Ibid, p. 195.

239 Ibid, p. 192.

240 Carlson, 1945, p. 56; *The Link*, December
1943, p. 17.

241 Nance, 1944, p. 195.

242 James, 1975, II, pp. 663–64, 891 note 2; *The
Link*, April 1943, p. 2.

243 *The Link*, April 1943, p. 35; James, 1975, II,
p. 859 note 32.

244 MacArthur, 1964, pp. 216–17.

245 Gannon, 1962, pp. 362–63.

246 1946, *History of Chaplains' Activities in the Pacific*, pp. 292–93; Jorgensen, 1961, p. 180.

247 Hastings, 2007, p. 586; 1946, *History of Chaplains' Activities in the Pacific*, p. 141; *The Christian Century*, 19 September 1945, pp. 1056–57.

248 MacArthur, 1964, pp. 275–76.

249 Considine, 1942, pp. 74–75.

250 MacArthur, 1964, p. 276.

251 Atkinson, 2007, p. 267.

252 Nance, 1944, p. 198.

253 Smith, 2006, p. 224.

254 Smith, 2006, p. 223; Atkinson, 2007, pp. 182–84, 376; Snape, 2005, pp. 72–76.

255 Gannon, 1962, p. 205.

256 Hastings, 2011, pp. 451–52.

257 Blumenson, 1972, II, p. 66; Atkinson, 2007, p. 59; Smith, 2006, p. 222.

258 Atkinson, 2007, p. 50.

259 Atkinson, 2002, pp. 465–66.

260 Eisenhower, 1948, p. 173.

261 *The Link*, March 1944, p. 66.

262 http://www.army.mil/d-day/message.html, accessed 10 January 2013.

263 Smith, 2006, p. 227.

264 Nance, 1944, p. 199.

265 Ibid.

266 *The Link*, December 1944, p. 66.

267 Mygatt and Darlington, 1944, p. 66.

268 Nance, 1944, p. 206.

269 Smith, 2006, p. 229.

270 *The Link*, April 1944, p. 44; Carlson, 1945, pp. 56–57.

271 Smith, 2006, pp. 223–32.

272 Preston, 2012, p. 443; Smith, 2006, pp. 232–33.

273 *The Chaplain*, August 1946, p. 7.

274 *Chicago Tribune*, 27 November 1943, p. 6.

275 Blumenson, 1972, II, pp. 268, 387–88.

276 Ayer, 1965, p. 48; Patton, 1995, pp. 18, 95; Blumenson, 1972, II, p. 357.

277 Blumenson, 1972, II, p. 357.

278 Ayer, 1965, pp. 9, 139, 210–11; Patton, 1995, p. xi.

279 Ayer, 1965, pp. 5, 48.

280 Blumenson, 1972, II, p. 102; *The Link*, September 1943, p. 17.

281 Nance, 1944, p. 207.

282 Atkinson, 2002, p. 433.

283 Patton, 1995, p. 384.

284 Ayer, 1965, p. 116.

285 Carlson, 1945, p. 57; Blumenson, 1972, II, p. 720.

286 Ayer, 1965, p. viii.

287 Blumenson, 1972, II, p. 266.

288 Metcalf, 1957, pp. 196–97.

289 Blumenson, 1972, II, p. 394; Mygatt and Darlington, 1944, p. 34.

290 Metcalf, 1957, pp. 183–84; Atkinson, 2013, p. 349.

291 Metcalf, 1957, pp. 183–84.

292 Patton, 1995, p. 185; VHP, James Meeks, VHP MSS Box 124. Folder 10/21.

293 Metcalf, 1957, p. 185.

294 Poling, 1959, p. 224.

295 D'Este, 1996, pp. 685–88.

296 Metcalf, 1957, p. 185.

297 *Chicago Tribune*, 27 November 1943, p. 6.

298 Ayer, 1965, p. 152.

299 Ambrose, 1998, p. 346.

300 Ayer, 1965, p. viii.

301 Ibid, p. 190.

302 Ibid, p. 4.

303 Poling, 1959, p. 223.

304 *The Christian Century*, 8 December 1943, pp. 1427–28; 10 May 1944, p. 580; 4 July 1945, p. 780.

305 Marshall, Pogue and Bland, 1991, p. 548.

306 Blumenson, 1972, II, p. 256.

307 Ibid, p. 268.

308 Metcalf, 1957, p. 258.

309 Ayer, 1965, p. 48.

310 NARA Record Group 247. Chief of Chaplains. Office Management Division Decimal File 1920–45. Box 194 250.1 Morals and Conduct – Language (Profanity). Lawrence E. Deery to William R. Arnold, 17 September 1943.

311 Ayer, 1965, p. 201.

312 Atkinson, 2007, p. 44.

313 Blumenson, 1972, II, p. 357.

314 Ayer, 1965, p. 202.

315 Metcalf, 1957, pp. 168–69, 173.

316 Ibid, p. 168.

317 Patton, 1995, p. 185.

318 Poling, 1959, p. 224.

319 *The Link*, July 1943, p. 4.

320 Ibid, November 1944, p. 15.

321 Weigley, 1968, pp. 421–23.

322 Nance, 1944, pp. 189–90; Marshall, Pogue and Bland, 1991, p. 81.

323 Marshall, Pogue and Bland, 1991, pp. 54–55, 72; Pogue, 1964, p. 21.

324 Marshall, Pogue and Bland, 1991, pp. 138, 548; Nance, 1944, p. 191;

325 Marshall, Pogue and Bland, 1991, pp. 199–200, 361–62; Pogue, 1964, p. 196.

326 Marshall, Pogue and Bland, 1991, pp. 481–82; Pogue, 1966, pp. 105–19.

327 Marshall and DeWeerd, 1945, pp. 92–93.

328 Nance, 1944, p. 189.

329 Marshall, Pogue and Bland, 1991, pp. 471–73.

330 Ibid, p. 324.

331 Ibid, p. 323.

332 Ibid, p. 472.

333 Marshall and DeWeerd, 1945, pp. 122–24; Bland, 1986, II, pp. 536–37.

334 Nance, 1944, p. 191.

335 *The Link*, August 1944, p. 1.

336 Spiller and Dawson, 1984, II, p. 564.

337 Ibid.

338 Wagner, Kennedy, Osborne and Reyburn, 2007, p. 301; Jeffries, 1996, p. 178; Spiller and Dawson, 1984, II, p. 565.

339 Claypool, 1944, p. 29.

340 Buell, 1980, p. 65 footnote.

341 Mygatt and Darlington, 1944, p. 27.

342 Buell, 1980, p. 89.

343 Dear and Foot, 1995, p. 651.

344 Buell, 1980, pp. 88–89.

345 Ibid, pp. 64–65.

346 Spiller and Dawson, 1984, II, p. 800.

347 Dear and Foot, 1995, p. 802.

348 Potter, 1976, pp. 26, 442–43, 456.

349 Wukovits, 1992, p. 173; Spiller and Dawson, 1984, II, p. 1034.

350 Spiller and Dawson, 1984, II, p. 428.

351 Merrill, 1992, p. 232; Hastings, 2007, p. 6; Dower, 1986, p. 36.

352 Love, 1992, p. 78.

353 *The Link*, January/February, 1943, p. 9.

354 Nance, 1944, p. 214.

355 Claypool, 1944, p. 53

356 Ibid, pp. 54–55.

357 Mygatt and Darlington, 1944, p. 27.

358 Ancell and Miller, 1996, p. 509.

359 1943, *Prayer Book for Catholic Service Men*, p. 76.

360 Willard, 1944, p. 183.

361 Tower, 1945, p. 136.

362 Ibid, p. 136.

363 Millett, 1991, p. 234.

364 Spiller and Dawson, 1984, I, pp. 157–58.

365 Ibid, pp. 158–59.

366 Blankfort, 1947, pp. 23–25.

367 Spiller and Dawson, 1984, I, pp. 158–60.

368 Blankfort, 1947, p. 12.

369 Ibid, p. 278.

370 Cameron, 1994, p. 22.

371 Mygatt and Darlington, 1944, p. 16.

372 Vandegrift, 1964, p. 25.

373 Ibid, p. 175.

374 Willard, 1944, p. 137.

375 *The Link*, November 1943, p. 28.

376 Nance, 1944, pp. 242–43.

377 Mygatt and Darlington, 1944, p. 29.

378 Vonnegut, 2010, p. 38.

379 1924, 'Army Regulations No. 60–5. Chaplains. General Provisions', par. 10.

380 Jorgensen, 1961, pp. 142–43; Bland, 1986, p. 343.

381 1945, 'Reports of the General Board. 68. The Army Chaplain in the European Theater', p. 28; Gushwa, 1977, pp. 175–76.

382 Donnelly, 1986, pp. 33–34.

383 Ibid, pp. 34–45.

384 *The Link*, March 1944, pp. 19–20.

385 Ibid, December 1944, pp. 46–47.

386 1945, 'Reports of the General Board. 68. The Army Chaplain in the European Theater', p. 29.

387 Nance, 1944, p. 142.

388 *The Link*, June 1944, pp. 28–29.

389 McGuire, 1993, p. 132.

390 Kertzer, 1947, p. 16.

391 Hale, 2004, p. 15.

392 Abbott, 1946, p. 62.

393 Ibid, p. 131.

394 1945, *American Chaplains of the Fifth Army*, p. 79.

395 *Yank*, 13 June 1943, p. 6.

396 Connelly, 1945, p. 19.

397 Ibid, 'The Author'.

398 Gushwa, 1977, pp. 176–77; 1945, 'Reports of the General Board. 68. The Army Chaplain in the European Theater', p. 29.

399 Wuest, 1953, pp. 17–19.

400 Jorgensen, 1961, p. 143.

401 1945, 'Reports of the General Board. 68. The Army Chaplain in the European Theater', p. 28; Jorgensen, 1961, p. 145.

402 1945, 'Reports of the General Board. 68. The Army Chaplain in the European Theater', p. 29.

403 1946, *History of Chaplains' Activities in the Pacific*, p. 80.

404 Jorgensen, 1961, p. 143.

405 Kimball, 1947, pp. 110, 122.

406 Bérubé, 1990, p. 62.

407 1946, *History of Chaplains' Activities in the Pacific*, p. 283.

408 *The Link*, April 1945, pp. 26–27.

409 Ibid, February 1945, p. 34.

410 Hale, 2004, pp. 14–15.

411 USAHEC, Charles E. Wilson Papers, 'Frail Children of the Dust', pp. 267–68.

412 Gushwa, 1977, pp. 176–77.

413 1945, 'Reports of the General Board. 68. The Army Chaplain in the European Theater', pp. 31–32.

414 Harrod, 1978, p. 65.

415 Drury, 1950, p. 78.

416 Martin, 'Meehling', p. 40.

417 Drury, 1950, p. 79.

418 Ibid, pp. 78, 80.

419 *The Link*, November 1944, p. 17.

420 Ibid.

421 Drury, 1950, pp. 80, 82, 84.

422 Tower, 1945, p. 146.

423 Ibid, pp. 146–47.

424 Ibid, p. 147.

425 Ibid, p. 149.

426 Drury, 1950, pp. 80–82.

427 Jorgensen, 1961, p. 72; Shindler, 1912, pp. 70, 91–94.

428 Jorgensen, 1961, pp. 39, 72.

429 Ibid, p. 72.

430 Ibid, pp. 73, 314.

431 Jorgensen, 1961, pp. 74–75; Gushwa, 1977, pp. 71–72.

432 Jorgensen, 1961, p. 74.

433 NARA Record Group 247. Chief of Chaplains. Office Management Division Decimal File 1920–45. Box 249. 333.1 Extracts from Reports of Inspectors. Volume I. Passim.

434 http://www.eyeonkansas.org/ncentral/geary/0603FortRiley.html, accessed 1 August 2012.

435 NARA Record Group 247. Chief of Chaplains. Office Management Division Decimal File 1920–45. Box 249. 333.1 Extracts from Reports of Inspectors. Volume I.

436 Jorgensen, 1961, p. 237.

437 RG 247 Records of the Office of the Chief of Chaplains. Records of Administration and Management General Records. Records Relating to the History of the Chaplains of the United States Army, 1941–58. Box 8. 'The Army Builds Chapels', War Department Press Release, 20 March 1941.

438 Ibid.

439 Lester, 1992, Reel 7, Box 60, 0827 et seq. Arnold to Marshall, 17 June 1941.

440 Ibid.

441 Ibid, Arnold to Marshall, 21 June 1941.

442 RG 247 Records of the Office of the Chief of Chaplains. Records of Administration and Management General Records. Records Relating to the History of the Chaplains of the United States Army, 1941–58. Box 8. 'The Army Builds Chapels', Descriptive.

443 Ibid, 'Introductory Address'.

444 Ibid, 'Remarks by Major General Edmund B. Gregory'.

445 Ibid, 'Remarks by General George C. Marshall'.

446 Ibid, 'Remarks by Chaplain William R. Arnold'.

447 Ibid, Arnold to CBS Program Manager, 28 July 1941.

448 Honeywell, 1958, pp. 265–66.

449 Ibid, pp. 265–66.

450 RG 247 Records of the Office of the Chief of Chaplains. Records of Administration and Management General Records. Records Relating to the History of the Chaplains of the United States Army, 1941–58. Box 8. 'The Army Builds Chapels', Descriptive and War Department Press Release, 20 March 1941.

451 Bureau of the Census, 1976, Series A 43–72, pp. 2, 11.

452 Wuest, 1953, pp. 33–34.

453 *The Link*, August 1943, p. 66.

454 Jorgensen, 1961, p. 237.

455 Ibid, pp. 238–40.

456 RG 247 Records of the Office of the Chief of Chaplains. Records of Administration and Management General Records. Records Relating to the History of the Chaplains of the United States Army, 1941–58. Box 8. 'The Army Builds Chapels', War Department Press Release, 20 March 1941; Jorgensen, 1961, p. 240.

457 RG 247 Records of the Office of the Chief of Chaplains. Records of Administration and Management General Records. Records Relating to the History of the Chaplains of the United States Army, 1941–58. Box 8. 'The Army Builds Chapels', 'Remarks by Major General Edmund B. Gregory'.

458 *The Link*, February 1944, p. 13.

459 Ibid.

460 Preston, 2012, pp. 349–50.

461 *The Link*, March 1944, p. 65.

462 Edel, 1994, p. 113.

463 Ibid.

464 Martin, 'Edel', p. 41.

465 *The Leatherneck*, January 1932, p. 27.

466 Edel, 1994, p. 113.

467 Ibid.

468 Drury, 1950, pp. 3–5; Edel, 1994, pp. 139–40; Martin, 'Edel', pp. 50–51.

469 Drury, 1950, pp. 7–8.

470 *Christian Science Monitor*, 13 November 1943, p. 11.

471 Drury, 1950, p. 8.

472 Ibid, pp. 123–31.

473 Ibid, pp. 125–26, 131.

474 Ibid, pp. 7, 134. There is a discrepancy in Drury's figures for the total of chapels functioning in July 1941.

475 Ibid, p. 125.

476 Edel, 1994, pp. 152–53.

477 Drury, 1950, p. 130.

478 Ibid, pp. 142–44.

479 Ibid, pp. 124–25, 127.

480 Ibid, p. 124.

481 Ibid, p. 128; Edel, 1994, pp. 152–53.

482 Cross and Arnold, 1945, p. 154.

483 1946, *History of Chaplains' Activities in the Pacific*, pp. 185, 199, 200, 213.

484 Ibid, pp. 504, 516–18.

485 NARA RG 492. Records of the MTO Headquarters. Chaplain Section. Box 1680. Folder 312.1 Circulars– Letter, Numbered. 3. Standard Operating Procedure for Production and Presentation of 'The Mediterranean Church of the Air', 29 July 1944.

486 1945, *American Chaplains of the Fifth Army*, p. 60.

487 1945, 'Reports of the General Board. 68. The Army Chaplain in the European Theater', p. 58.

488 Ibid.

489 Ibid.

490 Ibid.

491 Morley, 2001, pp. 85–86.

492 1945, 'Reports of the General Board. 68. The Army Chaplain in the European Theater', p. 58.

493 NARA RG 247 Records of the Office of the Chief of Chaplains. Records of Administration and Management General Records. Records Relating to the History of the Chaplains of the United States Army, 1941–58. Box 9. 'Helpful Hints and Other Information', May 1942, pp. 24–26; Office of the Chief of Chaplains, 1944, pp. 37–39.

494 Office of the Chief of Chaplains, 1944, pp. 42–43; Yost, 2006, p. 7.

495 Ibid, 1961, p. 256.

496 Jorgensen, 1961, p. 256.

497 1945, 'Reports of the General Board. 68. The Army Chaplain in the European Theater', p. 107.

498 Yost, 2006, pp. 139–40.

499 1946, *History of Chaplains' Activities in the Pacific*, pp. 440–47.

500 Ibid, pp. 179, 513.

501 Ibid, p. 225.

502 Ibid, p. 281.

503 Ibid, pp. 114, 513.

504 *Yank*, 5 September 1943, p. 9.

505 1945, 'Reports of the General Board. 68. The Army Chaplain in the European Theater', p. 117.

506 1946, *History of Chaplains' Activities in the Pacific*, p. 95.

507 Ibid, p. 417.

508 1945, 'Reports of the General Board. 68. The Army Chaplain in the European Theater', p. 117.

509 Kertzer, 1947, p. 116.

510 Tower, 1945, p. 75.

511 Ibid, p. 37.

512 Ibid, p. 39.

513 Drury, 1950, pp. 118–20.

514 Willoughby, 1943, pp. 16–21; Smith, 2006, p. 28.

515 Noll, 2002, p. 268.

516 Willoughby, 1943, pp. 31–32.

517 Ibid, pp. 27–29.

518 Ibid, p. 33.

519 Ibid, pp. 35–36.

520 Ibid, pp. 34–35.

521 Jorgensen, 1961, p. 256.

522 1942, *The New Testament of Our Lord and Saviour Jesus Christ. Prepared for Use of Protestant Personnel of the Army of the United States*, n.p.

523 Jorgensen, 1961, p. 257.

524 Ibid; Office of the Chief of Chaplains, 1944, p. 45.

525 Lester, 1992, Reel 7, Box 60, 0851 et seq.

526 Office of the Chief of Chaplains, 1944, p. 44; Jorgensen, 1961, p. 257.

527 Jorgensen, 1961, p. 256; Honeywell, 1958, p. 260.

528 Office of the Chief of Chaplains, 1944, p. 44.

529 Honeywell, 1958, p. 260.

530 NARA Record Group 247. Chief of Chaplains. Office Management Division Decimal File 1920–45. Box 262. 350.01 Testaments (Administration and Policy of). Correspondence, 27 September 1943 to 28 December 1944, passim; Honeywell, 1958, p. 260.

531 Jorgensen, 1961, p. 258; Office of the Chief of Chaplains, 1944, pp. 44–45; Hillenbrand, 2012, loc. 2065.

532 Office of the Chief of Chaplains, 1944, p. 44.

533 Willoughby, 1943, passim; *The Link*, June 1943, p. 22.

534 *Yank*, 6 December 1942, p. 15.

535 Honeywell, 1958, p. 261.

536 NARA Record Group 247. Chief of Chaplains. Office Management Division Decimal File 1920–45. Box 262. 350.01 Testaments (Administration and Policy of). *Christians, Awaken! F.D.R. Orders Bible Changes.*

537 *The Chaplain*, February 1945, p. 28.

538 Link and Hopf, 1946, p. 66.

539 1945, 'Reports of the General Board. 68. The Army Chaplain in the European Theater', pp. 106–7.

540 Drury, 1950, pp. 9, 290.

541 Ibid, pp. 9–10.

542 *Christian Herald*, April 1941, p. 73.

543 Drury, 1950, p. 280.

544 Ibid, p. 9.

545 Ibid, p. 290.

546 Ibid.

547 *Christian Science Monitor*, 1 March 1945, p. 2.

548 *Christian Herald*, November 1944, p. 26.

549 Honeywell, 1958, p. 236.

550 Poling, 1959, p. 189.

551 Ibid, pp. 73–74, 189–96, 206.

552 Nance, 1944, pp. 250, 253.

553 Ibid, pp. 250, 254.

554 *The Link*, June 1943, p. 2.

555 Poling, 1944, p. 135.

556 Jorgensen, 1961, p. 278.

557 1946, *History of Chaplains' Activities in the Pacific*, pp. 472–73.

558 Drury, 1950, p. 111; 1946, *History of Chaplains' Activities in the Pacific*, pp. 196, 474–76; *The Link*, February 1945, pp. 32–35.

559 1946, *History of Chaplains' Activities in the Pacific*, p. 483.

560 Ibid, p. 478.

561 *The Chaplain*, March 1945, p. 20.

562 Metcalf, 1957, p. 211.

563 Ibid, p. 212.

564 *The Link*, June 1943, p. 1.

565 Methodist Commission on Chaplains, 1948, p. 164; Reynolds, 1996, p. 104.

566 Nance, 1944, pp. 256–62; Jorgensen, 1961, p. 93.

567 *Berkeley Daily Gazette*, 14 November 1942, p. 5.

568 Gannon, 1962, p. 180.

569 Ibid, pp. 33–36.

570 Ibid, p. 181.

571 Ibid, pp. 193–95.

572 Spellman, 1943, pp. 1–2; Nance, 1944, p. 247.

573 Spellman, 1943, pp. 29–39.

574 Gannon, 1962, pp. 201–2.

575 Spellman, 1943, p. xii; Cooney, 1984, p. 136.

576 Spellman, 1943, p. 72; Cooney, 1984, p. 137.

577 Nance, 1944, p. 249.

578 Spellman, 1943, pp. 230–31.

579 Spellman, 1945, pp. 31–32.

580 Clark, 2007, p. 308.

581 Gannon, 1962, pp. 238–40.

582 Spellman, 1945, p. 62.

583 Drury, 1950, p. 112; Gannon, 1962, pp. 359–61.

584 Gannon, 1962, p. 361.

585 Ibid, pp. 362–63; 1946, *History of Chaplains' Activities in the Pacific*, pp. 502–3.

586 Gannon, 1962, pp. 363–66; 1946, *History of Chaplains' Activities in the Pacific*, p. 504.

587 Gannon, 1962, pp. 364–66.

588 Ibid, pp. 245–48.

589 Spellman, 1945, p. 107.

590 Blumenson, 1972, II, p. 548.

591 Gregg, 1945, pp. ix, 206–7.

592 *Baltimore Afro-American*, 22 August 1942, p. 5; Gregg, 1945, p. vi.

593 Gregg, 1945, p. vii.

594 Ibid, p. 200.

595 Ibid, pp. 34, 75, 90, 118–19, 133.

596 Ibid, pp. 104–5.

597 Ibid, p. 31.

598 Ibid, pp. 31–32.

599 1946, *History of Chaplains' Activities in the Pacific*, p. 399.

600 Gregg, 1945, p. 55.

601 NARA, RG 247. Chief of Chaplains. Box 199. 291.2. Race, Negro Volume 1, Memorandum 30 June 1943.

602 NARA, RG 493. Records of the China–Burma–India Theatre of Operations, US Army. Box 464. Trett to Arnold, 12 February 1944.

603 1946, *History of Chaplains' Activities in the Pacific*, p. 462.

604 Ibid, p. 398.

605 Nance, 1944, p. 263; Bernstein, 1971, p. 24.

606 1946, *History of Chaplains' Activities in the Pacific*, pp. 448–50.

607 Nance, 1944, pp. 263–65.

608 Nance, 1944, p. 263; Bernstein, 1971, p. 24.

609 Bernstein, 1971, p. 24.

610 1945, 'Reports of the General Board. 68. The Army Chaplain in the European Theater', Appendix 4, pp. 13–14.

611 Honeywell, 1958, p. 236.

612 Bernstein, 1971, pp. 24–26; 1946, *History of Chaplains' Activities in the Pacific*, pp. 490–91.

613 Gregg, 1945, p. vii; 1946, *History of Chaplains' Activities in the Pacific*, pp. 242–43; http://americanhistory.si.edu/archives/scurlock/about_the_scurlocks/notables/Jernagin.htm, accessed 11 October 2012.

614 1946, *History of Chaplains' Activities in the Pacific*, pp. 522–23.

615 Ibid, pp. 519–21.

616 Jernagin, 1946, pp. 118–19.

617 Ibid, pp. 121–22.

618 1946, *History of Chaplains' Activities in the Pacific*, p. 523.

619 1945, 'Reports of the General Board. 68. The Army Chaplain in the European Theater', p. 163.

620 Ibid, pp. 160–61.

621 Ibid, p. 161.

622 *The Chaplain*, September 1945, p. 23.

623 NARA, RG 493, Records of the China–Burma–India Theatre of Operations, US Army. Box 465, 'Reports– Chaplain History', p. 14.

624 Ibid., n.p.

625 Stewart, 1958, p. 27; http://maryknollmissionarchives.org/index.php/history/87-cummingsfrwilliamt, accessed 18 February 2014.

626 Nance, 1944, p. 104; Frillmann and Peck, 1968, p. xiii.

627 Grant, 1944, p. 90.

628 NARA, RG 247, Records of the Office of the Chief of Chaplains. Records of Administration and Management General Records. Records Relating to the History of the Chaplains of the United States Army, 1941–58, Box 3, 'Military History of the Second World War. The Corps of Chaplains', p. 103.

629 Ibid., pp. 103–4; Jorgensen, 1961, p. 139.

630 Gannon, 1962, p. 233.

631 *The Jewish Exponent*, 26 June 1942, p. 4.

632 1945, 'Reports of the General Board. 68. The Army Chaplain in the European Theater', pp. 161–62.

633 *The Chaplain*, December 1945, p. 47.

634 Coffey, 1991, p. 3.

635 Marshall and DeWeerd, 1945, pp. 93–94.

636 Coffey, 1991, p. 3.

637 Ibid, p. 5; United Service Organizations for National Defense, 1948, p. 2.

638 Kahn, 1973, 25–27 September 1941; 2 October 1941; 7 October 1941.

639 *The National Catholic Almanac*, 1943, p. 697; United Service Organizations for National Defense, 1948, p. 9; 1950, *Think Magazine's Diary of US Participation in World War II*, p. 292; Carson, 1946, p. xii.

640 *Los Angeles Times*, 26 March 1944, p. c7.

641 Coffey, 1991, pp. 5–7.

642 Carson, 1946, p. xi.

643 1944, *Technical Manual 16–205: The Chaplain*, p. 9.

644 Gannon, 1962, p. 196.

645 *The Link*, May 1943, pp. 30–31.

646 Carson, 1946, pp. xiii, 23, 26, 30, 121–24.

647 Ibid, pp. 48–49.

648 Carson, 1946, pp. 25, 54, 60, 93; United Service Organizations for National Defense, 1948, p. 9; Lynn, 1952, p. 79.

649 1950, *Think Magazine's Diary of US Participation in World War II*, p. 292.

650 *The Link*, November 1943, p. 6.

651 Ibid, March 1943, p. 38; Enjames, 2003, II, p. 210.

652 *The Link*, November 1943, p. 6.

653 Carson, 1946, p. 49.

654 *The Link*, May 1943, p. 37.

655 United Service Organizations for National Defense, 1948, pp. 20, 25.

656 Coffey, 1991, p. 23.

657 Hynes, 2005, p. 138.

658 Bassett, 1991, pp. 20–23.

659 Weatherford, 2010, p. 450.

660 Winchell, 2008, p. 140.

661 Carson, 1946, p. 25; Lynn, 1952, p. 78.

662 United Service Organizations for National Defense, 1948, p. 30.

663 1947, *The Story of Christian Science Wartime Activities*, p. 224.

664 Ibid, pp. 223, 227–40

665 Ibid, pp. 97, 357–58.

666 Ibid, p. 359.

667 *The Chaplain*, October 1944, p. 27.

668 *The Link*, October 1944, p. 26.

669 National Lutheran Council, 1949, pp. 7, 25.

670 Ibid, p. 25.

671 Ibid, p. 107.

672 Ibid, p. 107.

673 Ibid, pp. 26–27.

674 1945, 'Reports of the General Board. 68. The Army Chaplain in the European Theater', p. 116.

675 *The Link*, January/February 1943, pp. 29–30.

676 Tower, 1945, pp. 63–64.

677 *The Link*, June 1943, p. 24; March 1944, p. 46.

678 Hafer, 1947, pp. 38–53; Lunn, 1947, pp. 6–7; *Yank*, 12 December 1943, p. 17; *The Chaplain*, March 1945, p. 29.

679 Kennett, 1997, p. 31.

680 Hedstrom, 2013, p. 155; *The Link*, March 1944, p. 46.

681 *The Link*, March 1943, p. 38.

682 Berends, 1998.

683 Hedstrom, 2013, pp. 121, 167.

684 Nance, 1944, p. 274.

685 1945, 'Reports of the General Board. 68. The Army Chaplain in the European Theater', p. 116.

686 Bennett, 1942.

687 Drury, 1950, pp. 3–4, 121.

688 *The Naples Record*, 28 June 1944, p. 4; Nygaard, 1942, 11 November.

689 Hedstrom, 2013, p. 119; Fussell, 1989, pp. 235–36.

690 Lynn, 1952, pp. 82–83.

691 *The Chaplain*, October 1944, pp. 27–28.

692 Sperry, 1945, p. vii.

693 Lord, 1942, p. 40.

694 Cleveland Shrigley, 1943.

695 Brasted, 1944, title page.

696 Hedstrom, 2013, pp. 128–29, 184–88, 205.

697 VHP, Barilla, *It Happened This Way!*, p. 1, VHP MSS Box 1216. Folder 2/7.

698 Tullidge, 1944; http://www.abmc.gov/search-abmc-burials-and-memorializations/detail/WWII_58654#.U9fVi-NdXKM, accessed 29 July 2014.

699 Pyle, 2004, p. 39.

700 VHP, Russell Baldwin, online Complete Interview.

701 *Yank*, 23 January 1944, p. 18.

702 NARA, RG 247. Chief of Chaplains. Office Management Division Decimal File 1920–45. Box 312. 461 Books, Periodicals, Publications, Libraries etc. Volume VI. G.A. Emerich to William R. Arnold, 7 June 1942 and R.J. Honeywell to G.A. Emerich, 14 July 1942.

703 Lynn, 1952, p. 255.

704 NARA, RG 247 Records of the Office of the Chief of Chaplains. Records of Administration and Management General Records. Records Relating to the History of the Chaplains of the United States Army, 1941–58. Box 3. 'Military History of the Second World War. The Corps of Chaplains', pp. 155–56.

705 Tower, 1945, pp. 156–57.

706 Willard, 1944, p. 11.

707 Ibid, p. 76.

708 Ibid, p. 155.

709 Kimball, 1947, p. 23.

710 Ibid, pp. 61–62.

711 Ibid, pp. 109, 114, 120, 160, 184.

712 *The Chaplain*, August 1945, p. 48.

713 Van Schouwen, 1985, p. 150.

714 *The Chaplain*, April 1945, pp. 29–30.

715 Bernstein, 1971, p. 14.

716 Ibid, pp. 15–16; Eichhorn, 2004, pp. 71–72.

717 Drury, 1950, p. 292.

718 *Los Angeles Times*, 15 August 1944, p. A5; 4 October 1945, p. A5; 29 October 1943, p. A5; 26 October 1944, p. A4.

719 Metcalf, 1957, p. 18.

720 Yost, 2006, p. 7.

721 Bernstein, 1971, p. 15.

722 Ibid, p. 16; Cross and Arnold, 1945, p. 163.

723 Drury, 1950, p. 291.

724 Claypool, 1944, centre pages.

725 Drury, 1950, pp. 10, 291.

726 Jorgensen, 1961, p. 253.

727 Kimball, 1947, p. 326.

728 Bernstein, 1971, p. 14.

729 *The Chaplain*, February 1945, inside cover.

730 1945, 'Reports of the General Board. 68. The Army Chaplain in the European Theater', p. 59.

731 Proehl, 1942, p. 3.

732 *The Chaplain*, April 1945, p. 30.

733 Ebel, 2010, p. 8; 1945, 'Reports of the General Board. 68. The Army Chaplain in the European Theater', p. 68.

734 *The National Catholic Almanac*, 1942, p. 398.

735 *New York Times*, 20 December 1942, p. 46; Jorgensen, 1961, p. 211.

736 1945, 'Reports of the General Board. 68. The Army Chaplain in the European Theater', p. 59.

737 Ibid.

738 Ibid.

739 Poling, 1959, pp. 54–55; *The Link*, January 1945, pp. 28–29.

740 *The Link*, January/February 1943, p. 5; Jorgensen, 1961, p. 210.

741 *The Link*, January/February 1943, p. 5.

742 Nance, 1944, p. 275.

743 *The Link*, March 1943, p. 29; August 1943, p. 27.

744 Nance, 1944, p. 276.

745 *The Link*, June 1943, p. 3.

746 Ibid, January/February 1943, p. 34.

747 Ibid, April 1944, pp. 37–38; October 1944, pp. 41, 44–45.

748 Ibid, September 1944, pp. 47–48; December 1945, p. 37.

749 Ibid, June 1944, pp. 35–36.

750 Jorgensen, 1961, p. 211.

751 *The Link*, November 1943, p. 37.

752 Ibid, March 1943, pp. 26–27.

753 Ibid, April 1943, p. 10.

754 Ibid, November 1943, p. 4.

755 Ibid.

756 Ibid, January/February 1943, p. 4.

757 Ibid, November 1943, p. 5.

758 Ibid, January/February 1943, p. 67.

759 Ibid, March 1943, p. 22.

760 Ibid, October 1945, p. 45.

761 1945, 'Reports of the General Board. 68. The Army Chaplain in the European Theater', p. 59.

762 *The Link*, January/February 1943, p. 67.

763 Ibid, March 1944, pp. 2–3; June 1944, pp. 14 and 39; November 1944, pp. 29–30; December 1944, p. 50; *The Chaplain*, December 1945, pp. 33–34.

764 *The Link*, June 1943, p. 3; February 1944, pp. 42–43; July 1944, p. 24.

765 1945, 'Reports of the General Board. 68. The Army Chaplain in the European Theater', p. 59.

766 *The Link*, July 1943, pp. 54–57.

767 Carpenter, 1997, pp. 8–9.

768 *The Link*, April 1943, pp. 10–11.

769 Ibid, June 1943, p. 35.

770 Ibid, November 1944, pp. 28–29.

771 Ibid, p. 29.

772 Ibid, January 1945, pp. 29–30.

773 Rabey, 2002, pp. 166–72; http://www.navigators.org/us/aboutus/history, accessed 8 December 2012; Dennis, 1945, pp. 99–102.

774 1945, 'Reports of the General Board. 68. The Army Chaplain in the European Theater', p. 59.

775 Jorgensen, 1961, p. 211; 1946, *History of Chaplains' Activities in the Pacific*, p. 243.

776 1946, *History of Chaplains' Activities in the Pacific*, p. 526; Carpenter, 1997, p. 179.

777 NARA, RG 247. Chief of Chaplains. Office Management Division Decimal File 1920–45. Box 120. 200.6 Commissioned Officers and Enlisted Personnel Rewards, Medals, Citations, Etc. Volume I. 'Memorandum for Chief of Chaplains', 4 June 1943; http://www.tshaonline.org/handbook/online/articles/fho86. Hobby, Oveta Culp, accessed 11 December 2012.

778 Jorgensen, 1961, p. 212.

779 Jorgensen, 1961, p. 212; Grant, 1944, pp. 24–25.

780 Grant, 1944, p. 25.

CHAPTER 3

The Faithful in Arms

1 Loveland, 1996, p. 1.

2 Reynolds, 1996, p. 75.

3 Coffman, 2004, pp. 315–17.

4 Ibid, p. 300.

5 Ibid, pp. 333–35.

6 Rogers, 1946, p. 23.

7 Cameron, 1994, p. 45.

8 Martin, 'Meehling', pp. 44–45.

9 Harrod, 1978, Appendix, Table 9, pp. 191–95.

10 Ibid, p. x.

11 Ibid, p. 54.

12 Ibid, pp. 51, 101–2; Spector, *At War at Sea*, 2001, pp. 131–32.

13 Drury, 1949, p. 222.

14 *Christian Herald*, January 1941, p. 52.

15 Harrod, 1978, pp. 30, 213.

16 Ibid, pp. 56–57, 135–36.

17 Ibid, pp. 30 and 136.

18 Drury, 1949, p. 194.

19 VHP, Richard M. Becker, online transcript.

20 Harrod, 1978, pp. 159–63.

21 Tower, 1945, p. 81.

22 Carlson, 1945, p. 33.

23 Nance, 1944, p. 15.

24 Grant, 1944, p. 15.

25 Holland, 1946, p. 3.

26 Ibid.

27 Ibid, p. 6.

28 Ibid, p. 11.

29 *The Link*, October 1945, p. 11.

30 Coffman, 2004, p. 298.

31 Moore, 2006, p. 18.

32 Coffman, 2004, pp. 317, 319.

33 *The Link*, July 1943, pp. 15–17; Stanton, 2006, p. 539.

34 Sutherland, 2004, II, pp. 361–62.

35 USAHEC, World War II Veterans Survey, Armor Tank Battalions, Mark Henderson.

36 Faubus, 1971, p. 538.

37 Orr, 1948, p. 28.

38 Kimball, 1947, p. 137.

39 Ibid, p. 151. See also pp. 145, 148,154, 158.

40 Cross and Arnold, 1945, p. 104.

41 *The Chaplain*, September 1946, p. 45.

42 NARA, Record Group 247. Chief of Chaplains. Office Management Division Decimal File 1920–45. Box 199. 291.2 Race, Negro Volume I. Arnold circular letter, 13 November 1944.

43 Ibid, Memorandum, 30 January 1945, 'Whither Goeth Thou?'

44 Ibid, Pearce to Arnold, 8 December 1944.

45 Ibid, Peterson to Arnold, 17 November 1944.

46 Weatherford, 2010, pp. 497–98.

47 Treadwell, 1991, Appendix A, Table 1, p. 765.

48 http://www.history.army.mil/brochures/WAC/WAC.HTM, accessed 19 June 2013.

49 Ibid.

50 Treadwell, 1991, pp. 191–218; Hampf, 2004; Campbell, 1993, pp. 320–21; Costello, 1985, pp. 65, 69–71.

51 Treadwell, 1991, p. 203.

52 *The Link*, August 1943, p. 64; Kennedy, 1999, p. 404.

53 *The Link*, August 1943, pp. 23–24.

54 Treadwell, 1991, p. 216.

55 Kenneally, 1980, p. 197.

56 Treadwell, 1991, p. 197.

57 Ibid, pp. 206–7.

58 Nance, 1944, pp. 179–83.

59 Ibid, p. 174.

60 Ibid, p. 175.

61 http://www.history.army.mil/brochures/WAC/WAC.HTM, accessed 19 June 2013.

62 Ibid.

63 Nance, 1944, p. 177.

64 NARA, RG 247. Records of the Office of the Chief of Chaplains. Office Management Division Decimal File 1920–45. Box 120. *200.6* Commissioned Officers and Enlisted Personnel Rewards, Medals, Citations, Etc. Volume I. Hobby to Arnold, 4 June 1943.

65 NARA, RG 247. Records of the Office of the Chief of Chaplains. Office Management Division Decimal File 1920–45. Box 217. 319.1 Reports – General File Volume 3/3. Undated memorandum.

66 Drury, 1950, p. 260.

67 Drury, 1948, p. 180.

68 Spector, *At War at Sea*, 2001, pp. 273–74.

69 *The Chaplain*, March 1946, pp. 34–35.

70 Ibid, pp. 35–36.

71 Ibid, p. 36.

72 Stremlow, 1994, p. 25.

73 Millett, 1991, p. 374: Wickersham, 1998, p. 40.

74 Wickersham, 1998, pp. 39–40.

75 Chambers, 1999, p. 514.

76 http://www.history.army.mil/books/wwii/72–14/72–14.HTM, accessed 25 June 2013.

77 USAHEC , World War II Veterans Survey, Army Nurse Corps, Grace M. Emory Stewart.

78 Ibid, Gloria Sangermano.

79 Fredman and Falk, 1954, p. 105; Greenfield, Palmer and Wiley, 1947, Table No. 3, p. 203.

80 Kennedy, 1999, pp. 633–34; Kennett, 1997, pp. 14–15.

81 *The National Catholic Almanac*, 1942, p. 96.

82 *The Link*, June 1943, p. 4.

83 Harrod, 1978, pp. 57–62; Spector, *At War at Sea*, 2001, pp. 264–65.

84 Field and Bielakowski, 2008, pp. 206–12.

85 Millett, 1991, p. 374.

86 Grant, 1944, p. 155.

87 O'Callahan, 1956, p. 26.

88 Kershaw, 2003, p. 10.

89 Kahn and McLemore, 1945, p. 51; Stanton, 2006, pp. 117–18; Faubus, 1971, pp. 422–23.

90 Kershaw, 2003.

91 Pyle, 2001, pp. 52–53.

92 Crosby, 1994, pp. 208–9; Kahn and McLemore, 1945, p. 43; Stanton, 2006, pp. 110–11.

93 Wall, 2004, p. 190.

94 Stroup, 2000, pp. 23–25; Stanton, 2006, p. 521. Stroup's memoirs identify this unit as the 1112th Engineer Combat Group.

95 Stanton, 2006, p. 93.

96 *The Link*, August 1944, p. 16.

97 Donnelly, 1986, pp. 3–4.

98 Ibid, pp. 21–23.

99 Brown, 1986, p. 17.

100 Ibid, p. 18.

101 Kennett, 1997, pp. 33–37.

102 Wilson, 1997, p. 298; Kennett, 1997, p. 37.

103 Kennett, 1997, p. 35.

104 Wilson, 1997, p. 297.

105 Van Creveld, 1983, pp. 69–71; Wilson, 1997, p. 300.

106 Wilson, 1997, p. 302.

107 VHP, Norman Wesley Achen, online transcript.

108 Fahey, 1992, p. 3.

109 Martin, 'Craven', p. 11.

110 VHP, Norman Boike, transcript, pp. 2–3, VHP MSS Box 1853. Folder 3/3.

111 Fahey, 1992, pp. 6, 33.

112 Hynes, 2005, p. 112.

113 Grant, 1944, pp. 56–58.

114 *The Link*, June 1944, p. 5.

115 Gregory, 1944, p. 53.

116 Reynolds, 1996, p. 87.

117 Kennett, 1997, pp. 72–74; Wagner, Kennedy, Osborne and Reyburn, 2007, pp. 312–13; Blum, 1976, pp. 107–8.

118 Kennett, 1997, p. 72.

119 Reynolds, 1996, p. 87.

120 Promey, 2011, pp. 190–91, 205–6; McDannell, 1995, pp. 67–102.

121 Gaustad, 1989, p. 33; Promey, 2011, pp. 195–96.

122 Clare, 1945, p. 121.

123 Sampson, 1958, pp. 169–70.

124 *The Chaplain*, November 1946, p. 31.

125 *The Link*, October 1944, p. 6.

126 *Marine Corps Gazette*, November 1945, p. 26.

127 Rabey, 2002, p. 240.

128 Ibid, pp. 241, 247.

129 Ibid, p. 45.

130 Ibid, p. 48.

131 Adams, 1994, p. 70.

132 Brink, 1944, pp. 25–26.

133 *The Link*, September 1943, p. 2; Nance, 1944, p. 224.

134 *The Link*, September 1943, p. 3; Nance, 1944, p. 225.

135 Cross and Arnold, 1945, p. 70.

136 Carroll, 2007, pp. 45–46.

137 *The Link*, December 1944, p. 46.

138 Fahey, 1992, p. 182.

139 Jorgensen, 1961, pp. 172–79.

140 Society for the Propagation of the Faith, 1946, 'Christmas'.

141 *The Link*, December 1944, pp. 6–8.

142 Daniel, 1985, pp. 65, 84.

143 1945, *American Chaplains of the Fifth Army*, p. 28.

144 Reynolds, 1996, Tables 7.1 and 7.2, pp. 99 and 103.

145 *Stars and Stripes*, 24 December 1943, p. 2.

146 Ambrose, 1998, p. 229.

147 Huston, 2003, p. 167.

148 Atkinson, 2013, pp. 465–66; Blumenson, 1972, II, p. 606.

149 Hanford, 2008, p. 105.

150 Ibid, p. 106.

151 Connelly, 1945, pp. 46–47.

152 Moore, 2004, p. 138.

153 Keene, 2011, p. 110.

154 Moore, 2004, pp. 138–39; Moore, 1998, pp. 39–40.

155 Moore, 2004, p. 14.

156 Clare, 1945, p. 121.

157 Kertzer, 1947, pp. 90–92.

158 Ibid, p. 30.

159 *The Link*, November 1944, pp. 10–11.

160 Ibid, March 1945, p. 24; October 1945, pp. 23–24.

161 Donnelly, 1986, p. 24.

162 *The Link*, November 1944, p. 14.

163 http://www.history.navy.mil/photos/pers-us/uspers-f/r-flming.htm, accessed 1 February 2013.

164 Nance, 1944, p. 47.

165 Spellman, 1943, p. 159.

166 Dennis, 1945, pp. 146–51, 157–61.

167 *Stars and Stripes*, 26 July 1943, p. 3.

168 Hastings, 2005, p. 166.

169 Willard, 1944, p. 87.

170 Ibid, pp. 85–87.

171 Atwell, 1961, pp. 31, 35, 130.

172 Bassett, 1991, p. 60.

173 Hastings, 2007, p. 415.

174 Ancell and Miller, 1996, p. 422; 1946, *History of Chaplains' Activities in the Pacific*, p. 272.

175 Kertzer, 1947, p. 26.

176 http://www.usna.com/NC/History/ SeaStories/1942/ParsonsBible.htm, accessed 30 January 2014.

177 *The Link*, December 1945, p. 45.

178 *Christian Herald*, January 1945, p. 11.

179 *Stars and Stripes*, 30 October 1943, p. 2.

180 Sibley, 1945, p.1.

181 Ibid; Kennedy, 1999, p. 633; Dear and Foot, 1995, p. 263.

182 Sibley and Jacob, 1952, pp. 83–84.

183 Ibid, pp. 86–87.

184 Ibid, pp. 88–89.

185 Ibid, p. 91.

186 Linderman, 1997, pp. 132–36; Ambrose, 1998, pp. 311–12.

187 Ambrose, 1998, pp. 311–12.

188 Sibley and Jacob, 1952, pp. 86, 88.

189 Greenfield, Palmer and Wiley, 1947, p. 203 Table No. 3.

190 Sibley and Jacob, 1952, pp. 94–95; Perret, 1991, p. 462.

191 Stannard, 1993, p. 107; Fussell, 1996, pp. 130–31.

192 http://www.87thinfantrydivision.com/ Commentary/000030.html, accessed 1 February 2013.

193 Atwell, 1961, p. 135.

194 Ibid, pp. 93, 157–59, 274–78.

195 Taggart and Cross, 1943, pp. 7–8.

196 Kimball, 1947, p. 38.

197 *Yank*, 21 February 1943, p. 10.

198 *New York Times*, 21 September 1942, p. 10.

199 Willard, 1944, p. 114.

200 Noll, 2002, p. 262.

201 *The Link*, March 1943, p. 27.

202 *The Chaplain*, February 1945, p. 32.

203 Ibid, May 1945, p. 35.

204 Ibid, April 1945, p. 23.

205 Ibid.

206 Ibid, August 1945, p. 43.

207 Ibid, April 1945, p. 31.

208 Ibid, pp. 31–32.

209 Pyle, 2001, p. 391.

210 *The Link*, December 1943, p. 24.

211 Sledge, 2010, p. 2.

212 Ibid, p. 96.

213 Brink, 1944, pp. 21–23.

214 *The Link*, September 1944, p. 9.

215 http://www.audiemurphy.com/places018. htm, accessed 8 February 2013.

216 Cantril and Strunk, 1951, p. 39.

217 *The Link*, June 1943, p. 25.

218 Ibid, December 1944, p. 14.

219 Fussell, 1989, p. 234.

220 Kimball, 1947, p. 53.

221 Ibid, p. 58.

222 Taggart and Cross, 1943, p. 27.

223 Ibid, p. 40.

224 Abbott, 1946, p. 123.

225 *The Chaplain*, April 1945, pp. 46–47.

226 Atkinson, 2013, p. 122.

227 USAHEC, World War II Veterans' Survey, 32nd Infantry Division, Robert W. Teeples.

228 Yost, 2006, p. 54.

229 *The Link*, September 1944, p. 2; Daniel, 1985, p. 17.

230 *The Link*, September 1944, p. 3.

231 Cross and Arnold, 1945, p. 38.

232 Bergerud, 1996, p. 471.

233 Smith, 1967, pp. 488–89.

234 Hickcox, 1950, pp. 42–43.

235 *The Link*, September 1943, p. 42.

236 *The Chaplain*, January 1945, p. 21.

237 *The Link*, August 1944, p. 24.

238 Willard, 1944, p. 156.

239 Stroup, 2000, pp. 34, 71, 176.

240 Ibid, p. 176.

241 Carlson, 1945, pp. 20–21.

242 Ibid, pp. 69–72.

243 Atkinson, 2007, p. 224.

244 VHP, John Oliver Brixey, online transcript.

245 Whittaker, 1943, pp. 7–8.

246 Ibid, pp. 69–70, 80, 93, 102–3; Bartek, 1943, pp. 50–53.

247 Rickenbacker, 1943, p. 3.

248 Whittaker, 1943, p. 21.

249 Bartek, 1943, pp. 100–02.

250 Rickenbacker, 1943, p. 33.

251 Jorgensen, 1961, p. 258; Bartek, 1943, pp. viii, 80–81.

252 Whittaker, 1943, pp. 63, 67, 77–79, 82–83, 87, 99–100, 111, 115–16, 139.

253 1945, *American Chaplains of the Fifth Army*, p. 18.

254 1946, *History of Chaplains' Activities in the Pacific*, p. 405.

255 Taggart and Cross, 1943, p. 152; 1946, *History of Chaplains' Activities in the Pacific*, p. 408.

256 Martin, 'Craven', p. 28.

257 http://www.6juin1944.com/veterans/shumway.php, accessed 30 January 2014.

258 Yost, 2006, p. 7.

259 Grant, 1944, p. 22.

260 Nance, 1944, p. 56; Grant, 1944, p. 98.

261 *The Link*, August 1944, p. 37.

262 Ibid, April 1945, pp. 17–18.

263 Ibid, November 1943, p. 30.

264 Ibid, March 1944, p. 31.

265 Ibid, August 1944, p. 38.

266 *The Link*, November 1944, p. 36.

267 Drury, 1948, pp. 322–23; Mead, 1951, pp. 98–99.

268 *The Chaplain*, November 1946, p. 23.

269 Stroup, 2000, p. 142.

270 *The Chaplain*, December 1944, p. 6.

271 Stroup, 2000, p. 133.

272 *The Chaplain*, December 1944, pp. 6–8; May 1945, pp. 42–43.

273 Stroup, 2000, p. 145.

274 Ibid, p. 163.

275 *The Chaplain*, March 1945, p. 26.

276 Ibid, May 1945, p. 29.

277 Ibid, October 1944, pp. 18–20; November 1944, pp. 28–29; December 1944, pp. 27–30.

278 Ibid, October 1944, pp. 18–20.

279 Ibid, November 1944, p. 28.

280 Ibid, December 1944, p. 30.

281 Stroup, 2000, pp. 142, 175–76, 178.

282 Brasted, 1944, p. 140.

283 Lunn, 1947, p. 149.

284 *The Link*, April 1944, p. 36.

285 Carpenter, 1997, p. 179.

286 Leuschner, 1946, pp. 85–86.

287 1946, *History of Chaplains' Activities in the Pacific*, p. 107.

288 Ibid, pp. 107–8.

289 *The Christian Century*, 19 September 1945, pp. 1060–61.

290 Wickersham, 1998, p. 112.

291 Drury, 1950, p. 278.

292 http://www.gjenvick.com/Military/NavyArchives/Newsletters/NorfolkSeabag/1945-04-21-NavalTrainingCenterNewsletter.html#axzz2XQvtHY08, accessed 27 June 2013.

293 McGuire, 1993, pp. 50–51.

294 1946, *History of Chaplains' Activities in the Pacific*, pp. 400–1.

295 Ibid.

296 Ibid, pp. 401–2.

297 Hickcox, 1950, pp. 30–31.

298 NARA, Record Group 492. Records of the MTO Headquarters. Chaplain Section. Boxes 1680–1682. Box 1680. Folder 121.2 Apportionment and Allotment, Letters of–.

299 Hickcox, 1950, p. 31.

300 Ambrose, 1998, pp. 17–21.

301 Taggart and Cross, 1943, pp. 141–43.

302 Leuschner, 1946, p. 20.

303 *The Chaplain*, February 1945, p. 45.

304 Ibid, November 1944, p. 25.

305 1946, *History of Chaplains' Activities in the Pacific*, p. 80.

306 Drury, 1950, p. 145.

307 Ibid, p. 144.

308 Ibid., p. 26.

309 Hickcox, 1950, p. 48.

310 *The Chaplain*, January 1945, p. 26.

311 Ibid, p. 27.

312 Ibid, December 1944, p. 44.

313 1946, *History of Chaplains' Activities in the Pacific*, p. 369.

314 Jorgensen, 1961, pp. 246–47.

315 Cross and Arnold, 1945, p. 94.

316 *The Link*, February 1944, p. 43.

317 1945, *American Chaplains of the Fifth Army*, pp. 25, 58.

318 Ibid, p. 58.

319 *The Chaplain*, April 1945, p. 33.

320 1946, *History of Chaplains' Activities in the Pacific*, p. 368; *The Chaplain*, November 1944, pp. 24–25.

321 1946, *History of Chaplains' Activities in the Pacific*, p. 109.

322 *The Chaplain*, January 1945, p. 26; Drury, 1950, p. 152.

323 Hickcox, 1950, p. 48.

324 Cross and Arnold, 1945, p. 98.

325 Dear and Foot, 1995, p. 988.

326 *The Chaplain*, January 1945, p. 27.

327 http://www.history.navy.mil/museums/seabee/UnitListPages/NCB/096%20NCB.pdf, accessed 1 March 2013.

328 Drury, 1950, p. 150.

329 1945, 'The Soxos: 729th Railway Operating Battalion', pp. 5, 39; Cross and Arnold, 1945, p. 151.

330 *The Link*, March 1945, p. 35.

331 Moore, 2004, p. xi.

332 Vida, 1967, p. 3.

333 Moore, 2004, p. xi.

334 Lester 1992, Reel 7, Box 60, 0851 et seq. Declined invitation, 9 December 1942.

335 NARA, RG 217. Chief of Chaplains. Box 217. Reports–General File Volume 3/3. Undated memorandum.

336 Cross and Arnold, 1945, p. 158.

337 Ibid, pp. 158–59.

338 Wuest, 1953, p. 16.

339 Cross and Arnold, 1945, pp. 116–17.

340 Ibid.

341 Honeywell, 1958, p. 277.

342 Schultz, 2011, loc. 1271–78.

343 *The Link*, October 1944, pp. 25–26.

344 Ibid, p. 26.

345 Schultz, 2011, loc. 870–932.

346 Jorgensen, 1961, p. 209; Drury, 1950, p. 213.

347 Schultz, 2011, loc. 948–76.

348 Ibid, loc. 976–83.

349 Nance, 1944, pp. 88–89.

350 Tower, 1945, p. 168.

351 Ibid, p. 171.

352 Abbott, 1946, p. 145.

353 Nance, 1944, p. 76.

354 Cross and Arnold, 1945, p. 166.

355 Kertzer, 1947, p. 91.

356 Ibid, p. 11.

357 Ibid, p. 12.

358 Ibid, pp. 10–11.

359 Ibid, p. 10.

360 Martin, 'Craven', p. 11; Holifield, 2007, p. 255.

361 VHP, James Clevenger, online transcript.

362 Abbott, 1946, pp. 134–35.

363 Tower, 1945, p. 137.

364 Ibid, p. 144.

365 *The Link*, February 1944, p. 9.

366 Daddis, 2010.

367 Wuest, 1953, p. 45.

368 Murphy, 1949, pp. 162–63.

369 USAHEC ,World War II Veterans Survey, 32nd Infantry Division, Newman W. Phillips.

370 Ibid, United States Army Air Forces Bomber Groups, Clinton Rodefer.

371 Martin, 'Garrett', pp. 22–23.

372 Martin, 'Meehling', p. 93.

373 Ibid, pp. 77–78.

374 Rottman, 2006, p. 16.

375 Sampson, 1958, pp. 101–2.

376 Martin, 'Craven', p. 19.

377 Amoury, 1958, pp. 134–37; Crosby, 1994, pp. 237–38.

378 Sampson, 1958, pp. 24–26.

379 Ibid, p. 75.

380 Sampson, 1958, pp. 65–66.

381 Ibid, p. 66.

382 Yost, 2006, pp. 100 and 136.

383 USAHEC, World War II Veterans Survey, 24th Infantry Division, Roger Kenneth Heller.

384 Ibid, 34th Infantry Division, Julian Richard Jacobs.

385 Kertzer, 1947, p. 10.

386 Ibid, p. 40.

387 VHP, Edward Martinez, transcript, p. 8, VHP MSS Box 2082. Folder 1/1.

388 Clare, 1945, p. 45.

389 Ibid, pp. 57–58.

390 Ibid, pp. 116–17.

391 VHP, Muriel Rose Phillips Engelman, transcript, pp. 16–17, VHP MSS Box 1963. Folder 1/1.

392 Ambrose, 2001, pp. 23–24.

393 USAHEC, World War II Veterans Survey, 9th Infantry Division, Wilbert D. Goldsmith.

394 Eichhorn, 2004, p. 73.

395 Blumenson, 1972, II, pp. 782–86.

396 Ibid, pp. 783–84.

397 Ibid, p. 752.

398 Moore, 2004, p. 229.

399 Blumenson, 1972, II, pp. 759–60.

400 Ibid, p. 759.

401 Ibid, pp. 787–89.

402 Ibid, p. 790.

403 NARA RG 247. Chief of Chaplains. Box 199. Race–Jewish etc. Chief of Chaplains to Mrs ———, 4 October 1945.

404 National Lutheran Council, 1949, 'Chaplains Who Served', pp. 91–95.

405 NARA RG 247. Chief of Chaplains. Box 199. Race–Jewish etc. ——— to Chief of Chaplains, 11 October 1945.

406 Ibid, ——— to Prinz, 18 July 1944.

407 Ibid, Prinz to David de Sola Pool, 6 November 1944.

408 Ibid, Philip S. Bernstein to William R. Arnold, 30 November 1944.

409 Beard, Beard and Pinkerton, 2002, p. 228.

410 Ibid.

411 Bettelheim and Janowitz, 1950, pp. 189, 191.

412 Ibid, pp. 50–51.

413 Ibid, pp. 51–52.

414 Ibid.

415 Ibid.

416 Ibid, p. 166 n. 3.

417 Wickersham, 1998, p. 44.

418 *The Link*, January 1945, pp. 31–32.

419 Ibid, p. 32.

420 Ibid, May 1945, p. 23.

421 Ibid.

422 Ibid, p. 25.

423 Ibid.

424 Ibid, p. 26.

425 *The Chaplain*, May 1945, p. 29.

426 Ibid.

427 Stroup, 2000, p. 145.

428 VHP, Emma Delano Petengill, letter 23 April 1944, VHP MSS Box 1757. Folder 3/3.

429 Orr, 1948, pp. 68–69.

430 *The Chaplain*, July 1945, p. 43.

431 Glasser, 1946, p. 68.

432 Drury, 1948, p. 102.

433 Ibid; Drury, 1950, p. 100.

434 *The Chaplain*, November 1944, p. 47.

CHAPTER FOUR

Foxhole Religion and Wartime Faith

1 *The Christian Science Monitor*, 30 April 1943, p. 3.

2 Hickcox, 1950, p. 30.

3 Connelly, 1945, 1945, p. 49.

4 Nance, 1944, p. 52.

5 Lunn, 1947, p. 13.

6 1946, *History of Chaplains' Activities in the Pacific*, pp. 264–65.

7 Ardery, 1978, p. 92.

8 Clare, 1945, p. 122.

9 *The Christian Science Monitor*, 7 January 1944, p. 9.

10 Abbott, 1946, p. 51

11 Hastings, 2011, p. 290.

12 Martin, 'Meehling', pp. 66–67.

13 Pyle, 2001, p. 250.

14 1945, *American Chaplains of the Fifth Army*, pp. 33–34.

15 Sampson, 1958, pp. 24, 34, 51.

16 Ibid, pp. 10–11; Cross and Arnold, 1945, pp. 104–5.

17 Coffman, 2004, p. 400.

18 *The Link*, November 1943, p. 28.

19 Ibid, November 1944, p. 7.

20 Ibid, December 1944, p. 45.

21 Ibid, February 1945, p. 25.

22 Ibid, pp. 25–26.

23 Ibid, August 1945, pp. 5–6.

24 Bando, 2003, p. 34.

25 Ibid, p. 34.

26 USAHEC, World War II Veterans Survey, 101st Airborne, Leo Claude Martin.

27 Ibid, Richard E. O'Brien.

28 Ibid, Michael Zelieskovies.

29 VHP, Joe Baldwin, online transcript.

30 Crosby, 1994, pp. 26–27; *Los Angeles Times*, 6 October 1945, p. 7.

31 *Christian Herald*, September 1943, p. 17.

32 Gehring, 1962, pp. 10–11.

33 See, for example, the responses to Question 31a in the US Army Military History Institute's World War II Veterans Survey, 'How and to what extent were religious convictions expressed in your unit?'

34 Carroll, 2007, n.p.

35 Ibid, p. 48.

36 Robertson, 2006, pp. 134–36.

37 Taggart and Cross, 1943, p. 141.

38 VHP, Norman Wesley Achen, online transcript.

39 *The Link*, January 1945, pp. 13–14.

40 VHP, John Kempton, memoirs, p. 8, VHP MSS Box 1412. Folder 2/2.

41 Leach, 1987, p. 93.

42 Fahey, 1992, p. 402.

43 *The Link*, September 1943, pp. 20–21.

44 Ibid, April 1944, pp. 12–15.

45 Connelly, 1945, p. 45.

46 Atwell, 1961, p. 154.

47 Clare, 1945, p. 126.

48 Ibid, p. 127.

49 Willard, 1944, p. 27.

50 Grant, 1944, p. 101.

51 *Jewish Exponent*, 15 September 1944, p. 36.

52 Brasted, 1943, p. 190.

53 Hynd, 1943, p. 380.

54 Ibid, p. 379.

55 Braden, 1947, pp. 38–39.

56 Schneider, 1952, p. 167.

57 Runbeck, 1944, p. 78.

58 Hickcox, 1950, p. 42.

59 Cairns, 1919, pp. 7–8.

60 Committee on the War and the Religious Outlook, 1920, pp. 79, 82.

61 *Marine Corps Gazette*, August 1943, p. 20.

62 Glasser, 1946, p. 87.

63 Ibid, p. 88.

64 Leuschner, 1946, pp. 42–43.

65 Tregaskis, 1944, pp. 235–36.
66 *The Link*, August 1944, p. 18.
67 Rogers, 1946, p. 48.
68 Ibid, p. 154.
69 Ibid, p. 166.
70 Ibid, p. 96.
71 Cross and Arnold, 1945, p. 15.
72 Hedstrom, 2013, pp. 123, 133.
73 Daniel, 1985, p. 4.
74 Nance, 1944, p. 154.
75 Jorgensen, 1961, p. 279.
76 Brink, 1944, p. 53.
77 Carlson, 1945, pp. 24, 34, 80–82.
78 *The Link*, February 1944, p. 2.
79 *The Chaplain*, October 1944, p. 41.
80 Leuschner, 1946, p. 69.
81 *The Chaplain*, March 1945, pp. 30–31.
82 *Chicago Daily Tribune*, 4 September 1944, p. 21.
83 *The Link*, April 1945, pp. 6–7.
84 *The Chaplain*, August 1941, p. 41.
85 1946, *History of Chaplains' Activities in the Pacific*, pp. 440–47.
86 *The Christian Science Monitor*, 25 February 1943, p. 2.
87 *Los Angeles Times*, 11 April 1944, p. A3.
88 Kimball, 1947, pp. 58–60.
89 Tower, 1945, pp. 137–38.
90 Nance, 1944, p. 223.
91 Jorgensen, 1961, p. 284.
92 Miller, 2007, p. 389; Gilbert, 2007, p. xi; Atkinson, 2013, p. 488.
93 Gilbert, 2007, pp. 144–45.
94 1945, 'Reports of the General Board. 68. The Army Chaplain in the European Theater', note 8 p. 88.
95 Office of the Adjutant General, Statistical and Accounting Branch, 1953, p. 5.
96 Hastings, 2007, p. 375.
97 Wagner, Kennedy, Osborne and Reyburn, 2007, pp. 650–54; Burleigh, pp. 385–86.
98 Daniel, 1985, pp. 70–72.
99 Sampson, 1958, pp. 126, 133–34.
100 Crosby, pp. 148–49.
101 Daniel, 1985, pp. 38–39.
102 Carroll, p. 88.
103 1945, 'Reports of the General Board. 68. The Army Chaplain in the European Theater', p. 84, note 2 p. 87.
104 Ibid, pp. 85–86.
105 Drury, 1950, pp. 28–29.

106 Dorsett, 2012, pp. 205–6.
107 Honeywell, 1958, p. 280; Dorsett, 2012, p. 204.
108 Stewart, 1958.
109 Ibid, p. 105.
110 Ibid, p. 107.
111 Spivey, 2009, loc. 2911.
112 Sampson, 1958, p. 66.
113 Pyle, 2001, p. 54.
114 *Christian Herald*, December 1944, p. 63.
115 Runbeck, 1944, p. vi; dustjacket.
116 Tower, 1945, pp. 163–64.
117 Carlson, 1945, pp. 25–26.
118 Leuschner, 1946, p. 22.
119 *The Link*, April 1944, pp. 12–15.
120 O'Callahan, 1956, p. 39.
121 Hastings, 2005, p. 259.
122 Metcalf, 1957, pp. 120–21.
123 *The Chaplain*, September 1945, p. 37.
124 Sampson, 1958, p. 73.
125 O'Callahan, 1956, p. 38.
126 Ibid, p. 39.
127 Bassett, 1991, pp. 1–2.
128 VHP, Russell Baldwin, online Complete Interview.
129 *What the Soldier Thinks*, August 1944, pp. 8–9, 11.
130 Ardery, 1978, pp. 188–89.
131 Ibid, p. 92.
132 *The Link*, April 1946, p. 23.
133 VHP, William H. Schaefer, transcript, p. 17, VHPP MSS Box 778. Folder 4/4.
134 Bergerud, 1996, p. 470.
135 Atwell, 1961, pp. 51, 251–52.
136 O'Callahan, 1956, pp. 72–73.
137 1945, *American Chaplains of the Fifth Army*, pp. 35–36.
138 *What the Soldier Thinks*, April 1944, pp. 1–2.
139 Ibid, May 1944, pp. 6–11.
140 http://pattonhq.com/prayer.html, accessed 10 February 2014.
141 Moore, 2004, pp. 268–69, n. 19.
142 Dollard and Horton, 1944, passim.
143 *The Infantry Journal*, June 1944, pp. 59–60.
144 Stouffer, 1949, II, p. 185.
145 Ibid, Chart XII, p. 174.
146 Ibid, Chart XIII, p. 175.
147 Ibid, pp. 176–77.
148 Ibid, pp. 183–84.

149 Wansink and Wansink, forthcoming, p. 8.

150 Atkins, 1945, p. 105.

151 http://brothersinbattle.net/html/peleliu_chapter.html, accessed 10 February 2014.

152 Ardery, 1978, p. 92.

153 Robertson, 2006, p. 205.

154 Atwell, 1961, pp. 175–76.

155 Ibid, p. 434.

156 Faubus, 1971, p. 181.

157 Ambrose, 2010, p. 199.

158 Mygatt and Darlington, 1944, p. 85.

159 *Newsday*, 12 November 1943, p. 3.

160 Tapert, 1987, p. 199.

161 VHP Giarratano, transcript, p. 10, VHP MSS Box 1497. Folder 2/4.

162 Lewis, *Hell in the Pacific*, 2001.

163 Hickcox, 1950, p. 43.

164 See, for example, *The Link*, February 1944, p. 23; November 1944, p. 23; February 1945, p. 21.

165 Carlson, 1945, p. 59; *The Link*, June 1945, p. 49.

166 *The Link*, May 1943, p. 37.

167 *The National Catholic Almanac*, 1943, pp. 678–79.

168 Faubus, 1971, pp. 683–84.

169 Beard, Beard and Pinkerton, 2002, p. 95.

170 *The Link*, April 1943, p. 27.

171 Jorgensen, 1961, p. 212; *The Link*, September 1944, pp. 11–12.

172 *Stars and Stripes*, 3 July 1944, p. 2.

173 *The Christian Science Monitor*, 18 November 1944, p. 7; 12 March 1945, p. 3.

174 http://pattonhq.com/prayer.html, accessed 10 February 2014.

175 *The Christian Science Monitor*, 12 March 1945, p. 3.

176 Abbott, 1946, p. 81.

177 Ibid, p. 84.

178 *Stars and Stripes*, 7 June 1944, p. 1.

179 *The Link*, July 1944, p. 36.

180 Kershaw, 2003, p. 171.

181 Ibid.

182 Pyle, 2001, p. 254.

183 Clare, 1945, p. 133.

184 Abbott, 1946, p. 37.

185 Queen, Prothero and Shattuck, 2001, I, p. 126.

186 Eliot, 1943, p. 98.

187 Linderman, 1997, p. 66.

188 Murphy, 1949, p. 263.

189 Stouffer, 1949, II, p. 383.

190 Muirhead, 1988, pp. 127–28.

191 Wheal and Pope, 1995, p. 154.

192 VHP, William Thomas Barr, online transcript.

193 *The Link*, June 1946, p. 30; Thomas, 1991, pp. 724–34.

194 *The Link*, March 1944, pp. 54–56.

195 *Yank*, 13 December 1942, p. 10.

196 Spivey, 2009, loc. 3859.

197 Gavin, 2007, p. 111.

198 Crosby, 1994, p. 180.

199 Fahey, 1992, p. 77.

200 Ibid, p. 376.

201 Robertson, 2006, pp. 257–58.

202 *Chicago Tribune*, 4 September 1944, p. 21.

203 Stouffer, 1949, II, p. 188.

204 Ibid, pp. 188–89.

205 Robertson, 2006, p. 187.

206 *The Link*, August 1944, p. 26.

207 Ibid, December 1944, p. 37.

208 Ibid, August 1945, pp. 39–41.

209 Stouffer, 1949, II, p. 188.

210 Ibid, p. 88.

211 Pyle, 2001, pp. 207–8.

212 *What the Soldier Thinks*, August 1944, pp. 8–11.

213 Kimball, 1947, p. 33.

214 Cross and Arnold, 1945, p. 82.

215 Eliot, 2007, pp. 182–83, 188.

216 VHP Joseph Towell, transcript, p. 3, VHP MSS Box 512. Folder 2/3.

217 Feuer, 2004, p. 42.

218 Rabey, 2002, p. 110.

219 VHP, Jay S. Adams, online transcript.

220 VHP, Johann Carl Friedrich Kasten, online transcript.

221 VHP, Russell Baldwin, online Complete Interview.

222 Yost, 2006, pp. 97, 111, 141.

223 Ibid, p. 117.

224 Willard, 1944, p. 39.

225 Rogers, 1946, p. 162.

226 1945, *American Chaplains of the Fifth Army*, p. 36.

227 Ray, 1962, p. 86.

228 Gerth and Mills, 1964, pp. 139, 155.

229 Gregory, 1947, p. 420.

230 Stouffer, 1949, II, p. 188.

231 Muirhead, 1988, pp. 128–29.

232 Pyle, 2004, p. 232.

233 Pyle, 2001, pp. 143–44.

234 Pyle, 2004, pp. 90–91.

235 Pyle, 2001, p. 187.

236 Steinbeck, 1975, pp. 39–41.

237 Ibid, pp. 195–97.

238 *Yank*, 20 December 1942, p. 5.

239 Fussell, 1989, p. 51.

240 Eliot, 2007, p. 179.

241 VHP, Steve van der Weele, transcript, p. 5, VHP MSS Box 1855. Folder 3/3; Kenneth Kramer, transcript, p. 6, VHP MSS Box 1332. Folder 1/1; Carl W. Hardwick, transcript, p.2, VHP MSS Box 2180. Folder 2/3.

242 Steinbeck, 1975, p. 197.

243 Gavin, 2007, pp. 116–17.

244 Fussell, 1989, p. 49; Atkinson, 2002, p. 246.

245 McPherson, 1997, p. 63.

246 Promey, 2011, p. 196.

247 Dash Moore, 2004, pp. 49–50, 73; Enjames, 2003, II, p. 19; *Jewish Exponent*, 15 September 1944, p. 36.

248 Grant, 1944, pp. 21–22.

249 Atwell, 1961, p. 248.

250 VHP, Salvatore Tocco, transcript, p. 9, VHP MSS Box 1747. Folder 10/12.

251 Enjames, 2003, II, p. 19.

252 *Washington Post*, 23 March 1945, p. 5.

253 Atkins, 1945, p. 102.

254 Fry and Jessup, 1933, pp. 1025–6.

255 VHP, William Greene, transcript, p. 9, VHP MSS Box 663. Folder 2/2.

256 Chandler and Ambrose, IV, p. 2507.

257 Grant, 1944, p. 22.

258 Clare, 1945, p. 294.

259 Steinbeck, 1975, p. 195.

260 O'Callahan, 1956, p. 41.

261 Poling, 1959, p. 214.

262 *The Link*, February 1944, p. 31.

263 Ibid, October 1943, p. 67; April 1943, pp. 9–12; May 1943, pp. 40–41; June 1943, p. 64; September 1945, p. 61.

264 Ibid, June 1943, p. 64.

265 Ibid, July 1943, p. 56.

266 Steinbeck, 1975, p. 195.

267 Cross and Arnold, 1945, p. 95.

268 Fussell, 1989, p. 234.

269 1945, *American Chaplains of the Fifth Army*, p. 24.

270 *Stars and Stripes*, 28 December 1944, p. 4.

271 Carlson, 1945, p. 55.

272 Willard, 1944, pp. 156–57.

273 *The Link*, September 1944, pp. 14–15.

274 Cross and Arnold, 1945, p. 102.

275 Enjames, 2003, II, p. 211; Steinbeck, 1975, p. 195.

276 Atkinson, 2007, p. 62.

277 Kimball, 1947, p. 157.

278 *The Link*, April 1945, p. 25.

279 *The Chaplain*, April 1945, p. 11.

280 Dennis, 1945, p. 110.

281 Honeywell, 1958, p. 259.

282 Daddis, 2010, p. 115.

283 Gregory, 1947, p. 420.

284 Pyle, 2004, p. 107.

285 Ardery, 1978, p. 93.

286 Cross and Arnold, 1945, p. 80.

287 1947, *The Story of Christian Science Wartime Activities*, pp. 170–72.

288 *The Chaplain*, January 1945, p. 41.

289 Harrison, 1948, p. 26.

290 McDannell and Lang, 1988, pp. 276–92, 303–6.

291 Committee on the War and the Religious Outlook, 1920, pp. 35–36.

292 Marty, 1991, p. 201; Noll, 1992, pp. 375–76.

293 Cantril and Strunk, 1951, p. 310.

294 Ibid.

295 Rable, 2010, pp. 142–43, 177–78, 181; Ebel, 2010, pp. 147–58.

296 *Yank*, 14 February 1943, p. 15.

297 Ibid, 18 July 1943, p. 9.

298 Center of Military History, The U.S. Army Campaigns of World War II: Sicily, p.25, http://www.history.army.mil/brochures/72-16/72-16.htm, accessed 16 April 2013; Maddox, 1992, pp. 261–62; Murray, 2002, p. 164; Kennedy, 1999, p. 610.

299 Office of the Adjutant General, Statistical and Accounting Branch, 1953, p. 6.

300 Wagner, Kennedy, Osborne and Reyburn, 2007, p. 600; Perret, 1991, p. 507.

301 Rose, 2008, p. 217.

302 *The Christian Century*, 13 June 1945, p. 700.

303 Eliot, 1943, p. 96.

304 *Marine Corps Gazette*, June 1944, p. 57.

305 *The Leatherneck*, December 1945, p. 33.

306 Leckie, 2010, p. 233.

307 *The Chaplain*, February 1945, pp. 36–37.

308 Ibid, March 1945, pp. 5–8.

309 Ibid, p. 23.

310 *The Link*, May 1945, p. 28.

311 Ibid, March 1944, p. 6.

312 Ibid, October 1944, p. 60.

313 Ibid, April 1945, p. 15.

314 Ibid, pp. 15–16.

315 Ibid, p. 16.

316 Rable, 2010, p. 142.

317 http://lcweb2.loc.gov/diglib/ihas/loc.natlib. ihas.200000011/default.html, accessed 16 April 2013.

318 http://www.arlingtoncemetery.net/wgfarrow. htm, accessed 10 February 2014.

319 http://www.imdb.com/title/tt0035959/, accessed 29 July 2014.

320 Ebel, 2010, p. 147.

321 Muirhead, 1988, p. 155.

322 Faubus, 1971, p. 267.

323 *Yank*, 20 December 1942, p. 19.

324 1945, *American Chaplains of the Fifth Army*, Foreword.

325 1946, *History of Chaplains' Activities in the Pacific*, p. 134.

326 Poling, 1959, pp. 225–28.

327 Abbott, 1946, pp. 28, 48.

328 Ibid, p. 118.

329 http://www.presidency.ucsb.edu/ws/index. php?pid=16356, accessed 22 July 2013.

330 Kershaw, 2003, p. 174.

331 Faubus, 1971, p. 469.

332 Clare, 1945, pp. 141–42.

333 *The Chaplain*, May 1946, pp. 17–18.

334 Wuest, 1953, p. 100.

335 Mygatt and Darlington, 1944, p. 85.

336 Rose, 2008, p. 126.

337 *The Christian Century*, 22 August 1945, p. 954.

338 Wuest, 1953, p. 100.

339 Spellman, 1945, p. 81.

340 Ibid, p. 6.

341 Gannon, 1962, pp. 230–31; Spellman, *The Risen Soldier* 1944, passim.

342 Spellman, 1945, p. 79.

343 Ibid, p. 109.

344 Spivey, 2009, loc. 5526.

345 Carlson, 1945, p. 18.

346 Willard, 1944, p. 196.

347 Ibid, p. 50.

348 Ibid, p. 153.

349 Nance, 1944, p. 207.

350 Willard, 1944, p. 158.

351 *The Chaplain*, November 1944, p. 39; July 1945, pp. 30, 46.

352 Ibid, December 1945, p. 32.

353 Drury, 1950, pp. 51, 220.

354 *The Chaplain*, November 1946, pp. 19, 21.

355 Willard, 1944, p. 158.

356 *The Link*, July 1944, p. 2.

357 Ibid.

358 Ibid.

359 Glasser, 1946, pp. 5–7.

360 Ibid, pp. 62–63.

361 Nance, 1944, p. 46.

362 *The Chaplain*, July 1945, p. 44.

363 Ibid, November 1945, pp. 21–22.

364 Ibid, p. 21.

365 Nance, 1944, p. 45.

366 *New York Times*, 19 August 1941, p. 11.

367 Nance, 1944, p. 46.

368 Grant, 1944, p. 97.

369 Tregaskis, 1943, pp. 3, 21–22.

370 *New York Times*, 20 December 1942, p. 4.

371 *Los Angeles Times*, 30 December 1942, p. 7.

372 *The Washington Post*, 14 March 1943, p. 8.

373 *The Link*, January 1945, pp. 16–17.

374 Brink, 1944, Foreword.

375 Taggart and Cross, 1943, pp. 163–65.

376 *The Christian Century*, 13 December 1944, p. 1449.

377 Nance, 1944, p. 67.

378 Ibid, pp. 73–74.

379 *The Chaplain*, November 1946, p. 17.

380 Ibid, p. 18.

381 Ibid, pp. 21–23.

382 Nance, 1944, p. 14; Grant, 1944, p. 94.

383 *The Chaplain*, December 1944, p. 46.

384 Brink, 1944, p. 86.

385 Carlson, 1945, p. 80.

386 Nance, 1944, p. 74.

387 Ibid, pp. 78–79.

388 1946, *History of Chaplains' Activities in the Pacific*, pp. 454–55.

389 Nance, 1944, p. 265.

390 Johnson, 1945, pp. 48–49, 51.

391 *Yank*, 21 February 1943, p. 10; 1946, *History of Chaplains' Activities in the Pacific*, p. 318.

392 Martin, 'Meehling', p. 57.

393 Grant, 1944, p. 19.

394 Cross and Arnold, 1945, p. 83.

395 Sampson, 1958, p. 78.

396 Ibid, p. 147.

397 Smith, 1988, p. 91.

398 1945, 'Reports of the General Board. 68.

The Army Chaplain in the European Theater', note 4, p. 48.

399 Kertzer, 1947, p. 29.

400 *The Chaplain*, December 1945, p. 44.

401 Abbott, 1946, p. 146.

402 Kertzer, 1947, p. 29.

403 Sampson, 1958, p. 163.

404 Ibid, p. 170.

405 NARA RG 247 Records of the Office of the Chief of Chaplains. Records of Administration and Management General Records. Records Relating to the History of the Chaplains of the United States Army, 1941–58. Box 3. 'The Corps of Chaplains 1 July 1945 to 30 September 1946', p. 53.

406 Ibid, pp. 54–55.

407 1946, *History of Chaplains' Activities in the Pacific*, p. 265.

408 1945, 'Reports of the General Board. 68. The Army Chaplain in the European Theater', Appendix 14, p. 30.

409 Stanton, 2006, p. 310.

410 1945, 'Reports of the General Board. 68. The Army Chaplain in the European Theater', pp. 69–70.

411 Ibid, Appendix 15, pp. 32–33.

412 Ibid, p. 33.

413 Ibid.

414 Sherry, 1995, p. ix.

415 1945, 'Reports of the General Board. 68. The Army Chaplain in the European Theater', Appendix 15, p. 35.

416 Ibid.

417 Jorgensen, 1961, p. 101.

418 1945, 'Reports of the General Board. 68. The Army Chaplain in the European Theater', Appendix 15, p. 35.

419 Crespi and Shapleigh, 1946, p. 362.

420 Queen, Prothero and Shattuck, 2001, II, pp. 577–78.

421 Crespi and Shapleigh, 1946, p. 371.

422 Ibid, p. 367.

423 Ibid, p. 369.

424 Stouffer, 1949, I, p. 5; Merton and Lazarsfeld, 1950, p. 9.

425 Stouffer, 1949, I, p. 144.

426 Ibid, p. 112.

427 Ibid, p. 140.

428 Ibid.

429 Stouffer, 1949, II, p. 187.

430 Ibid.

431 Ibid, p. 172.

432 Ibid, p. 136.

433 Ibid, pp. 173, 175.

434 Ibid, pp. 176–77.

435 Ibid, pp. 180–81.

436 Ibid, pp. 183–85.

437 Ibid, p. 185.

438 Ibid, pp. 186.

439 Ibid.

440 Merton and Lazarsfeld, 1950, pp. 223–24.

441 Hyslop, 1945, p. 5.

442 Kimball, 1947, p. 168.

443 Martin, 'Craven', p. 24.

444 *The Chaplain*, July 1945, p. 31.

445 1945, 'Reports of the General Board. 68. The Army Chaplain in the European Theater', p. 60.

446 *The Chaplain*, April 1945, p. 13.

447 Ibid, p. 15.

448 *The Link*, August 1945, pp. 17–18.

449 Ibid, September 1945, pp. 24–26.

450 *The Chaplain*, July 1945, p. 23.

451 Ibid.

452 Ibid, August 1945, p. 23; January 1946, p. 46; NARA RG 247 Records of the Office of the Chief of Chaplains. Records of Administration and Management General Records. Records Relating to the History of the Chaplains of the United States Army, 1941–58. Box 3. 'The Corps of Chaplains 1 July 1945 to 30 September 1946', p. 40.

453 *The Chaplain*, August 1945, p. 30.

454 1945, 'Reports of the General Board. 68. The Army Chaplain in the European Theater', p. 60.

455 NARA RG 247 Records of the Office of the Chief of Chaplains. Records of Administration and Management General Records. Records Relating to the History of the Chaplains of the United States Army, 1941–58. Box 3. 'The Corps of Chaplains 1 July 1945 to 30 September 1946', p. 40.

456 *The Chaplain*, January 1946, p. 46.

457 Ibid, May 1946, pp. 19–21.

458 1945, 'Reports of the General Board. 68. The Army Chaplain in the European Theater', p. 69.

459 *The Link*, August 1945, pp. 18–19.

460 Holifield, 2007, p. 244.

461 Noll, 1992, p. 437.

462 Mason, 1986, p. 125.

463 Ibid, p. 136.

464 *The Chaplain*, December 1945, p. 32.

465 *The Link*, August 1945, p. 19; Adams, 1994, p. 152.

466 *The Link*, October 1944, p. 20.

467 *The Chaplain*, November 1945, p. 44.

468 *The Chaplain*, May 1946, pp. 19–20.

469 Casino, 1987, p. 61.

470 Ibid, p. 66.

471 Dolan, 2002, p. 181.

472 Ellis, 1969, p. 135; Dolan, 2002, p. 181.

473 Brink, 1944, p. 87.

474 Ibid, p. 91.

475 Abbott, 1946, p. 140.

476 Ibid, pp. 141–42.

477 Ibid, p. 147.

478 Stouffer, 1949, II, pp. 642–43.

479 Chamberlin, 1945, p. 18.

480 *The Link*, June 1944, pp. 19–20.

481 Nance, 1944, pp. 205–6.

482 Ibid, pp. 291–93.

483 Ibid, p. 294.

484 Ibid, pp. 295–96.

485 *The Chaplain*, July 1945, p. 48.

486 Burkhart, 1945, pp. ix, 51.

487 Ibid, passim.

488 Chamberlin, 1945.

489 *The Chaplain*, December 1945, p. 45.

490 Ibid, pp. 31–32.

491 Leuschner, 1946, p. 107.

492 *The Chaplain*, December 1945, p. 40.

493 Drury, 1950, pp. 245–46; Martin, 'Craven', pp. 30–31.

494 VHP, William Luitje, diaries and journals, folder 4, p. 1, VHP MSS Box 588. Folder 4/10.

495 Ibid, p. 2.

496 Ibid, pp. 8–9.

497 NARA RG 247 Records of the Office of the Chief of Chaplains. Records of Administration and Management General Records. Records Relating to the History of the Chaplains of the United States Army, 1941–58. Box 3. 'The Corps of Chaplains 1 July 1945 to 30 September 1946', p. 39.

498 *The Link*, March 1944, pp. 2–3; June 1944, pp. 14, 39; November 1944, pp. 29–30; December 1944, p. 50.

499 Ibid, March 1944, pp. 2–3.

500 http://www.cwv.org/default. aspx?pg=fff78b56-cc51–48f2–8077-bfa34fe2ac09, accessed 13 June 2013; Hennessey, 1981, p. 290.

501 *The Chaplain*, December 1945, pp. 33–34.

CHAPTER FIVE
Global Encounters

1 Yost, 2006, pp. 67–68.

2 Reynolds, 1996, p. 20.

3 http://www.nationalww2museum.org/learn/education/for-students/ww2-history/ww2-by-the-numbers/us-military.html, accessed 23 July 2014.

4 Glaser, 1946, p. 433.

5 *The Link*, January 1945, p. 47; Wuest, 1953, pp. 127–30; Yost, 2006, pp. 256–57; Kertzer, 1947, pp. 168, 179–80.

6 Sevareid, 1976, pp. 415–16.

7 Clark, 2007, pp. 297–98.

8 Lord, 1942, pp. 8–9.

9 Ibid, p. 9.

10 Ibid, pp. 9–11.

11 Ibid, pp. 11–12.

12 Carpenter, 1997, p. 93.

13 *The National Catholic Almanac*, 1942, p. 740.

14 Hoenicke Moore, 2010, pp. 59–60.

15 Ibid, pp. 91–92, 151.

16 Kennedy, 1999, pp. 469–70; Preston, 2012, pp. 324–25; Smith, 2006, p. 215; Overy, 1995, p. 285.

17 Hoenicke Moore, 2010, p. 172; Preston, 2012, pp. 366–67.

18 Hedstrom, 2013, Figure 4.4, p. 138.

19 http://www.presidency.ucsb.edu/ws/index.php?pid=16514, accessed 22 July 2013.

20 Sittser, 1997, pp. 1–2.

21 Carmer, 1943, p. xii.

22 Ibid, pp. xii–xiii.

23 http://www.elca.org/Who-We-Are/History/ELCA-Archives/Luth-Leaders-Collection/Stewart-W-Herman, 1943-Jr.aspx, accessed 13 August 2013.

24 Herman, 1943, p. xii.

25 Hoenicke Moore, 2010, p. 288

26 *Washington Post*, 20 February 1943, p. B4.

27 Wynn, 2010, pp. iii and 51; Fussell, 1989, p. 7.

28 *Marine Corps Gazette*, December 1943, editorial.

29 Sevareid, 1976, p. 402.

30 Schultz, 2011, loc. 941–47.

31 Stouffer, 1949, I, p. 50.

32 Hoenicke Moore, 2010, p. 161.

33 Stouffer, 1949, I, pp. 462–63.

34 Ibid, pp. 433–35.

35 Young, 1959, p. 310.

36 *The Link*, April 1943, p. 43.

37 Ibid, February 1944, pp. 11–12.

38 Ibid, July 1943, p. 63.

39 Ibid, January 1945, p. 45.

40 Ibid, April 1943, p. 51.

41 Ibid, February 1944, p. 33.

42 Ibid.

43 Ibid, March 1944, p. 47.

44 Ibid.

45 Ibid, January 1945, p. 44.

46 Burleigh, 2007, pp. 204–6; Bergen, 1996; Spicer, 2008; Conway; 1968, Lewy, 1964.

47 Kertzer, 1947, p. 141.

48 *The Link*, May 1943, pp. 36–37.

49 Ibid, March 1944, p. 49.

50 *The Chaplain*, December 1944, p. 39.

51 Ibid, May 1945, pp. 12–13.

52 Ibid, June 1945, p. 10.

53 Ibid, May 1946, p. 37.

54 Blumenson, 1972, II, p. 187.

55 *Warweek*, 12 May 1945, p. 1.

56 *Stars and Stripes*, 21 March 1944, p. 2.

57 *Warweek*, 7 April 1945, pp. ii–iii.

58 Tapert, 1987, pp. 83–84.

59 Ibid, p. 124.

60 Hastings, 2005, p. 241; Ambrose, 1998, p. 355.

61 Bando, 2001, p. 150.

62 Grant, 1944, p. 64.

63 Astor, 1998, pp. 479–80, 519.

64 Sampson, 1958, pp. 126, 134.

65 VHP, Johann Carl Friedrich Kasten, online transcript.

66 Schrijvers, 1998, p. 85; Zaloga, 1991, p. 34.

67 Linderman, 1997, p. 114.

68 Rogers, 1946, pp. 87–88.

69 Ibid, pp. 173–74.

70 Yost, 2006, p. 163.

71 Steigmann-Gall, 2003, pp. 218–20; Office of Strategic Services, Research and Analysis Branch, 1944, pp. 34–35.

72 Carlson, 1945, pp. 62–63.

73 Ibid, p. 63.

74 Sampson, 1958, pp. 63–64.

75 Ibid, p. 68.

76 Ibid, p. 112.

77 Ibid, pp. 133, 144–45, 150.

78 Kertzer, 1947, pp. 138–39.

79 Hoenicke Moore, 2010, pp. 159–60; Burleigh, 2007, p. 206; *The Link*, May 1943, p. 53; June 1943, p. 45; March 1945, p. 63.

80 *The Link*, November 1944, p. 7; Dennis, 1945, pp. 51–56.

81 *Yank*, 5 August 1942, p. 11.

82 http://www.history.navy.mil/faqs/faq87–30.htm, accessed 25 July 2013.

83 Atkinson, 2007, p. 477.

84 Kahn and McLemore, 1945, p. 114.

85 1945, *American Chaplains of the Fifth* Army, p. 41; Delaney, 1947, p. 55.

86 1945, *American Chaplains of the Fifth Army*, pp. 41–42.

87 Ibid, pp. 41–42; Brown, 1986, p. 93; Delaney, 1947, p. 55; *The Link*, September 1944, p. 14; Hale, 2004, p. 96.

88 1945, *American Chaplains of the Fifth Army*, p. 42.

89 1945, 'Reports of the General Board. 68. The Army Chaplain in the European Theater', p. 90.

90 Ibid.

91 Ibid, p. 96.

92 Ibid, p. 90.

93 1945, *Military Government Germany: Technical Manual for Education and Religious Affairs*, map: '"Greater Germany" percentage distribution of Roman Catholics', p. 88.

94 Burleigh, 2001, pp. 260–64; Grunberger, 1991, pp. 548–70.

95 NARA, RG 247, Records of the Office of the Chief of Chaplains. Records of Administration and Management General Records. Records Relating to the History of the Chaplains of the United States Army, 1941–58, Box 3, 'Military History of the Second World War. The Corps of Chaplains', p. 92.

96 1945, 'Reports of the General Board. 68. The Army Chaplain in the European Theater', p. 90.

97 Daniel, 1985, p. 41.

98 Ibid, pp. 51–52, 58–59.

99 Schrijvers, 1998, p. 138.

100 Ibid, p. 143.

101 Burleigh, 2007, p. 178.

102 Colby, 1991, pp. 459–60.

103 *Los Angeles Times*, 26 October 1945, p. 1.

104 *The Chaplain*, November 1945, p. 26.

105 Schrijvers, 1998, p. 143.

106 Office of Strategic Services, Research and Analysis Branch, 1944, p. iv.

107 Ibid, p. 29.

108 Ibid, pp. 90–91.

109 McClaskey, 1951, pp. 16–17.

110 1945, *Military Government Germany: Technical Manual for Education and Religious Affairs*, pp. 34–54.

111 Ibid, p. i.

112 Ibid, pp. 46–47; 1945, 'Reports of the General Board. 68. The Army Chaplain in the European Theater', p. 91.

113 Connelly, 1945, pp. 83–84.

114 Jorgensen, 1961, p. 224; Murray, 1955, p. 228.

115 Faubus, 1971, p. 633.

116 Ibid, pp. 661–62.

117 McClaskey, 1951, pp. 14–15.

118 1945, 'Reports of the General Board. 68. The Army Chaplain in the European Theater', pp. 92 and 97.

119 Schrijvers, 1998, p. 139.

120 USAHEC, Charles E. Wilson Papers, 'Frail Children of the Dust', p. 271.

121 1945, 'Reports of the General Board. 68. The Army Chaplain in the European Theater', pp. 91–92, 96–97.

122 Ziemke, 1975, p. 322.

123 Venzke, 1977, pp. 17–18.

124 Vida, 1967,p. 22.

125 Ziemke, 1975, pp. 323–25.

126 Ibid, p. 327; Willoughby, 1998, pp. 158–59.

127 Venzke, 1977, p. 17.

128 Ibid, p. 18.

129 *The Chaplain*, March 1946, p. 13.

130 Brink, 1944, p. 67.

131 Ibid, pp. 63–64.

132 *The Chaplain*, September 1945, p. 45.

133 Ibid, January 1946, p. 45.

134 Connelly, 1945, p. 15.

135 *The Chaplain*, October 1944, p. 26.

136 Office of Strategic Services, Research and Analysis Branch, 1944, p. 23.

137 Leuschner, 1946, pp. 77–78.

138 *The Chaplain*, September 1945, p. 22.

139 Venzke, 1977, pp. 7–11.

140 Burleigh, 2007, p. 171.

141 Steigmann-Gall, 2003, pp. 119–20, 162.

142 *The Chaplain*, January 1946, p. 45.

143 Venzke, 1977, pp. 7–10; Grossmith, 1998, pp. 48–49, 58–59, 72–76.

144 http://www1.umn.edu/humanrts/instree/1929c.htm, accessed 1 September 2014.

145 NARA, RG 247, Records of the Office of the Chief of Chaplains. Records of Administration and Management General Records. Records Relating to the History of the Chaplains of the United States Army, 1941–58, Box 3, 'Military History of the Second World War. The Corps of Chaplains', p. 92.

146 Ibid.

147 Office of the Chief of Chaplains, 1944, p. 35.

148 1945, 'Reports of the General Board. 68. The Army Chaplain in the European Theater', Appendix 1, p. 1.

149 Wagner, Kennedy, Osborne and Reyburn, 2007, p. 899. According to *The Link*, on 1 December 1944 'there were 359,247 prisoners of war being held in the United States'. Of these, 305,648 were German, 51,156 were Italian, and only 2,443 were Japanese. They were held in '130 base camps and 295 branch camps near current work projects'. *The Link*, March 1945, p. 26.

150 Ambrose, 1998, pp. 361–63.

151 1945, 'Reports of the General Board. 68. The Army Chaplain in the European Theater', p. 53.

152 Ibid; Ambrose, 1998, p. 363.

153 Delaney, 1947, pp. 237–38.

154 Venzke, 1977, p. 14.

155 Delaney, 1947, p. 236.

156 1945, 'Reports of the General Board. 68. The Army Chaplain in the European Theater', pp. 53–54.

157 Honeywell, 1958, p. 283.

158 1945, 'Reports of the General Board. 68. The Army Chaplain in the European Theater', p. 63.

159 Ibid, p. 54.

160 Honeywell, 1958, p. 283.

161 NARA, RG 247. Chief of Chaplains. Box 289. Prisoners of War (Axis) Vol. 2. 383.6 Prisoners of War (Axis) Volume I. F.W. Hagan to Commission on Aliens and Prisoners of War, 7 September 1943; NARA, RG 247, Records of the Office of the Chief of Chaplains. Records of Administration and Management General Records. Records Relating to the History of the Chaplains of the United States Army, 1941–58, Box 3, 'Military History of the Second World War. The Corps of Chaplains', p. 92; Wagner, Kennedy, Osborne and Reyburn, 2007, p. 899.

162 NARA, RG 247, Records of the Office of the Chief of Chaplains. Records of Administration and Management General Records. Records Relating to the History of the Chaplains of the United States Army, 1941–58, Box 3, 'Military History of the Second World War. The Corps of Chaplains', pp. 94–95.

163 NARA, RG 247. Chief of Chaplains. Box 289. Prisoners of War (Axis) Vol. 2. 383.6 Prisoners of War (Axis) Volume I. L. Meyer to W.R. Arnold, 11 September 1943.

164 Venzke, 1977, p. 15.

165 Honeywell, 1958, p. 282.

166 NARA, RG 247. Chief of Chaplains. Box 289. Prisoners of War (Axis) Vol. 2. 383.6 Prisoners of War (Axis) Volume I. Harry C. Fraser to W.R. Arnold, 21 September 1943.

167 Ibid., J.F. O'Hara to W.R. Arnold, 11 September 1943.

168 Society for the Propagation of the Faith, 1946, 'Prisoners of War'.

169 NARA, RG 247. Chief of Chaplains. Box 289. 383.6 Prisoners of War (Axis) Vol. 2. 383.6 Prisoners of War (Axis) Volume II. J.F. O'Hara to W.R. Arnold, 19 November 1943.

170 Ibid, W. Hartmann to J.F. Monahan, 2 December 1943.

171 NARA, RG 247, Records of the Office of the Chief of Chaplains. Records of Administration and Management General Records. Records Relating to the History of the Chaplains of the United States Army, 1941–58, Box 3, 'Military History of the Second World War. The Corps of Chaplains', p. 95.

172 Leuschner, 1946, p. 36.

173 *The Link*, November 1943, p. 34.

174 Ibid, June 1944, p. 15.

175 Ibid, p. 16.

176 Ibid.

177 Ibid, p. 38.

178 Ibid, February 1945, pp. 17–18.

179 *The Chaplain*, March 1945, p. 32.

180 Ibid, June 1945, pp. 44–45.

181 Ibid, November 1945, p. 41.

182 Ibid, June 1946, p. 16.

183 Ibid, November 1946, p. 30

184 See, for example, Dower, 1986; Burleigh, 2010; Linderman, 1997; Schrijvers, 2010; Cameron, 1994; Fussell, 1989.

185 Dower, 1986, pp. ix, 3, 11, 92, 94, 146, 161–62, 205–6, 314.

186 *Marine Corps Gazette*, November 1944, p. 17.

187 Embree, 1945, pp. 279–81.

188 Ibid, pp. 252–65; Dower, 1986, pp. 205, 275.

189 Minear, 1980, pp. 568–71.

190 Embree, 1945, p. 252.

191 Woodard, 1972, Appendix D:1, p. 305.

192 Embree, 1945, p. 240.

193 Herman, 1943, pp. 82–83.

194 1951, *History of the Nonmilitary Activities of the Occupation of Japan. No. 32. Religion*, pp. 5, 46.

195 Ibid, p. 45.

196 1951, *History of the Nonmilitary Activities of the Occupation of Japan. No. 32. Religion*, pp. 3, 45–46.

197 Ibid, pp. 46, 50.

198 *The Link*, December 1945, pp. 19–20.

199 *The Chaplain*, August 1945, p. 41.

200 Embree, 1945, p. 294.

201 Ibid, p. 293.

202 *The Chaplain*, March 1945, p. 37.

203 King, 2011, p. 303; *The Link*, August 1943, p. 16.

204 *The Link*, March 1943, p. 35.

205 Ibid.

206 *The Link*, March 1944, p. 49.

207 Ibid, April 1944, p. 9.

208 Carmer, 1943, p. 48.

209 *The Chaplain*, November 1944, p. 44.

210 Embree, 1945, pp. 290–92.

211 *The Chaplain*, December 1945, p. 37.

212 Ibid, pp. 19–21.

213 Ibid, January 1946, p. 45; February 1946, p. 13; September 1946, p. 28.

214 Ambrose, 1998, pp. 444–45.

215 Hastings, 2007, p. 406.

216 Stouffer, 1949, II, 30–36.

217 *What the Soldier Thinks*, July 1944, p. 8.

218 Ibid, pp. 8–9.

219 Jorgensen, 1961, p. 277; *The Link*, December 1943, p. 14.

220 Tapert, 1987, p. 238.

221 Stouffer, 1949, II, p. 157.

222 Kennedy, 1999, p. 401.

223 Price, 1945, pp. 142, 147.

224 *Marine Corps Gazette*, November 1944, p. 18.

225 Schrijvers, 2010, p. 215.

226 Burleigh, 2010, p. 19.

227 *Marine Corps Gazette*, November 1944, pp. 14–21.

228 Overy, 1995, pp. 299–300.

229 Fahey, 1992, p. 294.

230 Robertson, 2006, p. 259.

231 Ibid, p. 262.

232 Cross and Arnold, 1945, p. 23.

233 Sweeney, 1997, p. 188.

234 Rabey, 2002, p. 271.

235 VHP, Richard M. Becker, online transcript.

236 Leckie, 2010, p.89.

237 *Leatherneck*, April 1944, p. 26.

238 Linderman, 1997, p. 149.

239 Clear, 1942, p. 4.

240 Ibid, p. 6.

241 Dower, 1986, pp. 237–38;

242 Ibid, pp. 208, 210, 258–59.

243 Spector, *Eagle Against the Sun*, 2001, p. 217.

244 Cross and Arnold, 1945, p. 51.

245 Schrijvers, 2010, p. 215.

246 Feuer, 2006, pp. 7–8, 38, 52, 72–73.

247 Dear and Foot, 1995, pp. 244–45.

248 Feuer, 2006, pp. 72, 102, 93–98.

249 NARA, RG 247, Records of the Office of the Chief of Chaplains. Records of Administration and Management General Records. Records Relating to the History of the Chaplains of the United States Army, 1941–58, Box 3, 'Chaplains on Guadalcanal', p. 10.

250 Fahey, 1992, p. 25.

251 *Stars and Stripes*, 23 April 1945, p. 4.

252 Martin, 'Meehling', p. 52.

253 Donnelly, 1986, pp. 76–77.

254 Haggerty, 1946, pp. 150–52.

255 Hastings, 2007, pp. 249, 254.

256 Haggerty, 1946, p. xi.

257 *The Leatherneck*, December 1944, p. 80.

258 Willard, 1944, p. 111.

259 Ibid, pp. 115–16.

260 *The Chaplain*, December 1944, p. 46.

261 *Chicago Tribune*, 14 September 1943, p. 6.

262 Stroup, 2000, pp. 50–51; Schrijvers, 2010, p. 147.

263 *The Christian Century*, 21 April 1943, p. 476.

264 Schrijvers, 2010, p. 64; Spector, *Eagle Against the Sun*, 2001, p. 458.

265 Cameron, 1994, pp. 102, 110, 121.

266 Wagner, Kennedy, Osborne and Reyburn, 2007, p. 121.

267 Iokibe, 1987–89, 3–A–23, 'Interview with Rev. L.W. Moore, Presbyterian missionary from Japan'.

268 *The Chaplain*, August 1945, p. 41.

269 Haggerty, 1946, pp. 68,191.

270 *The Chaplain*, September 1946, p. 39.

271 Roper, 2003, Preface; Crosby, 1994, pp. 202–4.

272 Cross and Arnold, 1945, pp. 44–45.

273 Honeywell, 1958, pp. 278–79: Drury, 1950, p. 28.

274 Price, 1945, p. 147.

275 *Marine Corps Gazette*, April 1944, p. 74.

276 Ibid, pp. 74–75.

277 Robertson, 2006, p. 205.

278 Fahey, 1992, p. 45.

279 Ibid, p. 75.

280 Ibid, p. 232.

281 Ibid, p. 239.

282 Hastings, 2007, p. 185.

283 *Marine Corps Gazette*, November 1944, p. 18.

284 Iokibe, 1987–89, 3–D–4, 'Self-Immolation as a Factor in Japanese Psychology', p. 10.

285 Ibid, 3–D–8, 'Superstitions as a Present Factor in Japanese Military Psychology', p. 1.

286 Ibid, p. 25.

287 Ford, 2012, p. 120.

288 Iokibe, 1987–89, 3–D–9, 'Defects Arising from the Doctrine of Spiritual Superiority as Factors in Japanese Military Psychology', p. 1.

289 Ibid, p. 31.

290 VHP, Peter Bocko, online transcript.

291 Moore, 2004, pp. 24–25, 87.

292 Linderman, 1997, p. 160.

293 Willard, 1944, p. 190.

294 Hastings, 2007, p. 170.

295 Hopkins, 1966, p. 464.

296 *The Christian Century*, 21 March 1945, p. 358; Hastings, 2007, pp. 320–21.

297 *The Christian Century*, 23 February 1944, p. 229.

298 Hopkins, 1966, p. 471; Hastings, 2007, p. 321; Spector, *Eagle Against the Sun*, 2001, pp. 554–55; Woodard, 1972, Appendix I:6, pp. 373–74.

299 Willard, 1944, pp. 126–27.

300 *The Link*, February 1945, p. 14; Drury, 1948, p. 26.

301 Drury, 1950, p. 106.

302 *The Link*, December 1943, pp. 12–14.

303 *The Leatherneck*, August 1945, p. 38.

304 *The Chaplain*, October 1945, p. 49.

305 Ibid.

306 Carmer, 1943, pp. 46–48, 54–55; Iglehart, 1947, pp. 81, 84.

307 *The Christian Century*, 24 November 1943, p. 1359.

308 Iglehart, 1947, p. 82; 1951, *History of the Nonmilitary Activities of the Occupation of Japan. No. 32. Religion*, p. 49.

309 Woodard, 1972, p. 7.

310 Collie, 2012, loc. 675.

311 Hastings, 2007, p. 524.

312 Crosby, 1994, pp. 246–47; Preston, 2012, pp. 380–81.

313 Ray, 1962, p. 85.

314 Carpenter, 1997, pp. 92–93.

315 *The Leatherneck*, March 1943, p. 20.

316 Burleigh, 2007, p. 69.

317 Wagner, Kennedy, Osborne and Reyburn, 2007, p. 645; Burleigh, 2007, p. 199.

318 Parsons, 2008, pp. 92–94.
319 Stanton, 2006, p. 594.
320 NARA RG 247. Chief of Chaplains. Box 290. 383.6 Prisoner of War (Axis). Volume III. William R. Arnold to L.J. Lewandowski, 12 July 1944.
321 Pyle, 2001, p. 127.
322 Kerwin, 1946, p. 58.
323 Pyle, 2001, p. 142.
324 Sevareid, 1976, pp. 416–17.
325 Kertzer, 1947, p. 58.
326 Ibid, p. 59.
327 Grant, 1944, pp. 134–35.
328 Ibid, p. 160.
329 1945, *American Chaplains of the Fifth Army*, pp. 28–29.
330 Abbott, 1946, pp. 59–60.
331 *The Link*, March 1944, p. 43.
332 Yost, 2006, p. 45.
333 Ibid, p. 116.
334 *The Link*, March 1944, p. 49.
335 Yost, 2006, p. 248.
336 Ibid.
337 *The Chaplain*, March 1945, p. 46.
338 1945, *American Chaplains of the Fifth Army*, p. 58.
339 Leuschner, 1946, p. 12.
340 *The Chaplain*, September 1945, pp. 21–22.
341 Gushwa, 1977, p. 11.
342 Marshall, 2005.
343 Preston, 2012, pp. 349–50.
344 Reynolds, 1996, pp. 33–34.
345 Preston, 2012, p. 149.
346 *Leatherneck*, April 1942, p. 29.
347 Shindler, 1979, pp. 30, 49; Koppes and Black, 1987, pp. 229–30.
348 Schrijvers, 1998, p. 112.
349 Marshall, 2005, pp. 30, 32.
350 *New York Times*, 25 May 1942, p. 13.
351 Runbeck, 1944, pp. 62–63, 160–66.
352 *The Link*, October 1945, pp. 39–40.
353 Spellman, 1943, p. 72.
354 *The Link*, May 1943, p. 36.
355 Ibid, September 1946, pp. 15–18.
356 Ibid, June 1943, p. 21.
357 *The Chaplain*, November 1945, p. 37.
358 Daniel, 1985, p. 5.
359 Reynolds, 1996, p. 104; Stouffer, 1949, II, pp. 575–76.
360 *The Link*, April 1943, p. 36.
361 Schrijvers, 1998, pp. 32–41.
362 Spellman, 1943, p. 59; Snape, 2005, p. 152.
363 Spellman, 1943, p. 73.
364 *The Link*, December 1944, p. 63.
365 *The Chaplain*, September 1945, p. 16.
366 *The Link*, March 1944, p. 24.
367 *The Chaplain*, May 1946, p. 19.
368 *The Link*, August 1944, p. 14.
369 *The Chaplain*, July 1945, p. 43.
370 *Princeton Seminary Bulletin*, March 1943, p. 54.
371 *The Chaplain*, December 1944, p. 24.
372 *The Link*, January/February 1943, p. 18.
373 Jorgensen, 1961, p. 286.
374 *The Link*, April 1943, p. 19.
375 Ibid, July 1943, pp. 3–5.
376 Snape, 2005, p. 77.
377 Dear and Foot, 1995, p. 346.
378 Snape, 2005, p. 77.
379 *The Link*, March 1944, pp. 25–26.
380 Ibid, May 1945, pp. 7–8.
381 *The Chaplain*, March 1945, p. 20.
382 Dennis, 1945, pp. 168–71; Dobbie, 1945.
383 *The Link*, May 1945, p. 36.
384 Ibid, June 1944, p. 61.
385 *The Chaplain*, April 1945, p. 42; September 1945, p. 49.
386 Ibid, September 1945, p. 22.
387 1942, *Instructions for American Forces in Britain*, loc. 242.
388 Reynolds, 1996, pp. 108–12.
389 Kimball, 1947, p. 125.
390 Ibid, p. 124.
391 Ibid, pp. 141–43.
392 Ibid, p. 132.
393 Ibid, pp. 126–27.
394 Ibid, pp. 127–28.
395 Ibid, pp. 133–34.
396 Ibid, pp. 134–35.
397 Ibid, pp. 133, 152.
398 Ibid, pp. 152–53.
399 *New York Times*, 5 April 1943, p. 5.
400 Reynolds, 1996, p. 113; Balkoski, 1999, p. 56.
401 Metcalf, 1957, pp. 32, 44.
402 Ibid, pp. 140–43.
403 Ibid, pp. 156–57.
404 Ibid, p. 150.
405 Ibid, p. 153.
406 *The Chaplain*, February 1945, p. 46.
407 Ibid, August 1945, p. 46.

408 Jorgensen, 1961, p. 222.

409 USAHEC, Walter P. Plumley Papers, clippings.

410 Methodist Church Commission on Chaplains, 1948, pp. 168–69.

411 Lunn, 1947, p. 137.

412 Jorgensen, 1961, p. 222; Leuschner, 1946, pp. 74–75.

413 Leuschner, 1946, pp. 74–75.

414 Grant, 1944, p. 67; Sampson, 1958, pp. 4, 42–43.

415 Sampson, 1958, p. 47.

416 Ibid, pp. 48, 50, 82.

417 *Yank*, 26 December 1943, p. 10.

418 Rogers, 1946, pp. 26–27.

419 Ibid, p. 138.

420 Connelly, 1945, p. 20.

421 Ibid, p. 23.

422 Bowman, 2012, pp. 201–2.

423 Brink, 1944, p. 27.

424 *The Chaplain*, March 1945, p. 20.

425 Lunn, 1947, p. 66.

426 Connelly, 1945, p. 26.

427 USAHEC, Walter P. Plumley Papers, clippings.

428 *Yank*, 20 December 1942, p. 2.

429 *The Link*, June 1944, p. 65.

430 Reynolds, 1996, Illustrations.

431 Wilson, 1987, p. 253.

432 Rogers, 1946, pp. 124, 128.

433 *The Manchester Guardian*, 6 August 1942, p. 4.

434 Smith, 2006, p. 196; Preston, 2012, p. 366; Carpenter, 1997, p. 168; *The National Catholic Almanac*, 1943, pp. 679, 771; *Stars and Stripes*, 25 November 1943, p. 4.

435 *The Times*, 27 November 1942, p. 2.

436 Ibid, 18 November 1942, p. 4; Jorgensen, 1961, pp. 179–80; Honeywell, 1958, p. 273.

437 *Hull Daily Mail*, 27 November 1942, p. 3; *Gloucestershire Echo*, 27 November 1942, n.p.

438 *The Western Times*, 1 December 1944, p. 4.

439 *Stars and Stripes*, 25 November 1943, p. 2 and 23 November 1944, p. 1.

440 *Gloucestershire Echo*, 22 November 1945, p. 1.

441 Jorgensen, 1961, p. 223.

442 *The Times*, 12 October 1942, p. 2; Jorgensen, 1961, p. 222.

443 *The Times*, 31 August 1942, p. 2.

444 *The Link*, February 1944, pp. 36–37.

445 Metcalf, 1957, p. 50.

446 Brink, 1944, p. 28.

447 Montgomery–Massingberd, 1989, p. 162; Gardiner, 2005, p. 636; Beevor, 2009, p. 148; Gardiner, 1994, pp. 179–81; *Stars and Stripes*, 7 June 1944, p. 4.

448 *The Link*, June 1944, p. 41.

449 Ibid, August 1944, pp. 13–14.

450 *Yank*, 27 December 1942, pp. 4–5.

451 Metcalf, 1957, p. 155; *The Chaplain*, October 1946, p. 16.

452 Abbott, 1946, p. 20.

453 Ibid, p. 25.

454 Kimball, 1947, p. 5.

455 Ibid, pp. 10 and 118.

456 Ibid, p. 16.

457 Kertzer, 1947, pp. 23–24.

458 Daniel, 1985, pp. 47–48, 70, 74–75, 81, 98–99.

459 Hull, 2009, pp. 18–23.

460 Reynolds, 1996, pp. 115–16.

461 Lunn, 1947, p. 133.

462 Reynolds, 1996, pp. 125–26.

463 Lunn, 1947, p. 131.

464 USAHEC, Walter P. Plumley Papers.

465 Ibid, 'From Those in Service'.

466 *The Chaplain*, February 1945, p. 45.

467 Brink, 1944, p. 27.

468 *Gloucestershire Echo*, 28 December 1943, n.p.

469 Brink, 1944, p. 27.

470 Abbott, 1946, pp. 145–46.

471 Reynolds, 1996, p. 150.

472 *Somerset County Herald*, 8 August 1942, p. 7.

473 Leuschner, 1946, p. 56.

474 *The Chaplain*, August 1945, p. 47.

475 Leuschner, 1946, pp. 55–56.

476 *The Chaplain*, October 1944, p. 39.

477 Rogers, 1946, p. 131.

478 Ibid, p. 130.

479 Collins, 1998, p. 21.

480 Ibid, pp. 54, 58.

481 Reynolds, 1996, p. 197.

482 Rogers, 1946, p. 131.

483 Lunn, 1947, pp. 62–63.

484 Reynolds, 1996, pp. 209–15; Jorgensen, 1961, p. 187.

485 Figure based on Reynolds, 1996, pp. 420–22.

486 Collins, 1998, p. 74.

487 Ibid, p. 73. See also Reynolds, 1996, p. 415.

488 *The Chaplain*, July 1946, pp. 32–34; Eggen, 1976, pp. 93–108.

489 Snape and Parker, 2001, pp. 397–420.

490 *The Christian Century*, 12 April 1944, p. 451; *The Chaplain*, March 1945, p. 20.

491 Colby, 1991, p. 315.

492 Lunn, 1947, pp. 77–78: Metcalf, 1957, pp. 39 and 63.

493 *Yank*, 21 February 1943, p. 23.

494 *Stars and Stripes*, 23 December 1943, pp. ii–iii.

495 Ibid, 14 February 1944, p. 3.

496 Lunn, 1947, p. 75.

497 Ibid, pp. 75–77.

498 Rogers, 1946, pp. 133–34.

499 USAHEC, Walter P. Plumley Papers, 'Chorley Parish Church of St. Laurence. Suggested Outline of Service, 10.45 a.m. February 28th, 1943.'

500 *The Western Times*, 14 January 1944, p. 1.

501 *Christian Herald*, January 1945, p. 9.

502 *The Chaplain*, February 1945, p. 33.

503 *Somerset County Herald*, 16 June 1945, p. 8.

504 *The Chaplain*, November 1945, p. 42.

505 1952, *Britain's Homage to 28,000 American Dead*, p. 41.

506 Lester, 1992, Reel 6, Box 59, 0565 et seq, G.C. Marshall to Lord Trenchard, 16 November 1945.

507 Ibid, *The Times*, 15 November 1945, *The Daily Telegraph*, 15 November 1945; 1952, *Britain's Homage to 28,000 American Dead* , pp. 37–38.

508 1952, *Britain's Homage to 28,000 American Dead*, p. 53; http://www.angelfire.com/my/mighty8thlh/CHAPELUK.html, accessed 11 September 2013.

509 Potts and Potts, 1985, pp. 29–30.

510 Taggart and Cross, 1943, p. 69.

511 1946, *History of Chaplains' Activities in the Pacific*, p. 430.

512 Potts and Potts, 1985, p. 166.

513 Ibid, p. 167.

514 Spector, *Eagle Against the Sun*, 2001, pp. 401–2; Potts and Potts, 1985, pp. 166–68.

515 1946, *History of Chaplains' Activities in the Pacific*, p. 430.

516 Spector, *Eagle Against the Sun*, 2001, p. 400.

517 1946, *History of Chaplains' Activities in the Pacific*, p. 438.

518 Potts and Potts, 1985, p. 166.

519 Glasser, 1946, pp. 96–101.

520 Moore, 2006, p. 64.

521 Potts and Potts, 1985, pp. 187–93.

522 Moore, 2006, p. 70.

523 1946, *History of Chaplains' Activities in the Pacific*, p. 76.

524 Taggart and Cross, 1943, pp. 48, 67–69, 150–52: 1946, *History of Chaplains' Activities in the Pacific*, p. 159.

525 Glasser, 1946, p. 190.

526 Taggart and Cross, 1943, pp. 156–57.

527 Hill, Laws and Taylor, 1944, p. 10.

528 *The Chaplain*, October 1945, p. 46.

529 Ibid, September 1946, pp. 35–37.

530 Dear and Foot, 1995, p. 800.

531 Willard, 1944, p. 203.

532 Ibid, p. 201.

533 Ibid, p. 206.

534 Glasser, 1946, pp. 43–44.

535 *The Chaplain*, October 1945, p. 43; August 1946, p. 15.

536 Mitter, 2013, pp. 43–46, 240–41.

537 Jespersen, 1996, pp. 24–26.

538 Ibid, pp. 45–50.

539 Ibid, pp. 77–78.

540 Preston, 2012, p. 476.

541 Jespersen, 1996, pp. 78–79; Hastings, 2007, p. 216.

542 Burleigh, 2013, p. 112.

543 *The Link*, September 1946, p. 32.

544 Ibid, April 1943, pp. 9–11.

545 Ibid, November 1944, p. 12.

546 Ibid, January 1945, p. 45.

547 *The Chaplain*, October 1944, p. 14.

548 *The Link*, May 1943, p. 13.

549 Ibid, June 1943, p. 18.

550 Ibid, May 1946, inside front cover.

551 Schaller, 1979, pp. 120

552 Stilwell, 1948, pp. 132–33.

553 Preston, 2012, pp. 353–61.

554 *The Chaplain*, April 1945, p. 40.

555 Ibid, August 1945, p. 28.

556 Ibid, December 1945, p. 31.

557 Atkinson, 2013, p. 510.

558 Overy, 1999, pp. 162, 293.

559 *The Link*, April 1943, pp. 26–27.

560 Ibid, March 1944, pp. 48–49.

561 Ibid, June 1944, p. 58.

562 Ibid, June 1943, p. 21; March 1944, p. 48.

563 Ibid, June 1943, p. 21; *The Chaplain*, October 1945, p. 38.

564 Stouffer, 1949, II, Chart III, p. 566.

565 Stouffer, 1949, II, pp. 576–78.

566 1950, *112 Gripes About the French*, pp. 12, 27, 35.

567 Stouffer, 1949, II, pp. 576–78.

568 Ibid, p. 578.

569 Ibid.

570 1944, *A Pocket Guide to France*, pp. 29–30.

571 Burleigh, 2007, pp. 238–49; Burleigh, 2010, p. 203; Cobb, 2014, p. 327.

572 Gannon, 1962, pp. 238–39.

573 Kimball, 1947, pp. 172, 175; *The Chaplain*, September 1945, pp. 11–14.

574 Sampson, 1958, p. 70.

575 Ibid, pp. 69–70.

576 Ibid, p. 75.

577 Metcalf, 1957, p. 190.

578 Schrijvers, 1998, pp. 135–37.

579 Kimball, 1947, pp. 66, 81, 93, 107, 115, 122.

580 Ibid, pp. 180–81.

581 Sampson, 1958, p. 87.

582 Ibid, pp. 128–30, 133, 137–38, 146–47.

583 Sittser, 1997, pp. 234–43.

584 *The Link*, May 1943, p. 35.

585 Ibid, August 1943, p. 7.

586 Ibid, pp. 8–13; November 1943, pp. 45–47; March 1944, pp. 40–41.

587 Ibid, March 1944, p. 41.

588 Ibid, December 1943, pp. 4–7.

589 Ibid, October 1944, p. 9.

590 Ibid.

591 Ibid.

592 Drury, 1950, pp. 216–17.

593 Edel, 1994, pp. 162–63; Drury, 1950, pp. 216–17; *The Chaplain*, December 1944, pp. 46–47.

594 Eichhorn, 2004, p. 124.

595 Vida, 1967, p. 26.

596 NMAJMH, Kastenbaum Family. Marvin A. Kastenbaum, 'Memories of My Military Service May 1944–December 1945. A Diary', pp. 36–41.

597 Kertzer, 1947, pp. 57–58.

598 Slomovitz, 1999, pp. 101–4; Kertzer, 1947, p. 161; Vida, 1967, pp. 18–20.

599 Slomovitz, 1999, pp. 105–6; Grobman, 1993, pp. 76–77.

600 Kertzer, 1947, pp. 184–89; Grobman, 1993.

601 Grobman, 1993, pp. 111–21.

602 Kertzer, 1947, p. 188.

603 Grobman, 1993, pp. 1, 11–12.

604 Rogers, 1946, pp. 84–85; Kertzer, 1947, p. 79.

605 Hilberg, 1995, p. 265.

606 1945, *American Chaplains of the Fifth Army*, p. 47.

607 Kertzer, 1947, p. 56.

608 1945, *American Chaplains of the Fifth Army*, p. 47.

609 Kertzer, 1947, pp. 56–57.

610 *The Jewish Exponent*, 27 October 1944, p. 1.

611 Grobman, 1993, p. 29; Kertzer, 1947, p. 128.

612 Lunn, 1947, pp. 121–22.

613 Eichhorn, 2004, pp. 102–4; 107–9.

614 Cross and Arnold, 1945, p. 91.

615 Vida, 1967, pp. 23–24.

616 *The American Israelite*, 2 November 1944, p. 1.

617 Kertzer, 1947, p. 127.

618 Ibid, p. 128.

619 Ibid, p. 127.

620 Ibid, p. 127.

621 Ibid, p. 127.

622 Ibid, pp. 127–28.

623 Ibid, pp. 128–29.

624 Eichhorn, 2004, p. 130.

625 Bernstein, 1971, p. 39.

626 Kertzer, 1947, pp. 160–66.

627 Bernstein, 1971, p. 39.

628 Kertzer, 1947, p. 34.

629 Ibid, pp. 133–34.

630 Ibid, pp. 134–35.

631 Slomovitz, 1999, pp. 102–3; Grobman, 1993, pp. 49–50.

632 Kertzer, 1947, p. 190.

633 Ibid, pp. 30–31.

634 Ibid, pp. 59–60.

635 Ibid, p. 86.

636 Ibid, pp. 99–101, 105, 107–8.

637 Ibid, p. 65.

638 Ibid, p. 130.

639 Ibid, p. 191.

640 Ibid, p. 153.

641 Ibid, p. 154.

642 Bernstein, 1971, pp. 39–40.

643 Sittser, 1997, p. 204.

644 Willard, 1944, p. 91.

645 Leuschner, 1946, pp. 27–28.

646 *The Link*, November 1944, pp. 39–40.

647 Latourette, 1948, p. 64.

648 *The Link*, March 1944, p. 44; *The Chaplain*, March 1945, p. 21.

649 *The Link*, March 1944, pp. 44–45.

650 *The Chaplain*, October 1944, p. 29.

651 *The Link*, November 1944, p. 40.

652 Ibid, December 1944, p. 13.

653 Ibid, August 1945, p. 14.

654 Handy, 1960, pp. 4–5.

655 Carpenter, 1980, pp. 72–73.

656 Committee of Appraisal, 1932, pp. 326–29.

657 Van Dusen, 1945, p. 116.

658 Ibid.

659 Ibid, pp. 117–19.

660 Ibid, pp. 120–25.

661 Burleigh, 2013, p. 315.

662 Schrijvers, 2010, pp. 32–33; Burleigh, 2013, p. 315.

663 1943, *A Pocket Guide to India*, p. 5.

664 Ibid, pp. 7–8.

665 Ibid, pp. 14–15.

666 *Yank*, 6 December 1942, p. 8.

667 Pyle, 2001, pp. 242–43.

668 Muirhead, 1988, pp. 35–36.

669 *Yank*, 13 December 1942, p. 12.

670 Ibid, 16 January 1944, p. 22.

671 *The Link*, July 1945, p. 62.

672 1943, *A Pocket Guide to India*, p. 10.

673 Rooney, 2005, p. 155.

674 Clare, 1945, p. 55.

675 Ibid, p. 128.

676 Ibid, p. 189.

677 Ibid, pp. 189–90.

678 VHP, Wilbur Eugene Nickels, transcript, p. 44, VHP MSS Box 1743. Folder 6/7.

679 Clare, 1945, pp. 127–28.

680 Ibid, p. 82.

681 NARA, Record Group 493. Records of the China–Burma–India Theatre of Operations, US Army. Box 465, 'Christmas Observance in the Tenth Air Force, 1942'.

682 Jorgensen, 1961, p. 224.

683 Beard, Beard and Pinkerton, 2002, p. 220.

684 Clare, 1945, pp. 251–65.

685 Ibid, p. 255.

686 Ibid, p. 263.

687 *The Link*, December 1944, pp. 43–44.

688 *The Link*, July 1945, p. 48.

689 Coffman, 2004, pp. 338–40, 413–14.

690 Queen, Prothero and Shattuck, 2001, II, p. 466; Sibley and Jacob, 1952, p. 36

691 Carroll, 2000, pp. 102–3.

692 Gregg, 1945, p. 52.

693 *Yank*, 5 September 1943, p. 9.

694 Kimball, 1947, p. 76.

695 1943, *A Pocket Guide to North Africa*, pp. 5, 7.

696 Ibid, p. 7.

697 Ibid, p. 30.

698 Ibid, pp. 33–34.

699 Ibid, p. 34.

700 Ibid, p. 39.

701 Burleigh, 2013, p. 82.

702 1943, *A Short Guide to Iraq*, pp. 10–13.

703 1943, *A Pocket Guide to Iran*, p. 14.

704 Ibid, p. 12.

705 1943, *A Short Guide to Iraq*, p. 12.

706 Dear and Foot, 1995, p. 553.

707 Patton, 1995, p. 13.

708 *Yank*, 20 December 1942, p. 14.

709 Ibid.

710 Schrijvers, 1998, pp. 116–20.

711 Patton, 1995, p. 5.

712 Ibid, p. 25.

713 Ibid, p. 49.

714 Pyle, 2004, p. 36.

715 Ibid, pp. 48–49.

716 Wuest, 1953, p. 106.

717 Spellman, 1943, p. 49.

718 Grant, 1944, pp. 174–75.

719 Rogers, 1946, p. 97.

720 Ibid, p. 88.

721 Ibid, p. 89.

722 Ibid, p. 88.

723 Crosby, 1994, p. 90.

724 *The Link*, November 1943, pp. 23–25.

725 Van Dusen, 1945, pp. 23, 68.

726 *The Link*, April 1943, pp. 4–5.

727 Ibid, June 1943, p. 15.

728 Ibid, pp. 16–18.

729 Ibid, May 1943, p. 7.

730 Ibid, p. 8.

731 Ibid, July 1943, pp. 38–39.

732 Ibid, p. 39.

733 Ibid.

734 Van Dusen, 1945, p. 11.

735 Bergerud, 1996, pp. 109–11; Van Dusen, 1945, p. 12; Maahs, 1946, p. 8; *The Link*, November 1943, p. 65; April 1944, p. 5.

736 Bergerud, 1996, p. 109.

737 Van Dusen, 1945, pp. 12–14.

738 Maahs, 1946, pp. 8–9.

739 Van Dusen, 1945, pp. 39–40.

740 Ibid, p. 39; *The Link*, February 1944, pp. 3–4.

741 *The Link*, February 1944, p. 31.

742 Van Dusen, 1945, pp. 35–36.

743 *The Leatherneck*, August 1931, p. 45.

744 Orr, 1948, p. 55.

745 *The Link*, August 1945, p. 14.

746 Ibid, March 1944, p. 22; *Christian Herald*, May 1944, p. 7

747 *The Link*, November 1943, p. 28.

748 Van Dusen, 1945, pp. 41–42.

749 Ibid, p. 41.

750 Ibid, p. 20.

751 Willard, 1944, p. 114.

752 Van Dusen, 1945, pp. 64–65.

753 Ibid, p. 66.

754 Radike, 2003, pp. 123–28.

755 Schrijvers, 2010, p. 238; Moore, 2006, pp. 77–79.

756 Van Dusen, 1945, p. 65; *The Link*, November 1944, p. 40

757 Willard, 1944, p. 145.

758 Grant, 1944, pp. 91–92.

759 Radike, 2003, p. 127.

760 Cross and Arnold, 1945, pp. 176–77.

761 Orr, 1948, p. 55.

762 http://www.nytimes.com/1991/09/27/arts/james-j-Fahey, 1992-a-garbage-man-and-published-author-dies-at-73.html, accessed 19 August 2014.

763 *The Link*, March 1944, p. 30.

764 Grant, 1944, pp. 90–91; Leuschner, 1946, pp. 119–21.

765 *The Link*, March 1944, p. 38; April 1944, p. 41.

766 *The Link*, December 1944, pp. 9–10.

767 Society for the Propagation of the Faith, 1946, n.p.

768 Donnelly, 1986, pp. 121–25.

769 Glasser, 1946, pp. 162–64.

770 Orr, 1948, pp. 55–57.

771 *The Chaplain*, February 1945, p. 33.

772 Ibid, March 1945, p. 32.

773 Grant, 1944, pp. 85–85.

774 Ray, 1962, pp. 48–49.

775 1946, *History of Chaplains' Activities in the Pacific*, pp. 185, 285, 527.

776 Ibid, p. 286.

777 *The Chaplain*, March 1945, p. 32.

778 Jernagin, 1946, pp. 123–24.

779 Jespersen, 1996, p. 24.

780 Gaustad, 1990, p. 232; Schrijvers, 2010, p. 63.

781 Preston, 2012, p. 477.

782 Spector, *Eagle Against the Sun*, 2001, p. 369.

783 *The Chaplain*, July 1946, pp. 29–30.

784 Schrijvers, 2010, pp. 57–58, 65, 161.

785 *The Chaplain*, November 1945, p. 23.

786 Glasser, 1946, pp. 190–92.

787 *The Chaplain*, July 1945, p. 30.

788 Ibid, February 1946, p. 9.

789 Willard, 1944, pp. 161–62.

790 Dennis, 1945, pp. 130–31.

791 *The Link*, August 1945, p. 38.

792 1946, *History of Chaplains' Activities in the Pacific*, pp. 306–7.

793 Yost, 2006, pp. 168–70, 176.

794 Ibid, p. 117.

795 Ibid, pp. 63–64, 67–68, 130, 132.

796 Yost, 2006, p. 132.

797 *New York Times*, 3 February 1944, p. 9.

798 Martin, 'Craven', pp. 21–22.

799 *The Link*, December 1945, pp. 17–20.

800 Ray, 1962, pp. 96–97.

801 Ibid, pp. 108–15.

802 Donnelly, 1986, pp. 128–29.

803 1946, *History of Chaplains' Activities in the Pacific*, pp. 265–66.

804 Ibid, pp. 542–43.

805 Ibid, p. 432.

806 Ibid, pp. 286, 437; Orr, 1948, pp. 115–16.

807 1946, *History of Chaplains' Activities in the Pacific*, p. 431.

808 Ibid.

809 Ibid, p. 432.

810 Hickcox, 1950, pp. 76–78.

811 Ibid, p. 78.

812 Ibid, p. 75.

813 Ibid, p. 87.

814 Ibid, pp. 87–90.

815 Ibid, p. 90.

816 Woodard, 1972, p. 14, Appendix A:1, pp. 285–87.

817 1951, *History of the Nonmilitary Activities of the Occupation of Japan. No. 32. Religion*, pp. 1–10; Woodard, 1972, p. 16.

818 Woodard, 1972, Appendixes E: 5–6, pp. 319–21; MacArthur, 1964, p. 311.

819 Rabey, 2002, pp. 20–25, 119–20, 140–43, 228–35.

820 http://www2.wheaton.edu/bgc/archives/
bulletin/bu1203.htm, accessed 19 March 2014.

821 http://www.nytimes.com/2008/03/23/
us/23deshazer.html, accessed 19 March 2014.

822 Ibid; Spector, *Eagle Against the Sun*, 2001,
p. 4.

823 1951, *History of the Nonmilitary Activities
of the Occupation of Japan. No. 32. Religion*, pp.
11–12.

824 Woodard, 1972, Appendix G:4, pp. 355–59.

825 MacArthur, 1964, p. 310.

826 Poling, 1959, pp. 235–36.

827 Fussell, 1989, p. 162.

CHAPTER SIX
Religion, War and Morality

1 1945, 'Reports of the General Board. 68.
The Army Chaplain in the European Theater',
Appendix 17, p. 47.

2 *The Link*, March 1945, p. 25.

3 Ibid.

4 Ibid, pp. 25–26.

5 Ibid, p. 26.

6 Brink, 1944, p. 15.

7 Hynes, 2005, pp. 15, 18.

8 Ibid, pp. 72–73.

9 Ibid, p.74.

10 VHP, Howard Orr, typescript letter, 11
January 1945, p. 11, VHP MSS Box 2058. Folder
2/8.

11 Fussell, 1996, pp. 74–75.

12 VHP, Russell Baldwin, online Complete
Interview.

13 Ibid.

14 Kennett, 1997, pp. 18–19.

15 *The Link*, September 1944, p. 43.

16 Kertzer, 1947, pp. 37–38.

17 Brink, 1944, p. 83.

18 Lunn, 1947, pp. 57–58.

19 Ibid, pp. 93–96.

20 Leuschner, 1946, pp. 97–98.

21 Orr, 1948, pp. 105–6.

22 *The Link*, December 1944, p. 43.

23 Atwell, 1961, p. 271.

24 VHP, Nathan Robbins, letter 7 December
1944, VHP MSS Box 2098. Folder 3/6.

25 Hynes, 2005, p. 45.

26 *The Link*, October 1945, p. 35.

27 Smith, 2001, p. 197.

28 Lord, 1942, p. 20.

29 Ibid, p. 21.

30 Ibid.

31 Brasted, 1944, n.p.

32 Astor, 1994, p. 212.

33 Leckie, 2010, p. 150.

34 Hynes, 2005, p. 72.

35 Ibid, pp. 193–94.

36 Faubus, 1971, p. 378.

37 Ibid, pp. 377–78.

38 *The Link*, March 1944, p. 30.

39 Ibid, December 1944, p.23.

40 Atwell, 1961, p. 385; Stanton, 2006, p. 159.

41 Faubus, 1971, p. 562.

42 1946, *History of Chaplains' Activities in the
Pacific*, p. 128.

43 1947, *The Story of Christian Science Wartime
Activities*, pp. 98–99.

44 Hickcox, 1950, pp. 28–29.

45 Grant, 1944, pp. 137–38.

46 Kertzer, 1947, p. 28.

47 Bernstein, 1971, p. 60.

48 1945, 'Reports of the General Board. 68. The
Army Chaplain in the European Theater', p. 107.

49 Connelly, 1945, p. 8.

50 NARA Record Group 247. Chief of
Chaplains. Office Management Division
Decimal File 1920–45. Box 199. 291.2 Race
– General. G.E. Hopkins to W.R. Arnold, 17
January 1944; F.W. Hagan to G.E. Hopkins, 29
January 1944.

51 Ibid. E.W. Weber to L.B. Alder, 13 June 1945.

52 NARA Record Group 247. Chief of
Chaplains. Office Management Division
Decimal File 1920–45. Box 199. 291.2 Race,
Negro Volume I. G.F. Rixey to -----, 25 April
1945.

53 http://mlk-kpp01.stanford.edu/index.php/
encyclopedia/encyclopedia/enc_national_
council_of_the_churches_of_christ_in_america_
ncc, accessed 22 November 2013; Sittser, 1997,
pp. 181–85.

54 *The Link*, January 1944, p. 66.

55 Ibid, February 1944, p. 29.

56 Ibid, June 1944, p. 63.

57 Ibid, July 1944, pp. 58–60.

58 Ibid, November 1944, p. 25.

59 *The Link*, December 1944, p. 48; April 1945,
p. 27.

60 Ibid, July 1944, pp. 3–4; September 1944, p.
9; March 1945, p. 29.

61 *The Chaplain*, January 1945, p. 47; February
1945, p. 46.

62 Ibid, April 1945, p. 10; August 1945, pp. 21–23.

63 Ibid, August 1945, pp. 41, 46.

64 Ibid, March 1946, pp. 21–22.

65 Yost, 2006, pp. 35–36.

66 Wuest, 1953, p. 73.

67 Ibid.

68 *Baltimore Afro-American*, 12 August 1944, p. 11.

69 Willard, 1944, p. 76.

70 Ibid, p. 111.

71 Ibid, p. 124.

72 VHP, Russell Baldwin, online Complete Interview.

73 Pyle, 2004, pp. 241–42.

74 Bassett, 1991, pp. 14–15, 28, 83–84.

75 Ambrose, 1998, pp. 275–88; Linderman, 1997, pp. 286–90; Daddis, 2010, pp. 110–11.

76 Murphy, 1949, p. 208.

77 Sevareid, 1976, p. 388.

78 Abbott, 1946, p. 121.

79 Ibid.

80 The Link, December 1943, p. 7.

81 Ibid.

82 *The Chaplain*, April 1945, p. 46.

83 Ibid.

84 *The Chaplain*, November 1946, pp. 2–4.

85 Pyle, 2004, p. 86.

86 Ibid, p. 87.

87 Ibid, p. 195.

88 Ibid, pp. 195–96.

89 Holland, 2008, p. 390.

90 Sevareid, 1976, p. 388.

91 Ibid, pp. 388–89.

92 Faubus, 1971, p. 211.

93 Atkinson, 2013, pp. 612–14.

94 Eichhorn, 2004, p. 178.

95 Atkinson, 2013, p. 613.

96 Fussell, 1996, p. 124; Atwell, 1961, p. 131.

97 Atwell, 1961, p. 261; Sevareid, 1976, p. 407; Linderman, 1997, p. 119.

98 Linderman, 1997, pp. 130–32; Atwell, 1961, pp. 261, 349–50, 383–84.

99 Linderman, 1997, pp. 129–30.

100 Atkinson, 2013, p. 117.

101 Hanford, 2008, p. 54; Linderman, 1997, p. 127.

102 Costello, 1981, p. 401.

103 Cameron, 1994, p. 1.

104 Tapert, 1987, p. 71.

105 Fahey, 1992, pp. 118, 145.

106 *Yank*, 24 October 1943, p. 11.

107 Ibid, 7 November 1943, p. 11.

108 See, for example, Dower, 1986; Linderman, 1997; Schrijvers, 2010; Fussell, 1989; Cameron, 1994; Weingartner, 1992.

109 Schrijvers, 2010, p. 224.

110 Laurie, 1996.

111 Sledge, 2010, p. 119.

112 Fussell, p. 117; Weingartner, 1992, p. 57.

113 Hastings, 2007, pp. 280, 286.

114 Weingartner, 1992, pp. 57–58, 65–66.

115 Fahey, 1992, p. 192.

116 Ibid, p. 231.

117 Sledge, 2010, pp. 122–23.

118 VHP, John A. Carver, online transcript.

119 Fahey, 1992, p. 68.

120 Ibid, pp. 190–91.

121 Sledge, 2010, p. 1.

122 Ibid, pp. 53, 78; Lewis, 2001; Ambrose, 2010, p. 225.

123 Sledge, 2010, p. 146.

124 Pyle, 2001, pp. 188–89.

125 Murphy, 1949, p. 11.

126 Ibid, pp. 205–6.

127 Bassett, 1991, p. 30.

128 Ibid, p. 53.

129 Abbott, 1946, p. 121.

130 Carlson, 1945, p. 76.

131 Abbott, 1946, p. 120.

132 Daniel, 1985, p. 7.

133 Hale, 2004, p. 35.

134 Ibid, p. 41.

135 Ibid.

136 Ibid, p. 46; Marshall, 1947, pp. 54, 78.

137 VHP, Norman Wesley Achen, online transcript.

138 *New York Times*, 19 March 1944, p. 16; *Christian Science Monitor*, 20 March 1944, p. 18.

139 Jorgensen, 1961, pp. 195–99.

140 Hoyt, *Victory in the Pacific*, 2005.

141 Sweeney, 1997, p. 185; Collie, 2012, locs. 1952–57.

142 Sweeney, 1997, p. 185.

143 Ibid, pp. 185–89.

144 *The Link*, June 1943, pp. 9–11.

145 Ibid, p. 10.

146 Ibid, December 1943, p. 34.

147 Ibid, November 1944, p. 35.

148 Ibid, December 1944, pp. 19–20.

149 Yost, 2006, pp. 265–66.

150 Willard, 1944, pp. 33–34.

151 Ibid, p. 28.

152 *The Link*, December 1943, p. 14.

153 Ibid, October 1944, p. 54.

154 Brink, 1944, p. 66.

155 Abbott, 1946, pp. 131–32.

156 Ibid, pp. 64–65.

157 USAHEC, Charles E. Wilson Papers, 'Frail Children of the Dust', pp. 269–70.

158 Ibid, pp. 270–71.

159 Ambrose, 1998, p. 439.

160 Atkinson, 2007, pp. 116–21; Burleigh, 2010, p. 380; Wagner, Kennedy, Osborne and Reyburn, 2007, pp. 638–39.

161 Willard, 1944, p. 38.

162 Gehring, 1962, p. 157.

163 Donnelly, 1986, p. 98.

164 Stroup, 2000, p. 19.

165 Ibid, p. 49.

166 Ibid, p. 56.

167 Ibid, pp. 61–62.

168 Ibid, pp. 66–67.

169 Ibid, p. 137.

170 Ibid, p. 200.

171 *The Link*, February 1946, pp. 38–40.

172 Ibid, p. 38.

173 http://www.icrc.org/applic/ihl/ihl.nsf/Treaty.xsp?documentId=CD0F6C83F96FB459C12563CD002D66A1&action=openDocument, accessed 21 October 2013.

174 Atkinson, 2007, p. 432.

175 Atkinson, 2013, p. 74.

176 Kimball, 1947, p. 165.

177 Atkinson, 2013, p. 182; Beevor, 2009, p. 520.

178 Atkinson, 2013, p. 129.

179 *The Chaplain*, November 1944, p. 47.

180 Crosby, 1994, pp. 180–81.

181 Martin, 'Meehling', p. 74.

182 *Los Angeles Times*, 5 July 1944, p. 5.

183 Mauldin, 1945, p. 75.

184 Ambrose, 1998, p. 415.

185 Faubus, 1971, p. 473.

186 VHP, Johann Carl Friedrich Kasten, online transcript.

187 Carroll, 2007, n.p.

188 Atwell, 1961, pp. 222–24.

189 Connelly, 1945, pp. 66–67.

190 Steigmann-Gall, 2003, p. 249.

191 Hawkins, 1990, p. 66.

192 Ibid, p. 167.

193 Ibid.

194 Miller, 2007, p. 21.

195 *Stars and Stripes*, 3 June 1944, p. 1.

196 Atkinson, 2007, p. 433.

197 Ibid.

198 Gannon, 1962, pp. 225–28.

199 *New York Times*, 29 January 1944, p. 5.

200 Atkinson, 2007, pp. 436–39.

201 *Stars and Stripes*, 16 February 1944, p. 1.

202 Atkinson, 2007, pp. 433–35.

203 Cantril and Strunk, 1951, p. 1069.

204 Ibid.

205 USAHEC, World War II Veterans Survey, 34th Infantry Division, Giuliano Fregonese.

206 Atkinson, 2007, p. 433.

207 Ibid, p. 139.

208 See, for example, *Articles of War [1806], Military Laws, and Rules and Regulations for the Army of the United States... Revised, September, 1817*, Article 3, p. 9; 'Articles for the Government of the United States Navy, 1930', http://www.history.navy.mil/faqs/faq59–7.htm, accessed 4 November 2013; *The Link*, December 1943, p. 23.

209 Rabey, 2002, p. 228.

210 NARA Record Group 247. Chief of Chaplains. Office Management Division Decimal File 1920–45. Box 194 250.1 Morals and Conduct – Language (Profanity). W.R. Arnold to J.F. Welsh, 27 October 1943.

211 Fussell, 1996, p. 75.

212 'Articles for the Government of the United States Navy, 1930', http://www.history.navy.mil/faqs/faq59–7.htm, accessed 4 November 2013.

213 Fussell, 1989, p. 93.

214 Leckie, 2010, p. 4.

215 Ibid, p. 16.

216 Ibid, p. 17.

217 Atkinson, 2013, p. 31.

218 NARA Record Group 247. Chief of Chaplains. Office Management Division Decimal File 1920–45. Box 194 250.1 Morals and Conduct – Language (Profanity). W. Keisker to W. R. Arnold, undated.

219 Ibid, 20 September 1943 to 6 October 1943; Ancell and Miller, 1996, pp. 419–20.

220 Murphy, 1949, p. 102.

221 Burnham, 1993, p. 220.

222 *The Chaplain*, June 1945, p. 23.

223 Tapert, 1987, p. 43.

224 Murphy, 1949, p. 18.

225 Willard, 1944, pp. 15–16.

226 Tower, 1945, p. 94.

227 Ibid, p. 95.

228 Leuschner, 1946, p. 98.

229 NARA Record Group 247. Chief of Chaplains. Office Management Division Decimal File 1920–45. Box 194 250.1 Morals and Conduct – Language (Profanity). Eric G. Eklof to William R. Arnold,3 May 1944.

230 *The Link*, December 1943, p. 22.

231 Ibid, pp. 22–23.

232 Ibid, August 1944, p. 16.

233 NARA Record Group 247. Chief of Chaplains. Office Management Division Decimal File 1920–45. Box 194 250.1 Morals and Conduct – Language (Profanity). Herman H. Heuer to Carl Biar, 5 October 1943; J.F. Welsh to W.R. Arnold, 25 October 1943.

234 *The Link*, March 1944, p. 16.

235 Ibid, February 1945, p. 57.

236 NARA Record Group 247. Chief of Chaplains. Office Management Division Decimal File 1920–45. Box 194 250.1 Morals and Conduct – Language (Profanity). Addenda to Circular Letter 288,1 September 1944 and Memorandum To: All Unit Commanders, 77th Infantry Division, 3 August 1943; *The Link*, April 1944, p. 24; *The Chaplain*, September 1946, p. 21.

237 NARA Record Group 247. Chief of Chaplains. Office Management Division Decimal File 1920–45. Box 194 250.1 Morals and Conduct – Language (Profanity). G.M. Dougherty to W.R. Arnold, 31 May 1944.

238 Ibid, W.R. Arnold to E.G. Eklof, 11 May 1944.

239 *The Link*, January 1945, p. 9.

240 Grant, 1944, pp. 50–51.

241 NARA Record Group 247. Chief of Chaplains. Office Management Division Decimal File 1920–45. Box 194 250.1 Morals and Conduct – Language (Profanity). M.R. Miller to W.R. Arnold, 19 July 1944.

242 Ibid, G.M. Dougherty to W.R. Arnold, 31 May 1944.

243 Yost, 2006, p. 149.

244 Ray, 1962, pp. 32–33.

245 Ibid, p. 35.

246 Jorgensen, 1961, p. 271.

247 *The Link*, September 1943, p. 7.

248 *The Chaplain*, October 1944, p. 37; Jorgensen, 1961, p. 272.

249 Robertson, 2006, pp. 132–33.

250 Hynes, 2005, p. 213.

251 Ibid, pp. 213–14.

252 Schrijvers, 2010, pp. 211–12.

253 Reynolds, 1996, p. 233; 1945, 'Reports of the General Board. 84. The Military Offender in the Theater of Operations', Appendix 2, p. 34.

254 Reynolds, 1996, p. 232.

255 Schrijvers, 1998, pp. 183, 296, note 180; Roberts, 2014, pp. 195–261.

256 1945, 'Reports of the General Board. 84. The Military Offender in the Theater of Operations', p. 7.

257 Willoughby, 1998, pp. 169–70.

258 Atwell, 1961, p. 378.

259 Ibid, p. 381.

260 Ibid, p. 395; Schrijvers, 1998, p. 183.

261 Willoughby, 1998, pp. 160–61.

262 Lada and Reister, 1975, Table XXI, p. 38.

263 Reynolds, 1996, p. 208.

264 Atkinson, 2007, p. 449.

265 Holland, 2008, p. 243.

266 Kennett, 1997, p. 153.

267 Schrijvers, 2010, pp. 153–54.

268 Fahey, 1992, pp. 318–19.

269 Orr, 1948, p. 111.

270 Dower, 1986, p. 308.

271 Lada and Reister, 1975, Table XXI, p. 38.

272 Ellis, 1990, p. 306.

273 *The Chaplain*, October 1944, p. 32.

274 Polenberg, 1972, p. 151; Cantril and Strunk, 1951, pp. 997–98.

275 Boyer, 2001, p. 626.

276 Reynolds, 1996, p. 203; Costello, p. 290; Polenberg, 1972, pp. 150–51.

277 Costello, pp. 128–29, 289–91; Tower, 1945, p. 86.

278 Polenberg, 1972, p. 151; Costello, 1985, p. 128.

279 Kahn, 1973, 18 November 1941.

280 Costello, 1985, p. 302.

281 Coffman, 2004, pp. 318–19, 344, 368–69.

282 Pyle, 2004, p. 68.

283 Atkinson, 2007, p. 449; Costello, 1985, pp. 305–6.

284 Kennett, 1997, pp. 17–18.

285 Harrod, 1978, p. 126.

286 Costello, 1985, pp. 293–94.

287 *The Christian Century*, 15 November 1944, pp. 1309–10; *The Chaplain*, May 1945, p. 41.

288 Costello, 1985, pp. 302–3.

289 Ray, 1962, pp. 102–3.

290 Wickersham, 1998, p. 142.

291 Ibid, pp. 142–43, 157–58.

292 Ibid, p. 150.

293 Ibid, p. 146.

294 Drury, 1950, pp. 247–48.

295 *The Chaplain*, November 1944, p. 21.

296 Carpenter, 1997, p. 205.

297 Drury, 1950, p. 248.

298 Drury, 1950, p. 248.

299 *The Chaplain*, November 1944, p. 22.

300 Ibid, pp. 20–23.

301 Yost, 2006, p. 181.

302 Costello, 1985, p. 302.

303 *The Link*, March 1944, p. 14.

304 Ibid.

305 Ibid, pp. 14–15.

306 NARA, Record Group 247. Chief of Chaplains. Office Management Division Decimal File 1920–45. Box 261. 350.001 Lectures Volume II. Sex morality lectures from Camp Wheeler, Georgia, September 1943; Box 335. 726 Sex Morale Lectures; *The Chaplain*, January 1945, pp. 28–29; April 1945, pp. 26–27; June 1945, pp. 38–39.

307 *The Link*, October 1945, pp. 27–29.

308 Crespi and Shapleigh, 1946, pp. 368–69.

309 *The Link*, October 1945, p. 28.

310 Costello, 1985, p. 131.

311 Ibid, p. 149.

312 *The Chaplain*, June 1945, p. 38.

313 Burnham, 1993, p. 189.

314 *The Chaplain*, November 1944, p. 21; Lester, 1992, Reel 26, Box 78, 0516 et seq. and Reel 26, Box 78, 0534 et seq.

315 Martin, 'Meehling', p. 39.

316 http://articles.courant.com/1999–11–23/news/9911230135_1_falmouth-theology-divinity-degree, accessed 6 November 2013.

317 *The Chaplain*, October 1944, pp. 31–32.

318 Ibid, May 1945, p. 43.

319 Ibid, April 1945, p. 45.

320 Crosby, 1994, pp. 196–97.

321 Pyle, 2001, p. 192.

322 *Marine Corps Gazette*, November 1944, p. 15.

323 Willard, 1944, p. 48.

324 *Yank*, 6 December 1942, p. 16.

325 Ibid, 24 October 1943, p. 20.

326 Ibid, 31 October 1943, pp. 18–19; 7 November 1943, pp. 17–18.

327 Ibid, 31 October 1943, p. 18.

328 *Los Angeles Times*, 21 March 1943, p. 2.

329 *The Link*, September 1943, p. 64.

330 Costello, 1985, pp. 190–91; Fussell, 1989, p. 105.

331 Costello, 1985, p. 191; NARA, Record Group 247. Chief of Chaplains. Office Management Division Decimal File 1920–45. Box 194. 250.1 Morals and Conduct – Literature (Indecent).

332 Sampson, 1958, pp. 98–100.

333 Costello, 1985, p. 193.

334 *Stars and Stripes*, 'Special Supplement', 5 August 1943, n.p.

335 Ibid.

336 *Yank*, 23 May 1943, p. 7.

337 Muirhead, 1988, pp. 46–47.

338 *Stars and Stripes*, 5 August 1943, 'Special Supplement'.

339 Jorgensen, 1961, pp. 193–94; Atkinson, 2013, p. 564.

340 Brookes, 2000, cover illustration; O'Callahan, 1956, p. 41.

341 *The Link*, June 1944, p. 31.

342 *What the Soldier Thinks*, June 1945, pp. 4–5.

343 Yost, 2006, pp. 146–47.

344 Noll, 2002, p. 259.

345 McDannell, 1995, pp. 27–30, 189–90.

346 *The Link*, January 1945, pp. 40–41.

347 Ibid, January 1946, p. 49.

348 Grant, 1944, p. 24, illustrations.

349 Ambrose, 2001, pp. 36–37.

350 *Yank*, 27 June 1943, p. 20.

351 *Stars and Stripes*, 5 August 1943, Special Supplement.

352 Ray, 1962, pp. 29–30.

353 Clare, 1945, pp. 67–68.

354 Poling, 1959, p. 214.

355 *The Chaplain*, December 1944, pp. 32–33.

356 Record Group 247. Chief of Chaplains. Office Management Division Decimal File 1920–45. Box 193. 250.1 Morals and Conduct (Entertainment). O.C. Jensen to L. Philips, 4 September 1943.

357 Ibid, W.R. Arnold to Philips, 22 December 1943.

358 Pyle, 2001, p. 114.

359 Ibid.

360 *Yank*, 14 March 1943, pp. 22–23; 11 April 1943, pp. 22–23; 6 June 1943, pp. 22–23.

361 *The Christian Century*, 7 April 1943, p. 412.

362 Kimball, 1947. p. 113.

363 Leuschner, 1946, p. 98.

364 Atwell, 1961, p. 408.

365 *The Link*, November 1943, pp. 16–17.

366 Ibid, April 1945, pp. 23–24.

367 Fahey, 1992, p. 302.

368 Tower, 1945, pp. 42–43.

369 *The Link*, September 1944, p. 16.

370 Boyer, 2001, p. 298.

371 Donnelly, 1986, pp. 92–93.

372 Ardery, 1978, pp. 93–94.

373 Sampson, 1958, p. 31.

374 1945, 'Reports of the General Board. 84. The Military Offender in the Theater of Operations', p. 8.

375 Tower, 1945, p. 77.

376 Lord, 1942, pp. 37–38.

377 Sittser, 1997, p. 200.

378 *Infantry Journal*, May 1941, p. 69.

379 Polenberg, 1972, pp. 152–53.

380 Virden, 2014, pp. 80–81.

381 Sittser, 1997, pp. 199–200.

382 *The Christian Century*, 21 April 1943, pp. 479–80.

383 *Yank*, 21 February 1943, p. 15.

384 Ibid, 11 July 1943, p. 14.

385 Ibid, 5 September 1943, pp. 14–15.

386 Cantril and Strunk, 1951, pp. 687–88.

387 Lender and Martin, 1982, p. 171; Polenberg, 1972, p. 153; Rose, 2008, p. 38.

388 *The Link*, March 1943, p. 40.

389 Ibid, April 1943, p. 25.

390 Ibid, p. 19.

391 *The Chaplain*, November 1943, p. 14.

392 Ibid, May 1945, p. 38.

393 Whittaker, 1943, p. 137.

394 *Yank*, 11 July 1943, p. 9.

395 Costello, 1981, p. 601.

396 Chief of Chaplains. Office Management Division Decimal File 1920–45.Box 193. 250.1 Morals and Conduct – Beverages(Liquor). 'Information Regarding Manufacture and Sale of 3.2 Beer in the Army'; Fussell, p. 103; *Yank*, 14 February 1943, p. 15.

397 Pyle, 2001, p. 135; Record Group 247. Chief of Chaplains. Office Management Division Decimal File 1920–45.Box 193. 250.1 Morals and Conduct – Beverages(Liquor). F.D. Buxton to W.R. Arnold, 4 June 1945.

398 Hynes, 2005, p. 150.

399 *Yank*, 14 February 1943, p. 15.

400 Miller, 2007, pp. 87, 275; Robertson, 2006, p. 124.

401 Hastings, 2007, p. 113.

402 Fussell, 1989, p. 102.

403 Miller, 2007, p. 106.

404 Schrijvers, 1998, pp. 165–66.

405 Robertson, 2006, pp. 124–25.

406 Feuer, 2004, p. 115.

407 Chief of Chaplains. Office Management Division Decimal File 1920–45.Box 193. 250.1 Morals and Conduct – Beverages (Liquor). 'Information Regarding Manufacture and Sale of 3.2 Beer in the Army'.

408 1945, 'Reports of the General Board. 84. The Military Offender in the Theater of Operations', p. 8.

409 Schrijvers, 1998, p. 167.

410 Crosby, 1994, pp. 93–94.

411 Atkinson, 2013, p. 120.

412 Chandler and Ambrose, 1970, IV, pp. 2291–92.

413 Ibid, p. 2541.

414 Atwell, 1961, p. 400.

415 Lilly, 2007, pp. 96–97, 133–34; Fussell, 1989, pp. 102–3.

416 O'Callahan, 1956, pp. 124–25.

417 Fahey, 1992, pp. 100–01.

418 Ibid, p. 301.

419 Ibid, p. 306.

420 VHP, John Kempton, memoirs, p. 9, VHP MSS Box 1412. Folder 2/2.

421 Ibid, p. 6.

422 Sampson, 1958, pp. 88–89.

423 Pyle, 2001, p. 128; Atwell, 1961, p. 400.

424 Crespi and Shapleigh, 1946, pp. 369–70.

425 Robertson, 2006, p. 125.

426 *The Christian Century*, 10 May 1944, pp. 579–80.

427 Jorgensen, 1961, pp. 271, p. 305 n. 30.

428 Chief of Chaplains. Office Management Division Decimal File 1920–45.Box 193. 250.1 Morals and Conduct – Beverages(Liquor). J.C. Ensrud to D.E. Wineinger, 27 September 1943; W.R. Arnold to Director, Bureau of Public Relations, War Department, 28 March 1944.

429 Yost, 2006, pp. 8–9.

430 Martin, 'Meehling', pp. 32, 36.

431 Cantril and Strunk, 1951, p. 798.

432 Burnham, 1993, p. 101; Enjames, 2003, I, pp. 176–77, 182–83; II, pp. 145–47.

433 Rose, 2008, p. 39.

434 Spector, *Eagle Against the Sun*, 2001, p. 404.

435 Schrijvers, 2010, pp. 201–2.

436 Rose, 2008, p. 39.

437 Ellis, 1990, pp. 293–94.

438 Pyle, 2001, pp. 92–93.

439 Hynes, 2005, p. 189.

440 Kennett, 1997, pp. 201–5.

441 *The Christian Century*, 17 April 1946, p. 497.

442 Merridale, 2005, pp. 277–82; Longden, 2007.

443 *The Christian Century*, 9 May 1945, p. 573.

444 Atkinson, 2013, p. 559–61.

445 1945, 'Reports of the General Board. 84. The Military Offender in the Theater of Operations', p. 16.

446 1945, 'Reports of the General Board. 83. Military Justice Administration in Theater of Operations', p. 18.

447 Schrijvers, 1998, pp. 202–3.

448 1945, 'Reports of the General Board. 83. Military Justice Administration in Theater of Operations', pp.18–19.

449 Kennett, 1997, p. 201; Stouffer, 1949, II, p. 598.

450 Schrijvers, 1998, p. 203.

451 Atwell, 1961, pp. 161–62.

452 Ibid, p. 162.

453 Ibid, p. 294.

454 Ibid, pp. 295–96.

455 Murphy, 1949, p. 23.

456 Beevor, 2009, p. 153.

457 Lester, 1992, Reel 26, Box 78, 0534 et seq.

458 Feuer, 2004, p. 39.

459 Bassett, 1991, pp. 117–19.

460 Hanford, 2008, p. 96.

461 Kimball, 1947, p. 20.

462 Sledge, 2010, p. 242.

463 Astor, 1994, p. 215.

464 Parker, 2003, p. 367.

465 *The Link*, November 1943, p. 31; February 1944, pp. 20–21.

466 VHP, John Oliver Brixey, online transcript.

467 Atkinson, 2013, p. 600.

468 Ibid, p. 590.

469 Fussell, 2005, pp. 157–58.

470 Moore, 2006, p. xvii.

471 Preston, 2012, pp. 379–82; Sittser, 1997, p. 220.

472 *The Christian Century*, 29 August 1945, pp. 974–76.

473 Cantril and Strunk, 1951, p. 20.

474 Ibid, p. 21.

475 Preston, 2012, p. 380.

476 Rose, 2008, pp. 219–20.

477 USAHEC, World War II Veterans Survey, 1st Marine Division.

478 Ibid, Richard E. Milana.

479 Fussell, 1990, pp. 14–15.

480 Ibid, p. 19.

481 VHP, John Oliver Brixey, online transcript.

482 *Chicago Tribune*, 19 August 1945, p. 6.

483 *The Link*, January 1946, pp. 14–15.

484 *The Chaplain*, October 1945, pp. 26, 30.

485 Ibid, November 1945, pp. 2, 5–8, 30.

486 Yost, 2006, p. 257.

487 Fahey, 1992, p. 374.

488 Ibid, pp. 398–400.

489 VHP, Jack DeKorne, 24 March 2008 transcript, p. 10, VHP MSS Box 1857. Folder 4/4.

490 1945, 'Reports of the General Board. 68. The Army Chaplain in the European Theater', pp. 60–61.

491 Ibid, Appendix 17, p. 48.

492 Ibid, Appendix 17, p. 47.

493 Ibid, p. 61.

494 1951, 'Morale and Discipline in the European Command, 1945–1949', pp. i–ii.

495 *The Christian Century*, 17 April 1946, p. 495.

496 *The Christian Century*, 17 April 1946, p. 496.

497 Ibid.

498 Ibid.

499 Ibid, pp. 496–97.

500 *The Link*, August 1944, p. 57.

501 Gannon, 1962, p. 230.

502 Ibid, pp. 235–36.

503 *The Link*, January 1945, pp. 37–38.

504 Ibid, p. 38.

505 Faubus, 1971, p. 249.

506 Ibid, pp. 654–58; Linderman, 1997, pp. 231–34.

507 Kertzer, 1947, pp. 119–20.

508 Murphy, 1949, p. 56.

509 *The Link*, March 1945, p. 25.

510 *The Chaplain*, November 1945, p. 13.

511 Kertzer, 1947, pp. 22–23.

512 *The Chaplain*, March 1945, pp. 34–35.

513 Ibid, November 1945, p. 13.

514 Murphy, 1949, pp. 21, 162–64.

515 http://www.youtube.com/watch?v=LsCiaxPhtVY, accessed 18 November 2013.

516 Stouffer, 1949, I, pp. 545–50; Costello, 1985, pp. 147–48.

517 Stouffer, 1949, II, pp. 631–32; Adams, 1994, pp. 150–51.

518 *The Chaplain*, November 1945, p. 15.

519 Nance, 1944, p. 39.

520 VHP, Russell Baldwin, online Complete Interview.

521 Ambrose, 2001, p. 299.

522 Wansink and Wansink, forthcoming, pp. 9–11.

523 Ibid, p. 12.

524 Moore, 2004, pp. 47–48.

CONCLUSION

1 Herberg, 1955, p. 69.

2 Ibid, p. 274.

3 Ibid, p. 59.

4 Ibid, p. 276.

5 Ibid, p. 60.

6 Ibid, p. 62.

7 Ibid, p. 63.

8 Smith, 2001, pp. 196, 206–7.

9 Allitt, 2003, pp. 16–20.

10 Carpenter, 1997, p. 185.

11 Ibid, pp. 217–29.

12 Herberg, 1955, p. 64.

13 Cantril and Strunk, 1951, p. 790.

14 Preston, 2012, pp. 467–71; Allitt, 2003, pp. 22–25.

15 Herberg, 1955, pp. 73–74.

16 Preston, 2012, p. 441.

17 Ellwood, 1997, pp. 10, 26.

18 Herberg, 1955, pp. 74–76.

19 Ibid, p. 35.

20 Ahlstrom, 2004, p. 950.

21 Kennedy, 1999, p. 747.

22 Putnam and Campbell, 2010, p. 85.

23 Ibid, pp. 83, 85–86.

BIBLIOGRAPHY

Archival sources

Combined Arms Research Library Digital Library, Army Command and General Staff College, Fort Leavenworth, Kansas

'After-Action Report 82nd Airborne Division May 1945'.
'History of Military Training Chaplains: Chaplains Volume I – to December 1944', 1945.
'History of Military Training: Chaplains Supplement – to June 1945 (Volume 2)', 1945.
Sims, Lynn L. 'They Have Seen the Elephant: Veterans' Remembrances from World War II for the 40th Anniversary of V-E Day.' Fort Lee, VA, 1985.

National Archives and Records Administration, College Park, Maryland

Record Group 247. Chief of Chaplains. Office Management Division Decimal File 1920–45: Boxes 3, 7, 23, 119–20, 193–94, 199, 217, 219, 249, 254–56, 259, 261–62, 289–90, 298, 302, 310, 312, 316, 335.
Record Group 247. Records of the Office of the Chief of Chaplains. Records of Administration and Management General Records. Records Relating to the History of the Chaplains of the United States Army, 1941–58: Boxes 3, 8–9.
Record Group 492. Records of the MTO Headquarters. Chaplain Section: Boxes 1680–82.
Record Group 493. Records of the China–Burma–India Theater of Operations, US Army: Boxes 464–66.

National Museum of American Jewish Military History, Washington DC

Kastenbaum Family Marvin, Leon, Abraham.

United States Army Heritage and Education Center, Carlisle, Pennsylvania

Personal collections
22978032   Ole K. Davidson Papers.
22473076   Walter P. Plumley Papers.
24685287   Charles E. Wilson Papers.
US Army Military History Institute, World War II Veterans Survey
1st Marine Division
9th Infantry Division
24th Infantry Division
32nd Infantry Division
34th Infantry Division
101st Airborne Division
Army Nurse Corps
Armor Tank Battalions
United States Army Air Forces Bomber Groups

Miscellaneous

810736   Fowler, Arlen N. 'Research Material on the Religious Experience of Blacks in the Army', 1972.

275776   McClaskey, Beryl L. *The History of the US Policy and Program in the Field of Religious Affairs under the Office of the US High Commissioner for Germany*, 1951.

16945460   Speeches by Brehon Burke Somervell.

26859454   Van Schouwen, Cornelius. *The Life and Work of a Chaplain: Second World War (1943–1946)*, 1985.

Veterans History Project Collection, American Folklife Center, Library of Congress, Washington DC and http://www.loc.gov/vets/

Norman Wesley Achen Collection (AFC 2001/001/48504).
Jay S. Adams Collection (AFC 2001/001/151).
Joe Baldwin Collection (AFC 2001/001/9825).
Russell Baldwin Collection (AFC 2001/001/3541).
Robert Barilla Collection (AFC 2001/001/42420).
William Thomas Barr Collection (AFC 2001/001/10509).
Richard M. Becker Collection (AFC 2001/001/860).
Charles Luther Blount Collection (AFC 2001/001/6030).
Peter Bocko Collection (AFC 2001/001/38334).
Norman Boike Collection (AFC 2001/001/64307).
John Oliver Brixey Collection (AFC 2001/001/1602).
John A. Carver Collection (AFC 2001/001/10882).
James Clevenger Collection (AFC 2001/001/10457).
Jack DeKorne Collection (AFC 2001/001/64384).
Muriel Rose Phillips Engelman Collection (AFC 2001/001/68748).
Laverne C. Etshman Collection (AFC 2001/001/9810).
John Giarratano Collection (AFC 2001/001/53007).
William Greene Collection (AFC 2001/001/17465).
Carl W. Hardwick Collection (AFC 2001/001/62609).
Johann Carl Friedrich Kasten Collection (AFC 2001/001/12002).
John Kempton Collection (AFC 2001/001/50235).
Kenneth Kramer Collection (AFC 2001/001/47472).
William Luitje Collection (AFC 2001/001/12725).
Edward Martinez Collection (AFC 2001/001/74632).
James Meeks Collection (AFC 2001/001/1471).
Wilbur Eugene Nickels Collection (AFC 2001/001/51838).
Howard Orr Collection (AFC 2001/001/73751).
Emma Delano Petengill Collection (AFC 2001/001/57842).
Nathan Robbins Collection (AFC 2001/001/75983).
William H. Schaefer Collection (AFC 2001/001/23703).
Salvatore Tocco Collection (AFC 2001/001/56754).
Joseph Towell Collection (AFC 2001/001/11491).
Steve van der Weele Collection (AFC 2001/001/64360).

Published primary sources

1919, *Final Report of Gen. John J. Pershing Commander-in-Chief American Expeditionary Forces.*

1922, *Report of the Chief of Chaplains for the Fiscal Year Ended June 30, 1922.*

1923, *Army Chaplains Need Special Organization.* Washington DC: General Committee on Army and Navy Chaplains.

1923, *Report of the Conference on Moral and Religious Work in the Army.* Washington DC: Government Printing Office.

1924, *Army Regulations. No 60–5. Chaplains. General Provisions.*

1937, *Army Regulations No. 60–5. Chaplains. General Provisions.*

1941, *Technical Manual No. 16–205: The Chaplain.*

1942, *Instructions for American Forces in Britain.* War Department and the Department of the Navy.

1942, *The New Testament of Our Lord and Saviour Jesus Christ. Prepared for Use of Protestant Personnel of the Army of the United States.* Washington DC: Government Printing Office.

1942, *The Soldier and His Religion.* War Department, Bureau of Public Relations.

1943, *A Pocket Guide to Iran.* War Department and the Department of the Navy.

1943, *A Pocket Guide to North Africa.* War Department and the Department of the Navy.

1943, *A Pocket Guide to India.* War Department and the Department of the Navy.

1943, *Prayer Book for Catholic Servicemen.* Washington DC: National Catholic Community Service.

1943, *A Short Guide to Iraq.* War Department and the Department of the Navy.

1943, *A Spiritual Almanac for Service Men 1943–1944.* New York: Christian Commission for Camp and Defense Communities.

1944, *Etousa Special and Morale Services Guide.* ETOUSA: Special Service Division.

1944, *A Pocket Guide to France.* War Department and the Department of the Navy.

1944, *Technical Manual No. 16–205: The Chaplain.*

1945, *American Chaplains of the Fifth Army.* Milan: Pizzi and Pizio.

1945, *Military Government Germany: Technical Manual for Education and Religious Affairs.*

1945, *Reports of the General Board. 68. The Army Chaplain in the European Theater.*

1945, *Reports of the General Board. 83. Military Justice Administration in Theater of Operations.*

1945, *Reports of the General Board. 84. The Military Offender in the Theater of Operations.*

1945, *Reports of the General Board. 113. Special Services Organization.*

1945, *The Soxos: 729th Railway Operating Battalion.* Maastricht: Public Relations Section, 729th Railway Operating Battalion (reprint).

1946, *Historical Report for the Office of Military Government Berlin District. Volume V. Education and Religious Affairs.*

1946, *History of Chaplains' Activities in the Pacific.*

1947, *The Story of Christian Science Wartime Activities, 1939–1946.* Boston, MA: The Christian Science Publishing Society.

1950, *112 Gripes About the French.* Paris.

1951, *History of the Nonmilitary Activities of the Occupation of Japan. No. 32. Religion.* General Headquarters Supreme Commander Allied Powers: Allied Translator and Interpreter Service.

1951, *Morale and Discipline in the European Command, 1945–1949.*

1952, *Britain's Homage to 28,000 American Dead.* London: The Times.

2001, *Yearbook of American and Canadian Churches Compilation of Statistical Pages 1916–2000*. National Council of the Churches of Christ in the USA.

Abbott, Harry P. *The Nazi '88' Made Believers*. Dayton, OH: The Otterbein Press, 1946.

Abrams, Ray H. 'The Churches and the Clergy in World War II'. *Annals of the American Academy of Political and Social Science*, 256 (1948), pp. 110–19.

Abrams, Ray H. 'Foreword'. *Annals of the American Academy of Political and Social Science*, 256 (1948), p. vii.

Abrams, Ray H. *Preachers Present Arms; The Role of the American Churches and Clergy in World Wars I and II, with Some Observations on the War in Vietnam*. Rev. edn. Scottdale, PA: Herald Press, 1969.

Amoury, Daisy. *Father Cyclone*. New York: Messner, 1958.

Ardery, Philip. *Bomber Pilot: A Memoir of World War II*. Lexington, KY: University Press of Kentucky, 1978.

Arnold, Henry Harley. *Global Mission*. 1st edn. New York: Harper, 1949.

Arnold, Henry Harley and John W. Huston. *American Airpower Comes of Age: General Henry H. 'Hap' Arnold's World War II Diaries*. 2 vols. Maxwell Air Force Base, AL: Air University Press, 2002.

Atkins, Elisha. 'A Soldier's Second Thoughts', in *Religion of Soldier and Sailor*, ed. Willard Learoyd Sperry. Cambridge, MA: Harvard University Press, 1945.

Atwell, Leslie. *Private*. London: Transworld Publishers, 1961.

Ayres, Leonard P. *The War with Germany: A Statistical Summary*. Washington, DC: Government Printing Office, 1919.

Baber, Ray. 'Religion and the Family'. *Annals of the American Academy of Political and Social Science*, 256 (1948), pp. 92–100.

Baber, Ray. 'A Study of 325 Mixed Marriages'. *American Sociological Review*, 2, no. 5 (1937), pp. 705–16.

Bach, Marcus. *They Have Found a Faith*. Indianapolis: The Bobbs-Merrill Company, 1946.

Bartek, Johnny and Austin Pardue. *Life Out There, A Story of Faith and Courage*. New York: C. Scribner's Sons, 1943.

Bassett, John T. *War Journal of an Innocent Soldier*. New York: Avon Books, 1991.

Beard, Richard, Reva Beard and Elaine Pinkerton. *From Calcutta with Love: The World War II Letters of Richard and Reva Beard*. Lubbock, TX: Texas Tech University Press, 2002.

Bennett, Ivan Loveridge. *Song and Service Book for Ship and Field, Army and Navy*. Washington DC: Government Printing Office, 1942.

Bettelheim, Bruno and Morris Janowitz. *Dynamics of Prejudice: A Psychological and Sociological Study of Veterans*. New York: Harper & Brothers, 1950.

Bland, Larry I., ed. *The Papers of George Catlett Marshall. Volume 2. 'We Cannot Delay,' July 1, 1939–December 6, 1941*. Baltimore, MD: Johns Hopkins University Press, 1986.

Blumenson, Martin, ed. *The Patton Papers*. 2 vols. Boston: Houghton Mifflin, 1972.

Braden, Charles S. 'Christian-Jewish Relations Today'. *Journal of Bible and Religion*, 13, no. 2 (1945), pp. 94–105.

Braden, Charles S. 'Sectarianism Run Wild', in *Protestantism: A Symposium*, ed. William K. Anderson. Washington DC: The General Commission on Army and Navy Chaplains, 1944.

Braden, Charles S. 'The Sects'. *Annals of the American Academy of Political and Social Science*, 256 (1948), pp. 53–62.

Braden, Charles S. 'Teaching Religion in War Time: After One Year'. *Journal of Bible and Religion*, 11, no. 1 (1943), pp. 3–6.

Braden, Charles S. 'Why People Are Religious: A Study in Religious Motivation'. *Journal of Bible and Religion*, 15, no. 1 (1947), pp. 38–45.

Brasted, Alva Jennings. 'Religion of Our Soldiers: A Comparison of the Religious Attitudes and Needs of Men in the First World War and the War Today'. *Religious Education*, 38 (1943), pp. 188–94.

Brasted, Alva Jennings. *A Supplementary Study for Army Chaplains*. Fort Leavenworth, KS: Command and General Staff School Press, 1937.

Brasted, Alva Jennings. *A Symposium on the Work of the Chaplain in the Civilian Conservation Corps*. Fort Leavenworth, KS: Command and General Staff School Press, n.d.

Brasted, Alva Jennings and Edgar Allen. *'Az You Were!'*. New York: Morehouse-Gorham, 1944.

Breckinridge, S.P. 'The Actvities of Women Outside the Home', in *Recent Social Trends in the United States: Report of the President's Research Committee on Social Trends*, ed. Herbert Hoover, I, pp. 709–50. New York: McGraw-Hill Book Company, Inc., 1933.

Brink, Eben Cobb. *And God Was There*. Philadelphia: The Westminster Press, 1944.

Brownville, C. Gordon. *With Christ in a Shell Hole*. Grand Rapids, MI: Zondervan Publishing House, 1943.

Burkhart, Roy Abram. *The Church and the Returning Soldier*. New York and London: Harper & Brothers, 1945.

Cairns, David S. *The Army and Religion: An Enquiry and Its Bearing Upon the Religious Life of the Nation*. London: Macmillan & Co., 1919.

Cantril, Hadley. 'Educational and Economic Composition of Religious Groups: An Analysis of Poll Data'. *American Journal of Sociology*, 48, no. 5 (1943), pp. 574–79.

Cantril, Hadley and Mildred Strunk. *Public Opinion, 1935–1946*. Princeton, NJ: Princeton University Press, 1951.

Carlson, Alvin O. *He Is Able; Faith Overcomes Fear in a Foxhole*. Grand Rapids, MI: Zondervan Publishing House, 1945.

Carmer, Carl. *The War Against God*. New York: H. Holt and Company, 1943.

Carroll, Andrew. *Grace Under Fire: Letters of Faith in Times of War*. 1st edn. New York: Doubleday, 2007.

Carson, Julia Margaret Hicks. *Home Away from Home; the Story of the USO*. New York, London: Harper & Brothers, 1946.

Census of Religious Bodies, 1936. Bulletins 1–77. Washington DC: Bureau of the Census, 1939.

Chamberlin, J. Gordon. *The Church and Demobilization*. New York: Abingdon-Cokesbury Press, 1945.

Chandler, Alfred D. and Stephen E. Ambrose, eds. *The Papers of Dwight David Eisenhower: The War Years*. 5 vols. Baltimore: Johns Hopkins University Press, 1970.

Chesterton, G.K. *What I Saw in America*. New York: Dodd, Mead and Company, 1922.

Clare, Thomas H. and Irma Margaret Hempel Clare. *Lookin' Eastward, a G. I. Salaam to India*. New York: The Macmillan Company, 1945.

Clark, Mark W. *Calculated Risk*. New York: Enigma Books, 2007.

Claypool, James V. and Carl Wiegman. *God on a Battlewagon*. Philadelphia, Toronto: The John C. Winston Company, 1944.

Clear, Warren J. *Close-up of the Jap Fighting-Man*. Fort Leavenworth, KS: Command and General Staff School, 1942.

Cleary, William D. 'The Ministry of the Chaplain', in *Religion of Soldier and Sailor*, ed. Willard Learoyd Sperry. Cambridge, MA: Harvard University Press, 1945.

Cleveland Shrigley, G.A. *Prayers for Women Who Serve in Uniform and at Home*. Buffalo, NY: Council of Church Women, 1943.

Committee of Appraisal. *Re-Thinking Missions: A Laymen's Inquiry After One Hundred Years*. New York: Harper and Brothers Publishers, 1932.

Committee on the War and the Religious Outlook. *Religion Among American Men as Revealed by a Study of Conditions in the Army*. New York: Association Press, 1920.

Connelly, Kenneth A. *Chaplain's Assistant*. Seattle, WA: The Craftsman Press, 1945.

Considine, Robert, and Douglas MacArthur. *MacArthur the Magnificent*. London: Hutchinson & Co., 1942.

Crespi, Leo P. and G. Schofield Shapleigh. '"The" Veteran – a Myth'. *The Public Opinion Quarterly*, 10, no. 3 (1946), pp. 361–72.

Cross, Christopher and William Richard Arnold. *Soldiers of God*. 1st edn. New York: E.P. Dutton & Company, 1945.

Daniel, Eugene L. *In the Presence of Mine Enemies: An American Chaplain in World War II German Prison Camps*. Charlotte, NC: E.L. Daniel, Jr., 1985.

Daniel, Vattel Elbert. 'Ritual Stratification in Chicago Negro Churches'. *American Sociological Review*, 7, no. 3 (1942), pp. 352–61.

Dennis, Clyde H. *These Live On: The Best of True Stories Unveiling the Power and Presence of God in World War II*. Chicago: Good Books, 1945.

Dobbie, William George Shedden. *A Very Present Help, a Tribute to the Faithfulness of God*. Grand Rapids, MI: Zondervan Publishing House, 1945.

Dollard, John and Donald Horton. *Fear in Battle*. Washington DC: The Infantry Journal, 1944.

Donnelly, Thomas J. *'Hey Padre': The Saga of a Regimental Chaplain in World War II*. New York: 77th Division Association, 1986.

Douglass, H. Paul. 'Protestant Faiths', in *America Now: An Inquiry into Civilization in the United States*, ed. Harold E. Stearns. New York: Charles Scribner's Sons, 1938.

Edel, William W. *My Hundred Years, 1894–1994+*. El Cajon, CA, 1994.

Eggen, John M. *An Army Chaplain Sails the Seas*. Berryville, VA: Hudson's Printing Co., 1976.

Eichhorn, David Max, Greg Palmer and Mark S. Zaid. *The GI's Rabbi: World War II Letters of David Max Eichhorn*. Lawrence, KS: University Press of Kansas, 2004.

Eisenhower, Dwight D. *Crusade in Europe*. London: Heinemann, 1948.

Eliot, Thomas D. '– of the Shadow of Death'. *Annals of the American Academy of Political and Social Science*, 229 (1943), pp. 87–99.

Elkin, Frederick. 'The Soldier's Language'. *American Journal of Sociology*, 51, no. 5 (1946), pp. 414–22.

Embree, John F. *The Japanese Nation: A Social Survey*. Armed Services Editions, 1945.

Episcopal Church. Army and Navy Commission. *A Prayer Book for Soldiers and Sailors*. New York: Church Pension Fund, 1941.

Fahey, James J. *Pacific War Diary, 1942–1945*. Boston: Houghton Mifflin, 1992.

Faubus, Orval Eugene. *In This Faraway Land*. Conway, AR: River Road Press, 1971.

Feuer, A.B. *Packs On! Memoirs of the 10th Mountain Division*. Westport, CT: Praeger, 2004.

Fischer, Miles Mark. 'Organized Religion and the Cults', in *African American Religious History: A Documentary Witness*, ed. Milton C. Sernett. Durham, NC: Duke University Press, 1999.

Forgy, Howell Maurice and Jack S. McDowell. *'And Pass the Ammunition'*, New York and London: D. Appleton-Century Company, 1944.

Forrestal, James V. *The Forrestal Diaries*. New York: Viking Press, 1951.

Frillmann, Paul and Graham Peck. *China: The Remembered Life*. Boston: Houghton Mifflin, 1968.

Fry, C. Luther and Mary Frost Jessup. 'Changes in Religious Organizations', in *Recent Social Trends in the United States: Report of the President's Research Committee on Social Trends*, ed. Herbert Hoover, II, 1009–1060. New York: McGraw-Hill Book Company, Inc., 1933.

Furfey, Paul Hanly. 'The Churches and Social Problems'. *Annals of the American Academy of Political and Social Science*, 256 (1948), pp. 101–9.

Fussell, Paul. *Doing Battle: The Making of a Skeptic*. 1st edn. Boston: Little, Brown and Co., 1996.

Garrenton, John S. *The Flying Chaplain*. 1st edn. New York: Vantage Press, 1957.

Garrison, Winfred E. 'Characteristics of American Organized Religion'. *Annals of the American Academy of Political and Social Science*, 256 (1948), pp. 14–24.

Gavin, James M., Gayle Wurst and Barbara Gavin Fauntleroy. *The General and His Daughter: The Wartime Letters of General James M. Gavin to His Daughter Barbara*. 1st edn. New York: Fordham University Press, 2007.

Gehring, Frederic P. *A Child of Miracles: The Story of Patsy Li*. New York: Funk & Wagnalls, 1962.

Gellhorn, Martha. *The Face of War*. New York: Simon and Schuster, 1959.

Gerth, H.H. and C. Wright Mills, eds. *From Max Weber: Essays in Sociology*. London: Routledge and Kegan Paul Ltd, 1964.

Gillis, James M. 'The Radio and Public Service: The Radio and Religion'. *The Public Opinion Quarterly*, 2, no. 1 (1938), pp. 74–76.

Glaser, Daniel. 'The Sentiments of American Soldiers Abroad Towards Europeans'. *American Journal of Sociology*, 51, no. 5 (1946), pp. 433–38.

Glasser, Arthur F. *And Some Believed: A Chaplain's Experiences with the Marines in the South Pacific*. Chicago, IL: Moody Press, 1946.

Goldschmidt, Walter R. 'Class Denominationalism in Rural California Churches'. *American Journal of Sociology*, 49, no. 4 (1944), pp. 348–55.

Grafflin, Douglas G. 'Religious Education for Public Schools'. *The Phi Delta Kappan*, 28, no. 4 (1946), pp. 175–76.

Grant, Dorothy Fremont. *War Is My Parish*. Milwaukee, WI: The Bruce Publishing Company, 1944.

Gregg, John A. *Of Men and of Arms*. Nashville, TN: A.M.E. Sunday School Union Press, 1945.

Gregory, W. Edgar. 'The Chaplain and Mental Hygiene'. *American Journal of Sociology*, 52, no. 5 (1947), pp. 420–23.

Gregory, W. Edgar. 'The Idealization of the Absent'. *American Journal of Sociology*, 50, no. 1 (1944), pp. 53–54.

Hafer, Harold Franklin. *The Evangelical and Reformed Churches and World War II*. Boyertown, PA: Boyertown Times Publishing Company, 1947.

Haggerty, James Edward. *Guerrilla Padre in Mindanao*. New York, Toronto: Longmans, Green & Co., 1946.

Hale, Wallace M. *Battle Rattle*. Allen, TX: Timberwolf Press, 2004.

Harrison, Bernard. 'Judaism'. *Annals of the American Academy of Political and Social Science*, 256 (1948), pp. 25–35.

Hastie, William H. 'The Negro in the Army Today'. *Annals of the American Academy of Political and Social Science*, 223 (1942), pp. 55–59.

Hawkins, Ian, and United States Army Air Forces 95th Bomb Group (H). *B-17s Over Berlin: Personal Stories from the 95th Bomb Group (H)*. Washington DC: Brassey's (US), 1990.

Hazzard, L.B. 'Teaching Religion in War Time'. *Journal of Bible and Religion*, 11, no. 3 (1943), pp. 167–68, 191.

Herberg, Will. *Protestant, Catholic, Jew: An Essay in American Religious Sociology.* Garden City, NY: Doubleday & Co., 1955.

Herman, Stewart Winfield. *It's Your Souls We Want.* 1st edn. New York: Harper, 1943.

Hertzler, J.O. 'Religious Institutions'. *Annals of the American Academy of Political and Social Science,* 256 (1948), pp. 1–13.

Hickcox, Percy Merriman. *Mine Eyes Have Seen.* Boston: Mosher Press, 1950.

Hill, F.M., Gordon Laws and C. Vernon Taylor. *St. John-on-the-Hill, Port Moresby, 1943–1944.* Sydney: W.C. Penfold, 1944.

Hodgkins, Henry Bell. *A Charted Course for the Religious Life of a United States Ship at Sea with No Chaplain on Board.* Portsmouth, VA: Norfolk Navy Yard, 1944.

Holland, Jerome P. *Let's Talk It Over.* Milwaukee, WI: Bruce Publishing Company, 1946.

Hollingshead, August B. 'Adjustment to Military Life'. *American Journal of Sociology,* 51, no. 5 (1946), pp. 439–47.

Horton, Mildred McAfee. 'Women in the United States Navy'. *American Journal of Sociology,* 51, no. 5 (1946), pp. 448–50.

Huston, James A. *Biography of a Battalion: The Life and Times of an Infantry Battalion in Europe in World War II.* Mechanicsburg, PA: Stackpole Books, 2003.

Hynd, J. Hutton. 'How Fares Religion in the Fox Holes?' *Religious Education,* 38 (1943), pp. 379–83.

Hynes, Samuel. *Flights of Passage: Recollections of a World War II Aviator.* London: Bloomsbury, 1988 (2005 printing).

Hyslop, Ralph Douglas. 'The Right Men for the Ministry'. *Religious Education,* 40, no. 1 (1945), pp. 3–7.

Iglehart, Charles W. 'Current Religious Trends in Japan'. *Journal of Bible and Religion,* 15, no. 2 (1947), pp. 81–85.

International Committee of Young Men's Christian Association, *Summary of World War Work of the American YMCA.* New York: YMCA, 1920.

Iokibe, M., ed. *The Occupation of Japan: US Planning Documents 1942–1945 [Microfiche],* 1987–89.

Jenkins, Burris. *Father Meany and the Fighting 69th.* New York: Frederick Fell, 1944.

Jernagin, William H. *Christ at the Battlefront.* Washington DC: Murray Bros., 1946.

Jewish Welfare Board. *Final Report of War Emergency Activities.* New York: National Jewish Welfare Board, 1920.

Johnson, John E. 'The Faith and Practice of the Raw Recruit', in *Religion of Soldier and Sailor,* ed. Willard Learoyd Sperry. Cambridge, MA: Harvard University Press, 1945.

Kahn, Herman, ed. *Diaries of Henry Lewis Stimson in the Yale University Library* [Microfilm]. New Haven, CT: Yale University Library Manuscripts and Archives, 1973.

Kaplan, Diane Ellen, ed. *Papers of Henry Lewis Stimson (Not Including the Diaries) in the Yale University Library* [Microfilm]. New Haven, CT: Yale University Library Manuscripts and Archives, 1973.

Kertzer, Morris Norman. *With an H on My Dog Tag.* New York: Behrman House, 1947.

Kerwin, Paschal E. *Big Men of the Little Navy: The Amphibious Force in the Mediterranean, 1943–1944.* Paterson, NJ: St Anthony Guild Press, 1946.

Kimball, Clyde E. *A Diary of My Work Overseas.* Nashua, NH: E.E. Kimball, 1947.

Latourette, Kenneth Scott. 'The Present State of Foreign Missions'. *Annals of the American Academy of Political and Social Science,* 256 (1948), pp. 63–71.

Leach, Douglas Edward. *Now Hear This: The Memoir of a Junior Naval Officer in the Great Pacific War.* Kent, OH: Kent State University Press, 1987.

Leckie, Robert. *Helmet for My Pillow.* New York: Ebury Digital, 2010.

LeMay, Curtis E. and MacKinlay Kantor. *Mission with Lemay: My Story.* 1st edn. Garden City, NY: Doubleday, 1965.

Lester, Robert E., ed. *The Papers of George C. Marshall: Selected World War II Correspondence* [Microfilm]. Bethesda, MD: University Publications of America, 1992.

Leuschner, Martin Luther, Charles Frederick Zummach and Walter Edward Kohrs. *Religion in the Ranks.* Cleveland, OH: Roger Williams Press, 1946.

Lev, Aryeh. *What Chaplains Preach.* Washington DC: Corps of Chaplains, 1941.

Link, Henry C., Harry Arthur Hopf and Book Manufacturers' Institute (US). *People and Books: A Study of Reading and Book-Buying Habits.* New York: Book Industry Committee, Book Manufacturers' Institute, 1946.

Lord, Daniel A. *A Salute to the Men in Service.* St Louis, MO: The Queen's Work, 1942.

Lunn, Charles Edward. *Pilot to the Sky: The Experiences of an Army Air Forces Chaplain.* New York: The Hobson Book Press, 1947.

Lynn, Rita. *The National Catholic Community Service in World War II.* Washington DC: Catholic University of America Press, 1952.

Maahs, Arnold M. *Our Eyes Were Opened.* Columbus, OH: Wartburg Press, 1946.

MacArthur, Douglas. *Reminiscences.* 1st edn. New York: McGraw-Hill, 1964.

Maguire, William A. *The Captain Wears a Cross.* New York: The Macmillan Company, 1943.

Maguire, William A. *Rig for Church.* New York: The Macmillan Company, 1942.

Marshall, George C., Larry I. Bland and Sharon Ritenour Stevens. *The Papers of George Catlett Marshall.* Baltimore: Johns Hopkins University Press, 1981.

Marshall, George C. and Harvey A. DeWeerd. *Selected Speeches and Statements of General of the Army George C. Marshall.* Washington DC: The Infantry Journal, 1945.

Marshall, George C., Forrest C. Pogue and Larry I. Bland. *George C. Marshall: Interviews and Reminiscences for Forrest C. Pogue.* Rev. edn. Lexington, VA: G.C. Marshall Research Foundation, 1991.

Marshall, Peter J., ed. *The Wartime Sermons of Dr. Peter Marshall.* Dallas, TX: Clarion Call Marketing, Inc., 2005.

Marshall, S.L.A. *Men Against Fire: The Problem of Battle Command in Future War.* New York: William Morrow & Co., 1947.

Martin, Lawrence H. 'Captain Clifford Merrill Drury', Oral History Program, Chaplain Corps, United States Navy, 1980.

Martin, Lawrence H. 'Captain Frederick William Meehling', Oral History Program, Chaplain Corps, United States Navy, 1984.

Martin, Lawrence H. 'Captain Raymond Charles Hohenstein', Oral History Program, Chaplain Corps, United States Navy, 1983.

Martin, Lawrence H. 'Captain Walter Albert Mahler', Oral History Program, Chaplain Corps, United States Navy, 1985.

Martin, Lawrence H. 'Captain William Wilcox Edel', Oral History Program, Chaplain Corps, United States Navy, 1980.

Martin, Lawrence H. 'Martha Ellen Fondren Thomas', Oral History Program, Chaplain Corps, United States Navy, 1981.

Martin, Lawrence H. 'Rear Admiral Francis Leonard Garrett', Oral History Program, Chaplain Corps, United States Navy, 1984.

Mason, John T., ed. *The Pacific War Remembered: An Oral History Collection.* Annapolis, MD: Naval Institute Press, 1986.

Mauldin, Bill. *Up Front.* New York: H. Holt and Company, 1945.

McCanon, Rupert L. *Sometimes We Laugh, Sometimes We Cry or, 'Tell It to the Chaplain'.* New York: Vantage Press, 1969.

McClung Lee, Alfred. 'The Press and Public Relations of Religious Bodies'. *Annals of the American Academy of Political and Social Science*, 256 (1948), pp. 120–31.

McConahey, William M. *Battalion Surgeon*. Rochester, MN, 1966.

McDonagh, Edward C. 'The Discharged Serviceman and His Family'. *American Journal of Sociology*, 51, no. 5 (1946), pp. 451–54.

McGriff, E. Carver. *Making Sense of Normandy: A Young Man's Journey of Faith and War*. Portland, OR: Inkwater Press, 2007.

McGuire, Phillip. *Taps for a Jim Crow Army: Letters from Black Soldiers in World War II*. Lexington, KY: University Press of Kentucky, 1993.

McKinney, Madge M. 'Religion and Elections'. *The Public Opinion Quarterly*, 8, no. 1 (1944), pp. 110–14.

Merton, Robert King and Paul Felix Lazarsfeld. *Studies in the Scope and Method of 'The American Soldier'*. Glencoe, IL: Free Press, 1950.

Metcalf, George Reuben. *With Cross and Shovel: A Chaplain's Letters from England, France, and Germany, 1942–1945*. Duxbury, MA, 1957.

Methodist Church Commission on Chaplains. *Chaplains of the Methodist Church in World War II*. Washington DC, 1948.

Mones, Leon. 'Religious Education and the Public Schools'. *The Clearing House*, 15, no. 7 (1941), pp. 395–96.

Moody, Paul D. 'The Precedent of the First World War', in *Religion of Soldier and Sailor*, ed. Willard Learoyd Sperry. Cambridge, MA: Harvard University Press, 1945.

Morehouse, Maggi M. *Fighting in the Jim Crow Army: Black Men and Women Remember World War II*. Lanham, MD: Rowman & Littlefield, 2000.

Muckle, Coy. *Sermons of a Transport Chaplain*. Bristol, TN: The King Printing Company, 1946.

Muirhead, John. *Those Who Fall*. New York: Pocket Books, 1988.

Murphy, Audie. *To Hell and Back*. New York: H. Holt, 1949.

Murphy, T.F. *Religious Bodies: 1936. Volume I. Summary and Detailed Tables*. Washington DC: Bureau of the Census, 1941.

Murphy, T.F. *Religious Bodies: 1936. Volume II Part 1. Denominations A to J. Statistics, History, Doctrine, Organization, and Work*. Washington DC: Bureau of the Census, 1941.

Murray, John Courtney. 'The Roman Catholic Church'. *Annals of the American Academy of Political and Social Science*, 256 (1948), pp. 36–42.

Mygatt, Gerald and Henry Darlington. *Soldiers' and Sailors' Prayer Book. A Non-Sectarian Collection of the Finest Prayers of the Protestant, Catholic and Jewish Faiths, for the Men and Women of the United States Army, the United States Navy, the United States Marine Corps, the United States Coast Guard, the United States Maritime Service*. New York: A.A. Knopf, 1944.

Nance, Ellwood C. *Faith of Our Fighters*. St Louis, MO: Bethany Press, 1944.

National Lutheran Council. *By Their Side: A Memorial*. Washington DC: Bureau of Service to Military Personnel, 1949.

Nygaard, Norman E. *Strength for Service to God and Country: Daily Devotional Messages for Men in the Services*. Nashville, TN: Abingdon-Cokesbury Press, 1942.

O'Callahan, Joseph Timothy. *I Was Chaplain on the Franklin*. New York: Macmillan, 1956.

Office of the Adjutant General. *The Chaplain, His Place and Duties*. Washington DC: Government Printing Office, 1926.

Office of the Adjutant General, Statistical and Accounting Branch. *Army Battle Casualties and Nonbattle Deaths in World War II. Final Report. 7 December 1941–31 December 1946*, 1953.

Office of the Chief of Chaplains. *The Chaplain Serves*. Washington DC: Army Service Forces, War Department, 1944.

Office of the Chief Historian European Command. *The Second Year of the Occupation. Occupation Forces in Europe, 1946–47*. Frankfurt am Main, 1947.

Office of Strategic Services, Research and Analysis Branch. *Civil Affairs Handbook. Germany. Section 1b: Christian Churches*, 1944.

Office of the Theater Historian, European Theater. *Order of Battle United States Army World War II. European Theatre of Operations. Divisions*, 1945.

Ogburn, William F. 'The Family and Its Functions', in *Recent Social Trends in the United States: Report of the President's Research Committee on Social Trends*, ed. Herbert Hoover, I, pp. 661–708. New York: McGraw-Hill Book Company, Inc., 1933.

Orr, J. Edwin. *I Saw No Tears*. London: Marshall, Morgan & Scott Ltd, 1948.

Owens, Emiel W. *Blood on German Snow: An African American Artilleryman in World War II and Beyond*. 1st edn. College Station, TX: Texas A & M University Press, 2006.

Patton, George S. and Paul D. Harkins. *War as I Knew It*. Boston: Houghton Mifflin Co., 1995.

Poling, Daniel A. *A Preacher Looks at War*. New York: The Macmillan Company, 1943.

Poling, Daniel A. *Mine Eyes Have Seen*. 1st edn. New York: McGraw-Hill, 1959.

Poling, Daniel A. *Your Daddy Did Not Die*. New York: Greenberg, 1944.

Pope, Liston. 'Religion and the Class Structure'. *Annals of the American Academy of Political and Social Science*, 256, (1948), pp. 84–91.

President's Committee on Religion and Welfare in the Armed Forces. *The Military Chaplaincy*, 1950.

Price, Willard. *Japan and the Son of Heaven*. New York: Duell, 1945.

Proehl, Frederick C. *Service Manual for Lutheran Chaplains Serving with the Forces of the United States*. Chicago, IL, 1942.

Pyle, Ernie. *Brave Men*. 1st Bison Books edn. Lincoln, NE: University of Nebraska Press, 2001.

Pyle, Ernie and Orr Kelly. *Here Is Your War: Story of G.I. Joe*. Lincoln, NE: University of Nebraska Press, 2004.

Radike, Floyd W. *Across the Dark Islands: The War in the Pacific*. 1st edn. New York: Presidio, 2003.

Ray, Samuel Hill. *A Chaplain Afloat and Ashore*. Salado, TX: A. Jones Press, 1962.

Reddick, L.D. 'The Negro in the United States Navy During World War II'. *The Journal of Negro History*, 32, no. 2 (1947), pp. 201–19.

Reddick, L.D. 'The Negro Policy of the United States Army, 1775–1945'. *The Journal of Negro History*, 34, no. 1 (1949), pp. 9–29.

Rickenbacker, Eddie. *Seven Came Through: Rickenbacker's Full Story*. 1st edn. Garden City, NY: Doubleday, Doran, 1943.

Ridgway, Matthew B. and Harold H. Martin. *Soldier: The Memoirs of Matthew B. Ridgway, as Told to Harold H. Martin*. 1st edn. New York: Harper, 1956.

Robertson, Gordon Bennett. *Bringing the Thunder: The Missions of a World War II B-29 Pilot in the Pacific*. 1st edn. Mechanicsburg, PA: Stackpole Books, 2006.

Rogers, Edward K. *Doughboy Chaplain*. Boston: Meador Publishing Company, 1946.

Runbeck, Margaret Lee and Beatrice Atlass. *The Great Answer*. Boston: Houghton Mifflin Company, 1944.

Sampson, Francis L. *Look out Below! A Story of the Airborne by a Paratrooper Padre*. Washington DC: Catholic University of America Press, 1958.

Schneider, Herbert Wallace. *Religion in 20th Century America*. Cambridge, MA: Harvard University Press, 1952.

Scott, Emmett J. *Scott's Official History of the American Negro in the World War*. Chicago: R.L. Phillips Publishing Co., 1919.

Scott, Robert L. *God Is My Co-Pilot*. New York: Charles Scribner's Sons, 1943.

Sevareid, Eric. *Not So Wild a Dream*. New York: Atheneum, 1976.

Shedd, Clarence P. and Granville T. Walker. 'War-Time Adjustments in Teaching Religion'. *Journal of Bible and Religion*, 12, no. 2 (1944), pp. 72–82, 139.

Sibley, Mulford Quickert and Ada Wyman Wardlaw. *Conscientious Objectors in Prison, 1940–1945*. Philadelphia, PA: The Pacifist Research Bureau, 1945.

Silcox, Claris Edwin and Galen Merriam Fisher. *Catholics, Jews, and Protestants: A Study of Relationships in the United States and Canada*. Reprint. Westport, CT: Greenwood Press, 1979.

Sledge, E.B. *With the Old Breed*. New York: Ebury Digital, 2010.

Snyder, Robert Strong. *And When My Task on Earth Is Done*. Kansas City, MO: Graphic Laboratory, 1950.

Society for the Propagation of the Faith. *The Priest Goes to War: A Pictorial Outline of the Work of the Catholic Chaplains in the Second World War*. New York: The Society for the Propagation of the Faith, 1946.

Spellman, Francis. *Action This Day: Letters from the Fighting Fronts*. New York: Scribner's, 1943.

Spellman, Francis. *No Greater Love: The Story of Our Soldiers*. New York: C. Scribner's Sons, 1945.

Spellman, Francis. *The Risen Soldier*. New York: The Macmillan Company, 1944.

Spellman, Francis. *The Road to Victory*. New York: New Avon Library, 1944.

Sperry, Willard Learoyd. *Prayers for Private Devotions in War-Time*. New York and London: Harper & Brothers, 1943.

Spink, James F. *Service Men's Guide or, Helps Heavenward*. New York: Loizeaux Brothers, 1943.

Stannard, Richard M., ed. *Infantry: An Oral History of a World War II American Infantry Battalion*. New York: Twayne Publishers, 1993.

Steinbeck, John. *Once There Was a War*. London: Pan Books, 1975.

Stewart, Sidney. *Give Us This Day*. London: Pan Books, 1958.

Stilwell, Joseph Warren and Theodore H. White. *The Stilwell Papers*. New York: W. Sloane Associates, 1948.

Stimson, Henry L. and McGeorge Bundy. *On Active Service in Peace and War*. 1st edn. New York: Harper, 1948.

Stimson, Henry L., Leonard Wood, William Wallace Wotherspoon, Clarence Ransom Edwards, Hunter Liggett, George Henry Shelton and Robert Kennon Evans. *What Is the Matter with Our Army?* Washington DC: Government Printing Office, 1912.

Stouffer, Samuel Andrew. *The American Soldier*. 2 vols. Princeton, NJ: Princeton University Press, 1949.

Stroup, Russell Cartwright. *Letters from the Pacific: A Combat Chaplain in World War II*. Columbia, MO: University of Missouri Press, 2000.

Sweeney, Charles W., James A. Antonucci and Marion K. Antonucci. *War's End: An Eyewitness Account of America's Last Atomic Mission*. 1st edn. New York: Avon Books, 1997.

Sweet, William W. 'The Protestant Churches'. *Annals of the American Academy of Political and Social Science*, 256 (1948), pp. 43–52.

Taggart, William C. and Christopher Cross. *My Fighting Congregation*. New York: Doubleday and Company, Inc., 1943.

Talbot, Francis X. 'Catholicism in America', in *America Now: An Inquiry into Civilization in the United States*, ed. Harold E. Stearns. New York: Charles Scribner's Sons, 1938.

Tapert, Annette, ed. *Lines of Battle: Letters from American Servicemen 1941–1945.* 1st edn. New York: Times Books, 1987.

Taylor, Maxwell D. *Swords and Ploughshares.* Boston, MA: Da Capo Press, 1990.

Terkel, Studs. *The Good War: An Oral History of World War Two.* New York: Pantheon Books, 1984.

Thompson, Donald A. *American Army Chaplaincy, a Brief History.* Washington DC: The Chaplains' Association, 1946.

Tower, Hansel H. *Fighting the Devil with the Marines.* Philadelphia: Dorrance & Company, 1945.

Tregaskis, Richard. *Guadalcanal Diary.* New York: Random House, 1943.

Tregaskis, Richard. *Invasion Diary.* New York: Random House, 1944.

Tullidge, G.B. *A Paratrooper's Faith.* Staunton, VA, 1944.

Ulio, James A. 'Military Morale'. *American Journal of Sociology*, 47, no. 3 (1941), pp. 321–30.

United Service Organizations for National Defense. *Operation USO, Report of the President. February 4th, 1941–January 9th, 1948.* New York, 1948.

United Service Organizations, Inc. *Directory of USO Operations, March 15, 1944.* New York, 1944.

Van Dusen, Henry Pitney. *They Found the Church There: The Armed Forces Discover Christian Missions in the Pacific.* London: S.C.M. Press, 1945.

Van Dusen, Henry Pitney. *What Is the Church Doing?* London: Student Christian Movement Press, 1943.

Vandegrift, A.A. and Robert B. Asprey. *Once a Marine: The Memoirs of General A.A. Vandegrift, United States Marine Corps.* 1st. edn. New York: Norton, 1964.

Vanderbreggen, Cornelius. *Letters of a Leatherneck.* Philadelphia: Reapers' Fellowship, 1948.

Vida, George. *From Doom to Dawn: A Jewish Chaplain's Story of Displaced Persons.* New York: J. David, 1967.

Vonnegut, Kurt. *Slaughterhouse-Five.* New York: RosettaBooks, 2010. Kindle.

Wall, Max B. '*We* Will Be: Experiences of an American Jewish Chaplain in the Second World War', in *The Sword of the Lord: Military Chaplains from the First to the Twenty-First Centuries*, ed. Doris L. Bergen. Notre Dame, IN: University of Notre Dame Press, 2004.

Ward, Harry F. 'Organized Religion, the State, and the Economic Order'. *Annals of the American Academy of Political and Social Science*, 256 (1948), pp. 72–83.

Weigle, Luther A. 'Public Education and Religion'. *Religious Education*, 35 (1940), pp. 67–75.

Weinberg, S. Kirson. 'Problems of Adjustment in Army Units'. *American Journal of Sociology*, 50, no. 4 (1945), pp. 271–78.

Whittaker, James C. *We Thought We Heard the Angels Sing: The Complete Epic Story of the Ordeal and Rescue of Those Who Were with Eddie Rickenbacker on the Plane Lost in the Pacific.* New York: E.P. Dutton & Co., Inc., 1943.

Wickersham, George W. *Marine Chaplain 1943–1946.* Bennington, VT: Merriam Press, 1998.

Willard, Warren Wyeth. *The Leathernecks Come Through.* New York and London: Fleming H. Revell Company, 1944.

Williams, Lacy Kirk. 'Effects of Urbanization on Religious Life', in *African American Religious History: A Documentary Witness*, ed. Milton C. Sernett. Durham, NC: Duke University Press, 1999.

Willoughby, Harold R. *Soldiers' Bibles through Three Centuries.* Chicago, IL: University of Chicago Press, 1943.

Wilson, George. *If You Survive.* 1st edn. New York: Ivy Books, 1987. Kindle.

Wilson, Ruth Danenhower. *Jim Crow Joins Up: A Study of Negroes in the Armed Forces of the United States.* Rev. Edn. New York: Press of W.J. Clark, 1945.

Wilson, Woodrow. *Address of President Wilson at the Unveiling of the Statue to the Memory of Commodore John Barry.* Washington DC: Government Printing Office, 1914.

Wuest, Karl A. *They Told It to the Chaplain.* New York: Vantage Press, 1953.

Ylvisaker, Nils Martin. *Service Prayer Book, with Bible Readings, Hymns and Orders of Worship.* Minneapolis, MN: Augsburg Publishing House, 1940.

Yost, Israel A.S., Monica Elizabeth Yost and Michael Markrich. *Combat Chaplain: The Personal Story of the World War II Chaplain of the Japanese American 100th Battalion.* Honolulu: University of Hawaii Press, 2006.

Newspapers and periodicals

The American Israelite
Atlanta Daily World
The Baltimore Afro-American
Berkeley Daily Gazette
The Chaplain
Chicago Tribune
The Christian Century
Christian Herald
The Christian Science Monitor
Gloucestershire Echo
Hull Daily Mail
Independent [online]
Infantry Journal
The Jewish Exponent
The Leatherneck
The Link
Los Angeles Times
The Manchester Guardian
The Marine Corps Gazette
The Milwaukee Journal
The Naples Record
The National Catholic Almanac
New York Herald Tribune
New York Times
Newsday
Princeton Seminary Bulletin
Somerset County Herald
Stars and Stripes [London–New York edn]
The Times
Warweek
Washington Post
The Western Times
What the Soldier Thinks

Yank [British edn]

Secondary sources

Abercrombie, Clarence L. *The Military Chaplain.* Beverly Hills: Sage Publications, 1977.

Adams, Michael C.C. *The Best War Ever: America and World War II.* Baltimore, MD: Johns Hopkins University Press, 1994.

Ahlstrom, Sydney E. *A Religious History of the American People.* 2nd edn. New Haven, CT: Yale University Press, 2004.

Allitt, Patrick. *Religion in America Since 1945: A History.* New York: Columbia University Press, 2003.

Ambrose, Hugh. *The Pacific.* Edinburgh: Canongate, 2010.

Ambrose, Stephen E. *Band of Brothers: E Company, 506th Regiment, 101st Airborne from Normandy to Hitler's Eagle's Nest.* London: Pocket Books, 2001.

Ambrose, Stephen E. *Citizen Soldiers: The U.S. Army from the Normandy Beaches to the Bulge to the Surrender of Germany, June 7, 1944–May 7, 1945.* 1st Touchstone edn. New York: Simon & Schuster, 1998.

Ambrose, Stephen E. *D-Day, June 6, 1944: The Climactic Battle of World War II.* New York: Pocket Books, 2002.

Appelquist, A. Ray. *Church, State, and Chaplaincy: Essays and Statements on the American Chaplaincy System.* Washington DC: General Commission on Chaplains and Armed Forces Personnel, 1969.

Armstrong, Warren B. *For Courageous Fighting and Confident Dying: Union Chaplains in the Civil War,* Modern War Studies. Lawrence, KS: University Press of Kansas, 1998.

Astor, Gerald. *A Blood-Dimmed Tide: The Battle of the Bulge by the Men Who Fought It.* New York: Dell Publishing, 1994.

Astor, Gerald. *The Mighty Eighth: The Air War in Europe as Told by the Men Who Fought It.* New York: Dell Publishing, 1998.

Astor, Gerald. *Terrible Terry Allen: Combat General of World War II: The Life of an American Soldier.* 1st edn. New York: Presidio/ Ballantine Books, 2003.

Atkinson, Rick. *An Army at Dawn: The War in North Africa, 1942–1943.* 1st edn. New York: Henry Holt & Co., 2002.

Atkinson, Rick. *The Day of Battle: The War in Sicily and Italy, 1943–1944.* 1st edn. New York: Henry Holt, 2007.

Atkinson, Rick. *The Guns at Last Light: The War in Western Europe, 1944–1945.* 1st edn. New York: Henry Holt and Co., 2013.

Ayer, Frederick. *Before the Colours Fade: Portrait of a Soldier, George S. Patton.* London: Cassell, 1965.

Balkoski, Joseph. *Beyond the Beachhead: The 29th Infantry Division in Normandy.* Mechanicsburg, PA: Stackpole, 1999.

Bando, Mark. *101st Airborne: Screaming Eagles at Normandy.* Osceola, WI: MBI Pub., 2001.

Bando, Mark. *Vanguard of the Crusade: The 101st Airborne Division in World War II.* Bedford, PA: Aberjona Press, 2003.

Barish, Louis. *Rabbis in Uniform: The Story of the American Jewish Military Chaplain.* New York: J. David, 1962.

Beevor, Antony. *D-Day: The Battle for Normandy.* London: Viking, 2009.

Bellah, Robert N. 'Civil Religion in America'. *Daedalus,* 96, no. 1 (1967), pp. 1–21.

Berends, Kurt O. '"Wholesome Reading Purifies and Elevates the Man": The Religious

Military Press in the Confederacy', in *Religion and the American Civil War*, ed. H.S. Stout, C.R. Wilson and R.M. Miller. Oxford: Oxford University Press, 1998.

Bergen, Doris L. *Twisted Cross: The German Christian Movement in the Third Reich*. Chapel Hill, NC: University of North Carolina Press, 1996.

Bergen, Doris L. 'German Military Chaplains in the Second World War and the Dilemmas of Legitimacy', in *The Sword of the Lord: Military Chaplains from the First to the Twenty-First Century*, ed. Doris L. Bergen. Notre Dame, IN: University of Notre Dame Press, 2004.

Bergerud, Eric M. *Touched with Fire: The Land War in the South Pacific*. New York: Viking; London: Penguin, 1996.

Bergsma, H.L. *The Pioneers: A Monograph on the First Two Black Chaplains in the Chaplain Corps of the United States Navy*. Washington DC: Government Printing Office, 1980.

Bernstein, Philip S. *Rabbis at War: The CANRA Story*. Waltham, MA: American Jewish Historical Society, 1971.

Berube, A. *Coming Out Under Fire: The History of Gay Men and Women in World War Two*. New York: Free Press, 1990.

Biggs, Bradley. *Gavin*. Hamden, CT: Archon Books, 1980.

Blair, Clay. *Ridgway's Paratroopers: The American Airborne in World War II*. 1st edn. Garden City, NY: Dial Press, 1985.

Blaker, Gordon A. *Iron Knights: The United States 66th Armored Regiment, 1918–1945*. Shippensburg, PA: Burd Street Press, 1999.

Blankfort, Michael. *The Big Yankee: The Life of Carlson of the Raiders*. Liberty Book Club edn. Boston: Little, Brown and Company, 1947.

Blum, John Morton. *V Was for Victory: Politics and American Culture During World War II*. 1st Harvest/ HBJ edn. New York: Harcourt Brace Jovanovich, 1976.

Blumenson, Martin. *Mark Clark*. New York: Congdon & Weed: Distributed by St Martin's Press, 1984.

Booker, Bryan D. *African Americans in the United States Army in World War II*. Jefferson, NC: McFarland, 2008.

Booth, T. Michael and Duncan Spencer. *Paratrooper: The Life of Gen. James M. Gavin*. New York: Simon & Schuster, 1994.

Bourke, Joanna. *An Intimate History of Killing: Face-to-Face Killing in Twentieth-Century Warfare*. London: Granta, 1999.

Bowman, Martin W. *The American Bomber Boys: The US 8th Air Force at War*. Stroud: Amberley Publishing, 2012.

Bradley, Omar Nelson and Clay Blair. *A General's Life: An Autobiography*. New York: Simon and Schuster, 1983.

Brereton, Virginia Lieson. 'United and Slighted: Women as Subordinated Insiders', in *Between the Times: The Travail of the Protestant Establishment in America, 1900–1960*, ed. William R. Hutchison. Cambridge: Cambridge University Press, 1989.

Brinsfield, John Wesley. *Encouraging Faith, Supporting Soldiers: The United States Army Chaplaincy, 1975–1995*. Washington DC: Office of the Chief of Chaplains, Department of the Army, 1997.

Brinsfield, John Wesley. *Faith in the Fight: Civil War Chaplains*. 1st edn. Mechanicsburg, PA: Stackpole Books, 2003.

Brokaw, Tom. *The Greatest Generation*. New York: Random House, 1998.

Brookes, Andrew. *Air War Over Italy*. London: Ian Allan, 2000.

Brown, John Sloan. *Draftee Division: The 88th Infantry Division in World War II*. Lexington, KY: University Press of Kentucky, 1986.

Bruscino, Thomas A. 'The Analogue of Work: Memory and Motivation for Second World War US Soldiers'. *War and Society*, 28, no. 2 (2009), pp. 85–103.

Budd, Richard M. *Serving Two Masters: The Development of American Military Chaplaincy, 1860–1920*. Lincoln, NE: University of Nebraska Press, 2002.

Buell, Thomas B. *Master of Sea Power: A Biography of Fleet Admiral Ernest J. King*. Boston: Little, Brown, 1980.

Burke Smith, Anthony. 'America's Favorite Priest: *Going My Way* (1944)', in *Catholics in the Movies*, ed. Colleen McDannell. New York: Oxford University Press, 2008.

Burleigh, Michael. *Moral Combat: A History of World War II*. London: Harper Press, 2010.

Burleigh, Michael. *Sacred Causes: The Clash of Religion and Politics from the Great War to the War on Terror*. London: Harper Perennial, 2007. Kindle.

Burleigh, Michael. *Small Wars, Faraway Places: The Genesis of the Modern World, 1945–65*. London: Macmillan, 2013. Kindle.

Burleigh, Michael. *The Third Reich: A New History*. London: Pan Books, 2001.

Burnham, John C. *Bad Habits: Drinking, Smoking, Taking Drugs, Gambling, Sexual Misbehavior, and Swearing in American History*. New York: New York University Press, 1993.

Butler, Jon. 'Forum: American Religion and the Great Depression'. *Church History*, 80, no. 3 (2011), pp. 575–78.

Butler, Jon, Grant Wacker and Randall Herbert Balmer. *Religion in American Life: A Short History*. Updated edn. Oxford and New York: Oxford University Press, 2008.

Byers, Jean. *A Study of the Negro in Military Service*, 1950. Washington DC: Department of Defense.

Caldwell, Dan T. and B.L. Bowman. *They Answered the Call*. Richmond, VA: John Knox Press, 1952.

Cameron, Craig M. *American Samurai: Myth, Imagination, and the Conduct of Battle in the First Marine Division, 1941–1951*. Cambridge: Cambridge University Press, 1994.

Campbell, D'Ann. 'Women in Combat: The World War II Experience in the United States, Great Britain, Germany, and the Soviet Union'. *The Journal of Military History*, 57, no. 2 (1993), pp. 301–23.

Carpenter, Joel A. 'Fundamentalist Institutions and the Rise of Evangelical Protestantism, 1929–1942'. *Church History: Studies in Christianity and Culture*, 49, no. 1 (1980), pp. 62–75.

Carpenter, Joel A. *Revive Us Again: The Reawakening of American Fundamentalism*. New York: Oxford University Press, 1997.

Casino, Joseph J. 'From Sanctuary to Involvement: A History of the Catholic Parish in the Northeast', in *The American Catholic Parish*, ed. Jay P. Dolan. 2 vols (I). New York: Paulist Press, 1987.

Chapin, John. *Breaching the Marianas: The Battle for Saipan*. Washington DC: Marine Corps Historical Center, 1994.

Chatfield, Charles. *The American Peace Movement: Ideals and Activism*. New York: Twayne Publishers, 1992.

Cobb, Matthew. *Eleven Days in August: The Liberation of Paris in 1944*. London: Simon & Schuster, 2014.

Coffey, Frank. *Always Home: 50 Years of the USO – The Official Photographic History*. Washington DC: Brassey's (US), 1991.

Coffey, Thomas M. *Hap: The Story of the U.S. Air Force and the Man Who Built It, General Henry H. 'Hap' Arnold*. New York: Viking Press, 1982.

Coffey, Thomas M. *Iron Eagle: The Turbulent Life of General Curtis Lemay*. 1st edn. New York: Crown Publishers, 1986.

Coffman, Elesha J. *The Christian Century and the Rise of Mainline Protestantism*. New York: Oxford University Press, 2013.

Coffman, Edward M. *The Regulars: The American Army, 1898–1941*. Cambridge, MA: Belknap Press of Harvard University Press, 2004.

Colby, John. *War from the Ground Up: The 90th Division in WWII*. 1st edn. Austin, TX: Nortex Press, 1991.

Collie, Craig. *Nagasaki: The Massacre of the Innocent and the Unknowing*. London: Portobello, 2012.

Collins, F. and M. Collins. *Somewhere in the Midlands*. Studley: Brewin Books, 1998.

Conway, John S. *The Nazi Persecution of the Churches 1933–1945*. London: Weidenfeld and Nicolson, 1968.

Cooke, James J. 'The Experience of Being Abroad: Doughboys and GIs in Europe', In *The Great World War 1914–1945: Lightning Strikes Twice*, ed. John Bourne, Peter Liddle and Ian Whitehead. London: Collins, 2000.

Cooke, James J. 'America', in *The Great World War 1914–45: Who Won? Who Lost?*, ed. John Bourne, Peter Liddle and Ian Whitehead. London: Collins, 2001.

Cooney, John. *The American Pope: The Life and Times of Francis Cardinal Spellman*. New York, NY: Times Books, 1984.

Corbett, Michael and Julia Corbett Hemeyer. *Politics and Religion in the United States*. New York: Garland, 1999.

Costello, John. *Love, Sex and War: Changing Values, 1939–45*. London: Collins, 1985.

Costello, John. *The Pacific War*. 1st edn. New York: Rawson, Wade, 1981.

Craven, Wesley F. *The Army Air Forces in World War II. Volume 6. Men and Planes*. Chicago: University of Chicago Press, 1955.

Crosby, Donald F. *Battlefield Chaplains*. Lawrence, KS: University Press of Kansas, 1994.

Current, Richard Nelson. *Secretary Stimson, a Study in Statecraft*. New Brunswick, NJ: Rutgers University Press, 1954.

Curtis, Heather D. 'God Is Not Affected by the Depression: Pentecostal Missions during the 1930s'. *Church History*, 80, no. 3 (2011), pp. 579–89.

Daddis, Gregory A. 'Beyond the Brotherhood: Reassessing US Army Combat Relationships in the Second World War'. *War and Society*, 29, no. 2 (2010), pp. 97–117.

Dallek, Robert. *Franklin D. Roosevelt and American Foreign Policy, 1932–1945*. New York: Oxford University Press, 1979.

Davies, Norman. *Europe at War: 1939–1945: No Simple Victory*. London: Macmillan, 2006.

Davis, Richard G. *Carl A. Spaatz and the Air War in Europe*. Washington DC: Government Printing Office, 1993.

Daws, Gavan. *Prisoners of the Japanese: POWs of World War II in the Pacific*. 1st edn. New York: W. Morrow, 1994.

DeBenedetti, C. *The Peace Reform in American History*. Bloomington, IN: Indiana University Press, 1980.

Delaney, John Paul. *The Blue Devils in Italy: A History of the 88th Infantry Division in World War II*. 1st edn. Washington DC: Infantry Journal Press, 1947.

D'Este, Carlo. *Patton: A Genius for War*. New York: Harper Perennial, 1996.

Dolan, Jay P. *In Search of an American Catholicism: A History of Religion and Culture in Tension*. Oxford: Oxford University Press, 2002.

Donagan, Barbara. *War in England 1642–1649*. Oxford: Oxford University Press, 2011.

Dorsett, Lyle W. *Serving God and Country: United States Military Chaplains in World War II*. 1st edn. New York: Berkley Books, 2012.

Doubler, Michael D. *Closing with the Enemy: How GIs Fought the War in Europe, 1944–1945*. Lawrence, KS: University Press of Kansas, 1994.

Doubler, Michael D. and John W. Listman. *The National Guard: An Illustrated History of America's Citizen-Soldiers*. 1st edn. Washington DC: Brassey's, Inc., 2003.

Dower, John W. *War Without Mercy: Race and Power in the Pacific War*. New York: Pantheon Books, 1986.

Drury, Clifford M. *The History of the Chaplain Corps, United States Navy. Volume One. 1778–1939*. Washington DC: Government Printing Office, 1949.

Drury, Clifford M. *The History of the Chaplain Corps United States Navy. Volume Two. 1939–1949*. Washington DC: Government Printing Office, 1950.

Drury, Clifford M. *United States Navy Chaplains 1778–1945*. Washington DC: Government Printing Office, 1948.

Ebel, Jonathan H. *Faith in the Fight: Religion and the American Soldier in the Great War*. Princeton, NJ: Princeton University Press, 2010.

Ebel, Jonathan H. 'The Great War, Religious Authority, and the American Fighting Man'. *Church History*, 78, no. 1 (2009), pp. 99–133.

Ebel, Jonathan H. 'In Every Cup of Bitterness, Sweetness: California Christianity in the Great Depression'. *Church History*, 80, no. 3 (2011), pp. 590–99.

Eliot, Marc. *James Stewart: A Biography*. London: Aurum, 2007.

Ellis, John. *The Sharp End: The Fighting Man in World War II*. London: Pimlico, 1990.

Ellis, John Tracy. *American Catholicism*. 2nd edn. Chicago, IL: University of Chicago Press, 1969.

Ellwood, Robert S. *The Fifties Spiritual Marketplace: American Religion in a Decade of Conflict*. New Brunswick, NJ: Rutgers University Press, 1997.

Enjames, Henri-Paul. *Government Issue: U.S. Army European Theater of Operations Collector's Guide*. 2 vols. Paris: Histoire & Collections, 2003.

Farris, Marvin. *Do It Again ... Was It Luck or Prayer*. Fort Worth, TX: Branch-Smith, 1969.

Feldberg, Michael. '"The Day Is Short and the Task Is Great": Reports from Jewish Military Chaplains in Europe, 1945–1947'. *American Jewish History*, 91, no. 3–4 (2003), pp. 607–25.

Ferraro, Thomas J. 'Boys to Men: *Angels with Dirty Faces* (1938)', in *Catholics in the Movies*, ed. Colleen McDannell. New York: Oxford University Press, 2008.

Feuer, A.B. *Coast Watching in World War II: Operations against the Japanese on the Solomon Islands, 1941–43*. 1st edn. Mechanicsburg, PA: Stackpole Books, 2006.

Field, Ron and Alexander M. Bielakowski, *Buffalo Soldiers: African American Troops in the US Forces, 1866–1945*. Oxford: Osprey, 2008.

Finke, Roger and Rodney Stark. *The Churching of America, 1776–1990: Winners and Losers in Our Religious Economy*. New Brunswick, NJ: Rutgers University Press, 1992.

Fletcher, Marvin. *America's First Black General: Benjamin O. Davis, Sr., 1880–1970*. Lawrence, KS: University Press of Kansas, 1989.

Flint, James. 'A Chaplain's Diary: Reverend Victor Laketek, O.S.B., 1942–1946'. *The Journal of Military History*, 72, no. 3 (2008), pp. 853–867.

Folly, Martin H. *The United States and World War II: The Awakening Giant*. Edinburgh: Edinburgh University Press, 2002.

Ford, Douglas. 'US Perceptions of Military Culture and the Japanese Army's Performance During the Pacific War'. *War and Society*, 29, no. 1 (2010), pp. 71–93.

Ford, Douglas. *The Pacific War: Clash of Empires in World War II*. London: Continuum, 2012.

Fredman, J. George and Louis A. Falk. *Jews in American Wars*. 5th edn. Washington DC: Jewish War Veterans of the United States of America, 1954.

Freeman, Roger Anthony. *Experiences of War: The American Airman in Europe*. London: Arms and Armour, 1991.

Fridell, Wilbur M. 'A Fresh Look at State Shinto'. *Journal of the American Academy of Religion*, 44, no. 3 (1976), pp. 547–61.

Fugita, Stephen and Marilyn Fernandez. 'Religion and Japanese Americans' Views of Their World War II Incarceration'. *Journal of Asian American Studies*, 5, no. 2 (2002), pp. 113–37.

Fussell, Paul. *The Boys' Crusade: American GIs in Europe: Chaos and Fear in World War Two*. London: Phoenix, 2005.

Fussell, Paul. *Thank God for the Atom Bomb, and Other Essays*. New York: Ballantine Books, 1990.

Fussell, Paul. *Wartime: Understanding and Behavior in the Second World War*. New York: Oxford University Press, 1989.

Gannon, Robert I. *The Cardinal Spellman Story*. 1st edn. Garden City, NY: Doubleday, 1962.

Gardiner, Juliet. *D-Day: Those Who Were There*. London: Collins & Brown, 1994.

Gardiner, Juliet. *Wartime: Britain 1939–1945*. London: Review, 2005.

Gaustad, Edwin S. 'The Pulpit and the Pews', in *Between the Times: The Travail of the Protestant Establishment in America, 1900–1960*, ed. William R. Hutchison. Cambridge: Cambridge University Press, 1989.

Gaustad, Edwin S. *A Religious History of America*. New rev. edn. San Francisco: Harper & Row, 1990.

Gilbert, Adrian. *POW: Allied Prisoners in Europe, 1939–1945*. London: John Murray, 2007.

Gilmore, Allison B. '"We Have Been Reborn": Japanese Prisoners and the Allied Propaganda War in the Southwest Pacific'. *Pacific Historical Review*, 64, no. 2 (1995), pp. 195–215.

Gott, Kendall D. *The US Army and the Media in Wartime: Historical Perspectives: The Proceedings of the Combat Studies Institute 2009 Military History Symposium*. Fort Leavenworth, KS: Combat Studies Institute Press, 2010.

Greenawalt, Kent. *Religion and the Constitution*. 2 vols. Princeton, NJ: Princeton University Press, 2008.

Greene, Alison Collis. 'The End of "The Protestant Era?"' *Church History*, 80, no. 3 (2011), pp. 600–610.

Greenfield, Kent Roberts, R.R. Palmer and Bell Irvin Wiley. *The Organization of Ground Combat Troops*. United States Army in World War II: The Army Ground Forces. Washington DC: Historical Division, United States Army, 1947.

Gribbin, William. *The Churches Militant: The War of 1812 and American Religion*. New Haven, CT: Yale University Press, 1973.

Griffin, Martin I.J. *The Story of Commodore John Barry 'Father of the American Navy'*. Philadelphia, 1908.

Grobman, Alex and Judah L. Magnes Museum. *Rekindling the Flame: American Jewish Chaplains and the Survivors of European Jewry, 1944–1948*. Detroit, MI: Wayne State University Press, 1993.

Grossmith, F.T. *The Cross and the Swastika*. New edn. Stamford: Paul Watkins, 1998.

Grunberger, Richard. *A Social History of the Third Reich*. London: Penguin, 1991.

Gunn, T. Jeremy. *Spiritual Weapons: The Cold War and the Forging of an American National Religion*. Westport, CT: Praeger Publishers, 2009.

Gushwa, Robert L. *The Best and Worst of Times: The United States Army Chaplaincy 1920–1945*. Washington: Office of the Chief of Chaplains, 1977.

Hammond, Philip E., Amanda Porterfield, James G. Moseley and Jonathan D. Sarna. 'Forum: American Civil Religion Revisited'. *Religion and American Culture: A Journal of Interpretation*, 4, no. 1 (1994), pp. 1–23.

Hampf, M. Michaela. '"Dykes" or "Whores": Sexuality and the Women's Army Corps in the United States During World War II'. *Women's Studies International Forum*, 27 (2004), pp. 13–30.

Handy, Robert T. 'The American Religious Depression, 1925–1935'. *Church History*, 29, no. 1 (1960), pp. 3–16.

Handy, Robert T. *A History of the Churches in the United States and Canada*. Oxford: Oxford University Press, 1976.

Hanford, William B. *A Dangerous Assignment: An Artillery Forward Observer in World War II*. Mechanicsburg, PA: Stackpole Books, 2008.

Hangen, Tona J. *Redeeming the Dial: Radio, Religion, and Popular Culture in America*. Durham, NC: University of North Carolina Press, 2002.

Harrod, Frederick S. *Manning the New Navy: The Development of a Modern Naval Enlisted Force, 1899–1940*. Westport, CT: Greenwood Press, 1978.

Hastings, Max. *All Hell Let Loose: The World at War 1939–45*. London: Harper Press, 2011.

Hastings, Max. *Armageddon: The Battle for Germany 1944–45*. London: Pan, 2005.

Hastings, Max. *Nemesis: The Battle for Japan, 1944–45*. London: Harper Press, 2007.

Hedstrom, Matthew. *The Rise of Liberal Religion: Book Culture and American Spirituality in the Twentieth Century*. New York: Oxford University Press, 2013.

Hennesey, James J. *American Catholics: A History of the Roman Catholic Community in the United States*. New York: Oxford University Press, 1981.

Henry, Mark. *The US Navy in World War II*. Oxford: Osprey Publishing Ltd, 2002.

Herzog, Jonathan P. *The Spiritual–Industrial Complex: America's Religious Battle against Communism in the Early Cold War*. New York: Oxford University Press, 2011.

Hilberg, Raul. *Perpetrators, Victims, Bystanders: The Jewish Catastrophe 1933–1945*. London: Secker and Warburg, 1995.

Hillenbrand, Laura. *Unbroken: An Extraordinary True Story of Courage and Survival*. London: Fourth Estate, 2012.

Hodgson, Godfrey. *The Colonel: The Life and Wars of Henry Stimson, 1867–1950*. 1st edn. New York: Knopf, 1990.

Holifield, E. Brooks. *God's Ambassadors : A History of the Christian Clergy in America*, Grand Rapids, MI: William B. Eerdmans, 2007.

Holland, James. *Italy's Sorrow: A Year of War 1944–45*. London: Harper Press, 2008.

Holmes, Richard. *Firing Line*. London: Cape, 1985.

Honey, Maureen. *Bitter Fruit: African American Women in World War II*. Columbia, MO: University of Missouri Press, 1999.

Honeywell, Roy John. *Chaplains of the United States Army*. Washington DC: Office of the Chief of Chaplains, 1958.

Hönicke Moore, Michaela. *Know Your Enemy: The American Debate on Nazism, 1933–1945*. Cambridge: Cambridge University Press, 2010.

Hoopes, Townsend and Douglas Brinkley. *Driven Patriot: The Life and Times of James Forrestal*. 1st edn. New York: Knopf, 1992.

Hopkins, George E. 'Bombing and the American Conscience During World War II'. *Historian*, 28, no. 3 (1966), pp. 451–73.

Howard, David M. *From Wheaton to the Nations*. Wheaton, IL: Wheaton College, 2001.

Howarth, Stephen. *To Shining Sea: A History of the United States Navy 1775–1991*. London: Weidenfeld & Nicolson, 1991.

Hull, Michael D. 'Father Albert of the Rangers'. *Latin Mass*, 18, no. 1 (2009), pp. 18–23.

Hulsether, Mark. *Religion, Culture and Politics in the Twentieth-Century United States*. Edinburgh: Edinburgh University Press, 2007.

Hutchison, William R. 'Protestantism as Establishment', in *Between the Times: The Travail of the Protestant Establishment in America, 1900–1960*, ed. William R. Hutchison. Cambridge: Cambridge University Press, 1989.

Inboden, William. *Religion and American Foreign Policy, 1945–1960: The Soul of Containment.* 1st paperback edn. Cambridge: Cambridge University Press, 2010.

James, Dorris Clayton. *The Years of MacArthur: Vol. 2: 1941–1945.* Boston: Houghton, Mifflin, 1975.

Janowitz, Morris. *The Professional Soldier: A Social and Political Portrait.* New York: The Free Press, 1960.

Jeffries, John W. 'Mobilization and Its Impact', in *World War II and the American Home Front*, ed. Marilyn M. Harper. National Park Service: US Department of the Interior, 2007.

Jeffries, John W. *Wartime America: The World War II Home Front.* Chicago, IL: I.R. Dee, 1996.

Jessup, John E. 'The Soviet Armed Forces in the Great Patriotic War, 1941–5', in *Military Effectiveness. Volume 3. The Second World War.* New edn, ed. Allan R. Millett and Williamson Murray. Cambridge: Cambridge University Press, 2010.

Jorgensen, Daniel B. *The Service of Chaplains to Army Air Units, 1917–1946.* Washington DC: Office, Chief of Air Force Chaplains, 1961.

Kahn, E.J. and Henry McLemore. *Fighting Divisions.* Washington DC: Infantry Journal, 1945.

Kaplan, Julie B. 'Military Mirrors on the Wall: Nonestablishment and the Military Chaplaincy'. *Yale Law Journal*, 95 (1986), pp. 1210–36.

Karsten, Peter. *The Naval Aristocracy: The Golden Age of Annapolis and the Emergence of Modern American Navalism.* 1st Naval Institute Press pbk. edn. Annapolis, MD: Naval Institute Press, 2008.

Keegan, John. *Six Armies in Normandy: From D-Day to the Liberation of Paris, June 6th– August 25th, 1944.* London: Cape, 1982.

Keene, Jennifer D. *Doughboys, the Great War, and the Remaking of America.* Baltimore, MD: Johns Hopkins University Press, 2001.

Keene, Jennifer D. *World War I: The American Soldier Experience.* Lincoln, NE: University of Nebraska Press, 2011.

Kenneally, J.J. 'Eve, Mary, and the Historians: American Catholicism and Women', in *Women in American Religion*, ed. Janet Wilson James. Philadelphia: University of Pennsylvania Press, 1980.

Kennedy, David M. *Freedom from Fear: The American People in Depression and War, 1929–1945*, New York: Oxford University Press, 1999.

Kennett, Lee B. *GI: The American Soldier in World War II.* Norman, OK: University of Oklahoma Press, 1997.

Kershaw, Alex. *The Bedford Boys: One Small Town's D-Day Sacrifice.* New York: Simon & Schuster, 2003.

Kidd, Thomas S. *God of Liberty: A Religious History of the American Revolution.* New York: Basic Books, 2010.

Kindsvatter, Peter S. *American Soldiers: Ground Combat in the World Wars, Korea, and Vietnam.* Lawrence, KS: University Press of Kansas, 2003.

King, David P. 'The West Looks East: The Influence of Toyohiko Kagawa on American Mainline Protestantism'. *Church History*, 80, no. 2 (2011), pp. 302–20.

Klein, Maury. *A Call to Arms: Mobilizing America for World War II.* New York: Bloomsbury Press, 2013.

Klug, E.F. 'The Chaplaincy in American Public Life', in *Church, State and Chaplaincy: Essays and Statements on the American Chaplaincy System*, ed. A. Ray Appelquist.

Washington DC: General Commission on Chaplains and Armed Forces Personnel, 1969.

Krammer, Arnold. 'Japanese Prisoners of War in America'. *Pacific Historical Review*, 52, no. 1 (1983), pp. 67–91.

Koppes, Clayton R. and Gregory D. Black. *Hollywood Goes to War: How Politics, Profits, and Propaganda Shaped World War II Movies*. New York: Free Press, 1987.

Kurzman, Dan. *No Greater Glory: The Four Immortal Chaplains and the Sinking of the Dorchester in World War II*. 1st edn. New York: Random House, 2004.

Lada, John and Frank A. Reister. *Medical Statistics in World War II*. Washington DC: Office of the Surgeon General, 1975.

Laurie, Clayton D. *The Propaganda Warriors: America's Crusade against Nazi Germany*. Lawrence, KS: University Press of Kansas, 1996.

Laurie, Clayton D. 'The Ultimate Dilemma of Psychological Warfare in the Pacific: Enemies Who Don't Surrender, and GIs Who Don't Take Prisoners'. *War and Society*, 14, no. 1 (1996), pp. 99–120.

Lee, David D. *Sergeant York: An American Hero*. Lexington, KY: University Press of Kentucky, 1985.

Lee, Ulysses. *The Employment of Negro Troops*. United States Army in World War II. Special Studies. Volume 8. Washington DC: Office of the Chief of Military History, 1966.

Lender, Mark Edward and James Kirby Martin. *Drinking in America: A History*. New York: Free Press, 1982.

Lewy, Guenter. *The Catholic Church and Nazi Germany*. London: Weidenfeld & Nicolson, 1964.

Lilly, J. Robert. *Taken by Force: Rape and American GIs in Europe During World War II*. English edn. Basingstoke: Palgrave Macmillan, 2007.

Lincoln, C. Eric and Lawrence H. Mamiya. *The Black Church in the African-American Experience*. Durham, NC: Duke University Press, 1990.

Linderman, Gerald F. *The World within War: America's Combat Experience in World War II*. New York: Free Press, 1997.

Longden, Sean. *To the Victor the Spoils: Soldiers' Lives from D-Day to VE-Day*. London: Robinson, 2007.

Love, Robert W. 'Fleet Admiral Ernest J. King', in *Men of War: Great Naval Leaders of World War II*, ed. Stephen Howarth. London: Weidenfeld and Nicolson, 1992.

Loveland, Anne C. *American Evangelicals and the U.S. Military, 1942–1993*. Baton Rouge, LA: Louisiana State University Press, 1996.

Loveland, Anne C. *Change and Conflict in the US Army Chaplain Corps since 1945*. Knoxville, TN: University of Tennessee Press, 2014.

Loveland, Anne C. 'Character Education in the US Army, 1947–1977'. *The Journal of Military History*, 64, no. 3 (2000), pp. 795–818.

Loveland, Anne C. 'From Morale Builders to Moral Advocates: US Army Chaplains in the Second Half of the Twentieth Century', in *The Sword of the Lord: Military Chaplains from the First to the Twenty-first Century*, ed. Doris L. Bergen. Notre Dame, IN: University of Notre Dame Press, 2004.

Maddox, Robert James, ed. *Hiroshima in History: The Myths of Revisionism*. Columbia, MO: University of Missouri Press, 2007.

Maddox, Robert James. *The United States and World War II*. Boulder, CO: Westview Press, 1992.

Markkola, Pirjo. 'Patriarchy and Women's Emancipation', in *The Cambridge History of*

Christianity. Volume 9. World Christianities c.1914–2000, ed. Hugh McLeod. Cambridge: Cambridge University Press, 2006.

Marsden, George M. *Religion and American Culture*. San Diego, CA: Harcourt Brace Jovanovich, 1990.

Marston, Daniel. *The Pacific War Companion: From Pearl Harbor to Hiroshima*. Oxford: Osprey, 2005.

Martin, R.J. *The 101st Airborne Division*. Paducah, KY: Turner Publishing Company, 1995.

Marty, Martin E. *Modern American Religion. Vol. 1, The Irony of It All, 1893–1919*. Chicago, IL: University of Chicago Press, 1986.

Marty, Martin E. *Modern American Religion. Vol. 2, The Noise of Conflict, 1919–1941*. Chicago, IL: University of Chicago Press, 1991.

Marty, Martin E. *Modern American Religion. Vol. 3, Under God, Indivisible, 1941–1960*. Chicago, IL: University of Chicago Press, 1996.

Marty, Martin E. 'North America', in *The Oxford Illustrated History of Christianity*, ed. John McManners. Oxford: Oxford University Press, 1992.

Mathews, Donald G., Samuel S. Hill, Beth Barton Schweiger and John B. Boles. 'Forum: Southern Religion'. *Religion and American Culture: A Journal of Interpretation*, 8, no. 2 (1998), pp. 147–77.

Maurer, M. *Air Force Combat Units of World War II*. Washington DC: Office of Air Force History, 1983.

Maurer, M. *Combat Squadrons of the Air Force World War II*. Washington DC: Albert F. Simpson Historical Research Center and Office of Air Force History, 1982.

McDannell, Colleen. 'Christianity in the United States During the Inter-War Years', in *The Cambridge History of Christianity. Volume 9. World Christianities c.1914–2000*, ed. Hugh McLeod. Cambridge: Cambridge University Press, 2006.

McDannell, Colleen. *Material Christianity: Religion and Popular Culture in America*. New Haven, CT: Yale University Press, 1995.

McDannell, Colleen. *Picturing Faith: Photography and the Great Depression*. New Haven, CT: Yale University Press, 2004.

McDannell, Colleen and Bernhard Lang. *Heaven: A History*. New Haven, CT: Yale University Press, 1988.

McManus, John C. *The Deadly Brotherhood: The American Combat Soldier in World War II*. Novato, CA: Presidio, 1998.

McPherson, James M. *For Cause and Comrades: Why Men Fought in the Civil War*. New York: Oxford University Press, 1997.

Meacham, Jon. *Franklin and Winston: A Portrait of a Friendship*. London: Granta, 2005.

Mead, Gary. *The Doughboys: America and the First World War*. London: Allen Lane, 2000.

Merridale, Catherine. *Ivan's War: The Red Army 1939–45*. London: Faber and Faber, 2005.

Merrill, James M. 'Fleet Admiral William F. Halsey Jr', in *Men of War: Great Naval Leaders of World War II*, ed. Stephen Howarth. London: Weidenfeld and Nicolson, 1992.

Mets, David R. *Master of Airpower: General Carl A. Spaatz*. Novato, CA: Presidio Press, 1988.

Miller, Donald L. *Eighth Air Force: The American Bomber Crews in Britain*. London: Aurum, 2007.

Miller, Robert J. *Both Prayed to the Same God: Religion and Faith in the American Civil War*. Lanham, MD: Lexington Books, 2007.

Miller, Randall M., Harry S. Stout and Charles Reagan Wilson. *Religion and the American Civil War*. New York: Oxford University Press, 1998.

Millett, Allan R. *Semper Fidelis: The History of the United States Marine Corps*. Revised and expanded edn. New York: Free Press, 1991.

Millett, Allan R. 'The United States Armed Forces in the Second World War', in *Military Effectiveness. Volume 3. The Second World War.* New edn, ed. Allan R. Millett and Williamson Murray. Cambridge: Cambridge University Press, 2010.

Minear, Richard H. 'Cross-Cultural Perception and World War II: American Japanists of the 1940s and Their Images of Japan'. *International Studies Quarterly*, 24, no. 4 (1980), pp. 555–80.

Mitchell, George C. *Matthew B. Ridgway: Soldier, Statesman, Scholar, Citizen.* Mechanicsburg, PA: Stackpole Books, 2002.

Mitter, Rana. *China's War with Japan, 1937–1945: The Struggle for Survival.* London: Allen Lane, 2013.

Moellering, Ralph Luther. *Modern War and the American Churches: A Factual Study of the Christian Conscience on Trial from 1939 to the Cold War Crisis of Today.* 1st edn. New York: American Press, 1956.

Montgomery-Massingberd, Hugh. *The Daily Telegraph Record of the Second World War.* London: Sidgwick and Jackson, 1989.

Moore, Christopher Paul. *Fighting for America: Black Soldiers – the Unsung Heroes of World War II.* New York: Presidio Press/ Ballantine Books, 2006.

Moore, Deborah Dash. *GI Jews: How World War II Changed a Generation.* Cambridge, MA: Belknap Press of Harvard University Press, 2004.

Moore, Deborah Dash. 'Jewish GIs and the Creation of the Judeo-Christian Tradition'. *Religion and American Culture: A Journal of Interpretation*, 8, no. 1 (1998), pp. 31–53.

Morgan, Ted. *FDR: A Biography.* London: Grafton, 1986.

Morison, Elting Elmore. *Turmoil and Tradition: A Study of the Life and Times of Henry L. Stimson.* Boston, MA: Houghton Mifflin, 1960.

Morley, Patrick. *'This Is the American Forces Network': The Anglo-American Battle of the Air Waves in World War II.* Westport, CT: Praeger, 2001.

Morris, Charles R. *American Catholic: The Saints and Sinners Who Built America's Most Powerful Church.* 1st edn. New York: Times Books, 1997.

Motley, Mary Penick. *The Invisible Soldier: The Experience of the Black Soldier, World War II.* Detroit, MI: Wayne State University Press, 1987.

Muir, Malcolm. *The Human Tradition in the World War II Era.* Wilmington, DE: SR Books, 2001.

Murray, John. 'An Apostle of the Great City: Father Rupert Mayer, S.J. 1876–1945'. *Studies: An Irish Quarterly Review*, 44, no. 174 (1955), pp. 213–29.

Murray, Williamson. *War in the Air 1914–45.* London Cassell, 2002.

Nolan, Charles E. '"A Builder of Churches and Schools"', in *The American Catholic Parish*, ed. Jay P. Dolan. 2 vols (I). New York: Paulist Press, 1987.

Noll, Mark A. *Christianity in America: A Handbook.* Tring: Lion, 1983.

Noll, Mark A. *A History of Christianity in the United States and Canada.* Grand Rapids, MI: W.B. Eerdmans, 1992.

Noll, Mark A. *The Old Religion in a New World: The History of North American Christianity.* Grand Rapids, MI: Eerdmans, 2002.

Norton, Herman Albert. *Struggling for Recognition: The United States Army Chaplaincy 1791–1865.* Washington: Office of the Chief of Chaplains, 1977.

Norwood, Stephen H. 'Marauding Youth and the Christian Front: Antisemitic Violence in Boston and New York During World War II'. *American Jewish History*, 91, no. 2 (2003), pp. 233–67.

O'Connor, R.G. 'The American Navy, 1939–1941: The Enlisted Perspective'. *Military Affairs*, 50, no. 4 (1986), pp. 173–78.

Overy, Richard. *Russia's War.* London: Penguin, 1999.

Overy, Richard. *Why the Allies Won*. London: Pimlico, 1995.

Palmer, R.R., Bell I. Wiley and William R. Keast, *The Procurement and Training of Ground Combat Troops*. United States Army in World War II: The Army Ground Forces. Washington DC: Office of the Chief of Military History, Department of the Army, 1948.

Pappas, George S. *The Cadet Chapel: United States Military Academy*. West Point, NY: USMA Class of 1927, 1987.

Parker, Matthew. *Monte Cassino: The Story of the Hardest-Fought Battle of World War Two*. London: Headline, 2003.

Parsons, Gerald. 'A National Saint in a Fascist State'. *Journal of Religious History*, 32, no. 1 (2008), pp. 76–95.

Pellegrino, Nicholas. 'Embattled Belief: The Religious Experiences of American Military Combatants During World War II and Today'. *Journal of Military Experience*, 3, no. 2 (2013), pp. 156–76.

Perret, Geoffrey. *There's a War to Be Won: The United States Army in World War II*. 1st edn. New York: Random House, 1991.

Perry, J. *Pershing: Commander of the Great War*. Nashville, TN: Thomas Nelson, 2011.

Piper, J.F. *The American Churches in World War I*. Athens, OH: Ohio University Press, 1985.

Pogue, Forrest Carlisle. *George C. Marshall: Education of a General*. London: MacGibbon & Kee, 1964.

Pogue, F.C. *George C. Marshall: Ordeal & Hope 1939–42*. New York: Viking, 1966.

Pogue, Forrest C. *George C. Marshall: Organizer of Victory, 1943–1945*. New York: Viking, 1973.

Pogue, Forrest C. *George C. Marshall: Statesman, 1945–1959*. New York: Viking, 1987.

Polenberg, Richard. *War and Society: The United States, 1941–1945*. Philadelphia: Lippincott, 1972.

Pope, Steven W. 'An Army of Athletes: Playing Fields, Battlefields, and the American Military Sporting Experience, 1890–1920'. *The Journal of Military History*, 59, no. 3 (1995), pp. 435–56.

Potter, E.B. *Nimitz*. Annapolis, MD: Naval Institute Press, 1976.

Potts, E. Daniel and Annette Potter. *Yanks Down Under, 1941–45: The American Impact on Australia*. Melbourne: Oxford University Press, 1985.

Preston, Andrew. *Sword of the Spirit, Shield of Faith: Religion in American War and Diplomacy*. 1st edn. New York: Alfred A. Knopf, 2012.

Promey, Sally. 'Hearts and Stones: Material Transformations and the Stuff of Christian Practice in the United States', in *American Christianities: A History of Dominance and Diversity*, ed. Catherine A. Brekus and W. Clark Gilpin. Chapel Hill, NC: University of North Carolina Press, 2011.

Putnam, Robert D. and David E. Campbell. *American Grace: How Religion Divides and Unites Us*. 1st edn. New York: Simon & Schuster, 2010.

Putney, Clifford. *Muscular Christianity: Manhood and Sports in Protestant America, 1880–1920*. Cambridge, MA; Harvard University Press, 2001.

Rabey, Steve. *Faith Under Fire: Stories of Hope and Courage from World War II*. Nashville: Thomas Nelson Publishers, 2002.

Rable, George C. *God's Almost Chosen Peoples: A Religious History of the American Civil War*. Chapel Hill, NC: University of North Carolina Press, 2010.

Reynolds, David. *America, Empire of Liberty: A New History*. London: Penguin, 2010.

Reynolds, David. *Rich Relations: The American Occupation of Britain, 1942–1945*. London: HarperCollins, 1996.

Roberts, Mary Louise. *What Soldiers Do: Sex and the American GI in World War II France*. Chicago, IL: University of Chicago Press, 2014.

Rooney, David. *Stilwell the Patriot: Vinegar Joe, the Brits and Chiang Kai-Shek*. London: Greenhill Books, 2005.

Roper, Richard S. *Brothers of Paul: Activities of Prisoner of War Chaplains in the Philippines During WWII*. Odenton, MD: Revere Printing, 2003.

Rose, Kenneth D. *Myth and the Greatest Generation: A Social History of Americans in World War II*. London: Routledge, 2008.

Rottman, Gordon L. *US Marine Rifleman 1939–45*. Oxford: Osprey Publishing Ltd, 2006.

Schaller, Michael. *The US Crusade in China, 1938–1945*. New York: Columbia University Press, 1979.

Schmitz, David F. *Henry L. Stimson: The First Wise Man*. Wilmington, DE: SR Books, 2001.

Schrijvers, Peter. *Bloody Pacific: American Soldiers at War with Japan*. Basingstoke: Palgrave Macmillan, 2010.

Schrijvers, Peter. *The Crash of Ruin: American Combat Soldiers in Europe During World War II*. New York: New York University Press, 1998.

Schultz, Kevin M. *Tri-Faith America: How Catholics and Jews Held Postwar America to Its Protestant Promise*. New York: Oxford University Press, 2011. Kindle.

Schweitzer, Richard. *The Cross and the Trenches: Religious Faith and Doubt among British and American Great War Soldiers*. Westport, CT: Praeger, 2003.

Shattuck, Gardiner H. *A Shield and Hiding Place: The Religious Life of the Civil War Armies*. Macon, GA: Mercer University Press, 1987.

Sherry, Michael S. *In the Shadow of War: The United States since the 1930s*. New Haven, CT: Yale University Press, 1995.

Shindler, Colin. *Hollywood Goes to War: Films and American Society, 1939–1952*. London: Routledge and Kegan Paul, 1979.

Shindler, Henry. *Fort Leavenworth Its Churches and Schools*. Fort Leavenworth, KS: The Army Service Schools Press, 1912.

Sibley, Mulford Quickert and Philip E. Jacob. *Conscription of Conscience: The American State and the Conscientious Objector, 1940–1947*. Ithaca, NY: Cornell University Press, 1952.

Silk, Mark. *Spiritual Politics: Religion and America since World War II*. New York: Simon & Schuster, 1988.

Sittser, Gerald Lawson. 'American Christianity on the Home Front During the Second World War', in *World War II in Asia and the Pacific and the War's Aftermath, with General Themes*, ed. Loyd E. Lee. Westport, CT: Greenwood Press, 1998.

Sittser, Gerald Lawson. *A Cautious Patriotism: The American Churches and the Second World War*. Chapel Hill, NC: University of North Carolina Press, 1997.

Slomovitz, Albert Isaac. *The Fighting Rabbis: Jewish Military Chaplains and American History*. New York: New York University Press, 1999.

Smelser, Ronald M. and Edward J. Davies. *The Myth of the Eastern Front: The Nazi–Soviet War in American Popular Culture*. Cambridge: Cambridge University Press, 2008.

Smith, Gary Scott. *Faith and the Presidency: From George Washington to George W. Bush*. Oxford: Oxford University Press, 2006.

Smith, Graham. *When Jim Crow Met John Bull: Black American Soldiers in World War II Britain*. New York: St. Martin's Press, 1988.

Smith, Jeffery A. 'Hollywood Theology: The Commodification of Religion in Twentieth-Century Films'. *Religion and American Culture: A Journal of Interpretation*, 11, no. 2 (2001), pp. 191–231.

Smith, S.E. *The United States Navy in World War II*. New York: Ballantine Books, 1967.

Snape, Michael, *God and the British Soldier: Religion and the British Army in the First and Second World Wars*, Routledge: Abingdon, 2005.

Snape, Michael F. and Stephen G. Parker. 'Keeping Faith and Coping: Belief, Popular Religiosity and the British People', in *The Great World War 1914–45: Who Won? Who Lost?*, ed. John Bourne, Peter Liddle and Ian Whitehead. London: Collins, 2001.

Soffer, Jonathan M. *General Matthew B. Ridgway: From Progressivism to Reaganism, 1895–1993*. Westport, CT: Praeger, 1998.

Spector, Ronald H. *At War at Sea: Sailors and Naval Warfare in the Twentieth Century*. London: Allen Lane, 2001.

Spector, Ronald H. *Eagle Against the Sun: The American War with Japan*. London: Cassell, 2001.

Spector, Ronald. 'The Military Effectiveness of the US Armed Forces, 1919–39', in *Military Effectiveness. Volume 2. The Interwar Period.* New edn, ed. Allan R. Millett and Williamson Murray. Cambridge: Cambridge University Press, 2010.

Spicer, Kevin P. *Hitler's Priests: Catholic Clergy and National Socialism*. DeKalb, IL: Northern Illinois University Press, 2008.

Spivey, Larkin. *Stories of Faith and Courage from World War II*. Chattanooga, TN: God and Country Press, 2009.

Steigmann-Gall, Richard. *The Holy Reich: Nazi Conceptions of Christianity, 1919–1945*. Cambridge: Cambridge University Press, 2003.

Stephenson, Michael. *Patriot Battles: How the War of Independence Was Fought*. New York: Harper Perennial, 2008.

Stillwell, Paul. *The Golden Thirteen: Recollections of the First Black Naval Officers*. Annapolis, MD: Naval Institute Press, 1993.

Stover, Earl F. *Up from Handymen. The United States Army Chaplaincy 1865–1920*. Washington DC: Office of the Chief of Chaplains, 1977.

Stremlow, Mary V. *Free a Marine to Fight: Women Marines in World War II*. Washington DC: Marine Corps Historical Center, 1994.

Takaki, Ronald T. *A Different Mirror: A History of Multicultural America*. 1st rev. edn. New York: Back Bay Books/ Little, Brown, and Co., 2008.

Taylor, John M. *An American Soldier: The Wars of General Maxwell Taylor*. Novato, CA: Presidio Press, 1989.

Think Magazine's Diary of US Participation in World War II. New York: IBM, 1950.

Thomas, Keith. *Religion and the Decline of Magic: Studies in Popular Beliefs in Sixteenth and Seventeenth-Century England*. London: Penguin, 1991.

Thompson, Parker C. *From Its European Antecedents to 1791: The United States Army Chaplaincy*. Washington: Office of the Chief of Chaplains, 1978.

Tillman, Barrett. *Lemay*. 1st edn. New York: Palgrave Macmillan, 2007.

Tobin, James. *Ernie Pyle's War: America's Eyewitness to World War II*. New York: Free Press, 1997.

Treadwell, Mattie E. *The Women's Army Corps*. United States Army in World War II. Special Studies. Washington DC: Center of Military History, 1991.

Tsouras, Peter G., ed. *The Daily Telegraph Dictionary of Military Quotations*. London: Greenhill Books, 2005.

Van Creveld, Martin. *Fighting Power: German and US Army Performance, 1939–1945*. London: Arms and Armour, 1983.

Venzke, Rodger R. *Confidence in Battle, Inspiration in Peace: The United States Army Chaplaincy 1945–1975*. Washington: Office of the Chief of Chaplains, 1977.

Virden, Jenel. 'Warm Beer and Cold Canons: US Army Chaplains and Alcohol Consumption in World War II'. *Journal of American Studies*, 48, no. 1 (2014), pp. 79–97.

Wansink, Brian and Craig Wansink. 'Are There Atheists in Foxholes? Combat Intensity and Religious Behavior'. *Journal of Religion and Health* (forthcoming), pp. 1–28. See Copyright Permissions.

Ward, Geoffrey C., Ken Burns and Lynn Novick. *The War: An Intimate History, 1941–1945*. 1st edn. New York: A.A. Knopf, 2007.

Weigley, Russell Frank. *Eisenhower's Lieutenants: The Campaign of France and Germany 1944–1945*. Bloomington, IN: Indiana University Press, 1981.

Weigley, Russell Frank. *History of the United States Army*. London: Batsford, 1968.

Weingartner, James J. 'Trophies of War: US Troops and the Mutilation of Japanese War Dead, 1941–1945'. *Pacific Historical Review*, 61, no. 1 (1992), pp. 53–67.

Wells, Mark K. *Courage and Air Warfare: The Allied Aircrew Experience in the Second World War*. London: Frank Cass, 1995.

Wells, Ronald. *The Wars of America: Christian Views*. Macon, GA: Mercer, 1991.

Whitt, Jacqueline E. *Bringing God to Men: American Military Chaplains and the Vietnam War*. Chapel Hill, NC: University of North Carolina Press, 2014.

Willoughby, John. 'The Sexual Behavior of American GIs During the Early Years of the Occupation of Germany'. *The Journal of Military History*, 62, no. 1 (1998), pp. 155–74.

Wilson, Theodore A. 'Who Fought and Why? The Assignment of American Soldiers to Combat', in *Time to Kill: The Soldier's Experience of War in the West 1939–1945*, ed. Paul Addison and Angus Calder. London: Pimlico, 1997.

Winchell, Meghan K. *Good Girls, Good Food, Good Fun: The Story of USO Hostesses During World War II*. Chapel Hill, NC: University of North Carolina Press, 2008.

Wolk, Herman S. *Cataclysm: General Hap Arnold and the Defeat of Japan*. Denton, TX: University of North Texas Press, 2010.

Woodard, William P. *The Allied Occupation of Japan 1945–1952 and Japanese Religions*. Leiden: Brill, 1972.

Wukovits, John F. 'Admiral Raymond A. Spruance', in *Men of War: Great Naval Leaders of World War II*, ed. Stephen Howarth. London: Weidenfeld and Nicolson, 1992.

Wuthnow, Robert. *The Restructuring of American Religion*: Princeton University Press, 1988.

Wynn, Neil A. *The African American Experience During World War II*. Lanham, MD: Rowman & Littlefield Publishers, 2010.

Yellin, Keith. *Battle Exhortation: The Rhetoric of Combat Leadership*. Columbia, SC: University of South Carolina Press, 2008.

Zaloga, Steven J. *Blitzkrieg: Armour Camouflage and Markings, 1939–1940*. London: Arms and Armour Press, 1991.

Ziemke, Earl Frederick. *The US Army in the Occupation of Germany, 1944–1946*. Army Historical Series. Washington DC: Center of Military History, 1975.

Zinn, Howard. *A People's History of the United States: 1492–Present*. New edn. New York: HarperCollins, 2003.

Reference works

Ancell, R. Manning and Christine Marie Miller. *The Biographical Dictionary of World War II Generals and Flag Officers: The U.S. Armed Forces*. Westport, CT: Greenwood Press, 1996.

Bowman, Martin W. *USAAF Handbook, 1939–1945*. Stroud: Sutton, 1997 (2003 printing).

Boyer, Paul S. and Melvyn Dubofsky. *The Oxford Companion to United States History*. Oxford: Oxford University Press, 2001.

Bureau of the Census. *The Statistical History of the United States, from Colonial Times to the Present*. New York: Basic Books, 1976.

Carroll, Bret E. *The Routledge Historical Atlas of Religion in America*. New York: Routledge, 2000.

Chambers, John Whiteclay, ed. *The Oxford Companion to American Military History*. Oxford: Oxford University Press, 1999.

Chandler, D.G. and J.L. Collins, eds. *The D-Day Encyclopaedia*. Oxford: Helicon, 1994.

Dear, Ian and M.R.D. Foot, eds. *The Oxford Companion to the Second World War*. Oxford: Oxford University Press, 1995.

Forty, George. *US Army Handbook, 1939–1945*. New edn. Stroud: Sutton, 2003.

Forty, George. *US Marine Corps Handbook 1941–5*. Stroud: Sutton, 2006.

Gawne, Jonathan. *Finding Your Father's War: A Practical Guide to Researching and Understanding Service in the World War II US Army*. Havertown, PA, Casemate, London: Greenhill [distributor], 2006.

Gilroy, William F.R. and Timothy J. Demy. *A Brief Chronology of the Chaplain Corps of the United States Navy*. W.F.R. Gilroy, 1983.

Josephson, Harold, ed. *Biographical Dictionary of Modern Peace Leaders*. Wesport, CT: Greenwood Press, 1985.

Kull, Irving Stoddard and Nell M. Kull. *A Short Chronology of American History, 1492–1950*. New Brunswick, NJ: Rutgers University Press, 1952.

Mead, Frank S. *Handbook of Denominations in the United States*. New York: Abingdon-Cokesbury Press, 1951.

Mead, Frank S. *Handbook of Denominations in the United States*. 4th edn. New York: Abingdon Press, 1965.

Purvis, Thomas L. *A Dictionary of American History*. Oxford: Blackwell, 1995.

Queen, Edward L., Stephen R. Prothero and Gardiner H. Shattuck. *Encyclopedia of American Religious History*. 2 vols. Rev. edn. New York: Facts on File, 2001.

Renshaw, Patrick. *The Longman Companion to America in the Era of the Two World Wars, 1910–1945*. London: Longman, 1996.

Spiller, Roger J. and Joseph G. Dawson. *Dictionary of American Military Biography*. 3 vols. Westport, CT: Greenwood Press, 1984.

Stanton, Shelby L. *World War II Order of Battle*. Mechanicsburg, PA: Stackpole Books, 2006.

Sutherland, Jonathan. *African Americans at War: An Encyclopedia*. 2 vols. Santa Barbara, CA: ABC-CLIO, 2004.

Wagner, Margaret E., David M. Kennedy, Linda Barrett Osborne, Susan Reyburn and staff of the Library of Congress. *The Library of Congress World War II Companion*. New York: Simon & Schuster, 2007.

Weatherford, Doris. *American Women During World War II: An Encyclopedia*. 1st edn. New York: Routledge, 2010.

Wheal, Elizabeth-Anne and Stephen Pope. *The Macmillan Dictionary of the Second World War*. 2nd edn. London: Macmillan, 1995.

Young, G.R. *The Army Almanac: A Book of Facts Concerning the United States Army*. 2nd edn. Harrisburg, PA: Stackpole, 1959.

Unpublished dissertations

Rawson, Andrew. 'The Divisional Commander in the US Army in World War II: A

Case Study of the Normandy Campaign, 6 June 1944 to 24 July 1944'. University of Birmingham, M.Phil diss., 2011.

Rogers, R.J. 'A Study of Leadership in the First Infantry Division During World War II: Terry De La Mesa Allen and Clarence Ralph Huebner'. MA diss., US Army Command and General Staff College, 1965.

Skelly, Patrick G. 'The Military Chaplaincy of the US Army, Focusing on World War II Chaplains in Combat'. Norwich University, MA diss., 2007.

Television broadcasts

Hoyt, Austin. *Victory in the Pacific. Part One: Death Before Surrender.* PBS, 2005.

Lewis, Jonathan. *Hell in the Pacific. Episode Four: Apocalypse.* ITV Studios, 2001.

Websites

87th Infantry Division Legacy Association, http://www.87thinfantrydivision.com

About.com, http://usmilitary.about.com/

American Battle Monuments Commission, http://www.abmc.gov

American Ex-Prisoners of War, www.axpow.org/

The American Memorial Chapel, St. Paul's Cathedral, London, http://www.angelfire.com/my/mighty8thlh/CHAPELUK.html

The American Presidency Project, http://www.presidency.ucsb.edu/index.php

   Franklin D. Roosevelt: 'Letter to the Clergy of America,' September 23, 1935. Online by Gerhard Peters and John T. Woolley, *The American Presidency Project.* http://www.presidency.ucsb.edu/ws/?pid=14939.

   Franklin D. Roosevelt: 'Fireside Chat,' May 26, 1940. Online by Gerhard Peters and John T. Woolley, *The American Presidency Project.* http://www.presidency.ucsb.edu/ws/?pid=15959.

   Franklin D. Roosevelt: 'Fireside Chat,' December 24, 1943. Online by Gerhard Peters and John T. Woolley, *The American Presidency Project.* http://www.presidency.ucsb.edu/ws/?pid=16356.

   Franklin D. Roosevelt: 'Fireside Chat,' June 5, 1944. Online by Gerhard Peters and John T. Woolley, *The American Presidency Project.* http://www.presidency.ucsb.edu/ws/?pid=16514.

The American Spectator, http://spectator.org/archives/2011/02/14/eisenhowers-religion

Arlington National Cemetery Website, http://www.arlingtoncemetery.net

Army.Mil, http://www.army.mil/d-day/message.html

Audie L. Murphy Memorial Website, http://www.audiemurphy.com/index.htm

Billy Graham Center, http://www2.wheaton.edu/bgc/

Brothers in Battle, http://brothersinbattle.net/html/peleliu_chapter.html,

Catholic War Veterans of the United States of America, Inc, http://www.cwv.org/

D-Day: Etat Des Lieux, http://www.6juin1944.com

http://voices.yahoo.com/d-day-veterans-landed-normandy-remember-two-363691.html?cat=37

Evangelical Lutheran Church in America, http://www.elca.org/

Eye On Kansas, http://www.eyeonkansas.org/

GG Archives, http://www.gjenvick.com/

Hartford Courant, http://articles.courant.com/1999-11-23/news/9911230135_1_falmouth-theology-divinity-degree

ICRC Treaties and States Parties to Such Treaties, http://www.icrc.org/applic/ihl/ihl.nsf/Treaty.xsp?documentId=CD0F6C83F96FB459C12563CD002D66A1&action=openDocument

IMDB, http://www.imdb.com/title/tt0035959/

The Library of Congress, http://lcweb2.loc.gov/

The Martin Luther King, Jr. Research and Education Institute, http://mlk-kpp01.stanford.edu/

Maryknoll Mission Archives, http://maryknollmissionarchives.org/

National Museum of American History, http://americanhistory.si.edu/

The National WWII Museum, http://www.nationalww2museum.org/

Naval History and Heritage Command, http://www.history.navy.mil/index.html

The Navigators, http://www.navigators.org/us/aboutus/history

The New York Times, http://www.nytimes.com/

The Patton Society, http://pattonhq.com

Texas State Historical Association, http://www.tshaonline.org/

United States Naval Academy Alumni Association and Foundation, http://www.usna.com/

University of Minnesota Human Rights Library, http://www1.umn.edu/humanrts/instree/1929c.htm

US Army Center of Military History, http://www.history.army.mil

Youtube, 'Chaplain Song', https://www.youtube.com/watch?v=mvWuJgxxM7Y

Youtube, 'Tex Ritter- The Deck of Cards',
http://www.youtube.com/watch?v=LsCiaxPhtVY

Index

References to plates are in bold, eg **Pl.1, Pl.2** etc